THE McCARTNEY LEGACY

THE
McCARTNEY
LEGACY

VOLUME 1 | 1969–73

ALLAN KOZINN
ADRIAN SINCLAIR

DEYST.

An Imprint of WILLIAM MORROW

FOR PAULA & CAROLYN

Who helped us sing our song

FOR RICHARD & PHYLLIS, BOB & KIM

Who righted us when we were wrong

FOR GEORGE

Who makes his dad amazed at the way he really needs you

CONTENTS

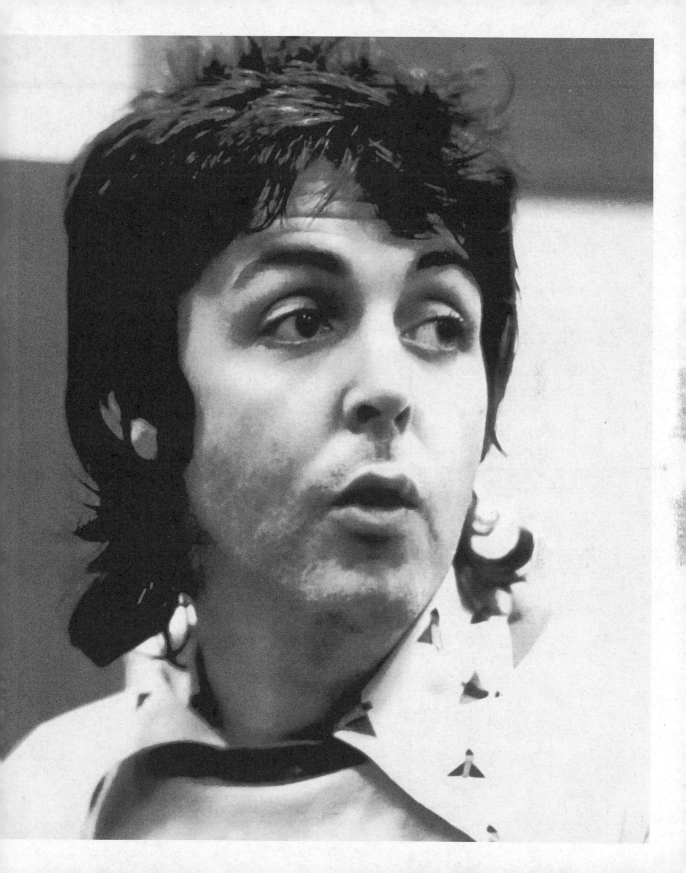

"I'M VERY GOOD AT FORGETTING WHO I AM, BECAUSE AS FAR AS I'M CONCERNED PAUL McCARTNEY IS A NAME I WAS GIVEN AT BIRTH AND AT THE BEGINNING OF THE BEATLES HE SPLIT OFF INTO A CELEBRITY, AND I REMAINED AS [ME]. I'VE GOT A VERY SCHIZO THING WITH THAT. WHEN HE GOES ONSTAGE HE'S AN ENTERTAINER. PEOPLE WHO ARE VERY BIG ONSTAGE ARE QUITE SHY IN THEIR PRIVATE LIVES. THAT DOESN'T COMPUTE; THEY SHOULD BE BIG IN THEIR PRIVATE LIVES. BUT THERE'S A CUTOFF. SO, WHEN YOU TALK ABOUT PAUL McCARTNEY, I TALK ABOUT THE GUY INSIDE ME, BUT YOU'RE TALKING ABOUT HIM—THE GUY WHO GOES ONSTAGE, AND MAKES RECORDS, AND STUFF. AND I THINK IT'S JUST A WAY OF PRESERVING MY SANITY REALLY, IS THINKING, 'I'M NOT REALLY THAT, I'M JUST SOME LITTLE KID FROM LIVERPOOL REALLY. I DIDN'T DO ALL THAT STUFF. IT'S A DREAM REALLY AND IT'S GONNA STOP SOON.'"[1]

INTRODUCTION

ALLAN KOZINN

—

There is something to be said for sitting in a room with Paul McCartney and watching him in action, up close, during an interview, an experience my years at the *New York Times* opened up for me on several occasions. And *experience* is the word: I probably conducted upward of 3,000 interviews during my 38 years at the *Times*, and though many interviewees are quite polished, no one comes close to McCartney in his ability to take control of the room. That's not to say that he hijacks your questions—if he finds those you ask engaging, he can be gratifyingly frank, although you have to be careful to avoid lines of inquiry that allow him to lapse into the many set pieces he has developed through decades of hearing the same questions over and over.

But the most striking thing about interviewing McCartney is his uncanny ability to make you feel as though you're old pals, and that there is nothing he'd rather be doing than answering your questions. As a journalist, you know that this isn't—cannot be—true, but there is no denying that there is something seductive about having what feels like a friendly chat—with jokes, asides, bits of gossip and clarifications of long-standing mysteries—with someone whose work you've admired all your life.

He also has a surprising memory for faces, given the huge number of people he encounters. In the fall of 1991, a year after my first one-on-one interview with him, he returned to New York for a press conference at Weill Recital Hall, to announce that his first classical work, *Paul McCartney's Liverpool Oratorio*, would have its American premiere at Carnegie Hall. As I left the hall when the press conference ended, one of Carnegie Hall's publicists stopped me to say that Paul had spotted me in the audience and wanted to speak with me about the review I had written after hearing the *Oratorio*'s world premiere, in Liverpool. I had enjoyed the work: its movements were, at heart, extended song forms, and if there's one thing McCartney handles better than most, it's the song form.

I was ushered backstage where Paul, with his wife, Linda, standing beside him, said, "I read your review of the *Oratorio*, and I just wanted to thank you for giving it a chance." He added that Linda's father, Lee Eastman, had read the review to him over the phone the morning after the performance and had been pleased that the work got a positive notice in the *Times*. "And you know," he added, "he died soon after that, so you did a good thing."

That is one side of Paul McCartney. The musicians and producers he works with see other sides of him, as do family members, colleagues, and functionaries at various levels.

He has, at times, spoken publicly about there really being two manifestations of himself, who he refers to as "Him" and "Me"—"Him" being the public Paul McCartney, the one you see onstage, on film and television, and in interviews, and "Me" being the private, "real" Paul McCartney, the man his family and closest friends know, and who does not need to project the unflaggingly cheerful, thumbs-up image that is central to being "Him."

We all have public and private selves, of course. But at the level of fame Paul McCartney inhabits, with millions of people constantly peering into the fishbowl, the distinction is more acute, by levels of magnitude. It is also exacerbated by his being a Gemini, and whatever one believes about the characteristics astrologers ascribe to those born under particular signs—Geminis are known for their duality—he has mentioned it in interviews (often jokingly), and Linda mentioned it as well.

In "Him" mode, McCartney is a consummate performer, charming and eager to please, but he is presenting an image that may have a shifting connection to reality. "Him," in other words, can proclaim publicly that he does not read newspapers (particularly reviews); "Me" reads them voraciously. "Him" can repeat, with a measure of wonder, a favorite anecdote of George Martin's, in which the producers of *Live and Let Die* thought the fully produced (by Martin) Wings recording of the title song was just a demo, and that wondered what female singer they should get to sing it in the film; "Me" was familiar with the details of his contract and knew that there was never any doubt that the Wings version would be used. So why did "Him" repeat the tale? It makes a great story, and since listeners are almost guaranteed not to have seen the contract, no one is likely to challenge it.

So is "Him" a liar? We don't see it that way. "Him" is a performer, and his performances are not only those he gives with an instrument in hand, but rather, the entire persona wrapped around the musician. His public statements, in other words, are part of the vast performance piece that is the Public Paul McCartney. Most of it is objectively true and can be taken at face value. But if it suits him to spin a story to make it more entertaining, or because a tweaked version makes a point he wants to get across, or merely to sweep away an embarrassing detail—well, that's just part of the construct.

"Me" is more complex, more natural. If he's angry, or just in a bad mood, "Me" will unload on you with little mercy, as fans hounding him for autographs or photos have sometimes found. It is McCartney's "Me" side, too, that pushes insistently for what he wants and how he wants it, whether musically or in his private life.

This duality comes through these pages, not because we've stressed it—we have not—but because different situations naturally demand different responses, and we have done our best to tell the story as it happened, neither idealizing it nor going out of our way to find a dark side within it.

But why, you may ask, have we opted to start our story in 1969 when James Paul McCartney was born in Liverpool on June 18, 1942?

The story of the Beatles has been told a great many times and from a great many perspectives, and for good reason: it's a ripping yarn about four colorful, supremely talented young men who made the most stunning pop music of the twentieth century and changed the way a generation (and then another, and another) saw, understood and responded to the world. But just about every telling of this tale ends in 1970, when musical, business, and personal tensions tore the Beatles apart. Some studies of the band continue for a chapter or two, summarizing the fallout of the breakup, and how John Lennon, Paul McCartney, George Harrison and Ringo Starr moved on, almost as a dutiful tying up of loose ends—like the text projected at the end of some films, telling the viewer what became of the characters after the main story ended.

Even biographies of the individual Beatles typically take that approach, devoting three-quarters of their pages, or more, to their subject's life through 1970 and touching lightly on their post-Beatles life and work. That may still have seemed a reasonable approach when John Lennon was murdered, in 1980, only a decade after the Beatles split. But now, more than 50 years after the split, it is untenable, particularly for an artist as prolific and adventurous as Paul McCartney.

Listeners who grew up during the Beatles' collective heyday sometimes have trouble recognizing that, but those born after, say, 1965, grew up in a world where the former Beatles' solo works were the hits they knew and loved; there are a great many people who say they came to the Beatles only after realizing that their favorite musicians had been in an earlier band. As early as the late 1970s, this was a truth said in jest—often in the form of a cartoon in which a child says to his parents, "You mean Paul McCartney was in a band before Wings?"

McCartney sometimes seems to have lived ten lifetimes in the span of one, and he remains as artistically driven, enduringly popular and relevant as ever. In artistic terms, he recognizes no boundaries, having moved beyond his principal pop music *métier* into electronica, short- and long-form orchestral and chamber works, visual art, poetry, children's books, films, and most recently, musical theater. Some of these efforts have been more successful than others, but what they have in common is McCartney's belief that if you love an art form, being a spectator and a consumer is not sufficient: you should learn how it's done, and try your hand at it.

In purely commercial terms, his success is quantifiable, and impressive: his post-Beatles recordings—26 studio albums (many now available in expanded archival editions), 9 live sets, 5 classical albums, 4 hits compilations, and 8 miscellaneous collections (electronic, soundtracks and nonclassical instrumental records) are estimated to have sold between 86.5 million and 100 million copies; his tours have set records for audience sizes and box office takes; and his two most recent albums, *Egypt Station* (2018) and *McCartney III* (2020), topped American sales charts, as did *McCartney III Imagined* (2021), an album of remixes and covers of songs from *McCartney III*.

McCartney's approach to creativity has made him an incessantly busy man, yet half a century after he ceased being a Beatle, there has not yet been a truly comprehensive, in-depth study of his post-Beatles work and how he creates it—or, for that matter, a look at his life, during those decades, in as close to granular detail as you can get without either being him or having a permanent perch on one of his shoulders.

To a great degree, his work and his life are inextricably entwined: you can enjoy his work without knowing a thing about him, of course; but there is a fascinating story in the way his life and attitudes, the things that please, anger or depress him, the interplay between confidence and insecurity in his psyche, the tension between his desire to collaborate and his need for control, and his way of seeing the artistic possibilities within anything from a newspaper headline to a random postcard all combine to make his work what it is.

Starting at page one of the book you have in your hands, we will address this woeful gap in the study of Paul McCartney's life and work beyond the Beatles, this first installment covering the period from 1969 (the Beatles' final year) through 1973 (the release of *Band on the Run*), including the full run of Wings Mark I, the first iteration of McCartney's first post-Beatles band.

Naturally, we invited Sir Paul to be interviewed for our project, but though he speaks freely and frequently to journalists, he tends to keep his distance from biographers. And the truth is, while it would have been useful to ask him to clarify details or resolve the inconsistencies and contradictions that invariably present themselves while researching someone's life, fresh interviews were not absolutely necessary. Our archives include thousands of radio and television interviews, and tens of thousands that have appeared in print. We know what he has to say—or what he has been willing to say, publicly—on most topics to do with his life and career. (And things he has not been willing to say need to be found elsewhere, in any case.)

Beyond that, we collected an enormous amount of source material, including thousands of unpublished documents (including contracts, legal papers, diaries, correspondence and recording information from tape boxes and studio documentation), as well as contemporaneous newspaper and magazine coverage. And we conducted hundreds of interviews with musicians, managers, recording engineers, producers, filmmakers, album jacket designers, roadies and others who worked closely with McCartney.

We should add that McCartney's disinclination to be a source notwithstanding, several interviewees mentioned that when they asked him directly whether they should speak with us, he gave them the go-ahead, for which we are grateful.

All this has allowed us to sweep away several myths and fictions that have become part of the lore, and to establish the timeline of his career accurately for the first time. Crucially, the timeline of events presented in this book was built from the ground up over a period of eight years, using firsthand sources. We found time and again during the research and writing of this first volume that aspects of the story as we had always known it were not quite right. The chronology of the Lagos sessions for *Band on the Run*, for example, has never been accurately told.

In telling this story, we have adopted an approach lately taken by Mark Lewisohn in his ground-breaking Beatles biography, *Tune In*, and Chip Madinger in his comprehensive *Lennonology*, of telling the story "without foreknowledge." That is, we discuss events essentially as the partici-pants experienced them, without telegraphing what the ramifications of specific actions would be (unless, of course, those ramifications were obvious at the time—for example, if you're a British citizen arrested for cannabis possession, it could reasonably occur to you—indeed, someone is likely to warn you—that you may have trouble obtaining an American visa). Lewisohn's *Tune In* demonstrated the attraction of this technique: as familiar as the Beatles story is, the book read like a thriller, assuming you were able to set aside your knowledge of what happens next.

In McCartney's case, it's a somewhat more difficult technique to maintain. For one thing, Mc-Cartney is a musician who often records far more than he needs (although that is true for only two of the five albums covered in this installment) and sets aside the extras, often revisiting and setting them aside again several times before finally releasing them, years or even decades later. As a writer, you imagine the reader wondering, *What happened to that song you just spent two pages describing?*—and you want to tell them, but if you do, you're violating the "no-foreknowledge" rule.

Similarly, McCartney often changed his mind about titles. In some cases, several titles were concurrent and interchangeable, so you could safely use the one everyone knows, referring to the others in passing. But throughout the recording of *Band on the Run*, for example, 'Mamunia' was listed on the tape boxes and session documents as 'Ma Moonia,' 'Mrs. Vandebilt' was listed as 'Mrs. Vanderbilt' (with an *r*, as in the common surname) and 'Picasso's Last Words (Drink to Me)' was just 'Drink to Me.' These songs took their final forms only when the final track listing for the album was decided. We can see knowledgeable readers wagging their fingers as they read the original titles, but in describing the sessions, we used the titles as they were at the time.

The same goes for EMI Studios. Even in the Beatle years, the studio complex was referred to colloquially as "Abbey Road," but its formal name was EMI Studios until 1976, when the company adopted Abbey Road as part of the name. So EMI Studios is what we call them; that will change midway through Volume 2. The television special and album the Beatles recorded in January 1969 was known at the time as *Get Back*, and we call it that until it was renamed *Let It Be*.

All that said, rules are made to be broken, and there are times we let the "no foreknowledge" rule slip. In our discussions of McCartney's recording sessions, we use a heading showing which studios were used, and their locations, as well as the dates and what songs were recorded, over-dubbed or mixed. While the text beneath such a heading may refer to 'Ma Moonia,' the heading will say: 'Ma Moonia' (Working title for 'Mamunia').

Footnotes were another escape valve, of sorts. For example, when we write that Hugh Mc-Cracken, the session guitarist who played on most of *Ram*, was in Florida recording with Aretha Franklin when McCartney first tried to reach him, the name and release date of the album Mc-Cracken was working on is given in a footnote. Footnotes look ahead in other ways, too, but we used them that way only when we felt it was necessary. We use footnotes to further explain things mentioned in the text; source citations are given as endnotes, at the back of the book.

We have tried to keep jargon to a minimum, but recording is a technical (and to a certain extent, ritual) process. So in discussing the mixes, we often refer to the numbers assigned to those mixes, which typically have the letters RS (for remix, stereo) as a prefix. So an entry might say that five mixes were done (RS1 to RS5) and that the third (RS3) was marked "Best," or chosen to be the master. Terms like "mastering"—the preparation of a master tape for pressing on vinyl—are either common parlance or self-explanatory in context; less familiar terms, and how certain pieces of equipment work, are explained in the text.

To avoid confusion on another technical front, all chart information (with few exceptions) comes from the Official UK Chart company, and *Billboard*. Monetary references are given in British and American currencies, using the prices of the time. Generally speaking, the 2022 equivalents of those prices are between six and ten times higher than the 1970s values.

We have included some musical analysis—relatively little, and only when a song's structure or harmonic backdrop is so unusual or extraordinary that we wanted to show what makes it so ingenious. In such cases, we have kept the language as nontechnical as possible. Granted, the language of musical analysis that has evolved over the centuries paints a clear picture of how a piece of music works, but general readers who have not taken music theory classes cannot be expected to navigate such discussions, and our goal was to show how the music works without readers' eyes glazing over. The descriptions work best, of course, if you play the songs while reading about them.

Actually, the rest of the book works best that way, too. If we've succeeded in what we've tried to do, you will come away from this volume with a deeper sense of how (and why) McCartney has created the music of the period we cover, and you will have discovered a few songs that you had previously overlooked, but will now regard as favorites.

1

THE KINTYRE MIST

—

t was a bad move, probably the worst thing he could have done at the moment. Paul McCartney, the most publicity-savvy of the Beatles, knew that the instant he hurled a bucket of kitchen scraps at a pair of unwanted visitors to High Park, his hard-to-find, harder-to-reach farm in the Scottish countryside, near Campbeltown.

As the vegetable scraps, dirty water, and dinner leftovers flew through the air, Paul focused on his targets and realized that he knew one of the intruders. Terence Spencer, a photographer best known for his war coverage, had shot the Beatles periodically, starting in 1963. Now on assignment for *Life* magazine, which had chosen him because of his relationship with the Beatles, Spencer was tagging along with Dorothy Bacon, who had been assigned to track down McCartney and get his response to a rumor sweeping the globe, to the effect that the doe-eyed bassist, singer and songwriter had been killed in an automobile accident in 1966, and that the Beatles, having suppressed word of his death, filled their post-1966 recordings with "clues" pointing to the truth.

Bacon had tried telephoning McCartney from London, with no luck, before driving to Scotland with Spencer. They arrived on Saturday, November 1, 1969, but their first attempt to reach High Park was fruitless. To get there, they had to cross the neighboring Low Park farm, whose owner, Ian McDougall, had agreed to prevent fans and reporters from reaching Paul's highland sanctuary. McDougall sent them packing, but later that afternoon, as they sat in a Campbeltown pub weighing their options, Spencer and Bacon overheard one of the locals tell another he would see him in church the next morning, and they realized that McDougall would likely be in church, too, leaving the way to High Park unguarded. So on Sunday at about 11:00 a.m., they tried again.

"Parking our hired car on the small road we started walking," Spencer wrote of the encounter. "We trekked over the hills, through bogs and waded across fast-flowing streams, arriving at the lonely farmhouse as unshaven Paul walked out of the front door carrying a slop pail. He took a startled look in our direction and the angel face distorted in creases of rage as he slung abuse at us. I had preset my camera and, when he turned to re-enter the house, I took a quick shot, knowing it would be my last. He heard the click, turned, and threw the slop pail at me. I took another shot of it in mid-air or rather tried to, since at the moment he charged me with flailing fists, and I was hit for the first time in twenty years of covering trouble around the world—by a Beatle!"[1]

Paul may have felt that his response was justified, if perhaps over the top. But it was also inconsistent. Nine days earlier, on October 24, he had granted an interview to Chris Drake, of the BBC, and it was probably Drake's report, broadcast the same afternoon on the topical news show *The World*, that put Bacon and Spencer onto Paul's whereabouts.

Where the *Life* team turned up unannounced, Drake had telephoned Paul and secured an invitation, arguing that the best way to short-circuit the rumor was to be heard robustly denying it, his voice recognizable to virtually anyone listening.

Paul gave Drake a brief but wide-ranging interview in which he asserted his continued existence and discussed a few of the clues that conspiracy theorists advanced. He added that he enjoyed being in Scotland with his family, and that since he was finished with his work as a Beatle for the year, he might not return to London until March.[2]

"I always used to do, sort of, an interview a week almost, for a newspaper, or for something, just to keep my name in the headlines," Paul explained, "because, I don't know, you just go through a phase of wanting to be up there in the limelight. But I'm going through a phase now where I don't wanna be in the limelight."[3]

Now he wanted what he came to Scotland for—peace and quiet, time to think. Paul had flown to Scotland on October 22 with his wife of just over seven months, Linda Eastman McCartney, their two-month-old daughter, Mary, and Heather, Linda's daughter from her first marriage (whom Paul adopted shortly after marrying Linda), hoping to get away from reporters and photographers, the other Beatles, and the staff at Apple, the Beatles' supposedly utopian company. Over the past year, Apple had been transformed into a spider's web of machinations, negotiations, and emotionally fraught battles with the other Beatles.

Looking back over the last 12 months, the Beatles seemed almost bipolar to Paul. They had released *The Beatles*, the eponymous double-LP better known as the *White Album* and had recorded two more albums and a couple of singles. During this same period, though, they had engaged the American businessman Allen Klein to manage them, and Apple, over Paul's vehement objections, and instead of Paul's choice, the upscale New York lawyers—and, not incidentally, his father- and brother-in-law—Lee and John Eastman. Klein had negotiated a substantially improved contract with EMI and Capitol Records, but thanks to squabbling between Klein and the Eastmans, and the Beatles themselves, they had lost bids to acquire Northern Songs, their music publisher, and NEMS, the management firm founded by their late manager, Brian Epstein.

Getting control of Northern Songs and NEMS would have been financially significant for the

Beatles: in both cases, percentages of their composing royalties and record sale income that were paid to others would instead remain in their pockets.

But all that paled beside their main source of pain for Paul. What he and only a few others knew was that the Beatles were finished—or at least, that was John Lennon's seemingly implacable view, and since unlike most bands, who could replace a member and carry on, the Beatles could only be those four guys. The death rumors were proof of that: inherent in it was the belief that instead of trying to carry on without their supposedly departed bassist, they had drafted a look-alike to preserve the impression that all was well.

Paul was in Scotland to tend to the psychic wounds that those battles left. So far, that tending took the form of anesthetizing himself with whisky and marijuana, which meant that the other major task at hand—sorting out his next chapter—was on hold. His funk was understandable: he had been a Beatle his entire adult life and being a part of that globe-striding phenomenon—the biggest, most beloved stars of the musical world—was not like holding a normal job. So the band's disintegration over the past year, and now its apparent collapse, felt like the earth evaporating under his feet.

Given the venom flowing through the corridors of Apple over the past year, he couldn't say he was surprised. And yet, *Abbey Road*, released on September 26, 1969, showed the Beatles at the height of their powers, sounding as together as a band could sound. There were those rich vocal harmonies on John's 'Because' and 'Sun King,' and the symphonic heft of the 'The End,' with its three-way exchange of guitar solos, and its charismatic drum break—both firsts for the Beatles on disc. And there was that exquisitely harmonized, philosophical finale: "*And in the end, the love you take is equal to the love you make.*" This was not the sound of a group on the verge of breaking up.

But that sound was a performance—an illusion. When the red recording light was on, the Beatles' musical connection was magical. That much they all admitted, even at their angriest. But outside the studio, Paul's relationships with John Lennon and George Harrison had frayed, especially when the future of the Beatles and Apple were discussed. There had even been a tense encounter between Paul and Ringo Starr, with whom everyone got along.

And then, on September 16, ten days before the album's British release, John announced that he was leaving the Beatles. "THE END," Paul declared in his diary—the two words, written in large, ballooning letters and flanking an Apple motif—before a scheduled dinner date with talent manager and friend Justin de Villeneuve, and his model girlfriend Twiggy Lawson.[4]

John had been saying things like that all through the year, and until now, everyone thought he was just being John—provocative and happy to shock. They had all walked out at one point or another. Ringo quit in frustration during the sessions for the *White Album*, in 1968, but was coaxed back. George quit in January, during the sessions for a television special and album, provisionally titled *Get Back*. He also returned, but only after John and Paul agreed to redress several festering grievances. And though Paul never actually quit, he had walked out on sessions in fits of pique on a few occasions.

But this was different. John was, more than ever, a wild card, someone who did as he wanted—and what he wanted, now, didn't involve his old friends from Liverpool. A keen observer of John and his moods in the 12 years they had known each other, Paul knew it was *possible* that John might change his mind again, and he held on to that for a while, as did the others. But John seemed to mean it this time; in fact, he seemed energized by his decision. All four agreed to say nothing publicly for a few months, until a lucrative new contract with EMI was ratified.

Having hightailed it to Scotland to get away from all that, the last thing Paul needed was a reporter quizzing him about the Beatles' business issues or their future plans. He was even less interested in discussing the idiotic "Paul is dead" rumor—although the rumor's upside was that it distracted reporters from getting to the real news.

This combination of circumstances taxed Paul's long-standing ability to project an image of friendliness and accessibility. Though the others had soured on the scrutiny that the Beatles' fame had brought them, Paul had always been comfortable with it. Under better circumstances, he took a different view of the Beatles' fame.

"It's what we wanted, for Christ's sake," said McCartney. "We came from Liverpool. We wanted to get out of Liverpool, number one—get out of the sticks, as we then perceived it. Get where the action is. Get famous. Get rich. And when that happens to you, it's very difficult to turn 'round and say, 'No, that's not what I meant.' We *wanted* to become legends. If you could get everything without the sort of overkill of the legend, maybe it would be better, but you kind of have to accept it as it's squeezed out of the tube.

"If you were that good, as the Beatles were, and if you were that interesting, as the combination of our four talents was, if you were that diverse—Lennon, McCartney, Harrison, Starkey*—and if you had the chemistry we had, you've got to expect to be picked over. I don't see too many bad sides to it. It certainly is what I set out to achieve. So having achieved it, I think it would be churlish to say, 'Oh, I don't want it.'"[5]

This public, gregarious side of Paul reasserted itself within seconds of hurling his bucket of kitchen slop at Spencer.

"They went away, and I thought, 'They've got a picture of me throwing a bucket; this is not what I want in my life,'"[6] explained McCartney.

He knew instantly how he would look if Spencer's photographs were published. Unshaven. Unkempt. Angry. Hungover. Maybe even a bit unhinged. And he knew that no matter what he was going through, this was not the Paul McCartney that he wanted the public to see.

He watched Spencer and Bacon hoof it toward the property line for a moment, then hopped into "Helen Wheels," his light blue Land Rover and caught up with them. By way of apology, he explained to the now wary Spencer and Bacon that he had come to Scotland for necessary and long overdue private time, to which, he was sure they'd agree, he was entitled. But he could offer a deal: Bacon could have a brief interview, and since Paul was not up for a photo session just then, he promised to provide *Life* with some family shots taken by Linda. In exchange, Spencer would hand over the compromising exposures in his camera.

Spencer surrendered his film, with its shots of an enraged Paul and a flying bucket. Bacon got her interview. And within a few days, a package of Linda's photographs arrived at *Life*'s New York headquarters.†

———— ➤ ————

The fraught state of the Beatles and Apple was far from Bacon's mind when she conducted her interview. Mostly, she wanted to know what he made of the "Paul is dead" rumor, and how he explained some of the more vivid clues sprinkled through the Beatles' post-*Revolver* singles and albums, all supposedly a sub-rosa confirmation of Paul's demise.

---

* The other Beatles rarely referred to Ringo Starr by his real name, Richard Starkey, except privately or in legal documents.

† *Life* published the photos, credited to neither Linda nor Spencer, but to Robert Graham. In an unpublished comment in an August 2008 interview with the author Peter Ames Carlin, Spencer (who died in February 2009) said he had no idea why Linda was not credited, or who Robert Graham was.

The rumor had started on September 17, when the Drake *Times-Delphic*, the campus newspaper at Drake University, in Iowa, published a front-page story by Tim Harper, that began:

"Lately on campus there has been much conjecturing on the state of Beatle Paul McCartney. An amazing series of photos and lyrics on the group's albums point to a distinct possibility that McCartney may indeed be insane, freaked out, even dead."[7]

Harper was not especially informed about Paul; he referred twice to his marriage to "Jane Eastman," conflating Linda with Jane Asher, Paul's girlfriend from 1963 to 1968. But he detailed some of the clues, and though the piece itself had no immediate national traction, a copy of the *Times-Delphic* made its way to Detroit, where on October 14, WKNR radio host Russ Gibb took an on-air call from a listener who said he had heard reports that Paul had died, and cited clues from Harper's piece.

By then, *Abbey Road* was in the shops, and Fred LaBour, a music reviewer at the University of Michigan's campus newspaper, the *Michigan Daily*, included a few new clues in his review of the album. Gibb read those on his show too. Soon reports of the discussion reached New York, where on October 21, WABC disc jockey Roby Yonge devoted much of his late-night show to the rumor and clues—until he was pulled off the air and summarily fired for irresponsibly spreading an unverified rumor and, as the station's switchboard operators could attest, creating hysteria.

But the rumor took on a life of its own, as Beatles fans with overactive and perhaps chemically enhanced imaginations began cataloging clues. Some were in plain sight, on the Beatles' record jackets—not least on the cover of *Abbey Road*, in which the Beatles, traversing the crosswalk outside the EMI Studios, were said to represent a funeral procession—John Lennon, dressed in white, was the preacher; Ringo Starr, in a suit and tie, was the undertaker; Paul, barefoot and out of step with the others, was the deceased; and George Harrison, in jeans, was the gravedigger.

Although the Beatles described the cover of *Sgt. Pepper's Lonely Hearts Club Band* as the fictional Pepper band and its many illustrious fans (including wax effigies of the Beatles circa 1964, from Madame Tussaud's) gathered in a park before a concert, the picture had been interpreted by many as a crowd of mourners gathered around a grave festooned with flowers that spell BEATLES. Under the last three letters of the group's name is a floral design that looks uncannily like Paul's left-handed Höfner bass. Indeed, the wax Beatles, looking down at the supposed grave, look particularly glum.

Flip the album over, and you find the four Beatles in their Pepper outfits, and the lyrics to the album's songs. Paul's back is turned to the camera, and George's right index finger points to the line "*Wednesday morning at five o'clock*," in the lyrics to 'She's Leaving Home,' supposedly the hour of Paul's fatal accident. And in the internal portrait of the group, a patch sewn onto Paul's left sleeve—a souvenir from a Beatles tour stop in Toronto, bearing the letters OPP, for Ontario Provincial Police—was widely misperceived as saying OPD, for "officially pronounced dead." And on the *Magical Mystery Tour* album, Paul is seen wearing a black carnation, where the other Beatles' carnations are red.

Among the aural clues, John's slowed-down, out-of-left-field *"cranberry sauce,"* in the coda of 'Strawberry Fields Forever' was said to be Lennon saying, *"I buried Paul."* The *White Album* was chock-full of hints, starting with Lennon singing *"here's another clue for you all, the walrus was Paul,"* in 'Glass Onion'—the walrus being, clue catalogers claimed, a Viking death symbol. Lennon's *musique concrete* soundscape, 'Revolution 9'—in reality, a portrait of society imploding during the revolution under discussion earlier in the album, in 'Revolution 1'—was repurposed as a sound-painting of Paul's fatal crash.

Backward masking made one of its first appearances in popular culture as well. Played backward, the repeated *"number nine"* at the start of 'Revolution 9' sounded uncannily like *"turn me on dead man,"* and John's mumbling at the end of 'I'm So Tired' was heard, if played backward, as *"Paul is dead, man—miss him, miss him, miss him."*

It was all a stunning study in how anything could seem to mean anything else, and how rumors, however flimsy, travel quickly, expanding along the way. At Apple, the staff was puzzled and a bit amused, but the reports left Derek Taylor, Apple's spokesman, spending his days issuing bemused denials and telling journalists who wanted to speak with Paul that he was on holiday with his family and did not want to be disturbed.

When Bacon asked about specific clues, Paul shot each down in a single, dismissive sentence. "I was wearing a black flower because they ran out of red ones . . . I was walking barefoot [on *Abbey Road*] because it was a hot day."[8]

The interview was so brief that Bacon wrote it up as if it were a prepared statement, just four uninterrupted paragraphs cobbled from Paul's responses—no questions, no description of Paul's farm (apart from an italicized note at the top, saying that Bacon had "waded through a bog in Scotland" to reach it), no independent observations, just Paul at his driest, sounding drained, bored, and humorless. *Life* published it as a sidebar to a longer story, "The Magical McCartney Mystery," by John Neary, who listed some of the clues, and quoted Louis Yager, the president of the Is Paul McCartney Dead Society at Hofstra University, stepping back from the idea his society was formed to explore: "We originally thought he was dead. But that's too emotional. We all ought to sit back and analyze this rationally."[9]

But there was something else in Bacon's piece, something more important than refuting the death rumor. Painting himself as a would-be recluse who just wanted to hang out with Linda and the kids, Paul let some big news slip, in an understated, matter-of-fact way.

"I have done enough press for a lifetime, and I don't have anything to say these days. I am happy to be with my family and I will work when I work. I was switched on for ten years and I never switched off. Now I am switching off whenever I can. I would rather be a little less famous these days. I would rather do what I began by doing, which is making music. We make good music, and we want to go on making good music. But the Beatle thing is over. It has been exploded, partly by what we have done, and partly by other people. We are individuals."[10]

Bacon had a scoop on her hands—"the Beatle thing is over"—and she seems not to have seen it. The bombshell went unnoticed by *Life*'s editors, as well. Had they understood its implications, they'd have spiked the death rumor story and made the Beatles' breakup the lead. Readers did not pick up on it, either: there are no references to the statement in the letters columns of the issues that followed, or in contemporaneous publications.

How did such momentous news get past everyone? Perhaps readers were confused by the fact that it immediately follows Paul's assertion that "we want to go on making good music." Or possibly, "the Beatle thing" was taken to mean Beatlemania, in the touring moptop sense, although that hardly needed saying, in November 1969, more than three years after the group's last tour. Nor does that interpretation explain the sentence that followed—"It has been exploded, partly by what we have done, and partly by other people."

So Paul was alive—it was the band that was dead. Once *Life* hit the newsstands, the clues were available, in plain sight, in black and white. You didn't have to read them backward or allude to Viking myths and symbology. And no one noticed.

———

It was about the ways "the Beatle thing" was exploded—not to mention how and by whom—that Paul was obsessing at High Park. In the weeks following John's announcement, Paul was angry, depressed, and bitter. To say that being a Beatle was the only life he'd known was not *literally* true—he'd had other ambitions as a child (being a teacher, for one), and he'd worked other jobs as a teenager. But the intensity of the experience turned everything before the Beatles into mere backstory. He was 15 when he joined the group. Now he was 27.

Paul later compared the Beatles' breakup to being sacked from a job—a comparison for which he took considerable criticism, given that the out-of-work laborers to whom he compared himself usually lacked the kind of golden parachute he had. But focusing on the financial implications inherent in such a comparison ignores the emotional depth of Paul's sense of loss. The Beatles *had* been his job, certainly, and creating music with the group gave him his primary sense of purpose.

But he was also mourning the loss of a unique community of friends with whom he had been close since adolescence, and who were the only three people on the planet who shared the pressures of Beatlemania. It was a group that had become so tightly knit and lived in such a sharply defined bubble of exclusivity that outsiders, including those who worked with them professionally, found their bond almost frightening.

"Individually, each of the Beatles was great to be with," recalled John Kurlander, a fledgling EMI engineer at the time of the *Abbey Road* sessions. "They were funny, warm, friendly—really a delight. If there were two of them, that was also great. If there were three, it could be a little dicey, but generally, it was fine. But when all four were together, they closed ranks, and it would be horrible. It didn't matter how any of them had treated you on his own; when all four of them were in the room, everyone else was treated as an outsider."[11]

Now that relationship was gone, and with it, Paul's internal compass and sense of self-worth.

"It was a barreling, empty feeling that just rolled across my soul," Paul said of this period. "And it was . . . I'd never experienced it before. I really was done in for the first time in my life. Until then, I really was a kind of cocky sod. It was the first time I'd had a major blow to my confidence.

"When my mother* died [when I was 14], I don't think my confidence suffered. It had been a terrible blow, but I didn't feel it was my fault. It was bad on Linda. She had to deal with this guy who didn't particularly want to get out of bed and, if he did, wanted to go back to bed pretty soon after. He wanted to drink earlier and earlier each day and didn't really see the point in shaving, because where was he going? And I was generally pretty morbid. There was no danger of suicide or anything; it wasn't that bad. Let's say I wouldn't have liked to live with me. So I don't know how Linda stuck it out."[12]

Deep within that pain and anger, but buried to the point where he could barely access it, was the knowledge that the path forward was through music. He doubted, at the moment, that he could work alone, but the evidence was otherwise: though all the songs he wrote as a Beatle were credited Lennon-McCartney, the reality was that most of the time, the two composers wrote on their own. Paul had also written a number of songs for other artists, and at the end of 1966, he wrote soundtrack music for *The Family Way*, the 1967 Boulting Brothers film, starring Hayley Mills. He recorded demos of his songs, with no help from his bandmates, and the fact that he was the only Beatle on the recording of 'Yesterday' led the group's producer, George Martin, to briefly consider releasing the track under Paul's name, rather than as the Beatles. There were tracks on the *White Album* that were Paul on his own, as well.

Moreover, he was arguably the most skilled instrumentalist among the Beatles. He was a peerless bassist, who rarely stuck to chord roots and traditional patterns; as far back as 'All My Loving,' he turned his lines into strands of counterpoint, as arresting as a song's melody. As a guitarist, though much of the world didn't know it, since the Beatles' album credits rarely mentioned who played the solos, he contributed some of band's most virtuosic playing, including the stinging solo on lead guitarist George Harrison's 'Taxman.' And if he lacked the sense of almost compositional

---

* Paul's mother, Mary Patricia McCartney, née Mohin, was born on September 29, 1909, in Liverpool, and died there on October 31, 1956, of breast cancer.

finesse that Ringo brought to his drumming, he was an able drummer, heard in that role on several tracks, including 'Back in the U.S.S.R' and 'The Ballad of John and Yoko.'

And then there was his flexibility as a singer. He was the one, among the Beatles, who could best carry off a wistful ballad like 'Yesterday' or 'I Will,' but he was also a top-drawer rock 'n' roll belter, who sizzled during performances of 'Long Tall Sally' and 'Helter Skelter.' A measure of that versatility was the fact that he recorded both the gentle 'Yesterday' and the high-energy 'I'm Down,' with its Little Richard–like screamed vocal line, at the same June 14, 1965, recording session.

Although he was unaware of it at the time, validation of his stature in other corners of the musical world arrived at Apple just as the McCartneys left for Scotland. On October 22, a telegram with a tantalizing offer landed on the desk of Peter Brown, for many years an associate of Brian Epstein, the Beatles' manager, and now Apple's managing director:

```
WE ARE RECORDING AN LP TOGETHER THIS WEEKEND IN NEW YORK
STOP
HOW ABOUT COMING IN TO PLAY BASS STOP . . .
PEACE JIMI HENDRIX MILES DAVIS TONY WILLIAMS[13]
```

Brown responded on Paul's behalf, saying that Paul had just left London for a holiday in Scotland.

Well into the Scottish trip, Paul remained disinclined to undertake the internal inventory of his musical strengths that Linda was trying to push him toward. But Linda understood that it was up to her to get him to embrace those strengths and move on. It was a task outside her experience, let alone her comfort zone: Who marries a Beatle with the expectation of having to nurse his psyche back to wholeness because the band imploded?

Moreover, she had Heather and Mary to take care of, and while the newborn Mary would be oblivious to the drama taking place, Heather needed to be shielded from the dark vortex engulfing her stepdad, as Linda worked to extract him from it.

"I was very scared," Linda said. "I didn't want to give up, but it was a mess, it was unreal, and I had to handle this all by myself. There was no choice. I had to try. We had two children, we'd just been married a year [sic] and my husband didn't want to get out of bed. He was drinking too much. He would tell me he felt useless. I knew he was torturing himself, blaming himself for the break-up, and I was sure that he could get beyond it, but if he didn't believe in himself, what could I do? I could only try, that's all I could do. Let me tell you, my hands were full."[14]

Paul and Linda married at the height of the Beatles' business mayhem, on March 12, 1969, in a low-key ceremony at the Marylebone Registry Office, in London. Paul's family was sparsely represented; only his brother, Michael,* who was pursuing his own performance career under the name Mike McGear, was on hand. There were two representatives from Apple—Mal Evans, the Beatles' longtime assistant, and Peter Brown, who Paul had asked to be best man when Mike's train was delayed, before Mike hotfooted up the steps of the Registry office to take that ceremonial role instead.

None of the other Beatles attended. Just as Paul and Linda were exchanging vows, George was being arrested for drug possession at his own home. He attended the reception. John and Yoko were in the studio completing their second joint LP, *Unfinished Music No. 2—Life with the Lions.* And Ringo Starr was filming *The Magic Christian*, with Peter Sellers. No other Beatles were present eight days later, when John married Yoko Ono in Gibraltar.

Linda Louise Eastman's background was utterly different from Paul's working-class childhood in Liverpool. She was raised in Scarsdale, New York, an affluent suburb, 30 miles north of New York City.

Her father, Lee Eastman (born Leopold Vail Epstein), was born in 1910 to Louis and Stella Epstein, Russian-Jewish immigrants. Leopold grew up poor, but worked his way to an education at Harvard University, and became a lawyer with many clients in the arts and show business. Her mother, Louise Sara Dryfoos Lindner, was from a wealthier family of German-Jewish immigrants who settled in Cleveland; Linda's grandfather, Max Lindner, was the founder of the Lindner Company, Cleveland's largest women's clothing store. Louise Eastman died on March 1, 1962, at age 50 (Linda was 18), in a plane crash.† (Losing her mother under such tragic circumstances left Linda with a lifelong fear of flying.)

By 1939, when their son, John,‡ was born, Leopold had changed the family name, as many upwardly mobile American Jews had done in the 1930s, the better to sidestep the currents of open anti-Semitism in American culture. Now known as the Eastmans, the family continued to grow: Linda was born on September 24, 1941, and had two younger sisters, Laura, born in 1947, and Louise, born in 1948. John Eastman followed in his father's footsteps, taking his law degree at New York University, and joining Lee's firm, then known as Eastman and DaSilva.

"My father was a Harvard man, my mother was a Smith girl," Linda said of her parents. "My brother and sisters went to Stanford University and Smith College, the best universities in America. I barely got out of high school. I was a typical 1950s rock and roll kid, not academically bright.

---

* Peter Michael McCartney, Paul's younger brother, and only sibling, was born in Liverpool on January 7, 1944.

† Louise Eastman was among the 95 people who lost their lives on American Airlines Flight 1. The jet, bound for Los Angeles, suffered an autopilot malfunction, rolled over, and crashed into Jamaica Bay two minutes after leaving Idlewild Airport, in New York.

‡ John Eastman died of pancreatic cancer on August 10, 2022. He was 83.

When my mother was killed in an air crash, I left home and I think it was to get away from my father's sadness."[15]

After briefly attending Vermont College, Linda transferred to the University of Arizona, in Tucson. Still uninterested in school, she developed a passion for horses, and an interest in photography that led her to take a course with the prominent photographer Hazel Larsen Archer. It was also in Arizona, on June 18, 1962, that Linda married Joseph Melville See Jr., a geologist. Their daughter, Heather, was born on the last day of that year.

The marriage did not survive long; by 1964, Linda had returned to New York with Heather (she and See divorced on October 18, 1965), where she took a receptionist job at *Town and Country* magazine for $65 (£24) a week. It was barely enough: her rent was $180 (£64) per month.[16] The shortfall could have been covered by the $200 (£72) monthly alimony called for in the divorce settlement, but Linda has said that she refused these payments. Caring for Heather alone gave Linda focus and determination to build a better life for the two of them.

"She was a brilliant single mother—completely together," Heather explained. "She would get me to school, go and do a full day's work, get me back home, make sure I had eaten. I was very lucky."[17]

Alongside her job at *Town and Country*, Linda began freelancing as a photographer, improving her skills by watching her sometime boyfriend, David Dalton, at his own photo shoots. Dalton, a writer as well as a photographer, was an editor at *Hullabaloo*, a youth culture magazine. When Linda pocketed an invitation, addressed to an editor at *Town and Country* who was not a rock fan, to a Rolling Stones press event on June 24, 1966—the Stones invited the press to join them on a yacht, the *Seawolf*, as they announced their fourth North American tour—Dalton told her that if she got some good shots, he would buy them.

As it turned out, the Stones' press handlers decided to allow only one photographer to board the *Seawolf*, and they chose the inexperienced Linda, who filled rolls of film with shots of the Stones, collectively and individually. Suddenly finding herself with a monopoly on photos from the floating news conference, Linda not only made her first sale, to Dalton and *Hullabaloo*, but was able to sell shots to all the newspapers and teen magazines that covered the event, many of which rewarded her with additional work. (In the course of the shoot, she also agreed to a date with Mick Jagger.)

"I was the only one who got pictures, so they got in every magazine and after that I quit my job and people started giving me freelance work. Groups would call and say, 'Can you take our pictures?' Or Elektra would call and say, 'Would you take Tim Buckley?' I took pictures of Jimi Hendrix the first time he came in."[18]

One editor who instantly piggybacked on Dalton's provisional assignment was Danny Fields,[*] the managing editor of *Datebook*. Linda and Fields also began a long-lasting friendship that day. When Fields left *Datebook* to become a publicist at Elektra Records, he hired her to shoot some of the label's artists, and more importantly, he introduced her to Jann Wenner, who was about to start *Rolling Stone*, a new rock publication that promised to look at the music more seriously than the teenybopper magazines that dominated the American pop music press. Linda's photographs of Cream were published in *Rolling Stone*'s first issue.

Over the next few years, Linda photographed virtually every top-flight performer in the rock world, from the Dave Clark Five, Herman's Hermits and the Animals, to Simon and Garfunkel, Jim Morrison, and Frank Zappa. Jimi Hendrix selected one of her photos for the cover of *Electric Ladyland*. Hendrix's British and American labels ignored his request, but the American edition included 31 of her black-and-white shots in the inner gatefold.

She also became a regular at the Fillmore East, where she could be found most weekends, photographing bands in performance.

"She was one of the three girls who used to hang out in my office," remembered John Morris, the Fillmore's managing director. "She and Blair Sable, who wrote for *Vogue*, and Robin Richmond, who wrote for *Time*. I knew Linda pretty well. On occasion, they invited bands over to the house to have fun, and a couple of times, Linda called me and said, 'Can you come up and rescue me?' I'd rescue them and chase whoever it was out the door. We had a nice relationship."

By then, Linda had become friendly with someone in the Beatles' circle, Peter Brown, who she met, along with Brian Epstein, when they were in New York on business.

"There were four or five guys that I knew very well, who lived in New York," Brown explained. "They were all gay, and I was, so we all hung out together. And Linda sort of attached herself to us because she thought they were cool, which they were. So we got to know each other, and I liked her a lot."[19]

In mid-May 1967, she flew to London to photograph bands for *Rock & Other Four Letter Words*, a book by the rock journalist J. Marks, for which Linda provided most of the photographs. One of her first stops was Brian Epstein's NEMS office in Albermarle Street where, portfolio in hand, she dropped in on Peter Brown, hoping to arrange a photo session with the Beatles. Brown asked her to leave her portfolio with him for a couple of days.

"I thought they were great pictures," Brown said, "and the most interesting were of the Stones on the yacht. There was a picture of Brian Jones, a very lovely picture. I was very close to Brian,

---

[*] A fascinating character in the American musical world, Fields (born Daniel Feinberg on November 13, 1939) moved from *Datebook* to publicity jobs at Elektra Records, where he was responsible for the Doors' early publicity, and Atlantic Records. He also managed the Stooges and later (in 1975) the Ramones; their relationship is commemorated in the Ramones' song 'Danny Says.'

and very fond of him, and I thought, 'I want this picture.' So when Linda came back to pick up her book, I said to her, 'I have to tell you that I've stolen one of the pictures, and obviously you have others, so I hope it doesn't matter.' She said, 'The one of Brian sitting on the bench?' I said, 'How could you have known that—there are dozens and dozens of pictures?' And she said, 'Oh, I just figured.' I thought, 'This woman is very interesting.'"[20]

Brown told her she would have an opportunity to photograph the Beatles on May 19 and handed her an invitation to the press party that Brian Epstein was hosting to celebrate the impending release of *Sgt. Pepper's Lonely Hearts Club Band*. As it turned out, Linda met Paul four days earlier, at the Bag O' Nails, a hangout for the Beatles and other bands.

Again, Brown was on the periphery. He and Paul had a business meeting on May 15, after which, Paul proposed going out for an early dinner.

"So, we went to the Bag O' Nails," Brown said, "and at the other end of the restaurant was Linda and a girlfriend. She came over to say hello, and I said, 'Great to see you—do you know my friend, Paul McCartney?'"[21]

Paul's telling of the story typically omitted Brown's introduction, picking up with a second encounter later that evening. By then, Brown had left, and Paul stayed on to hear a set by Georgie Fame and the Blue Flames. Linda remained as well and was by now sharing a booth with members of the Animals, whom she knew from photo shoots in New York. Paul spotted the attractive blonde, in a black-and-white blouse, and struck up a conversation, inviting her to join him and a group of friends, including the singer Lulu, who were about to leave for another club.

"I would always tease Paul," Brown said, "asking 'Why are you denying the fact that I introduced you to your wife?' And he'd say, 'No, no, no—I met her, nothing to do with you.'"[22]

Linda joined Paul's party that evening, stopping first at the Speakeasy, then back to Paul's house at 7 Cavendish Avenue for a nightcap. She did not stay long, knowing she would see him again at Epstein's *Sgt. Pepper* bash; her photos from that party are classic images of the Beatles from that time. But as she later estimated, she spent less than an hour with Paul in those first two encounters, with other people present in both cases.

Their flirtation would resume a year later, in May 1968, when Lennon and McCartney flew to New York to announce the formation of Apple at a news conference at the Americana Hotel, and in a handful of television interviews. Paul and Linda spent several afternoons together during that visit, meeting at the East 73rd Street apartment of Nat Weiss, Brian Epstein's and the Beatles' American lawyer and, as it turned out, a friend of Linda's father.

When Paul returned to the United States to give a presentation about Apple at Capitol Records' annual sales meeting in Los Angeles, on the weekend of June 21, he phoned Linda in New York and invited her to come out to see him. That weekend in Los Angeles was the real beginning of their romance: Linda arrived just after his convention appearance, and they remained locked in Paul's private bungalow at the Beverly Hills Hotel for much of the weekend, flying back to New York together on the 24th.

At the time, Paul was engaged to the actress Jane Asher. Not that he was in any way exclusive—certainly not when the Beatles were touring, and not even when he was in London, despite Jane's having moved into his house in 1966. Jane's acting career took her out of town frequently, and though that was a point of contention between them—Paul's preference was that she give up her career and become a more traditionally domesticated wife and mother—her absences also suited Paul, a man in his twenties with a seemingly insatiable libido and a black book full of willing playmates.

During much of the time he was romantically linked to Jane, he also carried on a clandestine relationship with Maggie McGivern, a model and actress he met in 1965, when she was working as a nanny to Marianne Faithfull's son. Their romance outlasted his relationship to Jane; although he saw her only sporadically, he didn't break it off until a couple of days before he married Linda.

There were others, too. When Jane was appearing in an out-of-town production, in July 1968, Paul invited Francie Schwartz, an American working at Apple, to stay with him at Cavendish Avenue, if not quite move in. Schwartz had arrived in London in June, clutching a screenplay she had written, and hoping Apple would produce it, but became one of McCartney's conquests instead. Jane's unexpected early return, and her discovery of Paul and Francie in bed, led to the end of Jane and Paul's relationship, although it was clearly the last straw rather than the cause.[23] On July 20, Jane announced that the engagement was off during an interview on *Dee Time*, a BBC interview show hosted by Simon Dee; Paul, who was unaware that she'd be discussing it, watched the interview at his father's home in Gayton, Cheshire, with Francie at his side.

During their brief relationship, though, Francie got to see a darker, more troubled side of Paul than the public knew, and a preview of the alcohol-fueled depression he would suffer when the Beatles broke up. One incident she has cited took place in Gayton, the same weekend as Jane's Simon Dee interview. Slipping out of a family party, Paul ended up at a relative's pub, obsessing about the amount of money he had given to his family, and about how people, including Francie, treated him as Beatle Paul, rather than as Paul McCartney, the person.

"You don't treat me like me," she quoted him complaining. "You treat me like *Him*, and I'm not him, y'know, I'm just me." Francie persuaded him to return to his father's house, but it was rough going, as she later described it. "When we got back to Birkenhead, where his father's house beckoned sleepily, he sobbed hopelessly on the floor, while the dogs climbed all over him. His trouble was deep, and nothing I said could set him straight."[24]

McCartney's worries, at the time, extended far beyond financial support for his family. There were tensions during the ongoing *White Album* sessions. Apple Corps was hemorrhaging cash. And although Francie didn't know it, the time Paul had recently spent in New York and Los Angeles with Linda Eastman, not long before hooking up with Francie, was increasingly on his mind.

By August 1968, Francie was out of Paul's life as well, and Linda was on her way into it. That month—possibly even before Francie left—Paul called Linda in New York and asked her to fly to London and stay with him. She did not go immediately—she had an assignment in Los Angeles for *Mademoiselle*, which included photographing Aretha Franklin, Judy Collins, and others. And she needed to arrange for someone to babysit Heather, who was about to start her first year at Dalton, a prestigious Manhattan prep school. She left for London in mid-September.

But it was not yet clear to him that Linda would be the one to bring his bachelorhood to an end. In early September—between Francie's departure and Linda's arrival—he hired a private jet and flew to Sardinia with Maggie McGivern, also taking along a male cousin and his girlfriend.

"We were lying on the beach just being young and in love," Maggie later recalled. "Paul turned to me, smiling, and out of the blue he just said, 'Have you ever thought about getting married?' I said, 'Yes, I suppose, one day . . .' and I thought nothing more of it. Looking back, it was obviously the wrong answer. When I said one day I meant in six months, maybe, but not never. But Paul was always slightly insecure and probably saw me as such a free spirit that he thought I was never going to settle down. . . . I suppose that, with the pressures of fame, Paul was craving security.

"I suppose I assumed we would end up together, but at that time I was just enjoying it all. In the Sixties, there was so much going on that I didn't have time to sit and think about the future. I suppose that, with the pressures of fame, Paul was craving security."[25]

After the trip, Paul and Maggie went their separate ways, which was normal in their relationship. The next time she telephoned him at Cavendish Avenue, Linda picked up, and Paul was evasive.

Linda was many things Jane Asher was not. Much as she enjoyed her career as a photographer, she didn't live for it, and could happily pursue it avocationally if she didn't have to make her living doing it. More importantly, she was an enthusiastic cook and a devoted mother, and happy to take on the domestic role that was so important to Paul. Yet she was also a free spirit. She could be stylish when the occasion demanded, but for the most part, her taste in clothes, and her disinclination to wear makeup, were rooted in a hippie sensibility that treated fashion as less important than comfort and practicality.

And, as Paul discovered in long hours of talking and playing records, she knew rock and roll—not only its contemporary manifestation, as performed by the bands and artists she photographed, but its historical roots. The music she loved as a girl, in the 1950s, was the same music that, half a world away, shaped Paul's tastes and fueled his dreams—and while Paul drank in early rock from afar, Linda saw his early heroes in concert.

"I'd take the subway into New York City and go to the old Brooklyn Paramount," she recalled, "where they had Buddy Holly, Little Richard, Fats Domino, the Everlys—everybody on one bill. In fact, I saw Chuck Berry do 'School Days' for the first time. He said, 'Well, I wrote this one last night, you know, I'll try it out.' And he's just 'Up in the morning and out to school.' I was mad on rock 'n' roll music when I was a kid."[26]

When Paul brought Linda into the Beatles' circle, during the *White Album* sessions, she was struck by the group's apparent disunity—or at least, the four musicians' independence from one another.

"When I got there, everybody seemed to be into their own songs. I mean, George would come in with his song and then he'd do what he wanted to do . . . John would be in one studio doing his song and Paul and Ringo would be in another studio. I think you reach a point when you have to be yourself rather than, well, 'John's the tough one; Paul's the sweet one; George is the . . .' You've got to have your own whole personality."[27]

As a photographer, she could not have asked for better access, and her photos of the Beatles during their final year capture fascinating, intimate glimpses of the band at work.

But her absorption into the Beatles' world also brought an introduction to the downside of being a Beatle's girlfriend—namely, the fans.

The girls who were virtually encamped outside both the EMI Recording Studios and 7 Cavendish Avenue had mixed feelings about Jane Asher—the complaint was that she could be snooty, but more to the point, she was with Paul, and they weren't. They took an immediate dislike to Linda, some for the same reasons they disliked Yoko: Whatever their issues with Jane, she—like John's first wife, Cynthia—was at least a proper Englishwoman. Linda was an American, and as one fan pointed out, in a piece of unaired news footage from the day of their wedding, she was Jewish. She was also a divorcée. And she dressed unfashionably.

"The press didn't seem to like me very much," Linda reflected, "and I had a bit of trouble with the people who lived outside our house. There were a lot of kids there who had hung around for years and kind of resented it when I moved in."[28]

The fans could be brutal. At one point, after not having been at Cavendish for some time, the McCartneys returned to find "Fuck Linda" painted on a wall across from their house. And the opprobrium was not always silent.

"When he first brought Linda back," one fan told a *Sunday People* reporter, "we would all stand in a row and scream abuse at her."[29]

From London, Linda kept in touch with Heather by phone and introduced her to Paul during these chats. By mid-October 1968, though, she felt it was time to bring Heather to London. Eager to meet Linda's family, and to see Linda in her own milieu—to get a sense of the texture of her life in New York—Paul flew to New York with her.

For Paul, there was another attraction, too. He had seen New York only as a member of the Beatles, so he never really saw it at all. Without the media alerting people that Paul would be in town, he had an opportunity to move through the city for a couple of weeks virtually unnoticed.

Linda took him all over Manhattan. They went to Harlem to see the Apollo Theater, to Greenwich Village clubs to listen to jazz, and to art museums and galleries on the Upper East Side. They walked through Central Park, browsed through secondhand shops on the West Side, and popped into neighborhood bars and restaurants. They also had a few evenings with celebrity friends—Bob Dylan, for one.

They almost always took the subway on these jaunts. When Linda went to appointments of her own, Paul explored New York alone, except when school was out, in which case Paul was Heather's minder. On at least one occasion early in the visit, Linda left Paul and Heather on the subway, assuring Paul that Heather knew the way to their apartment on East 83rd Street.[30]

One thing immediately caught Paul's eye in Linda's L-shaped, one-bedroom apartment: the framed, autographed manuscript of 'Linda,' a song that Jack Lawrence composed when his attorney, Lee Eastman, suggested that Lawrence write a song for his baby daughter.[31] 'Linda' was a hit for Buddy Clark and the Ray Noble Orchestra in 1946; other artists who recorded it include Frank Sinatra, Willie Nelson, Dale Hawkins, King Curtis and the surf duo Jan and Dean.

After years of being confined to hotel rooms as a touring Beatle, Paul found the visit thoroughly liberating.

"I had a full beard at that time, so I wasn't very recognizable as Beatle Paul. Linda would take me to thrift shops, and there was a big army and navy store that we went to on 125th Street where I picked up an old uniform with a couple of stripes, so I looked a bit like a Vietnam vet. I looked like the guy who would mug you rather than the guy you'd want to mug, so I was really quite safe on the streets with that disguise. Nobody was going to see me as me and nobody really knew Linda. She wore very casual jeans and a beige jacket, like a photographer, so it wasn't a couple of very rich people walking round New York, it was more the kind of people you'd want to avoid.

"It was good, we were very free consequently. We had a lot of fun together, getting together the first time. We were exploring each other and our surroundings and there was a lot of fun attached to that, just the nature of how we are. Our favorite thing really is just to hang, to have fun. And Linda's very big on just following the moment. We used to spend a lot of time just wandering around, going into bars, literally just exploring New York. New York has this great literary ambience. You could imagine Jack Kerouac or Norman Mailer or Dylan Thomas or William Burroughs hanging out in these little places rather than at the Carlyle. We never went to the Carlyle, it would more likely be Flanagan's Bar."[32]

The visit was precisely the immersion into Linda's world he wanted, and their interactions with Heather showed him that Linda could be the partner he was looking for—smart, funny, independent, and also a homemaker.

"She would have to take Heather to school, pick Heather up from school, cook the meal, certain things as a mother she had to do," he said, speaking about Linda in action. "And her womanliness impressed me, I'd never actually known anyone who was quite so much a woman. Linda was a very good mother. One of the things that impressed me about her was that she had the woman thing down, she seriously looked after her daughter. It seemed very organized to me, in a slightly disheveled way. She was very kind-hearted too, so that finished it all off. And there was this slight rebelliousness . . .

"I've been pretty open with most of my relationships, but with her I could be completely open. Our relationship has always been like that, painfully open sometimes. Sometimes you don't want the truth, but it's always a good idea."[33]

Paul returned to London with Linda and Heather on October 31, 1968. Within a week, all three, plus Paul's large sheepdog, Martha, were on another two-week road trip, this time to High Park, which Linda had not yet seen, with a stop in Liverpool.

———→

Stewing at his Scottish bolt-hole just a year later, Paul took the reports of his death no more seriously than anyone else in the Beatles' circle. But though he was able to shrug off the rumor, it had an unfortunate resonance at that moment. For all of 1969, after all, Paul had definitely been the odd man out, among the Beatles, in both creative and business matters. Now he was being portrayed in the media as possibly an impostor, a look-alike stand-in, when as he saw it, he had become the Beatles' driving force during the period when he was supposedly dead.

Although John Lennon formed the group and was, in the early days, its acknowledged "leader," he had been tuning out in recent years. Paul, by contrast, was constantly engaged with finding new things for the Beatles to do.

That the Beatles needed someone to hold the reins was clear by the end of 1966. John, by his own admission, had become lazy: he was happy to stay at home getting high, reading and making absurdist audio plays in his home studio. George was busy exploring Indian music and spirituality, and though Ringo was happy to work, if the others wanted to just hang out, that was fine too. *Somebody* had to come up with fresh ideas, because the Beatles' musical progression and sense of independence made it impossible to continue on the path they had taken so far.

Their experiments with electronics and Indian instruments had effectively closed the door on live performance—as had their experience on their bruising 1966 summer tour. They had experienced riots in Tokyo, led by nationalists who considered Western pop music at the Budokan to be sacrilege. After they failed to turn up at a televised children's party thrown by Imelda Marcos, the First Lady of the Philippines, their security detail was withdrawn, leaving them to get through the Manila airport by hiding among a group of nuns. And in the United States, Bible Belt fanatics were burning Beatles records because John asserted that the Beatles were more important to kids than Jesus.

Touring had lost its thrill by then, anyway. When the writer Alun Owen, in his script for the Beatles' first film, *A Hard Day's Night*, had Paul's grandfather complain, "*So far, I've been in a train and a room, a car and a room, and a room and a room,*" he captured the experience of Beatles themselves. Making films quickly lost its charm, too. They enjoyed making *A Hard Day's Night*, but *Help!* was a slog, and they refused to settle on a script for a third film, to which their December 1963 contract with United Artists obligated them.

In fact, the whole business of being the Fab, lovable moptops was something they were eager to jettison. Their music had moved beyond that—*Rubber Soul*, in 1965, and *Revolver*, in 1966, were musically and lyrically more sophisticated and varied than their earlier albums (although McCartney's 'Yesterday,' on the *Help!* album, pointed the way forward). And without tours or films to arrange, Epstein had little choice but to leave the Beatles to their own devices, since they had made clear early on that creative decisions were their province, not his.

Sensing what was, in effect, a creative management deficit, Paul sprang into action, coming up with projects that would keep the Beatles fresh, and would keep their fans guessing what they would be up to next. He did not regard this as usurping John's role as the group's de facto leader, but rather, as a logical extension of the success the Beatles had with songs he wrote on his own—from 'All My Loving' to 'Yesterday,' and 'Eleanor Rigby.' He had come a long way since his time as a junior partner in John's Quarrymen; now he was John's equal, not his subordinate, and if John was losing interest, Paul was happy to step in with ideas.

His first, early in 1967, was to propose that the Beatles adopt the persona of a fictional band as a way to put distance between themselves and their moptop past. Thus *Sgt. Pepper's Lonely Hearts Club Band* was born, the album being an idealized vision of the Pepper band in concert.

The follow-up, *Magical Mystery Tour*—a sparsely scripted film project—was Paul's idea, too, and was meant to expand the Beatles' horizons and bring filmmaking (not to mention the world of spontaneous "happenings") into their toolkit. That it proved a flop didn't faze McCartney: perhaps the 1967 audience was not ready for the Beatles' dreamy and druggie zaniness (which itself was undercut by the BBC's decision to screen it in black and white), but the film's time, Paul insisted, would come.

He next proposed promoting the *White Album* with a handful of live concerts, the Beatles' first public performances since August 29, 1966, when they closed their American tour at Candlestick Park, in San Francisco. They had filmed promotional clips for 'Hey Jude' and 'Revolution' at Twickenham Film Studios on September 4, 1968, singing live to an instrumental backing track, with an audience on hand. The performances were not truly live, but the Beatles enjoyed them and began discussing a limited run of concerts.

By early November, Jeremy Banks, Apple's photographic coordinator, told *NME* that the Beatles were planning three concerts at London's Chalk Farm Roundhouse in mid-December, shows that would highlight tracks from the not yet released *White Album*.[34] A week later, Derek Taylor told the paper that the concerts would be filmed,[35] probably by Michael Lindsay-Hogg, who had directed the 'Hey Jude' and 'Revolution' clips, as well as the Beatles' promo films for 'Paperback Writer' and 'Rain,' and their 1963 and 1964 appearances on the popular music show *Ready Steady Go!* But at the end of the month, Paul told an interviewer that negotiations with the Roundhouse had broken down, and that the concerts would be at the end of the year, perhaps in Liverpool.[36]

Soon, the concert idea gave way to a new plan of Paul's—a television special, to be directed by Lindsay-Hogg. The group would be seen rehearsing new material, as a prologue to a televised concert featuring their new songs. The live recording of that performance would be the group's new album.

Executing this idea required a change of musical direction. Until now, the trend had been toward greater complexity and sophistication, but for the new project, the Beatles would have to write songs they could perform live. That suited John, who was always one for upsetting the status quo, even if it was a status quo he helped establish.

"John actually said to me, 'I don't want any of your production crap on this,'" George Martin remembered. "I said, 'What do you mean by that?' And he said, 'This is going to be an *honest* album.' I said, 'Okay, what do you mean by *that*?' He said, 'We're not going to do any overdubbing. We're going to do it live. We're not going to do any editing. We're going to make sure it's good. We're going to do a fantastic album, where we really play beautifully.' John was very druggy, at that stage, and you never knew what he would be saying or doing. It was like living on the edge of a volcano."[37]

Before long the project acquired a philosophically appropriate working title, *Get Back*, after one of Paul's new songs.* This would be, as Derek Taylor put it in his advertising copy for the release of 'Get Back' as a single, "The Beatles As Nature Intended."

There was tremendous hubris involved. At the sessions scheduled to begin on January 2, 1969, the Beatles were to bring in their new songs, choose those to be included in the show and get them

---

* The project would undergo many changes by the time it was released, after long delays, in May 1970. The television special became a theatrical film, and both it and the album had a new name, *Let It Be*, after another of Paul's songs from the sessions.

concert-ready by January 19 and 20, when the shows were penciled in. The rushed schedule was dictated largely by the fact that Ringo was about to begin filming *The Magic Christian*, with Peter Sellers. That they had not played a public concert in nearly two and a half years hardly gave them pause. The fact that they had not settled on a venue was an issue as well, not least because John seemed most excited about the prospect of a live performance when the details were the most fanciful.

When Lindsay-Hogg pushed the idea of an outdoor amphitheater in Sabratha, Libya, for example, the others demurred, but John lit up. "Not only would we be doing it physically, making the album there, but it takes all that weight of, 'Where's the gimmick? What is it?' Cause, you just—you know, *God's* the gimmick. And the only problem we've got now is an audience. I'd be thrilled to do it, you know—just timing it so the sun came up, just on the middle eight, and all that!"[38]

There were other problems, too. Used to recording late in the day, and often through the night, the Beatles were unhappy turning up early in the morning to rehearse. They also disliked the large, acoustically imperfect soundstage at Twickenham studios, where the rehearsals were filmed. George, in particular, was uneasy having their rehearsals—including disagreements that, for any band of strong-willed musicians creating new work were an inevitable part of the creative process—filmed and recorded.

George also objected to Yoko Ono's constant presence at John's side, as she had been through the *White Album* sessions. Paul tried to be the peacekeeper here, arguing that if this was what John wanted, they had to accommodate it. Still, Paul found Yoko, an avant-garde artist who, in the early 1960s, had presented a series of legendary loft concerts in New York, more than a little intimidating.

"It simply became very difficult for me to write with Yoko sitting there," he explained. "If I had to think of a line I started getting very nervous. I might want to say something like 'I love you, girl,' but with Yoko watching I always felt that I had to come out with something clever and avant-garde. She would probably have loved the simple stuff, but I was scared. I'm not blaming her, I'm blaming me."[39]

Seven days into the sessions, on January 10, George decided he'd had enough and walked out of Twickenham, casually mentioning that he was quitting the band. When Lindsay-Hogg wondered how they would handle George's absence at the final concert—he proposed saying that George was ill—John nonchalantly suggested that if he didn't return the following week, they'd call Eric Clapton, the star guitarist of Cream (and before that, the Yardbirds), who George had brought in to play the solo on 'While My Guitar Gently Weeps,' during the *White Album* sessions.

Clapton, asked if he had heard about Lennon's suggestion, refused to take it seriously, except as an indication of the state of the Beatles' relationship.

"That would have been a quip, on John's part," Clapton explained. "You see, you get involved with a gang like that—they were a tough bunch of lads, you know. They'd say things like that to hurt one another. They could be very spiteful to one another. Because they were *trapped* with one another. I got used as a pawn quite a lot after George had asked me to do ['While My Guitar Gently Weeps']. John would use me to get back at Paul or get back at George. You didn't really *know* that this was going on, but you could presume it."[40]

George soon returned, but only after getting the others to agree to moving the sessions from Twickenham to the not yet completed studio in the basement of their Apple offices, at 3 Savile Row, and to give greater consideration to his songs, which Lennon and McCartney tended to overlook in favor of their own.

During the final two weeks of sessions, the Beatles bore down on the new songs, polishing and recording them. They even had a closing concert of sorts, with the "electric" songs filmed on Apple's rooftop on January 30, and songs that required a piano, or acoustic guitars, filmed the following day in Apple's basement studio.

Paul, curiously, chafed against the plan to play on the rooftop, arguing that anything less than a full-fledged public concert made Lindsay-Hogg's film little more than a documentary about making an album. The Beatles, he argued, should be doing something special, and unpredictable. But in the end, he climbed up to the roof with the others and gave his all.

Ringo then headed off to his sideline acting job, Lindsay-Hogg went off to edit his three weeks' worth of film, and the recordings were put in the care of Glyn Johns, who had undertaken a nebulous role as part engineer, part producer, and was now given the task of sorting through them and assembling an album.

By October 1969, when Paul was wandering the hilly terrain at High Park, the Beatles had recorded and released another album, *Abbey Road*. But the *Get Back* project remained on the shelf, its final form not yet decided. How its future would be determined if the Beatles were no longer a going concern was unclear. For the moment, though, it was not high on Paul's list of worries.

2

ROTTEN APPLE

—

Usually, Paul's trips to High Park were joyful, and though there seemed little chance of joy in the October 1969 visit, Paul found the clear, chilly air and the sense of earthy remoteness irresistible.

At the western edge of his Scottish estate, where Kilchenzie Burn marks the boundary of High Park, the endless landscape and panoramic view over the North Channel to the tip of Northern Ireland and the islands of Islay and Jura (both well known for whisky-making) transported Paul back to carefree days living at 72 Western Avenue, where the McCartney family resided from August 1947 to September 1950. Here in Speke, where his mother, Mary, worked as Municipal Midwife on a still expanding housing estate, five-year-old Paul enjoyed endless summers.

"As a kid I always used to like nature. I lived on the outskirts of Liverpool," Paul remembered. "For us kids, two miles down the road you could come into countryside, it was Lancashire rather than Liverpool. It was actually a village called Hale, which is a very pretty little village with thatched roofs, it was a real little paradise. And there were millions of woods around us, there was the Dam Woods, there was this place called the Chinese Farm where we always used to go, this place called Dungeon Lane. So, there was all these great romantic places for kids[1]. . . . To me that's precious. As a kid I used to get down on my hands and knees in dandelions and stuff. It's a huge part of my being all that stuff—smelling soil, and woods—it was a huge part [of my childhood]. When I grew up I thought I'd left it behind. I thought it had all gone. But I started to realize that if I got down on my knees in a field I'd smell it again; because it hadn't gone, it was just I'd moved away from it."[2]

Linda hoped that a reminder of the past would give him the calm he needed to bring the future into view. But it wasn't working. For Paul to catch one of the farm's most peaceful views—the mist rolling in from the sea, with the sound of the wind, the birds, and the distant ocean as its soundtrack—he would have to get up early and climb the hill, and that wasn't in the cards this trip.

Paul first visited High Park on June 14, 1966, accompanied by Jane Asher. A fairly ramshackle

sheep farm on a 183-acre estate, it had been granted to Archibald Campbell, the ninth Earl of Argyll, in 1667, and remained in the family until 1955, when the Duke of Argyll sold it to Charles Noel Beattie, a London barrister. Beattie had left the farm in the care of John and Janet Brown, who had managed it since 1947; it was their decision to retire that led Beattie to put the farm on the market.

High Park was ideally situated to become Paul's equivalent of Superman's Fortress of Solitude—a place he could go to escape the media fishbowl the Beatles had lived in since 1963. It was sufficiently difficult to reach and impossible to find without the help of a local guide, making a visit so onerous that, Paul hoped, most reporters and fans would give up the search.

Not that Paul was very secretive about it. Chatting with a couple of reporters backstage at a Beatles appearance on *Top of the Pops*, only two days after that first visit, he described the farm, mentioning its name as well as the two nearest towns, Campbeltown and Machrihanish.[3]

In Campbeltown, news of Paul's imminent purchase was splashed across the front page of the Campbeltown Courier, a week later, under the headline, "King Paul of Kintyre."[4] Several subsidiary stories described Paul's visit—one noting that he and Jane had flown to the area in a chartered

Piper Comanche and booked a taxi to the farm. On that trip, Paul used the pseudonym Taylor (most likely borrowed from Alistair Taylor, Apple's "Mr. Fixit," who would have made the arrangements). Having tried unsuccessfully to persuade the Browns to stay on as tenant farmers, Paul advertised (also pseudonymously) for their replacements. Beattie's sale of the farm to Paul for £4000 ($11,200)[*] was finalized and recorded on November 23, 1966.

Without chartering a private plane to Machrihanish, a typical journey to High Park begins with a flight from London to Abbotsinch airport (now Glasgow International) in Paisley, on the outskirts of Glasgow, followed by a four-hour drive down the Kintyre peninsula. The route takes you through the Trossachs National Park, around Loch Lomond—a wilderness of evergreens and remote villages, with heather, bracken, and huge fern trees everywhere you look. At night, streetlights are few and far between; the area is pitch-black but for lights from distant villages and other cars.

For the final stretch of the journey, the rugged coastline lies to the right, with the waves of the North Channel—that bridges the Irish Sea with the North Atlantic—crashing against the rocks and pebble beaches; to the left, hundreds of small farms dot the landscape.

Campbeltown sits on the southern tip of the Kintyre peninsula. It is a humble fishing town, with a distillery, a handful of pubs, a few shops, two hotels, an art deco cinema and Victoria Hall, where bands and touring discos entertain the locals. The town's focus is the harbor, where fishing boats come in, along with occasional cargo ships servicing the forestry industry. Small ferries move between the nearby Hebridean islands. The fishermen's wives work in the town's shops and hotels; the fishermen, when they're not at sea, are in the pubs. The mist, at sea level, can engulf the town and surrounding hills at times. Hours later it's gone.

About a mile before you reach Campbeltown, you pass a dirt track, just off the main road, and to the left. This rustic lane, with a surface made of mud and large stones, is not suitable for most vehicles; it was to navigate this perilous track that Paul bought "Helen Wheels."

Follow the road and you reach the top of the hill where High Park Farm sits, just over the crest, surrounded by open fields where Paul's 90 sheep and smaller herd of beef cattle graze. At the bottom of the hill's other side is a small loch that swells during the rainy seasons. And not far from Paul's doorstep is a megalith—a standing stone, placed there by the area's inhabitants millennia ago.

No other human habitation is visible from the house—nothing but green, rolling hills, tall evergreens, and low stone walls. Paul's nearest neighbor, at the time he bought the property, was Ian McDougall, whose Skeroblinraid (or Low Park) is three-quarters of a mile down the hillside. The other neighboring farms were High Ranachan and Low Ranachan.

Paul's feelings about High Park were complicated.

---

[*] The purchase price of £4000 is given in the Land Registry document (Wt. 73360).

"When we got married, Linda started saying 'Let's go to the countryside, let's get out of London'—anything to get out of London. And she's crazy, Linda, she'd say, 'let's get lost, try and get lost'—which was the total opposite of any other bird I'd ever met, who was always saying, 'don't get lost, whatever you do' . . . So she was like a new adventure for me, bring on back this nature thing.

"Anyway, I had the farm in Scotland, which I didn't really like. I'd never fixed it up at all, I just bought it and wondered why there were dead sheep in the field—you'd go, 'Ugh, dear me, that one's dead!' I never realized that the owner was responsible. It never occurred to me that if you didn't want them dead, you had to look after them. So, Linda said to me, we could do the place up, take down the old sheds and redo all the walls. Because the state it was in was exactly how it had been left, a real little hill farm that was quite down at the heel."[5]

To "do the place up," Paul built a homemade couch, cobbled together using wooden boxes from Sharps Express potatoes and a thrown-on mattress. Other furniture was bought secondhand in Campbeltown, as was an electric stove.

Paul made some cosmetic improvements, too, giving his front door a colorful paint job, with a psychedelic design at the center. Using wood from a demolished silo, he built a cupboard for the stone-floor kitchen and painted it electric blue. On some visits, he devoted time to painting and sketching, hanging the results in the kitchen. Otherwise, the house had two bedrooms and a bathroom (but no bathtub).[6]

Paul also took up the old farmer's tradition of building a wall, extending it gradually. But Paul's wall was unlike the standard model. He would put down a layer of wet cement, then push bottles into it—whatever he had around, from soft drinks to wine and whisky—before adding another layer of cement and bottles. Each visit, he added a bit more. The result was a cement wall that light passed through.

Linda's reaction to High Park was delight.

"Scotland was like nothing I'd ever lived in," Linda said. "It was the most beautiful land you have ever seen; it was way at the end of nowhere. To me it was the first feeling I'd ever had of civilization dropped away. I felt like it was in another era. It was so beautiful up there, clean, so different from all the hotels and limousines and the music business, so it was quite a relief, but it was very derelict."[7]

——

On November 5, 1969, the McCartneys observed the near 400-year-old—and somewhat morbid—tradition of Guy Fawkes (or Bonfire) Night on the hillside outside High Park. Deconstructed pallets and old floorboards were stacked high, and an effigy of Guy Fawkes—an old pair of jeans and pink jumper stuffed with straw—was placed at the top ready for the ceremonial torching. Guy

Fawkes, along with several coconspirators, was arrested on November 5, 1605, for trying to blow up the House of Lords in London, and as Paul lit a match under the jean-wearing effigy of Fawkes, he was likely considering his own desire to light a powder keg under the Beatles' contractual ties with Apple and watch their contract with Allen Klein smolder to ashes.

Paul had hoped the emptiness of the Scottish landscape would clear his head of thoughts of Apple, the Beatles' business concerns, and the sometimes Machiavellian, sometimes weirdly inept maneuvering involved in sorting them out. But it was impossible not to obsess. The fact was, Paul had made a crucial transition over the past year. No longer the teenage Liverpool rocker who didn't know or care much about business, he was now 27, married, and a father to two young girls. He was ready to uphold his responsibilities, and Apple, for better or worse, was his means of doing so.

It was also a symbol of everything he had built over the last decade, and it was in danger of vanishing into the pocket of a business manager hired by the other Beatles despite his opposition. Once so promising a project, Apple was now the main source of anxiety and turmoil in Paul's life, leaving him torn between wanting to walk away from it, and wanting to take back his share of control over its operation.

Apple's roots stretch back to the Beatles Ltd., a company Brian Epstein founded in 1963, and to Beatles and Company, which Epstein incorporated as a tax shelter for the Beatles on April 19, 1967, mainly as a result of a windfall due the Beatles from Epstein's renegotiation of the group's contract with EMI Records.

"Brian had taken 18 months to renegotiate the new EMI contract," Peter Brown explained. "With the original contract, Brian would have signed anything, just to get them on a label, so it was not very lucrative. When it came to an end, the Beatles were the world's most famous group, and Brian was intent on getting a decent contract, not only for new recordings, but looking back. So the money coming to them was a fucking mountain, I mean, an enormous, enormous amount. And in those days, the income tax for individuals was something like 85 percent. So what we ended up doing was starting this company, and we agreed with the accountants that 80 percent of the money coming from EMI would go into this company, and the other 20 percent would be divided equally among the Beatles. And that's how we proceeded."[8]

The Beatles wanted their new enterprise to have a less corporate name than Beatles and Company. "And everyone, sort of, hesitated about a name," Brown recalled. "Then Paul, in his efficient way goes, 'Let's go through the alphabet.' And he said, 'A is for Apple.' And he didn't have to go any farther."[9]

Beatles and Company became Apple Music Ltd. on November 17, 1967, and on January 12, 1968, they tweaked the name further, changing it to Apple Corps Ltd. By then, the idea of having a company began to evolve. It occurred to the Beatles that their company could be the hub not only of their own creative projects, but of projects of all kinds, which they would underwrite and market—not only in music, but also in every aspect of the culture they cared about.

There would be a record label, to which they could sign anyone they deemed worthy. There would be a film division, too, and a marketing arm that would sell everything from hip clothing to new electronic devices. Anything that appealed to them, they reasoned, would appeal to others too. René Magritte's painting "The Listening Room" inspired the company's green apple logo.

Exactly how they would run it came together in Paul's mind during the Beatles' February–March 1968 visit to Rishikesh, India, to study Transcendental Meditation with the Maharishi Mahesh Yogi. Paul remained in Rishikesh for five weeks, and immediately upon his return to London, on March 26, he began mapping out how the company should be set up, who should work for it, and other fundamentals.

"We wanted Apple to have a more charitable feel to it than big businesses," Paul explained. "We always felt there was an ugly side to capitalism and Apple was going to be the pleasant face of capitalism. And it was going to be 'business with pleasure' was one of our ideas at the time, and one of the dreams."[10]

Peter Asher, who had known Paul since 1963—apart from the fact that his sister, Jane, was Paul's longtime girlfriend, Paul's London headquarters until March 1966 was a room on the top floor of the Asher home—remembered long, philosophical discussions with Paul about what Apple could be.

"Apple was very substantially Paul's invention," recalled Asher, who soon became Apple Records' director of artists and repertoire. "I remember sitting with him in Cavendish Avenue, hearing him explain how he wanted Apple to work, and what it was going to accomplish. He wanted to build a company that would treat artists with the respect that he felt record companies didn't really give them. That was true at the time: record labels didn't treat rock and roll with any respect whatsoever. They regarded it as a sort of necessary evil to pay for classical music, or their electronics business, or whatever.

"What I noticed about Paul was the detail and energy of all his ideas—musically, businesswise, socially, and everything else. He was a man of extraordinary intellectual dexterity and ideas, and that, I think, remains true."[11]

When John and Paul announced Apple and its plans at a New York news conference, on May 14, 1968, Paul's idea of using the company to protect artists while giving the freedom they needed to complete their projects was high on the philosophical agenda.

"It's a business concerning records, films, electronics, and—as a sideline—manufacturing, or whatever it's called," John explained succinctly, if provocatively. "We just want to set up a system whereby people who just want to make a film about anything don't have to go on their knees in somebody's office, probably yours."

By the end of 1968, Apple was up and running, its record division naturally starring the Beatles, but also offering a roster of talented finds like the American singer-songwriter James Taylor, the Welsh folk singer Mary Hopkin, as well as a band of her countrymen, Badfinger, the Liverpool rocker Jackie Lomax, and the classical composer John Tavener. Ron Kass, who was lured away from Liberty Records to become director of the record division, also brought the label an already recorded but unissued album by the Modern Jazz Quartet and recorded a second with the group. The organist and singer Bill Preston was signed to the label, as was the R&B singer Doris Troy. And George Harrison signed on Ravi Shankar, as well as the Radha Krishna Temple. It was, in other words, a label that had everything—rock, pop, folk, jazz, soul, as well as Hindustani classical and devotional music.

McCartney was by no means an absentee boss. He played bass on 'Carolina on My Mind,' a track on James Taylor's eponymous album, in 1968. He also signed Mary Hopkin and produced both her debut single, Gene Raskin's 'Those Were the Days,' and *Post Card*, her first album. Paul also wrote Hopkin's second single, 'Goodbye,' for which he recorded a guitar-and-voice demo in his music room at Cavendish Avenue, calling in Richard Hewson to arrange it. At the session for 'Goodbye,' at Morgan Studios on March 1 and 2, Paul produced and played the lead acoustic guitar part, as well as bass, drums, and a brisk percussion part executed by tapping on his thigh.[12]

Apple's other divisions were decidedly less successful than its record label. The Apple Boutique, with clothing designed by the Fool, a Dutch artist collective, opened and closed in short order, with the Beatles deciding to give away the stock rather than hold a going-out-of-business sale. Apple Electronics, run by Alexis "Magic Alex" Mardas, a Greek television repairman and self-styled inventor who was tasked with building the Beatles a state-of-the-art recording studio (which he failed to do) and creating exciting gizmos for Apple to market (none of which materialized), was also a financial sinkhole.

Even in its day-to-day workings, Apple was supporting a lifestyle fit for the kings of pop, but alarming to the company's accountants. The building on Savile Row, which Apple bought in June 1968, had cost £500,000 ($1.2 million) and was lavishly furnished. Besides the money the company had wasted on Mardas's inept attempt to build a studio, Apple had spent £100,000 ($240,000) on a record-cutting lathe. Derek Taylor's press office was essentially an open bar, and Apple had a kitchen and staff, as well. Moreover, the Beatles personal accounts at Harrods and elsewhere were routed through Apple, and others on the staff found ways to charge hefty expenses to the company.

It was lovely if you could afford it, but the Beatles, despite their reputation for coining money, could not. As work on the *Get Back* project got underway in January 1969, Apple's accountants sent urgent word that the company was burning through money faster than it was coming in.

The Beatles all agreed that something had to be done. John proposed hiring a tough boss. His candidate was the Rolling Stones' manager and lawyer, Allen Klein.

Allen Klein began working as a business manager for musicians in 1960, when he was 29, building on experience he had gained working for an accounting firm during his student years at Upsala College, in New Jersey. The job involved auditing record companies, and what he learned about record industry accounting practices—specifically, the ways labels skimmed from the royalties due their artists—persuaded him that he could start an artist management business, with his skill at spotting record company mendacity and recouping plundered royalties as his selling point.

Klein quickly developed a reputation as a tough fighter who could spot chicanery in a label's ledgers at 50 paces. With the likes of Sam Cooke, Neil Sedaka and Buddy Knox on his roster, he quickly made a specialty of not only finding and recovering significant amounts of unpaid royalties, but also using his knowledge of this cheating as a lever to get his clients more favorable deals.

His connection to the world of British pop music began in 1964, when the record producer Mickie Most became a client, bringing with him his roster, which included the Animals, Herman's Hermits, Donovan and Lulu. By 1965, he had also taken over the American management of the Rolling Stones. It was Mick Jagger, in fact, who brought Klein to John Lennon's attention, telling him that Klein had negotiated a large royalty increase for the Stones from Decca Records.

That was a detail that irked Paul. John brandished Jagger's recommendation like a battle flag for Klein, yet he refused to heed Jagger's subsequent warning that Klein was less aboveboard than they thought. Once they began looking into their own finances, the Stones discovered that Klein had not only gained control of their publishing but had also bought the master tapes of their Decca recordings from their previous manager, Andrew Loog Oldham. Oldham, early in the group's career, had signed a deal with Decca whereby he owned the masters and leased them to the label. The arrangement gave him a 50 percent royalty on the Stones' recordings, the remaining 50 percent to be split by the band. Now Klein was receiving that 50 percent, and the Rolling Stones—and particularly Jagger—took the not unreasonable view that Klein had violated his fiduciary responsibilities to the band by not offering them the chance to buy out Oldham.[13]

This, McCartney argued, was the other side of Klein. Yes, he fought for his artists—but he also walked away with more than his fair share of the spoils, from which he would continue to benefit long after his managerial relationships ended.* Nor were the Stones the first to discover Klein's

---

* Klein's company, ABKCO, still owns the Rolling Stones recordings through *Let It Bleed* (1969), and CD compilations of hits by Sam Cooke, the Animals and Herman's Hermits have been issued either on the ABKCO label or bearing ABKCO copyright notices. ABKCO Records is a successor to Cameo-Parkway Records, which Klein also owned, giving him control of recordings by Chubby Checker, Bobby Rydel and other pre-Beatles hitmakers. Klein died in 2009; the company is currently run by his son, Jody Klein.

more self-serving side. Sam Cooke had come to a similar realization shortly before his untimely death, as had others.

Paul imagined things unfolding quite differently.

Linda's father, Lee Eastman, and her brother, John Eastman, were respected, experienced show business lawyers who represented the likes of the conductor Leopold Stokowski, the painter Willem de Kooning and the songwriters Hoagy Carmichael, Harold Arlen and Jack Lawrence.

At Paul's suggestion, the Beatles had engaged the family firm Eastman and Eastman as legal advisers. The Eastmans were, at that point, empowered to negotiate contracts for Apple, and to advise the Beatles on steps they could take to put Apple on a secure financial footing.

It was not lost on Paul that his relationship with the Eastmans might arouse, among his bandmates, the suspicion that he might receive favored treatment. George Harrison was quite direct on that point, in a radio interview with Howard Smith, on WABC-FM, in New York.

"You imagine that situation, if you were married and you wanted your in-laws to handle certain things. It's a difficult one to overcome because . . . well, you can think of the subtleties, you know. But he's really living with it like that, you see. When I go home at night I'm not living there with Allen Klein, whereas in a way, Paul's living with the Eastmans. And so it's purely . . . it's not really between Paul and us, you know, it's between Paul's advisers, who are the Eastmans, and our business adviser, which is Allen Klein."[14]

It would be unfair to say that Paul wanted the Eastmans, and only the Eastmans, to oversee the Beatles' affairs. He had, in fact, investigated other options. One was Dr. Richard Beeching, who in the 1960s reconfigured the financially troubled British Railways. Some found his methods draconian—he recommended closing about a third of the country's train stations—but his budget cuts saved £18 million (more than $43 million) per year.

It was decided that Lennon would be the point man, so he met with Baron Beeching at Apple's offices in November 1968.[15] But Beeching, after taking only a cursory glance at Apple's books, declared that the job was not for him. His advice to Lennon was that the Beatles should stick to making music—a wonderful twist on the admonition that John heard regularly from his aunt Mimi during his teenage years—"The guitar's all right, John, but you'll never make a living out of it."

John was so discouraged—and so freaked out by the possibility of everything he'd earned being swept away—that he gave a startlingly frank assessment of the state of Apple to Ray Connolly, of *Disc and Music Echo.*

"I think it's a bit messy and it wants tightening up. We haven't got half the money people think we have. We have enough to live on, but we can't let Apple go on like it is. We started off with loads of ideas of what we wanted to do—an umbrella for different activities. But like one or two Beatle things, it didn't work because we aren't practical, and we weren't quick enough to realize that we need a businessman's brain to run the whole thing. We did it all wrong with

Paul and me running to New York saying we'll do this and encourage this and that. It's got to be a business first. We know that now. It needs a new broom and a lot of people there will have to go. It doesn't need to make vast profits, but if it carries on like this all of us will be broke in the next six months."[16]

When Klein read Lennon's remarks, he saw a wide-open door. He had never made a secret of his desire to manage the Beatles. In 1964, he tried to persuade Epstein to wrest the Beatles away from Capitol Records, EMI's American affiliate, in favor of a deal with RCA, which Klein would broker. Epstein turned Klein down.

Klein had met Lennon in early December 1968, when he was in London for the taping of *The Rolling Stones Rock and Roll Circus*, in which Lennon performed with a supergroup that included him and Yoko, with Eric Clapton on guitar, the Stones' Keith Richards on bass, Mitch Mitchell, the drummer in the Jimi Hendrix Experience, and the classical violinist Ivry Gitlis. Klein had to content himself with an introduction and handshake, but the encounter was the furthest he'd reached into the Beatles inner sanctum.

Returning to London as soon as he read Lennon's *Disc and Music Echo* interview, Klein got a message to John and set up a meeting for January 26, 1969. That night, only eight days after John's public catastrophizing was published, Klein hosted John and Yoko for a macrobiotic vegetarian dinner—Klein had thoroughly researched his quarry—at the Dorchester Hotel.

Klein was a dogged researcher and arrived in London with a detailed overview of Lennon's background and tastes, experiences and attitudes. He was able to make his case in terms he knew Lennon would respond to—that is, without overtly making his case at all. He presented the meeting as just a matter of getting to know each other, a chance to explore common ground, like their passion for early rock, and their both having been abandoned by their parents. Klein knew the Beatles' music inside-out, and he had a clear understanding of the distinction between John's songs and Paul's. To Lennon, Klein was a kindred spirit.

By the time the meeting ended, at around 3:00 a.m., Klein wrote, and Lennon signed, a handful of letters informing Apple's accountants, EMI Records and Northern Songs—the company set up in 1963 by the publisher Dick James to oversee the Lennon-McCartney song catalog—that he had engaged Klein to look into his affairs, and that they should provide any cooperation or assistance he required.

The next day, during rehearsals at Apple Studios, he told the other Beatles that Klein now represented him, bigging him up in the process.

"I went there thinking, 'Oh fucking hell, well, I've got to see him. I put it off last time.' But I was sort of half-thinking all that time, you know, 'I keep hearing about him all these years, you know. So what? So, somebody says he's this or that, you know. . . .' But he . . . fuckin' hell, he knows about Isherwood [Beatles accountant], Bahamas [base of some Beatles finances], Strach [Beatles accountant] . . . Things that you can't believe, you know," John explained. "I said, 'He's going to look after me whatever . . .' Incredible guy. We [John and Yoko] were both just stunned."[17]

Within a couple of days, Klein had met with all four Beatles, and George and Ringo agreed that he should represent them as well. Only Paul demurred and his opposition grew firmer with every encounter.

For Paul, it was simply unbelievable that John, George and Ringo were unable to—*refused* to—look past Klein's studied veneer and see him as the gruff, fast-talking hustler he saw. John, Paul believed, was an easy mark for Klein. He had let his heart rule his head without considering the wider consequences and had made it far too easy for Klein to take control—in a single, supposedly preliminary meeting—of his business affairs.

"He's nothing more than a trained New York crook," was Paul's stark assessment. "To him, artists are money. To me, they're more than that. He has a very special gift for talking his way. Klein, so I heard, had said to John—the first time anyone had said it—'What does Yoko want?' So since Yoko liked Klein because he was for giving Yoko anything she wanted, he was the man for John. That's my theory on how it happened."[18]

But the objections Paul raised—and those raised by the Eastmans, in their meetings with the group, and to Klein's face—proved counterproductive. Lennon and the others defended Klein at every turn, and no matter how pointed Paul's criticisms were, they earned him nothing but hostility.

Concern spread through other precincts at Apple as well.

"Klein had a bad reputation from New York," Peter Asher recalled. "I'd heard about it from some people who worked for the Stones, and from some other friends who told me he was bad news. I was aware that Paul shared my feelings, although I don't remember talking to him about it a whole lot. I could well have told him that I'd heard bad things from New York. But there were others who thought he was good. He did get things done. And of course, Klein's argument was, 'Everyone's going to tell you I'm horrible, but the people telling you that are the record companies, and they're scared of me.' Or, 'People will tell you I'm a cunt, but I'm *your* cunt.' He was very good at disarming what he knew people were going to say."[19]

Klein's first move was to insinuate himself into negotiations in which the Eastmans were already engaged for the acquisition of Brian Epstein's Nemperor Holdings, which included the NEMS management firm. The Beatles held a 10 percent stake in NEMS; Epstein's majority share, upon his death, passed to his brother, Clive, who had nominally been part of the management team when Brian was alive, and was now managing director, and to his mother, Queenie. But Clive had little interest in running an entertainment company, and when he decided to sell, late in 1968, he offered the Beatles the right of first refusal.

John Eastman had shown the Beatles that it was in their interest to get control of NEMS, if

only because Epstein's company received a 25 percent management fee on the group's record royalties and would continue to do so until the end of their EMI contract, in 1976. Buying NEMS would put that 25 percent back into the Beatles' pockets.

Moreover, NEMS owned a stake in Northern Songs. Eastman had advised the Beatles to buy Northern Songs stock whenever possible, with an eye toward acquiring that company, as well. Here, too, buying Northern Songs would mean a substantial payday for the Beatles: as the publisher of the Lennon-McCartney team's songwriting output, Northern Songs took 50 percent (and more in some countries) of the royalties on the Lennon-McCartney songwriting catalog.

What ensued was open warfare between Klein and the Eastmans, with Klein objecting to the Eastmans' line of attack, and the Eastmans impugning Klein's business tactics and personal ethics, with the help of a stack of newspaper articles in which various financial misdeeds were alleged. Meanwhile, other suitors for both NEMS and Northern Songs—investors who saw the availability of these companies as a chance to tap into the Beatles magic, financially speaking—were making their plays. Klein's maneuvers also sowed distrust between Paul and the other Beatles.

In the Northern Songs fight, the Beatles biggest rival was Associated Television Corporation, Ltd. (ATV), the entertainment conglomerate run by the freshly knighted Sir Lew Grade. Grade had known Dick James since the publisher's days as a crooner whose 1950s Parlophone recordings were produced by none other than George Martin. James's biggest success as a singer was

'Robin Hood,' the theme song for a television series produced by Grade. When James started his publishing company, Dick James Music (of which Northern Songs was a subsidiary) in 1958, Grade bought a stake in the new venture.

"Dick James got his start in the music business through Lew Grade, and so [James] owed Grade a favor," explained Sam Trust, who was then head of publisher relations at Broadcast Music, Inc. (BMI), the performance rights organization, and would soon join ATV, "and Grade called it in."[20]

Grade made his move for the Beatles publishing while the Beatles' backs were collectively turned. On March 24, 1969, while both John and Paul honeymooned overseas—Paul was in New York, visiting Linda's family, and John was holding court from his bed at the Amsterdam Hilton—Sir Lew met with majority shareholder Dick James to discuss the possible sale. James had founded Northern Songs to handle the Beatles catalog in 1963 and took the company public in 1965.

Grade's ATV already owned 3 percent of the company's shares; James proposed to sell him a 32 percent stake, bringing ATV's total to 35 percent. Grade made the deal sound remarkably casual, describing it as having been "brewed up over a cup of coffee."[21] On March 28, Grade announced that ATV hoped to buy the company in its entirety, including the Beatles' shares. He had set aside a hefty £9.5 million ($22.8 million) war chest for that purpose, effectively starting a race with Klein to win control of the publicly held company by amassing 51 percent of its shares.

John and Paul were livid when they heard the news. So was George Harrison, who was so upset on his friends' behalf that he stormed into the offices of Dick James Music and asked James what he thought he was doing. James tried to shift the blame to the Beatles themselves, explaining that the public perception was that the Beatles were in trouble, and that he was afraid that a lack of confidence in the group's future would drive down the stock. Protecting his investment, he said, was a serious matter to him. To which George's angry response was, "It's fucking serious to John and Paul, is what it is."[22]

Klein quickly assembled a complicated plan that might have done the trick, but which required John and Paul to put up their shares as collateral. At a meeting on April 17, Paul refused to put up his shares, saying the Eastmans had advised him that Klein's plan was too risky. Klein then disclosed something he had discovered while perusing Northern Songs' shareholders list—that although John and Paul were given an equal number of shares when the company was founded, Paul had recently been buying up extra shares on his own.

John listened with astonishment that quickly turned to anger. As he saw it, he and Paul were equal partners, and Paul's undisclosed stock purchases were a betrayal, and a negation of the "all for one and one for all" pact that had existed between the Beatles from the start. George and Ringo agreed. In his defense, Paul argued that he had every right to invest as he saw fit, and that it made more sense to buy shares in Northern Songs than in another business.

The next day, John, George and Ringo signed a letter to Lee Eastman informing him that he was no longer authorized to act as the Beatles' or Apple's attorney. While recognizing that Eastman continued to represent Paul, they asked that all documents, correspondence, and files relating to the Beatles and their business interests be forwarded to Klein's ABKCO Industries, in New York.[23]

This was the charged backdrop when the Beatles and Klein gathered at Olympic Studios, on May 9, 1969, to hear engineer cum producer Glyn Johns's mix of the *Get Back* album. Earlier that day, John, George and Ringo signed a contract with Klein, giving him managerial control of Apple Corps Ltd. After listening to the proposed album, John, George, Ringo and Klein tried to persuade Paul to add his signature to the contract. Paul refused, raising several objections, not least Klein's demand of an across the board 20 percent commission, which Paul thought was at least 5 percent too high, given the Beatles stature.

Three signatures were enough, however, for the contract to take effect, so when it was clear that Paul would not be swayed, the others stormed out.

"It's more of a personal thing that's down to the management situation," George explained. "You know, with Apple—because Paul really, it was his idea to do Apple, and once it started going, Paul was really active. And then it got chaotic, and we had to do something about it and, when we started to do something about it, obviously Paul didn't have as much say in the matter. And then he wanted the Eastmans, his in-laws, to run it and we didn't want them. He's outvoted because we're a partnership where we all own 25 percent. If there's a decision to be made you have a vote, and if he's outvoted three to one and he doesn't like it, then it's really a pity. We're not trying to do what is best for Paul and his in-laws, you know."[24]

For Paul, this was a game-changing moment in his relationship with the other Beatles. Until now, the group had an all-or-nothing policy about decisions: unanimity, rather than a simple majority, was required. That changed when Apple's operating procedures were drawn up, and with Paul outvoted, the others proceeded without him.

As it happened, Glyn Johns was at Olympic that evening not only to play the Beatles his *Get Back* compilation, but also because he was producing the Steve Miller Band's *Brave New World* album. The project was close to complete—it was slated to be released in just over a month—and Miller planned to work alone that night. Walking into the studio moments after John, George and Ringo left, he found Paul still in the control room, intensely frustrated by the acrimonious meeting and its outcome, and venting freely to Johns. Paul liked Miller's first two albums, *Children of the Future* and *Sailor*, both released in 1968, and asked if he could sit in on Miller's session. Miller, delighted, readily agreed, and as Johns set up the microphones, Paul gave the American guitarist and singer some of the backstory.

"I thought, 'I'm just a little guy in this industry, but I have my own publishing, I own my own masters, but they have none of that,'" Miller recalled. "And now they are suggesting having Allen

Klein who is basically like a thief-as-manager. He's like an old-style music manager who is out to fleece the artist, so no wonder Paul is frustrated.

"Paul was an awesome musical presence. He was, like, 10 feet tall with music and it was everything: folk, rock, music hall, choral, it was all there."[25]

When Johns was ready to record, Miller picked up his guitar and Paul, to Miller's surprise, headed over to the drum kit. They jammed for a bit, and as Miller put it, "straight away I could sort of communicate with him.

"I told him about this song I was about to record, 'My Dark Hour.' And he said, 'Let's do it,' and it just sort of happened. He's on drums beating the hell out of them, and I'm on guitar, and then he plays bass and I'm on rhythm. We were popping tracks over and using techniques that the Beatles had developed for multitracking. Seven hours later and it's done, and he just sort of walks out the door."[26]

For Paul, the musical fruits of his session with Miller were eerily symbolic.

"That was the night we broke the Beatles. Really, that was the big crack in the Liberty Bell, it never came back together after that one," he later told an associate.[27]

Klein, empowered by his new contract, was intent on remaking Apple, and stanching the flow of money from its coffers. He swept through the offices like the Angel of Death, firing much of the staff, from division heads to secretaries, but—on the Beatles' instructions—sparing Neil Aspinall and Mal Evans, their longtime assistants (having formerly been their road managers).

Some Apple staffers, seeing the writing on the wall, quit before Klein could send them a pink slip. Peter Asher wrote a brief letter of resignation as soon as he heard that Klein would be in charge. Having signed James Taylor to Apple, and produced his eponymous album, Asher took Taylor with him—not difficult, since Taylor had become disillusioned with the disarray at Apple. Klein threatened to sue, but was talked out of it by Paul, with the support of the others, who argued that suing artists was not what Apple was about.

Through all this, the Beatles continued working together as a band. The *Get Back* project, now in the hands of Glyn Johns and Michael Lindsay-Hogg, was percolating slowly, but required their input. On July 19, all four Beatles attended a screening of Lindsay-Hogg's first rough cut, which ran about two and a half hours.

"A couple of days after we'd screened the rough cut," Lindsay-Hogg said, "Peter Brown called me and said, 'I think that went pretty well,' and I said, 'Yeah, I think it's pretty good, maybe we'll make it a bit tighter.' And he said, 'Don't you think maybe there's a little bit too much John and Yoko in it?' And I said, 'Oh, I'm not sure, I thought it was good,' and he said, 'Well, let me put it this way. I've had three phone calls this morning, saying maybe there was too much John and Yoko.'"[28]

At one point during the editing process, Paul thought it might be fun to give the film an experimental twist, suggesting to Lindsay-Hogg that it might be interesting if every fourth shot was shown upside down. "Well, we could," the director responded, "but I think it might be confusing to people. Why don't we look at it?" Lindsay-Hogg edited a short segment of the film as Paul proposed. On reviewing the sample, Paul immediately saw that it didn't work.

"It's a pretty fertile mind that Paul McCartney has," Lindsay-Hogg said of the incident. "Certainly, in terms of music, in terms of the songs he's written. But it's a restless mind, in a way, so he's got lots of thoughts, some of which he admits aren't all that good, but he likes to try them."[29]

Meanwhile, ad hoc recording sessions between February and May yielded the start of a new album. The Beatles kept their fans living in hope with the release of a pair of singles in quick succession—'Get Back' and 'Don't Let Me Down,' from the January sessions, and 'The Ballad of John and Yoko,' backed with George's 'Old Brown Shoe,' both recorded in April. After a break for holidays in June—Paul and Linda flew off to the Bahamas—the group reconvened, with George Martin at the helm, to complete the new album in sessions that ran from July 1 to August 25.

The Beatles considered naming the new album *Everest* and agreed to be flown to Mt. Everest to take the cover photo. But in the end, they couldn't be bothered. Someone suggested taking the photo on the crosswalk near the studio. Paul made a few rough sketches, and on August 8, with photographer Iain Macmillan perched on a ladder, the Beatles traversed the Abbey Road zebra crossing a half-dozen times, and just like that, the album had both a cover and a name, *Abbey Road*.

Martin and others in attendance characterized the *Abbey Road* sessions as energetic and friendly, but there were times when Paul's desire to direct the sessions, as he had done, on and off, since *Sgt. Pepper*, led to harsh words.

"I was beginning to get too producery for everyone," Paul admitted. "George Martin was the actual producer, and I was beginning to be too definite, and George [Harrison] and Ringo turned around and said, 'Look, piss off, we're grown-ups and we can do it without you fine.' People like me who don't realize when they're being very overbearing, it comes as a great surprise to be told."[30]

Three days after the sessions wrapped, Paul's private life took a new turn. On August 28, 1969, at 1:30 a.m., Linda gave birth to Mary Anna McCartney—named for Paul's mother—at the Avenue Clinic in St. John's Wood. With seven-year-old Heather already part of the household, fatherhood was not entirely a mystery to Paul. But having a newborn on hand was different, and he quickly found an efficient way to handle the demands.

"Mary was, of course, the first one born to us, and we brought her back from the hospital and put her in the cot in our bedroom. She was asleep and we were just about to go off when I heard 'hic, hic.' 'Oh no,' I thought, 'I'm not going to be able to make this.' So for the next night we managed to get hold of a night nurse. We had Mary all day until eleven, then the nurse would feed

Mary twice during the night. She did a really good job and by the time Mary was a few weeks old we didn't hear a thing from eleven to nine the next morning, she woke up starving and we'd had ourselves a good night's sleep."[31]

———

Some of the confusion Paul felt as he walked the dunes at Machrihanish in November 1969, Linda at his side with Heather in tow and ten-week-old baby Mary nestled inside his sheepskin coat, was to do with the oddly inconsistent approach John had taken to the Beatles in the weeks that followed the *Abbey Road* recording sessions—sometimes seeming to be planning for a collective future, sometimes wanting to put as much distance as he could between the Beatles and the next phase of his creative life.

John had made no secret of his desire to work on avant-garde projects with Yoko, to the point of suggesting that he and Yoko pursue some of their ideas within the context of the Beatles. That was a nonstarter for the other Beatles, although the Lennons had made some inroads during the *White Album* sessions. Yoko contributed vocals to 'Birthday' and 'The Continuing Story of Bunga-low Bill,' and though 'Revolution 9' was published as a Lennon-McCartney composition, a more accurate credit would have read, Lennon-Ono (with some help from George Harrison).

The fact was, Apple gave John ample leeway for projects with Yoko, and as Paul saw it, that should have been an ideal arrangement: Since November 1968 John and Yoko released *Two Virgins*, *Life with the Lions*, and *The Wedding Album*. They also completed several avant-garde films, and they performed publicly at the *Rolling Stones Rock and Roll Circus* (December 10, 1968); a Yoko concert at Lady Mitchell Hall, Cambridge University (March 20, 1969), and at the Toronto Rock and Roll Revival (September 13, 1969).

But John was also increasingly impatient with the Beatles' pop music format, and the "rules" that appeared to govern it. To him, the upside of all the hard work the Beatles had done—the long nights in Hamburg, and lunacy of Beatlemania, the claustrophobia of the touring years—was that they were now in a position where the norms of the pop music world were irrelevant. They could do what they wanted, and if that meant releasing an album full of music like 'Revolution 9' no one could stop them.

On September 9, John, Paul and George held a meeting at Apple to discuss their future and to air a few grievances. Ringo was hospitalized with stomach pains the previous day,[32] so the meeting was recorded for him. As it began, with Lennon evidently presiding, John brought up a proposal that addressed George's feeling, which had become acute by 1969, that his songs were consistently neglected in favor of John's and Paul's. Henceforth, their 14-song albums would include four songs each from John, Paul and George, and two from Ringo.

John then addressed the agreement under which he and Paul had worked since 1962, in which any song written by either of them was credited to Lennon-McCartney. They rarely collaborated anymore, and most fans could tell who wrote what. John proposed, with no objection from Paul, that their future songs be published under their individual names. Notably, Lennon made a point of saying that they had to find a way to announce this compositional de-linking in a way that would not lead to "Beatles Splitting" rumors.

After a bit more chat, including agreement on a plan for a new single, to be released around Christmas—John proposed that they each bring in their best new songs, and all choose the one to record—they turned to other matters, including George's development as a composer. Here, John found himself mediating between Paul, who argued that George's songs "weren't all that good" until *Abbey Road*, and George, who naturally defended his work, pointing out that the others had enjoyed his music all along. As a way of changing the subject, John brought up what he called Paul's "granny music," focusing on a comment Paul had made, to the effect that Paul himself wasn't that fond of the two songs that John particularly disdained, 'Ob-La-Di, Ob-La-Da' and 'Maxwell's Silver Hammer.'

"The thing is," John mused, "wouldn't it be better—because we didn't really dig them, you know—for you to do songs that you dug, and for 'Ob-La-Di' and 'Maxwell' to be given to people who *like* music like that—like Mary [Hopkin] or whoever it is that needs a song? Why don't you give them to them? The only time we need anything vaguely near that quality is for a single. For an album, we could just do only the stuff that we really dug. It just struck me, when I was thinking it over, it would be mad for us to put a song on the album that nobody really dug, including the guy who wrote it, just because it was going to be popular, you know? 'Cos the LP doesn't have to be popular, in *that* way. It just has to be an LP."[33]

Still, the meeting had been upbeat overall, and although Paul remained opposed to Klein, the group itself looked like it had a future. Yet when John proposed 'Cold Turkey' as the Beatles' next single, a couple of days later, he realized that not much had changed. Paul objected—and the others agreed—that its lyrics, about the horrors of getting off heroin, and the edgy dissonances of the guitar part (even in John's acoustic demo) did not suit the image the Beatles wanted to project.

John mulled over this when he flew to Toronto on September 13, having accepted an impromptu invitation to perform at the Toronto Rock 'n' Roll Revival, a daylong festival, on a bill with some of the Beatles' early heroes, like Chuck Berry, Little Richard, Jerry Lee Lewis, Bo Diddley, as well as contemporary stars, like Alice Cooper, the Chicago Transit Authority and the Doors. For the occasion, his band—to be billed as the Plastic Ono Band—included Yoko, Eric Clapton, Klaus Voormann and Alan White.*

It was a crazy idea, accepting a phone invitation on Friday for a concert on Saturday, halfway

---

* It was released on Apple Records as *Live Peace in Toronto* on December 12, 1969.

around the world, when you hadn't played a conventional concert set in public for three years and didn't have a rehearsed band, or a setlist. But given everything it had going against it, the concert went well, and it left Lennon energized and ready, at least for the moment, to get back on the stage. He also relished being the undisputed front man.

"I told Allen I was leaving, I told Eric Clapton and Klaus that I was leaving then, but that I would probably like to use them as a group. I hadn't decided how to do it—to have a permanent new group or what—then later on, I thought fuck, I'm not going to get stuck with another set of people, whoever they are. I announced it to myself and the people around me on the way to Toronto a few days before. And on the plane—Klein came with me—I told Allen, 'It's over.' When I got back, there were a few meetings, and Allen said, well, 'Cool it, cool it.' There was a lot to do, business-wise, you know, and it would not have been suitable at the time."[34]

Specifically, Klein insisted that John say nothing. And with good reason. On the Beatles' behalf, Klein persuaded EMI Records to reopen the contract that the Beatles had signed on January 26, 1967, and which ran through January 25, 1976. Even Paul had to admit that the results were impressive. The contract required the Beatles—as a group or individually—to produce two new albums, three singles and a compilation album each year between 1969 and 1976. The agreement is rich in complexities allowing the Beatles to release their music (including back catalog discs) on the Apple label in the United States, with Capitol manufacturing them. And it provides for the group's American royalties—which accounted for 75 percent of the Beatles income from record sales—to be paid to an American shell company, to avoid significantly higher British taxes.

But the main takeaway was that the Beatles' royalty increased from 17.5 percent of the wholesale price of each disc sold through 1969, to 25 percent of the wholesale price for sales through 1976, with another increase in 1972 if sales of the two most recent albums (group or solo) topped 500,000 copies. A 25 percent royalty was unprecedented in the record industry.

Klein persuaded John to remain silent until the EMI deal was ratified by both sides. John's news was no more welcome to Klein than it was to the other Beatles. But that was not the only reason Klein wanted John to keep mum. He knew that John could be volatile, and he thought there was a chance that John would reconsider once he'd weighed the pros and cons of going it on his own or continuing as a Beatle. But that was only likely to happen if John kept the plan to himself for a while.

Voormann, for one, was not surprised to hear John talk about leaving.

"It was not official to the public, but by 1969 it was more than clear that the band was disbanding," Voormann explained. "In other words, why would John call me and not only talk about forming a new band, but do it? The whole band was unhappy, and that wasn't just at the end of '69. But they still had contracts with EMI and were professional enough to put out all those wonderful songs, and that without spending much time together in the studio."[35]

For Paul, the new EMI deal, the agreements of September 9, and John's excitement about his Toronto experience all represented an opportunity for the Beatles to have a fresh start. When the Beatles (all but George, who was visiting his mother, Louise, who had been diagnosed with cancer) reconvened on September 16, he revived an idea he raised in January, when he suggested that the band consider returning to the stage. His idea had changed slightly over the months; now he envisioned performing unannounced concerts at small venues around England.

What Paul hadn't realized was that John made a clear distinction between performing as a Beatle, and going onstage with other performers, however starry. His takeaway from Toronto was that a single Beatle could perform on his own without the audience shrieking and causing mayhem, but his gut feeling was that if the Beatles performed, Beatlemania would erupt anew. George held that view as well; for both, touring had caused a form of post-traumatic stress disorder to which McCartney seemed to be immune.

So Paul was taken aback by John's response.

"I think you're daft," John said, and he didn't stop there. "Look, I might as well tell you, I'm leaving the group . . . I've had enough. I want a divorce, like my divorce from Cynthia."[36]

For John, the split was liberating, and he later explained it, after a bit of self-analysis, as something he had envisioned all along.

"Everything's fun off and on, you know," he later told Dick Cavett. "So, I suppose it could've gone on being fun off and on, or it could've got worse—I don't know. We don't want to be the Crazy Gang, being dragged onstage playing 'She Loves You' when we've got asthma and tuberculosis, when we're 50, you know . . . A long time ago I said that I didn't want to be singing 'She Loves You' when I'm 30, I said that when I was about 25 or something. Which, in a roundabout way, meant that I didn't want to be doing whatever I was doing then at 30."[37] (John turned 30 on October 9, 1970.)

For Klein, John's announcement was horrible news. He had come to London, and to the pressure cooker that was Apple, to get the Beatles on his management roster. He had succeeded, despite Paul's animus against him. Now it was all about to slip away. Klein's only option was to swear *all* the Beatles to secrecy for some indeterminate amount of time after the new EMI deal was in effect. The four Beatles signed the EMI contract on September 20, 1969, but it still had to be ratified by EMI.

But John added a proviso.

"Let me just say," Linda later remembered, "that John had made it clear that he wanted to be the one to announce the split, since it was his idea."[38]

September continued to rain misery on McCartney. On September 19, after a six-month tussle, Sir Lew Grade announced that his company ATV had secured a majority stake in Northern Songs.

All that was left, for John and Paul, was to determine what to do with their own shares. They took nearly a month to decide. On October 15, they sold their shares to ATV for loan stock worth £3.5 million ($8.4 million)—£1.5 million ($3.6 million) for Paul, £1.39 million ($3.34 million) for John. As they signed on the dotted line, they made an announcement of their own—not that they had broken up, just an assurance that when their Northern Songs contract expired in 1973, they would not renew it.[39]

This was a second blow to the Beatles' dream of putting Apple on a secure footing, and upgrading their own financial well-being: a few months earlier, they lost the battle for NEMS to Triumph Investment Trust, although in defeat, Klein negotiated a Byzantine deal with Triumph's chairman, Leonard Richenberg, in which Triumph acquired the Beatles' 10 percent share of the company, but agreed to take a much smaller cut of the Beatles' royalties than NEMS had taken—5 percent instead of 25 percent.

Paul was angry at John, and at Klein, but he was angry at himself as well. Having arrived in Scotland the clean-shaven Beatles seen on the cover of *Abbey Road* he stopped shaving once he arrived; by the time Linda took the photos seen in the November 7, 1969, issue of *Life*, he sported a week's growth. And he was partaking liberally of a locally produced remedy, scotch whisky.

"I exhibited all the classic symptoms of the unemployed, the redundant man. First you don't shave, and it's not to grow a groovy beard, it's because you cannot be fucking bothered. Anger, deep, deep, anger sets in, with everything, with yourself number one, and with everything in the world number two. And justifiably so because I was being screwed by my mates. So I didn't shave for quite a while. I didn't get up. Mornings weren't for getting up. I might get up and stay on the bed a bit and not know where to go, and get back into bed. Then if I did get up, I'd have a drink. Straight out of bed. I've never been like that.

"There are lots of people who've been through worse things than that but for me this was bad news because I'd always been the kind of guy who could really pull himself together and think, 'Oh, fuck it,' but at that time I felt I'd outlived my usefulness. This was the overall feeling: that it was good while I was in the Beatles, I was useful and I could play bass for their songs, I could write songs for them to sing and for me to sing, and we could make records of them. But the minute I wasn't with the Beatles any more it became really very difficult."[40]

This was difficult for Linda as well. For starters, she let Paul vent, as a supportive partner would. But Linda's position was a bit different from that of most spouses. Although the proximate cause of Paul's depression was the sudden loss of his band, he was also feeling battered by a year of business disputes that had been a live third rail within the band's dynamic, and he was terrified that Klein would walk off with it all. For Linda, Paul's side was also her father's and brother's side, and while she had normally kept clear of business concerns, particularly on the Eastman and Eastman level, now it was all around her, and Paul was its toxic ground zero.

Linda needed to yank Paul back into the world, and everything was at stake. In the process, she was also reconfiguring her own understanding of Paul's and the Beatles' situation to reflect her own change of circumstances—having gone from being an outsider who saw the Beatles as everyone else in the world did, to a member of the circle, who saw the dynamics within the Beatles' world at work.

"I remember Paul saying, 'Help me take some of this weight off my back,' and I said, 'Weight? what weight? You guys are the princes of the world. You're the Beatles.' But in truth Paul was not in great shape; he was drinking a lot, playing a lot and, while surrounded by women and fans, not very happy. We all thought, oh, the Beatles and flower power—but those guys had every parasite and vulture on their backs."[41]

Paul came to see it that way, too.

"It wasn't until she came along," he said of Linda, "that I realized what was happening to me. She made me see I was surrounded by conmen and leeches. I didn't need to be mollycoddled. Don't get me wrong. The Beatles gave me enough to do, what I want to do . . . play my own music and not worry about the rent."[42]

Gradually, Linda turned the discussion away from the Beatles, Apple and Klein, and toward what Paul's own abilities and accomplishments suggested as a logical road to the future he was so worried about. She adopted a strategy of encouragement, telling him that the Beatles breakup did nothing to change the fact that he was one of the twentieth century's greatest songwriters, and the rock world's most innovative bass player. He was an exceptionally inventive guitarist, and he knew his way around the piano and drums. And he still had a voice that women swooned over.

Paul's depression was about work, and Linda could see—better than Paul could, at the moment—that work was also the cure. If he had been, as he put it, "useful" as a member of the Beatles, why should he be less useful in any other context? What he needed was to pick up a guitar and get on with it.

"It's worked for you before, you know," she told him.[43]

All this made such complete sense that it can be difficult to see why Paul had such trouble imagining the leap from the Beatles to a solo career, until you factor in the degree to which he thrived under the pressure of the group dynamic.

What he missed was "the lack of great sounding boards like John, Ringo, George to actually talk to about the music. Having three other major talents around . . . I think that had quite a bit to do with it."[44]

Paul undertook one Beatles assignment in Scotland. Since the group had not recorded an independent single during the *Abbey Road* sessions, it was decided that George's 'Something' and

John's 'Come Together' would be paired as a double A-sided release on October 6. Given John's resignation, the group was not about to make a promo film, so Neil Aspinall assembled one himself, soliciting recent film clips of each of the Beatles and their wives, to be matched to 'Something.' It was, in its way, another clue to the breakup: although Aspinall alternated the film clips so that the promo moved from one Beatle and spouse to the next, no two Beatles are seen together.

Paul and Linda shot the required footage with a handheld Super 8 mm camera, with individual shots as well as a brief sequence of them snuggling in the pasture, the green rolling hills behind them. They also made a clip in which they romped through the pasture with Martha, Paul's large sheepdog, to be played back slightly faster than the filming speed to create a comic effect similar to that of the 'Can't Buy Me Love' sequence in *A Hard Day's Night*. They seemed in good spirits, although in his individual footage, Paul did not look especially healthy.

Having made the film, Paul failed to get it to Aspinall in time for the clip's first airing, on the November 13 edition of *Top of the Pops*. Aspinall improvised, using footage of Paul from the 'Fool on the Hill' sequence in *Magical Mystery Tour*, and film of Linda shot during the *Get Back* sessions. Shortly after their return to London, Paul sent the film to Aspinall, who edited in the new Paul and Linda sequences for subsequent screenings.

Ultimately, he had started contemplating what he had considered unthinkable until now—what a life outside of the Beatles might be like.

"I hung on wondering if the Beatles would ever come back together again, and hoping that John might come around and say, 'Alright lads, I'm ready to go back to work.' And natural enough, in the meantime I began to look for something to do . . . Sit me down with a guitar and let me go. That's my job."[45]

3

PLAYING WITH HIMSELF

—

As temperatures in Scotland began to drop, Paul and Linda agreed that a rustic farm in the unrelenting Scottish winter was no place for a newborn, and they returned to London shortly before the first snow fell in Campbeltown, on November 17, 1969. On the evening of November 18,[1] Allen Klein held a dinner meeting with Paul, George and Ringo (John, in Greece since November 11, had conferred with Klein in advance) to discuss the fate of the music recorded at the January 1969 sessions.

At that point, the album was still called *Get Back*, and the Beatles had not focused on it since that evening in May, when Glyn Johns played his mixes and proposed sequencing, and the other Beatles tried to persuade Paul to sign the contract with Klein. Johns had retained the spirit of the project as it had been articulated in January: his *Get Back* album sounded off-the-cuff, capturing a sense of the Beatles at work, with snippets of jams, oldies, quips, and count-ins punctuating live-in-the-studio versions of their new songs.

By now, the group's fans were wondering why the album was so long in coming to record shops. At first, Apple attributed the delay to the production of a softback book, packed with photos and some dialogue from the sessions, to be included with the album.

During the summer, it was announced that *Abbey Road* would be released in September, with *Get Back* following in November. As September approached, *Get Back* was moved to early 1970. The announcements and the inevitable backpedaling became a joke in the letters column of *Rolling Stone*, with readers periodically writing in to ask, "When is the *Get Back* album coming out?"

Worse, many fans had already heard the album, thanks to leaks of an acetate of Johns's mix to several radio stations in the United States. Capitol Records swiftly issued injunctions, but many a home tape deck was rolling when the tracks were played, and before long, bootleg albums drawn from these broadcasts could be found in American record shops. Those who hadn't heard the album could have read a detailed track-by-track report in the November 1 issue of *NME*.

But much had changed, starting with the band's breakup. Paul's comments in *Life* notwithstanding, the Beatles had kept their promise not to discuss the breakup publicly. Lennon, in interviews from this period, tended to obfuscate, saying that the Beatles were all busy with solo projects, and that decisions about future Beatles projects would be made as they came up.[2] Harrison continued saying, well into the spring, that the Beatles would work together again.[3]

Get Back was being rethought too. When the Beatles moved from Twickenham to their own Apple studio, after Harrison's brief resignation, they began speaking about Lindsay-Hogg's production as a film rather than as a television special—perhaps even as the third film owed to United Artists under the Beatles December 10, 1963, film contract.*

Klein thought he could persuade United Artists to agree to that idea, and when Paul wondered whether blowing the 16 mm footage up to 35 mm for theatrical presentation would degrade its visual quality, Klein had a 35 mm copy made and showed that the quality was satisfactory. The Beatles rejected Klein's second proposal—dumping Lindsay-Hogg and handing the project to Saul Swimmer, a director Klein was pushing.

Klein had ideas about the album, too. First, it should be configured as the film's soundtrack LP; songs performed in the film would be included, and those left on the cutting room floor would be dropped. When the Beatles agreed to that, Klein proposed bringing in another of his clients, the producer Phil Spector, to help assemble a more polished-sounding album.

"Allen Klein decided that the album was too bare," Paul explained, "[that] it wasn't commercial enough, so we ought to gloss it up a bit. None of us wanted to work on it, we'd had it with the whole project. So he brought Phil in."[4]

Spector was an unusual choice, given that the Beatles entire catalog (apart from a handful of early recordings they made in Hamburg) had been produced by George Martin. But Martin's feelings about the January sessions were largely negative, and it made sense to bring in a pair of fresh ears. The Beatles admired Spector's early-1960s "wall of sound" productions for the Ronettes, the Crystals and Darlene Love, and they had covered one of his compositions, 'To Know Him Is to Love Him'—a 1958 hit for the Teddy Bears—in their early-stage sets and during their unsuccessful January 1, 1962, audition for Decca. And they had met Spector. When he accompanied them on their flight to New York, on February 7, 1964, a nervous Paul quizzed Spector about their prospects in America, wondering, "What are we going to give them that they don't already have?"[5]

Thereafter, the Beatles and Spector ran into each other on occasion and struck up a friendship,

---

* The Beatles delivered the first two, *A Hard Day's Night* in 1964, and *Help!* in 1965, but they had tired of conventional filmmaking, and from 1966 on, they turned down all the scripts sent their way, including one by the then-hot playwright Joe Orton. *Magical Mystery Tour*, from 1967, was never envisioned as part of the deal, and United Artists did not consider *Yellow Submarine*, the animated 1968 feature film, an adequate fulfillment of the contract.

although Paul remembered Spector sometimes offering advice that ran against the group's own instincts.

"We were quite good friends in the beginning. We used to talk a lot, and we admired him because of his work, and his productions. And we did hang a little bit when he came to London. We thought he was one of the greats because of the records he'd made. He told us to not bother with B sides but to put 'Singalong with She Loves You' on the B side; put [out] the backing track. So, we said, 'No, Phil,' 'cos we remembered how much these records cost us when we were in Liverpool. And we went the other way—'Strawberry Fields' and 'Penny Lane'—we always tried to have really good value."[6]

The new plan suited the Beatles, who had not been able to agree whether the live-in-the-studio concept worked or simply yielded a collection that sounded half-baked. Spector was hired and given a free hand—so long as he understood that the finished album was subject to their approval.[7]

———

Upon their return to London, in November 1969, Paul and Linda set about giving the Cavendish Avenue house a long overdue remodeling, from bachelor pad to family home.* During their final days in Scotland, Linda had bid by proxy at a Sotheby's auction, acquiring a Tiffany lamp, with a dome in Tiffany's characteristic colored glass, sitting atop a stalklike stem in gilt bronze, for £700 ($1,680).[8] The lamp joined several others illuminating the ground floor of the Regency town house. Paul, meanwhile, initiated discussions with Arthur Bailey, a designer, about a new fireplace enclosure featuring a Louis XV marble mantelpiece they bought in September.

More importantly, Paul was reconsidering the technology in the modest home studio he had assembled in 1966. The heart of the studio, since then, was a pair of Brenell tape decks—all four Beatles had them[9]—on which he recorded demos and undertook musical/electronic experiments, some for practical use, others for his own amusement. He had used the Brenells to make the tape loops heard on John's 'Tomorrow Never Knows,' on *Revolver*, as well as the effects loops, with crickets, bells, and other atmospheric sounds, heard in the transition between 'You Never Give Me Your Money' and 'Sun King,' on *Abbey Road*.

Now Paul wanted a studio-quality multitrack deck, on which he could overdub instruments and vocals. Such a setup would allow him to produce sonically pristine recordings that he could take into the studio and mix. He was not, however, ready to go as far as George Harrison and John Lennon, who had each purchased a 3M eight-track deck like those in use at EMI.

———

* According to Land Registry documents, Paul completed the purchase of 7 Cavendish Avenue in the north London suburb of St. John's Wood on September 6, 1965, paying physician Desmond O'Neill £40,000 ($111,700). The three-story Regency town house sits on the edge of central London by Regent's Park and Lord's Cricket Ground, just a ten-minute walk from EMI's studios at Abbey Road.

Before his trip to Scotland, Paul discussed the prospect of a home studio upgrade with Eddie Klein, a sound engineer who joined EMI in 1967. They came up with a plan that involved borrowing one of EMI's Studer J37 four-track decks. Studer, the Swiss tape deck manufacturer, began marketing the J37 in 1964, and the following year, EMI bought four of them, at £8,000 ($22,320) apiece. They became EMI's main workhorses from 1965 until 1968, when the label acquired a pair of 3M M23 eight-track decks. The Beatles recorded everything from *Help!* through *Sgt. Pepper's Lonely Hearts Club Band* on the J37, as well as parts of the *White Album* and *Abbey Road*.[10]

With eight-track fast becoming the standard at EMI, putting a Studer at Paul's disposal was no sacrifice. Paul briefly considered adding a mixing board, but opted against it, deciding that he could plug instruments and a microphone (he owned only one) directly into the J37. This arrangement let Paul have it both ways: there was a romantically retro, do-it-yourself aspect that harked back to an earlier, simpler time, yet the recordings would be studio quality masters.

"It's a cool way to record because it's pure," was how he put it. "If, say, I was doing a drum track, I'd play the drums, record it with one microphone, listen to it back, move the mic a little if there wasn't enough high hat or cymbal, and then rerecord. Then I'd add bass by plugging the mic into track two and overdubbing while listening to track one through headphones. I'd do that with all with four tracks. It was a very hands-on, primitive way of working."[11]

Nevertheless, when the machine arrived, it was missing a few components that would make the J37 far more convenient to use. Without a mixer, he had no EQ (equalization, used to "sweeten" the sound of an instrument or voice by shaping its color and nuance) and no VU meters (which show the volume levels of the sounds being recorded). Before he left for Scotland, Paul wrote to EMI service and design engineers Ron Pender and Dick Sweetenham, requesting extra outboard units, but the additional equipment never arrived.[12]

When he returned from Scotland, Paul had an EMI team in to get the J37 set up, tested and ready for use. His presence was not required; the McCartneys' housekeeper, Rose Martin, could show the EMI engineers where he planned to use the deck.

Paul, Linda and the girls headed off for another fog-shifting vacation, this time to the West Indies, with a stop in New York for a holiday visit with the Eastmans. They left London on December 10, swapping the bleak British weather for the Curtain Bluff Resort, a luxury retreat wrapped in white sands, in southern Antigua. There they swam in the azure waters of Morris Bay, sunbathed, and sipped cocktails, Linda usually with a camera over her shoulder or at her eye. On an evening they would sit on the terrace, lining the white walls with candied fruit to tempt birds.

"We put cherries out for the birds," Paul remembered. "We'd get them from the bar, glacé cherries, and put them out, so there's pictures with loads of birds on there."[13] As Linda snapped the local wildlife, Paul doodled a family of cartoon mice (which he dubbed Bruce McMouse and family) on hotel stationery. Just as doodling had proven the perfect distraction from schoolwork during his days at the Liverpool Institute—where he would while away the hours copying characters from comics like *Radio Fun**—a world, and a lifetime, away in Antigua it occupied his restless mind.

When they returned to London, just before Christmas, the Studer was tucked into the corner of the living room,[14] ready to roll.

———➤

Recording Sessions

Tuesday–Tuesday, December 23–30, 1969.
Cavendish Avenue, Home Studio, London.
Recording: 'The Lovely Linda,' 'That Would Be Something,' 'Momma,' and 'Miss America.'

Refreshed from his time in the warmth of the Caribbean, Paul was eager to get to work, although it was not entirely clear what he was working toward. He resisted the idea that he was making an album for public release. That was a possibility, of course, but it made sense to see how the domestic recording went. In the meantime, he wanted the project shrouded in secrecy. Since Paul was still avoiding the press and had approached no other musicians to work with him, the likelihood of word leaking out was slim. If Paul was unsatisfied with his home recordings, they could disappear into his archives, with the rest of his demos and sound experiments.

"I didn't really think it was going to be an album," he later confessed. "It was just me recording for the sake of it."[15]

Recording was an escape, a form of self-therapy, and Paul quickly developed a comfortable way of working. "I'd get up and think about breakfast and then wander into the living room to do a track.[16] I had my little machine in there. I'd just go in for the day like Monsieur Magritte. It was like working in a sound laboratory. It was very interesting to do, and it had a certain kind of rawness."[17]

He enjoyed the intensity of focus involved in recording alone, and his experience overdubbing his bass lines—and sometimes guitar, drums and multiple vocals—on Beatles recordings assured him that he would be able to produce some useful work.

---

* Often noted by Paul as a childhood favorite, *Radio Fun* was a British celebrity comic book that ran from October 1938 to February 1961. Issues would capture in comic form celebrities like Benny Hill, Charlie Chester, Clark Gable, and Norman Wisdom.

As recently as July 24, during the *Abbey Road* sessions, he had done the one-man-band thing while waiting for the others to turn up. Commissioned to write some music for Ringo's film, *The Magic Christian*, Paul turned up at the studio with 'Come and Get It,' and asked Phil McDonald, the engineer on duty, to roll tape. Recording a lead vocal and piano first, he added a second vocal, while accompanying himself on maracas, then drums and finally bass. The whole production, including mixing, took him an hour. Paul regarded the recording as a demo and gave the song to the Apple band Badfinger to record properly. But he was happy enough with the performance that he demanded that Badfinger follow the arrangement on the demo precisely.

"Playing with yourself is a slower, more methodical thing," he explained. "When other people are involved, it obviously means that you have to listen a lot more to other decisions and weigh the decisions, and then come out with your own decision—unless you are capable of just agreeing with everything that everyone says, which I am not. It's less of a hassle playing with yourself than it is playing within anyone else. It's only a method of working."[18]

The question facing Paul as he powered up the Studer the first time was, what to record? In Scotland, he had started work on a pair of new songs. The first, 'The Lovely Linda,' was just a snippet, with a simple chord progression and some transitional chordal filigree between phrases, but only two lines of a lyric, including a syllabic placeholder for what could eventually be an opening phrase—"*La, la, la, la, la, the lovely Linda, with the lovely flowers in her hair.*"

Paul intended to do more with 'The Lovely Linda.' He jotted notes for a lively, Spanish-influenced section in his notebook, but ultimately scrapped it. But slight as the Campbeltown version of 'The Lovely Linda' was, it illuminated a few points about where Paul was, compositionally.

One was that Paul's gift for pulling simple but catchy melodies out of the air remained fully intact. More importantly, it was a declaration that Linda was by now so completely his muse that he didn't need to say much about her. Lacking a verb, his lyric was not even a single, complete sentence. In a way, it was a musical snapshot—a single image, its lyric more a caption than a proper song. It was, in effect, a tribute to Linda in a musical equivalent of her own artistic milieu.

"When you get married, things change, everything changes, and the way you look at things, you look at through a partner's eyes," he reflected on their time outside of the public gaze in Argyll. "I started to realize that I liked the warmth of a family. I started to realize that that's important. And warmth, and being kind of blatant about your feelings and investigating them rather than hiding them.[19]

"Get home, new baby, it was that joy, it transforms your life. I hadn't had a baby before—we had Heather from Linda's first marriage—so home was great joy and solace for me . . . The rest, outside, was shit. I'd go out the front door and face all the shit in the world, but coming inside was like a cocoon."[20]

The second Campbeltown song, 'That Would Be Something,' was also little more than a promising start—a catchy, blues-tinged riff that worked both as an instrumental figure and as a tune to hang lyrics on. Not that he had much in the way of lyrics—just the title and variants, with *"Meet you in the fallin' rain, Momma"* to tie up the verse.

He had a backlog of older songs, too, but for the moment, McCartney was keen on trying out his new creations, unfinished though they were. After setting up his single microphone, he threaded a fresh reel of BASF tape, breathing in the sweet aroma of Mylar that cries out "new project!" He made a few test recordings to check the levels (since in the absence of VU meters, this had to be done by trial and error) and picked up his 1967 Martin D-28 acoustic guitar. Pressing the record button, he went for a basic guitar-and-vocal take of 'The Lovely Linda,' giving the song a cheerful, 43-second run-through, ending in laughter.*

"You can hear the door squeak as Linda came in while I was recording," McCartney said of the finished track. "It was a good take, so we left it in."[21]

Satisfied with the song's foundation, he moved his microphone to the Studer's second track input and overdubbed another acoustic guitar part. On the third track, he played a basic rhythm, slapping his hands on the cover of a book.[22] With one track remaining, he added a simple bass line.

In the public's imagination, Paul's bass of choice was the distinctive Höfner 500/1 left-handed violin bass, the instrument he had used onstage from the Beatles' second Hamburg residency, in 1961, through the band's final tour, in 1966. But for these recordings, he opted for the Ricken-backer 4001S, a crisp-toned instrument that had been his favored bass for studio work since the *Rubber Soul* sessions in the fall of 1965. It had been given to Paul by the company's owner, Frances Hall, the previous August, when the Beatles performed in Los Angeles.

"Mr. Rickenbacker gave me a special left-handed bass. It was a freebie,"[23] he reflected on his encounter with Hall at the Los Angeles house they had rented from Burt Lancaster.[24] "By then I'd kind of made the Höfner my trademark . . . [But] Mr. Rickenbacker said to me, 'this will record better than what you've got.' It looked nice."[25] Nevertheless, Paul tinkered with its looks several times, its original fireglo (red starburst) finish giving way to a psychedelic paint job in 1967, and, by 1969, having it stripped back to bare maple.[26]

With 'The Lovely Linda' finished, Paul moved on to 'That Would Be Something,' in an arrange-ment that brought in new timbres to further test his setup. He began the same way he started 'The Lovely Linda,' with a guitar and vocal track—but with one notable engineering improvement. Because he was recording both his guitar and his voice through a single microphone, he had po-sitioned the mic for 'The Lovely Linda' midway between the guitar and his mouth. That yielded a

---

* Paul documented these recordings in colored pencil (black, red, green and blue) on a sheet of Apple stationery, his annotations sometimes including diagrams showing his ideas about where each element of the recording should be placed in a stereo mix. These annotations are, however, undated. And because he appears to have taken a thrifty approach to his use of tape, he did not keep takes that did not satisfy him, opting instead to wipe them while recording a replacement. Consequently, the number of takes he recorded for each song (and for each track within each song) cannot be determined.

sound in which the vocal was slightly distant. His solutions would have been either to redo it, or to use a second track to double the vocal. But this was a test piece, and the squeaking door and laughter gave it a quality he wanted to preserve.

For 'That Would Be Something,' he set the microphone at mouth level to capture a vocal with greater presence. Now the acoustic guitar was distant, but the part was less central than it had been in 'The Lovely Linda.' On the second track he added drums. Because the Beatles did not list Paul as the drummer on the tracks where he took over from Ringo, it was little known to the public that he was an avid stickman.

"For years I suggested to Ringo a lot of what he might play, and I heard drums well," he said. "I first got into it listening to 'Sweet Little Sixteen,' where there was a drum break around the kit. I would ask Ringo to play some variation on that. And at sessions I would climb on the drum kit and start having a go . . . In Hamburg, one week Tony Sheridan's drummer got sick, and I drummed for him, for the extra cash, for a week . . . I can hold quite a good beat."[27]

Holding a beat wasn't a problem, but properly recording an entire trap set—he set up his Premier[28] kit near the Studer—was nearly impossible without multiple microphones and a mixer. This time, he stripped the kit down to a tom-tom and a cymbal—a makeshift and not entirely satisfactory work-around that he had clearly settled on before he recorded the guitar and vocal track. With an idea of what the tom-tom and cymbal accompaniment would be, he included some vocalized drum sounds on the basic track, as a way of filling out the percussion layer. A bass guitar overdub onto track four completed the song's rhythm section.

On the third track, McCartney used his 1962 Epiphone Casino ES-230TD electric guitar to add some gloss, and to buttress the more interesting elements of the distantly recorded acoustic guitar part. Paul bought his Casino in December 1964, inspired by an evening listening to blues recordings at the London home of the guitarist and singer John Mayall. It was originally a right-handed model, with a Bigsby tremolo tailpiece—one of the things that attracted him to the model; Paul had it customized for left-handed play.[29] The distinctive clean sound of the Casino emphasized the song's bluesy character and transformed a loose acoustic soliloquy into an earthy rocker.

With his two new song fragments recorded, Paul was out of material from Scotland. He was still withholding judgment on whether these recordings might be the building blocks of an album—an unlikely prospect, given that of the two songs he had tracked, one was unfinished, and the other was pleasant but slight. He was, at that point, principally focused on learning how to record with the Studer, serving as his own engineer. To his ears, there were still technical problems to overcome.

His next step, therefore, was to create a series of improvised instrumentals, posing himself a set of escalating challenges. He announced the first as 'Rock and Roll Springtime' and laid down an easygoing, 12-bar drum pattern, with lazy accenting and occasional punctuating flourishes. After the first 12 bars (a verse, if it had lyrics), he played a brief two-bar fill, as a kind of section break. The rest was improvised, although the section marking in the drum track suggests that McCartney had a specific structure in mind. The full track ran just under two minutes.

On track two, he played a modified blues progression on the piano, starting in A minor and ending in A major. Paul's playing here is basic, mainly providing solid, open-voiced chords with a peppering of Romantic era bombast, in various ranges within the top half of the keyboard. Those flourishes aside, the piano mostly provides a backdrop for the electric guitar Paul would play on track four, after first adding a steady, bouncing bass line on track three.

Paul's arrangements for 'The Lovely Linda' and 'That Would Be Something' were straightforward, with each instrument heard from start to finish. This time, his plan was more intricate. During the first pass at the chord progression, the piano, drums and bass hold the focus, while the electric guitar, with a tremolo effect, was meant to add texture rather than substance. But after the drum break, the guitar is more assertive and more varied, with arpeggiated chords, light distortion and blues riffs.

The announced title notwithstanding, Paul listed the song as 'Momma' on his handwritten tracking sheet. The fate of this two-minute jam was not yet clear; it could be the basis of a song, or part of a larger track. What was apparent was the *feel* he wanted. With the title called out in advance—as if it were an engineer's voice, over the control room talkback—and the generally loose feel of the performance, the song seemed to embrace the spirit of the *Get Back* album.

"I just wanted to get back to absolute basics,"[30] he said of his home recording.

But 'Momma' did not entirely solve the problem of getting a good drum sound. Paul undertook a series of tests, using different settings on his microphone to record his drums. On his tracking sheet, he noted, for each test, which setting was used (they are described as "music" and "speech") and whether the sound was "live" (straight drum sound) or "dead" (with a sheet over the drums to damp the sound). If nothing else, the tests expanded the palate of drum sounds available to him, and he planned to explore that variety in a percussion piece called 'Keep It Together.' But he got only as far as a single take on track one before losing interest. He soon thought better of it entirely, erased the drum tests and 'Keep It Together,' and started a fresh piece.

This was another 12-bar, in G, and as with 'Momma,' not entirely a straightforward blues progression. Paul listed it on his tracking sheet as 'Instrumental,' with 'Miss America' added later in red pencil. As he had done with 'Momma,' he began with drums, adding an acoustic rhythm guitar on track two, a wonderfully fluid bass line on track three and electric lead guitar on track four, this time starting immediately after the short drum introduction, and using standard blues jam moves to create a line that was ear-catching but not especially showy.

This time, the innovation in Paul's "learning the Studer" self-tutorial was a midtrack instrument switch: the acoustic guitar fills in the texture for the first part of the song, and holds the spotlight with a rhythmic variation for about 10 seconds between electric guitar solos. But after a false (and somewhat ramshackle) ending, McCartney plays another drum fill and the song continues, this time with a piano replacing the acoustic guitar for the rest of the track.

Recording Sessions

Tuesday–Tuesday, December 23–30, 1969.
Cavendish Avenue, Home Studio, London.
Recording: 'Rupert,' 'Oo You,' 'Valentine Day,' 'Glasses,' and 'Suicide.'

McCartney's next recording was a fragment of a song he had started in August. He had only a chord progression with a slightly jazzy tinge—mostly A minor 7 and E minor 7, with C and G in the refrain and a passing D minor in its bridge—and the start of a beautifully arching melody. This recording, which Paul listed as 'Rupert,' but also referred to as 'Two Fingers' or 'When the Wind Is Blowing,' sounds more like a memo—a way of preserving the song's basic contours, while it was on Paul's mind—than a continuation of his Studer experimentation.

It does, however, show several aspects of McCartney's creative process. The seed of the idea came to Paul when Linda was convalescing at the Avenue Clinic in London after the birth of Mary, on August 28. On a wall in Linda's room hung a print of *The Old Guitarist*, Pablo Picasso's Blue Period masterpiece, painted in 1903.

"I'd looked at it all week," Paul said of the Picasso, speaking with his guitar in hand, ready to demonstrate. "And towards the end of the week, I thought, 'What chord's he playing?' I noticed he had just two fingers, here and here [at the fifth fret on the D and G strings], so I'll try and see what that chord is, if it sounds any good." He strummed the chord, an A minor 9, and continued, "Ooh, that's nice. So I used that inspiration to write a song that had only two fingers."[31]

The story is partly fanciful. Though the Picasso may have got Paul thinking in a way that led to a song, the guitarist in the painting is not playing a chord at all: his four fingers are lined up along the bottom E string, and his hand is not at the fifth fret, but at the nut, where the headstock meets the neck. Paul could be forgiven for missing that detail, since the headstock is only visible in an x-ray of the painting.[32] Picasso eradicated it (and the strings and frets) with a stroke of brown paint in the finished version.

Paul's story does, however, offer a window into how relatively mundane things—a reproduction of a famous painting, this time; a newspaper headline or a postcard, elsewhere—became the seeds of songs.

In this case, there was also another element at work. As a child, McCartney became acquainted, like millions of British children, with Rupert Bear, the star of a comic strip in the *Daily Express* since 1920 (and annual books since 1936). When Linda brought Heather into his life, he introduced her to Rupert and his family in the fictional town of Nutwood and was delighted that she loved the yellow-and-red-clad bear. Writing to Derek Taylor from Campbeltown in November 1968, he proposed an idea (the sometimes-odd punctuation is Paul's):

> While, reading to a friend of mines daughter the, Rupert book; gave me an idea.
>
> Instead of *Yellow Submarine*, it should have been *Rupert* with music by . . . [DONE RIGHT.]
>
> This could still happen and be a good project for good Apple Films. Before ANYTHING is done, the production must be checked out; but, before that happens (a months' time approx.) you could see the artist (a Mr. BESTALL) and tell him that you love him, so that if Beaverbrook papers don't like us or we don't like them, we still have the man behind it on our side. Of course, we may dislike <u>him</u> but I doubt it.
>
> If you do it, will you not tell ANYONE (wives excluded) s that it doesn't become an Apple event and trendy.
>
> It could be lovely if the right people got to do it—none of that psychedelic shit.
>
> Love and peace, brother.[33]

Paul signed the letter "Moon dog" and drew a picture of Rupert—complete with colored-in yellow checked pants, scarf and red sweater—and an elephant. Under the drawing, he wrote, "P.S. Mum's the word."

A year later, when Paul was no longer thinking in terms of projects for Apple, he asked the Eastmans to look into acquiring the film rights to Rupert, with an eye toward making an animated feature for which he would write the music. If the rights were available, that could be a project for the future—it made sense to start stockpiling them.

After his single pass at 'Rupert,' he set down two more improvised instrumentals. On the first, which he listed as 'Instrumental' on the tape box, but soon called 'Oo You,' he began with drums, but instead of the filled-out drum intros on both 'Momma' and 'Miss America,' here he played just four steady beats as the equivalent of a count-in,* and then right into the full track. To that he added bass and electric guitar, the two lines tightly intertwined and texturally transparent, the guitar and bass mirroring each other in a funky descending riff at some points. Elsewhere the guitar moves between

---

* Or a click track, common then in film, and used in some American studios, but not yet common in British recording studios.

chunky rhythmic accenting and a chordal melody, with slides and string bending that give it shape and create the impression that this improvised piece was carefully composed.

The second new instrumental was also untitled at first; McCartney later added 'Valentine' as a title on his track list, expanding it to 'Valentine Day' on the tape box. It included a few departures. One was a split drum track—a snare and a high-hat on track one, and a tom-tom on track three, allowing the possibility of a stereo drum effect. Picking up his Martin acoustic, he added a rhythm part with a peculiar structure.

Paul's introductory figure is built around a C chord sliding up to D and repeating, and a similar (sans slide) A-G-A pivot. But when he reaches the meat of the song—where the electric guitar begins a stuttering lead line—the acoustic rhythm guitar sits on an A minor chord. The opening figure returns briefly, again leading toward A minor, but this time played with a changing, deliberately shambolic rhythm, as the lead guitar settles into a stock blues ending. Thereafter, Paul signals a tempo shift with his cymbal and a gritty chordal figure on the electric guitar leads into a second jam that, in its unedited form, ran another 90 seconds.

There was one problem. Listening to the playback, Paul knew that the song needed a bass line. But he had used the four tracks available to him. Weighing the contents of each track, he opted to sacrifice part of track three, the tom-tom—but not all of it. At exactly the point where the listener's attention will naturally shift from the opening drum and acoustic guitar pattern to the electric guitar, Paul replaced the tom-tom with his bass, which continues to the end of the song.

———

Now McCartney was at a crossroads.

If this was to be the start of a solo album, he would have to dig into his stockpile of songs composed during the Beatle days, but never formally recorded by the band. He had done this kind of stocktaking in January, during the *Get Back* sessions. In a retrospective mood on January 3, the second day of the filming, he and John revived a few of their earliest collaborations—'Because I Know You Love Me So,' 'Wait 'Til Tomorrow,' 'Thinking of Linking,' and 'Won't You Please Say Goodbye,' songs they remembered well enough to play through a verse or two, sometimes with vocal harmonies. Only one proto-Beatles antiquity, 'One After 909,' was worked on further.

Among the early McCartney compositions played at the sessions, two now struck Paul as worth reviving—'Hot As Sun,' a cheerful instrumental dating to 1959, and 'Suicide,' a 1956 song in a cabaret style. Both would have been outliers in the Beatles' catalog, but connections could be drawn: 'Hot As Sun' had a distant kinship with 'Flying,' the instrumental on *Magical Mystery Tour* (which was credited to all four Beatles), and 'Suicide' in its channeling of prerock pop styles, had elements in common with 'When I'm Sixty-Four' and 'Honey Pie.'

'Suicide' was the kind of song Paul's dad, Jim McCartney,* enjoyed—the kind you could imagine Frank Sinatra or Dean Martin performing. Both singers had hits in 1956, even as the British skiffle master Lonnie Donegan (with 'Rock Island Line') and the American rockers Elvis Presley (with 'Blue Suede Shoes') and Bill Haley and the Comets (with 'Rock Around the Clock') were revolutionizing what a hit record could sound like. Paul was on both sides of that revolution, excited by nascent rock 'n' roll, but also fond of standards and show tunes.

"When I was growing up rock 'n' roll hadn't started," he explained. "Blues had started, but that was nowhere near as popular, and if anyone wanted to go into show business, probably being a Sinatra-type person was the most rocking you were gonna get.[34] Fred Astaire, Pearl Bailey, and all those people, I was brought up on a lot of that.[35] As a writer my heroes were Cole Porter, Rodgers and Hammerstein, that idea that a writer could turn his hand to this or that, as a craftsman."[36]

That dichotomy remained through the Beatles years. He was the one crooning 'Till There Was You' and 'A Taste of Honey,' but he was also the band's go-to singer for the vocal extremes of Little Richard's 'Long Tall Sally' and 'Lucille.'

Among McCartney's more recent unused compositions were 'Jubilee,' also known as 'Junk,' a wistful little meditation that Paul wrote in India, in February or March 1968. Slow and gentle, it evokes the London of a past era. Paul recorded a graceful, acoustic guitar performance at George's bungalow in Esher, as one of 23 songs the Beatles recorded on George's Ampex four-track as they prepared to start work on the *White Album*. 'Junk' did not make it to the formal sessions, and the Beatles did not pick it up subsequently.

'Every Night' was another promising leftover from 1968, written partly in London, partly during a visit to Corfu, Greece, in 1969. McCartney played through it a few times during the *Get Back* sessions, but like 'Hot As Sun' and 'Suicide,' it was never fully rehearsed. 'Teddy Boy,' another souvenir of Paul's time in India, got a more thorough workout at the sessions, and though it was never fully polished, Glyn Johns found one of the rehearsals charismatic enough to include in his *Get Back* album. Now that *Get Back* was being reimagined as a film soundtrack, Paul would have to find out, if he wanted to use it himself, whether the Beatles' ragtag version (with John calling out square dance moves—"*Swing your partner, do-si-do, hold your partner, don't let go, when you've got it—jump up!*"[37]—during an instrumental verse) would be included after all.

These were the songs Paul settled on as possibilities for his current project, but they were by no means the only potential solo tracks tried out during the *Get Back* project. Others McCartney ran through include 'Woman,' a song he wrote (under the pseudonym Bernard Webb) for Peter Asher's old folk-rock duo, Peter & Gordon; 'Another Day,' a jaunty tune with verses that needed work,

---

* Paul's father, James McCartney, known to his friends as Jim, was born in Liverpool on July 7, 1902.

and no hint of a bridge; 'The Back Seat of My Car,' a ravishing melody that owed something to *Pet Sounds*–era Brian Wilson; and an attractive keyboard instrumental, 'The Palace of the King of the Birds,' which Paul tried out on both piano and organ (the latter with contributions from George and Ringo).

Recording Sessions

Tuesday–Tuesday, December 23–30, 1969.
Cavendish Avenue, Home Studio, London.
Recording: 'Glasses' and 'Suicide.'

Paul followed his 'Valentine' instrumental with preliminary run-throughs of a couple of the older songs he was considering. When those takes were not keepers, he recorded over them, creating an experimental piece, 'Glasses.' However, nearly three minutes of 'Suicide' survived. Since the fragment is a single verse, repeated in a handful of treatments and tempos, it is impossible to say how much of the song was erased, or whether another song preceded it.

McCartney's description of 'Glasses'—"wine glasses played at random and overdubbed on top of each other"[38]—sounds almost dismissive, but it was part of a line of experimental projects that Paul began making in 1966, after Barry Miles and others at Indica Books and Gallery introduced him to the music of Karlheinz Stockhausen, Luciano Berio, Cornelius Cardew and other classical avant-gardists. It is possible that at one of the new-music concerts he attended at that time, Paul ran into the technique of making partly filled glasses "sing" by rubbing a moistened finger along their rims.

If not, he certainly ran into the technique in April 1967, when he flew to the United States to visit Jane Asher on her 21st birthday. Jane was on tour with the Bristol Old Vic, playing Juliet in Shakespeare's *Romeo and Juliet*. After a quick trip to Dallas, where they celebrated Jane's birthday on April 5, Paul, Jane and Mal Evans flew to Denver for a few days, then to Los Angeles (in a private Lear jet loaned to them by Frank Sinatra) on April 9. There, they visited the Laurel Canyon home of John and Michelle Phillips, of the Mamas and the Papas, and during the visit, Brian Wilson stopped by. As Evans noted in a dyspeptic diary entry:

> *Brian then put a damper on the spontaneity of the whole affair by walking in with a tray of water-filled glasses, trying to arrange it into some sort of session.*[39]

Not that playing music on water-filled glasses was a new concept. The Persians used water instruments as far back as the eleventh century, and the Italian composer Franchinus Gaffurius included a woodcut of a musician using a stick to strike partly filled glasses in his *Theorica musicae*, published in 1492.[40] The approach Paul took, of tuning the glasses by filling them to different levels, and creating sound with the stroke of a finger on the rim, was developed by an Irish musician, Richard Pockrich, who gave a recital on his "angelic organ" in Dublin in 1744.[41] Benjamin Franklin, who heard a water glass recital by Edmund Delaval in London in 1761, quickly produced his own sophisticated variation, the "armonica," by mounting the bottoms of different-size glasses on a horizontal rod, with a pedal to turn them as the player coaxed sound from their lubricated edges.[42]

'Glasses' was painstakingly set up, with each of the half-dozen wineglasses from Paul's kitchen cupboard filled to precise levels to play specific notes. Once the glasses were tuned (most likely using the piano as a point of reference), they produced the pitches A-sharp, another A-sharp an octave higher, A, B, C, D and E[43]—a set that would produce both consonant and dissonant combinations.

Paul filled all four tracks with the smooth tones of his tuned glasses, creating a slowly shifting, eerily atmospheric texture.

"My thing was always not to shout about it," McCartney said of his avant-garde experiments. "I used to have two Brenell recorders [and] I used to sit at home like a mad professor and make all these loops and carry them in [to Beatles sessions], in a little plastic bag. And I set John up in Weybridge with two Brenells and showed him how to do it. But he got noticed more, because he'd gone with Yoko and was wanting to do that stuff. I was a little reluctant to do it with the Beatles, I liked the idea of it being a side project. John wanted to do 'Revolution 9,' but that was all that Brenell, sound-montage kind of stuff. People didn't know because I kept quiet about it."[44]

Paul opted to preserve the partial performance of 'Suicide' that peeks through the end of 'Glasses,' creating an interesting juxtaposition of his latest composition and one of his first. At this point, 'Suicide' was a fairly sophisticated little piece, with rolling piano fill-ins between the lines that hint, with surprising fluency, at what a jazz pianist might bring to it.

For years, Paul had used this jazz ballad as one of several short ditties he would trot out at parties. Another was a faux-French boulevard song, which was eventually pressed into service, during the *Rubber Soul* sessions, as 'Michelle.' Their charm was in the way they parodied pop styles not typically associated with Paul. Though he presented them as comic throwaways, some of these songs had bigger potential.

Paul wrote 'Suicide' on his father's upright piano at 20 Forthlin Road, in Liverpool. In his younger years, Jim McCartney ran a local band, Jim Mac's Jazz Band, and though he never had a professional musical career, he enjoyed tickling the ivories at family gatherings, which invariably included a hearty sing-along. He encouraged Paul to cultivate that ability as well.

"I remember him saying to me when I was quite young, 'Learn the piano, you'll always get invited to parties.' That was the big thing about learning the piano. I think I did secretly think, 'That's a good idea.' I'd had piano lessons when I was a little kid from the local old lady that a lot of kids [went] to. And she was very nice, and very patient. But the thing I hated was that she gave homework."[45]

Though McCartney's lessons were short-lived, his interest in the piano was not, and he began to play Jim's upright whenever he had the chance, learning by ear what worked and what did not.

"My feelings were, then, that if you were ever going to be a songwriter, the height of it all was [to write for] Sinatra. That would be the greatest stuff you could do. Around the time I wrote ['Suicide'] I thought it would be a bit of a Rat Pack smooch."[46]

About the composition itself, he remembered lying in bed, getting ideas for lyrics. "I kept a paper and pencil by my bed, I'd just sort of lean out and try and not wake up, try and write them down."[47] What came to him this time was the tale of a young girl, stifled by her overbearing lover. Oddly, Paul's lyric does not characterize this stifling as "trouble" or "suffocating," but as "suicide."

What put the image in Paul's head? Several high-profile cases involving suicide were in the news in 1956, and it's possible that Paul was influenced by a story in Jim Mac's daily paper. One involved a suicide pact by two young lovers, Valerie Sparkes and Gordon Norris, whose story grabbed the headlines on May 9.[48] Forbidden by their parents to marry because of the four-year age gap between them, Norris suggested they take their own lives by gas poisoning. But Sparkes survived and was charged with Norris's murder. Her case played out in the press for two months, with the coroner ultimately recording a verdict of suicide. A second case flashed across the front pages in August—that of Gertrude Joyce Hullett, a wealthy widow who died after taking an overdose of barbiturates. "Rich Widow Drama—Suicide Verdict" read the *Daily Mirror*'s headline on August 22. "She was depressed, she had talked of suicide,"[49] the story explained.

Now that 'Suicide' was retired from Paul's party repertoire, he was thinking about finding its full potential, and in the surviving section of the take, he moves through various accompaniment and vocal styles, trying to find the right groove. But if he were to seriously revive it, he would have to add a few more verses, so it went back onto the "unfinished" stack.

Recording Sessions

Tuesday–Tuesday, December 23–30, 1969.
Cavendish Avenue, Home Studio, London.
Recording: 'Teddy Boy,' 'Backwards Guitar Piece,' and 'Hot As Sun.'

With only a few minutes left on his first reel of tape, Paul threaded a second BASF reel to record 'Teddy Boy,' one of only two songs recorded during these home sessions to survive in multiple takes (the other being 'Junk'). McCartney composed 'Teddy Boy' during his five weeks at the Maharishi Mahesh Yogi's Transcendental Meditation Academy. His daily schedule, and that of the other students, began with private contemplation in one of the compound's 84 six-by-four-foot "mediation caves," followed by a vegetarian breakfast and then mass prayers led by the maharishi. Lectures on Transcendental Meditation followed.[50]

Whether it was a benefit of meditation, or simply being away from London, the trip opened the creative floodgates for Paul, John and George, each of whom returned with a stack of new songs. Paul wrote 11 (that are documented): 'Back in the U.S.S.R.,' 'Blackbird,' 'I Will,' 'Mother Nature's Son,' 'Rocky Raccoon,' 'Why Don't We Do It in the Road?,' 'Cosmically Conscious,' 'Ob-La-Di, Ob-La-Da,' 'Honey Pie,' 'Teddy Boy,' and 'Junk.'

'Teddy Boy' reaches even further into Paul's childhood than 'Suicide.' It takes its name from a corner of British youth culture with roots in fashion—specifically, the revival of the Edwardian style—but with a dangerous air of toughness.

"The New Edwardian is a brave man, serving a lost cause," a writer for the *Tatler and Bystander* wrote in 1952. "He has done what hitherto has been done only by women—looking into the past to find the clothes of tomorrow. He has chosen his period, one of the most baroque and contradictory in men's dress as in many other things, and he is loyal to it."[51]

Reintroduced by Savile Row tailors, in 1949,[52] the Edwardian style suit, popular at the turn of the century, was enjoying a renaissance. By 1951, the look was embraced by a new generation of young Londoners, drawn to its characteristic "long jacket with high four-button front, waistcoat with step collar and the narrow 'drainpipe' trousers."[53] Tailors helped foment broader interest by making inexpensive versions: in October 1951, one West End tailor offered an Edwardian suit for £12 ($33.50)—a quarter the price of its Savile Row counterpart. And by 1953, the style was adopted by the fashion-conscious workingman; even dockworkers snapped up Edwardian suits as postwork attire, complete with the latest touch, an overcoat with a velvet collar.[54]

In four short years, the Edwardian look had transitioned from high society to high street, and was about to morph from a brand of fashion to a brand of violence as bands of teenage gangs in Edwardian attire became prominent.

The most infamous of these gangs were the Teddy Boys of Clapham Common, led by the 16-year-old Ronnie "The Masher" Coleman. In July 1953, Coleman and five members of his gang were charged with the murder of 17-year-old John Ernest Beckley, who they dragged from a bus to Clapham Common, where they savagely beat him, stabbed him 11 times, and left him to die.[55] Coleman's gang called themselves "The Edwardians," but their girlfriends referred to them as "Teddy Boys." That moniker made the front page of the *Daily Express* on September 23, 1953, and from that day forward, the term "Teddy Boys" was associated, on a national level, with hooligans in Edwardian dress.

Two years later, when rock and roll hit Britain like a thunderbolt, by way of director Richard Brooks's *Blackboard Jungle*, Britain's Teddy Boys went wild, tearing up theater seats, showering fellow cinemagoers with glass, and dancing in the streets.

"The main trouble is caused when the song 'Rock Around the Clock' is played during the film," one theater manager complained. "It causes a form of mass hysteria among the teenage element in the audience."[56] Teddy Boys embraced rock and roll, and for the older generation, the two became the embodiment of all the ills of society.

Except for its title, which inevitably brings this history to mind, McCartney's 'Teddy Boy' inhabits a different universe from the foppish teenage gangsters of fifties Britain. While Teddy Boys were associated with hostility and violence, McCartney's song is about a boy whose name actually is Ted, and who is devoted to his mother, a widow whose soldier husband was killed during World War II.

As the lyric tells us, "*When she said, 'Teddy be good,' he would*"—probably not the situation at Ronald "The Masher" Coleman's home; nor is it easy to imagine someone of Coleman's ilk singing the refrain, "*Momma don't worry, your Teddy Boy's here, taking good care of you-oo-oo*"—much less running away from home because he couldn't bear it when his mother found a new man.

Paul had the tune and most of the lyrics when he returned from India, but as the performances recorded with the Beatles in January 1969 demonstrate, it was structurally a bit amorphous. He polished it up in Scotland and London.

"There was always a song that'd lie around for a couple of years with one good part, and you'd mean to finish it one day. The words 'Teddy Boy' to English people had always meant what you might have called a 'hood' in America, a motorcycle type of guy. To us, it was these fellas in Edwardian long coats, a big fashion when I was growing up. I also have a cousin Ted, so he was the other meaning."[57]

Paul recorded two takes of 'Teddy Boy,' both with the same track layout: acoustic guitar on track one, lead vocals on track two, a lovely vocal counterpoint by Linda on track three, and bass on track four. He marked the first take "Master?" and the second "Another Version," but kept both for further consideration.

With 'Teddy Boy' complete, the urge to experiment grabbed Paul again. Using a technique similar to one the Beatles used during the *Revolver* sessions, most notably on 'I'm Only Sleeping' and 'Rain,' Paul recorded four guitar lines. He then cut the tape, spliced some white leader onto the end, and turned the recording upside down so that the leader was at the top, and the guitar music was heard running backward. Paul edited the recording onto his reel after take two of 'Teddy Boy.' In the absence of a better title, he listed it as 'Backwards Guitar Piece.'

The final recording McCartney made in his Cavendish Avenue living room before the end of the year was 'Hot As Sun,' the 1959 instrumental. When Paul revived it at a Beatles session on January 24, he sang a scat vocal and included a comic, tropical-themed spoken section: "*Welcome to the South Sea Islands, where the sound of a wave landing on the sand brings joy to the air, and the ears of the natives.*"[58]

This time he did it as a straightforward instrumental. Starting with an acoustic guitar guide track, he added a more precise rhythm guitar, a melodic electric guitar line and drums. But noting distortion on those tracks, he decided to abandon the song for the moment.

———

Surveying what he had recorded so far, Paul was convinced that his Cavendish recordings were the start of a respectable (and releasable) album.

"I had all these rough things and I liked them all," Paul reasoned. "And thought, well, they're rough, but they've got that certain kind of thing about them, so we'll just put it out."[59]

But a number of issues—running out of tracks to record extra instruments and vocals, the comparatively dry acoustics of his living room, the problem of getting a drum sound he liked, and of course, the irritation of working without a mixer or VU meters—suggested that he needed some time in a fully equipped studio.

He asked Linda to book him time at Morgan Studios in Willesden, and at EMI—but to do so under a pseudonym, to keep the project secret. Linda made the bookings under the name Billy Martin, an American baseball player and manager, who had managed (and been fired by) the Minnesota Twins that year.* Since Paul wanted to use Morgan's largest studio, which already had book-

---

* Although the choice of Billy Martin as a pseudonym was almost certainly Linda's, the name would have resonated with Paul as well, though in a different connection. Growing up in Liverpool, he would have been aware of the Martin School of Dancing, on Derby Lane. Membership cards to the school, which offered nightly lessons in ballroom dancing, carried a photo of a dapper Billy Martin and his dance partner, identified only as Pauline.

ings through January, and because he had other obligations for the first weeks of the year, the sessions would not begin until February.

Apart from a few brief interviews devoted mostly to whether or not he was still alive, Paul had been out of the public eye, and deliberately so, since October. The press, used to knowing where celebrities were and what they were doing, began to describe McCartney as a hermit and to wonder whether his scarceness on the London scene meant that something was amiss in the Beatles universe. He had hoped to circumvent such speculation by mentioning, in his BBC interview with Chris Drake, that the Beatles had no plans until midwinter, and that he might remain in Scotland until March, but it was to no avail.

With Paul not fielding questions, it was left to the others to deny that there were problems between them. John, not atypically, was all over the place, complaining that all his money was going into Apple,[60] leaving him without much to spend on his projects (films, most notably) with Yoko, and airing a few internal gripes, including the other Beatles' disinclination to record 'Cold Turkey.'[61]

He offered some telling comments about his collaboration with Paul, explaining what many Beatles fans already knew—that they rarely wrote together anymore, by saying that "we used to write mainly on tours. We got bored so we wrote. Today the Beatles just go into a studio, and *it* happens."[62]

Both John and George noted that the Beatles were all composing so prolifically, they needed other outlets like, in John's case, the Plastic Ono Band.

"The trouble is that we've far too much material," John explained. "Now that George is writing a lot we could put out a double album every month, but they're so difficult to produce. After *Get Back* is released in January, we'll probably go back into the studios and record another one. It's just a shame that we can't get more albums out faster."[63]

John and George also both noted a yen to tour again—John citing the energizing effect of his Toronto experience, and George enthusing about the recent tour he undertook with the American R&B band, Delaney and Bonnie and Friends—but worried that touring with the Beatles was problematic. About the Beatles' collective future, though, John expressed only optimism, tempered with criticism that mirrored his comments about Paul's "granny music" during the September 9 meeting.

"I can see it happening," he said of a new Beatles album in early December. "The Beatles can go on appealing to a wide audience as long as they make albums like *Abbey Road*, which have nice little folk songs like 'Maxwell's Silver Hammer' for the grannies to dig." He even suggested a new direction for the Beatles, saying that he "always wanted to have other people on our records, like the Stones and our other friends. But some of the others wanted to keep it tight—just the Beatles, you know? But you wait—it's starting to get looser, and there should be some fantastic sessions in the next few years. That's what I wanted all along."[64]

Even Ringo, it seemed, needed new outlets. *The Magic Christian* was his second film, after *Candy* in 1968. Now he was working on a solo album of standards—the songs he and his relatives sang at family parties when he was growing up. He had conceived the project as a gift for his step-father, Harry Greaves, who would be doing the singing. But throat problems kept Greaves from making the record, so Starr went ahead with the album, singing the songs himself.

But Ringo was not shy in voicing his opinion on the future of the Beatles, and his bandmates' sometimes provocative side projects.

"I don't particularly dig what John and Yoko are doing," Ringo noted of the couple's inclination toward mixing art and politics. "We all feel strongly about things. It's just a matter of how far you'll go. I mean, I just like to make my peace at home . . . You see we all have our part to play. We are four completely different people. We have all stopped doing things together. We are only together for meetings and recordings now. We are not all squeezed into the same room."[65]

No one was discussing Paul's musical future, much less other matters that weighed on him—Klein's plans for Apple, for starters, and what the business tensions between the Beatles were really about. And that suited Paul. He wanted his album to be a surprise, and he was less inclined than John to drag the Beatles' business relationship into the public domain.

As 1969 wound to a close, Paul, Linda, Heather and Mary took a quick trip to Liverpool to celebrate the New Year, and the new decade, with the McCartney clan.

4

ENTER BILLY MARTIN

—

The Beatles were three and a half months into their secret breakup, but there was still work to be done preparing the *Get Back* album for release. As Michael Lindsay-Hogg's film edit progressed, it became clear that the Beatles would be seen working on two songs that they had not completed in January—John's 'Across the Universe' and George's 'I Me Mine'—and that Paul's 'Teddy Boy,' included on the Glyn Johns–sequenced album, would not be used. That was fine with Paul, who wanted it for his own album and had already asked Johns to remove it from the LP sequence.[1]

The need for a finished 'Across the Universe' was easily solved: the version the Beatles recorded on February 4 and 8, 1968, could be revived. It had been included on *No One's Gonna Change Our World*, a charity compilation for the World Wildlife Fund. But Phil Spector could create a new version by remixing the song from the multitrack session tapes.

There was no easy solution for 'I Me Mine,' so Paul, George and Ringo—John was in Denmark—gathered at EMI Studio Two to record the song on January 3, 1970. It was the first time the three had worked together since John's September 16 bombshell, and George noted John's absence with deadpan comic obliqueness in an introduction to one of the takes.

George: You all will have read that Dave Dee's no longer with us. But Mick and Tich and I would like to carry on the good work that's always gone down in No. 2.*

Paul: *What Dozy says goes for me and Tich.*

[All three let out a nervous laugh.][2]

---

* The references were to the British band Dave Dee, Dozy, Beaky, Mick and Tich, whose most recent album, *Together*, had been released in September, and to EMI's Studio No. 2, where the Beatles had recorded most of their work.

But over the course of the session, which ran from 2:30 p.m. to 12:15 a.m., they also discussed John's departure and the group's future, as Paul remembered.

"I sat around wondering what I was going to do, and whether I was just going to be an ex-legend. I asked George and Ringo if they thought we might get back together again and they said we might, but we'd have to give John a bit more time. The time kept passing and I decided I wasn't going to sit around and do nothing."[3]

The three returned to EMI the next afternoon to work on Paul's 'Let It Be,' in a session that ran from 2:30 p.m. to 4:00 a.m. Paul had asked George Martin to write a score to flesh out the song, so a saxophonist, pairs of trumpets and trombones, and a small group of cellists were on hand for the session as well.

The take of 'Let It Be' they were filling out was recorded on January 31, 1969, and uniquely among the January recordings, it had already received a postproduction touch-up—a guitar solo, recorded by George on April 30. Glyn Johns used that version for his *Get Back* sequence, and that, combined with the new recording of 'I Me Mine,' and the planned refurbishing of 'Across the Universe' meant that the "no overdubs" rule for the album was truly abandoned. The overdubs undertaken on January 4 were extensive and included Linda's debut on a Beatles recording, singing backing vocals with George.

"It was supposed to be me and Mary Hopkin," Linda recalled, "but she'd gone home."[4]

Martin's orchestral score was recorded next, and by the time the session ended, Paul had added maracas, George played a new guitar solo, and Ringo added some touch-ups to the drums.

Paul attended the mixing sessions at Olympic Studios, on January 8, despite a stomach flu that hit him the previous night, after he and Linda had dinner with the model Twiggy and her boyfriend, Justin de Villeneuve. Pleased with the touch-ups, Paul and company decided to release this version of 'Let It Be' as a single, due March 6,[5] and to retitle both the film and the album *Let It Be*.[6]

Paul was also eager to return to his own album, but with his studio dates still a few weeks away, he and Linda flew to New York, on January 12, to celebrate Lee Eastman's birthday at a family dinner at Lee's apartment. Before returning to London three days later, Paul and Linda packed in some shopping at Saks, Bloomingdales and Colony music, and lunch with Hal David, Burt Bacharach's songwriting partner—the Beatles had recorded their 'Baby It's You' on their debut album, *Please Please Me*, in 1963—at Romeo Salta, an Italian restaurant on West 56th Street.

Back in London, Paul fired up the Studer in his living room studio for one last home session.

Recording Session

Saturday, January 17, 1970.

Cavendish Avenue, Home Studio, London.

Recording: 'Junk.'

After the intensive late-December sessions in his home studio, the novelty of multitracking on a machine without VU meters or a mixer had started to wear thin, and distortion on the last tracks Paul recorded led him to take a hiatus. But after a few weeks away from the Studer, he wanted to get back to work; specifically, he wanted to revive 'Junk.'

When he composed the song, in Rishikesh, he had the full melody and some of the lyrics—the first verse, part of the second, and the full bridge. Urged by Linda, he had completed the song in London[7] between early and mid-1969, adding two more verses, one of which—"*Caravans, boiler pans, Something old and new, Memories of you, and me*"—was crossed out, its last line pinched to complete the final verse.[8]

"Linda was very helpful," McCartney said of her role in finishing the song, "because she used to say, 'I love to hear you play the guitar.' I was no longer sitting in a room on my own, like I used to be. So I'd strum along, when I watch telly. 'Junk' came along that way. Handlebars, sentimental jubilee, jam jars—I like images like that. There are certain words you like. I always used to say that candlestick was my favorite word. Certain words either make colors in your head or bring up a feeling. So the song was a potpourri of nice words that I had to make some sense out of, so it was '*buy, buy, sell, sell, Junk says the sign in the yard.*' To lump it all together I got the idea of 'Junk.' It was a nice way to write a song."[9]

Paul recorded three versions. The first (take one) began with an acoustic rhythm guitar, to which he added a melodic guitar line, a piano part that, in its most interesting moments, played ornamental variations on the melody, and a bass line, yielding an instrumental that ran 2'35". Take two was arranged similarly, but with a vocal in place of the piano on track three, and significantly shorter, at 1'46". Take three was aborted after a single guitar track.

Paul spliced his three takes of 'Junk' to the end of his first four-track reel. His stash of home recordings now had the following running order:

TAPE NO. MAC 363

'The Lovely Linda'
'That Would Be Something'

'Rock and Roll Springtime ('Momma')
'Instrumental, 12-bar' ('Miss America')
'Rupert'
'Instrumental' ('Oo You')
'Instrumental' ('Valentine Day')
'Glasses'
'Suicide'
'Junk' (three takes)

TAPE NO. MAC 386

'Teddy Boy' (two takes)
'Backwards Guitar Piece'
'Hot As Sun'

Paul continued to keep his album under wraps, a secret from both the public and Apple. But he was pleased enough with the results to let Ringo in on it when the drummer and his wife, Maureen, visited the McCartneys for dinner on January 22, 1970. Ringo kept the news to himself, even when he was approached, nearly a month later by Alan Smith of *Melody Maker*, who was writing an article that wondered, in its headline, "Why Is Paul the Hermit of St. John's Wood?" Ringo was circumspect, telling Smith only that he and Maureen had been to the McCartneys' home for dinner recently, and that: "He's writing songs. He's doing things. He's happy."[10]

Recording Session

Saturday, January 24, 1970.
EMI Studios, Studio Two, London.
Mixing: 'The Lovely Linda,' 'That Would Be Something,' 'Valentine Day,' 'Momma,' 'Oo You,' and 'Teddy Boy.'

His between-takes discussions with George and Ringo on January 3 notwithstanding, Paul was no longer waiting to see whether John would return to the fold. His interest was now focused on completing his own album. When he learned that EMI had time available on January 24, he popped in with his home tapes, and with engineers Phil McDonald and John Kurlander at the desk, he made preliminary mixes of six of his Cavendish tracks. These mixes, designed only for review, would never see the light of day.

Apart from his obligation to help finish *Let It Be*, Paul kept his distance from Apple, and when he had to deal with the company, he could be short-tempered and distant. Neil Aspinall and Mal Evans discovered as much when they paid Paul a visit on January 27 and found him aloof, even critical. "Seem to be losing Paul," a downcast Evans noted in his diary. "Really got the stick from him today."[11]

Paul and Linda spent the final weekend of January visiting family in Liverpool, returning on February 2. Three days later, Paul telephoned Mal, and told him: "I've got EMI over this weekend—I would like you to pick up some gear from the house." Mal took heart from the news that Paul was recording again, but his expectation of settling into the general assistant and tea-brewer role he had always performed at Beatles' sessions was quickly dashed when Paul added, "But I don't want anyone there to make me tea, I have the family, wife and kids there."[12]

Recording Sessions

Saturday–Sunday, February 7–8, 1970.
EMI Studios, Studio Two, London.
Full details unknown.

It is unclear what Paul did during these two sessions, which were documented only in Mal Evans's and John Kurlander's diaries. The Evans entry, about Paul asking him to bring equipment to EMI, suggests that recording or overdubbing was planned. But no new recordings, overdubs or finished mixes can be attributed to these sessions.

Paul may have used the time for review and housekeeping—for example, checking the distorted recordings on his second reel to see if anything was salvageable, or making rough mixes that, like those he made on January 24, would help him decide which songs might benefit from instrumental or vocal overdubs.

It is possible, too, that in the process of reviewing the Cavendish tapes and the mixes he made on January 24, he had a nagging feeling that the home recordings might sound amateurish and was pondering remaking the tracks under optimum studio conditions.

"I remember thinking I could do this more professionally, and thinking maybe I ought to just use this as a demo album," he later confessed. "Maybe I ought to go and rerecord it. But it's a funny decision that, because you can sometimes go and do that, [and] you can lose a lot of the feeling by taking it in and trying to do it all very sophisticated and properly."[13]

By the middle of February 1970, reporters were hearing rumors that Paul was recording an album. *NME* reported in its February 14 issue that "Paul McCartney is to release a solo album of his own compositions. This is a long-awaited move from the Beatle who has so far been least interested in projects outside the group. Paul has been writing and arranging new material for some time in preparation for the venture."[14]

Melody Maker, following up in its next issue, added that McCartney has a small studio at home and was working on "songs which may be used in his first solo album." Seeking a comment from Apple, the paper was told that the company was "almost sure" that Paul would release an album—a response that underscores the degree to which Paul had deliberately kept Apple out of the loop.

Paul was not in London when those stories hit the newsstands. As a brief family getaway, to clear his mind before making the final push to complete his album, Paul took Linda, the girls and Martha, his sheepdog, for a drive south in his dark green Rolls-Royce Continental, stopping first at Bournemouth, on February 10. The weather was dismal, with snow and gale force winds, but that did not keep the McCartneys from walking along the breakwater: in Torquay, on the second day of the trip, Linda took a shot of Paul, holding Mary in his coat, as the waves crashed in the background. From Torquay, they drove to St. Ives, and then to Sidmouth on February 13, before heading home the next day.

The road trip was partly a scouting mission. As much as they loved the rustic charm of High Park, Linda and Paul were also looking for a country pile closer to home. Impromptu drives around the south coast of England were something they enjoyed, and the previous September, Linda had written to real estate agents in Berkshire, Sussex, Kent, and other counties in the southeast, saying that she and Paul were interested in a farm "in an unspoilable and secluded area within 70 miles of London."

More specifically, they were looking for a four- or five-bedroom farmhouse, perhaps with out-buildings, on land ranging from 50 to 500 acres, where they could stable (and ride) a few horses. "Ideally," Linda continued in one of the letters, "we would like the land to be natural—hilly—have its own wildlife and trees and if possible, be surrounded by national trust land."

"As you can see," she concluded, "we are looking for a home in 'the heart of the country.'"[15]

Their stop at Sidmouth excited interest from the local press. Linda had booked a suite at the Victoria Hotel, asking for "the best in the house." Her accent led the staff to expect an American family, but when the McCartneys arrived, even Paul's thick black beard failed to put the press off the scent. Mostly, they remained in their room, having melon, fish and fillet steak for dinner, and checking out the next morning. On the way out of town, they stopped at a newsagent's, where

Paul bought the week's music papers, a Valentine's Day card, and some postcards of Sidmouth. There were no other customers to bother him, and the salesgirl, Priscilla Maeers, was too discreet to trouble him for an autograph.

"He had a beard, but I recognized him from his photograph," she said. "I didn't like to ask him if he was Paul McCartney."[16]

The improvement in Paul's state of mind could be measured by the fact that once he realized that he still needed a few new songs to add heft to his collection, he reconnected completely with his muse. Instead of fleshing out 'The Lovely Linda' and 'That Would Be Something,' he revived a chord sequence he had come up with during the first flush of his romance with Linda, tweaked it further and wrote new lyrics. The song, 'Maybe I'm Amazed,' matched the quality of his best Beatles work.

"It's like when you write millions of love songs, and finally when you're in love you'd like to write one for the person you're in love with,"[17] Paul explained. "I was sitting in London, playing my piano, and the song kind of wrote itself—reflecting my feelings towards her.[18]

"Even though it had been a very heavy, difficult period, meeting Linda and starting a family was the escape. I could see that there was life out there.[19] We were getting to know each other, and I was getting the confidence that maybe I could do stuff outside the Beatles, and she was helping me with that confidence.[20] The two of us had this bond that we could fight the world. So in writing that, and in writing it for her, it kind of strengthened our bond, and gave me a bit of strength to go forward."[21]

If 'The Lovely Linda' was born of a crisis of confidence, 'Maybe I'm Amazed' was an expression of self-assurance and lucidity. And where 'The Lovely Linda' was a snapshot, 'Maybe I'm Amazed' filled in the details. The lyrics are purely confessional, a tentative, first-person exploration of love, loneliness, confusion and fear, laced with a blend of surprise and gratitude not only for "*the way you help me sing my song*," but also "*right me when I'm wrong*" in ways enumerated, in a kind of shorthand, throughout the song.

"'*Maybe I'm amazed at the way you pulled me out of time, hung me on the line*'," Paul explained, quoting his lyric, "these were things that were happening at the time, and these phrases were my symbols for them."[22]

It was not hard to decipher those symbols. Linda hung Paul on a line by sobering him up, and she pulled him out of time by reassuring him that the end of the Beatles was not the end of Paul McCartney. Though they had only been married nine months by early 1970, Linda had established herself as an important force in her husband's life. Now her influence could be heard on an artistic level, her bullish, unwavering support kick-starting McCartney's stalled songwriting engine.

Musically, the song does not sound revolutionary on a casual listen, but it boasts an unusual chord progression, full of surprising key shifts, major-minor pivoting (a characteristic of many Beatles songs) and a notably expressive melody.

McCartney wrote only two verses and one bridge for the song, but he wove them into a structure that makes the song's materials seem more expansive: the introduction, verse 1, bridge, verse (guitar solo), bridge, verse 2, bridge (instrumental), and then a coda in which the verse progression supports a second guitar solo that fades out as McCartney moves the song into its original D major home key.

Recording Session

Sunday, February 15, 1970.
EMI Studios, Studio Two, London.
Recording: 'Maybe I'm Amazed.'

Upon their return to London, Paul was keen to get his latest work on tape, and since he had already booked EMI Studios, he bypassed the home demo stage. 'Maybe I'm Amazed' was recorded in a single session, on the evening of February 15, with Paul working largely as he did at home, but without having to be both artist and engineer, and now having eight tracks available instead of four. EMI had assigned Phil McDonald as the balance engineer, with Alan Parsons, a newcomer on the EMI staff, assisting. Parsons had attended some of the *Get Back* and *Abbey Road* sessions, but he was startled at the ease and efficiency with which Paul worked.

"He played every single instrument, did all the vocals with one small contribution from Linda, but it was a song, 'Maybe I'm Amazed.' He did the whole thing, start to finish, every instrument, bass, drums, guitars, keyboards, everything, in a day, and I remember being so, so impressed with that."[23]

Taped in EMI's Studio Two, the large room where the Beatles did most of their recording, 'Maybe I'm Amazed' was a thoroughly polished production. Paul began with piano and lead vocal, recorded on tracks one and two. Drums were added on track three, then bass on track four and backing vocals, with Linda, plus hand clapping, on track five. The texture was filled out further with an organ and more backing vocals, all on track six, leaving the final two tracks for lead and rhythm electric guitar parts.

Within those eight tracks, Paul's arrangement strategies are ingenious. Consider his painterly use of the organ. It first appears supporting the sustained A major chord at the end of the introduction, and though it is subtle, it magnifies the drama of that pause before the vocal begins. It then slips into the background until the second of the song's three instrumental breaks—itself an unusual touch for McCartney—when it returns in full force.

In the first verse, McCartney accompanies his vocal with a sparse backdrop of piano and bass, bringing in the drums—first just high-hat taps and a muted bass drum (you hear, and feel, mallet strike the skin, but with no resonance) on the final two lines.

The arrangement expands further at the bridge, with full drums and backing vocals, and Paul's lead vocal changing from his ballad voice to the grittier sound he uses for tougher rock songs. That leads back to the verse, its chords supporting the first instrumental break, a melodic guitar solo, backed by scat vocals, a second guitar, and a hit of organ, providing a subtle counterpoint in the two closing lines. The bridge then returns, with McCartney's vocal more excitable than it had been in the first pass.

The second verse brings a change of texture provided by the percussive use of a toneless, rhythmically strummed electric guitar. Here, Paul overdubbed a second electric guitar playing a quickly repeating high B-flat, played in a stuttering rhythm that makes it sound like Morse code, and running through the verse. But he had second thoughts about this textural touch and mixed it out. The organ-dominated, instrumental version of the bridge follows, and seems, for a moment, to bring the song full circle, ending on a sustained A major chord, just as the introduction does. But it's a false ending; in the coda, McCartney offers an expansion on one of the earlier guitar solos.

Tracking the song took only a few hours, and McCartney, McDonald and Parsons made a preliminary mix that same night. In the process, McCartney captured four minutes of music that gave the impression of unbridled spontaneity.

"I think the musical results sound the same to me, because I'm aiming for the same thing," McCartney said, comparing working alone to working with the Beatles. "I still like the same kind of music, I still try to achieve the same kind of music as I would if I were playing with the Beatles. The same thing exactly in my mind. I still hear the same tune with its same arrangement and that tune and arrangement I then try and achieve. That's what it's about."[24]

———

Finally, it was time for Paul's five-day block at Morgan Studios. Booked into Studio One from February 16 through 20, 1970, he arrived just as Jethro Tull were nearing the end of two months of work on *Benefit*, the group's third album. Robin Black, Morgan's junior engineer, remembers Tull's front man, Ian Anderson, walking in for a session just as Paul was leaving, and asking, "Was that *Paul McCartney*?"[25] Anderson and Black were two of only a handful of people aware of McCartney's presence in North West London.

Recording Sessions

Monday–Tuesday, February 16–17, 1970.
Morgan Studios, Studio One, London.
Tape transfer and overdubbing: 'Teddy Boy.'

Measuring just 37 by 24 feet, and 13 ½ feet high, Morgan Studio One was roughly half the size of EMI Studio Two (McCartney described the room in Willesden as "cosy.")[26]

"We all used to work around the clock, all hours of the day," Robin Black recalled, noting that he sometimes slept behind the mixer, because late-night sessions would often run nearly to the start of the next day's earliest session. "You'd have to get up early, kind of grab some breakfast from somewhere, and get all the microphones set up and ready. We had a vocal booth so you could have a live vocal at the back of the control room."[27]

Black, just 21 at the time, had been working as an engineer for only a year, during which he engineered albums by the Incredible String Band, Blodwyn Pig (the band formed by Mick Abrahams after he left Jethro Tull) and Stone the Crows.* But he had never imagined he would record Paul McCartney until Paul turned up at the studio that Monday morning.

"When McCartney came in," Black said, "I thought Glyn Johns was supposed to be there. Paul said to me, 'Who's engineering?' I said, 'Well, actually I thought I was supposed to show Glyn how to work the desk.' He said to me, 'I don't think Glyn's going to turn up today. Can you do it?' With wobbly knees, and a quick prayer to God, I said, 'Yes please, I'd love to.' And it was great. He wanted a closed session. He didn't actually want an assistant. So, really it was just Paul, and Linda, and myself."[28]

At the February 16 session, McCartney and Black oversaw the transfer of Paul's four-track home recordings to an eight-track master, giving them four extra tracks for fresh overdubs, if necessary, on each song.

The next day, McCartney began adding to his home tapes, selecting 'Teddy Boy' as the first song to which new textures would be overdubbed. Paul's four-track recording was sparse—just guitar, lead vocal, harmony vocals and bass—but finishing it was easy work: apart from beefing up the lead and backing vocals by doubling them, he added three forms of percussion—drums,

---

* After the success of *Benefit*, Black became Jethro Tull's principal engineer, and subsequently worked, as either engineer or producer, with an array of artists, among them Steeleye Span, Fairport Convention, Black Sabbath, Gerry Rafferty, Cat Stevens, America, Ian Matthews, and Lou Reed.

clapping and tapping his leg with his hands, a technique similar to his book-slapping percussion on 'The Lovely Linda.'

———▶

A couple of years earlier, in his days as the bachelor Beatle, McCartney would have rolled out of the recording studio and into a favorite club, often the Bag O' Nails or the Scotch of St. James. These days, he was more likely to drive the four miles from Willesden to St. John's Wood, light the fire (and most likely an "herbal jazz cigarette," as he preferred to call reefers), and switch on the television. Domesticity was the new norm.

"I would rather be in bed than at the clubs," he claimed in early 1970. "For me life at home is what is interesting now. I have two kids, a wife of one year and everything at home. I love being at home."[29]

Sometimes, that meant renting a 16 mm film—often a Disney classic—to screen for Heather and Mary. More often, it meant watching TV. The night he polished off 'Teddy Boy' at Morgan Studios, McCartney settled in before the box, eager to indulge a guilty pleasure—watching two grown, heavily muscled men pummel each other until one falls down, in this case, the title fight between Joe Frazier and Jimmy Ellis for the world heavyweight championship.

"My dad and I liked boxing in Liverpool," Paul admitted. "We knew all the boxers, we watched a lot of it on telly.[30] I, sort of, almost don't like liking it, because sometimes you see some terrible stuff, but it's exciting. So I watch the big title fights and stuff."[31] (Paul had another link, if a tenuous one, to boxing: Johnny Best, the stepfather of Pete Best, the Beatles drummer from 1960 to 1962, was a well-known Liverpool boxing promoter.)

As boxing matches go, the Frazier-Ellis fight was big. It had taken place the previous evening, February 16, at Madison Square Garden, in New York City, and though a closed-circuit feed was shown live in arenas around the United States, people paid as much as $500,000 (£208,100)[32] for ringside seats. With the starting bell ringing at 10:30 p.m. in New York, British viewers had to wait for the delayed broadcast on BBC1, at 10:00 p.m. the next evening.

The fight lasted only four rounds, well under 20 minutes, with Frazier victorious. The BBC offered another 20 minutes of commentary, but Paul instead switched to ITV for the 10:30 p.m. broadcast of *The Tribe That Hides from Man*, a groundbreaking documentary by Adrian Cowell about an effort to contact the Kreen-Akrore Indians of the Brazilian rain forest.

As Cowell wrote, in a piece that McCartney would likely have read in the February 14–21 issue of *TV Times*, this extraordinary film follows representatives of the Brazilian government, plus members of other rain forest tribes, in search of the Kreen-Akrore—their name means skinheads, or short-haired people, in the Měbêngôkre language spoken by several Brazilian tribes*—in the hope of moving them to an area where they would be safe from forest-destroying prospectors and the diseases they brought.

The problem was that the Kreen-Akrore were fierce and decidedly nongregarious. They had no friendly relations with other tribes and were known to massacre any non-Kreen-Akrore visitors they encountered. By the end of the 66-minute film, the team had reached a wary standoff with the Kreen-Akrore but had not achieved communication or contact.

Paul was fascinated by the film and was particularly taken with its soundtrack, which included a rich variety of tribal music—drumming, melodies played on rough-hewn wind instruments, and war chants—recorded on location by Gareth Haywood, Bruce White and Mike Billing—as well as a tense, uncredited score.

A musical response began forming in McCartney's mind immediately.

Recording Session

Wednesday, February 18, 1970.
Morgan Studios, Studio One, London.
Overdubbing: 'Junk (Instrumental)' (working title for 'Singalong Junk') and 'Junk.'
Recording & Mixing: 'Kreen Akrore.'

Paul returned to Morgan on the 18th, and though a piece inspired by *The Tribe That Hides from Man* was still percolating, the first order of business was to complete the two versions of 'Junk' he had recorded at home. On take one, the instrumental version he would soon rename 'Singalong Junk,' he used the remaining four tracks to add electric guitar, bass drum, sizzle cymbal and an old Beatles favorite, the Mellotron.

The Mellotron Mark II is often described as a primitive synthesizer, but it would be more accurate to call it an early sampler. It was loaded with a library of tape loops made from recordings of real string, wind and brass instruments, a Spanish guitar (the flamenco flourish that introduces 'The Continuing Story of Bungalow Bill,' on the *White Album*, is a Mellotron loop) and other sounds. The loops were triggered by playing the Mellotron's 35-note keyboard, and their sounds could be shaped with a pitch control that allowed for extreme glissando effects. It was not inexpensive—the Mark II cost about £1000[33] ($2,400)—but it allowed artists to create rich soundscapes at the touch of its keys.

---

* Today the Kreen-Akrore are known as the Panará.

"Mellotrons have got a reality about them," McCartney said, explaining his interest in the instrument. "It doesn't sound synthetic. It's the kind of thing you can use as a color on a record . . . It's a world of possibilities, it makes making a record more fun."[34]

For 'Singalong Junk' McCartney used the Mellotron "strings" loop—a rudimentary string ensemble, approximating the sound of an orchestra. McCartney and Black then moved on to take two—'Junk,' the vocal version—to which Paul overdubbed drums (bass drum, snare, and cymbal), toy xylophone and harmony vocals.

Before breaking for lunch, Paul told Black that he planned to record a new, largely improvisatory song during the afternoon session and explained the dramatic essence of the Cowell documentary. Together, they gave Studio One a makeover to set the mood, building a fire at the center of the studio's hardwood floor, and recording the sounds of the twigs breaking in the flame.

Paul began his improvised piece by laying down a basic drum track. With relatively little recording experience under his belt, Robin Black remembers struggling to keep pace with McCartney's rapid flow of ideas.

"I was really very nervous," Black explained. "I was just trying to do my best to make sure everything sounded good, and Paul was happy. It was all in his mind—he just knew exactly what he wanted to do. So we set up a drum sound and he said what sort of sound he wanted. Once he'd got the drums down—of course that's the most important thing, because that's the kingpin to everything that comes afterwards—he just added to that."[35]

To enrich the rhythm section McCartney doubled the drum part. He then added two electric guitars, organ, piano, and a simple bass guitar part to create the song's rock sections—a move away from the tribal inspiration, serving not only as a change of musical perspective, but also as a kind of commentary on the tension between the Kreen-Akrore and the Brazilian and Indian team trying to contact them.

At this stage of the song's development, McCartney felt it sounded more like a rock instrumental than a tribute to an indigenous South American tribe. So he devised a series of overdubs meant to invoke the spirit of the jungle. These included a "stampede of animals,"[36] played by drumming his fingers on a guitar case; approximations of tribal chants, sung by Paul and Linda; and deep breathing, from Paul alone, sounding as if he were either a hunter chasing his quarry, or perhaps being chased. Also added were "animal noises"—actually, Paul and Linda screeching like monkeys, recorded at a slower speed so that on playback, they would be sped up and at a higher pitch.

To punctuate the drumming sections, Paul wanted an authentic hunting sound. Taking a break from the session, he and Linda headed to Whiteley's department store in Bayswater to search for suitably audible props.

"He came back with a bow and arrow, and a target,"[37] Black recalled, adding that Paul wanted to capture the sound of an arrow flying across the room and hitting the target. Capturing that sound was no easy task. To accomplish it, Black placed six or seven Neumann U67 microphones along the arrow's path.

"Everything was turned up full pelt, to try and get the 'whoosh' of the arrow," Black explained. "And of course, it would pick up absolutely everything. At one stage Paul had to go outside the room because somebody was laughing outside, and the sound was picking up on the mics."[38]

The arrow overdub took several takes to perfect, during which the bow broke.[39] Content that he had managed to emulate and put his own spin on the Brazilian rainforest's indigenous sound, Paul called it a day.

Recording Sessions

Thursday–Friday, February 19–20, 1970.
Morgan Studios, Studio One, London.
Recording: 'Hot As Sun.'
Mixing: 'The Lovely Linda,' 'Glasses,' 'Junk,' 'Momma,' 'Miss America,' and 'Oo You.'

McCartney and Black revisited 'Hot As Sun,' the old Quarrymen era instrumental, on February 19. Paul had noted on his tape box that there was distortion in the recording, and after a playback, he and Black agreed that he should record the instrumental afresh. Paul also saw an opportunity to improve it: as he recorded it in December, the song had no bridge, and the lack of a contrasting middle section now struck him as a flaw.

McCartney and Black followed the pattern of McCartney's home version, beginning with an acoustic guitar track. Working in a brighter acoustic setting than his living room, Paul decided to modify his Premier drum kit. Black put duct tape on the tom-toms and snare, turning their ringing sound into a less vibrant thud. The addition of maracas, bongos and a punchy bass line gave Paul's rhythm track a mildly Latin flavor, although this would largely vanish once Paul added the straightforward electric guitar melody, the song's focal point. The electric guitar and two more acoustic guitar tracks filled out the texture of the verses. For the contrasting bridge, Paul maintained the song's simple, three-chord structure, but riffed around the notes of those chords on the studio's Hammond organ.

The song was completed in a matter of hours.

"I had never seen anyone, ever, come in and play every instrument," Black recalled, "and after a few days you just took it as the norm, which was ridiculous. At the time I realized it was something pretty special. He knew what he wanted to overdub onto which tracks. I think it was all in his head. I can't remember any 'try and try again.' He just had this amazing knack of just getting it right. I can't remember doing more than two takes on anything. Quite amazing really. I think he just went by the feel, and if it felt right he'd just say, 'That's okay. I'm gonna do this overdub now.' It was just amazing watching a master at work, to be honest with you."[40]

Paul spent the afternoon session at Morgan on February 20 fleshing out 'Oo You,' which his January 24 mix convinced him was missing elements that could set it apart from the album's other bluesy instrumentals. As Linda prepared lunch that afternoon, an idea occurred to him. His first verse—"*Look like a woman / Dress like a lady / Talk like a baby / Love like a woman*"—was little more than observational stream of conscious. But in the second verse, he used a bit of Lennonesque wordplay: "*Walk like a woman / Sing like a blackbird / Eat like a hunger / Cook like a woman.*" All he needed was a refrain, for which he simply used the song's title, adding a short vocal flourish each time it appeared.

With the vocal recorded, Paul spiced up the track with another electric guitar line and additions to the rhythm section, including cowbell, tambourine, and what sounds like maracas but was actually an aerosol spray.

"That was the most amazing thing for me—we're gonna do an aerosol, we're gonna do a xylophone, were gonna do something else. Fantastic," said Black. "But then having done all the stuff with the Beatles, experimenting with different sounds, for him it was just natural. I'm a young engineer, and if Paul McCartney says were gonna do this—of course we're gonna do this! That's what was so interesting for me, this nonstop creativity."[41]

Paul and Black also made rough mixes of 'The Lovely Linda,' 'Glasses,' both versions of 'Junk,' and an edit of 'Momma' and 'Miss America,' making them a single track, 'Momma Miss America.' The mixes were most likely for Paul to listen to at home as work on the album continued; all were later discarded.

During his five days at Morgan, Paul made considerable headway, but he realized that there was a good deal still to be done. But Morgan was unavailable for the next six days, so he moved back to EMI for four days of mixing, as well as what turned out to be the final new recordings for the album.

Although word of his album had been reported in the press, Paul continued working as if the project were still secret. Phil McDonald and John Kurlander, both veterans of the *Abbey Road* sessions, had been sworn to secrecy; in his diary, Kurlander listed the sessions as "Billy Martin—Shhh." The fiction that Billy Martin was the artist was maintained all the way through the production of acetate test pressings of the album on both sides of the Atlantic.

In a small way, the note in Kurlander's diary perfectly captures the tension surrounding Paul's solo recording at EMI Studios, the Beatles' home turf. But he also noticed a shift in McCartney's mood, which he attributed largely to Linda's calming presence.

"For me, as a crewmember, Paul was the most accessible Beatle. He was friendly and easy to get on with. His relationship with Linda—and that was really at the beginning of it—was a very pivotal thing in his life. It was always 'Paul and Linda.' She was there for all of those sessions, taking photographs of everything."[42]

Recording Session

Saturday, February 21, 1970.
EMI Studios, Studio Two, London.
Mixing: 'The Lovely Linda,' 'Glasses/Suicide,' 'Momma/Miss America,' and 'Junk (Instrumental)' (working title for 'Singalong Junk').

On McCartney's first day back at EMI, he and McDonald began with a stereo mix of 'The Lovely Linda,' completing it in two attempts, and judging the second (RS2) as the keeper. They then moved on to the trial edit of 'Momma' and 'Miss America' that Paul and Black made at Morgan. The join, at 1'57", was not subtle, but it still worked for Paul: the solo drum introduction of 'Miss America' handily obscures the fact that the two instrumentals are in different keys. McCartney and McDonald made two mixes of the joined pair and marked the second (RS2) as "Best."

The day's third mix was also a joined pair, 'Glasses' with a few seconds of the 'Suicide' take that the 'Glasses' session partially erased. Paul concluded the eight-hour session with two mixes of 'Singalong Junk,' the second of which (RS2) was marked "Best."

———➤

At home between sessions, Paul sorted through his unfinished or unused songs, looking for neglected material that might work on the album he was shaping. One that was unquestionably suitable was 'Every Night,' a song Paul had vamped during *Get Back* session jams on January 21 and 24, 1969, both times singing the first verse and toying with a follow-up that began "*Every day*" and trailed off into mumbled place fillers.

Paul started composing the song during a tough period in the summer of 1968, between the end of his relationship with Jane Asher, and Linda's arrival in London, and he completed it in March 1969, when he and Linda were on their honeymoon.

Although the song's lyrics are entirely in the present tense, a definite "then versus now" aspect permeates them; in fact, they document two distinct periods in Paul's life, and corresponding changes in Paul's state of mind.

McCartney's opening verse—"*Every night I just wanna go out / Get out of my head / Every day I don't wanna get up / Get out of my bed*"—matches his own, and Linda's, descriptions of the fraught time following Lennon's "divorce" announcement. Yet it was written long before Lennon's decision to split the band, and given when it was composed, it seems likely that the verse is a remnant of what Francie Schwartz observed as a drinking problem that became particularly acute during Paul's visits to Liverpool.

"He had a hard time staying sober up there," she wrote, describing a couple of visits to Merseyside in July 1968. "We traipsed under the Mersey to the city to drink with his cousins and pals. Singing in a Liverpool pub could be fun. Even the autographs he gave were in good spirits. But he wasn't wearing it well."[43]

Out of this tumultuous period came the opening verse, concocted while Paul noodled around E major and E major 7 chords on his guitar—essentially, the chord progression for the entire verse.

"People say to me, 'How do songs start?'," Paul explained with an acoustic guitar in hand. "Sometimes it's an idea, sometimes it's something you've been thinking about. But sometimes it's a chord you like [plays an E major 7 chord.] That's like a variation of E, it's E7. So that sets up the mood of the song."[44]

For eight months, this autobiographical scrap remained in Paul's to-be-completed stack, but it came back to mind during his Corfu honeymoon. He finished it in their secluded cottage in Benitses, a fishing village.

"I remember sitting outside a Greek villa on a lovely night and playing it," McCartney explained, distancing the song's origins from his time with Schwartz. "I particularly associate it with first being with Linda."[45]

Paul and Linda's romantic getaway brought with it a conscious shift in McCartney's tone, from depression about the business squabbles that were beginning to characterize life in the Apple offices to the romantic contentment he enjoyed during his honeymoon getaway. That contentment informs the song's second section—not quite a bridge, but an expansion on the original E major—E major 7 verse progression that sounds brighter and more varied and supports an arching melody that fortifies a newer, more hopeful set of lyrics. Each of these B section verses ends with the couplet, "*But tonight I just want to stay in and be with you.*"

The rest of the verse was thin. "*Every morning brings a new day*" states the obvious but sounds like it might go somewhere; but the follow-up, "*Every night that day is through-ooh-ooh-ooh-ooh,*" accomplishes little beyond setting up the rhyme, "*be with you.*"

Still, 'Every Night' has an attractive melody that suits the more earnest side of Paul's ballad style, and an appealing acoustic feel that links it with 'The Lovely Linda' and 'Junk,' but otherwise expands the variety he is offering in this collection. There is even a nod, in the lyric of the second verse ("*Every day I lean on a lamppost / I'm wasting my time*") to 'Leaning on a Lamppost,' a Noel Gay song made famous by George Formby (the ukulele-playing actor, singer-songwriter, comedian George Harrison was fond of) in the 1937 film *Feather Your Nest*, and was revived by Herman's Hermits in 1966.

Recording Session

Sunday, February 22, 1970.
EMI Studios, Studio Two, London.
Recording: 'Every Night.'
Mixing: 'Every Night,' 'That Would Be Something,' 'Valentine Day,' and 'Maybe I'm Amazed.'

Paul turned up at EMI Studios at noon, for a ten-hour session that began with a review of two more songs from the Cavendish, 'Valentine Day' and 'That Would Be Something.' Deciding that neither required overdubbing, he and McDonald quickly made stereo mixes of both, as well as 'Maybe I'm Amazed,' leaving the rest of the day for a start-to-finish recording of 'Every Night.'

Paul made short work of laying down the song's instruments and vocals in a series of overdubs. The process this time began with lead vocals and acoustic guitar, followed by drums, bass, two acoustic lead guitar parts (the second was a harmony line that paralleled the first), and doubled vocals in some sections.

That left two free tracks. On track seven, Paul dubbed an electric guitar part. Track eight was left blank. McDonald and Kurlander produced a stereo mix during the final hour of the session.

Recording Session

Tuesday, February 24, 1970.
EMI Studios, Studio Two, London.
Mixing: 'Hot As Sun,' 'Every Night,' and 'Don't Cry Baby.'

February 24 began with an unwelcome distraction. Paul was used to fans loitering at the gates to his London home, documenting his every move in diaries and candid snaps. But neighbors were worried about a small group of girls sleeping on his driveway. One American fan, Carolyn

Mitchell, had been maintaining a vigil outside Paul's home for 13 months, not skipping a single day during that time. Since Paul and Linda wed, neighbor Evelyn Grumi, who lived opposite the McCartneys with her husband and two children, had noticed a conscious shift in the behavior of the fans.

"The girls sit on *our* wall," she told a reporter from the *Sunday People*, several weeks later. "I wouldn't mind if they just sat, but they play their transistors [radios] very loudly and shriek and giggle, and shout. If you try to talk to them reasonably, they just hurl abuse and bad language at you. Really awful language."[46]

And nothing was off-limits. The rabid crowd had taken to stealing Paul's mail, and on occasion breaking into his house, pilfering handfuls of Linda's photographs, and other trinkets as souvenirs with each sortie. Paul and Linda agreed action was needed. They called the local police, but when the constables arrived at Cavendish Avenue, they explained that since no laws had been broken, there was nothing they could do.

"We can only move them on by threatening an obstruction charge. They stand outside all night, sometimes in the bitter cold—I don't understand it,"[47] a local officer explained. Come rain, hail, or shine, the overzealous fans remained, 24 hours a day.

At EMI, that afternoon, Paul mixed the version of 'Hot As Sun' recorded at Morgan five days earlier. McDonald was away that day, so Kurlander oversaw the mix, assisted by John Leckie—a trainee, only nine days into his career at EMI. Leckie began with a proper measure of terror.

"This would have been my second week, and I was straight in at the deep end with Paul," said Leckie. "I always remember, Paul and Linda were making tea down in the studio. This was in the big room at Abbey Road, where the control room is upstairs. Paul looked up and said to me, 'Would you like a cup of tea?' and I said 'Yes, please.' And he said, 'It's orange pekoe, is that okay? Come and get it then.' And he had a teapot and a proper China cup."[48]

Kurlander's bold mix spread the acoustic guitar, bass, drums, maracas, and bongos across the stereo image, with the melodic elements in the center. After a lunch break, Paul asked for a playback of the previous evening's mixes of 'Every Night,' and impressed by Kurlander's mix of 'Hot As Sun,' decided to let him loose on 'Every Night,' too. He and Kurlander made five more mixes and marked the fifth—in which the electric guitar part was eliminated—as "best."

Before leaving, Paul asked the two engineers to transfer a short speech recording to the master reel and give it a stereo effect. In the snippet, Mary is heard crying, and Paul tells her: "*Don't cry, baby. Don't cry. Daddy's gonna play you a lullaby,*" which he counts in. This fragment was listed in the session documentation as 'Don't Cry Baby' and was later edited onto an alternate instrumental mix of 'Oo You,' although the pair of drumbeats heard after the count-in are from Paul's home recording of 'Hot As Sun,' suggesting that it may have been liberated from the distorted take.

Though Paul did not include 'Don't Cry Baby' on the album, it is possible that he was briefly considering sprinkling bits of family life verité between some of the tracks, much as Glyn Johns had included quips, count-ins, and jam fragments in his *Get Back* mix.

—

While McCartney was laboring on his album, his Beatle friends were keeping busy, and in the spotlight. Lennon remained in Denmark through most of January, visiting Yoko's daughter, Kyoko, who lived in Aalborg with her father, Tony Cox. But John grabbed a few headlines, first by announcing that his songwriting and recording royalties would henceforth be put toward the promotion of peace, and then by having his hair, and Yoko's, shorn to crew-cut length. The Lennons had legal troubles, too. An exhibition of John's lithographs—14 freehand drawings of himself and Yoko, several depicting sexual acts—had opened at the London Arts Gallery, on January 15; the police raided the show the next day, confiscating the eight most overtly erotic examples.

Upon his return to London, on January 25, Lennon dove back into the music business, embracing the notion that music was a species of journalism: his latest thoughts, embodied in song, could be recorded and released instantly, as if they were newspaper editorials. He demonstrated this concept with 'Instant Karma! (We All Shine On),' a song he dashed off on the morning of January 27 and recorded that afternoon with the Plastic Ono Band (this time with George Harrison playing guitar). Phil Spector, in London to work on the *Let It Be* album, produced the recording, which was in the shops on February 6. Five days later, Lennon performed 'Instant Karma!' on *Top of the Pops*.

By the time 'Instant Karma!' was released, Lennon was back in the headlines for his involvement with the activist and Black revolutionary Michael X and his Black House in North London. The Lennons traded their hair to Michael X for a pair of Muhammed Ali's boxing trunks, the plan being that each side would auction their side of the trade to raise money for their own causes.

Behind the scenes, John and Yoko began editing a documentary about their Bed-In for Peace in Montreal, where they had recorded 'Give Peace a Chance.' And John tussled publicly with the presenters of the Toronto Peace Festival, at which he was to appear in July. On February 25, he withdrew from the festival, which was soon canceled.

George, apart from playing on 'Instant Karma!' and producing 'It Don't Come Easy' for Ringo, was mostly lying low, probably because he was occupied with his acquisition of Friar Park, a 30-bedroom Victorian neo-Gothic mansion in Henley-on-Thames, to which he moved, with his wife, Pattie, on March 12.

Starr, though regarded by many outside the Beatles as the least likely to succeed on his own, was busily working to prove that opinion wrong. Since October he had been recording *Sentimental Journey*, his album of pop standards, for which a respectable group of musicians—from George Martin, John Dankworth, Quincy Jones and Elmer Bernstein to Maurice Gibb, Richard Perry and Klaus Voormann—provided arrangements. McCartney was also among the invitees: he supplied a stylishly jazzy orchestration of the Hoagy Carmichael–Mitchell Parish classic, 'Stardust,' which Ringo had recorded in November.

Between sessions, Starr flew to Los Angeles for the premiere of *The Magic Christian* on January 29, 1970; while there, he made an appearance on Rowan and Martin's *Laugh-In*, the popular American comedy television show, and flew to Las Vegas to catch an Elvis Presley concert. Back in London on February 3, he continued work on *Sentimental Journey*. After an evening-long session for the album on February 18, Ringo remained in the studio to work on 'It Don't Come Easy' with Harrison on guitar, Klaus Voormann on bass, and Stephen Stills, of Crosby, Stills, Nash and Young, on the piano. A second session took place the next evening, after which the song was shelved for the time being.

Paul kept tabs on all this activity but remained focused on his own solo project. As the sessions were winding toward completion, he composed one final song, although it was actually just a chorus and a single verse. Called 'Man We Was Lonely,' it was written at Cavendish Avenue in two casual sessions.

"The chorus," he explained, "was written in bed at home, shortly before we finished recording the album. The middle was done one lunchtime in a great hurry, as we were due to record the song that afternoon."[49]

That impromptu quality took a page from John's 'Instant Karma!' playbook, as if he were telling John, *I can match you, trick for trick*. Not that John would have known the circumstances of this album track's composition and recording; Paul was making the point for himself—if John could do it, so could he. That sense of self-assurance was not inconsiderable, given that only three months earlier, Paul's songwriting efforts yielded only fragments.

'Man We Was Lonely' had a country flavor, and although the vocal style he and Linda adopted for the recording suggests that it was more of a country music parody than a true bow to the style, Paul has said that he was channeling Johnny Cash[50] when he wrote it. Either way, it added another stylistic thread to an album that already had ballads, blues-rock, avant-garde experiments, and the inspiration (if not quite the substance) of Brazilian tribal music.

More crucially, it suited what was becoming apparent as the album's underlying theme of, as Paul put it in his press release for the album: "Home, Family, Love."[51] The loneliness in the title links the song with the "*lonely man who's in the middle of something*," in 'Maybe I'm Amazed,' and in both cases, that sense of isolation is dispelled by the love and strength of the right partner.

The song marked a decisive turning point in Paul's musical disposition since the Beatles' split. Despair turned to hope, depression to recovery—and not just for Paul. As the "we" in the title (and chorus) suggests, it is a joint statement from Paul and Linda: "*Man we was lonely . . . But now we're fine all the while.*"

For contrast, Paul switched back to first person singular in the song's verse, but Linda is very present in its lyric: "*I used to ride on my fast city line / Singing songs that I thought were mine alone / Now let me lie with my love for the time / I am home.*"

What no one knew, because the publishing credits attribute the song solely to Paul, was that 'Man We Was Lonely' was a collaboration between Paul and Linda, probably their first.

"We wrote a couple of things together for the *McCartney* LP," Paul later said, "but I didn't think to claim Linda as a coauthor. We wrote 'Man We Was Lonely' together. One of the main things about a collaboration is to have a 'bounce off'—somebody you can throw ideas at, and get their opinions and suggestions... We write just as John and I wrote in the beginning."[52]

Recording Session

Wednesday, February 25, 1970.
EMI Studios, Studio Two, London.
Recording & Mixing: 'Man We Was Lonely.'

'Man We Was Lonely' was recorded and mixed in a single session at EMI Studios on February 25. Beginning at 11:30 a.m., McCartney recorded 12 basic takes—vocals and acoustic guitar—of which only two (takes 10 and 12, the latter marked "Best") were complete. When the engineers broke for lunch, Paul and Linda took advantage of a quiet moment to finish the lyrics, over double egg and chips.

The afternoon brought almost six hours of overdubbing, as Paul fleshed out the basic track with bass drum, bass guitar, a second acoustic guitar and electric slide guitar (for which he used a drum peg as a slide[53]).

What followed was another step forward in the McCartneys' emerging musical partnership: just weeks after her vocal debut on a Beatles record, Linda and Paul gathered round a microphone in EMI Studio Two and recorded their first vocal duet. She had, of course, sung backing vocals on several of Paul's new tracks, including 'Maybe I'm Amazed,' 'Teddy Boy' and 'Kreen-Akrore.' This time, though, she and Paul sang the choruses in tandem, with Linda also contributing single-word ("*alone*" and "*home*") answering vocals in the verse. Not content with one vocal track, the couple doubled their efforts with a second pass.

As McDonald mixed the track to stereo, he selectively applied ADT (Artificial Double Tracking), an effect invented at EMI by Ken Townshend, in 1966, in response to the Beatles' fondness for double-tracking, combined with Lennon's impatience with having to sing a vocal line twice. It involved recording a voice (or instrument) and simultaneously sending it to a second tape deck. The recording from the second deck was then sent back to an empty track on the first, with a fraction of a second delay, creating the impression that the original sound was doubled.

McDonald used ADT on the electric guitar and second acoustic guitar, not so much to beef up their sound as to allow for a richer stereo image. During the final 14 seconds of the song, the ADT made the acoustic guitars dance from right to left. The two vocal tracks were panned hard left and right to create a vivid choral effect.

Recording Sessions

Thursday and Saturday, February 26 and 28, 1970.
Morgan Studios, Studio One, London.
Mixing: 'Junk', 'Teddy Boy,' 'Kreen Akrore,' and 'Oo You.'

Mixing was wrapped up during two sessions at Morgan in late February, with Robin Black at the desk. At the first, they completed 'Junk' (the vocal version), 'Teddy Boy' and 'Kreen-Akrore.' The second session was devoted to 'Oo You,' during which Black added tape echo at the points where Paul produced feedback on the guitar track, and used the effect to move the sound of the guitar howl across the speakers.

Recording Sessions

Saturday–Sunday, March 7–8, and Wednesday, March 11, 1970.
Morgan Studios, Studio One, London.
Mixing: 'Rupert,' 'Backwards Guitar Piece,' 'Junk' (take 3), 'Teddy Boy' (take 2), and 'Suicide.'
Album compilation.

With recording and mixing for the album complete, Paul took time to prepare rough mixes of the recordings that would not be included on the finished LP, compiling them on a reel for his archives. With that task completed on March 8, all that remained to be done was the album's final sequencing. Paul took copies of the mixes home for further listening, and to ponder the order in which they would appear on the album, and the McCartneys returned to Morgan on March 11, the day before their first wedding anniversary, to oversee the sequencing.

Sequencing an album involves considering everything from where in the running order the strongest songs are—usually an artist will want a solid opening track on each side of an LP, to draw the listener in—to whether songs should flow smoothly together or offer sharp contrasts. Other issues producers and artists consider are how each song's lyrics fit alongside those of the tracks that precede and follow it, as well as how the songs' keys and tempos work together, helping (or hindering) the flow of the album.

The sequence Paul and Black settled on was:

SIDE ONE (EMI MATRIX NO. YEX.775)

'The Lovely Linda'
'That Would Be Something'
'Valentine Day'
'Every Night'
'Hot As Sun'/'Glasses' [with a few seconds of 'Suicide']
'Junk'
'Man We Was Lonely'

SIDE TWO (EMI MATRIX NO. YEX.776)

'Oo You'
'Momma Miss America'
'Teddy Boy'
'Singalong Junk'
'Maybe I'm Amazed'
'Kreen-Akrore'

Paul was not inexperienced at album sequencing, but he made some radical choices. One was to open the album with 'The Lovely Linda,' an unfinished song that ran only 43 seconds. But the song represented the start of the creative rebirth from which the rest of the album flowed, so finished or not, it was important to Paul that it was the first song heard.

More crucially, it identified Linda both as his muse and as the album's central figure. As a song-writer for the Beatles, Paul wrote love songs that were abstract: its subjects were usually not named, and when they were, they were either fictional ('Michelle') or not actually women ('Martha My Dear' was named for his sheepdog). There was no mystery who this song was about, and how important she was to Paul.

On a more basic level—important for a musician who regarded a song's "feel" as a central characteristic, Paul was charmed by the sound of the track, not so much in spite of its flaws as because of them. He could have finished the song and rerecorded it; in his press release for the album, he said he eventually would, calling this version "a trailer." But he was presenting this album as a homespun production, and 'The Lovely Linda,' with its loud door squeak and its breakdown into giggles set the scene—as did an imperfection at the very start of the track, where the guitar bursts into action in the middle of a beat, giving the track (and the album) a starting jolt.

The rest of the sequence was a matter of alternating songs and instrumentals, with 'Man We Was Lonely' giving Side One a strong finish. Along the way, Paul decided to join 'Hot As Sun' and 'Glasses,' presenting them as a single track. Side Two worked similarly, with 'Oo You' providing a fashionably bluesy opening, and 'Singalong Junk' mirroring the vocal version on the other side.

The most puzzling of Paul's sequencing choices was to end the album with 'Kreen-Akrore' rather than the more powerful 'Maybe I'm Amazed.' The obvious solution—moving 'Kreen-Akrore' to the end of Side One, starting Side Two with 'Man We Was Lonely' and ending with 'Maybe I'm Amazed'—must have occurred to him and been rejected. It seems likely that the choice was conceptual.

Given the album's "Home, Family, Love" theme, 'Kreen-Akrore' is an outlier. That could be said of 'Teddy Boy,' too, but that song's chorus—Ted's loving interaction with his mum—veers close to the theme. No such connection can be made for 'Kreen-Akrore,' and perhaps that's the point of having it follow 'Maybe I'm Amazed.' The sequence that begins with 'The Lovely Linda' and runs through 'Maybe I'm Amazed' shows Paul looking inward, finding strength in his family circle. With 'Kreen-Akrore,' he closes the album with a look out at the world.

After completing the track layout, the McCartneys and Black gathered on the studio floor to look at dozens of snapshots that Linda (and, in a few cases, Paul) had taken in Scotland and on visits to Portugal, France, Greece and Antigua, as well as in London. There were shots of Paul at High Park, chiseling a window frame and walking through the hills. Also from Scotland were dusk shots of High Park's ancient standing stone.

From France, there were colorful shots of poppy fields. Greece, Portugal, and Antigua yielded shots of Paul on the beach, often clowning. Linda photographed Paul and Heather with a burro and a pony, in Portugal, and sledding in London. And there was a lovely sequence from Antigua in which birds feast on a bowl of cherries Paul and Linda put out for them.

The collection was filled out with several rolls of film capturing Paul at Cavendish Avenue, playing guitar, piano, bass and drums, and threading reels of tape on the Studer—or simply posing with his instruments, leaning out of windows or in the backyard.

"I remember her throwing down lots of photographs they'd taken on holiday, and I was asked to help point out any pictures I thought would look good on the album," Black reminisced. "There was one I laughed at, and he said, 'What's that?' And it was a picture of Paul in his swimming costume doing the macho-man arms. And it just made me really laugh."[54]

Paul and Linda also showed the photos to David Puttnam, a friend Paul met during the Beatle years, when he was part of Collett Dickenson Pearce, a prominent London advertising firm. Now Puttnam, the son of a photographer, was interested in moving to a career in film and was in discussions to become a partner in Goodtimes Enterprises, a film production company.

"Linda and I went out to dinner with him and his wife," Paul said, "and left him with some images and said, 'Just see if any of these are good for the cover.' And he got back the next day and said, 'There's only one.' 'Well, which one?' 'That one, you and the baby, in the jacket, that's incredible.' So we went, 'Oh yeah!' I like that, sometimes you need someone to show you."[55]

The main business of their dinner with Puttnam, however, was to engage him to produce a promotional film for the album, built from Linda's photos, including many that could not be accommodated on the record sleeve. For the soundtrack, Paul handed Puttnam a copy of 'Maybe I'm Amazed,' although there was no thought of releasing the song as a single.*

Paul and Linda showed the photo collection to other friends, too, setting aside those that people particularly liked, and going back and forth about their own preferences. In the end, they accepted Puttnam's choice for the cover, and Linda's shot of the cherries arrayed along the top of the wall in Antigua, along with the empty bowl full of cherry juice, for the back. During the production process, the front and back were switched, so that the cherry photo, with no other graphics, became the front, while the back showed Paul, with Mary in his coat, under the album's simple title—*McCartney*—with the song titles in the lower right.

Obvious as the album title may seem, Paul did not settle on it immediately. Toying, at first, with calling it *I'm the One It Hit the Most*,[56] a reference to the still unannounced Beatles split, Paul settled on *McCartney* after learning that a report he had read in the music press was either incorrect or misconstrued.

"I'd seen something that made me think, 'Oh, John's got a new record out, and it's called *Lennon*," he remembered. "I thought, 'Oh wow! That's great! Oh boy, I missed that boat.' And it turned out not to be so. So, I thought, that's a great idea, though, just call it your surname. So, I just made my first record *McCartney*."[57]

In the end, Paul and Linda chose a light-spirited family-centered selection of 21 photos for the gatefold, of which only one shot showed Paul with an instrument in his hand, his Fender Telecaster.

The whole production—the album and the artwork together—was a manifesto of sorts, a cele-

---

* The film, directed by Charlie Jenkins, had its first British airing on ITV on April 19, 1970, at 6 p.m., and its first American broadcast that same evening on the *Ed Sullivan Show*, on CBS at 8 p.m.

bration of the newfound joys of married life: domesticity and children, the farm with its remodeling projects and its animals, and a bit of globetrotting, not as a band member but as a husband and father, eager to take in both nature and tradition, wherever he went.

It was also, in several ways, a riposte to John Lennon. Where John was using his solo projects for either public commentary (about peace, mainly), radical experimentation (the *Two Virgins* and *Life with the Lions* albums) or as a confessional (as in the harrowing 'Cold Turkey'), Paul was arguing that peace begins at home, and that John did not have a patent on musical experiments.

Though never explicitly described as such, *McCartney* was Paul and Linda's equivalent of John and Yoko's *Wedding Album*. A boxed souvenir of the Lennons' honeymoon, released in the fall of 1969, the Lennons' *Wedding Album* included a facsimile of their marriage license, photos of their Amsterdam Bed-In, doodles and caricatures drawn by both John and Yoko, a booklet of press clippings from the time, a postcard, a strip of photo-machine portraits, a picture of a slice of wedding cake, and almost lost amid the goodies, an LP with an extended avant-garde sound collage on each side.

Paul's version was a more straightforward celebration of the power of love, and of 'The Lovely Linda' having pulled him out of his creative morass. He knew that some people would see that as corny, particularly when seen beside the tougher, hipper, in-your-face broadsides John was releasing. But as he had told Dorothy Bacon, from *Life*, three months earlier, "We are individuals—all different. John married Yoko, I married Linda. We didn't marry the same girl."[58] John told interviewers his releases were "honest." Paul was following suit.

As he looked through Linda's tableful of photos that March afternoon at Morgan Studios, Paul was in a reflective mood.

"He said, 'Robin, people think I just woke up one day and started writing hit songs,'" Black recalled. "They don't realize, I'd written a hundred songs before anybody said, 'Oh, that's quite good.' I thought that was really interesting. For somebody of that magnitude to be able to just say, 'I'm going to make an album and play every instrument' says a lot. I'm not sure what to read into that. But it says a lot about the man. It wasn't the Beatles. It was Paul McCartney."[59]

5

ONE GUY STANDING THERE
SHOUTING "I'M LEAVING"

—

Never having worked as his own producer—and, in effect, manager—Paul had not previously dealt with the administrative side of releasing an album. Those details were left in George Martin's hands, and from the Beatles' point of view, it just magically happened, nothing to concern themselves with. But now, Paul realized, it was up to him to arrange for the album's release and devise a plan to promote it.

All this was brought to Paul's attention by Peter Brown on March 17, 1970, when all the Beatles and their wives, as well as Brown, Neil Aspinall, Derek Taylor, and Klaus Voormann and their wives, attended a birthday party George threw for Pattie at Friar Park.

Shortly after the party, Paul telephoned Brown to further explore the publicity question.

"I talked to Peter Brown and asked him what we were going to do about press on the album. And I said, 'I can't deal with the press; I hate all those Beatles questions. I really don't feel like doing it, to tell you the truth.' But he told me that we needed to have something."[1]

Brown was still the managing director at Apple, having survived Klein's first purge, but only just: Klein had fired him, but the Beatles countermanded the order, Brown having been with them since the Liverpool days.

"It was a very, very difficult time for everyone, including me," Brown explained. "Because I was supposed to be running the Apple office, and my job was to run everything efficiently, but also being close to the Beatles. It was very awkward, because I was working for all four of them, and I had to give equal respect to all of them. And Paul was now expecting me to come up with a plan for what *he* was going to do. So I tried, but because the other three Beatles were really rather irritated by Paul's behavior—not for the first time—it was very awkward."[2]

Nevertheless, on March 23—the same afternoon EMI engineer Tony Clark made the production masters from Paul's reels of finished mixes, Brown and Paul had lunch in Brown's ballroom-size second-floor office* with its connection, by elevator, to Apple's cordon bleu kitchen.

McCartney and Brown discussed the possibility of holding a press conference to announce the album, but Paul wasn't interested in facing a roomful of reporters. He was not keen on individual interviews, either, but Brown persuaded him to choose a few publications he would speak with. Paul's selection included the *Daily Express*, *Billboard*, *Rolling Stone*, *Vogue* and a few British music papers. New publicity photos were a must, Brown told him, adding that it would also be a good idea to think about how he wanted advertisements for the album to look.

Brown's most striking idea, meant to keep personal interviews to a minimum, was to include a Question/Answer interview in the press kits that would be sent to writers with copies of the album.

"We decided to write up a list of questions that would be appropriate, which we could feed to the media. And Paul said, 'Well—you do it.' So I wrote up a list of questions, and he read it. I think he made some suggestions, though not many, because it wasn't difficult—it was obvious what kind of questions we wanted to ask."[3]

Question: Why did you decide to make a solo album?

Answer: *Because I got a Studer 4 track recording machine at home—practiced on it (playing all instruments)—liked the result, and decided to make it into an album.*

Question: Were you influenced by John's adventures with the Plastic Ono Band, and Ringo's solo LP?

Answer: *Sort of but not really.*

Question: Are all the songs by Paul McCartney alone?

Answer: *Yes sir.*

Question: Will they be so credited: McCartney?

Answer: *It's a bit daft for them to be Lennon-McCartney credited, so "McCartney" it is.*

Question: Did you enjoy working as a solo?

Answer: *Very much. I only had me to ask for a decision, and I agreed with me. Remember Linda's on it too, so it's really a double act.*

Question: What is Linda's contribution?

Answer: *Strictly speaking she harmonises, but of course it's more than that because she is a shoulder to lean on, a second opinion, and a photographer of renown. More than all this, she believes in me—constantly.*

Question: Where was the album recorded?

---

* Brown's office had been a ballroom earlier in the history of 3 Savile Row, which was built in 1733, and it could not be subdivided because the building was listed as Grade II* on the National Heritage List for England.

Answer:	*At home, at E.M.I. (No. 2 studio) and at Morgan Studios (WILLESDEN!).*
Question:	What is your home equipment (in some detail)?
Answer:	*STUDER 4 TRACK machine. I only had, however, one mike, and, as Mr. Pender, Mr. Sweetenham and others only managed to take 6 months or so (slight delay) I worked without V.U. meters or a mixer, which meant that everything had to be listened to first (for distortion etc. . . .) then recorded. So the Answer: STUDER, 1 MIKE, and nerve.*
Question:	Why did you choose to work in the studios you chose?
Answer:	*They were available. E.M.I. is technically good, and Morgan is cosy.*
Question:	The album was not known about until it was nearly completed. Was this deliberate?
Answer:	*Yes, because normally an album is old before it comes out. (Aside.) Witness Get Back.*[*]
Question:	Why?
Answer:	*I've always wanted to buy a Beatle's album like "people" do and be as surprised as they must be. So this was the next best thing. Linda and I are the only two who will be sick of it by the release date. We love it really.*
Question:	Are you able to describe the texture or the feel or the theme of the album in a few words?
Answer:	*Home, Family, Love.*
Question:	How long did it take to complete—from when to when?
Answer:	*From just before (I think) Xmas, until now. 'The Lovely Linda' was the first thing I recorded at home, and was originally to test the equipment. That was around Xmas.*
Question:	Assuming all the songs are new to the public, how new are they to you? Are they recent?
Answer:	*One was 1959 ('Hot As Sun'). Two from India, 'Junk,' 'Teddy Boy,' and the rest are pretty recent. 'Valentine Day,' 'Momma Miss America,' and 'Oo You,' were ad-libbed on the spot.*
Question:	Which instruments have you played on the album?
Answer:	*Bass, drums, acoustic guitar, lead guitar, piano and organ-mellotron, toy xylophone, bow and arrow.*
Question:	Have you played all these instruments on earlier recordings?
Answer:	*Yes—drums being the one that I wouldn't normally do.*
Question:	Why did you do all the instruments yourself?
Answer:	*I think I'm pretty good.*
Question:	Will Linda be heard on all future records?
Answer:	*Could be; we love singing together, and have plenty of opportunity for practice.*

---

[*] The *Get Back* album had already been renamed *Let It Be* by the time he wrote this. He mentions it later as well. Since Apple's press department did not proofread it, the error was not caught. Some journalists corrected it in their reports.

Question:	Will Paul and Linda become a John and Yoko?
Answer:	*No, they will become Paul and Linda.*
Question:	Are you pleased with your work?
Answer:	*Yes.*
Question:	Will the other Beatles receive the first copies?
Answer:	*Wait and see.*
Question:	What has recording alone taught you?
Answer:	*That to make your own decisions about what you do is easy, and playing with yourself is difficult, but satisfying.*
Question:	Who has done the art-work?
Answer:	*Linda has taken all the photos, and she and I designed the package.*
Question:	Is it true that neither Allen Klein nor ABKCO have been nor will be in any way involved with the production manufacturing, distribution or promotion of this new album?
Answer:	*Not if I can help it.*
Question:	Did you miss the other Beatles and George Martin? Was there a moment, e.g., when you thought: "Wish Ringo was here for this break?"
Answer:	*No.*
Question:	Assuming this is a very big hit album, will you do another?
Answer:	*Even if it isn't, I will continue to do what I want—when I want to.*
Question:	Are you planning a new album or single with the Beatles?
Answer:	*No.*
Question:	Is this album a rest away from the Beatles, or start of a solo career?
Answer:	*Time will tell. Being a solo album means it's "the start of a solo career" . . . and not being done with the Beatles means it's a rest. So it's both.*
Question:	Have you any plans for live appearances?
Answer:	*No.*
Question:	Is your break with the Beatles, temporary or permanent, due to personal differences, or musical ones?
Answer:	*Personal differences, business differences, musical differences, but most of all because I have a better time with my family. Temporary or permanent? I don't know.*
Question:	Do you foresee a time when Lennon-McCartney becomes an active songwriting partnership again?
Answer:	*No.*
Question:	What do you feel about John's peace effort? The Plastic Ono Band? Giving back the M.B.E.? Yoko's influence? Yoko?

Answer:	*I love John, and respect what he does—it doesn't give me any pleasure.*
Question:	Have you plans to produce any other artists?
Answer:	*No.*
Question:	Were any of the songs on the album originally written with the Beatles in mind?
Answer:	*The older ones were. 'Junk' was intended for* Abbey Road,* *but something happened. 'Teddy Boy' was for* Get Back *but something happened.*
Question:	Were you pleased with *Abbey Road*? Was it musically restricting?
Answer:	*It was a good album. (No. 1 for a long time.)*
Question:	What is your relationship with Klein?
Answer:	*It isn't. I am not in contact with him, and he does not represent me in ANY way.*
Question:	What is your relationship with Apple?
Answer:	*It is the office of a company which I part own with the other 3 Beatles. I don't go there because I don't like offices or businesses especially when I'm on holiday.*
Question:	Have you any plans to set up an independent production company?
Answer:	*McCartney Productions.*
Question:	What sort of music has influenced you on this album?
Answer:	*Light and loose.*
Question:	Are you writing more prolifically now? Or less so?
Answer:	*About the same. I have a queue waiting to be recorded.*
Question:	What are your plans now? A holiday? A musical? A movie? Retirement?
Answer:	*My only plan is to grow up.[4]*

Paul's responses to Brown's questions were terse, and in most cases, too short to be of much use to journalists seeking quotes. If the idea was to keep the press at arm's length, several of Paul's responses guaranteed the opposite, since amid the innocuous explanations of his aims, on *McCartney*, Paul took the occasion to air his sour feelings about the Beatles and Apple, and his outright disdain for Klein.

"At the time it just seemed to me that it was answers to questions, and I was being bitchy," Paul later reflected. "That's for sure. I'll admit that because we were all being bitchy. And that was my, sort of, weedy way of being bitchy. One of the questions is: What do you think of John and Yoko's thing? And I said, 'Well, it doesn't impress me very much.' And leave it at that. And it came off very weird."[5]

---

* It was actually demoed for the *White Album*. The Beatles did not attempt it at either the formal *White Album* sessions, or during the recording of *Abbey Road*.

There was some sleight of hand. Proclaiming that the composing credits would simply be McCartney, rather than Lennon-McCartney, looks like a unilateral reworking of a long-existing agreement; readers would not have known that the matter had been discussed, and agreed to, at the September 9 meeting. Lennon had already put that agreement into practice: the singles 'Cold Turkey' and 'Instant Karma!' were credited to him alone.

Moreover, the sourness of Paul's references to the Beatles—not missing their input while making the record, loving John but taking no pleasure in his peace efforts, the curt "No," to the question of whether a new Beatles recording was being planned—all give the impression that he is giving the band the back of his hand, and all but announcing his resignation. Yet he was cautious on that point: on the question about whether the break between him and the others was temporary or permanent, he refused to be definitive.

The other Beatles were not given an advance look at the interview, or the accompanying release; in fact, Paul might not have bothered informing his codirectors at Apple that he planned to release *McCartney* on April 17 (with the press kits going out on April 10), had he not been informed by EMI that according to the Beatles' new contract, which went into effect on January 12, the Beatles, collectively and individually, were Apple artists, and that EMI could not release the album without Apple's authorization.

Paul's proposed April 17 release date was a problem for Apple. Both Ringo's *Sentimental Journey* and the Beatles' *Let It Be* were already on the schedule for April. In a heated telephone exchange, George, irritated that Paul had stopped attending Apple business and planning meetings, asserted that release dates could not simply be imposed without considering the larger picture. Paul stood his ground.

The other Beatles' first reaction was to move up the release of *Sentimental Journey*, rush-releasing it on March 27.

"I put my album out two weeks before," said Starr, "which makes me seem like such a good guy but it wasn't really, because I needed to put it out before, or else it would've slayed me, Paul's album. And it did."[6]

Two days after *Sentimental Journey* was released, Ringo appeared on David Frost's ITV chat show *Frost on Sunday*. Between a short discussion of *Sentimental Journey* and an airing of the promotional film of its title song, Frost asked, "Will we ever see the four of you in concert, together again, or only on records?" Ringo quickly responded, "Only on record, up to now," adding, "At the moment, you see, what we're all doing—like, I'm doing my album. I've just finished it. Everyone else is doing albums. And maybe when we get all them out of the way"—at which point he paused and cast his eyes upward, then looked back at Frost before unconvincingly concluding, "we'll make a few more records."

But the conflict with Starr's release was only half of the problem. Lennon and Harrison believed that it was madness for Paul's album to compete directly with *Let It Be*. When they consulted Klein, he walked them through the relevant clauses of the EMI agreement and reminded them that the contract in which Apple was formed—and which all of them, including Paul, signed—tied the Beatles together until 1977 and required them to seek each other's permission for solo projects.

Assured that they were contractually within their rights, John and George sent a letter to Ken East, EMI's managing director, on March 31, asserting Apple's position:

> We have considered very carefully indeed the position concerning the release of Paul McCartney's album on 17th April. In all circumstances, we have arrived at the conclusion that it would not be in the interest of this company for the record to be released on that date and we have decided to re-schedule the release for the 4th June, to coincide with the Apple/Capitol Record [*sic*] Convention in Hawaii. The forthcoming Beatles album will be released as scheduled on 24th April, to tie in with the film release date in mid-May.[7]

The same day, John wrote a firm but conciliatory letter to Paul, which he and George both signed (with spiritual advice from George as a postscript):

> March 31
>
> Dear Paul,
> We thought a lot about yours and the Beatles L.P.'s—and decided it's stupid for Apple to put out two big Albums within 7 days of each other (also there's Ringo's and *Hey Jude**).
>   - So we sent a letter to E.M.I. telling them to hold your release date 'til June 4th (there's a big Apple-Capitol convention in Hawaii then)
>   - We thought you'd come round when you realized that the Beatles album was coming out on April 24th
>   - We're sorry it turned out like this—
>   - it's nothing personal,
>
>   Love
>   John
>   and
>   George
>   Hare Krishna
> A Mantra a Day keeps MAYA' Away[8]

---

* *Hey Jude*, an American compilation album bringing together ten songs the Beatles had released on singles, but which had never appeared on a Capitol LP, had been released on February 26.

John and George ran the letter past Ringo, who they felt could give them an unbiased opinion on whether their decision was fair.

"The real fighting had been going on between me and Paul, because of Eastman and Klein, and we were on the opposite ends of our bats," John later said. "Ringo had not taken sides, or anything like that, and he had been straight about it, and we thought that Ringo would be able to talk fairly, to Paul—I mean if Ringo agreed that it was unfair, then it was unfair."[9]

Ringo took the letter to Cavendish Avenue personally,* and as Paul read the letter, Ringo could see that he wasn't taking it well. In solidarity with John and George, he said that he agreed—that they had to run Apple as a company, not according to individual whim. That didn't help; in fact, Paul's thinking, since Scotland, had been moving toward getting away from the company—disentangling his assets that were tied up in it, and proceeding on his own. So while the note may have seemed reasonable to Ringo, to Paul, it represented Apple's tyrannical interference in his affairs.

"He told me to get out of his house," Ringo recalled. "He was crazy; he went crazy, I thought. I got brought down because I couldn't believe it was happening to me. I'd just brought the letter . . . He just pointed and shouted at me."[10]

Upon Ringo's departure, Paul took the fight back to EMI. In an extraordinary note to both EMI chairman Sir Joseph Lockwood and Capitol Records president Stanley Gortikov, he unilaterally scuttled the Beatles' promise to keep their breakup secret from EMI:

To E.M.I.

Dear Sir Joe and Stan Gortikov,
No matter what anybody tells you, The Beatles are no more (John and I, at least are pursuing our own careers). I think that the only thing to do in the circumstances is to dissolve the partnership, and the money and artistic control to go to each of us individually. I hope you can do something to help, because until this is cleared up, I'm on strike.

Paul McCartney.[11]

---

* John and Ringo had different memories of how Ringo came to take the letter to Paul. John's recollection was that he and George asked Ringo to do it. Ringo's was that they were going to send the letter by messenger, but he volunteered to take it himself. "I didn't think it fair that some office lad should take something like that 'round," he told *Melody Maker*. "I couldn't fear him then. But he got angry, because we were asking him to hold his album back and the album was very important to him."

The other Beatles, while annoyed at Paul's refusal to take a role in Apple or consider its plans and priorities, hoped to normalize the relationship. John's decision to write the note by hand, making his case with an apology rather than his trademark sarcasm, and Ringo's decision to hand carry John's note to Paul suggest as much. Hoping to keep the peace, once Ringo relayed Paul's reaction, John and George gave in, leaving Paul's release date as April 17, and moving *Let It Be* to May 8.

Ringo conveyed this news to Paul by telephone on April 2, two days after his visit, and sent over a letter from Apple authorizing the release. Paul immediately sent the authorization to Sir Joseph. But he was still fuming; four days later, he wrote again to Sir Joseph, demanding a copy of the January 12 contract.

And the battles continued. John Eastman released a press statement to American reporters on April 7, noting the imminent release of *McCartney*, along with the news that Paul had acquired the film rights to Rupert Bear from the chairman of Beaverbrook newspapers, Sir Max Aitken, and planned to make an animated feature film, to be called *Rupert*. Eastman's statement noted that these projects would keep Paul from working with the other Beatles indefinitely.[12] That led writers in the United States to conclude that the Beatles might be finished.

Klein fired back immediately with a statement on Apple's behalf, saying that: "Any individual Beatle cannot offer his services, appear alone, or with any other person in any branch of the entertainment industry . . . without the consent of Apple and the other Beatles."[13]

Slipping into promotional mode, Paul spoke with Jann Wenner, the founder and publisher of *Rolling Stone*, on April 9, for a story scheduled for the April 30 issue. Mainly, he wanted to discuss *McCartney*, which would be out by the time the story appeared. But the conversation also touched on the state of play at Apple. It was Paul's first in-depth interview in months, and he took the opportunity to lob a few salvos at Klein, who had recently told *Rolling Stone* that although Paul was initially reluctant, he had indeed joined the other Beatles in engaging him to manage the group and Apple. Paul did not mince words.

"The thing is," he told Wenner, "I am not signed with Allen Klein because I don't like him and I don't think he is the man for me, however much the other three like him. Allen Klein has me by *implication*, but that is a misapprehension. The truth is he has only three quarters of the Beatles and in fact he doesn't have the Beatles . . . I have read in *Rolling Stone* that he said those things, that he said I signed a contract with him, but it is not true."

He went on to downplay Klein's biggest accomplishment for the Beatles, the new EMI contract as "a deal that anyone would have done." About Apple, he said it was "a good organization," but it was a business, and neither businesses nor businessmen interested him. "For me, life at home is what is interesting now. I have two kids, a wife of one year and everything at home. I love being at home and I love music. That is largely what interests me and I am not looking for anything else to interest me."

Wenner also asked Paul about his relationship with John. "I don't know, really," Paul replied, adding that they hadn't spoken in awhile, but that there was no argument between them, and nothing to be read into their lack of contact.

"John is very busy at the moment. I don't like to be busy. I don't feel the need to," he said. "I will see him when I see him. And I love him just the same."[14]

After his interview with Wenner, Paul telephoned John. Their talk began as a retrospective heart-to-heart.

"I told him on the phone that at the beginning of last year I was annoyed with him," Paul said. "I was jealous because of Yoko, and afraid about the break-up of a great musical partnership. And it's taken me a year to realize that they were in love. Just like Linda and me."[15]

Eventually, Paul got down to business, telling John that he, too, was leaving the Beatles. As Paul remembered it, John's response was, "Good! That makes two of us who have accepted it mentally."[16]

Paul knew the ruckus that his self-interview would create; if Eastman's announcement of *McCartney* and *Rupert* sparked headlines about Paul leaving the Beatles, the effect of the interview would be seismic.

As it turned out, the world did not have to wait for the press kits to land. Don Short, the enterprising show business columnist for the *Daily Mirror*, was walking away from his desk, in the early evening of April 9, thinking he was finished for the day, when the telephone rang. Short had covered the Beatles since 1963; in fact, his story about John's assaulting the Cavern's disc jockey, Bob Wooler, was the group's first appearance in a national newspaper, and he claimed credit for coining the term "Beatlemania."

Short had an uncanny ability to learn about the Beatles' plans before they were announced, thanks to a network of sources close to the group. On the telephone that evening was an Apple contact with a scoop: "Paul is quitting, Don. It's definite. It's all over. The Beatles are breaking up."[17]

Short quickly phoned his higher-level Apple contacts, one of whom reluctantly confirmed the story. The *Mirror* scrapped its planned front page and led its early edition on April 10 with "Paul Is Quitting the Beatles," changing it to "Paul Quits the Beatles" once the press kit landed.

"By 11 a.m. the area outside Apple in Savile Row looked like a disaster zone," Apple's press officer Derek Taylor wrote when *Record Mirror* invited him to describe the day. "There were fans all over the place and all of Fleet Street seemed to have turned out."[18]

John was less amused by Paul's after-the-fact resignation when he saw Paul's press kit and Short's scoop. *He* was the leader of the Beatles. *He* was the one who decided to call it quits, and *he* wanted to be the one who broke the news, when *he* thought the time was right. Paul had usurped the moment.

"John wanted to be first [to announce the split]. But I didn't realize it would hurt him that much or that it mattered who was first,"[19] McCartney later admitted.

"No, I wasn't angry," Lennon claimed. "Shit, he's a good P.R. man, that's all. He's about the best in the world, probably. He really does a job. I wasn't angry. We were all hurt that he didn't tell us that was what he was going to do. I think he claims that he didn't mean that to happen but that's bullshit . . . I was cursing, because I hadn't done it. I wanted to do it, I should have done it. Ah, damn, shit, what a fool I was. But there were many pressures at that time with the Northern Songs fight going on; it would have upset the whole thing, if I would have said that."[20]

But Lennon *was* angry. Ray Connolly, a reporter for the *Evening Standard* who was on friendly terms with the Beatles, had known about John's "divorce" from the band since December, when John told him the news, but swore him to secrecy. When Connolly telephoned Lennon for a comment about Short's piece, Lennon demanded to know why Connolly hadn't written that John left the group when John confided in him. Connolly's reminder that John put the conversation off the record did not calm him down.[21]

The BBC, picking up on Short's piece, led its news report with footage of crying fans. Its coverage included an interview with Derek Taylor, who looked shell-shocked as he outlined the dispute between Paul and the others over Klein. Taylor noted the Eastmans' impeccable credentials and expressed some surprise, given the Beatles' tendency to consider one another's feelings, that John had not come around to Paul's point of view—a daring response, given that Klein was Taylor's boss.

Klein was interviewed, too, and was provocative as ever.

"Well, it's never pleasant when someone appears not to like you," he said. "I think his reasons are [long pause] are *sick*. They're his own personal problems. But unfortunately, he is obligated into Apple for a considerable number of years, so his disassociating himself with me has no effect."[22]

But John, the other Beatles, and Klein were soon distracted from that by another grenade from the McCartney camp.

The afternoon he spoke with Wenner and John, Paul sent word to Apple that he would not attend a board meeting, the next day, to discuss the *Let It Be* film, and a release and distribution deal Klein had worked out with United Artists. The agreement, which included details of the royalties that would accrue to Apple, and the management commission to be paid to Klein, was to be signed that day, and William Bernstein, of United Artists, had flown over to answer any questions or concerns the Beatles might have.

As the Beatles had hoped—and as Klein promised he could arrange—United Artists had agreed to consider *Let It Be* as the fulfillment of the Beatles' contractual obligation to the company, at long last tying up a loose end from the Brian Epstein days.

Paul's refusal to attend seemed, at first, a continuation of his recent policy of skipping Apple meetings. But a cable from John Eastman clarified his reasons:

```
Regret unable attend meeting upon such short notice
as McCartney representative. Examination of contracts
indicates no grant by McCartney or members of family to
Apple films or others. Apple films seemingly without right
or authority. Appreciate documentation of grant as well as
copies of all proposed agreements. Delighted discuss this
with you at convenience.23
```

Paul, Linda and Heather all appear in the film; Eastman was asserting that since none of them had signed a release, and that since films fell outside the Beatles' 1967 partnership agreement, neither Apple nor United Artists could release it. At the April 10 meeting, John, George, and Ringo signed. Paul never did. But this time, the others called Paul's bluff—and they knew it was a bluff, not only because *Let It Be* was, from start to finish, Paul's baby, because Paul had earlier told Peter Brown that he would do nothing to stop the release of the film.[24]

Still, Eastman's challenge kept the Beatles and Klein busy. Through the rest of April, letters went back and forth between Eastman, Klein, Harrison, and Starr (representing Apple Films Ltd.). Klein asserted that Paul had assented to the distribution agreement; Eastman demanded documents showing that to be the case, adding that Paul had assured him that there were no oral agreements to that effect.

But the film was released on schedule, on May 13 in the United States, and a week later in Great Britain. Paul and the Eastmans simply added the transaction to the growing list of what they considered Apple's and Klein's improper dealings.

Elsewhere at Apple, Paul's press release continued to generate press queries from around the world, and by the end of the day, with his secretary, Mavis Smith, arguing that the press had to be given *something*, Derek Taylor composed and released a statement, couched in his characteristically cosmic style:

APRIL 10, 1970

SPRING IS HERE, AND LEEDS ARE PLAYING CHELSEA TOMORROW*, AND RINGO AND JOHN AND GEORGE AND PAUL ARE ALIVE AND WELL AND FULL OF HOPE.

THE WORLD IS STILL SPINNING AND SO ARE WE AND SO ARE YOU.

WHEN THE SPINNING STOPS—THAT'LL BE THE TIME TO WORRY. NOT BEFORE. UNTIL THEN, THE BEATLES ARE ALIVE AND WELL AND THE BEAT GOES ON. THE BEAT GOES ON.[25]

As for Paul—he spent the afternoon riding Honor, a horse he bought on April 2. Then he, Linda and the girls headed off for a weekend in the country.

——➤——

With *McCartney* off his plate, Paul turned his attention to the acetate of the *Let It Be* album that Phil Spector left for him. He was shocked at what he heard. That Spector had elongated George's 'I Me Mine' by editing in repetitions of the verses, choruses and refrain didn't bother him—the song, as Paul, George and Ringo recorded it on January 3, was too short, running just over a minute. Nor was he troubled by the slowed-down version of 'Across the Universe,' with its orchestration and swelling choir—if John signed off on that, fine.

---

* Taylor is referring to the 1970 FA Cup Final, between Chelsea and Leeds United, at Wembley Stadium. The match ended in a 2-2 tie, which required it to be replayed, on April 29 at Old Trafford, the first such match to be replayed since 1912. In the replay, Chelsea prevailed, 2-1. The release is the last one Taylor wrote for the Beatles as a group; at the end of 1970, he left Apple to become Director of Special Projects at Warner Brothers Records.

But when he reached 'The Long and Winding Road' he was incensed. During the recording sessions, Paul remarked that the song might benefit from a wind arrangement, although at that point the ban on overdubs and production sweetening was still in effect. Spector thought the sparse piano ballad, with its gentle bass, guitar and drum backing, needed something, too, and engaged arranger Richard Hewson to write a score. Paul had worked with Hewson on Mary Hopkin's 'Those Were the Days,' and when Spector hired him to expand the textures of 'The Long and Winding Road,' Hewson consulted with Paul, to be sure his ideas matched Paul's vision of the song.

"I worked on the song originally alone in the studio with Paul at the piano," Hewson explained. "Then, when the orchestra tracks were put on the record, Spector took over. He kept adding more and more instruments on a huge scale, such as ten violins at a time. I ceased to count the number of musicians. There were not enough chairs and music stands for all of them. We had to send people home then Spector would bring in fresh ones. All the time I was writing scores for the new people. And Ringo Starr, the only Beatle who turned up for the session, just drummed his way through the whole thing."[26]

When Spector was finished, 'The Long and Winding Road' was an orchestral and choral extravaganza, both treacly and overwrought, and nothing like the graceful ballad McCartney composed, and the Beatles recorded.

Paul immediately fired off a letter to Klein:

Dear Sir,
In future no one will be allowed to add to or subtract from a recording of one of my songs without my permission.

I had considered orchestrating 'The Long and Winding Road' but I decided against it. I therefore want it altered to these specifications:

1. Strings, horns, voices and all added noises to be reduced in volume.
2. Vocal and Beatle instrumentation to be brought up in volume.
3. Harp to be removed completely at the end of the song and original piano notes to be substituted.
4. Don't ever do it again.

Signed,

PAUL McCARTNEY

c.c. Phil Spector, John Eastman

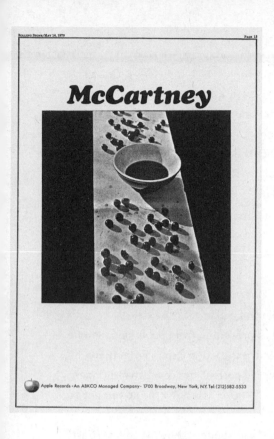

Klein insisted that it was too late to make changes to the recording, although with the release date four weeks away, there was ample time. But Paul's irate letter dictated Klein's next move in his tit-for-tat war with Paul: 'The Long and Winding Road' would be the Beatles' next single. A benign reading would be that, by releasing the song as a single, Klein was showing how completely he believed in the song, and the arrangement. But even if that were the case, Klein knew that a new Beatles single would get saturation airplay, and he could count on Paul being irritated afresh every time he heard it on the radio.

Another skirmish erupted around the cover and advertising for *McCartney*. Although the disc was pressed on an Apple label, the back cover lacked an Apple logo, and sported what Klein regarded as an incomplete EMI credit. John Lennon wrote to EMI's Ken East on the day of the release, asking that this detail be corrected on future pressings. The American pressings listed the album as an Apple recording, over ABKCO's New York address.

What truly incensed Paul, however, were the full-page advertisements Klein took out in *Billboard* and *Rolling Stone*.

"On the bottom was 'On Apple Records,' which was okay," explained Paul. "But somebody had also come along and slapped on 'An ABKCO Managed company.' Now that is Klein's company and has nothing to do with my record. It's like Klein taking part of the credit for my record."[27]

There was a dispute, as well, about whether American review copies of the album should include the four pages of press materials, including the self-interview. Paul thought it should; in fact, given the amount of information it contained about his instrumentation and recording methods, not to mention the lyrics, he wanted the four pages to be included in stock copies of the album, as well. But in the interview, Paul went out of his way, twice, to disclaim any relationship or involvement with Klein, and Klein was not going to have such effrontery included in a release from "An ABKCO Managed Company."

Paul's solution was to have the American press copies mailed by Eastman and Eastman, who included the press kit—and affixed a strip of black tape on the back cover, crudely covering ABKCO's address.

Disinclined as Paul was to give interviews, particularly now that the self-interview was causing such a commotion, he and Linda agreed to meet Ray Connolly for lunch at Wheeler's & Co., a fish restaurant in Soho, on April 16. It is likely that Paul chose to speak with Connolly—his first interview since announcing that he did not see much future with the Beatles—because Connolly knew the *real* story of the split, having heard it directly from Lennon, five months earlier. As Connolly told Paul, John had put their conversation off the record, back then; but now that Paul's news was out, he was in a position to tell the story, and perhaps deflect some fan anger from Paul. He kept his word.

"Paul McCartney did not kill the Beatles," Connolly wrote toward the top of a lengthy two-part piece about the McCartneys, published in the *Evening Standard* on April 21 and 22. "If the group is dead (and judging by what John Lennon has told me recently it is quite, quite dead) McCartney might have been seen as the last survivor. If he has quit, and he still hasn't said it, he was the last to go. (John Lennon, however, told me quite definitely last December that he'd finished with the Beatles forever—but asked me at that time not to make it known publicly.)"[28]

At a stroke, Connolly got to say he'd had a scoop he was prevented from publishing, and he exonerated Paul as the culprit behind the most popular band in the world's split. From there, he gave Paul a virtually open forum. That included the technically correct but somewhat disingenuous claim that his self-interview had been misunderstood: "I never intended the statement to mean 'Paul McCartney quits Beatles.'"

In fact, Connolly's assertion that Paul was "the last to go" was supported by the spin McCartney gave the group's recent history, running down everything from Ringo's and George's departures, to his plan to breathe new life into the Beatles with a tour of small venues, to John's telling him he was daft and wanted a "divorce." He added that the agreement not to discuss the split publicly had an end point of March or April, when *Let It Be* was about to be released. "But I got bored. I like to work."

From there, McCartney and Connolly discussed the intricacies of the Beatles' business concerns—Northern Songs, Eastman vs. Klein, Paul's dislike of the Spectorized version of 'The Long and Winding Road' (which had not yet been released) and his desire to remove himself from Klein's management—as well as his life as a family man.

"What I really would like to tell the people," he said, "is that I'm the same as anyone else. I love my family, I get up in the morning, have my breakfast, watch telly at night—do all the things everybody else does."

When a customer walked up to Paul and asked about the Beatles, as the McCartneys and Connolly were leaving Wheelers, Paul told him, "Just tell the people I've found someone I like enough to want to spend all my time with. That's me—the home, the kids and the fireplace."[29]

Record reviewers in Britain and the United States found themselves in an unusual position as they regarded their fresh press copies of *McCartney* and the accompanying information. Their sense of the state of affairs at Apple was sketchy: they knew from their own reporting that the rise of Apple had brought the Beatles' post-Epstein financial problems to a crisis point. They were aware of Apple's attempted purchases of NEMS and Northern Songs, and of tensions over Allen Klein's engagement to manage their affairs.

The more attentive among them—at least, those in New York—might have heard John's WABC-FM radio interview with Howard Smith, in December, in which he spoke about the frustrations of the unfinished *Get Back/Let It Be* album, and wondered why Lennon was so enthusiastic about the idea that the album would show the Beatles "with their suits off"—his way of saying it would break the myth. But they would not have heard about John's September 16 "divorce" announcement, or the depression it threw Paul into. There were rumors of internal squabbling; yet over the last 16 months, the Beatles had been as productive as ever.

Now, suddenly, Paul has announced that his future with the Beatles is doubtful—and, by the way, here's his debut solo album.

Those expecting something as polished as *Abbey Road* were either puzzled or disappointed, but generally buried their dismay in a deferential assessment of Paul's established strengths as a songwriter and player, and his accomplishments as a Beatle. A few put aside their expectations and sought to give the album the best possible spin; others turned cartwheels trying to find a fair balance. Only a few unloaded on the album without cutting Paul a break for his past work.

Judith Simons's review in the *Daily Express* was the first to see print, just two days after the press copies went out. Beginning with a backhanded compliment—"Only Paul McCartney's talent and charm could make this kind of thing enjoyable"—Simons captured her colleagues' confusion about what to make of the do-it-yourself production. But she concluded that "it is a beautiful album."[30]

William Mann, the renowned classical music critic for *The Times*—and a vigorous champion of the Beatles since 1963, when he cited the Aeolian cadences in 'Not a Second Time' among the charms of *With the Beatles*—described *McCartney* as "a relaxed, untidy, often unfinished collection." But he added: "Words like Genius should be sparingly applied but Paul's musical gift is for real."[31]

In the *Daily Mirror*, Don Short wrote that *McCartney* "conclusively confirms the suspicion that Lennon-McCartney are better together," but listed 'Every Night,' 'Junk' and 'Hot As Sun' as its "gems." Alan Smith, in *NME*, found the album "too harmlessly mild," on first listen, but "immensely warm and pleasurable" when he played it again, ratcheting up the praise by adding that "most of the sounds, effects and ideas are sheer brilliance; much of the aura is of quiet songs on a hot summer night."[32]

Among the British reviews, the two most contentious—and the two that got most firmly under McCartney's skin—were *Melody Maker*'s, by Richard Williams, and *Disc*'s, by Penny Valentine.

"*McCartney* contains the best and worst of an extraordinary talent," Williams wrote. "'Maybe I'm Amazed' would have become a classic, had it been included on, say, *Abbey Road*," but, he added 'Man We Was Lonely' "is sheer banality. If it had been sung by Dave Dee, Dozy, Beaky, Mick and Tich I (and you) would've sneered and turned it off. It's the worst example of his music-hall side."[33]

Penny Valentine liked 'Maybe I'm Amazed,' but found little value in the rest of the album. "It's a bitter disappointment," she wrote. "To have to say it's just 'nice' and nothing more should explain everything." She went on to say that "of all the Beatles I've always thought McCartney had the most to give musically. His work has always totally appealed to me—and to the world at large. Like that expectant world I too was breathless with anticipation at this first McCartney album. Truly, I thought, it would be magnificent. *McCartney* has managed to shatter all those hopes and illusions with about the same effort it takes to burst a balloon."[34]

Already treading a self-confidence tightrope, Paul was stung by the negative reviews. "I know that anyone who has to review 16 albums a week isn't gonna end up loving music, they probably end up hating it. I sometimes feel sorry for writers but normally I hate 'em, because they're slagging me off. But I am fully aware that they've got a tough job on their hands."[35]

Paul responded directly to both reviews. He sent *Melody Maker* a parody reader's letter, dripping in sarcasm:*

Who Does Paul McCartney Think He Is?

We don't see anything of him for a year, and then out he pops from his mysterious hermit-like existence, advertising his new record in a publicity-crazed manner.

Does he really believe that he played all the instruments? Let's face it, Mailbag, we're not suckers.

It's obvious George Martin had a lot to do with it. In fact, if you listen carefully to the end of the third track played backwards, you can almost hear him whistling.

Paul McCartney.[36]

---

* Taking the critical rough with the smooth was something Paul always found difficult. In an August 1963 review of 'She Loves You,' the disc jockey Brian Matthews, while predicting that the single would be a "big success," described the lyrics as "simple" and "idiotic." Matthews's critique crept so deeply under Paul's skin that he never let it go, bringing it up in interviews decades later, each time evolving and embellishing the original sentiment. He held on similarly to a *New York Times* review of *Sgt. Pepper's Lonely Hearts Club Band*, in which Richard Goldstein criticized what he saw as overproduction and thin inspiration, regularly adducing that review as a kind of shorthand proof ("Well, the *New York Times* panned *Sgt. Pepper!*") that critics don't know what they are talking about.

To Valentine, he fired off a telegram[37] that read:

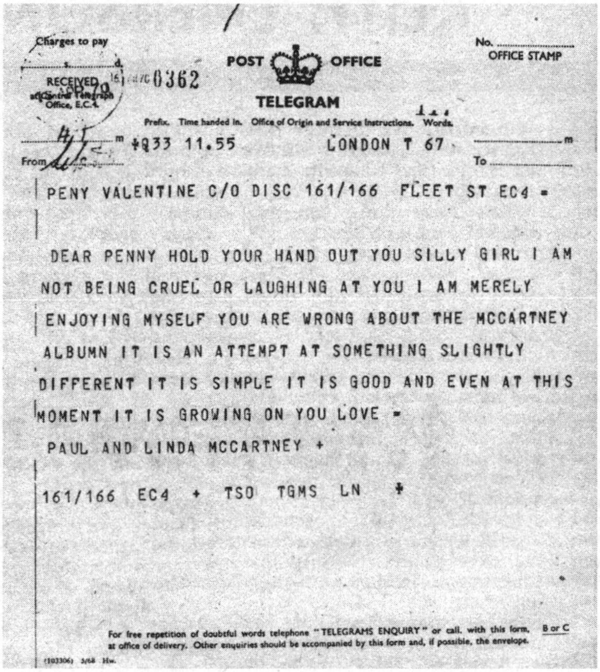

Charges to pay s. d.

RECEIVED at Central Telegraph Office, E.C.4.

0362

POST OFFICE

TELEGRAM

No. OFFICE STAMP

Prefix. Time handed in. Office of Origin and Service Instructions. Words.

m +Q33 11.55 LONDON T 67

From To

PENY VALENTINE C/O DISC 161/166 FLEET ST EC4 =

DEAR PENNY HOLD YOUR HAND OUT YOU SILLY GIRL I AM NOT BEING CRUEL OR LAUGHING AT YOU I AM MERELY ENJOYING MYSELF YOU ARE WRONG ABOUT THE MCCARTNEY ALBUMN IT IS AN ATTEMPT AT SOMETHING SLIGHTLY DIFFERENT IT IS SIMPLE IT IS GOOD AND EVEN AT THIS MOMENT IT IS GROWING ON YOU LOVE =

PAUL AND LINDA MCCARTNEY +

161/166 EC4 + TSO TGMS LN +

For free repetition of doubtful words telephone "TELEGRAMS ENQUIRY" or call, with this form, at office of delivery. Other enquiries should be accompanied by this form and, if possible, the envelope. B or C

(103306) 5/68 Hw.

The American reviews were similarly mixed, with the *Chicago Tribune* describing the album as: "Not terrible, not *really* bad—just very mediocre, and for a major star, that's tantamount to failure."[38] And Robert Hilburn, in the *Los Angeles Times*, found the album "a clear disappointment," but regarded 'Maybe I'm Amazed' as head and shoulders above the rest. It is, he wrote, a "totally uncontrolled free-wheeling story of the sometimes frantic, anguished side of love . . . sung with just the right spark of outrageous abandonment."[39]

Probably the oddest review was the 1,400-word dissection Langdon Winner wrote for *Rolling Stone*—a review that bears the seeds of the John-versus-Paul partisanship that was beginning to blossom in these early post-Beatles months. This was something Jann Wenner encouraged: when Winner filed his piece, it was more of a conventional album review, but Wenner told him, "This album is a political statement. This album is a weapon. This album is part of a feud. All that has to be taken into account."[40]

Winner reframed the review as a polemic, in which the music was almost incidental; in fact, he seems torn between admiring the album (he calls *McCartney* "a very beautiful and pleasing record" and is generous with praise for 'Maybe I'm Amazed') and hating it (he writes that "in both the quality of its songs and the character of its production, *McCartney* will no doubt be a disappointment" to Beatles fans who may have "hoped that Paul's album would be a gigantic leap 'beyond the Beatles'").

The review's main thrust is a stern lecture on Paul's recent behavior within the Beatles. "*McCartney* is an album that tries desperately to convince," he wrote. But what he sees, instead of a convincing argument, is "tawdry propaganda."

What he appears to have found most troubling, though, is the press kit. "The sheets contain even more assertions about how happy and peaceful Paul and Linda are these days, and some interview statement *[sic]* from Paul concerning his relationship to the Beatles—statements which drip a kind of unsavory vindictiveness." And he gives the impression that even the music is part of a sinister plot. "I like *McCartney* very much. But I remember that the people of Troy also liked that wooden horse they wheeled through their gates until they discovered that it was hollow inside and full of hostile warriors."[41]

Paul hardly had a monopoly on hostile warriors, of course, but that was the narrative that *Rolling Stone* presented. In the same issue, Jann Wenner wrote the lead story, essentially a challenge to, and clarification of, some of McCartney's comments in Wenner's April 9 interview, which had appeared in the biweekly's previous issue. The piece appeared to have been instigated by Lennon's and Klein's displeasure with some of Paul's comments, and perhaps also by Wenner's pique at Paul's not having given him a copy of the press kit that would be issued the day after his interview. (The full self-interview was also published in the new issue.)

It had not occurred to Wenner, for example, to check Paul's assertion that Klein did not represent him. Now he explained that the situation was more nuanced—that Klein managed Apple, and that the Beatles had a partnership agreement that bound them together, and to Apple, and therefore, to Klein.

In the same issue of *Rolling Stone*, under the headline: "One Guy Standing There, Shouting 'I'm Leaving'" Lennon gave Wenner *his* view of the state of affairs at Apple.

"It's John, George, and Ringo as individuals," Lennon said. "We're not even communicating with or making plans about Paul; we're just reacting to everything he does. It's a simple fact that he can't have his own way so he's causing chaos. I don't care what you think of Klein—call Klein something else, call him Epstein for now—and just consider the fact that three of us chose Epstein. Paul was the same with Brian, in the beginning, if you must know. He used to sulk, and God knows what. Wouldn't turn up for dates and bookings. It's always been the same only now it's bigger because we're bigger. It's the same old game.

"You know it's like this: four guys onstage with a spotlight on them; second picture; three guys onstage breezing out of the spotlight; third picture, one guy standing there shouting 'I'm leaving.' We were all out of it."[42]

Whichever side the public believed, *McCartney* was selling well. In the United States, it qualified for a RIAA Gold Record, representing 500,000 sales, within a week of its release.[43] By mid-May 1970, the album had sold 88,624 copies in Britain, and 887,965 copies in the United States.[44]

McCartney topped the *Billboard* 200 albums on May 23, where it remained for three weeks before being replaced by *Let It Be*. In the UK, the album peaked at No. 2 on May 2, denied the No.1 spot by Simon and Garfunkel's *Bridge Over Troubled Water*.

Paul was doing well as a Beatle, too: 'The Long and Winding Road' had sold 1.2 million copies in its first two days on the market, and the *Let It Be* album (released in the UK on May 8 and US on May 11) had sold 3.7 million.[45]

Two of Paul's Beatles tunes also won prizes at the 15th annual Ivor Novello Awards. 'Ob-La-Di, Ob-La-Da' was named the most-performed work of the previous year, and 'Get Back' won the award for the most sales. By the time the awards were handed out, in London on May 10, Paul was back in Scotland.

6

ANOTHER DAY,
ANOTHER DILEMMA

Though he may have been pleased with some reviews and angered by others, the real bottom line for Paul was that *McCartney* put him back in the game, with an album that sold well enough to be a useful career reboot, and right in time. What's more, during the final weeks of recording the album, the McCartney songwriting machinery kicked back into action, increasing his confidence that he could continue making records on his own. Musically, the umbilical cord to the Beatles was decisively cut. The troublesome business ties remained, chaining him not only to John, George and Ringo, but to Apple and Klein, as well.

To mull over all this, and to give himself space to write new songs, Paul returned to Scotland with Linda, Heather and Mary, on May 1, 1970, making the nine-hour journey in the Land Rover, with a brief break in Merseyside. He did not attend the world premiere of *Let It Be* in New York on May 13, or in either London or Liverpool, on May 20. Nor did the other Beatles.

"That didn't surprise me," Lindsay-Hogg said. "They had broken up, and they weren't really doing anything as Beatles anymore, so I didn't think anybody was going to turn up for the premiere. Also, by that time I would say that *Let It Be* became a slightly emotional issue for them, given that tempers were fraying. It wasn't the four of them in their normal, fairly happy, and humorous way. For some of them, the film represented a time when they weren't happy, and when they thought, perhaps, that Paul was trying to get them to do something which maybe they didn't want to do. They may have thought it might have been a pro-Paul movie—all sorts of, I would say, erroneous opinions, but things which would make them not want to attend the movie together, or representing the Beatles."[1]

Happily ensconced at High Park, Paul threw himself into the chores of spring, a busy time even for novice, part-time farmers like the McCartneys. They had six horses—Paul's own Honor,

Linda's Cinnamon, and three ponies, Cookie, Coconut and Sugarfoot, the last two being favorites of Heather's. The sixth, only recently moved to Scotland from stables near London, was Drake's Drum, the racehorse Paul gifted his father, Jim, upon his 62nd birthday, on July 7, 1964.

Jim was partial to a bet, and his horse enjoyed some degree of success, albeit short-lived. During the famous Grand National weekend at Liverpool's Aintree Racecourse on March 26, 1966, Paul and Jim watched on from the stands, betting slips in hand, as the "Beatle" horse (as it became known in racing circles) lined up for the Hylton Plate sprint race. With odds of 20–1, and stiff competition, Jim convinced Paul they should only back their horse to the tune of £2 (Paul was readying a £5 bet), but Drake's Drum overcame the odds, running in as the unlikely winner. Paul beamed with pride as his father walked into the winner enclosure on the biggest weekend of the horseracing calendar.

But Jim's treasured horse had not raced since picking up a shoulder injury in spring of 1967, and veterinarians had recommended to the McCartneys that the struggling nine-year-old be put down. Paul refused, giving him an early retirement in Scotland instead.

Linda had been riding since she was nine years old, when she took lessons at a stable in Scarsdale. She competed, as a child, and won a shelf full of ribbons and trophies, but could not persuade her parents to get her a horse of her own. Now she had a farm with six of them, with Cinnamon, a chestnut mare, as her favorite.

"She was very nervous, and didn't feel at all at home," Linda said of Cinnamon, when they first bought her. "Paul and I went for a ride along an idyllic river and decided to tie the horses up and sit in the tall grass by the river, just like in the movies. However, Cinnamon broke her reins and galloped off towards the main road. I jumped on Paul's horse and rode after her. We finally found her in someone's garden. She jumped the fence, and all the Dutch gardener there could say was 'Clean jump . . . she made a clean jump.'"

Paul was new to horse riding; when the Beatles were asked to ride horses in the promotional video for 'Penny Lane,' he had to work hard to look confident. But he took to it quickly, Linda said.

"He's a natural, his horse responds easily to him. One night after a drive to town and a bit of wine, we returned home to the horses who were waiting at the gate. Paul jumped onto his horse and galloped her up the field, guiding her with just the halter. What a beautiful sight that was!"[2]

There was serious farm work to be done, as well. Gardening, for example. The McCartneys had started growing all their own food, their crops including carrots, peas, spinach, cabbages, turnips, runner beans and melons—plus a bit of recreational cannabis in a Kencast greenhouse that they bought and assembled themselves.

"She's the lead gardener," Paul said of Linda. "I'm the rhythm gardener. We lead a very simple life there. We get up in the morning, I light the fire and Linda starts doing the cooking. Heather may lend a hand with the washing up. Then we may be busy about the garden or go out riding during the day . . . Then in the evening after supper, we'll all sit down and watch TV.* But we're not cut off from the world. We've never been hermits in the sense of the word, we're only ten minutes out of Campbeltown, and we can run into town in the Land Rover and get anything we need."[3]

And then there were the sheep. High Park, with its open but rough terrain, was better suited to sheep than to cows, and in 1970, Paul owned about 150 of them. Most of the time, the sheep were looked after by Duncan Cairns, a local farmer Paul had hired to oversee the farm when he was away. But there was a degree to which Paul enjoyed being a hands-on farmer, and he had Duncan teach him some of the necessary skills, including sheep shearing.

"Every year I do the shearing myself, using hand shears," Paul said. "We send the wool off to the Wool Marketing Board. The sheep don't mind. To them, it's just losing their winter coat because summer has arrived."[4]

Paul and Linda also bred their sheep, trying to limit each year's increase to about 30 lambs. But the joys of spring were delicately balanced against the realities of working the land, and they had to quickly come to terms with the fact that not all of their newborn lambs survived. The death of a lamb in the spring of 1970 was memorialized in a song Paul began on the spot.

"We were up in Scotland at my sheep farm—which all sounds very lovely on the postcards, until you get to lambing," Paul explained. "Of course, a few of them die; it's life and death and a lot of farmers just don't want to get involved. They say, 'Right,' and just chuck them over the wall. But you can't help it if you're a bit sensitive—particularly in a household full of children—and there was one lamb we were trying to save. The young ones get out into the weather and collapse from exposure; you find and bring them in. We stayed up all night and had him in front of the stove, but it was too late, and he just died.[5]

"So I had the happy job of clearing it up. When they go dead, they kind of go like a stuffed toy . . . these little lambs. It was very early in the morning, and no one was up, and I had my guitar there and I couldn't really say much to this lamb. But I started, '*I have no answer for you little lamb / I can help you out / but I cannot help you in.*' And it came from there. Just not being able to do anything about it was the idea of that song."[6]

Paul wrote down the opening section and set it aside, one of several new songs he was tinkering with during his spring-summer stay in Scotland. But another new song, 'Dragonfly,' gave him the means to complete it. In 'Dragonfly,' he directly addresses a dragonfly that flies past his window, just as he addresses the dying lamb. Both songs had uncommonly warm, attractive melodies, and it soon occurred to Paul that the two unfinished songs could work together in a joined piece, 'Little Lamb Dragonfly,' in which 'Dragonfly' became the song's extended bridge, with 'Lit-

---

* Television in Paul's region of Scotland was still black and white; color did not arrive until May 1971.

tle Lamb' supplying the outer verses, and a set of punctuating acoustic guitar figures connecting the two melodies.

Joining seemingly disparate songs had long been a part of McCartney's compositional toolbox. On *McCartney*, it was as simple as a splice between two instrumentals. Sometimes it was more complicated, but the list of works using the technique includes the Beatles' 'A Day in the Life,' in which verses by Lennon surrounded an unfinished McCartney song, and the medleys on the second half of *Abbey Road*, built of incomplete McCartney and Lennon fragments. Lennon complained that the *Abbey Road* medley was a cheat, nothing more than unfinished songs stitched together; but he didn't mind using that method himself when it was expedient—for example, in 'Happiness Is a Warm Gun.'

Still, 'Little Lamb Dragonfly' was nowhere near complete—each song had only a line or two of lyrics, enough to establish the basic theme, but not enough to fill out the already completed melody and structure. But McCartney made a basic recording of what he had so far, for a reel of demos he gradually compiled that spring and summer.

For the moment, he thought of 'Little Lamb Dragonfly' as a contender for the soundtrack of his planned Rupert Bear film, and he labeled it as such on the demo. Paul's demo reel also lists two more songs with a Rupert notation: 'Sunshine Sometime,' a laid-back piece with jazz harmonies and an almost bossa nova Brazilian feel, and 'Guitar Song Instrumental a.k.a. When the Wind Blows'—an expanded version, with a whistled melody, of the track he recorded during his Cavendish Avenue sessions under the name 'Rupert.'

Several other songs Paul worked on during this trip to Scotland also used this technique. One was 'Another Day.' Shortly after his arrival, he received a telephone call from the film director Bryan Forbes, who was also head of production at EMI Films. Wearing both those hats, plus that of a screenplay author, Forbes was in the process of making *The Raging Moon*, and he hoped Paul might consider writing a song to be played under the titles.

The film, which starred Malcolm McDowell and Nanette Newman (Forbes's wife) is based on Peter Marshall's novel about Bruce Pritchard, a footballer who contracted a mysterious degenerative disease. Confined to a wheelchair, he moves to a home for the disabled, where he meets Jill Matthews, also wheelchair-bound (with polio), and falls in love with her. Jill, however, was about to leave the home to marry her fiancé. She soon has a change of heart and returns to the home, where she and Bruce begin a romance. But their time together is brief: Jill contracts a virus and dies.

Forbes hoped Paul could write him a sad song to play under the credits, and Paul agreed to consider it, telling Forbes that he wanted to see the film before he would fully commit. Forbes arranged a screening in July, in Campbeltown.

Film themes were a lucrative avenue worth investigating for the newly freelance former

Beatle. He had already taken a couple of steps in that direction, writing (with orchestration help from George Martin) the theme music for *A Family Way*, in 1966, and more recently, 'Come and Get It,' for *The Magic Christian*.

Shortly after speaking with Forbes, Paul picked up an acoustic guitar and, taking the director's request at its most literal, composed a pretty yet downcast tune in E minor, the title and central lyric of which was 'So Sad.' Once again, the lyrics were fragmentary, just *"so sad, sometimes she feels so sad."*

As Paul told it, he soon transferred his original guitar idea to the piano and spent the next few days batting around ideas with Linda, whose role varied from that of a critical listener and sounding board, to coming up with occasional lines or melodic ideas, as she had done when Paul was composing 'Man We Was Lonely.'[7]

Paul's ideas about collaboration were fluid and often underpinned by pragmatic self-interest. With Lennon, the matter of songwriting credit was subject to an agreement that went back to the early Beatles years, and the collaboration was sometimes real, with each contributing ideas, and sometimes virtually nonexistent, with each composing separately—although Paul made a case for the importance of John's "bounce off" function.

"On 'Eleanor Rigby,' which I mainly wrote," Paul explained, "it was his opinion on my song that mattered. He didn't do much, but it came off."[8]

'Eleanor Rigby' was an odd example. According to John Lennon's childhood friend, Pete Shotton, who was visiting Lennon the weekend parts of the song were written, there were several other contributors, including Shotton himself. As Shotton remembered it, he and the other Beatles were present when Paul played the embryonic song, which lacked its final verse. Shotton himself proposed changing the name of the song's clergyman from Father McCartney to Father Mackenzie, so that listeners would not think Paul was singing about his own father, and Ringo suggested the image of Father Mackenzie *"darning his socks in the night."* The idea of ending the song with Eleanor dying and Father Mackenzie burying her was Shotton's as well.[9] Those are significant additions, yet the song is credited only to Lennon and McCartney.

It was not an isolated occasion. Paul openly acknowledged that the introductory and punctuating acoustic guitar line that George Harrison contributed to 'And I Love Her' was entirely George's creation. One can argue that George's four-note, repeating guitar figure was a matter of arranging, not composing, but for many listeners, it is an immediately identifiable element of the song, and it has been carried over into cover versions and orchestrations. Similarly, Mal Evans noted in his diary that he and Paul worked together on 'Fixing a Hole,' and that Paul promised him a royalty. In the end, he received neither a royalty nor credit,[10] but was reportedly paid a flat fee.

In those cases, Paul had nothing to gain by sharing the composition credit, and he would earn a lower royalty if there were other collaborators to split it with. But if he and Linda composed together, they stood to earn a higher share, since unlike Paul, Linda was not under contract to Northern Songs and could route her part in the collaboration through another publisher—specifically, McCartney Music, Inc., the publishing arm of the newly formed McCartney Productions Ltd.

Toward the end of the *Abbey Road* sessions, Paul had taken a step toward building a creative and business life outside the Beatles. Early in 1969, he had purchased a company registered under the name Adagrose Ltd., with an eye toward using it as a private production company, much as John and Yoko had formed Bag Productions that year.

Adagrose had been founded in December 1968, by Leonard Lewis, a theater director, and an associate, Francis Dean, with a broad remit that described the company as part arts agency and part sovereign government. Its stated purpose included: "to employ and exploit and turn to account the services of actors, composers, authors and other professional persons and to carry on business as theatrical employment and literary agents and artistes and author's personal representatives and managers" as well as "to construct, alter, remove or replace any buildings, erections, structures, roads, railways, reservoirs, machinery, plant, or tools, or works of any description . . . as may seem desirable in the interests of the company," and a great many other things as well.[11]

Paul applied to change the company's name to McCartney Productions Ltd., or MPL., on August 21, 1969, and the change was granted two weeks later. Though Paul remained signed to Northern Songs through 1973, any future music would be issued by his own publishing company. With Linda signed to McCartney Music, Paul and Linda would earn not only the full composer's royalty, but half the publisher's royalty as well.

But that was not the only attraction of collaborating with his wife. John Lennon figured into it as well. Though the other Beatles and their fans may have scoffed at John's demand that Yoko Ono be treated as his equal in the collaborative projects they undertook, Paul found that aspect of their relationship attractive, even enviable. He, too, wanted to be in a relationship so tight that they were perceived as inseparable in every way, including creatively.

That was partly what *McCartney* was about, but that album did not go far enough: it showcased Paul singing about his love for Linda, and Linda sometimes singing backup, but there was no indication that she was contributing anything beyond inspiration. Paul wanted Linda to be a cocreator, a comrade in the trenches.

What Paul wanted in a songwriting partner was someone intuitive, like him. Linda grew up loving the same music Paul did, and seeing performances in New York that Paul could only dream about. Moreover, because her father's clients were often at the Eastman home, she grew up in the presence of composers of an earlier generation and knew their music too. And as an adult, before she met Paul, she hung out with an extraordinarily creative crowd—rock royalty, really. In Paul's view, she had the background, if not the training, and training was something that Paul, as an untrained but astonishingly successful composer, did not particularly value.

All Paul had to do was show her how to make the leap from listener to creator. Teenagers in garage bands were doing exactly that, all over the world; there was no reason Linda couldn't become a songwriter too. Pulling her into the process with 'Man We Was Lonely,' and now 'So Sad,' was a start—and as far as Paul was concerned, she was a legitimate collaborator, anyway, by virtue of her role as a sounding board.

"One day," Paul recalled, "I just said to Linda, 'I'm going to strap you to the piano bench. I'm going to teach you my method, because I never 'write' music anyway. I just write by ear. And I like to collaborate on songs. I like company, not just going off alone in a quiet room—that's too much like doing homework, like school. If you work with me, then it's fun.'"[12]

When Paul described his songwriting process—always with the caveat that there was no formula, no single way to do it—he made it sound as easy as breathing.

"I'd sit down normally with just maybe a bit of an idea," he once explained. "And then I just start trying to sketch it in. Start at A: how's it gonna open then? And you think of an opening. Normally, if I'm on guitar, I'll just strum around on some chords I like for a little while. And then I may just be doing [he scats sings] and get maybe a half a melody or something. Sometimes, as you're working around on that little half melody, you find there's words there. This [he sings nonsense syllables] 'va-ze-za-za' is developed into 'washi saucer,' 'watch your saucer,' 'what you saw, sir,' 'what she saw there,' 'what she saw there was a man in a black suit.' And you've suddenly got a little idea.

"Then you carry it forward. Sometimes, you can go down a little alley that doesn't land anywhere. This 'man in the dark suit,' you go, oh God, he's terrible, I hate him. So you backtrack and get rid of him. And what she saw was a *face* in the mirror. Oh, that's better. And then you just go down that track, and you just hope that at the end of it, there's a chorus—that there's something's gonna get you out of this. That's one of the ways."[13]

Linda was keen to try, but musicianship and songwriting did not come easily to her, and she quickly discovered that she could not count on master classes from her highly accomplished husband.

"No, he is not a good teacher, Paul," she said in a frank moment. "He has no patience *what-so-ever* with somebody who doesn't know. He said, 'Here's C, now learn it, you know.' So, I've picked it up. I'm quite quick at picking things up, if I like them—like photography, nobody ever taught me."[14]

Linda noted, as well, that even for Paul, songwriting sometimes posed challenges. 'So Sad,' for example, presented Paul with a seemingly unsurmountable problem at this early stage. Set in three quarter ("waltz") time, it begins with what seems like a standard refrain: the words "so sad," sung twice, the first on a rising melody, the second falling, and continuing, "sometimes she feels so sad," on a gently ascending line with a melancholy descent on the final word. Two more lines follow, making the section long enough to be a verse. Paul then pivots to a second section, on a melody that begins with an ambitious arch before taking a dramatic turn in the form of shorter lines (the lyrics were not yet written) that lead back to the "sometimes she feels so sad" melody.

That was the difficulty: returning to the top (the rising and falling "*so sad*") was awkward, and it became clear that 'So Sad' would be better as a bridge than as a verse.

By mid-May, Paul found the solution by rummaging through some old, unfinished ideas. During the Beatles' sessions at Twickenham in January 1969, he had played through 'Another Day,' a fragment he tried both at the piano (on January 9—at the first of those sessions that Linda attended) and guitar (on January 25). It was mostly just a chord progression and a melody at that point, but its refrain had a lyric, "*it's just another day*," and there were a few lines of the verse, which vaguely outlined a song about a woman who worked in an office.

This was a song with a clear beginning and a viable verse structure, but without a bridge. The keys of the two fragments were close—'Another Day' was in G major, but quickly moves toward a wistful, E minor feeling, and 'So Sad' was in E minor. Where 'So Sad' was in 3|4 time, 'Another Day' was in 4|4—but that hardly mattered: rather than alter 'So Sad,' Paul would just shift at the point where the two sections meet, and then shift back when the verse returned.

With 'Another Day' as the main part of the song, and 'So Sad' as a contrasting middle section, Paul now had a structure that worked, and the basis of a song that would suit Forbes's needs. All that was needed now was for Paul and Linda to finish the lyric.

"This song, 'Another Day' is the story of Linda before she met me," Paul later noted.[15] He has also pointed out that the line "*Digging in the pocket of her raincoat*," in particular, was Linda's. By the time the song was finished, Paul had created a vivid portrait of a young woman, capturing her daily routine, her tentative romance, and the loneliness of her empty apartment. Paul even has her posting "*another letter to the Sound of Five*," a reference to a British radio show in the 1960s on which a panel discussed possible resolutions to problems listeners mailed in.

Other songs on the Summer 1970 demo reel show Linda's involvement more clearly. She sings on the demos for two incomplete songs, 'Long Haired Lady' and 'Love Is Long.' The first is a theatrical dialogue between a woman who wants to know if her man really loves her, or is just out for sex, and a man whose smooth responses are full of charming imagery ("*Who's the lady that makes that brief occasional laughter? / She's the lady who wears those flashing eyes*"); the second is less fully formed, more of a chorus carved out of wordplay centering on rhymes with "*long.*"

Another collaboration was 'Come on Little Lady (Eat at Home),' a simple rocker in which the second line—"*baby, let's eat at home*"—could be interpreted as a metaphor for oral sex. Paul dismissed that analysis, putting a more innocently literal spin on it.

"There are all the kind of things that, when you first get married, that you start to appreciate, you know, like home cooking," he said. "So that was just a song about home cooking and eat[ing] in bed. I mean, you know, that's not supposed to be *double entendre*, that's supposed to actually [be]—let's cook up something, go to bed and watch the telly."[16]

On the demo recorded that summer, 'Come on Little Lady' was the first section of a medley, sung by Paul and Linda. Little is known about the second song in the group, 'Buddy's Breakfast,' but it may have been the original bridge of 'Come on Little Lady,' which owes a clear debt to Buddy Holly, especially at the end, where the word *love* is sung with a Holly-like bit of "*OH-oh-oh-oh-OH*" scat singing. The medley's third song, 'Indeed I Do,' is a cheerful tune with the lilt of an Everly Brothers song.

———

Paul's hands-on (but part-time) involvement with the farm's sheep—and Linda's all-around love of animals—led the McCartneys to reconsider some basic aspects of their lives, not least, their eating habits. They were not quite ready to go fully vegetarian; Paul remained partial to his bacon and sausage. But dealing with animals directly put them in the position of understanding the degree to which they had the power of life and death: one day they might be shearing a sheep, the next, that sheep would be on its way to market, and a few days later, it could be on their dinner plates.

Taken aback as they were upon seeing farmers heaving lamb carcasses "over the wall," they came to realize that real farmers did not have the luxury of sentimentality; those animals were their livelihood. But as amateurs, Paul and Linda could redefine the relationship, turning their sheep into wool-producing pets, rather than eventual lamb chops.

They began talking about that realization almost immediately.

"We don't eat meat," Paul told an interviewer only a few months after an incident that, he said, brought him and Linda to that decision, "because we've got lambs on the farm, and we just ate a piece of lamb one day and suddenly realized we were eating a bit of one of those things that was playing outside the window, gamboling peacefully. But we're not strict. I don't want to put a big sign on me, 'Thou Shalt Be Vegetarian.' I like to allow myself."[17]

Through the spring and summer, Paul alternated the chores of maintaining a farm, as well as those of a new father, with a steady routine of writing new songs and diligently finishing older ideas. High on his list was 'Heart of the Country,' an idea that came to him as far back as the fall of 1969. Linda quotes from it in the letters she sent to estate agents that October, in her quest for a getaway in the south of England: "We are looking for a home in the 'heart of the country,'" she wrote, duly putting quotation marks around the title of a song no one else had yet heard.

Paul completed 'Heart of the Country' during an *al fresco* session—a habit he developed, when the weather was fine, of taking his guitar out to a field and sitting on the grass, playing with musical ideas. Closer to country music (in the Nashville sense) than to anything Scottish, the song is nevertheless an unabashed celebration of rural life.

"I love to find that, even in this day of concrete, there are still alive horses and places where grass grows in unlimited quantities and sky has got clear air in it," he explained. "Scotland has that. It's just there without anyone touching it. It just grows. I'm relieved to find that it isn't all pollution."[18]

A Nashville influence pervades other new songs, too. 'Country Dreamer' has a built-in twang and sounds tailor-made for Carl Perkins. The demo was probably recorded in the early evening: it has the added atmospheric attraction of insect noises. 'I Lie Around' envisions the day when, as Paul puts it in the song's refrain, "*furthermore in the country / I will lay my burden down.*" 'She Can't Be Found,' later retitled 'Hey Diddle' had similar country accents, along with the cheerfulness of a children's tune.

On the rockier side, but with a country influence that could be either magnified or submerged, depending on the arrangement and instrumentation, was the stomping 'Big Barn Bed.' 'Little Woman Love' was a lively rocker with country inflections as well. These country-rock hybrids were buoyed by a sense of humor that was not a notable element of the songs on *McCartney*.

That is not to say that the Beatles were far from his mind. In one of his new songs, 'Monkberry Moon Delight,' he tried to out-Lennon Lennon, as a lyricist, tapping into the same otherworldly, Lewis Carroll–inspired wordplay that drove such imagery-rich Lennon songs as 'Lucy in the Sky with Diamonds' and 'I Am the Walrus.'

Paul often said, when weaknesses in his lyrics were criticized, that he did not consider lyrics all that important. But that was partly defensiveness. He resented the conventional wisdom that held John to be the superior lyricist, much as he resented the idea that John was the adventurous avant-gardist, when his own experimental side predated Yoko Ono's unlocking of John's inner musical iconoclast. 'Monkberry Moon Delight' was explicitly meant to challenge the idea that John was the poet of the group.

"When we were in the Beatles, in the very early days, John had a book of his writings, *In His Own Write*, published. And I think that set it all, that single event made people think of John as a poet. I think if I had a book of poetry then, it might have been the other way around. But I don't mind, you know, I don't mind really what people think."[19]

But Paul had two almost contradictory aims in 'Monkberry Moon Delight.' The first was to go up against Lennon's nonsense lyrics with his own contender. But parts of the song sound more like a shopping list than a surrealist vision—ketchup, soup, purée, bananas, tomatoes, and honey (the last used as an endearment, rather than as a food, but he may have had both in mind) are all mentioned. And indeed, Paul has admitted that the title, and some of the lyrics, were inspired by food—and by his home life.

"When my kids were young they used to call milk 'monk,' for whatever reason that kids do—I think it's magical the way that kids can develop better names for things than the real ones. So, 'monk' was always milk, and 'Monkberry Moon Delight' was a fantasy drink, rather like 'Love Potion No. 9.'* Hence the line in the song '*sipping monkberry moon delight*.' It was a fantasy milk shake."[20]

A dismissive listener might suggest that only Paul McCartney would mix surrealism and baby talk—but of course, there was Lennon and his walrus, *goo-goo-ga-joob.*

Besides competing with John for respect as a poet, Paul undertook some lyrical jousting of another sort, in an embryonic version of 'Too Many People,' an open attack on what Paul saw as the self-righteousness of the Lennon-Ono camp.

"I felt John and Yoko were telling everyone what to do. And I felt we didn't need to be told what to do. The whole tenor of the Beatles thing had been, like, each to his own. Freedom. Suddenly it was, 'You should do this.' It was just a bit the wagging finger, and I was pissed off with it. So that one got to be a thing about them."[21]

Specifically, the line "*too many people preaching practices / don't let them tell you what you want to be*" was aimed at John and Yoko, their theatrical peace campaigning, and John's being celebrated as a god of hip culture. John's "divorce" announcement came in for a barbed refrain too: "*That was your first mistake / You took your lucky break / and broke it in two.*"

———

The Beatles may have been finished as a band—*broken in two*—but Apple remained a going concern, a clearinghouse through which they would each release their solo projects and could arrange whatever group efforts (compilations, for example) were required under their EMI contract. John, George and Ringo were prepared to use the company that way; Paul did so only because he was contractually required to.

The Beatles, including Paul, also saw Apple's potential as the "official" source of historical projects to do with the Beatles. One such project was *The Long and Winding Road*, a film history that Neil Aspinall had been assembling since the summer of 1969, when Paul suggested that he begin collecting all the Beatles footage from various television archives, before it disappeared.

"I got a researcher in and compiled footage from all sources, around the world—just as much footage as we could find at the time," Aspinall said. "And I just edited it down to about one hour and forty-five minutes and put the credits from the end of *Magical Mystery Tour* on the end so it would be clear when it finished, and I just sent it to everybody—John, Paul, George and Ringo—in a rough cut to see what they thought. They all quite liked it. And then it just got put on the shelf."[22]

By the summer of 1970, Paul scarcely saw any redeeming value in Apple. If the Beatles were no

* 'Love Potion No. 9,' a 1959 song by Jerry Lieber and Mike Stoller, was a hit for the Clovers the year it was written, and for the Searchers in 1963.

more, he reasoned, there was no point in Apple continuing to exist, with Klein taking a 20 percent fee on all their hard-won earnings. For Paul, there was no escaping Klein; he haunted Paul even in his sleep.

"I was having dreams that Klein was a dentist," Paul said. "I remember telling everyone and they all laughed but I said, 'No, this was a fucking scary dream!' I said, 'I can't be with the guy any longer. He's in my dreams now, and he's a baddie.' He was giving me injections in my dreams to put me out and I was thinking, 'Fucking hell! I've just become powerless. There's nothing I can do to stop this rot.' So I decided to just get out, but they wouldn't let me out, they held me to that contract."[23]

For Paul, the obvious and logical solution was—as he mentioned in his angry note to EMI a few months earlier—for the four Beatles to divide the spoils, go their separate ways, and send Klein packing. But that, as both Lee and John Eastman explained to him, was not an option unless the others felt the same way, a proposition Paul had already tested with disappointing results.

The problem, the Eastmans told him, was that the Beatles *were* Apple. They were bound together by the 1967 partnership agreement from which Apple emerged, and worse, that agreement governed aspects of their EMI deal—for example, how they were to be paid. Under the EMI agreement, whatever any of the Beatles recorded was considered "Beatle product," the proceeds paid to Apple.

Paul could not, therefore, simply declare that he was no longer a member of the Beatles and no longer an Apple artist, unless the others agreed, which they refused to do. Nor was there any way he could remain a member of the partnership without Allen Klein having a say in when his albums were released and how they would be promoted, not to mention taking a 20 percent fee.

McCartney's only way out, the Eastmans explained, was to have the Beatles' partnership legally dissolved, on the grounds that the partnership was based on the Beatles' working together as a performing or recording group, something that John, in September, and Paul, in April, said was unlikely to happen ever again. But the worst part of the Eastmans' analysis was that since the other Beatles wanted to keep the partnership going in order to run Apple, and had all agreed that Klein should manage it, Paul could only extricate himself by suing his friends and longtime partners.

"It was one of the most difficult things in my life," said Paul. "I had to sue the Beatles, which you just don't do . . . And it was much soul searching and many fog-shrouded days on a Scottish mountaintop.[24] All summer long in Scotland I was fighting with myself as to whether I should do anything like that. It was murderous. I had a knot in my stomach all summer. I tried to think of a way to take Allen Klein to court, or to take a businessman to court. But the action had to be brought against the other three."[25]

He was not the only one who found the idea worrying. When John Eastman raised the prospect with his father, Lee told him, "This is going to be a dirty battle and you're probably going to lose."[26] The younger Eastman had explored other possibilities, including trying to persuade Klein to let

Paul out of the agreement—something Klein had no reason to consider. In Klein's opinion, the partnership agreement would survive a challenge; as a tactician, he saw the possibility of a lawsuit as more of a nuisance than a threat.

Nevertheless, Eastman wrote to EMI on June 20, requesting that Paul's solo royalties be paid to McCartney Productions, rather than to Apple. He told Paul that it was unlikely that EMI would comply, since doing so would involve a change to the contract between EMI and Apple—and that would require Apple's agreement. But he thought it was worth a try. His pessimism was validated on July 29, when Peter Brown communicated Apple's refusal to consider such a change to Geoffrey Maitland Smith, Paul's financial adviser.[27]

Klein's recalcitrance and Lee Eastman's unencouraging analysis notwithstanding, John Eastman knew that Paul would be continually thwarted—the 'Long and Winding Road' orchestration and the dispute over the release of *McCartney* demonstrated as much—if he could not be freed from Apple and Klein. A lawsuit, however perilous, was the only option. He would explain this to Paul when he and his wife, Jody, visited High Park.

By the time the Eastmans arrived for a nine-day visit, on July 11, Paul understood (but was still a couple of arguments short of accepting) that there was no alternative. As soon as they settled in, Paul took his brother-in-law on a walk through the property, going over alternative possibilities one more time as they walked beyond the standing stone toward the hilltop with views of the ocean.

"My lawyer, John Eastman, he's a nice guy and he saw the position we were in, and he sympathized," Paul said. "We'd have these meetings on top of hills in Scotland, we'd go for long walks. I remember when we actually decided we had to go and file suit. We were standing on this big hill which overlooked a loch—it was quite a nice day, a bit chilly—and we'd been searching our souls. Was there any other way? And we eventually said, 'Oh, we've got to do it.' The only alternative was seven years with the partnership—going through those same channels for seven years."[28]

A lawsuit was fraught with ramifications for Paul, almost all negative. The suit would anger the other Beatles, and Paul would most likely take a public relations hit. He had already been criticized in the press for the *McCartney* self-interview, which some writers saw as dyspeptic and ungenerous toward the other Beatles. Now he was going to sue them?

"As you can imagine," Paul later explained, "that was horrendous, and it gave me some terrible times. I drank way too much and did too much of everything. And it was crazy, but I knew that was the only thing to do, because there was no way I was going to save it for me, because there was no way I was going to work that hard for all my life and see it all vanish in a puff of smoke. I also knew that, if I managed to save it, I would be saving it for them [the other Beatles] too. Because they were about to give it away. They loved this guy Klein. And I was saying 'He's a fucking idiot.'"[29]

Lennon, he said, seriously offered the argument that, "Anyone who's that bad can't be all bad."[30] By then, their debates simply moved in circles.

There was the possibility, however faint, that once the other Beatles received their writs, they would see that Paul meant business and would direct Klein to negotiate his release. But both Paul and Eastman knew that Klein liked a good scrap, and that even if the others were inclined to settle, they were susceptible to Klein's smooth talk, and he would dissuade them.

But the consequence of inaction was the perpetuation of an intolerable situation. He had to keep his eyes on the prize. By the time McCartney and Eastman returned to the farmhouse that Saturday afternoon, Paul had given the green light, and Eastman had walked him through the process, which would be handled not by the Eastmans themselves, but by a London legal team that they would engage.

———

Back at the farm, which, despite some sprucing up by Linda, was still decidedly more ramshackle than anything the Eastmans were used to, John and Jody wanted to know—and Paul and Linda wanted to tell them—how Paul's post-Beatles work was going. The upside was that Paul was writing up a storm, with Linda now pitching in.

They played the 'Another Day' demo and some of the others, presenting them as the probable basis of Paul's next album. Three months after *McCartney*, Paul was still smarting from some of the rougher reviews, and particularly criticism of the album's "homespun" quality. His next album had to be better written, better produced, and better sonically—a disc worthy of one of the architects of *Abbey Road*.

"I was able to take some time and start planning the kind of album I wanted next," said Paul. "Having done a homemade 'front parlour' album [*McCartney*], I now wanted to kind of expand a little bit. I was ready to open my horizons."[31]

Eastman offered a suggestion: why not record the album in New York, or Los Angeles. The Eastmans had contacts with studios and producers, should Paul want to work with one, in both cities. The producer Jim Guercio, for example, was a client of Eastman's who, apart from having been a backing guitarist for the British vocal duo Chad and Jeremy, and an early member of Frank Zappa's Mothers of Invention, had in recent years produced Chicago's first two albums and the second Blood Sweat & Tears album, all big sellers. If he wanted to produce the sessions himself, recording in the States would take Paul out of his comfort zone in a way that could lead to good things.

It was a proposal that appealed to Paul. He was used to EMI and a handful of London studios, but there were reasons to stay clear of them just now. George Harrison had started work on his own post-Beatles debut album in late May and was working at EMI, Trident and Apple. And though John was occupied with all manner of projects, many of them in Los Angeles where he was spending time with Phil Spector, undergoing primal scream therapy with Dr. Arthur Janov, and participating with Yoko in Fluxfest, an avant-garde festival with Yoko's old colleagues in the Fluxus movement, no doubt he would be recording again soon, most likely at EMI. Paul did not want to run into John or George casually in EMI's corridors.

"At the time," Paul said, "I felt that it was a bit too predictable, that everyone would leave the Beatles and go with old Phil Spector or the drummer, Jim Keltner. It was like a clique, and I just didn't want to join in that clique."[32]

By contrast, Paul was impressed with the approach Ringo was taking. Having gathered a varied field of respected arrangers, and having George Martin conduct a fine ensemble of session musicians and orchestral players for *Sentimental Journey*, he was now in Nashville, recording a country and western album with top-flight country players like the pedal steel player Pete Drake, the guitarists Charlie Daniels and Jerry Reed, Charlie McCoy on harmonica and D. J. Fontana—Elvis Presley's old drummer—holding down the beat.

What John Eastman proposed was something like that: Paul could work with American studio musicians he would handpick, in legendary rooms like the Columbia Studios in New York. The prospect excited him.

On July 22, two days after the Eastmans left High Park, Bryan Forbes brought a print of *The Raging Moon* to Campbeltown for a private screening at the Rex Cinema. Paul and Linda were not enthusiastic; mostly, they thought the lead roles were miscast.

"We then saw the film but didn't think the song fitted. So I said no,"[33] he explained. A few days later, Paul wrote a diplomatic note to Forbes saying that he didn't think the song he'd been working on was suitable.*

———

When McCartney was in composing mode, his creative antennae were always out, searching, unconsciously as well as consciously, for scenes, situations, or feelings that might inform a new song. The catalyst might be a news item, current or remembered, a conversation, or the quotidian turns of daily life, whether in London or in his new guise as a gentleman farmer. Often, this inspiration was passive, but he also went out looking for experiences that would fill out his ideas.

The last weekend in July 1970, Paul, Linda, the girls, and Martha the sheepdog set off in "Helen Wheels" for a road trip to the Orkney and Shetland Islands. It was partly for fun, a chance to see

---

* The title music for *The Raging Moon* was composed by Roger Cook and Roger Greenaway, a songwriting team that had composed several hits, including 'You've Got Your Troubles' (the Fortunes), 'Green Grass' (Gary Lewis and the Playboys) and 'I Was Kaiser Bill's Batman' (Whistling Jack Smith). Burt Bacharach and Hal David also contributed a song to the film, 'Long Ago, Tomorrow,' for which the film was renamed for its United States release.

a storied part of Scotland that they hadn't visited before. But Paul also hoped there might be something in the trip that would free up new ideas or provide detail and perspective for songs he was already working on.

Starting out early afternoon on Monday, July 27, they drove 225 miles north to Tain, in the Scottish Highlands, spending the night at the Royal Hotel, before driving the last 80 miles of available road to John O'Groats at the farthest tip of mainland Britain. After a night in the harbor town of Thurso, on July 29 the family headed to Scrabster to catch the ferry to the Orkney Islands. When the ferry stopped taking on vehicles, two cars ahead of them, Paul drove to the harbor town of Wick hoping to hitch a ride on a fishing boat.

"I went to a bunch of boats, but they weren't going to the Orkney Islands. So I went on this one and I went to this trapdoor sort of thing, and they were sleeping down below—the smell of sleep is coming up through the door. At first the skipper said no, and then I said there was 30 quid ($75) in it for him, and they say they'll take us."[34]

George Swanson, and the crew of his fishing boat *Enterprise*, took the family, Martha and what one witness described as "a guitar and other instruments" across the Pentland Firth to Stromness.

"As we steam out, the skipper gives us some beer, and Linda, trying to be one of the boys, takes a swig and passes it to me. Well, you shouldn't drink before a rough crossing to the Orkneys. The little one, Mary, throws up all over the wife, as usual. That was it. I was already feeling sick. I sort of gallantly walked to the front of the boat, hanging onto the mast. The skipper comes up and we're having light talk, light chit-chat, and I don't want it. So he gets the idea and points to the fishing baskets and says, 'Do it in there!' So we were all sick."[35]

At Stromness, they hired a car to take them to Kirkwall, where they caught a chartered Loganair flight (booked under Paul's *McCartney* session pseudonym, Billy Martin) for the 90-mile trip to Sumburgh, Shetland.

The McCartneys stayed for two nights at the Queen's Hotel in Lerwick (again booked as the Martins), and Paul and Linda spent the time walking through the wind and rain on the quay, and strolling through the town. Looking out from the first-floor window of Hays Shipping Agents, above the Clydesdale Bank on Commercial Street, photographer Dennis Coutts captured a rare snap of Paul deep in thought.

Friday afternoon, they flew back to Wick and caught a taxi to Thurso, where they recovered the Land Rover and drove south. They stayed overnight at the Corriegour Lodge—the name of the owners, Roddy and Betty MacLennan, must have raised an eyebrow—on the eastern shore of Loch Lochy, and made it back to High Park on Sunday night.

Like sightings of the mystical Loch Ness Monster, reports of Paul surfacing in towns and villages throughout northern Scotland were scattered throughout the region's newspapers. A front-page story in *The Orcadian*, a daily published in Kirkwall, noted that "one report is that he went by

sea to Orkney to get the atmosphere for a song he is writing."[36] Of the crop he was working on in the summer of 1970, the most likely candidate is 'Hands Across the Water,' given the imagery of its simple, anthemlike chorus, "*Hands across the water / Heads across the sky.*" A trip to the Orkneys hardly seems necessary for that much, but there was also an as yet untitled verse, which became the basis of 'Admiral Halsey,' for which Paul hoped to pick up some nautical inspiration.

Except for a quick trip to Edinburgh in mid-August—where, among other things, they bought themselves kilts at Andersons on George Street—Paul and Linda remained in Campbeltown until September 17, Paul focusing on writing songs and recording demos, energized by the new plan to record in New York.

The road trip to Shetland inspired a few new songs for the collection, besides 'Hands Across the Water.' A brisk, cheerful tune, which Paul alternately called 'Be a Gypsy' and 'Gypsy Get Around,' is the kind of travel tune parents might use to entertain a car full of children; on his demo, Paul sings it to ukulele accompaniment.

It also surfs on a wave of early Beach Boys style and energy and may have revived Paul's memory of another unfinished track from the Beatle days, 'The Back Seat of My Car.' The song dates back to the summer of 1968; Paul worked on it during his trip to Sardinia with Maggie McGivern that August,[37] but he hadn't finished it in time to be considered for the *White Album*—which, in any case, already had a Beach Boys–inspired song by Paul, 'Back in the U.S.S.R.'

It next appeared at a Beatles session at the Twickenham film studios on January 14, 1969.* Sitting at the piano, Paul played the heart of the song, with only Ringo present to hear it, George having quit the band four days earlier, and John and Yoko not yet arrived. The music for the song's verses was largely complete by then, including the exquisite melody that channels *Pet Sounds*–era Brian Wilson and traverses a vocal range from deep bass to falsetto. The lyrics were incomplete, but certain central images—"*We're just busy riding*" and "*sitting in the back seat of my car*"—were already present.

Now Paul refined it further, finishing off the lyrics and adding an anthemic chorus built around a single line of lyrical defiance—"*Oh, we believe that we can't be wrong.*"

Another of Paul's new concoctions was based on an oldie the Beatles played during the January 1969 sessions, 'The Walk,' a blues tune by Jimmy McCracklin and Bob Garlic that the Beatles knew from McCracklin's 1958 recording. The Beatles performance, slower than McCracklin's, covers only the chorus, which is where Paul's new song began, with the first line of McCracklin's refrain, "*When you walk*," changed to "*When I walk*" before heading off into a tale about a lopsided dog. Paul named his version '3 Legs.'

---

* In Peter Jackson's 2021 documentary, *The Beatles: Get Back*, Paul speaks of a song he wrote that morning, and is then shown playing 'The Back Seat of My Car,' giving the impression that the song was written that day. This was, however, an edit. The song he was speaking about was 'The Day I Went Back To School.' On the unedited tapes, 'The Back Seat of My Car' is played about 15 minutes later.

"When we went to Scotland, we had a very free, sort of hippie lifestyle," Paul said of the circumstances that gave rise to the song. "It meant I could sit around in the kitchen in the little farmhouse we lived in, with the kids running around and me just with my guitar, making up anything I fancied. '3 Legs' for instance was me jamming around with a blues idea, and then with no particular relevance I sang '*my dog, he got three legs, but he can run*,' meaning that everything doesn't have to be perfect, it can still work. And then I added the lyric '*a fly flies in*,' and I'm sure that happened, with the window open in Scotland! I'm sure a fly actually flew in, and I went 'okay—you're in the song! Fly flies in, fly flies out.' So yeah, it was a very free period and I think that found its way into the record."[38]

He mined the past in other ways, too. For 'We're So Sorry,' which he wrote and recorded after an afternoon with a bottle of whisky, he tapped family memories. The song was addressed to, though not directly about, Paul's uncle Albert—Albert Lolley Kendall, in full, born in 1902, married to Jim McCartney's sister Milly in 1927, and dead of a heart attack in 1966. Its opening verse begins as an expression of contrition for some unspecified misbehavior—"*we're so sorry if we caused you any pain*"—and ends with a touch of personal sorrow, "*I believe I'm going to rain*" (as in cry).

"I had an Uncle Albert," Paul said of the song's origins. "I was sort of thinking of him. He was an uncle who died when I was a kid, a good bloke who used to get drunk and stand on the table and read passages from the Bible, at which point people used to laugh. A lot. It was just one of those things—'Oh, Albert, don't get up and read the Bible again! Shut up! Sit down!' But he's someone I recalled fondly, and when the song was coming it was like a nostalgic thing. '*I think I'm gonna rain*' was the wistful line, really, and I thought of him. I say, I never can explain why I think of a particular person when I write. 'We're so sorry, Auntie Edna'—you know, it could have been her."[39]

Paul's ukulele demo of 'Gypsy Get Around' had a companion in another uke piece, 'Ram On.' A ditty rather than a full-fledged song, it shares with 'Gypsy Get Around' the sense of being intended to entertain Heather and Mary. Its lyric is sparse—a single phrase, "*Ram on / Give your heart to somebody soon / right away*"—and accompanied by a cheerfully quirky chord progression.

The song's title, though inspired most directly by the sheep at High Park, was also a pun: long before Billy Martin became his favored pseudonym, Paul styled himself Paul Ramon, first as a stage name during the Beatles 1960 tour of Scotland with the singer Johnny Gentle, and more recently in the credits for his contribution to Steve Miller's 'My Dark Hour.'

The song also fit Paul's idea of a possible title for his next album, something that came to him during the drive to Wick, en route to the Shetlands.

"As I'm driving I'm just thinking—Linda often used to say she could see my brain working. My face would get a look on it, and that would be me filing through ideas. And I just hit upon the word 'ram.' I thought, well, that's pretty cool, because it's strong, it's a male animal, and then there's the idea of ramming—pushing forward strongly. It's got a little double meaning, it's very short, a very succinct title you wouldn't forget, so that was nice."[40]

———

Though reachable by telephone, Paul was sufficiently far from London, physically and psychically, to keep business complications on the periphery. The handling of Northern Songs by ATV, for example, continued to evolve. On August 13, ATV teamed up with the promoter Don Kirshner to form a new company, ATV/Kirshner, to manage Maclen Music, the Northern Songs subsidiary that saw to their rights and royalties in the United States, Canada, Mexico, and the Philippines.[41] That move led Dick James, who had been managing Maclen through Dick James Music, to sue ATV for removing Maclen from his control and to resign as managing director of Northern Songs.[42]

Allen Klein, not one to stand on the sidelines when a battle was brewing, served Northern Songs with a High Court writ at the end of September, on behalf of John and Paul, requiring an accounting of all the money Northern Songs had made from the Lennon-McCartney catalog since 1963, and demanding 50 percent (plus 6 percent interest) on all the money earned by the company, or potentially earned "but for willful neglect or default."[43]

The McCartneys were also happily absent when, on August 31, 21-year-old Brett Solaries broke a window at Cavendish Avenue in the hope of gaining access to the house,[44] but was arrested while still in the enclosed garden.[45] Nor was Paul on hand to disavow any involvement with the producer Mickie Most's film project, *The Second Coming of Suzanne*—the story of a female Christ figure—in which, Most was saying, Paul would make his post-Beatles acting debut. The producer said he hoped to visit Paul in Scotland to discuss the role, but he may have foreclosed the possibility of Paul's involvement by telling the press that the music would be by Led Zeppelin, Julie Felix, and Jeff Beck, and adding that "I haven't thought about Paul as a writer, actually . . . I'm more concerned with persuading him to act than to write music."[46]

Most's approach was by no means a one-off. Offers of high-profile film roles had come Paul's way in the past. In 1967, the Italian director Franco Zeffirelli visited EMI Studios in an effort to cast McCartney in the role of Romeo in his film production of *Romeo and Juliet*. "It was amazing that he would ask me,"[47] was Paul's flattered response. But like Most, Zeffirelli received a polite refusal.

Paul did engage with John, briefly. Hoping to avoid the courtroom drama that seemed inevitable, he wrote to John a few weeks after John Eastman's visit to suggest once more that they "let each other out of the trap." John's response was a photograph of himself and Yoko, with a cartoon balloon coming out of his mouth. In it was written "How and Why?" Paul sent another letter with a straightforwardly minimalist explanation:

<u>How</u> by Signing a paper which says we hereby dissolve our partnership.
<u>Why</u> because there is no partnership.

John's response was flippant, but left the door open, a crack. "Get well soon," he wrote. "Get the other signatures and I will think about it."[48]

Paul had ample time for self-reflection during his four and a half months in Scotland, and an item that got him thinking was a profile by Alan Smith in the July 25 issue of *NME*. Smith had not interviewed McCartney for the piece, but he had known and covered him for years and had many past encounters to draw upon.

Smith liked and respected McCartney, but he noted that he had become "bitter, bored and bashed" by the politics at Apple, the presence of Klein, and the other Beatles' lack of support when he objected to engaging Klein. He had liked *McCartney*, but thought it lacked the spark that Paul brought to his work with the Beatles—which led him to conclude that Paul worked best when he could bounce his talent and artistry off other musicians. He described McCartney as the real leader of the Beatles: "Lennon is an erratic genius; McCartney has been the pusher, the steady inspirer, the most creatively consistent." But to Paul's chagrin, he concluded that if John would only reconvene the Beatles, "then I believe that Paul McCartney can find direction again."

What really stuck in Paul's mind, though, was a more personal assessment. "He is a man who likes to be liked," Smith wrote. "Inversely, he can be an exceptionally unpleasant person when those big wide eyes turn off their charm . . . There are those who find him deep and devious behind the instant smile and reassuring gaze." Smith went on to recall a conversation in which he told Paul that he found him "likeably insincere." In response, Paul tipped his hand, for just a moment.

"To you, possibly. Because I think, 'Here's *NME*, newspaper. I don't think Alan Smith—person—at all. I think I have to watch what I say because you just don't say certain things to papers. Maybe it's *NME*—Enemy! Whenever I've been faced with a pop press conference or a drink with reporters I couldn't be sincere.'"[49]

Shortly after Smith's piece appeared, Paul agreed to an interview with John Moss, for *Mirabelle*, and after the requisite questions about the Beatles, he turned to the question of his likable insincerity, in an oddly confessional way.

"This last year has been one of total honesty for me. I was once called insincere, and I realized I was. I tried to be nice to everybody, not to offend. Today I wouldn't mind admitting that something like starvation in India is something that I just accept. I'm not saying I don't sympathize . . . but I'm honest enough to realize that I'm just like everybody else. I'd rather sit at home, listening to a rock 'n' roll record, than helping the starving in India, or going to Vietnam to entertain troops. It's nothing to be proud of. I know one is morally better than the other, but I know I wouldn't get 'round to it. I'd be a hypocrite."[50]

Smith's characterization of him as bitter and bored notwithstanding, Paul was in far better spirits than he was during his last visit to High Park, in October 1969. His explosive creativity and the return of his sense of humor were signs; so was his relative forbearance with unexpected visitors. Three girls who found their way to the farm—past a shotgun-bearing McDougall—were told gently, by Paul, that he doesn't like uninvited visitors. But he chatted with them and let them take photos.[51]

A week later, Judith Simons of the *Daily Express* turned up, accompanied by Freddie Gillies, a local reporter who Paul befriended during his first trip to Campbeltown. Paul had known Simons for years, and unlike many music journalists and critics, she was not on his swerve-to-hit list. Paul greeted them both affably and gave Simons a casual interview—so casual that her editor cut her story to a few hundred words, just enough to describe him as "bronzed, barefoot and stripped to the waist," and to quote him saying that, "The Beatles will not get together again for financial or any other reasons. The reason should be perfectly plain to everyone."[52]

Simons had come to Scotland to pursue a suggestion raised in an interview with Apple press officer Derek Taylor in the August 15 issue of *Melody Maker*. Asked whether the fact that there were no plans for the Beatles to work together should be taken to mean that they would never work together again, Taylor said, "No. The fact that there are no plans doesn't mean anything. The group have never planned things much." That led the writer of the unsigned piece to suggest that "it appears there is a slight chance that we may hear from the world's most successful beat group again."[53]

To make sure his current feelings on the subject were widely seen, Paul fired off a letter to *Melody Maker*, which appeared in the paper's Mailbag column on August 29:

Dear Mailbag,
In order to put out of its misery the limping dog of a news story which has been dragging itself across your pages for the past year, my answer to the question, 'will the Beatles get together again'/. . . is no.

Paul McCartney (Smile)[54]

One point Paul made in his interview with Simons was that while he could happily stay at High Park indefinitely, he was still writing music and would continue to do so. And since he had a friendly relationship with both Simons and Gillies—and because Simons could be of some help when it came time to review the finished product—he played them a preview of his demo collection.

Of particular interest were a pair of late entries, 'Smile Away,' a straightforward, rocker with potential for a retro doo-wop vocal backing, and the musically more sophisticated and varied 'Get on the Right Thing.' After both, Paul and Linda are heard on the tape discussing the prospect of recording the songs with Jimi Hendrix. That was not an implausible hope. Paul and Hendrix played together on brother Michael's *McGough and McGear* album, in 1968, and it was less than a year ago that Hendrix invited Paul to play on his Miles Davis collaboration. If Paul was to record in New York, he could probably persuade Hendrix to play on a few tracks.

It had been an exceptionally productive summer for Paul. He had written more than 30 songs, and recorded 29 demos, a couple of which were medleys with parts of two or three tunes. That was enough for nearly three albums. As he prepared for another trip—from Campbeltown to Liverpool, to the south coast of France and from there to New York, all without stopping in London—he compiled the demos on a cassette to carry with him:

1.   'Heart of the Country'
2.   'Too Many People'
3.   'Why Am I Crying?'
4.   'The Back Seat of My Car'
5.   'So Sad (Just Another Day)'
6.   'Gypsy Get Around'
7.   'Ram On'
8.   'Rupert—Sunshine Sometime'
9.   'Rupert—Guitar Song Instrumental a.k.a. When the Wind Blows'
10. 'Rupert—Little Lamb/Dragonfly'
11. 'Smile Away'
12. 'Love Is Long'
13. 'Come on Little Lady (Eat at Home)'/'Buddy's Breakfast'/'Indeed I Do'
14. 'Monkberry Moon Delight'/'Frenzy'
15. 'Get on the Right Thing'
16. 'Little Woman Love'
17. 'Country Dreamer'
18. 'Long Haired Lady'
19. 'I Lie Around'
20. '3 Legs'
21. 'We're So Sorry'
22. 'A Love for You'

23.   'She Can't Be Found (Hey Diddle)'
24.   'Some People Never Know'
25.   'Hands Across the Water'
26.   'Tomorrow'
27.   'Big Barn Bed'
28.   'Great Day'
29.   'I Am Your Singer'*'

The plan was to go to New York to make the next album, taking a few weeks' holiday en route. Packing the Land Rover not only with what a family of four would need for an extended time away, but also with the gear Paul would need in the studio—including his Rickenbacker 4001S bass, a Gibson Firebird electric guitar, the trusty Martin D28, and a ukulele—the McCartneys drove from Campbeltown to Jim McCartney's Wirral home, Rembrandt,[†] on September 17, and visited for five days, some of which Linda spent on the phone making travel reservations and giving her brother an idea of their requirements in New York—studio time and musicians, for starters. They were at Rembrandt on September 19, when they heard the news that Hendrix had died the previous night, in London.

From Merseyside, they flew to Nice, where they hired a car and spent the next few days tooling around the Côte d'Azur, visiting Monaco on the 23rd, and checking into a lavishly appointed suite looking over the Ligurian Sea at the La Réserve de Beaulieu, in Beaulieu-Sur-Mer, where they celebrated Linda's birthday on the 24th.

Driving north, they spent a few days in Paris before heading, on October 2, to the port of Le Havre, where Linda had booked the family (this time under the name Paul Martin) on the S.S. *France*. The Compagnie Générale Transatlantique described the 1,037 foot long, 66,343 ton, 11-deck luxury liner as "the $80 million hotel that travels with you."[55]

"We had a great suite there," Paul said of their accommodations, which cost about $3,000 (£1,260) for the family. "You had a French maid with a little hat and apron. Like ooh-la-la! It was an adventure."[56]

Built in 1960, the ship was packed with modern conveniences. So when Paul wasn't assessing the staff, he had access to libraries and reading rooms, a 664-seat theater, ballrooms with resident dance bands, as well as smaller "retreats" with baby grand pianos (and taping services), as well as films, LPs and tapes, available by closed-circuit broadcast to individual staterooms.

---

* The cassette was lost until 2011, when it was discovered in a drawer, still in an envelope with the logo of the Compagnie Générale Transatlantique, the company that owned the S.S. *France*.

† Paul bought Rembrandt, 14 Baskervyle Road, Gayton, Wirral, for his father in July 1964. The five-bedroom house cost McCartney £8,750 ($24,420).

The cuisine, naturally, was French, and first class, in the two main dining rooms—the Chambord, where the chef was Henri Le Huédé, and the Versailles, with Chef Etienne Kraemer.[57] And the bar was sufficiently stocked to handle an average liquor consumption, during an Atlantic crossing, of 1,200 bottles of Champagne, over 1,000 bottles of fine wine, 2,400 bottles of spirits, and 18,000 quarts of beer.[58]

For someone who, over the past seven years, had learned to avoid fans when he was in public, and who now cherished his privacy, being on a ship with 2,000 people was not ideal. Paul's avoidance technique was minimal, and drew some unwanted attention.

"I wore shades a lot of the time and nobody bothered us," he said. "But there was one woman who got annoyed at me coming into the dining-room wearing them. I thought, 'What the hell. I'm on holiday, I'll do what I want,' and I didn't particularly want to have to relate to some of these people. She got annoyed, saying, 'Take your glasses off. Elizabeth Taylor is on this boat, and she doesn't wear them.' I said, 'Well I'm not Elizabeth Taylor!'"[59]

When the McCartneys disembarked at Pier 92, West 52nd Street in New York, at around 9:00 a.m. on October 7, Paul was energized and ready to make music. After settling into their suite at the Stanhope Hotel, just across Fifth Avenue from the Metropolitan Museum of Art, he put in a call to John Eastman, who had done the groundwork for the sessions.

The American Federation of Musicians, Local 802, had put Eastman in touch with Barry Kornfeld, a guitarist and banjo player who had worked with Bob Dylan, Dave Van Ronk, and Van Morrison. As contractor for the sessions, Kornfeld would send musicians Paul's way. Eastman also rented a couple of rooms Paul could use for auditions. And he booked time at CBS Studios, for six weeks of sessions, set to begin on October 12.

7

WORKING 9 TO 5

—

I t was embarrassing," Paul said of his first task in New York. "I'd never auditioned anyone be-fore."[1]

But without a band, or even individual players whose styles and strengths he knew, there was no way around it. The first day of auditions, on October 9, 1970, was devoted to finding a drummer. Linda called the players on the list Kornfeld provided, telling them that they were being considered for a jingle, or in some cases, a demo.

When the auditioning drummers arrived at 327 West 43rd Street, an apartment building be-tween Eighth and Ninth Avenues, they took the elevator down to a dingy basement, where Paul and Linda were waiting—Heather and Mary had been sent off with Linda's sister, Laura—with a cheap hired drum set.

Among those who auditioned were Herbie Lovelle, Donald MacDonald, Bill Lavorgna, Ronnie Zito, Alan Schwartzberg, Denny Seiwell, and Bernard Purdie, all experienced session players. Pur-die, who turned up at the audition wearing an admiral's hat, his trademark look at the time, had a tenuous Beatles connection: in 1964, Atlantic Records hired him to overdub drums on some of the recordings the Beatles made in Hamburg, when Pete Best was their drummer, backing the singer and guitarist Tony Sheridan. Purdie was hired to add some spice, but in the intervening years, his memory of the job expanded, to the point where he claimed he overdubbed drums on all the Beatles' early recordings.

"We tried lots of drummers," Paul said, "and most of them were really pissed off with these auditions. We hired this shitty little cellar—you could imagine—and a really shitty little drum kit. When each drummer came in, I apologized about the conditions and asked them to play a bit of rock."

The auditions were not a jam—Paul did not play a note, so the drummers were on their own, and some were uncomfortable playing just a rock beat, on a mediocre kit, with nothing to react to and a former Beatle judging them. Paul noticed that most went directly for the high hat, which struck him as more jazzy than rocking.

"Then Denny walked in," Paul said of Denny Seiwell, then 27. "Apart from everything else, he was a lot younger than the others. Denny, unlike the others, went straight for the tom-toms and within seconds the room began to throb. I was sold."[2]

Drumming was in Seiwell's DNA; during the Swing era, his father, Donald Hayden Seiwell, had been a drummer in the Tommy Dorsey Band. Growing up in Lehighton, Pennsylvania, where he was born on July 10, 1943, Denny first picked up the sticks when he was five, under his father's guidance. He later studied in Chicago with Roy Knapp, who had taught Buddy Rich and Louie Belson. When he moved to New York, in 1966, after a stint in the navy (playing in the Navy Jazz Band), he spent three years doing mostly club work at resorts in the Catskills and the Poconos, backing jazz players and comedians. A gig at Mount Airy Lodge with Russ Savakus, a bassist who also worked as a contractor, led to his move to New York.

"After he heard me play the show," Seiwell remembered, "he said, 'What are you doing up here? You should come to New York.' He took me to my first record date, just to see what it was like. It was Dionne Warwick, recording with Burt Bacharach, and they were doing 'Do You Know the Way to San Jose.' It was a small orchestra, with Gary Chester playing drums with a stick and a brush, and the violins almost next to him.

"It was a real eye-opener, and they started calling me on dates. Then the guitarist Joe Beck heard me on some session we played together, and he really had a big mouth—he told everybody about me. I give him credit for really getting me started. And I used to get a lot of Bernard Purdie's jobs, at the time: if Purdie couldn't make it, they'd say, 'call that white kid who plays like Purdie and smiles more.'"

Seiwell also played club dates in New York, including a regular gig at the Half Note, backing Zoot Sims and Al Cohn—and, at one of the club's Sunday night jam sessions, Judy Garland.

"Judy gave quite a nice little round," Seiwell recalled. "She did all her songs, you know, 'Rainbow' and 'April Showers'—the works. Two days later she died.* It was her last performance."[3]

By then, Seiwell was settling into studio work. Among his early session jobs were the 1969 J.J. Johnson and Kai Winding album, *Betwixt and Between*, and John Denver's *Take Me to Tomorrow*, released five months before Paul's arrival in New York.

As Seiwell remembered the audition for Paul, "He asked me to just play—he didn't have a guitar, so I just sat and played. He had a certain look in his eye—he was looking for more than a drummer,

---

* Judy Garland died on June 22, 1969, at age 47.

he was looking for a certain attitude too. I just played . . . I always say that if you can't get it on by yourself you can't get it on with anyone."[4]

Paul at first thought that the best plan was to have several drummers on tap, to accommodate the variety of styles his new songs embraced. He hired Seiwell for the first week of sessions, with Donald MacDonald booked for the second, and Herbie Lovelle penciled in for the third.

The next day, Paul moved to a loft on West 45th Street for guitar auditions. Among the busy session players Kornfeld recommended were the great jazz-rock guitarists Joe Beck, Dave Bromberg, Charlie Brown, Paul Metzke, David Spinozza and Hugh McCracken. They were not all available; McCracken, for one, was at sessions out of town. Of those he heard, McCartney was the most taken with Spinozza.

"Honestly, when I got the call, I didn't know it was an audition," said Spinozza. "It wasn't couched like that. My wife said, 'There's a Linda on the phone, she wants to talk to you about a session.' I just thought I was getting called for a recording session. She says, 'Hi, this is Linda. We'd like to hear you play.' I said, 'What do you mean, you'd like to hear me play?' And I said, 'Who is this?' She said, 'Linda McCartney.' And then it hit me, and I said, 'Well, what do you do?' She said, 'Well, we're staying in a loft on the West Side. Would you mind coming by?' I thought it was an informal thing. You'd come by and you'd play with them."[5]

The 22-year-old Spinozza was born in New York on August 8, 1949, and grew up in Mamaroneck, about 25 miles north of New York. He had been playing the guitar since he was eight and also studied the trumpet; by the time he began leading rhythm and blues bands, as a teenager, he had picked up the basics of piano and drums. He started playing sessions when he was 17, and concerned that his chart-reading skills needed polishing, he took up the classical guitar at 18.

In the months before he got the call from McCartney, he had played on sessions for John Denver's *Whose Garden Was This?*, the jazz saxophonist and composer Oliver Nelson's *Black, Brown and Beautiful*, and *Consummation* by the Thad Jones/Mel Lewis Orchestra, an all-star jazz band that also included Marvin Stamm on trumpet, Eddie Daniels on clarinet, and Roland Hanna on keyboards.

It wasn't until Spinozza arrived at the rehearsal space on West 45th Street and saw a handful of guitarists waiting for their moment with McCartney that he realized the call was for an audition, and like the other waiting guitarists, he found this irksome.

"At the time, I was a little headstrong," he recalled. "I'd played on hit records, and I'm doing 10, 15 recording sessions a week. I'm a little bit like, *I don't audition.* A lot of guys had an attitude like that back then. And honestly, I was not a Beatles fan. I thought they were a cute little harmony band; I didn't put them on the same level as, say, James Brown or Otis Redding. I was into an R&B thing."[6]

The invitation to audition became a topic of discussion among the guitarists in the waiting area.

"It seemed weird for him to come to town and audition the heaviest musicians in the business,"

Spinozza said in a fiery interview with *Melody Maker* a few months later. "Cats who had been in music for fifteen years and play with just about everyone and who, as musicians, the Beatles just couldn't stand next to as instrumentalists. You don't have to audition these cats; they can play anything under the sun."[7]

Still, hearing from the other players that some of the guitarists gave Paul and Linda a hard time about the auditions, Spinozza opted to hold his tongue, because Beatle fan or not, this was an opportunity too good to pass up, if only for the line on his still-growing CV. Eventually, Linda walked down the steps from the loft and invited Spinozza in. The room was empty but for a drum kit, a couple of bass amps, with a handful of guitars leaning against the wall in one of the corners.

Paul had not shaved since the S.S. *France*, so on Spinozza's first sight of him, he had a three-day beard and his hair swept back, fifties style. He was disarmingly apologetic about requiring an audition, explaining that it was the only way he could hear a good number of guitarists quickly. Spinozza mentioned that he and his colleagues could be heard on many hit records, but he couldn't argue with Paul's assertion, speaking as someone who'd made a few records, that what one heard on disc was a less accurate indicator of how they played than hearing them live.

Once Spinozza was set up, Paul asked him to play a bit in blues and folk styles. Then he picked up a guitar and showed Spinozza a chord progression in G major—the opening section of 'Another Day'—and asked the young guitarist to join him. After a few minutes, Paul asked if he played any other instruments, and when the guitarist said he played piano and drums, Paul asked to hear him play a bit on both.

Shortly after Spinozza returned to his apartment, Linda called to book him for the next four weeks.

With the sessions set to begin the next day, Paul had to reconsider his approach to recording. With the Beatles, members of the group drifted into EMI at all hours, regardless of the session's booked start time. Once they got down to work, a Beatle or two might find himself unneeded for several hours; Ringo said that he learned to play chess during these extended breaks. EMI was footing the bill, but since the Beatles were coining money for the label, no one was prepared to impose discipline or formality upon them.

But Spinozza and Seiwell, as top-tier session musicians, commanded $180 for a three-hour session, double the usual union scale. Though *McCartney* was selling well, Paul did not have carte blanche; EMI expected him to work efficiently. As a way around having a couple of expensive musicians sitting around with the clock running when they weren't needed, Paul planned to record the backing tracks with his hired players, and to overdub the bass lines, extra guitar parts, vocals and whatever else he deemed necessary on his own.

As the city burst into life on the morning of October 12, Paul, Linda, and the girls climbed into a yellow cab outside the Stanhope and rode the 29 blocks downtown to the CBS Studios Building, at 49 East 52nd Street.

As they made their way down Fifth Avenue, Central Park at their right, a piece of Paul's past was being readied for sale way downtown at the Fillmore East, where Bill Graham was organizing that day's "Rock Relics Auction," a superstar fundraiser to benefit the campaigns of politicians opposed to the war in Vietnam.

Among the treasures about to go on the block were a notebook of handwritten lyrics by Joni Mitchell, a pair of Ginger Baker's stage-worn drumsticks, a tape of Indian music selected by George Harrison, Roger Daltrey's fringed jacket, a blue trumpet played by Miles Davis, and a black Cadillac limousine used by the Beatles during the final American tour, in 1966 (and later by the Jefferson Airplane and Cream). Linda still had connections at the Fillmore, and upon hearing about the auction, she persuaded Paul to surrender one of the sweaters he had bought during their Shetland trip. It sold for $95 (£40). (The limo sold for $1,400 [£590].)[8]

Determined not to become a rock relic himself, Paul pulled up to CBS just before 9:00 a.m., his songbook brimming with fresh material he was eager to record. Fifty-Second Street was a busy thoroughfare, with fast-walking New Yorkers on their way to work, and unlike the EMI Studios on Abbey Road, where Apple Scruffs were a permanent fixture, the CBS Studios were blessedly free of waiting fans.

Columbia's 52nd Street building had a rich musical heritage. Formerly a lavish guesthouse built for the Dutch-American Vanderbilt family in 1908, it was sold to the Juilliard Musical Foundation in 1924, when it became Juilliard's graduate school. Juilliard unloaded it to the Columbia Broadcasting Service in 1938; for almost twenty years it was home to the CBS Radio Network. In the early 1960s, CBS converted it into recording rooms for its Columbia Records label.

Paul, Linda, and their girls (the full family attended all the sessions) were greeted by veteran studio attendant Albert Usher who escorted them up to Studio B on the second floor. Here Sinatra, Ellington and Dylan cut records; long before Paul set foot in the studio, Linda had been there for a 1966 photo shoot with Simon and Garfunkel.

Studio B boasted all the grandeur of EMI's Studio Two—a cavernous 43-by-58-foot space, with a 19-foot-high ceiling. The technical facilities were impressive too. The floor-level control room was kitted out with a 3M MM-1000 16-track recorder, and a custom-built, 30 input console. This was technology EMI had not yet adopted, having gone to eight-track recording only three years earlier. But doubling the available tracks offered significantly greater flexibility during both recording and mixing, and McCartney was eager to use it.

As on *McCartney*, Paul would produce the sessions himself, but he needed an engineering team. John Eastman called his client Jim Guercio to find out who to request at CBS and learned that Don Puluse had engineered the Chicago albums Guercio had produced, and that both Guercio and the band were pleased with his work. Eastman passed Puluse's name along to Paul.

"Paul McCartney had booked the studio and requested me," Puluse later recalled. "I couldn't get to do that because I was working with Chicago. So I missed the entire Paul McCartney sessions at Columbia Records, 'cos I was tied up with Chicago for a year and a half."[9]

In the end, Paul decided to go along with a team assigned to his sessions by CBS, with Tim Geelan at the board, and tape op Ted "Teddy" Brosnan assisting. Geelan was by no means an also-ran. Around the same time the embryonic Beatles (then called the Quarrymen) cut their first crude acetate at Phillips Sound Recording Services in Liverpool, Geelan was cutting pioneering jazz with Miles Davis.

"I started off at a little studio called Regent Sound Studios on 56th Street, where we recorded everybody all at once—back in the mono days—all in the same room. In fact, the first session I was ever involved in was the Flamingos' hit 'I Only Have Eyes for You.' I was running the tape machines, that was my first experience doing anything."

But he had no idea what to expect at these sessions with Paul McCartney.

"Usually with sessions, the engineering staff likes to know what's happening: how many musicians, what's the setup going to be, and so forth. We didn't have any of that information. So I showed up on Monday morning, and Paul, Linda, Denny Seiwell and David Spinozza arrived. And we just talked about how we were gonna handle it, and set up the microphones and got things going."[10]

———

Recording Session

Monday, October 12, 1970.
CBS Studios, Studio B, New York.
Recording: 'Another Day.'

The pounding beat of Denny Seiwell's kick drum, resonating through Studio B as Paul and Linda entered the room, stopped Paul in his tracks. The lanky American's newly acquired 1965 Ludwig Super Classic drum kit, finished in oyster black pearl, looked familiar.

"I had just purchased the Beatles' drum set, supposedly the one that Ringo used at Shea Stadium," Denny recalled. "It was purchased through the Museum of Famous People in New York,* who were going out of business. My buddy that owned a drum shop picked it up for me. So, Paul comes in and says, 'Hey Denny, are you ready to go?' I said, 'Yeah, ready to go.' And then he saw the drums and said, 'Oh shit!'"[11]

Sadly, Seiwell had been misled: the Ludwig kit was only a replica of Ringo's 1965 set. In fact, it was already a hybrid: Seiwell had replaced the snare in his faux-Ringo kit with the one his father had used during his drumming days, a deep-sounding Leedy Broadway model, with engraved hoops.

After outlining his plan for the day, Paul popped open his guitar case, lifted out his Martin D-28, and played through 'Another Day.' Spinozza recognized it as the song he'd played with Paul during the audition, but the song was fresh to Seiwell, who was floored.

"That song just blew my mind when I heard him singing and playing it on an acoustic guitar. As a studio man, you sometimes have to do what we call 'polishing a turd'—people bring in songs that aren't really great songs, but obviously, your job is to make them great songs. When he started playing 'Another Day,' and it went into the section in three—where it changes time signatures—on the first listen through, you knew you were in for a real treat. This was not *another job*, this was gonna be really special."[12]

Seiwell and Spinozza expected Paul, famed as the bass-playing backbone of the Beatles, to lay down the bass line on the rhythm track. Instead, he kept his Martin in hand as he prepared to join Spinozza on guitar. This puzzled both session men: the natural instrumental grouping for a rock rhythm track was bass, drums, and rhythm guitar. And given Paul's stature as a bassist, they were eager to hear him in action.

But Paul's approach to recording the bass had evolved during the Beatles years. Early on, when the songs were essentially live in the studio, he played with the rest of the band. But as their music evolved, and their recordings grew more complex, he sometimes played a basic line first, and developed more ornate ideas while he and the others built the song on tape. He would then add the finished bass line in an overdub.

"I was actually looking forward to playing, with him playing bass," says Spinozza. "But I never even heard him noodle on the bass the whole time I worked with him. Not one note."[13]

Spinozza and Seiwell were both in the habit of writing what Seiwell called "mini-charts"—reminders of the changes—at the start of a session. Seiwell wrote his without interference, but Spinozza remembers McCartney discouraging him from doing so.

---

* The Museum of Famous People, at 133 West 50th Street, was similar to Madame Tussauds. The museum seamlessly combined historic, often harrowing, New York scenes with models of famous celebrities. It closed in 1970 due to lack of business.

"I could've learned it a lot quicker if I'd just jotted down a chart for myself," Spinozza said, "but I could see he didn't want to do that . . . We wound up playing it for eight hours.

"He would sing along and just do a dummy vocal track. It wouldn't be the final vocal. I couldn't believe how many ways he could sing his own song. How he could change the melody every time and every one was better than the next. It really taught me about songwriting, how important songwriting is. Because, to me, he's a consummate songwriter. He's one of the best songwriters that probably ever lived. You know, melodist . . . That was a real eye-opener for me. That's where my respect for him really went up."[14]

CBS's 16-track studio gave Geelan the luxury of devoting three tracks to Seiwell's drums, putting the bass drum on its own track, the high hat, snare and small tom on a second, and the floor tom on a third—a setup he maintained through most of the sessions. McCartney and Spinozza—"Davey," as Paul took to calling him—played acoustic guitars, each on his own track, to create the song's backing.

Tracking two acoustic guitars was an old habit for Paul, a hangover from countless sessions with the only group he had ever known.

"When I worked with the Beatles there were at least two guitars, and when I played there were three," McCartney said. "We would often play a song through on acoustic, and sometimes we'd develop it from there on electric—or sometimes we just kind of liked it where it was, and it stayed acoustic. I didn't have the guys I developed things up with—John and George—and so things often remained acoustic. Of course, I also liked how it sounded."[15]

Linda watched from the control room, photographing the session, making tea, and occasionally commenting, while also keeping the girls—they brought a playpen for Mary—entertained.

Out on the studio floor, Paul, David and Denny committed the basic track to tape during the morning segment of the 9:00 a.m. to 5:00 p.m. session. Happy with the rich acoustic rhythm backing, Spinozza and McCartney spent the afternoon overdubbing electric guitar lines—one consisting largely of melancholy descending slides, played through a volume pedal to emphasize the effect, occasionally adding brighter ascending punctuation as well; the other built largely of short bursts of counterpoint, single-string lines, and arpeggiations that support the harmony, with occasional figures that were purely decorative.

Also among the overdubs, Seiwell beefed up the rhythm section with extra bass drum, and snare taps with a hollow but resonant sound that could easily be mistaken for the sound of coconut shells. The drumming, though not often the song's focus, is strikingly inventive—straightforward at first, with a galloping figure leading to the refrain that goes into the triple meter 'So Sad' section, to which Seiwell brought an almost jazzy character.

After a final playback that ended just before 5 o'clock, Spinozza and Seiwell clocked out. Still to be done were the vocals, but that would be left for another day.

"Paul had a great personality, very witty," Spinozza observed, "but when he came in and started working, it was 9 to 5. He was very serious about his music. He wasn't in New York to *hang*.[16] He's not a very loose cat, not eccentric in any way at all. In the studio, he's very prompt and business-like. No smoking pot, no drinks, or carrying on, nothing. Just straight ahead."[17]

Another thing Paul did not do was chat to his sidemen about the Beatles. There was no talk of the breakup, not even "how did you guys get that effect" technical banter.

"We were professional studio musicians who were there to do a job," is how Spinozza put it. "We didn't ask him about things."[18]

———

Paul also established the habit of visiting the studio on his own for overdubs.

"One day a week we'd do bass overdubs on what we had recorded already," Tim Geelan said, describing Paul's preference for "direct injection" recording—plugging the bass into the mixing board.

"Paul would come into the control room, and just work out his part. We didn't have to do a lot to get a good sound because he just knew how to do it. He's an excellent bass player. It was real easy—just plug in. I don't remember doing any drastic EQ [equalization], he just had that good sound. He'd stand in there [the control room] and that was a good way to do it because he didn't have to wear earphones. He could listen to the control room monitors, and that would be it."[19]

The overdubbing sessions are undocumented, but it is possible that Paul wanted to get his bass part for 'Another Day' down quickly. In any case, the night of the first session, he decided not to record on Tuesday. Linda called Seiwell and Spinozza to tell them that the Tuesday session was canceled and that they would pick up again on Wednesday.

Recording Session

Wednesday, October 14, 1970.
CBS Studios, Studio B, New York.
Recording: 'Get on the Right Thing.'

In the first few sessions, Paul and Geelan established a businesslike approach that would continue until the end of November. Paul would arrive at 9:00 a.m. and would go over the day's plan with Geelan, sometimes also listening to the previous day's work. When the other musicians arrived, between 9:00 and 10:00 a.m., they would record for two or three hours before taking a lunch break. After lunch, they would listen to the work completed in the morning, and either do more takes or overdubs, or move on to a new tune.

The song Paul chose for this second session, 'Get on the Right Thing,' is built around McCartney's interesting use of a common-tone harmonic trick: the chords accompanying the song's verses all contain an E natural, but the melody McCartney sings against them steadily rises, creating a subtle tension harmonically, and between stasis and movement.

Paul had already mapped out rough sonic sketches for most of his new compositions. On his demos, he can often be heard vocalizing guitar parts and whistling orchestral arrangements for later reference. But he maintains that he was always open to fresh ideas in the studio, even with session players.

"I would say: 'These are the chords. I'd like you to do this riff here, and this is the speed of the song, and this is how the words go,'" he explained. "I wouldn't say: 'This is *exactly* what you have to play.' So then within that framework people would then come up with their own ideas, and then once that was sounding okay you'd go and do a take."[20]

For the basic take, Paul played the piano and sang a rough vocal, with Spinozza on electric guitar and Seiwell on drums. He then had Spinozza add a simple, decorative guitar line to the intro, as well as some punctuating single-line figures during the verse. Spinozza also recorded a brief solo, and a track for which the tape was played backward at strategic points, so that when it was played normally, the guitar was backward—an old Beatles trick.

Though impressed by Paul's ability to simultaneously wear the hats of musician, producer, and arranger, Spinozza got the impression that he himself was going to have little input in the sessions.

"I think the whole album was done in the same form as the *McCartney* album," Spinozza observed, "only we played the parts for him. It was done in the way there was no freedom. We were told exactly what to play, he knew what he wanted, and he just used us to do it. He just sang us the parts he wanted, and the tune developed as we went along. We added things, we made suggestions, but I would say that two out of ten times he took one of our suggestions or at least if he did, he modified it and made it into a Paul McCartney–sounding thing. It always came out Paul McCartney."[21]

Perhaps because McCartney was principally a guitarist and bassist, and a drummer only when necessary, he was less hands-on with Seiwell.

"He never told me what to play, except for one song. I think that's why he hired me—he didn't *have* to tell me. I used to channel Ringo. I'd think, '*What would Ringo do here?*' And I listened to the way Paul played on the *McCartney* album. I knew what he liked as a drummer. I would always craft some sort of a part that was going to be down that vein at least. I knew he was going to like it."[22]

What Seiwell meant by channeling Ringo was that rather than simply keeping a solid beat and punctuating with fills at the obvious points, he virtually orchestrated his drum parts, changing both his beat and the combination of drums he used at given points in a song so that the drumming responds to the shape of the melody line, the section shifts, and other things happening in the texture. For McCartney, this sensibility reaffirmed the feeling he had at the drum auditions that Seiwell was the right choice for the project.

When the session wrapped up, Paul told Spinozza and Seiwell that he would not need them the next day. This was concerning for Spinozza, who had agreed to be available for four weeks on the assumption that he would be *working* every day. He had subsequently been offered a job for that Thursday, and had turned it down, thinking he'd be recording with Paul. This second cancellation in four days prompted him to ask Paul and Linda for a more definitive sense of when he was needed.

"I had to keep asking," Spinozza explained, "not to be a drag, but to keep my book straight and to know what other work I could take. I kept asking, but I wasn't getting a straight answer."[23]

Recording Session

Friday, October 16, 1970.
CBS Studios, Studio B, New York.
Recording: 'Come on Little Lady' (working title for 'Eat at Home') and '3 Legs.'

Still using the working title 'Come on Little Lady,' rather than the title suggested by the song's refrain, 'Eat at Home,' Paul set to work on the brisk, rollicking track, playing his Martin acoustic, with Spinozza on electric guitar and Seiwell drumming. The song was pretty simple— mostly a blues progression in B-flat major, with a hook in the form of a short, syncopated, almost fanfare-like electric guitar riff that introduces the song and reappears between verses, and Buddy Holly–style strumming in the bridge. Except for the hook, the basic track is energetic but pedestrian, one of countless pop songs based on a I-IV-V progression. But Paul could hear its possibilities: the bass line, and the lead and harmony vocals he had in mind would transform it.

After lunch, the trio took up '3 Legs,' an odd little song, with each verse cast in an A-B structure, the A-section built on a straight blues progression in A major—it seemed to be blues day at Studio B—and a call-and-response B section that sits firmly on an A major chord. The bridge is a variation on the A-section blues progression, but starting in D major, and revolving around the phrase "*When I fly above the crowd*," the first three words energetically repeated four times in each of the first two lines.

Its real peculiarity is lyrical rather than musical. The B-section of the first verse tells us, "*My dog he got three legs / But he can't run*" (a change from his optimistic original, "he can run") and in the next verse, we hear that "*Most flies they got three legs / But mine got one.*" Intended or not, these two refrains capture the strained relationship between Paul and the other Beatles—the group being the three-legged dog that can't run, with Paul as the fly, ready to soar above the crowd.

Another hint that Paul may have been thinking about his rift with the other Beatles, and particularly John, when he wrote the song, can be found in the second verse, which begins: "*Well I thought you was my friend.*" The couplet that follows was altered between the time Paul wrote it and the session. In Paul's handwritten manuscript (which he titled 'A Dog Is Here'), it is "*But you left me down / With a heart that never mend.*" [24] The crossed-out final line is replaced with "*Sent my heart around the bend,*" transforming its subject from heartbreak to madness. At the session, he changed "*left me down*" to the more straightforward "*let me down,*" more precisely echoing John's 'Don't Let Me Down.'

Paul presented the song to Spinozza and Seiwell as a leisurely, acoustic country blues, a style Spinozza knew well, and which gave him an opportunity to play a varied acoustic guitar part with alternations between straight chording and more melodic, fingerpicked variations, inspired by moves he would have known from recordings by Blind Willie McTell, Reverend Gary Davis, Brownie McGhee and Elizabeth Cotton.

Seiwell was comfortable with the style, too, and because drumming was rare on classic country blues recordings, he provided a subtle, straightforward beat that mostly faded into the texture, except for a few between-section fills.

McCartney opted not to play on the basic track, instead singing the song to Spinozza's and Seiwell's backing. On one take, Spinozza devised an unorthodox, rambunctious ending.

"The thing I came up with at the end of it—that he really liked—was at one point I'm pounding the guitar. I'm chording with my left hand, but I had a drumstick, and I was banging the guitar with the drumstick. That's why it sounds like it's going really compressed and going in and out."[25]

Much as Paul liked Spinozza's ending, he also liked the more conventional versions he played, with a fingerpicked ending. But choosing between them was a decision he could put off until he was ready to overdub.

Before leaving, Spinozza asked Paul about the schedule for the following week. Thinking he might devote the week to overdubbing, Paul told Spinozza that he might not be needed, and that at best, it would be loose. Spinozza had offers of studio work on Wednesday, Thursday and Friday, and decided to take them, not having been definitely booked by the McCartneys.

After working with Seiwell for a week, Paul was satisfied that he was a good fit; over the weekend, Linda canceled MacDonald and Lovelle.

When Paul and Linda returned to the Stanhope, they switched on the news and caught a report on the trial of Charles Manson, charged as the mastermind behind the murders of Sharon Tate (then eight and a half months pregnant) and six others over two nights—August 9 and 10, 1969—in Los Angeles. Manson, a failed musician who had befriended Dennis Wilson of the Beach Boys, had attracted a coterie of female followers who were willing to undertake his increasingly bizarre wishes, including murder, and who came to be known as the Manson Family.

At the trial that Friday, Gregg Jakobson, a songwriting partner of Dennis Wilson's who had underwritten a recording of Manson singing his own songs, testified as a witness for the prosecution and told the court that Manson believed that the Beatles were sending him messages in their songs. The titles of two *White Album* songs, Harrison's 'Piggies' and McCartney's 'Helter Skelter,' were scrawled in blood (with 'Helter' misspelled as 'Healter') at the murder scenes.

Paul found Manson's theory that 'Helter Skelter' was about an impending race war confounding and upsetting. He was used to reading bizarre interpretations of Beatles lyrics, but until now, Beatles songs had never been part of a murder investigation. To Paul, and to British listeners to the song, a helter skelter was a fairground ride, with a slide that spiraled downward around a tower. (Its closest American equivalent is a sliding pond.) The lyrics clearly evoke the excitement of sliding down it, then climbing back to the top for another ride.

To American ears, helter skelter meant chaotic and askew, a meaning Manson magnified in his perverse fantasy of a race war that would tear apart American society. The prosecution hoped to enlist Lennon and McCartney (the song was cocredited, like all their others) to explain what they meant, something they refused to do.

"Charles Manson interpreted that 'Helter Skelter' was something to do with the four horsemen of the Apocalypse," Paul recalled. "I still don't know what all that stuff is; it's from the bible, 'Revelations'—I haven't read it so I wouldn't know. But he interpreted the whole song . . . and arrived at having to go out and kill everyone. It was terrible. You can't associate yourself with a thing like that. Some guy in the States had done it—but I've no idea why. It was frightening because you don't write songs for those reasons."[26]

Over the weekend, Paul settled on his recording plans for the week, and on Sunday, Linda telephoned Seiwell and Spinozza to say that they would be needed after all.

Not so fast, Spinozza told her: he was an in-demand player, and when Paul told him he would not be needed, he accepted other jobs, the alternative being to sit home, unpaid, when Paul was not working. To Linda's astonishment, Spinozza told her he was available on Monday and Tuesday only.

Recording Session

Monday, October 19, 1970.
CBS Studios, Studio B, New York.
Recording: 'I Lie Around.'

McCartney's studio trio laid down a simple backing, in eight takes, with Paul and David on acoustic guitars—Spinozza playing a graceful, fingerpicked introduction—and Denny on drums. In an overdub, Denny scraped on a block covered with sandpaper, and Paul added piano. Unsure where he wanted to take the song from there, Paul set it aside.

As the session ended, Spinozza stopped in the control room to check in with Linda to make sure the next day's session was still on. It was, and Paul asked him to bring a nylon-string classical guitar, which he thought would be useful for the track he planned to work on.

Spinozza found Linda's presence at the sessions—not to mention that of Heather and Mary—puzzling, and slightly disconcerting.

"I thought to a certain degree it was distracting," he said. "It was a nice, loose atmosphere, but distracting. Linda, I really don't know what she did in the studio aside from sit there and make her comments on what she thought was good and what she thought was bad. My personal opinion is that everybody, especially in the music business, when they finally find an old lady that they really dig, they try to get her into everything, which I don't believe in. It just didn't make sense to me."[27]

There were other distractions, too. Among the other musicians recording in the CBS building were the Rascals, a band managed by Sid Bernstein, the man who presented the Beatles at Carnegie Hall in 1964 and at Shea Stadium in 1965 and 1966. Bernstein popped into Studio B one afternoon, ostensibly having forgotten which studio the Rascals were using.

Paul had mixed feelings about Sid. He had promoted stellar gigs for the Beatles in the United States, and indeed, he clamored to bring them over even before they had an American hit, based on reports in the British press. But he had also developed the unfortunate habit of making public appeals for big money stage comebacks—starting with a $1 million offer in 1967, a year after they gave up touring—that the Beatles had no interest in or involvement with, but for which they had to answer.

But he respected the Rascals. Paul's first encounter with them, billed at the time as the Young Rascals, was in November 1966, when he caught their shows at the Blaises Club and the Scotch of St. James Club, in London. He had met their keyboard player, Felix Cavaliere, three years earlier, when Cavaliere was a member of Joey Dee and the Starliters, for whom the Beatles opened at the Kungliga Tennishallen, in Stockholm, on October 26, 1963.

Between 1966 and 1968, the Rascals scored a number of hits—'Good Lovin',' 'Groovin',' 'I've Been Lonely Too Long,' 'How Can I Be Sure,' 'A Beautiful Morning'—but in 1970, the blue-eyed soul band from New Jersey had only two original members (Cavaliere and Dino Danelli) and was struggling to reestablish itself. In the album the Rascals were recording at CBS, *Peaceful World*, they were moving toward an amalgam of soul, jazz and funk.

"I saw Paul once at Columbia Studio B," Bernstein later explained, "when my own group, the Rascals, were recording there. I burst mistakenly into the wrong room and there were these strangers with a couple of kids and a big picnic lunch all over the control board, and I heard this heavy accent 'Eh, Sid Bernstein' and it was Paul—behind the beard that I hadn't seen before."[28]

Among the things they chatted about was a plan Bernstein had been hatching for a tour of the United States with Paul headlining and the Rascals supporting. Paul, he said, would walk away with half the tour's proceeds. Bernstein had mentioned this plan during an interview on a New York radio station, WMCA, in September. Now that he had "mistakenly" burst in on Paul in the studio, he presented the idea directly. Paul was diplomatically noncommittal.

Word of the meeting made it into the November 12 issue of *Rolling Stone*, where Bernstein disavowed any knowledge of a supposedly "off the record" report that Cavaliere and Danelli were playing on Paul's sessions.[29]

Recording Session

Tuesday, October 20, 1970.
CBS Studios, Studio B, New York.
Recording: 'When the Wind Is Blowing' and 'The Back Seat of My Car.'

At Tuesday's session, Paul turned his attention to 'When the Wind Is Blowing'—the tune inspired by the print of Picasso's *The Old Guitarist* that he had seen in Linda's hospital room, when Mary was born, and that he recorded a rudimentary version of during the home sessions for *McCartney*. At the time, Paul earmarked the tune for his *Rupert* film project, and so it remained. Both Seiwell and Spinozza were aware that the track was not for the album Paul was working on but for, as Spinozza recalled, "some cartoon he was scoring."[30]

With two guitarists and a drummer on hand, the new recording was more ambitious than the original, but simplicity remained its hallmark. Paul strummed the song's chords on his Martin acoustic, with David playing melodic filigree on his classical guitar and Denny contributing a light, steady beat.

That morning also saw an abortive first attempt at 'The Back Seat of My Car,' the ballad of teen-age sexuality and rebellion that Paul had been toying with since the summer of 1968. Everything about the song was a tip of the hat to Brian Wilson, from the wide vocal range demanded by its melody, the exquisite harmonic flow of its chord progression and its pocket-opera structure, to its sixties American teen imagery, centered around the car and all it represented—freedom, par-ticularly, including the freedom to speed along the highway, ignoring parental admonitions about staying out too late, and of course, premarital sex.

"Even though it was a long time since I was a teenager and had to go to a girl's dad and explain myself, it's that kind of meet-the-parents song," Paul explained, "with the stereotypical parent who doesn't agree, and the two lovers are going to take on the world: *We believe that we can't be wrong*.' I always like the underdog. . . . *We can make it to Mexico City*." I've never driven to Mexico City, but it's imagination. And obviously 'back seat' is snogging, making love."[31]

This first attempt at the song did not gel, so after a few hours Paul called the day's work to an end, opting to start again at the next session.

The problem was, he did not know when the next session would be. The Wednesday session was canceled because Paul was expected for a meeting with the Eastmans, but then, Spinozza was unavailable for the rest of the week—not that Linda didn't try to pressure him into throwing over his other gigs and continuing to work with Paul.

"When I told Linda I couldn't do it," Spinozza recalled, "she got a little pissy with me, like, 'Well, it's Paul McCartney.' I said, 'Linda, this is nothing against Paul McCartney, or you. It's just that when you go back to London, I have to stay here and work. These are people I work with all the time, and they booked me ahead of time.'

"She was a little insulted that I didn't just drop everything and continue with them. And I said, 'Welcome to New York. This is a freelance world, and when I take a job, I don't cancel it when a better one comes along.' That's how the New York studio scene worked. I don't think they under-stood that. I wasn't in the Beatles, you know? It wasn't like it was a Beatles session. I wasn't going to make a million dollars off this record."[32]

8

KEEP ON TRUCKIN'

—

Paul and Linda needed a new guitarist, and quick. Paul still had Barry Kornfeld's list of recommended musicians, and there were other guitarists at the auditions who impressed him. But having established a strong working relationship with Seiwell, Paul asked the drummer, at the end of the Tuesday session, which guitarists he liked working with.

"Well, I work with this other guy, Hugh McCracken," Seiwell told him, "and I'm sure you're going to like him. He's in the same league as Spinozza, if not better."[1]

McCracken had been on Kornfeld's list, but he was playing on an Aretha Franklin album* at Criteria Sound Studios in Miami at the time of the auditions. His credits, to that point, were more impressive than either Seiwell's or Spinozza's, and where their passions tilted toward jazz, McCracken's list of credits included a good balance of jazz, rock, pop, blues, and R&B.

McCracken, born in Glen Ridge, New Jersey on March 31, 1942, was 28, the same age as McCartney, and had an impressive résumé of studio and concert work. Paul would have heard plenty of the records he had played on, which dated back to King Curtis's *Trouble in Mind* (1961) and also included Van Morrison's 'Brown-Eyed Girl,' the Left Banke's 'Walk Away Renée' and 'Pretty Ballerina' (all 1967), Gordon Lightfoot's *Did She Mention My Name*, and Laura Nyro's *Eli and the Thirteenth Confession* (both 1968), B. B. King's *Completely Well* (1969), the bubble gum classic 'Sugar Sugar,' by the Archies, and the Insect Trust's decidedly more experimental *Hoboken Saturday Night* (1970).†

With some luck, Linda could sort that out the next day, and they could be back in business on Thursday, with no time lost.

But their first order of business on Wednesday morning was their meeting at Eastman and

---

* The album, *Young, Gifted and Black*, was released in January 1972.

† Hugh McCracken died on March 28, 2013, in New York.

Eastman. Hopping in a cab, they crossed Central Park, taking in the autumnal oranges, reds, and yellows of the park's foliage as they headed toward the Eastman and Eastman offices in a town house at 39 West 54th Street. The meeting was not with John and Lee Eastman alone; it was also Paul's first meeting with David C. Hirst, Q.C., the barrister the Eastmans had engaged to lead his London legal team. Together they would investigate whether a case to dissolve the Beatles business ties was viable or a legal dead end. Hirst had recently arrived in New York with two junior members of his firm, not only to coordinate with John Eastman and Paul, but also to gather information about the workings of the music business and practices of the record world, both in general and specifically where Allen Klein was involved. They intended to be thorough: they remained in New York for six weeks.

Hirst made his name as a libel lawyer but had lately shifted his interest toward commercial law. He had already briefed Eastman on Paul's position in the context of British commercial law, and as Eastman knew from speaking with other lawyers, it was not encouraging. It was likely, Hirst told him, that a British Chancery court judge would consider that Paul was one of four directors of a partnership, and that his three codirectors were within their rights to engage Klein. It was not certain that even if a judge proved sympathetic to Paul's grievances, he would rule that the company should be dissolved and that Paul should walk away with his 25 percent of it.

A possible strategy, Eastman and Hirst agreed, would be to show that Klein's malevolence toward Paul was not only demonstrable, but posed a significant threat to Paul's ability to pursue his career unimpeded—and that to the degree that Paul *could* continue to make music, Klein's track record suggested that his involvement in Paul's finances could be ruinous.

Walking Paul through the case, Hirst was clear about the potential hurdles, and the importance of building a case around what he considered Klein's interference with his artistry. He and Eastman also noted that Paul had several advantages. One was that since Klein was not named in the suit, his involvement in the trial would be limited: he could file an affidavit, giving his own account of his transactions with Paul and the other Beatles, but he could not testify, or otherwise respond to Paul's assertions.

Also, while Paul had known since July that the suit was in the works, and had ample time to prepare his case, the other Beatles would have to engage counsel and prepare their defense in relative haste.

When Hirst felt he had adequately caught Paul up on his planned strategy, he left to join his colleagues' researching. John Eastman had other business with Paul—mainly, setting up an American counterpart to Paul's MPL production company. Called McCartney Productions, Inc.—although its business stationery would say MPL, for consistency—the company listed Paul as president, Linda as vice president, and Lee Eastman as treasurer, in which capacity he took specimen cards with the principals' signatures to Chemical Bank when he opened the company's account on October 29.

Before they left the family firm's offices, Linda tracked down McCracken. His booking service told her he was playing a session, but that was not a barrier to Linda's determination: she persuaded his service to tell her where he was playing and phoned him at the studio. As McCracken recalled it, "I was at another session, and they said, 'There's an important call for you.'"[2] When McCracken took the receiver, Linda handed the phone to Paul. "Paul simply asked me if I could be in the studio the following morning at nine o'clock."[3]

Back at the Stanhope, Linda called a printer in Manhattan to order stationery for McCartney Productions Inc., adding an extra batch of headed paper to the order for her and Paul's amusement. "Linda had some note paper made up for herself, just for a laugh," remembered Paul, "which read: *Grin, Grin, and Bear It Solicitors*, like it was an official thing. She'd write to friends on it."[4]

Paul and Linda had lately adopted the phrase "keep on truckin'"—the opening line of an old Blind Boy Fuller record, 'Truckin' My Blues Away'—which they used as a form of encouragement during difficult times. Now they were truckin' indeed, with an immediate problem solved and the solution to a long-term problem in the works. It was not a bad day's work.

Recording Session

Thursday, October 22, 1970.
CBS Studios, Studio B, New York.
Recording: 'The Back Seat of My Car' and 'Rode All Night.'

Having heard from other freelancers that it was McCartney's practice to hear musicians before engaging them, Hugh McCracken thought his 9:00 a.m. appointment was part of another round of auditions, so he was surprised, upon entering CBS Studio B, to find McCartney and his old friend Denny ready to begin the day's work. Explaining that he thought he was there to audition, McCracken told Paul that he was only available until 2:00 p.m.

Paul must have wondered whether all New York session guitarists were only spottily available, but he briefed Hugh on the project and asked him to commit to exclusivity for the next month. Hugh agreed, and the session began.

A day away from the studio gave Paul time to analyze the problems with Tuesday's recording of 'The Back Seat of My Car.' For starters, he wanted a particular sound, and he, Seiwell and Spinozza had not quite captured it. But a larger problem was that the song was in several distinct sections, and Paul felt that they did not flow together as smoothly as they should.

"[I was] definitely trying to do something else," Paul said. "To have to invent something new was difficult. But I just felt like that was the way to go. So I tried to avoid any Beatles clichés and just went to different places. So the songs became a little more episodic. I took on that kind of idea a bit more than I would've with the Beatles. I suppose I was just letting myself be free."[5]

McCartney, McCracken, and Seiwell began the new version of 'The Back Seat of My Car' with Paul on the studio's Steinway Grand, Hugh playing his favored Gibson ES-335 electric guitar, and Seiwell on drums, working steadily until it was time for Hugh to leave. Paul and Denny took a late lunch, and then headed back to the studio, where they found Geelan and Brosnan taking down the microphones, thinking the day's work was finished.

"When we came back from lunch, Paul was all jazzed up," Seiwell said. "I don't know what was in him. He picked up that old black-and-green Firebird guitar of his and started jamming. I jumped behind the drums, so Paul and I are just slamming away, we're having fun, that's all we're doing—and letting off some steam. It was amazing, he was writing this song as we went. And he's looking at the booth, and these guys aren't recording it—they're out there, frantically trying to put the mics back in place, and get the sound correct.

"By the time they got everything ready to go again, we were spent, but we said, 'All right, they're ready—let's do take two.' We're in there just slamming and jamming, and having a great time, and he started singing, '*I rode all night 'til I finally hit the daybreak.*' That, to me—this is just to me, personally—was him saying, '*I can finally make music with someone other than John, George and Ringo.*' I thought, 'Wow, this is really a compliment to me,' and I gave it a bit more."[6]

Though Seiwell thought Paul's lyric was impromptu, it was not: Paul wrote the line on the S.S. *France*, on the same sheet of paper that includes fragmentary lyrics for 'Oh Woman, Oh Why,' and may originally have been intended for that song.[7]

The cathartic, nearly nine-minute second take of 'Rode All Night' survives as McCartney and Seiwell left it—too raucous and freewheeling to overdub, and apparently not enough of a basis for Paul to transform into a bona fide song.* But as it stands, it is one of the most aggressive, explosively energetic workouts McCartney ever committed to tape, thanks equally to the Little-Richard-on-steroids vocal style and the solid but agile guitar chording he brought to it, and to Seiwell's hard-edged, machine-gun drumming.

Moving to the control room, they sat back in the studio's swivel chairs, listened to the take and decided to keep it, if only to remember the spirit of the moment. Geelan handed Seiwell a tape copy as he left the studio for the day. McCartney remained to listen to the morning's recording of 'The Back Seat of My Car.'

It still lacked something, and Paul was unwilling to settle. They would start afresh on Friday.

---

* Paul later incorporated the melody and lyric into 'Giddy,' which Roger Daltry included on his third solo album, *One of the Boys* (1977).

Recording Session

Friday, October 23, 1970.
CBS Studios, Studio B, New York.
Recording: 'The Back Seat of My Car.'

"'The Back Seat of My Car' had the longest learning period," Seiwell recalled, "three hours or more to learn the whole song so that we could get the transitions to flow naturally, and everyone was familiar with the new tempo, when [it went] to another tempo. Then it was just a matter of getting a good performance."[8]

Ordinarily a producer, like George Martin or Glyn Johns, would be in the control room to spot flaws in the performance or arrangement and steer the musicians toward that one perfect performance. But having decided to self-produce his latest album, refining the sound and arrangement was on Paul.

"Most of the experimentation happened out in the studio," Geelan explained. "Since he was out there with them playing, it wasn't like most record producers who were behind your back in the control room, commenting on what's going on at the time. But he'd come in and listen to it, and we'd make a few adjustments here and there."[9]

After the trio's second failure to get a smoothly flowing basic track, Paul realized that it was not simply the episodic character of the song that presented difficulty, but the way the episodes were connected. In some cases, they were subtle variations rather than discrete section breaks.

Unlike 'Another Day,' with its meter shifts between 4|4 and 3|4, 'The Back Seat of My Car' is entirely in 4|4. But the tempos were fluid. The verses, which have a dreamy quality, contrast sharply with the driven section that follows the "*sitting in the back seat of my car*" refrain, and the "*we believe that we can't be wrong*" playout is brisker and more assertive than the short vocalise that precedes it.

Another of the song's appealing complications was that elements that are heard several times in the song are used differently each time. For example, the third line of each verse—"*But listen to her daddy's song*"—is accompanied by the same chord progression (E-flat major, B-flat major, C minor) that supports the very different "*We believe that we can't be wrong*" section at the end of the song.

That would have been clear to Seiwell and McCracken when Paul sang the song to them in a prerecording run-through, because in the final verse, he sings the defiant "*we believe that we can't be wrong*" instead of the expected "*don't stay out too long.*" In this verse only, the line is repeated, followed by a short section ending with a piano flourish and a dramatic pause—elements not heard in any other verse. It is an almost classical foreshadowing of the song's ecstatic playout. Once Seiwell and McCracken were able to map out those subtleties, the song took shape, and by the end of the day, they had it down.

McCracken, like Spinozza, has said that the parts he played were devised by Paul. On 'The Back Seat of My Car,' McCracken's part included an attractive chordal counterpoint, accompanying the "*don't stay out*" and "*we believe*" sections, and compressed, lightly syncopated chording in the insistent links between the verses.

Seiwell took a gradual approach, sitting out the intro and much of the first verse, then becoming increasingly present through the rest of the song, adding decorative touches at section shifts and going all out in the coda. Their instrumental backing weighed in at 5'15".

Completing the backing track was cathartic; Seiwell reports that the three musicians, with Linda, Geelan, and Brosnan, had a celebration in the studio before packing up for the week.

With two weeks of sessions, legal meetings and sorting out personnel changes in his studio ensemble behind him, Paul needed to unwind. Linda arranged for tickets for Friday evening's 11:30 p.m. late show at the Fillmore East, a bill headlined by Eric Clapton, fronting Derek and the Dominos, with Ballin' Jack and Humble Pie as the supporting acts.

Paul and Linda both considered Clapton an old friend. Paul met him in 1964 when, as a member of the Yardbirds, he was on the bill for the Beatles run of Christmas shows at the Hammersmith Odeon, in London; Linda had photographed him in both New York and London as a member of Cream.

Clapton and his band (Bobby Whitlock on keyboards, Carl Radle on bass, and Jim Gordon on drums) had just put the finishing touches on *Layla and Other Assorted Love Songs*, which was due out a couple of weeks hence. The sessions, at Criteria Sound Studios, in Miami, were concluded on October 2, the day the McCartneys set sail for New York on the S.S. *France*; McCracken missed crossing paths with Clapton at Criteria by only a few days.

At the Fillmore, the Dominos played a nearly two-hour set that included only 11 songs—five from the new album ('Key to the Highway,' 'Tell the Truth,' 'Why Does Love Got to Be So Sad,' 'Have You Ever Loved a Woman' and Jimi Hendrix's 'Little Wing'), along with a song each from his Cream and Blind Faith days ('Crossroads' and 'Presence of the Lord,' respectively), three from his debut solo album, released earlier in 1970 ('Blues Power,' 'Bottle of Red Wine' and 'Let

It Rain') and, as his opener, an outtake from the *Layla* sessions, 'Got to Get Better in a Little While."*

The next morning, the McCartneys drove a rented Oldsmobile out to Long Island, to spend the weekend at the Eastman family's getaway in East Hampton. Hanging out with Linda and her siblings Paul was feeling unusually appreciative of her efforts over the last few weeks, handling session grunt work (calling the musicians, scheduling, and being an extra ear in the control room) while also taking care of the girls. Musing on the positive changes she had brought to his life, he wanted to document that appreciation in song, but in a way that was not just another 'The Lovely Linda.'

An approach that occurred to him, and that, as far as he could tell, no other songwriter had taken, was to address the song not to his paramour, but to her ex—in this case, Linda's first husband, Joseph Melville See Jr., known to his friends as Mel.

"I was going out with a Princeton boy—a very attractive Hemingway man," Linda explained in one of her few interviews mentioning See. "My mother died in a plane crash, and I got married. It was a mistake. He was a geologist and when he graduated he wanted to go to Africa. I said, 'Look, if I don't get on with you here, I'm not going to Africa with you.' So he went. While he was there I really thanked God and said I'd get a divorce. So I wrote a letter and said I was getting a divorce. I got a letter back saying 'Let's not.' I said, 'Yeah, come on, let's get a divorce.' So luckily he agreed."[10]

The breakup of the marriage was civil and undramatic, and See made no attempt to get custody of Heather.† But Linda suggested, on one occasion, that there was a darker side to the marriage.

"Some men make women feel so guilty: they're their wives' worst enemies—and that is death. And these women keep saying to themselves, 'But I've got a good heart. I am good.' Imagine fearing your husband coming home! I don't like to talk about my first marriage, because it was crazed, and I started going crazy. All I know is that a woman has to say to a man, 'I have to love myself one hundred percent, and you have to help me love myself just as I am helping you to love yourself.'"[11]

The song Paul wrote, 'Dear Boy,' is simple at heart—an attractive melody in A minor, with dotted rhythms that give the lyrics a flowing, conversational quality, and a piano accompaniment in block chords. But Paul immediately saw the music's implications and began planning an arrangement—in particular, a complex web of backing vocals—that would elevate it considerably once he brought the song into the studio.

Because songwriters did not typically write epistolary works to their spouses' exes, Paul worried that listeners might think the 'dear boy' he was addressing was John Lennon.

---

* Derek and the Dominos would revisit the song in the April/May 1971 sessions for their prospective (but never completed) second album. Several performances from the show Paul and Linda attended, along with recordings from the Dominos' other shows that weekend, were included in *Derek and the Dominos in Concert*, released in January 1973, and *Live at the Fillmore*, released in February 1994.

† Joseph Melville See, a geologist when he was married to Linda, and later a respected anthropologist and ethnographer, died by suicide at age 62, on March 19, 2000, in Arizona.

When he was asked about it, Paul quickly clarified, "The thought behind that was that Linda's ex-husband—a very nice guy called Mel—I kind of felt like he had *missed* Linda—he'd not seen in her what I had seen in her—and so the song really was written to him. I had a person in mind that I was writing a letter to, and the 'dear boy' was almost harking back to Noël Coward: 'Dear boy!'"[12]

As often was the case, Paul did not rush into the studio with the song, but let it percolate as he continued to work through the material he was already planning to record.

Recording Session

Monday, October 26, 1970.
CBS Studios, Studio B, New York.
Recording: 'Hey Diddle' and 'A Love for You.'

The week began on a light note with 'Hey Diddle.' A weirdly charismatic doodle, the song has its lyrical roots in the old nursery rhyme about the cat and the fiddle. It had started a dual-purpose ditty—part country tune, part entertainment for Mary and Heather—but was completed as a minimalist torch song. It is virtually all chorus, the single line, "*Hey diddle, I want you back, diddle I want you back*" repeated many times over, with short, country-tinged verses occasionally interspersed without adding much more information about the relationship in question.

The song's attraction is that its chorus grows directly out of a folklike fingerpicked guitar lick with a rolling melody that matches the vocal line. McCartney and McCracken each play acoustic guitars, Paul starting with the song's signature riff, and Hugh entering on the riff's second statement with a single chord in natural harmonics (a ringing sound created by lifting the finger off the string as the note is plucked). Thereafter, the two guitar lines create a homey texture, the fingerpicked passages offset by a strummed accompaniment, with Seiwell supporting with an on-the-beat bass drum, a light shuffle and fills marking the shifts between chorus and verse.

When Paul recorded his bass line, during his next overdubbing session, it was simple, mostly just following Denny's bass drum beat, with some passing tones added only in the verses. For this session, he also brought in a handful of ocarinas—a simple wind instrument—and with Denny and Hugh joining in, he overdubbed a lightly harmonized ensemble, more or less in tune, onto one of the verses.

After lunch, Paul introduced 'A Love for You,' a midtempo rocker from his Scottish demo collection. Always looking for new ways to write a love song, Paul began this one by setting up oppositions—"*when you met me, everything was rosy . . . but when you go, everything that's rosy turns to pieces.*" The second verse is more self-regarding: "*if you get me, that could save a thousand conversations . . . but don't upset me, everything is cozy here tonight.*" As with 'Hey Diddle,' most of the song is a repetition of a musically catchy but lyrically lightweight chorus, largely built around a well-tread idea—"*Where will I run to / Where would I hide.*" This running and hiding is linked to the singer's paramour, who leaves him even though "*I really am, I really can, I really do, I really have a love for you.*" It is as awkward a way of saying "I love you" as Paul had yet devised.

What the song has going for it is an unmistakably McCartneyesque melody and the kind of attention-grabbing "feel" that helps so many McCartney songs pull you in. But after a full afternoon of performances, with Paul on his Martin acoustic, Hugh on his Gibson electric and Denny playing a richly detailed drum line, that feel remained elusive, and Paul called it a day.

Recording Session

Tuesday, October 27, 1970.
CBS Studios, Studio B, New York.
Recording: 'A Love for You' and 'Love Is Long' (working title for 'Long Haired Lady').

All three musicians knew that the key to 'A Love for You' was tightening up the playing while also pitching the song as an off-the-cuff rocker. At the morning session, they produced a 5'45" master take in which Paul strummed an acoustic guitar and sang a high-spirited guide vocal that alternately evokes Elvis Presley and Little Richard. Denny played a drum line rich in punctuating, section-marking fills, executed with a manic energy that evoked Keith Moon, and Hugh played an electric guitar part that alternately paralleled and harmonized with the vocal, with occasional bluesy lead figures and references to rock classics—most notably, Chuck Berry's 'Memphis, Tennessee.'

"It wasn't quick, it was a song a day," remembered McCracken. "He was pretty methodical; he knew what he wanted."[13]

That afternoon, Paul introduced a fusion of two songs from his Scottish demo, 'Long Haired Lady' and 'Love Is Long,' for which he was provisionally using the latter title. Both songs were in the key of G, and their tempos were similar, so joining them created no technical issues.

Structurally, 'Love Is Long' is just a four-bar phrase with a catchy, repeating melody, not unlike the *"we believe that we can't be wrong"* section of 'The Back Seat of My Car'—or, for that matter, the *"Na, na, na, na-na-na na"* finale of 'Hey Jude.'

'Long Haired Lady,' by contrast, has several distinct sections. The first, the theatrically exaggerated *"Well, well, well, well, well / Do you love me like you know you ought to do"* section, serves as an extended introduction. Paul abandons rock's standard eight-bar phrasing here. The introduction runs ten bars, heading into a five-bar refrain that departs further from the norm by starting with a single bar in 2|4 time; the rest is in 4|4. Its lyric (the title line) is sung on sustained notes, creating the impression that Paul has slowed the action.

From there, the song moves into the verse—the boyfriend's response to the *"well, well, well, well, well"* opening—cast as a bright, snappy section that, both musically and lyrically, calls to mind the cheerful theme songs typical of late-1960s/early-1970s American television sitcoms. Two of these toe-tapping verses follow, separated by a shortened version of the refrain, played twice each time. This is where the simple, musically repetitive 'Love Is Long' is joined to the composition. After its first appearance, McCartney brings us back to the *"Well, well, well, well, well"* introduction, but instead of moving from there to the verses, he returns to 'Love Is Long' for the song's remaining two minutes.

Like 'The Back Seat of My Car,' this was a song that needed a road map. It is likely that Paul knew they would not get a master take that day, but he had Geelan keep the tapes rolling while he, McCracken and Seiwell worked through it and got it under their fingers. Toward the end of the afternoon, the session was interrupted by a visit from another musician who had recorded in CBS Studio B, Bob Dylan, with whom Paul and Linda had a dinner date that evening.

Paul had been an admirer of Dylan's work since his 1963 second album, *The Freewheeling Bob Dylan*, and had known him personally since August 28, 1964, when Dylan and the journalist Al Aronowitz turned up at their suite in the Delmonico Hotel, in Manhattan, after the Beatles' show at the Forest Hills Tennis Stadium. The myth that has grown up around this visit was that Dylan introduced the Beatles to marijuana that evening; in fact, Lennon and Harrison had tried it as early as 1960. But it was probably new to Paul.

"We had a crazy party the night we met," Paul said of the evening. "I thought I got the meaning to life that night. I went around trying to get our roadie—'Hey Mal! Get a pencil and a paper! I've got it, I've got it!' And I wrote down my message for the universe, y'know. I said to Mal, 'Now keep that, keep that in your pocket.' The next morning, he said, 'Here Paul, do you wanna see that?' I said, 'What?' He said, 'That bit of paper.' 'Oh yeah!' And I'd written: There are seven levels."[14]

For Dylan, the Beatles were something of a guilty pleasure back then—one he could justify to his friends in the rock-phobic folk music world because they were so obviously gifted and original.

"I had heard the Beatles in New York when they first hit," he once said. "Then, when we were driving through Colorado, we had the radio on, and eight of the Top 10 songs were Beatles songs. In Colorado! They were doing things nobody was doing. Their chords were outrageous, just outrageous, and their harmonies made it all valid. But I just kept it to myself that I really dug them. Everybody else thought they were for the teenyboppers, that they were gonna pass right away. But it was obvious to me that they had staying power. I knew they were pointing the direction of where music had to go."[15]

That evening, Paul, Linda, and their daughters had dinner with Dylan and Sara, his wife of five years, and their children, Jesse, Anna, Samuel, Jakob, and Maria, at the Dylans' apartment at 94 McDougal Street, in Greenwich Village. Paul had not met Sara previously, but he knew that she was the inspiration for songs like 'Love Minus Zero/No Limit' and 'Sad-Eyed Lady of the Lowlands.' The evening was undoubtedly more sedate than Dylan's 1964 postshow visit with the Beatles, although it seems likely that a doobie or two was passed around after dinner.

Paul had told McCracken and Seiwell to take the Wednesday off, and it is possible that he used the day to catch up on bass overdubs. That same day, George and Pattie Harrison, traveling with Phil Spector, flew into New York, the master tapes for George's *All Things Must Pass* album in hand. Reporters at Kennedy Airport quizzed him about the Manson murders, asking whether he felt the Beatles' music was responsible for Sharon Tate's death. He gave the question the back of his hand, saying only, "I don't know about murder,"[16] before he walked to the limousine that was taking the party to the Plaza Hotel.

George was in town to edit and master his album and would be working just across town from Paul, at Mediasound, 311 West 57th Street. Work would begin on October 30; in the meantime, he spent time at Apple's New York office at 1700 Broadway—also the offices of Klein's ABKCO—discussing the album's marketing and promotion plans with Pete Bennett, a Capitol promotion man who had overseen Apple's American publicity since 1968 and had been a Klein associate since 1964.

———

Recording Session

Thursday, October 29, 1970.

CBS Studios, Studio B, New York.

Recording: 'Love Is Long' (working title for 'Long Haired Lady') and 'Sunshine Sometimes.'

After an afternoon of rehearsal and a day off, McCartney and his backing duo made relatively short work of 'Love Is Long.' On the master, which runs just over six minutes, Paul plays a casual acoustic guitar line—just the straightforward harmonic backdrop—leaving the nuancing to McCracken and Seiwell. McCracken, again on electric guitar, played—as on 'The Back Seat of My Car'—a beautifully organized part that moves between distinct musical accents (country, blues, rock, even a hint of jazz, by way of a solo figure in the refrain). Seiwell, increasingly comfortable in unleashing his inner Ringo, provides a thoughtfully "orchestrated" drum part, with clear section markers, and accents keyed to the vocal line. On that instrumental backing track, Paul can be heard off-mic, singing the vocal line, calling out the section breaks, and whooping it up during the long playout.

McCartney, at this point, was imagining how the finished recordings would sound, and for the two big production numbers in the can so far—this and 'The Back Seat of My Car'—he began compiling ideas for orchestral additions, which he would commission George Martin to write. Wanting to distance himself from the Beatles was high on his agenda, but Paul and Big George had a deep musical rapport, and Paul knew that Martin would produce scores that captured what Paul wanted.

For the moment, though, 'Love Is Long' joined the stack of recordings-in-progress, and Paul brought out another tune earmarked for *Rupert*, the Brazilian-jazz pastiche, 'Sunshine Sometimes.'* This was a comfortable change of pace for both Seiwell and McCracken. With Paul on acoustic guitar, Hugh on electric and Denny on percussion—mainly the bass drum and African tuned blocks—they quickly set down a basic track, to which they added a triangle overdub.

"They were really cool," Seiwell said of the *Rupert* tracks, "because they were real quiet. They weren't as hard as 'Get on the Right Thing' or 'The Back Seat of My Car.' This was kind of different. Musically, we had so much fun recording in that style."[17]

---

* Paul went back and forth between 'Sometime' and 'Sometimes' in the title. At these sessions, he listed it as 'Sunshine Sometimes.'

The star-and-sidemen arrangement served Paul well at first, but by now he realized that this distance was unnecessary; the nature of session work was that the hired guns played what (and how) the session leader wanted, end of story. Paul, Hugh and Denny had settled into a good, efficient working relationship, and they got on personally as well. To help lessen the sense of employer-employee distance, Paul and Linda invited Hugh and Denny, along with their wives, Holly and Monique, to dinner at La Scala, an Italian restaurant on West 54th Street.

Over several hours, and several bottles of red wine, the musicians traded stories of studio work and touring. An Associated Press reporter spotted them, but Paul declined to provide a bon mot, or to introduce his colleagues. So the sighting turned up as a single line in a gossip column, padded out with the incorrect claim that Paul and Linda had first met at the restaurant.[18] Indeed, restaurant sightings of the McCartneys were becoming a staple of New York celebrity columns. The same week, Ed Sullivan noted in his *Daily News* column, 'Little Old New York,' that Paul and Linda were seen dining with Burt Bacharach and his wife.[19]

Paul canceled the Friday session and took Linda and the girls shopping for Halloween costumes; Linda's sister Laura was taking them to a party, on Saturday. Paul, Linda and Laura hoped to go out as Popeye, Olive Oyl, and Wimpy, but while Linda found a Wimpy mask, Paul had to make do with a malevolent clown mask with a bulbous nose and spiky wings of hair.

Laura found a Marilyn Monroe mask, with molded blond hair and printed-on beauty mark. Mary, blithely unaware of Halloween, and subject to her parents' whim, was given a touch of geometric face paint. And Heather improvised a Native American costume, using a half mask with sharply angled, drawn-on eyebrows, a headband and a couple of feathers. All were wrapped in sheets borrowed from the Stanhope. Paul and Linda used a photo of themselves in their costumes as their seasonal ad in the music papers that year. Upon seeing it, John Lennon interpreted the narrow eyes on Linda's Wimpy mask as Asian, and took the photo as a sub-rosa insult to Yoko.*

Returning to the Stanhope after the party, Paul and company were spotted by a pair of fans, Joanne DiFilippe and Linda Rabe, who staked out a Paul-watching position near the hotel.

"After having no luck for most of the day," they wrote in a fanzine report, "we decided to try Fifth Avenue. As we crossed 81st Street, we saw two women and a man coming up toward Fifth. They were dressed in sheets with masks and the man was carrying a baby. As they were approaching us at the corner, the man hid the baby's face under the sheet, and as they came around the corner they were making these ghostly sounds. As they turned to go into the Stanhope Hotel we noticed the groovy Argyle socks and we realized we had been put on by a Beatle."[20]

Fans were, by then, becoming a nuisance for Paul and Linda, thanks to mid-October reports in *Disc and Music Echo*, *NME* and *Melody Maker* that Paul was in New York. The gossip column items

---

* Halloween would also have had a sad resonance for Paul, whose mother, Mary, had died of breast cancer on October 31, 1956.

about Paul's dinner outings verified his presence, and an article in *Billboard*'s October 31 issue reported that he was recording at CBS, further pinpointing his location. Resourceful fans like DiFilippe and Rabe soon learned that the McCartneys were staying at the Stanhope, so one of the visit's luxuries—freedom from fans, autograph seekers, and the press—had now vanished.

McCartney's relationship with fans blew hot and cold. When he was in the mood, he would spend a few minutes chatting amiably with those permanently camped outside 7 Cavendish Avenue. He was deeply aware that he was lucky to have them, particularly now, with much of the world believing that he had single-handedly scuttled the Beatles, and with some of the Beatles fan base splintering into John and Paul camps. But like all three of his former bandmates, he also found the fans' round-the-clock attention intrusive, at times even oppressive.

When he turned up at CBS to find fans wanting to take photos, he refused to oblige them, and when he left the building, he would try to make it into his cab without further interaction.

"When he first came in, the fans didn't know where he was," Tim Geelan said. "As time went along, they found him, and that got a little tense. He'd leave the studio in the evening with the family, and they'd be there. That got to be a little bit of a problem, after awhile."[21]

As Linda elaborated, "Twenty kids would follow us wherever we went. Everywhere—hotel, restaurant, studio. After awhile, I asked them to lay off, and one of them turned and said, 'Well what the hell did you expect?' I hadn't expected that."[22]

Moreover, the fans were publishing accounts of their sightings in fanzines, and they were by no means hagiographic. One fan, Tess Basta, had taken to cutting class and hanging around outside the studio with her friend Linda.

"We got there at 9:00 a.m., and no one was there," Basta wrote. "We couldn't figure this out. We found out later that he absolutely, positively does not want to see anyone there in the morning and he scared them enough that no one went . . . Finally, he pulls up in a cab with Linda and Mary and Heather. Both of us standing in front of the entrance and he is paying the driver and scowling at us from inside the cab. Everyone gets out and he stops directly in front of us—only 3 feet away. We say good morning to him, and not only does he not say good morning, he says absolutely nothing but continues to stare at us, and I mean really looking at us. We were a little uneasy and my friend Linda finally asks him if we can take a picture and he says, 'Not in the morning' and leaves it at that and walks in.

"Linda and I found out afterward that we were very lucky as there were a few bad incidents with girls there in the morning. Then we knew why he was staring at us the way he was. He was looking to see if he recognized us. If he had previously warned us not to be there at that time of day. Obviously realizing we did not know he did not go into a tirade. In spite of the fact that most of the time he was in a miserable mood, Linda and I were glad he didn't decide to randomly abuse us that morning considering we were innocent."[23]

———

Recording Session

Monday, November 2, 1970.
CBS Studios, Studio B, New York.
Recording: 'Oh Woman, Oh Why.'
Mixing: 'Sunshine Sometimes.'

Entering his second month in New York, Paul decided to uncork some of that pent-up fan-induced frustration and capture it on tape. Although he had a demo with 30 new songs in his suitcase, he continued composing during the crossing from Le Havre to New York, and he began the week's sessions with a tune from the voyage, 'Oh Woman, Oh Why.' What he had in mind was a gritty rocker, and with McCracken and Seiwell, he developed an arrangement that captured the tense energy necessary to support an upper range, screaming vocal.

The song, or as much of it as McCartney had written, was about a jealous man who murders his cheating wife. But it's hard to ignore the obvious lyrical connections with his legal concerns—for example, "*I can't get by, 'cos my hands are tied.*" Even a line as commonplace as "*what have I done*" takes on meaning in a context where he is about to sue his friends.

After a few hours' rehearsal, with lots of improvisation (some of which became part of the arrangement), no master take was captured, and the musicians agreed it would be best to start fresh the next day. Keen to keep a mobile working library of his *Rupert* material, Paul spent the rest of the session mixing 'Sunshine Sometimes,' and he left with a dub of a preliminary stereo mix.

Recording Session

Tuesday, November 3, 1970.
CBS Studios, Studio B, New York.
Recording: 'Oh Woman, Oh Why' and 'Monkberry Moon Delight.'

Having spent Monday arranging the song's contours and textures, Paul, Hugh and Denny quickly perfected the instrumental backing for 'Oh Woman, Oh Why,' polishing it off before lunch. Starting off with a four-bar drum introduction, the rocker is characterized by a tough drum sound, recorded dry to leave the option of thickening it with studio reverb. As always, Seiwell brought lavish detail to the track, switching the focus from bass and toms to cymbals in some sections, and ratcheted up the song's drive by moving to a double-time beat.

"I just punched it a little bit harder," Seiwell said, "and tuned [the drums] a bit lower. Maybe the engineers goosed it a little bit. It was a killer drum sound."[24]

Geelan's opinion was that the credit lies with the drummer and his kit, rather than anything he was doing at the mixing desk. "Fortunately, Denny had a good drum set and he had them tuned properly. So it was very little effort to get a good sound out of it. I used my usual compliment of mics that I'd had good experience with before. A mic on the bass drum. We used a Shure 57 on the snare drum. The overhead mics were Neumann U67s. It was pretty much the setup that most places used at the time."[25]

Paul and Hugh both played electric guitar, Paul contributing a straightforwardly chunky rendering of the chords, and Hugh playing a slide guitar part in which he adopted both the timbre and technique—and even, at times, a couple of the riffs that Ry Cooder used on 'Memo from Turner,' the Mick Jagger song from the soundtrack of *Performance*. The similarity cannot be coincidence: Jagger's single was released only 11 days earlier, on October 23, and had ample airplay on New York's FM stations.

With the basic track down, Paul and Hugh doubled their guitar parts, with Hugh adding a few more slide figures, and Denny overdubbing a shaker and cowbell before the lunch break.

At the afternoon session, Paul introduced his bizarre melding of Lennonesque stream of consciousness surrealism, and a decidedly unappetizing milk shake recipe, 'Monkberry Moon Delight'—a song that sent Paul back to the piano, while Hugh continued playing electric guitar.

The sound Paul sought here was a bit circuslike, an effect created largely by a continuously rising and falling guitar figure, woven around a piano line built mostly of block chords. The three musicians spent the rest of the afternoon working through this odd concoction, but when the day ended, they did not have a satisfactory master take.

Recording Session

Thursday, November 5, 1970.
CBS Studios, Studio B, New York.
Recording: 'Monkberry Moon Delight' and 'Uncle Albert.'

There was no session on Wednesday, so on Thursday morning Paul and company returned to 'Monkberry Moon Delight.' One question that had come up at the Tuesday session was, what kind of piano sound did Paul want? This was not going to be a ballad, like 'The Back Seat of My Car,' and given its unusual lyrics—the opening lines are, "*So I sat in the attic / a piano up my nose / And the wind played a dreadful cantata*"—it occurred to Paul that the lush tone of a concert grand would not be suitable. CBS Studios, like EMI at Abbey Road, had a collection of keyboard instruments to choose from, and hearing Paul's ideas about the song, Geelan knew exactly what was needed.

"The piano looked like something that came out of your grandmother's house—a nondescript, big old, upright piano. To make that rinky-tink sound, thumbtacks, or some kind of metal is put on the hammers. And that's what we used on that session."[26]

With Paul pounding out the piano part and screaming a scratch vocal, McCracken played the looping guitar lines, coloring its sound with a phase pedal. Seiwell added a tambourine to his arsenal, and once the basic track was complete, Paul and Hugh fleshed it out with additional guitar lines.

In the afternoon, Paul unveiled another of his multipart compositions, built of three songs from his High Park demos, plus some new material, linked together as a suitelike composition. The opening section was 'We're So Sorry,' the gently wistful tune inspired by memories of Paul's uncle, and now renamed for him, 'Uncle Albert.' The second part would begin with verses in a quasi-vaudeville style before pivoting to two souvenirs of the Shetland trip, 'Hands Across the Water' and 'Gypsy Get Around,' the first used as a lively refrain and a midsong shift of focus, and the second functioning as the song's playout.

Paul called this second section 'Admiral Halsey.' It might seem strange—or at least, random—for a British musician to name a song for the American admiral William Halsey, Jr., the commander of the Third Fleet in the Pacific during World War II. He could just as easily have named the song 'Captain Swanson' after the fishing boat owner who guided the family to the Orkney Islands in July. But he was reaching for an abstract name, and the McCartneys arrived in New York less than two weeks after the release of the war film *Tora! Tora! Tora!*, an American-Japanese coproduction starring James Whitmore as Admiral Halsey. Paul and Linda may have caught the film early in their visit, but even if they did not, they would have seen posters and newspaper advertisements for the film, and subliminally noted Whitmore's starring role.

"I don't know where I got Halsey's name," Paul explained, "but you read it in magazines and sometimes they just fall into your songs."[27]

Until now, Paul had made his joins compositionally and then recorded the composite works whole. This time, he wanted to record the song in two separate pieces and edit them later. The sections were in different keys, but close enough for easy modulations, and mostly in 4|4 time, although the 'Admiral Halsey' verse section moves between 4|4 and 3|4. There were tempo changes, too, which added to the complexity of learning the song.

At this first session, McCartney and company attempted, without success, to get a master take of only the 'Uncle Albert' section.

Geelan did, however, capture them letting off some steam in a quick-tempo jam, with Paul strumming briskly on his Martin, Denny playing a quick, rolling beat, and Hugh on electric guitar, playing jazz licks that inspired some classic McCartney scat-singing that coalesces, for no apparent reason, as a verse from the folk song 'Cumberland Gap.'

Recording Session

Friday, November 6, 1970.
CBS Studios, Studio B, New York.
Recording: 'Uncle Albert' and 'Admiral Halsey.'

With 'Uncle Albert' under their fingers, Paul, Hugh and Denny set down the basic track, with Paul on his Martin acoustic guitar, Hugh playing electric guitar and Denny executing a gentle drum part most notable for the gracefully rolling, punctuating figures that followed each line of the verse. Paul and Hugh overdubbed extra guitar lines, with Paul adding two more guitar parts, played through a rotating Leslie speaker, Hugh replacing his original part, and Denny adding a tambourine.

"That song represented a breakthrough in our musical relationship," McCracken said. "Paul is a genius. He sees and hears everything he wants and would give specific instructions to me and the drummer. But he didn't know what he wanted the guitar part to be like on this song. I asked him to trust me—and he did. After I came up with the parts, he was very pleased. For the rest of the record, Paul let me try things out before making any suggestions."[28]

The electric guitar part Hugh concocted brought together sweetly harmonized, occasionally jazz-tinged chords, punctuated with single-string figures that play off the melody and create much of the action between the vocal lines.

McCartney had more specific suggestions for Seiwell, who until now had been on his own in creating the drum parts. Paul was planning to ask George Martin to orchestrate the complete 'Uncle Albert/Admiral Halsey,' and he had ideas about how the drumming should fit into the larger picture.

"I wanna break that up and orchestrate it a little bit more," Paul told Seiwell after an early take, "so don't play a regular beat under it, try to play something that goes along with the vocal and leaves a lot of space."

It was the first time Paul had given Seiwell specific direction, and as the drummer recounted, "I fooled around a minute, and I came up with the part. He went, 'Oh that's brilliant!' And that was it."[29]

'Admiral Halsey,' the more complex and varied half of the song, came together at the same session. Paul switched to the tack piano he had used on 'Monkberry Moon Delight,' with Hugh remaining on electric guitar, and Denny continuing to play a drum part that bounced off the wordless melody Paul sang as a rough vocal.

At this moment, the lyrics for this multipart extravaganza were very unfinished: some of the words for 'Uncle Albert,' were sketched out, but Paul had nothing for 'Admiral Halsey' beyond the opening reference to the admiral, and the 'Hands Across the Water' and 'Gypsy Get Around' sections.

Toward the end of the session, Paul doubled his piano part on an electric organ (although when he mixed the track, he opted to drop this addition). Together, the two parts of the song ran about five minutes, and Paul could already envision them edited together as a miniature rock symphony:

Movement One: 'We're So Sorry' [0:00–2:16]
Movement Two: 'Hands Across the Water' [2:16–3:26]
Movement Three: 'Gypsy Get Around' [3:26–3:49]

Movement Four: 'Hands Across the Water (Reprise)' [3:49–4:22]
Movement Five: 'Gypsy Get Around (Reprise)' [4:22–4:50]

Given the song's complexities, and with that symphonic idea in mind, Paul added 'Uncle Albert/Admiral Halsey' to the list of songs to be sent to George Martin for orchestration. Among his instructions: the join would take place at the 2:17 mark, but there was no easy edit point, so Paul would need a connecting orchestral figure to cover the key and tempo shifts between the two pieces.

———

Though McCartney's legal team was hard at work collecting information and assembling their legal arguments, Paul clung to the sliver of hope that he could persuade the other Beatles to release him from the partnership—a hope Linda encouraged, as well.

"*Ram* was made during that period when everyone was very negative towards Paul," Linda later explained. "But I'm not saying that Paul is an angel either. If they had talked the thing out they would have seen what they thought about Paul wasn't true and what he thought about them wasn't true. It simply wasn't the three of them against Paul. It was four people who had to live. There were just too many personality problems."[30]

With George Harrison still in town, and staying at the Plaza, just over a mile south of the Stanhope, on Fifth Avenue, it seemed sensible to see if he could get George to better understand his position.

Paul and George had, at this point, a warily friendly, occasionally fraught relationship. They had met as schoolboys with a mutual interest in the guitar. Paul was a year older, but George was the better player. Paul brought George to John Lennon, who weighed the age gap (John was 17, Paul was 15, George was 14) against George's guitar skills and let George join the Quarrymen.

Lennon and McCartney continued to treat George as a junior partner, only rarely, and reluctantly, considering his songs worth recording, something George largely accepted until 1966, when he brought three songs to the *Revolver* sessions. The Beatles recorded all three, releasing three more of his songs in 1967 and five in 1968. But throughout the January 1969 sessions for what became *Let It Be*, he struggled to get John and Paul to focus on his songs, and it wasn't until 'Something,' late in 1969, that he was given the A side of a single for the first time (albeit as part of a double A-sided release, with Lennon's 'Come Together').

Paul's condescension toward George continued to the very moment George's complaints of his second-class treatment were about to be resolved—at the September 9, 1969, meeting, when Paul's response to John's proposal for more equitable song division on future albums was to comment that until that year, he did not think George's efforts were worthy.

Further complicating matters, the Klein dispute reconfigured the power distribution within the Beatles. Suddenly, John, George and Ringo were united in their belief that Klein was the man to help them dig out of their post-Epstein financial problems, and Paul was on his own, in the position of a supplicant, all but begging to be released from the partnership.

George had finished mastering *All Things Must Pass*, and its release date—November 27 in the United States; three days later in Britain—had been announced. Capitol Records had been creating a buzz about the three-disc set in the American press since September, but now it was time to begin marketing it in earnest. As McCartney and company were recording 'Uncle Albert' and 'Admiral Halsey,' on November 6, George hosted a group of music journalists at Apple/ABKCO to hear the album from start to finish.

Just as Paul was summoning up the courage to call George at the Plaza, George called him. "They talked for a while," according to an unsigned piece in *Rolling Stone*, "but it still looks like the Beatles need a new bass player."[31] Not only was nothing resolved, but in some ways, the tensions were exacerbated.

"I remember having one classic conversation with George Harrison," Paul said, speaking of this period. "I said, 'Look, George, I want to get off the label,' and as I say it now I almost feel like I'm lying with the devil's tongue, but I swear George said to me, 'You'll stay on the fucking label. Hare Krishna.' That's how it was, that's how the times were."[32]

Before the conversation ended, however, Paul and George agreed to meet in early December, when they would both still be in town.*

In the meantime, Paul got a glimpse of George's work when 'My Sweet Lord' and 'Isn't It a Pity,' the double A-sided single from *All Things Must Pass*, hit the airwaves on November 9.

'My Sweet Lord' was a catchy tune, George singing his interreligious (but mostly Hindu) Gospel in a cross between the Chiffons' 'He's So Fine' and the Edwin Hawkins Singers' 'Oh Happy Day.'†

But it was 'Isn't It a Pity' that caught Paul's attention. The slow, almost dirgelike song, thick with Phil Spector's Wall-of-Sound orchestration, lamented "*how we break each other's hearts / And cause each other pain.*" The song was not new to Paul: George had played it, in a gentle, acoustic

---

* *Rolling Stone* had reported in its November 26 issue that the phone call ended in a fight and that Paul and George did not meet. Since the meeting took place after the issue went to press, the magazine was not technically incorrect, but the article also asserted that Paul and George had not spoken in about a year, and that Paul and John had not spoken in two years, both wildly inaccurate. (In John's case, *Rolling Stone*'s estimate meant that they had not spoken since the release of the *White Album*.) In December, Lennon sent *Rolling Stone* an irritated, handwritten note (reproduced in the February 4, 1971, issue), saying that Paul and George *did* meet, and also noted the other errors before adding, "All the shit that fits is more like it," a reference *Rolling Stone*'s cover slogan, "All the News That Fits" (itself a parody of the *New York Times*' slogan, "All the News That's Fit to Print").

† George was sued in 1971 by Bright Tunes, the publisher of 'He's So Fine,' over similarities between the songs. By the time the long court saga ended, in 1976, Harrison and Allen Klein had parted ways, and Klein bought Bright Tunes, becoming his former client's legal adversary. Judge Richard Owen—a trained composer whose opera *Mary Dyer* was later performed in New York—ruled that Harrison had subconsciously plagiarized from 'He's So Fine.' But he also found Klein's acquisition of Bright Tunes inappropriate, and in an innovative ruling, he directed George to pay Klein the $587,000 he had paid for Bright Tunes and required Klein to transfer the rights to 'He's So Fine' to George.

guitar version, during the January 1969 sessions. But it was hard for Paul not to hear, in the arrangement George was about to release, a more specific message, directed to him.

The last half of the 7'10" song repeats the song's chord progression over and over—the same move that closes Paul's 'Hey Jude' (which was one second longer)—but with slide guitar and piano figures moving in and out of the thick texture while George first riffs on the lyrics and then settles into falsetto repetitions of *what a pity*." Around five minutes in, a male chorus joins the dense ensemble, and a minute later, the choral melody morphs into the *"Na, na, na, na-na-na na"* ending to McCartney's 'Hey Jude.'

Was this an innocent in-joke, or a barbed complaint? During the July 1968 recording sessions for 'Hey Jude,' George had followed Paul's vocal lines, in early takes, with short guitar responses. That wasn't how Paul envisioned the song,* and he asked George to stop. With Paul on piano and John on acoustic guitar, there was nothing for George to do, so he spent the session in the control room.

The matter arose again six months later, when the Beatles were recording Paul's 'Two of Us.' Finding George's guitar line unnecessarily fussy, Paul explained what he wanted, likening George's approach to when "you were playing guitar all through 'Hey Jude.'" George responded calmly, "I don't mind, I'll play whatever you want me to play, or I won't play at all. Whatever it is that will *please* you, I'll do it."[33]

And here it was again, 17 months later, evidently still a sore spot.

———

Recording Session

Tuesday, November 10, 1970.
CBS Studios, Studio B, New York.
Recording: 'Too Many People.'

McCartney gave McCracken and Seiwell a light week, telling them he needed them only on Tuesday and Friday, and spending the remaining days catching up with bass overdubs, including the plodding, four-square line that magnified the circus spirit of 'Monkberry Moon Delight,' and more fluid bass lines, with dotted rhythms and sliding figures, for 'Uncle Albert' and 'Admiral Halsey,' to which he also added another electric guitar and, near the transition between the two songs, a xylophone.

---

* It was not, however, without merit: Wilson Pickett, who is unlikely to have heard about the private dispute, recorded a soulful cover of 'Hey Jude' in 1969, with bluesy guitar figures—played by Duane Allman—following the vocal lines, as George had proposed.

On Tuesday, it was all hands on deck, and after a weekend partly spent sparring with George, both directly and through the apparent subtext of 'Isn't It a Pity,' Paul chose to work on 'Too Many People,' his most overt musical response to the battlefield that Apple had become. Though the song most specifically takes John and Yoko to task, George's position in the Klein camp made him an equal target of Paul's irritation.

'Too Many People' was not a hidden message, but rather, a vitriolic challenge to the public personas that John and Yoko were projecting. Paul did not discuss what he meant by "*preaching practices*" or "*your lucky break*" with Hugh and Denny nor did they ask whether the song was an attack on John when he played it to them, backing himself on acoustic guitar. Though Paul was beginning to break down the barriers with his sidemen, they intuitively understood that the Beatles remained a taboo subject.

"Our headspace was that we were in there trying to do the best job," Seiwell said. "We knew every one of these songs was going to be around for a long time, and we were just trying to do our very best. So we stayed away from all of that crap. Paul never brought it into the studio either. We respected him and he respected our professionalism—it was better left unsaid."[34]

Paul seemed intent on fitting out each of his songs with structural peculiarities, and in this case, it was a contrast between the straightforward verses, in G major, and the slightly more complex bridge, in A minor. The oddity here is that both times the bridge appears, it is used for guitar solos rather than vocals.

The song was set down quickly, with Paul on acoustic guitar, Hugh providing rising electric guitar figures between lines, and a bit of crunch in more emphatic sections, and Denny providing a driving beat.

With plenty of time left in the session, McCartney and Seiwell added extra percussion, including a shaker and a cowbell. And to Hugh's amazement, Paul recorded the two extended bridge solos in a single take.

Recording Session

Friday, November 13, 1970.
CBS Studios, Studio B, New York.
Recording: 'Little Woman Love.'

A full month into his New York sessions, Paul now had lots of basic tracks, and the makings of a varied collection, with everything from simple rockers to complex constructions. If one of the complaints about *McCartney* was that its homespun quality seemed a backward move from the burnished brilliance of *Abbey Road*, these new recordings were closer to the high expectations the critics had of him. (His focus on the negative reviews was scarcely offset by the fact that more than six months after its release, *McCartney* still held a place on the *Billboard* 200 album chart.)

The song Paul brought in on November 13, 'Little Woman Love,' was a slighter effort but its rockabilly sensibility added yet another touch of variety to the stack of tracks he was amassing. And he arranged a surprise: he invited the great jazz bassist Milt Hinton, then 60, to play on the session.

Hinton, who had worked with McCracken and Seiwell (and Spinozza, for that matter), brought the rounded, flexible sound of the acoustic double bass to the song, giving it a slinky quality that an electric bass cannot match, and which, more importantly, suited the spirit of Paul's rollicking, New Orleans–inspired piano part.

"In the days of acoustic bass, before the Fender bass came along, acoustic bass players in New York like Milt Hinton and George Devillier were much in demand as session players," Geelan explained. "Those guys you could put any microphone on, as long as it was decent quality, and they'd give you a great sound."[35]

Hinton recorded his part live with McCartney on the piano, and singing a rough vocal; McCracken playing melodic figures on electric guitar; and Seiwell combining a steady beat with layers of fleet figuration that filled out the texture.

Recording Sessions

Monday–Wednesday, November 16–18, 1970.
CBS Studios, Studio B, New York.
Recording: 'Heart of the Country' and 'Smile Away.'

Paul's booking at CBS Studios was coming to an end, but he was nowhere near finished. He began his final week with 'Heart of the Country,' another paean to country life, composed even before Paul had come to fully appreciate the charms of High Park—and a song he and Linda were so fond of that it seems strange that he held it back until now.

"That's the real life," McCartney told an interviewer in London about his farm. "I just have to get away from all this concrete. It's very rough up there, but it's the life I have always dreamed about.[36] I can breathe the air. It never ceases to amaze me that I put seeds in the ground, the sun shines at the right time, the rain comes on the right time, then something grows, and you can eat it. That's something to give thanks for."[37]

The recording had a simplicity that matched the song's subject and used only 6 of the available 16 tracks, one of which was Paul's bass, the song's only overdub. Paul played his Martin acoustic and sang, and Hugh, on electric guitar, contributed alternate voicings of the chords Paul played, and brief lead figures between the vocal lines. Denny, however, felt that a standard drum sound was not right for the song, so although the session tracking sheet assigns him two tracks—one listed as "bass drum," the other as "drums"—his setup was more complicated.

"We were approaching another genre of music," Seiwell explained, "so I looked around the studio to find some stuff that I could replace the drum set with. I found a plastic trash can and I hooked my bass drum pedal up to it, so that was the bass drum. I taped up my high-hat cymbals so that they made no noise whatsoever, and for the snare drum part I found a very thin sheet of sheet metal and I laid it down and played brushes on it. The kit was made up of all these weird things that I found around the studio."[38]

With the addition of bass guitar, which Paul recorded in a solo session the next day, 'Heart of the Country' was complete—the only song from the New York sessions about which that could be said.

'Smile Away,' the aggressive rocker Paul and his sidemen recorded that afternoon, is as different from 'Heart of the Country' as can be. Written in Scotland, and included among the demos he recorded during the spring, 'Smile Away' was another bit of Beatles fallout, a comment on those with whom he did not see eye to eye—or at least, that was how he explained it to Seiwell.

"With regard to 'Smile Away,'" Denny said, "Paul used to do this thing where you smile away with your mouth, but your eyes glare like you really hate the guy."[39]

The raw sound of the recording, right from the "1, 2, 3, 4!" count-in, preserved in the finished version, can be attributed to the fact that the heart of the song was captured live, with Paul and Hugh playing mildly distorted electric guitar lines, and Seiwell delivering a steady, solid rock beat. Paul's rough guide vocal with its patches of anger and sarcasm, along with ample falsetto whoops and woos, so completely captured the song's spirit that he decided to keep it.

Once the basic track was down, Paul had Denny doubled his drumming. He also added a third guitar track, with the song's solos, the first with light distortion and a touch of tremolo, the second cleaner and more fluid.

Paul devoted the Tuesday and Wednesday sessions to overdubbing bass lines on several tracks, including 'Smile Away,' for which Paul wanted a thick tone with a touch of distortion. He achieved it by plugging the bass into a preamp in the mixing console and turning up the gain until it began to distort, then sending the output of that first preamp into a second, which also overloaded.

"I love fuzz bass," Paul explained. "It helps you be a bit more lyrical because it makes the notes linger, gives you a bit more sustain. That used to really turn the whole thing around."[40]

Recording Session

Thursday, November 19, 1970.
CBS Studios, Studio B, New York.
Recording: 'Little Lamb Dragonfly.'

For his final day of recording with McCracken and Seiwell at CBS, Paul brought in 'Little Lamb Dragonfly,' the combination of his ode to a lamb that didn't make it, and his musings about a dragonfly that he saw hovering at his window. Paul earmarked this for his *Rupert* soundtrack. Notably, the songs set aside for *Rupert* were not throwaways or lesser melodies. 'Little Lamb Dragonfly' and 'When the Wind Is Blowing' are among the most ravishing tunes he had written in the last couple of years, and 'Sunshine Sometime' had an exotic accent that set it apart from most of his work.

Still, though the music for 'Little Lamb Dragonfly' was complete, the lyrics remained unfinished, with only a few lines sketched out. When Paul sang the song to McCracken and Seiwell—and when they recorded the basic track—he sang the words he had, and either hummed or sang "la, la, la" for the rest.

But the song's gentle spirit comes through the delicate textures of the nearly wordless performance recorded in the morning session. Paul and Hugh, on acoustic guitars—Paul playing a 12-string, Hugh playing 6-string—laid down the spine of the song, with Denny keeping time. The master take clocked in at an impressive 6'25".

That afternoon, Denny overdubbed extra percussion, including shakers, while Linda was lured out of the control room to add a triangle part, and Hugh and Paul doubled and then tripled their guitar lines. And with those overdubs, the six weeks of ensemble sessions at CBS Studio B came to an end.

Paul, however, had booked one more day for overdubs, and in addition to tying up loose ends on several tracks, he added piano to 'Little Lamb Dragonfly.'

With the basic tracking sessions at CBS's Studio B concluded, Paul reserved the upstairs section of a downtown restaurant and invited everyone who had been involved in the project—Denny Seiwell, David Spinozza, Hugh McCracken, Tim Geelan, Ted Brosnan, and their wives—to join them. "It was a wrap party," was how Spinozza described it. "He bought us dinner and thanked us for playing on the record."[41] Any lingering tension created by Spinozza's early exit from the sessions was put to bed that night.

As his New York sessions progressed, Paul began entertaining, if not actively exploring, thoughts of performing live—not on a Sid Bernstein–arranged tour with the Rascals, but in a one-off performance at Boston College's Alumni Stadium on April 18, 1971, for an audience of 35,000. The concert, which was the brainchild of Joe Maher, the chairman of the college's social committee, and Robert Chernov, a local promoter who was donating his services, was meant to raise money for a new concert venue at Boston College. McCartney was asked to donate his fee as well, but in return, the concert building would be named for him.

The obstacles were considerable. Although a letter of intent was issued by Robert Weinberg, Richard Sinnott, the special counsel to Boston's mayor, Kevin White, objected on the grounds that a Jefferson Airplane concert a couple of weeks earlier had devolved into what Sinnott called "near riot conditions."[42] Other forces in the city government were interested in helping the plan move forward, and by late November, mediation talks were underway.

Who McCartney would have used as a backing band was not discussed, but April was five months away, and if Paul were inclined, he could make it happen. He did not give Maher a flat no, and in mid-November, Maher and Chernov flew to London to meet with Peter Brown, who was acting as McCartney's manager. It is unknown when Paul and Brown might have discussed the prospective concert; Brown was in New York at the end of October, and Maher told *Rolling Stone* that Brown "sounded optimistic."[43]

The plan, though reported in several Boston and national publications, may have been out-right fiction. In mid-December, John Eastman told *Rolling Stone* that there was never a meeting between Mahler and Brown,[44] and that may be: Brown said he has no recollection of any such discussions.[45]

But even if the plan was entirely a fantasy of Maher's, the reports of Paul performing live "set Boston alight," as *Rolling Stone* put it, and Paul was certainly aware of the story. Given his tendency to file information away until he has a use for it, it may have occurred to him that when he was ready to return to the road, universities might be an interesting, relatively low-pressure place to start.

But for the moment, Paul had just completed six weeks of basic recording, and much work remained. There were lead and backing vocals to add—the latter to be recorded with Linda. Paul also had additional guitar and keyboard parts in mind for several tracks, and of course, there were the songs he had sent to George Martin for orchestrations, which he planned to record in New York as well.

Hanging over it all was the lawsuit, which John Eastman and David Hirst told him would be ready for filing in December.

What Paul needed now was some head-clearing and reinvigoration. On November 21, 1970, the McCartneys took off for some tropical downtime in Barbados. There, with the Sandy Lane Hotel as their headquarters, they went dancing, attended a motorcycle race at the National Stadium, and chilled out on the beach, Paul often with a guitar in hand.

9

BACK ACROSS THE WATER

—

While Paul was in Barbados, the Apple universe rumbled along under the Klein regime. George Harrison's *All Things Must Pass* was released to glowing reviews—Richard Williams, in *Melody Maker*, likened it to the Beatles' *Rubber Soul*, adding that it is "as good as having a new Beatles album."[1] Press copies of John Lennon's *Plastic Ono Band* were in critics' hands as well, and *Rolling Stone* was touting it, in its "Random Notes" column, as "the most powerful work of 1970."[2]

Mary Hopkin, one of Apple's most successful discoveries, announced in late November that she was leaving the label, noting that she had not seen Paul—who brought her to Apple and produced her early recordings—for more than a year. But Badfinger remained on the roster and flew to New York for a concert at Ungano's, on November 24, to promote their newly released *No Dice* album. Since George and Pattie Harrison were in attendance, George took to the stage to introduce the band. Asked by a reporter whether the Beatles might get back together—already a reflexive question for any journalist who spotted a Beatle—he cryptically replied, "stranger things have happened."

That was enough to lead *NME* to wonder, in a headline, "Could Beatles Reunite in '71 to Cut LP?"[3] while *Disc and Music Echo* splashed "Come Together!—The Beatles May Play Again—Live"[4] across the top of its front page. Both the *NME* and *Disc* stories were based on more than George's offhand comment. Both papers, as well as *Rolling Stone*,[5] reported that Paul had met with George and possibly John, and that further clear-the-air talks were planned. The British papers cited in-the-know (but anonymous) sources; *Rolling Stone*, noting that all four Beatles were in New York, attributed its information to Allen Klein.

There was a molecule of truth in this, and lots of exaggeration. Paul returned to New York on December 4 and met with George shortly thereafter. It was partly a social visit—Pattie and Linda were there, too[6]—but Paul and George had some time on their own to discuss Paul's desire to leave Apple, both as an artist and as a director. Rather than taking a hard line, George repeated the talking points Klein had given him (and John and Ringo) about the potential problems inherent in Paul's severing ties.

"No, Allen says there would be tax complications," Paul remembered George telling him. His response: "I don't give a damn about tax considerations, let me go and I'll worry about the tax considerations."[7] In the end, Paul and George agreed that everyone would meet in London, in January.

John and Yoko, meanwhile, landed in New York on December 1 and took up residence at the Regency Hotel. High on their agenda were meetings with Klein about the promotion of their twin *Plastic Ono Band* albums, and the freshly revived lawsuit in which Maclen Music, on behalf of Lennon, McCartney, and Apple, was suing Northern Songs for underpayment of royalties, to the tune of £5 million ($12.5 million), a saber Klein had been rattling since late 1969.

The Lennons met with D. A. Pennebaker, who screened *Sweet Toronto*, his film about the Toronto Rock and Roll Revival, at which the Plastic Ono Band had performed in September 1969. And with Yoko directing, they made two films, *Up Your Legs Forever*, for which volunteers dropped their pants so that their legs could be filmed, slowly, from toe to thigh, and *Fly*, in which a fly was filmed making its way around the body of a naked woman (with unseen sugar water keeping it on track).

Also on Lennon's schedule were a couple of interviews, both with journalists who were on friendly terms with John and Yoko.

The first, a nearly four and a half hour sit-down with Jann Wenner of *Rolling Stone* at the ABKCO offices on December 8, 1970, was entirely unbuttoned, and unfiltered: John, with occasional contributions from Yoko, discussed *Plastic Ono Band* and their recent involvement with Dr. Arthur Janov, the primal scream therapist (the experience of which inspired much of the album), and offered a dour survey of the Beatles—both their history and the current state of play, with descriptions of the boardroom battles between Klein and the Eastmans, and withering comments about Paul.

Asked about the *McCartney* album, Lennon described it as "rubbish" and likened Paul to the pop crooner Engelbert Humperdinck. Among his copious gripes about *Let it Be*, he complained that "I can't speak for George, but I pretty damn well know we got fed up being sidemen for Paul." He skewers Paul for being the last to take LSD but the first to announce it, and when discussing Klein and the Eastmans, he asserted that Lee Eastman had attacked Klein "with class snobbery," adding, "But Paul fell for that bullshit, because Eastman's got Picassos on the wall and because he's got some sort of East Coast suit; form and not substance. Now that's McCartney."

Even in more generous moments, he gave with one hand and took back with the other. "I think he's capable of great work and I think he will do it," he said of his former songwriting partner. "But I can't see Paul doing it twice."[8]

Rolling Stone published the explosive interview in two installments, in the January 7 and February 4 issues (which hit the newsstands on December 16, 1970, and January 13, 1971).

John's second interview was with Howard Smith on December 12, to be aired the next night on Smith's weekly show on WABC-FM. Smith, who wrote the "Scenes" column for the alternative weekly newspaper the *Village Voice*, had known Yoko during her New York avant-garde years, and his supportive coverage back then gave him an instant in with John. That meant frequent access for long, candid interviews. Smith had followed John and Yoko on their various errands during the week, including to the film shoots—his legs were among those filmed for *Up Your Legs Forever*, although it is unknown whether they made the final cut—so the 90-minute interview focused mainly on those activities and the new album, with none of the disparagement of McCartney that Lennon gave Wenner.

In the days between the interviews, John telephoned Paul, and they agreed to meet for dinner on Sunday, December 13. The chat was pleasant, with John mentioning that one reason he wanted to meet was to discuss the Maclen/Northern Songs dispute, focusing on the possibility that they might receive some back royalties (and gliding past the fact that Paul was not consulted before Klein filed suit in his name). He also asked if Paul had heard George's album, commenting, "He's the hip boy. Still, he's gotta follow it up! He-he-he-he!"[9]

Having been in New York since October, Paul was seeing the seasons change: when he arrived, it was warm enough to go out in a sport coat, but now there was snow on the ground. He was thinking about getting back to Scotland—not London—but he had an unfinished album on his hands, and he wanted to do more work.

"I got a call from Paul one day," Geelan recalled, "and he said, 'Can we get some more time?' And the studio just wasn't available, we had Columbia artists who had booked time well in advance. But we did have another studio downtown. The Columbia 30th Street Studio had a smaller room called Studio D. It was very, very small, but it was good for vocal overdubs. And for a few days Paul went down there with an engineer named Larry Keyes, and they did vocal overdubs."[10]

Recording Sessions

Monday–Friday, December 6–11, 1970.
CBS Studios, 30th Street, Studio D, New York.
Overdubbing: 'Monkberry Moon Delight,' 'Uncle Albert,' 'Oh Woman, Oh Why?' 'Three Legs,' 'Long Haired Lady,' and 'The Back Seat of My Car.'

The Columbia 30th Street Studios were in a converted church at 207 East 30th Street, between Second and Third Avenues. The building, dedicated in 1875, was used as a church until the early 1940s, when it briefly became the home of radio station WLIB. When Columbia took it over in 1948, the large sanctuary became Studio C, a room big enough to accommodate an orchestra. Countless enduring albums were made there, among them Glenn Gould's 1955 debut recording of Bach's *Goldberg Variations*; Leonard Bernstein's recording of the *West Side Story* Broadway cast album (1957) and many of the New York Philharmonic's recordings with both Bernstein and Bruno Walter; Billie Holiday's *Lady in Satin* (1958) and Miles Davis's *Kind of Blue* (1959).

Studio D, originally the church's sacristy, was an intimate room, suited to the vocal overdubbing Paul planned to do. For Paul, vocal overdubs were not always just a matter of waiting for the red light to go on and singing the tune. Often, he had a particular sound in mind, as if his song were being sung by a fictional character that Paul was playing, a character whose sound was not necessarily confined to the natural timbre and quality of his voice.

This was certainly the case for 'Monkberry Moon Delight,' one of the songs on his agenda for the week. Paul's vision for 'Monkberry' required a powerful, raspy sound that was well beyond even his Little Richard screaming voice. Jim Reeves, who was engineering other projects at 30th Street when Paul was recording there, has said that Paul sang 90 takes of the song's vocal to create that rasp. That was more or less true, if exaggerated.

"Larry Keyes told me at the time that Paul sang it a few times to get his voice hoarse," Geelan recalls, "which is the opposite of what most singers want to do. But that's what he wanted for that particular track. Then he recorded the master take."

'Uncle Albert' required a sonic trick that was easier on Paul's larynx. The main part of the song required straightforward ballad singing, with a touch of falsetto at the verse ends. But it occurred to Paul that in the final verse—shortly before the join with 'Admiral Halsey'—his vocal should sound as if it were being heard through a telephone. Paul would be two characters, as if he had telephoned his uncle in Liverpool to apologize because *"we haven't done a bloody thing all day"*—or, as it was understood by engineer Dixon Van Winkle, who would soon join Paul's New York recording team, a conversation between Uncle Albert and Admiral Halsey.

To get that sound, Geelan explained, "You would take the vocal track and put it through an equalizer, cutting off all the low frequencies and high frequencies to produce that telephone kind of sound. Every television cop show that you see, where someone is on the phone, that's how they do that sound."[11]

Van Winkle, listening to the tapes a few weeks later, spotted a mistake in that section. "If you listen carefully, you'll hear Paul gurgling right before the telephone voice comes in. That sound was his imitation of a British telephone ring. He was supposed to give the engineer a cue when he wanted the low-pass filter dropped in for the Admiral Halsey character. The engineer (Keyes) made the switch too early, and the filter came in on one of the gurgles! Paul didn't care, though. To him, it was all about the feel of the music."[12]

Also on Paul's dubbing schedule was 'Oh Woman, Oh Why?,' a track that needed a touch of the grit heard on 'Monkberry Moon Delight,' without straying so far from his standard rocker voice; 'Three Legs,' to which he brought several distinct vocal styles—a smooth blues voice, at first, and his harder-edge rock voice (to which a touch of reverb was added) in contrasting sections; and 'Long Haired Lady,' a song that relies heavily on Linda's vocal contributions, although for the moment, Paul recorded only his own lead vocal. And having recorded a bass line to 'The Back Seat of My Car' during one of the undocumented dubbing sessions in November, he now added the lead vocal.

At the weekend, the McCartneys decided to head back to High Park for the holidays. John had left a message canceling their Sunday dinner meeting and proposing Monday instead. Paul returned the call, but John and Yoko were out filming, so he left a message saying that he, too, needed to cancel on Sunday, and that he could not make the Monday meeting either. Irritated that Paul had not proposed another date, John called the Stanhope, but Paul had already left for Scotland.

That Monday, however, Lee and John Eastman met with Allen Klein, mainly to discuss the Maclen suit. The Eastmans' concern was that Klein was pushing the suit for the sake of his own fee, not to further John's and Paul's interests. Klein knew he would never persuade them otherwise, but also believed that he had the upper hand: if royalties were shaken loose, McCartney and his advisers/in-laws would not complain.

The Eastmans also raised a tax issue that was coming to a head. Four days earlier, Apple was notified that it was listed for a hearing before the General Commissioners of Income Tax on December 17. This, the Eastmans argued, was a consequence of Klein's unwillingness to provide a proper accounting of Apple's operations.

With their concerns about Klein's handling of those two issues duly conveyed, Lee Eastman returned to his Park Avenue apartment, and John Eastman cabbed directly to Kennedy Airport for the first leg of the long trek to join Paul and Linda at High Park.

Shortly after he arrived in Scotland, Paul got word that the first part of John's *Rolling Stone* interview was on the stands. *Rolling Stone*, then only three years old, and still considered an "underground" paper, was not easy to come by in Campbeltown, so Paul had a copy overnighted from London. Spreading out the issue on his kitchen table, he sat down to read the 11-page installment. Paging through and scanning for his name, the first things he saw were innocuous references to who played what at certain Beatles sessions, with hardly any criticism, even between the lines. He even gave Paul credit for the "newspaper taxis" image in 'Lucy in the Sky with Diamonds.'

Flicking on, he saw some snippiness that he could shrug off—John's response to a question about his slide guitar solo on 'Get Back,' for example. "When Paul was feeling kindly, he would give me a solo!" There was something, he had to admit, to John's complaint that Paul stepped in to run the Beatles after Epstein's death. Elsewhere in the interview, he even thanked Paul for doing it.

Until recently, all four had avoided public discussion of the Beatles' inner workings, and John's announcement that the Beatles were in dire financial straits in January 1969 was a departure that, in Paul's view, did more harm than good: for a shark like Klein, reading about the Beatles' financial troubles was like blood in the water. Now John was putting *everything* out there—not only in the interview, but on his new *Plastic Ono Band* album, too: in the song 'God,' he sings a long list of things he no longer believes in, a list that ends with the Beatles.

Paul continued paging and skimming, and there it was. Wenner asks John what he thinks of George's album, and he's lukewarm, but adds, "I don't want to hurt George's feelings." But asked, "What do you think of Paul's?" John says, flat out, "I thought Paul's was rubbish."

Paul was incensed. Yes, he had said in his self-interview that John's recent projects gave him no pleasure, but he didn't call them *rubbish*. Now, John's post–primal scream therapy candor made everything fair game. And this was only Part One, with another installment to come.

Paul knew, too, that however long he hid out in Scotland, he would eventually be asked for his reaction, and he would have to craft a response. How to play it? John's comments were too brutal to just brush off—that would seem glib. The reality was that he was livid, and hurt, and perhaps he should allow some of that to come through—it would be only human—without baring his feelings entirely. But that would be unseemly: however wounded he was by John's bitterness, anger and slice-and-dice style, that was his business. Plus, John knew him well enough to know how these comments would land; why publicly confirm that he had scored a direct hit?

For public consumption, he adopted a surprising spin, admitting that John's criticism touched on his own insecurities, and that he took it fully to heart, until others persuaded him that it was unreasonable.

"I hated it," he said, when he could put some distance between himself and the interview. "You can imagine, I sat down and pored over every little paragraph, every little sentence. 'Does he really think that of me?' I thought. And at the time, I thought, 'It's me. I am. That's just what I'm like.

He's captured me so well; I'm a turd, you know.' I sat down and really thought, 'I'm just nothin'. But then, well, kind of people who dug me, like Linda said, 'Now you know that's not true, you're joking. He's got a grudge, man; the guy's trying to polish you off.' Gradually I started to think, great, that's not true. I'm not really like Engelbert; I don't just write ballads. And that kept me kind of hanging on; but at the time, I tell you, it hurt me. Whew. Deep."[13]

He tried out another approach, too—a sober analysis that disarmed John's criticisms as fanciful, spur-of-the-moment quips.

"I know John," Paul said, "and I know that most of it was just something to tell the newspapers. He was in that mood then and he wanted all that to be said. I think, now, whilst he probably doesn't *regret* it, he didn't mean every single syllable of it. I mean, he came out with all stuff like I'm like Engelbert Humperdinck. I know he doesn't really think that."[14]

What he was not saying was that he was furious enough to skip the planned meeting with John, George and Ringo in London. Let them see him in court. The case was prepared, the paperwork was ready, and now John Eastman was there to explain that the Maclen suit and the new tax issue added greater urgency to Paul's lawsuit. All Eastman needed was Paul's go-ahead. Paul promised a final decision by Christmas.

For the girls' sake, he maintained a veneer of holiday cheer. He took them into Campbeltown, where Santa's Grotto was set up for three days at the Town Hall. At the Old Pier, they watched Santa's arrival on the fishing boat *Crimson Arrow*. On the way home, they stopped at an empty field, cut down a small fir tree and stuffed it into the Land Rover, to be set up as High Park's Christmas tree.

A Scottish goose was given the equivalent of a presidential Thanksgiving pardon in Campbeltown this Christmas, in line with the McCartneys' slow drift toward vegetarianism. The goose, ordered from Glasgow and picked up by local taxi driver Reggie McManus, was meant for the pot, but when it arrived at High Park alive, Paul and Linda could not face killing it and so set it free.[15]

Paul did not wait until Christmas to make his decision. On December 21, 1970, he gave Eastman the go-ahead to file suit. Ten days later, writs were served on John Ono Lennon, George Harrison, Richard Starkey, and Apple Corps Ltd., the defendants in a suit wherein James Paul McCartney sought to dissolve the partnership in which the Beatles had been bound since the agreement of April 19, 1967.

Most newspapers in the English-speaking world published brief reports on the lawsuit, noting that *this* is the end of the Beatles, as if the several apparent endings since September 1969—which, thanks to John's *Rolling Stone* interview, was finally public knowledge—were not sufficiently convincing. Those who sought a comment from the other Beatles were told that they were in discussions with their advisers. Only the *Daily Mail* got a comment from Paul, apparently by sending a reporter to Campbeltown on New Year's Day.*

"The other three could sit down today and write me out," he told the paper. "I would be quite happy. I would pick up my bags and get out."[16]

Notably, there was no breast-beating about how difficult the decision to sue was, or why a lawsuit was necessary. Nor were there recriminations, or even a comment, about John's *Rolling Stone* interview—just a bit of diplomatic bonhomie.

"I dig John. I like him. There is no rift between John and me. Our songwriting partnership finished over a year ago. But the Beatles' partnership has still seven years to go. This is why I want out. When the Beatles were working together 24 hours a day, we had no time to think about ourselves. But now we have stopped touring and we stopped being close. Maybe, when the partnership is dissolved, we could all meet together and have a drink. But not just now."[17]

———▶

Paul was keeping the legal profession busy in other ways, too. On December 31, the *Campbeltown Courier* reported that he had completed the purchase of Low Ranachan Farm, which adjoins High Park, from Archie Revie, whose family had owned the property since 1956. This land grab added 387 acres to Paul's Scottish holdings, increasing High Park's insulation from curious visitors. And for the £7,000 ($17,500) it cost him—nearly twice the cost of High Park—he also became the owner of the remains of an ancient (and landmark-protected) fort on Ranachan Hill.

And on either side of the New Year, there was good news about *McCartney*. Though some of the reviews had been harsh ("Rubbish!"—John Lennon, *Rolling Stone*), the album was a hit with buyers. In America, *Cashbox* reported in its December 26 issue that it was No. 9 on the Top Albums chart for 1970, and that Paul came in at No. 5 on the Top Male Vocalist list. The same day, *Record World* published its own results, in which *McCartney* placed at No. 6 among the year's Top Albums, and Paul was No. 2 in the Top Male Vocalists category.

Most of the British music papers published their 1970 overviews on January 2, 1971. *NME* put *McCartney* at No. 9 in its top 50 for 1970, and Alan Smith chose it as one of his top three albums of the year, the other two being *Let It Be* and *All Things Must Pass*. *Sounds*, using sales data from the British Market Research Bureau and *Record Retailer*, listed Paul's debut album as the year's

---

* The article describes Paul as bearded and wearing jeans and said that he was speaking in "his isolated farmhouse home in Campbeltown, Argyllshire." It gives the impression that a reporter was on the scene. But its relative brevity, its format (there is very little reporter narrative, just a heading for each topic Paul addressed) and the obvious absence of probing questions in a situation that demanded them, raises some question about how the interview was conducted—as does its title, "Why I Want Out—By Beatle Paul," and its byline, which reads "From *Daily Mail* Reporter."

fourth-biggest seller, after *Bridge Over Troubled Water*, *Led Zeppelin II*, and *Let It Be*. However, *Record Mirror*, basing its chart on the same sources as *Sounds* (although over a slightly different time period)* placed *McCartney* at No. 9 in its year-end chart, published on January 9, also noting that the album had spent 22 weeks in the top 20.

There was some news about Beatles sales as well—useful information for someone suing to break up the Beatles' partnership, with a lack of proper accounting records as one of his complaints. *NME*, using information from the Music Research Bureau, published an article on January 16 showing that the Beatles, over the course of their recording career, had sold more than 56 million albums, 74 million singles and 3 million EPs, worldwide. By comparison, Elvis Presley and Frank Sinatra had sold 25 million albums each—and they were tied for fourth place, with Mantovani in second (with 43.5 million) and Herb Alpert in third (with 30 million).[18]

———

Just after New Year's Day 1971, Paul and Linda flew back to New York to continue work on *Ram*, with sessions scheduled to resume on January 9 at A&R Recording. But Paul had some time to kill before the sessions began. On the night of January 6, he switched on the television in his room at the Stanhope and stumbled onto *The Johnny Cash Show*, then in its second season. Paul had always liked Cash's deep baritone and country twang, to say nothing of his legend: he was part of the "Million Dollar Quartet," the other three members being Elvis Presley, Carl Perkins, and Jerry Lee Lewis, every one of them a hero of Paul in his formative years. The four had recorded a jam session at Sun Records on December 4, 1956—a session that was the stuff of dreams until selections were released on disc in 1969.

As it happened, Johnny's guests that evening included another member of the quartet, Carl Perkins,† along with Paul's friend and countryman, Eric Clapton, with Derek and the Dominos. In an episode taped on November 5, Clapton and company played 'It's Too Late' and were joined by Perkins and Cash on 'Matchbox.' For Paul, *this was the stuff!* During his American visit, he watched the rest of the series, through to its final episode on March 24.‡ And it got him thinking about the next logical step after he completed his new album.

"The decision I made," he said, "was mainly to get a group together to play with because, with

---

* *Sounds* based its chart on information collected between January 5 and December 5, 1970; *Record Mirror*'s chart information was collected between January 10 and December 19.

† Although Paul was unaware of it at the time, only 19 days earlier, on December 21, another member of the Million Dollar Quartet, Elvis Presley, had met with Richard Nixon and, in his quest to be made a federal agent at large, denounced the Beatles as anti-American promoters of illegal drugs.

‡ The show, on the ABC network, was canceled as a result of the Network Prime Time Access rule, which went into effect during the 1970-71 television season and limited the number of hours of network programming a local affiliate could carry during the prime-time hours, 8 to 11 p.m.

the Beatles, we weren't really playing a lot. I thought of doing that after I had seen Johnny Cash on TV, and I wanted a similar group with a couple of guitars and drums, just to have a sing with."[19]

Paul and Linda also did some socializing while they waited for studio time. Linda had not been in touch with her New York friends since she moved to London in 1968. Some took her silence amiss; indeed, some of her women friends went so far as to characterize Linda as a talentless groupie-turned-gold digger who landed a Beatle.

But she wanted to reconnect, and her first call was to Danny Fields, a friend since the day of her *Rolling Stones* photo shoot in 1966. Back then, Fields was the managing editor of *Datebook*, and he had a Beatles connection neither Paul nor Linda knew about; it was he who extracted John Lennon's assertion that the Beatles were "bigger than Jesus," from a licensed version of Maureen Cleave's *London Evening Standard* profile, and put it on *Datebook*'s cover, igniting a furor during the Beatles' 1966 American summer tour.

Now Fields was working in the publicity department at Atlantic Records and managing the Stooges on the side. Paul and Linda cabbed to Fields's apartment on West 20th Street, where Linda quizzed Fields on people and places they both knew—the friends she had decided not to call, the Fillmore East, the Scene, Max's Kansas City—and Paul asked pointed questions about the workings of the American record industry.[20]

McCartney is a master of projecting a down-to-earth image that makes people feel comfortable and attended to, as if he were a friend of long standing. Still, Fields, who had spent plenty of time with rock stars, detected an aura of rock royalty, emanating as much from Linda as from Paul.

"Linda was now operating on MST, McCartney Standard Time," Fields observed. "In their own minds, and in their lives, the McCartneys were the Greenwich Meridian. As the Queen is the Fountain of Honor, they were the Fountain of Events."[21]

Paul, with his record business and publicity questions, may have been considering either hiring Fields to handle his American publicity or hoping he would recommend someone for the job. But he soon found another use for Fields. As the evening wore on, Fields mentioned that he missed seeing Linda's rock photos and wondered whether she had considered compiling some of them in a book—something Paul said he had been trying to persuade her to do, as well.

"The whole mood of the little get-together had changed," Fields recalled. "What Paul wanted was the rehabilitation of Linda in the public mind, as a photographer worthy of having her name on a book of her work, and he thought the world should know that he had married a person who was remarkably talented, an artist in her own right."[22]

Before the McCartneys and Fields said their farewells, Fields agreed to come to London, to sort through Linda's boxes of prints and negatives and to edit the book he suggested.

———

A&R was started in 1959 by Jack Arnold, a violinist, pianist, and accordionist who occasionally worked as a producer, and Phil Ramone, a Juilliard-trained violinist who was renowned for his engineering and production work. Originally, A&R was a demo studio, but by the time Paul hired it, it had become one of New York's most respected independent recording facilities, with space in two buildings: Studios A-1 and A-2 were at 799 Seventh Avenue, purchased in 1967 from Columbia Records; the smaller studios R-1 and R-2 were in the Leeds Music Corporation Building, 322 West 48th Street. Except for one mixing session in R-2, Paul worked in Studio A-1.

Columbia had designed the studio that became A&R's A-1 to mirror the acoustic qualities and floorspace of Studio C, in its 30th Street Studios. It was a big room, 40 by 50 feet, with a 30-foot-high ceiling, suitable for a 90-piece ensemble. For Paul, it offered another benefit: the building had a service entrance on West 52nd Street, so instead of walking in the main doors, where fans were most likely to congregate, he could go in the side and take an elevator that opened a few steps from the studio door.

Ramone, as the studio's owner, planned to oversee the sessions, with the fresh-faced Dixon Van Winkle, who Ramone had recruited right out of the Eastman School of Music in 1969, as his engineer and assistant. But since Paul was producing the sessions himself, Ramone quickly decided, with Paul's acquiescence, that Van Winkle could handle most of the work on Paul's agenda; Ramone would be on hand only for the orchestral overdubs.

"He was very confident of what he was doing," Ramone said of McCartney. "There wasn't any tentativeness to him or anything like that. You couldn't bullshit him. If something didn't sound right, you had to express your feelings. You might have been putting your head in the chopping block, but it was better than not speaking up."[23]

"Paul booked the big studio, A-1—that was the room of all rooms," Van Winkle said. "It was a wonderful-sounding, big warm wooden room, with an old console that, until this day, nobody knows what it was. An old wedge-shaped thing, with a big bunch of tube microphone pre-amps, sitting in big racks behind it—it was a big control room. All A&R Studios had four Altec 604E speakers in the control rooms. That's what that room was, and that's what he wanted."[24]

Van Winkle had one other responsibility, something not normally part of an engineer's purview.

"Mary was allowed to get out of her playpen," Van Winkle remembered, "and she used to crawl along the top of the console sometimes too. And I was kind of in charge of Mary at the time—you know, make sure she didn't move any faders."[25]

With some distance between himself and the recordings made in October and November, Paul and Van Winkle spent several days reviewing the CBS session tapes. Paul would have listened closely to confirm that the takes he had marked as "best" still struck him as the optimal choices; Van Winkle, who remembers the reviewing sessions taking place in the smaller studio A-2, in the same building, would have listened with a more technical ear.

"These boxes of 2-inch McCartney tapes all came in from CBS," Van Winkle said, "and we went through them all. At A&R, we were the independent guys in town, and we all looked at the record company–owned studios and thought that those guys were quite stiff, and square. We were more impressed by a lot of the British records that were coming in, because they sounded different—they weren't standard. But McCartney's tracks came in, and Phil asked me to go through them to see what we were up against, since Paul booked us to do all these overdubs. But they were really well-recorded at CBS."

Much of the overdubbing to be done was vocal work, including backing harmonies by Paul, Linda or both. Always an admirer of Brian Wilson's vocal writing for the Beach Boys, and proud of the Beatles' own vocal harmonizing, Paul had been mapping out complex vocal harmonies for some of his new material, and teaching the parts to Linda. There were tense moments.

"Linda hadn't done much singing before, and obviously there were some arguments about bum notes," Paul admitted. "We'd fight about Linda singing flat. I'd say she was flat, and she'd plead 'I know' in an exasperated voice. But it always worked out in the end."[26]

The dynamic was not lost on Van Winkle. "I just remember how sweet he and Linda were. They were just so good with each other, and he was very patient with her. Not just patient but helped her with her singing. He was wonderful working with her to get those background vocals, she was wonderful on a lot of those tunes."

Their first vocal session was on January 18. Paul started with something simple—'3 Legs,' which needed only a call-and-response approach, the responses simply mirroring the lead vocal that Paul recorded on October 16. To make it easier still, the responses did not require much vocal finesse—Linda sang it, in tandem with Paul, with a slightly jokey, country twang. At the same session, Paul added an electric guitar, closely following the acoustic parts he and Spinozza had recorded, at first, then adding pointed accenting and expanding to include some rockier textural touches and a few subtle lead figures.

Giving Linda a break, Paul added acoustic and electric guitar lines to 'Little Woman Love' on January 20 and the first part of the session on January 21. That afternoon he had Van Winkle thread up the master take of 'Another Day,' and added no fewer than six tracks of vocals—two devoted to Paul's lead and a doubling; a third for Paul and Linda's harmony vocals on the verses and bridge, plus a sound effect (five seconds of cheering and yelping, starting at 2'03"); a fourth for further harmonies and a high, wordless descant; and doublings of both the harmony tracks.

The parts were significantly more sophisticated than those Paul had Linda sing on '3 Legs,' which largely followed the main melody. Now Linda sang bona fide harmonies, at times multiple harmony lines when Paul wanted greater emphasis. She also had wordless lines at the start of each verse except the first, and the part Paul gave her for these sections ended with a short, swooping glissando. Other sections featured an ethereal, high-lying vocalise that contributes atmosphere: it's barely audible, but it would be missed if it weren't there.

Characterizing Linda's voice, and what he liked about it, Paul compared her to the singers in the 1960s American girl group the Shangri-Las.

"What I liked about Linda's singing was the tone of her voice," said Paul. "I'd never worked singing with a woman before, all my harmonies to that date had been with males, so I liked this idea of her range. But she wasn't a professional singer by any means. I put my part on and then encouraged Linda to just take it easy, relax, put a good performance in, which she did."[27]

They finished the week of overdubbing with light work, by comparison—a single vocal track for 'When the Wind Is Blowing,' sung by Paul and Linda on a shared microphone. The song has no lyric, although they sang the title where the refrain would naturally fall. For the rest, Paul wrote a graceful melody, which they sang wordlessly, and lightly harmonized, during the verses.

Paul continued working on vocal overdubs over the next few days. He was also awaiting a package from London that was necessary for the next phase of the project. At the end of the CBS sessions, Paul sent George Martin copies of the songs he felt would be enlivened by Martin's orchestrational wizardry—the not-yet-joined 'Uncle Albert' and 'Admiral Halsey,' 'Long Haired Lady,' 'The Back Seat of My Car,' 'Little Lamb Dragonfly,' and 'I Lie Around.'

Discussing the project by phone, Paul gave Martin an idea of what he had in mind for each.

"It was a shame the recordings happened in New York—I missed out on those," Martin later reflected. "Mostly the scores were straightforward. They are always templates which can be modified on the session. Quite often I would make on-the-spot changes to make the arrangements work better, and Paul had such a vivid imagination he could easily have done the scoring himself if he had a little instruction."[28]

Once the scores arrived, Paul asked Ramone to line up the necessary orchestral players—each song required a differently constituted ensemble—for sessions slated to begin on January 27. Ramone put the task in the hands of Emile Charlap, a Brooklyn-born trumpeter, arranger, and contractor.[29] Individual parts also had to be made for the players, from Martin's full scores, a task that may have fallen to the versatile Charlap, who also worked as a copyist.

Paul also caught up with Part 2 of John's *Rolling Stone* interview, which was published on January 13 (with a cover date of February 4), but although the second installment had its shockers—it was in the segment that John discussed the boardroom battles between the Eastmans and Klein, with considerable opprobrium heaped upon Paul and his in-laws—it affected him less viscerally than the first.

———

Neither Paul nor any of the other Beatles were present on January 19, 1971, when Hirst, representing McCartney, appeared in the High Court of Justice, Chancery Division, before Sir Edward Blanshard Stamp, to make his opening remarks in the case of *James Paul McCartney v. John Ono Lennon, George Harrison, Richard Starkey, and Apple Corps Ltd.*

Hirst told the court that the Beatles' finances were in such an appalling state that they did not have the money to pay their current tax bill—which, according to documents received only at 8:15 p.m. the previous evening, totaled £678,000 ($1,695,000) in tax, plus an estimated £500,000 ($1,250,000) surtax.

This, Hirst argued, was because Allen Klein, "a man of bad commercial reputation,"[30] had failed to provide audited accounts of the partnership and had prevented Apple's accountants from giving financial information to McCartney. This, Hirst continued, was one of several reasons McCartney felt that Klein was unsuitable as the Beatles manager. He went on say that Klein's appointment, over McCartney's objections; the artistic interference McCartney had experienced since the advent of Klein; and the fact that the Beatles no longer performed or recorded together were among the reasons McCartney wanted to dissolve the partnership and have a temporary receiver appointed to sort out the Beatles' finances.

After a two-hour hearing, Justice Stamp, adjourned the proceedings for a month, when the dispute would be taken up fully.[31]

Paul monitored the hearing from a distance of 3,000 miles, but did his best to focus not only on recording, but also on promotional plans for his new album. While he was waiting to add Martin's orchestral arrangements to the project, he sketched out plans for a television special that would include both straightforward performances (with a backing band and orchestra) and production numbers built around 'Monkberry Moon Delight,' 'The Back Seat of My Car' and 'Long Haired Lady.' Most of the show would be devoted to the new material, but 'Maybe I'm Amazed' appears in Paul's listing, as does 'Blackbird,' as part of a medley with non-McCartney tunes like 'You Are My Sunshine.'

Paul reportedly met with Greg Garrison,[32] who had produced specials starring Fred Astaire,

Gene Kelly and Dean Martin, to discuss the idea in the days before the orchestral sessions began. But nothing came of their discussions.

There was one point at which the lawsuit and the recording project intersected. As soon as Justice Stamp announced that the trial proper would begin on February 19, Paul thought it would be good to release a single that day—a way of saying, "the lawsuit's on, but it's not slowing me down." A call to EMI assured him that a February 19 release date was possible; the only question remaining was, what should he release? 'Too Many People' would certainly be thematically apt, but the news was already full of Combative Paul; he wanted something sweeter and more positive. He ran the question past Van Winkle, who had heard all the CBS recordings as well as the latest overdubs.

"Paul asked me, 'What do you think would be a cool single?' And I said, 'I think "Another Day" is just a gas.' And that's what he ended up going with."[33] McCartney chose the flip side, 'Oh Woman, Oh Why' himself.

———

Recording Sessions

Tuesday–Friday, January 26–29, 1971.
A&R Recording, Studio A-1, New York.
Orchestral overdubbing: 'Uncle Albert,' 'Admiral Halsey,' 'I Lie Around,' 'The Back Seat of My Car,' and 'Too Many People.'
Overdubbing: 'Oh Woman, Oh Why,' 'Smile Away' and 'I Lie Around.'

With orchestral sessions due to begin on January 27, Paul devoted Tuesday's session to overdubs on his chosen B side, 'Oh Woman, Oh Why,' adding his gritty lead vocal, a doubling of that vocal with falsetto harmonies in places, and three tracks of backing vocals with Linda, in which they repeated the final words of the first two lines in each verse.[34] The harmony vocals were bounced down and heavily compressed. Paul devoted another track to a maracas overdub before calling it a day.

On Wednesday morning, Paul, Linda, and the girls arrived at A&R to a chorus of instruments being tuned—the same warm texture that opened the *Sgt. Pepper* album—while Van Winkle and Ramone hurried around the studio floor putting microphones and pairs of cans in place for each of the assembled players.

It was later claimed that the New York Philharmonic performed on Paul's second solo album, but this can be put down to inaccurate press reports. Charlap engaged a starry ensemble from among New York's classical and jazz freelancers that included a contingent of current and former New York Philharmonic musicians who did session work. Among the Philharmonic players were David Nadien, who had been the orchestra's concertmaster from 1966 to 1970 (and was the concertmaster at these sessions); Joseph Singer, the orchestra's principal French hornist; and the harpist Myron Rosen. Others associated with the orchestra included the violinists Sanford Allen (the first Black musician to be hired by the Philharmonic, in 1962), Henry Nigrine, Joseph Bernstein, Michael Gilbert, and Morris Kreiselman; the cellist Lorin Bernsohn; and the bassist Homer Mensch.

Aaron Rosand, a violinist who had appeared as a guest soloist with the Philharmonic, was in the ensemble, as were Emanuel Vardi, a highly regarded violist in New York's chamber music world, and the trumpeter Ray Crisara, who had played in the Metropolitan Opera orchestra.

Among the top-flight jazzmen Charlap engaged were the flutist Hubert Laws, the violinist Joe Kennedy, the trumpeters Marvin Stamm, Mel Davis and Snooky Young, and the bassists Ron Carter and Richard Davis.*

"These were all handpicked people, he got the cream of the crop," Van Winkle observed.

"Back in the 70s, New York was still the center of the recording industry," said Nick DiMinno, A&R's studio manager. "There was so much talent in the city that even if you couldn't book your first call player, your second, third and even fourth call musician was amazing.† In midtown Manhattan between 39th Street and 59th Street, between 5th and 9th Avenues there probably was a recording studio on every block. Musicians would work 9:00 a.m. to 6:00 p.m. in the jingle biz, and then do record dates at night."[35]

Deeply curious about how music of all kinds worked, Paul had attended most of the orchestral sessions Martin had led during the Beatles years, and he had distinct ideas on how to make an orchestra sound the way he wanted it. He also had experimental ideas he wanted to explore, and he indulged some of them at these sessions.

"When we recorded the French horns," Van Winkle said, "I had them set up in our usual fashion—which was with the microphones in front of them, and a couple behind so you'd get the ambience. The French horn is a reflecting instrument. But Paul didn't like that, he wanted a microphone right close in on all the bells—right up inside them. And I can see why, as he wanted real detail."[36]

He had ideas about the strings, too, as Denny Seiwell discovered when, hearing that sessions

---

* McCartney never published a full list of the orchestral musicians who played on *Ram*, but in addition to those named, the roster included the violinist Harold Coletta; the French hornist Jim Buffington; the piccolo players Phil Bodner and Harvey Estrin; and the clarinetist Tommy Newsom.

† That said, it was a tough, competitive life: Emanuel Vardi, who played viola on *Ram*, has noted that although there were 40,000 members of the musicians' union in New York, 2,000 players got virtually all the jobs.

were underway at A&R, he stopped in and ended up accompanying some of the players to Jim & Andy's, a bar frequented by session musicians.

"They said, 'McCartney took about 40 minutes to tune the orchestra,'" Seiwell reported. "This was the David Nadien string section—these guys don't need more than three seconds to tune up. But Paul tuned it in a specific way, and when they heard the first playback, they said it sounded like the London Symphony."[37]

Once the ensemble was tuned and ready, someone had to conduct it. Paul expected that to be Ramone, but Ramone encouraged Paul to take up the baton. Paul protested that he wasn't trained to conduct—although he had tried his hand at it during the orchestral sessions for 'A Day in the Life,' on February 10, 1967, and during a June 30, 1968, session for 'Thingumybob' with the Black Dyke Mill Band. Ramone argued that since it was Paul's music, who could be better?

"Conduct it in a passionate way, based on what you hear," Ramone told him. "Wave your arms, and you'll be amazed."[38]

Wearing a sweater, jeans and Converse trainers, Paul stood on the studio floor—there was neither a podium nor a music stand—before an orchestra of predominantly middle-aged men in sport coats and ties sitting beneath a forest of microphones. Many had no idea who he was, having been booked for the session with no information about the artist involved, and not recognizing the heavily bearded figure before them as the moptop they had seen on their kids' record jackets.

On their stands, the musicians had Martin's score for 'The Back Seat of My Car.' Conducting without a baton, Paul duly cued the strings for the subtle chordal bed underlying the early verses, and then gestured to Myron Rosen for the harp glissando (at 1'12") that introduces a short but rich line of string counterpoint, and the swelling brass figure at the line, *"listen to her daddy's song."* Paul instinctively knew the gestures he needed to shape the string accompaniment to the wordless vocalise at 2'53", and to encourage a hefty brass sound to support *"we believe that we can't be wrong,"* as well as the descending string and brass chords in the song's final section, just before the coda.

After a few takes, Paul was satisfied, and turned to 'Uncle Albert/Admiral Halsey.' Martin's score—with the title 'Uncle Arthur,' unaccountably, on the title page—is written in two parts, reflecting the manner in which Paul recorded it. The orchestral overdubs would be recorded that way, too. At this first session, Paul presided over 'Uncle Albert,' which called for 16 violins, 4 violas, 4 cellos, double bass, 3 French horns, bass trombone and harp, leaving 'Admiral Halsey,' for the next day.

After the session players left, Paul had Van Winkle thread up 'Oh Woman, Oh Why' to record an effect suggested by a line in the refrain—*"Oh woman, oh where, where, where, where, where'd you get that gun?"* A studio assistant was dispatched to buy a starting pistol and a box of blanks, so that Paul could record gunshots. To avoid raising alarms at A&R, the overdub was recorded after hours, when the studios were empty. But McCartney and Van Winkle quickly discovered that Studio A-1, with its 30-foot ceiling, was too reverberant a space for recording gunshots.

"We practiced a lot so that it wouldn't distort," Van Winkle said. "We tried it in different spots, and with different mics."[39] During those rehearsals McCartney was photographed by Linda, holding the gun in firing position, his eyes closed. But the final overdub—seven shots—was recorded in the hallway outside Studio A-2, using a Shure SM57 microphone (a mic often used for percussion) to avoid distortion. McCartney got the sequence of shots down in two takes.

The orchestral session the morning of January 28 was devoted to 'Admiral Halsey,' which Martin scored for three flugelhorns or trumpets (with the opening solo marked "should be played à la Herb Albert [*sic*]"), three French horns (which, toward the end, are asked to "mumble at random starting low in pitch but ending on these definite notes," G, C and E) and bass trombone.

Because the flugelhorn solo at the start of 'Admiral Halsey' had been copied on a separate page from the ensemble parts, McCartney recorded the full brass section first. When he was satisfied, he walked over to the flugelhornists with the solo chart in hand, saying he had a tune he wanted someone to play. Mel Davis, the section leader for the date, said "Let the kid play it," indicating 31-year-old Marvin Stamm. Martin's score had all the notes and rhythms of the solo, but nothing in the way of dynamic or expression marks, beyond the suggestion to play it like Herb Alpert. As Stamm remembered it, Paul remedied that.

"Paul told me that he wanted the solo to sound a bit like it was coming through an old radio cone. Then he sang it to me. I played it back to him several times until he said it was the way he wanted it. Then we recorded the solo."[40]

The afternoon orchestral session on January 28 was devoted mostly to 'I Lie Around,' which required trumpets, trombones, French horns, cellos, and basses. The score's most notable moments included dramatic descending slides that create a sense of grandeur—an element that points up a current of self-effacing parody that would not be evident in a performance with just the basic rock instrumentation.

Paul also used the session for a touch of orchestral sweetening on a song that Martin had not scored, 'Too Many People.' Using only brass players, he led ad-libbed additions that included adding short, unison brass tones at the very start of the song and just before each of the two appearances of "*you took your lucky break.*"

With the third and final orchestral session scheduled for the following Wednesday, February 3, Paul took a break from his conducting chores and spent the Friday session putting the finishing touches on 'Smile Away.' A new electric guitar solo (most prominent toward the end of the song) and three vocal tracks did the job.

In the first, Paul replaced the scratch vocal he had recorded on November 16 (and had originally decided to keep) with a lead vocal that sometimes seemed to be channeling Elvis Presley, and elsewhere included unabashed whooping and falsetto vocalizing to emphasize the jam sensibility in the song's playout. On the two other vocal tracks, Paul and Linda sang a backing that includes a harmonized, doo-wop-style setting of the phrase, "*Don't know how to do that*," and a wordless setting ("bup-bup-*buuuuuh*") of the three rising and three falling chords within the verses.

Recording Sessions

Monday–Friday, February 1–5, 1971.
A&R Recording, Studio A-1, New York.
Orchestral overdubbing: 'Long Haired Lady' and 'Little Lamb Dragonfly.'
Overdubbing: 'Long Haired Lady' and 'I Lie Around.'
Mixing: 'Oh Woman, Oh Why.'

With the orchestral support for both 'Uncle Albert' and 'Admiral Halsey' in the can, Paul and Linda began the week by recording the backing vocals for the 'Hands Across the Water' segment of the latter. But the lyrics for the opening section of 'Admiral Halsey' continued to elude Paul, so they set the track aside.

They may also, on Monday or Tuesday, have tried to record the lead and simple backing for 'I Lie Around.' Paul was not entirely happy with his vocal in the verses, and he made a mental note to revisit it. Still, the day's work, combined with the orchestral overdub, transformed the song from a gentle, country-folk tune to a powerhouse with a comic edge.

Paul and Linda sang the refrain—the song's title—as if it were a grand proclamation, followed by a single unaccompanied line, "*all over the place*," with an Elvis-like tremble, and later in a falsetto scream. The Elvis imitation calls to mind 'Death Cab for Cutie,' the song the Bonzo Dog Doo-Dah Band sang in *Magical Mystery Tour*.

The orchestral session on February 3 began with Martin's sparse yet bold arrangement for 'Long Haired Lady,' using only brass (trumpets, horns, trombones) and woodwinds (piccolos, clarinets, bass clarinet). Standing before the orchestra in a sweater emblazoned with an elegant, long-horned stag deer, he first rehearsed the opening brass contribution a couple of times. It was pretty simple—just a single brass chord with a crescendo starting on the last "*well*" of the five in the opening line. Paul wanted a particular sound here (and each time the line returns)—a textured growl when the crescendo is at its loudest. The musicians picked it up quickly.

From there, it was easy work—chordal support on the slow refrain, winds accompanying parts of the final verse. There was one sticky point in the "*Love is long*" playout, Van Winkle recalled.

"There's a whole section of trumpet—that was played by two trumpet players who alternated notes, because no one could play that in one pass."[41] Their breathless performance stirred a deep reaction in McCartney. When Van Winkle spun back to tape and hit the play button, Paul stood motionless, his back to the console and his eyes closed, absorbing every last note to the song's abrupt finale.

After the lunch break, the ensemble's string complement (violins, violas, cellos, basses) arrived, joining the woodwinds and brass for the last of Martin's orchestrations, 'Little Lamb Dragonfly.' Paul had made no further progress on the song's lyric, but it was not an urgent matter, the track being for his *Rupert* project. The score itself was simple, mostly a matter of chordal accompaniment—a touch of atmospheric plushness—that grew richer toward the end.

Overdubbing two songs that both exceeded six minutes in length saw the session run over time. The orchestra was booked for a single session, and the meter was out of credit. "Phil [Ramone] managed to persuade everybody [to stay late]," said Paul, "but this one guy who got humpy and took the hoof."[42]

A few passes later, it was a wrap.

Paul took the next day to decompress by tinkering with a few songs, overdubbing an autoharp to 'I Lie Around,' and an acoustic guitar (with heavy reverb) and bass guitar to 'Long Haired Lady.' But there was a more pressing item on McCartney's to-do list. The deadline to conclude work on his first solo single in time for the start of the legal proceedings was less than two weeks away, and though he had finished recording both sides, neither had been mixed.

On Friday McCartney and Van Winkle picked up work on the B side, mixing 'Oh Woman, Oh Why.' The duo paid particular attention to the drums, which Paul wanted to be sure punched through the texture. A long afternoon's work saw them fill two reels each of mono and stereo mixes. At the end of the session, Paul was content that the B side, at least, was good to go.

Paul's response to the playback of 'Long Haired Lady' clearly reached far deeper than simple appreciation for Martin's orchestral work. By early February, the burden of producing music that would answer his critics, while mentally preparing himself for what was to come in London, was taking its toll. Like the gunshots that still resonated in his eardrums from the previous day's mixing, thoughts of the impending lawsuit circled through his mind on an endless loop. The confines of the Stanhope Hotel were becoming claustrophobic—Paul missed the fresh air and solitude of the Argyll countryside—and worryingly, he was still a long way from wrapping up his latest project.

"If you go to somewhere like New York," Paul later explained, "if you're in a hotel, there's someone above you, someone below you, and you can hear them turning on and off the radio and that. Someone to the left, someone to the right. It's like you're in a box. And every side has got people living, breathing. But you never see 'em, because there's only ever the one person you see at the lift. And I think that's a very dehumanizing thing."[43]

That weekend, Paul sought further lucidity in the streets of New York. After listening to cassettes Van Winkle had prepared of the recent orchestral sessions, he took advantage of the anonymity his thick beard provided to escape the family's stuffy hotel suite. Paul, Linda, and the girls strolled through Manhattan, west toward the Hudson, even down to Battery Park, where they could stare across the water to the Statue of Liberty. The McCartneys were later spotted on February 7 at Joe's Ice Cream Parlor on Pier 52, where they indulged in ice cream and milkshakes. Just as Paul and Linda had distanced the girls from his depression in October 1969, family life continued uninterrupted as they contemplated more difficult days ahead.

Recording Sessions

Monday–Friday, February 8–12, 1971.
A&R Recording, Studio A-1 and Studio R-2, New York.
Overdubbing: 'Too Many People,' 'Get on the Right Thing.'
Mixing: 'Another Day.'
Guest overdubbing: 'God Bless California' and 'Black Gypsy.'

On the evening of February 8, McCartney and Van Winkle met to conclude work on Paul's single, preparing the final mixes of 'Another Day.' Studio A-1 was unavailable, so the mixing session was moved to A&R's 48th Street facility. It seemed to go easily, but it turned out that the mixes had a fatal flaw.

"We mixed that single in Studio R-2," Van Winkle said, "using Altec 604E speakers. The 604Es were wonderful utility speakers, and Paul, having worked in British studios, was used to the big Tannoy speakers, which had a lot of bass. The 604Es didn't have that. So we pushed the bass up to where it sounded good in the room."

After filling two reels with stereo mixes and three reels with mono mixes, McCartney and Van Winkle chose a mono mix and brought it to A&R's cutting room. Dave Crawford, the studio's lacquer cutter, spent much of the following next day running off enough acetate discs—roughly 100 copies—for all of New York's radio stations. To McCartney's and Van Winkle's chagrin, when stations began playing it, the next day, the bass came pounding out, overemphasized to the point of distortion.

"It sounded terrible," Van Winkle said. "It was really a problem for me, and a problem for Paul as well, although he never said anything about it."[44] Van Winkle returned to the studio to try again on February 12, this time filling another reel with mono mixes. Paul chose a mix with a still prominent but not overpowering bass and sent the masters of 'Another Day' and 'Oh Woman, Oh Why' to

EMI in London. EMI assured him once more that the single would be in British shops on February 19; the American version was released on February 22.

John Eastman, at this time, was concluding negotiations with Chappell Music to publish sheet music for 'Another Day' in the United States, Canada and Great Britain. Paul was striking a blow against ATV, Apple's opponent in the long battle for control of Northern Songs. The view McCartney and Eastman took was that while Paul was signed to Northern Songs as part of the Lennon and McCartney composing team, he was a free agent when working as part of another team—in this case, Paul and Linda McCartney. But at the last moment, Chappell, or its attorneys, balked; ATV/Northern Songs published the sheet music after all.

Returning to Studio A-1 on February 10, Paul and Linda turned their attention to the vocals for 'Too Many People,' starting with a lead vocal from Paul, which he then doubled and tripled before calling Linda to the microphone. Together, they added backing to the ends of several lines—"*piece of cake*" and "*lucky break*," for example. These additions seem intended more to emphasize those lyrics than for purely musical reasons; they do not always occur at predictable points. When they reached the verse about John's "preaching practices," he and Linda doubled the entire second line ("*don't let them tell you what you want to be*").

Paul and Linda also added an in-joke, a response to John's *Rolling Stone* interview: instead of singing "*piece of cake*," they shout "*piss off* cake" in the backing vocals, and Paul added the phrase, on his own, to the song's introduction. There was one more last-minute amendment to the lyrics. In the lyric sheet used at the session, the end of the third verse included the line "*I find my heart awake and waiting to be.*" Paul struck out "*heart*" and replaced it with "*love.*"

They took two days to track the vocals for 'Get on the Right Thing,' with Paul recording the lead vocal on February 10, and Linda joining him the next day for backing vocals—an almost choral addition that includes atmospheric, wordless support for the early verses, and more complex variations and harmonies later. Boogying in the vocal booth at the end of the session, McCartney accidentally pulled his headphone's lead out of the patch bay, causing him to exclaim, "My plug came out!" (a comment he decided to leave in the finished mix).

McCartney still had work to do at A&R, but he was feeling sufficiently distracted to make an impromptu guest appearance. Leslie Fradkin, a guitarist and songwriter, then barely 20, had recorded an album's worth of tracks in July 1970 and had released a single from the sessions ('Song of a Thousand Voices,' as Fearless Fradkin) in September. When the single failed to chart, Fradkin's label, MGM/Sunflower, opted not to release the LP. Now Fradkin was reworking some of the tracks at A&R. The drummer at the sessions was Denny Seiwell.

When Denny and Paul ran into each other in the corridor, Denny quickly sold Paul on Fradkin's potential, and brought him, with Linda in tow, into the studio where Fradkin was working. "I have a bass player for you," Seiwell told Fradkin, who without looking up, pointed to a corner of the studio and said, "You can park your gear over there, I'll be with you in a minute."

Then he turned to look at the new recruit.

"He didn't look anything like what I remembered," Fradkin said. "He had aviator glasses on, and his hair was slicked back. And then I realized who it was, but I didn't pass out, I was preoccupied with getting my own thing done. So he introduced me to Linda, and said, 'Well, she can help out too, she can sing.'"

Paul plugged in and added bass to a pair of Fradkin's songs, 'God Bless California' and 'Black Gypsy.' He and Linda then recorded backing vocals on both.*

"She had a little trouble with pitch, I vaguely recall," Fradkin said. "But I thought if she wants to sing, that's fine. Paul seemed anxious about her confidence, and he encouraged her a lot."[45]

Now it was Linda's turn to reciprocate her husband's support, as the McCartneys returned to London for the first day of the court proceedings in Paul's lawsuit against the other Beatles and Apple.

---

* 'God Bless California' was released on the Thornton, Fradkin & Unger and The Big Band album, *Pass on This Side* (ESP-DISK' Records) in 1974; 'Black Gypsy' was included on Paul Thornton and Les Fradkin's *Godzology* (Renaissance Records) in 2000. For contractual reasons, the McCartneys were credited only as "Paul and Linda." Fradkin went on to play George Harrison in the original cast of *Beatlemania*, from 1976 to 1979, and appears on the show's soundtrack album. He also worked as a producer and session musician (on keyboards and guitars) and pioneered the use of MIDI guitars and guitar synthesizers, both in his production work and on his own recordings.

10

OF BEATLES AND BARRISTERS

—

The McCartneys had not been in London since May 1970, and they did not stay long. Paul's appearance in the Royal Courts of Justice on the first day—and only the first day—of hearings was little more than a matter of propriety: as the one bringing suit, it made sense that he attend, not least because the first day was entirely Paul's show.

Hirst began by restating the demands made in the December 31, 1970, writ, and in the hearing on January 19, 1971—that the Beatles' partnership be dissolved, and that a receiver be appointed to oversee the Beatles' collective and individual assets—and presented the main pillars of Paul's case.

He read the 1967 partnership agreement, nearly in its entirety, and then returned to several clauses—one describing the partners as "a group of performers," for example, and another specifying that "proper books of account shall be kept," with each member receiving an annual accounting—each either archaic, or not complied with, and therefore reasons Paul's demands should be acted upon favorably.

Hirst then described Paul's changing relationship with the Beatles over the past two years. He dissected the fees Allen Klein had taken so far, noting that "our confidence in Mr. Klein has not been enhanced" by his conviction, only 21 days earlier, on ten counts of tax fraud in New York. Transcripts of that ruling were included as an exhibit; it was as if Providence were smiling down upon Paul's cause.

"My Lord, these were not mere technical offenses," Hirst told the court. "They consisted of unlawfully, willfully and knowingly failing to make and file returns of Federal Income Tax which Mr. Klein was under a duty to make and file." He drew a direct line between the tax fraud case and Paul's lawsuit. "It seems that Mr. Klein has demonstrated towards the United States Federal authorities a willful failure to account comparable to that demonstrated towards the partners in Beatles & Company. The U.S. tax authorities can and have invoked criminal sanctions. We are dependent upon the civil sanctions available in this Court to enforce our rights."[1]

Hirst noted, too, that as a result of the dispute, EMI was holding £488,000 ($1,220,000) in royalties for the *McCartney* album—an album that Klein had nothing to do with, apart from trying to delay its release—awaiting the court's ruling on whether to pay the money to Paul, as he asserted was proper, or to Apple, as the Beatles EMI contract provided.

Paul did not take the stand, but he had his say in the form of a 12-page affidavit, summarizing the Beatles' history from Brian Epstein's death to the present, and touching on his reasons for distrusting Klein; Lennon's "divorce" announcement; the dispute over the release date of *McCartney*; Phil Spector's overzealous orchestral production on 'The Long and Winding Road,' and Paul's attempts to persuade the others, particularly John, to let him leave the partnership and Apple. Paul's April 1970 interviews with *Rolling Stone* and the *Evening Standard*, which he described as "substantially accurate," were included as supporting documents.

Hirst read Paul's affidavit to the court, while Paul and Linda sat in the first row holding hands, and an assembly of Beatles fans crowded into the back of the court. None of the other Beatles was present; they were represented by Morris Finer, Q.C.

Familiar as he was with the material, having hashed it over endlessly these last couple of years, and as calm as he appeared in the courtroom, dressed in a dark, double-breasted suit with a casual open collar, it was difficult for Paul to entirely push away the intensity of the moment as he watched the bewigged lawyers and judge publicly sorting through his business.

But on the radio, as his affidavit was being read, Paul could be heard sounding as if nothing could faze him, singing "*It's just another day, du-du-du-du-du-du, it's just another daaaaaay!*"

Speaking with reporters outside the courthouse, Paul seemed the picture of confidence. He told reporters that a member of his legal team had bet him 25p ($0.63) that Lennon would turn up; Paul collected his winnings at the lunch break. And there was happier news. The McCartneys were expecting another child, due in September.

As he had hoped, the release of 'Another Day' siphoned off some of the attention being paid to the lawsuit, with most of the music papers noting that it was rush-released as a "surprise single"—Paul's first under his own name. He was pleased to see that several papers took note of the composing credit on the green Apple label—Mr. and Mrs. McCartney, on British pressings, Mr. and Mrs. Paul McCartney, in the United States.

He felt a measure of relief, as well, when the first review appeared, the day of his court appearance. The always sympathetic Judith Simons grabbed the disc for review in the *Daily Express*, and after predicting that the single "may well unseat George Harrison's 'My Sweet Lord' at the top of the hit parade," she noted that the song joins 'Eleanor Rigby' and 'She's Leaving Home' as proof that Paul "seems to have great compassion for lonely women." She referred to Linda's cocomposer credit, but declared that "the spirit of the record is pure McCartney."[2]

When the rest of the music press weighed in, the following week, some were less kind.

"I was disappointed with McCartney's solo album many moons ago, and I must admit I feel rather the same about this single. When a man has written songs like 'Long and Winding Road,' 'Blackbird,' and 'Yesterday' is it mistaken to expect as much again?"[3]

Penny Valentine, *Sounds*

"A song that takes time to grow on you—but once its perception and beauty have registered, you're hooked on it."[4]

Derek Johnson, *NME*

"It arrived too late for review last week (because of the postal strike). It's been drubbed a bit by some critics, but after a few plays I'm sure it takes on vintage McCartney standards."[5]

Peter Jones, *Record Mirror*

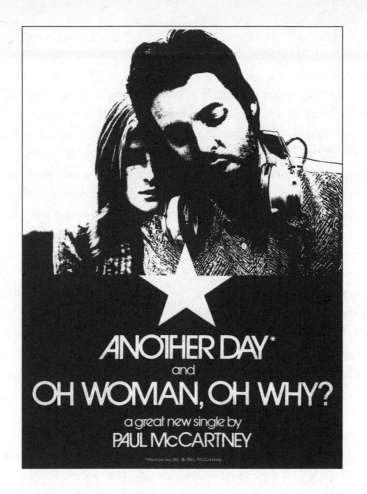

ANOTHER DAY*
and
OH WOMAN, OH WHY?
a great new single by
PAUL McCARTNEY
*Written by Mr. & Mrs. McCartney

The musicians and engineers working with McCartney in New York had seen the same level of confidence he showed in London, and indeed, the impression they had was that he was at the top of his game, coming into the studio daily to work on backing tracks and overdubs, and conducting the orchestral sessions. Between October and December, he had set down 20 songs, enough for two albums, and he had a few more that he wanted to record.

But those closest to Paul—Linda and her family—knew that the preparations for the lawsuit, and related affronts like John's *Rolling Stone* interview, weighed heavily on him. He had come to New York for a revitalizing change of scene, and that proved to be a good call. But now work was slowing down. Only a few tracks were complete; most still needed backing vocals or additional instrumental touches. Paul seemed to be losing focus, continually tinkering with tracks rather than finishing the album.

Paul agreed that another change of venue might help and found John Eastman's suggestion of

Los Angeles amenable. It was a city he knew slightly; the Beatles had played there in 1964, 1965 and 1966, and although they typically saw little of the cities they performed in, Los Angeles was among the few cities where they had downtime. He and Linda had some history there, too, their romance having blossomed while Paul was in town to get Capitol's executives fired up about Apple. That was in 1968, but it seemed a lifetime ago. Relocating to Los Angeles also gave Paul the option of attending the Grammy Awards ceremony at the Hollywood Palladium on March 16. The nominations had been announced on January 31, and the Beatles were up for several—Best Contemporary Vocal Group, Best Contemporary Song, Record of the Year and Song of the Year (all for 'Let It Be') and Best Original Score Written for a Motion Picture or Television Special (for *Let It Be*). On that prospect, Linda visited designer clothes shop Yaga on Madison Avenue, where she was fitted for three new dresses.

Not incidentally, the Eastmans had contacts in Los Angeles. They arranged for Paul to rent the oil tycoon J. Paul Getty's Malibu villa, and Linda booked time at Sound Recorders Studios, starting on March 1. Paul agreed, too, that working with a producer might be useful, so John Eastman telephoned his client Jim Guercio and asked him to oversee the final leg of the project. Guercio knew Linda fairly well, not only as his lawyer's sister, but also as a photographer: they met after she shot a session with Chad and Jeremy, in the mid-1960s, when Guercio was a guitarist in their backing band.

"I had a frantic call saying that the 'divorce' between John and Paul was not going well," Guercio said of John Eastman's invitation to work with Paul. As he remembered it, Eastman told him, "He can't focus—he's got all this material he keeps recording, but he can't finish. Will you come in and pull this together?"[6]

Guercio sympathized with Paul's view of Klein: Chad and Jeremy were ABKCO clients, and Guercio had seen Klein at work, close up. "It was my first job—I was a 17-year-old guitar player, back then. Allen was a crook—I learned what's wrong with the music business from Allen Klein."[7]

Producing a recording by one of the Beatles was high on Guercio's list of life goals—but there were complications, both professional and personal. As a staff producer for Columbia Records, Guercio had produced not only the Chicago and Blood, Sweat & Tears albums for which he was best known, but also recordings by the Buckinghams, the composer and street musician Moondog, and the satirical troupe Firesign Theatre. When Clive Davis, the label's president, got wind of Guercio's plan to work with McCartney, he threatened a lawsuit.

"I told him, 'What, you're going to sue me so I'm not going to work with a Beatle? Fuck you!' Yeah, he went ballistic." Davis did not file suit, but as a result of Davis's warning, he knew he would be unable to have a production credit on the finished album.

On the personal side, Guercio was about to marry the model and actress Lucy Angle—the wedding was scheduled for March 7, 1971, in Falls Church, Virginia, less than a week after the proposed start date for the sessions. From Virginia, the couple planned to fly to Paris for their honeymoon. Everything—flights, hotels—was booked.

Guercio flew to New York to meet with Paul and listen to all the session tapes, plus Van Winkle's rough mixes. Convinced that this was material he could work with, he agreed to produce the sessions when Paul came to Los Angeles, hoping that Lucy would understand that this was a once-in-a-lifetime opportunity. She did, more or less; she married Guercio, anyway, and flew to Paris with her best friend, Susan Forristal, another actress.

"This was a pivotal moment in my life," Guercio says.

Paul's remaining time in New York was devoted to tying up loose ends. A priority was the establishment of an MPL office in New York. Paul rented an apartment—rather than office space—at 257 Central Park West, on the southwest corner of West 86th Street.[8] Mostly, the office would handle publicity and promotion, and to oversee that, Paul hired an old friend of Linda's, Diane Brooks. Brooks, 24, had worked in media and music since she was 18, first at ABC-TV, where she was a publicity assistant, and later as a publicist for Mercury Records, where she knew Linda as a photographer.

While Paul was in London, Van Winkle assembled the 16-track masters from the New York sessions, compiling the best takes onto four reels. But with a couple of weeks between his return from London and his departure for the West Coast, and time still booked at A&R, Paul added a few new recordings to the collection.

Recording Sessions

Monday–Friday, February 22–26, 1971.
A&R Recording, Studio A-1, New York.
Recording: 'Ram On/Sleeping on a Big Barn Bed,' 'Now Hear This Song of Mine/Boogie/Sing-Along,' and 'Blues' (working title for 'The Great Cock and Seagull Race').
Overdubbing: Unspecified songs.

Paul spent much of this final week at A&R doing overdubs, touching up vocals and instrumental parts on the tracks-in-progress. He also devoted time during his Monday session to recording music for an advertising campaign he had dreamed up. The idea was to build a set of radio spots around the fragment of a new tune, 'Now Hear This Song of Mine.' Paul filled two reels recording its introductory bars, accompanying himself on the piano and singing a gradually rising line with the title as the only lyric. He then set it aside: since the advertisements would undoubtedly also include snippets from some of the songs that were actually on the album, unlike 'Now Hear This Song of Mine,' a decision about how to finish off this promotional track would have to wait until the album was completed.

He also brought in something new. Busy as he was with fleshing out the tracks he recorded with Seiwell, Spinozza and McCracken, McCartney had not recorded a new tune since November 19. Now, back from his appearance at the Royal Courts of Justice, and with a new single on the market, he wanted to add something fresh to the reels Van Winkle had just assembled for him to take to Los Angeles. A handful of songs on the Scottish demo tape had not been attempted, and there was 'Dear Boy,' composed just a few weeks earlier.

Given the choices, 'Ram On,' his selection for Monday's session, was decidedly idiosyncratic.

"We'd worked a lot of the day, I guess, and there was nobody there, everybody had gone," Van Winkle remembered. "It was like midnight or something, and Paul said, 'Can you set me up in the studio? I want to record a ukulele.'"[9]

The ukulele was not often heard on rock recordings, although the novelty singer Tiny Tim* had a mainstream pop hit with 'Tiptoe Through the Tulips' in 1968, accompanying himself on a uke, and singing falsetto. The Beatles were friendly with Tim, who appeared on their 1968 fan club Christmas message, singing 'Nowhere Man.' His use of the ukulele was undoubtedly part of the attraction; George Harrison was an avid player.

The other ukulele song on Paul's Scottish demo tape, 'Gypsy Get Around,' was reconfigured for standard pop instruments when Paul recorded it as part of 'Admiral Halsey.' But 'Ram On' still seemed most natural on the uke, with its trebly, transparent, homespun texture.

The song itself wasn't much—Paul had not added to its single line of lyrics since he recorded the demo. But there was that characteristically floating McCartney melody, the kind of tune Mc-Cartney could produce at will. When Paul ran through it for Van Winkle, as a medley with the more raucous but undeveloped 'Sleeping on a Big Barn Bed,' the engineer mentioned that McCartney's foot-tapping enhanced the track, much as it had done when he recorded 'Blackbird' during the *White Album* sessions.

"I put a mic on each of his feet," Van Winkle said, "and a vocal mic, and two on his ukulele, and that was it. I just hit the record button, and he came out with 'Ram On.' It was kind of a magic moment, so personal. And the beauty of it was, it was take one!"[10]

Linda was present, too; she can be heard singing along in the background, off mic. Later in the week, Paul added a second ukulele and fleshed out the rhythmic sound of his foot-tapping with a large tom-tom. He and Linda also added backing vocals. When it was clear that Paul would be adding nothing further to the track, Van Winkle affixed it to one of the compilation reels, using a strip of used two-inch tape as leader. Usually, A&R engineers used blank or wiped videotape as leader, but this piece of recycled tape was filled with rippling piano roulades, right up to the join,

---

* Tiny Tim, born Herbert Butros Khaury on April 12, 1932, was known for his long scraggly hair, a prominent beak, and ill-fitting clothes. Onstage, he cultivated his image as an eccentric warbler of antique pop songs, but he was also a serious scholar of that music. He died, at 64, on November 30, 1996.

where Van Winkle called the take number. Amused by the randomness of the join, Paul opted to keep the piano music as part of the song.

Monday's session crystallized Paul's feelings, those he first thought about during the long drive to Wick in the summer of 1970, that *Ram* could be the perfect title for his new collection of songs. Though only a single syllable, Ram so concisely captured all the album's central themes, from the couple's newly discovered bucolic bliss, to battling—ramming on—against the many obstacles thrown in their path (most notably the contract binding Paul with the other Beatles, and Klein until 1977). Paul's mind was quickly made up.

A second new addition, recorded on February 23, 1971, was a return to the spirit of the Cavendish Avenue *McCartney* sessions—a blues instrumental, with Paul playing all the parts. With a proper studio setup and an engineer, the performance was considerably more fluid than any of Paul's Cavendish recordings, and he surpassed himself with a crisp piano line that moved between a showy, New Orleans–inspired solo style and straight comping to support electric guitar solos. A solid, walking bass line and a steady drumbeat filled out the texture. It had neither a title nor lyrics; Van Winkle labeled it, simply, 'Blues."

In New York, Paul had worked in some of the city's best studios, places where legendary recordings were made, with experienced and respected engineers. If there were rocky moments with Spinozza, they had to do with scheduling, not with musical issues, and Paul understood that the problem was his own inflexibility—to which he felt entitled. Still, looking back at the sessions, he took a critical view of the differences between studios in London and New York.

"There are so many facilities here [in London]," he said during an interview at EMI, "and I think the engineers are better. In New York if you want a harmonium you have to order it, and pay for it, and then take a break for an hour until it is delivered. Here at EMI, you ask for it and five minutes later a porter brings it in for you. It's all big business in New York. It's a nicer atmosphere here."[11]

———

As Paul continued work on the album, the wheels of justice turned slowly in London, with sessions every day during the week of February 22. Paul was happily out of it: had he remained in London, he would have spent Monday listening to a debate about whether Allen Klein was famously disreputable, as per Hirst, or scandalously maligned and the Beatles' financial savior, as per Finer. In a lighter moment, Justice Stamp sent an usher to admonish a group of girls sitting at the back of the courtroom, telling them they would be removed if they did not behave better.

———

* Paul's generic choice of song title, 'Blues,' was perhaps a symbolic representation of his state of mind. While the Beatles' barristers tussled in London, he was in New York playing the blues.

That Tuesday, John, George and Ringo told the court, in written statements read by Finer, their versions of the various disputes within the Beatles and offered their own analyses of what they agreed was Paul's domineering behavior.

"To get a peaceful life, I always had to let Paul have his own way," Harrison said, "even when it meant that songs of mine weren't being recorded. At the same time, I was helping to record Paul's own songs, and into the bargain I was having to put up with him telling me how to play my own instrument." He described his dispute with Paul that was seen in *Let It Be* and noted that he briefly left the band at that time.

Lennon's statement was restrained and analytical, compared with his *Rolling Stone* interview. He spoke of the dispute between him and Paul as being mainly a matter of Paul preferring his in-laws to Klein, and he spoke frankly about the post-Epstein Beatles being "handicapped by our general ignorance of accountancy and business practice, and preoccupied with musical activities." He also noted a difference of taste that went back to the Beatles' early days, diplomatically (thanks, most likely, to Finer's editorial filter) updated: "Paul preferred pop-type music and George and I preferred what is now called 'underground.' But the contrast in our tastes, I am sure, did more good than harm and contributed to our success."

But it was Ringo's statement that touched a nerve. George had complained about Paul fighting with him before Lindsay-Hogg's cameras, but that was out there for anyone to see in *Let It Be*. And John's complaints were presented more brutally in *Rolling Stone*. Ringo, the Beatle everyone liked and got along with, described Paul as "the greatest bass guitar player in the world," but then added that "he goes on and on to see if he can get his own way," and characterized him as a spoiled child.

Ringo also gave an unflattering account of his visit to Cavendish Avenue to persuade Paul to move the release date of *McCartney*, an incident not yet in the public domain.

"He went completely out of control, shouting at me, prodding his fingers towards my face, saying, 'I'll finish you now' and 'You'll pay.' He told me to put on my coat and get out." And he called Paul out on his failure to meet with him, John and George in early January. "I trust Paul and know that he would not lightly disregard his promise."

This was what Paul always knew was the downside of his lawsuit—the likelihood that in the other Beatles' testimony, he would be made to look unreasonable to the public.

The rest of the week was taken up with financial discussions. Klein, who had no standing in the case, but filed an affidavit as manager of Apple, asserted on Wednesday and Thursday that he had more than doubled the Beatles' income over the past year, saying that the group had earned £7,864,126 ($19,660,315) in the six and a half years between June 1962 and December 1968, and another £9,142,533 ($22,856,333) in the 19 months between the start of Klein's contract, in May 1969, and December 1970.

Paul would leave the financial issues to others, but he needed to do damage control in light of John's, George's and Ringo's statements, all widely reported in the press. With the Eastmans, he prepared a letter for Hirst to read in court on Friday, in which he said that Harrison had left the Beatles temporarily not only because of his disputes with Paul, but also because he did not get along with Yoko—a point Lennon had alluded to in *Rolling Stone*. He insisted that the band had split mainly because they were all interested in their own solo projects. And he did a bit of transparent monkey-wrench lobbing, saying that Klein told him that "the real trouble is Yoko. She is the one with ambition," adding, "I wonder what John Lennon would have said if he had heard that remark."

———

At the end of February, the McCartneys flew from New York to Los Angeles, putting another 2,800 miles between Paul and Britain's Royal Courts of Justice. Settling into J. Paul Getty's huge villa, they quickly took advantage of one of the facilities unavailable to them in wintry New York—they stripped down and took drinks out to the pool, a form of relaxation that quickly became an important way to unwind during the Los Angeles sessions, along with catching the latest films. Paul also shaved off the thick beard he had cultivated over four months in New York. Even so, he was entirely unmolested by fans; it was weeks before the press realized he was in town, and his whereabouts had not registered on the fan grapevine, either.

Recording Sessions

Monday–Friday, March 1–5, 1971.
Sound Recorders Studio, Studio B, Hollywood.
Recording: 'Dear Boy,' 'Electric Piano,' 'Radio Spots,' 'Moment Recordings.'

Sound Recorders was founded in 1965 by Armin Steiner, an engineer who, like Phil Ramone, began his career as a classically trained violinist. But he was also fascinated with recording and ran a studio in his mother's house for several years using equipment he built himself. He produced hits for Motown, with the Supremes, Marvin Gaye and Stevie Wonder, backed by members of the Wrecking Crew, L.A.'s top-flight studio musicians.

Steiner started Sound Recorders when zoning laws forced him to close his home studio. The Turtles' 'Happy Together' (1967) and Richard Harris's 'MacArthur Park' (1968) were among the hits he recorded in his new quarters at 6226 Yucca Street, in Hollywood. Sound Recorders was close enough to the Capitol Records Tower, at Hollywood Boulevard and Vine Streets, that you could see the distinctive building rising like a giant stack of LPs—something Paul discovered as he and Linda walked from their rented green Cadillac convertible to Steiner's studio for their first session.

The McCartneys were booked in Studio B, a 43-by-20-foot room with an 18-foot ceiling. Steiner was on hand to engineer. And for the first time since the Beatles recorded *Abbey Road*, Paul put himself in the hands of a producer, handing Jim Guercio control of the sessions.

The most substantial work Paul did during the first week was 'Dear Boy,' at this point a straight-forward piano and vocal performance, with Paul accompanying himself on the studio's Steinway upright during the basic recording on March 1.[12]

Paul spent the rest of the session recording a series of electric piano improvisations and short cues, and a set of spoken word recordings, listed in the session paperwork as 'Moment Record-ings.' Among these were ad-libbed stories, some in British regional accents, as well as short comic bits and mentions of *Ram*, sometimes in an imitation of a sheep bleating. All this was raw material for the 'Now Hear This Song of Mine' spots. Stereo mixes were made of these improvisations, along with the music cues recorded on February 26, and they were compiled on a reel; the titles listed on the tape box are 'Rock No.1,' 'Rock No.2,' 'Boogie No.1A,' 'Boogie No.2B,' 'Boogie No.2,' 'Gospel,' 'Loose Talk,' and 'Come On Boogie.'

During a short session on Tuesday, a tambourine and more wordless (*"ooh"*) backing vocals were added to '3 Legs.'

Marketing *Ram* was on Paul's mind, and he began brainstorming ideas with Linda and Guercio, and at a meeting at the nearby Capitol Tower. 'Now Hear This' was one element of Paul's plan, and it was now beginning to evolve from a series of freestanding radio spots, into a promotional LP of 15 such spots, to be called *Brung to Ewe By . . .* The LP would be hand-delivered to disk jockeys by Capitol salesmen, with an instructions sheet suggesting that they use the spots whenever they play tracks from the album.

Other ideas—some Paul's, some proposed to him—included having Capitol produce *Ram* Fris-bees; a "speaking billboard," in which speakers would provide an aural counterpart to a large *Ram* advertisement; and a plan to hire the Goodyear blimp and fly it over major cities promoting the album. (The last was a nonstarter: Paul was told that the blimp was used only to promote Good-year tires and for public service announcements.)

Paul used the rest of this week reviewing tapes with Guercio, using the time to compile a list of outstanding instrumental and vocal parts. But with Guercio heading off to Virginia for his wedding, late in the week, songs that needed extensive backing vocal overdubs were put off until his return.

———

In London, the courtroom battle was expected to come to an end on February 26, or at least, that was what both sides told reporters. It did not. On March 1, the hearings moved into their second full week. Paul continued keeping tabs on the proceedings, but there was little in the current arguments likely to upset his equilibrium. The other Beatles and Klein had all made their statements, so all that remained was for the barristers to expand on their arguments.

On Monday, Hirst expounded on the messiness of Apple's accounts, and Klein's continual obstruction of McCartney's efforts to get clarity on the company's finances. The matter of McCartney's royalties going into the joint pot was revisited as well. A review of McCartney's justifications, artistic and financial, for filing suit followed on Tuesday, and on Wednesday, Finer began his summation with a defense of Klein's management—and the fees he took for it—and claimed that the appointment of a receiver would lead to the cessation of the Beatles' business operations.

Justice Stamp lost patience with that argument, and Finer walked it back. But it was clear, as well, that the judge felt that the proceedings had gone on too long. When Finer suggested taking Thursday off, because he was required to be elsewhere, Justice Stamp refused to consider it.

"This was going to be a five-day case, and then a six-day case. Where are we now? It is the ninth day. It seems to be going on since time immemorial."

In Finer's absence, his junior partner, W.A.B. Forbes took over the defense's argument that Klein had saved the Beatles from financial ruin, and that appointing a receiver was unnecessary. Finer returned on Friday, in time to hear Hirst shoot down Finer's and Forbes's defense as "clever but fallacious arguments" that were based on "a pure forensic frolic by Mr. Finer," rather than in law.

Finer proposed a compromise that would give McCartney control of his own recordings, and a say in any repackaging of Beatles recordings. But Justice Stamp wondered how McCartney could be expected to work with Apple, in light of everything that had been said in his courtroom since the hearings began.

And then it all blew up. Justice Stamp offered a proposal involving a receiver to be appointed by Apple—Klein, if they wanted—and another appointed by McCartney. Finer, to the judge's amazement, raised objections to his proposal and offered one of his own, in which there would be no receiver, but McCartney would have a representative on Apple's board to look after his individual interests. After listening to Finer's proposal for a moment, Justice Stamp interrupted:

Mr. Justice Stamp: Mr. Finer, the position is that you are not prepared to accept my proposal, and you put forth counter ones; is that correct?

Mr. Finer: *With respect, yes.*

Mr. Justice Stamp: Mr. Hirst?

Mr. Hirst: *Exactly the same objection, as your Lordship knows . . .*

Mr. Justice Stamp: Then I reserve my Judgment.

With that, Justice Stamp walked out of the courtroom, later sending word that he would have his verdict in a week.

For many Beatles fans, the legal arguments were less interesting than a battle shaping up between the former Fabs on the singles charts. On February 27, Harrison's 'My Sweet Lord' was at the top of the British charts for the fifth straight week, and McCartney's 'Another Day' made its chart debut at No. 24. On March 12, Lennon released 'Power to the People,' and on April 9, Starr joined the fray with 'It Don't Come Easy.' It was difficult not to see these four singles as a snapshot of these musicians' current interests—George praising Krishna, Paul singing a pretty ballad about a lonely secretary, John urging listeners into the streets to take up political causes, and Ringo (in a writing collaboration with George) making a genial call for peace and love.

Foremost on Paul's mind at the end of his first week at Sound Recorders was completing his arrangement for 'Dear Boy,' the latest addition to the album's prospective track list. Ideas about vocal harmonies, guitar lines and keyboard additions swirled around in his imagination, but one thing he was certain the track needed was drumming. The two most logical solutions would have been either to play drums himself, or to hire a local drummer, the best of whom was Hal Blaine, a member of the Wrecking Crew—the city's ensemble of premiere session players, who recorded backing tracks for the Beach Boys and countless others. Blaine was close at hand: during Paul's sessions, he was recording with Neil Diamond in another studio at Sound Recorders. A few weeks later, Paul stopped in on one of Diamond's sessions and had a bash on Blaine's "Monster Kit." Linda documented the moment in a snapshot showing Paul, in a blue vest, drumming with a cigarette dangling from his mouth.

Instead of bringing in Blaine, though, Paul telephoned Denny Seiwell and invited him and Monique to join him and Linda in Los Angeles.

Paul had been pleased with Seiwell's drumming in New York, but his decision to fly him to Los Angeles suggests that despite their considerably different backgrounds, they clicked as friends. And indeed, when the Seiwells were in Los Angeles, they and the McCartneys spent more time interacting socially than musically.

Denny and Monique landed in Los Angeles on March 6, and with Guercio away for a few more days, they took the time to cruise through the city, relax around the pool at Getty's house, and share a few spliffs. On the evening of March 8, they all attended a closed-circuit telecast of the Muhammad Ali–Joe Frazier heavyweight title fight, beamed from Madison Square Garden, in New York. The fight, the first between the two boxing titans and billed as the "Fight of the Century," went the distance, leaving Frazier the unanimous points victor, and World Heavyweight Champion.

Not having socialized previously with Paul on the McCartneys' turf (rented though it was), Denny was surprised at the freedom they allowed Heather and Mary.

"Getty's house was full of these priceless antiques, antique furniture, antique wallpaper, everything. Paul told me that he gave a $3,000 (£1,240) security deposit for any damage. And the kids would come out of the pool and lounge around these old sofas that were there, and they would write on the walls with crayons." (The McCartneys forfeited the security deposit.)[13]

Recording Sessions

Tuesday–Friday, March 9–12, 1971.
Sound Recorders Studio, Studio B, Hollywood.
Overdubbing: 'Dear Boy.'

In New York, the sessions had been disciplined and businesslike, but Los Angeles struck Paul as looser and more freewheeling in spirit, and the arrival of Denny gave him a confederate to help keep it that way—as Guercio learned, to his chagrin. Suddenly, Paul began slipping into Beatles rules, booking the studio, but not turning up until late in the afternoon, having smoked a joint on the way.

"I tied up the studio for the full day, and they wouldn't show up 'til five o'clock," said a frustrated Guercio. "And this was when Armin had other artists beating on him for studio time—he had cleared out other artists for me to work with Paul, and I'd be sitting there all day. It was hard."

Guercio spoke to Paul about the other artists trying to get studio time, and about how, having given up his honeymoon to work with him, he was surprised (as was Steiner) to find himself sitting in an empty studio all day. Nor was it particularly efficient for Paul himself, having studio costs mount while no recording was happening.

"But he said, 'No, I want it booked all day, you can't let [the other artists] record. And I want everybody ready to go, whether I come in at 10:00 a.m. or not.'"[14]

With Seiwell in tow, Paul arrived at Sound Recorders at 4:00 p.m. on Tuesday and worked until midnight adding drums and percussion to 'Dear Boy.' It did not go easily.

"Guercio took half the drum kit away," Seiwell recalls, "so I could just play the kick [bass drum] and the snare, on one take, and on the next take he'd take those drums away and I played the tom-toms. He did it for a stereo effect, but that really wasn't the way I normally recorded. It took away a little of the spontaneity and the realness of the drum part, although it came out okay. It was difficult, a real challenge."[15]

Paul and Denny also added a more unusual percussion part. "Paul was sitting with his guitar in his lap, and he would play the chords with his fingers, or a slide, and I would play triplets on the strings with very light timbale sticks. It was a very unique sound."[16]

Work continued on 'Dear Boy' with Paul adding a second piano part, electric guitar and bass guitar. (Seiwell was present for the Wednesday evening session but had no further drumming tasks.) All that was needed were backing vocals, which Paul and Linda began that evening and finished on Friday.

Paul had devised a set of interlinked, constantly moving, contrapuntal vocal lines that had one foot in the world of the Beach Boys and the other in late Renaissance polyphony. Included, too, was a vocalized bass line, with hard attacks ("*doom, doom, doom*"), sung by Guercio. All told, they added six vocal tracks, including the lead, four harmony and backing tracks, and the sung bass line.

Getting those harmonies and independent strands of vocals down involved patient coaching; this song's requirements were several steps beyond the harmonies Linda had sung so far.

"I do love harmonies, and always have," Paul later said. "With 'Dear Boy,' I had it obviously as an unharmonized thing because I was just singing the main vocal line myself when I wrote it. Because Linda and I both knew that she was a novice, and I was the veteran, almost, the question was how to manage those two ends of the spectrum."[17]

The finished vocal backing was stunning on its own; when set against the innocently cheerful solo vocal Paul had recorded on March 1, the harmonies transformed 'Dear Boy' from an attractive but not especially memorable parlor song into an arresting gem.

Paul's arrangement with Guercio, however, was beginning to unravel. Guercio had loved the tapes when he heard them in New York—they struck him as a dramatic improvement over the material on *McCartney*. And he was pleased with 'Dear Boy.' But he and Paul had already tussled over Paul's notion that the studio and its staff be available to him at any time, regardless of when he chose to turn up. And he was put off by Paul's and Denny's fondness for weed.

"Denny was a fine drummer," says Guercio. "I liked him, I worked with him—but he would smoke a lot, and it drove me nuts. I mean, listen—I work with people who have to just smoke a joint or have a drink, but I have never done any kind of drugs, I've never smoked dope. So I have a different perception. And that was my issue with Denny—and with Paul, too, at that time."[18]

Paul, for his part, was reconsidering his agreement to let someone else oversee the production. He had done his first album alone—for that matter, he was the producer in all but name on some of his Beatles tracks—and he was not keen on someone else having the last word.

"Next thing, I see Paul and Guercio sitting out in the lobby talking, and then he's gone,"[19] Seiwell said of Guercio's departure.

———▶

In London, Justice Stamp handed down his decision on March 12, 1971, and it vindicated virtually every clause of McCartney's complaint. Listening to his brother-in-law's summary of the verdict over the phone, McCartney felt the jubilation that comes from having an uninvolved third party listen to your argument and agree entirely—a striking contrast to the fruitless debates in which he engaged with John and George all through 1969.

Justice Stamp found that the appointment of Klein and ABKCO to run Apple without McCartney's agreement was "a breach in the terms of the partnership deed." Moreover, he noted that in several cases, Klein had taken fees greater than those to which he was entitled—or as he put it when addressing Klein's commission on EMI earnings, "ABKCO has made grossly excessive claims for commission and has received commission grossly in excess of that specified" in the agreement engaging Klein to manage Apple.

He found that decisions were made that Paul was not, but should have been, consulted about, and he gave the back of his hand to the other Beatles' argument that Paul sometimes could not be found, noting that if they could not reach him directly, they could have gone through his legal adviser, John Eastman. In one especially egregious case, he found that the Beatles and Apple had "acted in bad faith" by making a "covert oral agreement increasing ABKCO's commission" without McCartney's knowledge and consent—a "grave breach of duties" as McCartney's partners.

He also called out Klein's dishonesty in two sections of his affidavit and expressed irritation with Finer, who knew that those sections were inaccurate, but when challenged by Hirst, described them as "silly" and a mistake—something that, Justice Stamp argued, was a waste of the court's time. Klein's statements, he added, "read to me like the irresponsible patter of a second-rate salesman." Nor was he much impressed by Klein's explanation that his recent tax conviction was just a misunderstanding.

The bottom line was, Justice Stamp agreed that both business and personal considerations militated toward the dissolution of the partnership.

"Each of the Beatles has made and is making recordings otherwise than as the group of four referred to in the partnership deed. There is an issue whether the product of these separate recordings is or is not partnership property."

If so, he continued, this would cause "the odd situation" in which the four Beatles, "exercising their art separately, with inevitably varying degrees of skill and success" are contributing to the partnership in different proportions, all under the management of Klein, who McCartney distrusts. If, on the other hand, the income from solo work was *not* "partnership property," as McCartney argued, the Beatles would be competing against one another, and possibly against Beatles recordings. Either way, the judge wrote, the best solution was to bring the partnership to an end.

"The squabblings which are described in detail in the affidavit evidence may in truth be attributable primarily to the management situation but also to the situation in which the Beatles find themselves in the respects which I just mentioned. Confidence is gone; and although the discontinuance of joint recordings—and I am satisfied on the evidence the possibility of their being resumed is negligible—is not in theory destructive of the partnership, it may be thought as a practical matter that it would be inequitable to do otherwise than dissolve it."

Justice Stamp added a final nail to the partnership's coffin by noting that the other Beatles and Klein had treated McCartney unfairly, and that this was unlikely to change.

"The circumstances regarding the appointment of ABKCO and subsequent surreptitious increase of its remuneration point clearly to the conclusion that the Defendants are prepared, in conjunction with or at the instance of Mr. Klein, to make the most important decisions without regard to the interests of the Plaintiff."

Having ordered the partnership dissolved, Justice Stamp turned to McCartney's demand for the appointment of a receiver. "The financial situation is confused, uncertain and confusing," he wrote. "A receiver is, in my judgment, needed not merely to secure the assets, but so that there may be a firm hand to manage the business fairly as between the partners and to produce order."

He appointed James Douglas Spooner, a London chartered accountant with a reputation as a "company doctor," as receiver and manager. But he agreed to allow a week for the Beatles and Apple to prepare and file an appeal. They did so on March 19, but on April 26, they dropped their appeal, opting instead to negotiate Paul's exit from the partnership agreement.

Airing their dirty laundry in public view had not done the normally PR-savvy moptops any favors, but for McCartney it was a necessary first step to diminish Klein's control of Apple and, Paul hoped, turn John, George, and Ringo on to Klein's nefarious ways.

"I was doing something for them [the other Beatles]," McCartney explained. "I had to go after him [Klein], it was obvious I had to go after him, but I had to go after him in this incredibly crazed way. You know, after all that love and peace I had to turn 'round and sue my brothers. But no one could find any other way for me to make a stand against Klein, so I had to do that. . . . And obviously they hated me for a period after it because all they could see was me just trying to screw them."[20]

Recording Sessions

Monday–Tuesday, March 15–16 & 18, 1971.

Sound Recorders Studio, Studio B, Hollywood.

Overdubbing: Various songs.

When Paul and Linda returned to the studio on Monday, everything had changed, and the approach he had taken throughout the New York sessions had been restored. Guercio had gone, and Paul was once again the producer. Steiner took the opportunity of Guercio's departure to excuse himself as well, assigning Eirik Wangberg* to engineer the rest of the sessions. Paul quizzed the young engineer about the origins of his first name, and then gave him the nickname Eirik "the Norwegian."

Eirik may have assisted Steiner on a few of the earlier sessions—perhaps the ad-libbed material to go with 'Now Hear This Song of Mine,' which he has insisted he recorded—but now the project was, from an engineering point of view, all his. He would record the album's final overdubs, and it seemed likely that he would do the final mixing as well. Guercio said that when he left, he gave Eirik his proposed track sequence for the album; Eirik remembered him also giving another piece of advice.

"Paul," Guercio told him, "is not an artist you can direct or collaborate with. You kind of have to support his ideas."[21]

Eirik himself noted that he began working on the sessions on Sunday, March 14. Since Paul and Linda spent time with the girls on weekends, Eirik went to the studio alone to review the tapes. But Paul, knowing he would be there, stopped in at around 1:00 p.m. to assure himself that mixing was among Eirik's strengths by setting up a mixing test.

"He said, 'Eirik I have a tape with me that you can make a mix of. Let me hear what you can do.'" Paul handed him the master take of 'Dear Boy,' with no particular instructions about what he wanted. "I'm going to go for a walk along Hollywood Boulevard," Paul added, "and I'll come back, after a while, to see how you've done."

"It was quite a challenge for me," Eirik says. "But when it works, it's really lots of fun, especially if the arranger knows his job. As Paul really knew what he was doing, the harmonies and voice tracks did not step on each other or kill each other in the mix."[22] Paul gave him a couple of hours and declared himself pleased when he heard Wangberg's mix.

---

* Eirik had met Paul briefly, on April 10, 1967, when Paul, in Los Angeles to celebrate Jane Asher's birthday, stopped in on a Beach Boys recording session. He also assisted George Harrison, in 1968, when Harrison was unhappy with Capitol's mastering of the *White Album*, and remastered it himself at Sound Recorders, where he was also putting the finishing touches on Jackie Lomax's Apple album, *Is This What You Want?*

Unlike many engineers, Eirik did not note the dates of each mix that he made or overdub he recorded, so it is impossible to fully document all the work he and Paul did together.

One song Wangberg worked on during his first week with Paul—documented on Paul's own colorful tracking sheet—is 'Too Many People,' to which Paul and Linda added two more tracks of backing vocals on March 18, along with an unusual percussion effect. Paul asked Wangberg to buy a wooden pallet, like those used for shipping. When Wangberg brought it into the studio, Paul asked him to set up 'Too Many People,' and to mic the pallet. "Then he hopped onto the pallet and started jumping on each quarter [note]," Wangberg remembered. "What a sound it gave on tape!"[23] (In the final mix, however, the pallet is not heard until the song's final 30 seconds.)

A pallet was not the only thing Paul requisitioned. There was also Eirik's poodle, Snuffy, which the engineer brought into the studio at times. Paul took to Snuffy immediately, mentioning that he and Linda missed their sheepdog, Martha, and asking if he could borrow Snuffy for the remaining weeks of their stay.

Eirik agreed, but had reason to regret allowing his dog a few weeks of luxurious living in Malibu. The McCartneys fed him the same food they were eating, so when he was returned to Eirik, he turned up his nose at dog food. Worse, Eirik found that Snuffy was no longer responding to his call.

"Oh," Paul said, "I forgot to tell you—I've given him a new name. Henry."

Snuffy/Henry did make his way onto the *Ram* master tapes, and nearly made it onto the album. After recording new backing vocals (by both Paul and Linda) for 'Ram On,' Paul and Eirik made an experimental track that included Snuffy's barking, snippets of conversation, and whistling, to be inserted at various points in 'Ram On.' The idea was to give the track a more rustic, slightly eccentric quality, but in the end, Paul and Eirik agreed that it didn't work. Elements of the recording turned up instead in some of the 'Now Hear This' spots.

When Wangberg prepared to mix 'Ram On,' he was unaware that the tape leader spliced in by his New York counterpart, with its rippling piano, was not Paul, so he left it in, along with Van Winkle's take announcement. Sensing the song had thematic purpose to Paul, Wangberg also suggested splitting 'Ram On' into two sections—the first from 0'00" to 2'28", with a fade out, the second fading in at 2'21" and fading out at 3'15", after a few seconds of the unfinished 'Sleeping on a Big Barn Bed.' The overlap ensured that the full song was included, fade-outs and fade-ins notwithstanding.

Another song Eirik worked on during his first sessions with Paul was '3 Legs.' Paul was no longer satisfied with the lead vocal he recorded in New York—he wanted it a bit dirtier sounding, like an old blues disc. Eirik set up a pair of small Auratone speakers behind the microphone, facing Paul as he sang. The idea, originally, was that Paul could record the track without headphones, with the music resonating in the room. In the end, he used headphones as well.

"This way," Wangberg explained, "he would be able to feel the music, not just having the sound in some cans. He felt that being surrounded by the sound, he would sing better. The monitors created some (sound) leakage, and in the mix, I opened that leakage up at certain points, adding a special delay. I think it really rocks—it makes the mix a bit more magical."[24]

———

The end of the Apple lawsuit was not quite the burden lifted from his chest that Paul hoped it would be. There was still the matter of negotiating his exit from the partnership agreement. If he knew John—and who knew John better?—he would drag his heels and find all kinds of reasons not to just have papers drawn up, sign them, and be done with it. And relieved as Paul was that a receiver was appointed, sorting out the financial mess at Apple would take time as well.

But more than that, it seemed as if, now that the legal world had drawn him into its clutches, it was not going to let him go. No sooner than Justice Stamp handed down his decision in Paul's favor, legal troubles arose from another corner: ATV/Northern Songs was challenging the "Mr. and Mrs. McCartney" composing credit on 'Another Day.'

At stake was a percentage of the royalties. Northern Songs had Paul under an exclusive contract as part of the Lennon-McCartney songwriting team through February 1973. In practical terms, 55 percent of the royalties on a McCartney song was paid to Maclen Music, which was owned by John and Paul (40 percent each), as well as Apple (20 percent).

Paul now had his own publishing company, McCartney Music, Inc., based in New York, which was claiming royalties for Linda's share of the song, Linda not being party to the Northern/Maclen agreements. That meant that 50 percent of the royalties would bypass both Northern Songs and Maclen.

Northern Songs guessed, correctly, that Paul's joint writing credit with Linda was a harbinger of things to come—that the songs on the album he was known to be recording would be similarly credited. If that continued, the loss to Northern could add up.

"We will require Mrs. McCartney to prove that she is capable of composing such music if she persists in her claim," Jack Gill, the chairman of Northern Songs, told the press on March 15. "We find it extremely strange that a person who never wrote music before her marriage should have helped write 'Another Day.'"[25]

The challenge was not entirely unexpected; the Eastmans had told Paul it was possible, simply because no company likes to see an income stream siphoned off. But that made it no less galling, for Paul. Speaking about Northern's challenge, he offered the view that if he had communicated better—given interviews about writing with Linda, perhaps—their collaboration might have been better accepted.

"The main thing that's happened with Linda and me is that since the Beatles split, we didn't explain an awful lot of what we were doing. If we'd kind of really been very careful, like about *Ram* or something, and set up some kind of publicity machine before it all, and tuned all your minds onto it—maybe it would have been different. But we just bunged it on your desk and said, 'Look—love us or hate us.' And a lot of people said, 'Well, we hate you'—okay. And I think a lot of that's happened by default.

"Obviously, the Prince Rainier way of handling this would have been to say, 'Ladies and gentlemen, this is my lady wife, Linda' on ITN . . . like have a big press conference after we got married and saying, 'Please understand her, she's human.' Now the thing is, I didn't really feel like I needed to do that."[26]

News that Northern Songs might take the McCartneys to court coincided with reports that for the week ending March 17, 'Another Day' had reached No. 1 on the *NME* Top 30 chart.* George's 'My Sweet Lord' was at No. 5, and John's 'Power to the People' made its debut on the chart at No. 20.

Now, in a peculiar kind of symmetry, John, George and Paul were all in publishing disputes. Shortly after the release of *Abbey Road*, John had been sued by Morris Levy, whose Big Seven Music Corporation published Chuck Berry's 1956 'You Can't Catch Me,' to which John's 'Come Together' had striking similarities. Only days before the start of Paul's Apple lawsuit, George was sued by Bright Tunes Music over the structural and melodic resemblance of 'My Sweet Lord' to Ronald Mack's 1962 'He's So Fine,' a hit for the Chiffons.

Now Paul joined the club, although in his case, the threatened lawsuit was not about plagiarism, but pretty much the opposite: giving a partial songwriting credit to someone else when his publisher contended that he composed the song alone.

He was, in any case, confident that he and Linda would prevail, and that McCartney Music would be a useful subsidiary of MPL, not only for the administration of Linda's songwriting, but for Paul's music as well, once his contract with Northern Songs lapsed.

Lee Eastman, meanwhile, began searching for an executive to manage Paul's publishing. While visiting Paul and doing business with Capitol, in Los Angeles, Eastman made a stop at Beechwood Music, which had offices at the Capitol Tower. Beechwood had, only recently, lured Sam Trust to Los Angeles from New York to become its regional president.

Trust had become friendly with Eastman during the former's time as head of publisher relations at BMI, where he dealt with Eastman as the owner of several publishing companies. "He would confide in me, and he would call me 'Sam the Genius,'" explained Trust. Now Eastman had a plan to bring Trust back east.

"I didn't even have my offices [in Los Angeles] set up. I hadn't hired anybody, and I had a small

* The *NME* Top 30 was the only British chart 'Another Day' conquered. On the Official UK Singles Chart the song peaked at No. 2. In America, the song peaked at No. 5 on the Billboard Hot 100.

room in the [Capitol] Tower. And Lee made a beeline for me, all excited," Trust recalled, "saying, 'Look—here's what's going to happen. Now that [the Beatles have] broken up, I've convinced Paul to start a publishing company. For the time being, they're calling it McCartney Music, and I've told them all about you. And we want you to run their publishing!' I said, 'Lee—I just got out here. I signed a three-year contract. My kids are in school. I'm not about to pick up and leave.' He was startled. I said, 'I'm sorry, I can't do this.' After that [our relationship] was a little rocky for a while."[27]*

For Eastman, the search for a publishing executive for McCartney Music continued.

———

Paul had put off his decision about attending the Grammys until the last minute, not making up his mind until he knew that none of the other Beatles would be there. When Diane Brooks, who was in Los Angeles to join the McCartneys at strategy meetings for marketing *Ram*, called the National Association of Recording Arts and Sciences to arrange for tickets, she was told that Paul and Linda would be seated at a table with Capitol Records executives, toward the front of the theater. That was not Paul's preference, she told them: Paul wanted a table for five (the McCartneys, Brooks, and the Seiwells) toward the back.

The party arrived about 20 minutes before the ceremony's 5:30 p.m. start time and drove past the Palladium, waffling about whether or not to go in.

"We must have driven around the place where the awards were taking place four times. We were really leaping with nerves,"[28] Paul told a journalist a few weeks later. Other than their brief brush with the British press outside court in February, Paul and Linda had not openly courted reporters at an official event since attending the premiere of *Midnight Cowboy* on September 25, 1969. At the Grammys, he knew he would face American journalists as the guy who sued to split the Beatles, and won. His nervousness was apparent as the McCartneys posed briefly for photographers on their way into the theater.

Also striking was the group's unconventional dress for a formal occasion—and one that, as the first Grammy ceremony to be televised live, would be widely watched. Instead of a tuxedo, Paul sported a dark blue suit, with an open neck, a red flower print shirt, a yellow sweater and white sneakers; Linda wore a black flower print dress, with brown boots; Denny dressed festive, in a purple suede coat and a Peter Max tie, and Monique wore a gauzy dress.[29]

Making their way to their table, Paul ran into Peter Asher—James Taylor's *Sweet Baby James*,

---

* Trust's argument that he could not leave his new job at Beechwood notwithstanding, he left the publisher later in 1971 to start his own company, Trust Music Management, Inc. In 1973, he became president and CEO of ATV/Northern Songs.

which Asher produced, was up for a handful of awards (three of them in direct competition with the Beatles)—and chatted briefly,[30] before settling around their table at the back with Denny, Monique, and Diane, a bottle of scotch and some Cokes.

The evening was dominated by Simon & Garfunkel's *Bridge Over Troubled Water*, which took six of the seven categories it was nominated in, including Album of the Year. The Beatles—or, technically, Lennon, McCartney, Harrison and Starr,[*] as composers—won for Best Original Score Written for a Motion Picture or Television Special. When John Wayne broke the seal on the envelope and announced the winners, Paul, with Linda on his arm, walked through the crowd and onto the stage, accepted the trophies and said nothing more than, "Thank you. Good night."

Moments later, the Seiwells slipped out a back exit and returned to their motel, but Paul and Linda were asked to remain for press photos in a tent behind the Palladium. He was not at his most obliging. When the press gathered around, he answered only half a dozen questions.

Reporter: How are you going to get the awards to the other Beatles?

Paul: *Send them.*

Reporter: How long have you been in Los Angeles?

Paul: *A few weeks. Enjoying the sunshine.*

Reporter: Are you cutting an album here?

Paul: *Yes. Cutting an album . . . with a knife.*

Reporter: Is this your last act accepting on behalf of the Beatles?

Paul: *Yeah. Well . . . I don't know about that. I can't really talk about that, you know. I was here, so I accepted these.*

Reporter: Were you surprised that *Let It Be* didn't win more awards?

Paul: *Oh, no. The right records won.* Bridge Over Troubled Water *is too much.*

Reporter: What did you think of all the awards?

Paul: *Terrible. Terrible show. The whole thing was a flop.*[31]

He and Linda then hopped into their rented Cadillac and drove off, the cheering of about 200 fans fading into the distance.

---

[*] Ringo Starr, whose compositional contribution was as an arranger on 'Maggie May' and a cocomposer of 'Dig It' (both of which were credited to Lennon-McCartney-Harrison and Starr), was initially overlooked. When John Wayne announced the winners, he said, "John Lennon, Paul McCartney, George Harrison, for *Let It Be*." The oversight was NARAS's, not Wayne's: he had only three statuettes to hand to Paul and Linda.

The vocal arrangement, like that of 'Dear Boy,' was steeped in the Beach Boys' influence, with lines of counterpoint wrapped around the lead vocal. Paul recorded the harmonies mostly on his own, using three tracks, with Linda singing only on the refrain and in the "*We believe that we can't be wrong*" section.

The 24-second scat section proved complicated. Paul added it to the track that had otherwise been used for the lead vocal, and then he wanted to give it greater solidity by doubling it. Usually, that would mean singing it again on another track. But Paul was used to EMI's proprietary workaround, ADT, which created the double-tracking effect electronically. But the technique was not widely known outside EMI, so when Paul asked Eirik, "Can I have the ADT?" Eirik had no idea what he was talking about. They ended up phoning EMI, where an engineer explained the technique to Eirik.[32]

But that didn't help: even if Eirik had been able to do the wiring, a free track was required, and by now, the 16-track master of 'The Back Seat of My Car' was filled with the original rhythm track, bass and guitar overdubs, the orchestral score and vocals.

One solution, which the Beatles had used regularly, was to make a "reduction mix," in which several tracks were combined, or "bounced" to an empty track (or in this case, a new reel of tape), freeing up tracks for more overdubbing. But that meant a loss of flexibility in mixing (once tracks were combined, their balances could not be reconsidered), as well as a minor loss in sound quality, which Paul and Eirik preferred to avoid.

Instead, Eirik located space on adjacent tracks that were not used continuously—a few bars between guitar figures, for example—where he could punch in a few bars of Paul's second vocal, and punch out before the music on the punch-in track resumed. That approach gave Paul the opportunity to memorize the nonsense syllables he sang on the first pass and reproduce them exactly during the punched-in section. For Eirik, though, it was perilous: punching in and out required speed and precision if he was to avoid destroying an already recorded part.

"He would say to me, 'Eirik, you have to be faster!' I said, 'God, I must be as skilled as the world's fastest and most perfect surgeon to succeed in getting the short phrases into the narrow spots I have available!' And then we both laughed."[33]

When Wangberg mixed the track, he wondered whether the final seconds of the song—starting with Denny's short but decisive drum break—would sound better with the orchestra removed so that it was just Paul and company rocking on their own. He had already made a mix that he and Paul found satisfactory. Now he made another and cross-faded the original mix with the new, orchestra-free ending during Denny's break, creating the impression that the drums were double-tracked, an unintended sonic bonus.

Paul returned to the studio on Tuesday for instrumental touch-ups, adding lead guitar to 'Little Woman Love.'

The threat of a lawsuit over 'Another Day' meant that Paul would have to meet with David Hirst as soon as possible, in London. When he and Linda (with Mary and Heather in tow) landed at Heathrow, on March 25, a stringer for the *Daily Mail* was there to meet them, hoping to confirm a rumor, published five days earlier in a front-page *Daily Mirror* story by Don Short, that John, George and Ringo had met at Apple to discuss recording again. The story went on to say that Paul had been sent the proposed session dates, but because he had not responded, they were bringing in the Beatles' old Hamburg pal Klaus Vormann, to play bass.[34]

Short had been on target with most of his Beatles scoops over the years, but this time he was unable to get a comment from anyone, and the fact that the tale was exceedingly unlikely—he wrote the piece the day the Beatles and Apple filed its appeal against Paul's victory—did not slow him down. By the time Paul landed in London, an Apple spokesman had issued a denial. Yet here was Paul, suddenly in London. Could it be true after all, but with Paul actually returning to the fold?

Instead of asking Paul the question directly, the reporter asked whether he planned to see the other Beatles. "I think it is highly unlikely," he responded. "We are here for just two days and then we are going to France to do some recording for our latest album." By France, of course, he meant Los Angeles; it was part of a cat-and-mouse game he sometimes played with the press—fibbing to reporters and then criticizing them for getting it wrong. "I make it a habit not to read newspapers," he added, fibbing once more.[35]

At half past two on Friday, Paul and Linda sat down with Hirst and walked him through the history of 'Another Day,' starting with the phone call from Brian Forbes. They told him about sitting together at the piano in their bedroom at High Park, creating 'So Sad' and then writing out the lyrics, with 'McCartney and McCartney' at the bottom, and then recording the demo.

"Linda and I spent a week on this song," Paul said. Linda countered, "I think it took over two weeks."[36]

Paul explained that he often carried unfinished song ideas in his head—"I've got ten in my head at the moment"—and that he decided to combine his earlier 'Another Day' with 'So Sad,' with Linda helping to flesh out the lyrics.

Responding to Hirst's request for an analysis of who wrote what, they conceded that Paul wrote the music for the verses, but said that in each verse, Linda contributed lyrics, and that she also came up with some of the melodic ideas in the 'So Sad' section, which was now the bridge of the complete song.

Asked about her musical background, Linda said, "I sang at school and took piano lessons. I can play five chords on the guitar." Paul outlined his amorphous conception of collaboration, including the importance of having someone to bounce ideas off, a role Lennon and McCartney played for each other. He noted that on *McCartney*, though she was not credited, Linda helped him write 'Man We Was Lonely' and 'Kreen-Akrore,' and he said that of the songs he was currently recording, about half were collaborations with Linda.

During the consultation, Hirst pointed out that in his press statement, Jack Gill of Northern Songs had threatened to require Linda to prove she could compose a song, and that it might make sense for her to write one or more on her own, to disarm that part of Northern's strategy. Paul agreed.

Stopping in at Cavendish Avenue, Paul picked up another guitar that he thought might be handy in Los Angeles—his Epiphone Casino—and the McCartneys flew back to Los Angeles.

—

Recording Sessions

Monday–Friday, March 29–April 2, 1971.
Sound Recorders Studio, Studio B, Hollywood.
Overdubbing: Various songs.

Back at Sound Recorders, Paul was keen to push *Ram* across the finish line. Upon his return from London on March 29, he and Wangberg got down to business quickly, polishing off 'Monkberry Moon Delight' with two more vocal tracks, one for backing vocals on his own, the other with Linda. Paul's track was the addition of the scat vocal, starting at 2'55", which begins with him screaming "*monkberry moon delight*" and morphs into a passage featuring vocalized bass notes. (This overdub stands out in the final mix, not only because Wangberg boosted its level, but also because it was recorded using the same method as the backing vocals for '3 Legs'—placing a pair of Auratone speakers in front of Paul. This setup guaranteed that the playback of the backing leaked onto the vocal track, contributing to the track's odd, out-of-phase atmosphere.)

'Eat at Home' received no fewer than seven overdubs on March 30, including four lead vocal tracks (one marked "main," with Paul and Linda singing in tandem; a second for Paul's doubling, and two doublings for Linda), individual tracks devoted to guitar and cowbell, and lead guitar (on the Epiphone Casino). On reflection, Paul and Linda were not convinced by all these additions; Paul marked "erase" where the first guitar line and cowbell appear in their tracking notes.

They finished the day by returning yet again to '3 Legs,' to add a lead guitar line on the bridge.

April Fool's Day was dedicated to finishing one of the album's most complex compositions, the symphonic 'Uncle Albert/Admiral Halsey,' and it seems clear that a touch of the day's mischief was captured on tape. Having already laid down his vocal for the 'Uncle Albert' portion, Paul quickly tracked his lead vocal for 'Admiral Halsey.' Between Los Angeles and London Paul had finally completed the lyrics, and they were mildly eccentric: a single verse about the admiral needing a berth, and the song's narrator not doing much about it beyond having a cup of tea and a butter pie. The pie is a touch of Lancashire arcana—potatoes, onions, flour, salt, and a large amount of butter in a pastry crust, something Paul would have eaten as a child.

The final vocal parts for the coupled songs required some technical wizardry, so ahead of the session Eirik invited Paul Beaver, of the electronic music duo Beaver and Krause,* who wheeled in several modules from his synthesizer setup. Eirik proposed making the "answering" vocal (a repetition of the word "*water*") on the 'Hands Across the Water' section of 'Uncle Albert/Admiral Halsey' sound as if it were coming from underwater. Paul agreed to give it a try, and Beaver was on hand to show how that effect could be created by running that section of the vocal through the synthesizer.

"On Thursday afternoon I was scheduled to do a session at Sound Recorders in Los Angeles, but they wouldn't tell me what it was for," Beaver remembered with a smile. "I got there, set up the synthesizer and I sat in the recording engineer chair behind the console. Then this guy walked

---

* The other half of Beaver and Krause, Bernie Krause, had demonstrated the Moog synthesizer for George Harrison during a Jackie Lomax session at Sound Recorders, on November 10, 1968. To Krause's chagrin, Harrison recorded the demonstration session, later editing and releasing the tape as 'No Time or Space,' on his *Electronic Sound* album in 1969.

in the control room and with an intimidating English accent said, 'Who are you and what the hell are you doing here?' It was Paul!"[37]

One module Beaver used in his demonstration was a phase shifter, a device that creates the impression of a "whoosh" around a sound, as if it were coming from a different, magical reality. Paul was familiar with the sound—Jimi Hendrix had used it on 'Bold As Love,' and on parts of *Electric Ladyland*—and he liked its otherworldliness, so he ran the vocals for 'Dear Boy' through the module as well. They did not create the finished versions that day—Beaver would return the following week for that—but they filled a reel of tape with synthesizer experiments.

Paul also spent part of the day listening to a taped demonstration by the guitarist Geoff Levin of the Energy Bow, or Ebow. Invented by Greg Heet, the Ebow was an alternative to the guitar pick that allowed a player to draw sustained notes, as if the guitar were played with a violin bow rather than a plectrum.

With the end of the sessions in sight, Paul was planning for a mid-May release and began to focus on the LP jacket. Linda had brought to Los Angeles a collection of her photographs from Scotland, which joined a portfolio of session shots. Sorting through these, Paul chose a black-and-white photo Linda had taken during shearing season, showing Paul grabbing a ram by the horns.

Leaving the bottom part of photo intact, he clipped along the top of the fence and around his arms, shoulders, and head, and glued the photo onto a square piece of cardboard. Using a magic marker, he filled in a yellow sky, and drew zigzag designs in purple, red, yellow, and green around the left and right edges (also coloring in a torn piece of the cardboard, at the bottom left). To his left, Paul drew a rectangle bearing the album's name, in the same yellow as the sky, edged with the colors of the zigzag border. Midway down the right side of the zigzag, in a yellow stripe, he wrote L.I.L.Y, an acronym for "Linda I Love You."

On a second cardboard, he drew a yellow backdrop, with larger, looser versions of the border zigzag, with other patches of color and geometrical blotches, as well as a pair of lips at the bottom, and drawings of a pair of eyes, a row of teeth, and a freehand grid (the boxes numbered 1 to 15) at the top. At the center, he affixed a photo of the whole family leaning against a fence, with High Park's rolling land in the background. That was flanked by identical photos (one large, one small) of a pair of beetles copulating.

Like *McCartney*, the sleeve would be a gatefold, so for the inside, set against a blue background at the top and a green background below, Paul assembled a collage, with photos cropped around the edges of their subjects. Among these were several of Paul in headphones before a microphone, singing and playing his Firebird; a photo of Linda lying on a bed in the dress she wore to the Grammys; a bit of Paul and Linda in their Halloween costumes, and also recording backing vocals; several more casual photos of Paul; a reprise of the cover photo, and a shot of Paul's horse, Honor. Woven among all this were drawings by Heather and Mary, abstract designs by Paul, and—more easily visible on the original artwork than on the reproduced covers—blades of Los Angeles grass and strands of Heather's hair.

"We actually did the cover in LA, me just sitting around in the sunshine doing little drawings and things. The cover photo was Linda's, and the surrounding border was something I did. It was all very homemade and quirky, but I think that added to the charm of it. I remember when we were doing the layout for the gatefold, we put a little piece of grass from the garden and stuck it on. There were all sorts of little things that just came from our lifestyle at that moment. Linda took a photograph of two beetles copulating, or 'havin' it off!' Of course, this got totally misconstrued, because for us it was just an amazing wildlife picture. How often do you see beetles, and very colorful little iridescent beetles too? Linda just took it as a photo and we liked it, so we put it in. Of course, then people said, 'Oh, The Beatles are screwing each other—what's this mean?', and all sorts of hidden meanings got attached to things."[38]

In the finished version, the song titles and credits for the musicians (with Spinozza's name misspelled), engineering, artwork and production (only Paul and Linda; Guercio is among the engineers, who are listed by their first names only, except for Wangberg, as "Eirik the Norwegian") are on the left panel of the gatefold.

When Capitol called to say they needed new portraits, Paul and Linda hired Henry Diltz, a topdrawer rock photographer who had shot many of the same artists Linda had. They did a shoot on the grounds of the Capitol Tower, and another at J. Paul Getty's mansion. And Paul agreed to a couple of interviews.

One was with *Life* magazine, which sent Richard Meryman to tape an extensive interview at Sound Recorders that would be edited into a first-person, 4,400-word monologue by Paul. The cover story of the April 16 issue, it covered lots of ground—the Beatles split, the court case, John's *Rolling Stone* interview (which Paul says he ignored), the *McCartney* album, songwriting with Linda, and how much he enjoyed spending time on his farm.

Readers, who had not yet had a chance to hear *Ram*, were unaware that some of his stories—about the Shetlands trip, for example—explained the backdrop against which the songs on *Ram* were composed. But he did offer a hint of what listeners could expect of the album.

"My musical direction—I'm trying for music that isn't too romantic, yet contains a romantic thing. I personally don't like things to be too cute—except babies. My music comes off best, I think, when there's hard and soft together."[39]

Another interview was a matter of happenstance. As Paul pulled his Cadillac into a spot near the studio, he noticed that Allan McDougall, a writer for *NME* and other music papers, was getting out of the car in the next spot. McCartney and McDougall had not seen each other since the summer of 1967, around the time of *Sgt. Pepper*, but Paul had just read an article of McDougall's about Graham Nash. Nash, the former member of the Hollies who was then enjoying great success with Crosby, Stills, Nash and Young, had dinner with the McCartneys at the Getty villa only a few nights earlier and was given a preview of the *Ram* tracks.

"Hey," Paul asked Allan, "have you got a minute to come and hear some of me new album, eh, Allan, eh, eh?" McDougall walked into the studio with Paul and Linda, asking whether Paul minded if he wrote about the encounter—and the music—for *NME*. "So long as you don't mention song titles," Paul said, claiming it was a copyright issue, although a more likely reason was that he had not yet decided which tracks would be included.

As McDougall reported it, Paul offered his own review as they listened, regularly saying things like "ridiculous, isn't it?" and "real sweaty rock and roll, eh?" McDougall agreed, telling Paul that these songs were 100 times better than those on *McCartney*.

"Well, the *McCartney* thing was a whole different trip that I had to go through," Paul told him. "This one, though, this is really my music, this is really where I am."[40]

———

Recording Sessions

Monday–Friday, April 5–9, 1971.
Sound Recorders Studio, Studio B, Hollywood.
Overdubbing: Various songs.

In this final week of overdubs, 'Long Haired Lady' was finished off at last, with a track of backing vocals, another devoted to vocal harmonies, and a Wurlitzer electric piano part.

Wangberg remembers the mix being complicated—not a surprise, given the layers of vocals, the orchestral score, the rock instrumentation at its heart, and its unabashed theatricality, to say nothing of its frequent changes of tempo and texture.

"I had to make some tough choices," Wangberg said. "It is the longest piece of music on *Ram*. Paul made a repetitive loop at the end of the song with just the words, '*love is long*.' Meanwhile,

George Martin's score made this section a brilliant event. Both the band and ensemble run continuously over the same chord pattern for a long time, and I felt that this ran the risk of seeming 'thick' and 'blurred,' and perhaps boring."

One solution was to trim the section—but Paul wanted to retain its length, to embody the "*love is long*" idea. Eirik decided, therefore, to keep the section interesting by taking out several of the instruments (both symphonic and rock), then gradually restoring them: he added one instrumental strand, let it play for four bars, added another, and after four bars added a third.

"I wanted the listener to feel and hear the same as I, a growing magic until all the instruments are back—a great climax before the song ends."[41]

Paul Beaver returned with his stack of electronic boxes on April 7 to add the phase-shifting effects to 'Dear Boy,' and the underwater effects to 'Admiral Halsey.' Eirik also added sound effects to 'Uncle Albert/Admiral Halsey,' including a thunderstorm and rain effects. Eirik has claimed, in fanciful moments, that the storm effects were either field recordings he made himself at the edge of a cliff, or that they came from a sound effects tape he obtained from Universal Studios. The latter is more likely.

During the final overdubbing session, on April 9, Paul added a few vocal lines and another guitar part to 'I Lie Around,' before he and Eirik surveyed the materials intended for the disc of promo spots, which included takes of the 'Now Hear This Song of Mine' fragment, spoken word recordings, sound effects and Snuffy/Henry the poodle. Eirik added to these by having Paul and Linda go into the studio to answer questions from Eirik, piped in from the control room.

Paul, Eirik and Linda worked on the radio spots together: with bleating lambs, snippets of stories, sound effects and excerpts from some of the songs on the album all wrapped around 'Now Hear This Song of Mine,' they were very much in the spirit of the quirky sound experiments and humorous tracks Paul had made in his home studio all these years. The finished promotional tracks were issued to radio stations in America on a white-label 12-inch, which instantly became a collector's item.

———

The McCartneys also had a visit during their final week at Sound Recorders, from EMI's Len G. Wood, the company's managing director during the Beatles years, and now the label's group director. Paul had invited—summoned, really—EMI's chairman, John Reid, to come to Los Angeles, hear the album-in-progress and discuss marketing strategies. Reid decided that Wood was the man for that and dispatched him instead.

Wood arranged to meet Paul and Linda at Sound Recorders on April 6 at 3:00 p.m. On his way, he stopped at the Capitol Tower to collect Stanley Gortikov, Capitol's president, and wondered why, with the Capitol building—company territory—right around the corner, Paul was having them come to, as he put it, "some little studio."

"I was due to be there at three o'clock," Wood recalled, "so I got there a minute or two before three, and a little girl [the receptionist] answered the door. I explain who we are—'oh, yes, yes, yes'—and we sat there chatting, the two of us. It's a quarter past three, and no sign. It goes on towards half past three. No sign. So I said to the little girl, 'It is this afternoon that Mr. and Mrs. McCartney are coming in, isn't it?' 'Oh yes, yes, they usually come in about this time.' I thought, 'Usually? What's all this?' So I said, 'They're in here quite often, are they?'"[42]

When he was told that they had been there since March 1 and had been in nearly every day since, Wood's heart nearly skipped a beat, knowing that Paul had also been racking up studio time in New York since October, and having read news reports, just a few days earlier, in which Paul was quoted saying that he was recording in Paris. He remembered immediately thinking, *My God, this is going to cost!*

"But then Paul and Linda came in, quite bright and breezy, and we had a very nice talk—except that Paul had some rather elaborate ideas for promoting *Ram*. He wanted an airplane with a tow behind it, and billboards all over Los Angeles. But we had a sensible, nice conversation."[43]

But Wood was alarmed at the likely cost of the album. At a conservative estimate, considering studio rental costs, musician fees (including three sessions with orchestra), incidentals like instrument rentals, and overtime, recording *Ram* is likely to have cost in the neighborhood of $150,000 [£62,000] (about $1,050,800 [£888,120] in 2022 values). Wood immediately telephoned John Eastman, in New York.

"I said, we haven't seen a bill yet, but it's going to come in, and I really don't see why we should pay it," Wood told him. "Eastman said to me, 'Well, how many are you going to sell? I think you want to take these costs.' So I argued with him, and in the end, Eastman said, 'Look, you haven't had a bill yet. If you get those bills, you talk to me, and we'll work something out.'"[44]

Who covered the session costs is a mystery. Wood later said that EMI never received the bills. It is unlikely Capitol would have picked them up—they were not contractually required to do so, and if they had, Wood would certainly have known about it. Paul, feeling cash-strapped as Apple held his royalties from Beatles recordings and *McCartney*, is unlikely to have covered the tab himself—although if he did, he would have recouped the money relatively quickly, since in that case, EMI would not have been charging the expenses against his royalties. (But then, there was that pesky business of Apple sitting on those royalties while James Douglas Spooner, the receiver, sorted through the company's finances).

The most likely possibility, but one that is impossible to verify, is that the bills were sent to Apple. That would not have been unreasonable: John and Yoko frequently charged their expenses to Apple, and although Paul had just won his court case, he would remain an Apple artist until his separation took effect. Since Apple was receiving his royalties, it made sense for the company to deal with the billing as well. If nothing else, it would be an incentive for Apple to negotiate Paul's exit.

———

Recording Sessions

Monday–Friday, April 12–16, 1971.
Sound Recorders Studio, Studio B, Hollywood.
Mixing: Various songs.

After six months of recording, overdubbing, legal jousting, and periodic transatlantic travel, Paul was emotionally and physically spent. At this point, most but not all of the 23 songs he recorded since October were complete; a few, like 'Little Lamb Dragonfly,' still had holes in their lyrics, and therefore, lacked their final vocals. But there was more than enough to choose from.

That, in a way, was a problem for Paul. Having composed all the songs, and having spent months recording them, he was fond of them all. A few could be removed from contention. 'Another Day' and 'Oh Woman, Oh Why' were dropped from album consideration when they were released as a single, and 'When the Wind Is Blowing,' 'Sunshine Sometime' and 'Little Lamb Dragonfly' were intended for *Rupert*. 'Rode All Night' and 'Blues' were really just jams. So now there were 16 songs vying for 10 or 11 slots on the disc.

That's where the preview sessions for Graham Nash and Allan McDougall came in: Paul was not just showing off the new material—he was gauging listeners' reactions to the tracks he played them. Guercio had expressed his ideas and created a proposed track list. Eirik had ideas of his own. Paul was unwilling to relinquish the decision completely; getting a read on other people's reactions left him feeling more assured about his own.

"I say to people, 'Well—do you like it?' And that's how the decision gets made. Unless I'm very passionate about [a particular song]. With things like 'Get Back,' the Beatles record, I didn't spot it as a single. I didn't think it was anything special. It was the other guys who said, 'No, it's great—Jo-Jo, it's great, pure.' So, I don't really think of myself as a great spotter of what's good and what's not, in my work. You can't actually learn how to do it. It's all instinct."[45]

Certain inclusions were obvious for thematic reasons ('Too Many People,' for one), and there was never any doubt that the big production pieces ('Uncle Albert/Admiral Halsey,' 'Long Haired Lady' and 'The Back Seat of My Car') would find a place.

Some of the mixing had been done along the way, so at the April 12 session, Paul put the rest of the preliminary stereo mixing in Eirik's hands, along with tasks like joining the still separate 'Uncle Albert' and 'Admiral Halsey,' and executing Eirik's idea of splitting 'Ram On' into two sections, one for each side of the LP. A few days later, Paul returned to check on Eirik's progress and to do some tweaking of his own (countermanding Eirik's idea of putting the flugelhorn solo in 'Admiral Halsey' in a bed of ambient reverb, for example). Pushing the monitor faders to ear-bleeding levels during their final mixing session, McCartney was overtaken by a tsunami of more typically masked emotion.

"When I mixed 'Long Haired Lady' he never commented, he was just listening to what I had done," says Eirik. "He stood behind me, with his hands on the chair, with his head next to mine, because he wanted to hear exactly what I heard from the speakers when I mixed. And when it finished, I turned around and I saw a tear running down his face. Paul is a very, very sensitive person. Listening to his vocal work with Linda really got him into it. It was amazing."[46]

Paul and Eirik, sharing a glass or two of single malt whisky, then sequenced the album. And though he was open to suggestion, Paul was instantly set on one thing: the LP would start with 'Too Many People,' the McCartneys' melodic brickbat for John and Yoko, complete with its "*piss off cake*" backing vocals. He also chose to close Side One with an assertive rocker, separating the two with personal ruminations and fantasy tracks. Side Two was devoted almost entirely to songs that painted an alternately warm and goofy portrait of life with the McCartneys, ending with Paul's grand production piece and teen-spirit manifesto, 'The Back Seat of My Car.' Not coincidentally, the closing line of the LP, "*we believe that we can't be wrong*," was also directed at the pro-Klein camp.

SIDE ONE (EMI MATRIX NO. YEX.837)

'Too Many People'
'3 Legs'
'Ram On'
'Dear Boy'
'Uncle Albert/Admiral Halsey'
'Smile Away'

SIDE TWO (EMI MATRIX NO. YEX.838)

'Heart of the Country'
'Monkberry Moon Delight'

'Eat At Home'
'Long Haired Lady'
'Ram On (Reprise)'
'The Back Seat of My Car'

Of the 11 songs, 5 were credited to Paul alone ('Too Many People,' '3 Legs,' 'Ram On,' 'Smile Away' and 'The Back Seat of My Car'); the remaining 6 were listed as collaborations with Linda ('Dear Boy,' 'Uncle Albert/Admiral Halsey,' 'Heart of the Country,' 'Monkberry Moon Delight,' 'Eat At Home' and 'Long Haired Lady'). If ATV wondered whether its saber-rattling over the credit for 'Another Day' intimidated Paul, here was an answer: Keen to take the fight to Sir Lew Grade, Paul also had the Eastmans file a counter suit against ATV/Northern Songs, seeking a ruling that songs he composes with anyone other than John Lennon be exempt from his existing contract with the company.

Eirik took over for the final, mechanical tasks, which included assembling and banding the stereo masters (on April 22 and 23), and preparing a promo-only monaural mix for American radio stations (May 7). By then, Paul was long gone. When *Let It Be* won an Academy Award for Best Music for a Motion Picture, on April 15, Quincy Jones, deputizing for the Beatles, was at the Dorothy Chandler Pavilion to collect the Oscar. The McCartneys were on their way back to Campbeltown.

Fresh McCartney!

11

BATTERING *RAM*

—

Paul's relationship with High Park had changed fundamentally over the past year. Between 1966 and 1968, his visits were a matter of getting out of the limelight and going rustic for a few days. In 1969, the farm became a refuge from Apple politics, and his visit just after the release of *McCartney* started out that way too. But in 1970, the McCartneys had spent the spring and summer there, right up to the moment they left for France and the United States. That extended stay transformed the Scottish getaway into something much more like *home*.

Now, a year later, Paul planned to spend the spring and summer of 1971 at High Park once again. It was from there, not London, that he would oversee the release of *Ram*, an album that had been almost entirely written in Scotland, and which screamed *country life*, with a heavy undertone of the *McCartney* album's home and family theme.

Shortly after they arrived, Paul undertook maintenance chores, arranging to have hot water in the farmhouse for the first time (although the installation would not be until August), and he gave the corrugated roof a coat of green paint, with Linda providing entertainment by way of a new addition to their record collection, the first installment of the Trojan Records 'Tighten Up' series of reggae compilations. Paul and Linda were both taken with these tracks, which included a cover of Paul's own 'Ob-La-Di, Ob-La-Da' by Joyce Bond, and a sunshine rendition of a song the Beatles covered, 'Kansas City,' sung by Joya Landis. By the summer's end, they were determined to explore reggae more deeply.

Paul also oversaw a major improvement to his music facilities. In 1970, he used a small building attached to the barn as a studio of sorts. It was a comfortable and convenient place to work, and just big enough to accommodate a few other people, so he hired a builder to spiff it up with a corrugated tin roof and, except for a single stone wall, wall and ceiling paneling. Hefty shelving was built along the back wall to accommodate percussion instruments, boxes of recording tape, a four-track deck, and a pair of monitor speakers. Otherwise, the room was filled with guitars, an electronic keyboard, microphone stands and a drum kit. Paul and Linda called it Rude Studio.

Paul quickly got back to writing, first revisiting some of the 1970 songs that did not make it onto *Ram*—'Country Dreamer', and 'Indeed I Do,' for starters. At some point every day, he could be found in Rude Studio, tinkering with new tunes; his assertion to Hirst, that he had ten songs rattling around in his head, was not an exaggeration.

"The average day there would be get up, have breakfast with the family, then maybe go into my little studio," Paul explained of springtime at High Park. "I had a little four-track studio, which is what The Beatles always used to record on [between 1964 and 1968]. That's a real discipline recording on a four track, you've either gotta know exactly what you're doing, or you have got to start bouncing tracks. You can imagine, when you get into that, it's addictive."[1]

When he was not in the studio, Paul could regularly be found sitting on a stone wall or leaning against the barn, Martin acoustic in hand, entertaining Linda and the girls. 'Hey Diddle,' from the 1970 crop, was a favorite of Mary's, as was a new concoction, 'Bip Bop'—a blues progression in E major, overlaid with a simple tune built on a descending minor third, and lyrics that were mainly nonsense syllables that would catch a baby's ear. Indeed, on one tape he recorded over the summer, Mary can be heard singing the song's opening, while cartoons played on television in the background.

"I just had a very simple thing going on guitar," McCartney said of the tune, "just the bass string plonking away on the opening, like a sort of simple blues thing. And I put on the words '*Bip bop*.' And Mary could sort of understand it, she could sing it and stuff."[2] His girls, he said of his proclivity for writing child-friendly songs, are "the one audience I've got when I'm composing my songs. They're the ones who gather around the piano, so it's natural that a lot of my songs will turn out to be like that."[3]

He was also working on new songs that were decidedly for adults. '1882,' for example, is a Victorian tale of a boy who steals bread for his dying mother, with a grisly chorus: caught, tried and found guilty, the boy is both tarred and feathered and, in the final chorus, drawn and quartered.

That imagery is likely to have been inspired by a spate of news articles Paul would have seen throughout the first half of 1971, about the Irish Republican Army's practice of tarring and feathering those they regarded as traitors to their cause, including women in relationships with police or British soldiers. Paul was not comfortable commenting on the IRA directly, or on politics generally; "*preaching practices*" was best left to John. But he was fascinated that tarring and feathering—a gruesome form of torture that can be traced back to the twelfth century, when King Richard I instituted it as a punishment for sailors convicted of shipboard theft en route to the Crusades[4]—was still being practiced.

"I think I'm observant," he said of his ability to subconsciously mirror reality in the fictional worlds that his songs often occupy. "I think I notice stuff. Sometimes it's kind of awkward. But all these things, it's just stuff that happens naturally inside [of me]."[5]

With that barbarity as the song's most striking image, he built a story around it that could easily have been inspired by Victor Hugo's *Les Misérables*, which begins with Jean Valjean leaving prison after a 19-year term for stealing bread. Why Paul chose to place the song in 1882 is not clear, but his choice may have been more to do with rhyme than reason.

Other songs he was developing were firmly rooted in the here and now. During his time in the United States, he started 'Dear Friend,' a melancholy message to John Lennon, completed since he returned to High Park. Between the lines, and against a piano backdrop in C minor, he expresses his love for John and probes John's feelings about the issues that destroyed their working relationship and possibly their friendship. It has only two verses, each repeated, but its most arresting element is a set of questions: "*Is this really the borderline? Does it really mean so much to you?*" and "*Are you afraid, or is it true?*"—the last of which he changed to "*Are you a fool, or is it true?*" in the second verse.

At first, Paul offered an oblique interpretation of the song, presenting it in general terms. "Lyrically—I don't know really," he told David "Kid" Jensen, of Radio Luxembourg. "It's just about a dear friend, whatever it means to you. It's really, 'Dear friend quit messing about, let's throw the wine, have a good time and stop messing.' Like George says, '*Isn't it a pity that we break each other's hearts,*' well, that's me saying, let's not."[6]

But he later conceded that, much as 'Dear Boy' was conceived as a letter to Linda's ex, 'Dear Friend' was intended as a musical letter to John.

"Obviously it was a very difficult period, because the band I'd been in all my life had disbanded. And then came the meanness and the cruelty after it. I later heard that John, Yoko and Allen Klein would confab and think up mean things to say about me, and John would sometimes take it and put it in a song. John could be very cruel. He was wounded; he was a wounded pigeon. You know, his life was wounded from the start when his father left home and he had to live with his aunty, and his mother gone. And so, he had all sorts of tragedies. But as Liverpool guys you don't think about that, you just get on with it. And I'd lost my mother, so it was all part of getting on with it.

"Now this time round, after the Beatles, there was a new set of cruelties to deal with. So, sometimes I would think, 'Yeah, I'll get you back,' and probably more in my character was like, 'What are we doing this for? Why are we doing this?' And I could also see the side of John that was, 'Give Peace a Chance.' So I knew that side of John, I knew that, like most people, he's double sided. So if he was coaxed into being cruel he was good at it. Anyway, there were two options in responding to it, and the one in 'Dear Friend' was, 'Why don't we just sit down, shut up, and have a glass of wine. And, come on man, we've known each other too long to really get into this bullshit!' And so, I was glad to do that in the song."[7]

Linda devoted time to songwriting as well, since Hirst advised her to take seriously ATV's threat to "require" her to prove that she had that ability. Her first attempt was a 1950s-style blues progression in G major. Overcome with excitement, she pulled Paul to the piano and played it for him. "Been done, love," he told her, sitting down at the piano, and playing Paul Anka's 'Diana,' to which her song bore an uncanny similarity.

"I discovered a thing I thought was new," Linda said, "and it turned out that 'Diana,' and all those songs had used the chords I'd found."[8]

In her next attempt, Linda tried for a simple but appealing melody, but on the single known demo recording, in which she accompanies herself on the piano with a single line that mirrors the melody, she had not yet started to grapple with other elements, most notably rhythmic variety. Called 'This Time Next Year,' the song moves with the steadiness and simplicity of a Gregorian chant.

She next put her mind to emulating the sound that she was becoming increasingly fascinated with, reggae. On a pair of demos titled 'Pretty Woman,' Linda plays a basic piano part, built around a single chord, with bass notes (in octaves) struck twice, then the rest of the chord, also played twice. (John Lennon had used the same pattern in early versions of 'Mean Mr. Mustard.') Paul accompanies on drums and sings the title line, nonsense syllables, and lyric fragments about the titular pretty woman's long hair, and whether she'll go out with him. Linda occasionally sings an answering vocal.

After a couple of takes, they renamed the song 'Seaside Woman,' but continued along the same path. Paul, still on his perch behind the drums, ad-libbed a lyric in a Jamaican accent, with Linda singing the new refrain, '*Oh, seaside woman*,' and Paul sometimes repeating it, sometimes harmonizing.

———

Amid all this activity, the Big Event on the agenda remained the release of *Ram*. As with *McCartney*, Paul left the business of cultivating the press to nearly the last minute, and although he had set up McCartney Productions Ltd., he still lacked a publicist. Going through Apple was not an option; besides, Peter Brown had decamped to run the Robert Stigwood Organization's New York office, and Derek Taylor had left for Warner Brothers. Apple's current press spokesman, Les Perrin, was part of Klein's regime.

Surprisingly, given his preference for putting the Beatles behind him, he turned to Tony Barrow, an independent publicist now, but someone swimming in Beatles history. But Barrow was a special case: he had been there from the start, and just as importantly, he was *not* present at the end. When Epstein began managing the Beatles, he tried to persuade Barrow to cover the group in his *Liverpool Echo* record review column, "Off the Record," written under the pen name Disker, but Barrow told him he could do nothing for the band until they released a recording. By then, Barrow was living in London, writing sleeve notes for Decca Records; he helped Epstein arrange an audition with the label. By the end of 1962, shortly after EMI signed the Beatles, Epstein lured Barrow away from Decca, hiring him as a publicist for the Beatles and other performers on the NEMS roster.

Barrow held a firm place in Beatles history for other reasons, too. He wrote liner notes for some of their early releases and was credited with coining the nickname, "The Fab Four." It was Barrow who came up with the idea of having the Beatles record annual, fan-club-only Christmas discs. And when the Beatles played their last live concert, at Candlestick Park, in San Francisco, on August 29, 1966, Barrow stood a few feet from the bandstand with a cassette recorder, at Paul's request, documenting all but the final seconds of 'Long Tall Sally,' their closing number.* After Epstein's death, the Beatles distanced themselves from NEMS; Barrow, feeling marginalized, set up his own public relations company, Tony Barrow International.[9]

Those few years away from the Beatles kept Barrow in Paul's good books: he was untainted by any association with Apple or Klein. But there were problems that quickly doomed the relationship. One was distance. Paul meant to remain in Scotland, and Barrow found the long-distance relationship only created problems. The amount of time and effort Paul spent in Los Angeles envisioning and proposing spectacular advertising campaigns showed that he craved publicity for the new album. But he had no interest in popping down to London for interviews or press events.

"Our brief professional reunion failed to work out," Barrow later wrote, "not because of any issue with the album, but because Paul wanted to get me involved in a strange remote-control PR campaign for *Ram*. I was to play his LP tracks to journalists and DJs at my new company's London offices while he stayed on his Scottish farm some 538 miles away! I felt the least he could have done to support the campaign would have been to face the media in person and talk about the music. 'Can't you make it all up like we used to do?' he asked."[10]

It was a stunning misreading of the music press in 1971, and especially odd because Paul had not only witnessed, but taken part in, the changes the press had undergone since the Beatles' early days. There was scarcely a serious music press in 1963, when the Beatles released *Please Please Me*, their debut album. Trade magazines dutifully (and usually cheerfully) reported on new releases and backstage deals, and the major newspapers carried reviews and occasional interviews. Teen magazines covered pop stars with lots of photos and exclamation points, and the kinds of stories

---

* Barrow's recording is comparatively good quality for a non-soundboard tape, and it has been widely bootlegged. The end of 'Long Tall Sally' is absent because the cassette ran out. There is no other known recording of this historic show.

a publicist could, as Paul remembered, just make up. Pop and its stars were ephemeral, it was thought; building the short-term legend for the sake of immediate sales was more important than digging out the truth.

But even then, musicians—including musical royalty like the Beatles—made themselves available when there were records to promote, on the theory that a bit of glad-handing, witty chat and personal attention would transubstantiate into enthusiastic ink. When the Beatles released *Sgt. Pepper*, only four years earlier, the press launch was a lavish listening party at Brian Epstein's house, at which the Beatles mingled with writers.

By then, the Beatles had taken a hand in fostering a more independent music press by giving interviews and, toward the end of their touring years, news conferences at which they replaced banter about hair length and what kinds of girls they liked with criticism of the Vietnam war and racism, and other matters of concern to their maturing listeners. And by 1967, Paul had become a supporter of the *International Times*, one of the first "underground" publications, and a nexus of politics, art, and music.

Now the press was less interested in thumbs-up, thumbs-down reviews and cheering on favorites than in covering the ways music was linked to politics, to the broader sweep of musical history (rock was becoming venerable) and to what they knew about the musicians themselves. On the eve of *Ram*'s release, Paul found this newly muscular, independent press daunting.

That was partly because of his solution to getting press for *McCartney*. His self-interview was unquestionably an attention-grabber, but Paul came to regret the fallout. Instead of proactively defending his position, he retreated to Scotland, and then New York and Los Angeles, effectively surrendering the press to Lennon, who expertly put forth the narrative that Paul had usurped the leadership of the Beatles and had become unreasonable, bossy and spoiled. Talking to the press now meant playing defense, and facing the inevitable questions about his relationships with the other Beatles, and how his lawsuit might have affected them. Better to avoid that by having Barrow gather the press and play the album, without Paul and Linda.

Barrow held the press listening session as commanded, and it did not go well.

"Some around me were so gripped while [*Ram*] played," Alan Smith sarcastically reported in *NME*, "that for most of the time they called across the room to each other about old times and old friends."[11]

Still, Barrow soldiered on, announcing that the album would be in British shops on May 21 (though the UK issue was later delayed by one week), with an American release on May 17. And if Paul wasn't available for the stories he lined up, Linda photographs were. In fact, the incorrect claim that the New York Philharmonic played on the album was based on a Barrow press release accompanied by one of Linda's shots of Paul, in his deer sweater, conducting an orchestral session at A&R Studios. Though the orchestral players are not credited on the album, many of the reviews picked up on the Philharmonic's supposed involvement, and the *Daily Mirror*, on May 11, ran an "exclusive," using Linda's photo under the title, "Paul Goes It Alone with the Phil."[12]

Barrow consistently noted Linda's involvement, pointing out that she cowrote six songs and coproduced the album with Paul.

"To quote Paul," he told reporters, "Linda was very present throughout the making of the LP, both in the writing, recording and production. She sings harmony with Paul and is featured to a greater or lesser extent on all tracks. Instrumentally, I understand she plays simple percussion."[13]

Almost as if on cue, Northern Songs and Maclen Music filed suit, in New York, against Paul and Linda, claiming $50,000 in damages and $1,000,000 in punitive damages for violating Paul's exclusive publishing agreement with Northern Songs.[14]

On the other hand, Paul was entirely off the hook for the legal costs of his lawsuit against the other Beatles and Apple: when Apple dropped its appeal, on April 26, 1971, the court ruled that Lennon, Harrison and Starr would bear the costs, estimated at around £100,000 ($250,000).

———

With Barrow handling the rollout of *Ram*, the McCartneys took a day off to fly to Saint-Tropez for Mick Jagger's wedding to Bianca Pérez-Mora Macías, a Nicaraguan beauty who, commenters could not help noting, looked uncannily like Jagger. McCartney and Jagger enjoyed a friendly rivalry all through the Beatles years, and after the Beatles split, Jagger—who had just come through a difficult period with the Rolling Stones, having had to dismiss and replace founding member Brian Jones—suggested, in jest, that he and McCartney team up to form a new band.[15]

Paul put off the decision to attend the May 12 wedding until the last minute; when Jagger phoned him on May 11, McCartney tried to beg off, saying he was having trouble finding a nanny for the girls. "I will be your nanny," Mick said, "you just get here."[16]

But Paul's sidestepping likely had to do with more than simple childcare issues. John and Yoko, Jagger had explained, were also expected at the wedding reception, their suite at the Byblos Hotel already reserved. Ringo, too, was a definite, and though George was not fully committed, he was considering catching a late flight. Speaking to Don Short that afternoon, John confirmed that he would soon be on a flight to southern France.* John and Yoko were due at the Cannes Film Festival for the premiere of their latest short films *Apotheosis* and *Fly* on May 14, and they planned to attend Jagger's wedding in Saint-Tropez before hopping along the coast to Cannes.

---

* In a full-page piece published in the *Daily Mirror* on May 12, 1971, that carried the headline: "Jagger invites the Beatles to Make Up at His Wedding," Don Short claimed that Mick Jagger was playing peacemaker between the warring Beatles.

"It will be good to see Paul," Lennon told Short, "there will be no ill feeling between us."[17]

With the dust still settling on the Beatles' recent court case, Paul was left playing a game of wedding day roulette. If he failed to show, it was unlikely he would lose face. But there was a slim possibility of public fireworks. Whatever his decision, the presence of four Beatles under one roof so soon after tearing legal strips off of each other was not a welcome prospect. But finally, Paul came to a decision, and the McCartney clan flew from Machrihanish Airport to London Gatwick on the afternoon of May 12. Paul would front it out.

Jagger chartered a private jet, at a cost of £2,500 ($6,250) to taxi his guests from London to Nice. If the other Beatles did turn up as expected, the flight would give them a couple of hours to clear the air before Mick and Bianca's wedding reception.

Paul, Linda, and the girls arrived at Gatwick half an hour late, but the plane was still waiting for them on the tarmac, as were a pack of photographers and reporters. Strolling through the departure lounge, Paul spied Ringo and Maureen sitting alone. Without explanation—as was so often the case with Lennon—John and Yoko had bailed. George was also a no-show.

"Why have George Harrison and John Lennon not turned up?" reporter Sydney Curtis asked Paul as he took a seat at Ringo's table. "I cannot speak for the others," Paul replied. "Is there any chance of the rift being healed because of this wedding?" Curtis continued. "Look," Paul snapped back, "I don't want to talk about that, if you don't mind"[18] And with that, Jagger's guests were whisked away to the delayed jet.

On the runway, a BBC cameraman and reporter caught up with Paul and Linda as they walked to the plane, but Paul, not in the mood for a chat, lapsed into Beatles press conference patter:

Paul: Hello BBC.
Reporter: Are you looking forward to the wedding?
Paul: Oh yes.
Reporter: What are you taking for a present . . . ?
Paul: Don't push, chaps.
Reporter: What are you taking for a present?
Paul: My wife.
Reporter: As a married man yourself, can you recommend marriage?
Paul: Oh, definitely not.[19]

The McCartneys and the Starkeys were among the 100 or so friends and family members for whom Jagger chartered the jet to Nice. Others on the flight included Chris Jagger, Anita Pallenberg and Keith Richards, Eric Green, Ossie Clark, three of the Faces, Jo Bergman, Nathalie Delon,

Roger Vadim and Ricci Burns.[20] Paul and Ringo had not seen each other in person since Ringo's visit to Cavendish Avenue with the letter from John and George, asking Paul to postpone the release of *McCartney*. The encounter, as Ringo described it, was cordial.

"That was strange because we hadn't seen each other for a year, but we both knew everything was okay. I'm not gonna . . . none of us are gonna punch each other, or anything like that. It was just like, we hadn't seen him for a year, so it got like, 'Hello,' you know, and we had to get warm together."[21]

The wedding itself included two ceremonies, as dictated by French law—a civil marriage, performed by Marius Astetzan, the mayor of Saint-Tropez, at the city's council chamber, and a Roman Catholic ceremony at the seventeenth-century Chapel of St. Anne's. Few of Mick's guests attended those; the main event was the party in a hall near the Café Des Arts in Saint-Tropez's main square, with music by Freddie Notes and the Rudies, a reggae band, and the blues guitarist Terry Reid. Mick also sang with the soul singer (and Apple artist) Doris Troy.

Like the other celebrity guests, the McCartneys stayed at the luxury Byblos Hotel, and they were among seven couples (Keith Richards and Anita Pallenberg were another) who, believing that Jagger was picking up the tab, left without paying their bills, amounting to several hundred pounds. "This is, no doubt, a misunderstanding but it is an embarrassing one for us," said Claud Maret, the hotel's manager, who explained that he planned to send the bills to "the Rolling Stones organization."[22]

Paul and Linda were back in Campbeltown the next afternoon—the entire trip took less than 24 hours.

—

A between-projects break would have been tempting, but the quick jaunt to Saint-Tropez would have to do: the anxiety of awaiting the release of *Ram* militated toward staying put. But that did not stop Paul from grappling with future plans and prospects. High on his agenda was getting back onstage, and feeling the energy and embrace of a live audience. Paul's need to stand before an audience and work his magic had been deep in his soul since childhood, and it had been steadily on his mind since the end of 1968.

Now the question was, how to do it? He could enlist a few starry friends who were between bands and would relish playing in a group with a Beatle; for that matter, he could poach players from existing bands, the way the Beatles poached Ringo from Rory Storm and the Hurricanes. It could be a "permanent" band that toured and recorded, or it could be a different lineup for every project.

The solution Paul kept returning to was to build a band from the ground up.

"I did think now and again about getting in professional musicians, getting in the super session men. I could have asked the best in the world to play with me. But I wanted the amateur approach, something we could make ourselves and then work on."[23]

But who he would play with was only one of the questions Paul tussled with. Another was how he would balance playing in a band—presumably, a touring band—with his relatively new responsibilities as a husband and father. That was a question he had not had to deal with as a Beatle, and he had seen John and Cynthia Lennon grow apart under the pressures of pop stardom, something he was determined would not happen with him and Linda.

The downside of life with a touring pop star was not lost on Linda, either.

"I knew exactly what to expect if I married anyone who belonged to a group," she said. "It meant sitting around for months whilst the guy was on tour abroad or, if I went with him, I would still be lonely . . . So, it's not a piece of cake taking on a relationship in this business."[24]

For Paul, the solution was obvious: he would draft Linda into his prospective new group. She was already listed on record labels as a songwriter, and she'd sung backing vocals on *McCartney*, 'Another Day,' and *Ram*—which was credited not just to Paul, but as a Paul *and Linda* album.

"She had no musical experience," Paul reasoned, "but really my reason for doing it was a simple one. Linda and I had just got married and I had decided to continue making music. Now, when you're a musician, you're expected to leave your wife and kids at home when you go on the road. But I thought, 'No, we won't do it the usual way. Let's stick together and play music at the same time.'"[25]

All Linda needed to do, Paul figured, was learn her way around a keyboard. *Nothing to it*, Paul insisted. Linda had doubts. Singing backing vocals on a recording was one thing; getting out on-stage and being expected to perform with a band of experienced musicians was another. "The whole thing started because Paul had nobody to play with," was how Linda remembered their early discussions of her becoming a performer. "We were up on the farm in Scotland, and he started romanticizing about what it's like onstage. He made it sound so easy I just said, 'Yeah.' I must have been out of my mind. I never thought, '*Could* I learn piano? *Could* I sing?'[26]

"He went on and on about it," she added, inadvertently echoing Ringo's court deposition about Paul's method of getting his way in the Beatles, "saying he was dying to get back to performing, but wanted me to join in. We had a few rows as he tried to teach me. He really put me through it. I'd never realized how hard it all was.[27]

"We love being in each other's company and Paul was determined that I would be involved in everything from composing to playing. Now that might have been fine if I was a musician; but at that time, I wasn't. No way. I could pick out one-fingered notes on a piano. And yet here was my husband, former member of the Beatles . . . the greatest group ever . . . wanting me to be onstage alongside him. If you think that I was scared . . . you're right. I was absolutely petrified at the idea of going onto a stage before an audience. They'd think I was a fake."[28]

Another project on Paul's mind was the idiosyncratic notion of producing an instrumental version of *Ram*—one on which he would not play, and that would appear to be an independent tribute, a cover of the entire LP.

"At that time, a lot of substances were involved," Paul said, "so there were a lot of mad ideas that flew around, and it was a madcap idea that I just thought, 'Wouldn't it be great if an orchestra covered *Ram*?' It would just be an intriguing thing to happen. And then I thought, 'Well, that might involve me waiting around for someone to ring up, and the very unlikely event that they would say, Oh, by the way, I'd like to cover *Ram*.' So I thought, 'Well, that's a bit unlikely, so maybe I could do it?'"[29]

The project made business sense, too. All through the Beatles era, covers of Lennon-McCartney tunes—not only straightforward pop covers, but versions that ran the gamut of musical styles, not to mention translations into other languages—had provided a solid and steady income stream for the two songwriters. Why not encourage covers of his post-Beatles work?

The first hurdle was finding someone to orchestrate the songs, assemble an ensemble, and conduct the recording. George Martin was too obvious a choice; instead, Paul telephoned Richard Hewson, the arranger who scored James Taylor and Mary Hopkin recordings on Apple, as well as the Spector version of 'The Long and Winding Road.'

Hewson was surprised to hear from Paul. They had not spoken since Paul heard Spector's acetate of *Let It Be*. But Paul made a distinction between Hewson, as a hired hand, and Spector (with Klein behind him), as the producer responsible.

"I was called in by Paul even before *Ram* was released, to do a totally instrumental version of it," said Hewson. "He gave me an advance copy of the album, and said, 'Here you go. Just orchestrate that for me, in your own style. Anything you like—jazz, whatever you want to do. Go for it.' He never took any part in the arranging, he never advised or instructed me in any way. He just said, 'You can do whatever you like. Just make a totally instrumental record, with no limit to the orchestra,' though I didn't go mad, like Phil Spector. I don't, to this day, know why he wanted to do an instrumental album, even before his [version of *Ram*] had come out. But he did."[30]

Paul had no idea how he would market this cover album that no one was really desperate to make, and that no listeners were clamoring for, but in the months that followed, he and Linda would periodically return to the idea, concocting a tale involving the fictitious Percy "Thrills" Thrillington, an eccentric, socially well-connected conductor who they had signed as an MPL artist and who would be making his recording debut with this collection.

For now, he booked sessions at EMI for mid-June, giving Hewson about a month to do the arrangements. Paul paid Hewson £100 ($240) for each song he orchestrated.[31]

———

The release of *Ram* was decidedly less dramatic than the release of *McCartney*; apart from not being heralded by an incendiary self-interview, *Ram* had been announced well in advance, and press copies had gone out in enough time that reviews began appearing before the release.

There was a smattering of positive notices. Lon Goddard, in *Record Mirror*, wrote that "the 12 songs on *Ram* range from the incomparably complex to the delicately simple . . . Rarely does he ever stoop to a predictable progression and there is always a twist to his lines." Noting Linda's equal billing, he concluded, "We haven't lost a hero, we've gained a duo."[32]

Most of the upbeat reviews, however, worked hard to be positive without making great claims. *Billboard*, for example, chirpily reported that "Paul & Linda debut like the sweethearts of rock 'n' roll reborn, as the ex-Beatle continues to play the rock Romeo with little else on his musical mind."[33] And *Disc* and *Music Echo* called it "first-class musical entertainment," hardly the gold standard of acclaim at a time when musicians (John Lennon, chief among them) sought to make far-reaching statements in their work.[34]

The negative reviews were both more plentiful and more vehement. Robert Hilburn, at the *Times*, called it "a disappointing C plus at best."[35] David Wigg, in a thumbnail review in the *Daily Express*, found the 'Hands Across the Water' section of 'Uncle Albert/Admiral Halsey' "inspiring," but considered the album "disappointing inasmuch as it generally lacks the simplicity and beautiful, romantic melodies with which Paul has previously moved us."[36]

In the *Guardian*, Geoffrey Cannon took an arch approach to reconciling his generally pleasant experience at Barrow's listening session with his more critical response on hearing the disc at home. "*Ram* will sound very good against conversation at a party," he wrote, "but listen to it by itself, and it's little more than style, skill, and echoes of the days when the Beatles attended to the society of which they were a fulcrum. If you admire Paul McCartney, much better to once again listen to *Revolver*."[37]

Penny Valentine, having been rebuked by Paul for writing that *McCartney* wasn't very good, allowed that *Ram* was an improvement, but added that "whereas McCartney was once so warm, with such a broad sympathetic view of the human race, his outlook now appears to have turned a little hard." The album's most notable quality, she astutely observed, was what she called Paul's "man of a thousand voices technique." The result, she wrote, was a collection in which "snatches of Presley, Beach Boys, Buddy Holly, and the Stones, Hoagy Carmichael, 'Hey Jude' and 'Yellow Submarine' sift through continuously."[38]

In a review entitled "Mutton Dressed as Ram?" *Melody Maker*'s Chris Charlesworth found that the album "fails to match up to those of Harrison and Lennon," but attributed any disappointment with the disc to the difficulty of living up to the McCartney name.[39] But Alan Smith, in the *NME*, was uninterested in excuses: "What, in the name of all that has gone before, is happening to Paul McCartney?" he asked. "His newly-released second solo album, *Ram*, is an excursion into almost unrelieved tedium. The melodies are weak, the ideas are stale, the arrangements are a mess . . . Certainly it would be true to say that it contains not one worthwhile or lasting piece of music."[40] (Paul may have taken solace from the letters column in the following issue, when a couple of readers pushed back, sarcastically, against Smith's observations.)

There was even pushback from one of the musicians who played on the album, David Spinozza. In an interview in the May 29 issue of *Melody Maker*, Spinozza spoke about enjoying seeing how McCartney worked, and admiring him as a songwriter, but complained that the sessions weren't challenging for him as a player. He also aired his grievances about session scheduling and last-minute cancellations. What really stung, though, was Spinozza's dismissive assessment of Linda.

"She can sing fine," Spinozza said, "like any girl that worked in a high school glee club. She can hold a note and sing background. So Paul gives her the note and says, 'Here, Linda, you sing this and I'm going to sing this,' and she does it, and evidently feels creative or something. But it's all McCartney—Paul McCartney."[41]

For Paul, the tone of the reviews was painful, and deeply depressing. After reviewers' complaints about the homespun quality of *McCartney*, he took seven months and spared no expense to record an elaborate but not overproduced album using superb musicians, and choosing what he—and listeners he played this new music for—felt were the strongest tracks in a large collection of new songs, and his reward was to be treated like an underachieving cipher.

"I did get very depressed," Paul said of his reaction to the *Ram* reviews. "Everything I did was so slagged off by the critics and everyone that I began to think I had lost the knack. I thought, 'That's it—I've lost it and I won't get it back.' I began to believe all those people who were saying I wasn't very good and that I couldn't make decent records. Before that point I had thought very seriously about jacking it all in and spending the rest of my life just farming or something."[42]

He could console himself, to some extent, by joking about some of the reviewers' obtuseness. Not a single one noticed the message to John in 'Too Many People'; one critic wondered whether the song was about overpopulation. Even the positive reviews were irksome in that regard. One critic called 'Smile Away' the album's musical high point, but described 'The Back Seat of My Car' as unmemorable.

But there was no escaping it: he had made a major effort and been slapped down. And all those reviews were nothing compared with the slice-and-dice review Jon Landau published in *Rolling Stone*, a piece that looked as though Landau had paged through Nicolas Slominsky's 1953 *Lexicon of Musical Invective: Critical Assaults on Composers Since Beethoven's Time* and repurposed a parade of choice put-downs.

"*Ram* represents the nadir in the decomposition of Sixties rock thus far," Landau began. "For some, including myself, [Bob Dylan's critically pummeled] *Self-Portrait* had been secure in that position, but at least *Self-Portrait* was an album that you could hate, a record you could feel something over, even if it were nothing but regret. *Ram* is so incredibly inconsequential and so monumentally irrelevant you can't even do that with it: it is difficult to concentrate on, let alone dislike or even hate."

Landau offered an analysis of McCartney's role in the Beatles, characterizing his ability to write and sing both hard rockers and soft ballads as "schizoid," and noting that Lennon and McCartney each countered the other's extremes, with Lennon apparently keeping McCartney from lapsing into the rock equivalent of elevator music.

But his concluding paragraph was striking. The individual Beatles, he wrote, have not functioned well as solo artists, and now that they have tried, the weaknesses of each have become clear. "*McCartney* and *Ram* both prove that Paul benefitted immensely from collaboration, and that he seems to be dying on the vine as a result of his own self-imposed isolation. What he finally decides to do about it is anybody's guess, but it is the only thing that makes Paul McCartney's musical future worth thinking about and hoping for."[43]

Despite receiving a critical shellacking, *Ram* fared well in the *Billboard* 200. Thanks to pre-sales, the album entered at No. 6 on June 5, 1971, and strong sales kept it on the chart for 37 weeks, 24 of them in the top 10. But as with 'Another Day,' Paul had to settle for the No. 2 spot, where *Ram* peaked on August 21, unable to unseat Carole King's *Tapestry* at No. 1. The RIAA certified *Ram* Gold on June 9.

In Britain, despite the negative publicity stirred up by the Beatles' recent court case, support for McCartney's music was unwavering. *Ram* entered the chart at No. 1 on June 5 and remained in the top 100 British albums for 24 weeks, 15 in the top 10.

Paul knew exactly what he was going to do to avoid, as Landau put it, "dying on the vine of his own self-imposed isolation." On May 21, the day *Ram* was released, he phoned Hugh McCracken and Denny Seiwell, in New York, and invited them each to Campbeltown, with their wives, at the end of June.

"Hugh got a call from Paul," Holly McCracken recalled, "and he said, 'I'd like you and Holly and Denny and Monique to come.' In the very same call, he said that he'd already bought [flight] tickets for all of us, and was going to send them. We were all very excited, thinking, 'Wow! What's this about?'"[44]

Though Paul was not explicit, both Hugh and Denny suspected that putting together a band was what he had in mind. There was talk, after all, of bringing along their instruments, and doing some jamming. As Seiwell remembered it, "Paul didn't say, 'Come over and let's form a band,' he just said to come over and hang out. If it didn't work out, it would have been a nice vacation anyway."[45]

John Lennon had thoughts of his own about *Ram*. If the critics failed to hear 'Too Many People' as a message to John, John heard it loud and clear, and he suspected that the line '*We believe that we can't be wrong*,' in 'The Back Seat of My Car,' was intended for him too.

"I heard Paul's messages in *Ram*," Lennon fumed in an interview with *Crawdaddy* magazine. "Too many people going where? Missed our lucky what? What was our first mistake? Can't be wrong? Huh. I mean Yoko, me, and other friends can't all be hearing things."[46]

In response, he repurposed an unfinished song that had been kicking around since 1969, originally titled 'Since You Came to Me,' and fashioned a response. Composing new lyrics that put Paul directly, and identifiably, in the crosshairs, he transformed his old tune into 'How Do You Sleep?'

On May 26—just five days after *Ram* was released—John brought 'How Do You Sleep?' into Ascot Sound, the new recording studio built for him at Tittenhurst Park. Although the studio was not quite finished, Lennon had just started work on his next album there, with a band that included George Harrison on guitar, Klaus Voormann on bass, Nicky Hopkins on piano and Alan White on drums.

"*The only thing you done was* Yesterday," Lennon sang, "*And since you've gone you're just* Another Day." And it got harsher: "*The sound you make is Muzak to my ears / You must have learned something in all those years*." Harrison contributed a sizzling slide guitar solo, and in 11 takes, the song was complete but for a string section overdub, added in New York on July 4.

———

Up in Scotland, oblivious to the musical grenades that were soon to be launched in his direction, Paul considered ways to give his new album greater public exposure, without having to break cover. He had not made a promotional film clip to promote 'Another Day' (instead, when the song debuted on *Top of the Pops*, Pan's People, the BBC's resident dancers, awkwardly shuffled through it), and he had not settled on a single to be released from *Ram*, or whether to release one at all. But he knew from the Beatle days that supplying television shows with clips was a sensible practice, so he hired a film crew—Roy Benson, who had been an editor on *Magical Mystery Tour*, to direct, with cameraman Norman Langley—to come to High Park on June 5 and 6, to capture some footage that could be edited to a soundtrack of *Ram* cuts, to promote the album on *Top of the Pops*. The shoot yielded three clips, edited by Benson, with Paul nominally the producer.

In the first, footage of Paul and Linda riding their horses through the rugged farmland of High Park and Low Ranachan was edited to accompany '3 Legs.' More horse riding, intercut with film of Paul, Linda, and Martha the sheepdog playing on the beach at Machrihanish, became the 'Heart of the Country' promo. In neither clip do Paul and Linda attempt to lip-synch, and not much attention is paid to continuity, either: Paul and Linda are seen riding their horses in several outfits.

"There was a rush," Benson remembered, "so I went up to the BBC in person, straight from the edit suite in Wardour Street [in Soho, London], and delivered the film to the *Top of the Pops* office. I was hoping to have a few more days to work on it, actually, to do some special optical effects, doubling up images and that sort of thing, but there just wasn't time."[47] Both clips aired on the June 24 edition of the BBC's premier music show.

'Heart of the Country' had already been given a slight television boost—or, at least, a nod—by Kenny Everett, the DJ and longtime friend of the Beatles, whose satirical clip about his own recent firing by the BBC* aired on *Late Night Line-Up* on May 29. In the clip, Everett, wearing a Yoko Ono T-shirt, gives a tour of his country pile, stopping in his music room to play (and mime) a few seconds of the newly released song, which returned in a longer clip at the end of the show.

Langley's third clip was an 11-minute assemblage of unused footage showing Paul sitting out-

---

* Everett was dismissed by BBC Radio One on July 19, 1970, after suggesting on his weekend show that Mrs. Mary Peyton, the wife of the British transport minister, bribed her examiner to pass her advanced driving test. Everett continued to work as a DJ for Radio Luxembourg before joining Capitol Radio in 1973.

side the stone farmhouse playing a Gibson J-160e acoustic guitar, Linda harmonizing at his side, and Heather, Mary and Martha playing around them. He runs through five songs—Roy Brown's 'Good Rockin' Tonight,' which Paul knew best as an Elvis record; the new 'Bip Bop'; and two songs from the 1970 crop, 'Hey Diddle' and 'I Am Your Singer,' with a fragment of another new tune, 'She Got It Good,' sandwiched between them. Except for 'Good Rockin' Tonight,' Paul listed all these as part of the growing Paul and Linda McCartney composition catalog.

In mid-June, Paul and Linda made a lightning trip to London, with two goals. The first was to look at office space for MPL's new London digs. They had hired Shelley Turner, an American, from the West Coast offices of Warner-Reprise, to oversee publicity, but needed a proper head-quarters, and rather than paying an estate agent to locate vacant spaces, the McCartneys went knocking on doors in Soho.

Funding a central London base was a problem. With most of his money still in the hands of the court-appointed receiver, McCartney had to balance location with cost and settled for space at 1 Soho Square, above the offices of a film production company. Two dingy offices on the fourth floor were a step down from the lavish Saville Row base the Beatles had purchased almost exactly three years earlier, but it would do for the time being, and MPL was open for business by July.

More amusing, for Paul, were the Percy Thrillington sessions, led by Richard Hewson at EMI. In an unusual ceding of control—possible only because he enjoyed toying with the fiction that the project was not really *his*—Paul had given Hewson a free hand, and he had only a vague idea of what he would be hearing at the sessions.

Recording Sessions

Thursday–Sunday, June 15–18, 1971.
EMI Studios, Studios One & Two, London (Studio 1 on June 17).
Recording: *Thrillington* album (all songs from *Ram*), Richard Hewson, conducting.
Mixing (June 18): *Thrillington*.

When Paul walked into EMI's Studio Two, Hewson was already in the control room, giving Tony Clark, the engineer, and Alan Parsons, his assistant, an overview of the project, about which Clark had not been briefed.

"I was booked to do the sessions," Clark said, "and I set the studio up for the first day, which I think was a big lineup. I spoke to Richard Hewson, and said, 'Is Paul coming along? Is he going to sing on it?' Richard said, 'No, it's an instrumental version of *Ram*,' which I knew nothing about.

Great. Pressure. What am I supposed to be doing? And I remember, after the first session, not having heard *Ram*, thinking, 'Should I listen to *Ram*, to have some input?' But I chose not to. I just remember going home and thinking that the first sessions were so great, I don't want to put any barriers on the way I was feeling about them, by listening to the original. So I just went for it."[48]

Hewson had booked a starry ensemble, including a rhythm section with bassist Herbie Flowers, pianist Steve Grey, Roger Coulan on Hammond organ, Vic Flick on guitar, and several drummers, including Clem Cattini (who, long before his days as a session player, was a member of the Tornados), and drummer Dougie Wright, plus percussionists Chris Karan and Jim Lawless.

There was a string section (10 violins, 4 cellos) led by Tony Gilbert, and woodwind and brass sections that included the alto saxophonist Pete King, and Derek Watkins, a trumpeter who worked in both the jazz and classical worlds.

Hewson put together a packed schedule that included three sessions every day from Thursday morning to Sunday evening. The Swingle Singers, renowned for their bright-hued, bouncy vocal arrangements of Bach and other classical composers, were on hand for the Thursday afternoon session, with Mike Sammes Singers (who are heard on 'I Am the Walrus') recording that morning. Hewson also planned to use a quartet of recorder players from the Dolmetsch Consort—one of Britain's pioneering early music ensembles, which Hewson had also brought to Mary Hopkin's McCartney-produced *Post Card* sessions on Thursday evening.

"I hired the best jazz musicians I could find," Hewson said, "and because I was doing a lot of recording in those days, a lot of them were friends I'd worked with anyway. So that gave it a sort of jazzy flavor, but because I was a music student only a couple of years previously, I loved the classical side of things, so I brought in the Dolmetsch family, who I had been introduced to during my student days. And I loved choral sounds, so you've got a lot of different colors. I could have done it as a big band jazz thing, but there wouldn't have been the variety."

With Paul producing—in this case, mostly a matter of speaking up if something didn't work, for him—Hewson moved with impressive efficiency through the three days of sessions. This involved recording the rhythm section (or "pop combo," as it was called at the sessions) for all the songs at the very first session, on the morning of June 15,[49] and then adding the other instrumental and vocal timbres at sessions devoted to those parts of the ensemble. Strings and winds were overdubbed on the evening of the 15th, a boys' choir on the morning of the 16th, the Swingle Singers that afternoon, and strings and recorders that evening. Clark's recollection is that a few of the pieces were played live in the studio.

Some tracks—the brassy 'Too Many People' (with the guitar solo transferred to woodwinds), 'Eat at Home,' with its 'Ob-La-Di, Ob-La-Da' bass line and melodic brass, and the soft-focus 'The Back Seat of My Car'—veer toward middle-of-the-road symphonic pops arrangements. But most of the pieces have interesting orchestrational touches at their core. '3 Legs' has a sultry jazz sound of the sort you might run into in a smoky bar, a saxophone putting forth the song's bluesy melody. 'Dear Boy' and 'Heart of the Country' benefit from the Swingle Singers' "*do-do-do-do*" and "*wah-wah-weeeee!*" syllabic singing, and 'Long Haired Lady' owes its charm to a doubled soprano saxophone melody, and sharp-edged trumpets on the '*love is long*' sections.

Not everything went as planned. On 'Smile Away,' Hewson's score called for a cuíca, or "laughing gourd"—a Brazilian percussion instrument that is basically a bongo with a thin rod attached to the underside of the drum skin. It is played by rubbing one's fingers along the rod, and producing a squeaky timbre.

"I was looking for different sounds," Hewson said, "and I was mad about bossa nova, which had just come in. So I thought I'd use the cuíca on that track. Poor Chris Karan, the percussionist, had never seen the instrument, and never heard of it, so I told him what the principle was, and he played it. But it didn't come out anything like the sound Brazilians make with it, and all the band were laughing. He asked, 'Can I go behind a screen to play this?'"[50]

Hewson used the sound Karan produced on the track. It sounds like a barking dog or, as Hewson put it, "a grunty pig"—not what he envisioned, but interesting enough to keep.

"I don't think I've seen Paul quite so happy, away from the responsibility of making and producing his own music—just having a great, great bunch of musicians playing his music," Tony Clark said. "Paul would talk to the musicians, and be the producer in the box, with me engineering, and it all flowed. Paul was bopping around, and feeling great about his music. I reckon we all did."[51]

Clark produced a stereo mix of the album on June 18, along with Hewson's version of a contemporaneous B side that was not on *Ram*, 'Oh Woman, Oh Why.' For the moment, the recordings were filed away, awaiting Paul's decision about how and when to release them. The following day, the McCartneys paid a superfast visit to Italy to celebrate (belatedly) Paul's 29th birthday, jetting into Milan on Monday evening, and spending two nights at Villa d'Este, a five-star hotel on Lake Como. Paul and Linda were guests of EMI Italia, who laid on the hospitality in an effort to persuade Paul to return to the concert stage. Without a backing group, McCartney told his hosts, European concerts would have to wait.

———

Denny and Monique Seiwell flew into Glasgow Prestwick Airport on June 22. They quickly ran into problems at customs, where inspectors looked askance at the drum kit Denny brought, at Paul's request. When quizzed, Denny said he was on his way to Paul McCartney's house for a vacation, and to play some music. That, too, raised an eyebrow, but Denny handed over Paul's telephone number, and Paul told the inspectors, "Yeah, he's with me—send him down here." Pan Am arranged for a van to take the Seiwells, and the drums, on the five-hour trip to Campbeltown. There, they rented a car, checked into the Argyll Arms Hotel—"where," as Denny put it, "you needed to put a hot water bottle between your legs to sleep at night; I mean, it was cold"[52]—and drove up to High Park.

"We asked some of the villagers how to get to High Park Farm, and they said things like, 'Well, laddie, ye take the wee car . . .' and I'm thinking, 'What the hell are they talking about?' We finally found the right road, and they had said that we'd come to a farmhouse, which was on the edge of the McCartney property, but after that there was no real road to their house. Well, the sun was setting in the black hills of Scotland, and we beeped the horn, and this old guy came out, and we said, 'How do you find Paul's farm?' and his answer was nearly unintelligible, but he opened this old wooden gate and there were these boulders everywhere. We ruined the car. We ruined about three rental cars; they wouldn't rent us any more cars in this village. Finally, we got to the farm. Two bedrooms in the 'main house,' a kitchen, the kids, the horses, the sheep. Linda cooked up a dinner that was to die for, real simple stuff."[53]

The Seiwells spent the next day with the McCartneys, setting up Denny's drums in Rude Studio and tucking into scotch and Cokes. Hugh and Holly McCracken, fresh off a tour with Gary Wright, arrived at the Argyll Arms on June 24. After shedding their bags, they drove up to the farm with Denny and Monique. For the McCrackens, the Scottish countryside might have been another planet.

"It was absolutely beautiful," Holly McCracken said. "You were so far away from the gravity of the city. So we stopped the car, because I just had to run through one of the fields. I climbed over the fence, and just ran. And then I looked down and found myself covered in cow pies."[54]

Another day of socializing, and another of Linda's home-cooked dinners—this time a vegetarian meal built around baked red potatoes and creamed spinach—and plenty more scotch and Coke. When it was time for the Seiwells and McCrackens to leave, Linda buttonholed the drummer and guitarist and said, "Come back tomorrow, but leave your wives at home this time, we're going to make some music."

"Hughie and I said, 'Oh, what the hell, it's work,' and we made our way up there again," said Denny. "I'm not sure how the girls took it, but I don't think they took it too well, to tell you the truth."

They did not. "It was like, 'Okay, this is a much bigger reality now than I was aware of,'" recalled Holly, a professional singer who met Hugh when they were both performing on a television show. "They didn't know me, and they had no idea that I understand that work situation, and that I'm not there to be a member of the band. But I do remember being upset, and annoyed, and thinking, 'I'm out at the end of a peninsula in Scotland—am I supposed to take up knitting?'"[55]

But there was no point protesting; it was clear to everyone that this could be the start of something important. At High Park, the new band—Paul, Hugh, Linda and Denny—packed into Rude Studio and played through old rock classics, blues progressions supporting freewheeling jams, and some of the songs they had worked on together in New York. Denny reconfirmed his enthusiasm for 'Rode All Night,' the impromptu studio jam he recorded with Paul. They worked through some new things, as well, including 'Bip Bop,' which Paul told them was a song he composed for Mary.

"Everybody loved Mary the first time you saw her," Denny explained. "She had big, saucer eyes. But Mary used to go around the house when she was a baby, and she would just sing, 'Bip bop, bip bop, bip bop.' That's where the song came from. Paul heard her, and he said, 'Let me write a song around that.'"[56]

After only a couple of days of playing and talking, the satisfaction Paul felt while working with Denny and Hugh in New York was sufficiently bolstered that on June 25,[57] he popped the question.

"Paul sprung it on us," Denny recalled. "He said, 'This isn't just a holiday. I miss my old band. Do you want to form a band?'"[58]

Both musicians faced a tough choice: in New York, they were in demand and commanding multiple-scale session rates. But this was a chance to form a band with a former Beatle, and although there was not yet any discussion of finances, the possibilities were tantalizing.

Denny immediately agreed to join Paul, and misinterpreting Linda's presence on keyboards as a temporary stopgap, pending the engagement of an experienced player, he suggested that Paul get in contact with Paul Harris,* a keyboard player both he and Hugh worked with regularly in New York.

"He was a great piano player, and I thought, 'Wow, if we could put a band together with Paul, Hugh, Paul Harris, and myself, musically it should be very sound,"[59] Denny reasoned. The idea, he quickly learned, was a nonstarter.

Paul did, however, pick up on Denny's enthusiasm for 'Rode All Night,' and he found that 'Hey Diddle' and 'Blues' were growing on him. Having left the *Ram* multitracks at MPL's New York office, he had the relevant reels messengered to A&R and asked Dixon Van Winkle to make stereo mixes of these *Ram* leftovers.

Hugh shared Denny's enthusiasm about working with Paul, but he needed time to think about whether he wanted to join a band. Paul allowed Seiwell and McCracken some liberty to explore the charms of the peninsula with their wives as they made their decision, while he saw to farm and family tasks.

On one such off day, June 26, Paul, spotted Carolyn Mitchell, the 24-year-old who moved from

---

* A few months after Seiwell proposed his membership, Harris joined Manassas, the band led by Stephen Stills. Among the musicians he worked with in the studio were John Sebastian, B.B. King, Seals and Crofts, Nick Drake, John Martyn and ABBA.

Salt Lake City to London in March 1969, to be near Paul, and who regularly camped out in front of his house on Cavendish Avenue. She had spoken with Paul several times and appeared in several press articles about the girls who kept vigil at Paul's London home.

"I came from America to be with Paul and, just my luck, I arrived the week before he got married," she lamented to one reporter. "My feelings towards Paul are different from those towards a pop idol, really they are. They're as real as they can get. I don't often go out with boys. I just don't like them. Nobody could replace Paul for me. Maybe I will have to be an old spinster, like some people have told me. I can't help it. I just want a relationship with him that would mean I don't have to stand by the gate. I'd like him to be a friend."[60]

Paul recognized Mitchell when he saw her, perched on a rock just over the property line, looking down at High Park. Hopping into the Land Rover, he drove over to her and gave her a piece of his mind—as well as, she claimed, a clout on the nose.

"For three years now," Paul told the *Daily Express*, "I have been asking her politely—pleading with her—to leave me and my family alone. She refused to recognize that I am married with a family. When I saw her sitting, looking down on us, that was the end. This time I told her to go away, and not politely. I admit it. I was rude."[61]

"All I did was chase her away. I never touched her. If she's injured, she must have fallen on the way down the hill. I moved here for peace and quiet—not to have cranks and sightseers around. If I didn't try to stop girls invading the privacy of my home here, I'd never get rid of them."[62]

Mitchell lodged a complaint with the Campbeltown police, who sent an officer to investigate. Her complaint was later dropped.

In Campbeltown on their own, Hugh and Holly McCracken had their own glimpse of being stalked by fans, an experience that put Paul's invitation in an uncomfortable perspective and reminded Hugh that apart from other concerns, he had to decide whether, after a decade of mostly studio work, he was comfortable being in the public eye to the degree he would be in a band with Paul.

"I had long, straight blond hair," Holly said, "and Hugh had a beard, as Paul did at the time, and he looked a lot like Paul. So there were people following us around, and we figured they thought we were Paul and Linda. Hugh said it felt like someone had thrown cold water in his face, and he woke up to the reality that being in Paul McCartney's band would be huge. And that gave him pause. He loved Paul, and he loved working with him, but he didn't feel comfortable with that level of fame."[63]

But a more critical issue was that Hugh had two young children from a previous marriage. Joining Paul's band would mean moving to Britain, and not seeing his son and daughter grow up. He was enjoying jamming with this prospective new band. But after a couple of weeks, he realized that he could not resolve the tension between wanting to join the group and needing to be part of his children's lives. On July 4, he told Paul he could not accept his offer.

"Paul was very surprised, and upset," Holly said. "And Hugh felt awful. But they sat in the kitchen all night, talking, accompanied by a bottle of scotch. Then Hugh came back, and we left the next day. And Paul never spoke to him again."[64]

McCracken's departure meant putting the band on hold. Paul expected to play both guitar and bass, so a second guitarist was necessary. Without one, there was no point continuing to jam, so the Seiwells returned to New York on July 6, and Denny took up an offer to produce the debut album of a young New York singer-songwriter-pianist, Billy Joel.

Paul, pensively strumming his guitar in Rude Studio, returned to the drawing board.

12

GROWING WINGS

———

The false start disappointed McCartney, but eager as he was to start this new phase of his career, he knew that the chemistry had to be right. In the meantime, there were other projects to consider. A few weeks earlier, Ron Kass, the former head of Apple Records, called with a tantalizing commission.

Kass was working with Albert "Cubby" Broccoli, coproducer, with Harry Saltzman, of the James Bond film franchise. "Do you fancy doing a Bond thing?" Kass asked him. McCartney liked the idea. In 1965, he told a teen magazine that he was a big fan of Ian Fleming's James Bond novels; the first one he read, he said, was *Live and Let Die*.[1] Soon after he spoke with Kass, Broccoli called to propose that McCartney write the theme for *Diamonds Are Forever*, which had started shooting in April.

Nothing came of it, though. Several contradictory explanations have been offered. McCartney has said that he "tried to think of a tune for it. But then we couldn't do it because of some contractual things,"[2] specifically, Saltzman's prior contract with John Barry, the composer of most of the Bond themes to that point. Barry and Saltzman were going through a dispute early in the production of the film, but they settled it, and Barry composed the *Diamonds Are Forever* theme, which Shirley Bassey recorded for the film.

It's likely that signals were crossed, at this early stage in the production: in light of the production team's disputes with Barry, Broccoli saw an opportunity to get McCartney on board and pounced without checking with his partner, who typically oversaw the music for the Bond films.*

An alternative story was offered by Tony Bramwell, another Apple refugee working for Saltzman. As Bramwell told it, he chased McCartney for a year, in the hope that he would write the

---

* The confusion created by Kass's and Broccoli's approach to McCartney may have been among the reasons Harry Saltzman appointed Kass managing director of a new company, CDF Ltd., at the end of August 1971, and three months later, as the head of CDF subsidiary Hilary Music, which published the music heard in the Bond films.

Diamonds Are Forever theme, but that when McCartney submitted his track, it was too late to be included.[3]

July also brought a visit by Jim McCartney and his second wife, Angie,* plus Angie's 11-year-old daughter, Ruth. The Liverpool McCartneys were less fond of roughing it than Paul and Linda, so Paul tended to visit his dad in Heswall, and Jim, Angie and Ruth preferred to visit him in London.

"The Campbeltown farm did not have one decent guest bedroom for visitors to use," Ruth later complained. "The bathroom had no hot water when we were there. Angie and Jim, who was . . . arthritic, were given a mattress on the floor of a draughty garage [probably Rude Studio] to sleep on. I was luckier. I went in with Linda's kids, who had bunk beds. Paul and Linda loved to show what they had done with their remote farm. They grew their own lettuce and beetroot. Paul sheared and dipped his sheep. He took pride in showing his dad a concrete step he had made."[4]

But glitzy commissions and family visits aside, finding players for his new band was foremost on Paul's mind. A devoted reader of the British (and, lately, American) music papers, not only for reviews of his own work, but also to know what other musicians were doing, Paul had noted an article in the *NME*, back in February,[5] about the breakup of Balls, a Midlands band whose roster included an old friend, Denny Laine.

Paul had known Laine since July 1963, when the Moody Blues played as a support band during a Beatles tour of Britain. Paul was a fan of the Moodys' 1964 hit 'Go Now!,'[†] on which Laine was the lead singer. In the heady midsixties, they frequently ran into each other at the Ad Lib and other London clubs the Beatles and other bands frequented. Unlike Hugh McCracken, Laine was well accustomed to playing the fame game.

Born Brian Frederick Hines in Tyseley, Birmingham, on October 29, 1944, Laine took up the guitar as a child after hearing recordings by the Belgian jazz guitarist Django Reinhardt. He adopted his stage name, which combined a family nickname he was given because of his preference for the den in the Hines family home, and the surname of his sister's heartthrob, Frankie Laine, when he formed Denny and the Diplomats, a teenage band with brushed-back hair like the early Beach Boys. Also among the Diplomats was the drummer Bev Bevan.[‡]

In 1964, he was invited to join another Birmingham band that soon morphed into the Moody Blues. Brian Epstein managed the Moody Blues briefly, but did little for them; they were then taken on by Tony Secunda, who continued to manage Laine after he left the Moodys, late in October 1966.

---

* Jim McCartney and Angela Lucia Stopforth (born November 14, 1929) were married in North Wales on Tuesday, November 24, 1964. Neither Paul nor his brother Mike were present for the impromptu wedding. Jim was 62 and Angie was a 35-year-old widow with a daughter Ruth (born on February 15, 1960).

† The Moody Blues second single, 'Go Now!'—released in November 1964 in Britain (on Decca) and January 1965 in the United States (on London)—was a cover of a song released in January 1964 by the R&B singer Bessie Banks (whose husband, Larry Banks, composed it with Milton Bennett). On the Banks original, produced by Jerry Lieber and Mike Stoller, on Tiger Records, there is no exclamation point in the title. That was added by the Moodys or Decca.

‡ Bev Bevan went on to become the drummer for the Move and its spinoff, the Electric Light Orchestra.

Laine's next endeavor was the Electric String Band, a classical-rock hybrid with a lineup that included two violins and cellos, with guitar, bass and drums. Paul was in the audience when this band was among the opening acts for the Jimi Hendrix Experience at Epstein's Saville Theater, in London, on June 3, 1967.

While working with the group, Laine released a couple of singles on his own—'Say You Don't Mind,' backed with 'Ask People' (April, 1967) and 'Too Much in Love,' backed with 'Catherine's Wheel' (January, 1968). Laine left the Electric String Band in February 1968, complaining that its violinists and cellists were too frequently unavailable because of commitments to orchestral jobs. He hightailed it to the Spanish Canary Islands, where he spent several months studying flamenco and playing in ad hoc ensembles. By the end of 1968, he was back in London.

Early in 1969, Secunda brought Laine into Balls, a band that brought together musicians who had established themselves in other bands, including the guitarist Trevor Burton (late of The Move), the drummer Mike Kellie (from Spooky Tooth), and the singer and guitarist Steve Gibbons (of the Uglys). Jackie Lomax, who Paul knew from Liverpool, and more recently as an Apple artist, was briefly a member, as was Alan White, the drummer who played with several versions of Lennon's Plastic Ono Band, and on Harrison's *All Things Must Pass*.*

Balls had a rough time of it, and even while he was part of the band, Laine also kept his hand in elsewhere—specifically, Ginger Baker's Air Force, a supergroup built around Cream's former drummer. Laine performed with Baker's group and sang lead vocal on their only single, 'Man of Constant Sorrow.' But Air Force imploded even more expeditiously than Balls.

"The Balls thing, one by one people got the sack or left the band," Trevor Burton remembered. "It ended up with Steve, me and Richard Tandy for a while. Then it finished with just me and Steve, and then we split up. . . . Then Denny Laine appeared on the scene, and it was me and Denny Laine and Alan White . . . Basically we got an advance from Chess Records. We spent all that, and then broke up. And that was the end of Balls! (laughs) We were in the studio for almost a year, and nothing came out of that."[6]

Alan White took a more laid-back view.

"Bands are complex and I'm not sure anyone can give you a simple explanation as to why we didn't stay together for a longer period of time," White reminisced. "We spent about three months making the single we released but we never finished the rest of the songs we had planned to record for an album . . . I enjoyed working with both Denny Laine and Trevor Burton, we made some good music together and it was a memorable time in my life."[7]

Before the last of their breakups, Balls released one single, 'Fight for My Country,' backed with 'Janie Slow Down.' Oddly, it was released not by Chess, but by Secunda's Wizard Records imprint

---

* In 1972, Alan White became the drummer for Yes. He died on May 26, 2022.

in Britain, and Epic Records in the United States. No other tracks from their unfinished album were released, and when they broke up, they owed Secunda money, either because he had fronted recording costs, or to buy out the failed Chess contract. Several members released solo albums, the proceeds of which were meant to pay off Secunda.

That was Denny Laine's plan as well. Word of Denny's solo album was traveling through British music circles since *NME* mentioned it in its coverage of Balls' final breakup, but if it had not yet made its way to Paul, he would have seen a report on Laine's album-in-progress in the April 10 edition of *Sounds*, adjacent to a photo of Paul and Linda that illustrated a short piece announcing *Ram*.

Paul knew that Laine was not currently in a band, and thought that the breadth of his musical experience, plus the fact that he was a decent guitarist with a strong voice—and already a friend—made him an ideal prospect for the new band.

What Paul did not know was that Laine was broke, and homeless, and sleeping in the back room of Secunda's office, and that he was trying to keep body and soul together with a Tin Pan Alley job, writing songs and recording demos at Essex Music in the hope that other artists would record them and earn him some royalties. He was writing a song when Paul telephoned.

"The phone goes, and as though he'd been seeing me every day for the past 10 years, he says, 'Hi, man. What you doing?' I said, 'Who's that?' 'Paul.' 'Paul who?' He went, '*Paul!* You know!' And then I sussed who it was. I said, 'Well, what's happening?' And he said, 'Oh, well, I've just—you know, I've done this album, *Ram*,' as though he didn't know that I'd know he'd done an album. I says, 'Yeah, I have heard about it. Go on.'"[8]

After that tenuous start, Paul told Denny he was hoping to form a band, and had invited the studio players he had recorded with in New York, but that only the drummer wanted to do it. Then he asked, straight out, "Do you fancy doing something?"

"Basically, I was having trouble with my manager," Laine said, "trying to make it again but not really going out of my way as I was not getting the results—the kind that I wanted. Anyway, Paul just happened to call me up and it was the weekend that I had just finished some of the mixes from the album. So when he called I just said, 'Thank Christ for that'—I have somebody to work with that I haven't got to explain everything to, so that was the decider really. Just one of those things of fate."[9]

Denny Seiwell had been home from Scotland for just over a week and hard at work producing Billy Joel's *Cold Spring Harbor* when Paul called on July 14.

"Billy Joel was a confused kid," Seiwell recalled. "I started producing his very first solo album, *Cold Spring Harbor*. Michael Lang from the Woodstock festival asked me to produce Billy. I started in the studio with him, and he was very talented, very unique, very young, very troubled. A brilliant writer, piano player. But Paul called me halfway through the album and said, 'I need you back in

'London' and I had to leave that project, which broke my heart. I wanted to see it through, and it would have been my first opportunity to produce a new record."[10]

Still, it did not take much convincing to get the drummer to head back.

"I just loved playing with this man so much that I would've dropped everything anytime, which I did,"[11] said Seiwell. On July 19, he and Monique took the red-eye from New York to Glasgow, where they booked into the Excelsior Hotel and remained for a day before renting a car and driving to High Park on the 21st. Denny Laine flew to Glasgow and took a bus to Campbeltown, also arriving on July 21, and after 12 hours in transit, fell asleep on Paul's potato-box-and-mattress sofa.

Linda was happy to have Laine in the fold. "I think I was the only person in New York to have that first Moody Blues album," she said. "I remember they did this incredible Coca-Cola commercial. I always thought it would make a great single. I really wanted to photograph the Moody Blues, but I never got up the nerve."[12]

Denny, having imbibed Linda's flattering reminiscences, decided that she was okay.

The quartet spent all of July 22 in Rude Studio, jamming and learning some of the new songs Paul had been working on. He played them the unused songs from the 1970 *Ram* demos, and 'Tomorrow' and 'I Am Your Singer' went on the list. Band versions of 'Bip Bop' and 'Wild Life'—an ecology and animal rights song—were worked up as well. A couple of the jams, including a reggae workout they were calling 'Half Past Ten,' struck them as possible frameworks for new songs.

"The first time I went up to see them in Scotland, I only went up there for two days, and the first day I was that shattered I just slept," Laine recalled. "And then we were just talking about things and people and music—reggae and stuff—so I just learnt the chords to about three songs."[13]

Laine understood and accepted Linda's role in the band from the start.

"Linda was always around when Paul was writing," he reasoned. "He was testing his songs out on her; she would be there, and he would say, 'Try this harmony out.' Or he'd throw her ideas and she would say yes or no. Linda knew music, she knew what was good or bad, although she was not a musician and never professed to be. That led into her being in the band, just because she started with him. But she wasn't that happy about it because she was scared of being onstage and knew she wasn't that kind of person. It didn't come naturally to her. But Paul has this attitude of, 'Well, why not?' She was part of the whole scene, and that's the way I accepted that at the time."[14]

Denny Seiwell, the studio pro, took a more analytical and somewhat critical view after that day of rehearsals.

"You can imagine that, here we are in wellies, flannel shirts, and jeans, and we're showing up to work, up in the farm, putting this material together. And I think Paul had angst in his heart 'cos he was going through some of the Beatle crap, and at the same time, he'd just released this album that he put his heart and soul into, *Ram*, and it's getting mixed reviews, at best.

"And at the same time, it wasn't gonna be Paul Harris on keyboards, it was gonna be Linda playing piano. She was there as his security blanket, because of the emotional state that he was in, as far as I'm concerned. This is just my general opinion. But she wasn't there as a valid band member. She had great rock-and-roll knowledge, she knew what she liked, and she was very opinionated about stuff, and Paul liked her opinions. So Linda's there as his right-hand man. And instead of having Hugh McCracken, Paul, and I as the [musical] nucleus of the band, now it's just Paul and I, because Denny Laine—granted, he's a wonderful writer and singer, and he's a good guitar player. But he's not the quality I'm used to working with. So already we're kinda limited as to what we can do."[15]

Limits notwithstanding, there was some urgency to these rehearsals, because as soon as everyone assembled, Paul booked a week of studio time at EMI (under the pseudonym Sam Browne). The first session was scheduled for July 24, so Linda arranged for a private flight to take the musicians and their equipment to London on the 23rd. It was an extraordinary plan, with a touch of recklessness: with little more than a single day of rehearsals under their belts, this still unnamed group (Paul was pushing for the Dazzlers, at one point, and then Turpentine; "We laughed at him,"[16] Seiwell said) were about to record their first album in the same studio the Beatles used. That they were woefully underrehearsed was not lost on Paul, who later described their preparation as "the shortest rehearsals that any recording band had ever been through."[17]

Because the band's leader had been a Beatle, the album would inevitably come under scrutiny, and the press had already demonstrated that McCartney's Beatle past did not inoculate him from the harshest criticism. Laine had a public reputation to uphold, too, and although Seiwell, as a session player, was a drummer people had heard without knowing his name, working on *Ram* won him some name recognition. And then there was Linda—a mystery to everyone as a keyboardist. At a time when several hot bands were built around virtuoso keyboard players, from Elton John to Keith Emerson, Linda's rudimentary skills were guaranteed to attract criticism.

There was, of course, a fail-safe: if the recordings were unsatisfactory, they could go straight into Paul's archives and never see the light of day. But Paul's brief, for the sessions, allowed for a certain amount of looseness that militated against rejecting the recordings too easily. His plan was a modified version of the approach he wanted the Beatles to take during the *Get Back/Let It Be* sessions. The songs would be recorded live in the studio, and while overdubs were not precluded, Paul hoped there would be relatively few. The band's scant rehearsal notwithstanding, Paul was hoping the songs could be captured in very few takes, an approach, he claims, was inspired by press talk that surrounded Bob Dylan's latest release, *New Morning.*

---

* Bob Dylan's *New Morning* was issued on October 21, 1970, with reviews arriving in the music press during Paul and Linda's first recording stint at CBS. Having spent time with Bob in New York and having also auditioned guitarist Dave Bromberg who played on the record, it is likely Paul heard about Dylan's recording sessions firsthand. Most, but not all, of *New Morning* was recorded between June 1-5, 1970, at CBS Studios B and E.

"We heard he had been in the studio and done an album in just a week. So, we thought of doing it like that, putting down the spontaneous stuff and not being too careful."[18]

On the eve of their first session, the Seiwells, the McCartneys, and Denny Laine went to Ronnie Scott's Jazz Club, in Soho, where they took in a set by the Brazilian percussionist Airto Moreira, and his wife, the singer Flora Purim. The evening was going well until Denny Laine introduced the group to his latest flame, Maggie McGivern.

"It was a very emotional meeting," said McGivern, "we [Paul and I] had a great big hug. We were standing there gripping each other when there was a tap on his shoulder. We turned around and it was Linda. Paul told her who I was, and she said she had heard about me. There was, of course, an unfriendly atmosphere and we didn't get a chance to have a real conversation."[19]

Recording Session

Saturday, July 24, 1971.

EMI Studios, Studio Two, London.

Recording: 'Bip Bop,' 'I Am Your Singer,' 'Half Past Ten' (working title of 'Love Is Strange'), and 'Dear Friend.'

"We rehearsed the songs in Scotland, and when we got into the studio, bang, we got several in the first take," was Denny Seiwell's thumbnail synopsis of the sessions. "Paul would say, 'Wow, let's go with that.' I think he was trying to give the world a real, honest look at the new band—no frills, no 'let's fix this, this, and this.' One of his great lines was, 'Let's explore the accident, not fix the mistake,' which I thought was brilliant."[20]

Paul, Linda and the two Dennys filed into Studio Two just before 2:30 p.m., and exchanged greetings with Tony Clark and his assistant, Chris Blair.* Having grown used to seeing the bearded McCartney who turned up for the *Thrillington* sessions, Clark noted that Paul was now clean-shaven, with his hair swept back—the look he had just before, and shortly after, the New York sessions for *Ram*.

An important difference between *Thrillington* and this new project was that while Paul was the producer in both cases, he remained in the control room during Hewson's orchestral sessions, but would be on the studio floor, as both producer and artist, this time. The business of running the sessions was in Clark's hands.

"Inwardly I felt quite nervous," said Clark, explaining that shortly after he agreed to engineer the session, "I suddenly realized, it's the first *band* album that he's done since leaving the Beatles. It wasn't [a matter of pressure from] Paul at all, it was just me wanting to do the best job possible.[21]

"I wasn't the greatest lover of control rooms," Clark said of his recording technique. "I always liked to spend as much time as I could in the studio, to make sure that what I'm recording is what's happening. So to be part of the initial rehearsals, and the birth of the song, and to be with them and make sure they're all comfortable—but all the time, setting the mics up and actually listening

---

* Chris Blair assisted at only this first session. Subsequently, Alan Parsons took his place.

to the groove that's going on, so that when I went back in the control room I knew exactly what I'm supposed to be doing."[22]

Also joining the fold for Wings' first recording session were newly hired roadies Ian Horne and Trevor Jones. Horne, an accomplished sound engineer, joined on the recommendation of Denny Laine, bringing his brother-in-law sidekick Trevor, a graduate of Aston University, along for the ride.

Paul chose 'Bip Bop' as the first song to record. The band arrayed itself in the large studio, with Paul on electric guitar, Denny Laine on bass, Denny Seiwell on drums, and Linda playing tambourine. Laine was not an experienced or polished bassist, but he could handle the instrument. Three days at High Park had broken the ice, but he was still trying to work out how the band dynamic would work.

"He wanted to be in a band in a sense," Laine explained. "He wanted equality as musicians in the studio. But he would still have the final call. Obviously he'd been a Beatle and he had to be the boss, whether he liked it or not. I didn't have a problem with that. But I think his confidence was a little bit in question. Because trying to follow the Beatles, what are you gonna do?"[23]

For the first session at least, Laine took a relaxed approach. "I just play what he plays in the bass line or on keyboard,"[24] Denny explained. It was a measure of passivity that Paul could happily accept, given the tendency of the Beatles' front line to butt heads during sessions.

"I certainly prefer it very much to the last bit of the Beatles, with all the criticism of *Let It Be*, and people saying, 'He's bossing them all,'" Paul said. "I just felt that was my role—when everybody gets stoned, it needs somebody to pull it together. I felt the pressure of that and they [his new band] don't mind my telling them what to do. If I have an idea, I can just throw it out, and if it's dug, it's dug, if it's not, it's not. I'm not offended."[25]

The arrangement of 'Bip Bop' the band recorded was similar to the acoustic version captured on film in June, a midtempo, bluesy but upbeat children's song. McCartney offered a single instruction to Clark—to "keep it flat and funky"[26]—and gave the count-in.

Clark recorded the band in two takes of 'Bip Bop,' each with a lead vocal, but no backing vocals. The second take was marked "Best," and the band moved on to 'I Am Your Singer,' a sweetly melodic love song that pivots between G-sharp minor verses and E major choruses, and is built on a sweet metaphor, "*You are my song, I am your singer*." This time, Paul played bass, Denny Laine played a sparse electric guitar part—mostly one chord to the bar, with a heavy tremolo effect— and Seiwell provided an appealing, syncopated drum part. Linda did not play an instrument on the basic track. Ten takes were recorded (five of them false starts), the tenth marked "Best."

With the day's third selection, Paul decided it was time for Linda to make her debut as the group's keyboard player. He made it relatively easy on her, choosing 'Half Past Ten,' the gentle jam on a blues progression in E major, played in a reggae style, that the band had worked up during their day of rehearsals in Rude Studio. The keyboard part wasn't much—just two short answering chords at the end of every second bar. Paul, on bass, and Denny Seiwell, on drums, clicked into a tight groove, with Laine playing the changes in the short, off-the-beat accented bursts typical of reggae.

After a couple of takes, everyone climbed the stairs to Studio Two's control room and listened to playbacks. The jam sounded oddly familiar to Paul, as if it were a song he knew. Suddenly it came to him. The next time the top of the chord progression rolled around, he began singing 'Love Is Strange,' a song by Mickey Baker and Ethel Smith (the latter a pseudonym for Bo Diddley) that was a hit for Mickey & Sylvia in 1956.*

As the rest of the band joined in, they realized that for the lyrics to fit the jam more perfectly, the music needed a few nips and tucks. "We just arranged it a little bit here and there, put an ending on it and stuff, and 'Love Is Strange' was born,"[27] Paul said. One more take, and they were set, although they had left off the vocals: now that they were consciously recording a cover, Paul wanted time to revisit the original and decide what kind of vocal arrangement he wanted.

There was time to try one more song, and Paul was in the mood for a ballad that the band (excepting Linda) had not yet heard—his peace offering to John Lennon, 'Dear Friend.' Sitting at the piano, Paul played the song once for the band and Clark, and again for Laine and Seiwell to find their parts.

"'Dear Friend' was really a brilliant, brilliant song, and it was hard to find a part on it," Seiwell admitted. "There was a little beat that came in near the end of it, but all I remember doing was big cymbal swells."[28]

In fact, Seiwell kept the drum part subtle, joining at the instrumental break after the second verse, with accenting cymbal taps first, then a gentle swell at the end of the verse. Laine opted to make use of a vibraphone that was left in the corner of the studio after an orchestral session. Not being a master vibraphonist, he played a simple part—mostly just the chord roots—that is swallowed up in the piano timbre, except at the verse ends: as the piano's sustained chord fades, Laine's vibraphone can be heard ringing (and vibrating) out.

Paul signaled Clark that he was ready to try a take, and when the red light clicked on, he and the Dennys gave a performance that captured the song's spirit so completely that a second take was unanimously deemed unnecessary. As Clark later reflected, such moments are rare in the studio. "That was one of those magical, live recordings—and they *are* magical when they're like that. It's a fantastic track. It's very emotional."[29]

Paul added a simple bass line to 'Dear Friend,' and for day one of Sam Browne and the Dazzlers at EMI, that was a wrap.

---

* Paul is likely to have been equally familiar with the 1957 cover by Lonnie Donegan, and he would more recently have heard a version by one of his heroes, Buddy Holly. Holly had recorded the song in 1958, but his recording was not released until 1969.

After a single day of sessions, the idea of recording live in the studio, with minimal overdubbing, was already breaking down. Of the four songs the group had recorded, all but 'Dear Friend' needed lead and harmony vocals, and hearing the playbacks, Paul was imagining arrangement touches. For 'I Am Your Singer,' for example, he thought of bringing in the recorder players of the Dolmetsch Consort, having enjoyed their playing on *Thrillington*. With a call to the ensemble's office, five players were booked for a session on Thursday.

EMI was still hopping when Paul and company quit for the day. The Nigerian singer, composer, and multi-instrumentalist Fela Ransome-Kuti, and his band, Africa '70, were booked for afternoon and evening sessions in Studio Three on July 24 and 25. Each day's sessions produced a full album—*Afrodisiac* the first day, and *Live* (a studio concert before an audience of 150) the second. Ginger Baker, Denny Laine's former bandmate and boss, joined Kuti's ensemble for the live album. A longtime friend of Fela's, Baker had visited Lagos several times since 1969 and had already conceived the idea of building a recording studio there.

Tony Clark had worked with Kuti a few years earlier, when he was sent to Lagos to give the staff of EMI Nigeria a crash course in using newly upgraded equipment that EMI had installed. He was meant to head the engineering team for Kuti's sessions, which were produced by Mike Jarratt, but ended up splitting his time between McCartney and Kuti.

Clark would undoubtedly have mentioned the sessions to McCartney and company, partly because he hoped to be on hand for some of the engineering, but also because he knew that Laine had played in Air Force. The combination of McCartney's curiosity about music of all kinds, Seiwell's interest, as a drummer, in the rhythms of Afro-beat, Linda's fascination with African-rooted musics, from Motown to reggae, and Laine's curiosity about what Baker was up to these days, made it hard to resist having a look in on Kuti's sessions, which ran until 10:00 p.m.

RECORDING SESSION

Sunday, July 25, 1971.
EMI Studios, Studio Two, London.
Recording: 'Some People Never Know' and 'African Rhythm.'

Paul took a different approach to the second day of recording, focusing on a single song and undertaking overdubs once the basic track was captured. The song 'Some People Never Know' is an appealingly tender but clear-eyed love song for Linda. Composed in the summer of 1969, its simple message was that some people will never know what real love is. Paul recorded it for his collection of *Ram* demos in the spring of 1970, and as he thought about material for the new album, it bubbled up again.

Not having properly rehearsed it, the band spent an entire day arranging and tracking what would become a 6'35" epic. On the basic track, which was recorded in four takes (only the first and last were complete; take 4 was deemed "Best") McCartney played acoustic guitar, with Laine on bass and Seiwell drumming; Linda, again, did not feature.

To flesh out the song's texture, Paul overdubbed a harmonium and an electric piano, and Laine added another acoustic guitar before Paul recorded the lead vocals and, with Linda, the narrow, two-part harmonies. They worked hard to perfect those harmonies, leaving an impression on Clark, who noted that while Linda was timid in the studio, and had so far given no indication of her keyboard abilities, her singing had a strong appeal.

"There's something about Linda's voice. Had she not been in the band, you would have had just male harmonies. But it was obviously new to her, and Paul did encourage her to move in a bit [to the microphone], so that the vocal balance became a nice blend."[30]

Once those elements were added, the band settled back and recorded an impromptu jam using African drums from EMI's instrument closet, clearly influenced by the Fela Ransome-Kuti sessions unfolding elsewhere in the building. All four players took them up—bongos, maracas, bells, and claves—for a recording listed on the tape box as 'African Rhythm.'

———

The Seiwells and Laine stayed at Cavendish Avenue during the sessions and had their first glimpse of the fans who had taken up permanent residence out front. And some of the fans got to see that Paul, who had cultivated his image as the nice, friendly, approachable Beatle, had his limits.

One afternoon, as the two Dennys were chatting on the McCartneys' steps, Paul and Linda returned from an errand in their green Rolls-Royce convertible, heralded by some in the mostly female crowd of fans calling out, "Here he comes!"

"He and Linda looked quite good," Mike Sacchetti—a visitor, not one of the regulars—later wrote. "He had a denim jacket with black slacks and had long hair in the back. Linda was very pregnant. I walked in the yard, even though I was told I shouldn't, and took a few shots. Then a security guard [one of Paul's new roadies] came out and said everyone had to go, and that Paul wouldn't be out 'til very late."

Sacchetti and a friend returned the next afternoon. Feeling bold, they rang the doorbell, only to be confronted by Rose, who sternly told them to leave, adding that Paul was incensed with the fans "for what they did," referring to the recent "Fuck Linda" message painted on a wall across the road. Sacchetti protested that he had nothing to do with that, and Rose told him that Paul was "angry at everyone in sight."

As Sacchetti and his friend were about to leave, they heard Paul start the engine of his Rolls and turned to see the doors to the yard open. "There we were," he wrote, "face to face with Paul and Linda. We all smiled and waved, and he pulled out of the driveway like a madman and gave us the finger!"

Later that evening, Sacchetti and some of the other fans walked over to EMI, and Sacchetti caught Paul in the parking lot. When he asked for 30 seconds of McCartney's time, Paul stared at him and said, "Yeah?" Though Sacchetti had prepared a little speech disavowing all knowledge of those responsible for the "Fuck Linda" message, his mind went blank. Instead, he asked, "Are you recording a new LP?"

"Actually, we're just trying a few things out," Paul told him. Sacchetti said that he and his friends were looking forward to Paul's next album, and Paul cut the chat short, saying "Thanks. Gotta go— Good night, now."[31]

Paul was fed up with the persistence and aggressiveness of his fans, but he knew that Linda, not he, was feeling the brunt of their behavior.

"I can only say that when Paul and I first married, a lot of people were incredibly nasty and rude," Linda complained. "Before we'd met, I'd always felt able to cope with life, but the response was enough to make anyone vulnerable. I lost my confidence. But Paul helped me, though he never babied me along. He didn't sympathize, but he protected me.

"Sometimes—well, nearly always—we'd go home at night and find about 20 girls outside the front gate who seemed to have been standing there forever. They would almost spit at me and say, 'I hate you, you're horrible. Why didn't he marry Jane Asher?' These stupid kids painted nasty things—really crude messages—all over the walls and played the radio loud. If they saw Heather coming home from school they would shout out, 'Your mother is horrible.' Though I tried not to take any notice, all this got me down."[32]

She wondered at times, however, whether a different approach to fan hostility might defuse it.

"Looking back, I think I took on a battle when I should have just said that I understood, and tried to talk to the fans. But it was difficult. I had been a free woman in New York. When I married Paul I suddenly felt fenced in."[33]

Recording Session

Monday, July 26, 1971.
EMI Studios, Studio Two, London.
Recording: 'Wild Life,' 'Tomorrow,' 'Mumbo,' and 'Untitled Jam.'

The Cavendish scruffs were a nuisance, but Paul was not going to let them derail his new group's ongoing sessions. Four tracks—two proper songs and two jams—were recorded on the third day of sessions, starting with 'Wild Life,' another of the tunes they had rehearsed at High Park. Paul and Linda wrote the song after their return from the *Ram* sessions, but its roots go back to November 1966, when Paul visited Kenya with Jane Asher and Mal Evans, the memory of which was revived when Paul looked through photos he had taken at the Maasai Amboseli Game Reserve, in Kajiado County, Kenya.

"I was in a game park in Africa, called Amboseli, just doing the tour through it," Paul recalled a few months later. "And there's a big sign at the entrance that just says, 'Remember, all you people in motor cars, the animals have the right of way.' I liked that, you know, I liked the thought that somewhere they had a right of way over you. We don't stand up for millions of causes and stuff, you know. Conservation, and wildlife, we like to sing about that. The first song we've done which is saying something . . . is 'Wild Life.' And it just says that nature's all right. The wild state is a good state. So why are we getting rid of it? Let's not. And whatever happened to it? And the animals are in zoos instead of just actually running like they're supposed to."[34]

If Paul barely thought about animal rights in 1966, being married to a dedicated animal lover for a couple of years changed that. The song was strikingly simple: three descending electric piano chords—C minor, B-flat major, F major, in 3|4 time—repeated throughout the song. The keyboard part is the song's backbone, especially during the first two minutes, where the rest of the instrumentation is sparse. But this was a song Linda had been practicing, and if she was still nervous about that kind of exposure, she soldiered on through three takes, only the first and last of which were complete (and the last marked "Best"). For the basic track, Paul joined her on bass, with Laine on electric guitar and Seiwell drumming.

"She takes the whole intro of 'Wild Life,' and it's good," Paul noted after the session. "We were all surprised at the way she plays it—it's all up tempo and everything, and she hits it perfectly."[35]

McCartney's comment that his wife played the "intro" could allude to reports that her keyboard part were replaced with overdubs. If that were the case, Clark did not document it. More likely, Paul is referring to the fact that as the song's texture grows, with extra guitar parts and backing vocals—overdubbed later in the week—the piano fades into the texture. But in the intro, the keyboard part is fully exposed, and Paul admired the way Linda embraced the challenge of playing it, with little other instrumentation to hide behind.

The day's second song, 'Tomorrow,' had its roots in the McCartneys' holiday visit to the south of France in May 1969, just before the *Abbey Road* sessions began in earnest. It offers a touch of local color—"*Bring a bag of bread and cheese, and find a shady spot beneath the trees*"—that evokes some of Linda's photos from the trip, including Paul and Heather sitting in a field of bright red poppies. It could easily have sat beside his *Abbey Road* contributions: its bittersweet melody and its sophisticated harmonic backdrop were both closer in spirit to his late Beatles songs than to simpler pieces in the current batch.

It's likely that the song was unfinished then, although another reason he might not have offered it for *Abbey Road* was that lyrically, it explored an idea similar to the central impulse of one of Lennon's *Let It Be* contributions, 'Don't Let Me Down'—the combination of expectations and fears provoked by a new love affair, at least on the surface. A variant of Lennon's title, in fact, appears no fewer than a dozen times in the lyrics of 'Tomorrow.'

"I'd been let down a lot, in my mind," Paul explained. "I didn't want to be let down again . . . The idea was, in the future, let's make it better."[36]

Paul finished writing 'Tomorrow' at High Park in the spring of 1970 and included it among his *Ram* demos. But he bypassed it at the New York and Los Angeles sessions. Now its time had come, and Paul and company polished off the backing track in five takes—Takes 1, 2 and 5 were complete; Take 3 was a breakdown, and 4 was a false start; Take 5, deemed "Best," became the master—with Paul on piano, Denny Laine on electric guitar, and Seiwell drumming. Linda sat this one out.

In what was supposed to be a moment of blowing off steam between songs, Linda picked up a tambourine, Denny Laine switched to bass, Paul played what Clark listed on the tape box as an out-of-tune piano, and Seiwell was at his kit for what turned out to be the final keeper of the day, a song whittled out of a jam that Paul named 'Mumbo.'

"I'd never rehearsed 'Mumbo,'" McCartney told *NME* a few months after the session. "It was just something I'd done on piano, and they just fell in."[37] In a sidebar to the same story, Clark noted that 'Mumbo' was captured in a single take—something McCartney asserted in other interviews from the same time. Seiwell remembers it as a first take, too.

The tape box tells a different story. Two takes are listed—the first running 4'20", the second 6'13" and marked "Best." In fact, 'Mumbo' comes with layers of built-in mythmaking. Take 2 begins with an introductory drum figure that sounds as if it was in progress when Clark hit record, followed a second later by Paul shouting, "Take it, Tony!" as if he wasn't sure Clark was rolling tape.

Clark may have been unprepared for the band to start without signaling him that they were ready and awaiting his take announcement; in fact, the lack of an announcement, and the song's "indefinite start" were noted on the tape box beside the second take. But it stands to reason that after the first take—the truly improvised one—the band would have filed into the control room to hear it, and then decided that something could be done with it, just as they did with the reggae jam that became 'Love Is Strange,' and that they returned to the studio to record another take.

Clark would have been watching, waiting for Paul's signal. But when Seiwell hit the opening beat, Clark swiftly told Parsons to hit record. Paul would naturally want to alert Clark—but looking up, he would have seen that the red light was on, meaning that Clark was on it. So he knew when he called "Take it, Tony!" that the tape was rolling and that his instruction was being recorded— and that it would sound cool, and off the cuff, on the finished recording. What he would not have known is that because Parsons hit record after Seiwell began his introduction, the recording would have that "indefinite start" noted on the box. That was a bonus that would make "Take it, Tony!" sound that much more urgent.

The rest of the built-in myth was the performance itself. Once Paul and the band identified the strengths of the basic track, they intended to transform it into what sounds like a high-energy, live-in-the-studio jam. What they had for the moment, though, was just a basic track, with piano, bass, drums and tambourine, and Paul shouting in his best rock-screamer voice, pumping out a song's worth of nonsense syllables and somehow making them rhyme, as if he were singing actual lyrics with such passion that they could not be understood.

Making 'Mumbo' into a facsimile of a raucous, live jam would require more instruments, and listening to the playback, Paul mentally charted the overdubs necessary to make it work.

But for the moment, he was not convinced it was worth the bother, so the overdubs would wait. Laine, for one, argued that the track was a keeper.

"I said to him, 'I like the way you've ad-libbed the vocal—it sounds great just like that,'" Laine remembered. "It was mumbo jumbo, but it works! And so, we left it at that. If it worked, you kept it, simple as that."[38] When they finished playing Take 2, the band moved immediately into another jam. But they were only 2 minutes and 11 seconds from the end of the reel, so they were still playing when, in the control room, the leader at the end of the reel flopped onto the take-up reel.

All told, the group had recorded more than 40 minutes of music in their first three sessions, Having barely rehearsed before traveling to London, they already had an album's worth of music in the can.

Recording Sessions

Thursday–Friday, July 29–30, 1971.
EMI Studios, Studio One, London.
Overdubbing: 'I Am Your Singer' (July 29); 'Some People Never Know,' 'Wild Life,' 'I Am Your Singer,'
'Bip Bop,' and 'Tomorrow' (July 30).

McCartney and company ended their week of recording with two overdubbing sessions in Studio One, the largest of EMI's studios, typically used for symphonic recordings. There was not enough time to polish off the album, or even deal with all the songs, but they had made a solid start.

Members of the Dolmetsch Consort (also known as the Dolmetsch Family) had been booked to add recorders to 'I Am Your Singer' at the Thursday session. Five members of the group were engaged—Jeanne Dolmetsch and Brian, Peter, Christine and Paul Blood. Although improvisation plays a role in the early music repertoire the Dolmetsch players were known for, improvising parts for a pop song was outside their comfort zone. So Paul led them through it.

"Paul played what he wanted on the piano," recalled Brian Blood, "and we, being classically trained musicians, wrote out our parts from what he played, and recorded the results. More experienced pop session musicians would probably have picked up what he wanted and played without music!"[39]

The part Paul played them included a melodic section, with a light chordal accompaniment, for the instrumental break, as well as short figures to be played between each vocal line of the following verse, and another chordal section for the verse after that.

"Whilst placing the mics and setting up for the session, I listened to the interplay between Paul and the [Dolmetsch] players, and I just remember standing back and feeling privileged to hear it," said Clark, who also remembered the setup as fairly simple. "I had spot mics and two ambient mics, just to make [the recorders] sound as pure and as beautiful as they are."[40]

The second overdubbing session, on Friday, was devoted mostly to vocal additions, but it began with an odd touch: Picking up a trumpet from EMI's instrument closet, Denny Seiwell tapped into his inner adolescent, having taken trumpet lessons and played in his school marching band. He added a solo to 'Some People Never Know,' following the melody competently enough, but with the tenuous sound of a musician who had not played the instrument for several years. Paul eventually dropped it from the recording, and the solo was wiped when later overdubs replaced it—but not before a rough mix that was made, preserving Seiwell's handiwork.

Denny's solo was on Track 6 of the eight-track tape, and by the time the song was completed, several other overdubs were recorded as punch-ins on that same track. One immediate addition was a layer of African percussion at the end of the song. The band used the same instruments they had used on the 'African Rhythm' jam on July 25.

Not wanting to waste the few available tracks, Clark recorded the percussion ensemble in mono. "The percussion was all done in one go," he explained. "In fact, it's on one track of the multitrack tape. When we mixed it, we phased it at the end, and we spread it left and right and just moved the ADT so that it sort of traveled and phased as well,"[41] approximating stereo.

'Wild Life' was the next track selected for overdubbing, starting with Paul's raucous lead vocal—the source of much of the track's variety, as he vamps around the title and messes with some of the words (for example, changing animals to "aminals"). The choruslike backing vocals were tracked next, with Paul, Linda and Denny Laine sharing a mic, and Denny Seiwell in the control room overseeing the vocal balances. He retained vivid memories of this moment on the production side, and the band's camaraderie at the sessions.

"I used to say 'All right, guys, gather around the mic, let's get a blend. OK, that's good. Denny can you move back a little bit? Linda, I need you to move back.' She'd say, 'How far?' and I'd say, 'You got a car?' She'd laugh—we were just having fun."[42]

'I Am Your Singer' needed vocals, too. Paul and Linda split the lead and then added close harmony backing vocals. Lead and harmony vocals were also added to 'Bip Bop' with little fuss: Paul and Linda had been singing the song together at High Park for months.

That left 'Tomorrow,' on the day's schedule. Paul had recorded the lead vocal at the basic tracking session, but he felt he could better it. After a few passes, he was satisfied. His ideas for backing and harmony vocals were plentiful, but for now he was ready to call this run of sessions to an end, return to High Park, and consider how to proceed.

Alan Parsons, still a junior engineer, decided to stay on after Paul, the band, and Clark left the studio, and try some experimental mixes.

"I was fairly new to engineering at that time," Parsons explains, "and did a mix of 'I Am Your Singer' while no one was there, partly for my own amusement, and partly because they wanted some reference copies.[43] It was very difficult with the Beatles and Paul, I never got used to the notion that I was working with those people."[44]

During his after-hours mixing session, Parsons made the bold decision to add ADT to Denny Laine's electric guitar. This doubled the tremolo guitar part without the need for an overdub, and in the process created an appealing stereo effect. Before he left the studio that night, Parsons made rough mixes of the other seven cuts Paul and his charges had recorded.

Had he accepted Harrison's invitation, Paul would have been part of a three-quarter Beatles reunion at Madison Square Garden, in New York, on August 1, 1971, just two days after he and his band completed their week of London sessions.

In June, Harrison had been persuaded by the great sitarist Ravi Shankar to use his celebrity to bring attention to the humanitarian disaster taking place in Bangladesh, formerly East Pakistan. Bangladesh had declared independence from Pakistan in March, and its people were now suffering the effects of a brutal, ongoing war. Millions of Bangladeshis had fled into India, where flooding exacerbated sanitation problems that, in turn, led to starvation and outbreaks of disease.

George was producing Badfinger's *Straight Up* album at EMI when Shankar approached him. The sitar master originally planned to stage a concert of his own to raise money for a relief fund, but he realized that a sitar recital would raise a couple of thousand dollars at best; if George got involved, the scope of the tragedy could be brought to the attention of a much broader public, and much more money could be raised.

During a meeting in Los Angeles, Harrison and Shankar finalized their plans for a grand fund-raising show. Allen Klein booked Madison Square Garden, and George called dozens of musicians he knew. A mere six weeks before the concert, he rounded up an all-star roster that included Bob Dylan, Eric Clapton, Badfinger, Leon Russell, Billy Preston, Jesse Ed Davis, Klaus Voormann and Carl Radle, a gospel choir and a horn section. Ravi Shankar and the tabla virtuoso Ali Akbar Khan would play a short set of their own before the rock extravaganza began. Everyone would perform *gratis*; even Klein agreed to forgo his cut. The proceeds would go to the George Harrison–Ravi Shankar Special Emergency Relief Fund, to be administered by the United Nations.

Naturally, George invited his former Beatles bandmates. Ringo, in Spain filming *Blindman*, quickly agreed. John initially agreed, too, but withdrew when George made it clear that only John was invited, not Yoko.[45] Publicly, John said he was unable to join in because he and Yoko were in the Virgin Islands battling Yoko's ex-husband for custody of her daughter, Kyoko.

"The thing is," John told *Disc and Music Echo*, "we're really more involved at the moment with getting Kyoko back. If we were given the kid on a plate, we'd go running off and do the show."[46]

Paul told George he would think about appearing. But for him, the prospect was a nonstarter. If the show included a Beatles reunion, Allen Klein would take credit for it, and however important and lifesaving George's charity show may have been, it was not worth handing Klein a huge victory. Even if Klein were not in the picture, Beatles reunions were anathema to Paul.

"I knew for certain that if I'd taken part it would have been played up as 'the Beatles back together again,'" he explained. "It may have been only for one night, but the whole thing would have been perpetuated. When the truth is that it's definitely ended."[47]

For fans of the Beatles, collectively and individually, the contrast between George's activism and John's decision to sit this one out was surprising at first, given John's very public peace campaigning. But his efforts to find Kyoko were known, so the reason he offered for balking seemed understandable. McCartney's reasoning was harder to justify, given the lives at stake. Fans and critics noticed and commented.

"I have no quarrel with John Lennon's endless clattering around inside his psyche, or Paul McCartney's search for sweetness and light," the critic Don Heckman wrote in the *Village Voice*, shortly after George's concert, "but at the moment I have to have stronger feelings about George Harrison's active efforts to do something about the misery in the world around him. How surprising that the most introspective of the Beatles should be the one who, in the long run, takes the most effective actions."[48]

When Shankar enlisted George's aid, the first thing Harrison did, even before arranging the concert, was to write a song, 'Bangla Desh,' to be released as a single that would bring a popular voice to the cause. He recorded the song at Record Plant West, Los Angeles, on July 4 and 5, with a band that included Ringo and Jim Keltner on drums, Voormann on bass, Jim Horn on saxophone, Leon Russell on piano, and Billy Preston on organ.[49] As with the concert, all fees and royalties would go to the relief fund. The single was released on July 28, in the United States and two days later in Britain.

The BBC banned the song a week later, on the grounds that it took a political position on the recognition of Bangladesh as an independent nation. An Apple emissary was dispatched to the BBC with a lyric sheet and an explanation that the point was not to take a political side, but to raise money to provide refugees, principally children, with food and clean water in the wake of a dire humanitarian crisis. The ban was lifted, with the proviso that the song's title and beneficiaries not be mentioned on air. But that was an onerous restriction, and BBC airplay all but stopped.

Almost simultaneously, Paul released two singles from *Ram*, different selections in the United States and Britain, but both big production numbers. In America, 'Uncle Albert/Admiral Halsey,' backed with 'Too Many People,' was issued on August 2; the British single was 'The Back Seat of My Car' and 'Heart of the Country,' released on August 13. If the release of 'Uncle Albert' struck some listeners as predatory—a move to steal George's thunder, a day after the big concert—the timing was more likely coincidental: an edit had been made on July 20 to prepare for its single release. It did well, cruising to the top of the *Billboard* chart giving the McCartneys their first No. 1 single as a solo act; 'Bangla Desh' reached No. 23 in *Billboard*, and No. 10 on the UK Official Charts.

The British recording buying public was less inclined to purchase album-based singles so long after a record was issued, and the music press did little to provide a persuasive argument to the contrary. 'The Back Seat of My Car' stalled at No. 39 in the UK Singles Charts.

---

* In 1971, Bangladesh was typically written as two words, and that was the form Harrison adopted for both his single and for the album and film release, *The Concert for Bangla Desh*. When referring to these releases, we have spelled the name as it appears on the labels, jackets and advertisements; when referring to the country, we have used the updated, single-word version of the name.

"It's always something of a disappointment when an artist of the calibre of McCartney is content to release a couple of tracks from his latest album for a new single. . . . Whilst not so melodically memorable as some of his numbers, it's a ballad that's rich in atmosphere."[50]

Derek Johnson, *NME*

"As the Beatles, ex- or otherwise, seem so touchy these days, one does not wish to be rude, but it's about as exciting as the window display of the Scots House, Knightsbridge. It has a certain wistful charm, a few romantic touches, but it lacks intensity or the bittersweet qualities which make Paul such a fine writer."[51]

Chris Welch, *Melody Maker*

"Nice sensitive song which sort of ticks over through the first part; strings purring along with brass brashing. Clever arrangement, though curiously muzzy in parts. And a fair old soul-stirring finale. Obviously a giant chart cert."[52]

Peter Jones, *Record Mirror*

The other Beatles were all over the news, and Paul was always among the subjects they were asked about.

"It got better after the case," Ringo said of his relationship with Paul in the July 31 issue of *Melody Maker*. "We phoned each other and talked a bit. But while we were being hassled with the court case it was a bit strange. I was just thinking, 'What's he doing it to me for?' but then I realized he's gotta do it; to get what he wants it's the only way. So, I don't put him down for that. But as a person I can't help but love him. I really can't. He's very important to me."

Ringo also, however, expressed his disappointment in *Ram*. "I think it's such a pity that he doesn't get in there and do what I think he can do and I'm sure he knows he can do. He seems to be going strange. It's like he's not admitting that he can write great tunes. He picks the image of his choice, you know. I just feel he's let me down."[53]

Lennon gave several interviews, in which he noted how much he disliked all but a few tracks on *Ram*, complaining particularly about the lines directed at him in 'Too Many People,' and hinting that there would be a track ('How Do You Sleep?') on his forthcoming album that people *might* regard as being about Paul.

But he also gave a few hints about the state of play in the aftermath of Paul's lawsuit. "It's cost us quite a bit . . . trying to see it his way. It's like Monopoly, only with real money," he told Alan Smith in the July 31 issue of *NME*, adding that "Maybe about a year or two after all the money thing's settled, we might have dinner or forget about it, y'know. We might even celebrate getting it all over with ."[54]

In an interview with *Disc and Music Echo*, published the same day, John explained that the court-appointed receiver was dealing only with the 20 percent of Apple owned by the four Beatles (5 percent each); the other 80 percent of the Beatles' income went into Apple itself. And he held out a ray of hope for Paul, suggesting that they might do precisely what Paul had been arguing for all this time.

"If Paul wants out of Apple we'll buy his bit, simple as that, if he wants to sell."[55]

That *was* what Paul wanted, but whenever he suggested it to John or George, he quickly reached an impasse. Could John finally be seeing the light?

It wasn't just the other Beatles firing shots across Paul's bow; his ability to write a touching, conciliatory song like 'Dear Friend,' did not stop him from sniping when the others' comments put him in a foul mood. At the beginning of August, he informed the Beatles Fan Club that he was resigning his membership.

Dear People,

The time has come for me to withdraw from the Beatles Fan Club. As you may know, the band split up over a year ago and has not played together since. Each of us is getting together his own career, and for this reason, I don't want to be involved with anything that continues the illusion that there is such a thing as the Beatles.

Those days are over. In the past, you have been great supporters, and the idea of this letter is to let you know how I want it to be in the future, in case you wanted to know. Now I'm not a Beatle any longer, and want to get back to where I once belonged—living my own life, having my own family, my privacy, and getting on with my own music.

Thanks for everything . . .

Paul, Child-Bride Linda, Boy Prodigy Heather
And Baby Mary

A couple of weeks later, he had Shelley Turner, at MPL, issue a statement declaring, "He doesn't want the name McCartney linked with the names of the other Beatles." And he rounded on the Beatles Fan Club once again, after he received a note reminding him to let the club know when Linda delivered their new child, due in September, because the club always celebrated the births and birthdays of the Beatles' children. "Paul claims his children *aren't* Beatle children," lamented Freda Kelly, who had run the club since the start of the group's career. "I suppose that's fair enough. I've been waiting for someone to say something like this."[56]

Immediately upon the group's return to Scotland, the Seiwells went house-shopping, and found a farm house rental at Breakachy Farm, Kilchenzie, for £5 ($12.50) a week. A few weeks later, they agreed to let Laine stay there briefly as well.

"It was over the hill from Paul's place," Seiwell remembered. "We had an ocean view—it was a much nicer place than his, and it was fun. Paul, Linda, and the kids all showed up at our farm on horses. We had a nice dinner there and a good band hang. Denny was staying with us at the time. We had a little problem with him, and he moved on. My wife threw him out, actually."[57]

Aside from an ejection-worthy disagreement between Laine and Monique Seiwell, Paul and his new bandmates were getting on well. But it was a topsy-turvy arrangement. The group had already recorded the lion's share of an album, and the first week of August, Clark and Parsons sent rough stereo mixes of all eight songs to Campbeltown. But the band still lacked a name—they scratched their heads when the *NME* reported, in its August 7 issue, that "it is likely to be named the Paul McCartney Blues Band"[58]—and Paul had not yet conveyed to his colleagues his ideas about the nature of the group (would it be Paul plus sidemen, or a full-fledged band?) or the financial arrangements.

After a rehearsal in early August, Paul outlined his vision for the group. He was nostalgic for the days when the Beatles clawed their way into the music business, and while he did not want to go quite *that* far in his search for a new beginning, he encouraged Seiwell and Laine to think of themselves as equals, with as much of a stake in their collective future as Paul had.

"I would follow my heart musically," Seiwell said. "One of my credos has always been 'do it for love of art.' If you're doing any kind of music just to make money, it's probably gonna fail. Paul and I had this thing that didn't require any words. It was a nod, a look, a wink, and we knew we were on the same page musically. I never had that with anyone before, and I recorded with a lot of great, great people. But this was so special to me.

"Paul said, 'You guys are gonna be part owners of this band,'" Seiwell recalls. "Now, anytime you get a chance to be in a band with Paul McCartney and be a shareholder of the situation, I don't think money's gonna be an object."[59]

But in some ways money *was* an object, because even if the band members were to be equals, as Seiwell understood it, the recording sessions were underwritten through Paul's existing agreements; he owned the practice space and the equipment for recording high-quality demos; and he was, so far, paying the band's travel expenses. It would be that way for the foreseeable future—yet, his own cash flow was limited, since Apple still controlled it.

Moreover, he was wary of the kind of equal four-way split he had with the Beatles on recording royalties and performance fees. For one thing, though the new band would have to make its way, it had an advantage: its frontman was a former Beatle, a perpetual boldface name. Should the band generate lots of cash, and then have an angry breakup, he did not want to find himself in court again, battling for an equal share when he was the main draw.

So he didn't make it clear exactly what "part owner" meant—that, he told Seiwell and Laine, needed to be worked out with the Eastmans. For the moment, the agreement he and the two Dennys came to was that, for the time being, he would pay them each £70 ($175) weekly. There were no contracts—just what Seiwell described as "a hippie handshake."[60]

After a rehearsal and discussions on August 9, they had a party to celebrate their new agreement. Gathering outside Rude Studio, around Seiwell's kit, they raised a motley set of tumblers and coffee cups full of scotch and Coke, as Monique Seiwell snapped a few commemorative shots.

The next day, the band took a break. The Seiwells flew to Nice for a ten-day visit with Monique's family. At Prestwick Airport, in Glasgow, they were cornered by reporters from both the Scottish *Daily Express* and the *Campbeltown Courier*, who were eager to quiz Paul's new, six-foot four-inch, ginger-bearded American drummer about what the McCartneys, and company, were up to. Denny was already trained to the ways of celebrity; he told his interlocutors that the group was rehearsing at the farmhouse, "but we haven't come up with anything in particular yet."[61]

Linda was nearly eight months pregnant, but the McCartneys set out on a couple of trips, nevertheless. The first, on August 18, was a chartered European Falcon Services flight to Cork, Ireland, with both girls and two dogs (Martha and their new Dalmatian puppy, Lucky). Their mission was to start laying the groundwork for *Thrillington*. When the press caught up with them, they claimed they were in Ireland to visit the maestro—"What, you haven't *heard* him? Oh, dear!" Left to their own devices, they tried to create an untraceable, fictional backstory and iconography for the great conductor.

"We went around southern Ireland and found a guy in a field, a young farmer, and asked if he minded doing some photographic modeling for us," Paul explained. "We wanted to find someone that no one could possibly trace, paid him the going rate and photographed him in a field, wearing a sweater and then wearing an evening suit. But he never quite looked Percy Thrillington enough."[62]

They flew back to Campbeltown on August 21, and then four days later, they were off to Blackpool, the famous seaside resort just north of Liverpool, purely for a break. They were thrown out of a restaurant for not being properly attired and did a modest amount of fending off reporters. In one case, Paul filled in a journalist about his new band and then hectored him about his right to privacy. "I don't want my children automatically striking poses when they see a photographer," he said. "Get the message? If people think I'm a crabby old thing, it's too bad."[63]

Linda was more conciliatory this time, telling the reporter that like Paul, she was beginning to see most experiences in terms of their musical yield, noting that she came up with an idea for a new tune in Blackpool, inspired by "the raucous rhythm of the roundabout."

That tune, which Paul took up and finished, was 'Blackpool,' an acoustic blues, with a lyric—*"Blackpool, 38, 23, 38, Blackpool, That's the place for me"*—that seems cryptic until you realize that Paul's inspiration was a series of pictures of women, of all shapes and sizes, drawn by Philip W. Taylor and Brian Fitzpatrick for Bamforth & Co., a Yorkshire firm famous for its saucy seaside postcards.

Another part of the lyric, "*I like 'em heavy and tall, I don't like them skinny and small,*" may have been prompted by Linda's very pregnant state. But this was not, Paul later made clear, a song for which he imagined a great future.

"When Linda and I first got together we used to groove around a lot, and I had a number of songs which I would just sing but not really record. They were mess-around songs, and this was one of them."[64]

By the end of August, all hands reconvened at High Park, and though there was no formal rehearsal schedule, everyone naturally gravitated to Rude Studio to jam and work on existing material. Since there was a studio-grade four-track deck on hand, Paul often ran a tape while he and the band played, and they quickly filled three reels.

The first included versions of Linda's 'Seaside Woman,' a few old Elvis hits—'Mystery Train' and 'That's All Right,' the latter evolving into another Fela-inspired percussion jam, 'African Yeah Yeah'—plus the newly written 'Blackpool,' joined with a song called 'Poor Boy,' which gave way to 'Freight Train,' Chuck Berry's 'Little Queenie,' and Buddy Holly's 'Peggie Sue.' The Holly tune morphs into 'Seaside Woman,' bringing the reel to a close. The second reel included more takes of 'Seaside Woman,' plus a tune called 'Tea Bud.' On the third reel, McCartney and company stretch out on a wordless (but for the title) jam that, in the spirit of 'Mumbo' (from 'Mumbo-Jumbo') Paul named 'Oobu Joobu.'

The band flew to London on August 31 and returned to EMI Studios for more overdubbing.

Recording Sessions

Wednesday and Saturday, September 1 and 4, 1971.
EMI Studios, Studio Three, London; and Olympic Studios, Studio One, London.
Recording: 'Untitled.'
Overdubbing: 'Mumbo,' 'Tomorrow' (September 1); and 'Some People Never Know' (September 4).

It was time to begin transforming 'Mumbo' from a backing track into a more persuasive facsimile of a jam, but at this session, Paul took only a few steps in that direction, adding percussion and a lead electric guitar line before relegating the track to the back burner once again.

Clark then threaded up 'Tomorrow,' which needed plenty of work. To start, Paul added his melodic bass guitar counterpoint, which greatly opened up the song's texture. He added a low-lying, electric fuzz guitar solo as well, heard mostly in the song's coda. Paul, Linda and Denny Laine were then joined around the microphone by second engineer Parsons for the song's rich choral backing, which begins after the second verse and continues through the track.

The band finished off the session with another jam, listed as 'Untitled' and neither completed nor released.

Paul liked the rough mix of 'Some People Never Know' that Alan Parsons made on July 30, but by definition, rough mixes are not written in stone, and Paul had another idea—adding a woodwind section to fill out the sound, with a prominent solo oboe. The wind players convened at Olympic, on September 4, and added the parts, arranged by Richard Hewson. Paul was not convinced that they were an improvement, but he deferred that decision until the mixing stage.

"I remember thinking with *Wild Life* that Paul wasn't making such a perfect record that he might have made with the Beatles," Parsons observed. "It was a good sound, but he wouldn't spend quite as long getting guitar solos and harmonies right.

"As a producer, he's fairly demanding. He's often unable to describe that he wants and it's down to experimenting. He'd say, 'I want a better bass sound,' and I'd say, 'Where's the knob on the desk to get it?' Yeah, he was under so much criticism at the time. . . . But I've always regarded Paul as musically the cleverest of the four. It's just taste."[65]

———

Out in the Beatles universe, it sometimes seemed as though John were doing and saying things simply to irritate Paul. He told *Record Mirror*, for example, that he had been discussing touring with George and Ringo—that George, energized by the success of his Bangladesh concert, "had this idea to do a tour playing two concerts a night. The first concert would be normal, and everyone would pay, but the second would be in aid of some cause or foundation, or something. I liked the idea, so I'm going to do it. And we'll take Ringo with us and possibly Klaus Voormann and Eric Clapton and Jim Keltner." Where would this tour take place? "America, Britain, Russia, China—anywhere, I don't care," John said, adding, "I'd have speakers and leaflets and handouts and make it a real sort of happening—a left-wing circus."[66]

Not surprisingly, given the deep-seated loathing of life on the road that John and George shared—to say nothing of the focus that would have been required of John, who hated rehearsal and was now in a position where he could avoid it—nothing came of this plan.

On the brighter side, the September 4 issue of *Billboard* brought the news that 'Uncle Albert/ Admiral Halsey' had reached No. 1, and that *Ram* was holding the No. 3 place on the American album chart. And Paul had heard reports, confirmed in *NME* for the week ending September 11, that his suspicions of Klein were getting further (if belated) vindication: the Rolling Stones were suing him, in New York, for mismanagement of their business affairs and were seeking $30 million (£12 million) in damages.

Another dubbing session was booked for Trident Studios on September 6, but Paul canceled it. Instead, he invited Richard Hewson to Cavendish Avenue to discuss orchestration ideas for 'Dear Friend.' Paul envisioned the score in almost cinematic terms, "as if there was an orchestra just over the hill. It wasn't in your face. And when you're at the top of the hill, there it is, full blown."[67]

"I was handed the basic track that he'd done, and in this case he said he'd like some strings and a bit of brass towards the end," Hewson recalled. "He wasn't like a lot of the other producers I had to work for, he was very open to things. He'd let you have free hand, just to see what came out, basically. And I'm glad to say that what I did came out okay with him."[68]

An orchestral session was tentatively booked for September 10, but quickly canceled because of the advanced state of Linda's pregnancy. The band was essentially put on hiatus, which made it a good time for the Seiwells to fly to New York to tie up loose ends and complete their move to Scotland. That turned out to be surprisingly easy: the drummer Rick Marotta, then 23, but already making his way as a session player,* was searching for an apartment, so Seiwell sold him his, with all its contents, including the furniture, a television, and a piano. As a bonus, Seiwell also threw in all his contacts for jingles, TV, and film recording.

Linda had continued to travel and work with Paul nearly until she went into labor, but all was not well. She had been diagnosed with placenta previa, a potentially life-threatening condition in which the placenta blocks the cervix, posing problems during delivery. That meant that the birth would be by cesarean section.

Paul had observed Mary's birth, but he was barred from the delivery room this time. When Linda went into labor, three weeks early,[69] on September 13, 1971, Paul took her to Kings College Hospital in Denmark Hill, London.

"I sat next door in my green apron," Paul said, "praying like mad,"[70] as Linda gave birth to Stella Nina McCartney, a five-pound nine-ounce blonde, named for both of Linda's grandmothers.† The midwife, Sister Joan Piper, later took a photo of a spent-looking Linda holding Stella, as a wide-eyed Paul leaned over his wife's shoulder. (Piper was used to celebrity; in July 1970, she delivered Lord Nicholas Windsor, the youngest child of Prince Edward.)

"To be supportive, I stayed there with her, sleeping in a little camp-bed," said Paul. "It had been such a touch-and-go thing, such a drama, that I was imagining angels' wings. And I thought, 'That's

---

* Marotta became a prolific studio drummer; in 1973, he played on the sessions for John Lennon's *Mind Games*.

† Linda's maternal grandmother was Stella Dryfoos Lindner; her paternal grandmother was Stella Epstein.

a nice image—wings. I wonder if there's been a band called Wings?' That's how the name came about, in King's College Hospital, in London, as we recovered from the birth of Stella."[71]

There was, as it turned out, another band named Wings—an American group, formed in 1968, and fairly well-connected: its original members included Oz Bach, from Spanky & Our Gang, Pam Robins, from the Serendipity Singers, and Eddie Simon, Paul Simon's brother. By the time the band made its only album, *Wings* (ABC/Dunhill, 1968), Simon had departed, and the band expanded to a sextet, with the guitarist and songwriter Jim Mason (a cocomposer of the Peter, Paul & Mary hit, 'I Dig Rock and Roll Music"), the keyboardist Steve Knight, Jack McNichol on lead guitar, and former Jefferson Airplane drummer Jerry Peloquin. The band sounded like an amalgam of the Kinks and the Mamas and the Papas, but broke up before the end of 1968 so the name Wings was free and clear.

Paul and company spent some time batting the name around, trying it on for size. But Denny Seiwell, for one, could see that it had more emotional resonance for Paul than he was willing to admit to the group. "I think Stella's birth was a little dodgy," he said. "Paul said that she was delivered like on the wings of an angel or something. He took the word 'Wings' from that experience."

When MPL finally announced the name publicly, *NME* was the first to report it.[72] That seemed only right, if only to erase the paper's earlier report that the group would likely be called the Paul McCartney Blues Band. Asked for a comment on the McCartneys' new family venture, Mick Jagger quipped that he "wouldn't let *his* old lady in the band." Paul just shrugged it off.

"To most people, she was just some chick," said Paul in response to Jagger's put-down. "I just figure she was the main help for me on the albums around that time. She was there, every day, helping on harmonies and all that stuff. . . . So, I think all this business about getting Linda in the billing was just a way of saying, 'Listen, I don't care what you think, this is what I think. I'm putting her right up here with me."[73]

* Jim Mason also sang backing vocals on John Lennon's *Rock 'N' Roll* album, released in 1975.

13

WAR IS OVER, IF YOU WANT IT

—→

For Linda's 30th birthday, on September 24, 1971, Paul surprised her with a ring with a large, heart-shaped emerald in an antique, diamond-studded ribbon-and-bow setting—a gift they regarded as something private, entirely outside the down-to-earth image they had cultivated over the last two years. Though Linda was delighted with it, it struck her as something from another universe—the one she had rebelled against as a young girl in Scarsdale.

"I love emeralds, I must say," she told an interviewer for *Cosmopolitan* who spotted it on her ring finger in place of a wedding band. "But I never used to have a favorite stone before. I thought, it's ridiculous, all the fuss about diamonds. But they're beautiful, lovely—I can see now why diamonds are a girl's best friend. We're not into the big ones, though, we're not Dick and Liz."[*]

After another week of convalescence, on October 1, Linda rejoined Wings, and the band got back to work. The Seiwells returned to London just in time for a last-minute photo shoot that would yield the cover of the album Wings were about to finish. The couple landed at Gatwick with little time to spare; Monique Seiwell, who celebrated her birthday that day, remembered being driven directly to the shoot from the airport.

The idea was Linda's. Paging through the latest issue of *Vogue*, at the beginning of August, she was struck by a fashion spread, photographed by Barry Lategan.[2] She knew Lategan; he had discovered Twiggy, in 1966, and taken the earliest, most iconic shots of her. Twiggy was one of the first friends Linda made when she moved to London. But before she glanced down the page to find Lategan's credit line, her eye was drawn to a full-page photo of the model Marie Helvin, sitting on a fallen tree limb that stretches over a woodland lake, her legs dangling toward the water, and a leafy canopy above and around her.

---

[*] The reference is to the actors Richard Burton and Elizabeth Taylor, who were married from 1964 to 1974, and from 1975 to 1976. Among the jewels they owned were the 33.19-carat Elizabeth Taylor Diamond, which Burton bought for Taylor in 1968, and the 68-carat Taylor-Burton Diamond, which the couple bought in 1969.

Both Paul and Linda loved the setting, which captured something about the life they were pursuing, and offered an idealized version of the image they wanted to project to the public about that life. They could discuss the practicality and expense of transporting the band to the spot, once Linda asked Lategan where it was. It turned out to be in Osterley Park, in the Borough of Hounslow, West London, just a 12-mile drive from Cavendish Avenue. They engaged Lategan to shoot the Wings session—an hours-long affair, thanks to Lategan's focused discipline: he took as many as 20 Polaroids as part of his setup for each shot.[3]

With four musicians instead of a single model in the frame, Lategan took more distant shots than he had for the Helvin session, making the picture decidedly woodsier: the top half of the shot is leafy tree limbs—although, it being October, some of the green was fading toward yellow—and the bottom half is the lake, with the band perched on the same limb Helvin sat on. Lategan shot the band in several configurations, with doves flying around them in each shot.

In the one they chose, Seiwell, on the left, is wearing jeans and a black shirt with a red-and-white print design, and he smiles faintly at a dove flying between him and McCartney; Paul, second from the left, is standing in water up to his thighs, in brown pants and a light shirt with rolled-up sleeves, brandishing his Epiphone Texan FT-79 acoustic guitar (and strumming a C major chord). A dove, and Linda's right hand, rest on his left shoulder. Linda, in a long blue flower print dress, looks straight ahead as a dove flaps its wings to her left; and Laine, in a striped shirt and red tartan pants, balances himself on the log and smiles in Paul's direction, a dove sitting to his left, between his hand and his leg.

The woodland setting and the quartets of doves and rockers suggested taking the album's title from one of the songs, 'Wild Life,' although that was not yet fully decided.

A week after the cover shoot, Lennon's *Imagine* was released in Britain. In a way, the British release was anticlimactic: the album had been issued a month earlier in the United States, and copies had made their way across the Atlantic.

Still, the release was another stressor for Paul. Since early August reporters had focused on reports that *Imagine* would include a takedown of McCartney, even before its title, 'How Do You Sleep?,' was known. A surprise that had not leaked was John's inclusion of a parody of the *Ram* cover—a postcard with a photo of John holding a pig by the ears. Once the American release was available, critics and music reporters were able to write about these latest salvos in greater detail.

John, by now, was hardly gleeful about 'How Do You Sleep?,' his irritation at 'Too Many People' having waned since he wrote and recorded his riposte.

"There's a song which could well be a statement about Paul," he told *NME*. "It could be interpreted that way. But then, it could be about an old chick I'd known . . . Or Somethin'."[4] Speaking with *Sounds*, he implied that it might not be about Paul at all—and then said why it might be: "A perverted mind could think it is about Paul. I'll let you form your own opinion. It's surreal enough to be about anyone, like Dylan's 'Like a Rolling Stone.' Anyway, on *Ram* there are a lot of references to us, like in the line suggesting that George and I got a break in meeting him."[5]

George, who played lead guitar on 'How Do You Sleep?,' tried to mend fences during the October 3 opening party for the finally completed £500,000 ($1,200,000) studios in the basement of Apple's Savile Row offices and distanced himself from the song in the process.

"It's a bit sad now that Apple is in the position all four of us planned three years ago. I just wish Paul would use the studio if he wants. It's silly not to. I can't see the four of us together again. But I'd like us at least to be friends. We all own this business and it's doing well and I'd like all four of us to enjoy it now." Asked about 'How Do You Sleep?,' he said, "It doesn't help at all. I'm glad it wasn't about me. I said to John as we were recording it, 'It's pretty hard on him.'"[6]

Knowing he would be asked about *Imagine*, Paul opted for diplomacy. The first to ask was Judith Simons, of the *Daily Express*, in a chat about Wings' new moniker and impending album, now scheduled for a mid-November release. "That's all in the past,"[7] he told Simons when she wondered whether the new disc would include a response to John.

Recording Sessions

Saturday–Friday, October 2–15, 1971.
EMI Studios, Studio Two, London.
Recording: 'When the Saints Go Marching In.'
Overdubbing: 'Little Woman Love,' 'Love Is Strange,' 'Wild Life,' 'Tomorrow,' 'Mumbo,' and 'Some People Never Know.'
Mixing: All the above plus 'Mumbo Link' and 'Bip Bop.'

Two months had elapsed since Wings recorded the basic tracks for their debut LP, and in that time, they turned up for only a couple of dubbing sessions in early September. Now they were back to complete the album, which took them 10 more sessions over the next two weeks, bringing in the album in a total of 17 sessions.

During the band's time off, the 16-track masters for *Ram* were shipped from New York to London and logged into EMI's library. And on the first day back in the studio, Paul revisited one of those recordings—'Little Woman Love,' the tight, energetic country-rocker, with Milt Hinton on bass. Paul added extra guitar lines, and he, Linda and Denny Laine added vocals, making it a legitimate Wings track.

Paul was considering the song for a single or B side, but the idea was vague: there was talk in some of the music papers about Wings releasing a maxi-single before the album, with tracks that MPL's Shelley Turner said would be "specially recorded for this purpose," and not on the LP.[8] The EP never materialized.

The Saturday morning session was filled out with mixes of 'Little Woman Love' and 'Half Past Ten,' the instrumental version of 'Love Is Strange.' After lunch, Paul dubbed a lead guitar line on 'Wild Life.'

Listening to the playback, Paul realized that the top of the song needed something extra—an old-fashioned semisung, semispoken intro by Paul, accompanying himself on acoustic guitar. This edit piece—a single line "*the word wild applies to the words you and me*"—would be cross-faded with the master, which begins with Linda's piano, when the final mixes were made.

A by-product of the session—an attractive, fingerpicked guitar piece, recorded as a test while Clark was setting up the microphones for the edit piece—was also saved for later use as an unlisted link between two of the tracks on the completed album.* Paul referred to the new piece as 'Bip Bop Link.'

"I do remember when Paul was playing it ['Bip Bop Link']," noted Clark, "and I was mic'ing it up; I just used a couple of mics. And I thought crikey, what a fine musician he is. Because that's quite a complex piece of musicianship. It's just him and an acoustic guitar. That's not easy, and he played it fantastic."[9]

The mix of 'Half Past Ten' banished any lingering doubt Paul may have had about turning it into a cover of 'Love Is Strange,' so on Sunday, the band layered on the lead and backing vocals—loosely sung, deliberately avoiding locked-down precision with the intention of capturing a spur-of-the-moment vibe. Seiwell and McCartney added more drums and percussion, and Paul recorded a new guitar solo.

Wings returned to the studio on Tuesday to add another layer of harmony vocals to 'Tomorrow,' with Alan Parsons adding a fifth voice to the chorus. Clark then made stereo mixes of both 'Love Is Strange' and 'Tomorrow,' and Paul took away copies. By Friday morning, after a two-day break, he had decided that 'Tomorrow' was not quite satisfactory.

Knowing how to identify flaws, and whether to redo weak parts from scratch or find a way to strengthen them, was central to Paul's genius in the studio, as Seiwell observed from the start.

"If anything was weak we'd double and triple track it," Seiwell explained. "Even if it was a mistake, we wouldn't fix it. We'd just double and treble it. That was one of Paul's little quirks that he liked to do. And after a while it became your favorite part of the song."[10]

Clark, however, was running out of available tracks on the eight-track master. Bouncing the drums and bass to a single track freed up space, allowing Paul to double the guitar solo.

---

* On the original *Wild Life* LP, this short track was untitled and unlisted. The 1987 CD reissue presented it as a separate track, called 'Bip Bop Link,' as did subsequent releases, including the 2018 remastered archival set.

On Friday afternoon, Paul returned once more to 'Mumbo.' By this point only a lead guitar and percussion had been added, but now, Paul and Linda added a series of head-shakingly Beatlesque, high-pitched "ooohs" to the refrains, each preceded or followed by an assertive burst of organ, played by Paul. To that he and Laine added more electric guitar.

Filled out texturally, but retaining its shambolic energy, 'Mumbo' was finally ready to pass as a spirit-of-the-moment studio jam, so long as nobody wondered how a quartet managed to handle three electric guitars, piano, organ, bass, drums, and extra percussion. The full, completed track runs nearly seven minutes; Paul trimmed it to 3'58".

But he was not finished with 'Mumbo.' Having created a short acoustic link track to follow 'I Am Your Singer,' he wanted an electric link track as well. Instead of recording it fresh, he used two segments of the material trimmed from 'Mumbo,' everything faded out but Laine's bass and rhythm guitar, Seiwell's percussion overdubs and Paul's lead guitar tracks. Edited together, the two excerpts became the second link track.

This is a more daring interlude than the short, self-contained 'Bip Bop Link.' The snippets of 'Mumbo' are joined with deliberate crudeness and mixed more dramatically than on the main track, giving the 'Mumbo Link' an experimental aura.

Parsons again remained after hours to hone his mixing chops, producing a new mix of 'I Am Your Singer' and taking on 'Some People Never Know,' 'Bip Bop Link,' 'Tomorrow,' 'Dear Friend,' and the 'Mumbo Link.' His mixes for 'I Am Your Singer' and 'Mumbo Link' were retained for the final album sequence. For Parsons, it was another step toward earning the respect of his peers and becoming a full-fledged in-house engineer.

Like Seiwell, Paul had played the trumpet as a child, and at the October 9 session, he paid another visit to EMI's instrument closet, picked up a trumpet, and as Clark rolled tape, Paul played the one tune he learned on the instrument, 'When the Saints Go Marching In,' with Laine at the piano. It's hard to say what the point was: perhaps Paul thought an excerpt might be useful as another link track, or that if it turned out well enough, he might include it, going full circle to the period in his childhood just before he took up the guitar. But although Laine has some deft moments, Paul's search for the notes is not something he would have considered releasing on an album meant to introduce his new band.* Nevertheless, Clark made a stereo mix of the track at the end of the session.

The main work of the day was finishing 'Some People Never Know,' a track that already had plenty on it, but for which McCartney and Seiwell kept coming up with new ideas. The overdub-

---

* The two-minute recording was released as a hidden bonus track on the *Wild Life* Deluxe Edition, in 2018, tacked on (after a pause) to the end of the August 1971 Rude Studio recording of 'African Yeah Yeah.' Paul's only other known public performance of the song as a trumpeter was a notably more assured account with the Preservation Hall Jazz Band, Irma Thomas, Elvis Costello, Dave Grohl and others, in *Round Midnight Preserves*, a benefit for Preservation Hall on June 20, 2020. On that occasion, he played the song on a trumpet that had been owned by Louis Armstrong. With the Beatles, Paul played bass on a recording of 'The Saints,' a rocked-up version of the tune, backing the singer Tony Sheridan on June 22, 1961. It was released as the B side of 'My Bonnie' (Polydor) on October 23, 1961. It was that recording that brought the Beatles to Brian Epstein's attention.

bing began with a twin guitar solo, played in tandem by McCartney and Laine, as an alternative to Seiwell's trumpet solo. Backing vocals followed, this time with all four members of Wings—Linda singing soprano, McCartney and Denny Laine singing tenor, and Seiwell singing bass.

"Denny Seiwell has got a great bass voice," Laine told a journalist, a few weeks later, "so we can get these harmony things going. It opens it all up."[11]

Besides singing bass, Seiwell added higher frequencies too. On his way to the studio that morning, Seiwell saw a street vendor selling long, multicolored plastic Whirly tubes that, when swung in the air, produced high-pitched tones. Seiwell bought one, took it to the studio and showed Paul how it worked. By changing the speed with which he was swinging it, Seiwell got two notes out of it, an A, and a C. "Great, let's put it on here,"[12] Paul told the drummer.

With the eight-track master tape already full, this late addition posed a challenge for Clark. Instead of bouncing existing tracks to free up space, he used the same technique Eirik Wangberg used on 'Dear Boy,' punching in for the new addition on a track otherwise devoted to backing vocals. Seiwell added his whirring sound at 5'39", after a long, sustained vocal "aaahhh." Clark punched out mid-note, at 5'47", just in time for the "aaahhh" to resume.

"Luckily we were at EMI where the engineers were trained and really knew what they were doing," Seiwell notes. "Paul pushed them to the limits."[13]

With the rest of Wings around the console, McCartney and Clark spent the next day mixing. The final mixes for 'Mumbo,' 'Love Is Strange' and 'Tomorrow'—the last sped up by about 4 percent, making the finished mix a bit faster, and a half-step higher in pitch—were also completed on October 10.

Wings took most of the week off, turning up again on Friday, October 15, for more mixing, this time 'Wild Life' and 'Bip Bop.'

Recording Session

Saturday, October 16, 1971.
EMI Studios, Studio Two, London.
Overdubbing: 'Dear Friend.'

All that remained, apart from compiling the album, was adding Hewson's orchestration for 'Dear Friend.' The session was scheduled for October 16, an auspicious moment for it, because two days earlier, Paul had a phone call from John, the song's subject. The Lennons were in New York City, having spent John's birthday (on October 9) in Syracuse, New York, overseeing the opening of Yoko's *This Is Not Here* exhibition at the Everson Museum. During an interview with David Wigg, on October 15, John lamented the rift with Paul.

"I always remember watching the film with—who was it, not Rodgers and Hammerstein, those British people who wrote the silly operas years ago, who are they—Gilbert and Sullivan. I always remember watching the film with Robert Morley, and thinking, 'We'll never get to that,' and we did, which really upset me. I really never thought we'd be so stupid, but we [were]. Like splitting, and arguing, and they come back 20 years later and one's in a wheelchair. But we were naïve enough to let people come between us, and that's what happened."[14]

When Wigg wondered why John, the self-proclaimed peace activist, launched such a blistering attack on Paul in 'How Do You Sleep?,' John mentioned his attempt to hold out an olive branch.

"I spoke to Paul yesterday, and I said, 'I hope you weren't too upset about the song.' He says, 'No.' Okay? So that's that. Paul's version of it. The song isn't only about Paul, it is a song in its own right anyway, you know?"[15]

The conversation, however, was by no means dispute-free. John proposed a meeting without advisers to discuss their outstanding issues—liquidating Apple without having to send the lion's share of the proceeds to Inland Revenue, for one, and the still unresolved Maclen dispute, for another. Paul turned down John's proposal. He also told John that he would not, under any condition, sell his share of Apple to the others, one of John's proposed solutions.[16]

For the overdub, Hewson engaged a small ensemble with standard strings, trumpets and trombone, saxophones, oboe and flute, and harp. With Hewson conducting, Paul produced the session from the control room. As Hewson remembers it, "Paul had hands on everything. I don't think he would have let anything be done without him overseeing it."[17]

But Paul was not the only member of Wings with opinions. When the recording was finished, Clark made a stereo mix,* which led to a battle in the control room. Linda felt that the orchestra overwhelmed Paul's tender ballad, and that bringing it down in volume would not be sufficient—she wanted the orchestra wiped from the tape. A heated discussion ensued, and after a momentary crisis of confidence in which he nearly adopted Linda's view, Paul decided to keep the orchestration. Working into the early hours of the next morning, Clark filled two reels with mixes before finding a balance that satisfied everyone.

"With 'Dear Friend' there was quite a creative process with Paul and myself, with his ideas about how to place the orchestral sound into that track," Clark explains. "At the beginning, it's placed very low, and I think it's slightly phased as well, and it gives a really sort of mysterious sound—rather then it being a full, lush orchestra. Then, it just builds towards when the sax comes in, when the brass comes in. Making it feel just slightly tense. If you'd left it as a natural balance, that wouldn't have been the case."[18]

---

* Tony Clark's original mix of 'Dear Friend' (listed as "orchestra up") is available for review, released by McCartney via his website on December 24, 2018.

With the tracks complete, Wings and Clark took a day to sequence the album. It was not diffi-cult: just about everyone could see that the material broke down into tracks that were loose, both compositionally and as performances, and others that were more carefully wrought—and that there were four of each. Instead of interspersing weaker and stronger tracks, Paul followed essentially the same logic he conveyed to Seiwell about doubling up on mistakes rather than fix-ing them: he put the looser songs on Side One, starting with 'Mumbo,' and the more complex, thoughtfully textured songs on Side Two.

Paul's public explanation painted *Wild Life* as a party album.

"The way we think of the album is, a more hard side then a more romantic side, so if you're at a party and dancing you don't want to have to sit down because a slow number comes on in the middle of the fast ones. So you can just put one side on and dance to it all."[19]

SIDE ONE (EMI MATRIX NO. YEX.871)

'Mumbo'
'Bip Bop'
'Love Is Strange'
'Wild Life'

SIDE TWO (EMI MATRIX NO. YEX.872)

'Some People Never Know'
'I Am Your Singer'
'Tomorrow'
'Dear Friend'

That left the two link tracks. They clearly needed to go on Side Two, with the more sophisti-cated material. Clark added a phasing effect to the 'Bip Bop Link,' and spliced it to the end of 'I Am Your Singer.' It was not clear, at first, where the 'Mumbo Link' might fit, but Clark argued for putting it at the end of the side, after 12 seconds of silence. It was the perfect solution: not only did it turn 'Mumbo' into a frame for the album, with the link as a quirky reprise of the opening track, but thanks to its brusque edit, it would leave listeners wondering whether it was intended as an experimental tag, or was a serendipitous editing accident, like 'Her Majesty,' on *Abbey Road.*

---

* 'Her Majesty' was originally part of the medley of short songs on Side Two of *Abbey Road*, but Paul felt it was unsuitable. Deleted from

Unlike *McCartney* and *Ram*, *Wild Life* would have neither a gatefold nor a portfolio of Linda's photos—just a simple, old-fashioned LP sleeve. Lategan's photo would have the front cover to itself, with no graphics: the band's name and the album's title would be listed only on the spine and on the back cover, where they were printed in a large Bauhaus font. Beneath were the eight song titles, in two rows.

Under the song titles were liner notes, signed "Clint Harrigan,"[*] but written by Paul in a style that he later likened to Tony Barrow's and Derek Taylor's notes for the Beatles' early albums, but which were closer in spirit to Lennon's jokey prose style. The notes offer a potted history of Wings, some of it fictional. The assertion that "They rehearsed for a while, sang some old songs, wrote some new ones and in time headed for the big city studios," glosses over the group's scant preparation. Monique Seiwell rolled her eyes at the section noting that Denny arrived in Scotland "carrying his wife who was drunk again." Monique did not drink and was worried that her parents in France might get the wrong idea.

At the bottom of the cover was a pen-and-ink sketch, also by Paul, of Wings in performance, with angels' wings sprouting from their backs. Clark and Parsons are credited as engineers, and the recorder ensemble was credited as Dolmetsch. Lategan and EMI's Gordon House were credited for the cover photo and typography, but Hewson is overlooked.

A fresh start with a new group also meant taking a step away from Apple, visually if not contractually. Unlike *McCartney*, *Ram*, and Paul's trio of solo singles, which all carried Apple's distinctive Granny Smith vinyl labels, Paul wanted Wings' first album to be independent of the Beatles' brand. For the disc labels, Paul provided a photo of himself—or actually, his right eye, nose and mustache, with an overlaid poppy—taken by Linda, for Side One. The label for Side Two was a photo, taken by Paul, of Linda wiping water from her eyes as she steps out of a pool. (The shots were taken in France in 1970.)

Both labels carry a production credit for Paul and Linda McCartney, and publishing credits for the McCartney-McCartney songs list both Northern Songs (or Maclen, on American pressings) and rather than McCartney Music, Inc., a new publisher called Kidney Punch Music.[†] This aggressively titled business arm was Paul's latest gesture in his ongoing dispute with ATV over Linda's songwriting credit for 'Another Day.'

There were lots of messages here. If the two Dennys were still wondering to what degree they were shareholders in Wings, the labels on *Wild Life* provided a clue. And the Kidney Punch

---

the medley, the track was affixed to the end of the reel, after several seconds of leader. It was to have been removed later, but it was still present when the Beatles listened to the final sequence. Amused by its surprising appearance, they decided to keep it.

[*] Paul may have based the pseudonym on Barry Harrigan, a writer who joined *Melody Maker* in 1971.

[†] Kidney Punch Music was never registered as a trading company. However, on April 4, 1972, Hotheath Limited was registered by Paul and Linda as a 100-share company, designed to handle any royalties that should arise from Wings' early records.

Music credit was both an assertion that Linda would continue to be credited as a cocomposer who owned her own publishing, and a slight provocation. Northern certainly saw it as such and responded with advertisements proclaiming that they are "proud to be the exclusive publishers of the songs of Paul McCartney."[20]

While they were completing the *Wild Life* sessions and designing its sleeve, Paul and Linda were also preparing the ground for *Thrillington*. Their Irish trip had not yielded plausible photos of their fictional conductor, so they launched a whispering campaign in the columns of the British music papers. They announced, in the second week of October, that MPL had made its first artist signing, the Irish big band conductor Percy Thrillington—a musician they found "unusually flexible and inventive,"[21] and whose debut album would be an instrumental version of *Ram*. *NME* took the bait, as did *Melody Maker*, the *Daily Express*, and *Sounds*, which quoted Paul predicting that Maestro Thrillington is "capable of attracting younger listeners to the big band audience."[22]

With the album sequenced and mastered (by Peter Tackley, at EMI on October 20), the cover art settled, and a November 15, 1971, release date announced, Wings returned to Scotland on October 23, where Paul awaited the inevitable blowback from his demand that neither the disc nor the cover carry an Apple logo.

It was not long in coming. On November 2, Malcom Brown, in EMI's legal department, wrote to Gordon House, the typographic designer (with a copy to the McCartneys), saying that "It will be necessary to insert a small apple being a simple outline adjacent to the words 'An Apple Record' on the reverse of the sleeve."[23]

"I phoned the others up and asked them, 'Well, how about it?'" Paul said. "They ummed and aahed over the phone, but a couple of days later when I spoke to them they didn't like the idea. So, I asked them, 'Have you been talking to Klein?'"[24]

Paul pushed the point and reached a compromise: "An Apple Record" appears in very small print on each label, and at the bottom right of the back cover, and just beneath it, the American release says, redundantly, that the disc was manufactured by Apple, giving Klein's ABKCO address. But there are no apples of any kind to be found.

Still, the squabble over the Apple logo delayed the album's release, leading MPL to issue a statement, in early November, giving a revised but nonspecific release date that Wings hoped would be before December 1. When the last week of November rolled around, *Wild Life* was still nowhere to be found. EMI told reporters that they were unable to press the album because they had not yet been sent the labels and jackets. MPL shifted the blame back to EMI, saying in a press statement that the company had pressed a faulty matrix, producing a run of discs that skipped and had to be scrapped. An advertisement for the album, in the November 27 issues of some music papers, listed "as soon as possible" as the release date.

The situation was so chaotic that it is impossible to find a definitive release date, with contemporary British sources listing the UK release variously between December 3 and 10, and American sources giving the release date between December 6 and 13.

Incensed by the delays, Paul waited until the problems were sorted and the album was released, and then he reminded Klein who had won the lawsuit. On a piece of Kidney Punch Music stationery, bearing MPL's London and New York addresses and the publishing company's logo—a martini glass with a boxing glove in it—he dashed off a quick note, by hand, that read:

Dear Pig,
You have nothing to do with
    my affairs, so keep out of them!

Fuck off.

P.M.[25]

The labeling dispute was actually just the tip of the iceberg in the continued squabbling in the aftermath of Paul's lawsuit. J. D. Spooner, the court-appointed receiver, was still feeling his way in the job and felt hamstrung by the fact that he was getting most of his news about what the former Beatles were up to from the press, despite the court's order that all financial issues and decisions be run past him.

"I read in the press that Mr. McCartney may be forming a new Anglo-American pop group,"[26] Spooner wrote to Martin Lampard, Paul's representative in matters to do with Apple, on September 1—well into Wings' sessions for their debut album. It was not merely a matter of curiosity about Paul's activities; he sought confirmation that the group's recordings would be made for EMI, subject to the 1967 agreement, whereby royalties were paid to Apple (and were therefore under Spooner's care).

Sometimes his queries received tart pushback. When he wrote to Peter Howard, Apple's attorney, on July 27, seeking confirmation of press reports about George, John and Ringo working on new recordings, Howard provided the information—with the gruff preface: "Whilst in no way admitting your entitlement to the information you have asked for . . ."[27]

But keeping abreast of the former Beatles' plans was the least of Spooner's worries. Correspondence between Spooner, Lampard, Apple, and EMI, between late July and late October 1971, shows an array of issues that Spooner found himself in the middle of, some of which convinced him that he needed to consult the court for further instruction about what leeway he had.

Among them were questions about royalties for the Beatles pre-1967 recordings; issues surrounding costs and payments for the book that accompanied the original release of *Let It Be* in Britain and several other countries; questions about whether film royalties should be construed as part of the partnership agreement, and therefore payable to Apple; and a dispute between Apple and EMI over the Beatles' Hollywood Bowl recordings, which EMI wanted to release, and the Beatles opposed.*

The release of George's 'Bangla Desh' single, and a planned album recorded at the Madison Square Garden concert raised a handful of issues on their own: the court order had locked the royalties of the individual Beatles into Apple's bank account, pending Spooner's sorting of it all, but George and Ringo wanted their royalties donated, posthaste, to the Relief Fund. That would require special dispensation—and that, in turn, required the approval of McCartney, still reluctantly a partner in Apple. Paul had no problem with it, but Lampard took his time conveying McCartney's approval to Spooner—and when he did, the wording suggested that Lampard was dealing only with the single, not the concert album, so Spooner had to go back and wait several more months for a response.

———

For the most part, Paul kept out of these disputes, concerning himself only with those holding back *Wild Life*. Paul decided that the physical absence of the album should not slow his promotional efforts. After a four-day run of rehearsals at Rude Studio between November 2 and 5, Wings traveled to London—Paul, Linda, and the girls by sleeper train—for a lavish Ball that Paul and Linda threw at the Empire Ballroom, in Leicester Square, on November 8, a Monday evening. Originally meant to be both a release party for the album and a launch party for Wings, it was mostly the latter, although Paul brought an acetate of the album to play while guests danced; Wings did not perform live.

The introduction of McCartney's new band and their first album were guaranteed to draw press coverage, and he made an event of it. He produced a handwritten invitation, leaving space to write in the invitee's name, as well as a number, which would be used for a raffle drawing toward the end of the evening. (The prize was a magnum of champagne; the disc jockey Jeff Dexter was the winner.) Food and drink, music from *Wild Life* and dancing to the sounds of the Ray McVay Evergreen Dance Band were all promised.

The recommended dress was "glam." Paul had ordered a loud, plaid suit from Tommy Nutter,

---

* Because of the protracted dispute, and the Beatles' collective feeling that live recordings from the zenith of Beatlemania did not represent them at their best, *The Beatles at the Hollywood Bowl* was not released until May 1977.

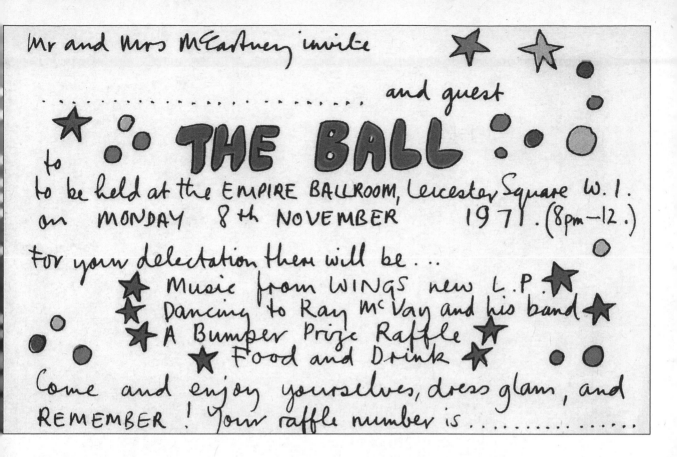

Mr and Mrs McCartney invite

. . . . and guest

to THE BALL

to be held at the EMPIRE BALLROOM, Leicester Square W.1.
on MONDAY 8th NOVEMBER 1971. (8pm—12.)

For your delectation there will be . . .
★ Music from WINGS new L.P.★
★ Dancing to Ray McVay and his band ←★
★ A Bumper Prize Raffle ★
★ Food and Drink ★

Come and enjoy yourselves, dress glam, and
REMEMBER! Your raffle number is . . . .

the London tailor. It was not completed in time, but he wore it anyway, over a gray turtleneck, with the in-progress stitching in plain view—another eccentric touch for the evening.

"His short hair, quaffed up with grease, black plimsolls and drape jacket gave him the appearance of a 'fifties teddy boy,'" Ray Coleman and Chris Charlesworth wrote in their joint report on the party for *Melody Maker*.[28]

The rest of the band was also casual, if not necessarily glam. Linda wore a red dress with a white dove print; Laine sported a bright red jacket and plaid trousers, and Seiwell, the most conservative dresser in the group, sported a gray jacket, black slacks, and a black turtleneck.

Some 800 musicians, reporters, friends of the band and music business honchos were invited. Among those who turned up were Jimmy Page, Elton John, Sandy Denny, Mary Hopkin, members of the Who, the Faces, and Deep Purple, Dave Clark, Peter Frampton, Ginger Baker, Grease Band guitarist Henry McCullough, Gilbert O'Sullivan, Graham Bond, Sandie Shaw, the Greek synthesizer wizard Vangelis, the actors Malcolm McDowell, and Terence Stamp, some of the Monty Python troupe, Sir Joseph Lockwood, the head of EMI, Allan Clarke, of the Hollies, and (Benny) Gallagher and (Graham) Lyle. None of the other Beatles were on hand, nor was anyone from Apple.

Security was tight. Invitations were checked against a master list and then punched. As always

at such events, there was ample carping, which a reporter for *Rolling Stone* duly cataloged. After describing the Empire Ballroom as decidedly unhip, a leftover from the days when the Joe Loss Orchestra would play foxtrots, and young ladies shopped for husbands among the dancers, the writer noted that while the wine and cheese were free, everything at the bar was for sale. Photographers complained that only Paul's authorized lensman could snap photos, with one complaining that it's harder to photograph Paul than the Queen.

Eyebrows were raised when, instead of a Wings performance, partygoers were treated to foxtrots, waltzes, quicksteps, and congas, played by McVay's band—along with what McVay remembered as arrangements of sixties and seventies hits, including a Beatles medley and some Beach Boys tunes.[29] They were raised higher still when the heavily sequined and coiffed Frank and Peggy Spence Latin and Ballroom Formation Dancing Teams filed onto the floor to demonstrate their artistry.

"I'm beginning to think that Paul actually digs all this," one guest quipped to the *Rolling Stone* reporter, "that he actually *likes* dance bands, ballrooms, and buffet food. That's incredibly camp, you know, incredibly camp. Have you seen his suit? It's like a clown's costume, the jacket is about five sizes too big, and it's not even been finished."[30]

Colin Burn, the general manager of EMI's Pop Division, was in charge of organizing the bash and keeping the budget under control. To begin with, there was some dissension in the EMI ranks about the party.

"Ron White (Marketing), Roy Featherstone (A&R) were there," Burn said, "but none of them wanted to have anything to do with it. I don't know why. Whether they were frightened of McCartney or not. It was all going to be vegetarian, and I had to go and meet with him at his office in Soho Square and fix it all up with him. Ron White and Roy Featherstone didn't want to go so I was left looking after McCartney with Linda. . . .

"I had to set the parameters, the sums in those days were really quite low. I said, 'EMI will obviously pay but it's not unlimited.' I was thinking of a ballpark figure of £1,000 ($2,500), [but] he wanted Ray McVay and his band to play dance music, the hire of the Empire Leicester Square, and all the food and booze, provided it was beer and wine. If they wanted spirits the guests had to buy their own. We worked all this out and I was saying, 'We can't do this, and we can't do this.' Linda was getting a bit twitchy, and Paul said to her, 'Linda love, you've got to remember that the days of the Queen Mary are really over for us.' I will always remember that line, such a great remark."[31]

All told, this shindig cost £5000 ($12,500), a bill Paul told reporters he was forwarding to EMI. Paul gave the label its money's worth, working the room like a veteran PR man, propagandizing for Wings and *Wild Life* and telling reporters that just the day before, he was in Scotland, shearing the sheep early in the day, and rehearsing with Wings later. Both on his own and with Linda, he persuaded skeptical reporters that the ball was the event of the season—as Coleman and Charlesworth put it in *Melody Maker*, "only an ex-Beatle could stage a glorified Saturday-night hop-style dance in the West End on a Monday night in cold November, and come up smiling like a winner."[32]

Seiwell, Laine and Tony Clark did their part, too, discussing agreed-upon talking points about the album's freshness and honesty, interspersed with tall tales about most of the songs being recorded in single takes. And Paul dangled the possibility of touring with Wings, offering two conflicting ideas—first, that he could not consider it until he was at last free of Apple, and alternatively, that he was thinking about driving around Britain with the band and giving unannounced performances.

But the real full-court press took place two days later, on November 10, when Paul invited critics to a listening session and interview at EMI Studios. McCartney's decision to release *Ram* at arm's length, Tony Barrow noted before they parted ways that summer, painted Paul as cold, distant, and evasive, an image that spilled into press reviews of the album. Paul was keen not to make the same mistake twice. Playback in the studio where the album was recorded was the optimal way to hear the album—better, certainly, than in a crowded ballroom—and when the playback finished, Paul was in a talkative mood, open to seemingly any question reporters threw at him.

Among the first questions was the perennial one about the state of Paul's relationship with Apple, some 11 months after he launched his lawsuit. Since nothing much had actually changed, in the aftermath of his victory, this was a hot button question for Paul, and he leaned into it. The situation, he said, was "way out of line with what I thought was going to happen. None of the Beatles have, to this day, seen any of that money. As far as the money of the Beatles' records is concerned, the Beatles still haven't got it. I'd like to see the four Beatles split up whatever is left of whatever the Beatles made. George calls it throwing a tantrum when I say things like that, but I only want what I earned. That's all I want. I'm not asking for a lollipop.[33]

"I just want the four of us to get together somewhere and sign a piece of paper saying it's all over, and we want to divide the money four ways. No one else would be there, not even Linda or Yoko, or Allen Klein. We'd just sign the paper and hand it to the business people and let them sort it all out. That's all I want now. But John won't do it. Everybody thinks I am the aggressor but I'm not, you know. I just want out."[34]

Paul was comfortable unloading, giving the press, which he regarded as being pro-Lennon, an earful of his side of things. "I don't wanna go putting the other three down particularly," Paul continued, "that's my trouble, I probably should. I probably should just rant and rave and call them the biggest shits on earth, you know, 'cos it's certainly not cool what they're doing."[35] If Linda's frequently laying her hand on his arm was meant as a message to cool it, he didn't notice; nor did he register the increasing discomfort Seiwell and Laine were feeling, sitting beside him at the control panel, with nothing to add to his litany of Beatles grievances. MPL's Shelley Turner, starting to panic, sidled up to *Melody Maker*'s Chris Charlesworth, as if he could somehow get Paul back on track.

"He's talking about money now," she whispered to Charlesworth. "That's one of his pet points. He'll never stop. Denny and Denny are protesting, but there's nothing I can do. Please get him talking about Wings. That's why we are here, after all. The others can't join in, talking about the Beatles. I wish he wouldn't go on like he does. There's really no stopping him."[36]

From there, everything was considered fair game. Paul offered his thoughts about *Imagine* ("I liked *Imagine*"[37]) and 'How Do You Sleep?' ("It's silly. 'The only thing you did was "Yesterday"'—That doesn't bother me. Even if that was the only thing I did, that's not bad, that'll do me. But it isn't, and he bloody knows it isn't, because he'd sat in this very room and watched me do tapes, and he's dug it."[38])

Eventually, he made his way to Wings, talking about having worked with Seiwell on *Ram* and inviting Laine to join. He defended Linda's keyboard playing, which had not yet been heard publicly and is barely heard on *Wild Life* ("I like what she does. Her style isn't like that old, hard pro thing that's got all the technique. It's got what children's drawings have got . . . innocence"[39]). He spoke at some length about touring, and the kind of touring band Wings would be—with a few odd rhetorical twists and more than a bit of waffling.

"With this band we play good together live because nobody's too hung up about what he's playing. We'll go 'round Denny's house and just sit there playing songs that we half-know. It's good. We don't want to be a media group—we don't want to go everywhere and plug everything and have knickers with our name on them and all that. That won't work for me now, it's all done—it was great while it lasted but it's over now. [40]

"Yes we'll go on the road, it may be next year, it may be two years' time, but it could be next week. But we'd just do it if and when we feel like it. There would be no tour. No announcement that Wings would be starting a tour at Slough Civic Hall on such and such a date. I'd just like to turn up and play unannounced. I'd even like to bill ourselves as something else like 'Rikki and the Redstreaks.'"[41]

And finally, he declared that *Wild Life* was exactly the album he wanted to make, the way he wanted to make it, and he did not expect that press criticism would change that.

"After the criticism of *McCartney*, I put so much into *Ram* to try and please myself and the critics. With Wings I don't care if people don't like it. I like it. I've got an awful lot to live up to, that's the problem. But I know *I'm* good. If I'm in the right mood I can write a solid gold hit."[42]

As the press conference broke up, Paul suggested to Linda and the two Dennys that they remain at the studio and listen to some tapes, with an ear toward choosing a single. They had already done touch-ups on, and mixed, 'Little Woman Love.' Now Paul wanted to check on the state of another *Ram* leftover, 'Get on the Right Thing.'

But upon playback Paul reverted to the insecurities that led him to set the track aside in 1971, and he was hesitant to revive it.

"He didn't think the lead vocals were any good," explained Laine, who lobbied on behalf of the Wingless song. "But it's great, I love it," he said. "If you change the vocal though, it won't be as strong."[43] In the end, Paul decided not to add anything to the song, but spent until 4:00 a.m. preparing mixes, two reels of them. The two songs were set aside for release as a single, and even assigned matrix numbers. But he ultimately decided that putting out two cuts from his New York sessions would be a backward step, and the single was never issued.

———

Wings were winding down for a holiday break. Paul and Linda would visit Jamaica and then fly on to New York, where they would visit the Eastmans. Seiwell and Laine would fly directly to New York, where they would see to some private errands before connecting with the McCartneys, and would then undertake some light promotional duties for *Wild Life*. The Seiwells, in fact, got a head start, flying to New York on November 16, and spending Thanksgiving (November 25) with Seiwell's family in Pennsylvania. Paul telephoned him there with an assignment.

"Pick up the tapes of *Wild Life* at Apple's offices on Broadway," he told Seiwell, "take them to Sterling Sound, and master the American release."

Never having mastered a recording, Seiwell was not sure he was the man for the job. "The guys at Sterling know what they're doing," Paul told him. "Just go up and sit with them, and make sure it sounds right—you know, if it sounds too thin, tell them to do it again."

Seiwell did as Paul asked, then took the tapes back to Apple, where he ran into John and Yoko. "He goes, 'Oh, you're Paul's new drummer, eh?' That was all he said."[44] Unknown to Seiwell, John had, a month earlier, worked with Hugh McCracken on the sessions for 'Happy Xmas (War Is Over).' Upon meeting Hugh, Lennon said, "I liked your work with Paul. But that was just an audition to get to work with me."[45]

Paul, Linda, and Denny Laine remained in London long enough for the first reviews. Because the physical album was unavailable—one publication noted that, as of the last week in November, even Paul couldn't get a finished copy—a few critics wrote their reviews based on the November 10 listening event at EMI—that is, after a single hearing, on studio-quality monitors, with Paul on hand to answer questions about his overall intentions or specific songs. After the lambasting of *Ram*, the tenor of these first reviews was overwhelmingly positive.

In *NME*, Richard Green adopted Paul's explanation of the rocker/ballad distinction between the LP's sides and heard the influence of Little Richard on 'Mumbo' and Carl Perkins on 'Bip Bop.' His reference point for 'Love Is Strange' was the Everly Brothers version, and he heard an Everly influence in 'Some People Never Know' as well.[46]

Peter Gavin, reviewing for *Disc and Music Echo*, found the album "an appealing mixture of fun, melody and excitement." He singled out 'Mumbo' as "a great, raucous, vulgar rock 'n' roll song" and characterized 'Love Is Strange' as "a skinhead's delight" with an imperfect harmony on vocals, which adds to the delight."[47]

Only Mike Hennessey among the reviewers at the listening session had any critical doubts. He began his *Record Mirror* review by calling *Wild Life* "unquestionably Paul McCartney's best solo album [sic] to date," and he praises 'Tomorrow' and 'Dear Friend' as "classic, vintage McCartney, sharply bringing into focus his flair for melody and harmony." It occurred to Hennessey that Paul's vocal on 'Wild Life' might be "a strident send-up of Lennon," but doubts that this was McCartney's intent. But after giving the album a thumbs-up, he ends with faint praise: "All in

---

* Ironically, though early reggae had given a voice to disillusioned black youths in Britain, by 1971 it had been adopted as the music of choice by British skinheads.

all the album is good but it still falls a long way short of the masterpiece Paul has the capacity to produce."[48]

As later reviews rolled in, that last sentiment—which also ran through several of the *Ram* reviews—became a standard refrain, regardless of whether the critic liked or hated the album. Having a name that guaranteed attention was a double-edge sword; it looked to McCartney as if his new work would forever be measured against expectations defined by his work with the Beatles.

Sometimes, the suggestion that Paul had something greater in him than he'd released so far was wrapped in strange verbal contortions. *Melody Maker*'s Roy Hollingworth sneered at McCartney's suggestion that *Wild Life* is for dancing, concluding that it is "a dream album for airline hostesses, but musically, and on the originality stakes, there's too many maracas around, and not enough balls. But he'll do something good, mark my words."[49]

In *Sounds*, Steve Peacock noted that McCartney works best with people around him "who can spur him on or give him something to get his teeth into." He found some of the songs overly long and chastised McCartney for hogging all the solos ("What is the use of having a player like Denny [Laine] in the band if you shove him out of the way all the time?"). Yet he found the disc "infinitely preferable to either *McCartney* or *Ram*" and opined that "this is an encouraging album, which shows that the McCartneys have found a way of working that could develop into something pretty exciting."[50]

The American reviews were generally rougher. The *Los Angeles Times* critic Robert Hilburn found it disappointing, as he had found *McCartney* and *Ram*, but still held out hope that "he may well produce an excellent album, even, perhaps, a masterpiece."[51] Lew Harris's review for the *Chicago Tribune* was unabashedly hostile, calling McCartney the "idiot child of rock," and expressing astonishment that "for some insane reason the people still buy his records." He did find the album better than *Ram*, which he found better than *McCartney*, and came up with a different spin on the idea that McCartney will someday make a great album. As he put it, "At this rate, he should match the quality of *Imagine*, *All Things Must Pass* and *Beaucoups of Blues* sometime in mid-1976."[52]

Rolling Stone was once again in a class by itself. "Like Paul McCartney's first two post-Beatles albums, *Wild Life* is largely high on sentiment but rather flaccid musically and impotent lyrically, trivial and unaffecting," John Mendelssohn wrote. "It lacks the exhilarating highs of *Ram* (which highs I, as one who found it as worthless as the next guy when it first arrived, can assure you are indeed present), and in the form of a track called 'I Am Your Singer,' contains the most embarrassingly puerile single piece of work Paul's been associated with since 'She's Leaving Home.'" But at least, Mendelssohn added, it is "unpretentious."

As it had done with *McCartney* and *Ram*, *Rolling Stone* approached *Wild Life* less as an album than as a political salvo in the McCartney-Apple war, and to that end, Mendelssohn advanced the theory that McCartney was deliberately making bland albums and would continue to do so for as long as he remains "contractually chained to an organization he has little desire to make wealthier." Alternatively—and a departure from *Rolling Stone*'s consistent championship of Lennon—Mendelssohn wondered whether McCartney was focusing on "the most banal imaginable themes" as a way of satirizing Lennon's earnestness and his devotion to causes.

George Harrison also weighed in at some length, to Paul's irritation. When *Record Mirror* asked what he thought of *Wild Life*, he maintained a diplomatic stance for all of two sentences—and then launched into an eviscerating critique.

"It really wasn't a very good album. To be kind to Paul, I'll just say that—it's not very good. I just can't believe it. Incredible. The songs are pretty poor—and the sounds! The recording was very bad. It's as if he's forgotten everything, I was really disappointed. The whole thing is crummy. Paul's first album never really knocked me out, but at least he did it on his own. Some of the songs were leftovers from Beatle days. The second I didn't really like, but *Ram* is sensational compared with the new one. If Wings was an unknown group, it would be a poor album. But by Paul it's just doubly poor."[53]

"I don't agree with the criticism, but it hurts," McCartney conceded soon after. "Any criticism hurts me, especially from George."[54]

In some ways, the continuing comparison of Paul's new work to work with the Beatles demonstrated that for the critics, the Beatles were immune to the changing zeitgeist. By the time the Beatles recorded *Abbey Road*, the rise of virtuoso rockers like Jimi Hendrix and all three members of Cream, along with jamming bands like the Grateful Dead, the Allman Brothers Band and Mountain, and prog-rock groups like King Crimson, Yes, and Emerson, Lake & Palmer, in which rock, jazz and classical influences were melded, had fundamentally expanded listeners' ideas about what a rock band could achieve. At the end of 1971, the Beatles had been gone for two years, and the rock world was moving on, on its own terms. While many critics continued to think in terms of the old hierarchy, record buyers—whose discretionary budgets forced them to make choices were thinking differently.

From the street-level perspective, the competition for *Wild Life* was not just the 1960s Beatles catalog and solo releases by John, George and Ringo, but also a raft of enduring 1971 releases including *Who's Next*, *Led Zeppelin IV*, the Rolling Stones' *Sticky Fingers*, Jethro Tull's *Aqualung*, T. Rex's *Electric Warrior*, Janis Joplin's *Pearl*, Carole King's *Tapestry*, Joni Mitchell's *Blue*, Alice Cooper's *Love It to Death* and *Killer*, Pink Floyd's *Meddle*, Rod Stewart's *Every Picture Tells a Story*, Elton John's *Madman Across the Water*, and Marvin Gaye's *What's Going On*.

Delays caused by the Apple vinyl label dispute diluted the fanfare built up by Wings' party at the Empire Ballroom and press launch at EMI Studios. *Wild Life* was released in early December with a whimper, rather than the explosion of excitement Paul had worked to create around his latest musical project.

The album entered the *Billboard* 200 at No. 25 on Christmas Day, clawing its way to a peak position of No. 10 on January 22. Though *Wild Life* only mustered an 18-week run in the *Billboard* album chart, Wings' debut sold in excess of 500,000 copies and was RIAA Gold certified on January 13, 1972. In Britain, *Wild Life* was commercially inert. It broke into the album chart at No. 11 (its peak position) on December 18 and vanished nine weeks later.

Still, there were signs that the public was taking satisfaction in McCartney's new work: on Christmas, the non-LP single 'Another Day,' released back in February, turned up on *Record Mirror*'s year-end chart, at No. 22. *Wild Life* was too new to figure in the year-end charts, but *Ram* placed at No. 10 on the *NME*'s 1971 album poll. Across the Atlantic, Paul and Linda took second place in a *Cash Box* survey (beaten only by the Carpenters), and Paul was ranked fifth among cast of male vocalists.

<hr>

Paul's talk of touring, at both the Wings Ball and the EMI session, caught the attention not only of fans, but also of music world professionals. The first offer, a tantalizing one, came from John Morris—Linda's friend from her Fillmore East days. The American producer had spent most of 1971 refurbishing the former Finsbury Park Astoria, transforming it into the Rainbow Theater, London's first auditorium devoted exclusively to rock presentations.[55]

Morris was an old hand at both rock presenting and turning movie palaces into concert venues. A former drama student, he joined forces with Bill Graham, the owner of San Francisco's legendary Fillmore Auditorium, to stage a week of rock concerts at the O'Keefe Centre, in Toronto. Morris went on to oversee, as production manager, European and American tours for the Jefferson Airplane. When Graham decided to expand his Fillmore franchise to New York, he took over the Village Theater, which had for many years been a Loew's movie palace, and hired Morris as its managing director.

Morris had several connections with the McCartneys. Both EMI Records and AIR London, the recording facility run by George Martin, were stakeholders in the Rainbow, both having come on board as principal investors. But it was Morris's friendship with Linda during her days as a freelance rock photographer that got Paul's attention. Now he was hoping to book Paul's new band for concerts at the Rainbow early in 1972.

PAUL McCARTNEY
REALLY IS DEAD!

The Dylan Liberation Front, whose demonstration-birthday party for Bob Dylan was an important factor in his singing his old songs at a benefit for the East Pakistanis held at Madison Square Garden has decieded to temporarily switch targets...our next victum is PAUL McCARTNEY.

Although the rumor that 'Paul is dead' started when he was still with The Beatles, it only became obvious that this was true after Paul came out with his last 2 solo L.P.s -McCartney & Ram-since they both are apparently written by someone whose brain just aint functioning....

McCartney's lyrics lack the slightest social committment and he's quickly becoming the Sinatra of the 70's. He lives like an aristocrat on a huge estate in England, never gives any money to any progressive organizations and hasn't done a benefit in years. So that's why the Rock Liberation Front (an offshoot of the D.L.F.) is going to hold a FUNERAL in front of McCartney's New York City residence at: SEVENTY NINTH STREET AND PARK AVE (895 Park) on THURSDAY, AUGUST 26, 1971 at ONE P.M. sharp to COMBAT McCARTNEYISM.

They'll be samples of McCartney's garbage, a special funeral ceremony, funeral dirges by Elecktra recording artists David Peel and the Lower East Side and many other surreal spontaneous happenings...(at the Dylan birthday party Yippie Abbie Hoffman, talk-jockey Alex Bennett & Screw Editor Al Goldstien all showed-up). After we get through with Paulie they'll be a march down to Rolling Stone Magazine (78E56th St) where we'll present them with documented evidence of their piggery!!!!

So truck on down to McCartney's pad and join the 500 or so people!

COMBAT McCARTNYISM!

for further information call
A.J. WEBERMAN at 477-6243

Morris met with Paul and Linda in late November for negotiations that were not entirely under wraps: *Melody Maker* reported in its December 4 issue that discussions were underway.[56] Morris's offer must have been tempting; at the time, he was paying headline acts up to $14,000 (£5,540) for a set of weekend shows.[57]

But for Paul, the timing wasn't right: he thought Wings should gain some stage experience out of town before appearing in London. He and Linda, in fact, had been concocting a romantic plot, based on the plan he presented to the Beatles moments before John said he wanted a divorce, in which Wings would cruise through England in a van, stopping at universities for impromptu concerts, and playing for a percentage of the door—fees closer to what they'd get by passing the hat than what Morris was offering.

Paul mentioned this plan in vague terms when he was cornered by a *Rolling Stone* reporter at the Wings launch party. "We want to start off real small. I think it'll be possible. We'll just turn up and play at small places completely unadvertised."[58] When he declined Morris's offer, Paul hinted that he would soon be in touch about a related project, without divulging the details.

Other comments Paul made during his early November 1971 interviews were noticed as well—not least by John Lennon. Like McCartney, Lennon was an avid reader of the music press, and when he saw Paul's comments in *Melody Maker*—that he wanted to sit down with others, sign a paper dissolving the Beatles, split up the money and go their separate ways, and that he liked *Imagine*, but considered John's other work too political—Lennon asked *Melody Maker* for the right of response and dashed off a three-page typed open letter to Paul.

> So, *you* think 'Imagine' ain't political, it's 'Working Class Hero' with sugar on it for conservatives like yourself!! You obviously *dug the words*. Imagine! . . . *Your* politics are very similar to Mary Whitehouse's*—saying *nothing* is as loud as saying *something*! . . . Join the Rock Liberation front† before it gets *you*.[59]

But Lennon closed his missive with a call for a truce, couched as an invitation:

---

* Constance Mary Hutcheson Whitehouse (1910–2001) was a conservative activist who argued that social liberalism of the kind long advocated by the Beatles and other rock bands, and, in her view, by the BBC, in television programs as diverse as *Till Death Do Us Part* and *Doctor Who*, was responsible for a breakdown of British morality.

† The Rock Liberation Front was headed by A. J. Weberman, a political provocateur best known for dumpster dives into Bob Dylan's garbage in a quest to prove that Dylan was both a capitalist sellout and a junkie. On August 19, Weberman added McCartney to his enemies list, staging a mock "McCartney Burial" outside Lee Eastman's Park Avenue apartment. His claim, reported in the *Village Voice* on September 2, was that McCartney had become "a good example of the capitalist, non-involved egotistical rock star."

No hard feelings to you either. I know basically we want the same, and as I said on the
phone and in this letter, whenever you want to meet, all you have to do is call.

Taking Lennon's response as an olive branch, or at least, an opportunity, Paul sent John a note saying he would be in New York soon and would get in touch. Although they had spoken by telephone, Paul and John had not met in person since the fall of 1969.

But before New York, Paul, Linda, and the girls flew to Montego Bay, Jamaica, where Linda could further explore her passion for reggae, right at the source. The McCartneys quickly found a hangout, a pub named the Jolly Roger, with a jukebox packed with reggae discs that were unknown in Britain. The locals took to Linda, calling her Suzy, after the 1957 Dale Hawkins song 'Suzie Q,' then current in Jamaica in a reggae version by Ken Boothe.

They also discovered RJR, a radio station that played reggae around the clock, and a favorite record shop, Tony's Record Centre, on Fostic Road in Montego Bay.

Tony's was a new experience for both Paul and Linda, who were used to the slick merchandising of the American and British record worlds. There, the bins weren't fussily organized: the 45s were unsorted, many without proper printed labels—just handwritten (and often enigmatic) titles, like 'Nic a Pipe' or 'Verjan'—waiting to be discovered by curious browsers.

'Verjan' turned out to be a variant spelling of "version," and through it, Paul and Linda discovered a local practice they were quite taken with.

"I must tell you, we picked up some great reggae singles when we were in Jamaica, which were just on the radio over there, things I haven't heard in Britain since," Paul said. "One of the greatest things they do in Jamaica is they have the record, and then on the B side they have the 'version.' The amazing thing being that the 'version' is the single without the vocal track, and possibly another take. But it's nearly always the same with just the vocals off.

"But the way they hear it there is different. We hung out with this Jamaican guy in Montego Bay, some hustler he was, a great little fella called Amos who kind of approached us and hustled. But we didn't mind being hustled, he'd take us to all the little bars where the tourist wouldn't get to. Little places with white rum, a jukebox, and fluorescent lights. We'd play those 'versions' and I'd say to him, 'But they've just taken the vocals off.' But he'd say, 'No man, you don't know man. Look, this is another song man, this the "version."' . . . To him it's just the band playing an instrumental, he kind of doesn't know it's just the same song."[60]

Curiously, this is the exact idea that Paul rejected in 1964, when Phil Spector proposed releasing Beatles singles with the instrumental backing track on the B side. Now encountering it in Jamaica, and in the context of reggae singles with handwritten labels, he saw its charm. That could be, too, because the McCartneys found their own use for "versions,"—singing along with them, not always with the lyric of the song on the A side. Paul noted that the lyrics and rhythms of 'Shortnin' Bread' fit nicely with one of the "versions" they sang with.

The McCartneys also discovered an acquaintance from London in Montego Bay, the photographer John Kelly, who had taken the portraits included with the Beatles' *White Album* and was the only photographer allowed into the registry office when Paul and Linda married. Kelly, en route to Jamaica with four models for a fashion shoot, was on the same plane as the McCartneys, although, as he put it, "Paul was flying first class and I was down in the back with the chickens and goats." Between trips to record stores and the beach, Paul and Linda paid him a visit.

"We had a mansion [in Montego Bay] and one day I had finished working and was sitting down having a drink, when suddenly this car pulled up outside the house," Kelly recalled. "I looked up and said, 'Oh, it's Paul.' I would have loved to have filmed the following scene. The girls were sitting around, looking like death all warmed up, a bit wrecked because I had them on their feet from early in the morning, photographing them. When Paul arrived, I heard some ahhs and squeaks behind me and when I turned around the room was totally empty, and doors were banging. So, Paul walks in with Linda. We sat down and had a drink and suddenly the girls come in looking like Miss World, sexy dresses, warpaint on, a total transformation from the moment they disappeared out of the room. He invited us all out for a meal. We went to a restaurant by the ocean where they serve fish, in particular king fish, a Jamaican specialty. We spent a nice evening there."[61]

The trip also further cemented the McCartneys' love for animals.

"If Linda takes Heather into one of the restaurants where you choose the lobster you want to be killed and cooked for you," Paul said, "Heather always wants to buy the lobster and take it home. On holiday recently, this fisherman came in with a giant turtle about three foot long. I must admit it had a magnificent shell on its back and all these Americans were standing about saying how good the shell would look in their living rooms. Anyway, I could tell Heather would have liked to set it free, so I offered the fisherman about twenty-five dollars for it.

"He took my money, but you know how superstitious fishermen are, they think if they let one fish live, everything in the sea is going to turn against them. So he gave me the money back and tied the turtle up. Heather just looked at us and said, 'Is he going to kill it?' There was nothing we could say, and Heather just sat there on this rock on the beach and burst into tears. She's going to get hurt a lot I know, but I'd rather have her like that than wanting the shell off its back for an ornament."[62]

Paul and Linda also discovered Red Stripe, a local lager they especially liked. They had several cases shipped to Scotland. Boxes of Red Stripe became fixtures in Rude Studio, and Linda borrowed the name, combined with the Jamaicans' nickname for her, to create a fictional alter ego, Suzy and the Red Stripes, which she kept in mind as she continued to tinker with 'Seaside Woman.'

Arriving in New York, the second week in December, Paul and Linda leased the Riverside Drive apartment of the actress Diahann Carroll and her current companion, the journalist David Frost,[63] a friend of Paul's from the Beatle days.

Denny Seiwell, in the United States for nearly a month, had spent his time in three states—New York, Pennsylvania for a family visit, and Illinois. Back in freelance mode, and needing to supplement his £70 weekly salary, he accepted a series of gigs drumming for singer-songwriter Bill Quateman, who had a residency at the Fifth Peg in Chicago. Quateman mostly performed his own material, and Seiwell, along with David Spinozza, had played on demos Quateman recorded at A&R Studios, in New York. But in his Chicago sets, he opened with a cover of 'Sgt. Pepper's Lonely Hearts Club Band,' as an homage to his drummer's boss.

That undoubtedly added fuel to rumors that McCartney would be in the audience—rumors started by the Amazing Gracers, a group of Chicago pranksters based at Northwestern University's Amazing Grace coffeehouse. The Gracers planned a prank for Quateman's third concert with Seiwell, on December 11. One of them, Walt Kelly, bore an uncanny resemblance to McCartney. Kelly went to the concert, taking a seat in the tenth row, and he fostered confusion by periodically casting what a *Chicago Tribune* reporter described as "bemused glances"[64] at different parts of the audience.

Soon enough, audience members gathered around Kelly, asking questions while Kelly protested that he was not McCartney. On the periphery, Carel Rowe, a member of Video Free Chicago, filmed Kelly's fan encounters, telling the *Tribune* that the hoax was his idea.

Quateman was as mystified as anyone. "I was not aware of it at the time. I heard about it afterwards, and I realized that the Gracers had put that thing into the wind to ramp up the activity. Paul was never going to be there. I knew that was the case afterwards. They were just out to create a buzz, and they were good at it. It was fun."[65]

Denny Laine used his first days in New York to visit a former girlfriend, Catherine James, and their son, Damian, in Lake Candlewood, Connecticut, a two-hour train ride north of the city. Denny and Catherine had a stormy relationship that both documented publicly—Laine in a string of solo recordings in 1967 and 1968, among them 'Say You Don't Mind,' 'Too Much in Love' and 'Catherine's Wheel,' and James in her memoir.

When Laine wrote to James that he would be in New York with McCartney and Wings, she was of two minds about allowing him to visit. She had no desire to reopen old wounds; but she thought it would be good for Damian to spend some time with his dad.

"Damian and I picked Denny up from the Brewster [New York] station. Seeing Denny on American soil felt strangely out of context . . . In the beginning it was actually nice to see Denny again. One admirable thing about him was that he was quite generous when he could afford to be. He took Damian shopping for winter clothes and filled my kitchen cupboards with all the amenities and nice things I'd been unable to afford."[66]

But, according to James, the visit ended badly after Laine began pressuring her to return to England, making that a condition for the continuation of the £100 ($250) monthly financial support he was sending her. James refused, and when Laine went outside to gather wood for the fire, she put his bags and coat on the porch and locked him out, leaving Laine to walk six miles to the Brewster train station, in a snowstorm.

———

When Seiwell returned from Chicago, Wings reconvened for rehearsals, a recording session, and a few interviews. Paul had left it to Seiwell to find a rehearsal space, since he was intimately familiar with New York's musical resources. Seiwell called David Lucas, a composer with whom he had become friendly during his freelance years. Lucas, along with another composer, Tom McFaul, owned the Warehouse Studio, a converted spice warehouse on West 46th Street. Mostly, Lucas and McFaul used the studio to record advertising jingles, although in October, Lucas produced Blue Öyster Cult's eponymous debut album there.

Paul's plan was to block book a comfortable rehearsal space in New York for the entire period Wings were in town, with the group popping in to work between other obligations.

"They were looking for a place to start rehearsing the band," Lucas remembered. "I had used Denny a lot on my sessions, and he was familiar with my studio. The Warehouse was a popular place—I did thousands of dates there, so I was not anxious to block book to someone outside; it would be like a guitarist renting his guitar to somebody, and then having to turn down a gig. But it was Paul McCartney, so I agreed."[67]

Paul added a few rules to the rental agreement. Only Lucas and his engineer could be present during the rehearsals, and the sessions were not to be recorded. The day of the first session, Lucas made the nearly two-hour drive into the city from his farmhouse in Dutchess County, arriving in plenty of time for the noon start time Paul had scheduled.

"I was very anxious to get there. And then—no Paul. Nervous waiting, nervous waiting. Eventually, I was so hyper, I went out into the studio and told my engineer to roll some tape." Lucas sat at the piano and improvised a song, 'Waiting for Paul,' with lyrics like, *"Driving down the Taconic Parkway, I feel good / Got Paul and Linda under the hood."* When the band finally turned up, Lucas was in the control room listening to a playback of the song. At its climax, a high, sustained vocal note, he turned to find Paul, standing over his shoulder, saying "Showing off, eh?"[68]

Though there were no concerts on the horizon, it was clear that live performance was Wings' next hurdle, and that serious woodshedding was in order. At the Warehouse, they ran through rock oldies like 'Long Tall Sally' and 'Lucille,' songs from *Ram* and *Wild Life*, Linda's 'Seaside Woman,' a new ballad Paul was tinkering with, 'My Love,' plus a pop adaptation of the nursery rhyme 'Mary Had a Little Lamb.'

Lucas, who had adored the Beatles, listened intently to the rehearsals, and—like Denny Seiwell who had suggested they hire keyboard player Paul Harris—questioned Linda's inclusion in the group. Linda, well aware of her own musical shortcomings, could probably tell that Lucas felt she didn't belong there, and she overcompensated with energy and a measure of regal condescension; in any case their relationship was frosty from the start.

"She was annoying, a complete pain in the ass," said Lucas, whose usual studio rules precluded allowing wives, girlfriends or children into the sessions. Lucas also struggled to understand the complex dynamics of Paul and Linda's public persona. "What bothered me most was, I watched Paul go way beyond acquiescing. He was subservient to this rude, indulged, entitled woman of little or no talent. I lost respect for him. I've since rebuilt it, but I had idealized him, and now suddenly I saw him as just a regular guy. When the sessions ended, and we were at the elevator saying goodbye, Linda's last words, as the doors closed, were, 'Don't think it wasn't nice, because it wasn't.'"[69]

———

Paul and Linda began December 17 with a cab ride to Greenwich Village for a visit with John and Yoko at their apartment at 105 Bank Street. They had some trepidation about how it might go—as Paul knew, predicting John's mood, especially when a subject as volatile as splitting the Beatles partnership was under discussion, was not easily done. Their recent phone conversations, after all, had hardly been sweetness and light.

"I used actually to have some very frightening phone calls," Paul said of his attempts to discuss the Apple situation with John. "I went through a period when I would be so nervous to ring him and so insecure in myself that I actually felt like I was in the wrong. It was all very acrimonious and bitter. I remember one time John said, 'You're all pizzas and fairy tales.' I thought, 'What a great album title!' I said, 'Well if that's what I am, I'm not wholly against that description of me. I can think of worse things to say.' But another time I called him, and it was, 'Yeah, yeah. Whadda ya want?' He suddenly started to sound American. I said, 'Oh, fuck off, Kojak,' and slammed the phone down; we were having those kind of times, it was bad news."[70]

But he had reason to think it might go well. Lennon had done some elaborate groundwork to ensure a pleasant meeting, including leaving Paul a rare bit of their mutual past. Early in December, the

Village Voice columnist Howard Smith had introduced Lennon to Dave Morell, a teenage collector with an impressive library of bootleg recordings, still a relatively new phenomenon in the rock world. Morell played Lennon *Yellow Matter Custard*, a collection of recordings the Beatles made during their *Pop Go the Beatles* series for the BBC, in 1963. Not having heard these performances since they recorded them, Lennon mistook them for the Beatles' January 1962 audition for Decca. He insisted on having Morell's copy, and Morell gave it to him, in exchange for a highly sought after *Yesterday . . . and Today* "Butcher" cover, which Lennon autographed for him on December 7.

Lennon had fresh acetates of the disc cut at Sterling Sound, and when Paul arrived in New York, a copy awaited him, packaged in a plain sleeve, with an attached note to Paul on a Sterling Sound sticker. Unable to resist promoting his latest single, Lennon began: "Happy Xmas! (war is over if you want it . . .)," followed by THE BEATLES, in capital letters, and a few musical notes. He continued:

> Dear Paul Linda et al. this is THE DECCA AUDITION!! I found the bootleg not the tape:
> They were a good group fancy turning THIS down! Love John + Yoko.

Paul could also, of course, find a clue about how it might go in John's 'Happy Xmas (War Is Over),' released in America barely two weeks earlier. Granted, its catchy chorus—"*War is over / if you want it*"—referred to actual shooting wars, like Vietnam; but to Paul, it could apply to anything—in fact, discussing his Apple woes during the *Wild Life* listening session at EMI, he told reporters, "I wanted to send him [John] postcards saying 'The war is over if you want it'—tell him that what he's saying is just crazy."[71] If John was being honest about peacemaking, including on a personal level, this was the solution: *The Beatles are over if you want it—just sign the paper!*

And indeed, the long friendship between John and Paul proved a balm that seemed, at the moment, to make anything possible.

John, Paul knew, had his own vulnerabilities, but Paul was not fully aware of the battles John was currently fighting. He and Yoko had been chasing Yoko's daughter, Kyoko, around the world, which is what brought them to the United States in the first place. But the United States government had stepped in to make that difficult, for political reasons. John's visa was set to expire at the end of February 1972, and when he and Yoko attempted to get the renewal underway early, they discovered that the 1968 drug bust that kept Lennon out of the country in May 1969 was suddenly a concern again.

The reason, this time, was that John's openly political activities, including his suggestion that he might tour in 1972 as part of an effort to protest Richard Nixon's reelection campaign, put him on the radar of Republicans in Congress, who decided that the best plan was to persuade the

Immigration and Naturalization Service that John was a danger and have him deported. The only way he could stay was to hire an attorney and challenge the INS's ruling, which he would do early in the new year. He could not be deported while his case was being fought—but he was also unable to leave the United States; if he did, he would not be allowed to return.

Paul and Linda sympathized, over a bottle of wine, and eventually the conversation turned to the relationship between John and Paul, and the world's perception of it. They resolved to put the preceding 18 months of sniping, in interviews and songs, behind them. Lennon put this peace plan into action—more or less—in an interview with *Sounds* a few days later. After reminding his interviewer about 'Too Many People,' he said that he'd gotten his anger at Paul out of his system.

"We met the other day and we decided to stop it all because we've both had enough—the four of us have, the four of us including the wives that is. But I don't regret it; to me the bit about Paul is all gone. The day I wrote ['How Do You Sleep?'], it was about Paul, but the day I was making the record I was just making a record. I groove on the music still. Maybe I'll change the words so I can sing it onstage without it all being about Paul."[72]

For the McCartneys, the major takeaway from the meeting was John's agreement to finally dissolve the Beatles' partnership. Whether Lennon would keep his word remained to be seen. But the discussion left Paul and Linda upbeat for a recording session with Wings that afternoon at A&R Studios.

Recording Session

Wednesday, December 17, 1971.
A&R Studios, New York.
Overdubbing: 'Blues' (now retitled 'The Great Cock and Seagull Race').

The *Ram* leftover 'Blues,' recorded on February 23 with Paul playing all the instruments, had popped into McCartney's mind several times in recent months, so he decided to see whether the two Dennys had anything to add. It wasn't much more than an amusing doodle, a blues progression with a rollicking piano part and a lightly fuzzed lead guitar, recorded as a way to distract himself as his lawsuit unfolded in London.

But McCartney saw some potential in it. Dixon Van Winkle, who engineered the original session (and sent a fresh mix to Paul in Scotland, in July) was on the board again as Wings set up in the studio. McCartney wanted to do an extensive revision, and before the session was over, he had replaced the electric piano part, added a more fluid guitar line, asked Denny to put on a weightier bass, and captured a bright-edged drum performance from Seiwell. The McCartney solo jam was now a Wings track—and its generic title was replaced, too. Now it was 'The Great Cock and Seagull Race.' As if to explain the new title, the sound of a crowing cockerel was added to the beginning. A rough mix was made, and Paul left with an acetate.

—————

Following a late lunch in Chinatown, Wings switched into promotional mode for an interview with CBS disc jockey Ed Williams. The discussion was a free-for-all, with the band sounding decidedly stoned. Denny Laine suggested that Williams distinguish him from Denny Seiwell by calling him Brian (his birth name). And Linda, unaccountably, reprised the joke about Monique Seiwell's drinking that Monique had objected to when Paul included it in his *Wild Life* liner note.

After playing cuts from *Wild Life* and a handful of reggae records from Montego Bay, Paul introduced the highlight of the hour-long visit, the just-completed and freshly cut acetate of 'The Great Cock and Seagull Race.' Offering the caveat that the recording was only a rough mix, Paul said it would probably be the B side of a forthcoming single.* Nervously fumbling at the controls—this was a McCartney world exclusive—Williams first set the turntable to the wrong speed, and the demo sounded like a bad acid trip. "This is actually us in a very heavy mood one morning, this is actually 7 o'clock in the morning on the Staten Island Ferry, a bit drunk," McCartney joked, before the speed was corrected to 45 rpm. "And now this is us when we got up and had breakfast, and ate our cornflakes."[73]

Wings gave another radio interview on December 20, for a special titled *Paul McCartney Now*, to be aired on WRKO in Boston, and other stations owned by RKO General, around the country. The discussion was held at MPL's New York office on Central Park West, and as he had done on the Ed Williams show, Paul offered an exclusive preview of another as yet unreleased song Wings had been toying with, 'Mary Had a Little Lamb.'†

Paul and Linda had been singing Paul's poppy arrangement to Mary, complete with a "*la, la, la*" chorus, and it occurred to Paul that just as he had transformed 'Bip Bop' into a Wings song,

---

* The Williams broadcast was the last the public heard of the song until 2012, when Dixon Van Winkle's earlier (July 13) mix, with only Paul playing, was included on the *Ram* archival reissue set. The December 17, 1971, mix, with Laine's and Seiwell's additions and Paul's new piano and guitar lines, was released in the *Wild Life* archival set, in December 2018, although this version lacks the introductory rooster.

† Apart from offering WRKO's listeners the treat of an unreleased McCartney tune, the song had a link to Boston that Paul most likely hadn't known about. Sarah Josepha Hale (1788–1879), the author of the original nursery rhyme, was a Bostonian, best known in the city for raising the money to complete the Bunker Hill Monument, a 221-foot obelisk commemorating the famous battle, and for undertaking a campaign to make Thanksgiving a national holiday.

WAR IS OVER, IF YOU WANT IT

perhaps this could make a similar transition. For the RKO broadcast, he played a rough rehearsal recording, with Paul at the piano and the rest of Wings gathered around to sing the chorus and clap along.

With that, their New York promotional duties were complete, and Wings returned to London in time for Christmas. On December 23, Paul spent some time at EMI, mastering a shortened edit of 'Love Is Strange' for release as a single, with 'I Am Your Singer' on the B side. He designed an attractive yellow sleeve, with Wings in the same Bauhaus typeface as on the *Wild Life* cover. But when sales of *Wild Life* proved disappointing, the single was scuttled.

After spending Christmas in London, the McCartneys traveled to Liverpool, to ring in 1972 with the extended McCartney clan. The two Dennys remained at liberty until January 11, when Wings reconvened for rehearsals at the Scotch of St. James Club, in London.

14

IRELAND, IT'S THE CAPITAL OF LIVERPOOL

—

Early in January 1972, Paul ramped up his plans to take Wings on the road, and he and Linda reconnected with resourceful American concert producer John Morris.

"They were putting a band together," Morris recalled, "and they thought they'd like to tour English and Irish colleges. I didn't know a damn thing about English and Irish colleges. I said, 'Okay, I'll figure it out,' and I started to make a couple of phone calls to people I knew, who knew people who were booking colleges."[1]

But Morris, apart from having little interest in the university circuit, was occupied with running the Rainbow Theater, and he soon excused himself from the university tour. Instead, he put Paul and Linda in touch with a booking agency in Soho run by Bag O' Nails owner Rik Gunnell, whose company had a wide network of contacts in universities across the country. There, they met June Whitting, the only female booking agent in London, and though Whitting's specialty was blues and R&B acts, she was happy to accommodate such a high-profile client. Since Paul anticipated turning up at universities unannounced, he asked Whitting to compile a list of addresses and telephone numbers that the group might use on the road. He also requested complete secrecy.

As the prospect of live performances approached, though, it became increasingly clear that something was missing from the band's four-piece lineup. As it stood, McCartney would be the lead singer and bass player, Laine would be the sole guitarist, with Linda on keyboards and auxiliary percussion (tambourine and maracas), and Seiwell on drums. Everyone would sing backing vocals as needed. In theory, Linda's keyboards might have filled the role that Lennon's rhythm guitar provided the Beatles, freeing Laine to play lead. But Linda was still a beginner, and game as she was, there was no point expecting her to fill out the texture with the flair an experienced player would bring.

Laine, too, felt that his abilities were overtaxed, once you added vocals to his combined lead and rhythm guitar duties. He agreed with Paul that another guitarist—ideally, a more dazzling lead player than Laine—would have a transformative effect on the band.

A guitarist who would fit the bill became available early in January, when the Grease Band, Joe Cocker's backing band from 1968 until he formed Mad Dogs and Englishmen in 1970, announced their breakup following an abandoned European tour during which the band's equipment was stolen, and their lead guitarist, Henry McCullough, broke his finger on the opening night in Paris. Laine was friendly with McCullough, who was now on the mend, and suggested him to McCartney. On January 17, McCartney dispatched roadie Ian Horne to invite McCullough to the group's rehearsal at the Scotch of St. James, Mason's Yard, the following day.

As it happened, McCullough had tentative plans. The day Horne contacted him, McCullough and Mick Weaver, a session keyboardist who had worked with the Grease Band, had announced that they were seeking a drummer and a singer for a new band. But the prospect of a job in Paul McCartney's band was not something McCullough could lightly dismiss, so on January 18, he turned up at the Scotch of St. James for a few hours of jamming. Though he was among the celebrity ranks at Wings' Empire Ballroom launch party, McCullough and McCartney had yet to cross paths.

"I'd never met McCartney before," the Irish guitarist recalled. "Once I got used to seeing him there in person, he turned out to be a great bloke. I guess I was a bit nervous, but I had a couple of pints of Guinness before I went along the first time. That helped."[2]

McCullough's curriculum vitae looked perfect. Born in Portstewart, Northern Ireland, on July 21, 1943, he had played lead guitar in several Irish bands in the mid-1960s before one of them, Éire Apparent, was signed by Jimi Hendrix's manager (and former Animals bassist) Chas Chandler and began touring as a support act for Hendrix, Pink Floyd, the Move, Eric Burdon and the Animals, and Soft Machine. McCullough left Éire Apparent in the middle of a Canadian tour, in 1968, and returned to Ireland, where he played briefly with Sweeny's Men, a traditional Irish folk band. He joined the Grease Band in 1969 and moved in and out of the group's orbit, serving briefly with Spooky Tooth, in 1970, but heading back to the Grease Band before the end of the year.

McCullough was invited back for another rehearsal on January 20, a five-hour session during which Wings worked to make songs like 'Smile Away,' 'Wild Life,' and 'Bip Bop' stageworthy, along with an assortment of oldies like 'Blue Moon of Kentucky' and Paul's favorites from the Little Richard songbook, including 'Lucille.' During the rehearsal, the band played a hard-driven jam that Paul turned into a song, tentatively called 'The Mess I'm In,' before the session ended. Watching the new song take form impressed McCullough.

"On one song, he was kinda playing away on a tune I hadn't heard before, so I asked him what to do. He said, 'We're all just trying it out,' and just continued playing. We all joined in, it went on a bit further, and in no time at all a song was written. It was written on the spot, and we all contributed."[3]

When the rehearsal ended, McCartney declared his intentions. "He says, 'Do you want the gig?' and I says, 'Aye,'"[4] was how McCullough described his hiring.

Like Laine, McCullough was bound by existing contractual obligations. Together with his former Grease Band bandmates, Henry was under contract with two labels—Shelter Records in America, and Harvest Records in Britain. Since Harvest was owned by EMI, extracting Henry from his British commitment did not prove difficult, but any records featuring McCullough released in America would need to carry a note that he appeared courtesy of Shelter Records, at least, until the Eastmans were able to sever his ties with the label.[*] Henry agreed to the same financial terms as the two Dennys, and before the day was out, MPL sent the music press a statement about McCullough's joining the band. The next day, Henry gave his first interviews as a member of Wings. He admitted to being a bit starstruck, at first, but he also offered a striking overview of how Wings was expected to work, as Paul described it to him.

"I do want to take part in the band as fully as possible," he said in his *NME* interview. "That's the way Paul wants it. He's leaving things pretty free. I'm sure he wants people to contradict him sometimes, just as you would in any group. He doesn't want it to be just Paul McCartney's band. He wants everybody to contribute as much as himself. I'm going into it with that thought in mind."[5]

In an interview with Johnny Moran for BBC Radio 1's *Scene and Heard* program, McCartney hinted at his immediate plans for the band.

"Musically, well, I like all sorts. I like modern music, and I like old-fashioned music. I like all the different kinds of sounds I've heard since I was a kid, from 'Blue Moon of Kentucky' to anything else. It's been a long time since I played live. That's why I want to get back, I've really decided I miss just playing to people. As far as performance goes, though, better than just playing in these great big seaters is to just turn up in a caravan and maybe open the back doors and just play to the people. That way, we'll be getting to the people, the people in the area—not those people standing there with notebooks, waiting to judge you."[6]

By now, McCartney was champing at the bit to play live. It irked him that while he was the one who pushed for a return to live performances, against the demurrals of the others (particularly John and George), he was, in 1972, the only former Beatle who had not performed in public since the split. Lennon had played with Yoko in Cambridge, and Toronto; Harrison had performed with Delaney and Bonnie, and he and Ringo had performed together at George's Concert for Bangla Desh.

But when Moran asked when the public might be able to hear McCartney's new band, the best

---

[*] McCullough departed Shelter Records in the spring of 1972.

Paul could do was tease. "When will we appear live? Sometime this year. I don't know where, or when. We're working up to it."[7]

By then, Paul had decided that the university tour would commence the second week in February. Paul's timing, however, was questionable. In a dispute over what Britain's coal miners regarded as a derisory working wage offer, on January 5, the miners declared "all out industrial war" on the British government. Three days later, the wheels stopped turning at Britain's 289 pits, and 280,000 miners went on strike. By late January many parts of the country were experiencing coal shortages. Schools and factories were forced to close, and the threat of power cuts loomed.

But Paul was resolute in his plan to tour, and he and Linda spent the rest of January brainstorming, on their own and with June Whitting, about the route, which universities to approach, and how the approaches would be made. Paul also booked a bigger rehearsal space, the 2,000-square-foot auditorium of the Institute of Contemporary Arts, better known in London arts circles as the ICA, for a week of rehearsals starting February 1.

——

The McCartneys were refining their tour plan at Cavendish Avenue on Sunday, January 30, 1972, when all hell broke loose in Londonderry, Northern Ireland. By midafternoon, they set aside their tour notes and focused on the BBC's increasingly grim reports and updates.

Three years earlier, the British government had sent troops to Londonderry for what was supposed to be a limited operation—restoring law and order amid escalating sectarian violence between the city's Protestants and Catholics. But many saw the British troops' presence as tantamount to military occupation, and civil rights organizations quickly took up the cause.

At around 2:45 p.m. on January 30, over 10,000 people, keen to make a stand against the British military presence, took to the streets in Derry, joining a march organized by the Northern Ireland Civil Rights Association (NICRA). But what started off as a peaceful protest soon became heated, and a violent confrontation broke out between protesters and troops, who used rubber bullets, CS gas and water cannons to disperse the crowds.

As tensions boiled over, British paratroopers were sent through the barricades lining the streets to regain control. But crowd control turned into slaughter, as 26 unarmed civilians were shot; 14 of them perished. Mid-Ulster MP Bernadette Devlin described the loss of life as "mass murder by the [British] army." The press dubbed it, "Derry's Bloody Sunday." It was a dark day in the history of the United Kingdom.

That evening, Denny and Monique joined Paul, Linda and the kids for dinner at Cavendish Avenue. Having only recently relocated from New York to London, the Seiwells regularly hung out with "the Macs" (as they called them) as they struggled to find a permanent base—the home comforts of Paul's house in St. John's Wood being vastly preferable to the Seiwells' room at the Swiss Cottage Hotel on Adamson Road, just around the corner from EMI Studios. They arrived to find Paul still monitoring reports of the tragic events in Derry.

"Paul was seething," Denny recalled.[8]

To take their minds off political matters, the two couples headed down to the Rainbow Theater, where John Morris had reserved them tickets to see the American guitarist Leslie West with his high-power group, Mountain. The newly formed Jimmy McCulloch Band were the support act. The performance wasn't to everyone's taste. "It was so fucking loud, we left,"[9] was Seiwell's succinct memory of the show.

The concert, in any case, was not enough of a distraction to get "Bloody Sunday" out of Paul's mind. On Monday morning, January 31, the headlines of the London papers screamed "Gun Fury"[10] and "Massacre,"[11] and front pages around the world were filled with black and white images of violent clashes, victims, and grieving families on the Bogside Estate. This only amplified Paul's anger, which—unusually, for a man who preferred to see his compositions more as timeless entertainments than topical or political comment—found an outlet at the piano.

"The morning after what they called 'Bloody Sunday,' I read the newspapers, and it just looked a bit wrong, what the British Army was doing in there. Me as a British citizen, I don't like my army going around and shooting my Irish brothers. It just isn't on, as far as I'm concerned. I mean, in Liverpool, we used to joke, it's the capital of Ireland, because there are so many Irish people living there. Suddenly we were killing them, and I just thought, 'Wait a minute, this is not clever, and I wish to protest on behalf of us people that this action of our government is way over the top.' So I just started on the piano and wrote a song. I'm sure I'm Irish way back somewhere. So, it just got very personal the whole thing."[12]

It was personal indeed, given Paul's Irish roots, and the likelihood that he had ancestors on both sides of Ireland's sectarian divide. Though his paternal roots have eluded researchers, beyond a direct link to James McCartney, Paul's great-grandfather, who made his first appearance in a Liverpool marriage registry in 1864, historian Mark Lewisohn has noted that the family name can be traced back to Scotland, as MacCartney. The MacCartneys were Catholic, before some of them moved to Ireland and became Protestants, sometime before the seventeenth century. Paul's mother, Mary Patricia Mohin, on the other hand, had clear Irish-Catholic roots. Her father, Owen Mohan (the family name saw several changes of spelling over the years) was born in Tullynamalrow, in Ireland's Ulster province, and lived briefly in Scotland before making his way to Liverpool, where he married Mary Theresa Danher, whose family came to England in the 1860s.[13]

The result of Paul's angry and anxious mulling over "Bloody Sunday" was a simple up-tempo rocker in D major, with a bridge that pivoted to B minor, and a ferocious, anthemic chorus calling for Prime Minister Edward Heath to *"give Ireland back to the Irish,"* the song's title.

A song embracing such an overtly political position was usually the province of John Lennon; indeed, only six months earlier, on August 11, 1971, John and Yoko attended a Northern Ireland peace march at Marble Arch, Mayfair and Piccadilly in London. Paul typically kept his songs free of politics, but he was thinking that could change. In the broader battle of public images, John's political involvements made him seem by far the hipper of the two, and much as Paul might deny it, John's comparing him to Mary Whitehouse in his December letter to *Melody Maker* stung.

Suddenly, here was an issue that so offended Paul's sense of right and wrong that he was passionate to respond. As a by-product, he could take his jousting with Lennon to Lennon's turf.

"Up to that point, whenever anyone said, 'Are you into protest songs?' and stuff, I'd say, 'Well, I like Bob Dylan, but I'm not really into protest songs, they're boring,' and I didn't like political songs. So, I'd always vowed I'd never really do that. I always used to think, 'God, John's crackers, doing all these political songs.' But this song came easily to me, and it is intended patriotically to Britain. It seems to me that the majority of Irish and British feel Ireland should be given back to the Irish.

"Really it was directed at [Edward] Heath, more than anybody. You see, I'm British and I love Britain. Since I was a kid onwards, I always thought this was a solid, truthful, good nation. I didn't realize we were knocking off every bloody country. Once you do realize it, you can either keep dumb or say something. I chose to say something."[14]

The situation also clarified, for Paul, John's notion that songwriting, particularly political songwriting, could function as a form of journalism, if it was undertaken quickly enough that consternation was still at a high pitch when the song was released.

Strangely, in the case of "Bloody Sunday," it was McCartney, not Lennon, who was determined to rush his response onto the market, and into the public discourse. While John's two songs about the situation in Ireland—'Luck of the Irish,' and 'Sunday Bloody Sunday'—went unheard by Lennon's fans until the June (September in Britain) release of *Some Time in New York City*, McCartney wanted his song out immediately.

On February 1, two days after the Bogside deaths, and less than 24 hours after he composed his response, McCartney decided to record 'Give Ireland Back to the Irish' at EMI Studios that very evening. He didn't bother to book studio time, hoping that the old magic was in effect—that if Paul McCartney turned up at EMI's door, he would not be turned away.

But first, the band needed to get the song under their fingers. He summoned the group to Cavendish Avenue, where they set up in his music room and worked through the arrangement. He also hired two filmmakers, Phil Mottram and Dick Spicer. Initially drafted to document the ICA rehearsals, scheduled to begin that afternoon, Mottram and Spicer were now asked to shoot the Cavendish rehearsal as well, with an eye toward gathering material for a possible promo.

"At first, Paul wanted it filmed in 35 mm, but Dick and I persuaded him that we couldn't really lay that on at six hours' notice," Mottram recalled. "We would have needed a larger crew and a major lighting rig. As it was, although I was nominally called the 'director,' I was really the camera-man. And Dick, although nominally the 'producer,' was really just the sound recordist. I also rigged up the lights. We had a basic three-man crew and what we shot was very much in the *cinéma vérité* style."[15]

From Cavendish Avenue, the band, along with Mottram and Spicer, moved to the ICA. The original agenda for that day's ICA rehearsal included two main items: working Henry McCullough into the band's routine and repertoire, and testing out a new PA system Paul had hired for the university tour. Now working out an arrangement for 'Give Ireland Back to the Irish' took precedence.

Less than a quarter of the 86 minutes of rehearsals Mottram and Spicer captured has been seen publicly—a pity, since the film not only documents the early stages of McCullough's integration, as lead guitarist, into the band's fabric, but also includes workouts of the material Wings would play on the university tour. Because of the pop-up nature of these first Wings concerts, audio recordings are few, and none of the shows were filmed, so the ICA footage is virtually the sole documentation of Wings at this early stage.

Included are the oldies and *Wild Life* cuts Wings rehearsed in New York and at the Scotch of St. James, as well as 'Seaside Woman,' three takes of Paul's new 'My Love,' 'The Mess I'm In,' and two takes of 'Give Ireland Back to the Irish.' The arrangement of 'Ireland' here is tight and energetic, but Henry's lead guitar part has not yet been fully refined.

That would change a few hours later, at Abbey Road.

Recording Session

Tuesday, February 1, 1972.
EMI Studios, Studio Three, London.
Recording: 'Give Ireland Back to the Irish.'

At 6:00 p.m., their fingertips still buzzing from a day of rehearsals, Wings and their roadies made the four-mile trip from the Mall to St. John's Wood to put 'Give Ireland Back to the Irish' on tape. Though no one at EMI knew they were coming, it turned out that Studio Three—the smallest of EMI's studios—was empty. Unfortunately, so was its control room, all of EMI's engineers having left for the day. But Mark Vigars, a technical assistant, was on hand, and he telephoned "*Take It Tony*" Clark.

"It was a very late booking," Clark remembered. "In fact, it wasn't booked. My parents had a bungalow down at Cliftonville in Kent, and I'd been there with my two daughters. My dad was teaching me to drive. We drove back, feeling very pleased, thinking I'll be all right, I'll pass my test here. Then, my wife's outside our house, waving, and she says, 'Mark Vigars has just phoned up and you've got to go into the studio.' I thought, 'But it's Tuesday afternoon—what do you mean, they want me in the studio?' I just didn't know what to do.

"Then I thought, 'Oh, sod it, I think it'll be worse, the repercussions of not doing it.' So, I decided to go. I came by train and the tube, and as I was walking down from St. John's Wood tube station towards the zebra crossing I could hear it coming out of the building. I thought—it's got to be loud in there—you could hear it outside. It was really loud."[16]

Now fully engaged with the music press once again, Paul invited Andrew Tyler, of *Disc and Music Echo*, to the session. It was unprecedented, for Paul: the Beatles rarely allowed the press into their sessions and in his own work, McCartney had often taken the precaution of booking his sessions under a pseudonym to keep the press off the scent. But now he was eager to raise his new band's profile, and to bring attention to the Irish cause—and, not incidentally, the fact that the heretofore nonpolitical Paul McCartney was taking a stand.

"It'll be our next single if it works out. If people want it. It's all about the mess in Ireland,"[17] Paul told Tyler upon his arrival, underplaying the fact that it was not really the "next" Wings single, but the first.

Sitting through several hours of rehearsals before the tapes rolled, Tyler chronicled an extraordinary scene in Studio Three.*

"There was the debris of stoned, sleep-hungry bodies strewn over chairs in the sound room. Linda was asleep across her husband's back; Henry and Denny S could have used matchsticks to prop open their eyes . . . 10:00 p.m. They try a take but listening in on the replay sense they've lost something. 'We should've done it this afternoon when it was still fresh,' says Denny Laine. Paul agrees, 'We've lost some of the feel but it's a better sound.' He calls through the monitor to Tony, 'Couldn't you make it sound like a record, something more electric? It sounds too much like a band.' By this time Henry has come through with a superb guitar line for the intro and verse. Denny supports with a compact rhythm that serves as a second lead and Linda backs with choppy chording on piano (a hired RMI Electra-Piano 300B.)"[18]

By 11:00 p.m., frustration had taken hold. Annoyed at the band's inability to re-create what had sounded so fresh at the ICA, Paul dispatched Ian Horne to pick up smaller amplifiers. Sensing the tension, Tony Clark took the opportunity to wheel out more baffles, to absorb the sound and keep the instruments separated, hoping that this would improve the recorded sound.

"I thought it sounded great and dirty," Clark said. "The playing wasn't great on it, but I just

---

* Neither Paul, nor EMI, had any editorial control over Andrew Tyler's article. Tyler's account of stoned and drunk musicians within the walls of EMI, given the squeaky-clean public image of both the record company and Paul McCartney, raised more than a few eyebrows.

thought, if that's what it is, that's what it is. It was one of those moments in studios that are so stressful. I had just stopped smoking, and I was so stressed that I felt I wanted to have a cigarette—but I was not gonna have a cigarette!"[19]

In the meantime, Tyler reported, the band tried to take the edge off with "more tea, dope and things."[20] As midnight approached, the new setup was ready, and a further six takes were recorded. "They sense they've found a suitable backing track among the half-dozen takes," Tyler related, "and gather round a couple of mics at the far end of the studio for vocals. But no, it's a compromise. They start the whole process again."[21]

Reverting to the punchier sound of their bigger amps—Henry's Fender Twin Reverb and Denny Laine's Sunn[22]—they settled on a preferred take just before 3:00 a.m. Paul then doubled his live vocal, and the rest of the band gathered around a microphone as Denny Laine conducted them through harmony vocals and handclaps. After nine hours of dope and whisky-infused recording, the musicians were "missing cues and giggling,"[23] but the resulting take was deemed satisfactory, and further overdubs were discussed.

Paul wondered whether a slide guitar might give the introduction the sense of anger and power it needed, so Henry slipped a bottleneck onto his finger, trying the intro a dozen times while Paul offered advice and direction over the talkback, suggesting at one point that Henry make it sound both simpler and more savage. Once Henry played a take that satisfied everyone, Paul decided to add a couple of new lead guitar lines to the song's ending, following a brief rehearsal with Henry and Denny playing rhythm guitar. After a few takes, Paul's additions were complete. By then, it was 5:30 a.m.; the band had worked around the clock. Any further overdubbing would have to wait until Thursday.

Recording Session

Thursday, February 3, 1972.
Island Studios, Studio Two, London.
Recording and Mixing: 'Give Ireland Back to the Irish' and 'Version.'

Wings did not return to EMI for overdubs; instead, a late booking was made at Island Records on Basing Street, in London's upmarket Notting Hill district. Here, in Island's Studio Two, engineer Brian Humphries oversaw sweetening and mixing, as well as preparing an instrumental mix, a tip of the hat to Linda's passion for Jamaican music, and the practice of putting a "version" on a single's B side.

But there was an ulterior motive behind the reggae-inspired choice. Should the lyric prove too hot for broadcasters, they could play the instrumental instead. If a radio station wanted to present Paul McCartney's latest work—and in 1972, few stations turned their backs on a former Beatle—they would have to play this song. And generally speaking, they would have to announce its title. So, lyrics or not, McCartney's protest would be heard.

To that end, the multitrack master was duplicated, the vocals were stripped away, and Paul and Henry overdubbed additional electric guitar lines—attractive, arpeggiated riffs that gave the song a cheerful, almost bouncy spirit that, at times, hinted at an Irish folk dance style. Paul, the two Dennys and Henry finished off the instrumental track with a countermelody, played on penny whistles.[24]

Brian Humphries and the members of Wings huddled over the board, mixing both sides late into the night. The A side was heavily compressed to make its deeply felt vocal and aggressive instrumental backing pop out all the more powerfully. And elements of studio chat were restored, just barely audibly, to the "version" mix, giving the B side a rough and ready feel.

There was also one final addition to the A side, designed to portray the sound of the British military oppression in North Ireland on record.

"He wanted what sounds like marching feet on [the record]," Brian Humphries explained. "So, my tape op had to find a bucket of gravel. And we all went out to the area outside the control room and put the gravel around the pillar, scattered it all over, set the microphone up, then recorded the sound of people marching."[25]

Paul continued to follow his intuition that press coverage was essential for this potentially controversial release and invited *Sounds* and *Melody Maker* to attend the mixing session. With the writers and the band crowded into the control room, and hovering over the board, Paul discussed his views on the situation in Northern Ireland, giving his guests a sense of how intensely he felt about the song and its message. Not lost in the discussion was the McCartneys' expectation that there would be pushback from radio stations disinclined to rock the boat with an overtly political track.

"It's going to run into a lot of trouble, and it'll have a hard time getting airplay."[26] Linda explained to the assembled reporters. "That's right," Paul broke in, "but it'll get played all the same—even if it's under the table or in dark corners—it'll get played all right."[27]

With all this discussion, added to actual work, the mixing session ran until 7 a.m. on Friday, February 4.[28] As the sun rose over London town, Humphries bicycled the master tapes to George Peckham at Apple Studios for mastering.

After a few hours' rest, Wings gathered once again at the ICA for rehearsals, where they were joined by journalist and DJ Kid Jensen of Radio Luxembourg. Jensen had played Paul's post-Beatles recordings regularly and enthusiastically on his late-night show, so McCartney, who had simultaneously been in both creative and publicity modes ever since he conceived the new song, invited him to the ICA for an interview and a glimpse of the band at work.

Paul hoped that the push for timeliness he had brought to the writing and recording of the song—not to mention his single-handed rounding up of publicity for the project—would see some follow-through by EMI, in the form of a quick release, much as the label had done for John Lennon when he wanted 'Instant Karma!' rushed out, almost exactly two years earlier. With that in mind, Jensen scheduled the interview for his February 12 broadcast, believing that the single would be out by then, or not much later.*

From the ICA, Paul took the band to the newly refurbished Apple Studios to master the single.

---

* Jensen later gave a partial transcript of the interview to *NME*, which published it in its 208 Radio Luxembourg supplement on April 8.

This was the first time Paul had embraced Apple's facilities since the Beatles split, having refused even to attend the opening gala, on October 3, 1971.

Given his soured feelings about Apple, it is a mystery why he chose to master the single there. Perhaps the truce he reached with John Lennon in December had softened his view, or perhaps he was just curious to know how the refurbished studio rated. He and Linda, Henry and Denny Laine were photographed leaving Apple that evening, acetates and master tapes in hand, by Arthur Murray of the *Daily Mirror*, so it is equally mysterious why, not long after the visit, Paul claimed never to have been there at all, telling *Record Mirror* that "I haven't ever used the studios and I don't use the offices now . . . I'm boycotting them."[29]

In any case, though he mastered the single at Apple, he was not ready for a public rapprochement. So as with *Wild Life*, he insisted that the label for 'Give Ireland Back to the Irish' not include Apple's Granny Smith design, although because Paul was still contractually tied to the label, it would bear an Apple catalog number. Instead, he commissioned a one-off design featuring five green shamrocks and the same split copyright: "Northern Songs Ltd. Copyright also claimed by Kidney Punch Music" that *Wild Life* carried. (In the United States, Maclen Music Inc. is substituted for Northern Songs.)

For the sleeve, McCartney planned to use the eye-catching yellow design he had planned for the scrapped 'Love Is Strange' single, but with variations for the British and American releases: the Wings logo in the UK; the Wings logo, plus the addition of the lyrics, on one side and the band members' names on the other, in the US. The songwriting credit was "McCartney and McCartney," a variation on the collaborative credit that had appeared on all of Paul and Linda's creative endeavors since *Ram*.

As much as Paul expected EMI to treat 'Give Ireland Back to the Irish' with the promptness it had accorded John's 'Instant Karma!,' Paul's song presented problems for the label that John's did not. When Sir Joseph Lockwood finally heard the song, he must have pined for the days when Lennon and McCartney were turning out tuneful love songs. This was no 'Please Please Me' or 'She Loves You,' and not only would Wings' new broadside have a fraction of those tunes' commercial appeal, it struck Sir Joseph as distinctly possible that it would face a blanket radio ban. He called Paul directly to deliver the bad news.

"I was phoned by Sir Joseph, explaining that they wouldn't release it. He thought it was too inflammatory. He said, 'Well, it'll be banned.' I told him I felt strongly about it and that they had to release it."[30]

With Sir Joseph eager to avoid the political fallout he was certain would occur—but also wanting to maintain the goodwill of one of EMI's most important artists, and Paul absolutely adamant that his statement reach the public, the conversation cannot have been easy. Sir Joseph undoubtedly would have reminded Paul that only six months earlier, the BBC's sensitivity to political comment in pop songs had been tested by George Harrison's 'Bangla Desh,' and even when the ban was lifted, the BBC's refusal to refer to it by name was, commercially, a poison pill.

In the end, Sir Joseph reluctantly gave in, and the single was scheduled for release in the UK on February 18, and in America on February 28. Still, not wanting to be associated with McCartney's stance on Northern Ireland, EMI issued a disclaimer, via press release, noting that the song was: "Simply Paul's comment on the situation."[31] When MPL was asked about the status of the release, they sent a contrasting message: "EMI are 100 per cent behind it," they declared, "and are very keen to put it out."

As advanced copies rolled off the presses at EMI's Hayes factory, it became clear to anyone who had not yet heard the song that McCartney's newest composition would be kicking a political hornet's nest.

By February 5, word of his protest song made the national press, leading the BBC to release a cautionary statement: "We have banned seven records since 1964. We won't ban this one unless we have to."[32]

Paul, confident that he would have his way, kept to his plan to introduce Wings to college audiences.

15

INTRODUCING . . . RIKKI AND
THE RED STREAKS

—

f Wings' first LP had been committed to wax after "the shortest rehearsals that any recording
band had ever been through," the band's approach to their maiden tour would be in the same
spirit. At Paul's request, Wings gathered in St. John's Wood just after lunch on February 8,
1972. Denny Seiwell arrived to find a three-ton Avis rental truck and a red Volkswagen minivan
parked across the driveway.

The low-key, unpublicized tour was on.

"I took a cab [to Cavendish Avenue]," Seiwell remembered as he paged through his wife's diary
from the time. "I didn't even have a car yet. I got up there and Paul says, 'Where's Monique?' I said,
'She's down at our place, you know, we're going on the road.' He goes, 'She's coming too. Tell her
to pack a bag and get her ass up here!' They needed her around, she was very close with the kids
and Linda. She was the only [woman] that, really, Linda felt safe around. Because we were married,
so Paul and Linda knew that Monique wasn't somebody with an ulterior motive, of hooking up with
Paul, or any of that stuff."[1] With Linda making her keyboard debut, and three kids in tow, an extra
pair of hands was much needed.

Roadies Trevor and Ian strapped down the hired PA system, amps, and guitars in the back of the
truck, and after one final group snap for posterity, the 11-strong touring party, plus the dogs, Martha and Lucky, bundled into the two vehicles. The rising diesel fumes were almost as intoxicating
as the prospect of playing to an audience—Rikki and the Red Streaks* hit the road.

Soon they were rolling north toward Britain's industrial heartlands—the epicenter of the min-

---

* Had Paul and his band turned up in Merseyside and played under the name "Rikki and the Red Streaks" there would have been no end
of confusion. Far from being a figment of Paul's imagination, Rikki and the Red Steaks were a real three-piece Mersey Beat group. John
Bancroft, Brendon McCormack, and Jeff Banford could be found entertaining crowds at venues like the Liverpool Jazz Society (LJS) and
Lathom Hall, until they disbanded in 1963. Long-serving Beatles confidant Tony Bramwell was their occasional roadie.

ing dispute. No eye-catching, logo-emblazoned tour bus. No agenda. No prebooked hotels. The man on the street had no idea they were coming.

"We were living like gypsies,"[2] Paul reminisced. "We just took off from London, heading north on the M1 [one of Britain's main highways]. We didn't want to go through the whole sort of established agent thing, managers, that kind of stuff. So, we just took off in a van, just like a gang of people going on a touring holiday. No publicity at all."[3]

Though not following a script, the trip wasn't entirely unplanned. Paul and Linda discussed possible low-profile venues with John Morris and with Rik Gunnell's booking agency and drew up a list of university towns and civic halls they might play. By late afternoon they came upon one likely destination—Nottingham University, where Henry had fronted a raucous Grease Band show a year earlier. But tempted by signs for the exotic-sounding town of Ashby-de-la-Zouche, they slipped off the M1 at Junction 21, heading west.

Even Ashby was a road too far, though. Just off the motorway were signs for the village of

Heather.* A geographical namesake to Linda's daughter, it was impossible to resist. Disappointingly, Heather was just a small mining village with a couple of pubs and no-frills corner shop. Hoping to snag a souvenir from the first stop on their road trip, Paul spied a pony tied to a post on a nearby village green. Thinking he might add to his growing highland herd, he tried to bargain with the owner, only to be sent packing.

With daylight vanishing fast, Wings reached Nottingham University campus at 5:00 p.m., and Trevor and Ian were dispatched in search of a concert hall. The burly roadies were welcomed by the Entertainments Committee's social secretary, Elaine Smith. Needless to say, she required convincing that they were secretly transporting Paul McCartney and his new band.

"I followed him outside and there was a red minibus parked in front of the Portland Building. He knocked on the window and the door slid back, and who should be sitting in the driving seat but Paul McCartney. Paul said, 'What's the chance of us playing tomorrow?'"[4]

The conditions were simple: no publicity, no press, and the university would take 25 percent of the door. Smith gleefully agreed, and the deal for Wings' first-ever gig, Paul's first public concert since Candlestick Park, in San Francisco, on August 29, 1966, was sealed over a pint in the campus Buttery bar.

With plans in place for the following lunchtime, the band retired to the Albany Hotel, Hyson Green—the only hotel in Nottingham with last-minute availability for a rock group, their wives, children, roadies, and two large dogs—six rooms in all. "We'd find the worst hotels you can imagine,"[5] joked Seiwell.

Before the day was out, Paul was spotted by students in the campus bar, and rumblings of impromptu Wings performances had already reached the *NME* news desk. When quizzed on whether Wings were set to play a series of surprise gigs, Shelley Turner told the paper: "If we confirmed this suggestion, they wouldn't be a surprise, would they?"[6]

As the band devoured a fish supper at the Albany, staying one step ahead of the press wasn't the only thing playing on Paul's mind. A swarm of butterflies had gathered in Linda's stomach. "Before [the gig] it was blind terror," he said. "All the sort of nerves she'd been suppressing all just finally came out. And she was just terrified, totally terrified."[7]

At 9:00 a.m., Trevor and Ian lugged the group's kit into the Portland Building Ballroom, a 600-capacity hall, usually used for dances and small functions. With less than three hours to advertise Wings' surprise appearance, the Entertainments Committee took to the campus public address system and threw together some crude posters and tickets, reading:

---

* Both local and national newspapers misreported their first stop as Hatherton, a town 50 miles west of Nottingham. Noticing their geographical blunder, the university newspaper, the *Gongster*, later attempted to correct the error, only to get the name wrong a second time, although Hathern, the town they cited, is much closer to Nottingham.

PAUL AND LINDA McCARTNEY

"WINGS"

SURPRISE DANCE...

Appearing in Portland Building Ballroom at 12 noon

TODAY

PRICE 40p.

Just as a metaphorical curtain was about to rise on Paul's second act, another descended on his Beatle days. Paging through the *Daily Mirror* over breakfast on February 9—the eighth anniversary of the Beatles' first appearance on the *Ed Sullivan Show*, in New York—an article about the closing of the Beatles Fan Club, launched in August 1961 by Bernie Boyle, caught Paul's eye. For a generation of young music fans, the dream was indeed over. As Paul's new band toasted the start of a new dawn, a dejected Ringo told *Mirror* reporter Kenelm Jenour, "We don't want to keep the myth going—because we are no longer together."[8]

McCartney's new group lacked polish, confidence, and stage time, but just as the Beatles had burnished their rough edges on the dimly lit stages of Liverpool and Hamburg, he was determined Wings would make their mistakes out of the spotlight.

"It wasn't like going back to square one, it was going back to square minus one. It was very awkward for me to suddenly go back to the roots, but it was necessary to get the group used to the idea of being a band. It takes time for any five people to understand each other. The idea was to build ourselves gradually, a sort of off-Broadway approach, without the enormous pressure of playing at major venues."[9]

With the paste still wet on the concert flyers, reports of an ex-Beatle on campus had already reached the farthest tip of Nottingham's legendary Sherwood Forest. Finally, after almost six performance-free years, "the Hermit of St. John's Wood" prepared to step out of the shadows. Hoping to recapture the magic of those early Hamburg days, and lose his musical virginity a second time, at midday Paul approached the microphone and ripped into a throat-wrecking rendition of 'Lucille.'* Bewildered students emerged from the cold to find the band already playing—an idea

---

* The Nottingham show is one of only two known recordings from the tour, the other being Hull. The tape begins partway through 'Blue

concocted the night before to settle Linda's nerves—and a primary schooler (Heather) and an infant (Mary) dancing in the wings.

The howl of McCartney's unrivaled Little Richard impression faded to find scarcely thirty people surrounding the stage. Outside, though, the collection bucket was ringing, and by the time Henry struck the closing chord to 'The Mess I'm In' the hall was brimming with 600 faces, staring up from the hardwood floor. Though cameras were strictly prohibited, student Nick Lambert captured five exposures of McCartney in a black sweater with a heart across his chest, and another small heart painted on his hand by Heather.[*]

From a Little Richard classic and an unknown original, Wings turned to Elvis Presley, and 'Blue Moon of Kentucky.' The flip side to the King's 1954 hit, 'That's All Right,' it was just one of the ingredients in the rock n' roll punch the Beatles, and countless other teens, had imbibed during their formative years. "Play 'Get Back!'" one impatient fan demanded, unaware that his Fab Four thirst would remain unquenched.

Much had changed in the six years since Beatlemania, and college crowds were a universe apart from the teenybopper circuit Paul remembered. The clash of styles was immediately apparent. Hysterical screaming had given way to quiet expectation and polite applause. Frenzy was replaced by hipsterish deliberation. Student audiences were not looking for pinups, but musical and lyrical depth. Those teenage girls who once threw jelly beans and knickers at four lads from Liverpool had grown up; their younger counterparts now fawned over the Osmonds and Marc Bolan.

Stunned by 600 silent, cross-legged students, Paul was overcome with nervous energy. "Has anyone in the audience got a harmonica?" Denny Laine called out to fill the silent void.

Even their latest politically loaded single, certain to stir a reaction with the young, educated crowd, was given a limp introduction: "We'd like to do a song we wrote earlier this week and recorded at EMI. It's called 'Give Ireland Back to the Irish.'" But what the band lacked in repartee, they made up for in vigor and musicianship—McCartney's protest song nearly blew the roof off Portland Ballroom.

The rest of the set combined tracks from the *Wild Life* LP ('Bip Bop' and 'Wild Life'), new compositions ('Thank You Darling' and 'My Love'), plus two McCullough blues originals ('You've Got to Help Me Darlin'' and 'Shuffle Blues'). "We haven't got that many numbers," Paul joked with the crowd. He wasn't lying. Following a ten-minute interval, the band repeated both 'The Mess I'm In' and 'Lucille,' pretending they were requests—an old trick from Paul's Cavern days.

As Wings fumbled through an artificially extended repertoire, that old McCartney magic was

---

Moon of Kentucky,' leading many to believe that this was the opening number. The university newspaper, however, noted that Wings began their set with 'Lucille' and 'The Mess I'm In,' both of which were repeated.

[*] Lambert's photo was later featured in *Sounds*, for which he was paid with a copy of *Bob Dylan's Greatest Hits Vol.2*.

slowly emerging. After 70 minutes, the students of Nottingham were up on their feet to see the group sign off with Little Richard's 'Long Tall Sally,' just as the Beatles had last done 1,990 days earlier in San Francisco. The show was little more than a glorified rehearsal before an audience, yet the wild applause that carried the band offstage was life-affirming, even a little inebriating.

On the steps outside, a single journalist from the *Nottingham Evening Post* anxiously pointed a microphone in Paul's direction, hoping to capture an inspired sound bite for tomorrow's edition. "It was very pleasing. They seemed to like us,"[10] Paul politely commented before slamming the van door.

After the university took its cut of the modest £200 ($520) purse, a bulging bag of small change was shared democratically among the band. "I'd never seen money for at least ten years," Paul marveled. "The Beatles never handled money. I felt like Duke Ellington, divvying out the money. We walked round Nottingham with £30 in coppers in our pockets."[11]

"It was the loosest thing I've ever done,"[12] glowed McCullough.

From the steps outside the Nottingham Portland building, the vans headed north, destination unknown. But whether it was the late-night fish supper, the Albany Hotel budget breakfast, or the tension of the first concert, both Henry and Linda were feeling the worse for wear, forcing an early pit stop at another unvetted lodge, the Forest Hotel on the edge of Sherwood Forest. There, they rested, took stock, and considered their next move.

The university's discretion had surprised Paul. Though one reporter flanked their exit, they slipped in and out of Nottingham like Robin Hood on a mercy mission, with a bag of loot to boot. Buoyant, he decided to take a punt and book their next gig in advance. A call was put in to Leeds University, seventy miles north, and rooms booked at the upmarket Metropole Hotel in Leeds city center.

The forward planning didn't end there. That afternoon, Barry Lucas, the Social Committee chairman at Lancaster University, took a call from June Whitting, at Rik Gunnell's Soho office. Lucas, an avid reader of *Melody Maker*, had seen Paul's interview with Chris Charlesworth back in November, when he touted the idea of playing anonymous gigs at venues like Slough Town Hall. Not one to miss a trick, he called Whitting—who had not yet signed on to Paul's plan but was a source of high-level talent for the university market—and told her she would have his undying gratitude if she could persuade McCartney to snub Slough in the south for Lancaster in the north.

Now Whitting was calling with good news. "I had a great relationship with June over the previous months," said Lucas, "she was an agent of the old school, we got on really well. June phoned me just to say, 'It's on!'"[13]

Wings were set to play the University of Leeds Refectory on February 10, while Lucas was told that Paul and his band could turn up in Lancaster at any time.

The hall where the Who's *Live at Leeds* LP was taped on February 14, 1970, Leeds Refectory was a dedicated concert venue with triple the capacity of Nottingham's humble ballroom. Entertainments secretary Paul Hurst was keen to add Wings to the university's starry presentation roster, which included the Rolling Stones, Elton John, and Rod Stewart, but he insisted on a formal contract, with a £250 ($650) fee, and minimum ticket price of 50p ($1.25). Paul, in turn, elicited a promise that Leeds would keep Wings' appearance under wraps.

In Nottingham that evening, the band broke out bottles of scotch and Coke and hung out at the Forest Hotel, smoking dope and jamming. Paul's 'Baby Dynamite,' a breezy blues number dedicated to baby Stella, was the song of the moment. That, along with two more lighthearted ballads, 'Mama's Little Girl' and 'Only One More Kiss'—a simple tune about Mary's growing embarrassment at parental doting—completed a new batch of family-centered compositions.

———

By Thursday morning news of McCartney's live return had already reached America. Fielding calls at Nottingham University, Mike Gleave insisted to *Rolling Stone*, "They asked for no publicity. I shouldn't even be talking to you. They asked me not to. Everybody else, I'm saying, 'no comment.'"[14] Unknown to Gleave, *NME* had promised the university a sizable payday for an exclusive on Wings' live debut; Gleave's colleagues, led by Geoff Liptrot, had already spilled the whole story.

Now en route to West Yorkshire, the band stopped at a local newsagent's, grabbing a fistful of music papers to brighten the short drive north. Paul's passionate, instinctive response to "Bloody Sunday" was now public knowledge. *NME*, *Melody Maker*, *Disc*, *Sounds*, and *Record Mirror* overflowed with features and comment on Wings' controversial single, including Andrew Tyler's fly-on-the-wall chronicle of the EMI recording session.

A somber, plain black page with a simple text advertised the group's first single.

The ad in *Disc and Music Echo* was also streaked with what appeared to be blood spatter—whether by design, or by a printing accident, it added drama to Paul's message.

Setting the papers aside, the band pulled up outside Leeds University. Flashbulbs erupted as the van door slid open, microphones and television cameras thrust in Paul's direction. Calling ahead, it seemed, was a big mistake.

"We had a few problems [in Leeds]," said Denny Laine. "The students had been getting a bit 'busy' and the moment that happened we just wanted to leave."[15]

Soon Leeds was a vanishing speck in the rearview mirror, the touring party trucking up the A64 out of the industrial city. It was time for a change of tack, and a change of scenery. To the fury of the promoter, the Refectory appearance was canceled, and Lancaster University also put on the back burner. Instead, Wings set their compass in the direction of the historic city of York, 30 miles away. Here Paul would make the university a take it or leave it offer: if a hall could be set up within

Give Ireland back to the Irish

wings

four hours, Wings would play a concert for students tonight.

When Paul walked into the Entertainments Committee's office, jaws hit the floor. But the timing could not have been worse. The university's Central Hall, where Free had played six days earlier, was already in use. All the committee could muster was a large dining room on the Goodricke College campus. Keen to keep the creative wheels in motion, McCartney accepted, though his musicians weren't thrilled by the room's lively acoustics. "It was a lunchroom, for Christ's sake!"[16] Seiwell objected.

While the band put their feet up, the undergraduates scrambled to erect a makeshift stage, and Paul checked in with Shelley Turner, in London. Promotional copies of 'Give Ireland Back to the Irish' had just been sent out, and he was looking for an update on when EMI might issue the single. Turner squirmed as she delivered the latest. EMI would issue the single in Britain, as promised, on February 18, but upon finally hearing the record the BBC decided to ban it, for much the same reason it had banned Harrison's 'Bangla Desh' six months earlier.

Mark White, the head of Radio One, was left to explain the BBC's stance. "We have decided not to play the record because the lyrics adopt a definite standpoint on the Northern Ireland situation and are therefore politically controversial. At a time when we are striving our utmost to remain impartial, this record can only be described as inflammatory." [17] (Such was the severity of the BBC's ruling, disc jockeys were not even allowed to name the single. Announcing the song's chart position on *Pick of the Pops*, Alan Freeman described it only as "a single by Wings."[18])

Top DJ John Peel lashed out at White's decision. "The ban disturbs me—the act of banning it is a much stronger political act than the contents of the record itself. It's just one man's opinion. There doesn't seem to me any reason why Paul McCartney shouldn't voice his feelings in the best way he can. It seems part of a general desire by some people to get pop music as trivial as possible."[19]

Political timidity as a programming policy was not limited to the BBC. Radio Luxembourg followed suit, noting that political comment breached the terms of their broadcasting license. With only independent stations like London-based Radio Jackie left to carry McCartney's message, the single, in Britain at least, was commercially damned.

Paul suspected a ban was coming, particularly after his face-off with Sir Joseph Lockwood, who was as good an indicator as any of the view the establishment would take. So he had a backup plan. Using rehearsal footage filmed by Mottram and Spicer at the ICA and Cavendish Avenue, he would produce a short promo film for commercial television. He asked Turner to buy advertising time on ITV and have Mottram and Spicer splice together a short TV spot. But Turner put the skids under that idea, too, telling Paul that the Independent Television Authority had also banned the single, noting that "political controversy"[20] was not allowed by the ITA Act of 1954. The ban even extended to the General Post Office's 'Dial-a-Tune' service.[21]

By now the phones at 1 Soho Square were lit up like Christmas trees, the world press desperate to hear Paul's response to the ban. Turner frantically scribbled down a statement.

"As a citizen of the UK, Paul feels a mistake is being made in Ulster. He is not a politician but believes the majority of British and Irish people think Ireland should be given back to the Irish. Paul is very patriotic and loves Britain, and this is his personal view. He and his wife have dedicated the single to Mr. Heath."[22]

Paul offered a less formal response to *Melody Maker*: "Up 'em! I think the BBC should be highly praised, preventing the youth from hearing my opinions."[23]

And the press releases kept coming. While backing their man, EMI wasted no time trying to dowse the political flames while shielding itself, and its valuable Beatles franchise, under its protective corporate armor.

"The song is not anti-British," the company's official statement read. "There is no incitement to violence. The lyrics represent a comment from Paul McCartney on the present situation in Ireland. As an international company, EMI does not hold any political views and is issuing the record in the usual way. The comments made by Paul McCartney are not necessarily those of the other three Beatles or that of Apple."[24]

Despite bitter cold and drizzle, at the University of York, a quarter-mile-long queue had formed around the Goodricke College dining room. Hundreds of freezing students, in a small way, collectively shared in Paul's misery.

The concert, at 8:00 p.m., was blighted by sound problems, the dining room's overly resonant acoustics frustrating the band and roadies. Desperate to catch a glimpse of Beatle Paul, those who didn't get inside pressed their faces against the windows. One overzealous fan went further, scaling the building and breaking in through an open window at the rear.*

After the gig, Paul and a member of the university's staff stood in the icy evening air, splitting

---

* Said fan was one Kevin Nixon, future manager of George Harrison's Britpop prodigies, Kula Shaker.

the door money. "Are you collecting for the IRA?" one student inquired. "We're simply playing for the people,"[25] Paul replied. The Irish debate, McCartney was coming to realize, was far from black and white. Though his song was intended as a comment on civil liberty, in the eyes of some, if he was against the British Army, he was pro-IRA.

Wading in on the Irish debate, John Lennon faced the same moral dilemma.

"I don't know how I feel about the IRA," Lennon told a reporter, "because I understand why they're doing it. And if it's a choice between the IRA or the British Army, I'm with the IRA, but if it's a choice between violence and non-violence I'm with non-violence. So, it's a very delicate line. Our backing of the Irish people is done really through the Irish Civil Rights which is not the IRA. Although I condemn any violence, if two people are fighting, I'm probably gonna be on one side or the other, even though I'm against violence."[26]

Back at the Chase Hotel the band tucked into a late supper of smoked salmon sandwiches. What happened next seemed to perfectly capture the mood of the day.

"In York, there was a night desk clerk by the name of Cyril. He wasn't all there," Denny Seiwell remembered. "We were all hanging out in this little room, and he comes up with a sand bucket, like a kid's sand pail. He says, 'One of you chaps own that black-and-white spotted dog?' Paul says, 'Oh yeah, that's Lucky. He's mine.' He says, 'Well, he shat in the hallway—you're gonna have to clean it up.'"[27]

Paul and Linda rose the next morning to a sobering Yorkshire breeze drifting in off York Race-course. News of the BBC ban had spread to newspapers from London to Los Angeles, the motives, and message, behind his political single picked over by journalists across the globe. One comment was still troubling Paul. Did people really believe he was supporting, or worse, funding the IRA? Or was his message simply lost in the dire dining room acoustics? Had his unifying message of freedom and peace fallen flat?

Behind the scenes, Denny Laine and Henry McCullough had their concerns about the song, too, concerns they chose not to communicate.

"Paul was quite innocently trying to solve a problem which just can't be solved overnight with a song like that," Denny Laine later demurred. "I anticipated there would be problems . . . because I certainly didn't know enough about the struggle and what the problem [in Northern Ireland] was, to be able to write that. Maybe Paul did. I don't know."[28]

An association with a song that could be interpreted as pro-Republican was a bigger problem for Northern Ireland–born McCullough. Soon after the single came out, his brother Victor, while drinking in a Kilburn pub, bore the brunt of his connection to McCartney's guitarist.

"He was asked if he was my brother, and he said he was. And he was asked again, 'Did he play on that record "Give Ireland Back to the Irish?"' And he said, 'He did.' And he ended up with a bottle in his face over it."[29]

The single provoked extreme reactions among Irish and Northern Irish natives, expatriates and those of Irish descent, and both sides were equally resolute. Wolverhampton-born, second-generation Irish musician Kevin Rowland's* experience in London was quite different from Victor McCullough's.

"I remember hearing 'Give Ireland Back to the Irish' in a club. I must have been 17. It was too fucking right of McCartney to release the song," says Rowland. "In this club, they normally played soul music, which you had to learn how to dance to, if you wanted to dance with a girl. And suddenly 'Give Ireland Back to the Irish' comes on at the end of the night. I told my parents about it, because the room erupted. I realized everyone there was like me: second-generation Irish. There were Irish people living all over London back then, in places like Harlow and Wembley."[30]

Settling the band's hotel bill in fifty-pence pieces, Paul realized that if his message *was* being lost, an interview at their next stop might help quell the flames.

By early afternoon on February 11, Wings had arrived at the East Coast fishing port of Hull. Paul strolled into the University of Hull's Entertainments office, and, following the model established at York University, asked if he could book their West Refectory Hall for the evening. The band then left campus to find accommodation and stumbled onto the Pearson Park Hotel, a tranquil auberge overlooking an ornate Victorian common with ornamental garden and fishing lake, just five minutes from the campus. Dumping their luggage, they returned to the university at 6:30 p.m. to rehearse. When the 800-strong crowd arrived, 90 minutes later, the band had just hit their stride, the rehearsal and concert merging into one.

"Henry went off his nut during his solo in 'The Mess I'm In' and leapt around," Paul remembered. "I wore baggy trousers for the first time. It felt better being on a stage than in a dining hall."[31]

Growing in confidence, Wings added three extra numbers to their set—Linda's 'Seaside Woman,' plus 'Smile Away' and 'Some People Never Know,' from *Ram* and *Wild Life*. The crowd was also treated to a double helping of the band's divisive new single. "You won't hear it on the BBC, this is probably the only time you're gonna hear it," said Paul as he introduced 'Give Ireland Back to the Irish' for a second time.

During the interval, Paul saw his chance for a quick word in the ear of a student writer. With only ten minutes before they were due back onstage, he told reporter Ian McNulty to press the record button on his tape deck so they could discuss the band's Irish single.

"You've got to be political when they start shooting them down," Paul explained, "you can't just sit on the fence. But of course, the BBC don't want to hear it said. The song could really apply

---

* Though born in England, Kevin Rowland lived in Ireland for three years (between ages one and four) before returning to the Midlands. His family moved to Harrow, in northwest London when he was 11 years old. Rowland formed Dexys Midnight Runners along with Kevin Archer in Birmingham in 1978.

to anything, it's about ownership. It says, *'give Ireland back to the Irish,'* but it could also be 'give Scotland back to the Scottish,' or 'Africa back to the Black Man.'"[32]*

The savvy young journalist didn't waste his opportunity, using his remaining interview time to quiz Paul on the state of play at Apple, and his relationship with the other Beatles. Distracted by McNulty's friendly juvenile features, Paul gave a cutting response, contradicting recent talk of peace between him and John.

"There's no hard feelings or anything, but you just don't hang around with your ex-wife. We've completely finished. 'Cos, you know, I'm just not that keen on John after all he's done. I mean, you can be friendly with someone, and they can shit on you, and you're just a fool if you keep friends with them. I'm not just going to lie down and let him shit on me again. I think he's a bit daft, to tell you the truth. I talked to him about the Klein thing, and he's so misinformed it's ridiculous."[33]

That night, as Paul hung up his baggy trousers, the roadies and band gambled away a freshly netted bag of fifty-pence pieces, their fingers still thick with grease from a late-night Chinese takeaway. Tumblers of scotch and Coke, liberated from the unmanned hotel bar, toasted the victors and drowned the sorrows of those who left empty-handed.

In the morning, Paul walked down the stairs to find the remnants of a boozy night scattered across the hotel lounge. The proprietor, enraged by the mess and missing drinks (though, in their defense, the band left payment), scorched Ian's ear at the reception desk. Indifferent about McCartney's superstar status, the owner had also taken exception to the two male roadies sharing a double bed and threatened to report them to the police under the Sexual Offences Act.[34] Linda documented the fiery climax to the argument in her diary.

"Dogs in the rooms!" the owner fumed.

"You let us," Paul protested.

"Mess in the rooms!" he shouted. "Your mob is most disgusting!"

THUMP![35]

Still seething from news of the BBC ban, Paul lost his head and clocked the hotelier.

"Paul was very pissed off but bit his tongue and didn't say anything, realizing the old boy didn't recognize him," Denny Laine said, minimizing the incident. "So, Paul nudged him in the nose with his elbow, accidentally on purpose . . . He just nicked him really. Of course, he threatened to call the police, but we just sort of breezed out like nothing happened."[36]

"We were thrown out,"[37] clarified Trevor Jones.

Wings were now a band on the run, taking flight up the east coast. Searching for a distraction, Paul tuned the van's wireless to Radio Luxembourg, hoping to catch the band's prerecorded in-

---

* German parody group Die Wingos released a parody version of McCartney's song to that effect. With German lyrics written by Gerhard Schmidt, Hans Herman Köper and Marius Müller-Westernhagen, 'Gebt Bayern Zurück An Die Bayern' called for Germany to 'Give Bavaria Back to the Bavarians.'

terview with Kid Jenson that was scheduled to air at 10:30 a.m. The conversation with Jensen was designed to set up a first play of their new record, but, owing to the ban, all mention of the contentious single was edited out; cuts from *Wild Life* were played instead.

Just up the coast was the traditional seaside town of Scarborough, where the Beatles had played concerts at the Futurist Theater in 1963 and 1964. Away from the seafront's penny arcades, fish and chip shops, and ice cream parlors, the town was a labyrinth of side streets and old smugglers' runs. The McCartneys and company lost themselves in the souvenir shops and thrift stores, Paul picking up a secondhand suit plus a fur coat for £3 ($7.50) and Linda buying a winter hat.

But February in Scarborough is not sunbathing weather. With the unforgiving wind and rain lashing in off the North Sea, the group found cover at the Prince of Wales Hotel overlooking the town's South Bay. Like a college band, they crowded around a tape deck to hear a crude cassette Ian had made of their Hull gig before switching on the television to catch the news. It made for grim viewing. Talks between the government and striking miners were going nowhere, and coal supplies at power stations were dwindling. Britain was at the breaking point. Worried that coal stockpiles could be gone within days, the government announced the biggest power switch-off ever ordered in peacetime: starting immediately, a ban was imposed on electric heating in offices, shops, restaurants, cinemas, theaters, and all other premises used for recreation and sport.

Then came a hammer blow for British industry. To protect power supplies for homes, factories would be restricted to a two-day working week. EMI was able to shield its recording operations from power cuts in Central London, thanks to the ingenuity of the engineers at its studios on Abbey Road, who built a heavily soundproofed petrol-fueled generator that enabled them to keep the studios open seven days a week. But the company's vinyl pressing plant in Hayes was subject to the same restrictions as other factories. The outlook for the music business was bleak; several small record labels announced they would cease pressing singles until the power crisis was over. Checking in again with Shelley Turner, Paul was reassured that the restrictions would not affect the release of his record.

Television was a welcome distraction. That afternoon the band crowded around the box to watch twenty-six men tear each other to pieces as England took on Ireland in a Five Nations rugby union clash. Winger Thomas Grace stole the day, running in a last-minute try as the Irish snatched a 16-12 victory. Not for the first time that week, Ireland took center stage.

On Saturday night a private bar was set up in Paul's suite by the hotel steward. This meant the family could maintain total privacy. Downstairs, the lord mayor of Scarborough hosted a lavish reception in the hotel's ballroom, blissfully unaware that Paul and his group were above them quietly watching *Match of the Day*.

Feeling refreshed after a Saturday by the sea on Sunday morning Henry took the wheel as Wings pushed farther north. The pretty shoreline, dotted with holiday spots like Robin Hood's

Bay, and the harbor town of Whitby (whose cottage-lined cobbled streets inspired Bram Stoker's *Dracula*), soon gave way to the harsh industrial skylines of Middleborough, Sunderland, and South Shields. Next on the touring list—Durham University.

In Durham, the university was in the thick of preparations for Rag Week, a period when students at British universities present fundraising events for charities. The school's main stage was set for a production of Shakespeare's *Hamlet*, so the students despondently waved away McCartney's band. Henry pointed the wheel north and they soon crossed the iconic green-clad Tyne Bridge into the North East's spiritual capital, Newcastle.

Eyes rolled when the troupe discovered that Newcastle University was closed for the weekend. But all was not lost.

"I was sitting outside the *Courier* office when two big vans drew up," said Stuart Prebble, a writer for the student newspaper. "The driver asked me for the ballroom, and I told him everything was locked up. I recognized him as Henry McCullough, and realized it was Wings."[38]

Thinking on his feet, Prebble told McCullough that there was a hall near his student dormitory at Castle Leazes, where folk bands would play on a Sunday night, and after a quick tour, Havelock Hall was given the thumbs-up. While Ian and Trevor unloaded the PA system (and explained to the band due to play, The Borderers, that their gig had been bumped to 10:30 p.m.), Paul and the band scored a bag of 45s at a local record store before settling at the Gosforth Park Hotel.

Meanwhile, students Dafydd Thomas and Steve Dresser barked announcements over the public address system, and students were soon clamoring for a chance to see McCartney in action. The band arrived to tune up at 7:45 p.m., before 400 students (the maximum hall regulations allowed) poured into the dining room for the latest of Wings' secret sorties. With the threat of power cuts looming, student Andi Brack hit the lights and Wings launched into what was by now a well-rehearsed, 70-minute set.

Unknown to the band, two *Newcastle Journal* staffers—photographer Ian Woodhouse and writer Philip Crawley—were lurking in the wings. Tipped off by someone at the university, Woodhouse snapped away at the side of the stage, while Crawley frantically scribbled notes in his pad.

"What do you think of the BBC banning your record?" Crawley queried as Paul and the band headed for the exit.

"I think it's great. It's the best thing that could happen to us," Paul replied sarcastically. "I wouldn't believe that they could be so stupid."

"Where will you be stopping next?" Crawley continued.

"Scotland. We're not sure where yet, but definitely Scotland,"[39] Paul concluded.

In the quiet Gosforth suburbs, Paul and Linda enjoyed a rare moment alone, the children left in Monique's care. In the absence of a late night off-license, they crept inside the Queen Victoria pub on the High Street, Paul slipping out with a bottle of whisky under his arm. Next door they queued up for Chinese takeaway. After chatting to, and signing autographs for, a handful of worse-for-wear pub regulars, Paul and Linda crashed on their bed with chow mein for two, and Ian's latest concert recording.

"It wasn't a fantastic gig or anything, but the tape sounded fabulous," Paul commented two days later. "Just a little band, that's all . . . We all worked well together, and we all enjoy it."[40]

Through Ian's cassette recordings, the group's increasing ensemble tightness was evident, and the backbone of a new album was emerging. 'The Mess I'm In,' played twice most nights, sounded studio-ready, while 'My Love' had obvious commercial potential that a string arrangement could magnify.

Now the traveling company was just an hour from the Scottish border, and Edinburgh was calling. But having announced Scotland as their next destination, Paul had a change of heart. Perhaps fearing his Irish message might fall flat with the Celtic crowd, he proposed heading west toward Carlisle, but crossed the destination off the list once he realized that the city had no university. Instead, they ventured south beyond the Lake District to Lancaster, where Social Committee chairman Barry Lucas had been waiting for Wings to turn up ever since his chat with June Whitting.

On Monday afternoon, while the band booted a football around a nearby playing field, Trevor and Ian trooped into Lucas's office.

"We all went over to the Great Hall," Lucas said. "On the grass by the Barbara Hepworth statue was a group of people—a lady, cradling a baby, and some guys playing football. Suddenly I could see Paul McCartney, Henry McCullough and Denny Laine. McCartney asked if it was okay to play tonight and of course I said yes but I would have to sort out the Great Hall porters."[41]

In Lancaster's Great Hall, ex-military porters Sid and Mick were preparing the room for a classical concert the next day when Lucas burst in.

"Stop! Sorry, you two," Lucas told them, "but there's a rock show on tonight."

"Piss off!"

"No, honestly, in a few minutes Paul McCartney will walk through those doors, he wants to play here tonight."

"Piss off, it's Rag Week."

"Look, honest . . ." Lucas was interrupted by Paul's arrival.

"Hi, are you two the guys I'm giving heart attacks to?" said Paul. "What kind of music do you have on here?"

"Proper music, classical, tomorrow. Not your pop rubbish,"[42] replied Sid.

Ice well and truly broken, the porters helped Wings' roadies clear the chairs and set the stage.

Leaving Lucas and his team to prepare the hall, the band drove to nearby Morecambe Bay to find a hotel for the night. Ringing the bell on the reception desk at the sleek, art deco Midland Hotel, Paul and Linda were greeted by the owner, Mr. J. Millar. Unacquainted with the popular music scene, Millar had no idea who they were, and when they asked to book six rooms, he insisted on a deposit. Linda's reaction, though likely politer in person, was captured in her tour diary, "Pay in advance? Up ya!"[43] Millar later remarked, "He didn't stay. I don't know why."[44]

Hopping back into the Volkswagen van, they stubbornly drove 30 miles inland to the Coniston Hotel on the edge of nearby Skipton. Luckily, the luxury lodge, set in a stunning 1,400-acre estate, was worth the drive.

A rich evening's entertainment was guaranteed for the Lancaster undergrads. That night 1,300 people witnessed Wings play their fifth concert in six days, the set taking a romantic, Valentine's Day detour as Paul serenaded Linda with an unidentified Elvis number.*

---

* The *John O'Gauntlet*, Lancaster University's student paper, noted the inclusion of an unspecified Elvis number. With no tape of the

"I nearly died of heart failure there and then," wrote 17-year-old Sheryl Pringle in an early Wings fanzine, guessing at the titles of the unrecorded songs. "The concert was really fantastic. They sang a lot of rock oldies like 'Lucille' and 'Long Tall Sally,' numbers off recent albums like 'Smile Away,' 'Bip Bop,' 'Some People Never Know' and 'Wild Life.' And loads of new numbers like 'Give Ireland Back to the Irish,' 'What a Mess I'm In,' 'Blues in A,' 'Say Darling,' 'My Love' and 'Sea Shore Woman.' They were laughing and joking all the time they were on-stage and when they went off Paul said hello to all the girls as they went past."[45]

At the interval, Paul took a back seat, giving his wife a rare chance to speak alone to the university paper. Or so she believed. As well as a lengthy tirade about the situation in Northern Ireland, she talked about being in a band with her husband, plus life on the road as a mother of three.

"We've only been playing together for five days and already I have confidence in the band," Linda beamed. "So far, the audience response has been good. Surprisingly perhaps, I am enjoying these one-night appearances—it's like a touring holiday. And the children love it too. We gave our elder child the choice of school or coming with us, and she chose the latter. Her teacher in London doesn't mind a bit—I mean—this is an education in itself, isn't it?"[46]

Two weeks later, Linda's comments showed up in an uncredited *Melody Maker* article titled "Bird on the Wing," the student paper having been persuaded to part with the interview tape for a modest fee.

The second Wings finished playing, the charged-up crowd piled down to the Bowland Refectory where another group, the Brother Lover Travelling Rock Group (who had kindly delayed the start of their own concert for Wings), were playing a benefit concert for the striking miners. In solidarity with their cause, Paul instructed Lucas to add Wings' door money to the miners' fund.

Back at the hotel, after her first interview as a musician, Linda was treated to a slice of life on the road with four sweaty rockers.

"Linda walked into Henry's room," recalled Seiwell. "We were all sitting on the bed playing guitars and hanging out after the show. She said, 'Oh my god. What's that smell?' He had his shoes off. He goes, 'It's feet. It's fucking touring feet. If you don't like it, get out of here.' Henry would tell you like it was."[47]

———————————————————————

concert available for review, there is no way to verify the account.

"We were like a bunch of kids really after the gig," Henry reflected, "that was the bonding period. We all wanted this to work, [and] we all got on really well. If you don't have a happy working group it doesn't work."[48]

—

"It's grim up north," is a good-humored saying among those from the south of England, but that Tuesday morning there was no disputing it. A bruised Lancastrian sky opened, pouring misery on everything and everyone below. Now traveling south, when Wings passed through West Yorkshire for a second time, the power was out, schools empty, and factories closed.

Still put out by the media scrum that greeted them at Leeds University a few days earlier, Paul planned to take the party to neighboring Bradford. Further frustration loomed. Every concert hall on campus was packed with tables and chairs for exams, due to take place the next day. A second rejection in as many days forced Paul's hand. "We went back to Leeds and fixed up a lunchtime gig for the next day [February 16]. We weren't all that pleased with it."[49]

In the afternoon, after booking into the Metropole Hotel, the band took the evening off and splintered, the two Dennys, Henry and Monique quickly settling at the hotel bar with the two roadies. Up in their suite, the McCartney girls caught snippets of *Play School* and *Jackanory* between blackouts. Ever-assiduous Paul captured the moment in a new composition with a resolutely foursquare beat, simply titled 'Power Cut': "*There may be a power cut and the candles burn down low / But something inside of me says the bad news isn't so / I may never tell you but baby you should know / There may be a miracle and baby I love you so.*"

Paul's return to Leeds hadn't escaped the attention of the local press. When the family sat down to dinner in the hotel restaurant, along with their main courses, the waiter delivered a business card from a BBC Radio Leeds reporter. Steve Haigh, 19, was the last man standing at the Radio Leeds news desk when a member of the public called in with a tip about Paul's stopover. Convinced he could secure what he mistakenly believed was McCartney's first interview since the Beatles' breakup, Haigh dashed down to the Metropole with a Uher tape recorder and a spool of ¼-inch tape.

Paul and Linda finished their dinner before retiring to a side room where Haigh nervously waited. "You must be Paul McCartney?" said Paul, confusing the young journalist. "I'm Steve Haigh." Slowly realizing the ex-Beatle was joking, Haigh hit the record button, desperate to find out why an ex-Beatle was touring the country in secret.

"We've had offers to play at Madison Square Garden, that kind of stuff, you know," Paul explained. "But I don't particularly want to do that kind of work at the moment, I like just being in a group, having a blow, and playing near to just a smallish-type audience—you know, that's the way I get my kicks."

"But the people want you to come back together, the people want the Beatles," said Haigh.

"As far as I'm concerned, I'm just some fella who used to be in a group called the Beatles," Paul responded. "The Beatles split up, that job's over, so quite naturally you don't hang out with all those people still, you look for something else. And that's all I'm doing. And it's a group called Wings and we're having a great time doing the kind of things the Beatles could have never done."[50]

Paul's local radio interview soon went national, guaranteeing that by lunchtime the next day 1,400 people were waiting outside the University of Leeds Refectory for Wings' 2:00 p.m. concert.

Here, for the first time, Linda's musical inexperience was laid bare.

Gazing across the intimidating crowd, her nerves got the better of her when Paul introduced 'Wild Life.' As he counted the song in, Linda's mind went blank, the opening chord progression having fled from her memory. Paul smiled at the audience before stepping across the stage to whisper the chords in her ear. By now, the murmurs of discontent were drowned only by the hum of a four-kilowatt generator propping up the hall's power supply.

"They thought it was part of the act. But that was embarrassing,"[51] Linda conceded. Her nerves shredded and her confidence shot, she abruptly stopped keeping her tour diary.

Like Linda's self-confidence, the element of surprise was fading. The crowd filed out, leaving a gaggle of Yorkshire pressmen seeking their pound of Beatle flesh, all of them (seemingly unaware of the state of play at Apple) under pressure from their editors to get the scoop on a possible Beatles reunion. Paul repeated his now well-practiced response—that the Beatles were finished—adding, for the Leeds-based reporters, that he would rather have played in nearby Bradford.

———

Thursday morning's newspapers delivered another helping of inevitable critique. Due for release the next day, 'Give Ireland Back to the Irish' received a mixed critical reaction.

"A real rough, raw and rugged item . . . Whatever you feel about the message, you'll find it difficult to resist the choruses, shouted loud, long and furious by Paul. . . . No finesse, but plenty of guts!"[52]

Andrew Tyler, *Disc and Music Echo*

"McCartney's Rebel Rouser Is Great!"[53]

Danny Holloway, *NME*

"Nice drum sound on the middle eight and the chorus hook is quite catchy. . . . It sounds like a number one chart hit."[54]

Chris Welch, *Melody Maker*

"This track does sound a bit rushed in the sense of McCartney's melodic content—the sort of thing you'd make up laying back in your bath."[55]

Penny Valentine, *Sounds*

"So-so composition . . . nothing particularly special."[56]

Lon Goddard, *Record Mirror*

The papers also brought coverage of Wings' Nottingham debut, which, by contrast, was wholly complimentary, the spectacle of a performing Beatle outweighing the group's musical shortcomings. But Rob Watkinson, a guest reviewer for *Record Mirror*, offered a scathing assessment of the York gig. "The concert was a bit of an anti-climax . . . The music was early 60s dance rock, with Paul playing elementary bass riffs and bellowing in that old familiar way. Linda held down some simple chords on the piano and sang very badly out of tune for the most part, as did Denny Laine."[57]

Seeing his wife's role in the group so swiftly dismissed was hard to stomach, but Paul was not going to let a few words derail his ambitions for the band. By 8:00 p.m. that night, another eleventh-hour concert had been fixed 40 miles away at the University of Sheffield's Lower Refectory, the 1,300 tickets selling out in just 80 minutes.

Speaking with fellow Scouser Heather Richardson of BBC Radio Sheffield the following morning, McCartney raved about the Steel City crowd. "Sheffield last night, it was great, you know. First half they just sat and watched, you know, to just sort of see what was what. Second half they were bopping up on their feet, dancing, and there was a big crowd outside the window—they were swaying like a football crowd."[58]

When Wings rolled out of town, David Bowie and his Spiders from Mars rolled in—the musical torch shining brightly that week on a city in the grips of the industrial dispute.

After the concert, the band spent an evening in the Peak District, at the Maynard Arms, Grindleford, before leaving for Salford on the outskirts of Manchester. Twenty-four hours after crossing the threshold of Sheffield University, an eighth date was penciled in at Salford University, and the band found lodgings at the Midland Hotel in Manchester city center.

"They'd been sent [to Salford] from Manchester University, who wouldn't put them on," explained Robert Conway, the university's Entertainments officer. "They said, 'We want to play here tonight. Get as many people as you can . . . In the space of two or three hours we managed to get 600 people in this hall."[59]

To toast the release of their debut single, Paul took the band for dinner at the hotel brasserie before the gig. By pure chance, the blind Puerto Rican guitar virtuoso and singer José Feliciano, in town for a concert at Manchester Kings Hall that night, was having dinner across the restaurant. Feliciano idolized the Beatles and had covered several of their songs. Nearly two years earlier, in a June 1970 interview in *Record Mirror*, entitled "I Got It From the Beatles," Feliciano discussed the influence the Fab Four had on his music. "I've never managed to meet any of them," he said, "but I wouldn't know what to say if I did. I'm completely awed by them."[60]

Feliciano summoned the courage to approach his musical idol, but shortly after he arrived at McCartney's table, the power went off. Feliciano was quick to find humor in the situation.

"We're in the middle of a restaurant having dinner and the lights went off," Denny Seiwell recalled. "We said, 'How the hell are we going to get back to our rooms?' And José Feliciano said, 'I'll take you guys back to your room, don't worry about it!'"[61]

That night the band made their way to Salford in the pitch-black. A month since the wheels stopped turning at Britain's pits, coal supplies were perilously low—two million streetlights the latest victims of energy cutbacks. Wings' gig nearly suffered the same fate.

"In Salford we had a big hall where a play was being produced and they were afraid the scenery would fall on us," Paul explained. "We just missed a blackout that time."[62]*

To the relief of the nation, a few short hours after the Salford concert, the picket lines stood down and coal trucks began rolling again. At 1:00 a.m. on February 19, 1972, union leaders voted 15 to 10 in favor of the Wilberforce settlement offer, and the monthlong strike was over.

When Wings checked out of the Midland Hotel the next day, José Feliciano was also at the counter. But again, his hope to have a serious chat with McCartney was dashed.

"In the hotel lobby [Paul's dog] Martha was 'overtaken' by their boy-dog," said Feliciano. "Everybody just tried to yield to decorum and ignore them both as if nothing were wrong. 'What of it? Paul McCartney's dogs doing it in the lobby of the Midland Hotel!'"[63]

Over the weekend Wings trucked on to Liverpool, spending a couple of days in Gayton with Jim and Angie. Checking in with his offices in New York and London, Paul got an update from John Eastman on the ATV legal action. On Thursday, a High Court judge in London dismissed a counterclaim filed by Northern Songs in Paul's case against them. Twelve months after the release

---

* Another future music impresario Wings entertained along the way was aspiring musician and songwriter Matthew Aitken. He was among the crowd at Salford University.

of 'Another Day,' a ruling that any songs written with anyone other than John Lennon would fall outside his 1965 contract, looked close.

Eastman also relayed news of ABKCO's annual general meeting on Friday, during which Allen Klein announced to shareholders that John, George, and Ringo would be making Paul an offer in the next two weeks for his 25 percent share in Apple. Klein went on to claim that if Paul's share was acquired by the other three, ABKCO would pursue negotiations toward fully acquiring Apple Corp Ltd. Paul knew this was just hot air. Klein was entering the final 12 months of his contract with Apple and trying to put a positive spin on his future relationship with the Beatles.

Klein's smoke-and-mirror tactics may also have been meant to distract Lennon, Harrison, and Starr from a Mick Jagger interview that ran in *Record World* on February 5. The Rolling Stones and Klein parted company in 1970, but nearly two years on, the band were still locked in litigation with ABKCO. In 1971, the Stones sued ABKCO for $1,250,000 over disputed royalty payments in America, while also attempting to regain control of their master recordings and copyrights from Klein's company. In early 1972, *NME* reported that the legal dispute had been settled, leaving the Stones' frontman incensed.

"It makes me sick to read his [Klein's] lies," fumed Jagger. "The article [in *NME*] infers that Klein settled out the dispute we had with him, where, in actual fact, he hasn't done anything to settle it. And not only has he not tried to settle anything, but companies which he is affiliated with are now claiming ownership of our masters and copyrights." In a final statement, fired firmly in the direction of the former Beatles, Jagger added, "I hope that other artists associated with him don't get the same treatment from Klein."[64]

Jagger also claimed that ABKCO had recently issued the double LP *Hot Rocks 1964–1971*, a compilation of the Stones' hits from that period, without the band's full cooperation, noting "Klein had never consulted with us as to what was going on the record or what the cover would be."

Though Klein had no claim on the Beatles master tapes or copyrights, their copyrights were now held by ATV, and their master recordings by EMI, leaving the former Beatles open to the same ill treatment. On the eve of Klein's contract with Apple expiring, Paul could only hope that Jagger's statement added further weight to his claim that Klein was bad news.

In London, Shelley Turner once again played doomsayer, delivering the news that two major retailers felt uneasy about Paul's protest song and had decided not to stock it. Record Merchandisers Ltd. (founded in 1966 by none other than EMI Records to supply discs to stores that did not typically focus on music) announced that they would not carry the single—meaning that it would not be available in the large Woolworths chain. Boots also refused to sell it.[65]

In response, Paul asked Turner to take out a full-page ad in Monday's *Daily Mirror*, saying:

Visiting Merseyside without trying to set up a concert was unthinkable, but cruising the streets of Liverpool unnoticed was impossible for one of the city's best-loved sons. On Sunday afternoon Paul asked his roadies to drive around town and sniff out a venue. Their mission did not go well. Being a Sunday, the University of Liverpool campus was deserted. Quickly devising a backup plan, the brothers-in-law figured one of Liverpool's many playhouses would roll out the red carpet for Paul and his group. Strolling into the Everyman Theatre, Ian found a carpenter fine-tuning the set for a new production of Shakespeare's *Measure for Measure*, due to open on February 23. He happily took a message to the theater's boss, Alan Dosser. "There's a group here called Wings who want to play a gig here tonight," the carpenter ventured. Dosser, not a follower of popular music, and having a schedule to meet, snapped, "Fuck off! Can't they see we're in the middle of a tech! Fuck off!"[66] Walking in late on the conversation, musician Terry Canning dashed out of the theater onto Hope Street to see the van disappearing around the corner.

McCartney's return to the Liverpool concert stage would have to wait.

By Monday morning, February 21, Paul was keen to get back on the road. From Liverpool they headed south to Denny Laine's hometown of Birmingham. It was here on July 5, 1963, that Paul and Denny first shared a stage, Denny and the Diplomats supporting the Beatles at what was then described as the "Mecca of the Midlands"—the Plaza Ballroom, Old Hill, Dudley. Just a few weeks before the concert, Denny's beat group had signed a contract with EMI Records. Eleven days after the concert, they made their first recordings, with A&R man John Burgess producing, at EMI Studios in London. Much to Denny's frustration, EMI decided that the songs didn't make the grade and let the band go.

Nine years on, the pair would revisit the stomping ground where Denny once hung out with the likes of future Led Zeppelin drummer John Bonham, and vocalist Bobby Davis (better known as comedian Jasper Carrott).

"John Bonham used to watch me and the Diplomats at the Wednesbury Youth Centre," Denny reflected. "Years later he stayed at my house, and we got drunk. He started singing 'Why Cry,' 'A Piece of Your Mind,' and a few other originals we used to do. He knew all the words and everything. Unbelievable."[67]

Coasting past Yardley Grammar School, where Laine took guitar lessons, they dropped in on Denny's parents, Herbert and Eva Hines, at 74 Holcombe Road, Tyseley.* Deep in conversation, they lost track of the time, and when their rental truck's headlights lit up the entrance to the Birmingham University campus, it was 5:15 p.m., and Paul was now debating whether they should return the following day. But the university Events Committee was desperate to please, hastily setting up the vacant Debating (or Deb) Hall, while the band refreshed themselves at the Priory Dean Hotel.

Getting to the Deb Hall a second time was trickier. Leaving the hotel at 7:30 p.m., they drove straight into stationary traffic. Navigating their way through the snow, 54,000 football fans were making their way toward Villa Park. Unknown to the band, local side Aston Villa were playing an exhibition match against Brazilian side Santos that evening. Wings would have to share the Birmingham spotlight with another visiting luminary—the South American footballing sensation Pelé.

As the whistle blew at Villa Park, the curtain went up on Wings at the Deb Hall. But rather than the two flames combining to burn brighter, both visiting idols had an off night: Brazilian maestro Pelé failed to shine, his team losing to Villa 2-1. Five miles away at the Deb Hall, the fading applause of 750 bouncing Brummies was no consolation for Paul's growing discontent.

"It wasn't the best gig,"[68] a downbeat Paul conceded. Nine dates in, the novelty had finally worn off. Paul and the band were losing confidence in the depth of their stage act and were keen to develop material for the follow-up to *Wild Life*.

"We had been planning to go on another week, but the last few concerts showed it was time to take a break from playing the same material, the same way, under those pressures,"[69] Denny Seiwell explained. Back at the Priory Dean Hotel, the band agreed to play one more date before heading back to London.

The next morning, they set a course for the port town of Cardiff in South Wales. Here, in the

---

* Herbert Edward Hines, a machine operator (born July 22, 1902) married Eva Lillian Bassett (born September 13, 1904) at St. Gabriel's Church, Birmingham, on June 6, 1925. Denny, christened Brian Frederick (for his grandfather, Frederick John) was one of five children (three daughters, two sons) born to the couple.

Welsh capital, a fourth rejection awaited. The reason is unclear: the local press reported that the University of Cardiff was staging a table tennis competition that afternoon, but Denny Laine has commented that late in the tour, the band was confronted by disgruntled students unimpressed with Wings' Irish record.[70] Neither story can be confirmed as the reason Wings did not perform.

Swansea University, just over an hour away in South Wales proved more fertile ground. Arriving in Swansea in the early afternoon, the band stopped in at Exchange and Mart, a music store run by Ivora and Graham Rowland, where they dropped several hundred pounds on three guitars—including a Höfner Senator, purchased by Denny Laine—as well as a violin and a stack of LPs.

Wings pulled into the university at 5:00 p.m., and three hours later, they were onstage at the Union House Hall. The pubs of Swansea emptied, and for two hours on February 22, the student population of South Wales, rarely visited by top-tier acts, basked in the glory of Wings in full flight.

"The venue was not known to promote any major bands performing in its small halls," said Andrew Lucas, one of the 800 fans who crammed into the small auditorium, "the only exception being Pink Floyd, who had played there a few years earlier and long before they were mainstream artists . . . The band started up and the rest of the evening rushed by at breathtaking speed. My head was in a whirl as I stood awestruck at being in the presence of a musical legend."[71]

"[When] we finished up at Swansea, I realized that it wasn't enough just saying, 'If anyone feels like having a dance, then have it,'" Paul remembered. "So, I said, 'These are our last three numbers now, GET UP!' And they all got up. If an audience isn't behaving the way I think they should, I'll tell them how to behave. Once they get up they love it; you just have to lead them."[72]

Fittingly, the road trip ended as it began, in an unknown guesthouse in an unvisited backwater. Overlooking Pwlldu Bay, the Ocean Meadows Hotel, Bishopston, was run by Mr. and Mrs. Norman Coleman. "Do I know you? Your face looks very familiar," Mrs. Coleman inquired as she checked in Mr. and Mrs. P. Martin. "Yes, I'm Dixon of Dock Green,"[73] joked Paul.

Discovering the true identity of her guests, Mrs. Coleman presented Mary and Heather with matching Welsh dolls in traditional dress. Paul and Linda promised to come back soon.

"We went on tour knowing it would either bring us together, or we wouldn't be able to stand each other, which was something we had to find out," Paul reflected. "We got on remarkably, wanting to do a common thing."[74]

On Wednesday, February 23, 1972, McCartney's wandering minstrels returned to London and turned their attention to the studio. Paul had secured recording time at Olympic Studios, in Barnes, West London, beginning March 6. He now had just two weeks to decide what would be on their next record.

---

* Many sources add an extra date at Oxford University. However, there is no mention of a concert in the university or local press, and Monique Seiwell's diary notes that the band returned to London on February 23. McCartney and Laine have also both said the tour ended in Swansea.

16

GETTING HIGH AND JAMMING

—

Back in London, the flames of controversy from Paul's Irish rallying call were still burning bright. After two weeks touring England and Wales, the McCartneys stepped through the door at Cavendish to an overflowing mailbox and a stack of unanswered telephone messages. Among them was a note from Dave Clark, a researcher for ITV's *Today* show, who tentatively sounded out Paul about a television appearance. Aware of the blanket ban on Wings' record, Clark explained that Thames Television—in which EMI was a substantial shareholder—was willing to make an exception and offer him a voice.

"We know that McCartney wanted to put out an ad on the channel and this was refused by our commercial department," Clark explained. "But our legal department has heard it and they're satisfied there's no harmful content as regards playing it."[1]

Today, a topical panel show hosted by Bill Grundy and Eamonn Andrews, encouraged Paul to join a studio debate of "points arising from his single." In return, the show's producers promised to give his song a rare play during the 6:00 p.m. broadcast. Paul turned down the request, explaining he was too busy to attend.

A more exceptional offer came from ex–Manfred Mann guitarist Tom McGuiness, who invited Wings to join him in the Irish capital of Dublin for a live television concert-cum-forum.* McGuiness shared common ground with McCartney. Both were of Irish descent, and a week after the Wings single was released, McGuiness's band, McGuiness Flint dropped 'Let the People Go'—a light-hearted folk tune in the model of Lennon's 'John Sinclair'—calling for the people of Northern Ireland to be set free. Unsurprisingly, McGuiness's record promptly joined 'Give Ireland Back to the Irish' on Mark White's BBC no-fly list.

---

* In Ireland, the record-buying public took 'Give Ireland Back to the Irish' at face value. Heavily backed by public service radio station RTE, it had advance orders of 3,000 copies. By March 25, Wings hit the No. 1 spot in the *Irish Hit Parade*, in spite of reviews like Tony Wilson's, in the *Irish Evening Herald*, which described the tune as "disappointing," and the lyrics as "trite."

"The song *is* anti-internment, but it seems strange that editorials can appear in the national press criticizing it—while they will not accept the same thing from a group," said McGuiness, blasting the BBC's heavy-handedness. "This is straightforward political censorship, which is as wrong as internment."[2]

Though tempting, the invitation came at a delicate time. Across London, Henry's brother Victor was still nursing a dozen stitches in his temple from the Kilburn attack, and Paul feared the band could also be targeted. John and Yoko had marched with Irish protesters in London, back in August 1971, but that was not an option for Paul and Linda. The assault on Victor McCullough rattled McCartney; he had gone from putting up a front for the press to feeling too intimidated to leave his comfort zone in London.

He was not giving up on the cause, though, paying for a third round of bordering-on-angry trade ads in the big five music papers.*

---

* This ad was followed up by another in the *Daily Mirror* on March 20, saying: "McCARTNEY BEATS BAN! Despite the BBC ban the record is in the Top 20 in every British chart—and going up. Have you heard it?"

While McCartney continued to protest the group's artistic and political castration at arm's length, Wings' only Irish-born member, Henry, kept out of the fray. Pressed for a comment by *Disc,** he seemed oddly aloof.

"If you really listen to the single, it's just a message from Paul to Mr. Heath. He doesn't have to know any more about the situation than he does already. We don't feel obliged to go over there. No one's *that* involved really."[3] Only months later did he confess that he "had to go through lots of little personal encounters because of what the song said."[4]

"He didn't return home for years after that,"[5] said Denny Seiwell of his bandmate.

But no number of trade ads could change the fortunes of Wings' debut single; the ban was the commercial death knell for 'Give Ireland Back to the Irish.' With potential buyers unable to hear it on the radio, sales were sufficient to keep it on the British Record Retailer's Top 100 chart for only eight weeks, entering at 49 on February 26, and peaking at 16, four weeks later.

In America, the sensitivities were not quite as raw as those in Britain. Though Americans followed news of the massacre with some alarm—the *New York Times*, in an editorial published on February 7, called the situation "Britain's Vietnam"—the dispute was well down a list of immediate concerns that was topped by Vietnam itself.

Moreover, while American networks might have exerted pressure to stifle political protest back in 1967, when CBS censors suppressed Pete Seeger's *Smothers Brothers Comedy Hour* performance of 'Waist Deep in the Big Muddy,' a clear Vietnam war protest, such censorship was rare by 1972. And that was where *American* politics was concerned; media outlets in America were unlikely to consider banning a song because it might offend the British government.

Around February 18, cutting engineer Lee Hulko mastered the US release at Sterling Sound in New York, and it was issued ten days later. And though controversy raged in Britain, the single, described by *Variety* as a "catchy rocker,"[6] received widespread airplay in the United States.

To promote their latest hit across the water, Paul and Linda agreed to an interview with the American Broadcasting Company (ABC), on March 2. Throughout the conversation, filmed late at night in his music room, Paul appeared nervous, repeatedly gazing at the ground as he answered the reporters' questions.

"I was born in Britain, and the song's written from a British point of view. I've had people saying, 'You shouldn't talk if you're not Irish,' but it's the British Army that's causing all the trouble. And the Irish got taken over about 800 years ago, a little bit of it, by the British, and they injected British people into there and made it a little bit of Britain. But I have always really thought of it as one place—Ireland. Me as a British citizen, I don't like my army going around and shooting my Irish brothers."[7]

---

* *Disc and Music Echo* became *Disc* in April 1972.

To lift the tenor of their news piece (and since the footage was of no use to him in London) Paul handed the film crew a reel of home rehearsal footage shot by Mottram and Spicer on February 1. The feature was broadcast five days later on ABC News.

But promotion and radio airtime didn't guarantee chart success. Wings' single spent only eight weeks on the *Billboard* Hot 100, entering at 78 on March 11, and peaking at 21 on April 8.

The single did, however, achieve unlikely success in Spain, where it reached No. 1 on May 27, displacing popular Spanish singer Mari Trini's 'Yo No Soy Esa' and holding off stiff competition from Chicory Tip's 'Son of My Father.'

———

On the morning of March 2, before his ABC News interview, Paul straddled the brown leather chair in his music room and made a list of the songs that might form Wings' second album. With his head resting on the spot where Ringo had so often looked for a beat, he ran his hand along the chair's left arm, fingering a puncture hole made by Lennon's mighty correction pencil. That antique brown chair had been the creative conduit for 'Hey Jude' and 'Michelle.' Now, on the page before him, Paul noted the latest songs by which his credibility as a songwriter would be judged.

In moments of brutally honest introspection, Paul was concerned about the trajectory of his recent work, having seen himself go from someone who could virtually do no wrong as a member of the Beatles, to a musician as susceptible as the next guy to critical laceration, as a solo artist.

"When the Beatles broke up," he said in a moment of tough self-analysis, "I personally think my music took a bit of a knock. I lost direction in songwriting.[8] I thought *McCartney* was quite good. . . . But then it didn't quite do it in every way. It did it sales-wise, but it didn't do it critically. . . . After it got knocked, I thought—it was very obvious in a way—I'll do just the opposite next time. So, *Ram* was with the top people in the top studio. I thought, 'This is what they want.' But, again, it was critically panned, though it did very well with the public. Then I thought, 'Oh, so they don't want the big production job.' So, I recorded *Wild Life* in two weeks. . . . But that was kind of critically panned. . . . So, we thought we'd get it together a bit."[9]

One thing he could say in behalf of his stack of recent compositions is that it took its strength from its eclecticism. Looking at 'The Mess I'm In,' 'Best Friend,' 'My Love,' 'When the Night,' 'Thank You Darling,' 'Country Dreamer,' 'Mama's Little Girl,' '1882,' 'Single Pigeon,' 'Mary Had a Little Lamb,' 'One More Kiss,' 'Power Cut,' and 'Baby Dynamite,' Paul saw the makings of an album that would cover considerable stylistic ground.

He also knew that, if necessary, he could lean on a bulging box of *Ram* rejects. 'Get on the Right Thing' and 'Little Woman Love' had been mixed for the aborted November 1971 single, and 'Hey Diddle,' 'The Great Cock and Seagull Race,' and 'Rode All Night' were solid B-side options.

There was greater strength in 'Little Lamb Dragonfly' and 'I Lie Around,' both of which had already been symphonically enhanced by an ensemble of New York freelancers.

But that Thursday morning, another *Ram* refugee entered Paul's thoughts as he coolly strummed a ukulele—'Big Barn Bed.' Composed at High Park and included on his Spring 1970 pre-*Ram* demo cassette, a few bars of the song were ad-libbed during the 'Ram On' session at A&R Studios, with a snippet appearing on *Ram* as an odd coda to the light-textured ukulele song. Now he imagined it with the full weight of a band behind it. A knock at the door meant he would soon have an answer, as Henry and the two Dennys arrived for rehearsals.

While the band tuned up, Paul dropped the news that he had drafted producer Glyn Johns to help shape Wings' next record at Olympic Studios. Though *Wild Life* had its honest charms, sales figures were poor, and he felt Johns would offer the group sharper musical direction. McCartney knew Johns well, and though he had a reputation for occasionally being difficult and headstrong, Paul felt he was equipped to strike a balance between glossy production and authentic live sound.

"I respected him and liked working with him. But he's serious," said Paul of Johns. "He doesn't just tell you what you wanna hear. If he doesn't like a thing, he'll just say he doesn't like it. That's a good thing. It's not easy to work with, but it's well worth persevering, because you know he makes you make a better record."[10]

Paul and Johns had worked together on the Beatles' abandoned *Get Back* album in 1969, the fruits of which only the bootleg buying public had sampled in its purest form.* Johns delivered the "naked" album that McCartney craved, presenting the Beatles at their most raw and vulnerable, before the album was given the Phil Spector "wall of sound" treatment.

Being removed from the helm by Allen Klein had not dented Johns's confidence. Between 1970 and the start of 1972, he produced albums for a who's who of rock nobility, including Bob Dylan (*Self Portrait*), The Band (*Stage Fright*), the Faces (*A Nod Is As Good As a Wink . . . to a Blind Horse*), Graham Nash (*Songs for Beginners*), the Rolling Stones (*Sticky Fingers*), The Who (*Who's Next*), and the Eagles (*Eagles*).

Johns shared McCartney's caution; only Jim Guercio had attempted to produce a Paul McCartney record, his tenure lasting less than two weeks. Talking to *NME* about the Wings project, just before recording began, Johns laughed off any suggestion that he could ever play puppet master to an ex-Beatle.

"Who me? I really doubt it. I mean, he knows more about producing his own records than I ever will. The reason I want to do it is because I want to learn. He's such an incredible dude to work with. It's just a buzz being around people who are that creative."[11]

---

* A version of the Glyn Johns mixed-and-sequenced *Get Back* album was included in the *Let It Be Super Deluxe Edition* in 2021. Curiously, though the included sequence is listed as the 1969 mix of the album, the American and British sets included a version of 'For You Blue' with extra overdubs from 1970. The *Let It Be Super Deluxe Edition* released in Japan, however, has the straight 1969 sequence.

Recording Session

Monday, March 6, 1972.
Olympic Studios, Studio One, London.
Recording: 'Big Barn Bed.'

A short stroll from the banks of the River Thames in Barnes, southwest London, Olympic Studios was to the Rolling Stones what EMI Studios at Abbey Road was to the Beatles. A treadmill for the Stones' blues strut, the group cut five consecutive albums there between 1966 and 1971.

Managed by engineer Keith Grant, the architect of mid-'60s hits for the Yardbirds and the Troggs, the Church Road facilities had entertained the Beatles on occasion (and famously, Yoko Ono in a double bed, as she recovered from a car accident in the summer of 1969). The basic tracks for 'Baby You're a Rich Man,' 'All You Need Is Love,' and 'You Never Give Me Your Money' were tracked in Studio One, as were guitar and bass overdubs on George's 'Something.' Much of the unreleased *Get Back* album was mixed, compiled, and recompiled at Olympic. And Ringo Starr joined B.B. King's all-star band (which included Steve Winwood, Gary Wright, Klaus Voormann, Rick Wright, and Jim Keltner) to track *B.B. King in London* at the former theater-turned-recording rooms in June 1971.

Of course, the studio held mixed memories for McCartney. Three years earlier, in this very room, the Beatles business differences came to a head when Paul refused to sign Allen Klein's management agreement, and he spent the rest of that angst-filled night recording with Steve Miller. Fittingly, the product of that session, Miller's 'My Dark Hour,' released as a single in the United States and Britain in 1969, was reissued on a British EP shortly before the impending run of Wings sessions.

But today, Paul was facing not his dark hour, but what he hoped was a new dawn with a new band.

The studios had been completely redesigned recently by Grant's architect father, Robertson Grant, to improve the acoustics and soundproofing. To lessen sonic leakage between the rooms, Studio Two, where McCartney and Miller jammed, had been rebuilt inside a floating box on rubber pads, and adjustable wooden slats (like Venetian blinds) were fitted to both studios to improve sound deflection. Grant's rooms were more in demand than ever.

Since the Beatles breakup Paul had seen Olympic as a solid fallback option, but when he added oboe overdubs to 'Some People Never Know' at Olympic Studio One the previous September, he began to think that a break from Abbey Road might help Wings find their own sound. Six months on, he entered the 60-by-40-foot space that gave birth to Jimi's *Are You Experienced?*, hoping some of that Hendrix stardust was still in the air.

Paul and Linda were welcomed to Studio One by Johns and in-house balance engineer Phil Chapman, who would handle the recording.

"The day after I finished with the Eagles, I went straight in with Paul McCartney and Wings,"[12] said Johns. "[I remember] him walking into the control room on the first day and saying, 'I want you to treat me like the bass player in the band, not Paul McCartney of the Beatles.'"[13] (Johns soon observed that McCartney's democratic impulse was wafer thin; when he started treating him like a lowly bass player, Paul quickly exerted his authority.)

Fresh from the road, Paul and the band soon found their groove jamming the newly absorbed 'Big Barn Bed.' As the musicians worked up a collective sweat, Johns and Chapman shifted baffles and microphones.

"Glyn got the best drum sound out of me at Olympic that I'd ever had," said Seiwell. "He only used three microphones—it was kind of a famous technique that he had. He'd place a fancy U67 Neumann mic up above, one behind, and one way out in front of the bass drum, and then he'd blend it. So, the drummer actually created his own sound, it's more of an acoustic sound."[14]

Johns's three-microphone system—one panned left, one right, and one centered—was revered by engineers the world over. But Johns later admitted that his signature recording technique happened by chance during a session with childhood friend Jimmy Page, and Led Zeppelin.

"I stole a microphone off the drums for Jimmy to overdub an acoustic guitar, and we did that in ten minutes, it was very quick. And then I put the mic back on the drums and we started running down the next number. I'd assigned that microphone to the left, normally the drums were all mono in the middle. By the time I got back into the control room they'd started to play again. I lifted the faders up on the drums, and this mic was still assigned to the left and I thought, 'Blimey, that sounds interesting.' So now the drums are coming from the middle and the left. And I thought, I wonder what would happen if I put that one to the right? So, it was a mistake!"[15]

Inside the cocoon of the control room, Johns and Chapman struggled to capture the spirit of Paul's bass performance. On review, the bass track sounded flat, lacking the bite of those early Beatles records. As Paul noodled on the studio floor, Johns picked his brain.

"My favorite bass sound, for years and years and years, was McCartney's bass on 'Paperback Writer.' Astonishing," explained Johns. "I'd never asked Paul anything about what they'd done in the past before. [But] I asked, 'Okay, how'd you get the bass sound on 'Paperback Writer'?' He said, 'Oh, the mic was a couple of feet away from the cabinet. The cabinet was a Fender. It was a [Neumann U] 67.' I'd never used a 67 on bass. I thought I'd give that a go."[16] After a few small adjustments the band was ready for a take.

Microphones and levels set, Chapman threaded up a fresh two-inch reel on the 16-track deck, and the sessions for Wings' second album were underway. With Paul playing bass, Denny Laine on acoustic guitar, Henry playing electric guitar, and Denny Seiwell and Linda delivering a thumping, percussive backing on drums and vibraslap, Wings ran through 'Big Barn Bed.'

Opening with a lyric and melody pinched from '5:10 Men,' the 1969 Masters Apprentices tune, and now led by mellow guitar licks courtesy of Henry's gold top Gibson Les Paul, 'Big Barn Bed' had been recast from a countryish ukulele tune into a blues-rock number that would not feel out of place on a record by the Band. Johns's job, as he saw it, was to capture its bluesy grit on tape; he looked to the musicians for a killer performance, rather than relying on studio trickery.

"It's essential for anyone that works with music to know what they're doing really," Johns explained, "because I want something good from them rather than me making it sound good, because it's lousy. You can't make a silk purse out of a sow's ear as they say."[17]

Luckily, touring had melded the band into a tighter unit than they had been a month earlier. McCartney's bass and Seiwell's drums instantly locked together, while Laine's energetic, jangling acoustic guitar blended seamlessly with McCullough's striking, dark-hued lead guitar lines. By midafternoon, Johns gave the basic track the thumbs-up, and they moved on to overdubs.

Onto the master take, McCartney added a vibrant piano part during the song's finale and Laine added a second acoustic guitar, before the band gathered around a microphone to countrify the choruses with four-part vocal harmonies. Content with what they had captured on tape, they set the song aside.

Recording Session

Tuesday, March 7, 1972.
Olympic Studios, Studio One, London.
Recording: 'When the Night.'

Though well acquainted with the pressures of the studio's red light from both the *Ram* and *Wild Life* sessions, Linda was still finding her feet as a studio musician, so she largely took a back seat during their first session with Johns. Not that Linda and Johns were strangers.

"During the first session she walked into the control room, and she said, 'Thank God it's you!'" Johns recalled. "Because we'd made friends while we were doing *Get Back/Let It Be*, and I was new to the band, and she was new as well. And we sort of buddied up, being the new kids on the block, as it were. She knew she had a friend in the control room."[18]

It is unlikely Johns was blind to Linda's challenges. With less than a year of dedicated keyboard playing under her belt (her only serious nonvocal contributions to *Wild Life* were unadorned keyboard parts on 'Love Is Strange' and 'Wild Life'), she was out of place in the ballroom-like studio space that had played home to some of the world's finest recording artists. And while the rest of the band had a solid musical rapport, Linda required frequent attention. But she never claimed to be Paul's musical peer.

"I learned chords, but that's not enough," Linda admitted. "You need a feel for it. I wasn't naturally rhythmic like Paul.[19] You get some painters who can recreate beautiful photographs. Others are abstract. I fall into the second category when it comes to music."[20]

Yet she had played to nearly 10,000 people across nine venues in February, and her chronic self-consciousness surfaced only once. Paul still believed that with encouragement and tutoring Linda could develop competence at the keyboard. The former he had no problem providing, but the latter was still proving elusive. Whenever the McCartneys sat down at the piano together their tinkering would frequently descend into a row, so Paul arranged for Linda to take lessons with an elderly neighbor, Mrs. Matthews, who lived in a basement flat opposite Paul's London home.

During their second session Paul encouraged Linda to free herself from the shackles of self-doubt. The most logical song for Linda's Olympic debut might have been 'The Mess I'm In,' a song she had played every night of the tour. But rather than risking an up-tempo number, Paul decided the moderately paced call-and-response ballad 'When the Night,' written at the beginning of the year, was a safer choice. Since the end of the tour the band had rehearsed the simple chord progression, and, with the help of her husband, Linda had plotted out a straightforward bass keyboard part.

'When the Night' had its roots in classic American Motown and doo-wop, but in a striking production touch, McCartney and Johns used nylon-string acoustic guitar figures, played by Laine and McCullough, to give the arrangement a slightly Spanish, melancholy twist. Paul led the session on grand piano, with Linda providing fuzz-toned bass accents on an electric keyboard. Offsetting Linda's bass figures, Seiwell tapped out a dense, hypnotic, high-hat beat.

"Most drummers tend to get a bit flash," Seiwell pointed out, "but good drummers never play a lot of fancy stuff. Buddy Rich is a fantastic drummer, but Elvin Jones plays a lot less and swings a lot more. Drums have to put a heartbeat, a pulse, into a song. I fell into this little loop, an odd drumbeat that repeated itself, and it worked so beautifully for the song."[21]

The basic track was completed in no time, leaving much of the afternoon free for arranging and overdubbing the song's rich choral harmonies. During the verses, each phrase sung by Paul (with the exception of the second line) was echoed by five voices: "*Well the night (well the night), was beautiful and mellow (mellow, mellow), and the light (and the light), of the night (of the night), fell on me (fell on me).*" That doo-wop style vocal arrangement was topped off with a second five-part chorus, harmonizing on "ooh" throughout, with Denny Seiwell's deep bass tones making the song a showcase for the group's broad collective vocal range.

Before wrapping for the day, Paul overdubbed his lead vocal, scat-vocalizing (in the style of a kazoo) ideas for Henry's guitar solo during the instrumental break.

Recording Session

Wednesday, March 8, 1972.
Olympic Studios, Studio One, London.
Recording: 'The Mess.'

In the two weeks since Swansea University, 'The Mess' had been trimmed in both name (edited from 'The Mess I'm In') and duration (cut from six to five minutes). For the song to work on record, Paul felt, it needed a more definitive arrangement, so what emerged from the Scotch of St. James on January 20 as a free-form jam was given tighter focus.

"Paul always had stuff structured, you know," McCullough elaborated. "And would never let guitar solos go past eight, twelve bars or something. There was no ad-libbing at all."[22]

During rehearsals—Paul on bass; Denny Laine and Henry, electric guitars; Linda, keyboard; and Denny Seiwell, drums—Johns and McCartney further decluttered 'The Mess.' The tour arrangement that had featured all five instruments throughout was simplified, with the coproducers opting to hold back Linda's keyboard part until the song's finale.

But structure and discipline rode roughshod over the raw unbridled energy of the version Wings had played in concert, and something in the studio version was not clicking. The red light flashed on and off as the band recorded take after take, trying to capture on tape the gritty, off-the-cuff sound that still rang in the ears of students across the country.

The master take was a stilted, near-lifeless recording that would mostly likely be consigned to Glyn Johns's "sow's ear" pile. Paul was unwilling to accept defeat, though, and as the band passed around a joint in the control room, he overdubbed a honky-tonk piano, organ swells during the refrains, and a throaty lead vocal. But on playback, it still sounded flat. What was once a vehicle for McCullough's dazzling guitar skills now lacked guts. McCartney decided to return to the song another time.

Recording Session

Thursday, March 9, 1972.
Olympic Studios, Studio One, London.
Recording: 'Single Pigeon.'

By the time Henry and the two Dennys sauntered into the studio on Thursday, Paul was settled at the piano playing his new anthropomorphic ballad 'Single Pigeon' for Glyn Johns. Written in London at the start of the year, 'Single Pigeon' is a colorful, yet tentative piano ballad, the tale of a pigeon cast out on the street by his lover after a fight. Images of a seagull—the song's other avian protagonist—gliding over Regent's Park ground the song firmly in Paul and Linda's backyard and give it an autobiographical hue.

Ignoring for a moment that they were in a recording studio, with the meter running, Seiwell picked up a bass guitar, Laine a pair of drumsticks, and Henry, sitting on his amp, merrily strummed along on guitar. Sensing there was an innocent magic in what they were playing, Paul signaled Johns and engineer Chapman to roll the tape.

Between takes the band shared smokes and laughs, and Linda abandoned the control room for Paul's side at the piano bench. McCartney's performance had an unassuming brilliance, but Johns was bemused by the rest. Seiwell could barely play a note on bass, plus the instrument was out of tune. Laine was so stoned he could only muster a solitary cymbal crash during the entire song. The mask of professionalism had taken only four days to slip.

"They wanted to enjoy themselves in the studio," Johns observed, with barely concealed scorn, a few weeks later. "They obviously like to take their time over recording. I'd say 'fantastic' if I could see a good end result emerging. Their idea of having a good time isn't mine necessarily, that's the point."[23]

In Johns's eyes, the sessions had become an extension of the group's recent touring holiday, and he was left a frustrated outsider. Now, the nomadic touring spirit that had brought the band close together was in danger of pushing their producer out the door.

"It was the time to go in the studio, because the band were tight," says Denny Laine. "We went in with Glyn Johns because he was well known as a producer. But then you're bringing someone new into the mix, so then you've got the difficulty of having to work with somebody you don't know. There's always a conflict there, always."[24]

Seven days earlier, Johns and Chapman were putting the finishing touches on the Eagles' nine-song debut album, which the American outfit recorded and mixed in just 14 days. "I was impressed by how professional and prepared the Eagles were,"[25] Phil Chapman noted of the country-rock combo. But four days into his stint with Wings, Johns was finding it difficult to detect that characteristic McCartney magic.

During the Eagles' sessions, Johns insisted on a no drink, no drugs rule, a policy that got a mixed reception with the Los Angeles quintet. Pushing the same restrictions on someone of McCartney's stature was an embarrassing prospect. Instead, he sat back and bit his lip.

Recording Session

Monday, March 13, 1972.
Olympic Studios, Studio One, London.
Recording: 'Tragedy.'

Sensing that Johns was losing patience with Wings, Paul returned to Olympic after a long weekend with renewed fervor. Captivated by the soulful vocal blend they had achieved on 'When the Night,' Paul stepped into the control room, placed an old 45 on the turntable, and dropped the needle on a record he thought the band might cover. The choice of song, even by his eclectic standards, was odd, but the assembled ears pricked up as the warm, nostalgic sound of Thomas Wayne's 1959 'Tragedy' piped out of the speakers.

Written by Fred B. Burch and Gerald H. Nelson, 'Tragedy' was the one and only hit for the Panola, Mississippi-born musician Thomas Wayne Perkins.* Recorded under the alias Thomas Wayne and the Delons (a made-up name for the trio of high school girls recruited to sing backing vocals), 'Tragedy' rose to No. 5 in the *Billboard* Hot 100 on March 23, 1959. The single's British release, late in 1958, had limited success. But Perkins's death in an automobile collision, as he was driving to a Memphis recording session in the early hours of August 15, 1971, led to a resurgence in airplay; the McCartneys were captivated by it when they heard it on the radio in New York a few months later.

---

* Thomas Wayne Perkins was the brother of guitarist Luther Perkins, who, along with Marshall Grant, was one of the founders of the simple, pounding, guitar and bass sound that characterized the early music of Johnny Cash. Luther perished under tragic circumstances, losing his life in a house fire, at his Hendersonville, Tennessee home, on August 5, 1968. Thomas Wayne's version of 'Tragedy'—the first recording of the song—was clearly the most decisive influence on the Wings cover, but versions by the Fleetwoods (1961), Brenda Lee (1961) and Brian Hyland (1969) were all available before Wings took the song into the studio.

"It was one of those songs that a lot of people would have picked up on hanging around amusement arcades in the summertime when they were younger," McCullough said of Wayne's hit. "It would have been in there along with Charlie Gracie; he had a record called 'Fabulous.'"[26]

Recording the backing track in essentially the same style producer Scotty Moore had used in 1958, McCartney played bass, Laine and McCullough acoustic guitars, and Seiwell drums. The intro was elongated, with pizzicato figures, plucked in tandem by Laine and McCullough, and the original's two-minute running time was extended to 3'21" by the addition of an extra middle-eight, verse, and chorus. The basic track was perfected in eight takes (Take 8 being the master), leaving the afternoon free to overdub Paul's lead vocal and a lavish chorus of harmony and backing vocals.

Though echoing the sentiment of the original production, Johns and McCartney simplified Moore's choral arrangement in places, allowing Paul's vocal more space to breathe; and the Delons' 1950s style "wa-ooh-wa-ooh" harmonies were updated with more contemporary "oohs." The result,- finished with a drop of tremolo guitar from Henry, is every bit as exquisite as Perkins's original.

Recording Session

Tuesday, March 14, 1972.
Olympic Studios, Studio One, London.
Recording: 'Mama's Little Girl.'

Continuing the model of recording a song per day, Tuesday was spent sketching out the basic track for Paul's pastoral folk tune 'Mama's Little Girl,' a recent addition to his growing archive of melodies written with his trio of girls in mind. Drawing inspiration from folk-pop masters Simon and Garfunkel, whose vocals always took center stage, McCartney and Johns stripped back the rhythm section to just acoustic guitar (McCartney), percussion (Seiwell) and bass guitar (Laine).

"I remember we brought a whole bunch of African drums in for that and I was clicking sticks on the side, and using the drum skin heads,"[27] said Seiwell.

The bare folk instrumentation shone a spotlight on Paul's sweet, family-centric lyrics, but consigned Henry and Linda to the shadows. Henry noodled a low-end electric guitar line (so low in frequency and volume that it's almost indistinguishable from the bass guitar) while Linda sporadically thwacked a snare drum.

The Beatles had given Paul a harsh schooling in group politics and the delicate balance between production and band morale. One of the toughest lessons he had to internalize was that his sometimes-overbearing nature, born of his perfectionism and a clear vision of his goals, could be off-putting, as each of his former colleagues had noted in their Apple lawsuit affidavits. He did not want to make the same mistake a second time. If Wings were to be a band, and not just *the Paul McCartney quintet*, he realized, he needed to loosen the reins.

But for Paul, that was much easier conceptualized than done, and whenever an opportunity to share the spotlight with his band members arose, the sense that Wings was an expression of *his* vision took over.

"In my mind, a band is a democratic unit," he reasoned. "Everyone has an equal vote, and in the Beatles for ten years that had been the case. There wasn't a leader in the Beatles. I think once or twice in Hamburg, in the early days, John said, 'I am.' But we got pissed off, so it became a democracy. But in Wings that wasn't the case. I was the ex-Beatle, so I saw myself as the leader of the group, which I'd never been in the Beatles. It wasn't a dictatorship, but we weren't all equal."[28]

The slow interlude midway through 'Mama's Little Girl' was potentially a place for Henry to stamp his creative authority, but Paul had other ideas, earmarking the break for an ensemble of clarinets. When the group gathered around a couple of microphones for yet another choral session, McCullough would not have been ill-judged for considering himself just a backing singer.

Still starstruck by the bandleader, though, McCullough held back his fiery Irish temper. "At present I'm still learning some of the numbers, but I think there could be scope for my own ideas eventually," he told a reporter a couple of weeks later.[29]

———

Stoking the fire back in St. John's Wood, Paul and Linda settled in front of the box on Tuesday night, knowing they could have, and probably should have, been in New York. 'Uncle Albert/Admiral Halsey' was nominated for a Grammy Award (McCartney's 31st nomination) and Paul and Linda had turned down the chance to attend the ceremony at the Felt Forum, in Madison Square Garden.

Being hard at work on his next album was as good a reason as any not to attend, but there were other forces at play, as well. One was that George's 'My Sweet Lord' and *All Things Must Pass* were nominated for Record and Album of the Year, and Paul's relationship with George was still shaky enough that Paul would not have relished an encounter. Another was that the Bacharach and David theme for *Long Ago Tomorrow* (the title used for the American release of Bryan Forbes's movie *The Raging Moon*) was nominated in the same category as they were. Win or lose, there was the possibility of an awkward brush with Forbes at the awards dinner, never mind the possible humiliation of losing out to the title song for a film Paul had passed up (not that his brief involvement with the project was public knowledge).

In the early hours of Wednesday morning, John Eastman rang with news from New York. At a ceremony dominated by Carole King's *Tapestry*—which scooped Best Record, Album and Song—Paul and Linda held off competition from Marvin Gaye's 'What's Going On,' the Carpenters' 'Superstar,' Bill Medley's 'Freedom and Fear,' and B.J. Thomas's 'Long Ago Tomorrow,' to win the Grammy for Best Arrangement Accompanying Vocalist(s).

Harrison, who also didn't show up for the awards, struck out entirely.

The victory was gratifying on many levels: though this was Paul's seventh Grammy,* it was the couple's first collective award; they had not been shown up by Bacharach and David, or by George, and the award vindicated Paul's feeling that the critics were wrong about *Ram*.

Recording Sessions

Wednesday–Friday, March 15–17, 1972.
Olympic Studios, Studio One, London.
Recording: 'Loup (1st Indian on the Moon)'

Strutting into the studio on Wednesday morning, Paul brought with him the spirit of a Grammys after-party; if he and Linda couldn't be in New York, they would bring the revelry to London. Trailing the beaming McCartneys, roadies Trevor and Ian carried Linda's brand-new £600 ($1,500) box of tricks—a Minimoog Model D monophonic synthesizer.

McCartney first clapped eyes on the Moog synthesizer in the aftermath of George Harrison's visit to Los Angeles in November 1968. Dazzled by Bernie Krause's and Paul Beaver's demonstration of the Moog One, George ordered one on the spot. "I had to have mine made specially, Robert Moog had only just invented it,"† explained Harrison, not entirely accurately. "It was enormous, with hundreds of jack-plugs and two keyboards."[30]

During the Beatles' *Abbey Road* sessions, Harrison's cabinet-like gadget took up residence at EMI Studios and was featured on the songs 'Maxwell's Silver Hammer,' 'I Want You (She's So Heavy),' 'Here Comes the Sun,' and 'Because.'

Unlike the multimodule, patch-cord-sprouting Moog One, the Minimoog's technological wiz-

---

* Paul first tasted Grammy success in 1964, when *A Hard Day's Night* won Best Performance by a Vocal Group. He also scored victories with 'Eleanor Rigby' (Best Contemporary Solo Vocal Performance, 1966), 'Michelle' (Song of the Year, 1966), *Sgt. Pepper's Lonely Hearts Club Band* (Best Contemporary Album and Best Album of the Year, 1967) and *Let It Be* (Best Original Score Written for a Motion Picture or a Television Special, 1970). This new addition to his shelf was his first Grammy for his post-Beatles work.

† Robert Moog, born May 23, 1934, died August 21, 2005, actually built his first synthesizer, a version of the Theremin, in the early 1950s, and founded the R.A. Moog company in 1954. He built the first modules for what became the Moog synthesizer in 1964, working with the electronic music composer Herbert Deutsch. By the time George Harrison bought his Moog One, the Monkees had already used the instrument on their *Pisces, Aquarius, Capricorn and Jones, Ltd.* album.

ardry was packaged inside a standard keyboard casing, and it was infinitely easier to program—no complicated patching required. "Just plug in and go, you can learn in just a few hours"[31] the trade advert boasted. By tinkering with the synthesizer's bank of oscillators and filters, a player could produce otherworldly sounds by striking a single key—perfect for a keyboard novice like Linda.

To test-drive Linda's new toy, the band fell in on a simple two-chord jazz progression in A minor. Fiddling with the controls on the Minimoog, Linda hit an A, and a deep, nearly distorted growl unexpectedly thundered out of the amplifier.

"Whoa! What the fuck was that?!" roared Henry. "I don't know whether she meant it to come out or not, or whether it just happened—but it's a mind-fucker!"[32]

A second twiddle of the frequency oscillator, and each note sounded like it had been captured by a NASA deep-space probe—sounds reminiscent of parts of 'Kontakte,' a seminal, 35-minute electronic work by the German avant-gardist Karlheinz Stockhausen. Paul often cited Stockhausen's 'Kontakte' (1959-60) and 'Gesange der Jungelinge' (1955-56) as works that particularly delighted him when he was discovering experimental music, around 1966, and he sometimes used bits of 'Kontakte' as soundtrack music for his late-'60s home movies.[33] Now the possibility of making those sounds himself was within his grasp; but for the moment, he left that to Linda.

Soon, the jam morphed into a fusion of jazz, prog-rock, sci-fi and Native American music (or at least, Wings' impression of it). Paul was in his element. Embracing this heterogeneous aural jigsaw puzzle, he tossed the sonic pieces in the air, and over a period of two days 'Loup (1st Indian on the Moon)' was born. Flying in the face of his "treat me like the bass player" plea, on the studio floor, Paul had taken complete control, relegating Johns to the role of an indifferent onlooker. Onto a basic track of drums, bass, electric guitars, and organ, McCartney oversaw percussion (tapping on a metal pan), further electric guitar and more Moog overdubs.

The finished track could happily have slotted into the track list for Pink Floyd's 1971 album *Meddle*, more Waters-Gilmour than Lennon-McCartney in style.

"The whole thing, it's like a plant," Paul mused about the track, like a hippie on a heavy trip. "I like the idea that it can just grow where it likes, and like any plant you don't know exactly where that shoot's going to grow to."[34]

Glyn Johns, by contrast, was flummoxed by the group's self-indulgent, two-day pot-infused trip. "They were just getting high and jamming,"[35] he grumbled. His disapproval was not lost on the band. According to Johns, when the session wound down, the two Dennys took him to one side to take him to task.

"They said, 'We're not happy with you as a producer. You're not taking any interest in what we are doing.' I said, 'When you do something that's interesting, I'm there. But if you think because you are playing with Paul McCartney that everything you do is a gem of marvelous music, you're wrong. It isn't. It's shite. Frankly it's a waste of tape and it's a waste of my energy.'"[36]

Recording Sessions

Monday–Tuesday, March 20–21, 1972.
Olympic Studios, Studio One, London.
Recording: 'Seaside Woman.'

To compound Paul's problems with producer Johns, his legal dispute with ATV/Northern Songs was still simmering. A demo of Linda's reggae composition 'Seaside Woman,' recorded on an old EMI four-track machine at Rude Studio, had already been given to his legal counsel as proof of her musical and lyrical skills. But Paul thought a more polished recording could add further weight to their case.

The band spent two days giving Linda's tune a complete overhaul. The tour arrangement was scrapped, a new intro added, plus fresh keyboard and electric guitar parts. From pop-reggae, the track became a shining tribute to the Caribbean 'Rock' of Jamaica.

A rough mix was run off for McCartney's legal team, and the tape set aside for future overdubs. If the song didn't make the cut, Paul and Linda planned to release it as a single under Linda's recently adopted reggae moniker, Suzy and the Redstripes.

Recording Session

Wednesday, March 22, 1972.
Olympic Studios, Studio One, London.
Recording: 'I Would Only Smile.'

On Wednesday, Wings' tour of the world's musical styles shifted from Jamaica to Nashville, as the band recorded the basic track for Denny Laine's lightweight country tune, 'I Would Only Smile.' In Denny, Paul saw a promising creative foil, but the McCartney-Laine partnership had yet to take off. By his own admission, Denny was not a prolific songwriter, and he was conscious that bringing half-baked songs to a (former) member of the most successful writing partnership in modern music was like presenting a Michelin-starred chef cheese on toast.

"I was just feeling my way—you always do," said Laine. "I was frustrated in some ways that I wasn't progressing enough with my own songs. But on the other hand, it was balanced by what I was doing with the band."[37]

But there was a bigger problem choking any possible writing partnership. Laine was still under contract with former Moody Blues manager Tony Secunda, who had no intention of cutting him loose. Secunda helped finance the fruitless Midlands supergroup Balls, and when the group failed to gel, he made it clear that he intended to recoup his lost investment. Denny had hoped to pay that debt with his solo album, but he set that aside to join Wings.

Not only would any McCartney-Laine composition face scrutiny from Northern Songs (with whom Paul remained under contract until February 1973), but Tony Secunda would also want his piece of the royalty pie. And though any payment to Secunda would come from Denny's cut of the song royalties, involving a third party would further muddy the waters when it came to music publishing.

"There are problems as far as publishing are concerned," Denny said. "That is the only hang-up with Wings. We could be doing many more things, but we had to go at a certain pace because of management problems. . . . You have to have a very professional attitude to it all, and that's the way we all are with Wings at the moment."[38]

Lee Eastman was visiting London that week, and as they put the finishing touches to Denny's song, Paul set up a meeting between the band and Eastman to discuss where they stood.

Recording Session

Thursday, March 23, 1972.
Olympic Studios, Studio One, London.
Recording: 'Thank You Darling.'

Wings had put nine songs on tape over the last 13 days, but Paul's latest crop of compositions left Johns cold, and their working relationship had degenerated to that of master and servant. During the recording of *Get Back*, Johns had a front-row seat to witness McCartney scale one of his highest creative peaks. He watched, for example, as Paul turned a messy bass riff into the basis of 'Get Back,' and then fleshed out the song over the next few days, as if plucking it out of the air. By contrast, 'Thank You Darling,' the saccharine love song chosen for Thursday's session, had none of the melodic muscle or enduring appeal of 'Let It Be,' 'The Long and Winding Road,' or 'Get Back.'

Johns's appraisal was typically British in its reserve: "There were a couple of songs that I thought were a bit iffy."[39]

But after their attempt to take him to task, Paul's sidemen were a bigger problem for Johns. Throughout the session, he watched in disbelief as Laine, Seiwell, and McCullough indulged McCartney's syrupy side, not one of them raising an objection to recording Paul and Linda's cutesy lovers' exchange. And when Phil Chapman cued a take devoted to a chorus of kazoos, Johns likely longed for John Lennon to suddenly stride through the door and take McCartney to task.

What Johns had perhaps failed to consider was Paul's less well-known Tin Pan Alley sensibility. For all his credibility as a rocker, McCartney had an equal measure of business savvy. Just as he had given away 'Come and Get It' to Badfinger, 'Love of the Loved' to Cilla Black, and 'Woman' to Peter and Gordon, among many other songs, some of the tracks recorded at Olympic were not destined for release by Wings. "We'll have to edit stuff down and chuck out some tracks, but then we'll maybe use those as demos*—get other people to do them,"[40] Paul noted soon after the Olympic sessions ended.

Johns was unaware of, and unconcerned by, Paul's publishing plan. And his patience was running out.

On Thursday night, the band had dinner at Paul's house with Lee Eastman, who was in town to see Linda and his granddaughters, and to strategize with Paul about a possible out of court settlement with ATV. But he had also agreed to update Seiwell, Laine, and McCullough on band contracts. For the two Dennys, the "hippie handshake" that sealed their membership in Wings was a distant memory. Now they, and Henry, wanted to know if Paul's talk of a percentages of recording royalties and box office takings, made over drinks in those distant days, would take bankable form.

Financially, the university tour had given McCartney's men a small taste of the high life. Dividing the door money from the two-week tour five ways gave each of them £550 ($1,375)—*eight times* the £70 a week retainer Paul was paying them. It was enough for Denny and Monique to put down a deposit on an apartment at 4 Alderville Road, Fulham.

But the situation was more complex than Paul had appreciated when he recruited his three Wingmen. Denny Seiwell, Eastman reported, was the only truly free agent in the band. Denny Laine was tied to his 1970 contract with Tony Secunda, and Henry remained bound to the 1971 deal that the post–Joe Cocker Grease Band signed with Leon Russell's and Denny Cordell's Shel-

---

* With no intention, originally, of putting the song out himself, a tape copy of 'When the Night' was later sent to soul queen Aretha Franklin. However, the biggest publishing success from this period was 'My Love,' covered by countless artists in 1973, including Tony Bennett, Cass Elliot, Brenda Lee, and Andy Williams.

ter Records. Russell and Cordell, Eastman reported, were happy to cut McCullough loose, but Secunda was playing hardball.

"We had a meeting with Lee Eastman at Paul's house," explained Seiwell. "We still hadn't had a contract as a band, even though we made verbal agreements that we would all be part owners of the band. We found out that Denny Laine had a horrible contract with his ex-manager, Tony Secunda. Apparently, that was such a problem, Lee Eastman said that we were going to have to figure out a way to end that contract before anything could be done with Wings. This was really the start of the demise of Wings, right there and then."[41]

But there was more. Even if Laine's contractual situation were resolved, Eastman continued, there was still the Apple hurdle to overcome. With EMI and Apple Corps still unable to agree how to distribute the cash from record sales, Paul had not seen a penny in recording royalties for Wings' *Wild Life* (not to mention, *Let It Be*, *McCartney*, *Ram*, or any of his or Wings' singles). McCartney and Eastman agreed to cover Seiwell's, Laine's, and McCullough's work expenses, such as travel costs, hotel bills, and airfares.[42] But for both Paul and his band, the outlook was bleak. Eastman was straight with them—issuing contracts was impossible.

Seiwell, Laine, and McCullough found themselves in an inconceivable position bandmates with an ex-Beatle, and living frugally. During recording sessions, their income was topped up at union rates, but in New York, Denny Seiwell earned in three hours what he took home in a week as a member of Wings. For him, sticking around was an unnerving financial gamble.

"The day that we actually met with Lee, my wife put in her diary, 'Still not paid. Recording session fees.' EMI was so slow paying us. We were living on very little money. I don't know how the hell we did it. I really don't. I used to have to fly to New York to do a couple of jingles and make some money so my dad could pay my American Express bill when it came in. It was awful. But we were committed to it, and we loved what we were doing."[43]

Though he was only just through the door, Henry found this a bitter pill to swallow too. In October 1969, Andrew Lloyd Webber and Tim Rice asked McCullough and other musicians working on the *Jesus Christ Superstar* album to accept a royalty percentage in lieu of session fees. Strapped for cash, and unconvinced that an album with *Jesus* in the title would sell, McCullough opted for payment in cash. Rice and Lloyd Webber's album went on to sell seven million copies worldwide and Henry knew Wings' records could be equally successful.

"We were still on this retainer, and we'd been told that as things progressed we could contribute material, become part of a 'band' as such, but it never ever came to that,"[44] McCullough lamented.

Downplaying his own management problems, and perhaps embarrassed to be the cause of the band not having contracts, Laine took the opposite attitude. He argued that signing a contract would make them employees of McCartney Productions Ltd.—working *for* Paul, rather than *with* him. And after spending much of 1971 sleeping in Tony Secunda's back room, Denny was content to live the life of a gypsy, dragging his beat-up caravan between Shepperton and Campbeltown.

"I learned a lesson from being in Balls. And I wouldn't have gone into Wings if I'd thought it wasn't going to work,"[45] said Laine, gambling his financial future on the band working out. "The money wasn't the reason [I stuck with Wings], because the money was useless to start with; it was the challenge: to get something going again and learn something from it. And I knew that eventually we'd be doing it on a proper level."[46]

One thing was clear: the meeting left Wings deeply divided.

———▶

Over the weekend, McCartney and Lee Eastman turned their attention to the ATV/Northern Songs dispute, which had been lining the pockets of lawyers in London and New York for over 12 months. Finally, after months of heated legal meetings behind closed doors, plus a fair deal of public posturing in the British press, senior figures at ATV advised Grade to drop the company's litigation against the McCartneys, accept Linda's coauthorship claims, and make peace with one of the company's biggest publishing assets.

Settling the dispute was a matter of some urgency, since Paul's contract with Northern Songs was due to expire in February 1973, only 11 months away. Grade actually had few bargaining chips. One was the knowledge that for Paul, the ownership of his songs was a matter of crucial importance. He hoped, as well, that Paul would want to avoid another potentially image-bruising day in court. If ATV allowed Paul to become a free agent once the contract lapsed, everything Paul had written to that point would remain in ATV's publishing catalog, but ATV would not stand to benefit from any of Paul's future work.

So Eastman and Grade negotiated an attention-grabbing offer: if Paul signed a copublishing deal with ATV, backdated to April 1971 and running through the end of 1979, then on January 1, 1980, ATV would relinquish control of everything McCartney had written from April 1971 onward—the publishing credits (and royalties) reverting to McCartney Music only.

In simple terms: sign the deal, extending ATV's interest in McCartney's music by another seven years, and in January 1980, the copyright for every song Paul had published since 'Another Day,' with the exception of the songs on *Ram* that Paul composed alone, would be exclusively his. Grade's deal included songs cowritten with Linda.

Moreover, beyond the matter of ownership, there was an immediate financial incentive: Paul's copyright royalties would increase by 25 percent. In 1972, copyright royalties accounted for roughly 6 percent of the retail price of a record, with 50 percent of this payment going to the publisher, and 50 percent to the composer. Under Grade's proposed copublishing deal, ATV would surrender half of its publishing royalty to Paul, meaning he would receive 75 percent of the copyright royalty in total (4.5 percent of each record sale, rather than 3 percent).

With two signatures on a new contract, the songwriting dispute, and the lawsuit it engendered, could disappear.

ATV was understandably keen to prolong its relationship with both Lennon and McCartney. The ATV Music group, which also included Pye Records, recorded turnover of $16,697,000 for the year ending March 1972, $4,623,000 of which was profit. By comparison, Northern Songs, operating before the ATV takeover in 1969, recorded operating profits of $2,400,000. The Lennon-McCartney catalog of songs had done a lot to bolster ATV Music's profits, and since both John and Paul were still under contract with Northern, they continued to do so with their solo projects.[47]

It had come down to two options: either ride out his contract with Northern Songs, face another lengthy, expensive court battle over the collaborations with Linda, and kiss goodbye the publishing rights for his post-Beatles recordings through 1973, or extend his deal with ATV Music for another seven years, smooth over the disagreement about Linda's compositions, and ultimately own his publishing.

"If you write a good song, I maintain, you should own it totally," Paul said of his dispute with Grade. "But no publisher will let you own the copyright. I wrote Sir Lew Grade a long letter saying, 'Don't you think I ought to be able to do this, and do that, and don't you think I've done enough, and don't you think I'm OK, and—hey, man, why have you gotta sue me?' He wrote me back a very rational letter. He's actually OK, Lew . . . he's a good businessman."[48]

Still, Paul was reluctant to accept a deal that looked good on the surface, but might have unforeseen consequences. He asked Lee for some time to consider Grade's offer.

Recording Sessions

Monday–Thursday, March 27–30, 1972.
Olympic Studios, Studio One, London.
Recording: 'Mary Had a Little Lamb.'

Faced with dwindling morale among his players, Paul decided over Sunday lunch to spend the next week recording and mixing a single for immediate release. That sounded fine to Johns and the band—but when he told them what he wanted the single to be, they collectively wondered whether he had taken a knock on the head over the weekend.

For their next single, he declared, Wings would release his musical reworking of 'Mary Had a Little Lamb.'

Being a parent had clearly changed Paul from a trendsetting, image-conscious rocker into a family man. But his band were not following his logic. Though they did not expect to climb the high diving board at every session, making records for schoolchildren was not a musical avenue they were expecting to tread, and three-fifths of the five-piece outfit worried that Paul's soft approach would tarnish the band's image.

"I didn't understand it," said Seiwell. "Henry and I, the two rebels in the band, we said, 'I thought we wanted to become a rock-and-roll band; what the hell is this 'Mary Had a Little Lamb' shit?'"[49]

"He's a strange guy like that," McCullough explained. "One would never query why we were doing 'Mary Had a Little Lamb.' Everybody would just tag along. He was the leader and had all the ideas, apart from odd bits here and there. If anybody had been let loose, it would have taken away from it. Somebody had to be in complete control. His personality is quite overwhelming, and it does tend to put dampeners on different things. If we were in the studio, we'd be inclined to be afraid to say, 'I've got this number here.' You'd shut up because of the personality."[50]

Even the typically indifferent Denny Laine was perplexed. "If I was running the band, which I wasn't, I wouldn't have put it out as a single. I would have picked something a bit more in line with what I like in music."[51]

Declaring they would rather emulate T. Rex than Tom Jones, much less *Sesame Street*, the trio aired their doubts, but brandishing a copy of that week's *NME*, Paul pointed out that the charts were dominated by ballads and novelty records. Harry Nilsson's 'Without You' topped the singles chart in Britain, and Don McClean's 'American Pie' had been in the Top 10 for 11 weeks. At the same time, Ringo's breezy 'Back Off Boogaloo' was gaining ground, Chelsea Football Club were riding high with 'Blue Is the Colour,' and a bagpipe cover of 'Amazing Grace' by the Military Band of the Royal Scots Dragoon Guard was destined for the top spot.

Just as the public had embraced the childlike singalong melodies of 'Yellow Submarine' and 'All Together Now,' Paul believed, people around the world would soon be humming the "*la-la, la-la, la-la-la-la-la-la*" chorus line of his enriched nursery rhyme.

To many who were inclined to give Paul the benefit of the doubt, the choice of 'Mary Had a Little Lamb' was interpreted as a reaction to the BBC banning 'Give Ireland Back to the Irish'— McCartney shouting from the rooftop, *You couldn't handle a political song; is 'Mary Had a Little Lamb' more your speed?*

Paul didn't see it that way.

"When I released 'Mary Had a Little Lamb,' after having been banned with 'Give Ireland Back to the Irish,' " McCartney later explained, "the automatic thought was he's done that to, sort of, stick a finger up to the people who banned him and say, 'Try and ban this! It's a children's song.' It actually wasn't like that. It just happened that I had this daft little children's song that I used to sing to my daughter Mary. I didn't put the thought into it that the analysts, quite naturally, would put into it."[52]

The selection, he further clarified, had more to do with his own eclecticism than anything else. And to the degree that 'Give Ireland Back to the Irish' entered his thinking, it had more to do with lightening the public's perceptions of him, and Wings, than with commenting on those who banned the single.

"I like to write melodic tunes, very old-fashioned ones like 'When I'm Sixty-Four,' it's very natural to me I was brought up on the Billy Cotton Bandshow and things like that. That's all gone into my head. Naturally, I like to write that sort of stuff, but it was getting a bit heavy, it was beginning to look daft—the humor had gone out of it, if you're an artist you like to create for people and it's not very nice if those people go 'urgh.' I just thought well, why not put out a record for younger people, instead of always putting records out for my age group?"[53]

Setting their personal feelings aside, Seiwell, McCullough and Laine put everything they had behind the playground melody. Paul and Denny Laine combined for the rhythm section on a pair of pianos, while Henry struck sparse electric guitar punctuations. The best take clocked in at 4'40", including an animated, minute-long coda.

Over the next three days, Wings added a chocolate box assortment of overdubs, including xylophone, mandolin, percussion, pennywhistle, lead, harmony and backing vocals, and bongos.

"Paul always entertained everyone's input during recording sessions," Phil Chapman noted, "and for some ridiculous reason I suggested we put the bongos through a wah-wah pedal. Paul just said, 'Oh, okay' and Glyn Johns was fine about it. So we went ahead and did it, with me operating the pedal by hand in the control room."[54]

But Johns, already parboiling after three weeks of recording music he considered indifferent at best, was fed up. Watching Paul splitting hairs over what he considered an average record was the final straw. In the midst of overdubbing, Johns's calm façade came tumbling down.

"Johns was going on a bit, and I was getting a bit fed up with him," Paul remembered. "And I said, 'Oh, you old tart.'"[55] Paul's banter fell on deaf ears. Johns cleared the control room, and behind the soundproof glass, three weeks of pent-up resentment spewed out.

"He was less than secure, really," Johns said of McCartney during the sessions he oversaw. "I admired him for what he was trying to do, but I think he was confused. He ended up with a bunch of sycophantic musicians who were all climbing up his backside. It wasn't a band, although he was constantly saying he wanted it to be one. The band itself was not very good.[56]

"My responsibility has always been to the artist. It's their career on the line every time they go into the studio to make a record. I'm very much aware of that."[57]

Johns gathered his things and filed through the band, right out the studio door.

"Paul was difficult to work with for a producer, because he held the reins so tight," said Seiwell. "He was a great producer himself. All the experimentation that he did with the Beatles and everything. He's difficult to work with, at times, because he took his music so personal."[58]

"I won't say that we didn't get along with Glyn," was Laine's final assessment. "We just didn't know him."[59]

17

PREPARING FOR LIFTOFF

—

Glyn Johns's criticism of Paul's new material, and his band, had cut to the bone and like a wounded animal, McCartney found cover and licked his wounds. Back at Cavendish Avenue, Linda rustled up a late supper as Paul scoured the pages of his little black book for a solution to the band's producer problem. But tracking down a gifted replacement for Johns, at short notice, was not a straightforward task. The levelheaded, gentle George Martin would have been the perfect fit, and likely more flexible to Paul and the band's needs and vagaries. But Paul was unwilling to entertain defaulting to a Beatle safety blanket. New band, new direction.

Perusing the pages of his address book the name of another hot British producer caught Paul's eye: former Olympic Studios tape op, Gus Dudgeon. Four consecutive Dudgeon-produced records had propelled former session musician Reginald Dwight to global success under his preferred sobriquet, Elton John, and Dudgeon's stellar work on David Bowie's 'Space Oddity' could not be ignored. Paul and Gus had often crossed paths on the London music scene, most notably in the summer of 1968, when Dudgeon was engineering-coproducing the Bonzo Dog Doo-Dah Band at Chappell Studios, with producer Gerry Bron.

Hanging out at the Speakeasy* in July 1968, Paul found himself on the receiving end of an extraordinary diatribe about Bron's budget-driven production methods from friend and Bonzo member Viv Stanshall. The Bonzos were due to record their next single, and Stanshall was worried that Bron's clock-watching ways would be to the detriment of their record. Sensing an opportunity to cause some mischief, McCartney offered to drop by the studio and lend a helping hand.

One evening in late July, Paul strolled down Maddox Street, on the edge of London's moneyed Mayfair district, to Chappell Studios, and walked in on the Bonzos' session unannounced. Bron was

---

* Taking its name and theme from American Prohibition-era speakeasies, the Speakeasy, or "The Speak," was a basement music venue and restaurant at 48 Margaret Street, London. The spirit of the place was captured by The Who in their song 'Speakeasy' (from the 1967 album *The Who Sell Out*), singing "Speakeasy, drink easy, pull easy."

stunned to silence, and with Dudgeon at the mixing desk, McCartney donned the producer's hat as the group laid down 'I'm the Urban Spacemen,' a colorful folk-style composition by Neil Innes, destined to be the Bonzo Band's next single.

Innes's song, for which Paul was given the producer's credit "Apollo C. Vermouth," secured the Bonzo Band a No. 5 hit in Britain and won Innes an Ivor Novello Award. "The record would have been nothing like [as successful] without Paul's touch,"[1] Innes later noted—although Dudgeon had a different view.

"I finished 'Spaceman' off, putting on the vocals, tuba, tambourine, drums and one or two other things, mixing the whole thing in my lunch-hour because it was easy to mix, only being a 4-track job," Dudgeon said. "But as they didn't want to upset McCartney—and I didn't want to either at that stage . . . the record went out as being produced by Apollo C. Vermouth."[2]

When Paul called him, Dudgeon had just returned from Strawberry Studios in the grounds of the Château d'Hérouville in central France, where he had recorded successive records with Elton John (*Honky Château*) and Joan Armatrading (*Whatever's for Us*). Though flattered by the offer, Dudgeon ended up talking McCartney out of employing him, or any other producer, to finish Wings' second album.

"I've never worked with big names," reasoned Dudgeon. "What puzzles me is if they're a big name and if they're being produced well, what the fuck difference can I make? I passed on a lot of big artists because I think they make great records anyway. I like to go into the studio with an artist no one's ever heard of, and I like to see success come out of it."[3]

Dudgeon's pep talk convinced McCartney to put some distance between himself and the tracks the band had cut at Olympic and travel to Scotland for a head-clearing spring break on the farm. But just before Easter weekend, the telephone rang at Cavendish Avenue; to Paul's surprise, it was Johns. "Meet me at Island Studios on Saturday morning," Glyn said.

Recording Sessions

Saturday–Monday, April 1–3, 1972.
Island Studios, Studio Two, London.
Overdubbing and mixing: 'Mary Had a Little Lamb.'

Storming out midsession was not the end Johns had envisioned for his time in the studio with McCartney and Wings. Though indifferent to Paul's glorified nursery rhyme, Glyn was keen to be professional, patch up his differences with the former Beatle, and finish work on Wings' latest single.

"Paul and I are on great terms," Johns later explained. "He and I made up after I told him to stuff it up his arse, and that was that."[4]

Just one small obstacle stood in the way of the duo tying up the loose ends on 'Mary Had a Little Lamb'—it was Easter weekend and Olympic Studios was closed, their staff having been given a long weekend with their families. Luckily, Johns was able to make a late booking at Island Studios and convince one of their in-house engineers, Phil Ault, to run the tape machines for a short run of closed sessions.

On April 1, Paul and Linda arrived at Basing Street with only Heather and Mary in tow, the rest of the band conspicuous in their absence. Whether their no-show was at Glyn's request, or a move by Paul to reduce friction, is unknown.

Threading up the master tape in the control room, engineer Phil Ault was as bemused as his producer when he rolled the tape on McCartney's latest production.

"The track was 'Mary Had a Little Lamb,' which I didn't take to," explained Ault, "but being professional, you leave your taste at the studio door."[5]

Following four days of basic recording and overdubbing at Olympic, 'Mary Had a Little Lamb' was all but complete, with only the final vocal parts outstanding. On Saturday afternoon Paul recorded his lead vocal with Linda joining him throughout, slightly off mic. He then doubled his lead in places, harmonizing with himself in the absence of Laine and McCullough. The session progressed quickly and without incident, any rift between artist and producer either well-hidden or quickly forgotten.

"We were overdubbing mainly vocals, and everything was relaxed and workmanlike," explained Ault. "When it was lunchtime, I stumped up the £10 for us all to eat, as they hadn't any cash. Two days later a cab arrived at Basing Street with £10 in an envelope for me, which I was impressed with—the mark of a true gent!"[6]

On Sunday, Paul and Linda were joined in the vocal booth by Heather and Mary (if it was good enough for the Von Trapp family, it was good enough for the McCartneys) as they giggled their way through "la-la" chorus overdubs. Finally, Paul added a short Moog part—bursts of fuzz-bass—during the song's finale, and the track was ready for mixing, which Johns and McCartney wrapped up on Monday afternoon. And with that McCartney and Johns shook hands and parted ways.

———

Looking for a quick fix for the B side, on April 5, tape copies of the November mixes of 'Little Woman Love' and 'Get on the Right Thing' were made at EMI Studios, Paul eventually choosing the former. Both sides were mastered for release on April 6[*]; provisional release dates were penciled in—May 5 for the UK, May 8 for America. "It's a song for spring to make people feel happy,"[7] said Paul, announcing his easygoing single to the music press a week later. When asked for an update on Wings' next album, he said it was coming in autumn.

But the truth was, with Glyn Johns gone Paul had no idea when the album might be finished. In mid-April, he pulled the plug on all future recording commitments and cut the band loose, telling them to reconvene in Scotland at the end of the month.

Troubled by the state of his bank balance, Denny Seiwell checked in with Local 802 in New York and was offered some session work with pianist Randy Edelman. He left London on April 10. Denny Laine, hoping to break his contractual standoff with Tony Secunda, reviewed the material he recorded before joining Wings, with a view to releasing a solo album on Secunda's Wizard label before the end of the year.

Henry was reunited with his former bandmates Chris Stainton, Neil Hubbard, Alan Spencer, and John Weathers for a Grease Band retrospective piece in *Disc*. Dispelling rumors that the five of them had fallen out as "bullshit," McCullough (now believing that Wings was to be a loose, contract-free arrangement) explained that the Grease Band were making plans for the future. Henry's comments, though likely missed by most, underlined his early frustrations with life in Paul's band.

"We've got another Grease Band album virtually finished. I've done quite a lot of work on it, and I've sent it to Chris to work on—he'll mix it in the States. We also hope to do another one sometime. Say if three or four of us are in the same place, we'll put down a track." In a veiled dig at McCartney he added, "Being in the Grease Band was always a great time because of the 'looseness' of it all. I wouldn't go into a group just for the sake of being there—I have to feel I'm contributing something."[8]

For Paul and Linda, it was business as usual. The couple remained in London for two weeks to organize the label and sleeve designs for 'Mary Had a Little Lamb.' Rejecting, for a third time, Apple's Granny Smith labels, Paul instead licensed an illustration by the American artist Clara Miller Burd[†] for Wings' latest release. Burd's sketch, depicting a young girl feeding a group of lambs, was used for the single label, sleeve front, and the first round of trade ads. In stark contrast to the broadly bellicose Ireland ad campaign, the text surrounding a photograph of Wings could not have been more flaccid:

---

[*] In the travel between three studios, two tape boxes were marked "master." When making tape copies for the German release, an engineer accidentally duplicated the wrong tape, meaning German fans were treated to an early mix, rather than the Island master.

[†] Born on May 17, 1873, Clara Miller Burd—a graduate of the New York National Academy of Design—worked as a stained-glass artist for the Tiffany Glass and Decorating Company in New York, before designing magazine covers for many major publications. But she was best known for her illustrations for children's books. A resident of Montclair, New Jersey, she died on November 11, 1933.

Mary Had A Little Lamb
a single record from your old chums Wings

Apple 1851

REGISTER TO VOTE/THE WORLD DEPENDS ON YOU

Before the band gathered again in Scotland, on Tuesday, April 25, Paul booked director Nicholas Ferguson to film a selection of videos to promote the single in mid-May.

Disappearing into the heavy highland mists on April 26, 1972, Paul took a lone stroll in the hills above High Park. Clambering up the knoll alongside the new season's lambs, he reached the ancient Ranachan fort, where Scotland's Iron Age settlers held off assaults from neighboring Celtic tribes, hoping to form his own plan of attack. Currently, the band seemed more at home on the road than in the studio, so rather than rushing back to Abbey Road and spending the hottest part of the year inside a dimly lit room, they would make the most of the warm summer weather by going on tour. A couple of months on the road would refine their repertoire and give Paul some breathing space to work on more material for their second album.

Wasting no time, Paul returned to the farmhouse, picked up the telephone and dialed John Morris.

"I was in London, and they were up in Campbeltown," said Morris. "He said, could I come up to Scotland and talk about a tour."[9] Morris jumped in a taxi to Heathrow Airport with technical manager Chris Langhart and made tracks toward Paul's country pile.

The start of 1972 had been disastrous for Morris. On Sunday, March 12, his firm, the Sundance Theater Company, declared bankruptcy, and the Rainbow Theater in Finsbury Park—the main reason for his relocation from New York to London—closed its doors.

The swift demise of Morris's rock theater came on December 10, 1971, when the American rocker Frank Zappa, playing the first of four sold-out concerts at the Rainbow, launched into a parody encore of the Beatles' 'I Want to Hold Your Hand.' Forcing his way past security staff, a disgruntled fan raced onto the stage, and after a scuffle, Zappa fell 15 feet, landing in the venue's concrete orchestra pit.

"A guy by the name of Trevor Howell had run up onstage, punched me and knocked me over into the pit. The band thought I was dead," Zappa later recalled. "My head was over on my shoulder, and my neck was bent like it was broken. I had a gash in my chin, a hole in the back of my head, a broken rib and a fractured leg. One arm was paralyzed."[10]

Zappa left the Harley Street Clinic in a wheelchair (in which he remained for the better part of a year); a crushed larynx also lowered the tone of his voice for life. Morris was forced to refund fans for the canceled concerts. In a press statement Morris blamed the Rainbow's financial woes on pop groups who charged unrealistically high fees, but he later acknowledged that the venue had been walking a financial tightrope, and the Zappa episode tipped them over the edge.

Across the hills that stretched out along the Kintyre peninsula, Paul and Linda spied a plume of dust trailing a taxi along the rocky road to their remote getaway, and they were on hand to greet Morris and Langhart outside Rude Studio, where the band had been rehearsing since April 29. As Linda poured orange pekoe tea into an assortment of broken mugs, Morris recounted the tale of the Rainbow's demise, adding that he had been keeping busy helping the Rolling Stones arrange an American tour. Paul's ears instantly pricked up, that instinctive Beatles versus Stones rivalry, friendly though it was, tough to pacify, even now.

"We talked about doing a tour together, which was perfect for me as I needed a direction and he became it," Morris said. "Talking to Paul and Linda about touring, very quickly they thought, 'If the Stones are doing America, we want to do more than just colleges in England and Ireland. They said, 'What can you do?' I said, 'Actually, to be honest, it's easier to do Europe for me than it is to do Ireland and England.'"[11]

Paul had last toured in Europe with the Beatles in 1966, playing concerts in the German cities of Munich, Essen, and Hamburg between June 24 and 26. European crowds, though not as wild as those in America, were less critical than British audiences, and the idea of cruising around the continent during the hot summer months was an easy sell.

"I said, 'I'll get ahold of all the people in the European Promoters' Association, and we'll have a meeting, and we'll talk,'" Morris continued. "'What kind of price do you think we should offer them?' We settled on $3,000 (£1,150) [per concert], and I went back to the hotel in Campbeltown."[12] For his part in producing, and managing the tour, Morris said he was offered $50,000 (£19,150).

In the cozy hotel bar at the Argyll Arms, Morris poured coins into the pay phone, calling every booking agent between Finland and France. A few days later he arrived in Switzerland to meet face-to-face with promoters Fritz Rau (Germany), Knud Thorbjornson (Denmark and Sweden), Claude Nobs (France, Belgium, and Switzerland), Norbert Ghamson (Finland and Norway) and Berry Visser (Holland), to finalize plans for Wings' European tour.

"We all sat around a big table in Montreux, and I said, 'Okay, it's real simple. It's Paul McCartney and Wings, his new band. They would like to have three grand a night, and let's book a tour.'"[13]

Spreading out a map of mainland Europe, each promoter juggled the dates that halls were available to them into an itinerary that would facilitate the movement of buses, trucks, and equipment in a logical manner. In just a few days Morris and his fellow promoters scheduled a 26-date, 27 concert tour, starting on July 9 at an amphitheater in the grounds of Châteauvallon, in southern France, and ending on August 24 at the Deutschland Halle, a structure built for the Nazis and inaugurated by Hitler in 1935, in West Berlin. Morris also arranged for Wings to use the Manticore rehearsal studios in Fulham—an abandoned Odeon cinema in London owned by Emerson, Lake, and Palmer—throughout June to hone their live act.

The proposed start date would mean taking nine-year-old Heather out of school before the end of the summer term. The children were the center of Paul and Linda's universe, and they had agreed, back when touring was only a theoretical prospect, that when they traveled, their children would travel with them. They had also agreed that their tours would, to whatever extent possible, take place during school holidays, but adjustments would sometimes have to be made.

Heather had already been excused from school during the university tour, and Linda felt that time with her family exploring the world was as valuable an education as any textbook could offer.

"Personally, I'm not interested in education at school," Linda later rationalized. "My parents were very interested in education, and I was more interested in rock and roll and didn't do well in school, whereas Heather—and we don't care how she does in school—really loves reading."[14]

Whether at home, in the studio, or on the road, Denny Seiwell stressed that no decision was taken lightly, and that Paul and Linda put their children's interests before anything else.

"As parents, they were the greatest parents I've ever seen," Seiwell enthused. "The kids were amazing. I really applaud them for the way they brought those kids up."[15]

Five hundred miles from London, Paul and the band put the vexations of Olympic Studios behind them. In London, however, *Melody Maker* got wind of the clash of personalities between McCartney and Johns and approached both for comment. Johns tactfully told their reporter that the band preferred having a good time to producing good music, cryptically adding: "We [Paul and I] now have respect for each other."[16] Paul had no desire to fuel the fire, and rather than face the prying eyes of Fleet Street in Scotland (as had so often happened when he and Linda ventured to High Park) he had Shelley Turner feed the press a false story that Wings were vacationing in Spain and unavailable for comment.

Paul instead channeled his frustrations into a new composition—an earsplitting rocker titled 'Soily,' whose somewhat confusing lyrics described a gathering of "*soily*," or dirty, characters. Written as a surreal vision of a gathering of low-life thugs and dangerous archetypes—among those mentioned are "*Hitler's son*" and "*a commie with a tommy gun*," as well as a "*cat in satin trousers*" as a kind of kingpin who declares everything "*oily*,"—the lyric also paraphrases the start of Mark Antony's eulogy in Shakespeare's *Julius Caesar* (an oblique shot in the direction of those he felt had betrayed him over the years).

'Soily' became an outlet for the group's collective musical therapy, with Seiwell bashing his drumskins raw, and McCullough and Laine thrashing their guitars until no string was left intact, the unruly din spilling out of Rude Studio into the neighboring hills. Though internal fissures had begun to surface, the band were firmly united.

"Going through that Scotland thing and living up there in the wilds, eating simply and working together, helped a lot," said Denny Laine. "We finished up pretty happy with the band when we're up there in Scotland rehearsing."[17]

Seiwell concurred. "We got to know each other a lot better, and the music started to happen. We found out what every member of the band really had to offer—and that's the thing that really takes time."[18]

Two weeks of rehearsals in early May also helped McCartney crystalize a rough 21-song setlist for their upcoming tour dates: 'Bip Bop,' 'Mumbo' (with added lyrics), 'I Am Your Singer' and 'Wild Life'; Paul's solo tracks 'Maybe I'm Amazed,' 'Smile Away' and 'Eat at Home'; the singles 'Give Ireland Back to the Irish' and 'Mary Had a Little Lamb'; Denny Laine's 'I Would Only Smile' and 'Say You Don't Mind'*; Henry's 'Henry's Blues'; Linda's 'Seaside Woman'; crowd pleasing overs of 'Blue Moon of Kentucky' and 'Long Tall Sally'; and the unreleased (and in most cases, not yet recorded) songs, '1882,' 'The Mess,' 'Best Friend,' 'Soily' and 'My Love.' But Morris, updating Paul on his Montreux meeting, asked for some last-minute additions.

---

* Written and released by Denny Laine on April 14, 1967, 'Say You Don't Mind' was covered by the former Zombies singer Colin Blunstone in February 1972. Blunstone's single did what Laine's original failed to do, spending nine weeks in the British Top 100, peaking at No. 15 on March 18. Fresh to the ears of the music buying public, it was included in Wings' touring set list. (Laine himself reissued his 1967 recording on January 6, 1972, but his single failed to chart a second time.)

Unsurprisingly, the European Promoters' Association thought the band would shift more tickets if (as Harrison had done at the Concert for Bangla Desh) they added a couple of Beatles numbers to their repertoire. Sensing Paul was uncomfortable with the idea, Morris offered up a compromise.

"[John Morris] said, 'At the end, you should just come on with a guitar and do "Yesterday,"'" said McCartney. "And I said, 'Oh, I can't do that, you know, oh blimey, it would be so embarrassing!'"[19]

In an attempt to assuage Morris's request, Wings worked on arrangements of 'The Long and Winding Road' and 'Yesterday,' but ultimately, revisiting his Beatle past was still too raw, and both numbers were dropped.

"I'll tell you the truth—it was too painful," Paul later admitted. "It was too much of a trauma. It was like reliving a sort of a weird dream, doing a Beatles tune."[20] Paul offered the same reason for refusing to be interviewed for the upcoming BBC radio series *The Beatles Story* (broadcast in 13 parts between May 21 and August 13).

"It's rather like an obituary for me. I don't like these old 'remember them' things. The only time I'd really like to talk about that is when I've got my new career together. I don't like talking about the old thing when inevitably anything I say I'm doing now won't match up to all the glorious things they'll show happened in the past. All I'm doing now with Wings is rehearsing. I'm not trying to do anything staggering, it'll be a good band that can play good music, that's good enough for me."[21]

Another spring visitor to High Park was the director Nicholas Ferguson. Paul had decided he wanted to launch 'Mary Had a Little Lamb' with a number of child-themed promo films. He had recently seen Ferguson's film of Emerson, Lake and Palmer's *Pictures at an Exhibition* and was impressed, so he asked Eastman to track down the former *Ready Steady Go!* director and invite him to oversee Paul's first music videos with Wings.

Like Morris, Ferguson trekked from London to Campbeltown to meet with Paul and Linda at High Park. Over tea and sandwiches in the farm kitchen they brainstormed ideas for the film shoot.

"I got a taxi to their place, and the taxi driver said to me that he wouldn't take me there," Ferguson wryly recalled. "I said to him, 'What do you mean?' And he said, 'Why can't you people leave him alone?' And I said, 'He asked me to . . .' 'Well how do I know that?' and I said, 'I've got an appointment with him this morning.' And he was really very protective. But anyway, he drove me up the hill.

"We sat around the kitchen table and chatted away, and Paul drew on a piece of paper what he wanted. We then fantasized about the four different versions; we did really collaborate. One was a circus tent. And he said he wanted one in a barn where he is sitting with [live] chickens and things. And I suggested at that point that we used Michael Wield [to design the sets]."[22]

On the eve of the British release* of 'Mary Had a Little Lamb,' the band flew out of Campbeltown's Machrihanish Airport by private jet, arriving in London as the sun began to set on May 11, 1972. Breaking cover out of necessity, rather than choice, they headed to the port town of Southampton two days later, where Ferguson had rented a soundstage at ITV's Southern Studios to film a collection of vibrant promo videos for 'Mary Had a Little Lamb.'

When the band entered the soundstage, the four backdrops that Ferguson and Wield had built for the shoot looked like the set of a low-budget Disney movie. Wield's design team had crafted a fake grassy knoll, a circus tent, a barn, and a blue screen background for special effects.

But there was method in this madness. Paul was hoping that his reinvigorated nursery rhyme would appeal to a diverse section of the record-buying public—children of all ages, from five to seventy-five—so he had plotted bespoke videos for *Top of the Pops*, the children's television show *Basil Brush*, and American television.

Lighting for the shoot was provided by John Morris's colleagues at Joe's Lights, formerly of the Fillmore East, latterly of the Rainbow Theater. "Hey man, that's heavy!" proclaimed the lighting engineer as the band set up against the blue screen, dressed like a chain gang in matching orange overalls and T-shirts. "Did you know, 'Mary Had a Little Lamb' was the first thing ever recorded by Thomas Edison?" he said to Paul, watching through the preview monitor as the production team used special effects to replace the blue backdrop with mind-expanding, spinning flowers.

The Joe's Lights crew weren't the only ones on a heavy trip. As the day wore on, the videos became ever more psychedelic. After a roll on the plastic grassy knoll, the band were joined by live chickens and sheep in the barn set, and the day ended in a circus tent with Paul dressed as a clown (complete with red nose and pointed hat), the band clad in equally ludicrous outfits. McCullough strummed a mandolin dressed as a circus master with fake beard, his hat reading "high"; Seiwell wore a similar outfit complete with fake muttonchop sideburns; Laine was dressed as a court jester with stick-on beard and black top hat; and Linda appeared on horseback wearing exotic gold clothing and headdress.†

"I was well aware of [the need for] discretion," Ferguson explained. "I arranged with Southern

---

* Trade ads in the British music press noted May 12, 1972, as the release date for 'Mary Had A Little Lamb', but since the single did not chart until May 27, it is possible the record did not arrive in shops until May 19. Either that, or (less likely) sales of the disc were slow.

† The barn promo was the first to air in England, playing on *Top of the Pops* on May 25. The grassy knoll promo was intercut with a stop-frame animation cartoon for the BBC's *Basil Brush Show* on June 24. The psychedelic film was shipped to America where it premiered on the *Flip Wilson Show* on October 12. And the circus promo was confined to the vault at MPL, 1 Soho Square until 2018 when it was released as a bonus film on the *Red Rose Speedway* archive reissue.

Television that I wanted nobody in the building at all except our crew, so they had complete secrecy. It's common knowledge that they all smoked joints, but I wanted that to be completely discreet—if they want to smoke a joint, they can smoke a joint. . . . It was a very relaxed atmosphere, very easygoing, everything went to plan. There was no temperament with anybody because they all seemed happy with what we were doing."[23]

Wield, who was gay, took a shine to Denny Laine during the shoot and spent the day chatting him up, the other band members playing along. With four videos in the can, at the end of the day, Paul and company headed north to London.

During the following week, Paul and Ferguson reviewed the four films at a postproduction house in Soho. No editing was necessary—the videos had been vision mixed on the day of filming.

The trip down Novelty Lane reminded Paul of another project that had been sitting on the shelf for almost a year, the still unissued *Thrillington* project. Paul and Linda had announced their artistic partnership with the fictional Irish bandleader a few months after making the album, but the tapes Tony Clark presented to Paul on his 29th birthday sat gathering dust.

With *Thrillington* again on his mind, Paul booked a few hours at De Lane Lea Studios, on Dean Street. Here, with a view to releasing a double A-side single, he mixed two cuts from the *Thrillington* sessions, the big-band reworking of 'Smile Away' and the Latin-marinated 'Uncle Albert/ Admiral Halsey.'

Meanwhile, 'Mary Had a Little Lamb' was attracting widespread ridicule in the British and American press, thanks in part to McCartney's former songwriting partner. On the same day the music press reviewed McCartney's cuddly children's melody, John Lennon entered the *Billboard* Hot 100 with his anthem for women's liberation, the boldly titled 'Woman Is the Nigger of the World.' The *Daily Express* was first to note the disparity in an impish article titled "Off-Beat," writing: "John Lennon and Paul McCartney have never been further apart lyrically than now."[24]

Discussing his provocatively themed single in New York, Lennon couldn't resist having a good-humored dig at his former bandmate.

"Whatever you put on top or whatever other problems there are, Woman's is the underlying problem, and children in a way, and probably children will be the next revolution. So, we wanted to make a point with it rather than just have an easy hit, ya know. We could have stuck 'Mary Had a Little Lamb' out, but we decided to go for 'Woman Is the Nigger.'" When the writer clarified that John was referring to the Wings single, John's sarcastic response was, "Yes, Paul's new wonderful effort."[25]

The British music critics were uncannily unified in their views on Wings' latest hit, most struggling to see past the glaring contrast between 'Mary Had a Little Lamb' and 'Give Ireland Back to the Irish,' and noting that the *Ram* era B side, 'Little Woman Love,' as the stronger of the two cuts (to a degree supporting Glyn Johns's assertion that Paul's most recent material was not up to scratch).

"I must confess a disappointment with 'Mary' although it's well done, with those fine little production details that Paul does so well, because it seems to lack any real vitality. The B-Side, on the other hand, is very good indeed. It has everything that 'Mary' lacks."[26]

John Peel, *Disc*

"After the highly controversial 'Give Ireland Back to the Irish,' the McCartneys return with a highly commercial song which incorporates the traditional nursery rhyme as lyrics. Wings will have no trouble finding radio play with this one."[27]

Danny Holloway, *NME*

"I have to admit this threw me into some disorder. Ostensibly it's a highly commercial track which will have no trouble conquering the market and certainly won't require an enormous amount of concentrated listening. They couldn't have moved further away from 'Give Ireland to the Irish' if they tried."[28]

Penny Valentine, *Sounds*

"After telling 'tremendous' Great Britain to get out of Ireland, Paul and Co. play it safe with a dreamy version of the well-known nursery rhyme. Flip is livelier."[29]

Peter Jones, *Record Mirror*

"Paul sings a coy but sincere, slightly tongue-in-cheek version of the old nursery rhyme. If you think 'Mary Had a Little Lamb' is a bit too far out, then cast an ear on the B-Side which is excellent."[30]

Chris Welch, *Melody Maker*

In America, where *Cash Box* described 'Little Woman Love' as a "Lady Madonna-ish rocker,"[31] radio stations took the same view, giving the B side significantly more attention than McCartney's novelty number. Neither side was able to find traction on US radio, though; between May and July 1972, the record only registered with one radio station (WRNO-FM, New Orleans) in *Record World*'s FM Airplay Report. After entering the charts at No. 85 on June 17, the single limped to No. 28 on the *Billboard* Hot 100. Three weeks later 'Mary Had a Little Lamb' disappeared completely, registering McCartney's poorest chart performance since 'From Me to You' fought its way to No. 41 on April 4, 1964, competing against more recent Beatles fare.

In Britain, the single faced a wall of Glam Rock resistance from T. Rex's 'Metal Guru,' Elton John's 'Rocket Man,' Slade's 'Take Me Bak 'Ome,' and Gary Glitter's 'Rock and Roll Parts 1&2,' stopping McCartney's song at the No. 9 berth where it arrived on June 24 and remained for two weeks. Asked to explain the group's musical U-turn—from politics to playground—Paul pinned the blame on the universe.

"I'm crazy. I've always been crazy from the minute I was born. Not kind of killing the teachers crazy, not that crazy, but there's just a certain kind of craziness I've always had, and that's the thing with me. Geminis' are supposed to be very changeable, and I don't know if that's true or not, but I'm a Gemini and I know one minute I might be doing 'Ireland' and the next 'Mary Had a Little Lamb.'"[32]

In defense of the single, Paul served up some chart facts, boasting that 'Mary' outsold the Rolling Stones' 'Tumbling Dice' (which managed three fewer weeks in the British Singles Charts during the same period), as well as celebrity endorsements (Pete Townshend's daughter had to have a copy). But the song was a commercial and musical embarrassment, and behind closed doors he was forced to concede that his band were right: the single took Wings in the wrong direction, even if he publicly pleaded ignorance.

"No one would say, 'No Paul that's a mistake,'" he told a reporter, no doubt picturing the reactions of Johns and his sidemen when they read it. "It was all a bit ropey."[33]

The press response to 'Mary Had a Little Lamb' snuffed out any hope of an imminent release for the equally quirky *Thrillington*. Revisiting the De Lane Lea mixes of 'Smile Away' and 'Uncle Albert/Admiral Halsey' at Island Studios on May 26, Paul made fresh mixes of the two songs, before deciding that a Percy Thrillington single was a novelty project too far. Both sets of mixes joined the *Thrillington* masters in the EMI archives. That afternoon Paul and the band hightailed it back to Campbeltown, where they would rehearse until June 12.

Bonding at Paul's Scottish pied-à-terre had created unity among the band, but the start of June provided the seed of further division. Paul had taken Lee Eastman's advice and accepted Sir Lew

---

* Paul's "Geminis" comment was a knowing wink in the direction of *NME* writer Alan Smith. On February 22, 1970, when commenting on Paul public withdrawal, Smith wrote: "Students of astrology may well recognize a typical Gemini reaction in this McCartney mystique . . . outward and sociable one minute; a hermit the next; good friendly guy one minute; distant guy the next." Expanding his astrological commentary on July 25, 1970, Smith continued: "And like the Gemini he is, his moods can jump from uncaring generosity to a crusading interest in good, honest, Northern value-for-money and the efficiency of others."

Grade's terms on an extension to his publishing contract with ATV/Northern Songs, and on June 1 the deal was revealed to the press. In a joint statement, ATV and McCartney Music announced that Paul and Linda had signed a new seven-year publishing deal with ATV, and that "all differences had been settled amicably."[34] A spokesman for ATV added: "This is a significant achievement. Everyone in the world was after Mr. McCartney."[35] The terms of the contract were not made public.

Taking Paul and Linda firmly under the ATV corporate wing, Grade introduced the McCartneys to the company's entertainment department, mooting a big budget Paul McCartney television special, and ATV Music offered Paul the opportunity to compose a theme tune for one of its television shows. Though neither offer was a condition of his new contract, both appealed to Paul. A television special featuring Wings could bolster the group's public image, and perhaps soften public perceptions of Linda, and the idea of waking up to the sound of milkmen whistling a TV theme tune he had composed tickled him.

On the same day, Reuters reported that John, George, and Ringo were meeting in New York to discuss their own futures under Allen Klein's management, but there was no truth in the story; John and Yoko were halfway across America, in Salina, Kansas. Lennon had, however, recently brushed shoulders with Lee Eastman at a BMI Awards dinner at New York's Americana Hotel, on May 25. Eastman and Lennon accepted awards for five Lennon and/or McCartney copyrights honored at the event ('Yesterday,' 'Let It Be,' 'Imagine,' 'Another Day,' and 'Uncle Albert/Admiral Halsey') and were photographed in conversation with Don Kirshner, the American publisher of the Maclen catalog.

Lennon, whose own contract with Northern Songs was also set to expire, was still musing over an offer from Sir Lew Grade. It is likely that Lennon and Eastman discussed Paul's new deal that evening, not least because, paralleling the Paul and Linda battle with Northern Songs, John and Yoko were locked in a dispute with the company over publishing rights on songs they had cowritten—a quarrel that was holding up the British release of their new album, *Some Time in New York City*. Of the 16 cuts on their double LP set, just 3 were credited to Lennon, 4 were by Ono, and the rest were cocompositions. When presented with the list of credits, Northern Songs reacted just as it had when Paul and Linda claimed coauthorship of 'Another Day.' As a consequence, *Some Time in New York City*, released in America on June 12, would not hit British stores until September 15. ATV/Northern Songs told John that the "door was still open"[36] for him to sign a new deal with them, as Paul had done, but the publishing dispute had soured Lennon's appetite for negotiation.

As the ink dried on the McCartneys' new joint publishing deal, the embargo on royalty payments to Linda for *Ram*, *Wild Life*, and their cowritten singles was lifted. Suddenly the mailbox at Cavendish Avenue was overflowing with royalty checks addressed to Mrs. McCartney.

"The joke at that time was that Linda was the only one getting paid in our household," Paul explained, "'cos we were all held up with Apple being subject to litigation. I wasn't seeing *any* money. I was literally having to say to all the Wings members, 'Don't worry, lads. One of these days we'll see some money.' It was ridiculous.[37] So, I didn't have much of a feeling of being that well off, although we spent it with great glee."[38]

Paul and Linda celebrated by splashing out on a secondhand Lamborghini Espada Series II. The metallic red 3.9-liter V12 Italian automobile—more at home on the Le Mans Circuit de la Sarthe than suburban London—had been snapped up by the couple at a London dealership as their family runaround, its cost offset somewhat by the sale of Paul's Aston Martin DB6, a car he took delivery of in March 1966. The previous day, the *Daily Express* also ran a piece claiming that the McCartney family were on the hunt for a holiday home in Los Angeles; the truth, that they were still seeking land in the south of England, was not as eye-catching.

Halcyon days for the McCartneys, but seeing Paul picking up groceries in a $20,000 (£7,660) sports car was galling to his band. Since their meeting with Lee Eastman money had become a taboo subject.

"We were too poor to even afford a car," says Seiwell. "Living in a furnished basement apartment that my wife found for us. I had no money in my pocket, we were just getting paid so little money, it was dreadful."[39]

Paul did share the spoils with his Wingmen, after a fashion, though not directly in their paychecks. Paul and Linda had planned a mid-June family getaway in southeastern Spain and invited the rest of the band to join them for Paul's 30th birthday celebrations. Through an elite London travel agency, Linda had booked the family into Montíboli Hotel, an exclusive five-star getaway in the quaint harbor town of Villajoyosa between Alicante and Benidorm, and secured the use of a private villa for the band in late June.

The McCartney family, together with their London housekeeper, Rose, arrived in Villajoyosa on June 14. At check-in, there was confusion over their reservation, made under the travel alias 'Mr. and Mrs. Martin.' The receptionist, Pilar, was among the relatively few Beatle-blind people in the Western world and was unable to reconcile the Martins with the people listed on their passports as McCartney. A worldlier manager sorted it out, and the family was led to its adjoining suites, 107A and B, the most expensive in the complex.

Wings were flying high in Spain. 'Give Ireland Back to the Irish' had been a No. 1 Spanish hit, the defiant political anthem striking a chord with young music fans living under the brutal regime of dictator Francisco Franco Bahamonde. As they touched down in Alicante, Paul was also stunned to discover that 'Mary Had a Little Lamb' had just topped the Spanish charts too.

Paul and Linda spent their days at the Montíboli playing with the kids on the resort's private beach and their evenings propping up the hotel bar, where they became friendly with Pepe, a waiter, Ramón, a receptionist, and the hotel's resident musician, Quique. Every night, after the barman called "last orders," Pepe would bolt the doors shut, prompting the delivery of a silver tray of contraband, and the Macs would jam into the night with Quique and the house band.

Denny Laine was the first of Wings to arrive, in time for Paul's birthday celebrations on June 18 (Henry was otherwise disposed, and Denny and Monique were visiting family in Nice), and that night, the after-hours fiesta stretched to sunrise.

In the early hours of the next morning, June 19, the dozing McCartneys were awoken by a disagreement outside their hotel window. Rubbing his eyes to check if he was still dreaming, or perhaps tripping, Paul spotted the hotel manager, José Manuel Castillo, arguing with a group of nuns and sheepish-looking children. The visiting sisters had ventured down from the Casa de Beneficencia de Alcoy (a nearby convent and school) hoping to treat their orphaned children to a rare day out, only to be turned away.

Pulling on a T-shirt and shorts, Paul dragged Denny Laine out of bed and ran outside clutching two guitars. And from facing eviction, the holy party suddenly found themselves the exclusive audience for an impromptu coastal concert with a former Beatle. News of McCartney's sunshine serenade soon spread, and photographer José Crespo Colomer was quickly on the scene to immortalize the moment on film, while a local journalist, Pirula Arderius, interviewed Paul for Alicante's *Información* newspaper.

The next day, the "Martin" family checked out, intent on continuing Paul's birthday celebrations with the rest of the band at a nearby villa.

Seiwell and McCullough touched down in Alicante on June 22. Settling in at the rented villa, the band relaxed around the pool, gorged on traditional Spanish tapas, drank, smoked, and jammed. "*We're gonna get high, high, high, in the midday sun,*" McCartney jawed, drowned by a chorus of distant cicadas.

Laine and McCullough instantly jumped on this spark of an idea, and in little time at all, a new addition to the Wings songbook was nearly complete. Its hedonistic, drug-saluting lyrics might not have gone down as well as 'Yesterday' with the sisters of Alcoy, but the song's rhythmic energy—a shuffle, partway between swing and straightforward rock and roll, with an upbeat swagger similar to that of Lennon's 'Revolution 1'—would have caught the attention of their young charges.

"It was very much a song of the times, long hair, flared trousers, macramé jackets and stuff," said McCartney. "To me that was my parting shot at those kinds of days really, it's all about '*we're gonna get high in the midday sun,*' very much what was going on at that time."[40]

While capturing the spirit of the time, the up-tempo rocker also scratched an itch Paul had been feeling during the group's recent rehearsals in Fulham. "We needed a rocker," he explained. "We wrote 'Hi, Hi, Hi' purposefully as a nice easy rocker for that very reason."[41]

The lyrics would be finished a few weeks later back in London. Keen to keep on the right side of the music censors, Paul worked hard to find a way to communicate his message of sex, drugs, and

rock and roll, without crossing the line. An obvious and entirely cost-free fix was to change the spelling of the title from the overtly druggy "High, High, High" to the cheery and nonintoxicant-suggesting 'Hi, Hi, Hi.' But there were other challenges.

"I put a line in 'Hi, Hi, Hi' where I said, 'Lie on the bed and get ready for my . . .' [And I thought] I wonder what I put here?"[42] he explained. "I used a really mad word from a surrealist play by a man called Alfred Jarry, a French playwright who wrote around 1900.* He was a real nutter who used to cycle around Paris on his bike, and he used to have this thing called the Pataphysical Society. It was nothing but a drinking club, but to be a Professor of Pataphysics sounds great. I used that term in 'Maxwell's Silver Hammer'—'he studied Pataphysical.' At any rate, Jarry wrote this theatre sketch called *Ubu Cocu*, which has this character called Peardrop, who's always going around worried about his 'polyhedron.' So I said, '*polygon*.'"[43]

---

* McCartney first encountered Alfred Jarry's *Ubu Cocu* (*Ubu Cuckolded*) in Cyril Connolly's English adaptation for BBC Network Three, on December 21, 1965. It made a clear enough impression on him that he bought a copy, and as he notes, he consulted it occasionally when searching for an odd word for one of his songs. In this case, he didn't look far: "polyhedron" is the sixth word in the play's opening scene.

In Spain, more than just music and sangria were flowing. Fame saw the Beatles forfeit some of life's simple pleasures. On November 26, 1964, when asked by Brian Matthew what he missed about life before Beatlemania, Paul simply replied "riding on a bus." Now, in the sun-bleached surroundings of the Costa Blanca, he tapped into his Liverpool past and uncorked an idea for their touring transportation that was destined to raise the blood pressure of road manager John Morris.

"We were on holiday trying to get healthy before our tour," said Paul, "and we suddenly thought, well wait a minute, if we're going to be in Europe in summer, going to places like the South of France, it's just silly to be in some little box all day gasping for air and stuff. So we came up with this idea to have an open top bus."[44]

Morris was in London, oblivious to the band's recent travels. One afternoon, he cabbed to Fulham to see how rehearsals were going and found an empty room full of equipment. "Nobody was there," says Morris. "They had gone to Alicante, Spain for an extended weekend and hadn't bothered to tell me."[45]

Morris and his business partner, Jean-Claude Kaufmann, swiftly boarded a flight to Alicante, where he found Paul enjoying a spot of water-skiing. "Fair cop," said McCartney. "You've found us!"

Quickly overcoming his annoyance at the band's disappearing act, Morris and Kaufmann took a siesta before discussing Paul's latest road plans over a bottle of Spanish red.

"I wanted to throttle him for having gone to Alicante, but it was a pretty good thing. That night, after dinner, we sat on the balcony of Paul's room and Paul and Denny Laine were just sitting there noodling with guitars. And we were talking about what we were going to do, and he said, 'You want to hear anything?' I said, 'Yeah, "Yesterday."' He and Denny played 'Yesterday' to Jean-Claude and me on that balcony, with the moon shining on the water, and that was one of the greatest thrills of my life."[46]

On June 26, the band traded Spain's white coast for southwest London as preparations for the tour intensified at Manticore. McCartney's first arranged tour in six years was a definitive declaration that he was moving on, but he also wanted to make a statement that he was moving with the times. What he had in mind was a visual accompaniment to the concert that would define the band's identity more than a drumskin motif.

For half a decade, Pink Floyd had provided evolving, often mesmerizing backdrops to their concerts, ranging from refracted light shows designed by their landlord and tutor Mike Leonard during their tenure as inhouse band at the UFO Club on Tottenham Court Road, to abstract films playing behind their 1972 *Eclipse: A Piece for Assorted Lunatics* tour. Paul decided to follow their lead.

John Morris passed McCartney's request for a visual component to Kaufmann, who, together with technical guru Chris Langhart, hired a 2,000-watt projector and a 30-foot screen, and edited a 45-minute film to play on a loop behind the band. At Paul's suggestion, the film juxtaposed man and nature, embracing some of the themes of the *Wild Life* album.

"Jean-Claude made this movie out of clips that he bought copies of," explained Langhart. "There was a long section on sun spots, several sections of Indian dancers hopping up and down and beating on drums. And there was other native dancing, things like that. We would start and stop it depending on what was going on, on the stage, try to sync it up best we could."[47]

The film was a strong statement against consumerism. Busy street scenes from New York and London were intercut with images of animals running free in Africa; airplanes taking flight and trucks dumping diesel fumes were juxtaposed with avian victims of oil slicks.

By contrast, the slick wardrobe Paul and Linda commissioned for the tour did not entirely line up with the moving images playing on the screen behind them, but did echo the flashy onstage dress of Britain's Glam rockers like Bowie and Bolan. At the end of June, D.A. Millings & Sons, the Soho tailor who had made stage suits for the Beatles from 1963 on, received an order for five matching black sequined suits, plus the same design in white. Matching blue T-shirts with a Wings logo across the chest—designed by Mike Ross at the London-based company Ritva—were another late addition to the band's touring wardrobe.

To document their time on the road, Paul was keen to secure the services of two photographers. The first name on the roster was Robert Ellis, a resident lensman with *NME*. With a view to putting together press packs, posters, and programs for the tour, Ellis had been engaged in late June to take some publicity shots of Wings during their rehearsals at the Manticore Theater. Linda was struck by Ellis's ability to capture sharp, characterful images in low-light conditions, and he was hired on the spot.

Soon after securing Ellis's services, Linda invited a snapper friend from her Fillmore East days to drop by the rehearsal space. Originally from New York, Joe Stevens—better known as "Captain Snaps"—was working in London as a freelance photographer and was quick to answer Linda's call. Laying out recent contact sheets from shoots with Marc Bolan and Alice Cooper on the studio floor, Linda was impressed and Stevens, too, booked his spot on the band's July flight to Marseilles. Paul seemed enthusiastic, too, for a few moments, but Stevens noted that his attention quickly moved elsewhere.

"Paul seemed very spaced, not just on grass, but distanced from what he was about to get into," said Stevens. "I got the impression that the idea of this tour would be that it was rock 'n' roll therapy for him. All the plugs from his switchboard had been pulled out, and he had to be courageous and put them back in."[48]

Controlling his and the group's public image was high on Paul's agenda. Ellis and Stevens were asked to sign a copublishing deal with MPL, relinquishing ownership of their photographs in exchange for a fee every time they were used. Image contracts would be handled by Samba Lessons, Ltd., a company Paul registered as an arm of McCartney Productions, at 1 Soho Square. Intended, at first, to handle Linda's photographs, Samba Lessons allowed them to track licensing and sales.

Not everyone was rushing to pack a suitcase for the July road trip, though. Having grown disillusioned with life as Paul's first line of defense, and wanting to focus on her writing career, Shelley Turner—the very first employee of MPL in London—left at the start of July.[49] In Turner's place, Paul hired two new secretaries—Rebecca Hinds and Jane Buck. Hinds, a German speaker, would accompany the band on the road.

Climbing the four flights of stairs to MPL's temporary offices later that year, *Jackie* writer "Sam"* gave an insight into why morale at MPL might be in short supply.

"There's nothing pretentious about the office," Sam wrote. "There are no carpets on the floor—just [plastic] lino. The desks are secondhand. There's a battered old filing cabinet against one wall. Photos of Paul and Linda, and of Wings are pinned to a board with little cartoons and snippets from papers."[50] The *Jackie* writer also noted that office hours stretched from the start of the working day in England, to the end of the working day in New York.

One thing was becoming clear: the demands of leading a band, writing and recording music, and running an office were too much for Paul to handle alone. Paul needed a manager, someone to run MPL. Shortly after Wings was formed he invited Wendy Hanson, Brian Epstein's personal assistant between 1964 and 1966, to take the job. "I remember what he said," Hanson recalled. "He said, 'I want you to be to Wings what Brian was to the boys.' In other words, when we arrive at the studio, you're there."[51]

When Hanson declined,† McCartney put the search on hold, reasoning that it was still early days. Until now, there were no tours to arrange, and contractual issues were being handled by the Eastmans. Shelley Turner had been able to keep MPL running smoothly in London, and Diane Brooks was overseeing things in New York. But the time was coming when a manager would have to be found.

Meanwhile, John Morris was managing the tour, and he was coming up against his first real hurdle. An open top bus, he had come to realize, was not only a bad idea, but also impossibly difficult to source. Scratching his head for a solution, he called in a favor from Tom Salter, a businessman

---

* Sam's full name was never given in issues of the weekly magazine.

† Wendy Hanson was born in 1935 in Fixby, West Yorkshire, and pursued a career mostly in the world of classical music. She ran the press office of the Metropolitan Opera in New York briefly and worked in various capacities (ranging from publicist to personal assistant) for the D'Oyly Carte Opera Company, the Philadelphia Orchestra, the Israel Philharmonic, the composer Gian Carlo Menotti and the conductors Leopold Stokowski and Lorin Maazel. She died after falling down a staircase at her home in Arezzo, Italy, in 1991.

and fixer based in Soho. Salter, owner of a dozen shops and boutiques between Carnaby Street and King's Road, had a wide network of contacts across the South of England.

"Originally John had asked me to talk Paul out of his idea to have a double-decker bus," said Salter. "But instead of me convincing *him* it was a bad idea, he convinced *me* what a great idea it would be."[52]

A few phone calls later, Salter had tracked down a likely candidate in Great Yarmouth, East Anglia: a double-decker bus, built in 1953 by Bristol Commercial Vehicles of Lowestoft, bearing registration number WNO 481. After 15 years of service ferrying holidaymakers to seaside towns on the east coast of England for the Eastern National Omnibus Company, the bus was retired from service in 1968 and sold. The new owners, Hall Coaches, gave it a new red-and-gray livery before renting it out to wedding parties, tourists, and racegoers. Still recovering from the initial shock of Paul's freethinking travel plans, John Morris nearly had a fit when Salter returned from the coast with the 20-year-old double-decker.

"I sent Tom off with them to get a bus, I was hoping for a Mercedes with a bathroom in it—a tour bus. He and Paul came back grinning like crazy with this open top London transport bus with a top speed of 38 miles an hour."[53]

With only six days to go before the start of the tour, Paul also requested a few modifications. His wish list for the tour bus included: bunk beds, a kitchen with fridge and stove, stereo equipment, a playpen for Stella, a clothesline for her nappies, and mattresses on the top deck for sunbathing. Surveying the bus's soporific red-and-gray paintwork at a London Transport garage in Staines, Middlesex, Paul also requested that they give the bus an eye-catching makeover. Local hippie Dave "DW" Wilson lent Salter a helping hand, working through the night to sand down the body of the bus for a fresh paint job the next morning.

On July 4, while a gang of tradesmen began revamping the bus interior, Salter enlisted the help of fellow Carnaby Street bohemians Neil and Georgina Dean, Charlie Smith, and Geoffrey Cleghorn to give the bus a radical new look. Fueled by a nearby greasy spoon café, and their local drug dealer, they went to work. After spraying on a sky-blue base coat, the three artists garnished the bus with vibrant clouds, flowers, and figures, plus bold, red-lettered "Wings Over Europe" banners down each side.

"We worked 18-hour days for three days," says Cleghorn. "And, without taking the Fifth Amendment, a couple of lines of cocaine helped."[54]

Marching powder also played a role in the iconic "W" logo that adorned the bus's rear. Though a band insignia was not on Paul's original list, artist Neil Dean took it upon himself to draft a Wings emblem, sketching the design on the back of an envelope. "Neil borrowed a Mickey Mouse ruler and pencil from Charlie's little girl Lucky," Neil's wife and fellow artist Georgina added, "and fueled with a few chemicals, a cup of coffee, and memories of the Matchless Motorcycles logo, designed the Wings logo."[55]

Dean's inverted Matchless Motorcycles logo was then fashioned out of five-foot-high, enamel-coated timber, and attached to the back of the bus, completing the design.

Speechless at the transformation, Paul invited the Carnaby crew to hop on board the beautified tour bus and join them in Toulon. There was one final request, though: to find a way to babysit a pound bag of Moroccan hashish across the British Channel, and through French customs. Former London bus driver Pat Puchelli grabbed the bag of hash and stuffed it the destination roller at the front of the bus, and on July 7 the overhauled double-decker rolled out of the Staines depot, destined for southern France.

Looking across at Morris as the bus crawled toward the South Coast, it struck Paul that the ever-resourceful American might be a useful person to have around on a more permanent basis.

"In the early days of it when I was pulling rabbits out of hats left, right and center, Paul came to me and said, 'Do you want to manage us? Would you like to be our manager?'" said Morris. "I thought for all of about 30 seconds and said, 'Thank you for asking. That's really polite. I have never managed anybody, and I think I'm going to say no. I'll always be able to help you any way I can producing stuff.' I think I kissed goodbye to a couple million bucks right then. But I also knew what I wanted, and that I didn't want to do it."[56]

18

"CHANTEZ A BIT IF YOU KNOW LES MOTS"

—

When we were thinking of going back on the road, I said to Linda, 'Do you think you could enjoy it?' You know, there's that feeling when you're behind the curtain waiting to go on and you get those terrible nerves and stuff. So I said, 'Do you think you could enjoy all of that?' And she said, 'Sure, show me the curtain!'"[1]

But now, on Sunday, July 9, 1972, with the curtain within eyeshot, Linda was having second thoughts. The stage was set at Châteauvallon, Ollioules, in southern France, for Wings' continental debut; the setting sun was perched between the pine trees and an eleventh-century fort that enveloped a beautiful open-air amphitheater built by Gérard and Colette Paquet in 1966.

Two thousand fans, paying a bargain 20 francs (£1.65/$4) per ticket, packed the arena's ascending stone tiers, eager to witness the first European concert headlined by a Beatle since 1966. But for all of the venue's magnificence and allure, Linda would happily have traded the French vistas for a grubby student dining room. Five months after the band's carefree British road trip—where the student throngs had not even expected their visit—Wings faced a crowd of paying punters expecting to hear the Beatles.

"I was scared stiff," said Linda of the band's European debut. "It would have been bad enough playing with an unknown group—but because of Paul being an ex-Beatle and everything, the eyes of the world were on him. Not really the kind of conditions to play your first [advertised] gig, believe me."[2]

Backstage, in a section of the ancient fort converted to a dressing room for visiting acts, Denny Seiwell consoled his anxious bandmate.

"I remember the first night backstage, she was crying on my shoulder. She said, 'I'm afraid. I don't want to be here.' She was so nervous about going out in front of the world and doing that. I said, 'It's a little late for that now, honey.'"[3]

For tour manager John Morris, it was easy to see that Linda was more at home behind a camera lens than a keyboard. Terrified that she might make a mistake in front of thousands of people, she had devised a fail-safe. Taking a cue from the inlays that mark the fifth, seventh, ninth and twelfth frets on Paul's guitars, she came up with a system that would let her see at a glance where she was on the keyboard.

"I was backstage and walked by Linda's piano," Morris recalled, "and almost had a heart attack, because the chords were color coded. There was a color-coded chord book on her piano."[4]

Linda's fears were amplified by news that a pack of British journalists was en route from Marseilles. Paul had not wanted to entertain the British press. Indeed, he went out of his way—750 miles south, to be precise—to avoid them. But knowing a handful of reporters would shadow the band across the English Channel regardless, he decided that he was more likely to win them over by being helpful than by trying to obstruct them, so he flew two dozen journalists from London to Marseilles, first class. At 9:00 p.m., as the band were about go onstage, likely to Linda's relief, stage manager Mike Leyburn burst into the dressing room to relay news that the press was running late.

The Air France jet transporting the traveling press pack left London at 4:30 p.m., touching down at Marseilles-Marignane Airport three hours later. The 11th-hour arrangements, made by MPL, left the press 90 minutes from the venue, pondering whether this was part of some cynical game of cat and mouse.

"Even the local taxi drivers had difficulty in finding the château," wrote *NME*'s James Johnson a few days later, "which would only be reached after a mysterious drive through the suburbs of Toulon, a half-built housing estate, and up a two-mile track through pinewoods."[5]

Johnson and his colleagues emerged from the nearby woods as the first half of the concert ended, the distant, muddy sound of Wings only becoming clear for 'Blue Moon of Kentucky,' the final number of their first set; the press had missed 'Bip Bop,' 'Smile Away,' 'Mumbo,' 'Give Ireland Back to the Irish,' '1882,' and 'I Would Only Smile.'

"'Blue Moon of Kentucky' sounded more like something from a local church hall group than a band led by a former Beatle,"[6] Johnson wrote in his review for *NME*.

Wings opened their second set more aggressively, with successive rockers 'The Mess,' 'Best Friend,' and the new 'Soily.' Three slow-tempo numbers followed, with 'I Am Your Singer' showing off Paul and Linda's soft vocal blend, 'Say You Don't Mind' showcasing Denny Laine's songwriting credentials, and 'Henry's Blues' providing a platform for McCullough's bluesy roots. But as Linda stepped up to follow Henry's unique brand of melancholy with her own reggae effort, a technical hitch left her exposed and embarrassed.

"My mic isn't working," Paul called out to the roadies a few bars into 'Seaside Woman.'

"*Give it to your missus then!*" a visiting American in the crowd yelled back.

A collective smile spread across the British press pack, each journalist noting the cutting quip for their forthcoming articles. Unperturbed by the heckler, Paul grabbed a working microphone and, adopting a Beatle-like swagger, uttered: "Chantez a bit if you know les mots," before moving on to 'My Love,' 'Mary Had a Little Lamb,' 'Maybe I'm Amazed,' and 'Wild Life.' With momentum back on their side, McCartney's band invited the French crowd to get 'High, High, High,' before signing off with a crowd-pleasing encore of 'Long Tall Sally.'

"onstage with McCartney in the South of France, playing 'Long Tall Sally,' I looked over and Paul was rocking like I had never seen anyone rock," said McCullough. "I thought I was hallucinating; it was like being onstage with the Beatles."[7]

At midnight, the band unwound at a small party in the backstage enclosure, with drinks laid out on trestle tables lit by floodlights in the evergreens. Slipping out of his stage outfit, Paul grumbled about the PA problems, but the band's performance, showy wardrobe, and slick stage production—all thrown together in a matter of weeks—underlined just how far Wings had come since Nottingham's Portland Ballroom, exactly five months earlier.

Paul and Linda emerged at 1:00 a.m., mingling with the press behind the château. Still fighting his post-Beatles reputation as a recluse—once they stick a label on you, it takes ages to peel it off—Paul sat down with a scotch and Coke in one hand, and Linda's hand in the other, and chatted with his press guests about why he was starting his comeback tour in such an out-of-the-way place.

"I think the British audiences and American audiences are a bit more cynical, unlike tonight's audience, who are just coming out for a good evening. And we're a new band, just starting out, no matter what we've been through before,"[8] Paul told the mob of pressmen pointing microphones in his and Linda's direction. "If you go and play Britain or America with a very new band you're really on the spot. You've got to be red hot. It takes a little time for a band to get red hot."[9]

The two Dennys and Henry rapidly became jaded onlookers to the press circus enveloping Paul and Linda. Rather than discussing the growing credibility of McCartney's new group, the reporters continued to press the Beatle button, questioning Paul's decision to keep his back catalog off the tour menu.

"The Beatles things are a bit close for me to do at the moment," said McCartney. "Although when we were on holiday recently I was rediscovering 'Yesterday,' playing it on an acoustic guitar. I love 'em, you know. I enjoyed it all. Fantastic thing while it lasted. But the Beatles will never get together again."[10]

Breaking away from a chat with journalist Chris Charlesworth about her obsession with reggae music, Linda launched into an unprompted attack on her husband's former bandmates, and the deadlock that was choking the family's finances.

"We have no income, it all goes to Apple, even from Paul's solo album *Ram*, we are stuck, let me tell you. What annoys me is the other three and their preaching. John goes around saying 'Join Rock Liberation—give the people what's theirs'—and he could get us out. We saw John and Yoko at Christmas, and it was all 'we're going to do it' and 'you'll be out by March,' and Yoko said, 'to hell with the contracts'—but nothing's happened."[11]

"I don't blame John or the others particularly. They're only puppets for Klein," Paul interrupted. "They're nice people, but they're being manipulated."

"Yeah, he'll get his, though. He'll get his in the end," Linda snarled.

"I've got a new band now. I'm more interested in that,"[12] concluded Paul.

And with that, the band and press retired to the Grand Hotel in Toulon.

———

The touring party moved 130 kilometers along the coast to Antibes, on July 10, for two rest days at the glitzy Hôtel du Cap-Eden-Roc, one of the most expensive resorts in the South of France—a hotel where the helicopter landing pad was as busy as the cocktail bar. At the very moment the luminescent Wings tour bus with its 30 scruffy rockers and crew broke through the pine trees that guard the entrance to this stylish playground for the deep-pocketed, the photographer, playboy, and art collector Gunter Sachs touched down with his model girlfriend, Mirja Larsson, for a lunch date.

That night the band quaffed champagne and dined on fine French cuisine and marked Denny Seiwell's 29th birthday with a party on the ocean view terrace.

"We stayed in these incredible places," says Seiwell. "As a band, we never got paid because we spent more than we made on that tour."[13]

Also celebrating *her* birthday with friends on the French Riviera was 19- soon to be 20-year-old Joanne LaPatrie. An up-and-coming model who had appeared in television commercials and on fashion magazine covers, Boston-born LaPatrie was already a fixture on the rock scene. The striking brunette boasted an impressive list of rock star conquests, having lost her virginity to Jimi Hendrix backstage at Woodstock in 1969, and having spent a wild night, soon after, with Jim Morrison who was, by her account, "already out of it and on a bottle of whisky a day."[14] She had dated Rod Stewart on and off for almost two years; according to LaPatrie, Stewart wrote 'You Wear It Well' about her.

Mingling in one of the many bars at the Cap-Eden-Roc, Jo Jo, as she preferred to be known, gravitated toward the Wings tour party, seducing one of the roadies before slipping inside the band's private get-together. She confessed to having sent love letters to Beatle Paul, as a teen, and as her daughter later averred, she had arrived in France "determined to marry"[15] her teenage crush. But the irresistible force soon met the immovable object, and Jo Jo, together with other circling female predators, quickly discovered that her presence was not welcome.

"Linda obviously hated groupies," said LaPatrie. "When I first met Denny, while they were touring the South of France in '72, she did not want me around."[16]

Jo Jo was by no means the first female admirer to fall foul of Linda's suspicions. "The actress Olivia Hussey had a crush on Paul and she was down at EMI Studios when we were recording one day. She was supposed to be just visiting, but when Linda walked in you could have cut the air with a knife,"[17] Laine verified. "Linda didn't like other chicks hanging around Paul. She thought—and so did Paul—that Jo Jo was after him. She was fascinated to meet him, but that soon wore off. Paul's not Jo Jo's type."

Captivated by the fierce young American, Denny—the only eligible bachelor in the band—handed Jo Jo tickets to Wings' next concert on July 12, and within 48 hours the two were inseparable.

"It was the ultimate groupie's dream. I was on the tour bus, going everywhere with them," remembered Jo Jo. "Linda wasn't happy at first. I told Paul once, 'I can't believe the way Linda puts me down all the time.' He just shrugged."[18]

Paul had bigger concerns than a clash between his wife and a young groupie. Following their second concert by the ocean at the holiday resort of Juan-Les-Pins, the band spent the night at another luxury retreat, the Hotel Baumanière, just outside of Arles. At breakfast on July 13, Jo Jo's 20th birthday, while a lovestruck Denny and Jo Jo fed each other grapes across the dining table, Paul was presented with a jaw-dropping bill for the first four days of tour expenses.

The group's spending was wildly out of control. The band's $3,000 concert fee, plus merchandise revenue, barely covered their hotel and travels costs—particularly when they were all bedding down in lavish hotels. Paul summoned Morris and his assistant, Sue Taylor, to his room to discuss some changes to the sleeping arrangements.

"He said, 'Look, we can't do this, paying all this money for these people,'" Morris remembered. "'We want all the crew to stay in pensions [small hotels] and we'll stay in four-star hotels.'"

But Morris was not happy with the prospect of asking the hard-grafting road crew to slum it and knocked back Paul's request.

"I said, basically, 'No fucking way. I'm not going to do that.' I just refused to do it. That's an attitudinal problem that I think Paul had that caused some of the friction on the tour."[19]

Morris's refusal only annoyed Paul further. That evening the band were scheduled to play their third concert at the historic Roman amphitheater in Arles, in southern France. Once the site of chariot races and bloody gladiator duels, it now became, in the hours before the concert's scheduled start, the stage for a spectacular bust-up between Morris and McCartney. It had become clear to Morris, as soon as Wings' wagons rolled into the arena, that adapting the ancient setting to their twentieth-century needs—particularly, hanging the thirty-foot film screen—was going to be a challenge.

"I said to Paul, 'I've got a problem. I don't know how the hell I'm going to hang the screen,'" said Morris. "He said, 'Nail it into the columns.' And I said, 'No way.' I could see the crew scurrying off the edge of the stage into the orchestra pit. He said, 'Nail it to the things,' and I said, 'No, I'm not going to do it. I'm not destroying antiquity just so we can hang a screen. If I can figure out another way, I'll figure out another way, otherwise we won't use the screen tonight.' I'm sure he thought I was being unreasonable, but I was not going to put nails into Roman columns."[20]

As McCartney and Morris retired to their corners, Chris Langhart stepped in with a solution, and the concert, with its film projection, went ahead as planned. Doubtless Paul had no desire to damage the UNESCO-listed site; the screen was never really the issue, but a regrettable manifestation of a failing relationship between talent and manager.

At the start of the tour, Tom Salter, the Carnaby Street businessman who had arranged the band's tour bus and subsequently hitched a ride on it to the South of France, had fallen into the role of accidental assistant to Paul and Linda. But four days of playing middleman and peacemaker between McCartney and Morris had worn Salter down, and he told Paul that he was leaving the tour—his departure coinciding with the amphitheater dustup.

"I left the tour after Arles," said Salter. "John Morris was getting slightly out of touch with Paul, they were not communicating very well. I knew Paul wasn't gonna be pleased with my leaving, but I also knew he needed to communicate with John."[21]

Wings were scheduled to play a concert in Lyon on Friday, July 14, but the show was canceled for logistical reasons, or more accurately, because of the tortoiselike tour bus: after Lyon, two Paris shows were scheduled, but at the bus's top speed of 38 mph, the drive would take 14 hours, at best. So the Lyon date was sacrificed to give the band and crew more time to travel north. As an added benefit, McCartney and Morris had some much-needed breathing space.

Struck down with glandular fever, photographer Robert Ellis joined Salter on a flight back to London. Henry was also feeling under the weather, having developed a bad toothache. Though they were kept company on the bus by their wives and children—Denny traveled with Monique; Henry with his wife, Sheila, and their son Jesse; and Denny Laine with his new love, Jo Jo—there were plenty of chemical and liquid distractions on board as well, so the Irish guitarist was able to anesthetize himself.

"The bus was really amazing," said McCullough. "There were a couple of gas fridges built into it stuffed full of cheese and beer and things like that."[22]

As he coasted through rural France on the top deck, a cheese and tomato baguette in one hand, a joint in the other, Paul felt the storm clouds hovering over his head beginning to clear. When the band stopped at a gas station, two hitchhiking Liverpudlians crept toward the double-decker, not believing their luck that they had crossed paths with McCartney. To the surprise of Malcolm Hughes and his brother, Paul waved them onboard.

"Hi, Paul, can I have your autograph?" said Hughes.

"There's no need to ask where you come from!" replied Paul, noting Malcolm's Liverpudlian accent. Hughes produced a Doors album from his rucksack, presenting it to Paul and Linda to sign. Confessing she was a big Doors fan, and had photographed Jim Morrison, Linda scrawled her name on the album sleeve, and Paul followed suit. Leaving the bus Hughes bumped into the other members of Wings who were, as he recalls, "a bit worse for wear."[23] But perseverance rewarded the young Scouser with a full set of autographs.

The band spent Friday night at Château St. Jean in Mâcon—halfway between Arles and Paris—completing the journey to the French capital on Saturday morning. Wings' matinee and evening concerts at the Théâtre de L'Olympia, on July 16, had sold out quickly, though times had changed since the Beatles last played there in 1964. Pulling up outside the venue at 28 Boulevard des Capucines, the band's eye-catching tour bus was greeted by only a handful of autograph hunters; the promoters had not even bothered to change the sign above the theater, which still read: *Tonight—Jesus Christ Superstar.*

"We were well pissed off by that, thank you very much,"[24] said Paul.

The McCartney family spent Saturday evening exploring the backstreets of Paris and shopping in the Left Bank, before settling at the five-star L'Hotel in the heart of the city, where Oscar Wilde spent his final three years. That evening, Paul and Linda sat for an interview and photo shoot with *Match*, the glossy French celebrity magazine.

The start of Henry's Parisian stay was less hassle-free. "I ended up with such a severe toothache that I had to go to have it fixed in France,"[25] said McCullough of the pain he had been self-medicating since Arles. John Morris arranged for Henry to visit an emergency dentist. The guitarist's dental struggles were soon immortalized, for the band's amusement, in the improvised lyrics of 'Henry's Blues.'

"We used to do a straight blues thing with Henry every night," explained Paul, "and halfway through the tour he got a terrible toothache, so he sang about that, 'Oh man, this tooth pain is killing me!' And the next night it was 'I've just been to the dentist.' So that was the saga of Henry's tooth."[26]

On Sunday afternoon, Wings played the first of their sellout gigs to 2,000 fans at the Paris Olympia. Backstage, Janet Horwood of *Woman's Own* magazine, together with a dozen other journalists, waited patiently for promised interviews. Fervent applause carried the band offstage, just as Sue Taylor hurried past with a handful of newspapers, dropping them off in the McCartneys' dressing room. As Paul and Linda began sifting through the press coverage of their Châteauvallon concert, Horwood was invited inside. The dressing room—until recently occupied by Stella, Mary, and Heather—was strewn with books, toys, games, and baby bottles.

Horwood sat in the corner, an awkward spectator to the McCartneys' first real dose of tour critique as a performing couple. Each newspaper feature included a healthy slice of their informal press conference at Châteauvallon, wedged between mostly negative assessments of the half of the concert the reporters managed to catch. "The two-hour concert amounted to little more than two hours of fair-to-goodish pop,"[27] opined James Johnson in *NME*. Scanning the collection of clippings for references to her own performance, Linda wilted into her chair. "To me," Johnson added, "Linda McCartney is still the weakest link in the group, with most of her contributions fairly ineffectual."

"Unfortunately, her voice lacks both depth and power, a fact which McCartney must know all too well,"[28] added *Melody Maker*'s Chris Charlesworth.

"As lovely and intelligent as Linda is, I do not think at present she is ready to give the band that bit of extra strength it needs,"[29] concluded Michael Wale in *Disc*.

The uncomfortable silence was broken by a small figure appearing from nowhere, flinging herself at Paul. A fan, eluding the French security, had crept through the stage door, and she wept with joy as her idol signed an autograph and kissed her on the cheek. Raising his eyes from the newspaper text to acknowledge Horwood, Paul offered a frank, if slightly throwaway response to criticism of his wife's playing and singing.

"I'm quite prepared for people to criticize us, and if they don't like us then they needn't listen to us again or buy our records," he said. "Most of the criticism says Linda is the weakest member of the group and if you are going to be like that, well, she is. . . . She is no Billy Preston, granted, but actually I would not like a very technical keyboard player in the group because they tend to take over. . . . Linda isn't a professional, but to have her with us is a great influence. As the song goes, she's getting better all the time."[30]

On the *Abbey Road* and *Let It Be* albums music critics saw the profound effect a skilled keyboard player could have on McCartney's musical output. 'The Long and Winding Road,' 'Let It Be,' and 'Get Back,' among others, all featured Billy Preston on Hammond organ, alongside Paul on the piano, and Preston's presence at the Beatles' sessions gave the band a fresh injection of soulful energy.

The French critics were no less brutal than their British counterparts, *Rock and Folk* magazine noting of Wings' Paris concert: "*L'incompetence de Linda peut etre la cause de cette faillite musicale de Wings*"[31] ("Linda's incompetence may be the cause of Wings' musical bankruptcy").[*]

Responding to the suggestion, in one article, that she might bow out of the group, Linda scoffed, "Quit the band?! I've only just joined."[32]

"American papers wouldn't have been so harshly critical of our European tour," Seiwell suggested. "But it didn't take much foresight to realize it would happen, what with Linda on piano."[33]

From Paris, the band took an Air France flight to Munich (München), West Germany, on Monday, July 17, the 520-mile journey once again proving too much for the psychedelic double-decker. McCartney and Morris, now in agreement about cutting costs while keeping the tour

---

[*] Press criticism was not limited to Linda. Yoko Ono was regularly on the receiving end of newspaper backlash for poking her nose in John's musical business. In the September 16, 1972, issue of *NME*, one journalist wrote: "I love them both [John and Paul], I really do, but I wish they'd leave their wives out of their music. To me it just sounds as though Yoko and Linda are interfering, and I think both of them are poor musical substitutions for what Paul and John were to each other."

party together, booked the band and crew rooms at the Hotel Grünwald, a modest Schlosshotel in the center of Munich.

By early evening, most of the road crew gorged on spit-roasted meat and steins of beer at the local Bierkellers. But five concerts into the tour, technical director Chris Langhart was unhappy with the quality of the pictures playing behind the band. So Langhart and a couple of roadies clambered up to the hotel rooftop with two tins of paint and the projection screen, hoping to remedy the problem.

"It was quite a big screen, like 30 feet, projected from the front," explained Langhart. "And to get enough light to reflect off it, we took the screen, which was sort of grayish, white plastic, on the top of the German building and we painted the whole thing silver, because that way you'd get more reflection off it."[34]

Down at ground level, Paul returned from an afternoon stroll with Stella on his shoulders. Outside the hotel he spied a familiar face and stopped in his tracks as he came face-to-face with actor and musical comedian Bernard Cribbins. Having recently finished work on Alfred Hitchcock's *Frenzy*, Cribbins was in town to direct actress Millicent Martin in a German television series; he was equally dumbstruck to see a famous face so far from home.

"Hey, I know you," said McCartney, "you're great!"

"You're great too,"[35] replied Cribbins.

After working as an actor on the stages of London's West End in the mid-1950s, Cribbins became a household name across Britain with a series of novelty records—the infectiously catchy 'The Hole in the Ground,' 'Right Said Fred,' and 'Gossip Calypso,' released on EMI's Parlophone label between February and December 1962. The man behind Cribbins's hits—whistled by every milkman from Land's End to John O'Groats—was a producer Paul knew well.

"Young Paul and I chatted away like old pals," Cribbins wrote in his memoir. "The main topics of conversation being our mutual friend and mentor Mr. George Martin, Abbey Road Studios, and a tune or two. Apparently, Paul had really enjoyed my cover of 'When I'm Sixty-Four' and was also a big fan of both 'The Hole in the Ground' and 'Right Said Fred.' I can't remember what I said in return, but it was definitely complimentary."[36]

Energized by his brush with Cribbins, Paul led his band in a concert for 3,000 fans at the Zirkus-Krone-Bau, a venue the Beatles filled twice in 1966. Not all the stalls were crowded for Wings' July 18, 1972, concert, though; the promoter, Fritz Rau, blamed the empty seats on a heat wave in Central Europe. When the fans filed out, Paul and Linda quickly followed, electing not to talk to the German press.

The last time Paul played in Germany he was feeling the heat in an altogether different way. Boarding a plane from London to Munich in June 1966, he was forced to deal with a paternity claim from Erika Huebers, a 22-year-old waitress working on the Große Frieheit in Hamburg—

ARLES
THEATRE ANTIQUE
JEUDI 13 JUILLET - 21 h.

Wings OVER EUROPE
PAUL MAC CARTNEY
Wings

PAUL MAC CARTNEY
LINDA MAC CARTNEY
DENNY LAINE
HENRY MAC CULLOUGH
DENNY SEIWELL

VENTE BILLETS :
BUREAU DU FESTIVAL - 35, Place de la République - Tél. 26.59

DISQUES APPEL   EMI · PATHÉ MARCONI

the Beatles' main haunt during their time in the West German port city—who maintained that McCartney was father to her daughter, Bettina. Paul vehemently denied Huebers's claim, but faced with arrest by the German Youth Welfare Department (and the negative press that would bring), he was advised by Brian Epstein and the Beatles' lawyer David Jacobs to settle out of court.[37]

"It was 1966 and we were due to do a European tour," Paul later explained. "I was told that if the maintenance question wasn't settled we couldn't go to Germany. I wasn't going to sign a crazy document like this, so I didn't. Then we were actually on the plane leaving for the tour when they put the paper under my face and said if I didn't sign the whole tour would be off. They said the agreement would deny I was the father, and it was a small amount anyway (£2,700 or $7,500) . . . So I signed."[38]

The next day, Wings escaped the searing heat of Munich, traveling north to Frankfurt for their second West German date. Unlike the Zirkus-Krone-Bau, the Stadthalle Offenbach was packed to the rafters, 2,500 fans filling the hall for a gig that nearly didn't happen.

Crawling along at 38 mph on the speed-limit-free autobahn, Wings got three-quarters of the way through the 250-mile journey when Morris realized they would not make the sound check, let alone the concert. Pulling up at a service station, Morris sent an urgent S.O.S. to German promoter Fritz Rau who, rather than face refunding 2,500 tickets, dispatched a fleet of Mercedes vans to whisk the band to Frankfurt. About 100 fans were still trying to get inside the convention center when—just an hour before the gig was due to start—Paul and the band burst through the stage door.

"They went on without a sound check, and without the film that night,"[39] Morris recalled.

Film backdrop or not, the adrenaline rush propelled Wings to one of the strongest performances of the tour. Leaving the Stadthalle stage to a standing ovation, the band received an unexpected invitation to bed down at Burg Hohenscheid, a twelfth-century castle on the outskirts of Düsseldorf, board and lodgings offered *gratis* by the generous castle proprietors. Their motives for their largesse became clear at breakfast, however, when a photographer and journalist arrived to document the McCartneys' visit. Two days later a curious photograph of Paul frying eggs, surrounded by castle staff, appeared in a German national newspaper with the headline, "*Lieber selbst macht ex-Beatle Paul McCartney seine Spiegeleier*" ("Ex-Beatle Paul McCartney Prefers to Make His Own Fried Eggs").

But after a marathon 375-mile drive to Zürich, Switzerland, the band were noticeably tiring. McCullough attributed the band's growing lethargy to the long journeys between venues, and postgig partying.

"We'd do the gig, come back to the hotel and get wrecked, and a bit pissed," said Henry, "then get up at half-past eight in the morning and take off in the bus again—traveling all day without a break."[40]

July 21 marked Paul's maiden concert in Switzerland. Though he and Jane Asher holidayed in the Swiss Alps in March 1966, the Beatles had never graced the stadiums or concert halls of the Swiss Confederation. It was also Henry's 29th birthday, and in tribute to McCullough's recent dental work the band tweaked the order of its setlist, opening the concert at the Zürich Kongresshaus with a short jam, 'Eat At Home' and 'Smile Away.'

Keeping tabs on Wings' progress for *Record Mirror* that night was Swiss-based journalist Bernie Sigg. His review described a performance of two contrasting halves.

"The first half of the concert featured mainly rock numbers, which won much acclaim from the audience," wrote Sigg. "After the interval the songs became softer. But, for some reason, the audience got visibly bored. They became vocally disapproving during 'Henry's Blues,' and the derogatory whistles blotted out the applause."[41]

Leaving the Kongresshaus, McCullough was visibly distant and was drinking more heavily than usual. Paul and Linda had put together a surprise birthday bash at a nearby fondue restaurant for the well-liked guitarist, but when they arrived it quickly became clear that tiredness, and irritation at the jeering, had left Henry in no mood to party.

"He was pretty volatile," says Seiwell. "We went upstairs to the fondue restaurant, right after the concert. Henry was smashed already. And he said to Linda at dinner, 'If you keep having that fucking hatchet face onstage, I can't look at you.' She looked scared all the time she was onstage, like she didn't want to be there. Paul went, 'Oh no, what the hell; is this going to happen now,' you know. Henry was the type of guy that, if he had a few drinks in him, he'd just tell you."[42]

McCullough chose the occasion of his 29th birthday to break a long-held band taboo, raising his head above the parapet and declaring that Linda was holding the band back. Henry's outburst was a worrying development for Paul, who maintained she was up to the job. Now the cynicism about Linda's place in the band was no longer restricted to outsiders, but was coming aggressively from within the band's ranks. Doubtless, in the morning, Henry blamed his outburst on the drink, and all was forgiven, but there was no taking it back.

"Linda, while proficient at picking things up on the keyboard, didn't have the ability to play freely," said Denny Laine. "If we'd had her and another keyboard player as well, we'd have been fine, but Linda was given too much to do. She was professional though, she got paid like the rest of us."[43] McCullough's soused outburst suggested that the criticism leveled at the band, though brushed off by Paul, was getting under Henry's skin.

"I could sense a feeling among the others of 'Linda's holding us back,'"[44] said Paul. "Two of the guys would say, 'What are we doing with her?' And I would say, 'I don't quite know. I can't put it into words, but I know there's a good reason for her being there.' I know that it is right, whether it is for the general confidence or to give some innocence to the group."[45]

"At the beginning people said, 'Oh, good grief, she can't play the piano.' And I wasn't good," Linda admitted. "But then I hadn't jumped up and down and said, 'Hey Paul, let me be in your band,' I was there because he'd asked me to join, and gradually I got into it, and began to enjoy it."[46]

The next day, Wings played the Montreux Pavilion—the final date of the first leg of the European tour—and after two nights at the Montreux Palace Hotel, the group flew out of Geneva Airport, bound for London and a tension-defusing midtour break.

———

Paul and Linda needed some respite from the demanding schedule, intraband squabbles, and media onslaught that the tour brought about, so on July 25 they took up an invitation from Mick Jagger to join him in New York for the final date of the Rolling Stones' American tour. On July 26, 20,000 fans filled Madison Square Garden for the Stones' fourth concert there in three days. At the end of the night, Jagger was presented with a double-tier cake for his 29th birthday, most of which ended up scattered across the stage as the gig descended into banana cream chaos.

The McCartneys were there to enjoy themselves, but inevitably, Paul also watched the show analytically, and from that perspective, it was hard not to see the Stones' onstage bravado and boisterous performance as a reminder of the flexibility that Wings still lacked. Still, he knew he was comparing apples and oranges. By 1972, the Stones had 10 albums and nine years of hits to pick from, but without Paul's solo recordings and Beatles hits, Wings had only 11 publicly known songs to their name—8 tracks from *Wild Life* and 2 singles, counting both A and B sides.

After the gig, the Stones threw an extravagant party at the New York St. Regis Hotel, where Paul exploited Mick's good mood to sweet-talk him into lending Wings the Rolling Stones' Mobile Studio truck for the end of their European tour. Back in London, with a view to recording a live single ('Hi, Hi, Hi' the likely candidate), Paul secured the services of EMI engineers Alan Parsons, Jeremy Gee, and Graham Fleming to record the tour's final concerts.

Paul's ambitions didn't stop there. As well as professionally recording the end of Wings' continental visit, he wanted the climax of their time on the road captured on film. Just around the corner from MPL's fourth-floor offices in Soho Square, former film editor Roger Cherrill, and his wife, Joan, ran a small production company. Paul and Linda dropped by their offices to discuss plans to film three of Wings' European dates. To oversee the project, Cherrill hired Barry Chattington, a young commercials director who had been assembling films for Pink Floyd's 1972 tour, and production manager Drummond Challis, who was tasked with putting together a team to accommodate their glamorous new clients.

Given only three weeks to put a crew together, Challis's staffing options were limited. Luckily, he was in the middle of gathering a team to film the Munich Olympics between August 26 and September 11, so he offered the cameramen already booked for the Olympics an extended engagement, starting a week earlier than originally planned. Director of photography Eric Van Haren Noman, plus camera operators Jurgen Wagner, Mike Delaney, Jaap De Jonge, Harvey Harrison, Ron Ford, and Geoff Glover, happily accepted. Sound recorders Rene Borisewitz and Paul Carr were drafted to coordinate syncing sound and pictures. Plane tickets were booked for the small crew to join up with Wings in Groningen, the Netherlands, three weeks later.

"It was a very last-minute thing," recalled Challis. "It was all pretty badly organized. I put the crews together, organized the transport, and the equipment. We really didn't have any production team on the film at all. We didn't have continuity. We didn't have any art department. It was just really me putting together a group of cameramen who could do that sort of thing, they were more newsreel cameramen-type guys."[47]

———

With batteries recharged and plans in place for a mind-focusing live single and film, Wings kicked off the second leg of the Wings Over Europe tour at the K.B. Hallen in the Danish capital of Copenhagen, on August 1. Expecting hysterical girls screaming and thrashing to the sound of a British beat group (as was the case when the Beatles played the K.B. Hallen on June 4, 1964), Scandinavian promoters laid on heavy security, blocking all the venue's exits, and employing guards and armed police in and around the 4,500-capacity arena. In the end, the iron-fisted security measures were unnecessary. The only obstacle blocking the path of Paul and Linda's black-out Mercedes en route to the venue was a half-dozen press cars, scrambling to capture their arrival. As Paul told a Danish reporter after the concert: "The pandemonium of the old days is over."[48]

During the band's two-hour show, bored guards chased down the few fans trying to make a break for the stage before Paul commanded the audience to stand on its seats for Wings' well-worn-in encore. Outnumbered a hundred to one, the guards were powerless to stop the sea of fans jumping up and down on their seats, and in the aisles.

Backstage in his dressing room after the show, Paul unwittingly set the wheels in motion for the formation of Wings' first fan club. Asked by Danish reporter Knud Orsted if he and Linda had a mailing list for followers of the group, Paul replied: "About the fan clubs—if someone wants to do it, that'll be okay. But we won't start it. That's for someone else to do."[49] His comment was published in the *Record Mirror* a week later, and within days a 16-year-old from Staffordshire—known only as Claire—established the *Paul McCartney and Wings Fan Club*.

Operating out of the back room of her parents' home in Kingswinford, Claire published a typed newsletter for Wings fans every other month, with news, reviews, wanted, and trade ads, all for the bargain price of 45p for five issues. The unofficial fan club proved so popular that it was hijacked by MPL a few months later and rebranded the *Paul McCartney and Wings Fun Club*. Taking over from Claire as club secretary was "Lucy," better known as Angie McCartney, Paul's stepmother, who had some experience of fan club newsletters, having helped sort Paul's fan mail for Freda Kelly of the Beatles Fan Club since her marriage to Jim in 1964.

"As my middle name is Lucia, we took the name 'Lucy' and made her the secretary," noted Angie of her adopted pen name. "We opened a post office box at Gayton Village Post Office,* and it didn't take much time before the word was out and the mail started pouring in. . . . As time went by, and Jim's poor health became more of an issue in our lives, Paul suggested we move the operation to his MPL offices in London."[50]

Wings drove out of Copenhagen on August 2, starting on a two-day journey, via Gränna and Stockholm, to the first of two dates in Finland. The group received a chilly reception at the Messuhalli, in the Finnish capital of Helsinki. The tame applause of 4,000 fans was enough to bring Wings back out for an encore, but frustrated with the hall's mediocre acoustics and damp atmosphere, Paul refused to meet with journalists and photographers. He did, however, grant Uma Aaltonen of Finnish radio a short interview with the band.[51]

Aaltonen talked briefly with each member of Wings before turning to Paul for comment. Not feeling inclined to answer Aaltonen's questions directly, Paul regressed to Beatlemania-era press conference quips.

Uma:	Paul, what do you aim to give to people that dig you?
Paul:	*Pleasure . . . music . . . that's it.*
Uma:	What's your message, do you have a message?

---

* Fan mail and Fun Club membership requests were sent to: The Secretary, The Official Wings Fun Club, P.O. Box 3, Wirral, Cheshire, L60 8QH. Paul charged an annual subscription of 75p.

Paul:	Non nobis solum sed toti mundo nati ("Not for ourselves alone, but for the whole world were we born"—the moto for the Liverpool Institute High School for Boys).

(The band double over with laughter.)

Paul:	That's the only Latin I know.
Linda:	That's his moto.
Uma:	Where do you think a pop band stands in the general culture?
Paul:	Onstage definitely. (Laughs.) Definitely onstage. Upright, facing front. In the culture? Well, it depends how cultured you are actually. We think it ranks top actually.[52]

Ten minutes of press patter later, the band were gone.

The following day, on August 5, Wings played the Kupittaan Urheiluhalli in Turku, the second Finnish date following the same pattern as the first.

"I'm not coming back," Paul had said at the very start of the tour. "I'm starting all over again and working upwards. It's like boxing. You don't fight Cassius Clay* your first time out. I know people still come and see *me* and not the band, which is why we don't do Beatles numbers. Will it work? Ask me in eight weeks' time."[53]

At the tour's midpoint, McCartney already had his answer. The *Observer*'s Tony Palmer described Wings' Copenhagen performance as "tight, almost brusque ensemble playing."[54] This was Palmer's polite way of noting that although stage time had sharpened the band's act, the comparatively meek audience responses in Scandinavia highlighted the band's "still developing" status, as well as listeners' disappointment at the absence of Beatles numbers.

But like the steadfast Muhammad Ali, McCartney rolled with the punches and the tour trundled on, crossing the border from Finland to Sweden on August 6. Taking advantage of an abundance of babysitters, Paul and Linda snatched a moment alone in Stockholm, slipping out of their hotel to a nearby club for a quiet drink. But as they sipped on cocktails, they were quickly reminded why they rarely ventured out to unfamiliar places. Their perceptions sharpened by hash-fueled paranoia, they experienced a bizarre incident that left the couple fearing for their lives.

"I walked into a club where I had arranged to meet Paul and Linda," remembered Denny Laine, "and found them sheet-white and shaking with fear. Paul stuttered out, 'There's a guy over there in the corner—he says he's got a gun and he's going to shoot me.' I'm not the bravest guy in the world, but there was only one way to handle it."[55]

Circling the club, Denny, Henry, and roadie Ian cornered the young Swede, pinned him against

---

* Paul's reference here is archaic: Cassius Clay changed his name to Muhammad Ali in 1964.

the wall, and turned out his pockets. No weapon was found. As Henry reached for a pocketknife he kept tucked in his boot, the rattled would-be mugger claimed he was having Paul and Linda on, and it was all a misunderstanding. Scrambling to his feet he made a dash for the club exit.

"It was one of those incidents that happens a thousand times on a Saturday night in any given city or time," McCullough observed. "People just get a little bit funny and if you don't get out of that quick it can get a little bit nasty. Paul needed a strong helping hand from whoever was around him."[56]

On edge after their Stockholm scuffle, Paul called his office in London the next morning, seeking chemical relief. Having jettisoned their smoke supplies just before crossing from Finland into Sweden, the band needed a fresh supply of hash. The McCartneys, cognizant of the danger of transporting drugs across European borders, had a system in place to keep them well stocked. With little consideration of the consequences of getting caught, Paul and Linda arranged for their office in London to mail packages marked "cassettes" to various hotels across Europe in advance of their arrival. The "cassettes" were, in fact, six-ounce parcels of hash, from which each member of the group was issued a daily pot per diem. On Paul's request, the latest bundle of contraband was sent to the Park Lane Hotel in Gothenburg, where they were due to arrive two days later.

"It's not like we were addicts walking around like, 'Oh, I can't play unless I'm high,'" said Seiwell. "It was all fun with us. And it's better that we were doing that than a lot of the bands just drinking to the point of blackout. You don't black out from smoking pot, you just fall asleep. So yeah, it wasn't a big deal."[57]

But having come through a death threat, and facing their biggest concert yet just 24 hours later, a shaken Paul and Linda were not in the mood to be smokeless as well. The band boarded two minibuses bound for Tivoli Gröna Lund, an amusement park on the seaward side of Djurgården Island, in Stockholm. By late afternoon on August 7, the park was already in chaos, and the band's minibuses struggled to break through a crowd far in excess of the venue's 20,000 capacity.

Once the ticketed enclosure was full it was a free-for-all, and tens of thousands of fans ran wild, clambering up trees, scaffolding, a carousel, and a Ferris wheel to get the best possible view of the stage. When there was nowhere left to stand, a group of young fans climbed on top of the stalls, nearly causing the roof to cave in on the people sitting below. Faced with a catastrophe, the chief of police, Bertil Ledel, was forced to call in extra officers and close the park, further aggravating those trapped on the outside.

"The enraged crowd threatened us with riots unless they could enter the area,"[58] Ledel later told a reporter. By the time the gates were slammed shut, 28,700 people—representing a diverse slice of the Swedish population—surrounded the stage for Wings' early evening concert.

"Right in the front row was this woman who must have been 70 if she was a day," Paul said of the crowd. "We were loud, and we were thinking, 'Oh blimey, she must have come for "Eleanor Rigby" or something,' but she was in there, rocking."[59]

According to the Swedish press, she wasn't the only member of the crowd expecting the band to break out some Beatles hits.

"I have no idea if the audience came expecting the Beatles or with the belief they were going to be served progressive rock like everywhere else," wrote Jan Nordlander in Swedish newspaper *Svenska Dagbladet*, "but one thing was sure: they seemed disappointed with what they got. Wings are certainly good performers, but others play just as well or even better."[60]

Henrik Salander, in *Dagens Nyheter*, damned the concert with the faintest praise. "Wings performed simple, straight-ahead music," he wrote. "The sound was surprisingly good coming from the troublesome stage of Gröna Lund. Paul McCartney seemed to enjoy playing and the band is definitely not bad. The music was competent but largely uninteresting; the music of Wings suffers from a lack of direction and personality."[61]

Backstage, the band, overcome with nerves, demolished two crates of Coca-Cola, two crates of beer, and several bottles of scotch. Still spooked by the previous night's prank murder threat, Paul refused to leave his dressing room until all fans, journalists, and photographers had been cleared from the amusement park. "I'll stay here all night unless you remove them,"[62] Paul commanded Gröna Lund manager John Lindgren. The next day, one Stockholm-based newspaper reported that several journalists and photographers had suffered bruises after being manhandled out of the park by the police.

And the McCartney's Swedish troubles weren't left behind in Stockholm. Three days later, following gigs at the Idretshalle, in Örebro, Sweden (August 8), and the Njårdhallen, in Oslo, Norway (August 9), their recklessness finally came back to bite.

Unknown to the band, when they arrived at the Park Lane Hotel in Gothenburg, on August 10, they were being watched by a team of plain-clothed narcotics officers, who mixed with them in the lobby, the on-site restaurant, and hotel bar.* The previous day, Swedish customs had found a suspicious package marked "cassettes," addressed to drummer Denny Seiwell, care of the hotel. Busting open the parcel they found 5.8 ounces (164.6 grams) of poorly concealed hashish. The discovery was quickly relayed to the national drugs unit who identified the American as part of McCartney's visiting group.

Initially tracking Seiwell on suspicion of drug smuggling, the true intended recipients of the parcel quickly became clear to the undercover officers when first Paul, then Linda visited the hotel reception desk asking for a letter addressed to the group's drummer. "They ran around like headless chickens and kept asking for the letter,"[63] one officer observed. The McCartneys' German assistant, Rebecca Hinds, also unwittingly implicated herself in the crime. Hinds had been

---

* Reports that Paul's and Linda's telephone conversations with their secretary at MPL had been recorded by Swedish police cannot be confirmed; there is no available evidence to suggest that they were.

sent to the hotel desk in search of a bundle of clothes Paul and Linda had dry-cleaned in Helsinki, and that were being forwarded on to the group in Sweden. Included were some of Paul's colorful shirts, and a few pairs of his underwear. When they failed to arrive, Hinds was flustered—a reaction the watching police mistook for distress over the nonarrival of the pot parcel. The lost clothes were never seen again.[64] That night as Wings entertained 3,600 fans at the Scandinavium Halle, the Gothenburg narcotics unit closed in. As wild applause called the band back onstage for the encore, sniffer dogs, armed police, and search teams flooded the arena. Standing in the wings, John Morris suddenly found himself caught in the eye of the storm.

"We were finishing the show in Gothenburg, I'm doing the settlement and look out the window and I saw two trucks and I went, 'Holy shit, what's this?' It turns out they were the drug squad from Gothenburg. The chief walked up to me, and I said, 'Yes, can I help you?' He said, 'I'm here to arrest Paul McCartney and Linda McCartney, and the band, for possession of marijuana.' I just started laughing. I said, 'Look, do me a favor. Let them go back and do their encore and then I'll hand them over to you.' He said, 'That's okay. We can do that,' because we didn't want to cause a great kerfuffle."[65]

Meanwhile, search teams scoured the double-decker tour bus for any other evidence of nefarious activities, and across town, at the Park Lane Hotel, a second team turned over the band's bedrooms. Between the bus and hotel, three hash pipes and a small quantity of cannabis resin were taken away. At 10:40 p.m., as Wings walked offstage, the hall's sound system pumped out the riotous rhythm of 'Rocks Off' from the Rolling Stones' *Exile on Main Street* album, Mick and the boys providing the rebellious soundtrack to the band's arrest.

"There must've been 40 cops there," Seiwell recalled, "and we did an extra encore, which screwed up the timing of their bust. Anyway, they took me offstage first, they grabbed me in my sweaty stage clothes, took me in a car downtown."[66]

"Get some pictures of this! It's great PR!"[67] Linda yelled out to photographer Joe Stevens, turning their arrest into an extension of the show. Stevens snapped away as Linda, Paul, and Rebecca Hinds were led to the back of a waiting police car.

"I had no idea what was going on," said Stevens. "I just did what Linda asked me to do. I didn't know how the police would react to me taking photos, so after taking a few shots I quickly pulled the film out of the camera and hid it in my sock."[68]

The four were placed in separate cells at the Gothenburg police station, where the only friendly face was a lawyer, Per-Olow Lewerth, sent from the British Embassy to defend them. Threatened with smuggling charges, Seiwell, Hinds, and the McCartneys were interrogated for three hours by Gothenburg's district prosecutor, Lennart Angelin. Seiwell protested that the package was a gift sent by a fan, while Paul and Linda took the "what's so wrong with smoking a little hash" defense. At 1:00 a.m., Angelin had all he needed.

"We presented the evidence for lawyer Lewerth who then had a long, serious conversation with Paul and the others," said Angelin. "After that they were ready to talk, and everything went smoothly from then on. They confessed to having made a deal with 'a man at their offices' in London to supply them with hashish by sending it by mail to Gothenburg. All of them are drug users, but they said the German [speaking] secretary was innocent. Paul McCartney was cool, calm and collected all of the time. No hysterics, no drama."[69]

The three bandmates were charged under Sweden's Incitement to Smuggling Act of 1960. But given their hasty confession, Angelin proposed an agreement in which they would pay the lowest possible penalty under Swedish law—an amount equal to what they would have to pay if they went to trial and were convicted. Paul was penalized 5,000 SEK (Swedish krona), Linda 1,000 SEK, and Seiwell 3,000 SEK—a total of 9,000 SEK (£720 or $1,700). The case would be tried in their absence, but in practical terms, they were free to go.*

"I went down to the police station, and they had put them all in separate rooms," Morris recalled. "And you could hear Linda saying, 'I want the American ambassador! I know my rights!' I was working it out with the prosecutor, and he said, 'What's going to happen is that you'll have to post a bond and we'll charge them back into your custody, and you'll leave the country in a couple of days.' We posted the bond, which wasn't a hell of a lot of money, and I said, 'I'll make you a deal. I'll give you twice as much if you'll keep her.' He said, 'No, no. I'll make you a deal. I will make it four times as much unless you take her.'"[70]

At 2:10 a.m., on August 11, Paul, Linda, and Denny were released from police custody. "It was a

---

* The trial, on November 14, 1972, was only a formality: Paul, Linda, and Denny Seiwell were convicted *in absentia* and fined the 9000 SEK that they had already paid.

big bother about almost nothing,"[71] a coy McCartney told assembled reporters outside the police station. Just a few hours later, thanks to a reel of film liberated from Joe Stevens's sock, their faces were already splashed across newspaper front pages around the world. One of Stevens's photos captured Linda making a "V" for victory sign, Paul grinning, and Denny flipping the middle finger. In a small way, Seiwell's single finger salute perfectly captured the band's disregard for the Swedish authorities. By the time they left Gothenburg for Lund, their dope supplies had already been quietly replenished.

"We had to sign a written promise not to use marijuana again while we were in Sweden," Seiwell said. "But the next morning I remember some hippie from Amsterdam brought us some weed and then we just went on about our business."[72]

But Sweden was not finished with the shamed band just yet. After the ignominy of their arrest and charge in Gothenburg, Wings still had a date to fulfill, on Friday night at the Lund Olympen. Outside of the four walls of the Gothenburg police station, few people knew the full details of Paul, Linda, and Denny's arrest. Paul was now faced with a choice: put out a denial and claim it was all a misunderstanding, or hold his hands in the air and admit they were caught red-handed.

At 1 Lily Place, Saffron Hill, the London offices of Paul's temporary press secretary, Christopher Maude-Roxby had been busy fielding calls from journalists keen to secure an exclusive interview with the ex-Beatle charged with pan-European drug smuggling. Speaking with Paul and Linda before the Lund show, Maude-Roxby nudged the couple in the direction of Anthea Disney,* a *Daily Mail* general assignment reporter. By the interval Disney was waiting backstage at the Olympen.

"I said to Paul, 'Look, you have an opportunity to just deal with it,'" Disney explained. "And he did. He was using whoever got there first as a mouthpiece for him, he just decided this was the easiest way to deal with it.

"Paul was extremely charming," Disney continued. "He's a man of several layers, I think, and certainly the superficial layer is immensely charming. He had that boyish, sort of raised his eyebrows and smiled at you, and looked right into your eyes, and said things as though, 'Gosh, I'm saying this for the first time ever and you're drawing it out of me.' I mean he's got a great act."[73]

Disney's piece, filed over an international telephone line that night at 10:30 p.m., was the talk of Britain by sunrise. In her article, headlined "Why I Smoke Pot—by Paul," the McCartneys were unrepentant about their arrest, and the embarrassment it had caused their families.† Rather, they used Disney's piece as a channel for a pro-cannabis manifesto.

---

* Born in Surrey, England, Anthea Disney started as a Fleet Street reporter in 1969, gaining acclaim for her first big story, about racial discrimination. After a career in journalism, she joined News Corp to oversee their magazine division in 1989. She later served as president and CEO of HarperCollins Publishers, and then as chairman and CEO of News American Publishing Group.

† Paul's arrest, according to stepmother Angie, did not go down well with his father, Jim, who had just turned 70. Paul's and Linda's liberal attitudes towards drug-taking caused Jim to stay indoors out of embarrassment.

"You can tell everyone that we're not changing our lives for anyone," Paul told Disney. "We told the police in Sweden the truth. We smoke grass and we like it, and that's why someone sent it to us in an envelope. Look, at the end of the day, most people go home and have a stiff whisky. They feel they need it. Well, we play a gig and we're exhausted, and we're elated, and Linda and I prefer to put our kids to bed, sit down together and smoke a joint. We also happen to like whisky, but it makes me feel lousy the next day.

"That doesn't mean we're heavily into drugs or anything. Neither Linda nor I have gone further than grass. You simply couldn't if you want to get out there and entertain people. But you can't expect us to pretend we don't smoke for the sake of our laws. We smoke. We like it. We think it's harmless. I don't go around preaching the gospel, but live my life quietly. But now that I've been caught I'll say, 'Yeah, it's true.' And in time things will change, you'll see, and all this will seem a fuss about nothing."[74]

Unfortunately, not everyone was on board with Paul's bohemian communiqué. Crossing the Danish border, the next morning, the "Wings Over Europe" embossed tour bus may as well have been spray-painted with the words *Convicted Drug Users*. Instead of the usual starstruck border guards grasping autograph books and sharpies, the band were met by a search team, and the bus, still thick with smoke, was boarded by sniffer dogs and armed police. The band and crew, their fingernails underlined with hash, were lined up along the bus as the dog passed along them and guards searched their pockets.

"We got off that bus saying, 'Oh no, we're all going to jail now,'" said Seiwell. "But the dogs didn't smell anything, I couldn't believe it. The whole band was like, *what*? We were free and clear."[75]

But $1,700 turned out to be not all Paul, Linda, and Denny left behind at the Gothenburg police station. With the band feeling emotionally drained, the postbust zeitgeist crystallized in two subdued performances at the Fyns Forum, Odense, and the Vejiby-Risskov Hallen, Aarhus, on August 12 and 14. Though downcast, Paul still felt obliged to hold court with the press.

Rather than quenching the establishment's thirst for his blood and the younger public's thirst for news of the former Fabs, Disney's *Daily Mail* exclusive had news editors clamoring for a follow-up on his European exploits. Awaiting Paul and Linda in Denmark was Paul Dacre,* a *Daily Express* writer who had tried hard to get the drug bust scoop, having phoned the Park Lane Hotel and the Gothenburg police station from London late on August 10 and having bought the rights to one of Joe Stevens's on-the-scene photographs to run with his story in the next day's paper. Now Dacre was in Denmark, keen to follow up on his remote sleuthing.

---

* Paul Dacre, who joined the staff of the *Daily Express* in 1971, moved to the *Daily Mail* eight years later. He was editor of the *Daily Mail* from 1992 to 2018, and was also editor-in-chief and chairman of Associated Newspapers, which owns the *Daily Mail*. As of June, 2022, he was reportedly being considered for a seat in the House of Lords, which he once described in a *Daily Mail* headline as the "House of Unelected Wreckers."

"There was a British reporter that met us right off the bus," remembered Seiwell. "He said to us, 'Now I'm here to do a feature story on you guys living as a family, traveling the way you travel,' and all of this stuff. 'I'm not here to talk about the bust, or to review the concert.' Paul said, 'Okay.' We gave him an interview. He came to a sound check for maybe 20 minutes or so; he was only there a very short time, then left. A few days later the story came out, he talked about the drug bust, he reviewed the concert, and everything that he said he wasn't going to do, he did."[76]

Dacre's piece, "Not So Magical—Paul and Linda's Mystery Tour," oozed negativity from first word to last. Describing Paul's tour "tantrums"; labeling the band "third-rate"; describing Linda's voice as "upsettingly flat," and her keyboard playing as "kindergarten" level, Dacre concluded: "Sadly I must report that Wings, musically, never takes off. At their best they are uninspiring. At their worst, mediocre. McCartney, wandering minstrel, hasn't made it."[77]

Having been true to her word, reporting Paul's response to the bust with a sympathetic, unfiltered ear, Anthea Disney was invited to travel with the band to two further dates on their European tour, during which she filed a second piece with her editor exploring the private lives of the McCartneys. Paul Dacre, on the other hand, received a more physical display of gratitude for an article Paul and Linda saw as a hatchet job.

"We were staying at some fancy hotel somewhere. They had those little plastic dishes that held the soap," said Seiwell. "Linda got a turd of Stella's, and they put it in this soap dish, wrapped it up and sent it to this guy. That was one of the cheekiest things I ever saw them do."[78]

By then, relations between band and crew were fraying too. The ominous sight of an auditor meeting with McCartney, Morris, and Kauffman in Denmark coincided with the abandonment of the agreement between Morris and McCartney that the band and crew would be treated as equals. Once the auditor cast an eye over the tour accounts, the crew was relocated to low-priced hotels.

"The crew was feeling out of sorts," Disney observed. "They weren't all staying at the same hotel with Paul, they were staying at some much less nice place. And they were all rather irritated with that because they were getting up every day and going somewhere else, and I think they were all feeling a bit pissed off that they weren't a little more comfortable than they were. That was certainly the impression I got from the people on the technical crew, and the roadies."[79]

Crew morale was not helped by the band's changing tour schedule. Beyond Denmark, Wings' entire concert itinerary had been thrown in the air: every date was shifted by 24 hours or more; a gig at the Cirque Royale in Brussels was moved to The Hague, and a concert in Breda was canceled completely. Wings' scheduled performance at the Hanover Music Hall (a former German submarine factory, built in 1939) was also scrapped, in favor of the Düsseldorf Rheinhalle (or

Tonhalle), heaping even more pressure on the already stretched road crew. Slumping out of their budget motel on August 15, the shift of destination from Hanover to Düsseldorf meant Morris's men faced a taxing 470-mile drive from Denmark to the center of West Germany—155 miles farther than originally planned.

With half a dozen dates still left to play, Paul feared that Wings Over Europe might limp to its conclusion. But the appearance of spirited film director Barry Chattington in Rotterdam on August 17 breathed life into the ailing tour.

"I first met Paul a couple of days before the Groningen shoot," said Chattington. "I went to shake his hand and he went, 'Oh, very German.'"[80] Chattington and director of photography Eric Van Haren Noman had come to see Wings' show before they filmed the band two days later. And Paul made sure the group put on a vigorous performance for their two filmmaker guests, inviting the already lively audience onstage for the finale of their concert at De Doelen, Rotterdam.

"We like the rowdy audiences," Paul later proclaimed. "In Rotterdam they were dancing onstage with us. It was great because they were all loving the music rather than ripping us apart."[81]

Two days later, photographer Robert Ellis rejoined the crew to see the tour over the line, and Alan Parsons, together with his team of EMI engineers, pulled up outside the Groningen Evenementanhal Martinihal in the Rolling Stones Mobile Studio, ready to record what could become a live Wings single.

Masterminded by the Stones' road manager and pianist Ian Stewart, the Rolling Stones Mobile Studio was purpose-built for portable recording in 1968. Originally fitted with an 8-track, 20-input Helios console designed by former EMI technical director Dick Sweetenham, the recording truck was upgraded to 16-track in 1971. Several classic albums were tracked using the Stones' truck, including Deep Purple's *Machine Head*, parts of the Who's album *Who's Next*, portions of Led Zeppelin *III* and *IV*, plus assorted tracks from the Rolling Stones' own *Sticky Fingers* and *Exile on Main Street*.

But the last-minute plans to film, and independently tape, the end of Wings' tour had not been properly thought through. Ordinarily, a multicamera shoot would involve hiring an OB (Outside Broadcast) Unit with a mobile gallery, allowing the director to see a live feed of what was being captured by each camera on the ground. But hiring an OB Unit, and transporting it to Europe, would have been extraordinarily expensive, and video cameras were bulky and captured low-quality pictures. To limit costs, and for greater mobility and quality, Chattington suggested they capture the concerts on 16 mm film.

But this created an even bigger issue—synchronizing 16-track audiotape and 16 mm film was uncharted territory. And the gig was only hours away.

"[The concerts were] shot on 16 mm Eclair film cameras," Chattington confirmed. "And Paul had a 16-track mobile truck recording sound. So how the fuck do we sync it up? How would it work?* So we invented, for this shoot, something that myself and sound recordist Rene Borisewitz ought to have patented, and we would have been very rich.

"The Eclair cameras were working on a crystal (installed in the camera to synchronize sound without the need for a cable). So, Rene says, 'If we put a tone on track 16 of the audiotape, you can synchronize to that.' So that's what we did. And of course, it caused complete confusion at Abbey Road, because this is an audio track with just a 'buzz' on it."[82]

With Alan Parsons and his crew rolling for sound, the cameramen used clapperboards positioned near Paul's vocal microphone, and the tone track being channeled to track 16 of the 16-track tapes, to make sure the sound and pictures could be lined up at an edit facility in London— though, as Chattington admitted, even with this custom-made system in place, the filming was done on a wing and a prayer.

"With five cameras, I didn't know what I had got. There was no way of knowing. It took a few weeks to sync it all up. In the end, it was a technical success, but it was very risky."[83]

After the concert, Paul, Linda, the band, and their partners, sat in the mobile recording truck late into the night, playing back their first professionally recorded concert.

"Listening to the tapes, it was obvious we were still pretty new as a band," said Paul. "I'm not going to deny that either, because it's stupid. There's nothing wrong with it, nothing to be ashamed of. We were very new."[84]

With a view to capturing the best possible performance for a live single, or cuts for their next album, Parsons and his EMI team were booked to record Wings' concerts at the Concertgebouw, Amsterdam, on August 20; the Nederlands Congresgebouw, The Hague, on August 21; the Ciné Roma, Antwerp, on August 22; and the Deutschlandhalle, West Berlin, on August 24. Chattington's run was extended to film pickups in Berlin, as well.

The Deutschlandhalle, a remnant of the fallen Nazi regime, provided a surreal backdrop for the end of Wings turbulent continental flight.

"It was in the hall that Hitler had for the youth organization," said McCullough. "It was a really big hall—like one of the big American theatres—and there was just fuck all happening, you know. Everybody was expecting great things with it being the last night, but it just didn't come off."[85]

That night the band and crew partied in West Berlin, with two notable absentees: Paul and Linda, who spent the evening with their girls at the hotel. The seven-week tour that had seen McCartney arrested, his life threatened, and his wife and band critically panned also had a cat-

---

* In the digital age, sound and pictures are synchronized (in most cases) using time of day timecode and a clapperboard, the sound of the clapperboard whack providing a point at which both sound and pictures can be lined up, and timecode, digitally burned into the video and sound, providing a perfect reference point for matching sound and pictures. Such technology did not exist in 1972; the film crew needed to improvise.

astrophic financial conclusion. According to Morris, the auditor found irregularities in the tour accounts, leaving both him and Paul heavily out of pocket.

"By the time we ended the tour, in Berlin, he and I were not getting along. I was supposed to be paid something like $50,000 for all the production costs and everything else. In the end, I didn't get it because Paul brought in an accountant who cheated me out of the 50 grand, cheated us out of a lot of expenses, and took Paul for a quarter of a million bucks. And of course, I didn't sue, because you don't sue somebody with as much money as a Beatle. You'll never win. I didn't want anything to do with him and he probably didn't want anything to do with me. We have not crossed paths since then."[86]

Trying to play composer, performer, producer, and businessman had become an impossible juggling act for Paul, as had balancing being a friend, bandmate, and manager to Laine, McCullough, and Seiwell. He was now fully convinced that he needed to put his trust in a full-time manager, a position Morris had turned down before the tour. He and Linda had, until now, largely handled their own affairs. But during their recent visit to New York, Paul turned to John Eastman for help, and the search for a manager was already in motion. Unfamiliar with the British music scene, Eastman scoured the Manhattan music business for a likely candidate, eventually settling on Vincent Frank Romeo, a 34-year-old booking agent for Creative Management Associates (CMA), the New York–based firm that handled management and tour bookings for high-profile bands and performers, including Eastman's clients Grand Funk Railroad.

Eastman felt the youthful, yet experienced music man was a good fit for Paul and his band. Romeo agreed to take up the post in October, allowing him time to find London lodgings and cast an eye over MPL's accounts and business papers.

"When I came to work for Paul in 1972, his financial affairs were very mixed up," said Romeo. "There was a lot that had to be done. He'd been running in twenty-seven different directions. He had to be brought together. As the Eastmans were in America, unable to coordinate his day-to-day affairs, I had to move over to England. . . . It was a full-time job."[87]

19

FROM THE AUTOBAHN TO THE
RED ROSE SPEEDWAY

—

Gliding above the clouds in a private jet bound for London in August 1972, Paul knew that, had things panned out differently, he and Wings could have been flying to New York for an appearance at Madison Square Garden. A year after shunning George's invitation to appear at his Bangladesh benefit, McCartney was handed another last-minute request that Wings join John and Yoko for "One to One," a benefit concert on August 30 spearheaded by New York reporter Geraldo Rivera to raise funds for Willowbrook, a Staten Island facility for children with severe mental disabilities.*

During an unannounced visit to the Willowbrook center, on January 6, 1972, Rivera and his film crew documented the deplorable conditions the 5,230 vulnerable residents were forced to suffer. A week later, *Willowbrook: The Last Great Disgrace* aired on American television, exposing how shameful budget and staff cuts had sent both Willowbrook and nearby Letchworth Rehabilitation Center into meltdown. Friendly with Rivera because of his coverage of John's ongoing US immigration case, the Lennons confessed their distress at his exposé, and after several months of courting by Rivera, John and Yoko agreed to throw the weight of their celebrity behind his "One to One" movement.

The lineup for "One to One," assembled in less than a month, featured 1950s revival act Sha Na Na, the jazz singer Roberta Flack, the multi-instrumentalist prodigy Stevie Wonder, plus headliners John and Yoko, backed by the Greenwich Village bar band Elephants Memory.

Paul was tempted to fly Wings over to New York at the end of the Wings Over Europe tour. But as strong as his desire to share a stage with John and Stevie was, his deep hatred of Klein, and

---

* 40,000 tickets were made available for the "One to One" benefit for a donation of between $5 and $10. Lennon himself bought $59,000 worth of tickets and gave them away to fans. According to press reports, $1.5 million dollars was raised for Willowbrook.

his annoyance with John for his constant delay in signing the papers that would end the Beatles' partnership, once again tipped the scales against a live reunion.

"John asked me to do a charity concert with him in New York, but I said no, because I knew Klein would have been in the background pulling the strings," Paul admitted a few months later. "It's a pity now that we didn't do it, but we will do things, I'm sure. I don't see any reason why all four Beatles shouldn't be onstage at some time, all playing together and having a good time. I think it's daft to assume that just because we had a couple of business upsets, we won't ever see each other again."[1]

Ultimately, it was academic: following his Gothenburg drug conviction, McCartney's chances of entering the United States, let alone playing concerts in America, were looking remote, although his visa had not yet been formally revoked. American immigration authorities were taking a tough stance on drugs and were refusing admission to anyone with a drug conviction, a ban that could last two years (but which authorities also had the power to waive).

Britain had a similar restriction, so instead of the heroes' welcome Wings might have expected, they were met at London Heathrow customs by a team of suits.

"They had a staff of lawyers waiting for us in London because Paul, Linda, and I were all busted," Seiwell remembered. "They didn't think that Linda and I, still being American, could get back into the country—we thought they were going to throw us out. [But] they whisked us right through customs. It was the quickest entry back into the UK I ever had. No problems."[2]

Settling in at Cavendish Avenue, Paul drew up a motivating end-of-year schedule, plotting out everything he hoped to achieve before the arrival of his newly hired American manager, Vincent Romeo, plus plans for the end of the year. His post-tour checklist included completing the band's second album by October, for a November release, a tour of Britain, and a live London residency before Christmas.

Aug 28. Tour Ends.
10 days off.
Sept 7. Recording album.
2 live gigs per week (London area).
One week off.
4 days recording.
Album finished, ready, mixed, and cover by October 7. Release date approx.
November 5.
November 12, approx., British tour (2 weeks).
Residency, beginning December.
Holiday. Xmas.[3]

Denny Seiwell took advantage of a ten-day break to reconnect with his recording contacts in New York and earn some money. On August 27, Denny settled behind a borrowed drum kit for a jingle session in Manhattan, as Monique found the couple temporary lodgings at the Warwick Hotel at 65 West 54th Street.

Back in England, Henry and Sheila spent time at their home, at 3 Sycamore Gardens, near the beach in Dymchurch. And Denny Laine introduced new love Jo Jo to the wholesome, down-to-earth digs a rock musician working with an ex-Beatle could expect to own: a caravan in Shepperton.

The young couple's low-key honeymoon period was quickly cut short, though. Hungry to pick up where they had left off at Olympic Studios five months earlier, Paul booked an extended block of time at EMI Studios, starting September 13. Until then, he secured a late booking at Morgan Studios, where he asked Wings to gather on September 1.

Denny Seiwell, not expecting to work with Wings again until September 7, had already lined up more lucrative recording dates in New York. But speaking with Paul from his room at the Warwick Hotel, Seiwell said he would be on the first plane out of New York on September 2.

Faced with the prospect of postponing his Morgan booking until Seiwell's return, Paul decided to busk it.

———

Recording Sessions

Friday–Wed, September 1–6, 1972.
Morgan Studios, Studio One, London.
Playback: 'Hi, Hi, Hi' (live in Groningen, Amsterdam, The Hague, Antwerp, and Berlin).
Recording: 'Hi, Hi, Hi' and 'C Moon.'

———

The McCartneys' red Lamborghini spun up Willesden High Road at 4:00 p.m., on September 1, greeted by a group of ardent fans who were tipped off by Rose that Paul and Linda were Morgan-bound.

Inside Studio One, Laine, McCullough, and in-house engineer Mike Bobak had already set up the group's equipment and were ready to record. But strolling into the control room, cradling a box of 16-track tapes, Paul explained that the first item on the agenda was to review a batch of their European tour recordings, specifically 'Hi, Hi, Hi.'

The world had already read McCartney's unrepentant response to his Swedish arrest in Anthea Disney's *Daily Mail* piece, but to make sure there was no element of doubt about his attitude toward cannabis use, he decided that a live version of his paean to sex, drugs and rock 'n' roll would be Wings' next single.

Bobak threaded up the first of the five concert recordings from the end of the European tour, and the band sunk into the control room sofas to listen to their performances of 'Hi, Hi, Hi' (noted at this time as 'High, Hi, High') from Groningen, Amsterdam, The Hague, Antwerp, and Berlin.

During playback Paul analyzed each recording, noting any weak elements that a little studio sweetening might straighten out. A couple of hours later, the band agreed their performance in Groningen was the strongest of the five, and Paul made a note to fix some issues with the bass and electric guitar parts.

Moving through to the studio, Henry and Denny tuned their guitars while across the room, Paul sat at the piano, playing a simple chord progression with a bouncy reggae beat, and vamping a few lines—"*C moon, C moon, C moon, is she / C Moon, C Moon, C Moon, to me*"—as Linda, sitting beside him, shook a tambourine.

Denny Laine swapped his electric guitar for a bass, and Henry found himself arbitrarily tapping away at Seiwell's unoccupied drum kit, momentarily taking up Paul's Caribbean jam. For the rest of the evening the four bandmates sculpted 'C Moon.'

At first glance, McCartney's reggae-pop fermentation seemed addressed to Linda. But once the superficial layers are scratched away, a swathed stab at society's killjoys is exposed. "*How come no one older than me, ever seems to understand the things I wanna do?*" McCartney sang, wagging his finger at the older generation for not cutting their kids some slack. As part of his lecture to the joy-sapping "squares" (including those who had taken the band to task in Sweden) Paul borrowed a phrase from Sam the Sham and the Pharaohs' 1965 novelty rock hit 'Wooly Bully.'

"Sam the Sham used the expression 'L seven,' which is L, and a 7, and means square," explained McCartney. "I thought C, and moon is like the opposite. So 'C Moon,' it just means 'cool.' So then the whole song is like, she's cool."[4] Though probably unintentional, the song also offered a response to Lennon's claim in 'How Do You Sleep?' that Paul "*lived with straights*."

Set on developing 'C Moon' from a studio jam into a polished recording, at Paul's request, Denny Laine invited his old Birmingham pal, Led Zeppelin's drummer, John Bonham, for a friendly jam during Wings' September 2 session. Fresh from Led Zeppelin's summer tour of America, Bonham riffed with four-fifths of Wings before Paul's conscience got the better of him. Working up a new track with an outside percussionist risked offending Seiwell.

Bonham was still keen to hear the band's latest tune, though. Replacing the 'Whole Lotta Love' and 'Black Dog' powerhouse behind the kit, a reluctant, and deeply self-conscious McCullough picked up the sticks and continued the previous day's reggae vibe. Digging the unsophisticated, laid-back workout the foursome was capturing—and egged on by Bonham—Paul told engineer Mike Bobak to roll the tapes.

"I was just sitting around the drums and McCartney was fluttering about on the piano, and the music started moving," said McCullough of the unexpected recording. "And then it was, 'OK, let's record this.' And so, I stayed on the drums."[5]

Six stilted takes later the basic track for 'C Moon' was committed to tape, Take 6 the standout and elected master. Lauding McCullough's efforts, Bonham resumed his position behind the kit, and the five musicians enjoyed a chemically enhanced jam into the early hours.

"John Bonham of Zeppelin was down the night we did 'C Moon' at Morgan Studios, which was a crazy night," McCartney later gloated. "He was down there, he brought some things with him, it was a good laugh—we had a crazy evening."[6]

Denny Seiwell returned from New York on September 3, and the band's collective noses were back to the grindstone. By now, Paul had second thoughts about the commercial viability of the Groningen recording of 'Hi, Hi, Hi' and believed the band could produce something better in the studio. A fresh 16-track reel was started, and the band tried to capture a sound that outshone their live performance. But just as had happened when they tried to track 'The Mess' at Olympic Studios, attempts to recapture the energy of their Groningen performance fell flat. The attempt to record a studio version of 'Hi, Hi, Hi' was abandoned.

On September 4 and 5, Wings returned their focus to 'C Moon'—now a firm contender for release as an album cut or B side—overdubbing lead and backing vocals onto Take 6.

———

Lightning supposedly never strikes twice in the same place, but Paul learned that metaphorically, at least, it can. In early September, he received an unexpected call from former Apple ally Ron Kass, now heading the English arm of Hilary Music, offering Paul another crack at composing a James Bond movie theme.

Harry Saltzman's and Cubby Broccoli's Eon Productions was gearing up to start filming *Live and Let Die*, the next installment in their series based on Ian Fleming's spy novels, with Roger Moore replacing Sean Connery in the role of 007. Once again, go-to Bond composer John Barry was at loggerheads with Saltzman and Broccoli and had taken a sabbatical, so this time there would be no confusion about whether the film composer's chair was vacant. McCartney didn't think twice.

"The fellow [Ron Kass] from James Bond rang me up and said would I be interested in doing the title song for their new film," McCartney said. "I agreed, so the fellow gave me the book, which I read and extracted from it pieces which I could pick up on musically. The thing about the

Bond themes is they've got to capture the spirit of the film and be sort of super memorable. The song had to be big and spectacular in keeping with the character of Bond."[7]

Ian Fleming's novel of *Live and Let Die* pits Agent 007 against American criminal mastermind Mr. Big (a role given to actor Yaphet Kotto), head of a Voodoo cult and high in the Smersh guild of terror, and his inquisitor, Solitaire (to be played by Jane Seymour), an exotic Creole beauty with the power to read a man's mind. Being a fan of Fleming's work, Paul was already familiar with the novel, but on the weekend of September 9, he read it again, refreshing himself with the narrative's finer points.

Four chapters in, Paul fell upon a first flash of lyrical inspiration—an exchange between Captain Dexter and Bond, spread over pages 37 and 38, with two lines of dialogue that supplied the novel its title and would form the backbone of Paul's new song.

"Don't go stirring up trouble for us," said Dexter. "The case isn't ripe yet. Until it is, our policy with Mr. Big is 'live and let live.'"

Bond looked quizzically at Captain Dexter.

"In my job," he said, "when I come up against a man like this one, I have another motto. It's 'live and let die.'"[8]

With "*Live and let live*" versus "*live and let die*" as his starting blocks, Paul was soon rifling through a stack of his and Linda's notebooks, in which the couple often jotted random song lyrics and titles. Here, he fell upon a doodle Linda made a year earlier. "*When you were young and your heart was an open home / You used to say live and don't moan.*" Though noted in Linda's hand, the idea might have come from either of them. In any case, replacing "*open home*" with "*open book*," and "*live and don't moan*" with "*live and let live*" provided Paul with the opening lines for his Bond theme.

With input from Linda, the lyrics quickly took shape. Come Sunday morning, Paul was at the piano exploring how the book's dramatic, mysterious, and exotic themes might translate into song. Through the course of the day, McCartney shaped a dynamic melody full of musical twists and turns, building from a slow piano introduction to an explosive, racing, instrumental bed vaguely reminiscent of sections of Richard Harris's 'MacArthur Park.' Paul also left yawning spaces for thundering orchestration, which he imagined having an almost balletic character—the musical equivalent of a fight scene, with orchestral kicks, punches and stabs.

Later that evening, Seiwell was on hand to provide one final, tropical addition, reflecting one of the book's principal locations, Jamaica.

"We got to this one bit when we were running the song down, 'So what does it matter to you,' and I thought, 'What a perfect place for reggae.' So I just played a reggae beat in there, and he turned around and loved it. And that was that."[9]

The result was an ambitious fusion of rock, reggae and space for kinetic symphonic elements and was unlike any Bond theme that had gone before. But Paul's basic piano arrangement only provided the foundations for the recording. A Bond theme called for bold, cinematic invention. Hoping to control all aspects of the song's production (rather than leaving orchestration to the discretion of the film's producers) Paul enlisted George Martin to write the orchestral score.

Having previously produced John Barry's title tracks for *Goldfinger* and *From Russia with Love*, Martin knew the franchise well. But as Martin remembered it, when they discussed the song over a cup of tea at Cavendish Avenue, Paul was not only uninterested in scoring that would make his song a John Barry soundalike but also seemed downright competitive with Barry.

"It all started with Paul ringing me up and saying, 'Look, I've got a song for a film. Would you produce it and arrange it for me?' I said, 'Sure,' and spent some time with him at his house going through the thing. He said, 'I want it to be really big.' And I said, 'obviously you want the same thing as John Barry.' He said, 'No, it's gotta be better than John Barry, it's gotta have much more kick in it!' So I said, 'Okay, I'll do my best.'"[10]

Martin suggested they use his AIR Studios for recording, and a tentative recording date of October 10 was added to Wings' growing schedule, giving Martin time to work on the score and hire musicians.

Writing to order was a lucrative business. Publishing and recording royalties aside, Lee Eastman negotiated Paul a $15,000 (£6,430) fee for composing 'Live and Let Die.' The terms of his joint deal with Eon Productions and United Artists (which would distribute the Original Motion Picture Soundtrack worldwide) are detailed in a memo sent by Ron Kass to Harry Saltzman.

The undated agreement* explained that *two versions* of McCartney's song would be recorded for the film: one by Wings, and the second by the American vocal group the Fifth Dimension (though their involvement had yet to be formalized).

MEMORANDUM

TO: HARRY SALTZMAN
FROM: RONALD S. KASS
MUSIC—"LIVE AND LET DIE"

---

* Though not dated, the absence of a composer for the rest of the soundtrack music noted in the first clause suggests that the memorandum was most likely sent between late September and mid-October.

The following are the arrangements which have been agreed upon with respect to the music and performance for "Live and Let Die."

Paul McCartney has agreed to write the title song entitled "LIVE AND LET DIE." He and his musical group WINGS will perform the title song under the opening titles. Besides using the basic Bond theme, any additional scoring necessary will be done by a composer and conductor to be decided upon.

THE FIFTH DIMENSION will perform a version of the title song in a live performance in the "Filet of Soul" scene.

Paul McCartney has agreed to produce THE FIFTH DIMENSION'S performance.

The original soundtrack album will be an extremely commercial package composed of Paul McCartney as composer, performer and producer, as well as THE FIFTH DIMENSION, who have had many number one records, and WINGS, McCartney's musical group.

The following are the financial arrangements which have been agreed to.

Paul McCartney is to be paid $15,000 for composing the title song. In addition, his father-in-law Lee Eastman has said he would be agreeable to splitting the music publishing with the administration of the publishing in the hands of United Artists, except in the U.K. where the publishing will be administrated by the company Paul McCartney is currently under contract to.

Since John Barry was paid $25,000 for "DIAMONDS ARE FOREVER," the $15,000 fee was negotiated in order to leave an amount of $10,000 to pay for the additional scoring necessary, as well as arranging and conducting services.

With respect to the performances, it is up to U.A. to negotiate a fee for the performance of WINGS. Lee Eastman has indicated that he would like to work this out with David Picker directly. The fee should be an advance of royalties not to interfere with the soundtrack royalties payable to Danjaq.

We are negotiating with Marc Gordon, manager of the FIFTH DIMENSION, for a fee which would include recording, as well as the performance on screen. They have agreed to a pro-rata artists royalty.

Please tell me who should be advised of the above information. R.S.K.[11]

The McCartneys' music publishing contract for the soundtrack album was also negotiated by Lee Eastman. A memo dated March 15, 1973, between Sydney Shemel (Foreign Operations

Director, United Artists) and Murray Deutch (Head of Music Publishing, United Artists) details the breakdown of royalty payments. This copublishing agreement notes "The McCartneys" (Paul and Linda) as the writers and sees publishing royalties split three ways: 50 percent to United Artists, 25 percent to Northern Songs and the final 25 percent to the McCartneys' publishing company. The agreement also states that the McCartneys "will use their best efforts to cause a single to be released by EMI between three and six weeks prior to the initial release in the USA and UK."[12]

With the plans and contracts in place for recording of 'Live and Let Die,' the band rehearsed Paul's song pending George Martin's input.

———

Recording Sessions

Wednesday, Friday and Saturday, September 13, 15 and 16, 1972.
EMI Studios, Studio Two, London.
Overdubbing: 'Hi, Hi, Hi' (live in Groningen, August 19, 1972).
Recording: 'Hold Me Tight' and 'Lazy Dynamite.'

Apart from the distractions of McCartney's spy song, Wings still had a single to prepare and an album to resurrect. Paul's original plan to have their next record ready by early October was already looking unlikely, though. On September 13, Wings returned to EMI Studios, hoping to wrap up their second LP and third single within four weeks. Unmoved by their attempts to track 'Hi, Hi, Hi' at Morgan Studios, the band revisited, once again, various European tour recordings of the song. At the console was 21-year-old junior engineer, and former *McCartney* sessions teaboy, John Leckie.

"The only reason I did the session was because Alan Parsons was away. I was shitting myself because I'd been there less than two years, really, and there I was doing that. The only thing I'd engineered was Roy Harper [his *Stormcock* album], which was acoustic guitar and voice. They'd just come back off tour, all a bit crazy, all a bit wild, drinking, partying, late nights, late starts—you know, they would often start at six or seven in the evening. But I was really keen."[13]

Breaking Leckie in gently, work began at 2:00 p.m. with four hours of playback, as Paul and the band auditioned the five live recordings for a second time. Again, the Groningen recording of 'Hi, Hi, Hi' stood out as the most energetic and well-rounded, but the guitars were ropy in places, so the master tape was duplicated for overdubbing. Taking to the studio floor, Denny and Henry replaced their original guitar parts, while Paul rerecorded his bass track. The new guitar lines replicated the live ones with added polish and studio precision. At 1:30 a.m., Leckie ran off a rough stereo mix of the upgraded live recording, which Paul took home on a cassette to assess.

Two days later, Paul returned to the studio with a concept to bolster the running time of the next album and shift a creative load off his shoulders. In the first nine months of 1972 he had stockpiled various song fragments that remained unfinished, among them 'Power Cut' and 'Lazy Dynamite' (originally called 'Baby Dynamite'), both written during the university tour, and two new ballads outlined on the European tour bus, 'Hands of Love' and 'Hold Me Tight' (not to be confused with the Beatles' song of the same name). Unfinished, the songs had no real merit, but combined as a medley, they suddenly became a vibrant macédoine of melodic pieces.

"I think laziness crept in," Paul later admitted. "So there's a lot of songs in there that are half finished. They were good ideas, but I don't realize them; I cop out around about the third verse."[14] It was a strategy he had used before, to stunning effect. "The idea for the [medley] at the end of *Abbey Road* had arisen out of a reasonably cynical idea, which was, 'We've got loads of these half songs. Instead of finishing them, why don't we just bung them together?' And so that became a method for disposing of half-finished songs."[15]

Setting aside 'Hi, Hi, Hi,' Paul and the band spent the first half of their September 15 session recording 'Hold Me Tight,' a sparse, yet dramatic piano ballad, with three short verses (the last of which was an instrumental break) and long repetitive choruses of "*hold me tight*." With Paul providing piano and vocals, both Denny Laine and Henry playing acoustic guitars, and Seiwell keeping time, the basic track was recorded in seven takes (two of which were false starts) and Take 7 was designated "master." Laine and McCullough then overdubbed a dual guitar solo during the refrain, before the group added three layers of harmony vocals.

"I remember doing all the vocals," said engineer Leckie. "Around one microphone you'd have Paul, Linda, and Denny Laine singing. And there's something about singing around one microphone, rather than singing around three. You do them around one microphone, and then they have to balance themselves. Whereas, if you've got three microphones, you're asking for trouble. Usually if someone's not loud enough, it's because they're not singing loud enough."

Leckie also noted his surprise at the strength and character of Linda's vocals, which he believes branded Paul's post-Beatles catalog. "The best thing about Linda was the texture of her voice. When you hear her voice in the backing vocals of the group, it's really distinctive. You know that it's Wings."[16]

At 6:30 p.m., after six and a half hours of recording, the band headed for the EMI canteen where they were briefly joined by Linda's parents, in town to finalize the contract with Eon Productions and plan for Vincent Romeo's imminent arrival. Charged up by the cafeteria grub, the band jammed for an hour before returning to the tedious business of finishing 'Hi, Hi, Hi.'

Still believing the song was lacking something, even with fresh electric guitar and bass parts, Paul had Denny Laine and Henry add two more guitar tracks to the live tape, and Leckie ran off a rough stereo mix for Paul to take home. The session ended at 3:30 a.m.

Nine hours later the band were back in Studio Two to track a second portion of the evolving album medley. 'Lazy Dynamite' is a sparse blues melody composed of verses built on a single, repeating lyric—"*oh lazy dynamite*"—and a lengthy refrain, building to a commanding falsetto conclusion. Alone, the melody was weak, but inserted between other song fragments it had an understated charm.

Searching for a musical motif to define the ballad, Laine suggested they record it in the style of an old blues number, with McCartney on piano and Laine waxing, like Sonny Boy Williamson, on harmonica.

The recording itself was unusually fragmented. Once Paul and Denny had recorded a basic track, with piano, guide vocal, and harmonica, in three takes (Take 3 marked "best") the rest of the recording was pieced together as a series of overdubs. Denny Seiwell first overdubbed his drums, then Paul added his lead vocal, and finally, the group superimposed two tracks of rising harmony vocals during the refrain. But according to John Leckie, the piecemeal recording method didn't sit well with some of the group.

"I remember it being really torture for the band doing 'Hold Me Tight' and 'Lazy Dynamite,'" said Leckie. "Because it's very empty. There's lots of space with just the voice on both 'Hold Me Tight' and 'Lazy Dynamite.' It's all vocal, almost a cappella."[17]

An electric guitar part, recorded by Henry on September 16, was later abandoned.

Recording Session

Monday, September 18, 1972.
EMI Studios, Studio Two, London.
Recording: 'Hi, Hi, Hi.'

So far, attempts to finalize 'Hi, Hi, Hi' had failed to raise Paul's artistic pulse. This was partly down to niggling imperfections in the live recordings, partly to the band's inability to capture the song's spirit away from the concert stage. One problem, Paul speculated, was the song's rhythm, a shuffle beat (an eighth-note rhythmic feel based on triplet subdivisions of the beat). On Monday afternoon, Paul tore up the original arrangement, asking Seiwell instead to play a standard rock beat, with McCullough and Laine playing economic, power chords.

"I originally wrote it with a shuffle beat, but we decided it didn't [work] as a record that way," McCartney explained soon after the session. "[So] we re-did it with a rockashake beat, kind of squared off a bit."[18]

Between 1:30 p.m. and midnight the four musicians made slow progress, battling through 24 takes of the revamped arrangement of 'Hi, Hi, Hi' (13 of which were complete) before finally settling for Take 24. Paul then donned the headphones to lay down an improved lead vocal, and Laine and McCullough provided detail with three tracks of lead guitar. But they remained unable to recapture the spirit of Alicante. Realizing, on repeated listening, that Take 24 was little better than run-of-the-mill, the band left EMI Studios deflated.

"Paul was just after that magic take, I suppose," reflected Leckie. "I remember endless shuffling around of sounds. They tried different amps, different guitars and different arrangements: faster, slower. There was no producer; Paul was trying to produce it himself. He'd come up and help me with the sound, so he'd be with me, tweaking sounds. He probably needed a producer for those sessions."[19]

Recording Sessions

Tuesday–Wednesday, September 19–20, 1972.
EMI Studios, Studio Two, London.
Recording: 'Hi, Hi, Hi.'
Overdubbing: 'Hi, Hi, Hi.'

Unwilling to accept defeat, Paul entered Studio Two on Tuesday morning determined to salvage something from the group's previous session. Short on numbers due to vacationing EMI staff, John Leckie arrived at the session after a morning shift with former Beatles engineer-turned-performer Norman "Hurricane" Smith* to find Paul sitting in the control room anxious to get going.

Revisiting Monday's session tape, Paul decided to ditch the existing master, Take 24, in favor of Take 17, and he wasted little time getting to work. With the band as his audience, Paul jumped behind the piano to add a track of keys, swiftly followed by two lead vocal overdubs. But it was all for nothing; Take 17 lacked guts, and it was back to the drawing board.

---

* Norman Smith worked as an engineer on the first six Beatles albums (*Please Please Me*, *With the Beatles*, *A Hard Day's Night*, *Beatles for Sale*, *Help!* and *Rubber Soul*) before being promoted by EMI to producer, with an A&R role, in 1966. Taking up the moniker "Hurricane Smith," in 1971, he embarked on a career as a recording artist in his own right. In 1972, he was working on what would become his third studio album, *Razzmahtazz Shall Inherit the Earth*.

Between 1:15 p.m. and 1:15 a.m., starting at Take 27, McCartney, Laine, Seiwell, and McCullough worked on a remake. But 12 hours, and 22 more takes, yielded nothing of worth, and the session was abandoned.

It was beginning to look like the end of the road for 'Hi, Hi, Hi,' but Wings finally made a breakthrough with the troublesome song on September 20. All attempts to record the song as a collective had failed, and fearing that one perfect band performance was beyond their reach, Paul chose to go back to basics and record the track as a series of overdubs. Beginning with only drums, bass, and rhythm guitar, Seiwell, McCartney, and Laine recorded a very basic rhythm track. The threesome tracked ten takes in total (five complete, five false starts), settling on Take 61 as "best." A mistake at the end of the master take was corrected with a short edit piece, spliced in at 2'36".

John Leckie's final afternoon working with Wings saw the group beef up the basic track with a dozen overdubs. Onto the freshly patched Take 61 they added seven tracks of electric guitar; two tracks of electric guitar played through a Leslie speaker; a double-tracked lead vocal; and a piano track. And with that, Leckie made a rough mix of the day's work and handed over proceedings to the returning Alan Parsons.

The band took the rest of the week off, paying a brief visit to AIR Studios on Thursday, September 21, to see where they would record Paul's Bond theme three weeks later.

———►

McCartney's fortunes inside the four walls of EMI Studios were finally starting to turn, but away from London, his cannabis call to arms had the ears of the law burning. On September 19, Norman McPhee, an officer from the Argyll crime prevention unit, drove up the private lane to High Park Farm to make sure that, in the McCartneys' absence, there were no signs of mischief. Local police had been keeping an eye on Paul's Scottish hideaway for two years after a tip from a neighbor that the farm was often left unsecured, and fans might break in.

Sniffing around the couple's Kencast greenhouse, though, McPhee spotted, among the tomatoes and cucumbers, some *florae* of a more exotic nature, bearing no fruit but long, thin, serrated leaves. Returning to Campbeltown's police station, McPhee compared the plant to an illustrated manual of illegal herbs and satisfied himself that the McCartneys were growing cannabis.

Revealing his discovery to the sheriff at Campbeltown court, McPhee was granted a warrant to search both of McCartney's Argyll properties. During a late-afternoon police raid five plants were seized from High Park and Low Ranachan, with formal charges pending the results of scientific tests on the cultivations. Word of the discovery quickly made the news, and Paul found himself at the center of a second bust in as many months. Asked for a comment on the story, Paul's spokesman gibed: "Maybe they were begonias. We shall have to wait and see what develops."[20]

This was especially distressing to Duncan Cairns, the farmer who looked after High Park. Cairns had his own suspicions that Paul was dabbling in horticultural dark arts in the greenhouse. After the Swedish bust confirmed that Paul was indeed involved with the demon weed, he wrote to Paul, suggesting that the McCartneys find a new overseer.

"I didn't get a reply,"[21] Cairns reported. So he stayed on. The McCartneys were ruffling feathers in St. John's Wood, too. In late September, the couple made an unwelcome appearance in the papers when a neighborly dispute was reported in London and picked up by papers around the world. Martha, Paul's aging sheepdog, had just welcomed the arrival of eight puppies and became the talk of Cavendish Avenue. But not in a good way. Martha's yapping pups were keeping the neighbors awake at night, so they wrote a polite letter to Paul and Linda asking for action. Unimpressed, the McCartneys sent a crudely scrawled, four-letter reply. The tactless note soon backfired, when three neighbors filed a formal complaint about the barking with the police. The McCartneys' response to reporters was equally cutting.

"They're all mad around here," said Paul. "They're a load of colonels—I don't care what they say."

"We're going to start a zoo next,"[22] Linda added, only partially in jest. The new canine arrivals joined a growing menagerie of wild and domestic residents at Paul's London pad. The couple had taken to keeping chickens in the garden and garage, along with other birds acquired from local rescue centers and farms.

"They kept their car outside at their home in St. John's Wood because their garage was full of rare livestock they planned to release into the Scottish hills to breed," Denny Laine observed. "Linda couldn't bear to see anything killed so she was heartbroken when the dogs got into the garage one night and killed some of her chickens. The survivors were taken up to Scotland and freed. But they just wouldn't leave. They just sat around in the front garden waiting to be fed. Eventually the dogs killed the lot."[23]

Recording Sessions

Sunday–Monday, September 24–25, 1972.
EMI Studios, Studio Two, London.
Overdubbing: 'Hi, Hi, Hi.'

Three weeks after returning to the studio, McCartney's band had very little to show for their time and effort. Countless recording hours had already been chewed up working on 'Hi, Hi, Hi,' making Alan Parsons's opening gambit on his return to the fold, on September 24, highly unpopular. Parsons strongly believed that the recordings he made during the European tour captured 'Hi, Hi, Hi' at its energetic best, and scanning the enormous pile of tape boxes in Studio Two control room—amounting to 61 takes of the song—he made his opinion known.

"It was a lot of takes," said Parsons. "He was just looking for some feel they were never gonna get. It was so much better live. The live version was very different. I preferred it, and I told him so.[24] I suppose I was one of the first not to be afraid of opening my mouth and making a musical suggestion. For whatever reason, it didn't seem to do me any harm. I can't say that I was booked as an engineer in order to give people lots of musical ideas, but I didn't ever feel that it was necessary to hold back what I thought."[25] Parsons discovered, however, that his opinion didn't have much sway with the band. Even after his promotion to engineer, Seiwell and Laine still saw Parsons as the teaboy from the band's *Wild Life* sessions, often winding him up by shouting, "Alan, get me a fucking cup of tea, would you?"[26]

Paul was in no mood to debate either. Sunday was Linda's birthday, and he was hoping to wrap up early and spend the evening with the girls. Ignoring Parsons's advice, Paul asked the young engineer to load up Take 61 of 'Hi, Hi, Hi' so they could get to work. Having filled the master tape during their previous session, Parsons first needed to bounce four tracks of electric guitars onto one track to make room for overdubs. By now, the recording had the makings of a Phil Spector production, with nine tracks of electric guitar creating an ear-bleed-inducing "wall of sound."

But Paul was still not content, and on Sunday afternoon, he had the band's guitarists overdub three new tracks of slide guitar, taking the total number of guitars to 12; deciding which overdubs to keep could wait until the mix.

Paul finished the session by replacing both of his lead vocal tracks, and at 5:45 p.m. the band headed to Cavendish Avenue to toast Linda's 31st birthday.

"[Paul] always had a strange attitude to the studio," Parsons observed. "He's not very good at describing what it is he's after, so we would spend a lot of time working out if the sound could be better."[27]

On Monday Wings returned for another round of overdubs, overwriting three of the existing electric guitar tracks with two new ones plus a third track of harmony vocals and percussion.

Recording Sessions

Tuesday–Wednesday, September 26–27, 1972.
EMI Studios, Studio Two, London.
Recording: 'Country Dreamer'
Overdubbing: 'I Lie Around.'

The band's pursuit of the perfect single had seen work on their follow-up to *Wild Life* all but grind to a halt. In late September Paul was left with no choice but to postpone the release date of their next album indefinitely. Taking a break from 'Hi, Hi, Hi,' on September 26, Paul placed the paddles of the defibrillator on their lifeless pursuit of a second LP by resuscitating 'Country Dreamer.' Written during his melodically fertile summer of 1970, the Nashville-inspired tune pictures Paul living the life of a country bumpkin, taking off his hat and boots, rolling up his trouser legs, and strolling across the fields, hills, and streams of the Scottish Highlands.

Embracing the rockabilly vibe, Paul arranged the song for drums, bass, acoustic, and pedal steel guitar. Rolling out the console-type pedal steel from an EMI storeroom, McCullough, Laine, and McCartney stared each other down, none of them entirely sure how to operate the plethora of pedals and levers that altered the pitch of certain strings.

The pedal steel guitar has roots in Hawaii but was made popular by country-and-western players like Lloyd Green and Buddy Emmons, making the horizontal guitar's distinctive glissandi (sliding notes) and vibrato tone synonymous with the Nashville scene. Now McCullough, as the band's lead guitarist, was given the task of getting a tune out of the table-size contraption.

The session was slow going while McCullough found his feet. Between 1:00 p.m. and 1:30 a.m. the band attempted 20 takes, with Paul on acoustic, Denny Laine on bass, and Seiwell using brushes to provide a soft rhythmic backing. Take 14 was eventually chosen as the master.

On Wednesday, Wings revisited another of Paul's pastoral themes, pulling the CBS master of 'I Lie Around' from the EMI vault. Playing back the *Ram* reject, Paul found little fault in the lush, orchestrated backing track, started in New York and finished in Los Angeles. But he was curious to hear how it might sound with Denny Laine singing the lead vocal. In an exercise in band diplomacy, Laine was thrust into the vocal booth with a sheet of scrawled lyrics, and the short afternoon session between 1:30 p.m. and 6:30 p.m. was dedicated to recording a new double-tracked lead vocal, while also retaining Paul's mock-Elvis performances of the refrain-ending line "*all over the place*" from the original.

On review, Laine's soft, easygoing tone fit the song's laid-back theme perfectly, giving the guitarist a faith-instilling ego boost, and a potential second lead vocal on Wings next album.

"It's great to sing someone else's song," said Laine soon after the session, "because I used to do that all the time, that's all bands ever used to do, and it's much more of a kick—you learn something. Whereas with my own stuff, I don't think I bother to do as much as I do with somebody else's. It's more of a challenge. It's more like going into a studio as a session man, sitting down and working something out in a way that I wouldn't do at home, and I really like that."[28]

———

Escaping EMI Studios for the evening, Paul and Linda drove across London to Soho, where Barry Chattington was ensconced in a basement edit suite, hacking away at thousands of feet of film shot during the last leg of Wings' European tour. Film reels were stacked high, and bins were brimming with trims, as Chattington and editor Gerry Hambling tried to make sense of the mountain of footage shot on five cameras across four different concert halls.

"It took a few weeks to sync it all up," said Chattington. "With five cameras there was a lot of footage. And there was no timecode, so there was a little cut of a flashing light where we used to synchronize the cameras; camera one went beep, camera two went beep, and all that sort of thing. And then we started looking at some of the material."[29]

Coming away from the shoot in August, Chattington confessed that while the cameramen were all briefed before each shoot, without any monitoring equipment he had no idea what had been caught on camera. And though they had filmed four concerts, quantity was no substitute for quality. Now, two months into the edit, Chattington and Hambling had pieced together rough edits of 12 of the 21 songs played live, and the problems were visible even to the un-trained eye.

Sitting down to view the first rough cut with Paul and Linda, it was obvious to anyone with a functioning pair of eyes that Hambling's shot options were limited. A lack of coverage during Wings' Berlin performance of 'The Mess' meant the young editor had to splice in shots from other concerts, in the process, introducing multiple jarring on-screen wardrobe changes. The links between numbers—often a time when the cameramen would reset—were poorly covered, and Chattington told Paul that they needed to arrange a pickup shoot to bridge the gaps.

Paul, however, was ready with an eccentric solution, one that he believed would melt away the problems and gloss over the technical imperfections. In a hash-energized moment, he came up with the idea of transforming the live action film into an animated musical, interspersing musical set pieces with the tale of a family of cartoon mice.

While vacationing in Antigua, in December 1969, Paul had dreamed up the character of Bruce McMouse, a rodent musical impresario and father of three, and captured them in a set of doodles. Now, in the back of a Soho edit suite three years later, Paul finally found a home for Bruce and his brood.

"We decided that it might be boring to watch a group in action for an hour or more," Paul said, proudly announcing the project to the music papers weeks later. "So we've added interest by incorporating a cartoon story about a family of mice who live under the stage."[30]

The reality of his animated venture was slightly less clear, though. Other than rough sketches and names for each of the cartoon mice—father Bruce; mother Yvonne; and kids Soily, Swooney, and Swat—Paul had no clue where the concept was headed. But confident he was on to something, he handed Chattington his rough drawings with instructions to hire a team of animators and writers to breathe life into his sketchbook doodles.

"You've got to remember that Paul owned [the film rights to] Rupert Bear; in fact, I had storyboards of Rupert Bear for years when we were doing this," said Chattington. "But very much the story came during the edit. Somehow the story evolved. I don't want to say Paul thought it up, or I thought it up, or the bloody cleaning lady thought it up, but it evolved."[31]

———

Recording Sessions

Thursday, September 28, 1972.
EMI Studios, Studio Two, London.
Recording: 'Night Out.'

Back in the studio on Thursday afternoon, the off-the-wall vibes continued, with the band exploring an improvised jam called 'Night Out.' Henry and Denny traded guitar licks to a thumping backbeat, as Paul pounded away on bass guitar while wailing the song's only lyric, "*Night out!*" Sixteen takes of the simple rock number were tracked, six of which went the distance. Take 16 was tentatively labeled "best." The session ended at 11:00 p.m., but not before the band added a solitary percussion overdub onto Take 16.

Recording Sessions

Friday–Sunday, September 29–October 1, 1972.
EMI Studios, Studio Two, London.
Recording: 'Only One More Kiss' (working title of 'One More Kiss'), 'Mood Music' (working title for 'Bridge Over the River Suite') and 'Hands of Love.'
Mixing: 'Mood Music' and 'Only One More Kiss.'

Following the brief freestyle interlude of 'Night Out,' the wheels of Wings' rockabilly wagon rolled into Friday's session when the band tackled another of Paul's county-pop hybrids, 'Only One More Kiss.' Written during the university tour, the gentle guitar melody breaks the typical McCartney ballad pattern, addressing daughter Mary rather than Linda.

"Mary was three at this time, so just a little kid," Paul later noted. "And you know how fathers often fuss over their kids? So, I was fussing over her, she was a really cute baby. And I'm fussing away going, 'Give me a kiss. Come on, give me a kiss!' And she'd get fed up with me and sort of go, 'Dad. All right. But only one more kiss.' So, I got one more kiss . . . and a song!"[32]

But like the grumpy toddler swatting away her father's playful affection, the band was not feeling the love for the song. With McCartney on acoustic guitar, Laine on bass, Henry playing electric guitar, Seiwell drumming, and Linda on electric harpsichord, the band filled three 16-track tapes with unfinished takes before the session stalled, after eight hours and ten minutes, at 9:40 p.m. Abandoning work on the ballad, Wings slipped into an experiment in lounge jazz, loosely labeled 'Mood Music.'

The next day, Wings continued work on 'Only One More Kiss.' Starting afresh with Take 60, the group recorded another 26 takes before Take 85 was chosen as the master. Henry added the only overdub of the day, doubling up his dominant lead guitar parts before the session ended.

Before heading into the studio on Sunday afternoon, Paul relaxed with the day's newspapers, where he found an unwelcome surprise. The *Sunday Independent* published a page-long interview with Paul, based on a backstage chat he had in Copenhagen, exactly two months earlier. The *Sunday Independent* piece, published without a byline, strung together a chain of quotes that portrayed Paul's transition from, as they called it "suave image-maker of the world's most famous group," to "an angry young man." The piece broke no new ground, but exposed a bitter, curmudgeonly side to Paul's personality that many believed had been left behind in 1971.

"Don't ever call me ex-Beatle McCartney again," Paul insisted. "That was one band I was with, now I'm not with them. I've got another band. . . . I just get irritated by people constantly harping on about the past, about the days when I was with that other band, the Beatles. The other Beatles get together and that is fine, but I'm almost always in another part of the world. The Beatles was my old job. We're not like friends, we just know each other. But we don't work together, so there's no point in keeping up old relationships. . . . And I'm downright angry with the people who keep trying to get me back with the others again."[33]

Paul didn't allow the unexpected exposure to sidetrack the band's recording, though. That afternoon, Wings tracked 'Hands of Love,' a third song fragment for the album medley. In this simple acoustic ballad, written on the road in July and August, Paul reflects on meeting and falling for Linda back in 1967. But it also echoes his distracted state of mind during the summer tour. He was not blind to the ballad's shortcomings and planned to bury it between 'Hold Me Tight' and 'Lazy Dynamite,' both already on tape.

Tracked in little over an hour on acoustic guitar (McCartney), electric guitar (McCullough), bass guitar (Laine), and drums (Seiwell), 'Hands of Love' took eight takes to perfect (four false starts and four complete passes); Take 6 was picked for overdubs.

Paul was still not completely convinced by the master take, though, and by the end of the session little of the original recording remained. Unhappy with the rhythm track, Seiwell overdubbed his drums, while McCullough added bongos, Laine's bass was wiped and overdubbed by Paul, and Laine and McCullough overdubbed a fresh set of guitar parts (three tracks of acoustic, and three of electric). Paul and Linda then replaced their joint lead vocals.

At the end of the session Parsons spliced together Take 6 of 'Hands of Love' and Take 3 of 'Lazy Dynamite,' readying them for stereo mixing.

Recording Sessions

Tuesday–Sunday, October 3–8, 1972.
EMI Studios, Studio Two, London.
Recording: 'Power Cut.'
Overdubbing: 'Hi, Hi, Hi,' 'Hold Me Tight,' and 'Lazy Dynamite.'
Mixing: 'Hi, Hi, Hi.'

The final portion of the medley, 'Power Cut,' was recorded on October 3 and 4. Tuesday's session produced three takes, none worth pursuing, so a further 17 takes were recorded the following day, the band settling on Take 12 for overdubs. With the clock ticking toward 2 a.m., Paul added a new lead vocal.

The rest of the week was dedicated to finishing off various half-completed tracks, starting on Thursday with 'Hi, Hi, Hi.' Still unhappy with the electric guitar sounds, McCartney asked a by now exasperated Laine and McCullough to overdub three new guitar lines. More percussion was added by Seiwell. At the end of the session, five rough mixes were made (RS1 to RS5), but none was chosen as the master.

Saturday's session was dedicated to sweetening 'Hold Me Tight,' onto which Paul overdubbed organ, and Henry added an electric guitar. They took another pass at mixing 'Hi, Hi, Hi,' on Sunday. Parsons and the band rode the faders for another three mixes, RS6 to RS8, but their efforts were in vain: the mix was scrapped and the single once again placed on a hiatus. Sunday evening was devoted to overdubbing drums, percussion, and electric guitar onto Take 3 of 'Lazy Dynamite.'

Recording Sessions

Monday–Thursday, October 9–12, 1972.
Island Studios, Studio One, London.
Overdubbing: 'Power Cut.'

Wings' still unnamed second album was slowly starting to come together. But endless, often unproductive, hours in the studio were taking a toll on morale, and the band grumblings that first surfaced in Zürich were worsening. In mid-October, *NME*, quoting a source close to McCullough, reported that the guitarist "may not be entirely happy with his job in Paul's band."[34]

The story wasn't without an element of truth. McCartney's three hired hands all had issues with the studio schedule and the incessant recording, rerecording, overdubbing, and mixing of 'Hi, Hi, Hi.' McCullough, the most unsettled of the group, and never shy about voicing his opinion, was the first to break the silence during an interview with *Sounds*' Ray Telford.

"Playing live with the band isn't all that much of a change from what I've done before," said McCullough of Wings' recent continental tour. "But in the studio, Wings work a lot different from most bands—or bands I've ever had anything to do with. The only time I get unhappy is just sitting around the studio waiting for something to happen."[35]

A passive observer to Paul's working methods during the group's time recording *Wild Life*, Alan Parsons noticed a similar pattern developing during sessions for Wings' second LP, only McCullough was less willing to play sideman than his fellow guitarist.

"Denny was very much manipulated by Paul," noted Parsons, "being told what notes to play. He hadn't got a lot of freedom, musically. I think Denny had a lot of respect for Paul, but he was like a puppet on a string at that time."[36]

Given Paul and Linda's domestic commitments, McCullough, Laine, and Seiwell had been spending a lot of time together away from the studio, taking in the occasional gig (like blues rock combo Uncle Dog at the Tally Ho pub in Finchley, in mid-October) and hanging out at Denny Seiwell's place, drinking, smoking, and venting their frustrations at the tedious cycle of recording.

"We were on call as a band, 24 hours a day, 7 days a week, 365 days a year,"[37] said Seiwell. "There were some problems, and you could feel the whole thing just fizzling out. The guys would sit around my place after [sessions], saying, 'Boy, things just aren't right here.' That was the period that was kind of dark."[38]

"He was fantastic in the studio, Paul," McCullough added. "But to do everything that he asked was just too much. Eventually, it got to us."[39]

In the preceding weeks, McCullough had also begrudgingly taken to subsidizing his weekly retainer with session work. Teaming up with in-demand jobbing keyboardist Mick Weaver, who had played with Henry on *Jesus Christ Superstar*, McCullough visited Nova Sounds Studios near London's Marble Arch, to back fellow Northern Irishman Jackie Flavelle. 'Sam' and 'Isle of Rab,' two cuts from Flavelle's late-1972 blues album *Admission Free*, would feature McCullough on guitar and harmony vocals.

As goodwill within the band was becoming exhausted, so was Wings' recording time at EMI Studios, forcing the players to shift their gear across town to Island Studios. Here the band spent four days adding a vast array of overdubs onto Take 12 of 'Power Cut,' including celeste, electric guitars, drums, Mellotron, bass guitar, lead and backing vocals. Among these were guitar overdubs on the long playout, during which the melodies of 'Hold Me Tight,' 'Lazy Dynamite' and 'Hands of Love' were reprised, giving the medley the illusion of unity.

Sensing that morale was slipping, Paul gave the band Friday off. That night they were treated to a night at Ronnie Scott's jazz club where American jazz-fusion group Return to Forever were playing a weeklong residency (an idea Paul also had for his group, but had yet to realize). Fronted by Armando "Chick" Corea, Return to Forever featured a stellar ensemble of jazz cats—Stanley Clark, bass, Joe Farrell, horns, Airto Moreira, drums, percussion and vocals, and Flora Purim, vocals and percussion. One reviewer described the band's sound as "electric Brazilian jazz-rock." Robert Fripp, Keith Tippett and McCartney all turned out to see Corea's group, which was the talk of London.

Recording Sessions

Saturday, October 14, 1972.
EMI Studios, Studio One, London.
Overdubbing: 'C Moon.'
Mixing: 'C Moon.'

Wings managed to get back to EMI for one final session, during which Denny Seiwell overdubbed two tracks of xylophone onto 'C Moon' between 3:00 p.m. and 11:30 p.m. on October 14. Before the session ended, Alan Parsons made five rough stereo mixes of the song for review, the third of which was chosen as "temporary best."

Recording Sessions

Monday–Wednesday, October 16–18, 1972.
AIR Studios, Studio One, London.
Playback: 'Loup (1st Indian on the Moon),' 'Tragedy,' 'Big Barn Bed,' 'When the Night,' 'Single Pigeon,' 'Thank You Darling,' 'The Mess,' 'I Would Only Smile,' 'Seaside Woman,' and 'Mama's Little Girl.'
Rehearsals: 'Live and Let Die.'
Overdubbing: 'Night Owl' (in Studio Three).

Sessions moved to George Martin's and John Burgess's AIR Studios, under the supervision of engineer Bill Price, on October 18. Price was highly regarded on the London studio scene. Starting as a tape op at Decca Recording Studios, in 1962, he graduated to engineer within a few months. At Decca he engineered sessions for Tom Jones, John Mayall (with Eric Clapton), and the Moody Blues. Price joined Martin at AIR in 1970 as chief engineer.

Wings spent their first two days with Price reviewing the Olympic Studios cuts with a view to sweetening all ten tracks in the coming weeks. But on Wednesday, October 18, the session was entirely dedicated to rehearsing 'Live and Let Die,' which was set to be recorded with Martin's handpicked orchestra on Thursday afternoon. When rehearsals wrapped, late on Wednesday evening, the band and roadies scattered to a nearby watering hole, while Paul and Linda remained at the studio to hammer out the fine details of Thursday's recording with George Martin. At around 11:30 p.m., they headed for the Oxford Street exit.

But Paul was restless and looking for a distraction, which materialized in the form of New York–born singer-songwriter Carly Simon. Simon had been in London since early September working on the follow-up to her breakthrough album, *Anticipation*. Though a rising star in America, she had yet to chart with a single or an LP released in Britain. But her powerful brand of folk-rock was firmly on the radar of journalists tuned into what was selling across the pond. Four weeks earlier, underground music champion and prescient Carly Simon fan Bob Harris invited her onto his late-night television show, *The Old Grey Whistle Test*. Conversation quickly turned to working in London.

"I did my last album here at Morgan Studios, and that was very warm, and I felt quite comfortable about that," Simon told Harris. "So, I thought I'd try Trident. Although it wasn't totally my decision, [producer] Richard Perry wanted to work there because of Robin Cable, who's just a mad and wonderful engineer. I just like London as a city better than New York as a city. I love London, I really love it."[40]

Better known for his work with American cabaret artists like Ella Fitzgerald and Barbra Streisand, producer Richard Perry was responsible for fashioning the laid-back swing arrangement for the title track of Ringo's debut solo album, *Sentimental Journey*. He had also scored Harry Nilsson a number one hit with his remarkable orchestral reworking of the Badfinger ballad 'Without You'—an achievement that had not gone unnoticed by Paul.

Simon had finished the bulk of her album at Trident with Robin Cable, but after a six-week stint, the studio was no longer available. "AIR Studios had become available thanks to its owner, George Martin," Simon explained. "We needed to replace some parts, especially background vocals, and a guitar solo on 'You're So Vain.'"[41]

As McCartney popped his head around the door to AIR's Studio Three, Simon was adding backing vocals to 'Night Owl,' a bluesy rocker penned by her fiancé—and former Apple artist—James Taylor. Around the microphone stood session guitarist Jim Ryan, and singers Doris Troy (another former Apple artist) and Bonnie Bramlett. Jim Ryan recalls McCartney gate-crashing the session.

"I looked in the control room and noticed Richard was talking to somebody—and it's Paul McCartney. Paul hits the talkback button and says, 'I hear you guys are having a little trouble out there, could you use some help?'"[42]

Perry welcomed the McCartneys with open arms, insisting they stay and join his A-list glee club. "We had this background chorus rehearsing the song consisting of Carly, Paul, Linda, Doris and Bonnie," Perry said. "It was quite a happening in the studio that night, very exciting, and totally spontaneous. Just a magical moment."[43]

Jim Ryan credits McCartney with arranging the backing vocals. But according to Carly Simon, there was only ever one man calling the shots.

"Richard Perry is like a movie director. He sees himself as holding the camera, as directing the players, as calling the final shots, as doing the theme."[44]

Keen to push the feel of the song from blues-rock to rhythm and blues, Perry choreographed a blend of all female and full chorus harmony and backing vocals. *"Oohs"* and *"ahhs"* from Carly,

Doris, Bonnie, and Linda bedded the verses, with Paul's unmistakable vocals punching through during the choruses.

Simon's track completed, McCartney couldn't resist a quick turn on the Steinway.

"We all got around the piano in the studio," said Ryan, "and he put his hands on the keys and played 'Live and Let Die.' But it got even better, he invited us to the session the next day."[45] A few glasses of wine and vodkas later, it was time to call it a day.

Recording Session

Thursday, October 19, 1972.
AIR Studios, Studio One, London.
Recording: 'Live and Let Die.'

Opening the music papers on Thursday morning, Paul noted that news of his Bond commission was now public knowledge, the announcement having been delayed to coincide with the recording sessions.

"I'm really chuffed to be doing the theme for Roger. I think he'll be great in the Bond role and I'm working on the right music for him. I'm also doing two or three songs for the film," said Paul, momentarily exaggerating his role. "We may use some Wings music. I'm not sure about writing the whole film score, we'll have to see how it goes."[46]

Asked for a statement on his replacement, John Barry, who had just written the music for *Alice in Wonderland* and was working on Richard Harris's musical version of *Gulliver's Travels*, told *Disc*, "I think a new musical approach to go with the new Bond is essential, and Paul's a great choice to write it."[47]

Almost a year after Ron Kass had first introduced McCartney to the Bond producers, hoping he might write the theme for *Diamonds Are Forever*, Paul's ambition to record a Bond theme was about to be realized.

Over 4,000 miles away, in New Orleans, the Bond film crew, headed by producers Harry Saltzman and Cubby Broccoli, were preparing to shoot one of the movie's bigset pieces: a complex high-speed boat chase on the Louisiana bayous. The plan was to send them acetates of 'Live and Let Die' for their consideration as soon as the recording was finished. Saltzman and Broccoli were well known in the business for their no-nonsense approach, as their periodic spats with John Barry made very clear. If they weren't happy with Paul's theme they wouldn't think twice about asking him to rewrite and rerecord it.

"The song had to be big and spectacular," McCartney explained at the time. "The band had been rehearsing it and when we got it as near perfection as possible we took it into the studio."[48]

Paul wasn't the only one wanting to make a good impression. When establishing AIR Studios as a recording facility, George Martin had equipment installed, at considerable expense, to cater for film clients, and he was hoping to attract Eon Productions to do its orchestral recording there. Martin was eyeing a filmscoring job, too: since John Barry had recently resigned his position at Eon Productions, the film composer's seat was empty. Martin hoped to be asked to write the orchestral score for *Live and Let Die*—and who knew, one job with Eon Productions might lead to more.

McCartney and Martin's ambitious plan was to record 'Live and Let Die' like an old mono record from the days before multitrack tape: with the band, singer, and orchestra playing together live (but with the benefit of 16-track technology). Wings would be backed by a 38-piece orchestra (primarily members of the London Symphony) together with local Watford lad, virtuoso percussionist Ray Cooper.

The orchestral musicians were scheduled to arrive at 7:00 p.m., but before then, George Martin and Bill Price wanted to tape an insurance policy: a backup rhythm track that could be used if the live recording didn't work out. "I said, 'This is the way we'll do it—we'll do it with Wings, and work on the session with just the group,'" explained Martin, "'and then in the evening, I'll bring in the orchestra, but we'll still keep Wings there, and try to do it live together, to try get a live feeling to it.'"[49]

Laine, Seiwell, and McCullough arrived at 2:30 p.m., and together with Paul and Linda, laid down ten takes of the basic arrangement: piano, organ, lead guitar, bass, and drums. When the orchestra arrived at 7:00 p.m., Martin and Wings were satisfied that they had a solid recording in Take 10 (but were hoping they wouldn't need to use it).

But after a few run-throughs with both band and orchestra, Martin and his team were on the verge of self-combusting. Though AIR Studio One, measuring about 60 by 40 feet, was large enough for Wings and the orchestra to fit comfortably, the rehearsals pointed up separation issues that screens and baffles could not correct.

"I found the pickup from the strings was too loud for Paul's voice," said Martin. "So, I took the strings outside."[50] In other words, since screens were insufficient, Martin moved the 20-strong string section to the adjacent Studio Two, putting a three-foot-thick wall between them and Wings.

Martin and his engineers were wading into unchartered waters. Recording between two studios was not an everyday practice; in fact, it had never been done before at AIR.* But Martin and

---

* Martin would, however, build on the experience, using the two-studio technique for the jazz guitarist John McLaughlin's *Apocalypse*—a collaboration between McLaughlin's Mahavishu Orchestra and the London Symphony Orchestra, conducted by Michael Tilson Thomas—17 months later, in March 1974.

Price knew it was possible, thanks to the "Synchronized Start System" devised by in-house technical boffin Dave Harries. The system worked by using an audio tone as a synchronization start link between the studios—the same system used by Barry Chattington, filming Wings on location in August.

Bill Price enlisted the help of engineer Steve Nye to record the strings in Studio Two, while he recorded the band and the rest of the orchestra in Studio One. "I was running out of channels on the desk as well," said Price. "[So] I asked Steve Nye to mix the strings down to a stereo pair and send them to me so they could go straight to a couple of tracks on my multitrack machine."[51]

What had started out as a "live" recording ended with Wings plus the woodwind, brass and percussion musicians in Studio One, and the strings in Studio Two. Not quite the spectacle McCartney was hoping to lay on for his guests—Carly, Bonnie, Doris, Jim, and Richard—up in the control room.

With everything finally in place, and the two rooms running in tandem, George Martin conducted Wings and the bifurcated orchestra through three takes of 'Live and Let Die.' Backed by almost forty musicians, McCartney and the band played with greater conviction than they had done during the afternoon session. Henry's guitar punched through the orchestra, then, like the speedboats racing down the Louisiana bayous that afternoon, the strings and brass chased down every pluck of McCullough's plectrum, and Ray Cooper's percussion matched every strike of Seiwell's sticks, to the song's last note.

Three takes was enough to leave Bill Price confident that he and Martin had enough material, between the live and band-only takes, to cover any editing eventualities.

———

Recording Session

Friday-Saturday, October 20-21, 1972.
AIR Studios, Studio One, London.
Overdubbing: 'Live and Let Die.'
Mixing: 'Live and Let Die.'

On playback, with fresh ears, the merits of the various incarnations of 'Live and Let Die' committed to tape the previous day became clear, and McCartney decided to throw Bill Price one final curveball: he wanted parts of various takes spliced together to create the master.

Price assembled the Frankenstein monster of an edit that Paul asked for, using a band-only take, and parts of several orchestral takes. Paul then set about overdubbing keyboards and extra lead vocals, with the rest of the band joining on backup vocals. Price's mix was so masterful that the edits are hard to detect and are not where you would expect them to be.

"There's one section where the orchestra stops and it goes into a reggae section, and that was actually done live; it wasn't edited in," Price noted. "We took it from a live take of Wings with the orchestra. And a lot of McCartney's vocal was live, some of it live with Wings, some of it live with the orchestra, a little bit of it overdubbed. But I do remember that I wasn't able to edit too much because there were so many tracks and so many different takes."[52]

The day ended in a hazy, smoke-filled control room, as the band gathered around the console to help Price mix their efforts from 16-track to stereo. In some ways the patchwork recording session meant the mix could be much more powerful. The strings were recorded clean, as were the brass and woodwind sections, meaning the horns pop, the strings surge and the timpani explode through the speakers.

McCartney was blown away. What had started out as a simple piano composition in his music room on September 9 had been given a cinematic treatment, the likes of which he had never experienced. 'Live and Let Die' was ready to take its place alongside enduring classics like 'Goldfinger' and 'Diamonds Are Forever.'

But not before it was signed off by Harry Saltzman and Cubby Broccoli. Acetates were cut at AIR Studios that evening and sent express to New Orleans.

The following day, on location in New Orleans, actor Roger Moore noted in his diary that Bond producer Cubby Broccoli had spoken briefly with lyricist Leslie Bricusse about one of the lyrics in Paul's song for 'Live and Let Die.' Music promoter Tony Bramwell claims he delivered the acetates to set, and the response to Paul's movie theme was overwhelming.

"I brought the track back for Saltzman and everyone involved with the film to hear the title song, and everyone was literally floored," said Bramwell. "This was the most powerful piece of music ever presented for a Bond film, as well as being a huge piece of music for Wings."[53]

On Monday, October 23, 1972, 'Live and Let Die' was mastered at EMI Studios and given the matrix number 7YCE.21722. The recording was never touched again after that date.

20

ROMEO, ROMEO

—

Despite McCartney's wish to exit the Beatles' long-drawn-out divorce with no further reputation-damaging fallout, as the end of 1972 drew near his past was ever present. Crawling out of the shadows, in early November, came former flame Francie Schwartz with her kiss-and-tell memoir, *Body Count*, which included a section exploring her three-month fling with Paul in undressed detail. Salacious extracts probing the couple's between-the-sheets adventures were also published in the gentleman's magazine *Penthouse*.

McCartney's relationship with Schwartz was all the more tantalizing for journalists, as it coincided with the early days of Paul's romance with Linda, in the summer of 1968. Asked her reaction to Schwartz's book by *Rolling Stone* writer Paul Gambaccini, Linda coolly dispatched her husband's former fling with a one-line put-down.

"She should flatter herself. She got one good lay. I'd never write about my sex life,"[1] Linda said with a hefty measure of scorn.

Someone at Apple was stirring the pot, too. On October 23, the British tabloid press turned heads with claims that the millionaire former Beatles owed the British government £162,000 ($381,000) in unpaid corporation tax. At fault for the late payment, an Apple spokesman declared, was McCartney, who (they claimed) was the only one of the four Beatles yet to authorize the settlement.[2]

The truth, of course, was less cut-and-dried. Apple *did* owe the taxman the amount cited, but (as with all monies owed both to the Beatles' creditors, and the Beatles themselves) the money was tangled up in the intricate financial web woven by the High Court when appointing a receiver to handle the group's financial affairs.

Though served up by an Apple spokesman, the information given to Nigel Benson of the *Daily Mirror* came straight from the desk of Allen Klein, the latest communiqué in his continued smear campaign against McCartney. Compounding the allegation against Paul, Lennon was still defending, and worse, enthusiastically promoting the divisive Apple boss.

"He was an orphan, he never had his parents," Lennon said of Klein in an interview with *Sounds* a few weeks earlier. "His mother died when he was a kid and he's as neurotic as me or any other person that's got no parents. He's capitalist, but that's all. That's his worst sin. Apart from that, I've got no proof he ever robbed anybody or did anything dirty."[3]

More nettlesome gossip filling newspaper column-inches concerned McCartney's James Bond theme. In early November, the question of who would sing the second version of 'Live and Let Die' in Saltzman and Broccoli's spy picture was still unanswered. Misinterpreting the search for another act to perform his movie opener, *Disc* ran a news piece titled "McCartney Bond Songs for Dimension," speculating that Paul would not perform his own Bond theme, but rather the vocal group the Fifth Dimension or Motown singer Thelma Houston would provide the lead vocals instead.

In an effort to tie down an act to perform the "as live" version of McCartney's movie theme, Ron Kass and Tony Bramwell had been in talks with Marc Gordon, the manager of both acts named in the *Disc* article. The Fifth Dimension were known for their intoxicating brand of champagne soul in hits like 'Aquarius/Let the Sunshine In,' 'One Less Bell to Answer,' and 'Wedding Bell Blues.' But while their knockout vocals ticked all the boxes for the filmmakers, a five-piece group did not fit director Guy Hamilton's vision. The scene called for a sultry soul singer, capable of playful interplay with Bond, not a male-dominant vocal group.

With the Fifth Dimension out of the running, Gordon offered up Thelma Houston as an alternative. But Houston was busy in the studio working on an album; moreover, she had just switched record labels and was in the process of reviewing her management situation.

"Around that time, I remember Marc Gordon telling me there was a possibility I was going to sing the song," Houston remembered. "I signed with Mowest Records in [late] 1972. I know that when I signed with Mowest, Marc no longer wanted to represent me. I never heard anything else about it after that."[4]

With Houston also ruled out, Ron Kass was keen on securing the services of Brenda (or B.J.) Arnau, an emerging soul singer from Cleveland, Ohio, who had recently signed a three-year contract with RCA Records in America.[5] Though her last two singles, 'I Wanna Go Back There' and 'The Big Hurt,' both produced by Jonathan King, had failed to make an impression on either side of the Atlantic, Arnau was a talented cabaret performer and had recently appeared in *The Two Gentlemen of Verona* on London's West End. Ultimately, the choice of female vocalist rested with producers Saltzman and Broccoli.

Deflecting press gossip was no longer a major worry for the McCartneys, though. At the start of November, Vincent Romeo was installed in MPL's 1 Soho Square offices, and a Kensington-based publicist, Tony Brainsby, had been hired to promote Wings or run interference between Paul and the press, as the need may be.

Brainsby was also tasked with imposing some order and sense of completeness on Paul's growing press archive by subscribing to Durrant's clipping service for a mere £10.45 ($24.50) a month. Two more fresh faces at MPL were Dave Golding, hired as an in-house press spokesman, and Jack Abbott, the new head of finance, appointments designed to prevent any repeat of the PR and financial fiascos of Wings' recent European tour.

Paul and Linda also briefly employed a PR agency run by American-born Carolyn Pfeiffer, at least partly, as Pfeiffer remembered it, "because the press was giving Linda a hard time,"[6] but also to work on band projects. Meeting at Pfeiffer's home office, at 10 Connaught Place, the publicist and Paul brainstormed ways to get the press on Linda's side. "I didn't like Linda initially, but grew to like her," Pfeiffer added. "She was nervous or uncomfortable."

The corporate spine of MPL finally matched Paul's ambitions for Wings as well as the company's growing business concerns, and Romeo offered a valuable tension-dispersing buffer between McCartney and his sidemen. Rather than airing their grievances with Paul directly, any business gripes would go through Romeo before landing on Paul's doorstep. And those gripes, Romeo soon discovered, had already taken root, driven, as he could see at a glance, by both financial and creative issues.

"I think Paul wanted to do something that no one has ever done: create a second super-group," Romeo noted of McCartney's post-Beatles vision. "He has a strict interpretation of what he knows is absolutely correct for his music. As a result, it is difficult for other musicians to work with McCartney, though, I must admit, I got along famously with him. He wanted to do everything—he always wanted to do everything. I loved Linda. She was more of an asset than anything else to me. She helped me communicate with him."[7]

Between repairing the financial damage the European tour had left, and bringing the band back onside, Romeo immediately had his hands full.

Paul, Linda, and the girls spent the weekend of November 3 in Merseyside, commemorating Guy Fawkes Night, on November 5, with family. Cousin Ian Harris, son of Paul's aunty Gin, hosted the McCartney clan in New Brighton, where they gathered around a burning pile of scrap wood with baked potatoes and sausages for a backyard firework display.

———

Recording Sessions

Monday–Wednesday, November 6–8, 1972.
EMI Studios, Studio Two, London.
Recording: 'Promotional Jam.'
Overdubbing: 'Hi, Hi, Hi,' and 'C Moon.'
Mixing: 'Hi, Hi, Hi.'

The McCartneys, and the rest of Wings, were back at EMI at 4:00 p.m. on Monday, hoping that the 12th session devoted to 'Hi, Hi, Hi' would, at long last, yield at least the basis of the band's next single. Alan Parsons loaded Take 61 onto the tape machine and the band filled the control room for a playback, desperately hoping this version would receive Paul's seal of approval.

But the recording still did not meet the high-water mark Paul had set for Wings' next release. The lyrics, though alluding to drug use, were deeply sexual, and Paul reasoned that this sybaritic anthem called for a breathless finale, a musical orgasm. With that in mind, during the final thirty seconds, when the song shifts into a faster tempo, Paul overdubbed manic organ flourishes, Seiwell doubled up his snare drum for added kick, Henry layered on yet another pounded rhythm guitar, and the group recorded frenzied, high-pitch, harmony vocals.

One other late addition is undocumented, but it is claimed that the group took the sexual theme one step further, overdubbed the pulsing sound of a vibrator after the line *"get you ready for my polygon."* (In the final mix this sound could easily be mistaken for the sound of a chainsaw or motorcycle.) By the end of the session, only six elements of the original Take 61 remained; the other ten tracks of the 16-track master had been wiped and replaced with overdubs. But finally, the results of the band's labor of love (as literally was the case) and frustration satisfied the boss.

Mixing 'Hi, Hi, Hi' turned out to be no less laborious than recording it. Intent on ensuring that the song would sound perfect on the radio, Paul became fussy and overcautious, much as he had during the preparation of 'Another Day.' Already at odds with the producer/bass player for overlooking the live recording, Alan Parsons butted heads with Paul once more.

"'Hi, Hi, Hi' took forever. We spent weeks, and weeks, and weeks [working on it],"[8] said Parsons. "I remember we spent a long time mixing it on small speakers trying to make it sound good for radio. I think we were going over the top on EQ as a result of that, and we'd play it on little speakers and they'd say, 'We can't hear the bass and the bass drum.' So you'd turn it up so you could hear the bass and the bass drum and then you play it on the big speakers and it would blow your head off! I wasn't too happy with it."[9]

But Paul *was* finally pleased. Four hours of mixing yielded eight attempts, RS10 to RS17; RS14 was sent for mastering (and assigned the matrix 7YCE.21692).

Ever since he announced himself as a solo artist with his unpretentious self-titled debut LP, McCartney's recordings had become part of a dialogue with his most severe critics, each release a direct response to what reviewers noted as the shortcomings of its predecessor. 'Hi, Hi, Hi' would be no exception. 'Mary Had a Little Lamb' had many critics baffled, speculating that parenthood had robbed McCartney of his edge, so he intended Wings' third single to be a double-barreled retort to his doubters. Poring over the options overnight, Paul and Linda concluded the relaxed Caribbean lilt of 'C Moon' provided the perfect contrast to the energetic A side. Moreover, the combined message of Wings' chosen cuts formed a decisive statement to establishment figures in Sweden and Scotland: "*don't be a square, get high, high, high.*"

Tuesday afternoon was spent fine-tuning 'C Moon' for release. Luckily, the easygoing reggae number was only lacking a few final touches. The band added two tracks of backing vocals, a short burst of electric guitar (later deemed unnecessary and dropped), and tambourine, before Denny Seiwell harnessed his navy band training to overdub a one-man horn section, comprising two tracks of cornet, a mellower, easier-to-play cousin of the trumpet.

Five hours of mixing, starting at 10:00 p.m., produced seven stereo mixes, RS10 to RS16, the last being the best. 'C Moon' was quickly mastered at EMI Studios and given the matrix 7YCE.21693. The band's third single was slated for release in Britain on December 1, and three days later in America.

On Wednesday, Wings spent from 4:00 p.m. to midnight recording, editing, and mixing a short musical skit to promote their impending release. The 'Promotional Jam' began as a one-take improvisation played by Paul on piano. Vocals, drums, and electric guitar were then layered on top, together with excerpts from both songs. Making light of his recent legal scrapes in Sweden and Scotland, in the midst of the sketch Paul shrieked: "*Now you know quite well, we've brought you here for questioning, and questioning is what's going to happen to you!*" Introducing an extract of 'C Moon' he continued his gibes, bellowing: "*L7 means square! Square—like you! Square! (repeated with echo).*" The message to those who had arrested Paul, Linda, and Denny Seiwell was loud and clear.

Unconcerned by the track's crude form, the 2'32" advert was mixed to stereo in one pass and copies were run off for British and international radio stations.

Recording Sessions

Thursday–Monday, November 9–13, 1972.
EMI Studios, Studio Two, London.
Playback: Wings live in Groningen, Amsterdam, The Hague, Antwerp, and West Berlin.
Mixing: All live recordings from Groningen, Amsterdam, The Hague, Antwerp, and West Berlin.
Recording: '1882' (studio version).
Sound Effects: 'I Lie Around.'

Eight months after the red light first flickered on at Olympic Studios, Wings had a wide-ranging collection of songs on tape, and Paul was beginning to view the group's follow-up to the rush-recorded *Wild Life* album with ambitious eyes. Rather than issuing a single record, he would surprise fans with a deluxe double LP set, offering an unfiltered look at the group's eclectic canon of new compositions. Wings, McCartney had asserted from the very start, was a *band*; to that end, their new long player would celebrate their collective strength in depth, while also affording each member a moment in the limelight.

Mindful that their tour recordings (much to the exasperation of engineer Alan Parsons, the engineer who recorded them) remained untapped, on November 9, Paul set out to salvage something from Wings' five concert recordings for inclusion on the double album.

A starting point was '1882,' Paul's moody period piece, which turned out to be one of the unlikely success stories of the European tour. Robin Denselow, writing in the *Guardian*, described the song as an "impressive, tuneful, narrative ballad,"[10] and the band liked it, too. As Denny Laine enthused, "The slow things like '1882' went down incredibly well."[11]

Embracing the approval of both the group and critics, Paul spent Thursday, Friday and Saturday making stereo mixes of all five recordings of this morose Victorian tale, in the hope of finding a live gem, and a cassette was made for him to pick over at home.

But the mixtape did nothing to improve Paul's confidence in the band's live cuts. The West Berlin recording of '1882' was note perfect, but the urge to sharpen the song was too much to resist, and the band soon set up for a studio run-through. On November 13, Wings tracked four "as live" takes of '1882' in Studio Two, none of which went the distance. Seeing potential in their final two attempts, Takes 3 and 4 were edited together as the master, and the tape was set aside for future overdubs.

Now the band had a single to promote, so the focus shifted from recording to lip-synching. Taking a break from the studio, Wings drove to Southern Television's studios in Southampton, on November 14, to film promotional videos for both sides of the upcoming single. Generally speaking, the flip side of a record would not be afforded a music video, but since Paul was releasing 'Hi, Hi, Hi' and 'C Moon' as a double A side, with equal billing for both, he planned near-identical videos for the two songs.

Here, Vincent Romeo's presence offered some level of accountability, and a shift in Paul's modus operandi. The days of self-indulgence were numbered. Unlike the costly, elaborate films made to promote 'Mary Had a Little Lamb,' the promotional videos for 'Hi, Hi, Hi' and 'C Moon' were put together at minimum expense. Both videos were more in line with McCullough's vision of Wings as a rock band—dark and edgy, filmed on a small stage with colorful, tightly focused spot lamps. Steve Turner, the award-winning director of the late-60s BBC 2 series *Colour Me Pop*, oversaw production.

"I had turned freelance, setting up my own Take One Productions company, when, out of the blue, I got a call saying that I'd been recommended, would I be interested in working with Paul," Turner remembered. "Paul's a great ideas man and was wanting to change things as we went along, which I was happy to do because his suggestions always fitted in. The only problem was the studio was being refurbished so I had to sit in an outdoor outside-broadcast wagon rather than in the control room. Paul likes his directors to work with him on the floor, but I couldn't because it took too long to go back and forth between the two places. Still, everyone was happy with the clips in the end."[12]

Simplicity ran through to delivery, too. Both promos were vision mixed on location (meaning no postproduction was needed) and handed to Paul at the end of the day on bulky U-matic videotapes.

———

Two men not afforded the luxury of such instant gratification were producers Harry Saltzman and Cubby Broccoli, who were still in the thick of shooting their spy feature *Live and Let Die*. On Monday, November 13, the Bond film crew traveled from New Orleans to Jamaica, arriving to a champagne reception laid on by the Jamaican Tourist Board. Seven days of filming began on November 20 in the port town of Ocho Rios.

During that week, George Martin flew out to Ocho Rios to meet with Saltzman, hoping to be engaged to write the film score. Martin's and McCartney's superbly atmospheric recording was already the toast of Eon Productions, so the meeting between veteran filmmaker and hitmaker was, to all intents and purposes, a formality.

But what happened during their lunch meeting left Martin deeply flummoxed. Martin relived their exchange as he remembered it, in his memoir:

Harry was straight to the point. He sat me down and said, "Great. Like what you did, very nice record, like the score. Now tell me, who do you think we should get to sing it?"

That took me completely aback. After all, he was holding the Paul McCartney recording we had made. And Paul McCartney was—Paul McCartney. But he was clearly treating it as a demo disc.

"I don't follow. You've got Paul McCartney . . . ," I said.

"Yeah, yeah, that's good. But who are we going to get to sing it for the film?"

"I'm sorry. I still don't follow," I said, feeling that maybe there was something I hadn't been told.

"You know—we've got to have a girl, haven't we? What do you think of Thelma Houston?"[13]

Assuming Martin was up to speed with the various recordings needed for the production, Saltzman was speaking about the film's *second* version of 'Live and Let Die,' to be sung during the "Filet of Soul" scene. It made perfect sense for him to ask Martin's advice, given that he had produced Bond-singer Shirley Bassey's recordings, and he undoubtedly knew which other female singers could be right for the scene. But Martin was unaware of the script's scene layout and planned music cues, nor was he privy to the details of the agreement between Lee Eastman and Eon Productions, so his confusion was understandable.

As Martin related the story, he told Saltzman that if he ditched the Wings recording, it was likely Paul would pull the plug on his involvement, and Saltzman, seemingly baffled by Martin's defensive response, offered no opposition.*

Martin remained in Jamaica for several days, joining the crew on location, and soon afterward, he signed a $10,000 contract to score the film. He was also engaged to produce the Brenda Arnau version for the "Filet of Soul" sequence, an indication that Saltzman was able to clarify the situation for him.

In London, Paul was taking more than a passing interest in the Bond project. As his song was woven into the fabric of the film, he oversaw development of the title graphics with designer Maurice Binder, the mastermind of the iconic red, white, and black film noir sequences that opened each of the Bond movies. The two met in Soho to see the first visualization of Wings' recording set to pictures.

---

* It is extremely likely that Saltzman explained the need for a second singer, but Martin always omitted that detail. Recounting the incident over the years, Martin consistently presented it as his having saved the day for Paul's recording, rather than as a misunderstanding on his part. Recognizing that it made a great story, McCartney, who knew the details of his own contract with Eon, latched onto Martin's version of the Ocho Rios lunch meeting years later, adding it to his canon of Wings-era tales.

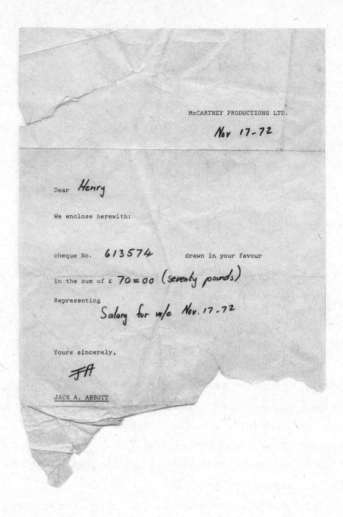

McCARTNEY PRODUCTIONS LTD.

Nov 17-72

Dear *Henry*

We enclose herewith:

cheque No. *613574*   drawn in your favour

in the sum of £ *70 = 00* *(seventy pounds)*

Representing

Salary for w/e Nov. 17-72

Yours sincerely,

JACK A. ABBOTT

"I rented out a viewing theater for Paul to see Binder's opening sequence," said Tony Bramwell, who continued to act as a go-between for Eon and MPL. "Paul and Binder worked together on the film's opening sequence making sure the right visual matched with the audio. The sequence evolved into being a tight little movie within the film itself."[14]

While they were in central London, the McCartneys mixed business with pleasure, catching up with theater productions in the West End. On the evening of November 15, Paul and Linda saw Tim Rice's and Andrew Lloyd Webber's *Jesus Christ Superstar* at the Palace Theater. The following night they were guests of honor for the opening night of Charles Strouse's and Lee Adams's *Applause*, playing at Her Majesty's Theater in Haymarket. Celebrations stretched into the early hours at Tramp nightclub on Jermyn Street, where the McCartneys mingled with Rod Stewart, Keith Richards, and Mick and Bianca Jagger.

Recording Sessions

Friday–Sunday, November 17–19, 1972.

EMI Studios, Studio Two, London.

Overdubbing: 'Mama's Little Girl,' 'Big Barn Bed' and 'I Lie Around.'

Mixing: 'I Lie Around.'

Eight months had elapsed since Wings had recorded 'Mama's Little Girl' at Olympic Studios. When he took it up again on November 17, the band members were merely spectators, since all Paul needed to add was a clarinet section. At Paul's request, EMI's Vera Samwell booked a small group of clarinetists to record a simple woodwind section for the song's refrain. Already set on what the clarinet line would be, Paul opted against engaging an arranger and was merrily whistling the clarinet part when the musicians walked through the studio door. Settling at the piano, Paul played the clarinet line as single notes for the musicians to transcribe and replicate. One take, one cup of tea, and one playback later, the jobbing musicians were gone, their business effortlessly executed.

Next on the checklist for final brushstrokes was 'Big Barn Bed,' a product of Wings' first session at Olympic. On playback McCartney picked up a tenseness in Seiwell's playing and the two agreed the drums should be reworked. Seiwell's second attempt at tracking the song's rhythmic backbone wrapped tightly around McCullough's riffing, and the closer microphone placement at EMI captured the thunder of the bass tom and kick drum with greater intensity than Johns's spatial three microphone setup. 'Big Barn Bed' was wrapped up at 12:45 p.m. with the overdubbing of backing vocals and percussion.

Saturday and Sunday were spent plundering the EMI sound effects library, as the band got creative with the introduction to 'I Lie Around.' Five stereo tapes of sound effects—riverbank atmosphere, birdsong, insects, sheep, and water splashes—were transferred to 16-track to form the building blocks for a rich soundscape underlying McCartney's and Spinozza's original fingerpicked introduction.

In the style of the long-running BBC Radio drama *The Archers*,* Paul also overdubbed a short

---

* Set in the fictional village of Ambridge, Borsetshire, *The Archers* was first broadcast on January 1, 1951, and is the BBC's longest-

scene of improvised dialogue to open the tune. Adopting a faux-Yorkshire accent, he took on the role of a father beckoning his nervous children to join him for a dip in a country stream. "*'Ere you are, come on, it's lovely! Come on, it's lovely init? This is the life in the country, it's lovely! Come on, 'ere you are. I'm going for a swim. Y' comin'?*" The scene concluded with a loud wail and a splash sound effect, as the fictitious character tumbled into the water.

Convinced that he now knew the song more intimately and could deliver the lead vocal with more conviction, Denny Laine overdubbed his vocals onto Take 8 for a second time on Sunday afternoon, and McCullough ripped through the acoustic-heavy rhythm track with effervescent stabs of lead guitar. At the end of Sunday's session, the sound effects and spoken-word intro was mixed to stereo in preparation for crossfading with the main track.

Recording Sessions

Monday–Wednesday, November 20–22, 1972.
Trident Studios, Studio One, London.
Overdubbing: 'Little Lamb Dragonfly.'
Recording: 'Captain of Love.'

A last-minute move on November 20 found Wings at Trident Studios in Soho, where the Beatles recorded 'Hey Jude,' lured there because it was one of the first studios in the country to introduce eight-track recording. At Trident, Denny Seiwell encouraged his boss to remove another lavish *Ram* leftover, 'Little Lamb Dragonfly,' from the short stack of songs reserved for *Rupert*. Complete but for its lyrics, the deliciously delicate ballad was one of 1970's most alluring outtakes.

"At Trident he broke out 'Little Lamb,'" remembered Seiwell, "and he said, 'We should finish this tune.' And I said, 'Yeah, it's a great song I really love that.' [But] he hadn't finished a lot of that song. I said, 'Come on, let us help you with this.' I wrote some background harmonies and stuff. I said, 'On the background vocals why don't we just do a little answer bit?' And I sang little parts to him as he was playing it, and he said, 'Yeah, that's great.'"[15]

"I tend to be a bit of a perfectionist about things is it good enough?"[16] Paul noted of the song a few days later, offering the outside world a glimpse of the crisis of confidence he suffered while trying to complete the lyrics in early 1971.

---

running radio drama.

Trident engineer David Hentschel put his feet up, supped tea, and read the morning paper, while Paul and Denny Laine fleshed out the song's scant existing lyrics, "*I have no answer for you little lamb, I can help you out, but I cannot help you in.*" Together McCartney and Laine shaped poetic, poignant lyrics befitting the vibrant, stirring orchestral backing.

A tale of tragedy, loss, reflection, and hope—a dying lamb taking its final breaths in Paul's arms, and a spirited dragonfly symbolizing rebirth and freedom—in Denny Laine's eyes, 'Little Lamb Dragonfly' was the first credible example of a McCartney-Laine cocomposition.

"I helped him with the words on 'Little Dragonfly,'"[17] explained Laine, soon after the session, momentarily forgetting the song's full name, but fully aware that such help did not necessarily yield recognition or remuneration. "I was contributing, but I wasn't credited for that. But that goes for lots of things that I've done,"[18] he acknowledged.

Paul blew hot and cold about collaborating with Denny. He had encouraged him to take a hand in writing for Wings, yet three years after the Beatles split, he doubted he could have a similar connection with another partner (apart, that is, from Linda).

"With John and I it was so special, so special, I think both of us knew we couldn't get that again," he later confessed. "We really were a complete fluke—just two kids who happened to meet up in Liverpool and share an interest and start writing songs together. And then developed, organically, together . . . All of these little awarenesses pretty much hit us at the same time over a period of years. And you really become soulmates when that happens."[19]

If he and Laine clicked, fine, but Paul was not willing to force a partnership. One thing McCartney did share with Laine was the lead vocal, recorded on Monday afternoon, with bass guitar and backing vocals completing the track. Clocking in at an impressive 6'20", the playback at Trident was a tender moment for those there to witness it.

"It was just the most magical experience of any of the Wings sessions I'd ever been in," Jo Jo LaPatrie remembered. "It was so beautiful I started crying. I had tears in my eyes and Denny came over to me and he kind of lifted my chin up and said, 'Are you crying?' And he just said, 'You soppy little girl.' Paul just smiled."[20]

During their brief stint at Trident, the band also worked on a new, not-quite-finished Denny Laine tune called 'Captain of Love.' But Paul decided that the undeveloped song didn't merit further attention and quickly abandoned it.

———

Lamb was no longer on the McCartneys' dinner menu under any circumstances, but when Paul and Linda invited the band to Cavendish Avenue for a Thanksgiving meal on November 23, Linda was willing to set aside her increasingly strong inclination toward vegetarianism to satisfy the appetites of her meat-loving bandmates and laid on a turkey dinner with all the trimmings. The overindulgent sample of Americana went down particularly well with Pennsylvania-born Denny Seiwell, whose memory is that the McCartneys had not yet gone fully vegetarian, a point Linda confirmed in an interview a week later.

"We're mostly vegetarian but we do eat meat occasionally. Eggs and bacon, sausages," Linda said of their struggle toward a meat-free diet. "One dish we both like is scrambled eggs on toast with smoked salmon on top."[21]

"Linda made a ferocious chicken dinner," Seiwell said of another of Linda's specialties. "And on Thanksgiving, we were up at the house in Cavendish, and she made a traditional turkey dinner."[22]

Thanksgiving was to be a double celebration. EMI's publicity machine had cranked into action and arranged for the band's new single to receive its first public spin during Tony Blackburn's BBC Radio One breakfast show. Paul, Linda, and the girls gathered around the wireless with toast, cereal, and fresh orange juice to hear Blackburn introduce 'Hi, Hi, Hi' to the nation.

Across London, another avid BBC radio listener, Radio One's executive producer, Derek Chinnery, also tuned in to Blackburn's show, and while the McCartney family bounced around their living room to the thunderous sound Wings had labored so long to harness, Chinnery grew enraged, calling his secretary into his office and dictating a hysterical memo to be sent to every DJ and producer working at Broadcasting House. McCartney's song, Chinnery declared, was "not suitable for airplay."[23]

Douglas Muggeridge, controller of the BBC's radio network, soon declared Wings personae non gratae for a second time, and press officer Rodney Collins was sent forth to explain the latest record ban to the press.

"It slipped through the net and was played once on Tony Blackburn's show, but you can take it from now it will not be played on Radio One or Two. It's nothing to do with drugs—the implications are more of a sexual nature," explained Collins, clarifying that a reference to a "body gun" was considered just too blatant for the BBC.[24]

Paul's attempt to distract the censors with an obscure Alfred Jarry reference had failed. The fault was later laid at the door of an EMI employee for wrongly noting the lyric as "body gun" rather than "polygon," but Chinnery's decision was made with his ears, without recourse to a printed lyric sheet.

Considering Wings' singles so far, it looked as though those who joked that only something as innocuous as 'Mary Had a Little Lamb' was safe enough for the BBC were right. 'C Moon,' however, was deemed sedate enough for the delicate sensibilities of BBC listeners. Radio Luxembourg had followed the BBC's lead in banning 'Give Ireland Back to the Irish' on political grounds, but took a different view of 'Hi, Hi, Hi,' gibing: "Far from banning it—we've made it our 'Power Play' of the week!"[25]

Glancing at the British singles chart, Paul found Chinnery's decision all the more mystifying: occupying the No. 1 spot, and high on the BBC's airplay list, was Chuck Berry's 'My Ding-a-Ling,' a song described by self-styled protector of public morals Mary Whitehouse as "as a vehicle for mass child molestation."[26] But in Chinnery's view, Berry's novelty song was "in the grand tradition of the music hall."[27]

Given Linda's plan for a traditional Thanksgiving dinner, it was perhaps an odd time to have scheduled press interviews, but before noon, the band trouped off to Tony Brainsby's offices at 23 Atherstone Mews for a series of prearranged appointments, leaving the turkey to roast under Rose's care.

Bad news traveling as quickly as it does, Paul had heard about the ban before his first interview, and took the opportunity to respond to what was starting to appear as a worrying pattern of banning tracks by the Beatles, collectively and individually: 'Hi, Hi, Hi' joined a list that included 'A Day in the Life,' 'Lucy in the Sky with Diamonds,' 'I Am the Walrus,' 'Give Ireland Back to the Irish' and 'Bangla Desh.'

"We were shocked because this is the second of the three records the group has made to get a BBC ban," Paul told Martin Jackson of the *Daily Express*. "We were not put out by the banning of our 'Give Ireland Back to the Irish,' but this new one had no political aspect. We were just making music and having fun. You'll see more sexual stuff in an evening's viewing on TV than you'll hear on my record. I was dejected when I heard of the ban, but I have decided not to change it. I write what I feel."[28]

But Paul's statement of shock was only a half-truth. It was now clear that the 'C Moon' promo film was not shot solely for posterity, but for this very eventuality.[*]

"Not being quite that thick, we all thought, you know, a ban might be possible,"[29] Paul confessed to *NME*'s Alan Smith, further down the day's interview schedule.

Sitting with his boots on Brainsby's desk, McCartney was a strange blend of composed and hyperactive. Between noon and 5:00 p.m., he offered an opinion on everything from Wings' latest cuts ("We heard some playbacks of the stuff we've been doing last night, and I think they're great."[30]) to musical disagreements with his wife ("We don't have any rows. I punch her. A good left hook does it. I put the rings on these fingers and let her have it. No, as far as the music goes, I'm the guvnor, the old pro. I don't always know what's right, but most of the time I *think* I do."[31]) before settling into the familiar pattern of fielding questions on his relationship with the other Beatles, and their chances of reuniting.

Referring to a recent telephone conversation with John, Paul let slip the reason for his smugness. The tide, he believed, was turning against Klein, and the American's tenure as Apple boss

---

[*] The promotional video for 'C Moon' would have its first airing on the BBC's *Top of the Pops* on January 4, 1973.

**Paul McCartney and Wings
invite you
to join them at-
Global Village
The Arches**
[off Villiers Street Charing Cross WC2]
**from 12noon to 2pm
Thursday November 30
for a drink, food and
to hear their new double 'A' side
Hi! Hi! Hi! and C. Moon**
by invitation only

might come to an end when his contract expired, in 1973.

"I still have connections with Apple but I'm hoping to get freed from it. My campaign is to get free from the Beatles partnership. Not the friendship," explained Paul. "I don't see why one day we couldn't have Wings onstage with the Plastic Ono Band. Anything like that can happen because there's no kind of hate between us, that's definite. Once it's all been settled—which I think might be in the next few months—we can go back to where, if John feels like playing, that's cool. Although I don't see the Beatles getting back together again."

"Wings are too good," added Denny Seiwell, staking a claim for his bandmates.

"That's true," continued Paul. "But what I can foresee is some concert, some time, where we all happen to be onstage together. I wouldn't rule that out. All that nastiness, that dirty linen in public had to happen because the contracts were there. Once we've cleared that up all will be cool. The relationship is dying to be friendly. I spoke to John on the phone recently and he now agrees that it was just done so stupidly, the break-up."

"He doesn't want Klein now," interrupted Linda, finishing her husband's thought.

"Of course, there are problems getting Wings away, they'll always be asking, 'Was he better with the Beatles?' Maybe. Who knows?" continued Paul, running with Seiwell's comment that the band was developing into a tight outfit. "I think we've got some songs as good as the Beatles. I think. I know Wings can do some things better than the Beatles. I wouldn't say we could be bigger. I wouldn't say we'd want to be bigger. It's getting nearer. I know the Beatles were so world-shattering, so huge, that it's daft to think they will be completely forgotten. But who knows, maybe Beatle music won't be so important in the years to come."[32]

The BBC's decision to censor 'Hi, Hi, Hi' on the grounds of taste and decency only served to stoke the fire in Paul's belly. After Thanksgiving he had Brainsby schedule a November 30 launch party to promote the single. The event, McCartney declared, would be a free lunch for the press: anyone who turned up with a working tape machine would be granted an interview. He also had Brainsby arrange one-on-one interviews with the music papers for every member of Wings.

All told, the single launch became the biggest public relations event the band had undertaken since *Wild Life*. For the event, Carolyn Pfeiffer arranged for the exclusive use of the Global Village, a brand-new—in fact, not yet open—two-tier underground leisure complex, complete with

cinema, restaurant, and two discotheques, tucked beneath the streets of central London in the Hungerford Arches, the colossal brick structures propping up Charing Cross Station.

Though the BBC's ban did nothing to halt the presses at EMI's Hayes vinyl plant, the corporation's ban could have an impact on sales of 'Hi, Hi, Hi.' But the label's sales manager, Ron White, and group director, Len Wood, were in attendance to lend support to the former Beatle they still considered one of their biggest commercial assets.

In the face of the ban, Paul greeted the press in an unusually happy mood, sporting the sort of eccentric attire he was getting into the habit of donning for such events—a red-and-white-striped shirt, tartan trousers with suspenders, and suede boots. Photographers snapped away as the band posed around a podium, at the top of which Denny Laine sat cross-legged and grinning. If the band had smoked something en route to Charing Cross to mellow their mood, it had done the trick.

Such was Paul's willingness to engage with any journalist willing to listen that the press interviews spilled into the next day. Groupies and hangers-on gathered outside Brainsby's Kensington offices as Paul, Linda, Henry, and the two Dennys filed in and out for solo interviews with *NME*, *Melody Maker*, *Disc*, *Sounds*, *Record Mirror*, *Music Scene*, *Pink*, *Petticoat*, and *Cosmopolitan*.

On the back of a day spent swatting away the latest Apple inquisition, Paul turned the spotlight on Wings' musical development, first touching on their eclectic catalog of singles. "With our stuff you can never tell really," Paul explained with tongue firmly in cheek. "One minute it's 'Ireland,' next minute it's 'Mary Had a Little Lamb,' next minute it's this ['Hi, Hi, Hi']. This is one of our new songs, but it doesn't mean that all our stuff's like that."[33]

He then went on to confirm the group's desire to issue a double LP in early 1973, showcasing Wings' year in and out of London's recording studios and on the road.

"At the moment we've got about 30 tunes—not all finished off of course," said Paul. "It's almost like a three-record pack or something, but I think the farthest we want to go is a double album, so we'll have to edit stuff down and chuck out some tracks. . . . We certainly want to get caught up, you know, because we've got so much material hanging around. . . . We've got quite a varied album too, because we'll be including some live stuff, though it won't be a live album, and we'll be including some stuff from before the tour."[34]

Paul McCartney, teen pinup and media darling, was back. And when 'Hi, Hi, Hi' hit record shops on December 1, the press, with the exception of Penny Valentine of *Sounds*, raised a critical glass to Wings' latest rocker.

"Put on your rock and roll shoes and shimmy to the rhythm. This is typically simple and down to earth, but not phenomenal or progressive in any way. A hit with airplay—and it certainly doesn't warrant the Beeb banning."[35]

Danny Holloway, *NME*

"The lyrics concern a lady being met at the station and the implication is that a certain amount of rudeness is about to take place. What is the world coming to, eh? Towards the end the tempo increases as everyone works to bring it home over swelling organ sounds. Very good stuff—and beautifully produced by our Paul."[36]

John Peel, *Disc*

"Mr. and Mrs. McCartney continue their strangely disconcerting habit of putting out tracks that are deceptively simple. Or maybe they're not deceptive at all. Perhaps it's time we stopped expecting McCartney to blitz our minds with a piece of Bernstein stature. Wings are, after all, just a band of rock and rollers it seems."[37]

Penny Valentine, *Sounds*

"Of all the vast pile of pre-Christmas releases, Paul and Linda's double-sided gem stands out as an excellent piece of pop making, filled with wit and originality. 'Hi, Hi, Hi' is a hard driving rock

Hi! Hi! Hi!

and
C. Moon

a new double 'A' side from
Paul
McCartney
and
Wings

opus, with a neatly executed double-tempo feature at the end. It is difficult to see who could find anything offensive in the song. A massive double hit."

Chris Welch, Melody Maker

Despite a significant drop in radio play, 'Hi, Hi, Hi' proved to be the group's most successful release of 1972. Faced with competition from David Bowie's 'The Jean Genie,' The Osmonds' 'Crazy Horses,' Carly Simon's breakthrough hit 'You're So Vain,' and teen favorite Jimmy Osmond's 'Long Haired Lover from Liverpool' (which boasted five weeks at No. 1), 'Hi, Hi, Hi' enjoyed a 13-week run in the British singles chart, entering at No. 40 on December 9, and cruising to No. 5 on January 13, 1973, where it remained for two weeks.

By December 30, 'Hi, Hi, Hi' was being played by 99 percent of pop and Top 40 radio stations in America. But despite saturation airplay, and being described by *Cash Box* as "a positive smash . . . good old rock 'n' roll as only the McCartneys can perform it,"[38] Wings' record managed only 11 weeks in the American singles charts, creeping into the *Billboard* Hot 100 on December 16, 1972, at the very bottom, and peaking at No. 10 on February 3, 1973.

Recording Sessions

Sunday–Wednesday, November 26–December 6, 1972.
AIR Studios, Studio One, London.
Recording: 'Jazz Street.'
Overdubbing: 'One More Kiss,' 'Single Pigeon,' 'When the Night,' 'Hands of Love,' 'Country Dreamer,' 'Thank You Darling,' and 'Tragedy.'
Mixing: 'Jazz Street.'

After the distractions of another censorship battle, McCartney still had a long list of tracks to see over the line for Wings' second album. Between November 26 and December 6, the band settled in at AIR Studios for a productive burst of studio time with engineer Bill Price, finishing seven more potential LP cuts. Bass guitar and lead vocals were added to 'Only One More Kiss,' and backing vocals to 'Single Pigeon.' McCullough then took center stage, adding electric guitar parts to 'Hands of Love,' 'Tragedy,' and 'When the Night,' with Laine overdubbing acoustic guitar on the latter. 'Country Dreamer' was treated to piano, electric guitar, lead vocals, backing vocals, and percussion. And 'Thank You Darling' was given new vocals, electric guitar, and kazoo.

Continuing their by now time-honored, pastime of stoned experimentation, on November 27 Wings recorded an untitled jam that was quickly abandoned, plus 'Jazz Street,' a largely shapeless eight-minute piano-driven improvisation. Paul led the session from the keyboard, Laine and Seiwell offered a thumping rhythmic backing on bass guitar and drums, and Linda played a variety of percussion found lying around the studio. McCullough riffed like a man possessed and Paul added texture with a gentle piano refrain. But the recording amounted to little more than an exercise in letting off steam. Paul attempted to add some elegance to 'Jazz Street' by recording an introductory burst of synthesizer and backwards guitar, but ultimately the track needed further work, and editing, and was set aside.

Recording Sessions

Monday–Wednesday, December 11–13, 1972.
EMI Studios, Control Room Four, London.
Mixing: 'The Mess,' 'Seaside Woman,' 'One More Kiss,' and 'Mama's Little Girl.'

Reports that Wings had been seen at Olympic, Island, Trident and AIR studios in recent months made their way to the always budget-conscious Len Wood, who vented about what he regarded as McCartney's profligacy to EMI in-house producer Wally Ridley, in the hope of enlisting Ridley to somehow keep tabs on the bills McCartney was racking up.

"He came to me and said, 'Will you look after this man McCartney because he's spending our money, hiring studios and we've got no idea what he's spending,'" Ridley recalled.[39]

So when Paul, desperate to make headway with stereo mixing, asked EMI for an engineer and a mixing room during an intensely busy period for the studio, the company accommodated him, putting Alan Parsons and the tiny Control Room Four at his disposal for Wings' final three sessions of 1972.

Unlike other artists and producers inclined to erase extraneous noises or accidental instrumental strikes on individual tracks, Paul would leave them as they were recorded, allowing the potential to "explore the accident, not fix the mistake" as Seiwell put it. Though aiding the creative process, for Alan Parsons this posed a problem.

"You try to keep the tracks clean and try to avoid having to pull down faders every time if there is a noise or a talking voice or something," he explained. "Whereas McCartney was notorious for never allowing engineers to wipe anything, so it always made the mix take twice as long."[40]

First on the list for stereo mixing was the studio version of 'The Mess'—the first song the five-piece band had developed together at the Scotch of St. James Club during Henry's audition. 'The Mess' was mixed in seven attempts on December 11, and RS7 was marked "best so far," implying that Paul intended to return to the song at a later date.

The following day, 'One More Kiss' was mixed to two-track in four passes (RS1 to RS4), the second of which was chosen as the master. Only two attempts were needed to mix 'Mama's Little Girl' on December 13. That afternoon Alan Parsons assembled the three new mixes, together with rough mixes of 21 other tracks Wings had recorded over the last 10 months. A set of four, single-sided acetate discs was cut, and copies were made for each member of Wings.

DISC ONE

'Big Barn Bed'
'When the Night'
'Single Pigeon'
'Tragedy'
'Mama's Little Girl'
'Loup (1st Indian on the Moon)'
'I Would Only Smile'

DISC TWO

'Country Dreamer'
'Night Out'
'One More Kiss'
'Jazz Street'

DISC THREE

'I Lie Around'
'Little Lamb Dragonfly'
'Get on the Right Thing'
'1882 (Live in Berlin)'
'The Mess (Live at The Hague)'

DISC FOUR

'My Love (Live at The Hague)'
'Seaside Woman'
'Best Friend'
'Medley: Hold Me Tight, Lazy Dynamite, Hands of Love and Power Cut'

The collection of tracks embraced polished studio cuts, jams, and live recordings—a reasonably comprehensive look at Wings as it was at the end of 1972. Now all they needed was a title for this ambitious double LP set.

———

Wings enjoyed their final get-together of 1972 at Cavendish Avenue on December 13. In the smoky haze of the McCartney living room, Paul handed Laine, Seiwell, and McCullough their own copies of the four freshly lacquered acetates. It was likely at this get-together that the band stumbled upon a title for the album.

"We were over at Paul's place one night and he got out this book called *Tales of the Truth*, or something like that," McCullough explained, "and we went through it to get a name. There was all these different words and phrases in it which were really good sounding, and Paul and Linda saw something about a 'Red Rose Speedway.' So that was it."[41]

"Yes, and it wasn't named after Rose, my housekeeper, to debunk another myth,"[42] Paul later confirmed.

Much had changed in 12 months. At the end of 1971, an image of Wings was just forming in the public's mind, on the strength of an album that combined the rough-hewn and the carefully wrought. But the group was still obscure enough that *Wild Life* was delivered to shops with a hype sticker to identify it as an album by Wings.

The band's university tour, despite the secrecy surrounding it, garnered enough international press that anyone with even a glancing interest in Paul heard about it, and after the full-fledged European tour, the idea that Paul had a new band was now firmly established.

In fact, if you discount the Plastic Ono Band, which John described as more a conceptual notion than an actual group, Paul was the first and only former Beatle to build a fixed-membership ensemble around himself. Add their two banned singles to the LP and the two tours, and not only were Wings gaining credibility, but Paul's musical rebirth was increasingly recognized as more than just a passing phase.

Slowly creeping out of the gargantuan shadow of the Beatles, Wings were voted sixth-best new band by readers of *Sounds*, and eighth-best vocal group by *Cash Box* subscribers in year-end polls.

"We've gone through all the bad side of it—McCartney has particularly," reflected Denny Laine at the end of 1972. "I mean Paul's gone through his put-down period for the last few years, and now he's starting to come up again—that's how we look at it. He's had his slagging. I really believe that, and he's going to use that, like we all use that, bouncing back off it. Like the band now is beginning just to level off and do it easier. Once you're together as a band, and you've

been through all that stuff like the busts, and first night reports and all that bullshit, you feel much more secure."[43]

After the get-together at Cavendish Avenue, the band dispersed for the festive season. Denny and Monique flew to New York; Henry and Sheila headed to Kent; and Denny Laine and Jo Jo to Shepperton. To honor Laine's loyalty and contributions to the group's upcoming record, Paul and Linda sent him a glistening steel dobro guitar for Christmas.

Gearing up for the double LP release, in mid-December Paul and Linda submitted the paper-work for Wings Music Limited, a new music publishing arm that would handle any tracks on *Red Rose Speedway* or future releases that might be credited to the whole band. Linda was appointed company secretary.

There were changes in the way ATV would be handling its publishing of Paul's music, as well. The transatlantic partnership that ATV had established with Don Kirshner, to market music in the

United States, expired at the end of the year, and in its place, ATV established a new company, the ATV Music Corporation, through which Paul's and Linda's music publishing in the United States would be handled.

Vincent Romeo had also been keeping busy, since his arrival in November, arranging for Wings' first properly scheduled and fully advertised British tour. To that end, he hired the London-based MAM (Management Agency & Music Ltd.) to book venues, oversee ticket sales and handle promotion. Details of the tour, which had yet to be finalized, had been kept under wraps, but between December 16 and 30, unconfirmed dates and details of a tour running from March 25, in Bristol, to April 14, in London, were prematurely leaked to the music press.

Furious about the leak, Romeo blamed Johnny Jones, who was running the tour for MAM. Jones was put on warning and told that all future press releases needed Romeo's sign-off before being made public. For good measure, Romeo also read the riot act to Dave Golding, MPL's in-house spokesman.

For all the positives the year served up, there were negatives in equal measure. Paul and Linda's seemingly insatiable appetite for the mellow, leveling buzz that marijuana and hashish gave them, and their stunning disregard for authority, meant they had to forgo their pre-Christmas visit to see the Eastmans in New York. On November 14, the couple were formally charged with smuggling drugs into Sweden, and Paul's American travel visa was revoked.

In Campbeltown, on December 22, Paul was charged with two counts of cannabis possession, and one count of cultivating the drug. Paul was not present at Campbeltown Sheriff Court when the charges were read; instead, his solicitor submitted a letter in which Paul pleaded not guilty to all charges. The trial was set for March 8, 1973, and Paul was ordered to appear in person.

One family custom was unwavering, though. New Year's Eve in Merseyside was a constant in the McCartney family calendar, and 1972 was no exception. Extending an olive branch to his unsettled bandmate, Paul invited Henry and Sheila to the family gathering at Rembrandt. Henry and Sheila helped themselves to drink and canapés laid on by Angie, while their son, Jesse, joined the growing McCartney brood for a concert with Uncle Paul. The young audience, Paul figured, was the perfect sounding board for his catalog of songs for the long-mooted *Rupert* movie.

"Every year we go back to Liverpool to see in the New Year and one of his cousins will say, 'Play guitar for us, Uncle Paul,'" said Linda, "and he'll come out with children's songs that nobody has ever heard outside the family, lovely songs, but whether they will ever be recorded I just don't know."[44]

Believing Klein's reign at Apple could soon be over, McCartney looked toward the New Year with growing optimism. The opposite could be said for McCullough, though. For Henry, 1972 began with an offer he found hard to refuse, but as the year progressed, he was questioning his decision to join McCartney's band. Henry had served his time in show bands back home in Northern Ireland, and he was concerned that Wings were simply a big-name version of the groups he toured with as a young musician, groups whose members had neither freedom nor creative input. Moreover, he was beginning to wonder whether there was really a pot of gold at the end of the Wings rainbow.

As the clock approached midnight, McCullough's mood continued to sink—matching, not coincidentally, the falling levels of the liquor in Jim's drinks cabinet. His frustrations came to a head outside Rembrandt, when in the quiet of suburban Gayton, Henry and Sheila tore strips off of each other, forcing Paul and Linda into the street to pull the couple apart.

"They went up to Paul's for New Year's Eve in Liverpool," said Seiwell of Henry and Sheila. "Paul called me—I was in the States, and he said, 'Jesus, Henry and Sheila had a big fight. They were out in the streets and everything. They were so drunk.' I said, 'He's not my problem man, sorry.'"[45]

Seiwell was right. Henry was Paul's problem. And while McCullough slept off the drink in Jim and Angie's back bedroom, McCartney was left pondering what 1973 had in store.

21

DOUBLE VISION

———

When the Seiwells and the McCartneys met for dinner at Albert and Michel Roux's luxury French restaurant Le Gavroche, on January 12, 1973, Paul was in superb spirits and full of news, having just hours earlier signed agreements with his new friends at ATV for two projects. The first was a commission to compose the theme for *Zoo Gang*, a new TV series ATV was planning with a glittering cast, including Brian Keith, John Mills, Lilli Palmer, and Barry Morse. The second, which had been in discussion for some time, was a TV special—an hour-long spectacular that was Paul's to do with as he saw fit, both on his own and with Wings.[1]

Paul had already mentioned the special to the press, but obliquely enough that it sounded like he might be speaking about expanding Wings' stage performance into a variety show. Most notably, he had floated the idea of having Denny Laine do handstands onstage between songs (Paul had recently learned that Laine, in addition to being a rock and roller and a flamenco guitarist, was a capable acrobat).

With the announcement of the special, though, his meaning became clearer: it was a chance for Paul to unleash his passion for the variety shows of his youth.

"We want to entertain people," he declared. "We'll fit in sketches and bits of dancing into our act . . . put on a real show. In other words, it was no point sitting around and complaining, as I did, about the poor quality of entertainment on television . . . it was up to us to get out there and do something about it."[2] Denny raised a congratulatory toast, and a cheerful smile, but having heard Paul brainstorm ideas for television and film specials in the recent past, he felt some trepidation. During the *Ram* sessions, Paul had filled him in on some of his ideas for a Rupert Bear film, which seemed charming—and in any case, would not involve Seiwell, apart from his drumming on *Rupert* songs.

But the filming of the final shows of the European tour, originally meant to yield a Wings concert film, was morphing into a hybrid concert special and cartoon, and Paul had mentioned to his bandmates—seemingly forgetting their near rebellion over 'Mary Had a Little Lamb'—that there could be scenes in which they would interact with Bruce McMouse and his family.

This was not a notion that filled Seiwell with joy, but it was right up Paul's street—and not only because he was a dad with three young daughters. He'd always loved cartoons, and in retrospect, he regretted that the Beatles had refused any real involvement with *Yellow Submarine*, in 1968. But the part of the film the Beatles participated in—the live ending, where they tell viewers that "newer and bluer Meanies" in the vicinity of the theater could be overcome by singing 'All Together Now'—had an element in common with Paul's new idea. As originally planned, the Beatles were to be filmed, and then the animators were to draw characters from the film crawling around them. The production company ran out of time and money before the animation could be executed.

Other films—most notably Disney's *Mary Poppins* (1964), and *Bedknobs and Broomsticks* (1971)—accomplished the melding of live action and animation, much to the delight of Heather, Mary and Stella (and himself). The Bruce McMouse film could be Paul's entry in that still wide-open field. But if Denny was going to be asked to don a frilly tux and do song-and-dance numbers, it might be time to demand a contract renegotiation (if only he had a contract).

Paul had been actively managing his public image, too, counterbalancing stories of drug busts and battles with neighbors and fans, with sizable interviews in which he shaped the portrait he wanted the world to have. Since 1970 he had successfully replaced his image as the cute bachelor Beatle and London bon vivant with that of a happily married family man and gentleman farmer in Scotland. Now he was offsetting (but not jettisoning) his conservative family-friendly public face with that of a protester on behalf of Ireland, and a champion of the rights of pot smokers everywhere. He had even created a theme song—'Hi, Hi, Hi'—for the generation that had made sex, drugs and rock and roll its catchphrase.

He was slowly making peace with his Beatles past, too—surprisingly, since his wished-for disengagement was still not settled.

"I'm still a Beatle and I always will be a Beatle," he told a Reuters reporter. "The Beatles thing happened, and I was a part of it and I'm glad. The fact that it no longer exists as a group does not mean I've stopped being a Beatle."[3]

In other interviews straddling the end of 1972 and the start of the new year, Paul offered telling glimpses of his current ideas about songwriting.

"I think you can get into music very critically, very analytically and stuff, but it really all just comes down to if it feels right," he explained to *Cosmopolitan*. "You can have the worst piece of music ever, but it gets you on your feet, it sounds nice—I like that. Music to get drunk to. I'd rather have that side of it, where everyone just sings some real dumb simple song but enjoys themselves doing it, rather than working for five weeks on a brilliant masterpiece and then never enjoying it."

His goal now, he continued, was to write "just kind of songy songs that the milkman can whistle."[4]

Heading into January, it was time for Paul to get back to his latest batch of songy songs, started in March and last touched in mid-December.

———

Recording Sessions

Monday–Saturday, January 8–13, 1973.
EMI Studios, Studio Two, London.
Mixing: 'Little Lamb Dragonfly,' 'Big Barn Bed,' 'When the Night,' 'Country Dreamer,' 'Loup (1st Indian on the Moon),' 'Hands of Love,' and 'Seaside Woman.'

———

The work at hand now was mostly a matter of mixing, but that could be a time-consuming task. With Alan Parsons at the console, John Kurlander assisting, and the band—or various combinations of its members, at different times—gathered in the control room, each with ideas about what should be prominent, what should be more subtly recessed, or what more a specific song might need, Paul set about giving the songs their final form.

"It really is just a balancing act," Parsons explained. "Paul was always very much a part of the mixing process. He would listen to each track and say, 'Make that sound better.' He wouldn't say what it is he didn't like about it, he'd just say 'make it sound better.' So, you'd always be pushed into trying effects, or trying drastic EQ, or some setup with a mic and a speaker in the studio. Anything to make it just a little bit different."

At times, Parsons said, Paul would, at least briefly, leave the process to him.

"He'd leave you to it for a while, and he'd go away, go for one of his 'walks.' And then come back and say, 'I think you're losing it, so start again.' So we'd start again. He'd say, 'Make it sound like Sly [Stone], make it sound like Stevie [Wonder],' all kinds of comments like that."

The week began with 'Little Lamb Dragonfly,' which proved surprisingly easy, given the number of elements that went into the song since Paul first took it up, with Seiwell and Hugh McCracken, in November 1970. Parsons made four mixes, and Paul declared himself satisfied with the last.

Tuesday saw 'Big Barn Bed' mixed in five passes (RS5 "Best") with ADT reinforcing Paul's vocals and a subtle touch of echo applied to the guitar solo, and 'When the Night' mixed in three attempts, with RS3 selected as the master. McCartney remained unconvinced that it was destined for his own album, but his hope that Aretha Franklin might cover it had dwindled in the months since he sent her a demo. Closer to home, the song had a champion in Denny Seiwell, mainly because he thought his drum part was transformational.

"It's one of my favorites," Seiwell said. "It's just some dumb song, nothing special. But my drumming on there was really pretty sensational. That little hypnotic drum part really made it a special song."[5]

'Country Dreamer,' the delicate rockabilly tune, was the first order of business on Wednesday, and it was dispatched in five mixes, RS5 marked "Best," before the band turned their attention to the experimental 'Loup (1st Indian on the Moon),' the peculiar instrumental that brought together standard and unusual timbres, and on which Linda made her synthesizer debut.

"He was never too bothered about where things were [placed] in the stereo," Parsons said of Paul. "That's always kind of been an engineer's prerogative, to spread the instruments from left to right. But he'd talk in terms of feel, you know, 'It's not quite hitting the mark, it's not quite happening, make this really sock through, this needs to pound through.' He basically wanted to hear everything, and that's the basis of the mixing process. But he knew that he got results by pushing, you know, 'Come on Alan, you can make it better than this.'"[6]

In the case of 'Loup,' however, the very nature of the track made it necessary to know what McCartney's broader ideas about sound placement were. Did he want synthesizer timbres moving across the soundstage, or something more settled, less open to being labeled "gimmicky"?

Painting a picture of 'Loup' for *Melody Maker* in late November, it was clear that Paul considered the jam to be a highlight of Wings' yet to be issued album.

"I love 'Loup,' although it's really not a commercial track at all," he raved. "It's sort of an instrumental with some moody sort of singing. It's just a thing really, really hard to explain about the first Red Indian on the moon called Loup. It's just a story but through his eyes."[7]

In the end, it took only three mixes (RS1–RS3) to find the sweet spot. Parsons and McCartney made the most of the song's sectional aspects, which alternated between the chantlike opening melody and more free-form sections. And they tapped into its thoroughly tactile qualities—for example, placing gentle guitar string bends to the extreme right side of the mix, and the responding, velvety synthesizer mewing to the left. Drums were split across the stereo image as well, with the bass grounding the track by holding the center.

At the end of the session, Linda's 'Seaside Woman' was also mixed to stereo in five passes, and a rough mix was made of 'Hand of Love' for Paul to take home during a two-day hiatus in recording.

On Saturday, happy with the elements in the basic rough mix, Paul tackled 'Hands of Love' afresh, with RS3 the last and best of the day's attempts to mix the song properly.

After the Saturday session, Paul and Linda unwound by catching Eric Clapton's set at the Rainbow Theater, his first live appearance since George Harrison's Bangladesh benefit. It was also an intervention: watching Clapton's talent waste away under the weight of his heroin habit, the Who's Pete Townshend had the idea of assembling a supergroup to support Clapton in his return to the stage as part of the Fanfare for Europe, a celebration of Britain's joining the Common Market (a political move Paul did not entirely support). Ron Wood joined Townshend on guitar, Steve Winwood played keyboards, Rich Grech was on bass, Jim Capaldi and Jimmy Karstein were the drummers, with Rebop Kwaku Baah on percussion. Besides Paul and Linda, the starry audience included Ringo Starr, Elton John, Joe Cocker, Ric Lee, members of the Faces, and Donovan.*

Paul was entirely behind Townshend's rehabilitation ploy. "I hope this thing comes off where he's going to play with a band again. That'll be the best thing for him. It'll make it all less precious. That's what I found in my case, anyway. You start off with all that, *'We are coming to witness a legend,'* type thing, and it turns into *'We're coming to see a band,'* and it's much nicer. I do think Eric needs to play in public a lot more regularly, just to kind of ease up the pressure. He played fine at the Rainbow."[8]

———▶

Recording Sessions

Sunday–Saturday, January 14–20, 1973.
EMI Studios, Studio Two, London.
Mixing: 'Hold Me Tight,' 'Lazy Dynamite,' 'Power Cut,' 'I Would Only Smile,' and 'Best Friend.'
Overdubbing: 'Rode All Night,' 'Why Do You Treat Me So Bad' (working title of 'Best Friend'), and 'I Would Only Smile.'

Paul began the second week of mixes with a more focused look at the medley. With 'Hands of Love' complete, McCartney and Parsons turned their attention on Sunday to 'Hold Me Tight,' completing it in four mixing attempts, and 'Lazy Dynamite,' finished in six. 'Power Cut,' which required seven mixes before Paul was satisfied, took up the Monday session, leaving Tuesday for the assembly of the medley—'Hold Me Tight'/'Lazy Dynamite'/'Hands of Love'/'Power Cut'—with the transitions from 'Hold Me Tight' to 'Lazy Dynamite,' and 'Hands of Love' to 'Power Cut' accomplished by crossfading, and 'Lazy Dynamite' and 'Hands of Love' joined with a splice.

---

* Clapton's two January 13, 1973, shows were recorded. Six of the 16 songs performed in the two sets were released on LP in September 1973 as *Eric Clapton's Rainbow Concert.* Another eight songs were added to the expanded 1995 reissue.

Running 11'18", the medley could account for most of an LP side. But Paul wanted everything mixed before he chose the material to include on the album, and everything was up for consideration—including 'Rode All Night,' the *Ram* sessions jam that Seiwell was so devoted to. Paul pulled that recording from the archives on Wednesday, and after giving it a listen, he added a bass part—and then sent it back to storage.

Taking Thursday off, he returned to sweetening tracks on Friday, adding an acoustic guitar, and having Seiwell beef up the drumming, on a live take of 'Best Friend' (listed as 'Why Do You Treat Me So Bad?'), recorded in Antwerp on August 22. And at another overdubbing session on Saturday, Denny Laine's 'I Would Only Smile,' which had languished since March, was taken up and given a fresh lead vocal by Laine, backing vocals by McCartney, Laine and McCullough, and another electric guitar part, also from Denny. The song was mixed the same day in four passes, none of which was marked for use.

With some time to kill, Paul had Parsons pull two reels of four-track Rude Studio recordings, taped shortly after the *Wild Life* sessions and deposited in EMI's archives. It was an eclectic collection of demos and rehearsals—'Seaside Woman,' 'Mystery Train,' 'That's Alright Mama,' 'Blackpool,' 'Freight Train,' 'Peggy Sue,' 'African Yeah Yeah,' 'Poor Boy,' 'Little Queenie,' and another 'Seaside Woman,' running 30 minutes on the first reel, and 12 minutes of 'Oobu Joobu,' on the second. Each complete reel was given a stereo mix in a single pass on Saturday afternoon.

———

While McCartney and Wings were working full throttle to complete *Red Rose Speedway* in Studio Two, Pink Floyd were working in Studio Three to complete their next album, *The Dark Side of the Moon*—a project that had been in the works nearly as long as McCartney's (and had also been interrupted by touring). Alan Parsons had engineered most of the sessions for *Dark Side* and had made a mix in December, before the band decided to add new elements. With Parsons now occupied with Wings, Chris Thomas took over, and made the final mix of the album.

"They were next door making *Dark Side of the Moon*," said Paul. "The engineers were quite interchangeable, so an engineer that'd work on their stuff would work on ours. And he did play us some of the *Dark Side of the Moon* stuff."[9] For an hour or so, during the weekend of January 19 and 20, Wings and Pink Floyd joined forces, on Pink Floyd's turf, when the latter were recording voices that would be woven into the fabric of several songs. It was, in a way, an avant-garde project in the spirit of John Cage.

"Roger [Waters] drafted a series of questions about madness, violence and mortality," Pink Floyd's drummer, Nick Mason, said of the project, "and I think I wrote them out on a set of cards.

These were placed, face down, on a music stand in Studio Three. We then invited into the studio whoever we could find around the Abbey Road complex: our crew, the engineers, other musicians recording there—anyone other than ourselves. They were asked to sit on a stool, read each card to themselves and then simply give their answers into a microphone."

The questions included: *"Does death frighten you?"* and *"When was the last time you were violent?"* *"Were you in the right?"* *"Do you ever think you're going mad?"* and *"If so, why?"* The contributors sat on a stool and were asked to respond openly and honestly with the first answer that came to them. Among those they drafted for the project were the EMI complex's doorman, Gerry O'Driscoll, their manager and his wife, Peter and Patricia Watts, and one of their roadies, Chris Adamson. Paul and Linda decided it might be fun to contribute, too, as did Henry and Sheila McCullough.

"This naturally induced a certain amount of paranoia," Mason reflected, "as a studio is a lonely place when everyone else is grouped in the control room peering through the soundproof glass. As it happened, some of the professional performers were a lot more stilted than the amateurs, who seemed quite happy to chat away at length."[10]

Mason remembered being thrilled to have "two such famous voices" as Paul's and Linda's, but alas, he and the rest of Pink Floyd found them to be too reserved to fully embrace the spirit of the exercise, so their responses went unused.

"He was too clever, too guarded," Roger Waters recalled. "He didn't want to give anything away. We needed people that were open and direct. He was the only person who found it necessary to perform, which was useless, of course. I thought it was really interesting, that he would do that. He was trying to be funny, which wasn't what we wanted at all."[11]

Henry and Sheila, by contrast, were just what Pink Floyd hoped for. When Henry turned over the card asking about the last time he was violent, he had to cast his mind back only as far as his New Year's Eve fight with Sheila at Rembrandt. Mason found them "frighteningly open," adding that "they went straight into a story of a recent and somewhat physically violent argument they had had."[12]

And so it was that a hazy recollection of McCullough's—"I don't know, I was really drunk at the time!"—found its way into 'Us and Them,' a track on one of the most revered albums in the history of rock.

——

McCartney and Parsons took up 'Night Out,' on Monday, agreeing that the fuzz-guitar dominated near instrumental lacked something. A new electric guitar part, extra backing vocals, and handclaps were added, further thickening the song's already dense texture. 'Night Out' was not mixed until the next day; in the meantime, McCartney took up 'Get on the Right Thing' yet again, adding compression (a studio process that reduces the distance between the loudest and softest sounds), and replacing the previous day's mix, on the compilation reel, with the new, compressed version of RS5.

The single cover tune Wings recorded for the album, 'Tragedy,' got another look—and several overdubs, including two tracks of lead vocal support, two tracks of backing vocals, and a piano. But Paul felt it still needed something, so it was set aside rather than mixed.

Earlier in the month, Paul had decided that a fresh studio recording of 'My Love' was warranted, having decided against using the recording from Wings' Hague concert he had been considering in December. Having been in Wings' repertory since early 1972, and in their setlist during both the university and European tours, 'My Love' was thoroughly under the band's fingers.

Paul recognized 'My Love' as a "smoochy"[13] love song—more so than most of his Linda-inspired tunes—but it had attracted enthusiastic comments in reviews of the European shows. And why not? Even on first hearing (as it was for both the audience and the reviewers), there was no denying that its shapely, soaring melody had all the characteristics of a McCartney hit.

And just as he had surveyed the British singles charts when issuing 'Mary Had a Little Lamb' in early 1972, Paul had done his homework. "Paul said to me, 'When Lennon and I got together we used to listen to the top ten singles on the charts and steal from all of them,'" explained Vincent Romeo. "Paul still gets the top ten every week."[14]

"To get commercial success I studied what was up with the moment,"[15] confirmed Paul.

In late 1972 and early 1973, "up with the moment" was another succession of ballads and bubble gum pop records, dominating the No. 1 spot in Britain for 15 consecutive weeks. Novelty singles by Lieutenant Pigeon ('Mouldy Old Dough') and Chuck Berry ('My Ding-a-Ling'), plus ballads by Gilbert O'Sullivan ('Clair') and Little Jimmy Osmond ('Long Haired Lover from Liverpool'), did what 'Hi, Hi, Hi' had failed to do—top the British singles chart.

Having decided against using the live recording, Paul now wanted 'My Love' to be cloaked in a rich orchestral fabric that would magnify its tender qualities. He invited Richard Hewson to Cavendish Avenue to discuss it, and while Hewson's wife and daughter went off to the kitchen to help Linda peel beans for a dish she was making for lunch, Paul played Hewson an acetate of the Hague recording and said he was thinking of strings—but did not preclude winds or brass.

"Most of the time, I would get the track and then start thinking about it," Hewson said, but this time, an idea occurred as soon as Paul played the recording. "While we were talking, I suddenly thought it would be good to start with a long note, just a single saxophone note and a brass section, all on that one long note, to start the record off."[16]

Paul had an idea, too. Convinced that the vitality of Wings' 'Live and Let Die' recording could be attributed to its having been recorded live in the studio, he wanted to record 'My Love' that way, too. Since Hewson would have a significantly smaller ensemble than George Martin had for the Bond song, he thought (or hoped) that working in a single studio would pose no problems.

Given the number of things that could go wrong, recording the band and orchestra together was in many ways a less efficient way to make a pop recording than the more typical practice of recording the backing tracks, adding the orchestra, and overdubbing vocal and instrumental lines as needed.

But there were distinct benefits.

"That way," Hewson explained of the all-at-once recording plan, "it all sounds live, and almost improvisatory—like we'd just started to play it, and there is was. A nice, natural, live-sounding thing, with people reacting to each other's playing. You can tell the difference between that and overdubbed sound. The overdubbed recording is crystal clear, very clean, no mistakes, no bum notes, but it's a bit antiseptic. I don't know why people didn't do that [record live in the studio] more, because it does have that edge."[17]

With Alan Parsons mixing voices, including Henry's, into Pink Floyd's latest mix of The Dark Side of the Moon, Richard Lush took over as engineer on January 26, with Mark Vigars assisting. Wings spent the afternoon rehearsing 'My Love,' and just as Martin had done with 'Live and Let Die,' Lush recorded a couple of band-only takes, just to be covered in case there were any mishaps at the live-with-orchestra session that evening.

When Hewson's 26-piece ensemble (eight violins, four violas, four cellos, three clarinets, bass clarinet, and pairs of horns, saxophones, and trombones) arrived at 7:00 p.m. Wings were ready to roll, with Paul playing electric piano and singing; Laine on bass; Henry on electric guitar; Seiwell on drums; and Linda, Denny Laine and Henry singing backing vocals; the organ part Linda played in concert was jettisoned. Hewson conducted.

Wings and the orchestra recorded 14 takes of the song, all but 2 complete (Takes 1 and 13 were breakdowns). After Take 13, Henry leaned on the piano for a word with Paul. 'My Love' had room for a spacious guitar solo, which in the live versions meandered around the organ chords, giving Paul some breathing space between verses without calling attention to itself as a solo. The solo Henry played was of Paul's devising, although as Hewson remembers it, Henry varied the solo a bit each time. Now, 13 takes in, Henry wasn't feeling it.

Henry and Paul took a fundamentally different approach to musicmaking. Henry was a blues guitarist, at heart, "organic and rootsy,"[18] as Seiwell described him, and in his element on an improvisatory tightrope. Paul took a more settled approach: once you had an arrangement that worked, the goal was to reproduce it, including the solos, the same way every time.

Paul was committed to the guitar solo he asked Henry to play, but for Henry, it became more irritating with each take—not least because this was by no means an isolated incident. Why engage a guitarist who had built his reputation on his inventiveness, he must have wondered, if he was just going to play phrases dictated by someone else?

"He does keep such a control over everything," McCullough summed up his frustration, "and that's how it's always been. I've never liked anybody humming notes in my ears to explain what they wanted. For a musician of my type, I have to have a bit of freedom too."[19]

As Paul remembered it, "Henry just sort of wanders over to me and whispers in my ear, 'I've got an idea for the guitar solo. Do you mind if I try it?' And my mind goes, 'No! We've got an arrangement! They're all here ready to go. It could be crap!' But something just told me to sort of say, 'Yeah, okay. Go for it!'"[20]

As saxophonist Peter King's time-suspending opening note led into Take 14, McCullough felt energized by the new, if no doubt temporary freedom McCartney had granted him, and when the moment arrived, he was stirred to deliver an inspired, stunningly beautiful, improvised solo.

"I don't know where it came from," Henry confessed. "But I was in a highly spiritual state at that particular time, because of the company [the orchestra]. The adrenaline was up and stuff, and it could have been out of fright as well. Before the guitar solo comes in, the orchestra comes in, and I'm there with a guitar and amplifier, and it was like being pushed over the edge."[21]

Paul was floored. "He plays this really signature beautiful solo. So I was glad I said yes! But it was quite the moment, you know. It was like, 'Well, here goes nothing!' Then we do the take, and I was amazed. I had never heard this solo, it was just something he'd come up with. And it was fabulous."[22]

Henry needed only the one take to wow everyone, and with Take 14 in the can by 10:00 p.m., Hewson's orchestra packed up and left, while Wings gathered in the control room to give the new track a few more plays. The next afternoon, some light overdubbing was undertaken to beef up the backing vocals. By the time the session ended, 'My Love' was mixed in five passes and added to a compilation reel.

———

As Wings plowed through their final overdubbing and mixing sessions, MPL was gearing up, under Vincent Romeo's direction, to deal with an increasingly hefty set of demands. Within that, preparing for the release of *Red Rose Speedway* was a project list on its own, including shoots for new publicity photos (set up for February 3 and 5), and coordinating the artwork, which Paul wanted built around images by the Scottish pop art pioneer Eduardo Paolozzi.

There was also the matter of planning for the ATV television special—some of which would be sketched out during an imminent working holiday in Marrakesh, Morocco—as well as overseeing the arrangements for Wings' British tour and keeping track of the hybrid Wings concert film and mouse cartoon, *The Bruce McMouse Show*.

Behind the scenes, in New York and Clovis, New Mexico, Lee and John Eastman were concluding negotiations for the purchase of Nor-Va-Jak Music, the publisher of Buddy Holly's music, for $100,000 (£40,620). The competition was stiff, with EMI and Chappell Music among the suitors. And there was another potential buyer who caught Paul's eye.

"Allen Klein was interested, and I think secretly that's what got me interested,"[23] Paul later noted, although it's likely that his love of Holly's music was sufficient reason for his eagerness to buy the catalog, even without adding spite to the equation.

The Eastmans, in their capacity as McCartney's business advisers, had moved beyond the Apple lawsuit to the logical question of what Paul should do with his money once Apple relinquished it, and in that regard, Paul saw his in-laws as both mentors and role models.

Their investment model was, essentially, buy what you're passionate about. The Eastmans themselves invested in paintings and music publishing catalogs, and to Paul, what could be better than art and music that blossomed in value?

"I thought, if you're gonna have to spend money on something it might as well be something you really love, rather than just, I don't know, a brush factory or something," Paul explained his path toward investing. "My business adviser was talking to me and said, 'What kind of thing do you love then?' and I mentioned Buddy Holly as being one of the things. And it so happened that Buddy's music came up for sale in America, so my business adviser said, 'Why don't you buy it?' And there was nothing I'd love more really, because that way I feel like I can protect the stuff [Buddy's music] so there's no big rip-offs for people like his widow, and also I can help popularize his music, too, just by being associated with it."[24]

Actually, though Paul credited the Eastmans with showing him that buying music catalogs could be a solid investment strategy, the concept was not entirely new to him. During the filming of the *Get Back* project, Michael Lindsay-Hogg's cameras captured a January 10, 1969, visit to Twickenham by Dick James, who brought the news that he had just bought the Lawrence Wright publishing catalog, with some 4,000 songs, on behalf of Northern Songs. As Paul and Ringo read through some of the titles—among them, Gene Autry's 'I Wish I Had Died in My Cradle (Before I Grew Up to Love You)' and 'Nobody Loves a Fairy When She's Forty,' made famous by Tessie O'Shea—James answers affirmatively when Paul asks, "All of these are ours?"[25]

Music, of course, doesn't grow in value on its own; it is the publisher's job to keep it in artists' and producers' ears, to encourage new cover versions and its use in everything from television and film soundtracks, to record reissues, to advertisements.

Buddy Holly was an important and beloved part of Paul's musical DNA, so Nor-Va-Jak was perfect as McCartney Music's first major catalog acquisition. Paul opted to keep Nor-Va-Jak's historical links intact by retaining its founder and president, Norman Petty—Holly's first manager and record producer—to oversee it and promote its holdings.[26]

———

Recording Sessions

Sunday–Wednesday, January 28–31, and Monday, February 5, 1973.
EMI Studios, Studio Two, London.
Overdubbing: 'Tragedy' and 'Single Pigeon.'
Mixing: 'Tragedy,' 'Single Pigeon,' 'Mama's Little Girl,' and 'Bridge over the River Suite.'

———

Although Henry had acquitted himself brilliantly at the session for 'My Love,' he had largely stopped attending the mixing and dubbing sessions. His absences registered with Paul and Linda, leaving Paul wondering, if only in passing, whether trying to run a proper band was worth the headaches.

"Paul got very nervous having to give everyone in the band a part to play," Linda complained in an interview. "Sometimes he wouldn't want guitar on a track, but Henry didn't like sitting around the studio. Because of that Paul started putting things on tracks on the

Red Rose Speedway album just to keep everyone happy, things he normally wouldn't put on the track."[27]

The mixing sessions allowed Paul to second-guess some of those pacifying, make-work decisions, and to eliminate tracks he considered superfluous (as he did with Henry's lead guitar part on 'Lazy Dynamite'); but he was more inclined to think of new things to add. He decided on Sunday, for example, that what 'Tragedy' really needed was a sitar. He played the part himself, mixed the track in two passes and appended it to a compilation reel. 'Single Pigeon' was given a short, improvised brass overdub—McCartney (trombone), Seiwell (cornet) and Laine (saxophone)—on Monday, and after six mixing attempts, it was complete.

The rest of the week was given to juggling track listings for the double album, for which several track orderings were tried. At this point, the songs that made the cut were: 'Night Out,' 'Get on the Right Thing,' 'Country Dreamer,' 'Big Barn Bed,' 'My Love,' 'Single Pigeon,' 'When the Night' (Denny Seiwell's advocacy having won the day), 'Seaside Woman,' 'I Lie Around,' 'The Mess,' 'Best Friend,' 'Loup (1st Indian on the Moon),' the medley 'Mama's Little Girl,' 'I Would Only Smile,' 'One More Kiss,' 'Tragedy,' and 'Little Lamb Dragonfly.'

At least one proposed sequence also included 'Jazz Street' and '1882,' and it is likely that other songs were swapped in and out as different sequences were attempted. In each case, however, the first tracks of each side remained the same: Side One opened with 'Night Out,' Side Two with 'Single Pigeon,' Side Three with 'Best Friend,' and Side Four with 'Mama's Little Girl.'

On February 5, Paul took a break from sequencing to polish off the two songs that still needed mixes, 'Mama's Little Girl' and 'Bridge Over the River Suite' (recorded under the title 'Mood Music,' on October 1). The following day, a few hours before the band left for Morocco, another two-disc sequence, with 18 tracks (or 21 songs, counting the components of the medley separately), was assembled.

———

Wings flew to Marrakesh on February 6 in style, meeting at London Heathrow to board a private Lear Jet and then flying to Morocco with a stop in Gibraltar. They checked into La Mamounia, the most exclusive and expensive retreat in Morocco, set within the walls of the old city, and quickly fanned out to explore the outdoor markets set among the palm trees. They bought colorful, loose-fitting clothing to wear during the rest of the visit and checked out the handwoven baskets, walking sticks, hash pipes and not least, the percussion instruments and flutes the vendors laid out on their carpets.

Part of the agenda for the trip was to work out plans for the television special, rehearsals for which were set to begin on February 22. But first, they had a few days of shopping, jamming

(McCartney, Laine and McCullough all brought acoustic guitars) and camel riding. Linda began writing two new songs, 'I Got Up,' which she described as "very sort of Fifties R&B, the Doves, the Penguins,"[28] and the Nashville-influenced 'Wide Prairie.' Paul juggled fresh ideas as well, including a song built around the hotel's name, *Mamounia*, which means safe haven in Arabic.

Several of the band's escapades involved the search for top-flight Moroccan hashish. In one, Paul, Linda and Denny Seiwell were approached by a dealer as they walked through the market-place. They followed him through the old city's narrow streets and back alleys to his apartment, where he handed them some hash. Denny Seiwell cut a sliver into a pipe and had a hit, but when Paul asked him if it was good, Denny said it was garbage. But Paul, feeling endangered on the dealer's turf, bought £250 ($625) worth, which they discarded on their way back to the hotel.

In a second attempt, Abdul, a worker at the hotel, approached the two Dennys at the hotel's discotheque and asked if they wanted some smoke. Repairing to Laine's hotel room, they sampled his hash and found it wanting, but Abdul was not standing for a refusal—he wanted cash. As the debate grew heated and seemed about to become physical, Laine spotted a magnum of Rémy Martin on the bureau and decided to smash the bottle against the wall and use what remained as a weapon. He picked up the magnum by the neck, swung it toward the wall. But instead of smashing, the bottle bounced and made a *booooiiiiinnng* noise, Laine not having noticed, in the heat of the moment, that it was plastic. It would not have mattered if it were glass; Abdul had a gun. They paid, and he left.

At the weekend, Gary Smith and Dwight Hemion, who were producing the show for ATV, arrived in Marrakesh to hear what Paul and Linda had in mind, and to present ideas of their own. Vincent Romeo was also present.

Smith and Hemion had worked together since 1963, when they directed episodes of the venerable Kraft Music Hall for NBC, and they had made specials with Judy Garland, Burt Bacharach, Liza Minnelli, Sammy Davis Jr., Perry Como, and Des O'Connor. Lew Grade had hired them to produce music specials for ATV in 1971, including a series that, though ATV branded, were meant for the American ABC network. Paul's special was part of the ABC series and would take advantage of the fact that filming a television show was considerably less expensive in England than in America.

"It is true that we make the shows with Americans in mind—but, after all, that's where the major audience is. We're talking now about 40 million viewers," Smith said. "Most of the shows are wrapped up in a couple of months, [although] the preparations for the McCartney show were extended because Paul wanted us all to talk the thing out thoroughly before we started work. That was a particularly difficult show, though, because although Paul is an all-around entertainer, the rest of his band isn't."[29] Indeed, Laine, Seiwell and McCullough had little interest in the details of the show, knowing that they would be little more than sidemen. They quickly made themselves scarce.

"We were supposed to spend the weekend talking about what we were going to do in the special," is how Denny Seiwell put it. "There was no talk. We laid around the pool. We went out, we had fun. We didn't do any discussion of anything."[30]

Paul and Linda, on the other hand, had plenty to say. Linda, for starters, had distinct ideas about the show's look, and who should create it.

"We saw a TV program about Erté," she said, referring to the Russian-born French artist and designer who worked in an art deco style, updated with a contemporary sensibility and a taste for the provocative. "I flipped out and turned to Paul and said, 'We really must meet this guy.' And we did! We talked for hours, just soaking up everything he said."

They had, in fact, convinced Erté (whose real name was Romain de Tirtoff; "Erté" was based on the French pronunciation of his initials) to do the designs for the special's sets and costumes before the trip to Marrakesh.

"He's going to dress Wings—yes, even Paul—to blend with the stage sets. He's a real master, and I can't wait to work with him because it's the opportunity of a lifetime."[31]

———

Because the shooting of the television schedule was clearly going to interfere with the planned British tour, the entire tour had to be rescheduled, and now that changes were necessary, Romeo fretted that the leak of the original itinerary, in December, made MPL look incompetent. He sent Golding out to deal with press queries, armed with virtually no information. "I understand the original tour dates were announced prematurely, and that MAM [Management Agency & Music Ltd., the promoter] are now setting up a revised schedule to commence in May," Golding told *NME* at the end of January.

Reconfiguring the tour schedule also put Romeo at odds, once again, with MAM's booker, Johnny Jones. Their relationship had been abrasive from the start, and Romeo was not shy about using his leverage as McCartney's manager to get him off the account. Jones soon turned over the Wings portfolio to Barry Dickins.[32]

Romeo also restated his demand that MAM say nothing about Wings without his approval. When *NME* sought a comment from the company, the best MAM's spokesman could manage was, "We are not allowed to say anything—we can't even tell you officially that the tour is postponed."[33]

Another task on Romeo's to-do list was to meet with EMI, partly to establish a relationship with McCartney's label, but more immediately, to discuss the release and promotion of *Red Rose Speedway*. He quickly found himself in a game of *Who Will Give the Bad News to Paul?*—the result being, *You're the new guy, you do it*.

The bad news was that the label was dead set against releasing *Red Rose Speedway* as a double album, for a host of reasons, some of them seemingly contradictory. It was suggested, for example, that consumers, particularly in Britain, resisted double albums; yet also among EMI's reasons for opposing a double Wings set was that the label was planning an April release for not one, but *two* double-LP Beatles compilations—*1962–1966* and *1967–1970*, known informally as the *Red* and *Blue* albums. Partly, these were cash trawls: with the Beatles no longer a going concern, EMI was keen to exploit the existing catalog—a move encouraged by ATV, the new(ish) owners of the Lennon-McCartney songbook. But they were also meant to combat a four-disc bootleg collection, *Beatles—Alpha Omega*, a set packed with Beatles hits plus a few solo tracks, like Lennon's 'Imagine' and McCartney's 'Uncle Albert/Admiral Halsey.'

George Harrison's *Living in the Material World*, due in May, figured into EMI's calculation, too: with albums from George and Paul, plus the *Red* and *Blue* sets, it was going to be a crowded time for Beatles product, and a double album, they told Romeo, would make Paul's release less competitive. EMI was also cold on the prospect of anyone other than Paul providing lead vocals.

Romeo met with Wings and forcefully stated EMI's position that *Red Rose Speedway* would fare best as a single disc.

"Hey, boys, we want you to put out a single album, I think that's the best idea," is how Denny Laine remembers him introducing the subject. "And we went, 'No. You reckon?' And we were pushing for the double one."[34]

But Romeo knew he could not back down. His EMI meeting left him convinced that insisting, on Paul's behalf, that EMI issue *Red Rose Speedway* as a double album would be a losing battle, and he could not afford one of those so early in his tenure. Explaining it later, he summarized his argument in a single, flimsy assertion. "I wanted him to reduce it," Romeo said, "because it didn't represent his current direction."[35]

But the double album, a freewheeling collection of ballads, rockers, country tunes, jams, and a bit of reggae, with showcase moments for everyone, either as a singer, a player, or a songwriter, represented that direction *precisely*.

None of the Wings musicians agreed with Romeo's arguments. Romeo later admitted that Paul was "furious that anyone should want to tamper with his music."[36] Laine and Seiwell both preferred the double album, but the most outspoken Wing was Henry.

"See, originally this was supposed to be a double album," Henry told *Sounds*, at the time, "because we'd put down enough tracks for one and everybody said great, a double would be a gas, and I think I was the most furious about it not being a double, because I wanted the band to be seen for what it could offer, you know, instead of just, like, being James Paul McCartney, you see what I mean?"[37]

Henry thought releasing the double album, with its stylistic breadth, would be to Paul's benefit as well.

"I was really excited about a double album," he insisted. "I was interested in letting it be known just what Paul was capable of. It was time for McCartney to branch out. It would have helped him lose that 'nice' image he had."[38]

———

Recording Session

Friday and Monday, February 16 and 19, 1973.
EMI Studios, Room Four, London.
Sequencing and Compilation: *Red Rose Speedway.*

After rehearsals at Cavendish Avenue, Wings trooped over to EMI to assemble the single-disc version of *Red Rose Speedway.* Cutting the track list in half, to nine cuts, was brutal work, and the rest of Wings had little input. Two quite different single-disc sequences were produced, and by the end of the session, Paul chose one to send off for mastering.

The first sequence preserved 'Seaside Woman,' 'Mama's Little Girl' and 'Tragedy,' but it seemed stylistically haphazard:

SIDE ONE

'Big Barn Bed'
'My Love'
'Get on the Right Thing'
'Country Dreamer'
'Medley: 'Hold Me Tight,' 'Lazy Dynamite,' Hands of Love,' 'Power Cut'

SIDE TWO

'One More Kiss'
'When the Night'
'Seaside Woman'
'Mama's Little Girl'
'Tragedy'
'Little Lamb Dragonfly'

Part of the problem was that the sequence retained aspects that worked well enough on a double album, but less so on a single disc. The medley, for example, was usually placed at the end of a side—often Side Three—in the various double-LP sequences, and in that case, it made no difference which side it ended, since the four-sided set was something like a four-act play, each with its own arc, and a distinct finale. On a single disc, however, a piece running 11'18" is weighty enough that it demands to be the album's finale.

One change that did work was placing 'Big Barn Bed' at the top. It had been a side opener in some iterations of the double album, but more typically, it was in the middle of a side. It was a strong opener, though, and starting with it emphasized its status as a link to Paul's past, having been previewed, however briefly, in the final seconds of 'Ram On.'

For the second sequence, compiled three days later, Paul kept 'Big Barn Bed' in the leadoff position, moved the medley to the end, and made several substitutions, including dropping 'Seaside Woman' and restoring the experimental 'Loup.' Each sequence had its strong points and deficits, and normally, Paul would have taken copies home to consider. Instead, he made the choice on the spot, opting for the new sequence:

SIDE ONE (EMI MATRIX NO. YEX.903)

'Big Barn Bed'

'My Love'

'Get on the Right Thing'

'One More Kiss'

'Little Lamb Dragonfly'

SIDE TWO (EMI MATRIX NO. YEX.904)

'Single Pigeon'

'When the Night'

'Loup (1st Indian on the Moon)'

'Medley: 'Hold Me Tight,' 'Lazy Dynamite,' 'Hands of Love,' 'Power Cut'

Though Henry's finest moment—his solo in 'My Love'—was retained, as was Seiwell's drumming favorite, 'When the Night,' Linda's 'Seaside Woman' and Laine's 'I Would Only Smile'—as well as his lead vocal on Paul's 'I Lie Around'—were all deleted, and deleted with them was Paul's twin goal of showing off the band's versatility, and further establishing it as a *band*, rather than a former Beatle with sidemen.

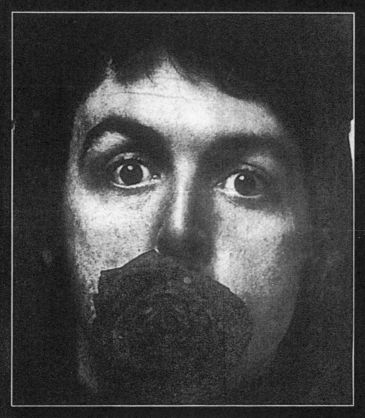

Red Rose Speedway

PAUL McCARTNEY AND WINGS

Side 1	Side 2
BIG BARN BED	SINGLE PIGEON
MY LOVE	WHEN THE NIGHT
GET ON THE RIGHT THING	LOUP (1ST INDIAN ON THE MOON)
ONE MORE KISS	MEDLEY: HOLD ME TIGHT
LITTLE LAMB DRAGONFLY	LAZY DYNAMITE
	HANDS OF LOVE
	POWER CUT

Includes 12 page booklet.

Apple Album SMAL-3409

Distributed by Capitol Records

Laine, for one, regarded the single disc *Red Rose Speedway* as a McCartney solo disc and distanced himself from the album and the decisions that went into it.

"It's just probably political that it ended up being just a solo thing," Laine later reasoned. "Maybe [EMI] weren't ready for it, didn't think it was gonna [sell] so many. I don't know. You gotta remember I wasn't involved in that. It was Paul's baby, really. I wasn't involved in that stuff. I just kind of turned up for work, and I had ideas obviously. But as far as the administration-record company discussions, I was no part of any of that."[39]

The surviving songs were all credited "McCartney" on the disc labels, but they were copyrighted as Paul McCartney and Linda McCartney collaborations. The way the band was listed morphed as well; indeed, the artist attributions on McCartney's album were becoming quite fluid. *McCartney* was presented as a solo album by Paul; *Ram* as a Paul and Linda McCartney album, *Wild Life* as a Wings disc, and now, *Red Rose Speedway*, with commercial considerations in mind (and with Romeo driving the change of name), was credited to Paul McCartney and Wings.

Meanwhile, Paul was making progress in his battle to minimize references to Apple on his releases: "An Apple Record" appears in small print on disc labels, on both British and American pressings. Apple Records is listed on the back cover of the US release, as the manufacturer of the discs. But ABKCO and its address are nowhere to be seen.

Where the artwork for *McCartney* and *Ram* had a homespun look, and *Wild Life* sported an elegant front cover and a simpler back, the art Paul had in mind for *Red Rose Speedway* was elaborate and overtly arty, and was packed with disparate elements that fall together as a kind of celebration of the world of pop art.

Significantly, having been shown all together on the *Wild Life* sleeve, Paul's bandmates are nowhere to be seen on the front gatefold cover of *Red Rose Speedway*. Instead, the cover sports a portrait of Paul with a rose in his mouth, shot by Linda, and re-creating a portrait of Paul she took in Morocco. In this version, Paul is wearing a black knit turtleneck sweater and is leaning against a Harley-Davidson motorcycle the McCartneys rented for the early March shoot on the roof of *The Times* newspaper group building.

"I remember the evening we did the album cover," Paul said. "Linda took that photo of me as I sat next to a motor bike with a rose in me mouth all evening, listening to Stevie [Wonder]'s album."[40]

The Harley offers a vague link to the *Speedway* of the title, but it may also be a private joke—an oblique reference to Neil Dean's having inverted the Matchless Motorcycle logo to create the Wings logo, which is seen, for the first time on an album, on the back cover, beside the address of the Wings Fun Club. The only text on the front cover is the album's title, in red script within an amoeba-shaped blue patch (which also appears, with the Wings logo, on the disc labels). In the

United States, a blue sticker was affixed, giving the newly expanded band name, listing the tracks, and promising a 12-page booklet.

The back cover was sparse: all black, but for the Fun Club message and manufacturing information (varying by country) across the bottom, and an egg-shaped photo in the center, showing a bouquet, wrapped in green plastic, at the foot of a microphone stand that sits on a pair of Persian rugs. The shot was taken in Paris, during Wings' summer tour, and beneath it was a message in Braille—"we love you baby"—intended principally for Stevie Wonder, although Paul later added that it might also entertain other blind fans.

The fun began when you opened the gatefold, both sides of which were devoted to a collage Paul commissioned for the album from Eduardo Paolozzi, an artist Paul had known about since his schoolboy days, having heard about Paolozzi's work from John Lennon and the Beatles' original bassist, Stuart Sutcliffe. Both were fans of Paolozzi's eye-catching, irreverent style. In Paolozzi's work, celebrities, product logos and other pop culture imagery were blended with abstract shapes and forms, a mashup that transformed the pop images into sometimes clear (but more typically ambiguous) metaphors.

Paolozzi was a founder of the Independent Group, a collective of like-minded artists, writers and critics who banded together in 1952, meeting to discuss their work and philosophy at London's Institute of Contemporary Arts (the ICA); among its members was Richard Hamilton, who later designed the cover and poster for the Beatles' *White Album*, in 1968.

Around the same time the Beatles undertook the first of their transformative residencies in Hamburg, in 1960, Paolozzi joined the faculty of the Hamburg College of Fine Arts. Sutcliffe enrolled there to study with him; the opportunity to continue as Paolozzi's student, along with his passion for Astrid Kirchherr, one of the Hamburg art students who befriended the Beatles, and to whom Sutcliffe became engaged, were among the reasons he left the Beatles, ceding the bass guitarist position to McCartney.

Paul made his own connection with Paolozzi during the Beatles years, when his London circle of friends included the art dealer Robert Fraser. Fraser had some of Paolozzi's work, including a sleek chrome piece, called *Solo* (1962), which he kept in his apartment. Paul especially liked that one and persuaded Fraser to sell it to him. He also wrangled an invitation to meet Paolozzi and later bought one of his wooden sculptures, as well.

"I once visited his Chelsea (London) studio and was impressed by his sense of humor, the twinkle in his eye and his generosity," Paul said. "I think his contribution to the British pop art scene (even though I don't think he liked that term) was extremely important."[41]

When Paul pondered artwork ideas for *Red Rose Speedway*, at the end of 1972, Paolozzi came to mind. Paul phoned him and proposed that they meet to discuss a project. At their meeting

Paul commissioned the gatefold collage, which includes images of Marilyn Monroe (her skirt blown upward in the famous scene from Billy Wilder's 1955 comedy, *The Seven Year Itch*), a coffee cup (with a tiny hand grabbing the edge), a few missiles and rockets, a rounded slice of the Periodic Table, and lots of geometric shapes and patterns. These elements were not exclusive to Wings' album artwork; they were plundered from *BASH* (1971) and *Mr. Peanut* (1970), two screen prints from Paolozzi's portfolio that had caught Paul's eye.

So far, Paul had an album cover with a commissioned artwork in its gatefold, and an attractive, stylishly information-free cover, with a Braille message on the back. But there was plenty more information Paul wanted included—the song titles, personnel lists for each song, and the lyrics, for starters, not to mention photos of Wings (remember Wings?). All that was accommodated in a 12-page booklet, which also included more Paolozzi collage images, plus a few pieces Paul commissioned from Allen Jones, another hero of the pop art world, whose sculptures were seen in Stanley Kubrick's *A Clockwork Orange*, in 1970.

Paul's request of Jones was that he produce works based on the titles of the album's songs, a list that Paul provided. Jones, whose works often have an erotic element, supplied provocative paintings, drawings and collages, to which Paul devoted full pages, for 'Hold Me Tight,' 'Power Cut' and—despite its absence from the single album—'Seaside Woman.' (Jones was rewarded for these contributions with a misspelled credit, as Alan Jones.)

The rest of the pages drew on photos of Wings in action, from the European tour, by Captain Snaps, along with pictures Linda took of Paul and the band in Marrakesh.

With the recording and artwork complete at last, Paul handed the album to EMI, which scheduled it for release on April 30, 1973, in the United States, and May 4 in Britain.

———

Shortly after *Ram* was released, Paul had put it about that he had recorded far more material than fit on the album, and that some might be released soon on a follow-up. That never happened, principally because the formation of Wings pushed Paul's career in a different direction. While assembling the trimmed sequence of *Red Rose Speedway*, Paul proposed a similar idea for the extra material—a prospect that placated Henry.

"I think there's something like that coming out as a summer album," Henry explained in his interview with *Sounds*, even before *Red Rose Speedway* was released. "There's some mindblowers on it, too, like there's a great song of Linda's—'Seaside Woman'—and another good one that Denny Laine's written, and both of them have been left off this album. But they have to come out because they're too good to just lie around and do nothing."

But this "summer album" never materialized.

22

FIVE OF THEM CAME UP ILLEGAL

—

We've been hammering ourselves into shape for a year, and I think this is the right time to show what we can really do," McCartney said of Wings during the preparations for his 1973 television special, to be called *James Paul McCartney* and carried by ITV in Britain and ABC in the United States. Looking ahead as production was about to begin, he added, "We've got a script, but we are playing it by ear. We want it to be as spontaneous as possible. We've got a lot of original ideas, but if they don't come off as well as we hope they won't be used. Especially the comedy. We hope there'll be a lot of laughs."[1]

Wings gathered on February 22, at Elstree Studios, in the London suburb of Borehamwood, to rehearse for the TV production—mainly a matter, at this point, of running through the songs that Wings would perform in the show, both in staged studio performances and in a concert sequence that was scheduled to be filmed live at Elstree on March 18. The studio performances were to be lip-synched, so these rehearsal sessions were recorded for the show's soundtrack. A letter from the Wings Fun Club went out on March 8, inviting members to request tickets for the live concert.

After another Elstree band session, on March 7, Paul gave Wings a couple of weeks off, while he and Linda were filmed on their own and attended to other responsibilities. As was increasingly the norm, McCartney was in constant motion.

There were contracts to be signed—one for the publishing of 'Live and Let Die,' another with ATV for the television show, which brought him "the sterling equivalent of $50,000" (£20,000) plus 50 percent of the net profits. The advance alone was enough to cover Seiwell's, Laine's and McCullough's salaries for 95 weeks.

There was a tour to announce, the revised schedule including 14 cities, starting in Bristol on May 11, and ending in Birmingham on May 27.[2] There were rumors to squelch, including reports that Paul was about to produce a film biography of Buddy Holly, speculation that Dave Golding described as "sheer rubbish."[3]

And on top of all that, Paul had a court date at the Campbeltown Sheriff Court on March 8, to answer the drug charges arising from the raid on his greenhouse and farms on September 19, 1972. He hired a private jet, for £1,000 ($2,500), to get him and Linda to the hearing and back.

No expense was spared assembling a legal team north of the border. Paul's London attorney engaged Len Murray, a Scottish solicitor with a sterling reputation, who in turn hired John Mc-Cluskey, who would appear for Paul at the hearing. Arriving in Campbeltown, Paul's first stop was Murray's office.

Murray and McCluskey had interesting news for Paul. Their original plan was to plead not guilty to the three charges brought against him—cultivating five cannabis plants in his greenhouse at High Park, and two counts of possession of cannabis at High Park and Low Ranachan. But Mc-Cluskey reasoned that the two possession charges were merely technical: the five plants were not mature enough to produce cannabis resin, and the resin was part of the law's description of the illegal substance under consideration. Moreover, all five plants could have yielded only a minus-cule amount of marijuana.

Convinced that the two possession charges could not stand, Murray and McCluskey met with the prosecutor, Alistair Iain Balfour Stewart, the evening before the hearing. After they made their case, Stewart agreed to drop both possession charges. Paul would now plead guilty to only the cultivation charge. Murray and McCluskey conveyed this to Paul an hour before the hearing. "He sat for a few moments," Murray later wrote, "looked at the ceiling and said with a trace of a Liverpool accent, 'Yes. Let's go with that and get it over with.'"[4]

The five rows of seats behind the dock, in which Paul sat alone, were tightly packed with jour-nalists and as many of the curious as could fit into the tiny, 65-by-40-foot wood-paneled court-room. McCluskey offered McCartney's guilty plea for the sole remaining charge, and then set about mitigating it, claiming that the seeds were sent by fans, unlabeled, and that Paul—like his father, an avid horticulturalist who raised tomatoes in his greenhouse and tended a vegetable garden—naturally planted them. He added that the plants were grown openly—that "there was no attempt to conceal them, as there could have been by whitewashing the windows, or putting in frosted glass"—and suggested that this was further evidence of Paul's innocence.

The argument skirted the edge of plausibility, but McCluskey's defense, and Stewart's having dropped the other charges, helped persuade Sheriff D. J. McDiarmid to fine Paul rather than jail him.

"I take into account that these seeds were given to you in a gift," the bewigged McDiarmid told Paul, who stood in the dock wearing a gray jacket and busy tie, with a fringed, white silk scarf thrown casually over his shoulder. "But I also take into account the fact that you are a considerable figure of public interest, particularly among young people, and you must be dealt with accord-ingly."[5]

McDiarmid set the fine at £100 ($250), and at McCluskey's request, he gave McCartney 14 days to pay it.

With Linda standing quietly at his side, wearing a bowler hat she had lifted from McCluskey, Paul held a short news conference outside the courthouse at the top of Castle Hill, looking down toward the harbor. You could see him and Linda suppressing a giggle as Paul repeated his mystery seeds defense—"We got a load of seeds, you know, in the post, and we didn't know what they were, and we kind of planted them all, and five of them, like—five of them came up illegal."[6]

He added that he was pleased with the outcome, but he had been prepared to spend time in jail, where he "planned on writing a few songs."[7] The humor in his fine being a tenth what it cost him to fly to Campbeltown was not lost on Paul. "Imagine arriving in a charter jet and asking 14 days to pay," he joked.

And as he had done in Sweden, he advocated for the legalization of cannabis.

"I look on it like Prohibition in the old days," he explained. "I think the law should be changed—make it like the law of homosexuality with consenting adults in private. I don't think that cannabis is as dangerous as drink."[8]

Murray and McCluskey warned him, though, that this conviction, like the Swedish one, could cause difficulties next time he tried to get an American visa. Nor was news of the conviction lost on General Motors, the sponsor for the American version of *James Paul McCartney*. Any hope the company had that Paul might come over to promote the show just went up in a puff of mellow smoke.

Paul and Linda flew back to London immediately and spent March 9 at Elstree, the first of five Wingless sessions (the others were on March 12, 15, 19 and 27) at which they filmed scenes that did not involve the band. A bomb scare and an evacuation on the 12th barely slowed them down.

The most musically expansive of the Paul and Linda scenes was a staged photo shoot. Paul sat on a high stool, surrounded by half a dozen pastel flash umbrellas, with his black Gibson J-180 Everly Brothers Signature acoustic, modified with a double pickguard—the same guitar he brought with him to Morocco. As he strummed and sang a handful of songs, Linda moved around him with her Nikon.

The raw recordings show him taking up a rich array of material—a few bars of Buddy Holly's 'That'll Be the Day,' 'Country Dreamer,' 'Mama's Little Girl,' the as yet unrecorded 'Bluebird,' which Paul composed in Jamaica, 'Hands of Love,' the 'Love Is Long' section of 'Long Haired Lady,' 'Heart of the Country,' and three Beatles tunes, 'Blackbird,' 'Michelle' and 'Yesterday.' Camera clicks were recorded on their own, to be overlaid on the scene. In the final edit, Paul is seen playing 'Blackbird,' 'Bluebird,' 'Michelle' and 'Heart of the Country,' with 'Bluebird' shown in the British cut, but deleted from the version shown in the United States.

The performances of 'Blackbird' and 'Michelle,' along with 'Yesterday,' in the show's final scene, were Paul's first public appearances playing songs he recorded with the Beatles, since the breakup.

No doubt ATV, and perhaps Chevrolet, insisted that Paul acknowledge his Beatle past in the program. But there was another reason Paul happily played these tunes. As he knew from his discussion with Lennon in November, Allen Klein's contract with Apple was due to expire on March 31, and sentiment among the former Beatles leaned toward not renewing it. By the time *James Paul McCartney* aired, on April 16 in the United States, and May 10 in Great Britain, Klein would be gone. For anyone seeking between-the-lines messages—and Klein would certainly be among them—the one Paul was sending here was clear and unequivocal.

The Paul and Linda sessions also included a concept video for 'Uncle Albert': a scene in which Linda makes tea while Paul does a crossword puzzle gives way to an office fantasy in which a demure-looking Linda takes notes as a bespectacled Paul, with a thin mustache, and pipe in hand, dictates. This dissolves to a room crowded with middle-aged men on the telephone, who, we see in a closing vignette, are speaking with Paul.

Paul recorded a couple of voice-overs during these sessions, too. For the introduction to what would be the first public airing of 'Live and Let Die,' he taped a cute, deadpan snippet in which he asserted that he regarded films as accompaniments to their soundtrack music, adding that the forthcoming Bond film would soon accompany his new song. This gave way to a brief disquisition on popcorn and was overlaid on footage of Paul and Linda sitting in a theater balcony, popcorn in hand. Eon Productions supplied clips from the film, to be interspersed with Wings' lip-synched performance.

The other voice-over was a brief autobiographical snippet about being born near the river Mersey, under which most of his relatives were buried (he did promise the press laughs), for a segment to be filmed there.

Paul's final solo task was an involved dance number based on 'Gotta Sing, Gotta Dance,' a McCartney song no one knew. It was written in the summer of 1972, commissioned by Twiggy for a film musical of the same name (the title pilfered from one of Gene Kelly's songs in *Singin' in the Rain*) that she and her paramour-manager, Justin de Villeneuve, were creating. It was not the first song Paul wrote with Twiggy in mind. Early in 1968, Granada Television planned to produce a documentary, *Twiggy in Russia*. The model asked Paul to write a song for the show, and he responded with 'Back in the U.S.S.R.' The production was scrapped when the team was denied visas to the Soviet Union, and the song found its way to the Beatles' *White Album*.[9]

When Linda and Heather moved from New York to London, Twiggy answered Paul's call to befriend his future wife, taking Linda shopping in Knightsbridge and to lunch at San Lorenzo, a nearby Italian restaurant. The two couples maintained their friendship ever since.

Twiggy described *Gotta Sing, Gotta Dance*, to be set on a cruise ship, as an homage to the songs and dance styles of the 1930s; indeed, McCartney's song was the only new work to be heard in the film. (A second song he developed for the project, called 'Tea and Sympathy,' was later withdrawn.)

"Paul McCartney wrote a title song for us, but for the rest we want to use the real songs of the time," Twiggy told the *Times* during preproduction of her movie. "Highly stylized we want it to be, but not all jokey and camp like *The Boy Friend*,"[10] she added, referring to the 1971 Ken Russell film, in which she starred.

But McCartney had shown, as early as 'When I'm Sixty-Four,' a tune he wrote as a teenager, and as recently as 'Honey Pie,' on the *White Album*, that he had mastered the art of writing convincingly in styles of past decades, and in 'Gotta Sing, Gotta Dance,' he channels the sound of the 1930s.

Twiggy had also invited Paul to appear in the film, which would be overseen by lesser-known commercials director Melvin Sokolsky. But the box office receipts for *The Boy Friend* did not meet MGM's hopes, so *Gotta Sing, Gotta Dance* was shelved, and Paul considered his song free to use for his own purposes.

For *James Paul McCartney*, it was recorded in two pieces: first, Paul recorded the slow, ornate piano and vocal intro. Then Jack Parnell, the show's music director, led his orchestra and the Ladybirds, a vocal ensemble, in an accompaniment to Paul's vocal on the song proper. Those sections were edited together, and Paul mimed to them.

The first part was easy enough: he sat at the piano, doing what he normally does, dressed in a dark jacket and open shirt, with no facial hair. But the body of the song was a big production number—an art deco fantasy with sets and costumes designed by Erté and made by Sue Le Cash. Paul donned a pink satin tux with, in some sections of the clip, a white cane (but no top hat), and sported a dark, trimmed mustache. He mimed the song while moving through an ensemble dance routine.

Or so it seemed. Actually, for most of the routine, Paul was filmed on his own against a blue screen, while the production's 35 dancers were filmed on the set. The two films were then composited. In some sections, they were sped up, to give their movements a Keystone Kops appearance, at which points Parnell's orchestral score grew brassier and more frenetic.

"Linda and Paul used to come to rehearsals occasionally, and just sit there and wind themselves around each other," Sue Weston, one of the dancers, recalled. "Paul never once danced with us. I mean, there were a horde of us, so many dancers, and he must've felt totally out of his comfort zone. What might've been a good idea in the production meeting, suddenly, oh goodness, you've got all these incredibly skilled dancers, and he wasn't going to make a fool of himself in front of us, I can quite get that. But he actually danced quite well. It's simple stuff he's doing, but he's doing it well."[11]

Paul's own estimation of his dancing was less generous. "They said to me, 'Oh, you can dance, right?' and they got a choreographer [Robert Iscove] in, and it was all sort of old-fashioned choreography. What I should have said is, 'I can leap,' or I should have told them they'd have to get me very drunk."[12]

Attentive viewers can see evidence of the film editors' sleight of hand. At a couple of points toward the end of the scene, Paul can be seen walking through the outstretched arms of several dancers. It seemed odd, too, that the dancers were wearing platform shoes in the tap scenes. Actually, Hemion took six of the best tap dancers and recorded them separately, overlaying their sound on the relevant sections of the clip.

Abstract as the scene was, it fell short of Paul's original plan.

"We had little things in there that would have been a bit mind-blowing," he later lamented. "Like we were gonna do a drag scene. I do a song and dance thing and in the middle of it we were going to change all into drag and I was gonna come on and do like a big Diana Ross bit. And Linda was gonna be a fella, and all the others were going to be girls. But Chevrolet sent a very heavy letter saying, 'Due to the sponsorship, blah, blah, blah.' Chevrolet were the money behind it."[13]

Chevrolet did not, however, object to Erté's costume designs for the dancers, who were half male, half female: one side of each costume was a black tux, and on that side the dancers' hair was short and dark, while on the other side, their costumes were glittery silver, with bare arms and legs, their hair long and blond. Depending whether they turned to the right or left, they appeared as men or women.

"Those costumes were so uncomfortable," Weston remembered. "The costumes, the wigs, the makeup, was all half-man, half-woman, so it took forever to get into them. And their construction, with so much weight on the male side and hardly any weight on the female side—it was extraordinary costume making.

"The whole concept sounded like a Moroccan spliff conversation,"[14] Weston said, not knowing how close to the mark she was.

———————

Some 5,500 miles to the west, John Lennon, George Harrison and Ringo Starr, along with Klaus Voormann, on bass, and Billy Preston, on organ, met at Sunset Sound Studio, in Los Angeles, on March 13. They had convened to record 'I'm the Greatest,' a song John wrote for the album Ringo had started recording at Sunset on March 5. Ringo had not made an album since *Beaucoups of Blues*, in 1970, and he might still have been sitting on the sidelines if not for an encounter at Tramp, a private London club. As Ringo downed tumblers of Southern Comfort, the producer Richard Perry matched him with shots of tequila, eventually working up the courage to pitch a project to the drummer.

"I convinced Ringo that it would be fun just to try out some stuff in a studio when he came to the States," Perry explained. "By the end of the [first week of recording] we had seven tracks down, such as 'Photograph,' plus one I'd brought along as a suggestion, 'You're Sixteen.' 'Step Lightly' was especially fun because that night Ringo showed up with some tap shoes; I don't know where he got them. And at 5 a.m., a drunken Ringo Starr, holding on to a music stand to keep his balance, made his tap-dancing debut."[15]

The gathering of Lennon, Harrison and Starr was partly happenstance: George was in town producing an album for Ravi Shankar, and John was promoting Yoko's new disc, *Approximately Infinite Universe*. Since they were all in the same city, Lennon, Harrison and Starr had a business meeting to discuss the Klein situation; John then met with Klein—who went to Los Angeles when he learned that the three former Beatles were there—to tell him that they would not renew his contract.

Naturally, reports that John, George and Ringo were working together, and that Klein would soon be out of the picture, combined with EMI's announcement on March 10 that it would be releasing its two double-disc Beatles compilations, led the press to speculate that a Beatles reunion was imminent.

John quickly stepped on such gossip, explaining to *Rolling Stone* that "the thing about 'they're all getting together' came out of the fact that we all had to get together to discuss this [Klein] thing, including the Paul situation, sooner or later. It just so happened that George had to be in L.A. to work with Ravi, and Ringo was there recording this album. So, we all timed it to be there to discuss our futures."[16]

John declined to discuss the reasons for the split with Klein, but hinted that Tony Cox was using his own dislike and distrust of Klein as a reason to keep Kyoko away from John and Yoko. Asked whether the Beatles were better off, post-Klein, than the Rolling Stones—who had lost both their publishing and master tapes to the manager—John offered an analysis that Paul could only have read as a long-belated vindication.

"Due to the presence of Lee Eastman looking over Paul's shoulder all the time—and therefore looking over Klein's shoulder—[Klein's] movements were hampered. We can now be thankful for that situation. We knew it was beneficial all the time playing one off against the other, and eventually we ended up here."

He went on to describe his relationship with Paul as "Distant physically. And mentally pretty okay."[17]

Elsewhere, John made an even fuller concession to the arguments Paul had made all through 1969.

"Well, there are many reasons to get finally given the push," he said of his abandonment of Klein as his manager. "Let's say that possibly Paul's suspicions were right."[18] Shortly after Klein's contract lapsed, Yoko offered a few more crumbs of insight into the failed relationship, in an interview with *Disc*.

"We really need someone who is an administrator, someone who can take care of our needs who also knows the legal side of things. In a way, Allen has a good head on his shoulders, but it fits his needs. It's not like the Beatles are just starting—John, George and Ringo are certainly established stars, they don't really need a 'manager'; what they need are accountants, lawyers. Not someone who wants to be a pop star himself.

"[Klein] was busy making those spaghetti westerns—he didn't promote Ringo in films as much as he should have. Ringo is fantastic in films, and often people would be intimidated about offering him things because they'd have to go through Klein. The same thing would happen with us. He would intimidate people. We used to sort of promote and protect him, but it just wasn't reciprocal. It was pretty hard for me—he's really a bit of a male chauvinist. Often, he would imply that my records were a real drain on Apple, and that just wasn't true. I was treated the same way that most non-Beatle artists are treated on Apple, and everyone knows that wasn't always the best. I mean, Billy Preston, James Taylor, they left Apple because of that."[19]

—————▶

With Paul and Linda occupied with filming, trouble was brewing in the Wings camp. Denny Seiwell and Henry McCullough took the opportunity to meet with Vincent Romeo on March 13 to discuss their financial worries, which remained unresolved a year after their meeting with Lee Eastman.

"Everyone in the band was paid £70 a week," McCullough summarized his concerns. "Paul said, 'Don't worry, we'll do a record, do a tour, then we'll sit down and work out what's what.' But we never did." [20]

Seiwell, with seven months seniority over McCullough, was making the same £70 salary, two years, two albums and two tours after the original "hippie handshake," and flying back to New York whenever possible to underwrite his Wings membership with freelance studio work. Together, Seiwell and McCullough told Romeo that this was unworkable. Nor was it lost on them that Paul and Linda had the money to expand MPL's staff, hiring David Minns, around this time, as their personal assistant. Romeo did not have the leeway to offer much encouragement; Seiwell and McCullough left his office without much hope that things would soon change.

That night, Paul and Linda took the band to Wembley Arena to watch the Liverpool-born boxer John Conteh fight Rüdiger Schmidtke for the European Light Heavyweight boxing title. Paul scored ringside seats to see the Scouser fight savagely against the West German defending champion, knocking out Schmidtke in 12 rounds.

"That was fun," Seiwell remembered. "I had never been to a prizefight before. We sat close enough; you'd get blood on you."[21]

But great seats at a prizefight weren't enough of a perquisite to keep Henry happy, and the next day he told Paul he was leaving the band. Still upset about the financial arrangements that had gone unresolved in the meeting with Romeo, he had other issues, too. He was angry about the transformation of *Red Rose Speedway* from an album that represented Wings to a showcase for Paul. He was happy with his solo on 'My Love' and pleased that Paul was impressed, but he disliked being in the position of having to beg to flex his musical muscles. And with a tour coming up, he was both perplexed and angry about Linda's continued membership in the band, since the inevitable criticism of her playing and singing reflected poorly on the band as a whole.

Paul understood Henry's concerns about Linda; it was not as if he hadn't heard such criticism frequently. "Everyone had to start somewhere,"[22] he would say, but he knew as well as anyone that "somewhere" was not typically onstage with former members of the Beatles, the Moody Blues and the Grease Band, and a top session drummer.

ATV Network Limited cordially invite you to

"PAUL McCARTNEY and WINGS"
IN A LIVE CONCERT

at **ATV ELSTREE** Studios
Eldon Avenue, Boreham Wood

Sunday, 18th March, 1973
Doors open 6.30 p.m.   No admission after 7.15 p.m.
Performance ends approximately 10.00 p.m.

Admit One
Studio D
Full particulars are given on reverse side of ticket

"Perhaps I did have doubts now and again about Linda on keyboard," Paul later admitted, adding that those doubts caused tension between them. "I did once say to her in a row that I could have had Billy Preston. It just came out. I said I was sorry about an hour later."[23]

Having a member of Wings quit in the middle of the television production, and four days before the concert at Elstree, obviously would not do, so Paul donned the mantle of peacemaker and lured Henry back to the fold with the offer of a £500 ($1,250) bonus for *Red Rose Speedway*, and a further £1000 ($2,500) loyalty bonus at the end of the year,* payments he would match for Laine and Seiwell. But Paul was on notice: Henry had grievances, and he felt strongly enough about them to walk.

Filming continued without either Wings or Paul and Linda on March 16, when Dwight Hemion, took a remote crew to Shenley Road, Borehamwood's main drag, and asked shoppers, as well as patrons of the Red Lion pub, to sing a bit of their favorite Beatles tune, giving the show a bit more Beatles content—and pointing up the music's centrality in the contemporary psyche—without troubling Paul to up the Beatles quotient of his own performances. The north London locals willing to chance a verse included, among countless others, local newsagent Pat May, a handful of schoolgirls—Tracy Callis, Jeanette Webb, Margaret Johnson, Julie Theobald, and Diane Lake—and housewife Pat Houton.

Actually, there was another helping of Beatles' music in the Wings concert segment, which was rehearsed on March 17 and filmed the next night. Before an audience in which Wings Fun Club members were heavily represented, the band took to the stage at 7:45 p.m. and launched into 'The Long and Winding Road'—Wings' first public performance of a Beatles tune, heard in

---

* An internal MPL memo notes Denny Laine's income for 1973 as £5730, of which £3640 was retainer fees. A further £500 was a bonus for *Red Rose Speedway*, leaving £1590 in additional payments for the calendar year. Whether Laine paid a cut of his income to Tony Secunda is unknown, but possible.

its pre-Spector arrangement, with Paul at the piano, Laine on bass, Henry on guitar and Seiwell on drums.

Linda did not play on the song; instead, she drifted around the stage photographing the band. She moved to her keyboards (but sometimes played tambourine rather than electric piano) for the rest of the set, which included 'Maybe I'm Amazed,' 'When the Night,' 'The Mess' (which, having fallen off *Red Rose Speedway*, was announced the next day as the B side of Wings' next single, 'My Love'), 'Wild Life,' Denny Laine singing 'Go Now,' and a closing section with 'Hi, Hi, Hi' and 'Long Tall Sally.'[24]

"It was a short set," Wings Fun Club member Den Pugsley reminisced. "My friend and I were seated on the studio floor, just six feet to the right of the stage. It was fabulous." Pugsley was particularly impressed by "a blistering 'Long Tall Sally,'" which was followed by the announcement that "there had been some 'technical issues' and that Wings would return and play exactly the same set again. Of course, we didn't mind one bit!"[25]

The second show, which included two performances of 'Hi, Hi, Hi' (the second at a slower tempo) but skipped 'Long Tall Sally,' ran until 10:00 p.m.

Wings were not finished for the night, however. Paul had committed to play a late set at the Hard Rock Cafe, in London's West End. The show was the Hard Rock's "Charity Brawl," a benefit for Release, an organization founded in 1967 to provide legal advice and support for people charged with possession of drugs. If anyone could have been a poster boy for the cause, it was Paul, but he was listed only as "Mystery Star" in the Hard Rock's advertising.

"Paul insisted that we didn't let on that he would be appearing, and we weren't sure that he would, in fact, turn up," Mick Smallwood, Hard Rock's general manager explained. "We had a couple of other star acts lined up, just in case."[26]

While trusty roadies Ian and Trevor carted the band's equipment over to the Hard Rock, Wings and their entourage of about 20 arrived early enough to catch a set by pub rock favorites Brinsley Schwarz, a band Paul liked enough to invite them to join Wings on their British tour in May. Wings went onstage at about 12:45 a.m., and performed until 1:30 a.m., making their London concert debut unannounced and in the dead of night. With tickets going for £5 ($12.50), about £1,500 ($3,750) was raised for Release.[27]

———

With Paul's solo turns and scenes with Linda mostly complete, Wings spent several days filming their mimed performances to recordings made during the first couple of Elstree sessions.

They began, on March 20, with the clip that Seiwell and McCullough were the least eager to appear in. Dressed in matching white suits (Linda wore a nineteenth-century full-length dress and

hat and is seen on a swing with a tambourine) they set up in Hampstead Heath to mime 'Mary Had a Little Lamb.' To give the clip variety, they also did some rowing and bridge crossing, as a small flock of sheep wandered past.

"There I was," Henry recalled unhappily of the shoot, "leaned up against a tree, singing 'Mary Had a Bloody Little Lamb!' It was one the many instances where I thought: 'How long will this last?'"[28]

A version of 'Big Barn Bed,' with Wings onstage playing to a wall of television screens showing an applauding audience (from the concert shoot), as well as close-ups of the band members, was shot on March 24. This would become the special's opening scene; in the finished edit, responses to a fanzine-like questionnaire (birth date, hair color, eye color, etc.) were overlaid on close-ups of each player. Once 'Big Barn Bed' was in the can, the band shot the show's finale, a backstage setup in which Wings gathered around Paul and listened to him reclaim 'Yesterday' and an improvised piece entitled 'Well, That's the End of Another Day.'

Studio performances of 'Live and Let Die' and 'My Love,' for which Wings were surrounded by the Jack Parnell Orchestra, were filmed on March 25, in a session that bordered on cataclysmic. The performance of 'Live and Let Die' would be the song's premiere, so Paul wanted the clip to be memorable. Taking advantage of the music's grand gestures and its provenance as the theme for a spy film, he devised a surprise for the finale. A special piano was made, using balsa wood in some sections (it did not have to be playable, since the performance was mimed), and explosives were placed inside it. As the song ended, a shadowy figure in a trench coat and fedora is seen pushing a plunger, whereupon the piano explodes.

"They told us, 'When we get to the end of the song, there's going to be a blast—the piano is going to break apart in the middle and fall in on itself, so be aware of it,'" Seiwell explained. "But I don't think they told the violin section, which was behind the piano. These are all old guys, with toupees, holding their Stradivariuses. Well, the blast was bigger than they expected. The piano broke in half, and it was like a ball of flames, and pieces of wood went up and over these violin players' heads. I'm surprised somebody didn't have a heart attack. It was such a blast that Henry was standing next to Paul, and it swept him off his feet. I was hiding behind the cymbals, trying not to get hurt."[29]

Between the first and second Wings miming sessions, on March 22, the band and the film crew traveled to Liverpool to film a family and friends get-together in a pub, complete with a sing-along—the kind of thing Paul sometimes spoke of in interviews, when reminiscing about his family and his youth (although such stories were more typically set over holiday dinners than in pubs). Hemion and his crew settled on two locations, in Wallasey and New Brighton, across the River Mersey from Liverpool: the exteriors were shot at the Ferry Inn, with the interior of the Chelsea Reach as the setting for the crowded scenes of Paul and his friends drinking, smoking, chatting, and singing.

During the Liverpool visit, Paul and Linda stayed at Rembrandt, where the makeup crew turned up a few hours before the shoot. "Paul was very nervous and irritable that day and even yelled at Martha (the dog) for standing in front of the TV,"[30] Angie reported. And he was certainly not pleased when he arrived at the Chelsea Reach to find a crowd of more than 500 trying to wedge their way into the pub, some climbing in through the bathroom windows.

The plan for the shoot, originally, was that Paul, Linda and Wings would be surrounded by about 20 relatives—among them, Jim and Angie, several of Paul's aunts and uncles (Millie, Gin, Joe and Joan) and cousins (Johnny Mac, Bette Robbins, Kath and Reg Stapleton)[31]—and a few dozen friends, including a handful of Liverpool celebrities like Gerry Marsden, of Gerry and the

CHELSEA REACH

THE PROMENADE, NEW BRIGHTON, WALLASEY

A.T.V. WILL BE FILMING AN INFORMAL EVENING

WITH

Paul McCartney

AND HIS FRIENDS

on THURSDAY, 22nd MARCH, 1973

ARRIVE . . . WHEN YOU NORMALLY WOULD

DRESS . . . AS YOU NORMALLY WOULD

FREE BEER ALL NIGHT   ADMIT ONE.

Pacemakers, the bantamweight boxer Alan Rudkin and the artist and sculptor Arthur Dooley (who would later, in a drunken state, accuse Paul of not being working class).[32] But an advance piece in the *Liverpool Echo* on March 21, the day before the shoot, pointed the way for fans.

As perturbed as Paul was, his instincts before a running camera remained infallible, and he looked as though he were having a grand time during the four-hour shoot, heartily joining in with the crowd on a broad collection of time-honored pub favorites like 'April Showers,' 'It's a Long Way to Tipperary,' 'Nothing Could Be Finer Than to Be in Carolina' and several more, plus 'Hey Jude,' 'You'll Never Walk Alone' (later cut from the special due to its association with Liverpool FC—Paul's family were Everton FC fans), and 'Maggie Mae'—most sung several times to allow the three cameras to capture the performances from many angles.[33]

When the shoot ended, Paul and Linda stayed overnight at Rembrandt, while the rest of Wings returned to London in a limousine.

"That was horrible," Denny Seiwell said of the trip. "Everybody was drunk—we'd spent the whole day there, sitting around, singing old songs, and drinking, mainly—hanging out in a pub getting blotto. Henry, Denny [Laine] and I were in a limo, going back to London, and the limo driver drove about two blocks, opened the window and threw up. I said to him, 'Okay, you hop in the back here, I'm driving.' That night, Denny [Laine] and Henry got into it, sitting in the back, putting out cigarette butts in each other's faces. It was the longest night of my life."[34]

After the first Wings miming session, Paul and Hemion agreed that the band recordings made in late February and early March needed some touching up. Because ATV's producers were used to the demands of recording television sound, but not those of balancing rock recordings, Paul invited Richard Perry to oversee the rerecording of the Wings tracks. He knew Perry from the Carly Simon session at AIR, the previous fall, and he was aware that Perry was producing Ringo's new album.

The touch-up session with Wings was on Saturday, March 24, and during one of the play-backs, Perry felt out Paul's willingness to contribute to Ringo's album. He wondered, for starters, whether Paul might add something—a backing vocal, perhaps[35]—to 'I'm the Greatest,' Ringo's all-but-Paul Beatles reunion. Paul declined, but he was amenable to contributing a song. He did not have any unused songs lying around that would suit Ringo, but he knew he could write one if he had a deadline. He asked Perry to give him one.

"So I said 'Wednesday,' and he came up with his tune 'Six O'Clock,'" Perry recalled.[36] On Sunday, Wings did their final miming session, to the new tracks they recorded with Perry at the helm. Before Perry left, Paul agreed to attend the session for 'Six O'Clock.'

Ringo could not have been happier. "George and John were in town and George wrote 'Photograph' with me," he told a reporter. "John then said that he had a song and I thought, fantastic! Then we thought, 'Well, we've got to hit Paul.' I mean, we just can't break up the band!"[37]

The shooting for *James Paul McCartney* wound up with a Paul and Linda session on March 27. That day, Paul also made time to speak with Derek Johnson of *NME*, who came to Elstree Studios to ask what Klein's imminent departure meant for his relationships with the other Beatles.

"I've been talking to John recently," Paul confided. "I'm not sure what's going to happen to Apple, as everyone keeps changing his mind. But the only thing that has prevented us from getting together again has been Allen Klein's contractual hold over the Beatles' name. When he is out of the way, there is no real reason why we shouldn't get together."[38]

Johnson added that "an unnamed member of the Beatles' entourage" had mentioned the possibility of a concert, but that logistics militated against that: McCartney's recent drug convictions would keep him out of the United States, while Lennon's visa problems meant that he could not leave, for fear of not being readmitted.

Paul, in any case, was not at all consumed with thoughts of a Beatles reunion. More important to him, at the moment, was the release on March 30 of 'My Love' and the live Hague recording of 'The Mess'—the former a preview of *Red Rose Speedway*, the latter an advertisement for Wings' live sound (and peace offering to McCullough) just under six weeks before the start of its British tour. Paul's selection of 'The Mess' both pleased and frustrated Alan Parsons.

"We went around Europe in the Rolling Stones truck taping concerts," Parsons later complained. "Out of all that stuff came one song—'The Mess'—out of five days. He's very good at spending money for things like that and then doing nothing with it."[39]

The A side, according to Apple's PR man Pete Bennett, was also put out under duress. 'My

Love,' Bennett explained, fell down the recording pecking order as Paul was not convinced that the crooned ballad represented the direction of his band (Paul's change of heart was likely underpinned by a sudden surge of Glam Rock hits in the British singles chart. Since recording 'My Love,' the Sweet's 'Blockbuster' had snatched the top spot from Little Jimmy Osmond and had been at the summit for five consecutive weeks. Slade's 'Cum on Feel the Noize' was destined for a similar run at the top). Moreover, 'My Love' played into John's assertion that he had turned into Engelbert Humperdinck. But Bennett, together with Romeo, convinced Paul the song would be a hit.

"I first heard 'My Love' when a tape was shipped to me from London," explained Bennett, "and my gut feeling was that Paul McCartney did not feel that it would be a No. 1 record. I was so excited about this record's potential that I had acetates made that were sent to every major radio station in the country. I received a phone call from the Eastmans asking me what I thought of the record. I told them that this was a No. 1 record."[40]

Reviews of Wings' follow-up to 'Hi, Hi, Hi,' their racy, banned third single, were generally favorable, praising the composition, Hewson's arrangement, and McCullough's guitar work. McCartney's ballad even received faint praise from his critical nemesis Penny Valentine, in her final column for *Sounds*.

"Paul and his mates have produced another good strong pop record and one that should be safe enough for radio plays unless the words, 'My love does it good' are considered too wicked for a super sensitive British public. In particular there is a most agreeable burst of activity from the lead guitar."[41]

Elkie Brooks, *Disc*

MY LOVE
and
THE MESS

PAUL McCARTNEY AND WINGS

"He's played it safe and put out a piece of glush that's tailor-made for your most senile old aunt and just ripe for covering by Andy Williams or Perry Como. Apart from Henry McCullough's slashing guitar solo, it's just as wimpy as anything you'd expect from Des O'Connor."[42]

Charles Shaar Murray, *NME*

"A grand ballad from Paul, rather in the tradition of songs that turned on the troops in the days of the Cyprus crisis and other manifestations of the Fifties. Its appeal is timeless, and it certainly rates among his seemingly unstoppable flow of classics [with] a splendid, gutty guitar solo."[43]

Chris Welch, *Melody Maker*

"This is the first track Paul has put out that's likely to delight all his devotees of yesteryear. A tender, misty vocal with nice solid unobtrusive backing from Wings and a good guitar solo midway. Lovely and romantic it is too."[44]

Penny Valentine, *Sounds*

Critical applause did not translate to British chart success, though. 'My Love' enjoyed an 11-week run in the British Top 100, entering the chart at No. 43 on April 7, 1973, but rising only as far as No. 9 on April 28.

Upon the single's American release, on April 2, *Cashbox*'s anonymous reviewer pronounced 'My Love' "a fine ballad," delivered "as only [Wings] can," but added a puzzlingly backhanded compliment: "Though it is thin on melody, Paul's added sentiment and crooning will soon make this a classic."[45] Elsewhere in the same issue, *Cashbox* noted that 42 percent of American radio stations had added it to their playlists the week it was released.[46]

Singers, apparently, did not find it "thin on melody." By November, Tony Bennett, Cass Elliot, and Brenda Lee had recorded cover versions. The single gave Wings their first ever American No. 1 hit, entering the *Billboard* Hot 100 on April 14 at No. 73, topping the chart on June 2 and holding the No. 1 spot for seven weeks. 'My Love' finally dropped out of the Hot 100 after an 18-week run.

Paul made good on his promise to attend the sessions for 'Six O'Clock,' making his way on March 28 to, of all places, Apple Studios on Savile Row. An exquisitely tuneful song, with a cathartic descending chorus melody and a contrastingly rising bridge, 'Six O'Clock' is driven by the major-minor key shifts that had long been classic McCartney fingerprints. But it was also, in a way, a vote of confidence in Ringo's ability to put across a more complex song than people usually associated with him.

Paul played piano on the basic track, as well as the song's two synthesizer solos, and he arranged the backing strings and flutes. He also provided background vocals, with Linda, and before leaving for the night, he added a kazoolike, buzzing solo to 'You're Sixteen.'

"It's not kazoo. It sounds like a kazoo, but it's me doing an imitation of a saxophone player," Paul later revealed. "It was put through a fuzz thing. It's a bit daft, really, because it winds up sounding like a kazoo. I could have just done it on a kazoo. The idea was to make it sound like a great big funky sax."[47]

Strangely, it was Ringo, whose new album was the first project all four Beatles had participated in since *Abbey Road*, who issued the most vehement denial that a reunion was likely. Caught at London Heathrow, en route to Los Angeles on April 3, he told the *Times*, "We must get the picture straight—there is hardly any chance at all of us appearing together again. We are still good pals, but it's just not on.

"The papers drummed it up today that we are going to get together again, that is a load of absolute rubbish. Apart from anything else, we are doing quite well on our own. [Problems within the group] were nearly all over management. But although we haven't got Klein, Paul has still got Eastman. Let's face it, I'm quite happy. I'm busy all the time and I'm making money. As I say, we're all good friends but it's crazy to start up some campaign about us getting together again in public. And for my part, I want this record put straight."[48]

When the round of denials about a possible Beatles reunion failed to stop speculation in the media, John released a satirical press release, under the headline NEWSWECANALLDOWITHOUT:

Although John and Yoko and George, and George and Ringo have played together often, it was the first time the three ex-Beauties have played together since, well, since they last played together. As usual, an awful lot of rumours, if not downright lies, were going on, including the possibility of impresario Allen De Klein of grABKCo playing bass for the other three in an 'as-yet-untitled' album called *I Was a Teenage Fat Cat*. Producer Richard Perry, who planned to take the tapes along to sell them to Paul McCartney, told a friend, "I'll take the tapes to Paul McCartney." The extreme humility that existed between John and Paul seems to have evaporated. "They've spoken to each other on the telephone, and in English, that's a change," said a McCartney associate. "If only everything were as simple and unaffected as McCartney's new single 'My Love' then maybe Dean Martin and Jerry Lewis would be reunited with the Marx Bros., and Newsweak [*sic*] could get a job," said an East African official—Yours up to the teeth—John Lennon and Yoko Ono.[49]

McCartney slipped into promotional mode, or tried to, on April 4, when Wings were scheduled to record a performance of 'My Love,' with Paul singing live and Wings miming to a recorded track, for the edition of the BBC's *Top of the Pops* scheduled to air the following day. That morning, EMI prepared a mono mix of the backing track and sent it over to BBC Television Centre.

Paul and Linda arrived that afternoon, Paul with a hand-stitched strawberry jacket, with the word *Macca* across the front. The jacket, designed by the London-based Wonder Workshop, was specially commissioned for the *James Paul McCartney* special, and hand-stitched by Molly White, Carol Walsh, and Pamela Keats. Based on John Claridge's famed 1968 pop-art Strawberry Cut 'n' Sew design, the silk blazer, referred to by Paul as the "Strawberry Fields Jacket," was a televised, if subtle, message to his former writing partner that, with Klein gone, the war was over.

Paul had agreed to interviews with both Steve Gaines, of *Circus*, and Andrew Tyler, of *Disc*, and invited them to meet him backstage before the taping. When they arrived, the two Dennys and Henry were already an hour late, Romeo had not turned up, and Paul was in a foul mood. Both Gaines and Tyler quoted him saying, "I'm enthusiastic about nothing at the moment. It's not the kind of thing you tell journalists, but I'm not in that kind of mood, so I'm spilling the beans."[50]

He was not specific about what the beans were, and Gaines barely quoted him further. But Tyler did, and from the context of his remarks, he seemed troubled and even a bit confused by the prospect of a phoenixlike rebirth of the Beatles, post-Klein, and the steady but slow development of Wings, and what it would all mean for his future.

"It's just kind of happened," he said, speaking of the possibility of working with the other Beatles, "and that's where it still is, you know. The Beatles thing is loosening up. There's no kind of bitterness there anymore, so it means if everyone is really keen and fancies like mad getting a band together, you know, great! There are a few headaches which are, like, where can you go?

"To Bangladesh? Do the Madison Square big-return-of-the-Beatles concert? Or are you gonna keep going on with Wings and keep Wings going and do Wings concerts and do, like Wings and Beatles concerts? I don't know. There are possibilities there, but I can't put my finger on any plan. I haven't got any plans."

Aware that such remarks were at odds with his image as the cheerful, thumbs-up master of publicity, Paul pulled back the curtain further.

"Talking to a newspaper, I never know what to say. I'm conscious that I should be saying: 'Yes, our new album is a total gas. Yes, wow, it's just great to work with Ringo. We sure as hell are getting these Beatles together. Wings, shit, man, we've got the greatest potential in the world. There's no band can touch us. That's what I think, too.' It just depends what mood I'm in."[51]

But there was more to Paul's dark mood than uncertainty about the Beatles and Wings. Paul seems to have been having a crisis of confidence. Linda hinted at it when she told Gaines, "We need a little encouragement. Wings, and especially Paul, need people to say if we're good." In his chat with Tyler, Paul expanded on his insecurities.

"I feel like I've got so much in me I haven't even hinted at yet. I'm just keeping cool and waiting for it to happen. . . . I've felt I could make a better record than I'm making. That's just me. That's my personality. I always feel like I still haven't made the record I'm waiting to make.

"Even after 'Eleanor Rigby,' 'Yesterday,' 'All My Loving,' whatever, 'Michelle,' 'Sgt. Pepper.' I mean, I thought *Revolver* was out of tune. I was really annoyed with it for a couple of days. I thought 'Hey Jude' went on too long. I thought they'd never play it. I'm that, you know. I never think I'm much good."

When the rest of Wings turned up, Henry was drunk—so drunk he appears not to have realized that he needed only to mime. "I was totally langered," he confessed. "As we got to the solo, I knew I was going to throw up. I only had time to leap off stage and dive behind scenery—still playing the solo as I was being sick. The worst of it was I'd sent my mother a postcard: 'Watch *Top of the Pops* on Thursday.' McCartney was very tolerant and never said anything. He'd seen everything in his Beatle days, so nothing shocked him. I think he just thought I was having an alcoholic burst out and being typically Irish."[52]

Perhaps Henry had developed a physical aversion to the song. Four days later, while filming multiple takes of director Mick Rock's promotional video for 'My Love'—a performance clip with the band enveloped in smoke, and Paul and Linda dancing during Henry's solo—Henry again threw up on the set, this time overcome by the oil-based output of the smoke machine.

By now, Paul was fully in need of a break, so he and Linda arranged for a return visit to Montego Bay, in Jamaica, where they could update their reggae collection directly from the source. They left London on April 12, but the day before their departure, Paul gave an interview to Nicky Horne, for the BBC Radio One's *Scene and Heard* program. Naturally, the prospect of a Beatles reunion came up again, and his response, unlike the one he gave at Television Centre, was direct and to the point.

"Now [Klein]'s gone out, the main obstacle to people working together has been removed," Paul said, cautioning that "it doesn't mean necessarily the Beatles are going to re-form. It might mean that I'll play a concert with John in New York, somewhere, and George might roll in, Ringo might roll in, and you find that the Beatles are onstage, kind of thing. But at the moment, there's no great plan to get back together. I know as much as you, really.

"But as I say, there's no kind of anger anymore, none of that. See, you've gotta remember, in our position, all that has to happen is for John to write a snidey song about me, or to do a snidey article about me, and I'm expected to jump down his throat. And whilst I was a bit cheesed off, I tried not to [respond], and we eventually kind of held off. And after a couple of months, we were chatting away on the phone, and kind of talking quite peacefully between each other, and happily, you know.

"So, I mean, there was a bit of the business, but now it's great, you know. I just worked with Ringo, and I've spoken to John and George pretty recently."

By the time the interview aired, on April 13, 1973, Paul, Linda and their girls were enjoying the sun and the sand, and prowling Montego Bay's record shops.

23

DUSTIN' OFF THE COBWEBS

—

The McCartneys rented a small house just outside Montego Bay, and shortly after they arrived, they read in the *Kingston Daily Gleaner* that Dustin Hoffman and Steve McQueen were in the vicinity, filming *Papillon*, a $7 million prison drama that was being shot in 37 locations along Jamaica's northern coast, and in Kingston.[1] Paul thought it would be fun to meet Hoffman, so Linda sprang into action, finding out how to reach the actor, and telephoning him. Hoffman was an avid Beatles fan,* and invited the McCartneys to the house he and his wife, Anne Byrne, were renting. (They also spent time with Steve McQueen, who Linda photographed with his wife, Ali.)

Over dinner, the discussion turned to the artist Pablo Picasso, who had died on April 8. McCartney loved Picasso's work; he owned a couple of his sketches, and he likely told Hoffman that he had based one of his songs, 'When the Wind Is Blowing,' on Picasso's *The Old Guitarist*.

The conversation soon meandered to the creative process, with McCartney and Hoffman comparing notes on how they did what they did, and about the difference between creative artists, like painters, composers and novelists, and interpretive artists, like actors and performing musicians.

"To be able to write a song is an incredible gift,"[2] Hoffman enthused.

"But it's the same as any gift," countered McCartney. "It's the same as you and acting. When the man says, 'Action!' you just pull it out of the bag, don't you? You don't know where it comes from, you just do it. How do you get all your characterizations? It's just in you."

Hoffman made the obvious distinction—actors generally have a script, and a director; writing a song is *creatio ex nihilo*. "You mean," he asked Paul, "you can just do it, like that?"

---

* Several of Hoffman's films include striking Beatles references. In *Tootsie* (1984), for example, Jessica Lange's bedroom has a poster for the Beatles' Palladium show on her wall. In *Rain Man* (1988), the film's central emotional revelation takes place while its main characters reminisce about their childhood and sing 'I Saw Her Standing There.' And in *Hook* (1991) Wendy's bedroom is filled with Beatles memorabilia.

Later in the week,* the McCartneys and the Hoffmans dined together again, and Hoffman returned to the subject of songwriting.

"I've been thinking about this," he told Paul. "I've seen a little thing in *Time* magazine about Picasso, and it struck me as being very poetic. I think this would be really great set to music." He handed Paul the latest issue of *Time*, dated April 23, 1973, which included a seven-page appreciation of Picasso, and pointed to an anecdote on page 93, in a sidebar about the artist's final days:

> "Later that evening Picasso and his wife, Jacqueline, entertained friends for dinner. Picasso was in high spirits. 'Drink to me; drink to my health,' he urged, pouring wine into the glass of his Cannes lawyer and friend, Armand Antébi. 'You know I can't drink any more.' At 11:30 p.m. he rose from the table and announced: 'And now I must go back to work.'"

The article goes on to say that Picasso painted until 3 a.m., then went to bed.

> "On Sunday morning Picasso awoke at 11:30 a.m., his usual hour, but this time he could not rise from his bed. His wife, Jacqueline, rushed in and then called for help. At 11:40 a.m., before a doctor could get there, Pablo Picasso was dead."

Paul reached for the guitar he brought with him, gave it a strum to check its tuning, and then, as he later remembered, "I strummed a couple of chords I knew I couldn't go wrong on." The chords were G major, B minor, E minor and A minor (the first three are also the opening chords of 'A Day in the Life'), against which he sang a wistful melody, rising on "*Drink to me*," and falling on its continuation, "*Drink to my health*."

"Annie! Annie!" Hoffman called to his wife. "The most incredible thing! He's doing it! He's writing it! It's coming out!"

"He's leaping up and down, just like in the films," McCartney remembered. "And I'm knocked out because he's so appreciative."

Paul rewarded that appreciation with an informal concert, which he allowed Hoffman to record

---

* In some tellings, Paul condenses the story to a single dinner. Hoffman has told it as having taken place in one visit as well. This two-visit account is based on Paul's earliest and most detailed discussion of the event, reconciled with elements of Hoffman's version.

on a portable cassette machine. With Mary and Stella playing noisily in the room, Paul warmed up with a single-string blues riff, then documented the newly composed refrain for 'Drink to Me,' as well as the start of a verse—"*Three o'clock in the morning, I'm getting ready for bed*." He mumbled through the last two lines of the verse, returned to the refrain, and slowed down for the finale. He then moved directly into another new tune he had been working on, 'Getting Closer.' Linda sang impromptu but suitable harmony lines on both. Paul continued with slow and fast versions of the children's song, 'Baa-Baa Black Sheep,' 'Hands of Love,' chords for an unfinished and unidentifiable song, and a short sample of Buddy Holly's 'Peggy Sue,' followed by some instrumental noodling.

—

With McCartney on holiday, Denny Laine flew to Los Angeles to spend a week at Wally Heider's Studios at 1604 North Cahuenga, Hollywood, trying to finish the album he started before Paul invited him to join Wings. In a deal negotiated by Secunda, Laine's trip was paid for by Mo Ostin, the head of Warner Brothers Records.

Everyone had an agenda here: for Ostin, underwriting Laine was part of a long-term strategy to lure McCartney to Warner. For Secunda, it was a way of getting Laine to complete a project from which he would take a managerial cut. And for Laine, it was a step toward finishing an album that had languished since 1971, discharging his final debt to Secunda, and getting the manager out of his life so that he could sign a contract with McCartney and Wings, and collaborate on songs with his boss.

But in a way, spending time in Los Angeles only set Laine back. "I redid a lot of [the album]," he said, "in fact, everything except the rhythm tracks, which I felt just could not be any better." He described the project almost as if he were embarrassed by it. "The album is all very simple, easy chord songs, but for me it's a bit old, even though it's been tarted up. It's a low-budget album which I like."[3] In any case, he did not complete it and scheduled further sessions for after Wings' British tour.

Tony Brainsby went into action, too, making sure Wings were in the spotlight as their triple shot—the new album, the television special and the tour—was about to burst over Britain, and seeing to it that the non-McCartney members of the band grabbed some of the spotlight. This was, seemingly, what they wanted, but when Paul encouraged them to take turns introducing songs, during the European tour, they were reluctant.

"He wanted each band member to be known by the public, like John, Paul, George, and Ringo," Seiwell said. "It was just one of those things. That never happened, that's for sure."[4] With Brainsby scheduling the interviews, they had to step up. But when they did, they did not always toe the MPL/Wings line. In his lengthy interview with *Sounds*, published in the April 14 issue, Henry pulled back the curtain on the band's disappointment that *Red Rose Speedway* had been trimmed from two discs to one, and his frustration that the single disc focused on Paul rather than the band.

But McCullough also used the interview for a touch of diplomacy, conveying his enthusiasm about Wings' potential and trying to tamp down the generally accurate rumors that he was discontented.

"It sounds really good," he said of the group's musicmaking in concert. "Wings are a live band, and that's the truth. See, the band's been through a lot of changes, and it's beginning to get right because everybody wanted it to get right. There's been a lot of hard work. . . . To me the band has become better in every way because we're playing together all the time, you know, without it being like a TV show or something, we just have a blow in between and these are the times when I know I'm happy to be playing with Wings. We've played enough good music up to now for me to say, yeah, it's been worth sticking with."[5]

Denny Seiwell told Deborah Thomas of the *Daily Mirror* that "We didn't want to tour Britain in a shabby state, but now we're ready. We really shine as a live band. Paul makes most of the decisions, but the rest of us have something to offer." If that veiled complaint went unnoticed, his response to questions about a Beatles reunion would have surprised readers. "It would be healthy for everyone if they got together," he said. "Wings hasn't made a penny, because of McCartney's contractual problems."[6]

Seiwell spoke with *Record Mirror* as well, saying that the recent gig at the Hard Rock was the best Wings had played, but noting that the show was only an hour long, whereas "on tour we'll be doing a rather extravagant affair—probably playing for two and a half hours." Looking back on Wings' development during their first two years, he said that "it's hard work for a band to come together. It's similar to a marriage—there are the five of you and you have to find out what makes each of you tick, and that learning takes time.

"It was especially true in our case, as Paul purposely chose musicians who came from very separate types of backgrounds, so we'd all have different influences and inspirations to bring into the band's music. It might have been quicker and easier to have chosen five people who'd all been through the same sort of experiences and been playing similar music, but if you do that there's less chance of creating anything original; the music would tend to be very predictable."[7]

Brainsby's biggest win was a special Wings section in the April 21 issue of *Melody Maker*, that included an interview/profile for each member, a detailed listing of the equipment the band would use during their British tour, and a discography listing the band's singles and albums, with full track listings. Mostly, they covered the same ground as in other interviews, but there were a few surprises.

Henry, for example, revealed that he had recently played on recording sessions for a new album by his former group, the Grease Band—a point of only minor interest to many readers, but one that underscored his simmering disgruntlement in Wings. Yet he was enthusiastic about Wings' "progress as a team," adding that the battle, as he saw it, was to keep working as a band, rather than as sidemen for Paul. "I'm there 100 percent. I know we've got a lot to offer."

And Linda spoke more openly than usual about her insecurities, saying of her presence in Wings that "because Paul is so good it might even be wrong now, maybe I am holding them back. I like being in Wings, but if Wings would be better without me I'd definitely step down. I'm not interested in the fame bit, I just like being with Paul. But it's gotten a bit heavy because I don't really know where it's at."[8]

The Wings production line, meanwhile, continued to roll along even in Paul's absence.

Recording Sessions

Monday–Wednesday, April 16–18, 1973.
EMI Studios, Control Room Four, London.
Mixing: Live recordings from Wings' 1972 European tour.

Though it had slipped down the priority list during the completion of *Red Rose Speedway* and *James Paul McCartney*, Wings' concert film was still in the works, and at these sessions, stereo mixes were made for use in what Paul was now referring to as *The Bruce McMouse Show*. Starting from the top of the set, on Monday, mixes were made of the 'Intro' and 'Eat at Home,' from the Hague, 'Bip Bop' from the same show, and 'The Mess' recorded in West Berlin. But the guitar solo in the Amsterdam performance of 'The Mess' had been deemed superior to the one recorded in West Berlin, so a mix was made of the solo only, and edited into the West Berlin recording. All the mixes were completed in a single pass, except for the West Berlin 'Mess,' which required two, plus a third covering only its introduction.

The Tuesday session took up the Hague performance of 'Wild Life,' with two mixes completed (neither marked "best," a choice Paul could make later). The Hague recording of 'Mary Had a Little Lamb' was mixed twice as well, the second of which had the final section slowed down. Single mixes of the Groningen and Amsterdam performances of 'Blue Moon of Kentucky' completed the day's work.

That left the more complicated mixes for the final session. Starting with 'I Am Your Singer,' from the Hague, which got three complete mixes, plus a fourth to bring out the maracas in one section of the song, and a fifth devoted to the postperformance applause. 'My Love,' also from the Hague, was mixed twice, and 'Maybe I'm Amazed,' from Groningen, was mixed once, with edit pieces from The Hague and West Berlin performances each mixed once, as well. 'Hi, Hi, Hi' and 'Long Tall Sally,' each mixed once, completed the mixes for the film.

—

Chevrolet's sponsorship of *James Paul McCartney* bought it the first global screening of the show, on ABC television in the United States, on Monday, April 16, 1973. It also bought at least a limited right to interfere. Besides nixing Paul's notion of performing 'Gotta Sing, Gotta Dance' in drag, the company insisted that 'Hi, Hi, Hi' be removed from the concert sequence, because its message was inconsistent with the family-friendly spirit Chevrolet believed it was paying to project. That meant that in Britain, where the BBC had banned the single, 'Hi, Hi, Hi' would be included in the ITV broadcast, but in America, where there had been no such ban, it was absent.

Inevitably, quite a few songs were dropped from the photo shoot and concert sequences when the show, which reportedly cost £200,000 ($495,000),[9] was edited to fit a one-hour time slot (or 53 minutes in the American version, to allow for commercials). The final running order [with Britain-only clips in brackets] was:

OPENING SEQUENCE

ATV logo, Introduction
'Big Barn Bed'—Wings

PHOTO SHOOT SCENE

'Blackbird,' ['Bluebird,'] 'Michelle,' 'Heart of the Country'—Paul and Linda

OUTDOOR SHOT

'Mary Had a Little Lamb'—Wings

STUDIO PERFORMANCES (MIMED)

'Little Woman Love' and 'C Moon' medley—Wings
'My Love'—Wings and Jack Parnell Orchestra

CONCEPT VIDEO

'Uncle Albert'—Paul and Linda

LIVERPOOL PUB SCENE

'It's a Long Way to Tipperary,' 'April Showers,' 'California Here I Come,'
'Pack Up Your Troubles' and 'You Are My Sunshine'—pub crowd

DANCE ROUTINE

'Gotta Sing, Gotta Dance'—Paul, Dance Ensemble, Ladybirds, Jack Parnell Orchestra

CINEMA SCENE

'Live and Let Die'—Wings and Jack Parnell Orchestra

BEATLES MEDLEY

'When I'm Sixty-Four,' 'A Hard Day's Night,' 'Can't Buy Me Love,'
'She Loves You,' 'Ob-La-Di, Ob-La-Da,' 'Yellow Submarine'—Men and Women in the Street

CONCERT SEQUENCE (LIVE)

'The Mess,' 'Maybe I'm Amazed,' ['Hi, Hi, Hi,'] 'Long Tall Sally'—Wings

FINALE

'Well, That's the End of Another Day' (fragment), 'Yesterday'—Paul

It was, all told, an old-time variety show, but corny moments aside, it offered several treats for McCartney fans, not least a handful of previously unheard songs—'Bluebird,' 'Gotta Sing, Gotta Dance,' and 'Live and Let Die.' (The fragment preceding 'Yesterday' was an ad-lib that Paul did not pursue further.) *Red Rose Speedway* would be in the shops before the British airing on May 10, but it had not been released in time for the American broadcast, so viewers in the United States also had their first hearing of 'Big Barn Bed' in its full-band version.

There was a downside to the 24-day gap between the American and British broadcasts: American-based writers for British papers could send back advance word—and indeed, Linda Solomon filed a long review to *NME* from New York, in which she concluded that "although there were some fleeting musical diversions, the overall production was low level rubbish, a waste of time, energy and money."[10]

Michael Watts, filing from New York for *Melody Maker*, liked the show better, but his praise was backhanded. "McCartney, perhaps realizing he's ill-equipped for intellectual aspirations, has rather astutely followed a natural bent and become, in that well-worn expression, an 'entertainer.'"[11]

Nor were American reviewers especially generous. Robert Hilburn offered a calmly reasoned slam in the *Los Angeles Times*, wistfully comparing the "traditional, middle of the road, decidedly 'show business' stance of the special" with the vigor and originality of the Beatles television appearances. "Unlike the Beatles at their best, McCartney has adapted himself to television rather than try to adapt television to himself in any imaginative way." With a measure of contrarian perverseness, he proclaimed the pub scene and the street performances the show's "most effective moments."[12]

The *New York Times* assigned the show not to a music critic, but to its television reviewer, John J. O'Connor. Taking McCartney's artistry as a given, O'Connor praised the 'Big Barn Bed' opener and the concert segment, but found the production as a whole little more than "a series of disconnected routines." McCartney, he wrote, "really doesn't need a nonstop flow of gimmicks."[13]

But the review that drew blood was the one Lillian Roxon wrote for the *New York Sunday News*. Roxon, an Australian based in New York, was the author of the 613-page *Lillian Roxon's Rock Encyclopedia* (1971), the most comprehensive rock reference book of its time, and an influential columnist for the *New York Daily News*. She had also been one of Linda's closest friends—Linda had, in fact, taken the jacket portrait for her encyclopedia—and she was deeply hurt when Linda moved to London to be with Paul and failed to keep in contact with the New York circle. "We used to gossip a lot," Roxon told an interviewer in 1970. "I wonder if she has someone to gossip with these days? I don't. I miss her."[14]

Three years later, her feelings toward Linda were angrier, and rather than recuse herself, she reviewed the show and went directly for her former friend's jugular. In the pub scene, she wrote, Linda seemed "positively catatonic with horror at having to mingle with ordinary people," adding that "she didn't marry a millionaire Beatle to end up in a Liverpool saloon singing 'Pack Up Your Troubles in Your Old Kit Bag' with middle-aged women called Mildred."

For Roxon, Paul ("congenial and friendly as all get out") was a secondary focus. "Not a soul I talked to afterwards could remember the names of most of the songs in *James Paul McCartney*, but they certainly had names for Linda's varied hair arrangements—her Stevie Wonder multi-braid, her Los Angeles groupie Moulin Rouge topknot, her modified Bette Midler 40s page-boy, and her quite unforgettable David Bowie split-level crewcut"[15]—the last of which would have particularly stung, since Linda had mixed feelings about the Bowie-like results of a haircut Paul gave her in Marrakesh.*

---

* Lillian Roxon died at age 40 on August 9, 1973, less than four months after the review was published. Craig McGregor, in a 1970 *New York Times* article about *Lillian Roxon's Rock Encyclopedia*, described her as "the mistress of the put-down and the send-up, the come-on and the come-uppance, the double-faced about-turn and the blunt, uncompromising insult. She blurts out what she thinks with impossible, calculating honesty, reels off aphorisms, bon mots and salacious insights like a virtuoso and treats life as an exercise in instant improvised Drama, a Hairy happening."

By the time of the British airing, on May 10, Paul had absorbed the spanking that American critics had administered and prepared a response that distanced him from the show without quite disowning it.

"I suppose you could say it is fulfilling a very old ambition," he said. "Right at the start I fancied myself in musical comedy. But that was before the Beatles. Then I forgot all about it until we were deciding what to do in the show. But don't get me wrong, this is just a lark. I'm no Fred Astaire or Gene Kelly, and this does not mean the start of something big. I do not want to be an all-rounder: I'm sticking to what I am."[16]

Some of the British reviewers, who were more *au fait* with the dry British humor presented in the show, were open to Paul's song-and-dance man side. "If ever there was a man who understood what pop is," Rick Sanders wrote in *Record Mirror*, "it must be him—nothing ever gets too heavy, there's always a touch of the mickey-take to prevent a complete topple into dreadful schmaltz. The show, which is basically light entertainment and no more, is a showcase for Paul's amazing ability to be all things to all men, women and little lambs." [17]

Alan Coren, in *The Times*, seemed actually offended by the show. Referring to the amateurs singing Beatles' tunes, he wrote, "When, derisorily almost, snatches of that good music were played last night, parodied, shrugged over, thrown away, what could one feel but cheated by an artist so obviously bored with his own best material? Paul McCartney may wish to shake his old persona, and good luck, but to do it at the expense of the affection most of us feel for that early identity amounts to something very like an insult."[18]

Clive James, in the *Observer*, was too aghast to devote more than half a paragraph to the show, simply noting in passing that "the monstro-horrendo, superschlock-diabolical special on McCartney (ATV) burgeoned before the terror-stricken eye like a punctured storage tank of semolina."[19]

For anyone who wondered what John Lennon thought of the show, he offered his opinion, briefly and in passing, later in the year. "I liked parts of his TV special, especially the intro," he told *Melody Maker*. "The bit filmed in Liverpool made me squirm a bit, but Paul's a pro. He always has been."[20]

———

Recording Sessions

Wednesday–Thursday, April 25–26, and Monday, May 7, 1973.
EMI Studios, Studio Two, London.
Recording: 'Zoo Gang,' 'Rock and Roll Rodeo,' and 'Leave It.'

Wings were technically still on hiatus, but as soon as Paul returned from Jamaica, he wanted to discharge his other obligation to ATV by recording his theme for 'Zoo Gang.' Given that both the theme and the television special were essentially sweeteners for Paul's new publishing deal with Lew Grade's company—which itself was McCartney's and Grade's settlement of ATV's lawsuit alleging that Linda could not have cocomposed 'Another Day'—Grade's announcement of the project was extraordinary.

"This will be the first theme music that Paul and Linda McCartney have written for any television series," Grade crowed to the press, "and we are delighted that we have been able to get this exceptionally talented couple to be associated with the series."[21] (Grade was less eager to publicize the ATV/Northern Songs lawsuit against John Lennon and Yoko Ono that paralleled its earlier suit against the McCartneys.)[22]

Paul publicly embraced the idea of writing a television theme, no doubt with an eye on the residuals likely to accrue once the show began to air. "I like writing-to-order," he said, "particularly TV signature tunes and theme music. The idea of it being heard every week at the beginning of the program appeals to me."[23]

Paul booked two days at EMI, with Alan Parsons engineering. Besides 'Zoo Gang,' he wanted to produce and play on a couple of tracks with his younger brother, Michael, who had pursued his own musical career under the name Mike McGear—a name he chose in the early years of the Beatles' fame, arguing that "If I remained Mike McCartney, it would have been like being Mike Presley, or Mike Sinatra."[24] His band, the Scaffold, formed in 1962, mixed music, comedy, and even a bit of poetry—the Liverpool-born poet Roger McGough was a member—and was best known for oddball hits like 'Lily the Pink' and 'Thank U Very Much.'

In 1971, the Scaffold joined forces with Neil Innes and Viv Stanshall of the Bonzo Dog Doo-Dah Band to perform and record as Grimms, an acronym for the names of its members, (John) Gorman, (Andy) Roberts, Innes, McGear, McGough and Stanshall. By then, Mike had also released an album with McGough (*McGough and McGear*, 1968) and one on his own (*Woman*, 1972). *Woman* failed to breach the Top 40 albums in Britain, and Mike was worried that his contract with Island Records would not be renewed. Though he was not quite ready to record a follow-up, he and Paul agreed to work up a few songs that would serve as a showreel in his search for a new label.

Paul would have to work without the benefit of Wings for these sessions. Laine was still in Los Angeles, having extended his stay when singer-songwriter Dave Mason, late of Traffic, agreed to play on his album. McCullough was also unavailable, either because he was working with Chris Stainton and other members of the Grease Band, or simply because neither 'Zoo Gang' nor the Mike McGear recordings were Wings projects, and Henry was feeling sufficiently abused, financially and musically, that he was unwilling to surrender his downtime to play on Paul's side projects. Only Denny Seiwell agreed to participate.

Apart from its opening flourish—a winding descent in a French café style that returns twice as a section break—'Zoo Gang' is simple and direct, with a repeating two-note melody (a descending minor third—F and D) played on Linda's Minimoog, over a backdrop in which the chords shift with each repetition, giving the two-note theme a constantly changing harmonic context. But the real action is in the accompaniment, which alternates between a funky rhythmic figure, driven by Paul's bass, with bass drum pedal support (and sharp cymbal punctuation) from Denny, and short sections in which the focus is on the light-textured, twangy electric guitar chords, also played by Paul.

In a single session, on April 25, the basic track was perfected in 15 takes (the last being the keeper); an unused jam, 'Zoological Blow,' was recorded as well. Paul returned to the track on May 7 (with John Leckie taking over from Parsons) and finished it off with an accordion overdub that gave the introduction (and its reappearances) its French character—a necessary component, signaling the show's setting in World War II France. Stereo and mono mixes were made at AIR Studios on May 14, when the mono mix was also edited for television use—a version running just over a minute for the opening credits, and a 30-second version for the end of each episode.

The April 26 session was devoted to Mike, who invited a saxophonist, Tony Coe, to round out a lineup that included McGear on vocals, Paul on guitar and, with Linda, backing vocals, and Seiwell drumming. The first of the two songs they attempted, 'Rock and Roll Rodeo,' was abandoned after a few takes. But 'Leave It,' an upbeat, melodically catchy pop tune with a pun in its opening line—"*I dearly love her artichokes*," the vegetable also heard as "*arty jokes*"—had a more direct appeal.

"We went to my brother's house in London," Mike said of the song's genesis, "and sat around, the three of us [Mike, Paul and Linda] in his lounge, strumming a guitar. And, *ching-a-ching-ching*, [singing the chorus] '*leave it, leave it, leave it.*' Lin would come in with her bits, and I'd do my bits. And we thought, 'Right, we'll go into Abbey Road, and we'll just do it like a record.' So that song just came out of heaven, down to us."[25]

Mike's part in the composing process notwithstanding, 'Leave It' was published as a Paul and Linda McCartney song. It was not the first collaboration in which Mike's contribution went uncredited.

"I have one of the most unique pieces of paper," Mike explained, cryptically, "with one of my brother's most famous songs written on it. And he's left out a verse. It was on one of my school papers, it was that long ago. And if you flip it over, there in *my* schoolboy writing, in blue pen, are the rest of the words to that song."*

---

* Michael McCartney refuses to divulge the name of the song in question. But he was born on January 7, 1944, so if he was a schoolboy, the song would have been written in the late 1950s. Paul had written several songs by then, including 'I Lost My Little Girl,' 'Hot As Sun,' and 'Suicide,' but Mike's assertion that it was one of Paul's "most famous" songs eliminates most of those, leaving 'When I'm Sixty-Four'—

The basic track for 'Leave It' was completed in 12 takes, the last becoming the master. Paul and Mike returned to the song on May 7, after completing overdubs on 'Zoo Gang,' finishing the track with vocals, bass guitar, piano, acoustic guitar, backing vocals and percussion overdubs (some replacing the tracks recorded 11 days earlier). The song was mixed in sessions on May 23 and 30.* Though both Paul and Mike considered it a likely single (the May 30 mixes were labeled as such), 'Leave It' was shelved until Mike's contractual situation with Island Records was resolved.

———▸

To Paul's annoyance, *Red Rose Speedway* had been hanging fire for more than two months, mainly because EMI did not want too many new Beatles-related releases on the market at once, and its principal interest was shifting copies of *The Beatles 1962–1966* and *The Beatles 1966–1970*. The fact that EMI's plans to release those sets also factored into the reduction of the Wings album to a single disc made the delay even more galling, particularly as MPL had to explain the delay to fans who were expecting the album. Paul announced, through the Fun Club, that complications to do with the album's cover art and booklet had held up the release.

The upside of the delay, for Paul, was that by the time *Red Rose Speedway* was released, on April 30 in the United States, and four days later in Britain, 'My Love' was getting a tremendous amount of airplay; *Cash Box* reported that the single was on the playlists of 99 percent of the top-40, pop, rock stations in the United States,[26] piquing interest in the album.

Though it had detractors, the *Red Rose Speedway* fared generally well with critics who had largely slammed *McCartney*, *Ram*, and *Wild Life*. The weekly music trade press was typically cheerful, with *Cash Box* describing McCartney's latest work as "somewhere between quaint and romantic," and guessing it would "succeed in pleasing critics of [*Wild Life*] who missed the 'Yesterday' wistfulness of McCartney in it."[27] *Billboard*'s reviewer found it the "best effort from McCartney since his break with the Beatles, featuring powerful rock material as well as the great ballads he was so well known for."[28]

Among the dailies, Ian Dove, reviewing the album for the *New York Times*, found it McCartney's "best album to date, showing his busy little mind at work in many corners, from rock to country, all a little laid back, a little personal." Dove heard soul influences in 'My Love,' lightly rocked coun-

---

written around 1958—as a prime candidate.

* It is unclear whether Paul attended the May 23 session. He was in London, between concerts on Wings' British tour, but he flew to Edinburgh that day for early and late shows at the Odeon. Unless the mixing session was held at an uncommonly early hour, and was relatively short, it is unlikely (though not impossible) that he could have overseen the mixing and flown to Edinburgh in time for a sound check and an early concert.

trthe in 'One More Kiss' and pure sentiment (but also a "winsome melody") in 'When the Night.' And he admired the simplicity of 'Single Pigeon,' which he found "the best title on the album."[29]

But Robert Hilburn, at the *Los Angeles Times*, took a dyspeptic view, not least because the album frustrated Hilburn's hunch that after three disappointing albums and "that bland television special," *Red Rose Speedway* was likely to be worthy, McCartney being "simply too proven a talent to continue producing material so far below expectations." Alas, the album struck him as "a careful, cautious, low-keyed effort, one that repeatedly tells us McCartney is in love, but doesn't offer any fresh or inviting treatment of the theme." Still, he found two highlights: 'Get on the Right Thing,' for its "steady, snappy background vocal that bites out the title phrase," and 'Single Pigeon,' which he found the album's most poignant song.[30]

In the *Chicago Tribune*, Lynn Van Matre, intent on offering a contrarian view that represented a particular corner of the rock world, opened her review by declaring, "To tell the truth, I don't give a damn whether the Beatles get back together or not." Characterizing McCartney's post-Beatles work as "continuing in the tradition of those songs that didn't work on the *White Album* and turning out bland ballady banalities and bubble gum that smacks no less of stickiness for being Beatle-blown," she found that his new album "continues along the same track, for better or worse—mostly worse." Among Van Matre's few specific complaints are McCartney's repetitive lyrics—for example, "'Get on the Right Thinking' [*sic*] repeated several score in several minutes" (though not enough, apparently, for her to get its title right).[31]

Lenny Kaye's thoughtfully analytical review for *Rolling Stone* suggested that the publication had declared a cease-fire in its war on McCartney. Though he is not without criticism for McCartney's lyrics, and his "basic reliance on a rotating riff," he admires Paul's "skill as an arranger, his placement of instruments and the succession of movements he notches within any given tune. The hooks are never obvious, certainly not on the order of those soaring Beatlesque choruses, but after a while you might find yourself waiting for that pristine guitar figure, the drum interjection, the wash of background harmonies that are meticulously set in each piece."[32]

Of the British reviews, Henry would have given a thumbs-up to Caroline Boucher's observation, in *Disc*, that it seemed as if "those incredible musicians—the two Dennys and old Henry" were being "rather curbed—bloody shackled in fact." Citing only 'Hold Me Tight' ("the only song that lets go and rocks") and 'Little Lamb Dragonfly' (the only song in which "Paul's voice stretches to its full heights") as favorites, she concluded that "technically the album is very good, everybody plays very nicely and sings very nicely, but for the first couple of hearings it lacks light and shade and the repetitive technique of the songs hits you between the eyes."[33]

Tony Tyler took on the album for the *NME*, describing *Red Rose Speedway* as "lightweight," but hastening to add that this was a *good* thing: "With all the current heaviness and after-me-the-apocalypse brainstuds around, I for one am bloody pleased to discover a lightweight record that not only fails to alienate, but actually succeeds in impressing via good melodic structure, excellent playing and fine production." Calling it McCartney's best "since the Great Demise," he concludes: "Paul makes his stand here and as far as I'm concerned he's proved his point. And I also think that in the future he's going to be able to look back on the last three years without cringing—which is more than I suspect Lennon will be able to do."[34]

The album pleased listeners, too, giving Wings their first No. 1 album on the American charts. *Red Rose Speedway* broke into the *Billboard* 200 at No. 127, on May 12, and quickly ascended to the top spot, three weeks later. Wings' second LP stayed at the summit of the *Billboard* 200 for three weeks, and enjoyed a 31-week run in the top 200. In Britain, however, McCartney's post-Beatles hangover continued. *Red Rose Speedway* managed only 16 weeks in the British Top 100 albums, peaking at No. 5 on May 26.

———

At the end of April, Wings returned to the Manticore Theater, the Fulham rehearsal space they used to prepare for the European tour. There was now plenty of material to choose from—two albums, a handful of singles and a few unreleased tunes (including the hard-rocking 'Soily' and Linda's reggae workout, 'Seaside Woman'), plus a couple of Denny Laine songs, and Little Richard's 'Long Tall Sally,' a proven favorite on Wings tours, not only because it offered a connection to the Beatles (without being a Beatles original), but also because Paul's high-energy delivery was never less than sizzling.

In the post-Klein era, Paul's insistence on avoiding the Beatles songbook was wavering, and Laine, Seiwell and McCullough all let it be known that they would enjoy having a bash at those classics. At Manticore, Paul let them give it a shot. They revisited the version of 'The Long and Winding Road' they had played during the *James Paul McCartney* concert set (but was omitted from the broadcast), as well as 'Let It Be.' But Paul soon called that exploration to a halt.

"We just couldn't get behind it," he said of Wings' attempt to work up a few Beatles songs, "it just wasn't good. You see, you have the danger of developing a second-rate Beatles. Even if you developed an incredible McCartney act, you could blow it by not keeping up with the times. Then you would get, 'Oh, they're a very nice nostalgic group,' and I don't want that . . . With this band I am tending to write things to perform."[35]

For this tour, Paul wanted to present a more expansive show than Wings played in Europe. For starters, he wanted to bring along a support band and had settled on Brinsley Schwarz shortly after he saw them at the Hard Rock Cafe. He was introduced to the band then but did not spend much time with the five musicians—guitarists Brinsley Schwarz and Ian Gomm, bassist Nick Lowe, keyboardist Bob Andrews and drummer Billy Rankin. Known for rich vocal harmo-

MᶜCARTNEY PRODUCTIONS LIMITED
I SOHO SQUARE
LONDON WIV 5DE
01-437 1659

Dave Robinson Esq.,
Wilton Park Farm,
Beaconsfield,
BUCKS

12 June 1973

Dear Dave,

Please accept this letter as confirmation that we would
like to engage Brinsley Schwartz for the forthcoming
WINGS tour, commencing 4th July in Sheffield. We also
confirm that we will pay you £125.00 each night and I
enclose our list of the tour dates and venues.

Sincerely,

Vincent Romeo
VINCENT ROMEO

nies in the style of Crosby, Stills and Nash, and for a combination of original songs and oldies, Brinsley's sound was distinctive, but not miles away from the esthetic Wings were exploring. Romeo contacted Dave Robinson, the band's manager—formerly the manager of Eire Apparent, Henry's old band—offering Brinsley Schwarz £125 ($310) per show.[36] That came out to £25 ($62) per player (before Robinson's fee), so in effect, every three shows, the Brinsley players each topped the weekly salary McCartney paid Seiwell, Laine and McCullough. During the tour's final week, when there were seven shows, the Brinsleys each earned £175 ($435), compared with Wings' £70 ($175).

Paul also wanted the shows to have an old-time variety atmosphere, so he needed something more than a pair of bands. His plan included engaging a local comedian at every stop, who would do short sets before Brinsley Schwarz and Wings and serve as compere. And he hired the O'Keefes, a husband-and-wife circus act, whose routine included juggling, tap dancing and acrobatics with their poodle, to entertain while the roadies reset the stage between the Brinsley Schwarz and Wings sets.

Expanding on the Paolozzi and Jones commissions for the group's latest LP, Paul personally contacted Derek Bamforth, the owner of Bamforth & Co.—the postcard firm whose titillating handiwork had inspired the unreleased McCartney song 'Blackpool'—to commission an eye-catching concert poster. Paul was reminded of the firm on November 6, when BBC One aired a documentary about the West Yorkshire company's historic filmmaking past and provocative postcard-making present. Paul simply requested that the design exude Britishness.

The poster Bamforth produced was designed by Philip W. Taylor and featured a quintessentially British seasider—a bald, corpulent man in a blue suit and gold waistcoat, with rolled-up trousers, carrying a bucket with sand pouring from it, and a spade—with the sea behind him and seagulls in the sky. The right side of the poster had a portrait of Wings and the legend, "Paul McCartney & Wings on Tour." Any effort to market the tour on the group name alone was abandoned when Romeo insisted that the former Beatle's name be included on the bill.

Two program books were produced. The first, a monochrome, eight-page pamphlet, included three full-page photos (Paul, both McCartneys and a band portrait), an outdated biography (it is updated to include *Red Rose Speedway*, but notes that Wings was formed "last summer"), individual photos of each player with the same "vital statistics" that were projected during the 'Big Barn Bed' sequence of *James Paul McCartney*, and a page with both the tour itinerary and a truncated discography. The second, with the Bamford beachgoer on the cover, was a 12-page color production, illustrated with elements from the *Red Rose Speedway* jacket and booklet. It included an interview with the band, a more up-to-date biography and pages devoted to the itinerary and a more expansive discography.

There would be no messing about with antique, slow-moving double-decker buses this time. Paul ordered a coach from Foxes of Hayes, the company that supplied the one the Beatles used in *Magical Mystery Tour*, to ferry Wings, Brinsley Schwarz and the O'Keefes (dog included) from city to city.

———

The rehearsal period had a few interruptions. Realizing that David Bowie was also rehearsing at the Manticore Theater, Paul and Linda stopped by to watch him work. Wings also spent a few days at Twickenham Film Studios. Roger Cherrill had booked Twickenham to shoot material for *The Bruce McMouse Show*. The set was built over a 48-hour period on April 30 and May 1, and Wings spent May 2 through 4 shooting the between-songs links and the band-and-rodent conversations that would be edited with European tour footage.

Since Paul's edit suite epiphany of enlivening his concert film with the exploits of the animated McMouse family—Bruce, his wife Yvonne, and children Soily, Swoony, and Swat—the director, Barry Chattington, had hired a five-strong team of animators, to sketch out the (as yet unclear) story. The team, led by former Walt Disney trainee Eric Wylam, included Eddie Radage, Richard Cox (both of whom worked on *Yellow Submarine*), George Jackson, and Alan Gray.

With the animators busy designing the characters and backgrounds, McCartney and Chattington got to grips with a loose narrative for the rodent family. Illustrator and cartoonist Gray Joliffe, creator of *Chloe & Co.* for the *Daily Mail*, was brought in to develop the story, but soon found himself marginalized, and his services unneeded: Paul was keen on devising the plot himself.

"I had a couple of writers on it at one point," Chattington explained. "[But] none of the writers seemed to work out. I mean, they all wanted it to go in some way or other. And I think, in the end, we wrote it ourselves."[37]

McCartney's and Chattington's concept was uncomplicated: Bruce McMouse, an old-time music business impresario shares stories of his past with his family below the stage, when his son runs in to announce Wings are playing a concert above them. A couple of tunes later, Bruce declares his intention to produce Wings and visits the group onstage.

But when it came time for man and mouse to come face-to-face, things got complicated. Blending live action and animation in the same frame required precision filming and animating. And for the band, it meant interacting with invisible characters.

"Yeah, my acting debut, I've been trying to block that all these years," Seiwell unwillingly remembered. "We had dialogues with these imaginary cartoon characters standing in our hands, and it was really hard to do, with 50 people around, and cameras. And the director would say, 'Do it again. Again. Keep going.' I had no idea what they wanted. I had no training in it. It was awful."

There was, however, an upside.

"One day they needed Linda to do something on the set," Seiwell continued, "and Paul came into the dressing room, with just the guys. It was probably the only time, ever, that he was alone with us, without Linda, and we had a right hang. He told us about some of the stuff that went on behind the scenes with the Beatles—picking out the girls at the end of the night, stories he couldn't tell with Linda around. It was kind of cool."[38]

———

Wings' final rehearsals for their British tour were on May 8 and 9. Paul worked out an hour-long set list that was actually a series of two- and three-song segments, occasionally separated by single-song palette cleansers. The show would begin with a burst of hard-stomping energy, by way of 'Soily' and 'Big Barn Bed,' before lightening up for the bittersweet pop of 'When the Night.'

'Wild Life' and 'Seaside Woman,' holdovers from the European tour, made a handful of points that were important to Paul and Linda: the first brought their animal conservation message into the set, the second put the spotlight on reggae, and not incidentally, on Linda as a songwriter and singer.

The B side medley of 'Little Woman Love' and 'C Moon,' worked up for the ATV special, followed, adding some rollicking rock and another taste of reggae; and 'Live and Let Die,' due out soon as a single, brought some musical drama to the set. A pair of Paul's songs for Linda, 'Maybe I'm Amazed' and 'My Love' (the latter still cruising up the chart) gave way to two songs with Laine as the front man, the Moody Blues hit, 'Go Now,' and his 'Say You Don't Mind.'

The rocking home stretch—'The Mess,' 'Hi, Hi, Hi' and, as an encore, 'Long Tall Sally,' with a bluesy solo guitar intro by Henry—brought the mood full circle. And reviving a quirky moment from the university tour, an a cappella rendering of a folk song (usually 'Turkey in the Straw,' sometimes the melodically similar 'The Wee Tobacco Box'), lasting under a minute, was placed between two of the song groups, usually after 'Seaside Woman,' sometimes after Laine's miniset.

There is a sub-rosa protest against the trimming of *Red Rose Speedway*, here: three songs from the single album were included, as were three that had been discarded.

Wings took the day off on May 10, while Ian and Trevor loaded the group's equipment into a truck that would travel in tandem with the tour bus. Paul brought his Rickenbacker bass, an Acoustic 360 bass amp, and a Marshall speaker stack. He also had an Epiphone semiacoustic guitar that was not used in the show, but kept on hand for the kind of offstage noodling that sometimes led to new songs.

Henry would play his signature Gibson Les Paul Custom electric guitar through an Ampeg V2 amp and V4 cabinet. Laine's guitar was a Fender Telecaster, but since he played bass when Paul was at the piano, he brought both a Fender Jazz bass and a Fender Mustang, which he would play through an Ampeg combination that matched Henry's. Seiwell brought his 24-inch Gretsch kit, and Linda's keyboard setup included an RMI electric piano, Paul's Fender Rhodes, her Minimoog and a Mellotron M400, played through a Fender Twin Reverb stack.

The Mellotron was an odd addition to the band's kit. Linda would be using the model 400, a portable form of the instrument, introduced in 1970. The 400 could not only play sampled orchestral instruments from its built-in library, but could also record new sounds.

But Wings did not use the Mellotron to replicate the orchestration on 'My Love' or 'Live and Let Die.' Those parts, especially the latter, with its jagged rhythms, quick figuration and need for precision timing, were well beyond Linda's technique. But her experience on the European tour—the savage reviews she received for singing out of tune, and especially, the memory of the wag in Châteauvallon who, when Paul complained of a nonworking microphone, called out "give it to your missus"—inspired Paul to use the Mellotron as a fail-safe.

"What he did was, he had a Mellotron with them with all their vocal harmony parts on it," explained Brinsley Schwarz guitarist Ian Gomm. "So, you press a key and they go, '*Ahh.*' On a bad night, he'd look at her and say, 'Mellotron,' and she'd mime to the recorded part. The other boys would be happy then, because she was in tune."[39]

Also carted along in the equipment truck was the band's new custom-designed PA system, built for the group by RSE (Rodgers Studio Equipment); a strobe light setup, for use during the energetic instrumental sections of 'Live and Let Die,' and boxes of giant balloons and Frisbees, emblazoned with a Paul McCartney and Wings logo, to be thrown to the audiences by Ian and Trevor on either side of the O'Keefes' set and at the end of the show.

Wings' mainstay roadies were joined on the tour by a British road crew, put together by a man who knew a thing or two about lugging Paul's guitars and amps around concert halls: former Beatles aide Mal Evans.

———

Because some of the dates were within striking distance of London, there were nights when the coach returned to the city, although in most cases the performers stayed at hotels. That meant that Heather, Mary and Stella could, individually, sit out a few stops, staying with Rose at Cavendish Avenue and rejoining the tour later. When Wings and Brinsley Schwarz stayed in London, everyone but Paul and Linda would meet at the Notting Hill tube station.

"Someone worked out," Gomm explained, "that it was the only tube station with a bar that was open all day, and of course, Henry had to have his first fix in the morning."[40] They would then swing by Cavendish Avenue to pick up Paul and Linda.

But on the first day of the tour, May 11, 1973—the morning after ITV's airing of the *James Paul McCartney* special—Paul and Linda were on the bus before anyone else, ready to greet each of the Brinsley Schwarz players by name, Paul saying how happy he was to have them along. Billy Rankin, Brinsley's drummer, vividly remembers his reaction. "There he was, your idol, sitting right in front of you. Wow."[41]

Ian Gomm was less starstruck. "After a while," he said, "the novelty wore off and it was just like going to work. Paul and Linda would sit at the back of the coach, and I would, too, because I wasn't a drinker or a gambler, and the rest of the Brinsleys would be playing cards to while the time way. So one day, I thought, 'Why don't I just go have a chat with him? When will I ever have this chance again?' We'd sit there talking for hours, not about music, just about life in general and things like that. We got on really well."

Well enough, in fact, for Paul to designate Gomm as his stash-minder.

"He was saying, 'I'm really worried, because if I get done again . . .' and all that. I said, 'I'll look

after it for you.' He must have trusted me, because he thought it was a good idea. I said, 'Just tip us a nod and I'll slip it to you right when you need it,' and I added, 'All right if I have a bit?' He said, 'Yeah, fine.' So I'm on this bloody tour, smoking Paul McCartney's dope!"[42]

The opening gig was at the Hippodrome, in Bristol. Upon arrival, Paul and Linda did their best to dodge the press, but a couple of reporters caught up with them and were granted a short interview. Mostly, they were asked about the Beatles, and Paul gave his standard response—"We are all doing our own thing now, and enjoying it"—but suggested that Wings might play acoustic versions of a few Beatles tunes.[43]

James Belsey, a reporter from the *Bristol Evening Post*, also caught up with Denny Laine and was given a hint of one of the frustrations within Wings. After a set piece about how much the band was looking forward to playing for British audiences, Laine mused about the group's billing, as Paul McCartney and Wings. "Paul is who he is, and you can't get away from a name like that. None of us would want to, either. We accept it. But we're all hoping—Paul included—that at the end of the tour we'll be known as Wings and nothing else."[44]

Reporters from both the local and national press were plentiful. They noted that the Hippodrome was packed with McCartney fans from as far away as Texas, and that the show was orderly but for a surge into the aisles that security tried in vain to stop.

"McCartney showed that he's got the lungs and the onstage ability to keep the spotlight without much bother," Belsey reported in the Bristol paper, adding that Wings "kept up a driving wall of sound with few surprises, but lots of quality."[45] But the highlights, for him, were not the McCartney songs, but Denny Laine's 'Go Now' and 'Say You Don't Mind,' which he performed from the keyboard.

By contrast, Judith Simons, one of the British critics most consistently supportive of Paul, fawned over his star power (which, she said, overshadowed the rest of the band) and his "matey smile and intimate linking patter," and described his overall effect as "pleasant, polished and polite rather than wild."[46] But Simons did not mention a single song and concluded her review with plea for a Beatles reunion.

The most in-depth coverage of the show was Tony Palmer's review in the *Observer*. "Certainly, Wings on stage is an altogether different sound from Wings on record. The latter is tame, even lame, whereas the former is undeniably vigorous and invigorating. The music is determined to be rock 'n' roll and, if nothing else, Wings give a superb parody of an old-style rock 'n' roll band: shrieks, runs down the keyboard and all. It's a solid bash all the way."

Palmer had seen Wings perform in Europe and found those performances more promising. In Europe, he wrote, "Wings seemed also to be striving towards a new, free-flowing contrapuntal rock 'n' roll, but that has been abandoned. Now it's playing-to-the-gallery time, with McCartney bopping like fury from start to finish," to which he added: "When McCartney runs out of rock 'n' roll steam and accompanies himself on piano in an exquisite number like 'C Moon,' the man as a songwriter stands head and shoulders above all his contemporaries. But when he leaps around the stage in an ever-increasing frenetic attempt to make energy a substitute for artistry, there is cause for regret."

Only Palmer, among the reviewers, lit into Linda. "And, though McCartney's wife clearly gives him a good deal of moral support, should he allow her into the band? Her sole contribution as a keyboard player during the opening number was one note."[47]

As a way of discouraging the national press from covering the first show, so that Wings could work through opening-night jitters without the glare of publicity, EMI laid on buses from their offices at 20 Manchester Square ("leaving at 5 p.m. sharp") to bring about 30 journalists to the second show, the following evening at the New Theater, in Oxford. A postconcert press conference and party at the Randolph Hotel (also on EMI's dollar) were an added inducement.

Apart from a few amusing blunders—Seiwell causing a momentary timing glitch when a stick flew out of his hand during 'My Love,' and Henry, already inebriated, falling over at the end of 'Live and Let Die'—the show went well, and the audience, which at first responded sedately, grew increasingly energized, eventually flooding toward the stage for the closing group of rockers. Long after the final chords of 'Long Tall Sally,' the crowd remained, calling for more, until Paul came out to say, "Listen, we haven't got any more songs for you, so thanks a lot for being a great audience, and we'll see you when we come back—Ta."[48]

The critics were happy, too. Chris Charlesworth admitted in *Melody Maker* that he had gone expecting the worst, partly because he had found the band disappointing in Europe, but mostly because the *James Paul McCartney* special had left him feeling that McCartney was now "a rather bland show business artist angling for a place in the Tom Jones field of music." The Oxford show changed his mind enough to declare that "Paul has, at last, shaken off the post-Beatles stigma which has hampered his every move over the last three years," and that Wings proved themselves "a group to reckon with."[49]

Rick Sanders, of *NME*, was similarly won over after having all but written off McCartney after the TV special. "Any fears that Paul might follow his TV spectacular on the schmaltzy side of his talents," he wrote, "were dispelled as the show rolled on and it became increasingly apparent that what Wings are all about is good, tightly-rehearsed rock and roll. Just as they promised, there's no ego-tripping solo virtuosity but the traditional short, well-arranged song. It's like turning the clock back to hear vocals that aren't running a poor second to a thunderous roar of amplification, and, unlike most bands, Wings paced their act to perfection—fast and slow, meaty and lighter numbers were blended to maximum effect."[50]

But at the postconcert party at the Randolph Hotel, things went off the rails. The party was to include a press conference, for which Paul and Linda arrived an hour late, giving the assembled journalists ample time to down drinks at the open bar and mingle with Henry and the two Dennys.

Among the assembled writers was Paul Gambaccini, attending on behalf of *Rolling Stone* and not impressed by his British colleagues.

"The Beatle and the Wings seated themselves on a couch with a wall behind them and a table in front, and immediately got swarmed by uncounted reporters," he wrote. "It was an extremely rude performance by the press, who treated the McCartneys the way vultures regard carrion."*

The questions were mostly the usual ones about whether the Beatles are getting back together, what Paul thought of John's work ("Good luck to him . . . We'd rather listen to Stevie Wonder, or reggae"), or John's attacks on him ("When John said those things after we broke up, I said, he's really slagging me, but then I realized it was his problem and not mine"), or even

---

* After covering Wings in Oxford, Gambaccini began working to persuade Tony Brainsby that Paul should sit for a lengthy interview with *Rolling Stone*, like the one Lennon gave the publication in December 1970. "Paul, who was very familiar with the paper and with John Lennon's interview, agreed to my suggestion," Gambaccini wrote to Adrian Sinclair, in July 2017. But it took a while: the interview was conducted in six one-hour sessions, in London and New York, in Autumn 1973.

what he felt was "the most representative" Beatles album ("*Please Please Me*—Fourteen hours, boom, done").

But with the press already well-oiled, and apparently interested in one-upping each other with tough questions, the interview turned unusually aggressive. "You don't expect Wings to be as big as the Beatles, obviously not," one reporter asked Paul.

"Crap, 'obviously not,'" Paul responded. "The Beatles were guys coming down from Liverpool who wanted it a lot. Now I've got the lot. I want to play; I want to live; I want to have some fun."

With Paul clearly unfazed, reporters began tossing grenades at Linda.

"What do you say to people who say you're nothing, musically?"

But Linda was not biting either.

"I'm learning," she said, "I realize I'm starting, but the Beatles started at one point and learned to play and got better. I didn't get these criticisms before I married Paul, so they don't bother me now."

The follow-up was harsher. "Some people say you've destroyed Paul. How have you helped?" to which a stunned Linda said, "I helped him most when the Beatles broke up. He went through a bad period; his whole band was gone. I was there to help him."[51]

But the real fireworks started when the press conference ended, and the party resumed. The hotel had commissioned an ice sculptor to make a large centerpiece—an eagle, painted gold, its wings spread as a reference to the evening's honored guests, and plates stacked around it on the serving table. Henry took a dinner plate, and inspired by the Wings Frisbees, sent it sailing across the room, where it connected with Brinsley Schwarz's upper lip.

"It split Brinsley's lip wide open and there was blood pouring out everywhere," Ian Gomm recalled. "So, Brinsley got rushed to hospital, at which stage our drummer, Billy Rankin, goes up to this golden eagle. Everybody's looking at it, saying, 'Is it ice or not? It can't be, can it?' So Bill put his finger on it, to see if it was, and he knocked the bloody thing off the table."

The ice sculptor, who had spent days perfecting his now shattered eagle, came running over, cursed a blue streak, threw his beer mug to the floor, and stormed out of the hotel.

"Then a fight started between him and Billy on the pavement outside the hotel," Gomm added. "It was like bedlam."[52]

That was not the end of it for Brinsley Schwarz. Back in London, Romeo had taken an anguished call from the hotel manager, and since disciplining Henry would have involved tangling with Paul over one of his band members, he laid the full blame for the evening's mayhem at the feet of the support band. When they arrived in Cardiff, Wales, to play at the Capitol Cinema and Theater, the next day, a note from Romeo awaited the Brinsleys, bearing the terse message, "I've made sure you boys never work in show business again."[53]

The show went on without a hitch that night, Wings filling the theater's 2,500 seats, and winning an enthusiastic review from the local critic—who, nevertheless, took the time to wag a finger at Linda as the show's "only disappointment," noting that she "hardly justified her presence in the hard-working group."[54]

With no concert scheduled for May 14, the troupe returned to London after the show. Paul spent the day at EMI, mixing 'Zoo Gang,' and the five members of Brinsley Schwarz, on the advice of their manager, made their way to Soho Square and filed into Romeo's office. "We had to apologize to him on bended knee," Gomm recalled. "He forgave us, I think."

The Wings and the Brinsley musicians met the next morning at the Notting Hill tube station for travel lubrication, then hopped on the coach and rode to Cavendish Avenue. They waited for Paul and Linda, and then waited some more.

"We would all be sitting in the coach for a quarter of an hour," Gomm said, "and you'd start to say, 'What's happening?' [Rose] would come out and say, 'They'll be out shortly. They're just doing something.' Then another 10 minutes would go past, and she'd come out again. We'd say, 'Can we go? We're getting late now. Can we go?' She'd say, 'They'll be out in five minutes.' Then she'd come out again and say, 'They're nearly ready.' Eventually I said, *What the bloody hell is going on?*' and she said, 'Well, they're having a row in the kitchen.' A few minutes later they made it onto the coach, saying 'Morning! Morning!' They didn't know we'd been told what was going on."[55]

Wings and company traveled to Bournemouth for a performance at the Winter Gardens on May 15. Three concerts into the tour, the show was running smoothly—most of the time. Part of the O'Keefes' act involved their dog doing tricks, something the animal would only do if it was properly rewarded, typically with a pork pie. O'Keefe was in the habit of buying day-old pies at a discount, from pubs in the towns they visited, and storing them in the coach's refrigerator.

"One evening, he had an old stale pork pie for the dog," Gomm remembered. "Dave Robinson, our manager, was with us, and he comes in and says, 'God, I'm hungry today,' and he eats the pork pie. The O'Keefes went bananas. 'Where's the pork?' And the dog was going bananas, too. '*You ruined our act!*'"[56]

That night, after the concert, the Brinsleys were able to tap into some McCartney/Beatles magic. One of the roadies, playing armchair psychologist, told the group that McCartney had what he perceived as a mental block about playing Beatles songs. That was a misreading; it was a policy, not a block, but the Brinsley boys bought it.

"We hatched this little plan," Gomm explained. "After the show that night, we went to one of our rooms at the hotel, and Paul came around. I think it was two bottles of whisky mysteriously appeared. Of course, I'd been boning up on my Beatles songs, just in case. I was a big Beatles fan. So we were all sitting around, playing old rock and roll, this, that and the other. I started playing 'Love Me Do.' There were just two acoustic guitars—I had one, Paul had the other. He's left-handed, but he knew how to play a right-handed guitar upside down, a kind of mirror image. I think he was a bit pissed, to start, but he started playing it. When we got to the middle eight, I realized he was looking at me to see how it went. And I thought, 'Hang on, this is good! I think we've cracked it!' We took away the mental block."

They drew on the McCartney magic in a more practical way, too. One song Brinsley Schwarz were hoping to add to their set list was 'Please Don't Ever Change,' a Gerry Goffin–Carole King song that had been a hit in England for the Crickets—Buddy Holly's backing band—in 1960 and that was a staple of the Beatles repertory through 1963. But they were having trouble with it, and although they rehearsed it during sound checks, they did not consider it stage ready.

"It's a catchy tune but not straightforward," Nick Lowe remembered. "It was probably a bit ambitious for us back then. Nevertheless, we burnt a lot of our allotted sound check time wrestling the song's tricky harmonies and fancy chords into something we hoped would please the larger crowds. Unsettlingly, at first anyway, Paul would occasionally sit out front in the empty theater, listening to our efforts.

"One evening, after about a week of this, he stopped me in the corridor. He asked if I knew that one live performance was worth two days' rehearsal. I said I did (I didn't). He then suggested we stop fucking about and do the tune that night. I whinged about how we could play it and we could sing it but doing both at the same time was a bit of a stretch.

"Then he said, 'We used to do that song . . .'—I presumed by 'we' he meant the Beatles—'. . . so I know what you mean. But whenever this kind of problem cropped up with us, we had a little trick you could try. Stand at the back until just before you've got to start singing, then run up to the microphone and give it whatever you've got. It might still sound like shit, but it looks so cool that no one'll notice.' We followed his advice. It worked a treat that night, and I've been doing it ever since."[57]

From Bournemouth, the company moved on to Manchester for two shows (May 16 and 17) at the Hard Rock Concert Theater.

"He treated us to a banal string of Beatles oldies, other people's oldies, and the odd Wings original, including their current top twenty ditty, 'My Love,'" an unimpressed Barry Coleman shrugged in the *Guardian*. "Were it not for its author, this would be just another bad song, oozing cheap sentimentality. As it is, it comes as a firm statement that McCartney has moved out of the area of worthwhile music."

Exactly what songs were included in the "banal string of Beatles oldies" is anybody's guess, since the closest McCartney came to the Beatles repertoire was the Little Richard cover, 'Long Tall Sally.' Coleman found Wings, as a band, just okay, except for Linda, who came in for the full measure of opprobrium. "Linda McCartney, photographer, sang in a painfully flat howl," he wrote. "Her piano playing is crudely inept, and she was frequently defeated by the simple tambourine. No amount of kisses from the prince will turn her into a musician, and her unnecessary and ungainly presence on the stage amounts to contempt for the paying public."[58]

The emotional heart of the tour for Paul—and somewhere he could expect a warmer reception—was his hometown. Having failed to find a Liverpool venue to host Wings during the university tour, Wings scheduled two shows at the Empire Theater on May 18—Paul's first public performances in the city since he last played there with the Beatles, on December 5, 1965.

At one point during the show, he pointed to the upper reaches of the Empire's balcony and told his listeners, "I used to sit up there and listen to Cliff Richard." After the first show, he repaired to his dressing room, where he gave an interview to George Harrison (no relation), a *Liverpool Echo* reporter who had covered the Beatles when they were a hot local band.

"It's a funny feeling, coming back to Liverpool after so long away from the scene," Paul admitted. "I wasn't even sure how the folk would take me. But they were marvelous tonight. Fantastic. And when they started jiving in the aisles and jumping on the seats I just thought, 'This is where it all began.'"[59]

Between shows, members of the two bands took the opportunity to smoke a few "herbal jazz cigarettes" in the large dressing room several of the players shared. Within that dressing room was another, for Paul and Linda.

"There were joints being rolled on the table in front of us," Gomm recalled, "and I looked up to see a police sergeant and four constables walking in. I thought, 'This is it. This is all over.' But the door was open to Paul's dressing room, and all those guys just looked in at Paul. They didn't even bother looking at the table, and we had time to put it all away. That's the sort of effect he had on people."[60]

One man who missed the drama was guitarist Nick Lowe, who was in a pub around the corner drinking with the aspiring Scouse singer-songwriter Declan MacManus,* who Lowe met when the Brinsleys played at the Cavern the previous year. Distracted by the bottom of an empty beer glass, Lowe arrived at the Empire Theater late, leaving his bandmates to fill in for him until he walked onstage midway through the set.

Leeds Refectory was the only venue on the current tour that Wings had visited during the university tour. The appearance was noted, on posters for concerts at the Refectory, as Wings' "only university date in the country," and drew an audience of over 2,000.

This was where Linda froze, during the earlier visit, having forgotten the introductory chords to 'Wild Life.' Not so this time: she played the introduction confidently, and as Seiwell's drum roll crescendo gave way to Henry's power chords—the arrangement was now beefier than on the recording—that ghost was laid to rest.

Chris Oadkley, the *Yorkshire Evening Post*'s reviewer, remembered the earlier visit well enough

---

* Declan McManus, though unknown at the time, became globally famous as Elvis Costello after he was signed to Stiff Records and adopted his stage name in 1976.

to marvel at how far the band had come, and if he did not compare them directly, his description made the difference between the shows clear. "Wings don't just amble on and play, their whole show is a well-presented package from support group through to jugglers and an old-style rock 'n' roll compere to giant balloons floating down for the audience to play with in the interval."[61]

As in the other shows, the pacing of Paul's set list guided the temperature of the audience response, and by the end of the show, the crowd packed the aisles and pushed toward the stage, its calls for an encore beyond 'Long Tall Sally' particularly insistent. Paul's announcement that "We haven't got any more songs for you—that's the truth!" did nothing to quiet the audience, let alone persuade the crowd to leave, so he led Wings in a second, shorter performance of 'Long Tall Sally,' singing the first couple of verses and having the audience shout along with the bridge.

After a night off, the coach pressed on for Preston, where officials at the Guild Hall stopped the show early in the belief that concertgoers' foot-stomping was causing cracks in the ceiling of the foyer below the auditorium. It turned out to be nothing to do with Wings. When Colin Hotch-kiss, the consulting architect, inspected the hall and the foyer, the following day, he explained that the cracks were caused by the stage mechanism, which allowed sections of the platform to be raised and lowered. (It had been lowered for the show.)

"There is absolutely no cause for alarm. This fault is not in the concrete superstructure. It is just in the acoustic plaster," Hotchkiss told the *Lancashire Evening Post*, which made light of the incident in an article headlined "Wings Bring the House Down."[62]

Paul Rickman, the critic for the *Preston Evening Post and Chronicle*, was one of several critics to offer advice that Paul, by now, found as tiresome as it was predictable. "You can't help but conclude," Rickman wrote, "that to become great again, McCartney needs one thing. To work again with his fiercest critic. To have just the edge of his essential charm eroded away by the acid cynicism of John Lennon."[63]

———

With a concert in Newcastle postponed because of a scheduling conflict at the venue, Paul and Linda returned to London after the Preston show, spending May 22 in town and hiring a private jet to fly to Edinburgh, where the rest of the band awaited them. For £1,000 ($2,550), the McCartneys—Paul, Linda and all three girls—had the 79-seat BAC 1-11 jet, with two pilots and three stewardesses, to themselves. "It's the only way to travel," Paul quipped to a reporter at Gatwick Airport before boarding the plane.[64]

Wings and company played two shows at the Odeon before driving to Glasgow for a concert at Green's Playhouse, where Wings were given what Paul later described as a "ridiculous welcome there—kind of, really, a bit like the Beatles. Police outside, and crowds and stuff, the whole bit."[65]

Yet in Glasgow, as in several cities on the tour, there was no local news coverage of the concert—something that would have been unthinkable in the Beatle days.

The Brinsley Schwarz players, by now, had ample time to assess Wings close-up. In drummer Billy Rankin's estimation, "Denny Laine was a treat, such a sweet guy—absolute magic as a person, and a brilliant singer and great guitarist. Henry McCullough—you know, bit of a heavy drinker. Great guitarist, but a bit irrational, a bit too 'all over the shop' sometimes. And Denny Seiwell—super pro, incredibly expert. And I, being a drummer, it used to blow me brains out, how good he was.

"And then there was Linda, who couldn't—let's say she had a little trouble with her intonation is the nice way of putting it, and I would say she was a gifted amateur on keyboards. The rest of the guys were trying to be superprofessional, and then you'd hear this little bit of twee warbling for the keyboard. It wound them up. Well, it didn't wind Denny [Seiwell] up. He didn't care—he'd rock anywhere."[66]

Rumors that Wings were on the verge of a breakup trickled in during the tour. *Disc*, in its May 19 issue, quoted an anonymous source saying that Henry would be getting together a new band to back Joe Cocker. That might have been a belated and slightly skewed report about Henry's brief departure threat during the filming of *James Paul McCartney*.[67] A second rumor, reported in the May 26 issue of the *NME*, had both Henry and Denny Laine about to quit to form a new band, to be called the Rats. An MPL spokesman dismissed the report as "nonsense."[68]

The tour's home stretch was a three-night residency in London, at the Hammersmith Odeon, May 25 through 27. Wings abandoned the coach for the trip home, flying from Glasgow instead, and taking a bar-equipped coach from Heathrow into central London. The final night, actually, had been added at the last minute, after a concert planned for the 27th in Birmingham was canceled because of an electrical hazard at the Hippodrome. (A 15-ton water tank had been installed in the stage for a summer production, and the owners concluded that amplifiers and water were not a good mix.) The newly added London show sold out in a day.

Wings' set for the three shows was unchanged, but the final concert—to be followed by a party at the Café Royale—was a starry event, with some of the party invitees (among them, Rod Stewart and Elton John) spotted in the audience.

Reviewing that show for *Melody Maker*, Mark Plummer noted that "from their long tour of Britain, Wings have emerged as one of the most enjoyable and pleasing live bands around," praising the stylistic breadth of the band's setlist, as well as "McCartney's high-class vocals," and praising the strengths of each player, including Linda, whose "piano, Moog and Mellotron playing, along with her vocal harmonies," he wrote, have become "an important part of Wings' sound."[69]

As Wings played that last Hammersmith Odeon show, the Cavern—the Liverpool cellar club

where the Beatles (and their earlier incarnation, the Quarrymen) played nearly 300 shows between 1958 and 1963—closed its doors for the last time, as the original building was to be destroyed to make way for British Rail to build a ventilation shaft for a planned underground train.

Paul had received an invitation, during Wings' stop in Liverpool, to pay a final visit to the iconic venue before the bulldozers moved in, but he could not face crossing the threshold after a five-year absence, his last visit having occurred on October 25, 1968.

One Merseyside newspaper reported Paul had been spotted outside 20 Forthlin Road, the former McCartney family home, during the group's time in Liverpool. But descending the steps to the damp basement where the Beatles found fame was a reminiscence too far, and Paul made his excuses in an open letter to the *Liverpool Echo*.

"If it had been physically possible, I would certainly have gone along to the old Cavern to kiss goodbye. When I heard the Cavern had to go in the near future, I wanted to take the group with me on a farewell surprise visit for an hour, after our Empire show. But there just wasn't the time available. I'd have loved to have done it. After all, for the Beatles and a lot of other folk who eventually made it, the Cavern was where it all began."[70]

Paul was not looking backward. With the first leg of his British tour now concluded (more concerts, in July, were about to be announced), it was time to party. Or at least, for Wings, it was;

the Brinsley Schwarz crew played their set at the Hammersmith Odeon, then traveled to a pub in Kensington, where they performed for a few hours before returning to the tour-wrap party at the Café Royale.

"We went in, and it was a room full of *everybody*," Ian Gomm reminisced. "Imagine *Melody Maker* had come to life." Sipping pink champagne, Gomm and his colleagues took a quick inventory. Besides Elton John and Rod Stewart, there was Neil Sedaka, Cat Stevens, Keith Richards, Marc Bolan, Keith Moon, Gary Moore, Ronnie Wood—the list went on.

"I remember doing some bad stuff with Ronnie Wood," remembered Seiwell. "We drank them out of cognac, I know that. That was one hell of a party."[71]

Noticing a stage at one end of the café, and aghast that no music was being played, the Brinsleys made the audacious decision to provide some. Their two Glaswegian roadies, having already set up for the band twice that night, quit on the spot, leaving the Brinsleys to haul their own gear—although they were soon joined by other partygoers. "I remember seeing Marc Bolan carrying the tom-toms,"[72] Gomm recalled. The Brinsleys played a few songs, and then asked everyone to join them in a jam—an invitation several partyers took up, with Elton on the piano, McCartney playing bass, Keith Moon drumming and Gomm and Gary Moore wrestling for the lead guitar spot.

"That [tour] was a great number for us," Nick Lowe told an interviewer, soon after the tour concluded. "We really enjoyed it, and they were really nice to us. . . . They had a kind of poppy show, which is something we like, we're all pop fans, really, and they had this feel of being a very high-class pop band. We learnt a lot about that side of it."[73]

24

"HOW DARE YOU INCONVENIENCE US?"

—

Wings did not bother meeting for a posttour analysis, nor did they take a few days to decompress. Denny Laine flew to Los Angeles to continue work on his album at the Wally Heider Studios, and upon his return, in early June 1973, he would continue working at AIR. The Seiwells left for New York, by ship from Southampton, so that Denny could pick up a few weeks' freelance income. Henry returned to his cottage in Dymchurch, and Paul and Linda, after the May 30 mixing session for Mike's 'Leave It,' flew to Scotland. The group would meet again at the end of June.

Paul's first order of business was to celebrate the British release of Wings' new single, on June 1. (The American release followed on June 25.) This was a pairing of recordings that had been lying around for a while—understandably, in the case of the A side, 'Live and Let Die,' which had been completed in October 1972 but could not be released until the film was about to hit theaters. With the release now imminent, it was time to get Paul's theme onto the market. Brenda Arnau's version, on RCA Records, was released the same day.

For the B side, Paul selected 'I Lie Around,' finally ending that song's long gestation, which began at High Park in the spring of 1970, with basic recording in New York that October, orchestral additions in January 1971, further overdubs three months later in Los Angeles, and others, including a fresh vocal from Denny Laine, in September 1972.

As B side choices go, 'I Lie Around' ticked several boxes. It provided a gently laid-back contrast to the more explosive Bond song. Like 'Live and Let Die,' it sported an orchestration by George Martin. And it gave the loyal, (mostly) uncomplaining Laine a moment in the spotlight. Shortly before Wings embarked on the British tour, Paul sent it for mastering; it was assigned the matrix number 7YCE.21723.

Having had glowing praise from Eon Productions, and from the audiences and critics during Wings' British tour, Paul had every reason to expect enthusiastic reviews. But as ever, the critical reaction was mixed.

"A bit of distinctively sweet McCartney melody, a sudden booming uproar of massed symphony orchestra, a snatch of reggae and some more bombast a la '1812 Overture.' The best 007 movie theme of all and one of McCartney's two or three most satisfying records ever."[1]

Uncredited, *Billboard*

"This composition compares favorably with other Bond themes and illustrates the extraordinary versatility of McCartney's songwriting talent."[2]

Beverley Legge, *Disc*

"It's not intrinsically very interesting, but the film will help to sell it or vice versa. The B-Side, 'I Lie Around,' is a cute seasonal offering, with sounds of picnicking families and dads diving into rivers shouting, 'It's lovely, it's lovely!' S'arright."[3]

Ian MacDonald, *NME*

"McCartney's made what is obviously a good title song for a James Bond film . . . It's a nice piece of work, but hardly great music."[4]

Steve Peacock, *Sounds*

The reviews were offset by the news, on June 2, that 'My Love' and *Red Rose Speedway* had reached No. 1 on *Billboard*'s singles and albums charts. It was the first time a former Beatle topped both charts simultaneously.[5] The single and album topped their respective charts in *Cash Box* the following week.

Paul's recent releases put him in direct competition with George Harrison, whose 'Give Me Love (Give Me Peace on Earth),' backed with 'Miss O'Dell,' was released on May 25 and was in the top 20 in both American trade magazines when Paul's discs reached the top of their charts. Within a month, 'Live and Let Die' would climb into *Cash Box*'s top 10. And in the June 23 issue of *Cash Box*, the Beatles, collectively and individually, held four of the top five spots, with *Red Rose*

Speedway at No. 1, Harrison's *Living in the Material World* at No. 3, and *The Beatles 1967–1970* and *The Beatles 1962–1966* holding the fourth and fifth spots. (The interloper at No. 2 was Paul Simon's *There Goes Rhymin' Simon*.)

'Live and Let Die' scored Wings another hit in America, peaking at No. 2 in the *Billboard* Hot 100 on August 11. In Britain, where fans had been treated to a live preview of the track, 'Live and Let Die' managed 14 weeks in the Top 100, peaking at No. 9 on June 30. The appetite for Wings' music, it was becoming clear to Paul, was healthier across the Atlantic than at home, making the band's inability to tour there all the more frustrating.

As brief as this visit to High Park would be, Paul and Linda quickly settled into country life, with Paul trying out a new toy—a tractor Linda bought him for his birthday, midway through their stay. The rhythms of nature continued apace as well: shortly after their arrival in Scotland, their Labrador, Poppy, gave birth to seven puppies. The McCartneys kept one, which they named Captain Midnight, and gave the others to friends,[6] including Brown Meggs, named for the vice president of Capitol Records, and the liveliest of the litter, which they named Jet, for his solid black color.

Paul had already started writing songs for the next Wings album, and Jet's name struck him as a useful song title and refrain.* The fact that the word itself—a single syllable, starting on a soft sound and ending with a hard *T*, and with a meaning that suggests energy and speed, as well as blackness—made it the perfect staccato attention grabber.

"We were sitting in a field in Scotland, and it was a nice day," Paul said of the song. "I was just sitting there, and I was trying to think of a song to write. You know, just playing around on my guitar, picking in the sun. And one of our dogs had just had a litter of black Labrador puppies, and one of them we named Jet. And this little dog was coming around and playing at me and gnawing at my guitar and stuff. So, I just started making this song up about Jet. As the song went on it eventually came to be about this fellow's girlfriend and got a bit more involved."[7]

To some degree, "this fellow's girlfriend" was based on Linda.

"I just started to think of this thing of when Linda and I had first got married," Paul explained. "I had her father to deal with. He was a great man, a lovely man, but he definitely was a father figure. He could be a little bit serious, a little bit restrictive, so this whole idea came into my mind, 'Jet, your father was a sergeant major.' I started going off down that track."[8]

Besides 'Jet,' Paul had another rocker in his back pocket. Built around a rip-roaring guitar riff that Paul had been jamming, 'Let Me Roll It' was essentially a love song, but the chorus—"*let me roll it, let me roll it to you*"—gave the song undertones of Paul and Linda's guilty pleasure.

Paul's new crop of compositions, finished or in process, was beginning to stack up nicely. There

---

* A few years later, in 1976 or 1977, Paul and Linda bought a black pony, which they also named Jet. The pony is sometimes mistakenly (and anachronistically) cited as the source of the song title.

was 'Ma Moonia,' a folksy tune that would lend itself to rich vocal harmonies, composed during the Marrakesh visit, its title taken from the name of their hotel there, but in an eccentric spelling.

He had started 'Mrs. Vanderbilt" in January, amused by a reference to Linda's privileged upbringing in a *Cosmopolitan* piece about her, published that month: "But Scarsdale has left its mark [on Linda]—you could take Amy Vanderbilt's *Complete Book of Etiquette* in hand and never fault her."[9] 'Drink to Me,' the souvenir of the McCartneys' dinners with Dustin Hoffman in Jamaica—was coming along. And there was 'Piano Thing,' built around an energetic keyboard figure and the lyric "*No-one ever left alive in nineteen hundred eighty-five will ever do*," in which Paul seemed to be channeling Marvin Gaye's 'Trouble Man' through his own stylistic filter.

These joined two songs Paul had completed and performed publicly—'Bluebird,' which he previewed in the British version of *James Paul McCartney*, and 'Soily,' a fixture of Wings' live setlist on the European and British tours.

Early in his stay at High Park, he also added a bespoke song to his list of new compositions. During Wings' unruly press conference at the Randolph Hotel in Oxford, Paul had joked with the press that, after writing 'Six O'Clock' for Ringo, he would happily satisfy any songwriting requests from close friends, and he mentioned Rod Stewart as an example. At the Wings posttour bash at the Café Royale, Stewart picked up on this throwaway comment and prevailed upon Paul for a song. True to his word, he wrote 'Mine for Me' for the spiky-haired, raspy-voiced singer, shortly after arriving in Scotland.

The song was typical Paul, but channeling Stewart's personality—a graceful love song, offered by a singer who'd been onstage just an hour earlier and was looking forward to driving home to his love. A touch specifically for Rod was the passing dismissal of a groupie—"*save your breath, sweet painted lady, it won't be me*" because "*over the mountain and under the sea, there will never be another one like mine for me*.' Also with Rod in mind, he wrote a more constricted melody than he might have written for himself—but one that allowed for a lot of impromptu interpretive decoration.

"'Mine for Me' was easy to write for Rod's precise vocal requirements 'cos he's got such a distinctive voice," Paul said. "You can hear him singing it as you're doing it. I wrote it up in Scotland, and sent it to him on one of these [pointing to a cassette]. With all the kids shouting and screaming over it."[10]

Down in London, both EMI and MPL were busily at work on Paul's behalf. The stereo mix and two alternate edits of 'Zoo Gang,' completed in May, were mastered on June 7, and the full-length version was assigned the matrix number 7YCE.21747, indicating that EMI and McCartney foresaw releasing it as a single, presumably once the television show began airing.

A week later, MPL announced a second leg of Wings' British tour, including make-up dates for the canceled Birmingham and Newcastle concerts, plus shows in Sheffield, Stoke-on-Trent

---

* The title eventually lost its "r," but is spelled this way all through the writing and recording process.

(although this show was canceled, once MPL realized that it conflicted with the Royal World Premiere of *Live and Let Die*) and Leicester. Romeo invited the Brinsleys back, at the same fee. The O'Keefes signed on for the short tour as well.

Paul's office also handled some of the publicity for Denny Laine's album, in the works since 1971 and finished at last. Though it did not yet have a title, the album was scheduled for release in September by Wizard, an EMI imprint run by Tony Secunda, in Britain, and by Reprise Records, a subsidiary of Warner, in the United States (though the US release was later delayed until November). A single, 'Find a Way Somehow,' would precede it on July 27.

During the last week in June, the McCartneys packed their Land Rover and headed back to London. It was a productive drive: they were not on the road long before Paul hit on the idea of using the name he had given the vehicle, "Helen Wheels," as a song title, and before long, he and Linda were tossing lines back and forth, creating a fanciful chronicle of the drive from Campbeltown to London, noting stopping points (Glasgow, Carlisle, Kendal, Liverpool, and Birmingham) along the way.

"That song described a trip down the M6, which is the big motorway to get from Scotland down south to England," Paul explained. "So that song was my attempt to try and put England on the map."[11]

One of those stopping points was Sunset, Mike McCartney's house in Heswall overlooking the river Dee on the border between England and Wales. Mike and his wife, Angela, were expecting a child and gave Paul and Linda the happy news, so when Paul picked up a guitar and started strumming, the idea of writing a song about the baby seemed to occur to everyone at once.

"All we did was the three of us sat down 'round Our Kid [Paul] and his guitar," said Mike. "Lin was on vocals, and I was just singing, and we just wrote a song about a baby Angela and I were having at the time.* And then we recorded it in my back room, all just on my Revox [tape deck]—you can probably hear the birds on it. And then I just overdubbed and overdubbed."

Originally, the brisk toe tapper was called 'All My Loving,' after the refrain, which is repeated plentifully throughout the song—'*All my loving, all my loving, how can I give you all my loving . . .*' "Then," Mike joked, "somebody mentioned that there's a group that had a record with that name." The title was changed, first to 'All My Love,' then to 'Sweet Baby.'

During the following week, Mike met Paul at Island Studios, on Basing Street, to work on the song. Instead of recording it afresh, Mike brought his home recording so that Paul could add extra instrumentation as well as harmony and backing vocals with Mike and Linda.

As engineer Richard Digby Smith remembered it, the session did not last long.

"Mike brought a reel of tape in, a 7 ½ [inches per second] plastic spool, so we transferred that

---

* Abigail Faith McCartney was born to Angela Fishwick and Michael McCartney in January 1974.

over to 16-track. I just remember Paul, being the expert that he is, as quick as I could change tracks and adjust the microphones, he was ready with another overdub, so I had to be right at the top of my game. We got a lot of work done in a short space of time. Paul recorded bass and electric guitars, Linda did percussion, they all did backing vocals, and everybody added handclaps and all sorts of silly nonsense in between drinking lashings of tea."[12]

Acetates of both 'Leave It' and this second McCartney-McGear collaboration were cut at EMI Studios and shipped to the Eastmans in New York, who were helping find a new recording deal for Mike.

―

The Seiwells returned from New York on June 28, and four days later, Wings assembled for rehearsals, to blow a month's worth of cobwebs off the unchanged setlist before embarking on the final concerts of the British tour. Reuniting with Brinsley Schwarz and the O'Keefes on July 4, the troupe drove to Sheffield in South Yorkshire for the opening concert at a packed City Hall. An unnamed but starstruck reviewer for the *Sheffield Star* wrote that Wings "seems like the best rock 'n' roll band in the world," and enumerated McCullough's, Laine's and Seiwell's bona fides, adding that Linda's "back-up harmonies cannot be dismissed lightly."[13]

After the show, McCartney gave the paper an interview, seemingly after relaxing with a post-concert spliff. He began the discussion, which took place as he autographed photos for waiting fans, by claiming that he was no longer a superstar.

"I'm not really big time anymore," Paul told his puzzled interlocutor. "I've had my fame. The aura of the Beatles still sticks—but the Beatles don't exist any longer . . . Performing hasn't changed much since I last went out. It's just a different band and different material. It never could change. It's just you singing a song."[14]

If the Sheffield interview seemed eccentric by Paul's standards, he topped it with an odd sartorial display at the Royal World Premiere of *Live and Let Die*, the next evening. A benefit for Children's Play, a campaign organized by the National Playing Fields and a celebrity charity for the disabled, the event was expected to raise £63,000 ($162,150).[15] Fans and reporters waiting to spot celebrities outside the Odeon, in Leicester Square, would have seen the film's stars, Roger Moore and Jane Seymour, as well as Princess Anne, David Bowie, Lulu, Peter Sellers, Burt Reynolds, Michael Caine, Gregory Peck, Cilla Black, Liza Minnelli, David Frost, Brian Forbes and Nanette Newman—a seemingly endless, glittering parade.

Amidst it all, Wings' limo drove up and out poured Denny and Monique Seiwell, the drummer looking like a cool TV cop, in a light suit and black open collar; a content-looking, dressed-down Henry and Sheila; Denny Laine, in a white suit and satin shirt, with a seven-months pregnant Jo

Jo; Linda in her David Bowie haircut and a dark, abstract pattern dress, and Paul, wearing a tuxedo jacket and trousers, a loose bow tie and . . . no shirt. As dressing for the occasion goes, it was a step beyond the unfinished suit Paul wore to Wings launch at the Empire Ballroom in November 1971. The *Daily Express* ran a picture of Paul and Linda, with a caption that read, "McCartney and Wife, Expecting Laundry?"

The *Live and Let Die* soundtrack album, with Paul's song and George Martin's film score, was released the next day in Britain (it had been out since July 2 in America). By then, Wings were back on the tour bus, headed for the Odeon in Birmingham, Denny Laine's hometown.

Tony Brainsby had rounded up a sizable contingent of reviewers from the music press and brought them to Birmingham, among them, writers for the *NME*, *Melody Maker*, *Sounds* and *Record Mirror*. And they seemed pleased, overall, *NME*'s reviewer, Ray Telford, going so far as to say that "most people are only beginning to understand what McCartney was aiming for, and that probably explains the recent lessening off of the wild criticism the band were subjected to a year ago."[16]

Howard Fielding, in *Sounds*, wrote that Wings' sound was "tighter than it used to be," and offered a defense of Linda. He noted that she "made it easy to see how those unkind people said she was only onstage to assert her conjugal rights," and he admitted that "she doesn't do much." But he added, "I rather liked the quality of her voice, singing solo on 'Seaside Woman' and harmonizing strongly on most of the others."[17]

After the show, Brainsby herded the press into Paul's dressing room, where, as Tony Tyler wrote in the *NME*, "[Paul's] kids are running 'round and both he and his lady are being cool with them, giving friendly prods and pushes, and generally letting them get on with it." Still, recent events pushed the interview in an unusual direction.

Two days earlier, Don Powell, the drummer for Slade (and a Midlands local), was seriously injured in a car crash; his girlfriend, Angela Morris, was killed. The story still dominated the British rock world, and Slade's decision to continue their tour with a substitute drummer had become the subject of debate. In a chat with Dennis Detheridge, of *Melody Maker*, Paul weighed in.

"It's a terrible business but Slade were right to carry on with a stand-in drummer. We used a dep for Ringo [Jimmie Nicol] in Australia. I think how Slade have done it is great. They've done it very well. It's one of those things—either they lay off and lose momentum or they keep going with a dep, someone not as good, obviously. But the kids will dig it. They'll understand. That's the great thing about audiences. That's the good thing about working live. That's the kind of thing people do understand. They will think it's great of Slade to have even turned up. They'll appreciate that they did it."[18]

The discussion led Paul to muse on his own driving habits. "I've never worried at all about driving. If I crash, I crash, but I've been lucky so far. I don't drive as fast as I used to. I used to have an Aston Martin and bomb down the motorway at 140 [mph]. And you'd see some little fella in his Ford Prefect suddenly pull out about a mile down the road thinking he was doing a bomb doing 65. And you'd come roaring up on him and you'd got to brake from about half a mile out. So the thrill went after a couple of those. I've got a Lamborghini now, slightly faster, but with three kids I've cooled it a bit."[19]

Paul also tipped his hand, if only slightly, about his immediate plans.

"After we've finished the tour, we're going to take a small break and get some material together. I've written a few new songs. I've got about four, a couple half-finished and we'll put that all together for the next LP. We're planning to make it ace, that's all I can say. Ace, cool, okay. I think it will be a bit different from stuff we've done. Nothing you can put into words. I just hope it will be a bit better. I can't say it any other way. It's not in any particular musical direction. It won't be kind of 'no strings' or 'lots of strings.' I know in my head where I want it to get to, and I'm working up to it, as they say."[20]

Riffing further on those plans, Paul threw in a sop for the boys in the band, or at least one of them; but he did so in such a vague, waffling way that a reader had to wonder if he had mixed feelings about surrendering some of the spotlight.

"What we'd like to do is get Denny Laine a bit more into it," he said. "We'd like to get Denny a bit more material with the band because it's silly, he doesn't do that much with the band at the moment. I'd like to do more so it's just a question of waiting to get around to it. But we're not in any screaming hurry. We'll just take it easy and work on the stuff and see what comes out. I'm going to try to get Denny to write something for the next LP. That is something I'm trying to do. I don't know whether we'll do it on the next LP."[21]

NME's Tony Tyler came to his assignment with a perspective different from any of the other journalists in the room. Tyler had grown up in Liverpool and played in bands there when the Beatles were coming up. He knew them, both on- and offstage, from Liverpool and Hamburg. Tyler had been taken with the show and with Wings. He did think that Henry seemed slightly drunk, but that was nothing—"ask anyone from Joe Cocker down, and they'll tell you that Henry plays great when he's pissed." During the postconcert interview, Tyler was curious about Paul's response to the other Beatles not renewing Allen Klein's contract.

"I'm not smug, and I don't want to say, 'I told you so,'" was Paul's response, "but I knew I was right then, and it's been proven. I'm just glad it's all over and we can get down to playing again."

That last sentence seemed to embody some stunning news, but Paul quickly threw a wet blanket on it. "People have gotta remember that it's over. It really is. What we did was what we did. I was in that band. Now I'm in another band, playin' different music. It's over."[22]

But if the Klein episode was largely over for Paul—there was still the unfinished matter of the partnership dissolution—a new phase was beginning for the others. In New York, a few days earlier, Klein's ABKCO Industries filed suit against Lennon, Harrison, Apple Films and Apple Records, to recover what Klein said were loans and advances totaling about $780,000, and suggested that he would soon file suits for unpaid royalties and commissions as well. (When the suit was filed, John and Yoko were in Washington, D.C., attending the Watergate hearings in the United States Senate.)[23]

While Tyler was with the press group interviewing Paul, Ray Telford, also from *NME*, popped into Henry's dressing room for a chat. Telford noticed what he described as "a gap between McCullough's highly individual approach and the rest of the group, which is not necessarily unhealthy," and he speculated that this may have given rise to the recent rumors that Henry might leave the band.

Telford was clearly on to something. He guessed that any discontent on Henry's part might have arisen from what he described, not quite accurately, as "Wings' long period of inactivity just before the first leg of the tour"—a conclusion encouraged by an observation of Henry's that can be read several ways. "I hate to be stagnant all the time," the guitarist said, continuing with a list of musicians (including Joe Cocker) he felt were "stuck now," and were "doing [fuck] all."

Henry continued with another ambiguous remark, couched with sufficient diplomacy that Telford presented it as evidence of his contentment, but which the small coterie of people who knew of his musical and financial frustrations, and Seiwell's—a group that included the rest of Wings, Romeo, a few EMI engineers, members of Brinsley Schwarz, and probably his Grease Band friends—would have read differently.

"Yeah, there's enough for me to do with Wings," he said. "I dig it musically and I'm just doing my own thing *within* it, which suits me fine. I know Denny Seiwell thinks the same as me. We've got the same opinions about being with Wings."[24]

After a weekend in London, it was back on the coach for the trip to Leicester. Again, Brainsby shepherded reporters, this time from *Record Mirror* and *Beat Instrumental*. That part of the transaction did not go well: Brainsby's car broke down on the M1, and although it was back in action in ample time to get to the show, Brainsby discovered, upon their arrival that he had forgotten the tickets. The bouncer at the backstage door of the Odeon would not allow them entry, but he was persuaded to send for Romeo, who ushered the group inside.

The concert was not exemplary, partly because of amplification problems and what the critic for the *Leicester Mercury* described as "out-of-tune instrumentation,"[25] particularly during 'My Love,' but mostly, according to *Record Mirror*'s Peter Harvey, because of a "peculiarly staid audience who showed very much a start-of-the-week attitude (it was Monday night) and didn't start bopping until the last few numbers."[26]

When Wings reached 'Long Tall Sally,' Harvey reported, "Leicester was rocking, clapping, shouting, and even screaming." Thankful for that belated burst of energy, Paul sang 'Long Tall Sally' a second time.

Brainsby persuaded Paul to do interviews before and after the show this time, partly because Fred Robbins, an American reporter, was planning to do an in-depth interview with both Paul and Linda for the inaugural issue of *Viva* magazine, a woman's spinoff of *Penthouse*, and would need more time than the others. Robbins, who had interviewed Paul several times over the years—starting with an interview in Paris, in January 1964—was given the preshow slot. He conducted a mostly historical interview, so Paul and Linda revisited the formation of Wings, Linda's background as a rock fan and her passion for reggae, and how Paul persuaded her to join the band, as well as the university tour and parenthood. Once readers of the new glossy were sated with beefcake photos, they could catch up with the last three years of the Cute Beatle's life.

After the show, Brainsby took Peter Harvey, from the *Record Mirror*, and a reporter for *Beat Instrumental* (whose publication did not print a byline) to Paul's dressing room, tucked away at the top of the building. As they approached, they could hear Wings singing a nicely harmonized version of 'When Irish Eyes Are Smiling.' Deciding not to interrupt until the singing ended, the writers kept still to hear Wings' a cappella rendering of the old Mills Brothers classic 'Down by the

Old Mill Stream," knocking when nothing followed. Letting him in, Paul quipped, "You've heard of a warm-up? Well, that was a cooldown."

Their questions, which covered the tour, Wings' chemistry and whether the Beatles might reunite, gave Paul an opportunity to take stock in a more reflective way than usual, albeit with a modicum of spin. He suggested, for example, that on the British tour, "people are looking at us critically for the first time," and explained that this was because he had done his best to limit press coverage of the university and European tours.

"Early on, there were one or two dodgy nights," Paul said of the tour, "but that was the idea of doing it the way we did it. If we'd gone straight on to do Earls Court you can imagine, you know, bands that have been together a few years have problems there and we didn't fancy that, we just fancied playing around, and we managed to pretend that we were a small-time group. It was easy for us. But it was great because it meant we really were in the deep end, and we had to kinda solve everything for ourselves."[27]

Exploring the kinds of things that needed to be "solved" led into a discussion of the band's internal politics, and how Paul expected the band to evolve. There had been moments of friction, he admitted—"a few kinda arguments and stuff like 'I don't like the way you do that.' It's a bit democratic," he said, "but if we're looking for a decision, I'll just make it." Talk of expanding that democracy followed, with Paul asserting that "as we go on, we're going to take the center of attention off me and let Denny [Laine] come through more."

Laine, still present after the vocal warm-up, chimed in to say—oddly, for a musician who had just completed an album—"It's just that I haven't got any numbers." Paul gently reminded Denny that there may be songs Wings could do on his forthcoming record, but then stepped back, saying, "we don't want to push Denny just for the sake of saying 'Hello folks it's not just me,' you know, we're trying to keep it on what they want."

Eventually the two journalists asked why Paul thought the Leicester show took so long to ignite.

"Our buzz is to play to people," Paul said. "Some nights you don't get good audiences, but there is nothing to match the nights when you do. If you are a performer, it is in your blood . . . The ballsier towns were better, of course, places like Glasgow, Newcastle and Birmingham.[28] I like 'em rockin.'"[29]

McCartney's reference to Newcastle-Upon-Tyne, during his postshow interview, was informed (and perhaps, wishful) guesswork; Wings would close the tour at Newcastle City Hall the next evening, although the group had performed in the city during the university tour. He was, in any case, proven correct. The 2,100 seats for the July 10 concert were sold out, and hours before the

---

* Though Paul would probably have known the song from the Mills Brothers' 1959 recording, it was composed by Tell Taylor, published in 1908, and recorded by Bing Crosby (1939) and many others over the years.

show, fans were lined up in the streets adjacent to the hall, those without tickets searching for scalpers. Some fans on the lines snaking around the building peered into the basement windows and discovered Paul's dressing room. When they shouted to him, Paul accommodatingly stood on a chair to chat with them.[30]

McCartney, wanting a well-recorded sample of the British tour for his archives—or for release, if it proved good enough—had arranged for a 16-track recording of the show to be made.*

Inside the hall, the atmosphere was electrifying. Henry was spotted dancing in the wings during the Brinsleys' set, and the audience patiently indulged the O'Keefes, who a local described as "unbelievably pathetic and totally uncalled for."[31] But when the lights dimmed and Laine, Seiwell, McCullough and Linda walked onstage, the crowd roared, and then roared louder when Paul followed a few seconds later.

The set unfolded without a hitch, but with a couple of surprises. Henry, plainly inebriated and chafing against Paul's control of his solo lines, adorned several of the songs with improvised blues licks not heard at the other shows, and he reconfigured his solo in 'My Love.' As Ian Gomm remembered it, Henry performed the solo from the stage floor.

"In the middle of 'My Love,' he was so pissed, he'd actually fallen," said Gomm. "He was on his back. He was lying on the stage on his back looking up at the lights playing his solo. And I'm looking at him thinking, 'Does he know he's fallen down?' . . . Anybody who can start drinking special brew in the morning and still carry on and manage to do everything is a better man than me because I couldn't."[32]

Between 'Go Now' and 'Say You Don't Mind,' one of the roadies brought out a cake to celebrate Denny Seiwell's 30th birthday, and Henry played him a bluesy version of 'Happy Birthday.' And at the end of the show, when Wings returned for their encore after two minutes of shouting, stomping and whistling, Brinsley Schwarz joined them for the most raucous and freewheeling 'Long Tall Sally' of the tour, with repeated verses, extra guitar solos, and even some vocal improv from Paul.

Seiwell's later recollection of the show was that it was not particularly good, saying, "some of the tempos were really weird, which is usually *my* fault."[33] But Seiwell made a strong impression on *Disc*'s Peter Erskine that evening and was singled out for lavish praise. Early in the set, Erskine wrote, "you realize how good Denny Seiwell really is. His playing is so damn forceful and incisive. He manages to combine an intrinsically-sensitive black style—that arrogant laid-back ease, say, of someone like Bernard Purdie, with all the edge and attack of the best white drummers—Aynsley Dunbar, for instance."[34]

---

* The full concert was mixed to stereo in EMI's Control Room Four, on July 29, overseen not by Paul but by Ian Horne, his roadie with a background in sound engineering. Cassettes were made for Paul on August 9, and after he let EMI know what he wanted trimmed—the band's a cappella rendering of 'The Wee Tobacco Box,' Laine's 'Say You Don't Mind' and Seiwell's birthday celebration were deleted—acetates were made for the band and members of Brinsley Schwarz.

Erskine's review of the Newcastle concert, titled "They're the Best Band in the Land," underlined Wings' growing credibility, and a slowly shifting opinion among the music press. McCartney's much maligned group were finally gaining momentum.

———➤

On July 12, two days after the tour ended, McCartney found himself at Apple's Savile Row offices, accompanied by John Eastman, for meetings with Harrison and Starr, and their advisers (David Braun, for Harrison, Hilary Gerrard, for Starr) to work out the details of the partnership dissolution agreement. (Lennon, unable to leave the United States, was absent.) The meeting stretched on for a second day, during which Klein's lawsuit against Apple was also discussed, John Eastman offering to arrange for top-flight representation for Apple, in the person of David Warner Peck, a retired judge who was a senior partner in the New York firm Sullivan and Cromwell.

As much as Paul disliked business meetings, this one yielded the basis of a song.

"I happened to be talking to George at a meeting—we were sorting out some of the Apple business," Paul later recalled. "Someone said something, and George just said, 'Well, we're all prisoners, kind of inside ourselves,' or, you know, 'inside every fat man, there's a thin man trying to get out.' I just took up that theme of, we're all prisoners in a way, so I kind of wrote a prison song. And as I say, you can take it symbolically or straight, it works on both levels."[35]

Getting from George's comments to a prison song took some doing, however, and as Paul turned over the remark in his mind, his first thoughts reflected his own sense of still being trapped in the Beatles partnership agreement—and at an Apple legal meeting. The first verse he wrote,[36] *"If we ever get out of here / Thought of giving it all away / To a registered charity"* is the kind of internal bargaining one does when stuck in circumstances—a business meeting, say—and hoping for liberation. Another verse moves closer to the prison metaphor—*"Stuck inside these four walls / Sent inside forever / Never seeing no-one nice again."*

While John Eastman was with Paul at Apple, Lee Eastman was across town at EMI, working to improve his son-in-law's recording situation. McCartney's relationship with EMI was governed by the Beatles-EMI agreement that Klein negotiated in 1969, and that ran until 1976. Eastman reasoned that because EMI's contract was with Apple, not the individual Beatles, once the partnership was dissolved, Paul would be a free agent.

Eastman had written from New York to EMI's group director, Len Wood, to open discussions on June 21. Wood made his offer on July 12: a £5,000 ($12,750) advance on McCartney's next album. Characterizing the offer as laughable, Eastman urged Wood to consider making a more serious one. Wood also suggested that Paul might collaborate with EMI's Italian affiliate, as part of a Wings tour of Italy (an idea first floated in 1971, when EMI Italia executives courted Paul and Linda at

Lake Como); Eastman said he would mention the proposal to Paul but wanted to see specifics. In the meantime, Wings agreed to a one-shot performance at EMI Italy's Festivalbar, on August 25.

Six days later, Wood had not upgraded his offer, so Eastman wrote again, saying he wanted to confirm "that EMI is prepared to advance solely £5,000."

"I am about to undertake negotiations for a major production deal on behalf of Paul McCartney," he continued. "I take it from your conversation that it would be pointless to discuss this with EMI."[37]

That, for the time being, was where the matter rested. But Eastman knew, and had reason to believe that EMI did as well, that other labels were hearing that Paul might not be content with his EMI contract and were gingerly making their moves. Warner Records, for one, was starting to build relationships with people in Paul's circle, including Denny Laine.

The Eastmans met with Wings at Cavendish Avenue on July 19, to discuss the band's continued financial concerns. It may have been a point of pride, but in practical terms it was cold comfort to learn that, just a few days earlier, 'My Love' was certified Gold, for 500,000 sales in the United States,[38] for which Seiwell, Laine and McCullough received no royalties or other tangible benefits.

They had each received their £500 bonuses for *Red Rose Speedway*, but the occasional few hundred quid and the promise of a year-end loyalty bonus was not enough to keep the three musicians happy.

Seiwell, who had just turned 30, and Henry, whose 30th birthday was in two days, were both married, and Laine, 28, was expecting a son in August. And the longer their £70 retainer prevailed, the more demeaning it felt to them. Moreover, Laine had completed the album he owed Secunda—the principal impediment to a contract the last time they met with Eastman—and it was due out in the fall.

But they could not counter Eastman's argument that much of Paul's money was tied up in Apple, including payments for Wings' records. That made the band's desire for royalties on Wings recordings—one of their principal asks—impractical, since EMI was obligated to pay Wings' royalties directly to Apple.

Eastman also reminded them that Paul had borne the expense of running the band. When they toured, everything from the coach, the support acts, the custom PA, the equipment, transportation, and the hotel rooms to the Frisbees and balloons, was on Paul's tab. There was also the staff at MPL to pay, and most of the activity at MPL had to do with Wings. Because of all those expenses, the company's ledgers showed an annual loss.

From the band's perspective, it seemed odd to plead poverty when you were driving a Lamborghini or going for shopping sprees, as Paul and Linda had done recently, at Fortnum and Mason, which billed itself as "the most luxurious department store in the world." But Laine, Seiwell and McCullough simply had no bargaining chips, and they left the meeting dejected, once again.

Amid all the financial tussling, Paul caught Tony Palmer's Omnibus documentary, *Ginger Baker in Africa*, on BBC One on July 15. The film follows Baker as he drives south through the Sahara in a Range Rover, from Algeria to Lagos, Nigeria. Baker had built his Batakota Studio, also known as ARC (Associated Recording Company) in Lagos, and it had been fully up and running since January 1973.

The drummer is seen riding a camel, feeding mountain monkeys, and trying traditional instruments, like the West African talking drum. But most of the hour-long show captures Baker's encounters with a broad array of African music and musicians. Intercut throughout the film is footage of Baker jamming with local Lagos musicians who play guitars, keyboards, reeds and brass, amid rhythmically complex layers of African percussion.

Presented as well are performances by traditional ensembles and dancers—among them Chris Olude's Nigerian Cultural Group, a dance troupe; the Lijadu Sisters, a vocal group; and the Sweet Things, a dance trio. Nigeria's biggest international star, Fela Ransome-Kuti performing with his band, Africa '70, and a group of female dancers, is the subject of an entrancing segment.

Paul remembered Kuti and Africa '70 from their visit to EMI Studios during Wings' sessions for *Wild Life*. For a musical omnivore like Paul, all this was exciting and inspiring. In a few of the interviews he gave during the British tour, he floated the possibility that Wings might record in Marrakesh—but he was vague, and his comments seemed little more than an example of something unpredictable that Wings might do.

There was, in fact, a vogue among British musicians to record in exotic locales in 1973. Cat Stevens's *Foreigner* album and the Rolling Stones' *Goats Head Soup* were recorded in Jamaica that year, and Elton John had gone there to record *Goodbye Yellow Brick Road*, only to be thwarted by what he considered inadequate studio facilities.

Paul noted the trend, and it made sense to him: recording outside the familiar round of London studios might kick the band toward a fresh approach. Given his and Linda's passion for reggae, and Jamaica's status as one of their favorite vacation places, recording there had a certain appeal, but it might have seemed like following the crowd.

He was looking for two things in a getaway recording location: atmosphere, including warm weather (and ideally, an opportunity to spend time on the beach between sessions), and a strong local musical culture.

"If you record in the same place all the time, music can become work, and you want it always to be play," said Paul. "[So] I rang up EMI, my record company, and asked where else they'd got studios. The list included Rio de Janeiro, China, and Lagos."[39]

---

*Other EMI worldwide locations included Argentina, Peru, Mexico, Chile, Venezuela, Uruguay, the Republic of Congo, South Africa,

Until he saw the Baker documentary, Paul had been leaning toward Rio de Janeiro, which boasted both magnificent beaches and a distinctive, vibrantly rhythmic local musical style. But Lagos was on EMI's list as well, and as he watched Palmer's documentary, he became persuaded to go there instead, and perhaps work at Ginger's studio. In purely musical terms, it made sense: after all, much of the rhythmic character of Brazilian music had its origins in Africa. Why not go to the source? Baker had been road-testing the Lagos scene since 1971—what could go wrong?

It did not take Paul long to make a definite plan. He dispatched Romeo to Lagos to check out Baker's ARC in the Ikeja district of town, as well as the EMI Lagos Studios, in Apapa—and Lagos, generally, as a place to work.

"He thought it would be camp to go down there and maybe get an African influence," Romeo explained, "like when Dustin Hoffman was going to play a prisoner for *Papillon* and he went to prison to soak up the influence."[40]

EMI weighed in as well, letting Paul know that as a cost issue, while the label would not prohibit him from using Baker's studio, using EMI's own facilities would be an internal charge, and greatly preferable.

A week after the Palmer film aired, the trip to Lagos was a talking point: when *Melody Maker* interviewed Laine on July 22, the guitarist mentioned that Wings would record their next album at EMI's Lagos studio ("it's free," he explained), adding, "but you never know, we might end up at Ginger's."[41]

Laine had devoted the day to preparation for the release of his LP, starting with a photo shoot at his caravan, parked in Shepperton, Surrey, where photographers from a handful of music papers snapped him playing guitar on the caravan's step, sitting on his motorcycle, and posing with Jo Jo. There was some curiosity about the caravan, not quite the typical rock star crib.

"I've never owned a house of my own because I don't like mortgages and borrowing money and being in debt," Denny said, "and whenever I've rented anywhere, I've always ended up giving the landlord a cheque for £500 because somebody's dropped ash on the carpet, or whatever. So, I thought to myself how silly it was to pay all that rent—so I moved into a caravan."[42]

After barbecuing steaks and potatoes for his guests, Denny settled into an interview, giving *Melody Maker*'s Mark Plummer a look inside Wings, offering a diplomatic overview of some of the band's unresolved tensions.

"Wings was formed to be a band. The first thing Paul said to me was that everybody had to be equal, as equal as possible anyway. In a way he can't help being where he is, but it's a bit embarrassing if you've got just one person in a band. Obviously, he's had a hard time of it. It was Paul's

Thailand, the Philippines, Hong Kong, India, Lebanon, Australia, New Zealand, Pakistan, Yugoslavia, and most countries in mainland Europe.

idea to get Wings together, but I know the problems because they were similar for me with the Electric String Band and Balls, obviously people like a focal point. It can get really boring after a while unless everyone can feel on the same level."

Some of the equality issue, he suggested, was about to be redressed.

"Now I'm off to Scotland for five weeks to start writing with Paul. Yeah, we'll be writing together because we live so closely as a group in Scotland. Paul's got Henry together now, and he's coming up with some really good ideas. Henry just needs encouragement to bring them out, much more so than me because with one of my songs ['Find a Way Somehow'] taking off this year, I've been thinking a lot more about songwriting."[43]

The following week, Secunda arranged for a room on the 15th floor of the Park Towers Hotel, with a panoramic view of London. With ample scotch and vodka laid on for visiting journalists, Laine held court for two days, speaking with *Disc*, *Sounds*, *Record Mirror*, *Beat Instrumental*, and just about anyone else Secunda could persuade to pop by. The point, of course, was to promote Laine's new album, to be called *Ah . . . Laine!*, and due in the fall. But the discussions inevitably touched on Wings as well; in fact, Laine wore a pink Wings T-shirt to the session.

The interviews painted Laine as an odd duck, alternately engaging and ornery, ambitious and lackadaisical. He bragged about his adventurousness, telling *Record Mirror*, "I'm always trying something new. I seem to have a gift, musically. I could get a tune out of a lampshade."[44] He said that if one of his own songs was not on the next Wings album, "I'll thump somebody,"[45] but he also spoke about songwriting as "a hobby," adding that his best songs "come while I'm sitting around fiddling about."[46]

Laine insisted that "the single was Tony's idea. I didn't really want to put a single out. I mean the last thing I want is to push myself as a solo artist. I don't get any kicks out of that, and I don't want to do any gigs on my own."[47] But he told another interviewer that: "Apart from Wings I want to put out two albums a year myself, as a songwriter displaying my stuff for other people really."[48]

Henry gave an interview on his own, too, with Nicky,* the new secretary of the Wings Fun Club. James Johnson, a reporter from *NME* and Tony Brainsby were also present. He was decidedly uncomfortable with the fanzine side of the chat. Sitting across the table—and across a row of empty Long Life beer cans—he stared into space for a moment when Nicky asked if he had a message for the fans.

"I know all this [fandom] is going on around me," he said, giving exactly the wrong answer for a publication catering largely to teenage hero-worshippers, "but I just can't relate to it at all. I'm just a musician, you know."[49]

NME's Johnson, who had known and respected McCullough since his Grease Band days, won-

_____

* Like her predecessors, "Claire" and "Lucy," "Nicky" did not use her full name.

dered whether life in Wings had tamed the guitarist, and whether his talents were being wasted in the group. It was a question that stung, but Henry did his best to give his answer a positive spin.

"I've never been the kind of guitarist to play 20-minute solos anyway. I don't feel restricted or anything like that. I think it's also down to the numbers we're playing. They're quite highly structured, not very free, and on stage I'm just playing what I played on the record. Perhaps I would like the band to be a little freer. It's just been kept that way so far. But I could never be just Paul McCartney's backing guitarist. I'd leave if it was like that.

"Over the last eighteen months we've had to sort out the slight differences we had musically. At the start I wasn't really aware of what I was doing. It only came after I got to know the lads in the band. Now I think Wings have reached the point where the music is really starting to come out of the band. Everybody's contributing and the results are a five-piece product. That's what it's going to and it's great."[50]

—

Paul and Linda were in Campbeltown by July 23, and apart from a day trip with the girls to Betws-y-Coed, Wales, and a brief visit to have a look at Strawberry Studios in Stockport, they focused mostly on finishing off the songs for the album—with the Lagos sessions booked to begin on August 31, they had just over a month—and winding down by riding their horses.

Paul had grown used to thinking a step or two ahead, and that meant the next tour, for when the album was finished—or even, as in the case of *Red Rose Speedway*, if it wasn't. With the United States out of reach because of Paul's cannabis convictions, he set his sights on the next most frenzied locale during Beatlemania, Australia. Paul directed Romeo to begin planning for a tour in January 1974, the middle of summer Down Under.

Finishing off songs had been a leisurely business in the immediate post-Beatles years, when Paul left songs unfinished for weeks or months—or even years, and well into the recording process, in the case of songs like 'Little Lamb Dragonfly.' But his response to a question an interviewer asked during the British tour—that his writing process usually begins with the thought that he had to write 12 songs for an album—put him in mind of his working method during the Beatles years, when the prospect of an approaching recording session had him turning them out quickly. Granted, he could no longer bring in an incomplete lyric and hope that Lennon would finish it, but Linda could come up with a good line, and Laine had lately shown both interest and ability.

Where Paul was most efficient was in creating structures and melodies, with lyrical ideas (if not necessarily all the words) to hang on them. Sitting down with what he had, he was acutely aware that the "prison song" he started after the Apple meetings needed intensive work—not because

THE McCARTNEY LEGACY

he disliked what he had, but because as soon as he wrote those verses, he knew they'd be an effective opener for the album.

Songwriters don't always know whether the song they are writing will open or close an album, or dwell somewhere in the middle, but when they know they are writing the first music that will be heard, they think differently about the music at hand. In this case, the two verses he had written—"*If we ever get out of here*" and "*Stuck inside these four walls*"—could become distinct compositions. They were in different keys (in the order he wrote them, the first is in A minor, the second in D major), and each with its own feel (rocky and insistent for the first, quietly introspective for the second). That was fine; joining disparate pieces had become a favorite songwriting strategy.

It soon occurred to him that if he switched those fragments around ("*Stuck inside*" first, "*If we ever*" second), they began to delineate a narrative, starting with a single prisoner lamenting his incarceration, then raising the temperature as a group of prisoners (the narrator switches from "*I*" to "*we*") imagine getting out. It worked musically, too, moving from calm dejection to more insistent and driven, and the fact that the "*if we ever get out of here*" verse is in five-bar phrases, rather the more typical eight bars, increases the tension by toying with the listener's expectation of where the cadences will be.

Thinking about where to go from there, Paul realized that among his unfinished songs was a fairly developed piece, with verses and a chorus, that could easily be grafted onto this one. Its existing verses were impressionistic, with some nice imagery—"*the rain exploded with a mighty crash / As we fell into the sun*"—but new lines could be added to advance the jailbreak story. And its chorus, "*Band on the run*," suited the jailbreak theme.

The first two sections were only fragments, but Paul gave them form by adding an introduction to the first, and a playout to the end of the second. The playout would lead into the new addition, and once joined, the three pieces were like a compact, cinematic pop symphony. Paul named the song for the third section's chorus, and since it was to be the album's opening track, he thought of *Band on the Run*, at least provisionally, as the album's title.

The two Dennys and Henry were back in Scotland in ample time for the start of rehearsals on July 31. For the rehearsal period, Paul and Linda decided to put up the two Dennys and Henry at their second farm, Low Ranachan. But though Paul and Linda had made High Park more habitable than it had been in 1969, Low Ranachan was unfit for civilized habitation—a point immediately noted by the eight months pregnant Jo Jo.

"The band had to stay in outhouses with stone floors," Jo Jo complained. "We got the impression they had only ever been used for animals. True, they had been swept out, but I was most unhappy. . . . We had an old-fashioned bathtub, and we had to fill it with hot water from pots and pans. [Even though] I was eight months pregnant, I was never offered a wash or a bath in Paul and Linda's place."[51]

Jo Jo's issues with the accommodations notwithstanding, Denny enjoyed life on the McCartneys' farm. Just before the rehearsals for the new album began, he spoke about his living situation to a reporter from *Jackie* magazine.

"Though the work is disciplined, it's still kept very loose," he said. "When we're rehearsing at the farm, if it's a nice day then we'll just as likely spend the day working in the vegetable garden, watching birds, or wandering the hills. And then we'll catch up with our rehearsals in the evening. That's the thing with Paul. He'll relax and take things easy. But the work always gets done."[52]

To keep Jo Jo comfortable, Denny rented a caravan, having left his own in Shepperton. Henry and Sheila, and Denny and Monique, along with Ian and Trevor, shared a cottage, but it was damp and dreary, and they were not much happier than Denny and Jo Jo. "Everyone," Jo Jo later wrote, "got uptight and uneasy."[53] By August 9, Denny and Monique returned to their rented farm in nearby Kilchenzie.

Paul had a stack of new songs for the band to learn, and Denny Laine, having internalized the encouragement Paul gave him in the tour interviews, brought along a song, too—actually, half a song, which Paul helped him finish by grafting on an unfinished song of his own.

Denny's 'No Words,' a song about a romance going through a rough patch, moves like a George Harrison tune. Its melody, like many of Harrison's, begins cheerily but quickly takes an unexpected turn toward the lachrymose, with phrases that sound as if they are in minor keys, even when the accompanying chords are major. The opening line, for example, is a gently rising melody over an A major chord; but a sudden drop from C-sharp to G, transforming the accompanying chord into an A7, gives the melody a dark, thoroughly Harrisonian lilt.

The bridge, by contrast—Paul's principal contribution—is bright and outgoing and reaches up into the falsetto range.

"I would help him finish off a lot of stuff," Denny said of collaborating with Paul. "You get together and say, 'I haven't got this bit yet, I haven't got that bit' and you kind of finish the thing off. He comes in with the initial idea and then says to me 'have you got anything you want to add?' And I'd have some ideas as well, and we'd join 'em together. 'No Words,' for example, was two songs that became one song.[54] I wrote the first few verses and couldn't get any further. I took them to Paul, and he added his little bit of magic."[55]

During the first two weeks in August, Wings gathered daily at Low Ranachan, where Paul set up a rehearsal room even ruder than Rude Studios and drilled the band in his arrangements. As the songs took shape, the band recorded demos on Paul's 4-track deck, eventually getting recordings of nearly all the tracks proposed for the new album.

There was extracurricular jamming, as well. When the Hertfordshire band Babe Ruth played at

Victoria Hall, in Campbeltown, on August 8, Henry and the two Dennys attended the concert and invited the band back to Low Ranachan. Babe Ruth were a fundamentally different kind of band than Wings; they played a hybrid of blues, jazz and progressive rock, with an occasional touch of soul. But like Wings, they were EMI artists and had made their recordings (the second, *Amar Caballero*, had just been released) at the label's London studios. For the Wings players, it was an opportunity for a free-blowing jam, a refreshing change after rehearsing Paul's airtight, unvarying arrangements for just over a week.

"We got to Campbeltown," recalled Ed Spevock, who had only recently signed on as Babe Ruth's drummer, "and the three of them were in the front row. We went back to the farm where they lived, and they had a load of gear set up in a barn. I would get up and play with Denny and Henry and our bass player would get up and play, and then I'd get off and Denny Seiwell would get up and play with our guitarists. It was just a big band jam. We played most of the night, and when everyone was knackered, our tour manager took us back to the hotel."[56]

Wings' rehearsals had their ups and downs, as rehearsals do. But from McCullough's point of view, a lot of it was the 'My Love' session all over again, except without Paul relenting and letting him try out his own ideas. During a rehearsal of 'No Words,' on August 14, Paul was intent on Henry playing the solo he had mapped out. Henry had an idea of his own that he wanted to try, but Paul was not having it.

Laine understood Paul's desire to have the band learn his arrangement and press on. "Henry always took a long time to get exactly what he wanted. He liked to go through all these trial things, and we couldn't afford that."[57]

But for Henry, it was hard to see Paul's refusal as reasonable.

"Give me a chance," the guitarist begged, "if it doesn't work out, we'll do it your way."[58]

McCullough had been telling interviewers that he was fine with his role in Wings, but he knew he was mainly trying to persuade himself that this was so. He had hoped that the acclaim his solo on 'My Love' brought would help Paul see that allowing him some creative input could be a good thing. Now he realized that this would be a never-ending battle.

"I had been too long on the road to be told like a child to play this or that. I had come from working with Joe Cocker and somehow ended up singing bloody nursery rhymes.[59] I felt it was time he allowed the musicians to have some of their own ideas used as part of this 'group' vibe. But all that was slowly being lost. . . . I was trying desperately to hold onto it because I wanted it not just for the band but for him as well—for him to show people that he wasn't namby-pamby all the time, that he really had balls. And he does have an awful lot of balls, he just doesn't seem to get it down on record."[60]

But here was Paul, holding on to his Rickenbacker, shouting "You'll fucking do this," and Henry finally reached his limit. He looked Paul in the eye, unstrapped his Les Paul, and said, "We'll see about that, you cunt."[61] The band looked on in stunned silence as Henry angrily packed his guitar, unplugged his amp, threw them both into the back seat of his car, and drove off. Even Paul felt things had gone too far, though he also knew this moment was inevitable.

"We all got a bit choked about it," Paul remembered.[62] Romeo said that "Everyone cried when Henry left, including Henry."[63]

Henry and Sheila headed into Campbeltown where Henry could down a few beers and ponder whether to return or just get on with his life. But rather than calming down, Henry realized that being told what to play was not the only issue. Discussions of the financial situation always reached an impasse. The Wings songbook, varied as it was, veered too far toward chart-oriented pop for a self-respecting bluesman to be seen playing. And there was Linda, who he believed had no business playing on the same stage as the experienced and seasoned players in Wings.

"It just wasn't going to work out for the rest of us in Wings—unless, of course, you had an apron on, if you know what I mean,"[64] he concluded.

"I was cheating myself in the long run. . . . If I had stayed, I would have been prostituting my own art of music by doing something that I didn't believe in. I know Paul understands that. I wanted to get out and do rock and roll and blues. What we did was done the exact same way every night. It was never set free, and I like to branch out here and there when the situation arrives."[65]

In the morning, Henry felt no differently about it and telephoned Paul to say he was quitting.

"When Henry left, I was really brokenhearted," said Seiwell, "because Henry and I were very close. He was close as you could get with Paul and Linda; I mean, we were tight as a family, we spent a lot of time together. Henry and I were kind of like the rebels. We hung out with the roadies, and we had our own little side relationship going on there."[66]

Denny Laine understood Henry's frustrations, too; in fact, when he was in an ambitious mood, he felt he was underachieving in Wings. "I'm kind of the odd job man in this group. It's not my songs, and I'd like to feel more involved, and contribute as much as *they* [Paul and Linda] do."[67]

Paul's immediate response was to suspend the rehearsals and consider how to proceed. He had Romeo cancel the group's August 25 Festivalbar appearance. The reason MPL gave was that the band had a bad reaction to antimalaria vaccinations for their upcoming trip to Lagos.

Paul then drafted a statement for Brainsby to read to the press.

H. McCullough has left Wings due to the usual musical differences and by mutual agreement. Everybody thinks it's for the best and wish each other well in the future.

At the bottom of the sheet, Paul doodled a fuzzy, smiling caricature looking upward at the text, as if to suggest that nothing should be read into the dismissively pro forma character of the statement. The music press picked it up for their issues dated August 25, some adding an MPL spokesman's confirmation that the trip to Lagos was still on.

With rehearsals halted, the Seiwells flew back to London on August 15, with Denny Laine and Jo Jo preparing to follow on August 25, and the McCartneys shortly thereafter. But Jo Jo went into labor on the 24th; their son, Laine Hines, was born in Campbeltown that day.

Young Laine's birth led to an altercation between Denny and the McCartneys.

"We were planning to leave the next day and were clearing out the caravan in preparation when Jo suddenly said, 'This is it—the baby is on its way!' I had to lay her down in the back of the van and drive to the nearest town," Denny later wrote. "When I eventually got back from the hospital, next day, I found Linda and Paul very angry about all the stuff that had been left lying around. They actually thought I'd driven off leaving a pile of rubbish behind. They seemed far more concerned about that than the baby we had just had."[68]

Hurt as he was, Denny attributed Paul's gruffness to the disarray in Wings' plans caused by Henry's departure, exacerbated by Linda's enduring dislike of Jo Jo. He was not about to make a fuss, though: thanks to the McCartneys, he had a position in a hit band, and with a song of his own about to be recorded for Wings' new album, he would finally share more fully in the rewards.

With the word out that Wings were in the market for a guitarist, MPL was soon flooded with inquiries. One player with an early inside track was Jimmy McCulloch, a young guitarist who lived around the corner from Wings roadie Ian Horne. Though only 20, McCulloch had an impressive résumé: he had been a founding member of Thunderclap Newman, and when he left that band, in 1971, he formed the Jimmy McCulloch Band; Paul had seen him perform at the Rainbow Theater, supporting Mountain, in January 1972—on Ireland's "Bloody Sunday." More recently, he played briefly with Blue, an offshoot of the Scottish band Marmalade.

Back when all was well within Wings, Ian had given Jimmy tickets to hear the band in Leicester and brought him backstage to meet Paul. "I was really knocked out with them," McCulloch later remembered. "The thing I was impressed with was how much like his records Paul sounds—there are no effects on his voice or anything, it's just him. I met him and the band too—they were really nice."[69]

Now Ian called Jimmy with more news. "He told me they were going out to Lagos to cut *Band on the Run*," McCulloch said, "and that there was a possibility of me getting a gig when they returned."

The story of Henry's departure, meanwhile, took on a life of its own: soon rumors circulated to the effect that during their Low Ranachan row, Paul had punched Henry, or that Henry had pulled a gun on Paul, or smashed a bottle over his head. On August 29, Paul put these tales to rest, telling reporters outside Cavendish Avenue that they were all nonsense.

To Denny Seiwell, the Wings saga was quickly becoming a circus, and as he saw it, it was time to cancel all future plans and regroup. For starters, he told Paul, going to Lagos without a lead guitarist was folly: Wings had rehearsed the new material and had it under their fingers, and in his view it made far more sense to find a new guitarist, rehearse the new songs until they were as polished as they had been at Low Ranachan, and then make the record.

"We were a band," Seiwell contended. "We'd just done all this touring, we'd knit as a unit, and at the rehearsals in Scotland, everybody was giving their all. So I said to Paul, 'Can't we just postpone this for a month? That studio in Lagos will still be ready for you, but let's first break in a new guitarist, so we can go down and record the album as a band.' And he said, 'No, I don't want to do that. Let's just go down, and it will be like *Ram*—we'll just get the basic tracks and do overdubs.' That didn't sit well with me."[70]

When Laine returned to London, Seiwell did his best to enlist the guitarist to his point of view. But Laine had other concerns, which he confided to Seiwell. As Seiwell remembers it, "Denny came over to my place and told me more things that had been going on since Henry left. He'd just had his baby, in Scotland, and he told me about some ugly shit that had happened."

———

Laine flew to Lagos on August 29, with Geoff Emerick, the former EMI engineer who the Beatles had hired to run the Apple Studios, and who had recently left Apple to become a staff engineer at AIR. He had been at AIR only a couple of weeks when Paul invited him to engineer the Wings sessions in Lagos and follow-up sessions at AIR. Emerick, naturally, called Paul to ask whether the trip was still on, and he remembered Paul telling him, "We'll still do it, even if we have to make an acoustic album."[71] Seiwell was scheduled to leave the next day, with Paul, Linda and the girls. But he had been mulling over his feeling that the recording plan did not do Wings justice, as a band, as well as Laine's complaints, and his own growing belief that Paul's original promise of band equality, contracts and percentages would never be honored.

"The night that we were going to Lagos, there was a car [sent by Paul] in front of my place, and I just thought, 'You know what? I've got to put an end to this.' I just said, 'That's it, I think I'm going to leave.' My wife and I were both having tough times trying to keep all the plates in the air, the way things were. I'm in one of the top bands in the world, and we're living in a dingy, one-bedroom, furnished apartment. It was just really a rat hole. The toilet had a big tank above it, where you'd pull the chain to flush it, and the [manufacturer's] name on the toilet was Thomas Crapper and Sons. But this was the straw that broke the camel's back.

"I picked up the phone and called Paul, and I said, 'I'm done. I can't do this anymore.' It was hard to do, really, extremely hard to do. And he was shocked."

An argument ensued, both Seiwell and Paul becoming increasingly incensed, until Paul slammed down the phone. Five minutes later, Seiwell's phone rang, and as soon as he put the receiver to his ear, he heard Linda, shouting, *"How dare you inconvenience us?"*

"Inconvenience *you*?" Seiwell replied. "How about the last three years of *my* life? You took me out of a great career [in New York]. I don't want to hear this," and he hung up on her.[72]

The next day, both Vincent Romeo and Mike McGear phoned Seiwell to try to persuade him to take the next available flight to Lagos. "But I was done," Seiwell said.

Paul later offered an analytical view of McCullough's and Seiwell's departures, but his analysis showed that he had not quite internalized the lesson of the band's disintegration; in fact, he remained in denial about the musical issues behind McCullough's and Seiwell's resignations.

"When I came out of the Beatles, I got slated for being a bit too heavy with the other guys in the band," he said. "It was a bit as if I was taking over as the manager. I thought with the new band, I'll give them total freedom, so no one can accuse me of that again . . . and you can't do that either. You started to have people saying, 'Hey man, c'mon, produce us.' No one would take up the baton, the role. So I came back to that.

"The whole of 'Wings Mark I' was to see if that could be done. But there was too much indecision, and I wasn't willing enough to take the thing by the scruff of the neck and say, 'Look, I think we've gotta organize the solos you're gonna play.' It was a bit like we're gonna be the Grateful Dead and we're just gonna play what comes up. But to do that you've gotta know each other for a long time."[73]

Paul and Linda were deeply wounded by Seiwell's rebellion. In Henry's case, they knew what the problems were, and they knew he would leave eventually, having already quit once. They even, to a degree, respected him for standing up for his own artistry. But their relationship with Seiwell was not just that of band colleagues. It went back to the *Ram* sessions and had quickly become a real friendship.

The degree to which that wound quickly became a callus can be seen in Paul's response to the press questions about the two departures. Paul explained that in Henry's case, there were legitimate musical differences. But he skated over Seiwell's objections to recording the album as an overdubbing project, rather than as a band, saying only, "It's simple, really, Denny didn't want to go to Africa."[74]

"I was definitely not cool about it, are you kidding? I was livid,"[75] Paul admitted.

But the McCartneys did what they had to do: they hopped into the Lamborghini, headed to Gatwick Airport, boarded their flight to Nigeria, and tossed back a few stiff drinks.

25

STEP SOFTLY, THIS TOWN IS JINXED

———

Even down a guitarist and a drummer, Paul and Linda were determined to follow through with the sessions in Nigeria. Laine and Emerick were already in Lagos, the studio was booked, and the trio's instruments were en route. Paul had already resolved to account for Henry's absence by overdubbing the lead guitar lines himself; Seiwell's leaving complicated that plan only slightly, since Paul was also an able drummer.

Mostly, though, the defections activated one of Paul's strongest internal motivators—prevailing against the odds and the *I told you so*'s. It was the same impulse that led him to record *McCartney* on his own after the shock of the Beatles' breakup. Four years later, he was driven to make *Band on the Run* a success, not just for the sake of creating a hit, perhaps even a classic—although those drives were as powerful as ever—but because in the aftermath of two-fifths of his band walking out, he needed to show those former bandmates, and the world, that he could do it without them.

"After feeling completely deflated and bummed-out for a couple of hours, I just thought, 'Right, okay, we'll show you.' We will now make the best album, and when these guys hear it, they'll go, 'Shit, we should've gone.'"[1]

The trip to Lagos, on August 30, 1973, proved more eventful than Paul would have liked. As the flight neared Lagos International Airport, the captain, who had recognized Paul when he boarded, invited him to watch the landing from the crew's point of view. Considering the invitation one of the perks of fame, Paul accepted and headed to the cockpit, leaving Linda with the girls.

As the flight descended, Paul could see the jungle canopy, permeated with a thick layer of mist. "It's perfect, it's Africa," was his response to the aesthetically stunning view. But he quickly discovered that, at several hundred feet, aesthetics weren't everything.

"Can you see it?" the pilot said to his copilot, in search of the runway.

"I think it's over there, now," the copilot responded calmly.

"No, that's not it," the pilot said.

Watching from the cabin window, Linda saw the plane descending toward the trees that envelop the city, with no airport in sight, and turned white, her lifelong dislike of flying kicking in, while Paul, knowing that she was probably digging her fingernails into the armrests, commiserated at a distance, thinking *Oh my God! Are we even going to land?*

But soon the runway appeared, the plane landed, and Paul got his first glimpse of Nigeria. "The impression was, okay, this is very underdeveloped," he said. "It was a bit of a shock."[2]

Lagos was, in fact, still on the road to becoming a modern city, thanks to a boom driven by the nation's rich natural resources, and international trade connections. But its infrastructure remained rudimentary, as Ginger Baker noted.

"They built this great motorway in Nigeria, it's about sixty feet in the air," Baker said. "When they first opened it all they put across the end was a fence about two foot high. And they just put a sign saying: 'Branch Off.' First day they opened it a guy went bombing up and he went straight off the end into a swamp. They never saw him again. Then they thought, 'Well, perhaps we'd better block it off.'"[3]

Formerly a British colony, Nigeria became a republic on October 1, 1963, but three years later, a coup led by Major Chukwama Kaduna Azeogwu brought the country under military rule. At the time of the McCartneys' visit, General Yakubu Gowon was the head of state, and a civil war that raged between Nigeria and the breakaway state of Biafra, from 1967 to 1970 was still fresh in the memory. Nigeria's prosecution of the war had been brutal, with a blockade that led to the starvation of as many as two million Biafrans.

Britain's support of Nigeria, in the conflict, was one of the reasons (along with the British government's support of the United States in Vietnam and, as a flippant afterthought, "'Cold Turkey' slipping down the charts") John Lennon included in his letter to the Queen upon returning his MBE (Member of the Order of the British Empire award) on November 25, 1969.

McCartney had an unfortunate family connection to Nigeria. William Stapleton, Paul's uncle by marriage,* was a steward on the *Apapa*, a Nigerian liner that regularly sailed between Liverpool and Lagos in the 1940s. Stapleton was on board the ship when it sailed out of Liverpool on September 6, 1949; Paul was seven years old. While at sea, Uncle Will, along with pantryman Thomas Davenport, and ship's baker Joseph Edwards, stole £10,000 ($27,900) in African currency from the liner's strong room.

The theft was discovered when the *Apapa* docked in Ghana, five days later, and when the ship arrived at Lagos, it was reported to the captain. Learning that a search team was about to board, Stapleton and his confederates dumped the stolen cash in Lagos Lagoon. Nevertheless, the three were arrested on September 11, and on the way back to Liverpool, one of the conspirators confessed.

---

* William Stapleton married Paul's aunt, Edith ("Edie") Kathleen McCartney, on January 5, 1924.

They were taken into custody upon arrival, charged with larceny on the high seas, and sentenced to three years imprisonment. The case was described, at the time, as "a great blemish on the Merchant Navy's reputation"[4]—and was considered a family disgrace among the McCartney clan.

Twenty-four years later, Paul would be working daily at EMI's Lagos studio, at 7 Wharf Road, overlooking the lagoon in the port of Apapa; for all Paul knew, his uncle's purloined loot was buried in the silt nearby.

As Paul quickly discovered, the street-level reality of life was nothing like the colorful picture Tony Palmer's culture-focused film painted. Sanitation was basic, with clean drinking water only available to a minority. Cholera, yellow fever, typhoid and other diseases were rife. Emerick remembered driving through the city center in a cab and seeing someone walking along the road, bound in white sheets. "Leprosy," his cabdriver told him.

Before the trip, the entire Wings party visited London's Tropical Disease Hospital to have shots for the diseases that were rampant in Nigeria. Only two years earlier a major cholera outbreak killed nearly 3,000 people. Paul and company were also required to take antimalarial drugs throughout their stay.

Odion Iruoje, EMI Lagos's studio manager, and the head of EMI's operations in Nigeria, arranged for a car to take the McCartney party from Lagos International Airport[*] to a secure villa complex on the outskirts of the Ikeja district. The complex, known as a GRD, or Government Residential District, was a safe haven for wealthy tourists and locals. Paul, Linda and the kids shared one villa; Denny, Geoff, Trevor and Ian shared another.

September was the end of Nigeria's rainy season, but temperatures were in the mid-80s, and humidity was high. Lack of clean water meant that swimming pools were uncommon. Astonishingly, the McCartneys had booked their visit to Lagos without having researched the city, or even looked into what kind of weather to expect.

"We thought great—lying on the beach all day, doing nothing, breeze into the studios and record," Paul said of his fantasy vision of the trip. "It didn't turn out quite like that. It was at the end of the rainy season. We thought it was going to be tropical, warm and fantastic. It turned out to be a torrential monsoon."[5]

Iruoje, who added to his many jobs the role of point man and facilitator for McCartney while he was in the country, gave the celebrity visitors a crash course in what they should and should not do. The streets of Lagos and its surrounding districts, he told them, were barely safe for locals, and not at all for tourists, especially white tourists. Though they were staying in a secure compound, Iruoje advised them against traveling alone, particularly at night.

---

[*] The airport was later renamed Murtala Muhammed International Airport, after a military head of state who came to power in 1975 and was assassinated a year later. At the time the McCartneys visited, it had a single terminal and a single runway.

"Paul's [villa] was about a mile down the road from ours," Laine recalled. "We were all warned about going out after dark because there were lots of robberies. And for robbery out there, because it's a military setup, they take the guys down to the beach and shoot them publicly. Execute them tied to a pole. In other words, it was just as much to their advantage, if they were going to rob you, to kill you, because then you couldn't recognize them in a lineup."[6]

"They had an execution one day on the beach!," remembered a dumbstruck McCartney. "They just take this guy out, tie him to an oil drum, and go, *pop*. And then they sell wooden souvenirs of the dead guy, little carvings. We said, 'Er, we're not used to *this*, lads.' The next day it was a beach again—'Hooray! Come and swim!' *Weird*. It was pretty different from all we expected."[7]

Geoff Emerick took an instant dislike to the villa he shared with Denny and the roadies, and he found his first glimpses of jungle life downright creepy, partly (but not entirely) because of Denny's inclination to prank him.

"I opened the door to the pantry," Emerick remembered, "and nearly jumped out of my skin: somebody had stored their collection of dead spiders there, all stuck on a big polystyrene whiteboard with pins. When I went to sleep that night and pulled the covers back, I found that Denny had discovered the collection, as well, and had put several of the dead spiders in my bed, as a practical joke. Suddenly I didn't like Mr. Laine quite so much . . . but luckily, I'd seen the spiders beforehand, so I didn't react nearly as severely as he'd obviously hoped I would.

"The next morning, I woke from a deep, refreshing sleep, and in the warmth of the sun everything seemed a lot brighter. This place isn't so bad, I was thinking as I gazed out the bedroom window. At least the villa was gorgeous, the company tolerable, the impending project full of promise. Just then, this huge lizard popped up from the tall grass, staring right at me. It had a big red head and a green neck . . . it was terrifying! I didn't know if it was dangerous or poisonous; I didn't know what to think. Then I began looking around the bedroom and realized that I was sharing my space with a family of translucent 'jelly lizards,' scuttling all over the walls, ceilings, and floors. One night in that villa was quite enough for me."[8]

Emerick quickly phoned Iruoje, who found him a hotel room in the city center. (That did not turn out to be much better; his hotel room was infested with cockroaches.)

———➤

As the McCartneys were settling into their villa in Ikeja, about 13 miles from the studio—but an hour by car, taking into account the heavy traffic in the city center—Geoff Emerick was at the studio to familiarize himself with its setup. It was a compact facility: attached to the studio was a pressing plant, where EMI (Nigeria) Ltd. had pressed and distributed Beatles records since 1963; the Nigerian 45 of 'Love Me Do' carried the same typo as the British promo pressing, with Paul's surname misspelled 'McArtney.' Iruoje, who EMI hired to oversee its Nigerian operations shortly after his graduation from the Imperial College, in London, ran it all.

Emerick was shocked when he got out of his taxi and had his first glimpse of Iruoje's domain.

"[The studio was] very primitive. EMI Lagos was virtually a shed and an eight-track with one stereo machine and no spares. If anything went wrong it meant switching cards [circuit boards] around all the time... [It was] about 20 by 30 feet with about a 17-foot ceiling, and about 13 by 16 feet for the control room. The board was an EMI transistor board. But the studio [was] very busy. There were about six groups a day going in there—seven days a week."[9]

The studio had a standard (if aging) EMI console, and all the necessary cables. But it lacked some important items. Apart from a couple of Neumanns, like those EMI in London used, most of the microphones were mediocre. The tape deck had a troublesome limitation as well. Usually, an artist adding overdubs to a recording did so while hearing, through headphones, a mix of the existing tracks. But at the Lagos studio, it was possible to play only a few recorded tracks while adding a new one, so a musician recording a new track could not hear all the other instruments or voices already captured on tape.

It turned out, Emerick discovered, that this was not an issue for EMI Lagos. The recordings made there were live in the studio—ensembles came in and performed, their sound spread across the eight tracks, from which a stereo mix would be made. To Emerick's amazement, overdubbing was not part of the local staff's world.

Most crucially, though, Emerick discovered that isolation booths and acoustic screens, used to keep groups of instruments and voices sonically separated—standard in his world—were unknown in Lagos. Emerick described what was needed to Iruoje, who hurried in carpenters to quickly construct what their famed client needed.

Consequently, when Paul and Linda stopped by the studio to orient themselves the next day, what they found was a construction site. This was a matter of some concern, since sessions were scheduled to begin in two days, on Monday, September 3.

"When we first went to have a look at the studio," Paul said, "there was about four or five black carpenters who were building booths because they don't use them out there apparently.

"These guys were boppin' about to a record and smoking some native weed I think!"[10]

Everyone, including Paul, pitched in to help building; by Monday everything was ready to roll.

Until then, Paul and Linda saw to the details of the vacation side of the trip—something that was part of deal, in their minds, ever since the idea of recording in a distant locale first occurred to them. Intent on finding a place for the family to swim, Paul asked Iruoje for a recommendation. Iruoje advised joining the Lagos Country Club, not far from their villa. Paul's Beatles past status paid dividends there: when he asked what was involved in membership, the manager pointed to a photo of the Beatles on his wall and told Paul that if he signed it, he and his family were members.

1) JAIL NOISES,
2) LAUGHTER.
3) "
4) "
5) DA "
6) FRENCH BROADCASTER
7) PARTY NOISES
8) CANNON SHOTS
(ALTERNATIVES

MONO ☐   STEREO ☐   CM/S. ☐
I.P.S.

QM 09 22 05 503   3M and 'Scotch' are trade marks of 3M Company

Paul's other goal for the trip was to soak up some African sounds. He did not know a lot about African music, beyond recordings by Fela Ransome-Kuti, and occasional World Music programs on the BBC. But what he heard in the Ginger Baker documentary made him eager to learn more. Perhaps he could assimilate some ideas he could transform for his own use, as he had done in Jamaica, and even watching the documentary on the Kreen-Akrore. He would keep an eye out for performances, and he asked around for recommendations of players who might add some local flavor to his music more directly.

"We went there intending to use some of the local musicians—thought we might have some African brass and drums and things."[11]

Recording Sessions

Monday–Friday, September 3–7, 1973.
EMI Studios, Apapa, Lagos.
Recording: 'Ma Moonia' (working title for 'Mamunia'), 'Band on the Run,' and 'Helen Wheels.'

The McCartneys quickly established a working pattern. They began each day with a morning swim at the Lagos Country Club. By 3:00 p.m., Paul and company were picked up in a Mercedes and brought to the studio, where they generally worked until 10:00 p.m., but sometimes continued until 4:00 or 5:00 a.m.

Firm believers that atmosphere was important, the McCartneys adorned the studio's drab walls with Wings posters—most notably one for 'Mary Had a Little Lamb,' either as inspiration to do better, or as a way of asserting that Paul will do as he pleases—and an eclectic selection of album sleeves. Among them were Fela Ransome-Kuti's *London Scene*, as well as an album of Glenn Miller Orchestra arrangements, recorded by the Syd Lawrence Orchestra at the Royal Festival Hall in

London on November 17, 1969, and *Hammond Sound* by Howard Blake. Originally released in 1966 and reissued in 1972, Blake's album—which included an organ rendition of 'Till There Was You'—was a taste of home on foreign soil, perfectly capturing the sound of the Great British seaside holiday.

These pinups joined a poster for the Nigerian artist Peter Okoh and his Patience Rhythm Dance Band, an act so obscure that they released only two singles in Nigeria. They went beyond decoration. The sounds of the Glenn Miller album informed Paul's thoughts about the orchestration he wanted for 'Bluebird,' and Kuti's album, which draws on funk, jazz and African influences, informed the rhythm section of what was then still called 'Ma Moonia,' as well as the brass arrangement he would later apply to 'Jet.'

"I'd taken a bunch of American soul records that I liked," remembered McCartney, adding another genre of music to the assortment pinned to the studio walls. "And I'd say [to Geoff Emerick], 'I really love the snare on this one' or 'the space on that one.' We knew we'd got the essence of the album [in our demos] and could add to it—the orchestration and overdubs and so on."[12]

Having rehearsed their new songs as a five-piece band, the core of Wings now had to decide how to record them as a three-piece. Paul considered finding a drummer. Ginger Baker would make a magnificent substitute, as would Baker's business partner, Bayo Martins. But the famously irascible Baker was unhappy that Paul was using EMI's studio rather than his, and in any case, he was a decidedly *busier* player than Paul preferred. There was the possibility of finding a more pliable local player, but after brief consideration, he dismissed that idea, too.

"I didn't want to break in an African drummer 'cos it would have taken hours to tell him exactly what I wanted. I knew basically that I could do most of it,"[13] he explained. "I'm an okay drummer, I mean, I'm not a great drummer, but I've got a kind of style, I've got a feel, and I like playing drums. I knew if I kept it simple I would be able to cover it."[14]

Emerick was assigned two local assistants, who he knew only by their first names, Monday and Innocent, who would help him get around hitches that were evident from the start. As Denny Laine put it, "I can remember exactly what happened when we got there. Half of the equipment at EMI Lagos didn't work. It was there, but it wasn't plugged in. It was just kind of starting again and a challenge, you know. It was great, I enjoyed it."[15]

It was also not quite the climate-controlled setting the musicians were used to. The studio's control room was air-conditioned, more to prevent the equipment from overheating than to keep the staff comfortable. The studio itself was somewhat cooler than the control room, but if you opened the door to the adjacent pressing plant, a blast of sweltering, damp air poured in as you peered at shirtless workers, ankle-deep in water.[16]

For the first session, Paul chose 'Ma Moonia,' a light-textured song that did not require a drum

---

* Because the recording dates were not noted by Emerick's assistants, the date each song was recorded cannot be verified. However,

kit, and would therefore be an entirely nonstressful introduction to the sessions. It struck Paul as a good choice for other reasons, too. Its lyrics are full of rain and rain cloud imagery, and the fact that a tropical rainstorm began as they arrived at the studio seemed a good sign. So was the fact that, although the title is taken from a hotel in Marrakesh, Paul spotted a pair of plaques in EMI Lagos, one of which had the same word, in an alternate spelling.

"The funny thing is," he added, "there was a plaque next to it, which advertised a local carpenter. It read, 'Son of always.'"[17] Paul briefly considered using *Son of Always* as the album title, but soon reverted to the original plan.

For the basic take, Paul played a simple acoustic guitar part and sang a guide vocal, with Laine accompanying on congas. Once they had a solid take, they moved on to overdubs, with Laine adding a second acoustic guitar, this one with delicate filigree meant for the foreground, and Paul playing a bass line that dominates the instrumental texture. Two more tracks were devoted to Paul's doubled lead vocal (erasing the guide vocal in the process), and another captured Linda playing a synthesizer line throughout the song (all but the end of which would be faded out in the final mix).

That left one track free. Rather than bounce down to free up more tracks, Paul decided it would be best to record the backing vocals at the 16-track AIR Studios in London, where they planned to finesse the album on their return from Nigeria.

"They were very bare [recordings]," Laine observed. "We put the backing track down first, and we had to remember the arrangement, but just play the drums and the guitar part. So you're now learning the songs in little pieces, rather than as a song."[18]

For reference, Paul had brought along cassette copies of the demos the full band had made at Low Ranachan, and they consulted them when necessary. But mostly, Paul had the arrangements in his head.

Pleased with the basic recording of 'Ma Moonia,' Paul turned to a more complex track, 'Band on the Run.' Because of the song's sectional nature and changing textures, it would be recorded in two sections—the introduction and the song's first two verses made up Part 1; the section beginning with "*well the rain exploded*," was Part 2.

Emerick used three tracks for Paul's drums, a setup similar to that used by engineers in New York and London to record Seiwell. For the basic recording of Part 1, Paul's drums, Denny's electric guitar and Linda's keyboards (mainly, the prominent synthesizer part), together used five of the eight available tracks. Paul and Denny then added electric guitars, and on the final track, Paul added the bass line, preferring as always (going back to the Beatle days) to record the bass only after the other instruments were recorded, so that he could shape the line around the broader

the tape boxes and other internal documents show the order in which the songs were recorded and mixed, and other sources—diaries, interviews, newspaper reports and photographs—helped establish a definite Lagos timeline.

texture. The setup for Part 2 was similar, except that here, Denny played acoustic guitar on the basic track. The overdubs were acoustic and electric guitars and bass.

With all eight tracks now filled, Paul had Emerick bounce the percussion to a single track, freeing up two for Paul's lead vocal, and backing vocals by Paul, Linda and Denny. During the overdubs, the three improvised a spoken word section for Part 1, which Paul later dropped:

Denny: As I was walking along the bay . . . I'd sit and watch all the children . . .

Linda: . . . Walking by . . .

Denny: She seemed to say to me . . .

Paul: I couldn't tell what she was thinking, but I knew it was through.[19]

Laine, for one, was warming to the process, which gave him a more significant role than anything since *Wild Life*.

"It was a challenging album for us," Denny said at the time. "I'm more pleased working this way, because I can contribute more, whereas with Wings [as a 5-piece] I could only contribute certain things and I was sitting around the studio doing nothing a lot of the time. My main contribution has been in being able to pick up and understand exactly what Paul wanted. I sing a lot of backings, and I play a couple of long guitar solos, and that's great for me, I love having more of a combined effort than anything I've done before—it's a good direction."[20]

Paul closed out the first week of recording with 'Helen Wheels,' his play on words ("hell on wheels") song about his Land Rover. This had a special complication: it was a shuffle, a beat style that tested the limits of Paul's drumming skills. But he found a way: with Linda acting as a human metronome, calling out "1-2-3-4" (in the final mix, she can be heard toward the end of the song) and also playing cowbell, Paul played the triplets on a cymbal, while Denny Laine hit the bass drum. The overdubs included two more tracks of electric guitar (played by Paul and Denny in tandem), Linda creating synthesizer swells, and Paul's lead vocal. A bounce-down of the drum tracks freed up a track for the backing vocals.

'Helen Wheels' and 'Band on the Run' included a little word game for fans to discover. Both songs mention, in passing, "Sailor Sam," a name that would not have meant much to American listeners, although British listeners, and anyone close enough to Paul to know the details of his expanded project list, recognized Sailor Sam as a Rupert Bear character—the sailor who lived on the edge of Nutwood and took Rupert on rides in the sidecar of his motorcycle.

After a week in Lagos, Paul had three complete songs, or at least, recordings as complete as he could make them in Lagos. The occasional technical glitch was handled without losing much time, and there were neither musical nor interpersonal problems to grapple with. The only uncomfortable issue to arise was to do with Ginger Baker's dismay that Paul was recording at EMI. "There was a little political thing which we hadn't realized," Paul explained, "in that Ginger was slightly in competition with EMI."[21]

In an effort to pacify Len Wood—who was still seething about the recording costs for *Red Rose Speedway*—Paul was using EMI's Apapa facilities to keep recording costs down. But somewhere between London and Lagos, wires with Ginger Baker had become crossed.

"There was a bit of a kerfuffle at one point," Emerick wrote in his memoir, "because somehow Ginger Baker had gotten the impression that we were going to record the album at his Nigerian studio, ARC. There were lots of phone calls flying back and forth, but Paul was adamant that he had never promised to work anywhere but at the EMI studio."[22]

That "impression" was most likely created by Vincent Romeo, who had met with Baker, and who may himself have believed that this was Paul's intention.

"An American representative for Paul McCartney had a look around and was very impressed," Baker later wrote. "I was knocked out because a booking from Paul would really put us on the map. Through our contacts in the government, we arranged for Paul, Linda, Denny and the rest of Wings to get visas to come to Nigeria."[23]

"I am fuckin' angry," Baker later added. "The actual truth of the matter is that *Band on the Run* would never have been recorded if it wasn't for me."[24]

———

The McCartneys took the weekend off, but quickly discovered that there was little they could do in Lagos, in light of the admonitions to be careful going out alone, and the fact that there were not many tourist attractions in the city. Nor, for that reason, were there many tourists. Whiling away a few hours at the Lagos Country Club, it was hard not to second-guess his choice of Lagos over Rio de Janeiro. Rio had its dicey sections, but also areas filled with tourists, modern hotels and pristine beaches. It was hard to keep 'The Girl from Ipanema' from running, unbidden, through his head.

Iruoje, fully aware of the limitations on what the McCartney family could do in their downtime, arranged for a visit to the private estate of Chief Moshood Abiola. Abiola was one of Africa's richest businessmen, although local folklore magnified that distinction, holding that he was the richest African who ever lived.

Whether or not that was so, Abiola's story was fascinating. He started a business selling firewood when he was nine years old, and as an adult, parlayed a job as a bank clerk into better things, including a university education in Glasgow, and jobs at a number of international companies before becoming manager of the Nigerian arm of ITT. At the time of Paul's visit, he was working with the military government to upgrade Nigeria's rudimentary infrastructure, and putting together a deal to supply phone lines for the entire country. [25]

Normally, such a meeting would have generated some press, but Paul had told Iruoje that he did not want any press coverage while he was in Lagos, a request Iruoje honored. His principal memory of the meeting was that Abiola called him 'Mac' and mocked his monogamous ways.

"Mac," Abiola asked, "why you no have four wives?"

"One's enough trouble, Chief," Paul told him.[26]

Recording Sessions

Monday–Friday, September 10–14, 1973.
EMI Studios, Apapa, Lagos.
Recording: 'Mrs. Vanderbilt (working title for 'Mrs. Vandebilt'), 'No Words,' and 'Let Me Roll It.'

'Mrs. Vanderbilt' had been on Paul's song stack since early in the year, but a slight lyric tweak toward the end ("*Leave me alone Mrs. Washington / I've done plenty of time on my own*") not only linked the song to the title track's prison narrative (albeit very loosely) but also made that version of the refrain into a lightly veiled protest against the American government's refusal to grant him a visa. And along with the reference to doing time, the "*Ho Hey Ho*" section evokes the work songs of a chain gang.

Otherwise, the song remained true to its original inspiration: "*When your light is on the blink / You never think of worrying*" and "*When your bus has left the stop / You'd better drop your hurrying*," to say nothing of "*When your pile is on the wane / You don't complain of robbery*" are an over-the-top parody of Amy Vanderbilt's etiquette guide, and a dismissal of it, in the form of "*what's the use of worrying . . . hurrying . . . anything?*" Its opening line, "*Down in the jungle, living in a tent*," might have seemed like a reference to working in Lagos, but although his surroundings perhaps suggested the image to Paul, he lifted it from a gag made famous by the British music hall performer and comedian Charlie Chester.*

When Paul, Linda and Denny turned up to begin work, there was a problem—not a tropical storm, this time, but a power cut that sent the studio into darkness midway through a take. It was like the Midland Hotel in Manchester, all over again, but without José Feliciano to guide them. EMI Lagos had a generator, however, and Monday and Innocent got it running, leaving

---

* The opening lyric was plundered from the BBC radio sketch show *Stand Easy*, which ran from 1945 to 1950. One of the sketches featured on the show, entitled "Tarzan of the Tape" included the chant: "*Down in the jungle / living in a tent / Better than a prefab—no rent!*"

Paul hoping the microphones would not pick up its hum. A few tests showed that recording could continue unimpeded.

The basic backing for 'Mrs. Vanderbilt' had Paul drumming, Denny playing a steady folk strum on acoustic guitar, and Linda playing a sparse but interesting electric piano part. A second acoustic guitar, bass and lead vocal were overdubbed, the end of the vocal track giving way to laughter, at what sounds like a rehearsed level of madness. Emerick again surrendered the possibility of a stereo drum effect, bouncing the three drum tracks down to one so that Paul could double his lead vocal and add a lead guitar line.

The Laine-McCartney collaboration, 'No Words,' was taken up gingerly; this was the backdrop of Henry McCullough's final confrontation with Paul, after all, and it had not been rehearsed since then. Paul got behind the drums, Denny played the rhythm guitar part on an electric guitar with a wah-wah pedal, and Linda played the electric piano, to complete the basic track. Paul and Denny then undertook a series of electric guitar overdubs, Denny on slide.

"It became a slightly different song from the way it was before," Denny said of the recorded track's differences from the version the five-piece Wings had rehearsed. "It's still the same melody, the same lyric, but the approach to it was based on what the backing track was like."[27]

One difference, Denny explained, was serendipity—a mistake that turned out well. "Paul was playing the drums and he forgot where to come in. So he stopped and then came in a bar later. And we thought, 'Well, that's unusual,' and kept it in. All these little things that happened accidentally, suddenly became part of the song."[28]

Paul and Denny agreed to record the vocals in London, so in Lagos, 'No Words' had no words; it also clocked in a 4'29".

'Let Me Roll It,' a slow rocker with an arresting guitar riff, rounded out the second week of sessions. That riff, however, was not recorded during the Lagos sessions, nor were the vocals. On the basic track, Paul played drums, with Denny on electric rhythm guitar, and Linda playing electric organ. Three tracks remained available, but Paul decided to leave it at that.

———▶

The group's session wrapped early on Friday, September 14, when Paul, Linda, Denny and Geoff decided to venture into the Nigerian musical world. Ginger Baker, still keen to make inroads with the McCartneys, had told Paul that Fela Ransome-Kuti and Africa '70 were performing that night at the Afrika Shrine, Kuti's "music sanctuary." Originally called the Afro-Spot, the Shrine had until recently been based at the Luna Nite Club in Calabar, where Fela was filmed for the Baker documentary. Now it was based in the courtyard of the Empire Hotel, in the Surulere district, about six and a half miles from Ikeja.

Paul and Fela had never formally met, but Paul knew and admired his work even before Wings eavesdropped on his London sessions in 1971. Now he was eager to experience Fela and his band in a concert setting on their home turf.

But he was also there as a talent scout, looking for a few players he might hire for overdubs. The choice was ample: Kuti's group included more than a dozen percussion, reed and brass players, including Tony Allen (drums), Tunde Williams (trumpet), Eddie Faychum (trumpet), Igo Chico (tenor sax), Lekan Animashaum (baritone sax), Peter Animashaum (rhythm guitar), Maurice Ekpo (bass guitar), Henry Koffi (congas), Friday Jumbo (congas), Akwesi Korranting (congas), Tony Abayomi (sticks) and Isaac Olaleye (shekere, a West African percussion instrument).

Though Paul was not entirely unknown in Lagos, as he had discovered at the Lagos Country Club, he was not the pinup idol he was in most of the world; Fela was far more famous here than he was. "[In Nigeria,] Fela was like a prince,"[29] explained Laine. At the Shrine, Paul immediately began

To-nite At The
SHRINE

to feel uncomfortable, even though Baker—who was well known locally—had joined Paul and company at their table.

"I think we were the only white people there, and there was a lot of tension,"[30] Paul explained, adding that he had told his companions that because they were unfamiliar with the setting, it might be a good night to abstain from pot smoking.

"So, we're sitting there . . . and this guy comes up, he's crouching, and he's got a packet of Rothman cigarettes. And they're all joints. So he says, 'Want one of these?' And I go, 'No thanks, man.' The guy carries on around and he gets to Ginger Baker, and Ginger goes, 'Yeah, yeah, man, sure.' And he's lighting up and Fela goes, 'Ginger Baker—the only man I know who never refuses a smoke.' And I go, 'Okay, I'll have one of those.' Man, I tripped out. I mean, it was so strong. I mean, it was stronger than anything I'd ever had."[31]

The cocktail of antimalaria drugs, Nigerian grass and pent-up frustration, mixed with the ecstatic energy of Fela's music, exploded into a torrent of emotion for Paul.

"When Fela and his band eventually began to play, after a long, crazy buildup, I just couldn't stop weeping with joy. It was such a fantastic sound, to hear this African band playing right up your nose, because we were sitting right by them. The rhythm section was so hot, so unusual, that it was a very moving experience for me."[32]

Still, Paul's sense that his party was not welcome turned out to be correct. During the break, Baker had gone off to speak with one of the African musicians, so he was unavailable to intervene in what Emerick remembered as a tense encounter.

"Some of the musicians came over to say hello. We assumed it was going to be the usual kind of camaraderie that goes on at live gigs everywhere—swapping road stories, talking music, telling jokes. But it was anything but. To our surprise, our visitors were angry and hostile. I could see Paul getting alarmed; this was not the reception he had been expecting. Somehow, he managed to talk his way out of it and got the musicians calmed down enough to leave us alone."[33]

Fortunately, Fela noticed the fracas and further defused it by inviting Paul onto the stage and held his right arm aloft as Paul gestured toward Fela with his left hand. The moment was captured in a photo published in the *Lagos Evening Times* on September 18. Feeling reassured, Paul chatted with the musicians after the performance ended. Word quickly filtered back to Fela that Paul was trying to poach some of his players, and another apparent change of mood among Fela's ensemble was enough to persuade Paul that it was time to leave.

That was not the end of it, though. On Saturday, Paul decided to continue working at EMI Lagos, lacking anything else to do. While he, Denny and Linda were setting up, Fela and a sizable group of bodyguards walked into the studio. Paul, for a couple of seconds, was excited to see him, having been so completely taken with the concert; but a glance at the evident anger on Fela's face reminded him that the usual expectations did not apply here.

"You are trying to steal the Black African's music," was Fela's accusatory greeting.

"What are you talking about," Paul responded, "I've written it all myself."

"Yes, but you have come to steal the vibe," Fela continued, "and the African, we get no money. This is our music. If there's any money to be made, we must make it." [34]

Fela explained that there had been a precedent: the jazz trumpeter Hugh Masekela had come to Lagos, and according to Kuti, he used elements of his band's music in a recording he made in the United States. This was a slightly confusing explanation, since Masekela was an African as well. Granted, he was from South Africa, but although the regions have distinct musical traditions, they are not without points of contact.

"[Kuti was] really sensitive about the idea of people ripping off their music," Paul said. "They couldn't understand why we had come to Lagos. We told them there was no dirty motive behind it. It's just that we thought it would be sunny. We thought it would be sort of a holiday while we recorded. That's all we wanted."[35]

As Paul and Fela debated, Laine went into the control room and telephoned Baker, who drove over to talk Fela down.

"I got a phone call that Fela and the army—this is about 40 strong—had arrived at EMI studios and stopped the session," Baker said. "They took over EMI. I said [to Fela], 'It's Paul McCartney, we really can't do this.'"[36]

As Kuti sat stone-faced at the back of the control room, Paul offered to prove the music was his own and uninfluenced by Afro-beat. Emerick threaded up one of the session reels and played a couple of songs, and Kuti seemed persuaded that McCartney had not lifted his rhythms, melodies, forms or even timbres. Hoping to create further goodwill, Paul promised Fela that when he returned to London, he would promote Fela's music in his own interviews.

"Just as swiftly as it had begun, the entire matter was dropped,"[37] Emerick noted. He took a few snapshots of Fela and Paul with Fela's bodyguards, everyone smiling.

But the matter was not dropped. As Paul privately lamented that his notion of fusing rock and African rhythms was now shattered, Fela made his way to a local radio station to express his outrage in an interview that soon found its way to the BBC World Service.

"Just in case Paul McCartney is over here in order to steal African music," he declared, "or in order to help African music to gain a wider audience than it has, I would like to make it clear that if he wants to steal it, we will fight him, and if he is under the impression that we need a wider audience to carry on with what we are doing, he is mistaken. We have enough people right here in Africa who enjoy and appreciate our music to keep us satisfied, and with our two studios in Lagos, we don't even need to travel abroad to record."[38]

From the radio station, Kuti drove to the offices of the *Lagos Evening Times*, where he continued to unload, this time to the columnist A. B. Attah. Attah listened, but before writing, he phoned EMI to get a comment from Paul, who was still at the studio, but was getting little done in the aftermath of Kuti's dramatic visit.

"Looks like you don't want me here," Paul responded. "I have not come to steal Afro rhythms, though Fela's music blew my mind."[39]

That evening's paper carried Attah's truly bizarre column. Under the title, "Step Softly, This Town Is Jinxed," he began by shattering Paul's incognito status, asking, "What is former Beatle Paul McCartney doing hiding out in Ikeja? Don't let your eyes pop, dear reader. I mean, Ikeja, Lagos, Nigeria. And I mean Paul McCartney, former bassist of the Beatles, author of 'Mean Mr. Mustard.' The same one [who] called a press conference some years back to announce his own death and give a eulogy." He went on to issue a variation of the warning in his headline—"Step carefully, this town kills big stars."[40]

—

Recording Session

Monday, September 17, 1973.
Batakota (ARC) Studio, Ikeja, Lagos.
Recording: 'Drink to Me' [Working title for 'Picasso's Last Words (Drink to Me)'].

As a way of rebuilding bridges with Baker, and thanking him for intervening with Fela, Paul scheduled a session at the drummer's studio in Ikeja—closer than EMI's studios to the family's villa, and not far from the airport.

"I thought, we can't let old Ginger down," said McCartney, glossing over the events of the previous day, "so we went and worked there too just to show no favoritism."[41]

The song he chose for the session, 'Drink to Me,' had developed in an unusual way since he vamped the chorus for Dustin Hoffman.

It now included four distinct sections—the opening verse, which sets up the song by reporting Picasso's death; the '*Drink to me*' refrain; another verse, distinct from the first, taking us to 3 a.m., when Picasso put down his brushes and went to bed; and an instrumental section in a French style, to evoke the music Picasso might have heard on the radio the night he died.

Either intimidated by Baker's presence, or keen to put on a creative master class, Paul began with an unorthodox backing track. Rather than putting down a basic rhythm section, Paul recorded a loop of backward drum sounds, and processed cowbell (also looped) that provided a skeleton framework on which instruments and voices could be hung. Paul and Denny then overdubbed two acoustic guitars, Paul added bass, and the trio overdubbed lead and backing vocals, with Denny and Paul splitting lead vocal duties between them.

Paul's ideas continued to evolve during the session. Since Baker's studio was a 16-track facility, they had ample room for additions. Next, he wanted to add the sounds of homespun shakers, made by filling tin cans with gravel from outside the studio. Paul, Denny, Linda, Ginger and a few others who were hanging around the studio recorded a track of these gravelly shakers, along with other percussion instruments Baker had in the studio.

It also occurred to Paul that it might be interesting to attempt a sonic equivalent of Picasso's collage technique.

"We started off doing ['Picasso'] straight," Paul explained. "Then we thought, Picasso was kind of far out in his pictures, he'd done all these different kinds of things, fragmented, Cubism and the whole bit. I thought it would be nice to get a track a bit like that, put it through different moods, cut it up, edit it, mess around with it—like he used to do with his pictures. You see the old films of him painting, he paints it once and if he doesn't like it he paints it again, right on top of it, and by about 25 times he's got his picture. So we tried to use this kind of idea, sort of a Cubist thing."[42]

Emerick cut the tape into roughly six sections and then joined them, in various sequences, until he found one that worked. "We were just making it up as we went along," Paul said. "We didn't have any big concept of it in mind at all. I just thought, we'll mess it up, keep messing it up until it sounds good, like Picasso did, with the instinctive knowledge you've got."[43]

And finally, he decided that since 'Drink to Me' was now meant to be both sound collage and song, it might make sense to include fragments from a couple of the album's other songs—a move that would give the album a sense of thematic unity and perhaps create the impression that it was a concept album. Throughout a light, tactile percussion section during one of the segments meant to evoke French radio, Paul, Linda and Denny sang the refrain of 'Jet,' a song they had not yet recorded outside of Paul's elementary Scottish studio. And over the gravel shaker section, they sang the "*Ho hey ho*" vocals from 'Mrs. Vanderbilt,' after which Paul launched into a scat-singing section, using the lyrics of 'Day-O' (The Banana Boat Song), but in a freewheeling melodic style inspired by African improvisatory singing.

With that, Paul called it a day, and he, Denny and Linda returned to their villas.

———————

That evening, Paul and Linda decided to go for a stroll, despite the warnings about going out at night. Their reasoning was stunningly naïve: Paul argued that people in New York had always told him it was unsafe to visit Harlem on his own, but when he did it, anyway, during his first long visit to New York with Linda, it turned out to be fine.[44] As their time in Lagos wound down, Paul felt that they hadn't really experienced the place. They expected to go out for only half an hour; the odds were in their favor.*

But as they walked along an otherwise deserted dirt track, a car drove up, slowing down along-side them. Paul's first thought was that they were offering him a ride.

"Listen, mate," he said, "it's very nice of you, thanks very much, but we're out for a walk."

The six people in the car were confused; usually people understood that they were being robbed and did not stop to glad-hand them. After a short conference, they rolled down the window again, and one called out, "Are you travelers?"

"No," Paul said, "we're out for a walk. We're on holiday—we're tourists."

That was all the mobile posse needed to hear. The doors flew open, and all six occupants jumped out, the smallest of them brandishing a knife. Linda began screaming, "Don't kill him! He's a musician! He's a soul brother! Leave him alone!"

Paul said, "What do you want, money? Here, take it," and handed over his cash.

"Give us the bags," one of the muggers said, and they handed over their carrying bags, with Linda's camera and film, Paul's cassette player, and copies of the Low Ranachan demo tapes.†

The bandits drove off—and then terrified Paul and Linda further by turning around and heading back toward them. Just as they were about to dive into the bushes, evidently not considering the potentially lethal wildlife those bushes might harbor, the car made a turn and drove away, tires screeching.

A shaken Paul and Linda walked the rest of the way to the villa as quickly as they could and made themselves coffee to calm their nerves. At that moment, there was another power cut. "We thought they'd come back and cut the power cables," Paul said. "It was just like Kojak, only the African version."[45]

———————

* In some accounts, Paul said they were walking home from Denny's villa. Both villas were in the GRD, which was supposed to be a secure zone.

† Although Paul and Linda mentioned the mugging in interviews shortly after their return to London, the detail of the demos being stolen was not mentioned until the 1980s. In various versions, Paul noted that the loss of the demos meant that he had to reconstruct the songs from memory at the sessions. But, in fact, 'Picasso's Last Words' was the last song recorded in Lagos. The four-track master of the demo remained in London or Campbeltown, and could be consulted, if necessary, before the continuation of the sessions at AIR.

Hearing the story, the next afternoon when Paul, Linda and Denny arrived at EMI, determined to continue working, Odion Iruoje told Paul that he had a lucky escape. But Iruoje was terrified and angry: it would not do to have one of EMI's biggest stars murdered in his territory, on his watch.

"If you had been Black, they'd have killed you," he told Paul. "But as you're white, they know you won't recognize them."[46]

Suddenly, the studio seemed stuffier than usual to Paul. He stepped outside for air, but it was even worse—hot, humid, foul-smelling. Back in the studio, he began feeling a pain in his chest and was unable to breathe.

"He turned as white as a sheet," Emerick explained, "finally fainting dead away at our feet. Linda began screaming hysterically; she was convinced that he was having a heart attack. Odion dashed out and quickly assessed the situation; we were pleading with him to call an ambulance, but he coolly explained that he could get Paul to the local hospital in his car a lot sooner than any ambulance could. Paul was starting to come around by this point, but we lifted him off the ground and gently deposited him in the backseat. Then Linda and one of the roadies piled into the car and they went roaring down the street."[47]

At the hospital, a doctor assessed Paul calmly, assured Linda that it was not a heart attack—that it might be bronchial—and sent him home to rest.

Paul had come to Lagos with ten songs to record, and at this point he had brought seven close to completion. The three that remained—'Jet,' 'Bluebird' and 'Piano Thing'—were among the best of the new batch. And there was a new song, too—'Oriental Nightfish,' which Linda composed in Lagos, and Paul put on Wings' to-do list.

But Lagos was not fun for Paul anymore. At the Nigerian doctor's command, he spent two days at the villa, preparing to bring this adventure to an end. He placed calls to Romeo and Brainsby, asking them to make arrangements for his family, Laine and Emerick to fly back to London on September 22. He would hold a press conference at Gatwick upon his arrival.

Brainsby sent Romeo a memo with a detailed itinerary and arrangements for a coach to take the press to and from the Post House Hotel, just north of Gatwick Airport. It was a six-hour plan all told, with a coach to bring the reporters to the hotel, a 90-minute press conference, and the coach ride back into town.

The memo also included questions Paul should expect reporters to ask, among them a couple about Henry's and Denny's resignations; Paul's immediate plans for Wings; the decision to record in Lagos, and how the sessions went; the Fela incident; Paul's negotiations for an American visa and the possibility of an American tour; whether Paul and Denny might form a permanent song-writing partnership; and of course, whether the Beatles might get back together.

Paul paid one last visit to the EMI Lagos Studios, on September 21, most likely to compile the master tapes he was taking back to England. That afternoon, EMI laid on a farewell party that began with a riverboat cruise and ended with a barbecue on the beach. Ginger Baker was among the guests and brought Paul a copy of Fela Ransome-Kuti's latest LP, *Shakara*. Its jacket included three groups of women—48 in all, all topless—the first arrayed in the shape of Africa, the second making up the numeral seven, and the third a zero with Fela sitting at the center.

Just when it seemed that nothing else could go wrong, the plane the McCartneys, Laine and Emerick were to fly out on suffered brake failure, delaying the flight by 10 hours. They arrived in London at 3:00 a.m. on Sunday. The carefully orchestrated press conference was canceled, but Brainsby arranged for several reporters to be on hand.

Tired as he must have been, Paul gave a first-class performance. Asked how the trip to Lagos went, Paul went into cheerful, thumbs-up Macca mode without even batting those long eyelashes.

"It was a great experience," he said, "and we had no problems whatsoever."[48]

The Lamborghini was brought around from the car park, the McCartneys hopped in, and they were back at Cavendish Avenue before sunrise.

26

RESTLESS MOMENTUM

—

Sorting through the month's worth of mail awaiting him at Cavendish Avenue, Paul found a letter from EMI's group director Len Wood that arrived at the end of August, apparently just before they left, but which had gone unnoticed in the uproar caused by Seiwell's resignation. Unfolding the single sheet, he read:

> Dear Paul, I understand you're taking your family to our Lagos studios. Would advise against your going there as there's just been an outbreak of cholera.[1]

It was possible, in other words, that things in Lagos could have gone worse; as Odion Iruoje had put it just a few days earlier, they had a lucky escape.

Paul and Linda were so happy to be home and safe that they felt friendly even to the fans outside who had ignored his plea, published in the June *Fun Club Newsletter*, that they refrain from gathering in St. John's Wood.

As usual, there was a small group out front, among them the sisters Pat and Janet Dees and their mom, from New York, and two girls from Maine. They had been standing outside since about noon and had already enjoyed an eventful day, as loitering outside a star's house goes: they had seen Heather, Mary and Stella peek out the front gate; they had caught a glimpse of Martha; and they watched a couple of local kids return Poppy, who had run off on her own.

But around 5:00 p.m., there was some real excitement. Mother Dees, famished and tired of standing around, walked up the steps and rang the bell. Rose told them that Paul was still in bed, but a moment later, the door opened, and out he stepped—unshaven and tousle-haired, wearing a blue-and-white-striped short-sleeve shirt with a Wings button, followed by Linda in a blue top and orange skirt. They signed autographs, posed for photos, and engaged in light banter. Paul responded to a request that he show one of the girls his wedding band by also holding up his hand to show that he had drawn a horse on it. Linda told one of the Maine girls that as a teenager, she had been a camp counselor in Washington, Maine.

Pat Dees, intent on extending the encounter, peppered Paul with questions about the Lagos trip ("It was quite hot, but we were beginning to like it") and asked if his new album would be out soon ("Yes"). Two more girls, who had been watching from across the road, joined the crowd. After a few moments, Paul spotted more fans heading toward the house and brought the encounter to an end.

"He started to close the gates," Pat Dees later wrote, "then pulled them open saying, 'Now, you're not going to hang around the house all night, are you?' looking at my mom as if to get us going. We had already begun to walk away, so she said, 'We're leaving!' He gave us one of those sexy smiles and closed the gates. So, we left quite content."[2]

Paul took a week to get back into London life, and to catch up with MPL business. The Australian tour would have to be canceled, for starters. Someone had to take the fall for the Lagos trip, too, and it might as well be the guy who went for an advance look and apparently promised Baker that Paul would use his studio. So, farewell, Vincent Romeo. For the next few months, David Minns, the McCartneys' assistant, and Jane Buck, their secretary, would run the office.

Minns, for one, approached this interim arrangement with only modified enthusiasm, as it would mean "long hours and low pay again; who needs it?"

"McCartney," Minns later wrote of his boss, "is notoriously tight with money but after Apple and Allen Klein who can blame him? Linda was the opposite; she was great and generous—of heart as well as pocket—and Jane and I forged a good relationship with her. Paul was more guarded and never let you in on very much that was going on in his head. When he did he was magic, but I just wish one could have seen more of it. I guess he's too suspicious of everyone and most alarmingly, incredibly naïve at times."[3]

At the end of September, Paul decided he should make things right with Henry McCullough—not to persuade him to rejoin Wings, but to see whether he could take a sad song and make it better. Henry had not been idle; a couple of weeks after quitting Wings, he was in the recordings studio, working on Donovan's next album. He also began work on an album of his own,[*] and he was seen playing around town: when Frankie Miller performed at Finsbury Town Hall, on October 8, Henry was in his backing band. As for having a band of his own, the music press

---

[*] McCullough's album *Mind Your Own Business!* was released on George Harrison's Dark Horse Records label on October 31, 1975.

speculated that he planned a group with Seiwell and members of the Grease Band and Free—reports that Henry told *Melody Maker* were "a load of crap."[4]

Henry was surprised when Paul telephoned, but he agreed to a meeting at MPL. They smoked a couple of joints and downed half a bottle of whisky, while Paul asked Henry what he was up to and told him some tales of Lagos.

"Look," Paul said, "I know we've had our differences, but I really appreciate the time you've been with the band, and I want you to have this." He handed Henry a check for £5,000 ($12,000) and a flight case full of guitar strings. McCullough was touched by the gesture, but he was bemused by Paul's indifference to whether the fracturing of Wings suggested problems with his approach to running a band.

"Two of the band members in Wings walked out in the same week for different reasons, and he never asked why," Henry mused. "You can take from that what you want."[5]

Paul seems not to have sought out Seiwell, either because he thought he had already returned to New York, or because the personal aspect of Seiwell's departure still stung. The drummer remained in London, trying to decide what to do next. For Seiwell, the gut-wrenching decision to leave Wings was compounded by a telephone call, on September 28, relaying news that his father, Donald Seiwell, had died suddenly of a heart attack at age 57, having collapsed while attending a Friday night football game. The Seiwells immediately flew back to the United States. The combination of cutting ties with the McCartneys and losing his father hit Denny hard.

"Leaving the band was the hardest decision I ever had to make in my life," the drummer said, "and it was one that affected my life profoundly. The years that followed were not pretty; for many, many years, they weren't pretty. I didn't know what to do with the situation. I had a problem with alcohol over it, which I solved. It was a very, very difficult journey for my wife and I to go through."[6]

———

* Seiwell moved to San Francisco after his father's death and briefly formed a band with Henry. When that split up ("there was a lot of drinking going on, it wasn't fun," Seiwell said), he moved to Los Angeles to resume his career as a session player. When McCartney played in Anaheim in 1993, Seiwell sent a note backstage and was taken back to Paul and Linda's dressing room. "The kids were there, which we hadn't seen in years, and it was just a beautiful, beautiful reunion, and everything was forgiven and forgotten." When McCartney's *Wingspan* documentary was in production, in 2001, he hired Seiwell as a consultant, making up for the years of low wages.

Recording Sessions

Tuesday–Friday, October 2–5, 1973.

AIR Studios, Studio One, London.

Recording: 'Jet,' 'Bluebird,' 'Oriental Nightfish,' and 'Piano Thing' (working title for 'Nineteen Hundred and Eighty Five.')

Mixing: 'Helen Wheels.'

It was important to Paul to keep up the momentum on *Band on the Run*. Even before he left London for Lagos, he had booked time at George Martin's AIR Studios, in Oxford Circus. AIR was hopping that week: besides McCartney, Roxy Music were there to mix their *Stranded* album, and Procol Harum were at work on *Exotic Birds and Fruit*.

Paul had expected to use AIR for the album's final touches—orchestral sweetening, last-minute overdubs, and mixing. But the limitations of the EMI Lagos Studios meant that there were more overdubs to be recorded in London than he expected, and his illness and early departure from Lagos meant that there were songs to be recorded from start to finish.

From that point of view, he was behind schedule. On the other hand, he had completed most of the album in three weeks, and though he was intent on efficiency, he was not going to ruin it by rushing.

Paul's first order of business was to release a single from the Lagos sessions, to show that Wings were still a going concern, even in their current, drummerless (there were still a couple of excellent guitarists) incarnation. Of the Lagos recordings, 'Helen Wheels' was the only fully overdubbed track, and the most commercial, and the group spent the first day at AIR mixing it, with Geoff Emerick engineering and Peter Swettenham assisting. (Swettenham had been a guitarist in Grapefruit, one of the first bands signed to Apple, before he moved to the other side of the glass.)

While Paul, Denny, and Geoff Emerick rode the faders on Tuesday afternoon, Mike McGear dropped by the studio. Mike was in town with Grimms to rehearse for a tour of British universities, starting in Swansea on October 17, and Paul invited him to hear a preview of Wings' next LP, and to discuss expanding the two songs they had recorded together ('Leave It' and 'Sweet Baby') into a full album at the start of 1974. Mike found Paul's desire to release 'Helen Wheels' as a single puzzling.

"I went down to the studio," Mike remembered, "and there they were, Paul and Wings, all dancing around. Paul was saying, 'Isn't it great?!' and bopping up and down. I just had to sit down and say nothing because it did absolutely nothing for me. It was a nice little pop tune but not where that man's head's at, at all. He's a very clever boy, so to waste it on that seemed a shame."[7]

For the B side, Paul continued his practice of reviving orphans from previous projects, in this case choosing 'Country Dreamer,' a song he had demoed before the *Ram* sessions but only got around to recording properly during the sessions for *Red Rose Speedway*. Alan Parsons had mixed 'Country Dreamer' on January 10, 1973, but it did not make the album's final cut. Revisiting Parsons' mix, McCartney decided to use it untouched. Both tracks were mastered the next day at EMI and assigned the matrix numbers 7YCE.21734 and 7YCE.21735.

Paul devoted the first part of the Wednesday session to the clerical task of transferring the 8-track recordings from EMI Lagos Studios to 16-track for the addition of vocals and other overdubs. ('Drink to Me,' recorded at Baker's Batakota Studio, was a 16-track recording and did not need to be copied.)

But new recordings were made that day as well: Paul and Denny made a first attempt to record 'Jet,' but were unsatisfied with the results and set it aside.

Instead, they picked up acoustic guitars and recorded the straightforwardly simple backing track—just the two guitars and a scratch vocal—for 'Bluebird,' a graceful tune with sweetly poetic lyric that continued the series of metaphorical avian fantasies that already included 'Blackbird' and 'Single Pigeon'—subliminal echoes, perhaps, of Paul's childhood days as a devoted reader of S. Vere Benson's *Observer's Book of Birds*.

Here, the bluebird is a stand-in for love, or being in love: a single bluebird flies through his lover's door in the dead of night, giving her a magic kiss that makes her a bluebird, too, whereupon they fly across the sea to a desert island together. The chorus, in that final scene, shifts from "*I'm a bluebird*" to "*we're the bluebirds*." With the acoustic backing in the can, Paul called it a moderately productive day.

Although she had not pushed her own material, Linda had written more songs since 'Seaside Woman,' and Paul wanted to get some of her music on tape. So Paul, Linda and Denny devoted the entire October 4 session to recording the song Linda wrote in Lagos, 'Oriental Nightfish.' As Paul remembered it, Linda had a basic demo with lyrics, but the music took shape during the course of the session.

"It was one of those, 'Let's make up something, shall we?' It was Linda's idea, so we made up a little bit of backing," said Paul, "and Linda got into a bit of a Shangri-La's kind of mode, and that was it really. It just kind of took one evening to make up."[8]

The song was mainly a straightforward chord progression that unfolded at a moderate tempo, with a bridge built from fragments of the verse progression, and short, briskly played four-chord blocks used as dramatic punctuating figures at section breaks. Strikingly, it does not have a melody, as such: the lead vocal is spoken, a stream of impressionistic images—colors, descriptive passages and references to the mysterious creature of the title. It is more a quasi-cinematic mood piece than a conventional song.

Paul and Linda did most of the work, starting with Paul on drums and Linda on piano, with Linda overdubbing a Moog synthesizer and the vocal, and Paul adding electric guitar figures, mellotron and bass. Denny Laine's contribution was a flute line, following the contours of those chordal punctuation figures.

For the final session of the week, on October 5, Paul brought in the song he had been calling 'Piano Thing,' based as it is around an insistent, funky piano figure. Creating the song's lyrics had proved daunting for Paul.

"With a lot of songs I do, the first line is it," he explained. "It's all in the first line, and then you have to go on and write the second line. With 'Eleanor Rigby' I had *'picks up the rice in the church where the wedding has been.'* That was the one big line that started me off on it. With this one it was *'No one ever left alive in nineteen hundred and eighty-five.'* That's all I had of that song for months.[9] But the words just came to me the day we were due to record."[10]

Now the song was finished and ready to record, but that first line remains the most interesting—the hint of an apocalyptic vision, with 1985 guaranteed to put George Orwell's dystopian *1984* in listeners' minds (even though, as Paul's comment suggests, the year was chosen for its rhyming possibilities). In his completed lyric, though, the dark imagery of the opening line evaporates into a mundane love song, and not even the McCartney standard model. With neither arching melodies, nor phrases dripping with treacle, the lyrics are quick and riffy, wound around the piano figure, which embodies much of the song's energy. The only place where Paul's usual melodic strength bursts out is in a short connecting figure within the verse, when he sings variations on the words "*Oh I,*" like a jazz improviser, melismatically threading his way around them before the verse's final couplet.

But constricted melodies and throwaway lyrics are not the whole story here. In its finished form, the song's freewheeling structure and its evolving (and sometimes suddenly changing) instrumental textures make it an exceptionally magnetic track, greater than the sum of its comparatively simple components, and in many ways the most brilliant (if also the most overlooked) piece of music on the album.

The most central of those components is the C minor piano riff that opens the song—a short, repeating cell, pounded out in a steady rhythm, and building on a descending, sparsely harmonized figure that dances over a bass line in alternating octaves. In the introduction and verses, this riff comes to rest on an A-flat major chord, a surprising harmonic shift after so many repetitions of the C minor riff, and is supported by synthesizer growls and steady organ chords.

The riff returns to anchor the first verse, and Paul's vocal plays off it, sounding (except for that dark opening line) more like a vocal vamp than a formal verse. Another surprise follows—a section Paul marked as an "Interlude," in which the forward-driven repetition of the piano riff grinds to a halt, replaced by a smooth, sustained organ tone over a calmly descending chord progression (C minor, B-flat major, A-flat major, G major), with a contrasting piano riff (this one rising and insistent, repeated without alteration over the changing chords). The effect calls to mind, of all things, the Supremes' 1966 hit, 'You Keep Me Hangin' On.'

A repeat of that short section lands on a C minor chord that Paul holds for an extra bar before shifting up a half-step to D-flat minor—another harmonic surprise—to support a soprano and alto chorus singing a wordless passage.

In an ingenious touch, this vocal passage uses the same notes as the rising piano riff in the first part of the "Interlude." But where the piano version rumbles in the background, the vocal version holds the spotlight. The choral passage heads toward an A-flat major chord, accented by the organ—an arresting touch that has an effect like that of a slashing brushstroke of bright red paint in the middle of a blue and green canvas. From there, Paul heads back to C minor, the song's opening riff, and the next verse.

Paul would assemble this richly layered texture over the next few days, working mostly on his own, with sparse contributions from Denny and Linda. At the October 5 session, though, the task was to assemble the basic track. The rhythmically driven piano part being so central to the song, Paul recorded it first. He then added drums. Linda overdubbed the simple but ear-catching synthesizer swells, with Paul adding the organ and Denny contributing a rhythm guitar part. That was where Paul let it stand for the moment.

Paul and Linda also found time to make a guest appearance during their time at AIR. An old acquaintance of Paul's, Terence Nelhams-Wright—"Tel" to his friends, although the public knew him as the 1960's teen idol Adam Faith—was working at AIR on *I Survive*, an album inspired by an automobile accident two months earlier. As Faith remembered it, Paul and Linda popped into his studio to say hello.

"I was down at AIR Studios one day and Paul was recording there," Faith recalled. "He and Linda came in and we got chatting. He asked me what I was doing, and I said I was just making an album. He said, 'You don't need a bass player, do you?' So, I said, 'Yeah, Christ!' It all came from there. I asked Linda if she'd do some singing on the album 'cos I love her voice."

Paul never got around to playing bass for Faith, but he did contribute to his album, adding Moog to 'Change,' 'Never Say Goodbye,' 'Goodbye' and 'Star Song,' as well as vocals, with Linda, on the last.[11]

Faith and his wife, Jackie, invited the McCartneys to dinner at the RAC Club (Royal Automobile Club) on Pall Mall, a first-class members-only haunt normally frequented by automobile enthusiasts. Sitting in the club's lounge drinking coffee after dinner, with no other customers in the room, Faith asked Paul whether he would mind playing 'Let It Be' on the grand piano sitting on a stage, beneath a portrait of the Queen. Paul agreed, and sharing the piano bench with Faith, he sang the old Beatles favorite—or part of it. As Faith reported the incident to his producer, the songwriter David Courtney, the concierge "stormed into the room and instructed Paul to stop playing immediately."[12]

Recording Sessions

Monday–Friday, October 8–12, 1973.
AIR Studios, Studio One, London.
Recording: 'Jet' (Remake).
Overdubbing: 'No Words,' 'Bluebird,' 'Piano Thing' (working title for 'Nineteen Hundred and Eighty Five'), 'Let Me Roll It' and 'Drink to Me' [working title for 'Picasso's Last Words (Drink to Me)'].

Fela Kuti's claim, less than four weeks earlier, that McCartney and his group had traveled to Lagos to "steal the Black African's music," was still ringing in Paul's ears on October 8, when Denny Laine bumped into an old friend, Afro-pop percussionist Remi Kabaka, at AIR Studios. Laine knew Kabaka from his time in Ginger Baker's Air Force, and together with multi-instrumentalists Steve Winwood, and Abdul Lasisi Amao (another former member of Air Force), Kabaka had formed the London-based Afro-pop trio Third World. After finishing their debut album *Aiye-Keta* in August, Kabaka was gigging and doing session work.

Setting up to begin overdubs on 'Bluebird,' McCartney invited Kabaka to join Wings for the afternoon. Paul's desire to hire African musicians during the Lagos sessions was frustrated by local hostility, so the irony of Kabaka's African heritage was not lost on his host.

"This old friend [of Denny Laine's] from the past named Remi Kabaka turns up. And he's from Lagos!" Paul chaffed, "so he's the only one [African musician] who ended up doing anything on the album."[13]

Kabaka added some light percussion—sticks, guiro and conga—to 'Bluebird.' That was the highlight of Monday's overdubbing session, which also included replacing the song's scratch vocal with a fresh lead vocal, with harmonies from Denny and Linda.

One song remained to be recorded—or rerecorded, since an earlier attempt came to grief. The trio devoted Tuesday's session to a remake of 'Jet,' a straightforward rocker with a sinewy melody, and a driven rhythm. Much of the song was completed at this session with Paul and Denny creating the basic track on drums and rhythm guitar, respectively. Paul and Denny then both added more interestingly textured electric guitar lines—Paul playing a new Ampeg Dan Armstrong guitar he was breaking in during these sessions—and Linda played a synthesizer part consisting mostly of single sustained notes, deep in the bass, with a filtering effect that makes each note morph from a dark bass tone to a brighter, more complex sound. As part of the synthesizer overdub, Linda also played a solo line that traced the shape of the song's melody.

With ample time left, Paul added his lead vocal, and the trio recorded several tracks of backing vocals. One pass was devoted to the exuberant shouts of the title during the refrain (delivered with the same bite as the final syllable of Bowie's 'Suffragette City'—the word *suffragette* being, perhaps not coincidentally, among the McCartney song's lyrics). Another focused on the harmonies that support selected lines of the lead vocal. The day's work ended with Paul adding rippling piano figures at various points, and finally, his bass guitar part.

After the aborted attempt to record 'Jet' the previous week, this second version seemed to go smoothly—or at least, it seemed that way to Paul, Linda, and Denny, out in the studio.

In the control room, though, Emerick was on the verge of a meltdown. During one of the playbacks, he noticed that the cymbals had lost their bright top end. When Emerick asked Swettenham what was going on, the assistant had a look at the tape heads and discovered an unusually thick oxide buildup.

This was distressing, because it meant that the oxide on the master tape was shedding at an unusually fast rate—the consequence, Emerick theorized, of tape manufacturers using new formulas to bind the oxide to the tape's Mylar backing (although it could simply have been a defective reel).

"Not only was it irreversible, each time you played back or even rewound the tape, it got worse," Emerick explained. "The only thing you could do was to quickly make a second-generation copy of the audio on a good reel of tape and hope that the sound hadn't deteriorated too badly by that point. It was just our luck to have this one bad reel of tape just as we were recording such a great song."

Emerick's immediate dilemma was whether to tell Paul about the situation, breaking the energy and upbeat mood of the session, but allowing him to get the tape copied before it disintegrated further. The trio had, by then, recorded the basic track and quite a few overdubs, so Emerick opted to play the odds, hoping the session would end soon.

"I decided to try to mask the problem, which was becoming most noticeable on the crack of the snare drum and sizzle of the high hat. Every time we'd play the tape back, I would add more treble to the monitors so that Paul couldn't hear that the top end was disappearing. We finally did what I thought was the last overdub of the night. Breathing a sigh of relief, I looked over at Pete and said, 'Thank God!' Then, of course, Denny said, 'How about if we just add one more guitar?' and I thought, 'Oh no!' We had almost gotten to the point where you could see through the tape—

that's how much oxide had been shed. But to my relief, Paul vetoed the idea, and everyone packed up for the night."[14]

On Wednesday, it was back to overdubbing. 'Piano Thing' was revisited, with Paul replacing his rough vocal, and Linda and Denny contributing the backing and harmony vocals. Paul's bass line and a wiry guitar solo from Denny finished Wings' contributions to the track.

Also polished off that day was 'Let Me Roll It,' which had in common with 'Piano Thing' a repeating instrumental riff—in this case, a bluesy, slightly distorted guitar figure—as its spine. Something like the figure that runs through Lennon's 'Cold Turkey,' the 'Let Me Roll It' riff called for a distinctive atmosphere, which Paul and Emerick created by putting the guitar through a PA system rather than a guitar amp, giving it a bright, high-power sound.

Paul brought more juice to that sound by double-tracking the part. The bass line, nearly as characterful as the lead guitar part, was overdubbed, too, as were the vigorous lead vocal—with a hefty amount of slapback echo—and backing vocals for the refrain. These vocals were heartier, less artfully rarified than usual; they sound like a full-band singalong with Paul's lead.

Riding a wave of momentum, Wednesday's session tipped into Thursday, when Paul took up the experimental 'Drink to Me.' The track recorded at Baker's ARC studio was a brilliant start, but it was also quite loose: the rough lead vocal would need replacing, possibly some of the guitar work as well. Some of Emerick's on-the-spot section editing would need smoothing over by way of overdubs, and the track as a whole, running nearly six and a half minutes, would undoubtedly need a trim. Drumming, however, was the song's most pressing need, and Paul added it on Thursday morning.

The rest of the week was dedicated to vocal work. 'No Words' needed vocals, which Paul, Denny and Linda added, essentially singing lead in tandem, at times virtually in unison, with tight harmonies elsewhere. 'Drink to Me' also received fresh lead and backing vocals.

Checking through the list of songs, most were now complete, apart from orchestrations that Paul had yet to commission. With that in mind, Emerick ran off rough mixes of everything to date.

———

Paul wanted orchestral sweetening for seven of the songs—'Band on the Run,' 'Jet,' 'Bluebird,' 'Mrs. Vanderbilt,' 'No Words,' 'Drink to Me' and 'Piano Thing'—and he scheduled a session on October 17 for that purpose. But he had not yet engaged an arranger. Wanting to use someone he had not worked with before, and who could give him an up-to-date sound, he settled on Tony Visconti, a New Yorker whose work with David Bowie and Marc Bolan's T. Rex made him one of the hotter producers on the London scene. Laine had worked with Visconti before he joined Wings;

Visconti wrote the arrangements for Denny's classical-rock hybrid, the Electric String Band. And Paul knew him slightly—he had married Mary Hopkin in 1971.

McCartney telephoned Visconti on Saturday, October 13, and after catching up briefly with Hopkin, he suddenly realized that he was not entirely sure about Visconti's bona fides as an orchestrator. So he conducted a brief interview.

"Hi, Tony," he said, "I love the strings on the T. Rex, did you write them?"

"Yes," Visconti replied. Paul continued the quiz.

"Can you really read and write music?"

"Yes."

"In that case," Paul asked, "will you write strings for the album I've just finished?"

Visconti quickly accepted, and Paul invited him to Cavendish Avenue the next evening to listen to Emerick's rough mixes and discuss the details. Visconti brought Hopkin and their ten-month-old son, Morgan, with them, but once Paul and Tony began to discuss the orchestrations, Linda, Mary and the children took over the other end of the music room, far enough to be out of the way, but close enough for Linda to keep tabs on the discussion.

As Visconti remembered the meeting, Paul sat at the piano with two portable cassette machines. On one, he played the songs he wanted Visconti to score; on the other he recorded his comments about what he had in mind. In some cases, he played his arrangement ideas on the piano.

Visconti, like most arrangers, was not used to his orchestration ideas being preempted, or dictated to him as if he were simply an assistant, hired to notate someone else's musical lines. But there was some flexibility within McCartney's instructions.

"Some ideas he wanted me to strictly adhere to, and some were just sketches that I was asked to improve upon. For a song called 'Drink to Me (the Picasso song)' he said, 'Just do your thing, but in the style of Motown strings.'"[15] On hearing the tracks, Visconti had some ideas of his own. Hearing 'Band on the Run,' he proposed a high string part to shadow the synthesizer figures.

"Oh no you're not," Linda called from across the room. "I played that part, and you're not going to step on my part!"

Then came the kidney punch: Paul needed Visconti to complete the arrangements, hire the musicians and be ready to conduct the already scheduled session in three days.

"I was thrilled to be doing this for one of my idols but not so thrilled when he told me he needed all seven arrangements by Wednesday."[16]

Visconti completed the seven arrangements in 48 hours. He engaged David Katz to contract the string players, and Phil Kenzie—who came to the project through Mal Evans—to round up the necessary winds and brass. Because the needs of each song were different—'Band on the Run' used the 60 players of the Beaux Arts Orchestra; 'No Words' used only a string quartet—it also fell to Visconti to "strategize" the order in which the orchestrations would be recorded, so that players were not sitting around collecting fees when they weren't needed.

"When I turned up with the arrangements [at such late notice]," Visconti noted, "he was ecstatic about them and asked me to co-produce his brother's album,"[17] Visconti recalled.

Recording Sessions

Monday–Friday, October 15–19, 1973.
AIR Studios, Studio One, London.
Overdubbing: 'Band on the Run,' 'Mrs. Vanderbilt' (working title for 'Mrs. Vandebilt'), 'Ma Moonia' (working title for 'Mamunia'), 'No Words,' 'Bluebird,' 'Piano Thing' (working title for 'Nineteen Hundred and Eighty Five'), and 'Drink to Me' [working title for 'Picasso's Last Words (Drink to Me)'].

Wings and Emerick began the week by making a stereo mix of Linda's 'Oriental Night Fish,' which was set aside for another project Paul and Linda were planning, an album by Linda under the moniker Suzy and the Red Stripes. The team spent Tuesday compiling 16-track tapes, assembling reels of the best takes of several of the nearly completed songs for both the orchestral session and further overdubs.

The orchestral session was on October 17, and Visconti turned up at 10:00 a.m., looking bedraggled, but ready to conduct, for what turned out to be eight hours.

"The sixty musicians are already there, and I braced myself to begin the tedious arm waving (my bad style of conducting) and note correcting. The very first thing we did was the interlude between the first and second parts of 'Band on the Run'; it proved to be very difficult because the first section is in an entirely different tempo from the next. We just kept doing take after take, until we got the transition to work smoothly. Only some of the sixty musicians were wearing headphones, so it was a genuine job of conducting to bring them in and to keep them together. The rest of the day went a lot smoother. For the most part Paul acted the jovial perfectionist, which made it all seem like fun."[18]

The string sessions were scheduled for the morning, with the winds and brass in the afternoon. Among the horns, which included Geoff Driscoll, Dave Coxhill, Jeff Daly, and Phil Kenzie, was Howie Casey, a name from Paul's past. Paul knew Casey from Liverpool and Hamburg as the saxophone-playing front man of Howie Casey and the Seniors (formerly Derry and the Seniors). These days, Casey was a highly regarded London session man.

"The first number was 'Jet,'" Casey remembered. "And that consisted of two tenor saxes, a baritone sax, and a bass sax. I was one of the tenor sax players. They asked me to stay behind to do a couple of other numbers. I said, 'Yeah, fine.'"

Casey's solos are on 'Mrs. Vanderbilt' and 'Bluebird.'

"I did that in one take," Casey said of his 'Bluebird' solo. "Paul said, 'That's it. It's great.' I said, 'No, no, no. Come on, I can do better than that.' You know, because you are sort of feeling your way through it [on the first take]. He said, 'You can put a couple more takes down if you'd like.' So, I did. And then he said, 'No, the first one. Definitely, the first one.' That was neat."[19]

Paul also wanted to give Casey a solo on 'Jet,' beyond the part he recorded as one of the ensemble. That proved more complicated and required some orchestrational ingenuity from Visconti.

"He sang [the solo] to Howie, but the melody started higher than the upper limit on the tenor sax. . . . I solved the problem by writing out the phrase and gave the first half to the alto sax player. The first half was easy on alto sax but ended lower than the alto's range. Paul would not accept alternative notes once he had this part in his head, but he liked the idea of Howie playing the final handful of notes on the tenor sax. After several tries, the two sax players made the transition perfectly and helped make the song's end so much better."[20]

At the orchestral session, McCartney projected a clear sense that he knew what he wanted and, as Visconti noted, would not deviate from his goal once he set it. But there was also a hint of insecurity about whether he was hearing everything the musicians were hearing, as Phil Kenzie observed.

"Paul was directing everything. In fact, he was quite a stern taskmaster in the studio. I mean, at one point we were all coming in for a listen back, and I remember him putting everyone on their toes because he turned around and said, 'Okay, that's great, that was it.' And then he looked around the room at everyone and said, 'Wasn't it?' In other words, 'if you know anything I don't know, don't let us find it later—that had better be it.' So everyone just sort of went, 'Hmm, yeah!' And that was the last we saw of Paul, he bid us farewell and we all trouped out. And Linda was there taking Polaroid pictures; she was a lovely lady, I liked Linda a lot."[21]

During the final two days at AIR, Paul, Denny and Linda returned to the title track, untouched since Lagos but for the orchestral overdubs. It was still lacking vocals, so Paul added his lead and was joined by Denny and Linda for tightly arranged harmony vocals to support selected lines. Listening to the playback, Paul decided that the song needed another keyboard part, either electric piano or organ. Opting for the dryer sound of the electric piano—mostly, it would double one of the rhythm guitar parts—Paul added that himself.

All that remained to be done were vocal touch-ups on 'Ma Moonia' and 'Mrs. Vanderbilt,' which the group dispatched quickly. By the end of the Friday session, *Band on the Run* was fully recorded and ready to be mixed.

———

'Helen Wheels' and 'Country Dreamer,' credited to Paul McCartney and Wings, were released in Britain on October 19, 1973, the day recording for *Band on the Run* was completed; the American release was not until November 5. Also released in Britain that day (and in the United States on September 24): the first single from Ringo Starr's *Ringo* album, 'Photograph,' putting Paul and

Ringo (and, in a way, George Harrison, who cowrote 'Photograph' with Ringo) in direct competition. A few weeks later, John Lennon joined the fray, releasing his *Mind Games* album, and its title track as a single, on November 16 (October 31, in the United States).

The reviews for 'Helen Wheels' were enthusiastic, most reviewers relieved to hear McCartney rocking rather than crooning; the only demurral was from a critic who preferred 'My Love.'

"With a cranking, tubular-metal, Canned Heat–style guitar, Macca boogies into a slice of rock'n'roll primitivism that has everyone here jugging about and saying things like 'Now this I like' and 'Straight from the fridge, daddy-o.'"[22]

Ian MacDonald, *NME*

"McCartney the truck drivin' man. After a string of soppy ballads and the heavy production job on 'Live and Let Die,' Paul, with his amputated Wings (Paul, Linda and Denny Laine) have remembered their rockin' roots."[23]

Richard Green, *Record Mirror*

"A good rocking single from the prolific pen of Mr. McCartney . . . But I must say his ballads are usually more classy and characteristic than his other compositions. . . . Perhaps we could have a ballad next time."[24]

Rosemary Horide, *Disc*

"I'm racking my pointed head to think of something deep and profound to say about it but can think of nothing. It's just a good record. The 'B' side, 'Country Dreamer,' is sort of Brinsley/rural . . . It's light and airy, lovely harmonies on the sort of song that others may record."[25]

John Peel, *Sounds*

But 'Helen Wheels' proved to be only a moderate hit, entering the British charts at No. 33, on November 3, peaking at No. 12 on December 1, and remaining in the top 50 for 12 weeks. In America, it debuted on *Billboard*'s Hot 100 chart at No. 66, on November 24, reached No. 10 on January 12, 1974, and remained in the Hot 100 for 13 weeks. Ringo's 'Photograph' outperformed

PAUL McCARTNEY & WINGS

Photo. by Linda McCartney

HELEN WHEELS

apple single R5993
Marketed by EMI Records

EMI Records Limited.
20, Manchester Square. London W1A 1ES.

EMI

the Wings disc on both sides of the Atlantic, reaching No. 8 in Britain and No. 1 in the United States.

When 'Helen Wheels' rode into the charts, it became necessary to promote it on television, but this presented a dilemma: with two members of the band gone, a conventional performance video was out of the question, and a live appearance impossible. Paul's solution was to hire a cameraman to drive in front of his dark blue Rolls-Royce convertible, and film as they barreled down a country lane with Paul at the wheel (which did not stop him from standing, miming and mugging for the camera). With the single blasting out of the Rolls-Royce speakers, a second pass was shot using a car side-rig—easier and safer for the McCartneys to stare down the camera lens and mime lyrics.

"The footage came into the editing suite daily, over two or three days," said Roy Benson, who edited the promo. "Paul would simply bring in the latest cans of film, saying 'This is today's lot.' It was all very seat-of-the-pants."[26]

Realizing, after a couple of days, that this might not yield an irresistible video, Paul hired a studio and had the cameraman film Wings miming individually, with Paul seen playing drums, bass and guitar, Linda twiddling the controls and pressing the keys of her Moog, Denny playing guitar, and Denny and Linda singing backing vocals. A final shot captured the trio unfurling a Wings banner, to bookend the production: they open the banner at the start of the clip and close it at the end.

Benson's film premiered in Britain on *Top of the Pops*, on November 15.

Recording Sessions

Thursday–Friday, October 25–26, 1973.
Kingsway Studios, London.
Mixing: 'Band on the Run,' 'Bluebird,' 'Ma Moonia' (Working title for 'Mamunia'), and 'No Words.'

Emerick had expected to mix the album at AIR, but by the time Paul was satisfied that overdubbing was complete, the time he had booked was at an end, and the studio had been booked by producer Gerry Bron for his prog-rock quartet, Tempest. Bron, who Paul had sidelined back in 1968 when he stepped in to produce 'I'm the Urban Spaceman' for the Bonzos, also insisted on using Emerick for his sessions, beginning on Monday, October 29, leaving him only four days to mix *Band on the Run*.

But Paul was not about to hit the pause button. Having taken most of a year to produce *Ram*, and a year to complete *Red Rose Speedway*, he had completed *Band on the Run* in a mere eight weeks, and he was eager to get it into the stores. It would be his second album of the year, a Beatles-era level of productivity. Apart from the obvious benefits of having the album on the market in time for Christmas, he was sending a message—"I'll show you!"—to *all* his former band-mates: Lennon, Harrison, Starr, Seiwell and McCullough.

With AIR unavailable, he cast around for somewhere to mix. But *everyone* was getting releases ready for Christmas, so all his favorite studios—EMI, Olympic, Trident, Island—were booked. He found a berth at Kingsway Studios, a facility that was not high on his list: he last worked there in 1968, on *McGough and McGear*, his brother's duo project with Roger McGough, and he hadn't thought much of it.

But Kingsway had changed considerably since then. It had recently installed a Studer 24-track deck and a custom Raindirk console,[27] becoming the first studio in Britain to offer 24-track recording. Even so, McCartney felt hamstrung by the absence of certain effects that were available at EMI and AIR—most notably, ADT. He ended up renting a couple of extra decks so that Emerick could rig up an approximation of EMI's time- and effort-saving faux-double-tracking device.

Waiting for McCartney and Emerick at Kingsway was an effects compilation, prepared at Emerick's request by London-based Theatre Projects Sound Limited. The seven-inch stereo reel of Scotch audiotape, marked "20a," contained sound effects that Paul wanted to add to several tracks.

For the sections of 'Drink to Me' meant to evoke the French radio broadcast Picasso heard the night he died, for example, Paul wanted spoken French fading in and out of the texture, much as the Beatles had done with fragments of *King Lear* on 'I Am the Walrus,' broadcast by the BBC the night they mixed the track and incorporated as "found sound."

For this, Theatre Projects supplied a recording from the BBC French Language Service program, "Le Flash Touristique." The full text of the section reads (in translation):

> "I hope that, thanks to this campaign, many French people will rediscover the charms. So, let me remind you that our tourist help service is there for you. As you know, we send free of charge a variety of guides, lists of addresses . . . London and its suburbs, in French of course. Recommended guides on Great Britain. Guides of farms offering a room for the night. Guides of the inns. Lists of organizations specialized in au pairs for hire . . . as a paying host. Guides for motorized tourists, featuring a translation of the English driving book, in French."

Other segments on the tape were labeled 'Party Noises,' also for 'Drink to Me,' and four tracks of laughter to bolster the cackling at the end of 'Mrs. Vanderbilt.' 'Jail Noises' (guard and prisoner footsteps and a jail door slamming) and 'Cannon Shots' were intended for 'Band on the Run,'[28] Paul's idea being that they would give the track a measure of cinematic depth.

"I thought it should start off very kind of moody, and quiet, and sort of inside a cell," Paul later said, "with this fellow kind of just cursing things and just thinking, you know, what he'd do if he gets out. And there's a little bit there which you call the kind of production bit where there's a massive orchestra comes in just for a couple of bars and that's the breakout, and then he gets out and then it goes into the main song of 'Band on the Run,' which is about these fellows, you know, rabbits on the run kind of business. And then he's sought after by a multitudinous throng."[29]

In the end, Paul opted not to use the jailhouse sounds. The footsteps and jail noises were lost in the mix, and the slamming cell door sounded too much like the effect the Rolling Stones used to open 'We Love You,' the 1967 B side (to 'Dandelion') to which McCartney and Lennon had provided backing vocals. Cannon shots announcing the jailbreak between the two sections of 'Band on the Run' also proved overly theatrical.

In their two days at Kingsway, Emerick and McCartney completed mixes of both sections of 'Band on the Run,' and edited them together. The mixes for 'Ma Moonia' and 'No Words' were quickly dispatched as well, with 'No Words' getting a trim from 4'29" to 2'36".

While at Kingsway, Paul again ran into the young guitarist Jimmy McCulloch, who was working on an album of his own. He was still a contender for Henry's position in Wings—not that Paul had spoken with anyone else. Linda, in fact, was hinting to the press that she and Paul might head in another direction entirely, with ideas about a new percussion section, seemingly influenced by the Fela Ransome-Kuti concert.

"We'll definitely get a new act together," she told *NME* at the time. "Use our imaginations a bit as well. We can either get a new guitar player and drums or congas section, something like that. I think we'll sort it out once we get the album done—hopefully at the end of the month. We'll start really thinking about what kind of live act we do want—because we want to play the stuff on this album. I don't know how soon it will be. Remember, we spent two years getting Wings together. That's the only drag for me about Wings, all that work in getting it together and then you get personality problems."[30]

The mixing sessions would continue for another few days, after a move to EMI. But by now Paul was also obsessing about the cover art. He wanted something cutting-edge—the kind of covers the high-flying Pink Floyd had, for example.

Looking into it, he learned that Pink Floyd's covers were done by Hipgnosis, a London design group run by Aubrey Powell and Storm Thorgerson. As students at the Royal College of Art, in 1968, they were friendly with Pink Floyd, and designed the covers for all the group's post-1967 LPs, starting with *A Saucerful of Secrets*. Most recently, they designed *The Dark Side of the Moon*, and the worldwide success of that album brought them to Paul's attention. In between, they had done covers for the Pretty Things, Led Zeppelin, the Nice, Argent, T. Rex, and the Electric Light Orchestra, all eye-catching and quirkily innovative.

"He'd been watching the progress of Pink Floyd, and *Dark Side of the Moon*," said Aubrey Powell, known to his friends as Po, "and he basically saw what Hipgnosis was doing and what we were capable of, and we had a call from his office to say, would you go and talk to him?"[31]

When Thorgerson met with Paul and Linda, in mid-October, they outlined their idea for the cover, which was to reflect the prison escape motif of the title song. Paul handed Thorgerson a list of celebrities who he wanted to pose as the escapees (an idea Linda cooked up in bed one morning), with the members of Wings.

"It was quite a long list," Powell said. "There were people like Warren Beatty, Rod Steiger, Sydney Poitier, Michael Partridge, Kenny Lynch, all sorts of characters, of which he hoped we could get a dozen.

"Now, we didn't normally work for people where we did what they wanted to do—it was normally our ideas. But we were so enamored to be working for a Beatle. We fell into that groupie trap, I'm afraid, and said, 'Yeah, sure. Whatever you want, we'll do it.' And also, it was kind of fun to think that we'd be phoning all these agents in Hollywood."[32]

Powell and Thorgerson made the calls and reported to Paul with a short list of those who had agreed and were available, in London, at short notice. Paul and Linda made calls of their own as well. In the end, the photo would include the television host Michael Parkinson, the pop singer Kenny Lynch, the actors Christopher Lee and James Coburn, Liverpool-born boxer John Conteh, and Clement Freud, a polymath (and a neighbor of the McCartneys) who, apart from being Sigmund Freud's grandson, had already had careers as a chef, writer, and broadcaster and had recently become a Member of Parliament.

"Well, listen, the next thing is," Paul asked, "will you organize the shoot?" To which he quickly added that he wanted the cover to be photographed by Clive Arrowsmith. Paul knew Arrowsmith from Liverpool; he had been a classmate of John Lennon's at the Liverpool College of Art. They connected again after the Beatles became famous, and Arrowsmith was the art director for *Ready, Steady, Go*.

Arrowsmith had only recently changed careers, to photography, but he had already done shoots for *Vogue* and other publications, one of which caught Linda's eye. When she showed the photos to Paul, he said, "Oh, I know him," and just like that, mirroring the hiring of Barry Lategan for the *Wild Life* cover, Arrowsmith became their choice to shoot the *Band on the Run* cover.

Arrowsmith, McCartney and the Hipgnosis team talked through the escaping prisoners concept. Arrowsmith suggested that everyone wear black prison uniforms, which were quickly ordered. The photographer also ordered a large spotlight, from a theatrical production company, to be used as a searchlight, throwing an oval beam on the escapees.

"I just pulled together Paul's ideas," Arrowsmith said. "When you work with Paul, you know, he has very strong ideas about what he wants."[33]

On October 28, the participants in the cover shoot met for lunch at San Martino, an Italian restaurant in Knightsbridge. Plenty of red wine was consumed before the cast headed over to Osterley House in west London—a Georgian manor house set in the country park in which the *Wild Life* cover was captured—where the shoot took place.

Arrowsmith quickly discovered that his rented spotlight was not quite powerful enough. There was no time to find another; the only solution was to increase the exposure time to something over two seconds, during which everyone in the shot had to be absolutely still to avoid blurring.

"Two seconds may not sound like a long time," Arrowsmith said, "however, they did have a party before the shoot and everyone was very much the worse for wear, but still enjoying each other's company to say the least. Trying to get everyone to stay still and play the part of escaping prisoners was proving extremely difficult, amid the laughter, jokes and substance haze; I arranged them all together so they could lean against each other and the wall.

"Now, because they had all become a little unsteady on their feet—Denny Laine fell over a couple of times laughing hysterically—everyone was having a great time. I had to have a megaphone to get their attention, I had even positioned myself up to the top of a ladder, next to the spotlight and barked instructions persistently, which the most part everyone ignored, until I finally snapped and screamed 'Stay Still!'"[34]

The session ran about an hour and was filmed for posterity on 8 mm. Arrowsmith shot two rolls of film, and of the 24 exposures, there were only 4 in which everyone had stood still enough to remain sharp.

Michael Parkinson remembered the shoot as "a lovely day, a family day," and said of his coparticipants that "even though we resembled a motley crew we genuinely knew each other and liked the idea of posing together." He recalled a funny incident at the end of the shoot.

"We were encouraged to bring our kids along and I took my three sons who had a marvelous time. At the end of the shoot, which resembled a kindergarten party, Paul's wife, Linda, who had been taking Polaroid pictures throughout, laughingly suggested I take a look at the display of about 200 or more on a trestle table near where we did the shoot. She said, 'I want you to have a look at these because in every shot I took one of your sons somehow managed to appear'—which was true. Mike somehow managed to get his mug in every single shot she took. He was about six at the time."[35]

Recording Sessions

Saturday–Monday, October 27–29, 1973.
EMI Studios, Studio Three, London.
Mixing: 'Jet,' 'Mrs. Vanderbilt' (working title for 'Mrs. Vandebilt') 'Let Me Roll It,' 'Piano Thing—1985' (working title for 'Nineteen Hundred and Eighty Five') and 'Drink to Me' [working title for 'Picasso's Last Words (Drink to Me)'].

Recording time in EMI's small Studio Three became available on October 27, so Paul and Geoff transferred the mixing operation from Kingsway to more familiar turf. That day, in a session that ran from 2:00 p.m. to 4:00 a.m., Emerick mixed 'Jet,' editing parts of RS4 and RS5 together to create an optimum mix. 'Mrs. Vanderbilt' was mixed in a single pass, and three mixes of 'Let Me Roll It' concluded the evening.

During a break in the mixing session, Paul ran into Bobby Elliott, the drummer for the Hollies, who were at work on their *Hollies* LP. Inviting Elliott into Studio Three, he played one of his fresh mixes—Elliott, who mentioned the encounter in his memoir, could not recall which—and then invited the drummer to join Wings. Elliott, happy as a member of the Hollies, politely declined.[36] Whether there was a serious intent behind McCartney's proposition is debatable.

On Sunday, Paul, Linda and Denny arrived at EMI at 8:00 p.m., after spending the afternoon at Osterley Park, for the cover shoot, and this final mixing session ran until 6:45 a.m. It began with a last-minute overdub: Paul felt he could improve on the lead vocal to '1985' (documents note the title change) and replaced it. The song was then mixed and edited (the finished mix used parts of RS5 and RS8).

**is
Paul McCartney and Wings**

OUT NOW.

PAS 10007

Mixing Paul's paean to Picasso was tricky, since Emerick added the party sounds and French broadcast recording live during the mix. Consequently, it took 14 attempts to achieve a mix McCartney liked, and even so, the final version (faded out 20 seconds early, removing Paul's 'Day-O' scat vocal in the process) was an edit of RS13 and RS14. The final mix made great use of Visconti's Parisian, Left Bank–influenced clarinet lines, and rich string arrangement to mask the rough Lagos edit points.

Paul had decided that '1985' would close the album, and though Visconti's arrangement gave the song a robust, conclusive orchestral finale, Paul wanted to link the song to the title track. So as a final touch, Emerick copied a section of the refrain from 'Band on the Run' and attached it to the end of the track by way of a crossfade, adding echo as the fragment of the title track was faded out. Staggering out of the studio (as Geoff Emerick put it) on Monday morning, Emerick hailed a taxi to AIR Studios where he was scheduled to begin work with Tempest in little more than three hours' time.

Paul and Linda returned to EMI alone on the afternoon of October 29 to assemble the master, in its final running order, opening with the concept-defining 'Band on the Run,' and closing with the swelling majesty of '1985' and its brief reprise of the title track. In the process, Paul tweaked the spellings of a few song titles: 'Ma Moonia' became 'Mamunia,' 'Mrs. Vandebilt' lost its R, 'Drink to Me' was expanded to 'Picasso's Last Words (Drink to Me),' and '1985' took on its spelled-out form.

SIDE ONE (EMI MATRIX NO. YEX.929)

'Band on the Run'
'Jet'
'Bluebird'
'Mrs. Vandebilt'
'Let Me Roll It'

SIDE TWO (EMI MATRIX NO. YEX.930)

'Mamunia'
'No Words'
'Picasso's Last Words (Drink to Me)'
'Nineteen Hundred and Eighty Five'

The album was sent off to be mastered, but there were complications. John Smith, at Apple, produced a master that Emerick signed off on. But EMI's cutting engineer, Harry Moss, thought it could be improved. He remastered it himself with, Emerick reported, slightly greater punch.[37] (That punch may have been too much: customers returned a significant number of British first pressings because of a flaw that made their styluses jump out of the grooves.)

With the record complete, all that remained was for Hipgnosis to complete jacket art. The front cover was given fully to Arrowsmith's prison escape photo, with *Band on the Run* across the top in lettering designed by Hipgnosis in-house designer George Hardy. Though illustrating a Wings LP, Arrowsmith's cover shot also symbolized Paul's feeling of contractual imprisonment with Apple. The seed of an idea sown by George at their July business meeting had now been captured in both song and photograph, and a veiled illustration of Paul's desire to finally shed his legal ties with John, George, and Ringo would soon be in the hands of music fans.

The back cover, also snapped by Arrowsmith, was assembled with the wry humor Hipgnosis was known for. It shows the desktop of a law enforcement officer trying to track down three fugitives, Paul, Linda and Denny. Arrowsmith had taken black-and-white portraits of the band, individually and together. Choosing a solo shot of each player, the Hipgnosis team rubber-stamped each with a circular passport stamp in which LONDON was printed on top, LAGOS on the bottom, and SEPT 73 in the center.

The portraits are placed, with studied haphazardness, at the center of the desk, atop a red dossier with a sticker reading PAUL McCARTNEY AND WINGS, and what looks like a passport. Also on the desk—a cup of cappuccino, a fountain pen, a cigar, a paperweight, a rubber stamp, a pencil, a ruler, and some paperwork, including a mocked-up surveillance report listing Wings' Lagos and London activities, and a photocopied document on EMI letterhead.

The album's credit list, at the bottom-right corner of the back cover, is as revealing for its omissions as for what it includes. The album's title is followed by Paul's, Linda's and Denny's names; Wings is not mentioned here. The track listing follows, and beneath it, Geoff Emerick's engineering is credited, as are Howie Casey's sax solos. Remi Kabaka's percussion on 'Bluebird' is not mentioned.

Under "Special Thanx To," EMI Studios (Lagos and London) and ARC Studio Lagos are listed; AIR and Kingsway are not. Clive Arrowsmith, Tony Visconti, Ian and Trevor, Gordon House (EMI's typographer) and Storm Thorgerson are also included, their contributions not specified.

Tony Visconti took issue with this vague listing, which offers no hint that he wrote and conducted the orchestrations. And though Thorgerson (but not Powell) is included, Hipgnosis is not mentioned. The final credit, common to the British and American releases was, "And Paul would love to thank Linda and Linda would love to thank Paul and thanx Denny"—not quite the wording one would expect from musicians trying to project a group image.

Hipgnosis appears to have had some fun with transatlantic differences in the cover art, which are minor but plentiful. For starters, the order of the portraits differs: on the British version, the order is Paul, Linda, and Denny. On the American edition, it is Paul, Denny, and Linda. The fountain pen is in a slightly different position on each, and less of it is visible on the American cover. The American version also has a coffee stain on the surveillance report (at the tip of the pen) that does not appear on the British cover.

Transatlantic differences crop up on the disc labels, too. On both sides of the Atlantic, the labels were black, with the portraits from the back cover arrayed across the top half. On the British release, the order is Paul, Denny and Linda on Side One, Paul, Linda and Denny on Side Two; the American labels use the two portrait sequences as well, but the sequence on the British Side One appears on the American Side Two, and vice versa. The album title is given beneath the portraits. The British version then lists the song titles, followed by the composition and publishing credits (McCartney Music, ATV Music), PAUL McCARTNEY AND WINGS, and Paul's production credit. The American labels put the Wings listing directly under the album title, followed by the song titles, the composition credit (no publisher listed, just "All Selections BMI") and the production credit.

The inner sleeve has the song lyrics on one side, a black-and-white photo of Paul, Linda and Denny with a group of eight Nigerian children (taken during their final day in Lagos) on the other. And Hipgnosis assembled a poster, with Linda's Polaroid snapshots, mostly from Lagos, and mostly session shots, but a few from AIR Studios (including a casual shot of Bryan Ferry, Roxy Music's singer) as well.

With Klein out of the picture, Paul's stance toward Apple softened, and there were no disputes about Apple's name or logo—'Helen Wheels,' in fact, was issued with the standard, Magritte-inspired Apple labels. But Paul still appears inclined to avoid Apple references where possible. The British cover and inner sleeve are Apple-free, but the disc labels sport an Apple logo, off to the right.

On the American release, a tiny Apple logo is part of the notation, "Manufactured by Apple Records," that runs across the top edge of the disc labels. That note is repeated at the bottom right of the American edition's back cover, with the address of Capitol Records' New York offices, 1370 Avenue of the Americas.

When the album arrived at Capitol, Al Coury, the company's vice president in charge of marketing and publicity, was puzzled. 'Helen Wheels' was receiving healthy radio play in America and would be in the ears of listeners when Wings' latest LP hit American record stores. But it was nowhere to be found in the track listing.

"He had a visa problem and couldn't come to America," said Coury. "He'd send us tapes through the mail. The next thing, the label copy for the album *Band on the Run* came, and it didn't include this hit. I couldn't understand that."[38]

Paul was still thinking of singles and albums as he did during the Beatles' days, and as many British groups (and record labels) did in the 1960s—as separate releases, with no crossover. With few exceptions, when the Beatles released a song as a single, it was removed from consideration as an album track. They explained this as a value-for-money issue: fans who already bought a single should not have to buy those tracks again on the next LP.

It was different in the United States. Singles were considered teasers for albums. Record executives like Coury considered albums more marketable when they had hits on them, and American consumers considered it a convenience to have the songs they knew as singles on albums as well. In the Beatles' case, because Capitol LPs typically included 12 songs, compared with 14 on their British counterparts, putting both sides of a single on an LP meant removing four songs from the British configuration, so every three British albums yielded a fourth LP for Capitol, bringing together the orphaned tracks—a practice the Beatles disdained.

But times were changing. Now it was becoming common on both sides of the Atlantic not only for singles to be included on albums, but for album tracks to be spun off as singles even after the album was on the market, as well. Coury knew how effective a marketing tool a single could be: when Capitol released Pink Floyd's 'Money,' after the release of *The Dark Side of the Moon*, the album surged back up the *Billboard* chart. He was intent on persuading Paul to adopt this approach.

Coury telephoned Paul on November 3 to make his case, and like a true marketing professional, he gave Paul numbers, demonstrating that several hit albums sold more copies when they were associated with a hit single. He may also have reminded Paul that he had agreed to release 'My Love' as a single, shortly before the release of *Red Rose Speedway*, and that it not only went to No. 1, but undoubtedly helped push the album to the top of the charts as well.

Paul made his counterargument, telling Coury that 'Helen Wheels' didn't fit into the album's "concept," but agreed to speak again the next day. When Coury called back, Paul agreed to add 'Helen Wheels' to the American *Band on the Run*, slotted between 'No Words' and 'Picasso's Last Words (Drink to Me).' But the British version would remain untouched. "He allowed me to put it on the LP based on the fact I was very strong and demanding," said Coury.[39]

When Paul spoke with BBC Radio 1, three weeks later, he was still rationalizing his decision.

"I don't normally do that myself, you know, I like the idea of making an album which is just an album, and singles which are just singles. But I don't have any real hard and fast rules for it, so if someone rings me up and says it would be good to put the single on the album, which the American record company did, I said, 'Okay,' but we won't do it on the British one just 'cos I didn't really think it fitted too well. One way you look at it, it's more value 'cos you got an extra track in there. Another way you look at it, well, you've got a single on an album."

Hipgnosis was asked to amend the artwork and labels for the American version, and the matter was settled.

27

THE KING OF POP

—

It was just a matter of weeks until the release of *Band on the Run*, and the time-honored ritual that releasing an album involves—the rounds of interviews to promote and explain it, the anxious wait for the reviews (followed by a denial of any interest in reviewers' opinions) and the weeks of chart-watching. But even after the intense, nonstop exertion of making *Band on the Run*, Paul was loath to just sit back and wait.

With Linda's 'Oriental Nightfish' newly recorded, and 'Seaside Woman' languishing in the archives, he decided on a lightning visit to Paris to record something else for her Suzy and the Red Stripes project.

"We're doing a thing with Linda, not like 'I am Linda McCartney, come and listen to me, I'm going to be a big star,' and all this big hype," Paul told *Melody Maker* at the time. "That she doesn't want, and I don't fancy it either because it's too pompous. She's not ready for it, she's still an apprentice, which is cool because she doesn't mind. It's the right position for her. So we're doing this thing called Suzy and the Red Stripes. And she is Suzy! So Linda will have an album, but not plugged hugely as Linda's album. We're not trying to hide the fact that it's her, but it'll be like Derek and the Dominos, a slight anonymity."[1]

With Christmas coming, the McCartneys could also use the trip to do some shopping in Paris. But more critically, the trip was an opportunity to try out new musicians out of the spotlight. And because the music they were going to record was Linda's, the sessions would give Paul a glimpse—after all of McCullough's complaints about Linda's musicianship—of how the new guys responded to her, as both a player and a songwriter.

Paul had David Minns telephone Jimmy McCulloch and Davy Lutton, until recently the drummer for Ellis (and before that, Eire Apparent, Henry's old band), to invite them to Paris to cut some tracks with Paul, Linda and Denny. They immediately agreed, McCulloch putting his own plans on ice (as Denny Laine had done when Paul came knocking in July 1971) to brush shoulders with one of his musical idols.

"I was getting a solo album together, but I had to shelve that because Paul asked me to go to Paris to do a project of Linda's,"[2] McCulloch explained. "I was delighted, it was unbelievable. We all piled into this Mercedes truck and hit the road for Paris."[3]

Ian Horne drove the McCartney entourage (including, as always, the children) to Dover, where they took the ferry to Calais and then made the four-hour drive to Paris. They checked into the George V Hotel, where the Beatles stayed during their 1964 and 1965 visits to the city, and all went out for dinner, after which they were picked up in a black Cadillac and driven to EMI Pathé Marconi Studios in Boulogne-Billancourt.

The studio had Beatles ghosts, too: Paul was last there on January 29, 1964, when the Beatles recorded the German versions of 'I Want to Hold Your Hand' (as 'Komm, Gib Mir Deine Hand') and 'She Loves You' (as 'Sie Liebt Dich'), and began work on 'Can't Buy Me Love.'

Recording Sessions

Tuesday–Thursday, November 20–22, 1973.
EMI Pathé Marconi Studios, Studio Four, Boulogne-Billancourt, France.
Recording and Mixing: 'Wide Prairie,' 'I Got Up' and 'Luxy' (jingle).

Paul could not have designed a better trial by fire for McCulloch and Lutton than to have them do an all-night session—they began work at 12:45 a.m. and didn't get back to the George V until 8:30 a.m.—playing Linda's 'Wide Prairie,' after a long travel day.

That was not their only trial. The band's equipment was held up at Calais, and after waiting a few frustrating hours for it to turn up, Paul called Duncan Richards, the newly appointed press chief at Pathé Marconi-EMI. Richards shrugged off the problem, telling Paul, "Ça ne fait rien"[4] (or "It does not matter," more loosely translated as "Don't worry, we'll sort it"). Paul and Linda heard Richards's comment as "San Ferry Anne," a phrase they adopted to mean "don't worry," and true to form, McCartney began toying with the phrase as the title for a new song.

When the McCartneys and company arrived at the EMI Pathé Marconi Studios, the equipment still was nowhere to be found. As they hung out in the studio with little to do, a member of the

French band Les Variations popped into the control room to see whether rumors that Paul McCartney was on the premises were true.

Les Variations were in the studio adjacent to Paul's, working on their third album, *Moroccan Roll*.

Paul was fascinated by Les Variations' sound. Three of the band's five players were Moroccan Jews, and they were creating a hybrid of high-energy rock with North African and Sephardic Jewish folk music, playing Moroccan instruments along with guitars, keyboards, bass and drums.

"As soon as I knew Paul was in the studios," recalled Marc Tobaly, the band's guitarist and singer, "I dropped by to say hello. We were talking about his trip to Marrakesh, and more generally about Morocco and Moroccan music. If I recall, Paul dropped in once or twice to chat with us. Did we jam? Unfortunately, not. It would have been a blast."[5]

Les Variations may not have played with McCartney, but their instruments did: once the French band finished for the evening, shortly after midnight, they agreed to lend Paul their guitars, drums and keyboards. That was only necessary for the Tuesday evening (or, by then, Wednesday morning) session, which was reportedly the first all-night session in the history of the Pathé Marconi Studios. On Wednesday, the British musicians' own gear arrived.

Linda's sessions began with 'Wide Prairie,' a country tune with something of a plot about a girl who was born in Arizona, grew up in Ashtabula (Ohio) and raised a family in Albuquerque (New Mexico)—although her memories, mostly, are of her parents putting her on their saddle while they rode the wide prairie. With Paul on bass, Denny on acoustic guitar, Jimmy on electric and Davy drumming, Linda sang the tune in a parody country voice, with an overstated twang.

"I always thought of this song as Linda's fantasy," said Paul. "Her tongue in cheek attitude and what we called her 'twangy' voice joined to make this a joyful little record."[6]

In the absence of a bridge, she grafted on a section of a somewhat rockier, unfinished song, and added a long, slow atmospheric outro that evolved into a free-form, 11-minute jam. During this extended section, she and Paul recorded a topical, quasi-cinematic spoken passage: Linda begins, saying "*I was in Paris / waiting for a flight / when this guy came up to me and said . . .*" Paul responds: "*Have you got a light?*"

Distant as the exchange was from the main business of the track, Paul made a copy of that dialogue fragment and affixed it to the top of the song. It was a crucial touch: the spoken intro, over slow, hazy music, plus the extended, slow outro, help clarify the fantasy character of the song itself.

On Wednesday, the group tracked Linda's 'I Got Up,'—a 1950s-style rocker with a spoken intro (as with 'Oriental Nightfish,' she was channeling the Shangri-Las' 'I Can Never Go Home Any-more') and a defiant lyric that at times seems a retort to her musical critics, and at others a re-sponse to her disgruntled pre-Paul New York friends: "*I got up and I ain't goin' down again.*" Paul, on piano, set down a backing track with Jimmy and Davey, and Linda sang a scratch vocal.

Paul added organ and bass, and Linda and Denny overdubbed the backing vocals. But by the time they got around to the finished version of Linda's lead vocal, her energy was flagging, so they opted to save that for a later session.*

The two songs filled a reel each of 16-track tape, and Paul devoted the Thursday session to mixing them, returning from Paris with five reels of mixes.

Paul also used his time at Pathé Marconi to record 'Luxy,' a jingle for Radio Luxembourg. Ac-tually, it was part radio station jingle, part Wings promotion: the lyrics of this 2'14" boogie jam were mostly, "*I heard it on Luxy,*" but peppered through it were the titles of *Band on the Run* tracks, dressed up as listener requests. With some editing, the station could use part of it as a generic jingle, and other parts to introduce songs from the new album.

———

Back at the George V, Paul discovered that the Osmonds, who were performing in Paris that week, were fellow guests. Mary was a big fan, so in his capacity as an indulgent dad, Paul took Mary up to the Osmonds' rooms to meet them.

"There's a knock on the door, and I open it up and there's Paul standing there," Donny Osmond recalled. "He was holding hands with his little daughter, Mary, who apparently was a big Donny Osmond fan at the time. And he said, in his Liverpool accent, 'Can I get your autograph, please, for my daughter?' I said, 'Yeah, sure,' and he handed me a picture of me, and said, 'Put, To Mary, Love Donny.' She was so excited."[7]

They chatted briefly, Osmond telling Paul he enjoyed *James Paul McCartney*, and Paul asking whether the Osmonds were going to sing 'Long Haired Lover from Liverpool'—which had been

---

* It turned out to be much later—she did not record the final version of the lead vocal until 1998.

at No. 1 when Wings issued 'Hi, Hi, Hi'—at their show that evening, which Osmond said they would.

"When the door closed," Osmond continued, "I said, 'That was friggin' Paul McCartney standing at my door! And he asked me for *my* autograph! To this day, I kick myself for not getting his."

Paul and company planned to leave Paris on Friday, but Paul had asked the studio to make cassettes of his sessions to listen to on the journey back to London. When they stopped by to pick them up, the tapes were not ready, and they ended up missing the ferry. Paul and Linda took that opportunity go out to a club, and on Saturday, they did some shopping, Linda buying jewelry as well as sunglasses in the shape of Christmas trees and tennis racquets. They caught the 9:00 p.m. ferry on Saturday night.

Publicly, Paul was downplaying the urgency of finding a new guitarist and drummer for Wings, and it may be that he really had doubts about it. He spoke with interviewers about the difficulties of forming a band, noting that the evolution from the Quarrymen to the Beatles took several years and quite a few personnel changes, and that expecting a band to instantly gel—not only musically, but as personalities—was unrealistic. At times, he seemed to despair of that ever happening again.

Yet, he wanted to tour, and that required a band. And he wanted to make records, and for that, too, the band context was what he was used to, even if his headstrong approach to the material created resentments within the ranks, and at least partially negated the benefits of having first-rate, creative players around him. So the most he could say, when interviewers wondered about the state of Wings, was that he was taking his time.

"There's no real need to have a new band at this second," he told Rosemary Horide, of *Disc*. "We're going to have a holiday, then Christmas, and think about that after. We're just quietly looking around for a really nice guitarist."[8]

As guitarists went, Jimmy McCulloch still had the inside track. Paul mentioned the Paris trip, and McCulloch's role in it, in several interviews. Davy Lutton was mentioned in none of them. At the end of 1973, Lutton was looking at two potential futures, one with McCartney and Wings, the other with Marc Bolan and T. Rex. He took the Glam Rock route and disappeared from the McCartney narrative.

———

The search for band members aside, there were administrative tasks to be seen to at MPL. Paul filled Romeo's position with two newcomers—Brian Brolly would become MPL's managing director, and Alan Crowder would become band manager, effective in early December.

Both appointments were seen as major coups for McCartney. Crowder had worked his way up from the sleeve department at Decca Records to international coordinator for MCA Records in Britain. Brolly was vice president of the MCA label, and within the business it was widely known that he was responsible for getting Andrew Lloyd-Webber's *Jesus Christ Superstar* recorded when theater companies and record labels were looking askance at the project. Now Brolly would be overseeing the McCartneys' flourishing publishing, photography, and recording interests.

"Paul owns the company, and our role is to provide a secure basis for him to work," is how Brolly described his job. "He can compose, record, make concert tours with Wings and generally concentrate on his creative life in the firm knowledge that the benefits will accrue to him and the other members of the band. What all of us do—managers, lawyers, financial and business experts of all kinds—reflects their needs. And we aim to produce a structure which does this honestly, morally and with integrity."[9]

Crowder's view of his job was equally utilitarian, if more prosaic—an adaptation, it seems, of Alistair Taylor's "Mr. Fixit" role during the Beatle years.

"When I joined McCartney Productions," Crowder said, "I asked Brian Brolly what I should call myself. He said 'Oh . . . what about management executive?' So that's what I am. Basically . . . you pick up the phone, you deal with the problem—whatever it may be."[10]

Paul was also persuaded that it was time to go big-time with his publicity in the United States. After assessing the public relations business, John Eastman engaged Solters/Sabinson/Roskin as McCartney Music's national press representatives, right in time to promote *Band on the Run*.

Eastman was also working hard behind the scenes to settle Paul's visa problems, calling on political connections—most notably, Jacob Javits, a Republican (but liberal) senator from New York—to see what could be done. He was also in touch with Phoenix House, a drug rehabilitation center, which agreed to write a letter in support of Paul's visa application, if Paul would commit to playing a benefit for the center. Sir Joseph Lockwood, at EMI, joined the battle, too, asking Walter Annenberg, the American ambassador to the United Kingdom (with whom he was on friendly terms) to put in a good word for McCartney.

A few unfinished projects needed the McCartneys' attention, too. Bruce McMouse reared his furry cartoon head once again. In mid-November, Paul and Linda returned to AIR to record dialogue for *The Bruce McMouse Show*. Wings, including Seiwell and McCullough, had already been filmed and recorded; now Paul and Linda were voicing two of the mice. Derek Guyler, Pat Coombes, and Derek Nimmo were drafted to do the others. And Paul was beginning to speak about the project publicly.

"We filmed the last four concerts of the European tour, and we're currently making them into a film," he told *Record Mirror*. "But it's not just us performing. The story is that there's a family of animated mice living under the stage we're working on."[11] In the same interview he mentioned that he planned to "do an album with my brother Mike in January and spend a bit of time back up

North sinking a few jars." And he promoted the composing-for-hire sideline that he increasingly enjoyed, mentioning that he was writing for several people, among them Twiggy, who was reviving her *Gotta Sing, Gotta Dance* film project, for which Paul had agreed to write more songs.

One of the songs he composed by request, 'Mine for Me,' made the transition from the page to tape at the end of November, and Paul was on hand to help, joining Rod Stewart at Morgan Studios and contributing backing vocals. And although there were no collaborations mooted, Paul and Linda had a friendly dinner with Elton John in late November, Linda handing over the Christmas tree and tennis racquet sunglasses she had bought in Paris.

But with *Band on the Run* due imminently, Tony Brainsby had set up a raft of interviews for Paul in London, starting on November 24 with a visit to the amusingly eccentric Capitol Radio show hosted by Kenny Everett and an American, Dave Cash.

Everett had a great many scoops on his show during the Beatles years. They occasionally allowed him to do his interviews at EMI while they were working, and at times, they played things especially for him—John performing 'Cottonfields,' for example, and Paul playing his otherwise unheard 'All Together on the Wireless Machine,' which he half jokingly proposed as a theme for Everett (who is mentioned in the lyrics). Paul brought along another treat for today's show, too—the AIR recording of Linda's 'Oriental Nightfish.'

As Paul and David Minns walked into the Capitol Radio offices on Euston Road, Paul was handed an envelope by a waiting process server. Opening it and quickly scanning its contents, Paul rolled his eyes and kept walking. He handed it to Cash as he sat down to begin the interview.

"What is this piece of paper," Cash asked, "this *amazing* piece of paper from the Supreme Court in the State of New York—is this for me?"

"No, this is for me," Paul replied. "On the way in just now, I just got handed it by a man who didn't want to embarrass me. It's a writ for $20 million (£8.5 million)."[12]

Paul had half expected it. The writ was from Allen Klein. Klein had filed suit against the other Beatles and Apple, in April, claiming he had made loans to the Beatles and Apple, for which he was seeking repayment, and saying that he would soon also sue them for the percentage due him on EMI and Capitol royalties. In the past week—as reported in the current issue of *Billboard*, dated that very day—Lennon, Harrison, Starr and Apple countersued Klein, at the High Court in London, claiming damages for misrepresentation. Harrison provided the perfect mood music in his song 'Sue Me, Sue You Blues.'

For Paul, the suit against Klein could not have been richer: Lennon and company were now arguing that their May 1969 contract with Klein—the contract they tried to strong-arm Paul into signing at Olympic Studios—should be considered invalid "because they did not understand the nature and effect of it."[13] They argued, too, that an amendment to that contract should be rendered invalid on the same grounds, plus misrepresentation, by Klein, of its meaning.

The writ Paul now received was the next volley in a legal tennis match: Klein had sued the Beatles, the Beatles sued Klein, and now it was Klein's serve. Just when Paul thought he was out, Klein pulled him back into the game.

For some of his music press interviews, Paul revived a practice that was common in the Beatles' early days but had been abandoned in 1963—visiting journalists at their offices. But after a visit to *Melody Maker*, with Stella in tow, he reconsidered this approach. Stella, bored with the proceedings, began wailing near the end of the interview, whereupon Paul decided it would be better to hold court at MPL, where he had greater control of the circumstances.

When *Record Mirror*'s John Beattie turned up at MPL, Paul was ready with some unusual show-and-tell. Walking into Paul's office and finding him "jiggin' about the floor, clapping his hands and stompin' his feet," Beattie quoted Paul's enthusiastic assessment.

"Have you heard this album?" he asked the reporter, handing him the jacket of Fela Ransome-Kuti's *Shakara* LP (and making good on his promise to Fela to promote his music to British journalists). "It's the Nigerian fella who was on the Ginger Baker program, he's great, very funky. It's incredible, this guy actually lives with all these women, a kind of harem."[14]

So eager were the McCartneys to promote *Band on the Run* that no publicity opportunity seemed too slight. In late November, Paul and Linda posed, dressed in 1950s garb (with Paul as a Teddy Boy) for the *Cosmopolitan* Celebrity Calendar. (They were the February 1974 celebrities.) A second image of the McCartneys featured Linda lying inside an illuminated new moon with Paul at her side with a dove on his shoulder. Paul liked the moon shot so much that it was printed in several of the music papers, including a center spread in *Disc*, and he had it on the wall inside MPL's London offices. The photos were taken by John Kelly, the photographer they ran into on their way to Jamaica in 1971.

A couple of days later, they turned up at the Piccadilly Headquarters of the Toy for a Sick Child Fund, where Stella donated Fruity, her teddy bear. They even agreed to be filmed introducing Disney films and characters for a *Disney Time* Boxing Day special. It was all a universe away from Paul's decision to lie low when the *McCartney* album was released.

Linda fielded a few interviews as well, and in one, with Romany Bain of the *Daily Mirror*, a question about whether marriage had changed Paul elicited an unusually thoughtful response not only about how Paul had changed, but how their relationship had evolved as well.

"Not really," was her direct response to the question. "Except that he used to club it and chase chicks and now he's very involved with his family. He's still a boy with a very Beatle sense of humor. He's a bit moody, being an artist and Gemini. I'm calmer. I'm Libra and we're supposed to be together. Paul brings out the maternal in me and I definitely mother him. Yet he is my strength. I don't blow up as easily as I used to. We don't seem to say all those negative truths which are so hurtful. Our fights are brought on by outside pressures—not personal bitches. And they always end happily."[15]

———

Paul's frenetic activity in the weeks since *Band on the Run* was sequenced was both a way to lay the groundwork for the album's release and to siphon off the nervous energy that comes with waiting. But now, at the close of November 1973, the album was out in Britain (the American release was five days later, on December 5). Finally, Paul could power down and relax. He and Linda attended a concert by the New York Dolls at the Rainbow Room above the Biba Department Store, in London, making them probably the only people on the planet to attend concerts by the Osmonds and the Dolls within a month of each other. They found the high-energy, down-and-dirty performance eye-opening. But they were also so taken with the Biba building that they began thinking about approaching its designers to remodel MPL's Soho Square offices in a similar art deco style.

On December 1, they headed to what had become their favorite vacation haunt, Jamaica. There was no denying that a break was necessary: in nearly every way—from the fracturing of Wings, to the nonstop parade of mishaps in Lagos and the self-imposed pressure to complete the album and get it out—the last few months had been bruising.

But the experience was also fulfilling: Paul's new album had the variety that was his hallmark, with ballads and rockers, acoustic tracks, and high-energy electric cuts. But most importantly, where each of his post-Beatles releases had tracks that Paul knew were throwaways—throwaways that he liked, or that struck him as having a personality that earned them a place on an album, but throwaways all the same—*Band on the Run* had an energizing consistency, track for track.

Beyond all that, the McCartneys' early December trip to Jamaica was the perfect way to close the loop: although he had already written a few of the songs that appeared on *Band on the Run*, it was during his last Jamaican holiday, in April, that Dustin Hoffman spurred him to write one of the album's most adventurous tracks.

The first reviews appeared before Paul left for Jamaica, and they continued through December and into the New Year. As they poured in, Paul was pleasantly surprised not only that the consensus was positive—more than positive, enthusiastic, with "his best album yet" a common refrain—but that he was no longer being treated as the Underachieving Bad Guy of the Beatles, let alone as Lennon's hapless inferior.

Pretty much the only major critic who published a demurral was Robert Hilburn of the *Los Angeles Times*, although he, too, considered the album an improvement over its predecessors. As in his pans of McCartney's previous albums, Hilburn couched his disappointment in terms of "what we all know McCartney should be able to provide." But there was ample praise. "McCartney's vocals are bolder and his arrangements are more confident and tailored" than in his past work, Hilburn said, and though he was unimpressed with most of Side Two, he singled out 'Bluebird' and 'Let Me Roll It' as the album's strongest attractions.[16]

Chris Welch told *Melody Maker* readers that "the feeling expressed throughout is one of happy, almost exultant freedom, in which the music is open, unpressured and eminently satisfying."[17] In *Sounds*, Steve Peacock declared *Band on the Run* a "brilliant and completely uninhibited album which lays waste to anything he's done since the Beatles in terms of creativity and awareness." Peacock had liked *Red Rose Speedway*, but found *Band on the Run* "grander and more arrogant, with all the highs brightly polished and gleaming."[18]

Disc's Rosemary Horide took an unusual approach, interspersing her own assessment among a track-by-track explanation drawn from an interview with Paul. Her own conclusion: "This is an outstanding album, with a lot more of Paul's individual sound than his previous albums have had— and for my money there can't be enough."[19] (Two weeks later, Horide listed it in her top three albums of the year.)[20]

Critics who focused on specific tracks made some striking observations. Loraine Alterman, in the *New York Times*, wrote of 'Band on the Run' that "there is so much going on within this one cut that it is almost a mini-rock opera, yet there is nothing pretentious about it."[21] 'Picasso's Last Words (Drink to Me)' struck Robin Denselow, of the *Guardian*, as akin to "a New Orleans–style funeral celebration transferred to the Mediterranean."[22] And in *NME*, Charles Shaar Murray described 'Let Me Roll It' as sounding "exactly like Plastic Ono period Lennon," and advised listeners, "If anybody ever puts down McCartney in your presence, bust him in the snoot and play him this. He will thank you for it afterwards."[23]

But the publication McCartney was waiting for was *Rolling Stone*. He had good reason to feel that he had not been treated fairly by the American biweekly, especially in the early days, when the magazine's reviews were dissections of the Beatles' internal politics, with an unmistakable bias toward Lennon. That had been slowly changing; the magazine's *Red Rose Speedway* review seemed to have put all that aside, at long last.

These, it seems, were different times. Jon Landau's 1,900-word review appeared in the January 31, 1974, issue, which had Paul and Linda on the cover and also included Paul Gambaccini's long interview with McCartney. It was as if Jann Wenner, the magazine's founder and editor, was declaring Paul fully rehabilitated and the King of Pop.

Landau's review could have been the summary of a doctoral thesis about how artists' creations are inevitably autobiographical, a theme he traced through recordings by Dylan, the Band, the Eagles, Steve Miller, the Who, the Beatles, Lennon and Harrison before even mentioning McCartney (some 500 words in).

"*Band on the Run*," he wrote, "finds McCartney walking a middle ground between autobiograph-ical songwriting and subtle attempts to mythologize his own experience through the creation of a fantasy world of adventure . . . He does it by uniting the myth of the rock star and the outlaw, the original legendary figure on the run."

He added, "I'll take a chance and say that *Band on the Run* is an album about the search for free-dom and the flight from restrictions on his and Linda's personal happiness. It is about the pursuit of freedom from his past as a Beatle, freedom from the consequences of the drug busts that have kept him from the United States and forced him into thinking of himself as an outlaw (witness the album cover, as well as the title). It is also about two people becoming what they want to be, trying to decide what they want to do, and asking to be accepted for what they are now rather than what they were then."

All of which led to the money quote: with "the possible exception of John Lennon's *Plastic Ono Band*," he wrote, *Band on the Run* is "the finest record yet released by any of the four musicians who were once called the Beatles."[24]

The most caustic comments about the album came from the members of Wings. Denny Seiwell admired the finished album when he heard it, but he pointed out that for the most part, Paul, Linda and Denny Laine played the music—including his own drum parts—almost exactly as the full band had rehearsed it, but not quite as well. "Somewhere in the universe," he said, tantalizingly, "is the demo we made, and that's better than the record, I'll tell you that," he said.[25]

And Denny Laine, just weeks after the LP was released, had developed a sour view of the proj-ect, and Wings generally.

"I look on *Band on the Run* as definitely their [Paul and Linda's] album," he complained to *Disc*'s Caroline Boucher, while promoting *Ahh . . . Laine!*, finally released on December 7. "We're not a group anymore. I'm one of the three, or I'm an individual. If it was Wings I'd feel more a part of it. But it's not my songs and I'd like to feel more involved and contribute as much as they do."[26]

———

The McCartneys' trip to Jamaica was brief. Shortly after popping into a local cinema that was showing *Live and Let Die*—"I wanted to stand up and say, 'I wrote that music!' but they'd probably have told me to shut up and sit down so I didn't"[27]—Paul received word that his American visa had been approved. So instead of lounging at the beach and spending leisurely afternoons looking for new reggae discs, Paul and Linda shepherded the girls onto a plane and flew to New York for a wholly unexpected holiday visit with the Eastmans.

While in Manhattan, Paul and Linda reached out to thank Phoenix House for supporting Paul's immigration case, visiting their East Harlem branch. Here, a choir run by the center sang a short program, and the McCartneys were shown what the facility does.

"It's a good cause," Paul said at the time. "I wasn't thinking it would be much, I thought it would be a bit depressing. But it's a beautiful place. There's a lot of love in that place. . . . There's discipline, too, but the discipline comes out of love. That way no one minds the discipline. If you just start off with discipline and nothing else, a lot of the kids find it hard to do it. But they're all very self-supporting now. It's a great place, I must say."[28]

The details of the concert Paul had promised to play for Phoenix House remained vague, though. "Obviously, that is dependent on getting a band together. If we can get something together in the early months of 1974, then we're hoping to come to the States, do a nice tour here."[29]

While he was in New York, and enjoying the buzz of a successful album, Paul decided it would be good to get the Beatles together for a meeting. Since John's immigration problems made it impossible for him to leave, it would have to be in the United States.

"I rang John up," he said during an interview session with Paul Gambaccini in December, "and John was keen to do it. He was going to fly in today from L.A. to New York. Great! I was going to be here, John was going to be here. Then I rang Ringo, and Ringo couldn't figure out what we were going to actually say, outside of 'Hi, there.' And he didn't want to come all the way to New York from England, he was just getting settled for Christmas. So he was a bit down on it, that kind of blew it out. Then I called John and he said he was talking to George and George was having some kind of visa problems. So it's a bit difficult to get the four of us together. But it will happen soon."[30]

Desperate though McCartney was to meet with his former bandmates in the hope of finally dissolving their lingering business ties, Paul knew he had to bide his time. As it turned out, meeting with John would have been a bad idea. On September 22, when the McCartneys were stuck on the runway at Lagos International Airport, Lennon and his personal assistant, May Pang, flew to Los Angeles, where John was fast developing a taste for cocaine and excessive drinking. Rumors were gathering pace that John and Yoko's marriage was over, now that John and May were living openly, and seemingly happily, as a couple in Los Angeles. Paul refrained from interfering in his former writing partner's business.

Paul and Linda returned to London in mid-December. They had committed to record their contributions to *Disney Time*, at the BBC's studios on December 16. Three days later, they tuned into the Granada Television children's show, *Lift Off with Ayshea*, to watch an airing of the promo clip for 'Helen Wheels.'

For Christmas, Paul presented Linda with 12 pheasants—they were less noisy than 12 drummers drumming, and Linda intended to breed them in the garage at Cavendish Avenue until she could get them to High Park. The *Disney Time* appearance aired on December 26, 1973, exactly six years after (and a universe away from) the BBC's airing of the Beatles' *Magical Mystery Tour*, a decidedly more personal and adventurous project of Paul's. And as was their habit, all the McCartneys made their way up to Merseyside for New Year's Eve.

For light reading, Paul brought along the music papers, which published their annual reader polls in their December 29 issues. The deadlines were too early to gauge reader interest in *Band on the Run*, but in each publication, Paul charted in several categories:

CASH BOX POLLS

Groups Singles—No. 8, Wings

Male Vocalists Single—No. 6, Paul McCartney

Top 100 Albums of 1973—No. 35, *Red Rose Speedway*

Groups—Albums—No. 20, Paul McCartney & Wings

Top Singles—No. 6, 'My Love' and No. 33 'Live and Let Die'

BILLBOARD POLLS

Top Singles Artists—No. 4, Paul McCartney & Wings

Top Album Artists—No. 60, Paul McCartney & Wings

Top Singles Vocal Duos and Groups—No. 2, Paul McCartney & Wings

Top Singles Easy Listening Artists—No. 14, Paul McCartney & Wings

Top Pop Singles—No. 5, 'My Love' Paul McCartney & Wings

Top Easy Listening Singles—No. 8, 'My Love' Paul McCartney & Wings

Top Pop Producers—No. 29, Paul McCartney

Top Popular Albums—No. 33, *Red Rose Speedway*

RECORD WEEK POLLS

Top 45 Record 1973—No. 2, 'My Love'

Top Vocal Combination Singles—No. 1, Paul McCartney & Wings

Top Record 1973—No. 16, *Red Rose Speedway*

Top Vocal Combination Album—No. 1, Paul McCartney & Wings

RECORD MIRROR POLLS

British Male Singer, No. 9, Paul McCartney

British Groups, No. 4, Wings

British Single, No. 6, 'My Love'

British Album, No. 2, *Red Rose Speedway*

British Guitarist, No. 8, Paul McCartney

British Keyboard, No. 6, Paul McCartney
Miscellaneous Instruments, No. 5, Paul McCartney
International Male Singer, No. 10, Paul McCartney
International Group, No. 10, Wings

The one thing Paul knew about how the public was responding to *Band on the Run* was that it had sold enough copies in the United States—half a million—to be certified Gold by the RIAA after only a week on the market.

With a critically lauded, Gold-certified hit album on his hands, Paul found himself in a very different position at the end of 1973 than he'd been in at the end of 1969. Four years earlier, he was crawling from the wreckage of the Beatles, unsure of himself and his future. But he had also been nursed, coaxed, and sweet-talked by Linda into recognizing his strengths sufficiently to borrow a Studer four-track from EMI and set down some tunes, taking his first steps toward reinventing himself.

But what he recorded then was a motley batch, assembled largely of belatedly finished songs from the Beatle days, revived and polished juvenilia from the late 1950s, and jams molded into instrumentals. He started with only two new songs; others had sprouted as he worked, including the enduring 'Maybe I'm Amazed.' But the music on *Band on the Run* was fresh—its oldest songs were written during the *Red Rose Speedway* sessions—and the album was fully conceived before the first session.

Making *McCartney*, he was like a survivor of a shipwreck, hanging on to bits of detritus to stay afloat. With *Band on the Run*, he was looking to what appeared to be a bright future.

Yet in some ways, Paul had come full circle. At the turn of 1974, like the turn of 1970, he was essentially without a band. Technically, Wings were still a going concern, just awaiting the selection of a new lead guitarist and drummer. But for the moment, it was just a name; Denny Laine had a point when he said that *Band on the Run* was made by Paul and Linda with a utility guy, recorded in much the same way as *McCartney*, but in a studio, with an engineer, rather than at home on his own, without VU meters or a mixer.

For Paul, the situation was maddening. Even before Wings, he had established a distinctive sound, built around the combination of his and Linda's voices. The addition of Laine's harmonies expanded that sound, and in their two years together, Wings had become a formidable live band, in which Seiwell's fluid drumming and Henry's sleek lead playing were crucial. Paul was dying to tour Australia and America, huge markets for both the Beatles and himself, but he held off until Wings were ready. At the end of the British tour, they were. And then they were gone, just as he was about to record a hit album to take on tour.

Henry was right to observe that two players left Wings, and Paul hadn't asked why. But Paul hadn't asked why because he knew the answer. The dispute that led to McCullough's departure mirrored fights he'd had with Harrison over what to play and how to play it, as well as Lennon's complaint, in that painful *Rolling Stone* interview, about Paul treating them as sidemen. He was, once again, accused by his bandmates of being a control freak.

But Paul could justify that. Though he had been open to collaborating on arrangements during the early Beatle years, greater experience made him less willing to tolerate, or even to consider, contributions at odds with his own vision. Consciously or not, he had adopted a fundamentally nineteenth-century classical model of creating music, in which a composer conceived a work and expected musicians to play it as written. Different performers might bring their own expressive nuances to the music, but Paul was also the performer here—a composer-conductor, in effect, who expected his ensemble to execute his interpretive and expressive ideas.

Studio musicians were used to that approach, which is why there was no pushback during the recording of *Ram*. So are sidemen, in the star-with-backing-group model. And it was hardly unknown in other popular music circles, including soul and R&B, where groups adhered carefully to both musical arrangements and choreography; in fact, Paul's approach was positively lackadaisical when compared to a performer like James Brown, who was known to impose fines on his players for wrong notes or deviations from the arrangements.

But this was alien to the freewheeling rock band aesthetic that Paul thought he wanted when he formed Wings. In that model, players were expected to make contributions on an almost compositional level, and they expected the freedom to do so. Both approaches are legitimate, historical models, and though one could argue that allowing band input might yield greater vitality (think of Harrison's 'And I Love Her' guitar figure and McCullough's 'My Love' solo as Exhibits A and B), Paul was most comfortable having both the first and last word.

What he needed to do now was recognize that, and assemble a new version of Wings with that in mind. With the band's first incarnation, he wanted it both ways and promised Seiwell, Laine and McCullough that Wings would be a band of equals. It was an idealistic view, and either he lacked the self-awareness to see that it was unlikely to work, or he believed that with a new band, he could reset the impulses that created friction in the Beatles. But that promise became the powder keg that blew the Wings Mark I to bits.

In the New Year, he would consider what kind of band he wanted Wings to be, and what kind of guitarist and drummer he was looking for. They would have to be musicians who smiled and did as they were told, and impressed as he was with Jimmy McCulloch, he could not tell, yet, whether he fit the bill. He would invite him to work on his brother's album, in January, to see what more he could learn.

As for *Band on the Run*, the album would have a life of its own over the next year. The American version entered *Billboard*'s album chart at No. 33 on December 22 and crept up to No. 1 on April 13, 1974. Al Coury's strategy of spinning off album tracks as singles—first 'Jet' and 'Let Me Roll It,' then 'Band on the Run' and 'Nineteen Hundred and Eighty Five'—helped keep the music in listeners' ears, so after dropping down the charts, the album returned to No. 1 for a second time on June 8, and for a *third* time on July 6. All told, it spent 74 weeks in the Hot 200.

In Britain, *Band on the Run* entered the UK Album Chart at No. 45 on December 15. It did not reach No. 1 until July 27, 1974. But had a longer chart run than it did in America, remaining in the Top 40 for 100 weeks, and spending 124 weeks in the Top 100.

By the time it vanished from the British charts, the McCartneys and Wings had other tofu to fry. But that's another story.

To be continued . . .

ACKNOWLEDGMENTS

—

In many ways, this volume is the literary equivalent of Richard E. Grant standing in the pouring rain in Bruce Robinson's British comedy *Withnail and I*, telling a bemused farmer: *"We've gone on holiday by mistake!"* Originally, this series was meant only to be a sessionography of McCartney's music beyond the Beatles, but somewhere between 2014—when Adrian conceived the idea of penning the equivalent of Mark Lewisohn's *The Complete Beatles Recording Sessions* for Paul's catalog of solo work—and now, we wrote a biography . . . by mistake. And this is only the first installment.

As we pieced together the events that formed the backdrop for McCartney's musical rebirth between 1969 and 1973, we discovered for ourselves that his life and music are inseparable. The story of one cannot be told without the other, and each is better understood when the other is in full view. Telling that story, five decades on, was not a straightforward task, and we have a long list of people to thank for providing the pieces to help us assemble this 50-year-old jigsaw.

Outside of our own extensive research, our ability to transform black-and-white stories into technicolor is largely thanks to the foresight of a handful of people who chronicled their day-to-day lives in the early 1970s in diaries and journals and retained those precious books in their possession to this day. Most notably, Denny and Monique Seiwell. Monique's astonishing personal diaries for 1971–73, together with Denny's own session logs, offered us a portal to the early '70s without which we would not have been able to tell this story so accurately and vividly. *The McCartney Legacy Vol. 1* would not have been possible without their generous and candid contributions.

One criticism often leveled at Beatle biographers is that we "weren't there" to witness the events we chose to write about, but the ensemble of colorful characters listed below were. For their original contributions, time, memories, diaries, and knowledge, without which the pages of this book would be empty, we would like to thank: Alan Murray, Alan Parsons, Andy White, Angie McCartney, Anthea Disney, Aubrey Powell, Barry Chattington, Barry Dickins, Barry Lucas, Bill Quateman, Billy Rankin, Brian Blood, Brian Humphries, Chris Charlesworth, Chris Langhart, Danny Fields, David Lucas, David Spinozza, Dennis Coutts and his son John, Dick Barnatt, Dixon

Van Winkle, Donny Osmond, Dougie Wright, Drummond Challis, Ed Spevock, Eirik Wangberg, Eric Clapton, Geoff Britton, Geoffrey Cleghorn, Georgina Dean, Glyn Johns, Gray Joliffe, Holly McCracken, Howie Casey, Ian Gomm, Jim Guercio, John Kurlander, John Leckie, John Morris, José Feliciano, Josie McCullough, Kevin Nixon, Klaus Voormann, Les Fradkin, Marc Tobaly, Mike McCartney, Neil Aspinall, Nick DiMinno, Nicholas Ferguson, Paul Gambaccini, Peter Asher, Peter Brown, Phil Ault, Phil Chapman, Phil Kenzie, Ray & Sue McVay, Richard Digby Smith, Richard Hewson, Robin Black, Sam Trust, Sir Michael Lindsay-Hogg, Sir Michael Parkinson, Steve Haigh, Stuart Prebble, Sue Weston, Thelma Houston, Thomas Salter, Tim Geelan, Tony Clark, and Willy Russell. Several sources asked to remain anonymous, but also deserve our thanks.

We are also eternally grateful to an army of academics, historians, collectors, fans, and fellow authors who have offered us their knowledge, expertise, and advice along the way. The trio of people who top that list are John Lennon expert Chip Madinger, who was present at the conception of the series and granted us use of several unreleased archive interviews, including those with the late Henry McCullough and Hugh McCracken, McCartney collector and expert Benoît Dumetz, who gave us access to his extraordinary collection, and the world's foremost Beatles expert, Mark Lewisohn, who encouraged us to expand our sessionography project into a full-fledged biography.

In 2014, we considered the possibility of engaging a mainstream publisher as fanciful as bottling a rainbow. But five years later, when we were introduced to our tireless, like-minded agent (and by that we mean Beatle-obsessed) Matthew Elblonk, everything changed. Based on only snippets of research and text—shown to him over a pint in a backstreet New York pub—he helped us assemble a pitch that would win over one of New York's finest book editors, Carrie Thornton, who in turn welcomed us onto her roster at Dey Street Books. We feel incredibly privileged to be working under such an extraordinarily gifted wordsmith, and to be on the roster at Dey Street alongside legends like Dave Grohl, Joni Mitchell, Sinéad O'Connor, Debbie Harry, Peter Hook, Gene Simmons, and Johnny Marr. Thanks, as well, to Laurie McGee, our discerning copyeditor, and the amazing staff at Dey Street: Liate Stehlik, publisher, Benjamin Steinberg, associate publisher, Leah Carlson-Stanisic, interior designer, Andrea Molitor, production editor, Owen Corrigan, art director, Allison Carney and Heidi Richter, directors of marketing and publicity, Kyran Cassidy, legal counsel, and Chelsea Herrera, intrepid editorial assistant. If newspapers have mastheads, why shouldn't books?

Without the input of the wider Beatles community, a project like this one would never "come together," so we would also like to doff our hats to: Andrew Lucas, Andy Pitchford, Antonio Martinez, Axel Korinth, Barbara Gardner, Bjorn Jarsson, Bruno MacDonald, Carl Magnus Palm, Dan Kirby, Darren DeVivo, Edward Eikelenboom, Edward Malevani, Eoghan Lyng, Freddy Gillies, Ian McCarthy, James MacMillan, Jim Keyes, Jim Reeves, JoAnne Jimenez, Joe Russo, John Winn,

Jon Burlingame, Joseph C. Self, Ken Michaels, Linus Törnqvist, Luca Perasi, Mark Davey, Mark Malevani, Matt Ingham, Michael Ayr, Nick Lambert, Nina Antonia, Paul Gorman, Peggy Morgan Keyes, Peter Ames Carlin, Richard Buskin, Richard Davis, Richard Lawrence, Richard Royston, Rob Geurtsen, Rosa Ana Crespo Picó, Sara Schmidt, Sheryl Warmsley, Stephen Katz, Steve Marinucci, Stuart Cameron, Sunny Hanley, Thomas Desisto, and Víctor López Heras.

We also extend our thanks to the British Library (most notably, Bev Wise, Tamsyn Chadwick Lynn Townend, Julie Berry, and Jacqui Wake), ITV Archives Leeds, the Newcastle Film Archive, BBC Film Archive, Scotland's Land Information Service, the British Land Registry, Lancaster University, Leeds University, Manchester University, Newcastle University, Nottingham University, Salford University, Swansea University, and York University.

Finally, for enduring endless McCartney and Beatles talk for almost a decade during the making of this book (and for a lifetime beyond that), we would like to thank the Sinclair and Kozinn clans, plus our wonderfully patient and forgiving friends and colleagues.

ILLUSTRATIONS

—

i: *Adobe Stock*; **ii:** Paul McCartney onstage with Wings in Arles, France, July 13, 1972. Joe Stevens **vi–vii:** © *Michael Putland/Getty Images*; **viii, 656:** © *Pictorial Press/Alamy Stock Photo* **9:** Linda, Paul, Mary and Heather board a taxi outside Glasgow Abbotsinch Airport, October 22, 1969. *AP/Shutterstock* **18:** Paul, Linda and Heather outside Marylebone register office, March 12, 1969. *Globe Photos Inc.* **32:** Linda's first visit to Campbeltown, together with Paul, Heather and Martha, November 8, 1968. Freddy Gillies **42:** Ringo, Paul, George and John by the Thames, London, April 9, 1969. *Globe Photos Inc.* **102:** Paul and Linda pose for a press photo at Cavendish Avenue, April 1970. *Associated Newspapers/Shutterstock*; **113:** London's newspapers respond to Paul's self-interview, April 10, 1970. **117:** McCartney album trade ad with ABKCO credit. **121:** Telegram sent to journalist Penny Valentine on April 16, 1970. **140:** Paul lost in his thoughts, with Linda by his side, Lerwick, Shetland, July 30, 1970. *Derek Coutts* **141:** Paul, Linda, Heather and Mary pose for a shot at Wick Airport, July 31, 1970. *Robert MacDonald* **148:** Paul, Linda, Heather and Mary arrive in New York on the ocean liner S.S. *France*, October 7, 1970. *Globe Photos Inc.* **179:** Paul and Linda evade fans outside CBS Studios in New York, November 1970. Linda Aiello **202:** *Mirrorpix/Alamy Stock Photo* **219:** Paul and Linda take a stroll by the London law courts, February 19, 1971. *Associated Newspapers/Shutterstock* **221:** Black-and-white trade ad for 'Another Day' single, March 1971. **253:** Colorful trade ad for the *Ram* album, May 1971. **262** Paul and Linda share a joint at Mick and Bianca Jagger's wedding, Café des Arts, St. Tropez, France, May 12, 1971. *Globe Photos Inc.* **283:** Paul, Linda, Ian, and the two Dennys arrive at EMI Studios for Wings' first recording session, July 24, 1971. Mike Sacchetti **317:** Unused invitation to Wings' launch party at the Empire Ballroom on November 8, 1971. **318:** Denny Seiwell, Linda, Paul and Denny Laine at the Wings launch party, Empire Ballroom, London, November 8, 1971. *Monty Fresco/Daily Mail/Shutterstock* **326:** A. J. Weberman's Rock Liberation Front taunt McCartney in the lead up to their anti-McCartneyism event on August 26, 1971. **338:** An early advert for Wings' debut album, *Wild Life*, its release date unknown. Published in NME on November 27, 1971. **348:** Mary, Denny Laine, Henry, Paul and Linda outside Apple's offices on Saville Row, London, February 4, 1972. *Trinity Mirror/Mirrorpix/Alamy Stock Photos* **352:** Wings' first concert at Portland Building Ballroom, February 9, 1972. *Nick Lambert* **354:** Paper ticket issued for Wings' first concert appearance at Nottingham University's Portland Building Ballroom, February 9, 1972. **358:** Trade ad for Wings' first single, 'Give Ireland Back to the Irish,' with accidental blood spatter, published February 12, 1972. **364:** Paul, Linda, and the McCartney girls, Scarborough, February 13, 1972. *Stuart Cameron* **367:** Paul and Linda onstage at the Great Hall, Lancaster University, February 14, 1972. *Sheryl Warmsley* **373:** McCartney responds to the banning of 'Give Ireland Back to the Irish' in the British press. Advert placed on February 21, 1972. **377:** 'Give Ireland Back To The Irish' "Banned Everywhere" trade advert, published February 26, 1972. **405:** Trade ad for Wings' single 'Mary Had a Little Lamb,' May 1972. **417:** Paul, Linda, and Denny entertain the children and nuns of the Casa de Beneficencia of Alcoy, June 19, 1972. *Crespo Colomer* **418:** Wings Over Spain, circa June 20, 1972. *Benoit Dumetz* **419:** The McCartneys and Denny Laine at Montíboli Hotel, Villajoyosa, mid-June 1972. *Antonio Martinquez* **420:** Wings Over Spain, circa June 20, 1972. *Benoit Dumetz* **426:** McCartney and his Wings pose by their tour bus, Zürich, Switzerland, July 20, 1972. *Bob Aylott/Daily Mail/Shutterstock* **437, top:** Paul and Linda onstage in Arles, France, July 13, 1972. *Joe Stevens, Globe Photos Inc.* **437, bottom:** Paul onstage, Arles, France, July 13, 1972. *Joe Stevens, Globe Photos Inc.* **438, top:** Paul and Linda at the K.B. Hallen, Copenhagen, Denmark, August 1, 1972. *Jan Persson* **438, bottom:** Denny Laine, Henry and Paul perform at the K.B. Hallen, Copenhagen, August 1, 1972. *Jan Persson* **439:** Paul with his Rickenbacker bass guitar, K.B. Hallen, Copenhagen, August 1, 1972. *Jan Persson* **446:** Swedish newspaper *Aftonbladet* announces Paul's arrest on smuggling charges, August 11, 1972. **490:** Henry McCullough's paycheck for the week ending November 17, 1972. **496:** Wings launch their single 'Hi, Hi, Hi' and 'C Moon' in London, November 30, 1972. **497:** Paul and Linda court the press at the launch of 'Hi, Hi, Hi' in London, November 30, 1972. *Globe Photos Inc.* **499:** Quirky trade ad for the double A-Side release 'Hi, Hi, Hi' and 'C Moon,' December 1972. **504:** Wings pose for a publicity shot in November 1972. *AP/Shutterstock* **525:** *Red Rose Speedway* album trade ad, May 1973. **534:** Paul poses with dancers at Elstree Studios during the filming of the *James Paul McCartney* special, March 1973. *David Dagley/Shutterstock* **538:** A ticket for the live segment of the *James Paul McCartney* special, filmed on March 18, 1973. **540:** Wings mingle with gamboling lambs, London, March 1973. **542:** Invitation to a day of filming at the Chelsea Reach, New Brighton, March 22, 1973. **544–45:** Paul and Linda with the McCartney clan, Chelsea Reach, March 22, 1973. *David Dagley/Shutterstock* **546:** 'My Love' trade ad, late March 1973. **552:** Wings land at London Heathrow Airport, May 25, 1973. *Daily Mail/Shutterstock* **567:** Brinsley Schwarz contract for British tour, dated June 12, 1973. *Ian Gomm* **572:** Wings and Brinsley Schwarz kick back on the tour bus between concerts, May 1973. *Ian Gomm* **581:** Wings at the Hammersmith Odeon, London, May 25, 1973. *Dick Barnatt* **589:** Wings and wives attend the premiere of *Live and Let Die*, London, July 5, 1973. *Harry Myers/Shutterstock* **613:** Unseen sound effects tapes used during the Band On The Run sessions, September–November 1973. Adrian Sinclair **620:** Fela Ransome-Kuti enjoys a herbal jazz ciggie in his dressing room, Lagos, Nigeria, undated. William Campbell **621:** "Fela To-Nite At The Shrine"—a local newspaper advertises Fela Ransome Kuti's concert on September 14, 1973. **640:** Paul and Linda during the AIR Studios sessions for Band On The Run, November 1973. Michael Putland **643:** 'Helen Wheels' trade ad, November 1973. **650:** *Band on the Run* album trade ad, December 1973. **659:** Paul at EMI Pathé Studios, Paris, France, November 1973. *Marc Tobaly*

BIBLIOGRAPHY

Abiola, Jamiu: *The President Who Never Ruled* (self-published, Nigeria, 2016).

Babiuk, Andy: *Beatles Gear* (Backbeat, New York, 2015).

Badman, Keith: *Off the Records 2—The Dream Is Over Volume 2* (Omnibus Press, London, 2002).

Baker, Ginger, with Baker, Ginette: *Ginger Baker Hellraiser* (John Blake, London, 2009).

Barrow, Tony, with Bextor, Robin: *Paul McCartney Now & Then* (Carlton, London, 2004).

Benitez, Vincent P.: *The Words and Music of Paul McCartney* (Praeger, Santa Barbara, 2010).

Boyd, Pattie, with Junor, Penny: *Wonderful Tonight* (Harmony, New York, 2007).

Braun, Michael: *Love Me Do! The Beatles' Progress* (Penguin, London, 1964, reprinted 1995).

Burlingame, Jon: *The Music of James Bond* (Oxford University Press, Oxford, 2014).

Carlin, Peter Ames: *Paul McCartney: A Life* (Touchstone, New York, 2009).

Cavendish, William: *His Master's Voice* (Unicorn Publishing Group, London, 2017).

Collins, Judith: *Paolozzi* (Lund Humphries, Farnham, 2014).

Connolly, Ray: *Being John Lennon—A Restless Life* (Pegasus Books, New York, 2018).

Courtney, David: *Oh Wot a Life: Nothing in This Book Is True, But It's Exactly the Way It Happened* (Courtney World Music Ltd., London, 2020).

Cribbins, Bernard: *Bernard Who?* (Constable, London, 2018).

Davies, Hunter: *The John Lennon Letters* (Little, Brown and Company, London, 2012).

Doggett, Peter: *You Never Give Me Your Money* (Harper Studio, New York, 2009).

Du Noyer, Paul: *Band on the Run* Archive Edition (MPL Communications, London, 2010).

Du Noyer, Paul: *Conversations with McCartney* (Hodder & Stoughton, London, 2015).

Du Noyer, Paul: *McCartney* Archive Edition (MPL Communications, London, 2011).

Elliott, Bobby: *It Ain't Heavy It's My Story* (Omnibus Press, London, 2020).

Emerick, Geoff; Massey, Howard: *Here, There and Everywhere: My Life Recording the Music of the Beatles* (Gotham Books, New York, 2006).

Evans, David, with Minns, David: *This Was the Real Life: The Tale of Freddie Mercury* (Tusitala Press, London, 2008).

Fields, Danny: *Linda McCartney—A Portrait* (Renaissance Books, Los Angeles, 2000).

Fleming, Ian: *Live and Let Die: James Bond 007* (Pan Book Limited, London, 1966).

Flick, Vic: *Vic Flick, Guitarman: From James Bond to the Beatles and Beyond* (BearManor Media, Oklahoma, 2014).

Flippo, Chet: *McCartney the Biography* (Sidgwick & Jackson, London, 1988).

Frinke, David: *Wild Life Archive Edition* (MPL Communications, London, 2018).

Gambaccini, Paul: *Paul McCartney: In His Own Words* (Omnibus Press, New York, 1976).

Gillies, Freddy: *From the Blue Sea to the Black Country* (Ardminish Press, Isle of Gigha, 2012).

Giuliano, Geoffrey, *Blackbird: Life and Times of Paul McCartney* (Penguin; Reprint Edition, New York 1992).

Giuliano, Geoffrey, *The Beatles in Their Own Words: A Rockumentary: The Lost Beatles Interviews* (Laserlight Audiobook, Santa Monica, 1995).

Goodman, Fred: *Allen Klein—The Man Who Bailed Out the Beatles, Made the Stones, and Transformed Rock & Roll* (Houghton Mifflin Harcourt, New York, 2015).

Grundy, Stuart, with Tobler, John: *The Record Producers* (BBC Books, London, 1982).

Harper, Colin, with Hodgett, Trevor: *Irish Folk, Trad & Blues—A Secret History* (The Collins Press, Ireland, 2004).

Harper, Simon: *Ram Archive Edition* (MPL Communications, London, 2012).

Harris, John: *Dark Side of the Moon—The Making of the Pink Floyd Masterpiece* (Da Capo, New York, 2005).

Harris, John (Editor): *The Beatles: Get Back* (Callaway Arts & Entertainment, London, 2021).

Helvin, Marie: *The Autobiography* (Orion Books, London, 2007; Phoenix ebook).

Hogan, Joe: *Sticky Fingers—The Life and Times of Jann Wenner and Rolling Stone Magazine,* (Alfred A. Knopf, New York, 2017).

Howlett, Kevin: *Abbey Road 50th Anniversary Super Deluxe Edition* (Apple/Universal, London, 2019).

James, Catherine: *Dandelion; Memoir of a Free Spirit* (self-published, 2007, eBook).

Jarry, Alfred: *Ubu cocu or Cuckold Ubu* (Nick Hern Books Limited, London, 1997).

Johns, Glyn: *Sound Man* (Blue Rider Press, New York, 2014).

Kehew, Brian, with Ryan, Kevin: *Recording the Beatles* (Curvebender, Houston, 2006).

Lawson, Twiggy: *Twiggy* (Granada Publishing Limited, St. Albans, 1975).

Lawson, Twiggy: *Twiggy in Black and White* (Simon & Schuster, London, 1997).

Leng, Simon: *While My Guitar Gently Weeps* (Hal Leonard, New York, 2006).

Lewisohn, Mark: *The Beatles Recording Sessions* (Harmony, New York, 1988).

Lewisohn, Mark: *The Beatles: All These Years, Vol. 1—Tune In* (special ed.) (Little Brown, London, 2013).

Lewisohn, Mark: *The Compleat Beatles Chronicle* (Pyramid, London, 1992).

Lucas, Barry: *Rock Goes to College: Legends Live at Lancaster University, 1969-1985* (Palatine Books, London, 2019).

Madinger, Chip, with Raile, Scott: *Lennonology: Strange Days Indeed* (Open Your Books, Chesterfield, Missouri, 2015).

Martin, George, with Hornsby, Jeremy: *All You Need Is Ears* (St. Martin's Press, London, 1979).

Martin, George, with Craske, Oliver: *Playback—An Illustrated Memoir* (Genesis Publications, Guildford, 2002).

Mason, Nick: *Inside Out: A Personal History of Pink Floyd* (Chronicle Books, San Francisco, 2005).

Massey, Howard: *The Great British Recording Studios* (Hal Leonard Corporation, Milwaukee, 2015).

McCabe, Peter, with Schonfeld, Robert D.: *Apple to the Core* (Pocket Books, New York, 1974).

McCartney, Angie: *Angie McCartney: My Long and Winding Road* (ROK Books, Los Angeles, 2013).

McCartney, Angie: *Your Mother Should Know—From Liverpool to Los Angeles* (Probablistic Publishing, Los Angeles, 2019).

McCartney, Paul (Lewisohn, Mark, ed.): *Wingspan* (Bulfinch Press, London, 2002).

McCartney, Paul (Muldoon, Paul, ed.): *The Lyrics 1956 to the Present* (Liverlight Publishing Corporation, New York, 2021).

McGee, Garry: *Band on the Run* (Taylor Trade Publishing, New York, 2003).

McNab, Ken: *And in the End—The Last Days of the Beatles* (Polygon, Edinburgh, 2019).

Miles, Barry: *Paul McCartney—Many Years from Now* (Henry Holt and Company, New York, 1997).

Moore, Carlos: Fela: *This Bitch of a Life* (Omnibus Press, London, 2011).

Murray, Len: *The Pleader—An Autobiography* (Mainstream, Edinburgh, 2002).

Norman, Philip: *Paul McCartney—The Life* (Little Brown & Company, New York, 2016).

O'Dell, Chris, with Ketcham, Katherine: *Miss O'Dell* (Touchstone, New York, 2009).

Pascall, Jeremy: *Paul McCartney & Wings* (Phoebus Publishing, London, 1977).

Petrusich, Amanda: *Red Rose Speedway Archive Edition* (MPL Communications, London, 2018).

Rosen, Craig: *Billboard Book of Number One Albums: The Inside Story Behind Pop Music's Blockbuster Records* (Billboard Books, New York, 1996).

Sadie, Stanley, ed.: *The New Grove Dictionary of Musical Instruments* (Macmillan Press, London, 1984).

Salewicz, Chris: *McCartney The Biography* (Futura Publications, London, 1987).

Schwartz, Francie: *Body Count* (Straight Arrow Books/Quick Fox, New York, 1972).

Shapiro, Marc: *Behind Sad Eyes* (St. Martin's Press, New York, 2002).

Shotton, Pete, with Schaffner, Nick: *John Lennon in My Life* (Stein and Day, New York, 1983).

Simon, Carly: *Boys in the Trees—A Memoir* (Constable, New York, 2016).

Smith, Howard Smith: *The Smith Tapes*, edited by Ezra Bookstein (Princeton Architectural Press, New York, 2015).

Sounes, Howard: *Fab: An Intimate Life of Paul McCartney* (HarperCollins, New York, 2011).

Southall, Brian, with Perry, Rupert: *Northern Songs* (Omnibus Press, London, 2007).

Spencer, Terrence with Lesley: *Living Dangerously* (Percival, London, 2002; reissued privately by Cara Spencer, 2012).

Taylor, Derek: *Fifty Years Adrift* (Genesis Publications, Guildford, 1984).

The Beatles: *The Beatles Anthology* (Chronicle Books, San Francisco, 2000).

Wincentsen, Edward: *The Moody Blues Companion* (Wynn Publishing, Pickens, 2000).

Zappa, Frank with Occhiogrosso, Peter: *The Real Frank Zappa* (Pan Books, London, 1989).

SELECTED DISCOGRAPHY

Albums

PAUL McCARTNEY, *McCARTNEY*

UK: Apple PCS 7102, April 17, 1970
USA: Apple STAO-3363, April 20, 1970
Reissued: Paul McCartney Archive Collection, Hear Music, HRM-32799-00, June 2011
Original tracks: The Lovely Linda/That Would Be Something/Valentine Day/Every Night/Hot As Sun/Glasses/Junk/Man We Was Lonely/Oo You/Momma Miss America/Teddy Boy/Singalong Junk/Maybe I'm Amazed/Kreen-Akrore
Additional music tracks with reissue: Suicide (Outtake)/Maybe I'm Amazed (From One Hand Clapping)/ Every Night (Live at Glasgow, 1979)/Hot As Sun (Live at Glasgow, 1979)/Maybe I'm Amazed (Live At Glasgow, 1979)/Don't Cry Baby (Outtake)/Women Kind (Demo)

PAUL & LINDA McCARTNEY, *RAM*

UK: Apple PAS 10003, May 21, 1971
USA: Apple SMAS-3375, May 17, 1971
Reissued: Paul McCartney Archive Collection, Hear Music, HRM-33450-00, May 2012
Too Many People/3 Legs/Ram On/Dear Boy/Uncle Albert-Admiral Halsey/Smile Away/Heart of the Country/Monkberry Moon Delight/Eat at Home/Long Haired Lady/Ram On/The Back Seat of My Car
Additional music tracks with reissue: Another Day/Oh Woman, Oh Why/Little Woman Love/A Love for You (Jon Kelly Mix)/Hey Diddle (Dixon Van Winkle Mix)/Great Cock and Seagull Race (Dixon Van Winkle Mix)/Rode All Night/Sunshine Sometime (Earliest Mix)
Plus the mono promo mix of *Ram*, and stereo mix of *Thrillington* (1977)

WINGS, *WILD LIFE*

UK: Apple PCS 7142, December 3, 1971 (date cannot be confirmed due to label dispute)
USA: Apple SW-3386, December 6, 1971 (date cannot be confirmed due to label dispute)
Reissued: Paul McCartney Archive Collection, Capitol Records, B0028224-00, December 2018
Mumbo/Bip Bop/Love Is Strange/Wild Life/Some People Never Know/I Am Your Singer/Bip Bop Link/Tomorrow/Dear Friend/Mumbo Link
Additional music tracks with reissue: Mumbo (Rough Mix)/Bip Bop (Rough Mix)/Love Is Strange (Version) (Rough Mix)/Wild Life (Rough Mix)/Some People Never Know (Rough Mix)/I Am Your Singer (Rough Mix)/Tomorrow (Rough Mix)/Dear Friend (Rough Mix)/Good Rockin' Tonight (Home Recording)/Bip Bop (Home Recording)/Hey Diddle (Home Recording)/She Got It Good (Home Recording)/I Am Your Singer (Home Recording)/Outtake I/Dear Friend (Home Recording I)/Dear Friend (Home Recording II)/Outtake II/Indeed I Do/When the Wind Is Blowing/The Great Cock and Seagull Race (Rough Mix)/Outtake III/Give Ireland Back to the Irish/Give Ireland Back to the Irish (Version)/Love Is Strange (Single Edit)/African Yeah Yeah/When the Saints Go Marching In (Hidden track)/Dear Friend (Orchestra Up; *free download only*)

PAUL McCARTNEY & WINGS, *RED ROSE SPEEDWAY*

UK: Apple PCTC 251, May 4, 1973
USA: Apple SMAL-3409, April 30, 1973
Reissued: Paul McCartney Archive Collection, Capitol Records, B0028225-00, December 2018
Big Barn Bed/My Love/Get on the Right Thing/One More Kiss/Little Lamb Dragonfly/Single Pigeon/When the Night/Loup (1st Indian on the Moon)/Medley: Hold Me Tight, Lazy Dynamite, Hands of Love, Power Cut
Additional music tracks with reissue: Night Out/Country Dreamer/Seaside Woman/I Lie Around/The Mess (Live at the Hague, 1972)/Best Friend (Live in Antwerp, 1972)/Mama's Little Girl/I Would Only Smile/Tragedy/Mary Had a Little Lamb/Little Woman Love/Hi, Hi, Hi/C Moon/Live and Let Die/Get on the Right Thing (Early Mix)/Little Lamb Dragonfly (Early Mix)/Little Woman Love (Early Mix)/1882 (Home Recording)/Big Barn Bed (Rough Mix)/The Mess/Thank You Darling/Mary Had a Little Lamb (Rough Mix)/1882 (Live in Berlin)/1882/Jazz Street/Live and Let Die (Group Only, Take 10)/ Hands of Love (Take 2; *free download only*)

PAUL McCARTNEY & WINGS, *BAND ON THE RUN*

UK: Apple PAS 10007, November 30, 1973
USA: Apple SO-3415, December 5, 1973
Reissued: Paul McCartney Archive Collection, Hear Music,

HRM-32565-00, November 2010
Band on the Run/Jet/Bluebird/Mrs. Vandebilt/Let Me Roll
It/Mamunia/No Words/Helen Wheels (**US release only*)/
Picasso's Last Words (Drink to Me)/Nineteen Hundred and
Eighty Five
Additional music tracks with reissue: Helen Wheels/Country
Dreamer/Bluebird (From One Hand Clapping)/Jet (From One
Hand Clapping)/Let Me Roll It (From One Hand Clapping)/
Band on the Run (From One Hand Clapping)/Nineteen
Hundred and Eighty Five (From One Hand Clapping)/
Country Dreamer (From One Hand Clapping)/Zoo Gang
(Single mix)
Plus audio documentary on the making of *Band on the Run*

Singles

**PAUL MCCARTNEY, 'ANOTHER DAY'
B/W 'OH WOMAN OH WHY'**

UK: Apple R 5889, February 19, 1971
USA: Apple 1829, February 22, 1971

**PAUL & LINDA MCCARTNEY, 'THE BACK SEAT
OF MY CAR' B/W 'HEART OF THE COUNTRY'**

UK: Apple R 5914, August 13, 1971

**PAUL & LINDA MCCARTNEY, 'UNCLE ALBERT-
ADMIRAL HALSEY' B/W 'TOO MANY PEOPLE'**

USA: Apple 1837, August 2, 1971

**WINGS, 'GIVE IRELAND BACK TO THE IRISH' B/W
'GIVE IRELAND BACK TO THE IRISH (VERSION)'**

UK: Apple R 5936, February 18, 1972
USA: Apple 1847, February 28, 1972

**WINGS, 'MARY HAD A LITTLE LAMB'
B/W 'LITTLE WOMAN LOVE'**

UK: Apple R 5949, May 19, 1972
USA: Apple 1851, June 5, 1972

WINGS, 'HI, HI, HI' B/W 'C MOON'

UK: Apple R 5973, December 1, 1972
USA: Apple 1857, December 4, 1972

PAUL MCCARTNEY & WINGS, 'MY LOVE' B/W 'THE MESS'

UK: Apple R 5985, March 30, 1973
USA: Apple 1861, April 2, 1973

**PAUL MCCARTNEY & WINGS, 'LIVE AND
LET DIE' B/W 'I LIE AROUND'**

UK: Apple R 5987, June 1, 1973
USA: Apple 1863, June 25, 1973

**PAUL MCCARTNEY & WINGS, 'HELEN
WHEELS' B/W 'COUNTRY DREAMER'**

UK: Apple R 5993, October 26, 1973
USA: Apple 1869, November 12, 1973.

Note: All release dates are based on chart information rather
than dates printed in the news columns of period music
papers, which were often estimated dates for when buyers
might expect to pick up 45s, and LPs in record stores. Even
trade ads often carried misleading release dates.

SELECTED VIDEOGRAPHY

Promo Films

All promotional films are available on the MPL box set *The McCartney Years* (MPL/Warner Music Group, 2007), Paul McCartney's archive series deluxe edition sets, and many are widely available through McCartney's official YouTube channel (in some cases, offered in 4K or HD). The *James Paul McCartney* TV special was released on the *Red Rose Speedway* archive edition in 2018.

PAUL MCCARTNEY, 'MAYBE I'M AMAZED'

Filming date: April 1970
Director: Charlie Jenkins
Producer: Paul McCartney

PAUL & LINDA MCCARTNEY, 'HEART OF THE COUNTRY' AND '3 LEGS'

Filming date: June 5-6, 1971
Director: Roy Benson
Producer: Paul McCartney

WINGS, 'MARY HAD A LITTLE LAMB' (#1, CARTOON)

Filming date: May 13, 1972
Director: Nicholas Ferguson
Producer: Paul McCartney

WINGS, 'MARY HAD A LITTLE LAMB' (#2, BARN)

Filming date: May 13, 1972
Director: Nicholas Ferguson
Producer: Paul McCartney

WINGS, 'MARY HAD A LITTLE LAMB' (#3, PSYCHEDELIC)

Filming date: May 13, 1972
Director: Nicholas Ferguson
Producer: Paul McCartney

WINGS, 'MARY HAD A LITTLE LAMB' (#4, CIRCUS)

Filming date: May 13, 1972
Director: Nicholas Ferguson
Producer: Paul McCartney

WINGS, 'C MOON'

Filming date: November 14, 1972
Director: Steve Turner
Producer: Paul McCartney

WINGS, 'HI, HI, HI'

Filming date: November 14, 1972
Director: Steve Turner
Producer: Paul McCartney

PAUL MCCARTNEY & WINGS, 'MY LOVE'

Filming date: April 8, 1973
Director: Mick Rock
Producer: Paul McCartney

PAUL MCCARTNEY & WINGS, 'HELEN WHEELS'

Filming date: October 1973
Director: Roy Benson
Producer: Paul McCartney

Television Specials

PAUL MCCARTNEY & WINGS, *JAMES PAUL MCCARTNEY* (ATV, 1973)

Filming date: March-April 1973
Producer: Gary Smith
Director: Dwight Hemion

CONCERT TOURS

University Tour (February 9–22, 1972)

February 9: Portland Building Ballroom, Nottingham University, England
February 10: Goodricke College Dining Room, York University, England
February 11: West Refectory Hall, Hull University, England
February 14: The Great Hall, Lancaster University, England
February 16: University of Leeds Refectory, Leeds University, England
February 17: Lower Refectory, Sheffield University, England
February 18: Maxwell Hall, Salford University, England
February 21: Deb Hall, Birmingham University, England
February 22: Union House Hall, Swansea University, Wales

Wings over Europe (July–August 1972)

July 9: Centre Culturelle, Châteauvallon, France
July 12: Juan-Les-Pins, France
July 13: Theatre Antique, Arles, France
July 16: Théâtre de L'Olympia, Paris, France (two shows)
July 18: Zirkus-Krone-Bau, Munich, West Germany
July 19: Stadthallle Offenbach, Frankfurt, West Germany
July 21: Kongresshaus, Zürich, Switzerland
July 22: Pavilion, Montreux, Switzerland
August 1: K.B. Hallen, Copenhagen, Denmark
August 4: Messuhalli, Helsinki, Finland
August 5: Kupittaan Urheiluhalli, Turku, Finland
August 7: Tivoli Gröna Lund, Stockholm, Sweden
August 8: Idretshalle, Örebro, Sweden
August 9: Njårdhallen, Oslo, Norway
August 10: Scandinavium Halle, Gothenburg, Sweden
August 11: Olympen, Lund, Sweden
August 12: Fyns Forum, Odense, Denmark
August 14: Vejiby-Risskov Hallen, Aarhus, Denmark
August 16: Düsseldorf Rheinhalle, Düsseldorf, West Germany

August 17: De Doelen, Rotterdam, The Netherlands
August 19: Evenementanhal Martinihal, Groningen, The Netherlands
August 20: Concertgebouw, Amsterdam, The Netherlands
August 21: Nederlands Concertgebouw, The Hague, The Netherlands
August 22: Ciné Roma, Antwerp, Belgium
August 24: Deutschlandhalle, West Berlin, East Germany

Benefit Concert for the Charity Release

March 18: Hard Rock Cafe, London, England

Wings Tour of Britain (May–July 1973)

May 11: Hippodrome, Bristol, England
May 12: New Theatre, Oxford, England
May 13: Capitol Cinema & Theatre, Cardiff, Wales
May 15: Winter Gardens, Bournemouth, England
May 16: Hard Rock Concert Theatre, Manchester, England
May 17: Hard Rock Concert Theatre, Manchester, England
May 18: Empire Theatre, Liverpool, England (two shows)
May 19: University of Leeds Refectory, Leeds, England
May 21: Guild Hall, Preston, England
May 23: Odeon, Edinburgh, Scotland (two shows)
May 24: Green's Playhouse, Glasgow, Scotland
May 25: Hammersmith Odeon, London, England
May 26: Hammersmith Odeon, London, England
May 27: Hammersmith Odeon, London, England
July 4: City Hall, Sheffield, England
July 6: Odeon, Birmingham, England
July 9: Odeon, Leicester, England
July 10: City Hall, Newcastle-Upon-Tyne, England

NOTES

INTRODUCTION

1   Wonfor, Geoff: Video interview with Paul McCartney for *Flaming Pie* press kit, May 5, 1997.

1 THE KINTYRE MIST

1   Spencer, Terrence and Lesley: *Living Dangerously* (Percival, London, 2002; reissued privately by Cara Spencer, 2012), pp. 284–5.

2   Drake, Chris: Radio interview with Paul McCartney, BBC Radio 2, October 24, 1969; information taken from a rebroadcast on "The World This Weekend—Late Night Extra," broadcast October 27, 1969.

3   Drake, Chris: Radio interview with Paul McCartney, BBC Radio 2, October 24, 1969.

4   McCartney, Paul, and Muldoon, Paul (ed.): *The Lyrics 1956 to the Present* (Liverlight Publishing Corporation/ W.W. Norton & Company, New York, 2021), p. 111.

5   McCartney, Paul: Author interview (Kozinn), October 19, 1990.

6   Cavanagh, David: "Suddenly I Was Unemployed!," *Uncut*, June 2012, p. 20.

7   Harper, Tim: "Is Beatle Paul McCartney Dead?" Drake *Times-Delphic*, September 17, 1969, pp. 1, 3.

8   Bacon, Dorothy: "I Want to Live in Peace," *Life*, November 7, 1969, p. 33.

9   Neary, John: "The Magical McCartney Mystery," *Life*, November 7, 1969, p. 33.

10   Bacon: "I Want to Live in Peace."

11   Kurlander, John: Author interview (Kozinn), January 19, 1987.

12   Goodman, Joan: "*Playboy* Interview: Paul & Linda McCartney," *Playboy*, December 1984, p. 96.

13   Telegram to Paul McCartney, care of Apple, October 22, 1969.

14   Fields, Danny: *Linda McCartney—A Portrait* (Renaissance Books, Los Angeles, 2000), p. 132.

15   Wood, Franklyn: "The McCartney Marriage Hasn't Gone to Pot," *Woman's Own*, July 26, 1980, p. 12.

16   Pumer, Eddie: "A Snap Decision," *Club Sandwich*, No. 64, Winter, 1992, p. 12.

17   O'Brien, Catherine: "Linda's Most Fragile Legacy," *Daily Telegraph*, February 4, 1999, p. 21.

18   Webb, Julie: "Wings in the Air," *NME*, October 27, 1973, p. 11.

19   Brown, Peter: Author interview (Kozinn), May 1, 2020.

20   Ibid.

21   Ibid.

22   Ibid.

23   Schwartz, Francie: *Body Count* (Straight Arrow Books/ Quick Fox, New York, 1972), pp. 72–93.

24   Schwartz, Francie: "He Loved Me, Yeah, Yeah, Yeah," *Penthouse*, November 1972, p. 60.

25   O'Riordan, Maggie, and Harris, Paul: "Paul McCartney's Secret Affair," *Daily Mail*, April 12, 1997, p. 25.

26   Nightingale, Anne: Audio interview with Linda McCartney for Rock Around the World, BBC Radio One, December 1976.

27   Ibid.

28   Mills, Nancy: "I Think I Must Be Extraordinary—Linda McCartney on Herself—and Paul," *Family Weekly*, December 7, 1975, p. 20.

29   Uncredited staff writer: "Give Her a Break, Paul," *Sunday People*, April 5, 1970, p. 9.

30   Fields: *Linda McCartney—A Portrait*, p. 19.

31   Uncredited: "Linda," *Scarsdale Inquirer*, September 26, 1947.

32   Miles, Barry: *Paul McCartney—Many Years from Now* (Henry Holt and Company, New York, 1997), pp. 514–5.

33   Ibid., pp. 517–8.

34   Uncredited: "Beatles—Three Live December Concerts," *NME*, November 9, 1968.

35   Uncredited: "4,500 Seats At the Beatles' Concerts," *NME*, November 16, 1968.

36   Uncredited: "Beatles Shows: Venue Switch," *NME*, November 30, 1968.

37   Martin, George: Author interview (Kozinn), May 11, 2003.

38   Discussion during the *Get Back/Let It Be* recording sessions, January 8, 1969, unissued.

39   Connolly, Ray: "The Party's Over But None of Us Wants to Admit It," *Evening Standard*, April 21, 1970, p. 24.

40   Clapton, Eric: Author interview (Kozinn), June 7, 1990, unpublished.

2 ROTTEN APPLE

1   Ross, Robin: Audio interview with Paul McCartney for the Press album release, August 1986.

2   Williams, Richard: Audio interview with Paul McCartney for the *Times*, December 28, 1981.

3   Interviews published in the *Daily Sketch* and the *Daily Mirror*, June 17, 1966.

4   Uncredited: *Campbeltown Courier*, various articles, June 23, 1966.

5   Lewisohn, Mark (Ed.): "Mac and 2 Veg," *Club Sandwich*, No. 57, Spring, 1991, p. 6.

6   Description taken mostly from Chris Drake's narration for his October 24, 1969, interview with Paul for BBC Radio 2. Bathtub: comment by Linda in a Paul McCartney interview with Ray Connolly, *Evening Standard*, April 21–22, 1970.

7   Miles: *Paul McCartney—Many Years from Now*, p. 522.

8   Brown, Peter: Author interview (Kozinn), May 1, 2020.

9   Ibid.

10 Smith, Joe: Audio interview with Paul McCartney for the Library of Congress, October 22, 1987.

11 Asher, Peter: Author interview (Kozinn), October 9, 2019.

12 Howlett, Kevin: *Abbey Road 50th Anniversary Super Deluxe Edition* (Apple/Universal, London, 2019), p. 62.

13 Goodman, Fred: *Allen Klein—The Man Who Bailed Out the Beatles, Made the Stones, and Transformed Rock & Roll* (Houghton Mifflin Harcourt, Boston, New York, 2015), pp. 198–9.

14 Smith, Howard: Radio interview with George Harrison, WABC-FM, New York, circa May 1, 1970. An edited version appears in *The Smith Tapes*, edited by Ezra Bookstein (Princeton Architectural Press, 2015), p. 212.

15 Uncredited: "4,500 Seats at the Beatles' Concerts," *New Musical Express*, November 16, 1968.

16 Connolly, Ray: Untitled piece, *Disc and Music Echo*, January 18, 1969.

17 Harris, John (Editor): *The Beatles: Get Back* (Callaway Arts & Entertainment, London, 2021), p. 181.

18 Goodman, Joan: "Paul and Linda McCartney: The *Playboy* Interview," *Playboy*, December 1984, p. 95. Gambaccini, Paul: *Paul McCartney: In His Own Words* (Omnibus Press, New York, 1976), p. 40.

19 Asher, Peter: Author interview (Kozinn), October 9, 2019.

20 Trust, Sam: Author interview (Sinclair), April 13, 2022.

21 O'Connor, Gillian: "ATV Bids £9.5m for Northern Songs," *The Times*, March 29, 1969, p. 13.

22 Goodman: *Allen Klein—The Man Who Bailed Out the Beatles, Made the Stones, and Transformed Rock & Roll*, p. 171.

23 Letter from John Lennon, George Harrison and Richard Starkey (Ringo Starr) to Lee Eastman, April 18, 1969, reproduced in Davies, Hunter: *The John Lennon Letters* (Little, Brown and Company, New York, Boston, London) p. 162.

24 Smith, Howard: Radio interview with George Harrison, WABC-FM, New York, circa May 1, 1970. An edited version appears in *The Smith Tapes*, edited by Ezra Bookstein (Princeton Architectural Press, New York, 2015), p. 211.

25 Miller, Steve, essay in Barrow, Tony, with Bextor, Robin: *Paul McCartney Now & Then* (Carlton, London, 2004), pp. 78–79.

26 Ibid.

27 Lewisohn, Mark: Interview with Paul McCartney in 1991, quoted by Lewisohn in interviews and on Twitter, May 9, 2019.

28 Lindsay-Hogg, Michael: Author interview (Sinclair), May 24, 2020.

29 Ibid.

30 Salewicz, Chris: "Paul McCartney—An Innocent Man?" *Q*, October 1986.

31 Coxhill, Gordon: "Paul and Linda and Togetherness," *Petticoat*, February 17, 1973, pp. 28–30.

32 Uncredited: "Ringo Taken III—Rushed to Hospital," *Melody Maker*, September 13, 1969, p. 1.

33 Beatles meeting at Apple, London, September 9, 1969, unpublished tape.

34 Wenner, Jann: Recorded interview with John Lennon for *Rolling Stone*, December 8, 1970. The interview was published January 7 and February 4, 1971, and in book form as *Lennon Remembers*.

35 Voormann, Klaus, email exchange with author (Sinclair), January 14, 2020.

36 Affidavit of James Paul McCartney in *James Paul McCartney v. John Ono Lennon, George Harrison, Richard Starkey and Apple Corps Limited*. In the High Court of Justice, Chancery Division Group B 1970 No. 6315, December 1970.

37 Cavett, Dick: Interview with John Lennon and Yoko Ono for *The Dick Cavett Show*, ABC-TV, broadcast September 11, 1971. Available on *The Dick Cavett Show—John and Yoko Collection* (Shout Factory, DVD, 2005).

38 Goodman: "The *Playboy* Interview, with Paul and Linda McCartney," pp. 75, 110.

39 Mackie, Roy (Editor): "Yeah, Yeah for ATV," *Daily Express*, October 16, 1969, p. 19.

40 Miles: *Paul McCartney—Many Years from Now*, pp. 568–9.

41 Heyn, Dalma: "The Alarmingly Normal McCartneys," *McCall's*, August 1984.

42 Cass, Alain: "McCartney's Circus," *Daily Express*, July 14, 1972, p. 7.

43 Fields: *Linda McCartney—A Portrait*, p. 141.

44 Goodman, Joan: "The *Playboy* Interview, with Paul and Linda McCartney," *Playboy*, December 1984, pp. 75, 110.

45 Connolly, Ray: "The Party's Over But None of Us Wants to Admit It," *London Evening Standard*, April 21, 1970.

3 PLAYING WITH HIMSELF

1   Affidavit of Allen Klein in *James Paul McCartney v. John Ono Lennon, George Harrison, Richard Starkey and Apple Corps Limited*. In the High Court of Justice, Chancery Division Group B 1970 No. 6315, December 1970.

2   Smith, Howard: An example is John Lennon's interview with Howard Smith on WABC-FM, New York (although the interview was taped in Mississauga, Ontario, Canada), December 17, 1969. Also in *The Smith Tapes*, edited by Ezra Bookstein (Princeton Architectural Press, New York, 2015), pp. 153–8.

3   Smith, Howard: Radio interview with George Harrison, WABC-FM, New York, circa May 1, 1970. Also in *The Smith Tapes*, edited by Ezra Bookstein (Princeton Architectural Press, New York, 2015), p. 211.

4   Black, Johnny: Audio interview with Paul McCartney for *Mojo* magazine, March 6, 2003.

5   Braun, Michael: *Love Me Do! The Beatles' Progress* (Penguin, London, 1964, reprinted 1995), p. 91.

6   Black, Johnny: Audio interview with Paul McCartney for *Mojo* magazine, March 6, 2003.

7   Court Transcript, *James Paul McCartney v. John Ono Lennon, George Harrison, Richard Starkey and Apple Corps Limited*, March 4, 1971, p. 10.

8   Keen, Geraldine: "Not-So-Antique Sale," *The Times*, November 12, 1969, p. 2.

9   Lewisohn, Mark: *The Beatles Recording Sessions* (Harmony, New York, 1988), p. 72.

10 Kehew, Brian, with Ryan, Kevin: *Recording the Beatles* (Curvebender, Houston, 2006), pp. 227–8.

11 McCartney, Mary: Filmed interview with Paul McCartney for *Wingspan* documentary (MPL Communications, 2001).

12 *McCartney* album press release and self-interview, April 10, 1970.

13 Du Noyer, Paul: *McCartney Archive Edition* (MPL Communications, London, 2011), p. 54.

14 McCartney, Paul (Lewisohn, Mark, ed.): *Wingspan* (Bulfinch Press, London, 2002), p. 20.

15 Du Noyer: *McCartney Archive Edition*, p. 9.

16 White, Timothy: "Farewell to the First Solo Era," *Musician*, February 1988, p. 47.

17 Du Noyer, Paul: Interview with Paul McCartney for the World Tour Program, November 1989, p. 14.

18 Wenner, Jann: "Paul McCartney," *Rolling Stone*, April 30, 1970, p. 20.

19 Garbarini, Vic: *The McCartney Interview*, Capitol Records, 1980. Available in print as, Garbarini, Vic: "Paul McCartney—Lifting the Veil on the Beatles," *Musician*, August 1980, p. 98.

20 Du Noyer, Paul: *Conversations with McCartney* (Hodder & Stoughton, London, 2015), p. 98.

21 McCartney (Lewisohn, Mark, ed.): *Wingspan*, p. 20.

22 *McCartney* album press release and self-interview, April 10, 1970.

23 Garbarini: "Paul McCartney—Lifting the Veil on the Beatles," p. 51.

24 Babiuk, Andy: *Beatles Gear* (Backbeat, New York, 2015), p. 314.

25 Mulhern, Tom: "Paul McCartney," *Guitar Player*, July 1990, pp. 16–32.

26 Babiuk: *Beatles Gear*, p. 321.

27 Welch, Chris: "Paul McCartney Interview," *Melody Maker*, December 1, 1973.

28 Assaf, Ali, with Tovey, Rob, directors: *The Making of McCartney—The Album Story*, video *McCartney* Archive Edition (MPL Communications, London, 2011).

29 Babiuk: *Beatles Gear*, pp. 273–4.

30 Assaf with Tovey: *The Making of McCartney—The Album Story*.

31 Parkinson, Michael: Filmed interview with Paul McCartney for *Parkinson*, BBC1, broadcast December 3, 1999.

32 The x-rayed version can be seen at Pablopicasso.org/old-guitarist.jsp#prettyPhoto.

33 Reproduced in Taylor, Derek: *Fifty Years Adrift* (Genesis Books, Guildford, 1984), pp. 356–7. The letter is undated; Taylor ascribes it to late summer 1968, but given the density of the Beatles' recording schedule at that time, it seems more likely a product of Paul's first visit to High Park with Linda and Heather.

34 White, Timothy: *Timothy White's Rock Stars*—"Put It There, 20 Years of Paul McCartney," audio interview, 1990.

35 Rice, Tim: Filmed interview with Paul McCartney for *Meet Paul McCartney*, ITV, broadcast May 19, 1980 (also available on *McCartney II* Archive Edition DVD).

36 White: *Timothy White's Rock Stars*.

37 The Beatles: *Get Back/Let It Be* recording sessions, January 24, 1969, unissued. An edited version, combining takes from January 24 and January 28, was included on the Beatles *Anthology 3* (EMI/Apple, 1996).

38 *McCartney* album press release and self-interview, April 10, 1970.

39 From Mal Evans diaries, quoted on the beatlesnumber9.com website (http://beatlesnumber9.com/mal.html).

40 Sadie, Stanley, ed.: *The New Grove Dictionary of Musical Instruments* (Macmillan Press, London, 1984), Vol. 2, pp. 725–7.

41 Uncredited: "The Musical Glasses," *Belfast News Letter*, May 19, 1947, p. 3.

42 Sadie: *The New Grove Dictionary of Musical Instruments*.

43 Spectral analysis by author (Sinclair). In addition to the notes, the analysis showed the hum of, possibly, a refrigerator, suggesting the possibility that Paul rolled the Studer J37—EMI had its units fitted with wheels—into his kitchen for the recording.

44 Du Noyer: *McCartney Archive Edition*, p. 10.

45 Reid, Mike: Radio interview with Paul McCartney for "McCartney On McCartney," Part 1 of 8, BBC Radio 1, broadcast March 25, 1989.

46 Du Noyer: *McCartney Archive Edition*, p. 22.

47 Ibid.

48 Uncredited: "She Is Accused of Killing Him," *Daily Mirror*, May 9, 1956, p. 1.

49 Longmuir, Harry: "Rich Widow Drama—Suicide Verdict," *Daily Mirror*, August 22, 1956, p. 1.

50 Hazelhurst, Peter: "Beatles Begin Their Career as 'Sages,'" *The Times*, February 21, 1968, p. 6.

51 Croft-Cooke, Rupert: "The New Edwardian," *The Tatler and Bystander*, November 1, 1952, p. 16.

52 Uncredited: "Notebook," *Daily Herald*, September 15, 1950, p. 4.

53 Uncredited: "The Way Men Look," *The Tatler and Bystander*, August 1, 1951, pp. 230–1.

54 Uncredited: "Every Man Wants to Be a Gay Dog," *Daily Mirror*, September 12, 1953, p. 7.

55 Uncredited: "Davies Reprieved After 91 Days. New Evidence?" *Daily Herald*, January 22, 1964, p. 1.

56 Uncredited: "Trouble Film Cinemas Seek Police Aid," *Birmingham Gazette*, February 27, 1956, p. 5.

57 White, Timothy: "Farewell to the First Solo Era," *Musician*, February 1988, p. 47.

58 The Beatles: *Get Back/Let It Be* recording sessions, January 24, 1969, unissued.

59 Gambaccini, Paul: "The *Rolling Stone* Interview: Paul McCartney," *Rolling Stone*, January 31, 1974, p. 23.

60 Skan, David: "The Thoughts of Chairman John," *Record Mirror*, October 4, 1969, pp. 6–7.

61 Williams, Richard: "John and Yoko," *Melody Maker*, December 6, 1969, p. 20.

62 Skan: "The Thoughts of Chairman John."

63 Williams, Richard: "The Beatles Wealth Is a Myth," *Melody Maker*, September 20, 1969, p. 19.

64 Williams, Richard: "John and Yoko," *Melody Maker*, December 6, 1969, p. 20.

65 Klan, David: "Why Ringo Gets All the Old Ladies . . . ," *Record Mirror*, November 5, 1969, p. 9.

4 ENTER BILLY MARTIN

1 Johns, Glyn: *Sound Man* (Blue Rider Press, New York, 2014), p. 142.

2 Beatles, The: *Let It Be [Super Deluxe Edition]* (Apple, 2021) CD2, Track 14.

3 Coleman, Ray: "Paul, the Beatles Who Goes On," *Boston Globe*, July 6, 1980, p. 72.

4 Du Noyer, Paul: Interview with Paul and Linda McCartney for the World Tour Program, November 1989, p. 11.

5 Uncredited: "New Beatles Single, LP," *Record Mirror*, February 21, 1970, p. 5.

6 Uncredited: "Solo Album by Paul," *New Musical Express*, February 14, 1970.

7 *McCartney* album press release and self-interview, April 10, 1970.

8 McCartney and Muldoon (ed.): *The Lyrics 1956 to the Present*, p. 390.

9 Lewisohn, Mark: "The Paul McCartney Interview," *Club Sandwich*, No. 58, Summer, 1991.

10 Smith, Alan: "The Big Beatles Query: Why Is Paul the Hermit of St. John's Wood?" *New Musical Express*, February 21, 1970.

11 Edmonds, Mark: "With a Little Help from Their Friend," *Sunday Times Magazine*, March 20, 2005, p. 39.

12 Ibid.

13 Peebles, Andy: Radio interview with Paul McCartney, BBC Radio 1, broadcast May 26, 1980.

14 Uncredited: "Solo Album by Paul," *New Musical Express*, February 14, 1970.

15 Letter from Linda McCartney to William Parker & Son, real estate agents in Reading, Berkshire, September 30, 1969. A small item in the Hickey's Side Lines column of the *Daily Express*, on October 2, 1969, also noted the McCartneys' search, quoted a similar letter to a real estate agent in Kent.

16 Burgess, Frank: "Talk of the Town," *Sidmouth Herald and Directory*, February 21, 1970.

17 Gambaccini: *Paul McCartney: In His Own Words*, p. 51.

18 McCartney, Paul (Lewisohn, Mark, ed.): *Wingspan* (Bulfinch Press, London, 2002), p. 12.

19 Assaf with Tovey: *The Making of McCartney—The Album Story*.

20 Reid, Mike: Radio interview with Paul McCartney for "McCartney on McCartney," Part 5 of 8, BBC Radio 1, broadcast April 22, 1989.

21 Wilson, John: Filmed interview with Paul McCartney for "Mastertapes," BBC Radio 4, broadcast May 28, 2016.

22 White, Timothy: "Farewell to the First Solo Era," *Musician*, February, 1988, p. 47.

23 Bruce, Ken: Radio interview with Alan Parsons for "The Tracks of My Years," BBC Radio 2, broadcast September 27, 2019.

24 Wenner, Jann: "Paul McCartney," *Rolling Stone*, April 30, 1970.

25 Black, Robin: Author interview (Sinclair), April 28, 2016.

26 *McCartney* album press release and self-interview, April 10, 1970.

27 Black, Robin: Author interview (Sinclair), April 28, 2016.

28 Ibid.

29 Wenner: "Paul McCartney."

30 Miles: *Paul McCartney—Many Years from Now*, p. 132.

31 Long, Janice: Radio interview with Paul McCartney for "Listen to What the Man Said," BBC Radio 1, broadcast December 22, 1985.

32 McCulley, Jim: "Tonight, at Last, 1 Champ—Frazier or Ellis," *New York Daily News*, February 16, 1970, p. 69.

33 Awde, Nick: "Mellotron: The Machine and the Musicians That Revolutionized Rock," *Desert Hearts*, 2008.

34 Radcliffe, Mark: Radio interview with Paul McCartney for "Sampledelica the History of the Mellotron," BBC Radio 4, broadcast August 7, 2014.

35 Black, Robin: Author interview (Sinclair), April 28, 2016.

36 *McCartney* album press release and self-interview, April 10, 1970.

37 Black, Robin: Author interview (Sinclair), April 28, 2016.

38 Ibid.

39 Ibid.

40 Ibid.

41 *McCartney* album press release and self-interview, April 10, 1970.

42 Kurlander, John: Author interview (Kozinn), July 28, 2016.

43 Schwartz: "He Loved Me, Yeah, Yeah, Yeah," p. 60.

44 Wilson, John: Filmed interview with Paul McCartney for "Mastertapes," BBC Radio 4, broadcast May 28, 2016.

45 Lewisohn, Mark (Ed.): Interview with Paul McCartney about the *Unplugged* album, Club Sandwich 58, Summer 1991.

46 Uncredited staff writer: "Give Her a Break, Paul," *Sunday People*, April 5, 1970, p. 9.

47 Police statement taken from *The Desert Sun* (through the UPI), February 25, 1970.

48 Leckie, John, email exchange with author (Sinclair), July 19, 2017.

49 *McCartney* album press release and self-interview, April 10, 1970.

50 Steinblatt, Harold: "Yesterday and Today," *Guitarist*, December, 2004, pp. 36–44.

51 *McCartney* album press release and self-interview, April 10, 1970.

52 Legal notes regarding the composition of 'Another Day,' offices of David Hirst, Q.C., March 26, 1971, p. 1.

53 Drum peg noted in the *McCartney* press release and self-interview, April 10, 1970.

54 Black, Robin: Author interview (Sinclair), April 28, 2016.

55 Du Noyer: *McCartney Archive Edition*, p. 54.

56 Hilburn, Robert: "He Finally Satisfied Fans AND Critics," *Los Angeles Times*, May 12, 1974, p. H-11.

57 Rubin, Rick: *McCartney 3,2,1!* Episode 5 (Hulu, 2021), broadcast July 2021.

58 Bacon, Dorothy: "I Want to Live in Peace," *Life*, November 7, 1969, p. 105.

59 Du Noyer: *McCartney Archive Edition*, p. 54.

5 ONE GUY STANDING THERE SHOUTING "I'M LEAVING"

1   Bonici, Ray: "Paul McCartney Wings It Alone," *Music Express*, April 1982, p. 9. Plus, Goodman, Joan: "*Playboy* Interview: Paul and Linda McCartney," *Playboy*, December 1984, p. 95.

2   Brown, Peter: Author interview (Kozinn), May 2, 2020.

3   Ibid.

4   *McCartney* album press release and self-interview, April 10, 1970.

5   Williams, Richard: audio interview with Paul McCartney for the *Times*, December 28, 1981.

6   Watts, Michael: "Ringo," *Melody Maker*, July 31, 1971.

7   Letter taken from: Cavendish, William: *His Master's Voice* (Unicorn Publishing Group, London, 2017), Kindle Edition, Location 3898-3905.

8   Davies, Hunter (ed.): *The John Lennon Letters* (Little Brown & Co., New York, 2012), p. 180. Davies presents both the handwritten note and a transcription, and appears to have mistaken John's date, giving it as March 5 rather than March 31. It appears here with the punctuation as given in the handwritten version.

9   Wenner, Jann: "Lennon Remembers, Part Two: Life With the Lions," *Rolling Stone*, February 4, 1971, p. 41.

10 This and the quote in the footnote, about how Ringo came to take the letter to Paul, are from Watts, Michael: "Ringo," *Melody Maker*, July 31, 1971.

11 Letter taken from: Cavendish, William: *His Master's Voice* (Unicorn Publishing Group, London, 2017), Kindle Edition, Location 3905-3915.

12 United Press International report, carried in the Washington Post, New York Daily News and other papers on April 8, 1970.

13 Uncredited: "McCartney Film Project," *New Musical Express*, April 11, 1970.

14 Wenner, Jann: "Paul McCartney," *Rolling Stone*, April 30, 1970.

15 Connolly: "The Party's Over But None of Us Wants to Admit It," p. 24.

16 Affidavit of James Paul McCartney in *James Paul McCartney v. John Ono Lennon, George Harrison, Richard Starkey and Apple Corps Limited*, in the High Court of Justice, Chancery Division Group B 1970 No. 6315, December, 1970 (specific date not given). Paul also quotes John's reaction, using the same words, in Meryman, Richard: "The Ex-Beatle Tells His Story," *Life*, April 16, 1971, and Brayfield, Celia: "They Are an Unlikely Couple But . . . Linda and Paul McCartney Are Still Madly in Love," *Cosmopolitan*, January, 1973.

17 Short, Don: "The Beatles Behind the Scenes—by Mirror Reporter Who Became Fab Four's Friend," *Mirror* (online), March 15, 2020.

18 Taylor, Derek: "Paul McCartney: Your Friendly Press Agent Knew That The Day Would Not Be Easy," *Record Mirror*, April 18, 1970.

19 Goodman, Joan: "*Playboy* Interview: Paul and Linda McCartney", *Playboy*, December 1984, p. 95.

20 Wenner, Jann: Recorded interview with John Lennon for *Rolling Stone*, December 8, 1970. The interview was published January 21 and February 4, 1971, and in book form as *Lennon Remembers*.

21 Connolly, Ray: *Being John Lennon—A Restless Life* (Pegasus Books, New York, 2018), p. 324.

22 BBC News: Coverage of Paul McCartney's press release, April 10, 1970.

23 Court papers from *James Paul McCartney vs. John Ono Lennon, George Harrison, Richard Starkey and Apple Corps Limited*, in the High Court of Justice, Chancery Division Group B 1970 No. 6315, March 2, 1971, p. 15.

24 Ibid.

25 Taylor, Derek: *Fifty Years Adrift* (Genesis Books, Guildford, 1984), p. 392.

26 Simons, Judith: "Backroom Richard Is Out in Front Row," *Daily Express*, January 27, 1976, p. 10.

27 Meryman, Richard: "The Ex-Beatle Tells His Story," *Life*, April 16, 1971, p. 54.

28 Connolly: "The Party's Over But None of Us Wants to Admit It," p. 24.

29 Ibid., p. 21.

30 Simons, Judith: "Disc—McCartney," *Daily Express*, April 13, 1970, p. 12.

31 Mann, William: "Paul Goes Solo and Shows Talent," *The Times*, April 17, 1970, p. 17.

32 Smith, Alan: "*McCartney* Is a Warm Pleasure," *New Musical Express*, April 18, 1970, p. 3.

33 Williams, Richard: ". . . And That Album" (sidebar to

"Paul McCartney: The Truth"), *Melody Maker*, April 17, 1970, p. 18.

34   Valentine, Penny: "Paul, What a Bitter Blow!" *Disc*, April 18, 1970.

35   Carr, Roy: "The Trial of James Paul McCartney," *NME*, April 29, 1978, pp. 33–35.

36   McCartney, Paul: "Who Does Paul McCartney Think He Is?" *Melody Maker*, May 2, 1970.

37   Telegram from Paul McCartney to Penny Valentine, April 16, 1970 (the newsstand date of her April 18 review).

38   Baker, Robb: "Paul's Solo Disk Disappointing," *Chicago Tribune*, April 21, 1970, p. 3.

39   Hilburn, Robert: "McCartney Album First Solo Effort," *Los Angeles Times*, May 4, 1970, p. 24.

40   Wenner's instruction is quoted by Greil Marcus in Hogan, Joe: *Sticky Fingers—The Life and Times of Jann Wenner and Rolling Stone Magazine* (Alfred A. Knopf, New York, 2017), Kindle edition, location 2825.

41   Winner, Langdon: "Records: *McCartney*," Rolling Stone, May 14, 1970, p. 50.

42   Wenner, Jan: "One Guy Standing There, Shouting 'I'm Leaving,'" *Rolling Stone*, May 14, 1970, p. 1.

43   Uncredited: "McCartney Gold," *Disc and Music Echo*, May 9, 1970, p. 8.

44   Uncredited: Untitled article giving Apple as its source, *Music Now*, May 16, 1970, p. 1.

45   Uncredited: "Beatles Album Hits American Jackpot," *Disc and Music Echo*, May 23, 1970, p. 6.

6 ANOTHER DAY, ANOTHER TOUGH DECISION

1   Lindsay-Hogg, Michael: Author Interview (Sinclair), May 24, 2020.

2   Reprinted in Wings Official Fun Club newsletter, No. 5, 1973 (December), originally in *Lucky Rider*.

3   Uncredited: "Pete Meets Paul McCartney: Ram On," *Jackie*, November 1972.

4   Ibid.

5   White, Timothy: "Farewell to the First Solo Era," Musician, February 1988, p. 50.

6   Robbins, Fred: "Viva interview: Paul and Linda McCartney," January 1974, pp. 122, 124.

7   Legal notes regarding the composition of 'Another Day,' offices of David Hirst, Q.C., March 26, 1971.

8   McCartney, Paul and Linda: Legal statement regarding 'Another Day,' March 26, 1971.

9   Shotton, Pete, with Schaffner, Nick: *John Lennon in My Life* (Stein and Day, New York, 1983), pp. 122–4.

10   Edmonds, Mark: "Here, There and Everywhere," London *Sunday Times* Magazine, March 20, 2005. Evans diary entries of January 27 and February 1, 1967, p. 35.

11   Registration filing for Adagrose Limited, December 18, 1968.

12   Von Faber, Karin: "Paul McCartney: Goodbye, Kicks; So Long, Birds," *New York Daily News*, April 7, 1974, p. 24.

13   Read, Mike: audio interview, McCartney on McCartney, Program 7, BBC Radio 1, broadcast May 6, 1989.

14   Nightingale, Ann, audio interview with Linda McCartney for *Rock Around the World*, BBC Radio One, December 1976.

15   Legal notes regarding the composition of 'Another Day,' offices of David Hirst, Q.C., March 26, 1971.

16   McCartney, Paul: Press Conference, Nashville, Tennessee, July 17, 1974.

17   Meryman, Richard: "I Felt the Split Was Coming," *Life*, April 16, 1971, p. 57.

18   Ibid.

19   Uncredited: "Paul McCartney Interview," *Let It Rock*, September 2008.

20   Lewisohn, Mark: "The Paul McCartney Interview," *Club Sandwich*, Issue 72, Winter, 1994.

21   Du Noyer, Paul: "Paul McCartney Interview," *Mojo*, July 2001.

22   Aspinall, Neil: Author interview (Kozinn), October 11, 1995.

23   Miles: *Paul McCartney—Many Years from Now*, pp. 570-1.

24   Williams, Richard: audio interview with Paul McCartney for the *Times*, December 28, 1981.

25   Meryman: "I Felt the Split Was Coming," p. 54.

26   Goodman: *Allen Klein—The Man Who Bailed Out the Beatles, Made the Stones, and Transformed Rock & Roll*, p. 205.

27   Noted in Leggatt, Andrew, and Drake, Charles: Reply, in High Court of Justice, Chancery Division, Group B, *Paul McCartney v. John Ono Lennon, George Harrison, Richard Starkey and Apple Corps Limited*, signed by Andrew Leggatt and Charles Drake, served May 3, 1972.

28   Goodman: *Allen Klein—The Man Who Bailed Out the Beatles, Made the Stones, and Transformed Rock & Roll*, p. 205.

29   Jones, Dylan: "At Home With Paul McCartney: His Most Candid Interview Yet," *GQ UK* (online), August, 2020.

30   Ibid.

31   Harper, Simon: "Taking Life by the Horns," *Classic Rock*, June 2021, p. 30.

32   Bonici, Ray: "Paul McCartney Wings It Alone," *Music Express*, April/May 1982, p. 8.

33   Legal notes regarding the composition of 'Another Day,' offices of David Hirst, Q.C., March 26, 1971.

34   Meryman, Richard: "The Ex-Beatle Tells His Story," *Life*, April 16, 1971, pp. 52–58.

35   Ibid.

36   Uncredited: "Paul McCartney in Orkney—Comes Across Firth with Family in a Fishing Boat," *The Orcadian*, August 6, 1970, p. 1. Details of the trip are taken from this, as well as reports in the *Shetland Times*, August 7, 1970, and Meryman: "The Ex-Beatle Tells His Story," p. 59.

37   Norman, Philip: *Paul McCartney—The Life* (Little Brown & Company, New York, 2016), p. 340.

38   McCartney, Paul: "You Gave Me the Answer—RAM Special!," Paul McCartney Official Website, May 16, 2021.

39   White, Timothy: "Farewell to the First Solo Era," *Musician*, February 1988, p. 48.

40   Harper, Simon: *Ram Archive Edition* (MPL Communications, London, 2012), p. 69.

41   Simons, Judith: "Beatle Songs Get New U.S. 'Backing,'" *Daily Express*, August 14, 1970, p. 7.

42   Gooding, Kenneth: "Beatles Song Row: James to Sue ATV," *Financial Times*, August 15, 1970.

43   Uncredited: "Lennon, McCartney Write Seeks Account of Northern Monies," *Cash Box*, October 3, 1970, p. 53.

44   Uncredited: "Man on Beatle Home Charge," *Daily Express*, September 1, 1970, p. 7.

45   Metropolitan Police District report, September 1, 1970. Solaries was charged with violation of Section 4 of the Vagrancy Act of 1824, "being found in an enclosed garden for an unlawful purpose."

46   Uncredited: "Paul in Christ Film?" *Disc and Music Echo*, September 12, 1970, p. 4.

47   Rivers, Bobby: Video interview with Paul McCartney for the VH-1 Meet McCartney special, broadcast between June 10 and 12, 1989.

48   Affidavit of Paul McCartney in *James Paul McCartney v John Ono Lennon, George Harrison, Richard Starkey and Apple Corps*.

49   Smith, Alan: "Paul McCartney," *New Musical Express*, July 25, 1970.

50   Moss, John: "Paul McCartney So Very, Very Real," *Mirabelle*, September 5, 1970, p. 22.

51   L.W. (full name not given): "Looking Back I Had a Dream," *McCartney Ltd* (fanzine), April/May/June 1972.

52   Simons, Judith: "Beatles Are Finished, Says 'Hideaway' Paul," *Daily Express*, August 27, 1970, p. 5.

53   Uncredited: "The Beatles—The Facts," *Melody Maker*, August 15, 1970.

54   McCartney, Paul: Letter to Mailbag, *Melody Maker*, August 29, 1970.

55   This and the accommodation costs from the brochure "S.S. *France* transatlantic and cruise sailings 1969-70."

56   Du Noyer, Paul: *Conversations with McCartney* (Hodder & Stoughton, London, 2015), p. 93.

57   Menus from the S.S. *France* literature, circa September 1970.

58   Baim, Harold: S.S. *France* promotional film, Harold Baim Motion Picture Productions, Ltd., London, 1970.

59   McCartney (Lewisohn, Mark, ed.): *Wingspan*, p. 23.

7 WORKING 9 TO 5

1   Petrie, Gavin: "Wings Take Off," Disc, November 20, 1971, p. 3.

2   Ibid.

3   Katz, Robin: "Denny Seiwell—One Time Session Man, Out on a Wing," *New Musical Express*, January 6, 1973.

4   Boucher, Caroline: "Desperate Den," *Disc*, December 16, 1972.

5   Spinozza, David: Author interview (Sinclair), June 15, 2019.

6   Ibid.

7   Wickham, Vicki: "Playing for Paul," *Melody Maker*, May 29, 1971, p. 8.

8   Uncredited: "McCartney Sweater Brings $95 at Auction," Associated Press, via *Central New Jersey Home News*, October 13, 1970, p. 16.

9   From an oral history interview with Don Puluse, Berklee College of Music Archives, April 30, 2010.

10 Geelan, Tim: Author interview (Kozinn), February 2, 2017.

11 Seiwell, Denny: Author interview (Kozinn), June 9, 2016.

12 Ibid.

13 Spinozza, David: Author interview (Sinclair), June 15, 2019.

14 Ibid.

15 Steinblatt, Harold: "Yesterday and Today," *Guitarist*, December 2004, pp. 36–44.

16 Cavanagh, David: "Escape to the Country," *Uncut*, September 2020, p. 60.

17 Wickham, Vicki: "Playing for Paul," *Melody Maker*, May 29, 1971, p. 8.

18 Cavanagh, David: "Suddenly I Was Unemployed," *Uncut*, June 2012, p. 22.

19 Geelan, Tim: Author interview (Kozinn), February 2, 2017.

20 Harper: Taking Life by the Horns," p. 32.

21 Wickham, Vicki: "Working with Paul—A Session Musician Speaks," *Hit Parader*, November 1971, p. 40.

22 Seiwell, Denny: Author interview (Kozinn), June 9, 2016.

23 Wickham: "Working with Paul—A Session Musician Speaks," p. 40.

24 Paul's handwritten lyrics for "A Dog Is Here," reproduced in Harper: *Ram Archive Edition*.

25 Spinozza, David: Author interview (Sinclair), June 15, 2019.

26 The Beatles: *The Beatles Anthology* (Chronicle Books, San Francisco, 2000) p. 311.

27 Wickham: "Working with Paul—A Session Musician Speaks," p. 40.

28 Block, Adam: "The Makka Material," McCartney: Beatle on Wings, K.49569, 1976, p. 57.

29 Untitled and unsigned extended caption for a photo showing the McCartneys arriving in New York. *Rolling Stone*, November 12, 1970, p. 8.

30 Spinozza, David: Author interview (Sinclair), June 15, 2019.

31 Du Noyer, Paul: "Alone Again, Or." *Mojo*, July 2001, p. 62. White, Timothy: "Paul McCartney on His Not So Silly Love Songs," *Billboard*, March 17, 2001, p. 94.

32 Spinozza, David: Author interview (Sinclair), June 15, 2019.

8 KEEP ON TRUCKIN'

1   Seiwell, Denny: Author interview (Kozinn), June 9, 2016.

2   McCracken, Hugh: Interview with writer Chip Madinger, November 22, 1998.

3   Eskow, Gary: "Classic Tracks: Paul McCartney's 'Uncle Albert/Admiral Halsey,'" *Mix* (online), August 1, 2004.

4   Dombal, Ryan: "The Rock 'n' Roll Icon Talks About the Making of his Homespun 1971 Album *Ram*," *Pitchfork*, June 7, 2012.

5   Doyle, Tom: "Paul McCartney Starting Over," *Guitar World*, Holiday issue (December-January) 2010, p. 65.

6   Seiwell, Denny, Composite from author interviews (Kozinn/Sinclair), June 9, 2016, and September 13, 2016.

7   McCartney and Muldoon (ed.): *The Lyrics 1956 to the Present*, p. 542.

8   Seiwell, Denny: Author interview (Kozinn), June 9, 2016.

9   Geelan, Tim: Author interview (Kozinn), February 2, 2017.

10   Mills, Nancy: "John, Paul, George, Ringo . . . and Linda," *Guardian*, December 18, 1974.

11   Heyn, Dalma: "The Alarmingly Normal McCartneys," *McCall's*, August 1984.

12   Paul McCartney interview for *Ram* Deluxe edition book, MPL, 2012, p. 42.

13   McCracken, Hugh: Interview with writer Chip Madinger, November 22, 1998.

14   Paul McCartney in *The Beatles Anthology*, TV and DVD documentary, Apple, 1995.

15   Scaduto, Anthony: "Where the Music Had to Go," in Rowlands, Penelope: *The Beatles Are Here!* (Algonquin, Chapel Hill, N.C., 2014), p. 176.

16   Uncredited: "Beatle Brush-Off," Associated Press, via the *Rochester Democrat and Chronicle*, October 29, 1970, p. 21.

17   Seiwell, Denny: Author interview (Sinclair), September 13, 2016.

18   O'Brian, Jack: "Roger Vadim Introduces Five New Cuties in His First US Flick," Associated Press, via *Rockland County Journal News*, Nyack, N.Y., November 3, 1970, p. 13.

19   Sullivan, Ed: item in "Little Old New York," *New York Daily News*, October 30, 1970, p. 62

20   DiFilippe, Joanne and Rabe, Linda: "5 Bites of the Apple" (fanzine), September/October 1972.

21   Geelan, Tim: Author interview (Kozinn), February 2, 2017.

22   Boucher, Caroline: "Side by Side by Side," *Disc and Music Echo*, December 1, 1973.

23   Basta, Tess: reminiscences in "With a Little Help from My Friends" (fanzine), April 1982.

24   Seiwell, Denny: Author interview (Sinclair), October 31, 2016.

25   Geelan, Tim: Author interview (Kozinn), February 2, 2017.

26   Ibid.

27   White, Timothy: "Farewell to the First Solo Era," *Musician*, February 1988, p. 48.

28   Eskow, Gary: "Classic Tracks: Paul McCartney's 'Uncle Albert/Admiral Halsey,'" *Mix* (online), August 1, 2004.

29   Seiwell, Denny: Author interview (Kozinn), June 9, 2016, including the preceding comment from Paul.

30   Charone, Barbara: "Linda McCartney: Silly Love Songs," *Sounds*, April 3, 1976.

31   Uncredited: "Three New Beatle Albums by Xmas," *Rolling Stone*, November 26, 1970, p. 6.

32   Miles: *Paul McCartney—Many Years from Now*, p. 570.

33   George's response ("I don't mind. . . . I'll do it") is included in the film *Let It Be*; the full discussion is included in The Beatles: *Get Back/Let It Be* recording sessions, January 6, 1969, unissued.

34   Seiwell, Denny: Author interview (Kozinn), June 9, 2016.

35   Geelan, Tim: Author interview (Kozinn), February 2, 2017.

36   Connolly, Ray: "The Home, the Kids and the Fireplace," *London Evening Standard*, April 22, 1970, p. 21.

37   Petrie, Gavin, "McCartney on Wings and Things," *Disc and Music Echo*, November 27, 1971, p. 18.

38   Harper: *Ram Archive Edition*, p. 49.

39   Ibid.

40   Mulhern, Tom: "Paul McCartney," *Guitar Player*, July 1990, p. 23.

41   Spinozza, David: Author interview (Sinclair), June 15, 2019.

42   Murphy, Brendan: "McCartney Waiting on City Hall," *Boston City Heights*, November 24, 1970, p. 1.

43   Uncredited: "Random Notes," *Rolling Stone*, December 10, 1970, p. 4.

44   Uncredited: "Random Notes," *Rolling Stone*, January 7, 1970, p. 4. (The issue was on the stands on December 17, 1970.)

45   Brown, Peter: Author interview (Kozinn), May 1, 2020.

9 BACK ACROSS THE WATER

1   Williams, Richard: "Forget the Beatles, Listen to George," *Melody Maker*, December 12, 1970.

2   Uncredited: "Random Notes," *Rolling Stone*, December 24, 1970, p. 4.

3   Uncredited: "Could Beatles Reunite in '71 to Cut New LP?" *New Musical Express*, December 12, 1970.

4   Uncredited: "Come Together! The Beatles May Play Again—Live," *Disc and Music Echo*, December 12, 1970, p. 1.

5   Uncredited: "Random Notes," *Rolling Stone*, December 24, 1970, p. 4.

6   Boyd, Patti, with Junor, Penny: *Wonderful Tonight* (Harmony, New York, 2007), p. 169.

7   Gambaccini: "The *Rolling Stone* Interview: Paul McCartney," p. 22.

8   Wenner, Jann: "Lennon Remembers, Part 1: The Working Class Hero," *Rolling Stone*, January 7, 1971, and February 4, 1971.

9   Brown, Geoff: "McCartney: Life After Death," *Melody Maker*, November 30, 1974, p. 8.

10   Geelan, Tim: Author interview (Kozinn), February 2, 2017.

11   Ibid.

12   Eskow: "Classic Tracks: Paul McCartney's 'Uncle Albert/Admiral Halsey.'"

13   Gambaccini: "The *Rolling Stone* Interview: Paul McCartney," p. 22.

14   Ibid.

15   Norman, Philip: *Paul McCartney—The Life* (Little Brown, New York, 2016), pp. 498–9.

16 Uncredited: "Why I Want to Get Out—By Beatle Paul," *Daily Mail*, January 2, 1971.

17 Ibid.

18 Uncredited: "Beatles' Total: 56 Million LPs," *New Musical Express*, January 16, 1971, p. 10.

19 Bonici, Ray: "Paul McCartney Wings It Alone," *Music Express*, April-May 1982, p. 8.

20 Fields, Danny: Author interview (Kozinn), December 7, 2019.

21 Fields: *Linda McCartney—A Portrait*, p. 153.

22 Ibid.

23 Bosso, Joe: "Production Legend Phil Ramone on 15 Career-Defining Records," *Music Radar* (online), November 15, 2012.

24 Van Winkle, Dixon: Author interview (Sinclair), January 8, 2017.

25 Ibid.

26 Charone, Barbara: "Paul Reliving the Beatles' Struggle with Wings," *Los Angeles Times*, August 31, 1973, p. 19.

27 Harper: "Taking Life by the Horns," p. 34.

28 Ibid., pp. 32–33.

29 Van Winkle, Dixon, email exchange with author (Sinclair), February 2, 2017.

30 Uncredited: "Eye Funds, McCartney Asks Court," *New York Times*, January 20, 1971, p. 22.

31 Uncredited: "Beatles Finances 'Grave,'" *Guardian*, January 20, 1971, p. 6.

32 Haber, Joyce: "Double Trouble in Valley of the Dolls," *Los Angeles Times*, January 28, 1971, Part IV, p. 8.

33 Van Winkle, Dixon: Author interview (Sinclair), January 8, 2017.

34 Ibid.

35 DiMinno, Nick, email exchange with author (Sinclair), February 25, 2017.

36 Van Winkle, Dixon: Author interview (Sinclair), January 8, 2017.

37 Seiwell, Denny: Author interview (Kozinn), June 9, 2016.

38 Myers, Marc: "Interview: Phil Ramone," *JazzWax* (online), November 12, 2010.

39 Van Winkle, Dixon: Author interview (Sinclair), January 8, 2017.

40 Myers, Marc: "Interview: Marvin Stamm," *JazzWax* (online), August 16, 2012.

41 Van Winkle, Dixon: Author interview (Sinclair), January 8, 2017.

42 White, Timothy: "Farewell to the First Solo Era," *Musician*, February 1988, p. 48.

43 Long, Janice: Audio interview with Paul McCartney for BBC Radio, November 1985.

44 Van Winkle, Dixon: Author interview (Sinclair), January 8, 2017.

45 Fields: *Linda McCartney—A Portrait*, p. 148.

10 OF BEATLES AND BARRISTERS

1 All quotations from and information about the hearings are from the Court Transcript, *James Paul McCartney v. John Ono Lennon, George Harrison, Richard Starkey and Apple Corps Limited*, in the High Court of Justice, Chancery Division Group B 1970 No. 6315, February 19 through March 12, 1971, and from daily coverage in the *Daily Express*, the *Guardian*, the *Daily Mirror*, the *New York Times* and the *New Musical Express*.

2 Simons, Judith: "Disc—Another Day," *Daily Express*, February 19, 1971, p. 10.

3 Valentine, Penny: "Single Reviews," *Sounds*, February 27, 1971, p. 25.

4 Johnson, Derek: "Paul—It's Been Worth the Wait," *NME*, February 27, 1971, p. 8.

5 Uncredited: "Paul McCartney—Another Day", *Record Mirror*, March 6, 1971.

6 Guercio, Jim: Author interview (Sinclair), July 25, 2019.

7 Ibid.

8 Uncredited: "McCartney Prod. Sets New York Office," *Cash Box*, February 20, 1971, p. 7.

9 Van Winkle, Dixon: Author interview (Sinclair), January 8, 2017.

10 Ibid.

11 Charlesworth, Chris: "McCartney," *Melody Maker*, November 20, 1971.

12 Wangberg, Eirik, email exchange with author (Sinclair), May 26, 2016.

13 Seiwell, Denny: Author interview (Sinclair), November 2, 2016.

14 Guercio, Jim: Author interview (Sinclair), July 25, 2019.

15 Seiwell, Denny: Author interview (Kozinn), June 9, 2016.

16 Ibid.

17 Harper: *Ram Archive Edition*, p. 42.

18 Guercio, Jim: Author interview (Sinclair), July 25, 2019.

19 Seiwell, Denny: Author interview (Kozinn), June 9, 2016.

20 Williams, Richard: Audio interview for *the Times*, December 16, 1981.

21 Wangberg, Eirik, email exchange with author (Sinclair), May 26, 2016.

22 Ibid.

23 Wangberg, Eirik, email exchange with author (Sinclair), January 8 and 31, 2017.

24 Wangberg, Eirik, email exchange with author (Sinclair), May 26, 2016.

25 Shamoon, Stella: "Beatle Paul's Wife in Storm Over Hit Song Earnings," *Daily Telegraph*, March 16, 2020.

26 Smith, Alan: "McCartney—Linda: The Facts," *NME* December 16, 1972, p. 16.

27 Trust, Sam: Author interview (Sinclair), April 13, 2022.

28 McDougall, Allan: "My New LP Is Sweaty Rock!" *NME*, May 8, 1971, p. 3.

29 Seiwell, Denny: Author interview (Sinclair), June 9, 2016.

30 Hilburn, Robert: "They Let It Be a McCartney Grammy Affair," *Los Angeles Times*, March 18, 1971.

31 Van Ness, Chris: "The Thirteenth Annual Grammy Awards," March 19, 1971, p. 2.

32 McCartney, Paul: Information from an interview with *Paul McCartney in the 80s*, audio CD, Wienerworld, 2017.

33 Wangberg, Eirik, email exchange with author (Sinclair), May 26, 2016.

34 Short, Don: "The New Beatle," *Daily Mirror*, March 20, 1971, p. 1.

35 "Paul Blows In . . . And Blows a Raspberry," *Daily Mirror*, March 26, 1971, p. 3.

36 Legal notes regarding the composition of 'Another Day,' offices of David Hirst, Q.C., March 26, 1971, p. 3.

37 Eikelenboom, Edward: *Maccazine*, Ram Special Part 2, Volume 42, Issue 1, p. 56.

38 McCartney, Paul: "You Gave Me the Answer—RAM Special!", Paul McCartney Official Website, May 16, 2021.

39 Meryman, Richard: "I Felt the Split Was Coming," *Life*, April 16, 1971, p. 56.

40 McDougall, Allan: "My New LP Is Sweaty Rock!" *NME*, May 8, 1971, p. 3.

41 Wangberg, Eirik, email exchange with author (Sinclair), May 26, 2016.

42 Buskin, Richard: Audio interview with Len Wood of EMI Records, March 9, 1987.

43 Ibid.

44 Ibid.

45 McCartney, Paul, Author interview (Kozinn), October 19, 1990.

46 Dirani, Claudio: Interview with Eirik Wangberg, published online May 25, 2007. Skavlan, Fredrik, radio interview with Eirik Wangberg for *Ramming On Skavlan*, June 5, 2017.

11 BATTERING RAM

1 Adams, Sean and Draper, Paul: "Paul McCartney Discusses Songwriting and Ram," *Drowned in Sound*, May 28, 2012.

2 Williams, Ed: Radio interview with Wings for WCBS, New York, recorded December 15, 1971.

3 Sky, Rick: "Paul McCartney—He's Still Flying High!" *OK*, March 26, 1977, p. 9.

4 Yale Law School, Lillian Goldman Law Library: The Avalone Project—Documents in Law, History and Diplomacy (online), https://avalon.law.yale.edu/medieval/richard.asp.

5 Ahmed, Samira: Paul McCartney in Conversation, audio interview at the Royal Festival Hall, November 5, 2021.

6 Jensen, David, "Kid": "The McCartney Interview," 208 *Times* (*NME*), Vol. 3, No. 2, March/April 1972, p. 4.

7 McCartney, Paul: *Wild Life and Red Rose Speedway Radio Special*, MPL Communications, January 2019.

8 Webb, Julie: "Linda the Unloved," *NME*, May 19, 1973, p. 5.

9 Kozinn, Allan: "Tony Barrow, Beatles Publicist Who Coined the Term 'Fab Four,' Dies at 80," *New York Times*, May 16, 2016, p. A16.

10 Barrow, Tony, with Bextor, Robin: *Paul McCartney Now & Then* (Carlton, London, 2004), p. 123.

11 Smith, Alan: "Paul, What a Mess You've Made of It!" *NME*, May 22, 1971, p. 7.

12 Uncredited: "Paul Goes It Alone with the Phil," *Daily Mirror*, May 11, 1971, p. 7.

13 Uncredited: "McCartney's *Ram* Out This Month," *Sounds*, May 8, 1971.

14 Uncredited: "£830,000 Claim Against Paul," *Daily Express*, May 6, 1971, p. 2. (It appears that the *Daily Express* writer miscalculated the currency translation; the amount in Sterling should have been £420,000.)

15 Britton, Geoff: Author interview (Sinclair), April 2, 2020.

16 Ellison, John: "The Settling Stone," *Daily Express*, May 12, 1971, p. 2.

17 Short, Don: "Jagger Invites the Beatles to Make Up at His Wedding," *Daily Mirror*, May 12, 1971, p. 3.

18 Badman, Keith: *The Beatles: Off the Record 2—The Dream Is Over* (Omnibus Press, London, 2009), pp. 52–53.

19 BBC news footage compilation, May, 1971.

20 Guest information from reports in NMC, May 15/22, 1971, and *Australian Women's Weekly*, June 2, 1971.

21 Watts, Michael: "Ringo," *Melody Maker*, July 31, 1971.

22 Ellison, John: "'Who's Paying' Row as Mick Sails," *Daily Express*, May 15, 1971, p. 2.

23 Davies, Hunter: "Paul McCartney: Confessions of an Unemployed Beatle," *Sunday Times*, April 4, 1976.

24 Uncredited: "Linda McCartney—Why She Loves Paul and Why His Fans Hated Her for It," Star Beat #1, 1979, pp. 9–10.

25 Bonici, Ray: "How Paul McCartney Has Spread His Wings," *Look Now*, September 1980, p. 26.

26 Charone, Barbara: "Linda McCartney: Silly Love Songs," *Sounds*, April 3, 1976.

27 Davies, Hunter: "Paul McCartney: Confessions of an Unemployed Beatle."

28 Uncredited: "Linda McCartney—Why She Loves Paul."

29 Harper: *Ram Archive Edition*, p. 89.

30 Hewson, Richard: Author interview (Sinclair), December 3, 2016.

31 Simons, Judith: "Backroom Richard Is Out in Front Row," January 27, 1976, p. 10

32 Goddard, Lon: "Paul, Linda—The New Bag," *Record Mirror*, May 22, 1971, p. 24.

33 Uncredited: "*Billboard* Album Reviews," *Billboard*, May 29, 1971, p. 24.

34 Ledgerwood, Mike: "It's Diabolical . . . er, No, It's Brilliant!" Disc and Music Echo, May 22, 1971, p. 3.

35 Hilburn, Robert: "McCartney's New Album," *Los Angeles Times*, May 18, 1971, Part IV, p. 8.

36 Wigg, David: "Disc: *Ram*," *Daily Express*, May 19, 1971, p. 12.

37 Cannon, Geoffrey: "Pop on Record," *Guardian*, May 21, 1971, p. 10.

38 Valentine, Penny: "Album Reviews," *Sounds*, May 22, 1971, p. 26.

39 Charlesworth, Chris: "Mutton Dressed as Ram?" *Melody Maker*, May 22, 1971.

40 Smith, Alan: "Paul, What a Mess You've Made of It!" *NME*, May 22, 1971, p. 7.

41 Wickham, Vicki: "Playing for Paul," *Melody Maker*, May 29, 1971, p. 8.

42 Blake, John: "He's A Star Again . . ." *Liverpool Echo*,

September 19, 1974, p. 6. Plus, Petrie, Gavin: "McCartney: I Know I'm Good," *Disc and Music Echo*, November 20, 1971, p. 3.

43   Landau, Jon: "Record Reviews: *Ram*," *Rolling Stone*, July 8, 1971, pp. 42–43.

44   McCracken, Holly: Author interview (Kozinn), August 10, 2019.

45   Boucher, Caroline: "Desperate Den," *Disc*, December 16, 1972, p. 7.

46   Uncredited: Unpublished interview with John Lennon, *Crawdaddy*, late 1971.

47   Lewisohn, Mark: "Mining the Film and Video Archive: Heart of the Country," Club Sandwich, No. 58, Summer, 1991.

48   Clark, Tony: Author interview (Sinclair), February 17, 2017.

49   Flick, Vic: *Guitarman: From James Bond to the Beatles and Beyond* (BearManor Media, Oklahoma, 2014), pp. 131-2.

50   Hewson, Richard: Author interview (Sinclair), December 3, 2016.

51   Clark, Tony: Author interview (Sinclair), February 17, 2017.

52   Seiwell, Denny: Author interview (Sinclair), June 9, 2016.

53   Fields: *Linda McCartney—A Portrait*, pp. 135–6.

54   McCracken, Holly: Author interview (Kozinn), August 10, 2019.

55   McCracken, Holly: Author interview (Kozinn), August 14, 2019.

56   Seiwell, Denny: Author interview (Kozinn), June 19, 2016.

57   Date provided by Monique Seiwell, who noted the invitation to form a band in her diary.

58   Seiwell, Denny: Author interview (Kozinn), June 19, 2016.

59   Ibid.

60   Kasson, Celia: "Vigil of Fan Who Loves a Beatle," *Daily Mail*, May 10, 1971, p. 13.

61   McCallum, Andrew: "Beatle Off: Paul 'Caught Me on the Nose,' Says Carolyn," *Daily Express*, July 2, 1971, p. 1. Also, reports from UPI (via the *Los Angeles Times*) on July 3, and the *Campbeltown Courier*, on July 8.

62   *Daily Mail* Reporter [uncredited]: "Beatle 'Didn't Hit Girl,'" *Daily Mail*, July 2, 1971, p. 3.

63   McCracken, Holly: Author interview (Kozinn), August 10, 2019.

64   Ibid.

12 GROWING WINGS

1   Uncredited: "Your Instant Guide to Paul Beatle," *Jackie*, January 16, 1965, p. 19.

2   Rosen, Steve: Backstage interview with Paul McCartney, Birmingham, July 7, 1973. This story was also confirmed in an interview with the *Los Angeles Times*, interview with Paul and Linda McCartney, August 31, 1973. "I was asked to do 'Diamonds Are Forever' originally, but John Barry was already contracted."

3   Mabbs, Val: "Ex-Beatles Boy Recruits Colonel Bagshot," *Record Mirror*, January 20, 1973.

4   McCartney, Ruth: "My Stepbrother Was a Beatle," *19 Magazine*[ital], March 1983, p. 56.

5   Uncredited: "Balls Supergroup in Surprise Breakup," *NME*, February 20, 1971, p. 11.

6   Uncredited: "Trevor Burton Interview", Ugly Things No. 28, March 16, 2009.

7   White, Alan: Author interview (Sinclair) by email, July 19, 2021.

8   Giuliano, Geoffrey: "In Conversation with Denny Laine," *Author's Republic* audiobook, recorded October 1989.

9   Unedited interview with Denny Laine for the *Holly Days* album press kit, May 6, 1977.

10   Reinartz, Joe: "Denny Seiwell Talks Jazz Trio, Paul McCartney, A Young Billy Joel, Etc.," Celebrityaccess. com, November 19, 2018.

11   Seiwell, Denny: Author interview (Kozinn), June 6, 2016.

12   Charone, Barbara: "Linda McCartney: Silly Love Songs," *Sounds*, April 3, 1976.

13   Peacock, Steve: "But Life Goes on for Denny Laine," *Sounds*, October 2, 1971, p. 6.

14   Garr, Gillian: "Ready for Take Off: The Early Years of Wings," *Goldmine*, February 2019, p. 61.

15   Seiwell, Denny: Author interview (Kozinn), June 6, 2016.

16   Seiwell, Denny: Author interview (Sinclair), November 2, 2016.

17   McCartney, Paul: Interview with Paul McCartney for the Wings 1973 British tour program, p. 9.

18   Badman, Keith: *The Beatles: Off the Record 2—The Dream Is Over* (Omnibus Press, London, 2009), p. 72.

19   O'Riordan, Maggie and Harris, Paul: "Paul McCartney's Secret Affair", *Daily Mail*, April 12, 1997, p. 25.

20   Seiwell, Denny: Author interview (Kozinn), June 6, 2016.

21   Clark, Tony: Author interview (Sinclair), February 16, 2017.

22   Clark, Tony: Author interview (Sinclair), March 23, 2017.

23   Doyle, Tom: "The Great Escape", *Q Magazine*, June 2010, pp. 96–97.

24   Uncredited: "Denny Laine—A Special Musical Gift," *Record Mirror*, August 11, 1973, p. 26.

25   Green, Richard: "Paul McCartney Is Like a Man Who Has Dodged a Death Sentence," *NME*, November 20, 1971, p. 6.

26   Petrie, Gavin: "McCartney: I Know I'm Good," *Disc and Music Echo*, November 20, 1971, p. 3.

27   Wings interviewed for "Paul McCartney Now," WRKO Radio Network, taped December 20, 1971, at MPL, New York; broadcast on January 13, 1972.

28   Seiwell, Denny: Author interview (Kozinn), June 9, 2016.

29   Clark, Tony: Author interview (Sinclair), February 16, 2017.

30   Ibid.

31   Sacchetti, Mike: "Encounters in July 1971," *The Write Thing*, June-July 1984.

32   Oliver, Sally: "What It's Like Being Married to a 36-year-old Ex-Beatle for Nine Years," *Woman's World*, June 1978, p. 45.

33 Evans, Jim: "Faster Than Concorde—The Story of Wings," *Record Mirror*, April 16, 1977, p. 17.

34 Wings interviewed for "Paul McCartney Now," WRKO Radio Network, taped December 20, 1971, at MPL, New York; broadcast on January 13, 1972.

35 Charlesworth, Chris: Audio recording of interview with Wings, EMI Studios Two, London, November 10, 1971.

36 Fricke, David: *Wild Life Archive Edition* (MPL Communications, London, 2018), p. 46.

37 Green, Richard: "Paul McCartney Is Like a Man Who Has Dodged a Death Sentence."

38 Garr, Gillian: "Ready for Take Off: The Early Years of Wings," *Goldmine*, February 2019, p. 61.

39 Blood, Brian: Author interview (Sinclair), October 28, 2016.

40 Clark, Tony: Author interview (Sinclair), February 16, 2017.

41 Ibid.

42 Seiwell, Denny: Author interview (Sinclair), October 31, 2016.

43 Cummings, Howard: "Alan Parsons," *Recording Engineer*, October 1976, pp. 29–32.

44 Haskell, Duncan: "Interview: Alan Parsons," *Songwriting Magazine* (online), October 11, 2015.

45 Shapiro, Marc: *Behind Sad Eyes* (St. Martin's Press, New York, 2002), p. 115.

46 Ledgerwood, Mike, with Shipston, Roy: "John Lennon Still Searching for Peace," *Disc*, July 31, 1971, p. 10.

47 Johnson, James: "Wings on Wheels," *NME*, July 15, 1972, p. 29.

48 Heckman, Don: "The Event Wound Up as a Love Feast," *Village Voice*, August 5, 1971.

49 Leng, Simon: *While My Guitar Gently Weeps* (Hal Leonard, New York, 2006), p. 112.

50 Johnson, Derek: "Paul & Linda McCartney," *NME*, August 21, 1971, p. 8.

51 Welch, Chris: "Paul & Linda McCartney—The Back Seat of My Car," *Melody Maker*, August 21, 1971.

52 Jones, Peter: "Paul and Linda—a Soul-Sitter," *Record Mirror*, August 21, 1971.

53 Watts, Michael: "Ringo," *Melody Maker*, July 31, 1971.

54 Smith, Alan: "Lennon—Doing the Rounds for Publicity," *NME*, July 31, 1971, p. 3.

55 Ledgerwood with Shipston: "John Lennon Still Searching for Peace."

56 Uncredited: "McCartney: Don't Call Me a Beatle Again," *Disc*, August 14, 1971.

57 Seiwell, Denny: Author interviews (Kozinn/Sinclair), June 6, 2016, and September 13, 2016.

58 Uncredited: "McCartney's Blues Band Debut Soon," *NME*, August 7, 1971, p. 12

59 Seiwell, Denny: Author interview (Kozinn), June 6, 2016.

60 Ibid.

61 Uncredited: "'Break of My Life'—Says Paul's New Drummer," *Campbeltown Courier*, August 12, 1971, p. 1.

62 Lewisohn, Mark (Ed.): "The Other Me," *Club Sandwich*, Spring 1992, p. 4.

63 Uncredited: "Ex-Beatle Paul Wants His Privacy," *Daily Gleaner*, August 26, 1971, p. 4.

64 Lewisohn: "The Other Me."

65 Doherty, Harry: "Parsons Knows," *Melody Maker*, July 10, 1976, p. 13.

66 Uncredited: "Beatles Tour Again," *Record Mirror*, August 21, 1971.

67 Free Downloads: 'Dear Friend (Orchestra Up)' and 'Hands of Love,' quote from paulmccartney.com, December 24, 2018.

68 Hewson, Richard: Author interview (Sinclair), December 3, 2016.

69 Uncredited: "Beatle Baby," Associated Press (via *Washington Post*), September 18, 1971, p. 6.

70 Pascall, Jeremy: *Paul McCartney & Wings* (Phoebus Publishing, London, 1977), p. 14.

71 McCartney (Lewisohn, Mark, ed.): *Wingspan*, p. 33.

72 Uncredited: "McCartney's Wings," *NME*, October 2, 1971, p. 6.

73 Gambaccini: *Paul McCartney: In His Own Words*, p. 51.

13 WAR IS OVER, IF YOU WANT IT

1 Brayfield: "Linda and Paul McCartney Are Still Madly in Love," p. 67.

2 Uncredited: "Naturals for Your Beauty Life," *Vogue*, August 1971, p. 59.

3 Helvin, Marie: *The Autobiography* (Orion Books, London, 2007; Phoenix ebook), p. 66.

4 Smith, Alan: "At Home with the Lennons, Part 2," *NME*, August 7, 1971.

5 Mabbs, Val: "At Home with the Lennons, Part 2," *Record Mirror*, August 14, 1971, p. 5.

6 Wigg, David: "Give Peace a Chance—By George," *Daily Express*, October 4, 1971, p. 12.

7 Simons, Judith: "Dove Paul Takes Wings," *Daily Express*, October 1, 1971, p. 17.

8 Uncredited: "Paul's Group—Maxi Single Prior to November Album," *NME*, September 18, 1971.

9 Clark, Tony: Author interview (Sinclair), March 23, 2017.

10 Seiwell, Denny: Author interview (Kozinn), June 9, 2016.

11 Peacock: "But Life Goes on for Denny Laine," p. 6.

12 Seiwell, Denny: Author interview (Kozinn), June 9, 2016.

13 Seiwell, Denny: Author interview (Sinclair), October 31, 2016.

14 Wigg, David: Radio interview with John Lennon for BBC Radio 1, recorded on October 15, 1971, from *The Beatles Tapes: From the David Wigg Interviews*, Polydor CD, 1976.

15 Madinger, Chip, with Raile, Scott: *Lennonology: Strange Days Indeed* (Open Your Books, Chesterfield, Missouri, 2015), pp. 274–5.

16 Details of the conversation are included in John Lennon's letter to Paul in the pages of *Melody Maker*, December 4, 1971.

17 Hewson, Richard: Author interview (Sinclair), December 3, 2016.

18 Clark, Tony: Author interview (Sinclair), February 16, 2017.

19   Green: "Paul McCartney Is Like a Man Who Has Dodged a Death Sentence."

20   Northern Songs advertisement, *Melody Maker*, November 27, 1971.

21   Uncredited: "McCartney Signs Irish Bandleader!," *NME*, October 9, 1971, p. 4.

22   Uncredited: "Thrilling Instrumental," Sounds, October 16, 1971, p. 10.

23   Letter reproduced in Fricke, David: *Wild Life Archive Edition* (MPL Communications, London, 2018), p. 72.

24   Uncredited: "Paul McC. Throws Swank Party," *Rolling Stone*, December 9, 1971, p. 15.

25   Letter from Paul McCartney to Allen Klein, undated.

26   Letter from J.D. Spooner of Dixon, Wilson & Co., to M. R. Lampard of Ashurst, Morris, Crisp & Co., September 1, 1971.

27   Letter from P.J. Howard, for ABKCO Industries, to J.D. Spooner of Dixon, Wilson & Co., July 29, 1971.

28   Coleman, Ray, with Charlesworth, Chris: "A Strange Day's Night," *Melody Maker*, November 13, 1971, p. 10.

29   McVay, Ray, email exchange with author (Sinclair), by way of Sue McVay, October 7, 2018.

30   Ibid.

31   Hughes, David: "A Personal History of the British Music Business Pt. 15—Colin Burn 7," *Vinyl Memories* (online), March 25, 2015.

32   Coleman with Charlesworth: "A Strange Day's Night."

33   Green: "Paul McCartney Is Like a Man Who Has Dodged a Death Sentence."

34   Charlesworth, Chris: "Paul McCartney," *Melody Maker*, November 20, 1971.

35   Charlesworth, Chris: Audio interview with Paul McCartney, recorded at EMI Studios on November 10, 1972.

36   Charlesworth: "Paul McCartney."

37   Peacock, Steve: "Trying to Keep Things Loose," *Sounds*, November 20, 1971, p. 14.

38   Ibid.

39   Ibid.

40   Ibid.

41   Petrie, Gavin: "McCartney: I Know I'm Good—If I'm in the Right Mood I Can Write a Solid Gold Hit," *Disc and Music Echo*, November 20, 1971, p. 3.

42   Ibid.

43   Giuliano, Geoffrey: *Blackbird: Life and Times of Paul McCartney* (Penguin; Reprint Edition, New York 1992), pp. 363–4.

44   Seiwell, Denny: Author interview (Sinclair), September 13, 2016.

45   McCracken, Holly: Author interview (Kozinn), August 10, 2019.

46   Green, Richard: "Two Sides of McCartneys," *NME*, November 20, 1971, p. 17.

47   Petrie, Gavin: "Wings Take Off," *Disc and Music Echo*, November 20, 1971, p. 3.

48   Hennessey, Mike: "Wings: Aggressive Simplicity," *Record Mirror*, November 20, 1971, p. 4.

49   Hollingworth, Roy: "Do You Wanna Dance with Paul?" *Melody Maker*, December 11, 1971.

50   Peacock, Steve: "McCartney Shows His Teeth," *Sounds*, December 18, 1971, p. 23.

51   Hilburn, Robert: "McCartney's Third Disappointment," *Los Angeles Times*, December 12, 1971, p. 56.

52   Harris, Lew: "Pity Poor Paul, 'Idiot Child of Rock'," *Chicago Tribune*, December 1971, p. 26.

53   Hennessey, Mike: "Pop Now Is Very Boring," *Record Mirror*, December 18, 1971, p. 3.

54   Orsted, Knud: "McCartney—I'm Boycotting Apple," *Record Mirror*, August 19, 1972, p. 11.

55   Partridge, Rob: "U.K. and Europe—Wide Open for Rock Theater," *Billboard*, December 18, 1971, p. 51.

56   Uncredited: "Wings Cut," *Melody Maker*, December 4, 1971.

57   Partridge: "U.K. and Europe—Wide Open for Rock Theater."

58   Uncredited: "Paul McC. Throws Swank Party," *Rolling Stone*, December 9, 1971, p. 15.

59   Lennon, John: Letter to Paul and Linda McCartney via the music press, *Melody Maker*, December 4, 1971.

60   Plummer, Mark: "Mary Had a Little Lamb—Those Lyrics Are a Heavy Trip," *Melody Maker*, December 2, 1972.

61   Mathezing, Arthur, with Stoop, Fran: "A Chat with John Kelly—Part 2," *Beatles Unlimited Magazine*, July/August 1991, p. 12.

62   Coxhill, Gordon: "Paul and Linda and Togetherness," *Petticoat*, February 17, 1973, p. 26.

63   Haber, Joyce: "David Frost's New Hero Does Himself In," *Los Angeles Times*, November 28, 1971, p. 16.

64   Berler, Ron, "Was It Paul?," *Chicago Tribune*, December 14, 1971, p. 2.

65   Quateman, Bill: Author interview (Sinclair), October 16, 2018.

66   James, Catherine: *Dandelion; Memoir of a Free Spirit* (Self-published, 2007; Kindle Edition), Locations 1787-1793.

67   Lucas, David: Author interview (Sinclair), August 5, 2020.

68   Ibid.

69   Ibid.

70   Miles: *Paul McCartney—Many Years from Now*, p. 588.

71   Peacock: "Trying to Keep Things Loose," p. 14.

72   Pulin, Chuck: "Talking Straight to America," *Sounds*, February 12, 1972, p. 5.

73   Williams, Ed: Radio interview with Wings for WCBS, New York, recorded December 17, 1971.

14 IRELAND, IT'S THE CAPITAL OF LIVERPOOL

1   Morris, John: Author interview (Kozinn), November 17, 2017.

2   Johnson, James: "McCartney's New Man," *NME*, January 29, 1972, p. 9.

3   Ibid.

4   Harper, Colin, with Hodgett, Trevor: *Irish Folk, Trad & Blues—A Secret History* (The Collins Press, Ireland, 2004), p. 174.

5   Johnson, James: "McCartney's New Man," *NME*, January 29, 1972, p. 9.

6   Moran, Johnny: Interview with Paul McCartney for *Scene and Heard*, BBC Radio 1, January 22, 1972.

7   Johnson: "McCartney's New Man" (Reference to "Scene and Heard" last Saturday.)

8   Seiwell, Denny: Author interview (Sinclair), October 31, 2016.

9   Ibid.

10   Uncredited: "Gun Fury—13 Shot Dead in Bogside," *Daily Express*, January 31, 1972, p. 1.

11   Garrod, Joe: "Ulster's Bloody Sunday," *Daily Mirror*, January 31, 1972, p. 1.

12   ABC News: Interview with Paul and Linda McCartney, ABC News Report, recorded on March 2, 1972 (broadcast March 7, 1972). White, Timothy: *Timothy White's Rock Stars*—"Put It There, 20 Years of Paul McCartney," audio interview, 1990. And Peacock, Steve: "Paul McCartney in the Talk-In," *Sounds*, December 2, 1972, pp. 22–23.

13   Paul's genealogy is discussed at length in Lewisohn, Mark: *All These Years—Tune In (Special Edition)*, (Little Brown, London, 2013), pp. 32–41.

14   White: *Timothy White's Rock Stars*. Plus, Gambaccini: "The *Rolling Stone* Interview: Paul McCartney," pp. 20–28. And Uncredited: "BBC Ban Beatle Song of Protest," *Irish Independent*, February 11, 1972, p. 1. And Johnson, James: "Wings on Wheels," *NME*, July 15, 1972, pp. 28–29.

15   Lewisohn, Mark: Interview with Phil Mottram, *Club Sandwich* 74, Summer, 1995, pp. 12–13.

16   Clark, Tony: Author interview (Sinclair), February 16, 2017.

17   Tyler, Andrew: "Paul on the Wing," *Disc and Music Echo*, February 12, 1972, p. 8.

18   Ibid.

19   Clark, Tony: Author interview (Sinclair), March 23, 2017.

20   Tyler: "Paul on the Wing," p. 8.

21   Ibid.

22   Melbourne, Harry: "Wing Man McCullough—Always Solid, Never Flash," *Disc Music and Echo*, December 9, 1972, p. 23.

23   Tyler: "Paul on the Wing," p. 8.

24   Seiwell, Denny: Author interview (Sinclair), October 31, 2016. (Denny still has his whistle.)

25   Humphries, Brian: Author interview (Sinclair), July 8, 2020.

26   Uncredited: "Paul and Linda Make Their Stand," *Sounds*, February 12, 1972, p. 17.

27   Ibid.

28   7 a.m. reference from Monique Seiwell's diary, she was babysitting the McCartney girls.

29   Orsted, Knud: "McCartney: I'm Boycotting Apple," *Record Mirror*, August 19, 1972, p. 11.

30   McCartney, Paul (Lewisohn, Mark, ed.): *Wingspan* (Bulfinch Press, London, 2002), p. 40. (McCartney also discussed this in a 1989 interview with the BBC.)

31   Ledgerwood, Mike: "Paul: A TOTAL Ban!" *Disc and Music Echo*, February 19, 1972, p. 2.

32   Uncredited: "Wings Single Date," *Disc and Music Echo*, February 12, 1972, p. 1.

15 INTRODUCING... RIKKI AND THE RED STREAKS

1   Seiwell, Denny, Compound of author interviews (Sinclair/Kozinn), September 13, 2016, and June 9, 2016.

2   Charone, Barbara: "Paul Reliving the Beatles' Struggle with Wings Group," *Los Angeles Times*, August 31, 1973, p. 19.

3   Ibid. Plus Richardson, Heather: Radio interview with Paul McCartney for BBC Radio Sheffield, February 17, 1972.

4   Woodhams, Elaine: "The Magical Mystery Tour," Nottingham University online exchange, April 6, 2001.

5   Seiwell, Denny, Compound of author interviews (Sinclair/Kozinn), September 13, 2016, and June 9, 2016.

6   Unknown: "Single by McCartney on the Irish problem," *NME*, February 12, 1972, p. 3.

7   Peebles, Andy: Radio interview with Paul McCartney for BBC Radio 1, May 16, 1980.

8   Jenour, Kenelm: "Signing Off . . . the Beatles Fan Club," *Daily Mirror*, February 9, 1972, p. 11.

9   Quotes taken from: Williams, Mark, "Wings Taking Off at Last," *Melody Maker*, June 16, 1979. Charone: "Paul Reliving the Beatles' Struggle with Wings Group." Brace, Reginald: "Ex-Beatle Paul Takes His Wings on a Magical Mystery Tour," *Yorkshire Post*, February 17, 1972, p. 1. And Humphries, Patrick: "The Other Side of McCartney," *Record Collector*, May 2001, p. 29.

10   Uncredited: "Paul Gives Live City Concert," *Nottingham Evening Post*, February 9, 1972, p. 1.

11   Davies, Hunter: "Paul McCartney: Confessions of an Unemployed Beatle," *Sunday Times*, April 4, 1976.

12   Turner, Shelley: "Wings First Flight" interview with Henry McCullough for the Wings over Europe tour program, July 1972.

13   Lucas, Barry: *Rock Goes to College: Legends Live at Lancaster University, 1969-1985* (Palatine Books, London, 2019). Quotes taken from Lucas's unedited manuscript.

14   Uncredited: "Paul McCartney Throws 2 Curves," *Rolling Stone*, March 30, 1972.

15   Hennessey, Mike: "Living in a Shadow," *Record Mirror*, August 12, 1972, p. 3.

16   Seiwell, Denny: Author interview (Kozinn), June 9, 2016.

17   Uncredited: "Paul: A TOTAL Ban!" *Disc and Music Echo*, February 19, 1972, p. 3. And Uncredited: "McCartney Disc Banned by BBC," *NME*, February 19, 1972, p. 4.

18   Uncredited: "Banned—Why?" *Melody Maker*, February 21, 1976, p. 21.

19   Peel, John: "Political Censorship—Now New BBC Irish Ban," *Melody Maker*, February 26, 1972.

20   Uncredited: "Irish Song by McCartney Banned by BBC," *The Times*, February 11, 1972, p. 2.

21   Wilson, Tony: "Ex-Beatle says 'Give Ireland Back to Irish," *Irish Evening Herald*, February 17, 1972, p. 7.

22   Goddard, Lon: "Paul's Irish Disc Banned," *Record Mirror*, February 19, 1972, p. 7.

23   Uncredited quote taken from the front page of *Melody Maker*, February 19, 1972, p. 1.

24   Uncredited: "Paul McCartney Throws 2 Curves," *Rolling Stone*, March 30, 1972.

25   Chippindale, Peter: "Paul Beatles Back," *Arts Guardian*, February 17, 1972, p. 10.

26   Skoler, Ron: "John and Yoko—Some Time in New York City," *Sounds*, September 2, 1972, pp. 18–19.

27   Seiwell, Denny: Author interview (Sinclair), September 13, 2016.

28   Giuliano, Geoffrey: "In Conversation with Denny Laine," Author's Republic audiobook, August 3, 2019.

29   McGee, Garry: *Band on the Run* (Taylor Trade Publishing, New York, 2003), p. 159.

30   Lyng, Eoghan: Interview with Kevin Rowland provided by email to author (Sinclair), August 2, 2020.

31   Turner, Shelley: "Wings First Flight" interview with Paul McCartney for the Wings Over Europe tour program, July 1972.

32   McNulty, Ian: "The Beatle Who Found Some Wings," *Hull University Torch*, May 1972, pp. 13–18.

33   Ibid.

34   Lewisohn, Mark: Wingspan press kit interview, May 7, 2001. Paul noted: "Hotels were called at the last minute. Consequently, when one small hotel in the north of England was fully booked, two Wings roadies had to share both a room and the only bed in it. The hotel reported the roadies to the police, thinking the roadies to be gay, which was apparently offensive at the time."

35   Extracts of Linda McCartney's diary published in Fricke, David: *Wild Life Archive Edition* (MPL Communications, London, 2018).

36   Giuliano, Geoffrey, *Blackbird: Life and Times of Paul McCartney* (Penguin; Reprint Edition, New York 1992), p. 15.

37   Turner, Shelley: "Wings First Flight" interview with Trevor Jones for the Wings Over Europe tour program, July 1972.

38   Prebble, Stuart: "Wings Fly to Havelock Hall," *Courier*, February 16, 1972, p. 1.

39   Ibid.

40   Vallely, Paul: "No Time for Klein," *Leeds Student*, February 25, 1973, p. 5.

41   Lucas: *Rock Goes to College*. Quote taken from Lucas's unedited manuscript.

42   Ibid.

43   Extracts of Linda McCartney's diary published in Fricke: *Wild Life Archive Edition*.

44   Uncredited: "Ex-Beatle Paul's Campus Concert," *The Morecambe Visitor*, February 23, 1972, p. 11.

45   Warmsley (nee Pringle), Sheryl: "Letter from Lancaster," *Beatles Kingdom Fan Club*, 1973, pp. 3–4.

46   Uncredited: "Bird on the Wing," *Melody Maker*, February 26, 1972, p. 5.

47   Seiwell, Denny: Author interview (Sinclair), October 31, 2016. Marinucci, Steve: "Wing Wild Life and Red Rose Speedway—Denny Laine and Denny Seiwell Talk New Box Sets," *Billboard* (online), December 26, 2018.

48   Harper with Hodgett: *Irish Folk, Trad & Blues*, p. 174.

49   Turner: "Wings First Flight" interview.

50   Haigh, Steve: Radio interview with Paul McCartney for BBC Radio Leeds, broadcast February 16, 1972.

51   Uncredited: Filmed interview with Linda McCartney for *Cool Cube*, Channel 4, broadcast December 7, 1992.

52   Uncredited: "The Irish Problem—Just for the Record," *Disc and Music Echo*, February 19, 1972, p. 8.

53   Holloway, Danny: "Singles—McCartney's Rebel Rouser Is Great," *NME*, February 19, 1972, p. 11.

54   Welch, Chris: "A Drop of the Irish," *Melody Maker*, February 19, 1972.

55   Valentine, Penny: "McCartney's Message," *Sounds*, February 19, 1972, p. 32.

56   Uncredited: "Wings' Irish Rush Disc," *Record Mirror*, February 19, 1972.

57   Watkinson, Rob: "Live! Wings at York University," *Record Mirror*, February 19, 1972.

58   Richardson, Heather: Radio interview with Paul McCartney for BBC Radio Sheffield, broadcast February 18, 1972.

59   Wilkinson, Damon: "The Forgotten Salford Music Hall Which Played Host to Paul McCartney, U2, Blondie and a Legendary Gig by the Smiths, *Manchester Evening News* (online), April 2, 2022.

60   Uncredited: "José Feliciano: I Got It from the Beatles," *Record Mirror*, June 13, 1970, p. 7.

61   Seiwell, Denny: Author interview (Kozinn), June 9, 2016.

62   Turner: "Wings First Flight" interview.

63   Feliciano, José, email exchange with author (Sinclair), via wife Susan Feliciano, October 22, 2018.

64   Uncredited: "Jagger, ABKCO Trade Verbal Punches", *Record World*, February 5, 1972, p. 49.

65   Information taken from *Billboard*, February 26, 1972.

66   Russell, Willy: Story relayed to author Adrian Sinclair by Russell, May 14, 2020.

67   Uncredited: Quote taken from brumbeat.net, page dedicated to the history of Denny and the Diplomats.

68   Turner: "Wings First Flight" interview.

69   Ibid.

70   Giuliano, Geoffrey: "In Conversation with Denny Laine," *Author's Republic* audiobook, August 3, 2019. Laine said, in the fall of 1989: "As a result of it [the Ireland single], we did get a lot of picketing, you know, at gigs and things. And I mean, at one point, I had to sort of put my toe down and drive through people, not knocking people over literally, but forcing them to jump out of the way, to get out."

71   Lucas, Andrew, email exchange with author (Sinclair), November 27, 2018.

72   Turner: "Wings First Flight" interview.

73   Uncredited: "Yes, It Was Paul McCartney," *South Wales Evening Post*, p. 7.

74   Uncredited: "Wings . . . and Their Incredible Journey," *Mirabelle*, July 14, 1973, p. 24.

16 GETTING HIGH AND JAMMING

1   Uncredited: "Paul, Somebody Wants You," *Melody Maker*, March 25, 1972.

2   Ledgewood, Mike (Editor): "My Goodness, McCartney, McGuinness," *Disc and Music Echo*, February 26, 1972, p. 4.

3   Boucher, Caroline (Editor): "Who Killed Off the Grease Band?" *Disc*, April 22, 1972, p. 4.

4   Telford, Ray: "On the Wing with Henry," *Sounds*, October 14, 1972, p. 7.

5   Seiwell, Denny: Author interview (Sinclair), October 31, 2016.

6   Uncredited: Review of Wings' 'Give Ireland Back to the Irish,' *Variety*, February 23, 1972.

7   ABC News: Filmed interview with Paul and Linda McCartney for ABC News, filmed March 2, 1972, broadcast March 7, 1972.

8   Haber, Joyce: "High Hopes for a One-Day Wonder," *Los Angeles Times*, March 28, 1974, p. 16.

9   Hilburn, Robert: "He Finally Satisfied Fans AND Critics," *Los Angeles Times*, May 12, 1974, p. H-11.

10 Petrusich, Amanda: *Red Rose Speedway Archive Edition* (MPL Communications, London, 2018), p. 13.

11 Holloway, Danny: "The Producers: Glyn Johns," *NME*, February 26, 1972, p. 12.

12 Johns, Glyn: *Sound Man* (Plume, 2015), p. 192.

13 Petrusich, Amanda: *Red Rose Speedway Archive Edition* (MPL Communications, London, 2018), p. 13.

14 Seiwell, Denny: Author interview (Kozinn), June 9, 2016.

15 Goldman, Scott: Filmed interview with Glyn Johns for the Grammy Museum, shared on YouTube November 17, 2014.

16 Crane, Larry: "Glyn Johns,", *Tape Op Magazine* No.109, September-October 2015, p. 62.

17 Goldman, Scott: Filmed interview with Glyn Johns for the Grammy Museum, shared on YouTube November 17, 2014.

18 Petrusich, Amanda: *Red Rose Speedway Archive Edition* (MPL Communications, London, 2018), p. 13.

19 Evans, Jim: "Faster Than Concorde—The Story of Wings," *Record Mirror*, April 16, 1977, p. 17.

20 Cain, Barry: "Wings' Linda Speaks—Sob Story," *Record Mirror*, March 25, 1978, p. 17. And Davies, Hunter: "Paul McCartney: Confessions of an Unemployed Beatle," *Sunday Times*, April 4, 1976.

21 Boucher, Caroline: "Desperate Den," *Disc*, December 16, 1972, p. 7. Plus Seiwell, Denny: Author interview (Kozinn), June 9, 2017.

22 Uncredited: Radio interview with Henry McCullough by "Kevin" (surname unknown), US radio, July, 2011.

23 Uncredited: "Producing Problems," *Melody Maker*, April 22, 1972.

24 Prism Films: Filmed interview with Denny Laine for Prism Film, published in multiple parts on YouTube, June 9, 2012.

25 Chapman, Phil: Author interview (Sinclair) by email, July 10, 2019.

26 McCullough, Henry: Interview with writer Chip Madinger, April 20, 2000.

27 Seiwell, Denny, Author interview (Kozinn), June 9, 2016.

28 Du Noyer, Paul: "Alone Again, Or," *Mojo*, July 2001.

29 Boucher, Caroline (Editor): "Who Killed Off the Grease Band?" *Disc*, April 22, 1972, p. 4.

30 Uncredited: Information from https://www.moogmusic.com/news/beatles-use-moog-synthesizer-abbey-road-sessions.

31 Minimoog Model D trade advertisement, *Beat Instrumental*, June 1972.

32 Telford: "On the Wing with Henry," p. 7.

33 Jewell, Derek: "We Can Work It Out . . . Alone," *Sunday Times* Magazine, January 22, 1967.

34 Peacock: "Paul McCartney in the Talk-In," pp. 22–23.

35 Petrusich, Amanda: *Red Rose Speedway Archive Edition* (MPL Communications, London, 2018), p. 13.

36 Sounes, Howard: *Fab: An Intimate Life of Paul McCartney* (HarperCollins, 2011), p. 505.

37 Peacock, Steve: "Denny Laine—The Talk In," *Sounds*, December 16, 1972, pp. 10–11.

38 Hennessey, Mike: "Living In a Shadow . . ." *Record Mirror*, August 12, 1972, p. 3. And Peacock: "Denny Laine Talk In."

39 Rosen, Craig: *Billboard Book of Number One Albums: The Inside Story Behind Pop Music's Blockbuster Records* (*Billboard* Books, New York, 1996), p. 161.

40 Peacock: "Paul McCartney in the Talk-In," pp. 22–23.

41 Seiwell, Denny: Author interview (Sinclair), September 13, 2016.

42 Payment of expenses noted in Denny Seiwell: Author Interview (Sinclair), September 13, 2016.

43 Seiwell, Denny: Author interview (Sinclair), September 13, 2016.

44 Harper, Colin: "Hello, Goodbye: Henry McCullough & Wings," *Mojo*, September 1977.

45 Peacock: "Paul McCartney in the Talk-In," pp. 22–23.

46 Wincentsen, Edward: *The Moody Blues Companion* (Wynn Publishing, Pickens, 2000), p. 71.

47 ATV financial information taken from *Billboard*, 23 September 1972, and *Billboard*, April 12, 1969.

48 Gambaccini: "The *Rolling Stone* Interview: Paul McCartney." And Welch, Chris: "All Paul," *Melody Maker*, December 1, 1973.

49 Seiwell, Denny: Author interview (Kozinn), June 9, 2016.

50 Doherty, Harry: "Spreading His Wings," *Melody Maker*, January 15, 1977, p. 35.

51 Peacock: "Denny Laine—The Talk In," pp. 10–11.

52 McCartney, Paul: Author interview (Kozinn), October 3, 1995.

53 Peebles, Andy: Radio interview with Paul McCartney for BBC Radio 1, broadcast May 26, 1980.

54 Massey, Howard: *The Great British Recording Studios* (Hal Leonard Corporation, Milwaukee, 2015), p. 169.

55 Petrusich: *Red Rose Speedway Archive Edition*, p. 13.

56 Rosen, Craig: *Billboard Book of Number One Albums: The Inside Story Behind Pop Music's Blockbuster Records* (*Billboard* Books, New York, 1996), p. 161.

57 Crane, Larry: "Glyn Johns," *Tape Op Magazine*, No.109, September-October 2015, p. 56.

58 Seiwell, Denny, Compound of author interviews (Kozinn/Sinclair), June 9 and October 31, 2016.

59 Prism Films: Filmed interview with Denny Laine for Prism Film, published in multiple parts on YouTube, June 9, 2012.

17 PREPARING FOR LIFTOFF

1   McQuarrie, Fiona: "Natural Exuberance: The Bonzo Dog Doo-Dah Band's 'I'm the Urban Spaceman,'" *Writing on Music* (online), March 13, 2016.

2   Dellar, Fred: "The Producer: Gus Dudgeon," *Sound International*, May 1978, p. 38, 41.

3   Tiven, Jon: "Gus Dudgeon," *International Musician*, October 1975.

4   Johns, Glyn: Author interview (Sinclair), May 30, 2021.

5   Ault, Phil: Author interview (Sinclair) by email on September 23, 2021.

6   Ibid.

7   Uncredited: "Wings 'Happy' Song," *Sounds*, April 15, 1972, p. 3.

8   Boucher: "Who Killed Off the Grease Band?"

9   Morris, John: Author interview (Kozinn), November 17, 2017.

10 Zappa, Frank with Occhiogrosso, Peter: *The Real Frank Zappa* (Pan Books, London, 1989), p. 114.

11 Morris, John: Author interview (Kozinn), November 17, 2017. And email exchange with author (Sinclair), June 28, 2020.

12 Morris, John: Author interview (Kozinn), November 17, 2017.

13 Ibid.

14 Coxhill, Gordon: "Paul and Linda and Togetherness," *Petticoat*, February 17, 1973, pp. 30–31. And Uncredited: "Bird on the Wing," *Melody Maker*, February 26, 1972, p. 5.

15 Seiwell, Denny: Author interview (Sinclair), October 31, 2016.

16 Uncredited: "Producing Problems," *Melody Maker*, April 22, 1972.

17 Hennessey, Mike: "Living in a Shadow," *Record Mirror*, 12 August 1972, p. 3.

18 Uncredited: "McCartney Spreads His Wings," *Beat Instrumental*, June 1973, p. 6.

19 Capitol Radio: Radio interview with Paul and Linda McCartney for Capitol Radio, broadcast September 1975. And Fong-Torres, Ben: "Yesterday, Today & Paul," *Rolling Stone*, June 17, 1976.

20 Fong-Torres: "Yesterday, Today & Paul."

21 Connolly, Ray: "The Crunch That Had to Come," *Radio Times*, May 18, 1972, pp. 52–53.

22 Ferguson, Nicholas: Author interview (Sinclair), March 9, 2022.

23 Ibid.

24 Uncredited: "Off-Beat," The *Daily Express*, May 1, 1972, p. 13.

25 Skoler, Ron: "John and Yoko, Some Time in New York City," *Sounds*, September 2, 1972, p. 18.

26 Uncredited: "Wings Sad Nursery Rhyme Song," *Disc*, May 20, 1972.

27 Holloway, Danny: "Bolan Slip as McCartney Rips," *NME*, May 6, 1972.

28 Valentine, Penny: "Simple, Wings 'Mary Had a Little Lamb,'" *Sounds*, May 20, 1972, p. 15.

29 Jones, Peter: "Paul Plays It Safe," *Record Mirror*, May 20, 1972.

30 Welch, Chris: "Wings: Mary Had a Little Lamb," May 20, 1972.

31 Uncredited: *Cash Box* review of 'Mary Had a Little Lamb,' *Cashbox*, June 17, 1972.

32 Peacock: "Paul McCartney in the Talk-In," pp. 22–27.

33 Brown, Geoff: "Wings", *Melody Maker*, November 30, 1974, p. 28.

34 Simons, Judith: "Beatle Paul Signs Up for Sir Lew," *Daily Express*, June 2, 1972, p. 4.

35 Jenour, Kenelm: "Ex-Beatle Paul in a Deal," The *Daily Mirror*, June 2, 1972, p. 3.

36 Simons: "Beatle Paul Signs Up for Sir Lew."

37 White, Timothy: "Farewell to the First Solo Era," *Musician*, February, 1988, p. 48.

38 Salewicz, Chris: Audio interview with Paul McCartney for *Q Magazine*, September 1986.

39 Seiwell, Denny, Compound of author interviews (Kozinn/Sinclair), June 9, 2016, and October 31, 2016.

40 White, Timothy: *Timothy White's Rock Stars*—"Put It There, 20 Years of Paul McCartney," audio interview, 1990.

41 Plummer, Mark: "Mary Had a Little Lamb, Those Lyrics Are a Heavy Trip," *Melody Maker*, December 2, 1972, p. 10.

42 White, Timothy: "Farewell to the First Solo Era," *Musician*, February, 1988, p. 50.

43 Ibid.

44 Paul and Linda McCartney in conversation at the Châteauvallon press conference, France, July 9, 1972.

45 Morris, John: Author interview (Kozinn), November 17, 2017.

46 Ibid.

47 Langhart, Chris: Author interview (Kozinn), September 13, 2018.

48 Salewicz, Chris: *McCartney: The Biography* (Futura Publications, London, 1987), pp. 227–9.

49 Shelley Turner's departure from MPL was reported in *Record World* on July 22, 1972.

50 Sam [no surname given], "The Girl Behind Paul and Linda," *Jackie*, January 1973, p. 9.

51 Coleman, Ray: Unpublished interview with Wendy Hanson, circa 1986.

52 Salter, Tom: Author interview (Sinclair), November 21, 2017.

53 Morris, John: Author interview (Kozinn), November 17, 2017.

54 Cleghorn, Geoffrey: Author interview (Sinclair), November 8, 2018.

55 Dean, Georgina, email exchange with author (Sinclair), November 2, 2018.

56 Morris, John: Author interview (Kozinn), November 17, 2017.

18 "CHANTEZ A BIT IF YOU KNOW LES MOTS"

1 Gambaccini: "The Paul McCartney Interview," pp. 20–28.
2 Uncredited: "Meet Linda McCartney—Linda's Lovely," *Tina*, September 29, 1973.
3 Seiwell, Denny: Author interview (Sinclair), September 13 and October 31, 2016.
4 Morris, John: Author interview (Kozinn), November 17, 2017.
5 Johnson, James: "Wings on Wheels," *NME*, July 15, 1972, p. 28.
6 Ibid.
7 Uncredited: "The Man Who Played Alongside the Legends of Rock Releases Powerful New CD," *Ulster Herald*, December 24, 1998, p. 4.
8 Wale, Michael: "McCartney Getting Ready for Criticism," Disc, July 15, 1972, pp. 2–7. And Charlesworth, Chris: "Chantez a Bit If You Know Les Mots," *Melody Maker*, July 15, 1972, pp. 12–13.
9 Wale, Michael: "Paul's Return," *The Times*, July 11, 1972, p. 13.
10 Charlesworth, Chris: "Chantez a Bit If You Know Les Mots," *Melody Maker*, July 15, 1972, pp. 12–13. Wale: "Paul's Return."
11 Denselow, Robin: "Paul McCartney on Tour in France," *Arts Guardian*, July 11, 1972, p. 10.
12 Johnson, James: "Wings on Wheels," *NME*, July 15, 1972, p. 29.
13 Seiwell, Denny: Author interview (Sinclair), September 13, 2016.
14 Uncredited: "Jo-Jo Laine Obituary," *Sunday Independent*, November 12, 2006.
15 Johnson, Angella: "Mum Was Beautiful, Wild . . . The Ultimate Rock Groupie," *Mail on Sunday*, November 5, 2006, p. 38.
16 Stewart, Gloria: "Inside the Strange World of Paul McCartney," *Sunday People*, April 17, 1983, pp. 21–23.
17 Laine, Denny: "All That Money But They Just Nick Things for Fun," *The Sun*, January 31, 1984, pp. 15–17. Laine, Denny: "I'd Be Rich If Paul Wasn't So Stingy," *The Sun*, February 1, pp. 14–15.
18 Stewart: "Inside the Strange World of Paul McCartney."
19 Morris, John: Author interview (Kozinn), November 17, 2017.
20 Ibid.
21 Salter, Tom: Author interview (Sinclair), November 21, 2017.
22 Telford, Ray: "On the Wing with Henry," *Sounds*, October 14, 1972, p. 7.
23 Hughes, Malcolm, email exchange with author (Sinclair), April 22, 2020.
24 Peacock: "Paul McCartney in the Talk-In," p. 22.
25 McCullough, Henry: Interview with writer Chip Madinger, April 20, 2000 (unpublished).
26 Peacock: "Paul McCartney in the Talk-In," p. 22.
27 Johnson, James: "Wings on Wheels," *NME*, July 15, 1972, p. 28.
28 Charlesworth: "Chantez a Bit If You Know Les Mots."
29 Wale, Michael: "McCartney Getting Ready for Criticism," *Disc*, July 15, 1972, p. 7.
30 Horwood, Janet: "The Second Coming of the McCartneys," *Woman's Own*, September 23, 1972, p. 48. Uncredited: "Linda: Quit the Band! I've Just Joined," *Record Mirror*, July 22, 1972, p. 5.
31 *Rock and Folk* magazine headline quoted in *Melody Maker*, August 12, 1972.
32 Uncredited: "Linda: Quit the Band! I've Just Joined."
33 Boucher, Caroline: "Desperate Den," *Disc*, December 16, 1972, p. 7.
34 Langhart, Chris: Author interview (Kozinn), September 13, 2018.
35 Cribbins, Bernard: *Bernard Who?* (Constable, London, 2018), p. 239.
36 Ibid.
37 Details of Erika Huebers Settlement taken from editorial by Warschauer, Harry: "Why Paul Had to Pay in Love Child Wrangle," *Sunday People*, April 24, 1983, p. 2.
38 Warschauer: "Why Paul Had to Pay in Love Child Wrangle."
39 Morris, John: Author interview (Kozinn), November 17, 2017.
40 Telford, Ray: "On the Wing with Henry," *Sounds*, October 14, 1972, p. 7.
41 Sigg, Bernie: "Live! Wings in Zürich," *Record Mirror*, August 5, 1972.
42 Seiwell, Denny: Author interview (Sinclair), October 31, 2016.
43 Clayson, Alan: "Denny Laine," *Record Collector*, July 1995, pp. 48--53.
44 Davies, Hunter, "Paul McCartney: Confessions of an Unemployed Beatle", *Sunday Times*, April 4, 1976.
45 Pearce, Garth: "The McCartney Memoirs," *Daily Express*, February 9, 1977, p. 17.
46 Telford, Ray: "Wings Fly Home Intact," *Disc and Music Echo*, December 1, 1973, p. 7.
47 Challis, Drummond: Author interview (Sinclair), December 13, 2018.
48 Jessen Jørgen: "Paul McCartney: John og jeg ikke uvenner, men vi går aldrig sammen igen," *Danish Press*, August 2, 1972.
49 Orsted, Knud: "McCartney: I'm Boycotting Apple," *Record Mirror*, August 19, 1972, p. 11.
50 McCartney, Angie: *Angie McCartney: My Long and Winding Road* (ROK Books, Los Angeles, 2013), p. 125.
51 Helopati, Kari: "Live Wings," *Record Mirror*, August 19, 1972, p. 11.
52 Aaltonen Ulla-Maija: Audio interview with Wings for YLE Finland, broadcast on August 5, 1972.
53 Cass, Alain: "McCartney's Circus," *The Daily Express*, July 14, 1972, p. 7.
54 Palmer, Tony: "Paul's Tour," *The Observer*, August 6, 1972, p. 24.
55 Laine, Denny: "The Real McCartney," *The Sun*, January 31, 1984, p. 17.

56 McGee, Garry, interview with Henry McCullough quoted in *Band on the Run* (Taylor Trade Publishing, 2003), p. 164.

57 Seiwell, Denny: Author interview (Kozinn), June 9, 2016.

58 Martin, Sverre: "De vågade livet för att få se sin idol," *Aftonbladet*, August 8, 1972, pp. 10–13.

59 Peacock: "Paul McCartney in the Talk-In," p. 22.

60 Martin: "De vågade livet för att få se sin idol."

61 Ibid.

62 Ibid.

63 Widén, Britta: "Beatlen skuggad dag och natt," *Aftonbladet*, August 11, 1972, pp. 6–7.

64 Callan, Paul [editor] "Was It Wandering Underwear Which Landed Paul McCartney with His Fine for Pot?," *The Daily Mail*, August 18, 1972, p. 13.

65 Morris, John: Author interview (Kozinn), November 17, 2017.

66 Seiwell, Denny: Author interview (Kozinn), June 9, 2016.

67 Widén: "Beatlen skuggad dag och natt."

68 Naffredaktion: "Paul förs bort I Scandinavium", *GT extrabladet*, August 11, 1972, pull out supplement.

69 Widén: "Beatlen skuggad dag och natt."

70 Morris, John: Author interview (Kozinn), November 17, 2017.

71 Choate, Roger: "McCartneys Fined on Drug Charge in Sweden," *The Times*, August 12, 1972, p. 1.

72 Seiwell, Denny: Author interview (Kozinn), June 9, 2016.

73 Disney, Anthea: Author interview (Kozinn), September 10, 2018.

74 Disney, Anthea: *Daily Mail*, "Why I Smoke Pot—by Paul," *Daily Mail*, August 12, 1972, p. 3.

75 Seiwell, Denny: Author interview (Sinclair), September 13, 2016.

76 Dacre, Paul: "Not So Magical—Paul and Linda's Mystery Tour," *Daily Express*, August 14, 1972, p. 6.

77 Ibid.

78 Seiwell, Denny: Author interview (Sinclair), October 31, 2016.

79 Disney, Anthea: Author interview (Kozinn), September 10, 2018.

80 Chattington, Barry: Author interview (Sinclair), December 15, 2018.

81 Boucher, Caroline: "Look Out Showbiz, Here Come Wings," *Disc*, December 2, 1972, pp. 18–19.

82 Chattington, Barry: Author interview (Sinclair), December 15, 2018.

83 Ibid.

84 Smith, Alan: "McCartney Talking to Alan Smith," *NME*, December 23, 1972, p. 25.

85 Telford: "On the Wing with Henry," p. 7.

86 Morris, John: Author interview (Kozinn), November 17, 2017.

87 Block, Adam: "The Makka Material," McCartney: Beatle on Wings, K.49569, 1976, p. 62.

19 FROM THE AUTOBAHN TO THE RED ROSE SPEEDWAY

1 Connolly, Ray: Interview published in the sheet music for 'Hi, Hi, Hi' and 'C Moon', issued November 1972, p. 2.

2 Seiwell, Denny: Author interview (Sinclair), September 13, 2016.

3 Paul McCartney, handwritten memo, dated August 28, 1972.

4 Smith, Alan: "Linda: The Facts," *NME*, December 16, 1972, p. 16.

5 Harper with Hodgett: *Irish Folk, Trad & Blues*, p. 194.

6 Plummer, Mark: "Mary Had a Little Lamb—Those Lyrics Are a Heavy Trip," *Melody Maker*, December 2, 1972, p. 10.

7 Marks, Laurence: "McCartney and Price—Knowing the Score," *19 Magazine*, December 17, 1972, pp. 14–15. And Jones, Dylan: "At Home with Paul McCartney—His Most Candid Interview Yet," *GQ* (online) August 4, 2020.

8 Fleming, Ian: *Live and Let Die: James Bond 007* (Pan Book Limited, London, 1966), pp. 37–38.

9 Seiwell, Denny: Author interview (Kozinn), June 9, 2016.

10 Grundy, Stuart, and Tobler, John: *The Record Producers* (BBC Books, London, 1982), pp. 121–2. And *James Bond's Greatest Hits* documentary, Channel 4, broadcast in 2006.

11 Burlingame, Jon: *The Music of James Bond* (Oxford University Press, Oxford, 2014), p. 108.

12 Internal United Artists memo between M. Deutch and S. Shemel, March 15, 1973, p. 2.

13 McNay, Ian: Radio interview with John Leckie, published online November 23, 2016.

14 Smith, Joe, Audio interview with Paul McCartney for the Library of Congress, October 22, 1987.

15 Doyle, Tom: "Paul McCartney Starting Over," *Guitar World, Holidays* issue, 2010, p. 69.

16 Leckie, John: Author interview (Sinclair), December 1, 2016.

17 Ibid.

18 Peacock: "Paul McCartney in the Talk-In," pp. 22, 27.

19 Leckie, John: Author interview (Sinclair), December 1, 2016.

20 Uncredited: "Paul's Posy Probe," *Daily Mirror*, 22 September 1972, p. 5.

21 Gradon, John and Grylls, James: "Paul Fined for Growing 'Pot' in His Greenhouse," *Daily Mail*, March 9, 1973, p. 15.

22 Uncredited: "Newsmakers," *Los Angeles Times*, October 1, 1972, p. A.

23 Laine, Denny: "The Real McCartney," *The Sun*, January 31, 1984, p. 16.

24 Parsons, Alan: Interview with writers Chip Madinger and Mark Easter, August 17, 2002.

25 Buskin, Richard: "The REP Interview: Alan Parsons," *Recording Engineer Producer*, August 1990, p. 28.

26 Seiwell, Denny: Author interview (Sinclair), October 31, 2016.

27 Doherty, Harry: "Spreading His Wings," *Melody Maker*, January 15, 1977, p. 35.

28 Peacock: "Denny Laine—the Talk-In," p. 10.

29 Chattington, Barry: Author interview (Sinclair), December 15, 2018.

30 Smith, Chris: "McCartney Right Back in His Stride," *NME*, December 9, 1972, p. 5.

31 Chattington, Barry: Author interview (Sinclair), December 15, 2018.

32 McCartney, Paul: "You Gave Me the Answer—*Red Rose Speedway Special*," paulmccartney.com, November 26, 2018.

33 Uncredited: "An Ex-Beatle Confesses," *Sunday Independent*, October 1, 1972, p. 11.

34 Uncredited: "News," *NME*, November 4, 1972, pp. 2–3.

35 Telford, Ray: "On the Wing with Henry," *Sounds*, October 14, 1972, p. 7.

36 Doherty, Harry: "Spreading His Wings", *Melody Maker*, January 15, 1977, p. 35.

37 Seiwell, Denny: Author interviews (Sinclair), September 13 and October 31, 2016.

38 Cecchetti, Simone, with Bonfanti, Cristiana: "*Paul McCartney.fm* Interview with Denny Seiwell," *Paul McCartney.fm* (fanzine), January 16, 2002, p. 8.

39 Deriso, Nick: "*Something Else!* Interview—Henry McCullough, Formerly of Wings," *Something Else!* (online), August 24, 2011.

40 Harris, Bob: Filmed interview with Carly Simon for the *Old Grey Whistle Test*, BBC1, September 16, 1972.

41 Simon, Carly: *Boys in the Trees—A Memoir* (Constable, New York, 2016), p. 253.

42 Ryan, Jimmy: Filmed interview for "The Hit Men," published on YouTube, February 15, 2017.

43 Grundy, Stuart, with Tobler, John: *Record Producers* (BBC Books, London, 1982), p. 67.

44 Harris, Bob: Filmed interview with Carly Simon for the *Old Grey Whistle Test*, BBC1, September 16, 1972.

45 Werbin, Stuart: "James Taylor & Carly Simon," *Rolling Stone*, January 4, 1973, p. 35.

46 Uncredited: "McCartney Music for Bond Film," *Disc*, October 21, 1972, p. 3.

47 Ibid.

48 Marks, Laurence: "McCartney and Price—Knowing the Score," *19 Magazine*, December 17, 1972, pp. 14–15.

49 Grundy with Tobler: *Record Producers*, pp. 121–2.

50 Ibid.

51 Massey, Howard: *The Great British Recording Studios* (Hal Leonard Corporation, Milwaukee, 2015), p. 217.

52 Ibid.

53 Tony Bramwell account of playback from: http://www.tonybramwell.com/liveandletdie.html.

20 ROMEO, ROMEO

1 Gambaccini, Paul: "The McCartneys Meet the Press," *Rolling Stone*, June 21, 1973, p. 8.

2 Benson, Nigel: "Taxman Wants a Bite of the Beatles' Apple," *Daily Mirror*, October 23, 1972, p. 7. Uncredited:

"Beatle's Tax 'Hangar'," *Daily Express*, October 23, 1972, p. 1.

3 Skoler, Ron: "John & Yoko—Some Time in New York City," *Sounds*, September 9, 1972, p. 16.

4 Houston, Thelma: Author interview (Sinclair), May 31, 2017.

5 Brenda Arnau's deal with RCA Records reported in *Billboard*, September 16, 1972.

6 Lewisohn, Mark: Interview with Carolyn Pfeiffer, June 15, 2011.

7 Block, Adam: "The Makka Material," *McCartney: Beatle on Wings*, K.49569, 1976, p. 62.

8 Cummings, Howard: "The Rise of Engineer/Producer Alan Parsons," *Recording Engineer Producer*, October 1976, p. 30.

9 Ibid.

10 Denselow, Robin: "Paul McCartney in Berlin," *Guardian*, August 26, 1972, p. 8.

11 Plummer, Mark: "Wings and Things," *Melody Maker*, October 28, 1972.

12 Lewisohn, Mark (Ed.): "Mining the Film and Video Archive—Hi, Hi, Hi", *Club Sandwich*, Christmas, 1991, p. 8.

13 Martin, George, with Hornsby, Jeremy: *All You Need Is Ears* (St. Martin's Press, London, 1979), p. 231.

14 Tony Bramwell account of events taken from: http://www.tonybramwell.com/liveandletdie.html.

15 Seiwell, Denny, Compound of author interviews (Sinclair/Kozinn), September 13, 2016 and June 6, 2016.

16 Peacock: "Paul McCartney in the Talk-In," p. 22.

17 Uncredited: "Denny Laine—A Special Musical Gift," *Record Mirror*, August 11, 1973, p. 24.

18 Giuliano, Geoffrey: "In Conversation with Denny Laine," *Author's Republic* audiobook, August 3, 2019.

19 Binelli, Mark: "Return of the Macca," *The Independent Magazine*, October 22, 2005, p. 16.

20 Giuliano, Geoffrey: In conversation with Joanne Laine during the audio documentary *The Beatles in Their Own Words: A Rockumentary: The Lost Beatles Interviews* (Laserlight Audiobook, 1995).

21 Uncredited: "Paul McCartney—Home Sweet Home," *Pink*, May 19, 1973, p. 33.

22 Seiwell, Denny: Author interview (Sinclair), September 16, 2016.

23 Uncredited: "Wings Single—BBC Ban," *Disc*, December 2, 1972, p. 2.

24 Uncredited: "Wings Single Hit by BBC's Airplay Veto," *NME*, December 2, 1972, p. 3.

25 Ibid.

26 Ibid.

27 Ibid.

28 Jackson, Martin: "Surprise Ban on McCartney," *Daily Express*, December 1, 1972, p. 12.

29 Smith, Alan: "Linda: The Facts," *NME*, December 16, 1972, p. 16.

30 Peacock: "Paul McCartney in the Talk-In," pp. 22–23.

31 Coxhill, Gordon: "Paul and Linda and Togetherness," *Petticoat*, February 17, 1973, pp. 30–31.

32 Boucher, Caroline: "Look Out Showbiz—Here Come Wings," *Disc*, December 2, 1972, pp. 18–19.

33 Plummer: "Mary Had a Little Lamb . . . ," p.10.

34 Peacock: "Paul McCartney in the Talk-In," p. 22.

35 Holloway, Danny: "Wings Fly Hi," *NME*, December 2, 1972, p. 21.

36 Peel, John: "Wings Beating on Both Sides," *Disc*, December 2, 1972, p. 22.

37 Valentine, Penny: "Wings: 'C Moon'/'Hi, Hi, Hi'," *Sounds*, December 2, 1972, p. 37.

38 Uncredited: Review of 'Hi, Hi, Hi' from *Cash Box*, December 16, 1972.

39 Hughes, David: "A Personal History of the British Record Business 92—Walter J. (Wally) Ridley Pt. 3", *Vinyl Memories* (online), March 25, 2015.

40 Uncredited: "Alan Parsons on Dark Side: 'Roger Knew Something Great Was in the Making'," *Rolling Stone*, September 28, 2011 (online).

41 Telford, Ray: "Henry McCullough in the Talk-In," *Sounds*, April 14, 1973, p. 12.

42 White, Timothy: "Farewell to the First Solo Era," *Musician*, February 1988, p. 50.

43 Peacock: "Denny Laine—The Talk-In," p. 10.

44 Tremlett, George: "The Other McCartney," *Sunday Telegraph*, 14 August 1977, pp. 27–28.

45 Seiwell, Denny: Author interview (Sinclair), October 31, 2016.

21 DOUBLE VISION

1 Davis, Clifford: "Paul McCartney Signs a Deal," *Daily Mirror*, January 13, 1973, p. 10.

2 Uncredited: "Paul McCartney—A Living Legend," Press Association (via the *Kingston Gleaner*, Jamaica), January 10, 1973, p. 6.

3 Backshall, Paul: "Paul McCartney Is Still a Beatle," Reuters (via the *Kingston Gleaner*, Jamaica), January 1, 1973, p. 6.

4 Brayfield: "Linda and Paul McCartney Are Still Madly in Love," p. 67.

5 Seiwell, Denny: Author interview (Kozinn), June 9, 2017.

6 Parsons, Alan: Interview with writers Chip Madinger and Mark Easter, August 17, 2002.

7 Plummer, Mark: "Mary Had a Little Lamb . . . ," p. 74.

8 Welch, Chris: "All Paul," *Melody Maker*, December 1, 1973.

9 Rubin, Rick: McCartney 3,2,1! Episode 4 (Hulu, 2021), broadcast July 2021.

10 Mason, Nick: *Inside Out: A Personal History of Pink Floyd* (Chronicle Books, San Francisco, 2005), pp. 175–6 (Kindle Edition).

11 Harris, John: *Dark Side of the Moon—The Making of the Pink Floyd Masterpiece*, (Da Capo, New York, 2005), p. 132.

12 Mason: *Inside Out: A Personal History of Pink Floyd*.

13 McCartney, Paul: Press Conference, Nashville, Tennessee, July 17, 1974.

14 Block, Adam: "The Makka Material," McCartney: Beatle on Wings, K.49569, 1976, p. 62.

15 Gilchrist, Roderick: "McCartney Tells of the 'That Day Linda Nearly Left Me'," *Daily Mail*, June 12, 1980, p. 13.

16 Hewson, Richard: Author interview (Sinclair), December 3, 2016.

17 Ibid.

18 Seiwell, Denny: Author interview (Sinclair), October 31, 2016.

19 Telford: "Henry McCullough in the Talk-In."

20 McCartney, Paul: "You Gave Me the Answer—*Red Rose Speedway Special*," paulmccartney.com, November 26, 2018.

21 McCullough, Henry: Interview for BBC Radio 1, October 29, 2014.

22 McCartney, Paul: "You Gave Me the Answer—*Red Rose Speedway Special*."

23 Scott, Roger, audio interview with Paul McCartney and Denny Laine for Capitol Radio, November 11, 1977.

24 McCartney, Paul: Audio interview for *Paul McCartney in the 80s* (MVD Audio, 2016).

25 Part of the conversation is included in Peter Jackson's documentary, *The Beatles: Get Back*, 2021.

26 Uncredited: "McCartney Acquires Nor Va Jak Catalog," *Variety*, February 7, 1973, p. 65.

27 Charone, Barbara, "Linda McCartney: Silly Love Songs," *Sounds*, April 3, 1976.

28 Gambaccini: "The *Rolling Stone* Interview—Paul McCartney," p. 22.

29 W. Watson: "Spectacular—It's the American Connection," *Aberdeen Evening Express*, March 19, 1974, p. 2.

30 Seiwell, Denny: Author interview (Sinclair), September 13, 2016.

31 Uncredited: "Linda—Winging Her Way," *Music Star*, March 17, 1973.

32 Dickins, Barry, email exchange with Adrian Sinclair, via Yasmin Purshouse, September 6, 2018.

33 Uncredited: "Wings Tour Delayed—All Gigs Off Till May," *NME*, February 10, 1973.

34 Laine, Denny: Interview conducted by Rogers & Cowan, Wings mid-1970s publicists, June, 1977 (unpublished).

35 Block, Adam: "The Makka Material," McCartney: Beatle on Wings, K.49569, 1976, p. 62.

36 Ibid.

37 Telford: "Henry McCullough in the Talk-In."

38 Doherty, Harry: "Spreading His Wings," *Melody Maker*, January 15, 1977, p. 35.

39 Edelson, Howie: "Winging It with Denny Laine," *Beatlefan*, July-October 2006.

40 White, Timothy: "Farewell to the First Solo Era," *Musician*, February 1988, p. 50.

41 Uncredited: "Paintings on the Wall—Eduardo Paolozzi (1924-2005), paulmccartney.com, August 23, 2019.

22 FIVE OF THEM CAME UP ILLEGAL

1   Uncredited: "James Paul McCartney—Paul McCartney in His First Post-Beatles Television Special," ITV press release, early 1973.

2   Uncredited: "Wings Set to Fly," *Disc*, March 3, 1973, p. 3.

3   Uncredited: "New Itinerary Set by Wings," *NME*, March 3, 1973, p. 3.

4   Murray, Len: *The Pleader—An Autobiography* (Mainstream, Edinburgh, 2002), pp. 151–5.

5   Uncredited: "Paul McCartney Had Five Cannabis Plants at Farm," *Guardian*, March 9, 1973, p. 9.

6   BBC News: Filmed interview with Paul McCartney for BBC Scotland, broadcast March 8, 1973.

7   Uncredited: "Paul McCartney Had Five Cannabis Plants at Farm."

8   Ritchie, Murray: "Drugs Conviction May Put U.S. Ban on McCartney," *Glasgow Herald*, March 9, 1973, p. 3.

9   Twiggy: *In Black and White—An Autobiography* (Simon & Schuster, London, 1997), pp. 139–40.

10 Champlin, Charles: "Twiggy's Talent Filling Out," *Los Angeles Times*, April 20, 1973.

11 Weston, Sue: Author interview (Sinclair), May 11, 2018.

12 Welch, Chris: "Paul: The TV Act I Couldn't Watch," *Sun*, October 20, 1975, p. 22.

13 Rosen, Steve: Backstage interview with Paul McCartney, Birmingham, July 7, 1973.

14 Weston, Sue: Author interview (Sinclair), May 11, 2018.

15 Thegze, Chuck: "Richard Perry's Way with an Album," *Los Angeles Times*, March 24, 1974, p. 52.

16 Werbin, Stuart: "Lennons Discuss Deportation, Allen Klein, Beatles 'Reunion,'" *Rolling Stone*, May 10, 1973, p. 10.

17 Ibid.

18 Fielding, John: Filmed interview with John Lennon for the Weekend World show, first transmitted April 8, 1973.

19 Tyler, Andrew: "Spilling The Beans," *Disc*, April 14, 1973, p. 9.

20 Price, Stephen: "Rock—Henry McCullough," *Sunday Times* (online), August 27, 2006.

21 Seiwell, Denny: Author interview (Sinclair), October 31, 2016.

22 McCartney, Paul, with Pearce, Garth: "The McCartney Memoirs, Part 1—The Crushing of the Beatles and Take Off of Wings," *Daily Express*, February 9, 1977, p. 17.

23 Davies, Hunter: "Paul McCartney: Confessions of an Unemployed Beatle," *Sunday Times*, April 4, 1976.

24 Claire: "Paul McCartney and Wings Fan Club Newsletter," No. 1, April, 1973.

25 Pugsley, Den, email exchange with author (Sinclair), January 4, 2018.

26 Uncredited: "Paul Plays London Gig for Charity," *Disc*, March 24, 1973, p. 3.

27 Uncredited: "Wings: TV/Tour," *Sounds*, March 24, 1973, p. 1.

28 Deriso, Nick: "Something Else! Interview—Henry McCullough, formerly of Wings," *Something Else!* (online), August 24, 2011.

29 Seiwell, Denny: Author interview (Kozinn), June 6, 2016.

30 McCartney, Angie, email exchange with author (Sinclair), June 3, 2019.

31 McCartney, Angie: *Your Mother Should Know—From Liverpool to Los Angeles* (Probablistic Publishing, Los Angeles, 2019), p. 132.

32 Uncredited: "Paul Stars in a Pub Sing-Along Spectacular," *Birkenhead News*, March 30, 1973.

33 Uncredited: "No Room at the Inn for Paul," *Birkenhead News*, March 28, 1973, p. 5. ITV paperwork for the show.

34 Seiwell, Denny, Compound of author Interviews (Kozinn/Sinclair), June 6, 2016 and September 13, 2016.

35 Gaines, Steve: "Will *Red Rose Speedway* Snap McCartney's Slump?" *Circus*, July, 1973, p. 6.

36 Thegze, Chuck: "Richard Perry's Way with an Album," *Los Angeles Times*, March 24, 1974, p. 52.

37 Alterman, Loraine: "Ringo's Agenda: Movie, Music, But No Beatles", *Rolling Stone*, May 23, 1973, p. 16.

38 Johnson, Derek: "Way Is Open for Beatles Reunion," *NME*, April 7, 1973, p. 3.

39 Cummings, Howard: "The Rise of Engineer/Producer Alan Parsons," Recording Engineer Producer, October 1976, p. 30.

40 Badman, Keith: *Off the Records 2—The Dream Is Over Volume 2* (Omnibus Press, London, 2002), p. 98.

41 Brooks, Elkie: "Wings' Work of Clean Simplicity," *Disc*, April 7, 1973.

42 Murray, Charles Shaar: "Singles," *NME*, April 7, 1973, p. 17.

43 Welch, Chris: "New Pop Singles—Paul McCartney & Wings: 'My Love,' *Melody Maker*, April 7, 1973.

44 Valentine, Penny: "Wings Bring Romance," *Sounds*, April 7, 1973, p. 27.

45 Uncredited: "Cashbox/Singles Reviews," *Cashbox*, April 14, 1973, p. 20.

46 Uncredited: "Cashbox/Radio Active," *Cashbox*, April 14, 1973, p. 24.

47 Gambaccini: *Paul McCartney: In His Own Words*, p. 86.

48 Uncredited: "Ringo Says Reunion 'Remote,'" *Los Angeles Times*, April 5, 1973, p. 18.

49 Badman, Keith: *The Beatles: Off the Record 2—The Dream Is Over* (Omnibus Press, London, 2009), p. 98.

50 Gaines, Steve: "Will *Red Rose Speedway* Snap McCartney's Slump?" *Circus*, July, 1973, p. 6. And Tyler, Andrew: "Spilling the Beans . . ." *Disc*, April 14, 1973, p. 9.

51 Tyler: "Spilling the Beans . . ."

52 Harper with Hodgett: *Irish Folk, Trad & Blues*, p. 174.

23 DUSTIN' OFF THE COBWEBS

1   Uncredited: "Equipment Come for Shooting of $7m Film," *Kingston Gleaner*, February 3, 1973, p. 33.

2   The details of McCartney's conversation with Hoffman are from Gambaccini: "The *Rolling Stone* Interview: Paul McCartney," p. 21. Plus, *The Story of* Band on the Run, documentary disc from *Band on the Run Special Edition*, EMI, 2010.

3   C.P. (full name not given): "Long and Winding Laine," *Beat Instrumental*, September 1973, p. 31.

4   Seiwell, Denny: Author interview (Sinclair), October 31, 2016.

5   Telford: "Henry McCullough in the Talk-In."

6   Thomas, Deborah: "Wings Swing into Spring," *Daily Mirror*, April 17, 1973, p. 11.

7   Sanders, Rick: "WINGS: They're All Set for Take-Off!" *Record Mirror*, April 28, 1973, p. 23.

8   Plummer, Mark (compiler): "Wings—MM Band Breakdown," *Melody Maker*, April 21, 1973.

9   Thomas, Deborah: "Wings Swing into Spring," *Daily Mirror*, April 17, 1973, p. 11.

10   Solomon, Linda: "McCartney: A Teenybopper with Wife and Kids?" *NME*, April 28, 1973.

11   Watts, Michael: "McCartney, the Family Favourite . . . ," *Melody Maker*, April 28, 1973.

12   Hilburn, Robert: "A Traditional McCartney," *Los Angeles Times*, April 16, 1973.

13   O'Connor, John: "TV: McCartney and His Group on A.B.C. Tonight," *New York Times*, April 16, 1973, p. 75.

14   McGregor, Craig: "Roxon's Rock: From A (Acide) to Z (Zombies)," *New York Times*, May 17, 1970.

15   Roxon, Lillian: "An Undistinguished McCartney Special," *New York Sunday News*, April 22, 1973.

16   Uncredited: "New Look for McCartney," *South Wales Echo*, May 10, 1973, p. 5.

17   Sanders, Rick: "McCartney Lets It All Hang Out," *Record Mirror*, May 5, 1973, p. 11.

18   Coren, Alan: "James Paul McCartney (ATV)," *The Times*, May 11, 1973.

19   James, Clive: "Clive James's Television Week," *The Observer Review*, May 19, 1973, p. 34.

20   Charlesworth, Chris: "Inside the Mind of an Ex-Beatle," *Melody Maker*, November 3, 1973.

21   Uncredited: "Lennon and McCartney Stories Denied," *Record Mirror*, January 20, 1973.

22   Uncredited: "Court Denies Lennon, Ono, Et Al, Motion," *Cash Box*, April 21, 1973, p. 7.

23   Legge, Beverley: "When the Questions Begin to Paul," *Disc*, June 2, 1973.

24   McCartney (McGear), Michael: Author interview (Kozinn), May 19, 2019.

25   Ibid.

26   Uncredited: "*Cash Box*—Radio Active," *Cash Box*, May 5, 1973, p. 24.

27   Uncredited: "*Cash Box* Album Reviews," *Cash Box*, May 5, 1973, p. 30.

28   Uncredited: "*Billboard*'s Top Album Picks," *Billboard*, May 5, 1973, p. 60.

29   Dove, Ian: "Records: By McCartney," *New York Times*, May 2, 1973, p. 37.

30   Hilburn, Robert: "A Hunch Cracks Up on McCartney's *Speedway*," *Los Angeles Times*, May 13, 1973, p. 48.

31   Van Matre, Lynn: "Along McCartney's Muddy *Speedway* Track," *Chicago Tribune*, May 20, 1973.

32   Kaye, Lenny: "Paul McCartney: *Red Rose Speedway*," *Rolling Stone*, July 5, 1973, p. 68.

33   Boucher, Caroline: "Clipped Wings," *Disc*, April 28, 1973, p. 23.

34   Tyler, Tony: "Nice One, Paul," *NME*, April 28, 1973, p. 6.

35   C.P. (full name not given): "High on Wings," *Music World's Beat Instrumental*, September 1973.

36   Letter from Vincent Romeo to Dave Robinson, June 12, 1973. The letter covers the arrangements for the second leg of the tour, but the rate of pay was the same for the first leg.

37   Chattington, Barry: Author interview (Sinclair), December 15, 2018.

38   Seiwell, Denny, Compound of author interviews (Kozinn/Sinclair), June 9, 2016, and September 12, 2016.

39   Gomm, Ian: Author interview (Sinclair), July 26, 2019.

40   Ibid.

41   Rankin, Billy: Author interview (Sinclair), August 6, 2019.

42   Gomm, Ian: Author interview (Sinclair), July 26, 2019.

43   Bath, Michael: "The Beatles Have Split Up Forever," *Western Daily Press*, May 12, 1973, p. 1.

44   Belsey, James: "Shy Paul and Wings Fly West," *Bristol Evening Post*, May 11, 1973.

45   Belsey, James: "Paul (and Wings) Off to a Flying Start," *Bristol Evening Post*, May 12, 1973, p. 4.

46   Simons, Judith: "Paul Is Back on the Wing with a Swing," *Daily Express*, May 14, 1973, p. 10.

47   Palmer, Tony: "O, For the Wings . . ." *Observer*, May 20, 1973.

48   Observations based on an audience recording of the concert.

49   Charlesworth, Chris: ". . . But Wings Fly High," *Melody Maker*, May 19, 1973.

50   Sanders, Rick: "Wings at Oxford: At Last the Old Magic Works," *Record Mirror*, May 19, 1973.

51   All the press conference coverage is from Gambaccini, Paul: "McCartneys Meet Press: Starting Over Again," *Rolling Stone*, June 21, 1973, p. 6.

52   Gomm, Ian: Author interview (Sinclair), July 26, 2019.

53   Ibid.

54   Nifield, Philip: "Beatle Paul Still Big Hit," *South Wales Echo*, May 14, 1973.

55   Gomm, Ian: Author interview (Sinclair), July 26, 2019.

56   Ibid.

57   Bonner, Michael with Hughes, Rob & Watts, Peter: "McCartney at 80," *Uncut*, May 2022, p. 126.

58   Coleman, Barry: "Wings," *Guardian*, May 18, 1973, p. 40.

59   Harrison, George: "Ten Years On—And Rock Is Still Top," *Liverpool Echo*, May 19, 1973, p. 7.

60   Gomm, Ian: Author interview (Sinclair), July 26, 2019.

61   Oadkley, Chris: "Wings Soar to Blast Out Rock," *Yorkshire Evening Post*, May 21, 1973, p. 4.

62   Uncredited: "Wings Bring Down the House," *Lancashire Evening Post*, May 22, 1973, p. 1.

63   Rickman, Phil: "The Magic of McCartney," *Preston Evening Post and Chronicle*, May 26, 1973, p. 8.

64   Uncredited: "Yesterday—Seems So Far Away," *Edinburgh Evening News*, May 24, 1973, p. 9.

65   Robbins, Fred: "The Viva Interview: Paul and Linda McCartney," *Viva*, January 1974.

66   Rankin, Billy: Author interview (Sinclair), August 6, 2019.

67   Uncredited: "McCullough to Quit Wings?" *Disc*, May 19, 1973, p. 4.

68 Uncredited: "Two Leaving Wings? The Reply Is 'Rats,'" *NME*, May 26, 1973.

69 Plummer, Mark: "Caught in the Act," *Melody Maker*, June 2, 1973.

70 Harrison, George: "Playing for Kicks—by Paul," *Liverpool Echo*, May 22, 1973, p. 10.

71 Seiwell, Denny: Author interview (Sinclair), September 13, 2016.

72 Gomm, Ian: Author interview (Sinclair), July 26, 2019.

73 Telford, Ray: "Brinsley Schwarz's Nick Lowe in the Talk In," *Sounds*, March 30, 1974, p. 11.

24 "HOW DARE YOU INCONVENIENCE US?"

1 Uncredited: "Top Single Picks—Wings—'Live and Let Die,'" *Billboard*, June 30, 1973, p. 56.

2 Legge, Beverley: "Paul's Bond Movie Theme," *Disc*, June 9, 1973, p. 19.

3 MacDonald, Ian: "McCartney Lets It Be," *NME*, June 9, 1973, p. 12.

4 Peacock, Steve: "Singles," *Sounds*, June 9, 1973, p. 25.

5 Uncredited: "Chart Talk," *Billboard*, June 2, 1973, p. 61.

6 "Nicky," editor: "Run Down on the Latest Wings Activities," *Paul McCartney and Wings Fun Club Newsletter*, August 1973, p. 1.

7 Stone, J.: Radio interview with Paul McCartney, KSLQ, St. Louis, February 1974.

8 Rodgers, Nile: Audio interview with Paul McCartney for Deep Hidden Meaning podcast, January 8, 2021.

9 Brayfield, Celia: "They Are an Unlikely Couple But . . . Linda and Paul McCartney Are Still Madly in Love," *Cosmopolitan*, January, 1973, p. 66.

10 Burgess, Michael, "McCartney, Wings & Things", *Musician and Recording World*, March 14, 1975.

11 White, Timothy: "Farewell to the First Solo Era," *Musician*, February 1988, p. 52.

12 Digby Smith, Richard: Author interview (Sinclair), June 30, 2020.

13 Uncredited: "A Superb City Hall Show from Wings," *Sheffield Star*, July 5, 1973, p. 3.

14 Strong, Keith: "Ex-Beatle Superstar Just Wants to be a Singer in a Rock 'n' Roll Band!" *Sheffield Star*, July 6, 1973, p. 4.

15 Hickey, William: "The Night the World (and His Wife) Went to the Pictures," *Daily Express*, July 6, 1973, p. 9.

16 Telford, Ray: "Over the Rainbow," *NME*, July 21, 1973, p. 16.

17 Fielding, Howard: "Live Sounds—Wings," *Sounds*, July 14, 1973, p. 30.

18 Detheridge, Dennis: "They Were Right to Use a Stand-In Says Paul," *Melody Maker*, July 14, 1973.

19 Ibid.

20 Ibid.

21 Ibid.

22 Tyler, Tony: "The Renaissance of Dirty Macca," *NME*, July 14, 1973, pp. 20–21.

23 Watts, Michael, and Wickham, Vicki: "Hot News from America" column, *Melody Maker*, July 7, 1973.

24 Telford: "Over the Rainbow."

25 C.B. (full name not given): "A Million Miles Away from Sergeant Pepper," *Leicester Mercury*, July 10, 1973.

26 Harvey, Peter: "Live—Wings," *Record Mirror*, July 14, 1973, p. 16. (Peter Harvey's review and John Clegg's Birmingham review were published back to back in the same article.)

27 All the quotes in this and the next four paragraphs were published in Harvey, Peter: "Paul's Wings Find Their Identity On Stage," *Record Mirror*, July 21, 1973, pp. 14–15.

28 C.P. (full name not given): "High on Wings," Beat Instrumental, September 1973.

29 Harvey: "Paul's Wings Find Their Identity on Stage."

30 Uncredited: "Paul Replies to the Fans," *Newcastle Journal*, July 11, 1973, p. 5.

31 Pollard, Ken: "Wings Fly High," *Newcastle Evening Chronicle*, July 11, 1973, p. 6.

32 Gomm, Ian: Author interview (Sinclair), June 26, 2019.

33 Denny Seiwell: Author interview (Sinclair), November 2, 2016.

34 Erskine, Peter: "Concert Review—Wings," *Disc*, August 4, 1973.

35 McCartney, Paul: Press Conference, Nashville, TN, July 17, 1974.

36 Gambaccini: *Paul McCartney: In His Own Words*, p. 72.

37 Letter from Lee Eastman, of Eastman & Eastman to L.G. Wood, of EMI Limited, July 18, 1973.

38 Uncredited: "'My Love' Gold," *Cash Box*, July 21, 1973, p. 27.

39 White: "Farewell to the First Solo Era," p. 51.

40 Block, Adam: "The Makka Material," *McCartney: Beatle on Wings*, K.49569, 1976, p. 62.

41 Plummer, Mark: "Country Laine," *Melody Maker*, July 28, 1973.

42 Sam [surname not given]: "Down Memory Laine," Jackie, November 10, 1973.

43 Plummer: "Country Laine."

44 Uncredited: "Denny Laine—A Special Musical Talent," August 11, 1973, p. 24.

45 Harvey, Peter: "Denny Spreads His Wings," *Record Mirror*, August 4, 1973, p. 25.

46 Erskine, Peter: "Denny Laine It All on the Line," *Disc*, August 4, 1973, p. 17.

47 Uncredited: "Denny Laine—A Special Musical Talent."

48 Erskine: "Denny Laine It All on the Line."

49 Johnson, James: "H. McCullough Meets the Wings Fan Club," *NME*, July 28, 1973, p. 8.

50 Ibid.

51 Laine, Jo Jo: "Living Like Peasants Down on Millionaire Paul's Farm," *Sunday People*, April 17, 1983, p. 22.

52 Sam (surname not given): "Down Memory Laine," Jackie, November 10, 1973.

53 Laine: "Living Like Peasants Down on Millionaire Paul's Farm."

54 Laine, Denny: Filmed interview and Q/A session, Fest for Beatle Fans, Chicago, May 14, 2016.

55 Uncredited, "An Exclusive Interview with Denny," *Wings Official Fun Club*, June 1974, p. 6.

56 Spevock, Ed: Author interview (Sinclair), May 14, 2018.

57 Johnson, James: "Right, Now Let's Number That Best McCartney", *NME*, August 17, 1974, pp. 7–8.

58 Harper, Colin: "Hello Goodbye—Henry McCullough and Wings," *Mojo*, September 1997.

59 Deriso, Nick: "Something Else! Interview—Henry McCullough," *Something Else!*, August 24, 2011.

60 Harper: "Hello Goodbye—Henry McCullough and Wings."

61 Harper with Hodgett: *Irish Folk, Trad & Blues—A Secret History*, p. 175.

62 Gambaccini: "The *Rolling Stone* Interview: Paul McCartney," p. 33.

63 Stein, Kathleen: "Paul McCartney—Seven Trials Inside *Band on the Run*," *Circus Raves*, April 1974, p. 62.

64 Deriso: "*Something Else!* Interview—Henry McCullough."

65 Doherty, Harry: "Spreading His Wings," *Melody Maker*, January 15, 1977, p. 35.

66 Seiwell, Denny: Author interview (Kozinn), June 9, 2016.

67 Boucher, Caroline, "Denny Laine Is the Lazy Star Who Doesn't Want a Hit or a Glitter Suit", *Disc*, December 29, 1973, p. 21.

68 Laine, Denny: "The Real McCartney," *Sun*, January 31, 1984, p. 16.

69 Horide, Rosemary: "Take Off—Wings in Full Flight," *Disc*, November 2, 1974, p. 13.

70 Seiwell, Denny: Author interview (Kozinn), June 9, 2016.

71 Doherty, Harry: "Spreading His Wings," *Melody Maker*, January 15, 1977, p. 35.

72 Seiwell, Denny: Author interviews (Kozinn, Sinclair), June 9 and October 31, 2016.

73 Brown, Geoff: "Wings," *Melody Maker*, November 30, 1974, p. 29.

74 Beattie, John: "McCartney on the Run," *Record Mirror*, December 1, 1973, p. 11.

75 O'Leary, Dermot: Filmed interview with Paul McCartney for the documentary *Paul McCartney & Wings: Band on the Run*, ITV, first broadcast October 31, 2010.

25 STEP SOFTLY, THIS TOWN IS JINXED

1 Du Noyer, Paul: *Band on the Run* Archive Edition (MPL Communications, London, 2010), p. 18.

2 O'Leary: Filmed interview with Paul McCartney for *Paul McCartney & Wings*.

3 Salewicz, Chris: "People Thought We Were Only Good for One Album," *NME*, November 1, 1975, p. 45.

4 Uncredited: "Great Blemish on Merchant Navy's Reputation," *Liverpool Echo*, November 23, 1949, p. 5.

5 Welch, Chris: "Paul McCartney," *Melody Maker*, December 1, 1973.

6 Giuliano, Geoffrey: Audio interview with Denny Laine for "The Beatles in Their Own Words, A Rockumentary, Paul McCartney Beyond the Myth," *Author's Republic*, August 3, 2019.

7 White: "Farewell to the First Solo Era," p. 52.

8 Emerick, Geoff, with Massey, Howard: *Here, There and Everywhere: My Life Recording the Music of the Beatles* (Gotham Books, New York, 2006), p. 341.

9 Cummings, Howard: "Geoff Emerick", Recording Engineer Producer, December 1978, p. 38.

10 Beattie, John: "McCartney on the Run," *Record Mirror*, December 1, 1973, p. 11.

11 Horide, Rosemary: "Side by Side," *Disc*, December 1, 1973, pp. 18–19.

12 Hogan, Phil: "Paul McCartney: 'Suddenly It Just All Came Together'," *Observer* (online), November 7, 2010.

13 Beattie, John: "McCartney on the Run," *Record Mirror*, December 1, 1973, p. 11.

14 O'Leary: Filmed interview with Paul McCartney for *Paul McCartney & Wings*.

15 Du Noyer: *Band on the Run*, p. 19.

16 Emerick with Massey: *Here, There and Everywhere*, p. 340.

17 Badman, Keith: *Off the Records 2—The Dream Is Over Volume 2* (Omnibus Press, London, 2002), p. 121.

18 Prism Films: Denny Laine interview with Prism Film, published in multiple parts on YouTube, June 9, 2012.

19 Dialogue taken from: Rubin, Rick: *McCartney 3,2,1!* Episode 2 (Hulu, 2021), broadcast July 2021.

20 Peacock, Steve: "Ahh . . . Laine," *Sounds*, January 5, 1974, p. 8.

21 White: "Farewell to the First Solo Era," p. 52.

22 Emerick with Massey: *Here, There and Everywhere*, p. 345.

23 Baker, Ginger, with Baker, Ginette: *Ginger Baker Hellraiser* (John Blake, London, 2009), p. 179.

24 Hooper, Joseph: "Harmonic Convergence? Ginger Baker's Crazy Story," *Observer* (online), June 7, 1999.

25 Information on Moshood Abiola taken from Abiola, Jamiu: *The President Who Never Ruled* (self-published, Nigeria, 2016).

26 McCartney and Muldoon (ed.): *The Lyrics 1956 to the Present*, p. 39.

27 Prism Films: Denny Laine interview with Prism Films, published in multiple parts on YouTube, June 9, 2012.

28 Ibid.

29 Doyle, Tom: "The Great Escape," *Q Magazine*, June 2010, p. 96.

30 Wright, Michael: "A Time To Heal," *Classical FM Magazine*, March 2000, p. 33.

31 Moron, Marc: Radio interview with Paul McCartney for "WFT Podcast with Marc Maron," August 8, 2018.

32 Lewisohn, Mark: "The Club Sandwich Interview," *Club Sandwich 72*, Winter 1994, p. 4.

33 Emerick with Massey: *Here, There and Everywhere*, p. 348.

34 Du Noyer: *Band on the Run*, p. 27. And Horide, Rosemary: "Side by Side," pp. 18–19.

35 Hilburn, Robert: "McCartney on Beatles Breakup—Let It Be," *Los Angeles Times*, April 21, 1974, p. 52.

36 Hooper, Joseph: "Harmonic Convergence? Ginger Baker's Crazy Story," *Observer* (online), June 7, 1999.

37 Emerick and Massey: *Here, There and Everywhere*, p. 349.

38 Wheeler, Paul: unpublished piece about Paul McCartney and Fela Ransome Kuti in Lagos, October 1973, p. 3.

39 Attah, A.B: "Step Softly, This Town Is Jinxed," *Lagos Evening Times*, quoted by the *Irish Press*, September 17, 1973.

40 Ibid. And *Melody Maker*, September 29, 1973.

41 White, Timothy: "Farewell to the first solo era", Musician, February 1988, p.52.

42 Gambaccini: "The *Rolling Stone* Interview: Paul McCartney," pp. 21–28.

43 Gambaccini: *Paul McCartney: In His Own Words*, p. 79.

44 Du Noyer,: *Band on the Run*, p. 22.

45 McCartney has told the story of this encounter many times, with slightly varying details. This account is pieced together from several of those sources, most notably: Uncredited, "Homes Sweet Homes—Tina Talks to Paul McCartney," November 17, 1973; Welch, Chris: "Paul McCartney," *Melody Maker*, December 1, 1973; Pearce, Garth, "The McCartney Memoirs—Band Almost on the Run," *Daily Express*, February 10, 1977; and Du Noyer, Paul: *Band on the Run* Archive Edition (MPL Communications, London, 2010).

46 Pearce, Garth: "The McCartney Memoirs—Band Almost on the Run," *Daily Express*, February 10, 1977, p. 7.

47 Emerick with Massey: *Here, There and Everywhere*, p. 347.

48 Uncredited: "No Problems—Paul," *Record Mirror*, September 29, 1973, p. 4.

26 RESTLESS MOMENTUM

1 Du Noyer: *Band on the Run*, p. 30.

2 Dees, Pat: Fan account from McCartney Ltd. (fanzine), November-December 1973.

3 Evans, David, with Minns, David: *This Was the Real Life: The Tale of Freddie Mercury* (Tusitala Press, London, 2008), p. 30.

4 Brown, Geoff: "McCullough's Solo Plans," *Melody Maker*, September 15, 1973, p. 10.

5 Deriso, Nick: "Something Else! Interview—Henry McCullough," *Something Else!*, August 24, 2011.

6 Seiwell, Denny: Author interview (Kozinn), June 9, 2016. (The quote in the footnote was also from this interview.)

7 Read, Lorna: "Multi-Media McGear (OK, Mike?)", *Beat Instrumental*, October 1974, pp. 20–21.

8 McCartney, Paul: Self-interview for *Wide Prairie* webcast, broadcast online on December 18, 1998.

9 Gambaccini: *Paul McCartney: In His Own Words*, p. 83.

10 Horide, Rosemary: "Paul's Run on the Run," *Disc*, December 8, 1973, p. 20.

11 Ward, Jeff: "Faith: Return of a Survivor," *Melody Maker*, August 24, 1974, p. 3.

12 Courtney, David: *Oh Wot a Life: Nothing in This Book Is True, But It's Exactly the Way It Happened* (Courtney World Music, Ltd., 2020), Kindle location 1437.

13 Gambaccini: *Paul McCartney: In His Own Words*, p. 83.

14 Emerick with Massey *Here, There and Everywhere*, pp. 350–51.

15 The details of the meeting are from Visconti, Tony: *The Autobiography: Bowie, Bolan, and the Brooklyn Boy* (HarperCollins Publishers, London, 2007), Kindle location 2798 of 5637. And Tobler, John, with Grundy, Stuart: *The Record Producers* (BBC Books, London, 1982), p. 181.

16 Ibid.

17 Parade, James: "All in a Little Name," *Record Mirror*, September 22, 1979, p. 9.

18 Visconti: *The Autobiography: Bowie, Bolan, and the Brooklyn Boy*.

19 Casey, Howie: Author interview (Sinclair), October 19, 2019.

20 Visconti: *The Autobiography: Bowie, Bolan, and the Brooklyn Boy*.

21 Kenzie, Phil: Author interview (Sinclair), April 24, 2020.

22 Uncredited: "Paul McCartney and Wings: Helen Wheels (Apple)," *NME*, October 20, 1973.

23 Green, Richard: "Helen Wheels b/w Country Dreamer," *Record Mirror*, October 20, 1973.

24 Horide, Rosemary: "McCartney's Rockin' Rover," *Disc*, October 27, 1973.

25 Peel, John: "Wings' Double Sided Winner," *Sounds*, October 27, 1973.

26 Lewisohn, Mark: "Mining the Film and Video Archive: Helen Wheels," *Club Sandwich*, No. 70, Summer, 1994.

27 Uncredited: "It's All Here If You Want It," *Sounds*, March 23, 1974, p. 36.

28 The information is taken from the effects reel, sold by Geoff Emerick's estate in 2021.

29 Gambaccini, Paul, Audio interview with Paul McCartney for *Birth of a Band* show for BBC Radio One, circa September 1975.

30 Webb, Julie: "Wings in the Air," *NME*, October 27, 1973, p. 11.

31 Powell, Aubrey: Author Interview (Sinclair), May 15, 2020.

32 Ibid.

33 Du Noyer|: *Band on the Run*, p. 47.

34 Arrowsmith, Clive: "Band on the Run—The Great 'Wrong Film' Debacle," *Clive Arrowsmith* (online), January 13, 2014.

35 Parkinson, Michael: Author interview (Sinclair), August 9, 2019.

36 Elliott, Bobby: *It Ain't Heavy, It's My Story* (Omnibus Press, London, 2020), Kindle Edition, pp. 220–22.

37 Cummings, Howard, "Geoff Emerick", Recording Engineer Producer, December 1978, p. 40.

38 Fong-Torres, Ben: "Al Coury Owns Number One," *Rolling Stone*, October 5, 1978.

39 Ibid.

27 THE KING OF POP

1 Welch, Chris: "Paul McCartney," *Melody Maker*, December 1, 1973.

2   Pike, Jeremy: "The Best Is Still to Come: Jimmy McCulloch," *Guitar*, January, 1975, p. 20.
3   Evans, Jim, "Faster Than Concorde—The Story of Wings," *Record Mirror*, April 16, 1977, p. 18.
4   Richards, Duncan, Audio interview (in French) with French press, December 1973.
5   Tobaly, Marc, email exchange with author (Sinclair), August 5, 2019.
6   Quote taken from the press release for Linda's posthumous album *Wide Prairie*, issued on October 26, 1998.
7   Osmond, Donny: Author interview (Sinclair), February 4, 2020.
8   Horide: "Side by Side," *Disc*, December 1, 1973, pp. 18–19.
9   Gelly, David & Sykes, Homer: The Facts About a Pop Group (Whizzard & Deutsch, London, 1976), p. 27.
10 Ibid., p. 28.
11 Beattie, John: "McCartney on the Run," *Record Mirror*, 1 December 1973, p. 11.
12 Everett, Kenny, with Cash, Dave: Radio interview with Paul and Linda McCartney for "Kenny and Cash," Capitol Radio, broadcast November 24, 1973.
13 Uncredited: "3 Ex-Beatles File Suit Vs. Klein, ABKCO," *Billboard*, November 24, 1973.
14 Beattie: "McCartney on the Run," p. 11.
15 Bain, Romany: "Linda—My Life with a Legend," *Daily Mirror*, November 29, 1973, p. 7.
16 Hilburn, Robert: "John and Paul: Artistic Barometer Is Up," *Los Angeles Times*, December 16, 1973.

17 Welch, Chris: "Band on the Run: Wings Soar Sunward," *Melody Maker*, December 1, 1973.
18 Peacock, Steve: "Albums: Paul McCartney and Wings: *Band on the Run* (Apple)," *Sounds*, December 1, 1973, p. 34.
19 Horide, Rosemary: "Paul's Fun on the Run," *Disc*, December 8, 1973, p. 30.
20 Horide, Rosemary: "Albums of the Year," *Disc*, December 22, 1973, p. 20.
21 Alterman, Loraine: "Paul's Grooves Will Grab You," *New York Times*, December 2, 1973, p. 32.
22 Denselow, Robin: "Rock Records," *Guardian*, January 12, 1974, p. 10.
23 Murray, Charles Shaar: "Paul Rolls It Home," *NME*, January 19, 1974, p. 12.
24 Landau, Jon: "Reviews—*Band on the Run*," *Rolling Stone*, January 31, 1974.
25 Seiwell, Denny: Author interview (Kozinn), June 9, 2016.
26 Boucher, Caroline: "Denny Laine Is the Lazy Star Who Doesn't Want a Hit of a Glitter Suit," *Disc*, December 29, 1973, p. 21.
27 Lewisohn, Mark (Ed.): "James Bond," *Club Sandwich* 76, Winter, 1995.
28 Gambaccini, Paul: "The *Rolling Stone* Interview: Paul McCartney," *Rolling Stone*, January 31, 1974.
29 Ibid.
30 Ibid.

DEYST.

THE MCCARTNEY LEGACY. Copyright © 2022 by Allan Kozinn and Adrian Sinclair. All rights reserved. Printed in the United States of America. No part of this book may be used or reproduced in any manner whatsoever without written permission except in the case of brief quotations embodied in critical articles and reviews. For information, address HarperCollins Publishers, 195 Broadway, New York, NY 10007.

HarperCollins books may be purchased for educational, business, or sales promotional use. For information, please email the Special Markets Department at SPsales@harpercollins.com.

FIRST EDITION

DESIGNED BY LEAH CARLSON-STANISIC

Endpaper art by Evgeny Turaev/Shutterstock, Inc.

Library of Congress Cataloging-in-Publication Data has been applied for.

ISBN 978-0-06-300070-4

22 23 24 25 26   LSC   10 9 8 7 6 5 4 3 2 1